Y0-DFB-403

Detroit
street guide

Contents

Introduction

Maps

Lists and Indexes

RAND McNALLY
Rand McNally Consumer Affairs
P.O. Box 7600
Chicago IL 60680-9915
randmcnally.com
For comments or suggestions, please call
(800) 777-MAPS (-6277)
or email us at:
consumeraffairs@randmcnally.com

NAVTEQ ON BOARD™

Legend

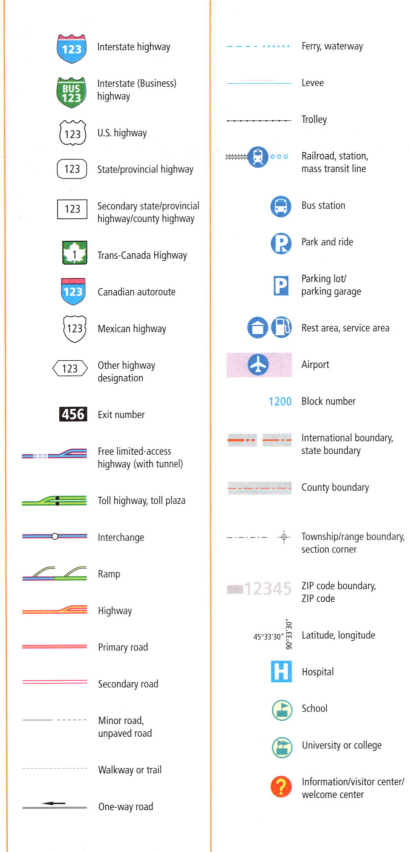

Interstate highway

Interstate (Business) highway

U.S. highway

State/provincial highway

Secondary state/provincial highway/county highway

Trans-Canada Highway

Canadian autoroute

Mexican highway

Other highway designation

Exit number

Free limited-access highway (with tunnel)

Toll highway, toll plaza

Interchange

Ramp

Highway

Primary road

Secondary road

Minor road, unpaved road

Walkway or trail

One-way road

Ferry, waterway

Levee

Trolley

Railroad, station, mass transit line

Bus station

Park and ride

Parking lot/ parking garage

Rest area, service area

Airport

Block number

International boundary, state boundary

County boundary

Township/range boundary, section corner

ZIP code boundary, ZIP code

Latitude, longitude

Hospital

School

University or college

Information/visitor center/ welcome center

Police/sheriff, etc.

Fire station

City/town/village hall and other government buildings

Courthouse

Post office

Library

Museum

Border crossing/ Port of entry

Theater/ performing arts center

Golf course

Other point of interest

we've got you COVERED

Rand McNally's broad selection of products is perfect for your every need. Whether you're looking for the convenience of write-on wipe-off laminated maps, extra maps for every car, or a Road Atlas to plan your next vacation or to use as a reference, Rand McNally has you covered.

Street Guides

Detroit Metro/w CD

Detroit/including Wayne County

Oakland & Macomb Counties

Western Michigan

Folded Maps

EasyFinder® Laminated Maps

Ann Arbor/Ypsilanti

Detroit & Vicinity

Michigan

Paper Maps

Ann Arbor/Brighton/Howell

Detroit/North Wayne County

Detroit/Southeastern Michigan Regional

Macomb County

Oakland County South

Michigan

Wall Maps

Detroit/Southeastern Michigan Regional Wall Map

Road Atlases

Road Atlas

Road Atlas & Travel Guide

Large Scale Road Atlas

Midsize Road Atlas

Deluxe Midsize Road Atlas

Pocket Road Atlas

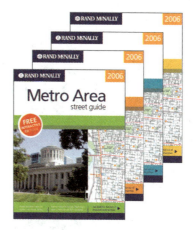

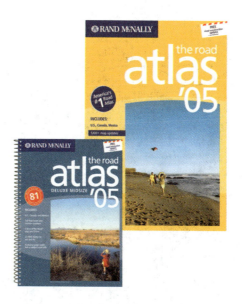

Wherever Rand McNally products are sold or at

www.randmcnally.com

DOWNTOWN DETROIT

Note: This grid references this map only

1 in. = 1400 ft.

0   0.25   0.5

miles

MAP
4186

1:24,000
1 in. = 2000 ft.
0   0.25   0.5
miles

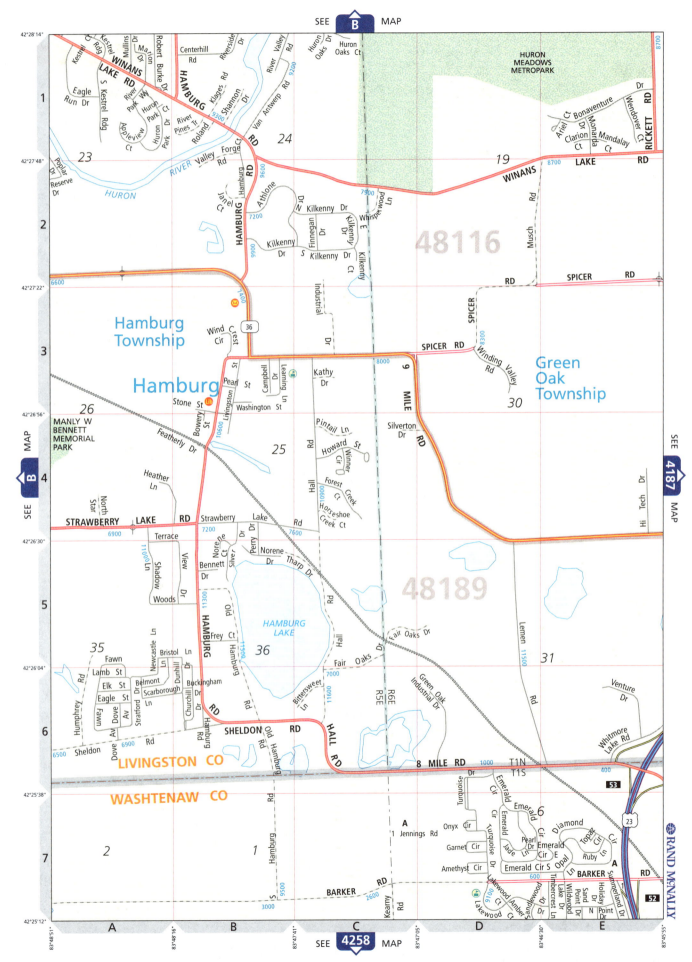

SEE **B** MAP

HURON MEADOWS METROPARK

WINANS LAKE RD

Hamburg Township

Hamburg

MANLY W BENNETT MEMORIAL PARK

HURON

48116

Green Oak Township

SPICER RD

SEE **4187** MAP

STRAWBERRY LAKE RD

HAMBURG LAKE

48189

SHELDON RD

HALL RD

LIVINGSTON CO

WASHTENAW CO

8 MILE RD

BARKER RD

SEE **4258** MAP

RAND McNALLY

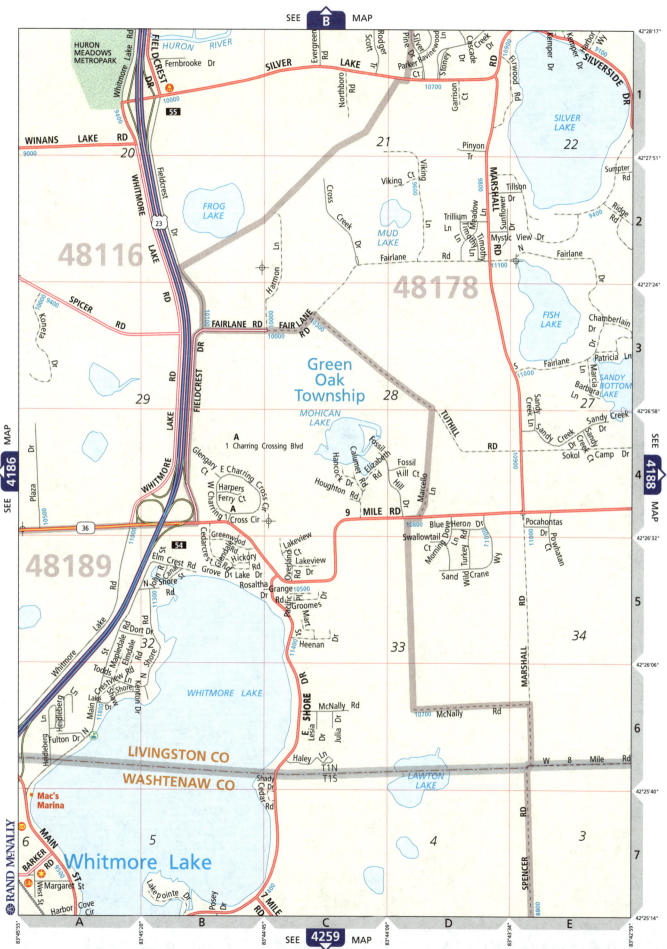

MAP
4187

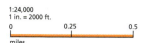

1:24,000
1 in. = 2000 ft.

0   0.25   0.5
miles

N

SEE B MAP

42°28'17"

HURON MEADOWS METROPARK

HURON RIVER

FIELDCREST DR

Fernbrooke Dr

Whitmore Lake Rd

SILVER   LAKE   RD

Evergreen Rd

Northboro Rd

Scott Tr

Rodger Dr

Parker Ravinewood Ln

Pine Ln

Silver Ct

Stoney Dr

Cascade Dr

Creek Dr

RD

Elmwood Rd

Garrison Ct

10700

10900

Kemper Dr

Kemper Dr

Harbor Vw

9100

SILVERSIDE DR

10000

55

42°27'51"

SILVER LAKE

22

1

WINANS   LAKE   RD

9000

20

WHITMORE

21

Pinyon Tr

MARSHALL

9800

Sumpter Rd

9400

Ridge Rd

42°27'51"

48116

FROG LAKE

LAKE

23

SPICER   RD

10000   9400

Koneta Dr

Fieldcrest Dr

Cross Creek Dr

Ln

Viking Ct

Viking Ln

9600

MUD LAKE

Trillium Ln

Meadow Ln

Timothy Ln

Timothy Ln

Sunflower Dr

Tillson Dr

Mystic View Dr

N

RD

11100

11000

Fairlane

48178

Fairlane Dr

42°27'24"

Chamberlain Dr

FISH LAKE

Patricia Ln

Marcia Ln

SANDY BOTTOM LAKE

Barbara Ln

42°26'58"

RD

FAIRLANE RD

10101

10000

FAIRLANE RD

10300

Harmon Ln

FIELDCREST DR

LAKE

RD

29

Green Oak Township

28

TUTHILL

Sandy Creek Ln

Sandy Creek Dr

Sandy Creek Dr

Camp Dr

Sokol Ct

27

SEE 4188 MAP

42°26'58"

MOHICAN LAKE

A
1 Charring Crossing Blvd

Glengary Ct

E Charring Cross Cir

W Charring

Harpers Ferry Ct

A
1 Cross Cir

Fossil Pl

Calumet Rd

Hancock Dr

Houghton Rd

Elizabeth Rd

Fossil Hill Ct

Fossil Hill Dr

Marcello Ln

RD

11000

Pocahontas Ct

Powhatan Ct

SEE 4186 MAP

Plaza Dr

10500

Whitmore Lake Rd

36

9 MILE RD

10800

Blue Heron Dr

Swallowtail Ct

Morning Dove Ln

Turkey Rd

Sand Ppl

Will Crane Rd

11100

10000

Wy

42°26'32"

11000

42°26'32"

48189

54

Greenwood Rd

Glendale Rd

Hickory Rd

Lakeview Dr

Overland Pl

Lakeview Dr

Elm Crest

Cedarcrest Ln

Grove Dr

Canal St

Lake Dr

Rosaltha Dr

Grange Rd

Pacific Rd

10500

Groomes Dr

Mart Dr

S

Heenan Dr

11400

34

33

42°26'06"

Lake Rd

Whitmore

Mapledale Rd

Elmdale Rd

N Shore Dr

Dort Dr

S Shore Dr

Kenton Dr

11300

WHITMORE LAKE

E. SHORE DR

McNally Rd

Lesia Dr

Julia Dr

MARSHALL RD

McNally Rd

10700

Todds St

Crestview Rd

St

Main St

11800

Heidleberg Ln

Heidleberg Dr

Fulton Dr N

42°25'40"

LIVINGSTON CO

WASHTENAW CO

Haley Ln

T1N
T1S

LAWTON LAKE

W 8 Mile Rd

Mac's Marina

Shady Dr

Cedar Rd

42°25'40"

6

MAIN ST

BARKER RD

9500

5

Whitmore Lake

West St

Margaret St

Lakepointe Dr

Posey Dr

7 MILE RD

7400

4

3

SPENCER RD

8800

7

RAND MCNALLY

Harbor

Cove Cir

A   B   C   D   E

SEE 4259 MAP

83°45'55"   83°45'20"   83°44'45"   83°44'09"   83°43'34"   83°42'58"

MAP
4188

1:24,000
1 in. = 2000 ft.

0   0.25   0.5
miles

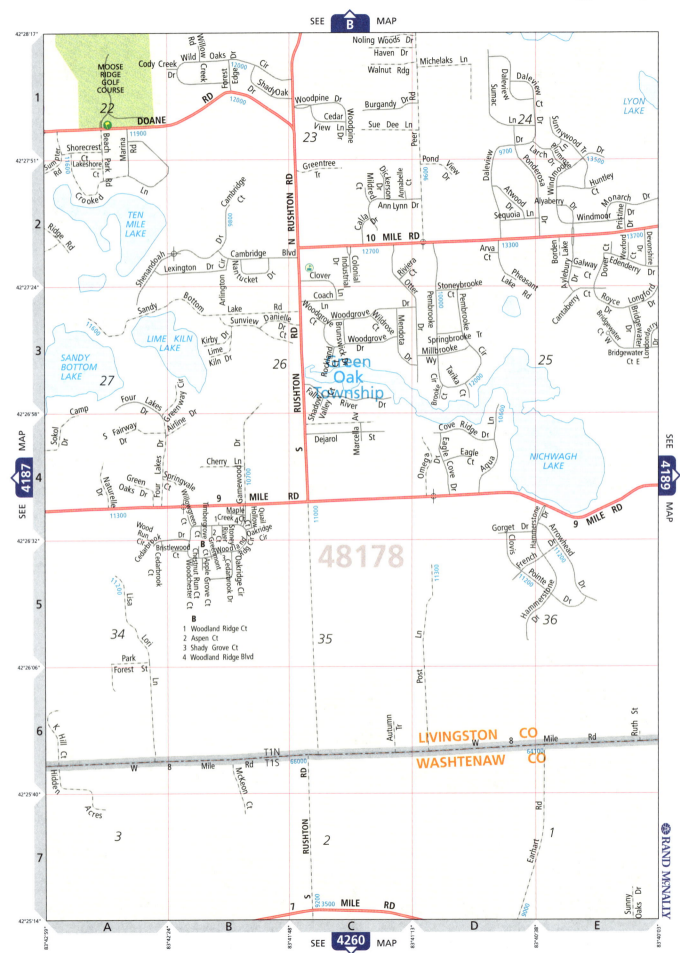

SEE 4187 MAP

SEE 4189 MAP

RAND MCNALLY

MAP
4189

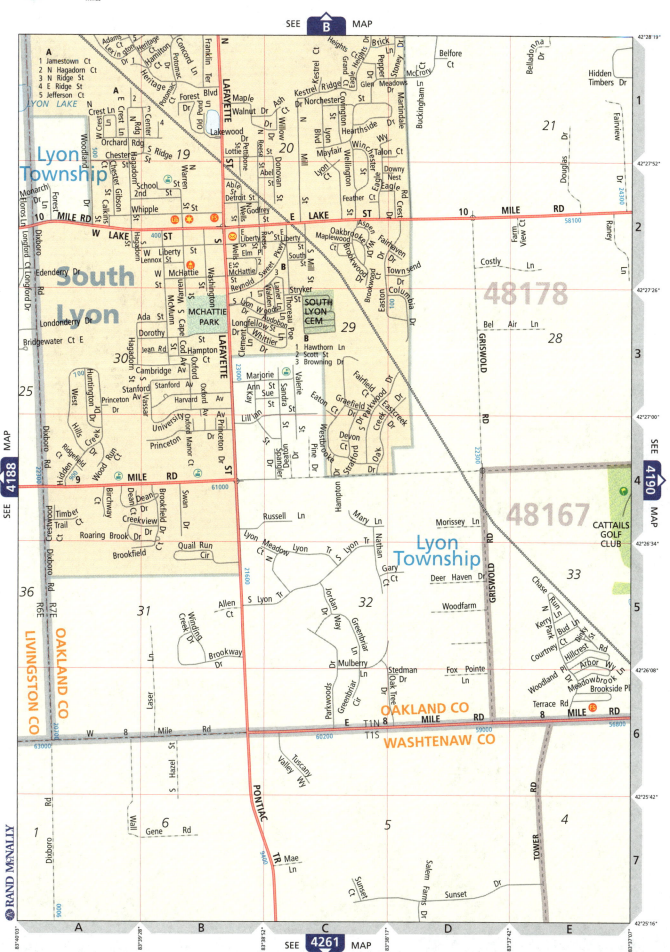

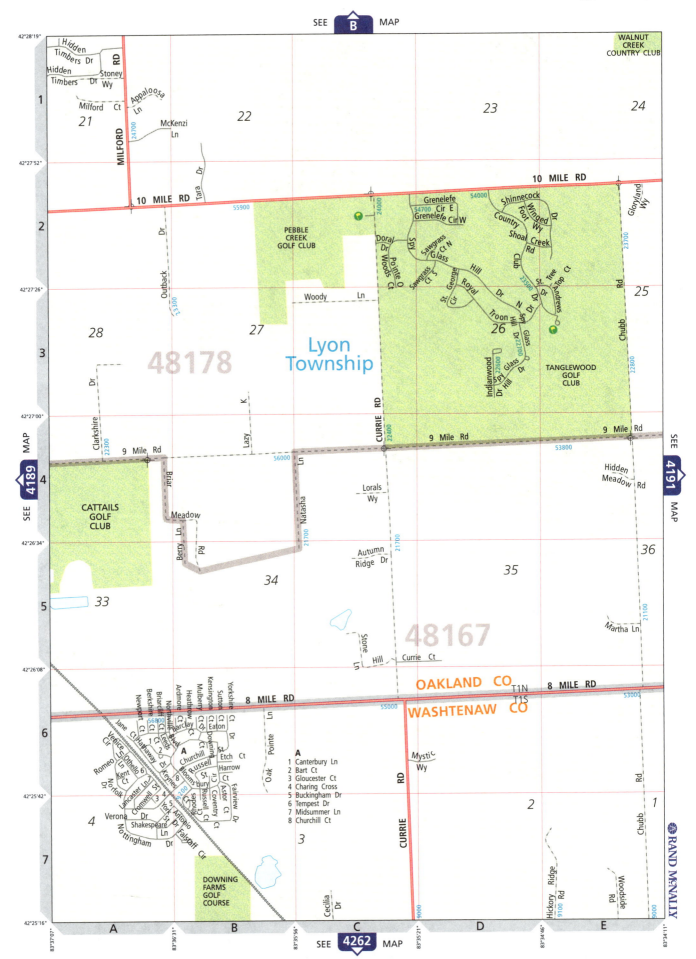

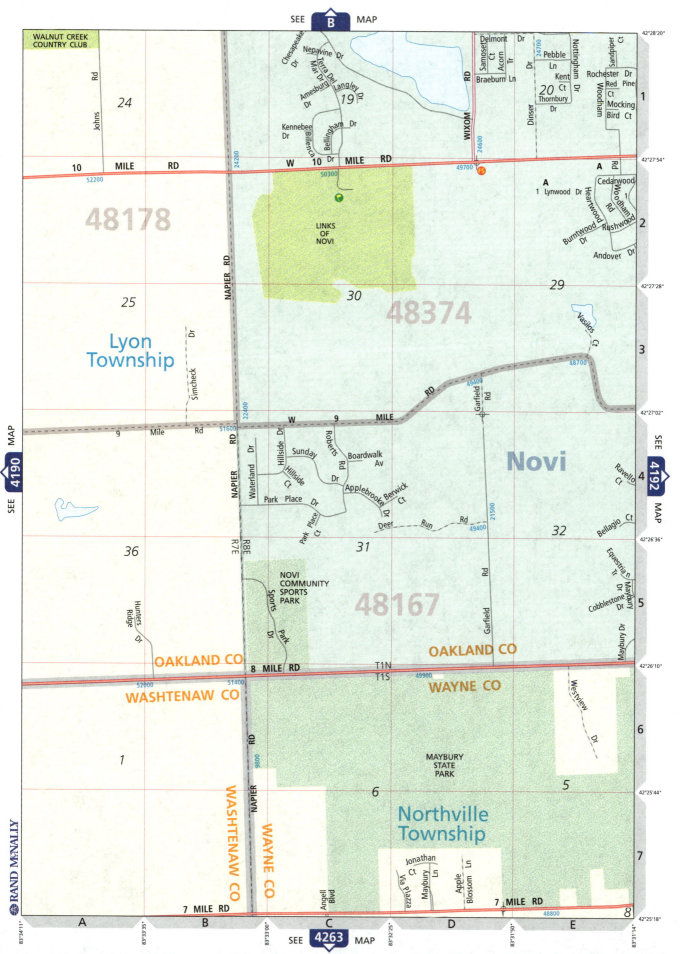

MAP
4191

SEE **B** MAP

1:24,000
1 in. = 2000 ft.
0   0.25   0.5
miles

WALNUT CREEK
COUNTRY CLUB

24

Johns Rd

10   MILE   RD
52200

W 10   MILE   RD
24200

48178

25

Lyon
Township

Simcheck Dr

NAPIER RD

9   Mile   Rd
51600
22400

36

R7E R8E

Hunters
Ridge
Dr

OAKLAND CO
8   MILE   RD
52000   51400

WASHTENAW CO

1

NAPIER RD
9800

WASHTENAW CO
WAYNE CO

7 MILE RD

Chesapeake Dr
Nepavine Dr
Terra Del
Mar Dr
Amesburg Dr
Langley Dr
19
Kennebee Dr
Billenca
Bellingham Dr

Delmont Dr
Samoset
Ct   Acorn
Tr
Braeburn Ln
24700   Pebble
Ln
Kent   Nottingham Dr   Sandpiper Ct
20   Ct
Thornbury   Rochester Dr
Dr   Woodham   Red   Pine
Dinser   Ct
Mocking
Bird Ct

WIXOM RD
24600

49700   F5

50300

LINKS
OF
NOVI

30

48374

29

A   Rd
Cedarwood
A
1 Lynwood Dr   Woodham
Heartwood   Rd   1
Burntwood   Rd   Rushwood
Dr
Andover Dr

Vasilos Ct
48700

RD
49400   Garfield Rd

W   9   MILE   RD
42°27'02"

Hillside Dr
Sunday
Waterland Dr   Hillside
Ct
Park   Place
Park
Place   Dr
Ct

Roberts Rd
Dr
Boardwalk
Av
Applebrooke
Deer   Dr
Run
Berwick
Ct
Rd
49400

Novi

Ravello
Ct

21500

32

Bellagio Ct

Equestrian
Tr
Dr   Maybury
Cobblestone
Dr
Maybury Dr

31

NOVI
COMMUNITY
SPORTS
PARK
Sports
Park
Dr

48167

Garfield Rd

OAKLAND CO

OAKLAND CO

T1N
T1S   49900   WAYNE CO

Westview
Dr

6

MAYBURY
STATE
PARK

5

Northville
Township

Jonathan
Ct   Maybury Ln
Via Plazza   Apple
Blossom Ln
Angell
Blvd   7   MILE   RD
48800

SEE **4263** MAP

SEE **4190** MAP

SEE **4192** MAP

42°28'20"
1
42°27'54"
2
42°27'28"
3
42°27'02"
4
42°26'36"
5
42°26'10"
6
42°25'44"
7
42°25'18"
8

A   B   C   D   E

83°34'11"   83°33'35"   83°33'00"   83°32'25"   83°31'50"   83°31'14"

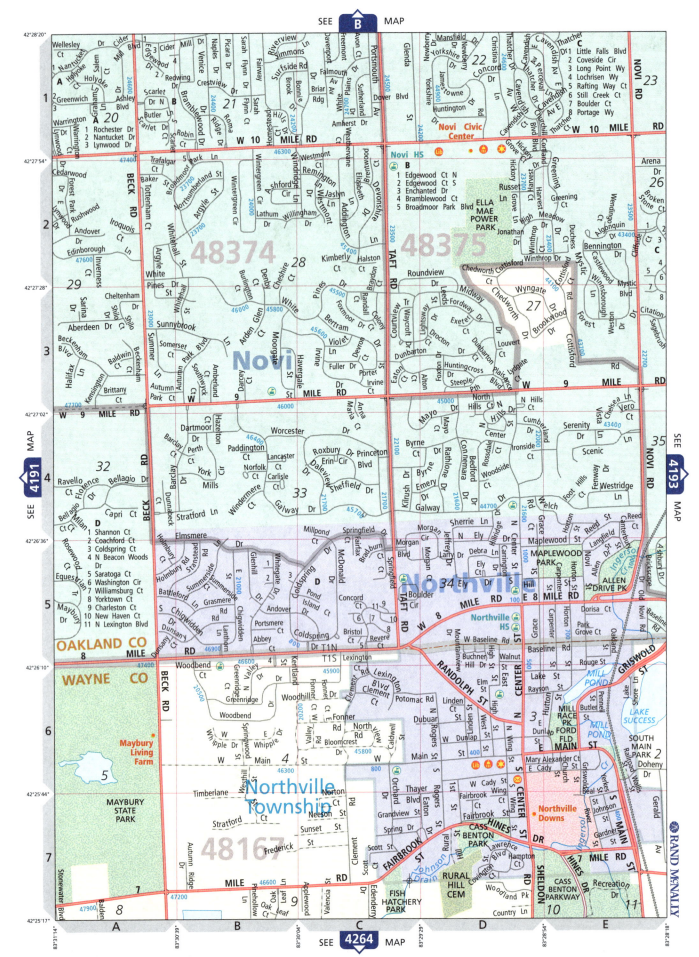

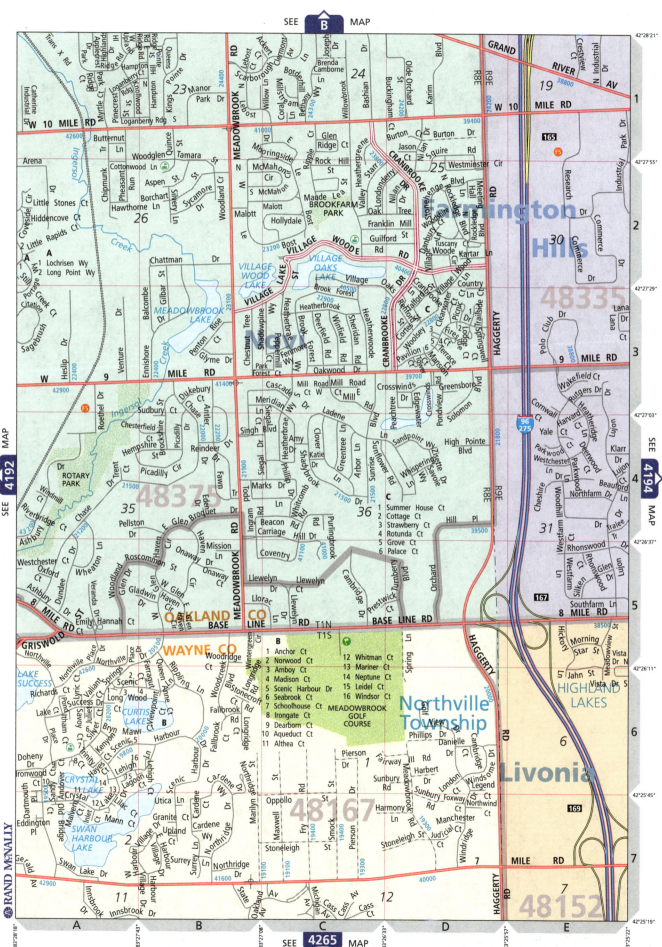

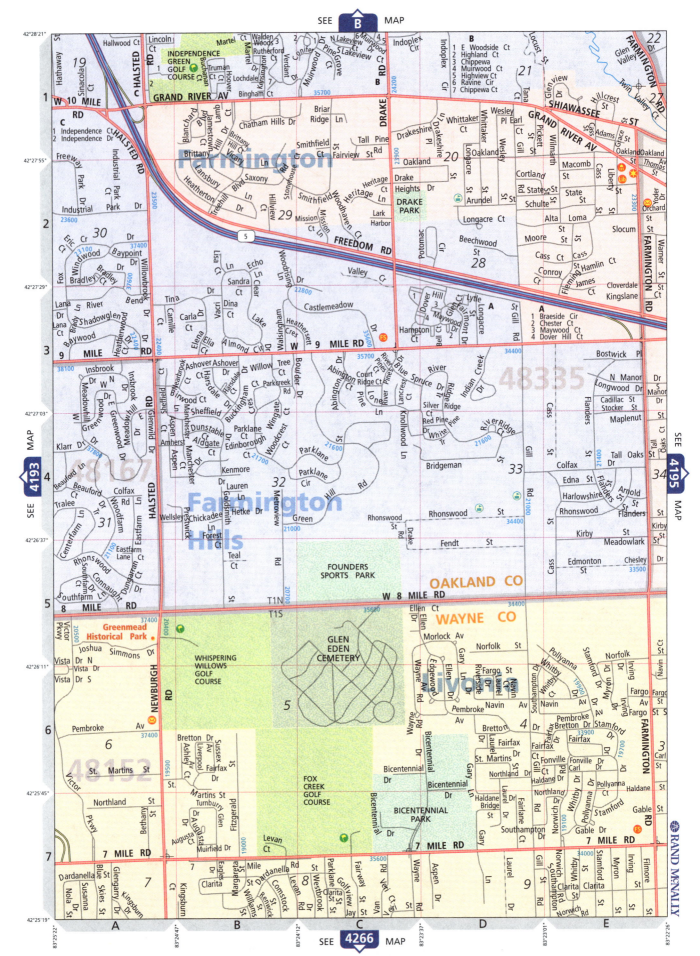

MAP
4194

1:24,000
1 in. = 2000 ft.

0   0.25   0.5
miles

SEE **B** MAP

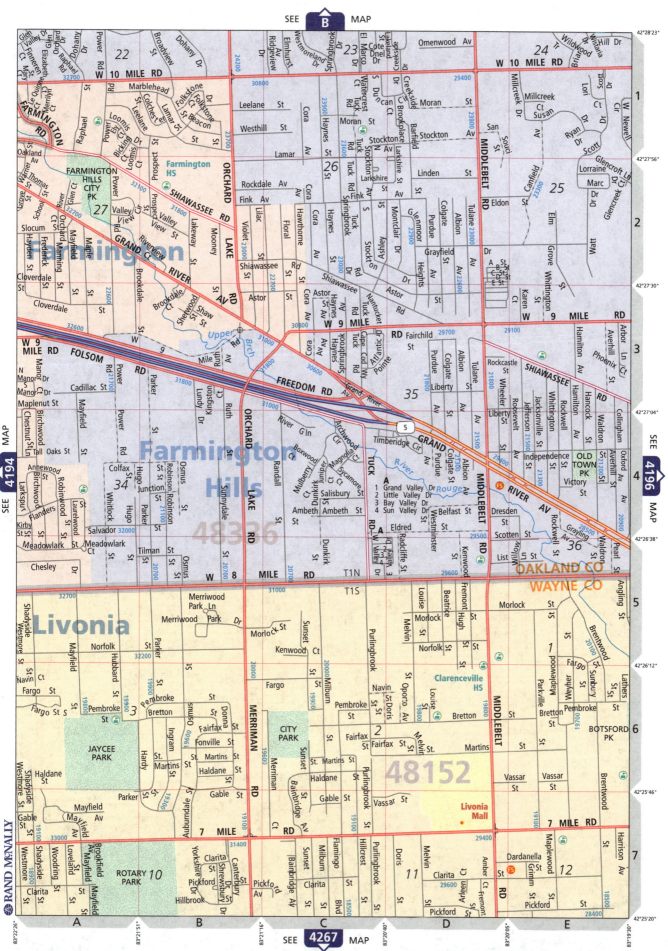

MAP
4195

1:24,000
1 in. = 2000 ft.

0   0.25   0.5
miles

SEE **B** MAP

SEE **4194** MAP

SEE **4196** MAP

SEE **4267** MAP

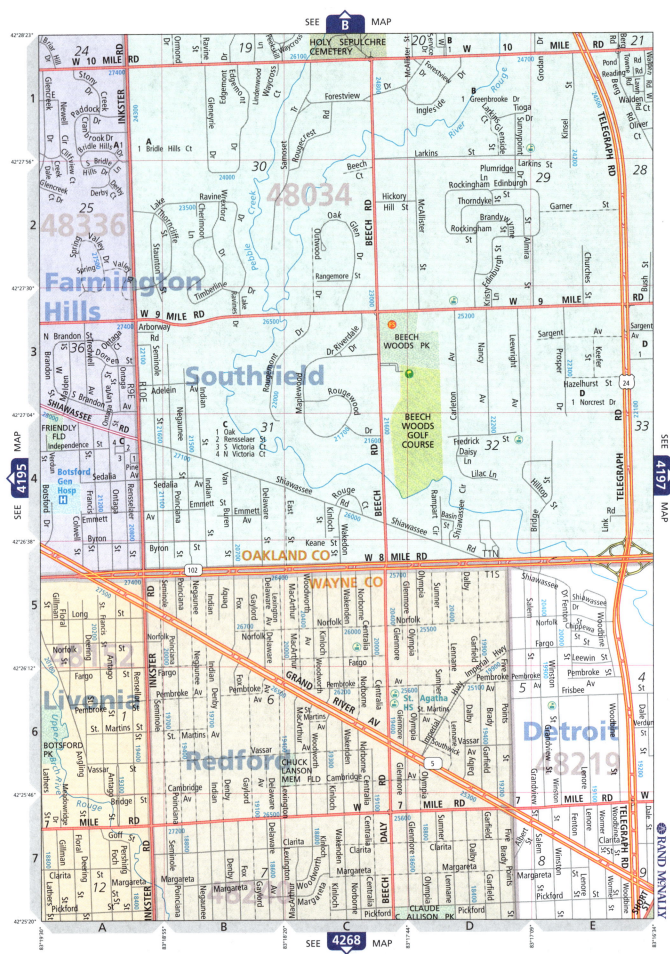

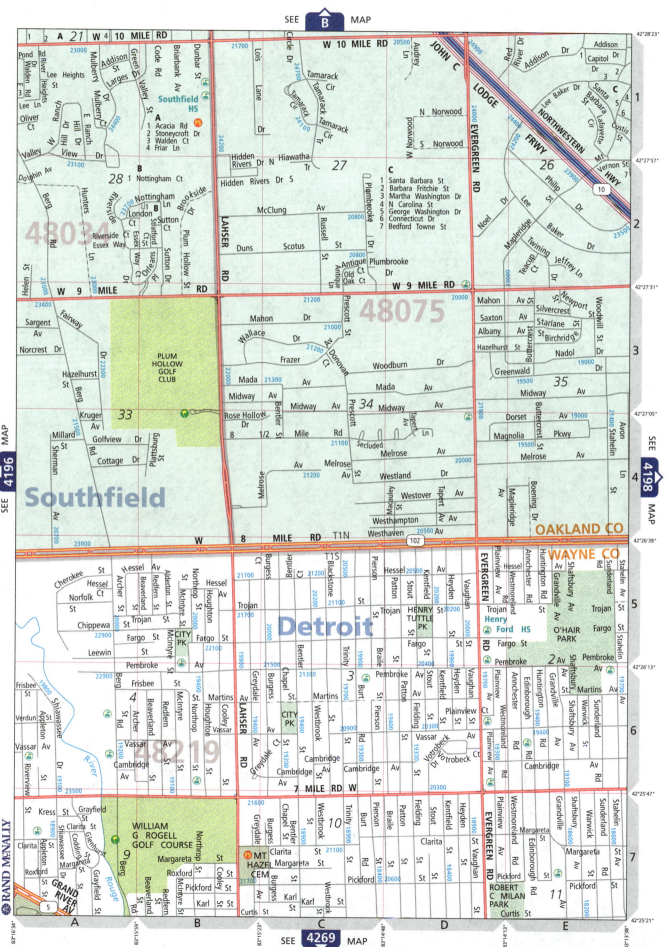

MAP
4197

1:24,000
1 in. = 2000 ft.
0   0.25   0.5
miles

SEE B MAP

SEE 4196 MAP

SEE 4198 MAP

SEE 4269 MAP

48034

48075

48219

Southfield

Detroit

OAKLAND CO

WAYNE CO

Plum Hollow Golf Club

William G Rogell Golf Course

Southfield HS
A
1 Acacia Rd
2 Stoneycroft Dr
3 Walden Ct
4 Friar Ln

C
1 Santa Barbara St
2 Barbara Fritchie St
3 Martha Washington Dr
4 N Carolina St
5 George Washington Dr
6 Connecticut Dr
7 Bedford Towne St

Henry Ford HS

O'HAIR PARK

HENRY TUTTLE PK

MT HAZEL CEM

ROBERT C MILAN PARK

CITY PK

RAND McNALLY

MAP
4198

1:24,000
1 in. = 2000 ft.

0   0.25   0.5
miles

SEE B MAP

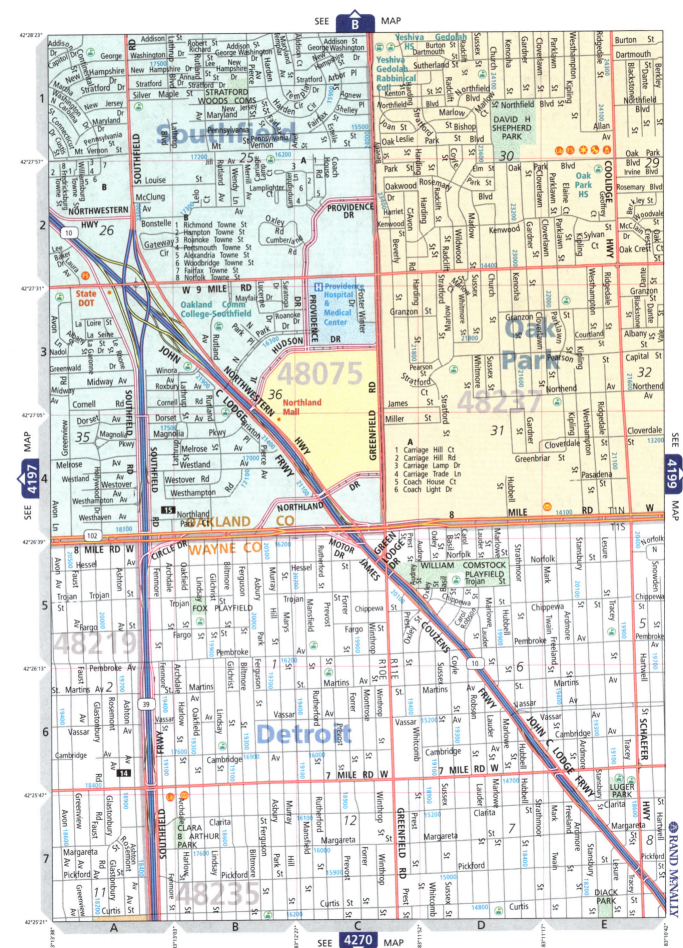

SEE 4197 MAP
SEE 4199 MAP
SEE 4270 MAP

RAND McNALLY

MAP
4199

1:24,000
1 in. = 2000 ft.

0   0.25   0.5
miles

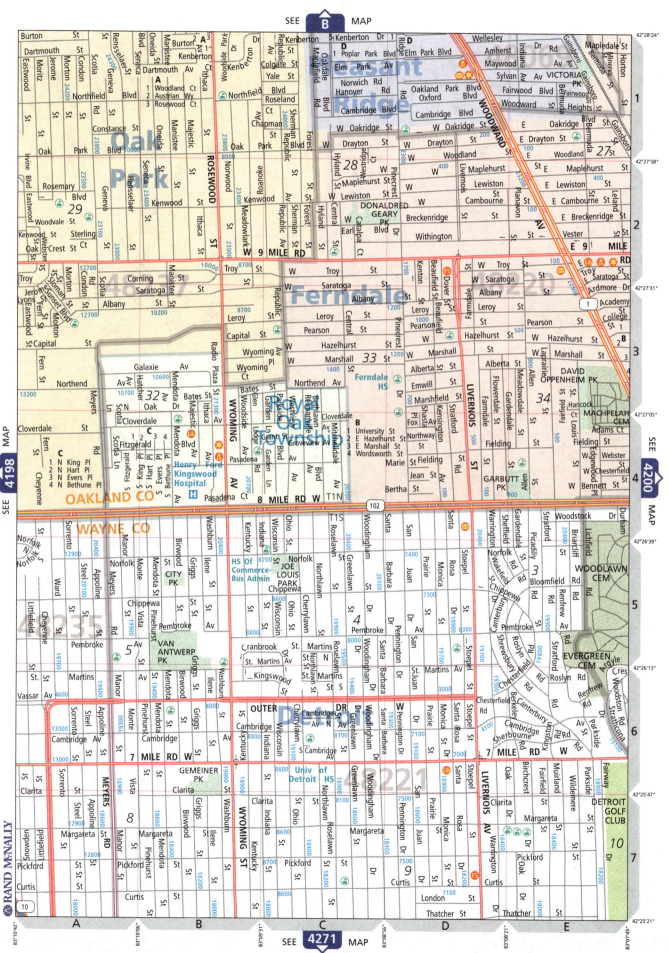

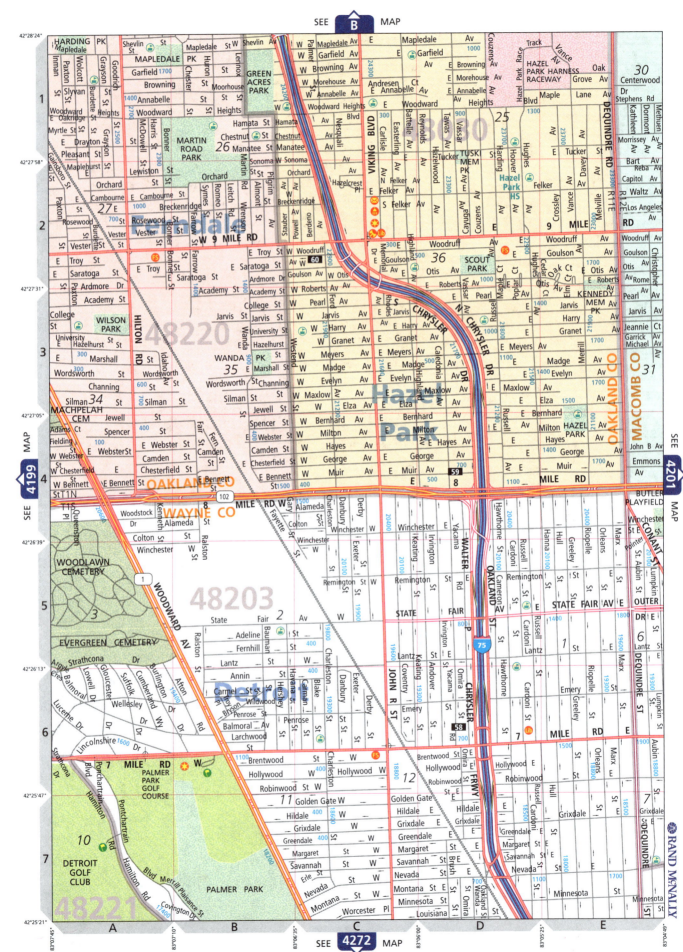

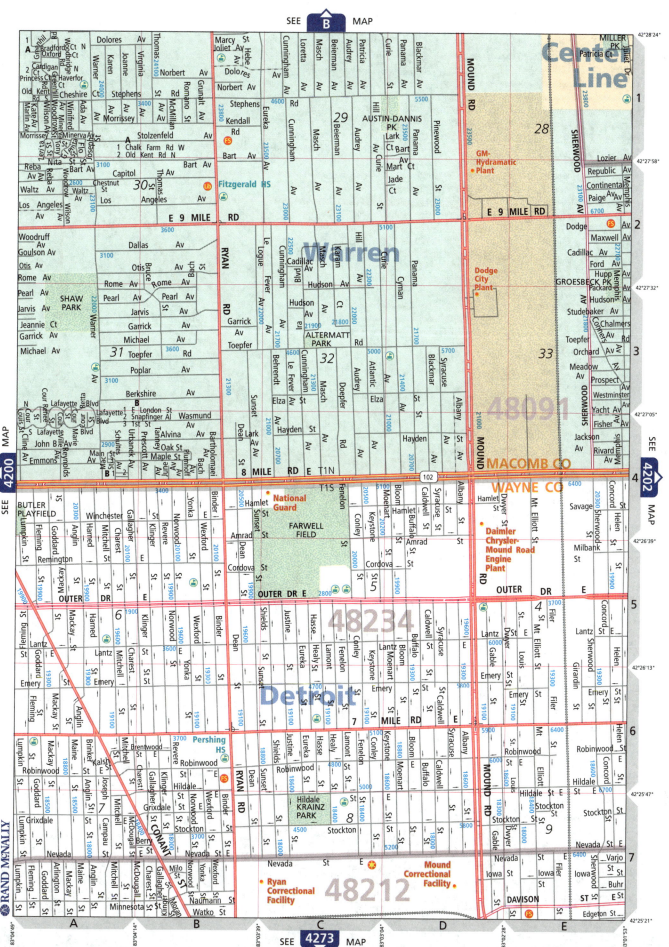

MAP
4201

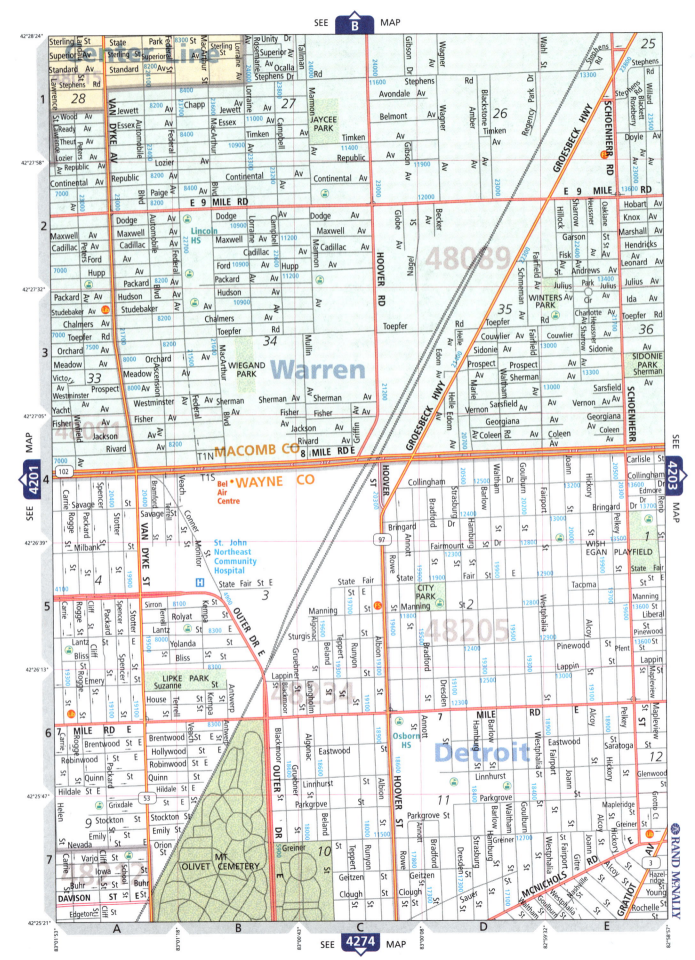

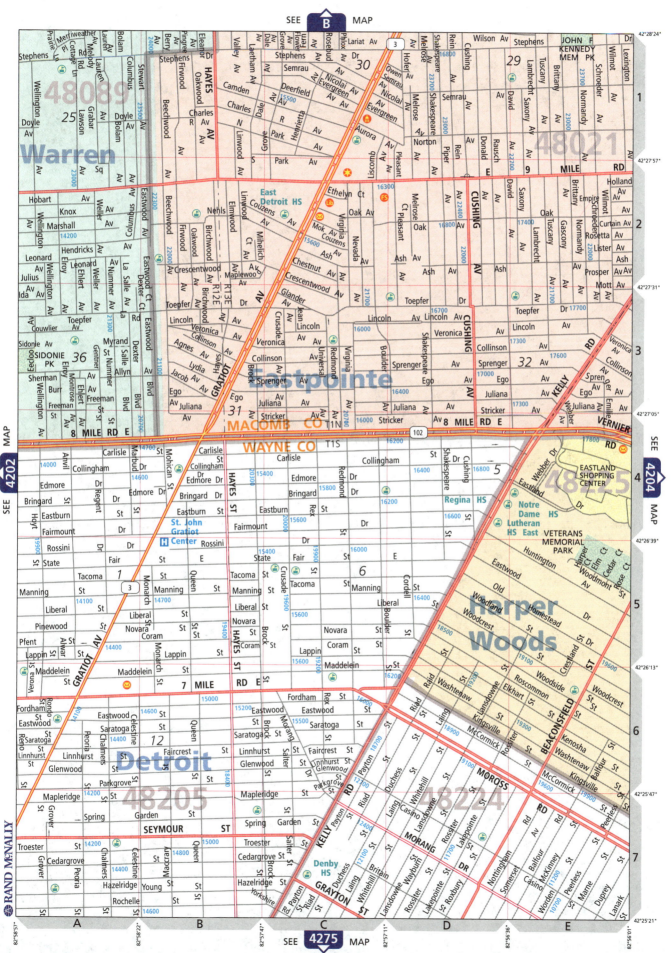

MAP
4203

1:24,000
1 in. = 2000 ft.

0   0.25   0.5
miles

SEE 4202 MAP

SEE 4204 MAP

48089
Warren
48021
Eastpointe
MACOMB CO
WAYNE CO
48225
EASTLAND SHOPPING CENTER
Harper Woods
Detroit 48205
48224
VETERANS MEMORIAL PARK
JOHN F KENNEDY MEM PK

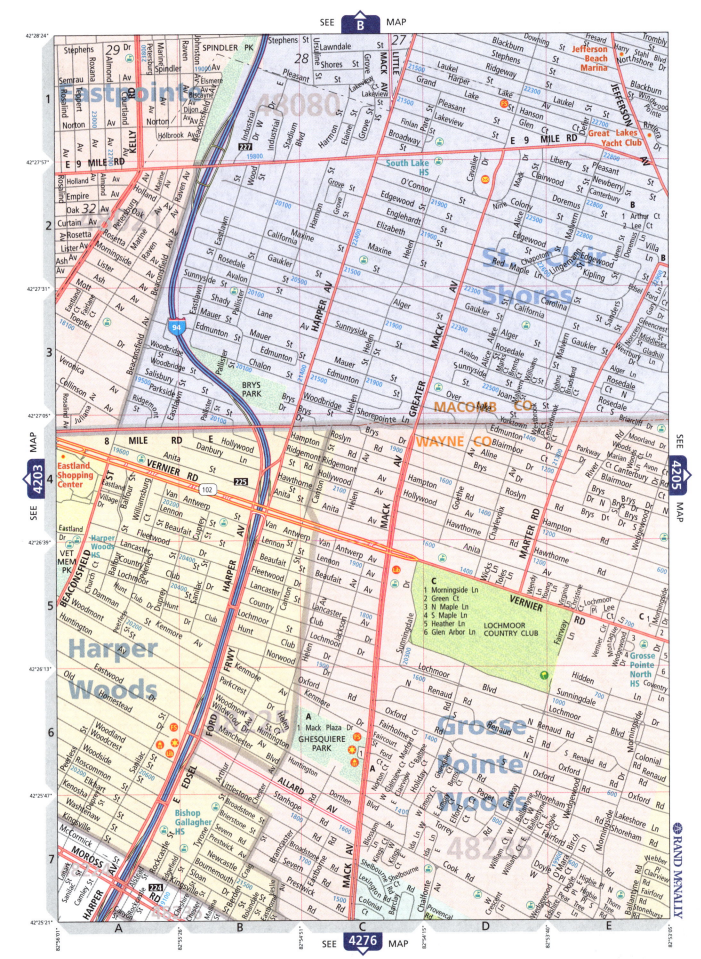

1:24,000
1 in. = 2000 ft.

0   0.25   0.5
miles

MAP
4205

SEE **B** MAP

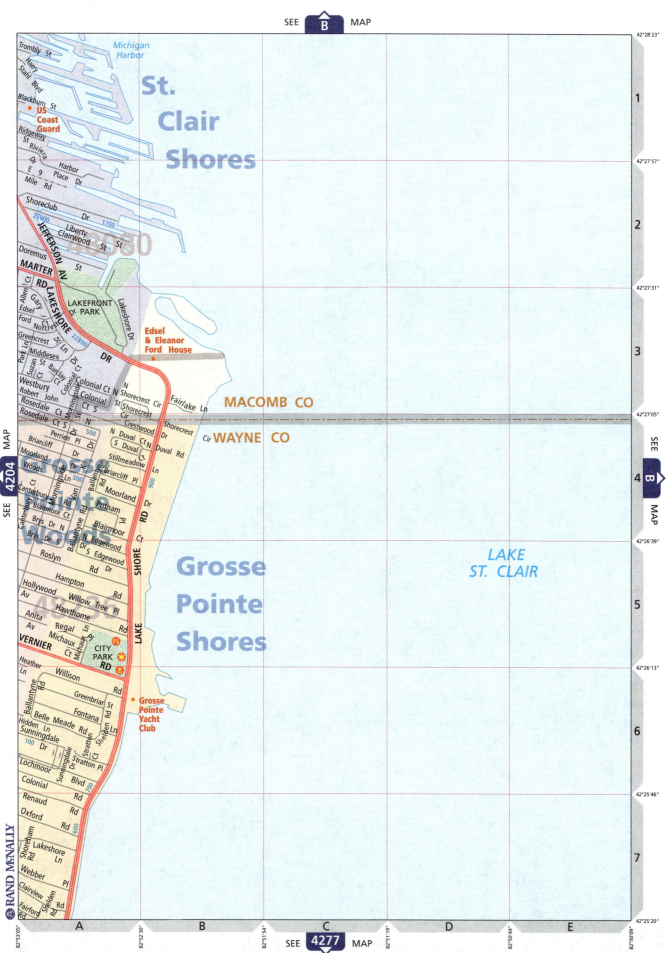

Michigan Harbor

Trombly St
Harry
Stahl Blvd
Blackburn St
• **US Coast Guard**
Ridgeway
St Riviera
Dr
E 9
Harbor
Mile Rd
Place Dr

St. Clair Shores

Shoreclub Dr
22800   1700
Liberty
Clairwood St
Doremus St
MARTER AV
MARTER RD
LAKESHORE
Allen Ct
Gary
Edsel
Ford St
Norcrest St Ln
22800
Greencrest
Middlesex
Park
Suzan St
Barclay Ct
Westbury
Robert John Ct
Rosedale
Rosedale Ct

LAKEFRONT PARK
Lakeshore Dr
Edsel & Eleanor Ford House

N Colonial Ct
Morningside
Colonial
Colonial
N Shorecrest Cir
N Shorecrest
St Shorecrest
Cir
Crestwood
Shorecrest
Fairlake Ln
MACOMB CO

N Duval Ct N
S Duval Ct
Shorecrest
Cir **WAYNE CO**

Briarcliff
Moorland
Woods Ct
Ln 500
Briarcliff Pl
N
Perrien Pl
Canterbury Ct
Morningside Rd
Blairmoor Ct
Brys Dr N
Brys
Dr
Roslyn
Canterbury Rd
Ballantyne Rd
Duval Rd
Stillmeadow Ln
Ballantyne Rd
900
Moorland
Putnam
Blairmoor
N Edgewood
Ct
Dr S Edgewood
Dr
Rd

Grosse Pointe Woods

Hampton
Hollywood Av
Willow Tree Pl
Hawthorne
Anita Av
Regal Pl
Michaux Ln
Michaux Ct
VERNIER RD
Heather Ln
Willison

SHORE RD
LAKE

LAKE ST. CLAIR

Grosse Pointe Shores

FS
CITY PARK
Rd

Willison Rd
Greenbriar St
Ballantyne Rd
Fontana
Belle Meade Rd
Hidden Ln
Sunningdale
100 Dr
Lochmoor
Colonial
Renaud
Oxford
Shoreham
Lakeshore
Webber
Clairview
Fairford
Rd

Sunningdale
Stratton Pl
Stratton Ct
Shelden Rd
Blvd 700
Rd
Rd
Rd
600
Rd
Ln
Pl
Shelden Rd

• **Grosse Pointe Yacht Club**

SEE **B** MAP
SEE **4204** MAP

RAND MCNALLY

42°28'23"
42°27'57"
42°27'31"
42°27'05"
42°26'39"
42°26'13"
42°25'46"
42°25'20"

1
2
3
4
5
6
7

A   B   C   D   E

82°53'05"
82°52'30"
82°51'54"
82°51'19"
82°50'44"
82°50'08"

MAP
4258

1:24,000
1 in. = 2000 ft.

0   0.25   0.5
miles

SEE **4186** MAP

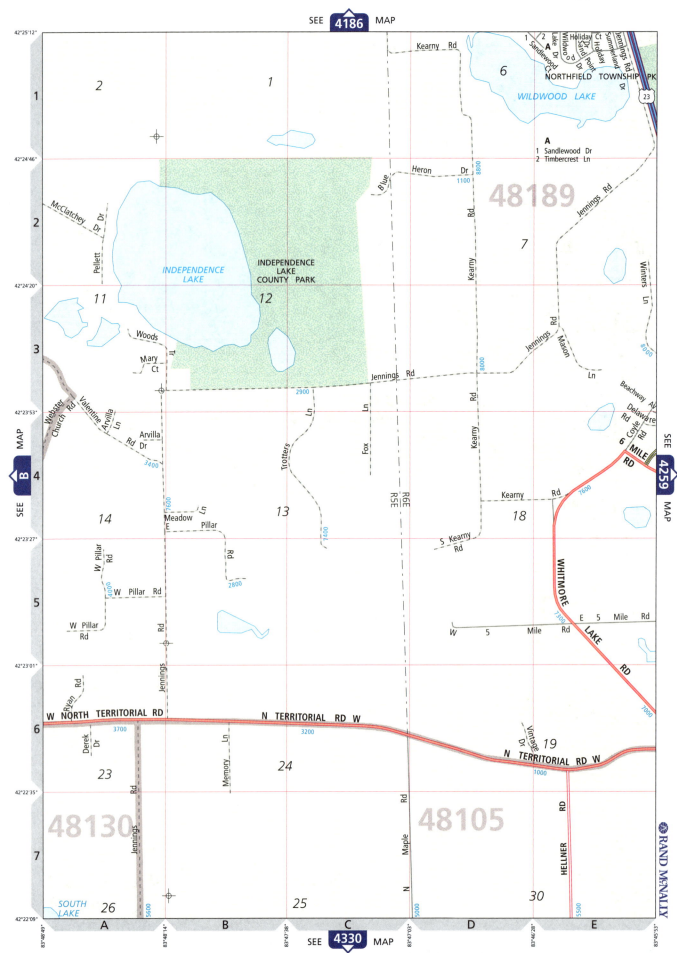

42°25'12"

Kearny Rd

2

1

6

NORTHFIELD TOWNSHIP PK

WILDWOOD LAKE

A
1 Sandlewood Dr
2 Timbercrest Ln

23

42°24'46"

Heron Dr
Blue
1100   8800

48189

McClatchey Dr

2

7

Pellett Dr

42°24'20"

INDEPENDENCE LAKE

INDEPENDENCE LAKE COUNTY PARK

11

12

Kearny Rd

Winters Ln

8000

Woods Tr

Jennings Rd
Mason Ln

3

Mary Ct

Jennings Rd
2900

Kearny Rd
8000

Beachway Al
Delaware Rd
Coyle Rd

42°23'53"

Webster Church Rd

Valentine Rd

Arvilla Ln

Ln

Ln

6 MILE RD

SEE **4259** MAP

Arvilla Dr
3400

Trotters

Fox

Kearny Rd
7600

4

13

R6E
R5E

Kearny Rd
1400

Kearny Rd

18

14

Meadow E

Pillar

S Kearny Rd

42°23'27"

W Pillar Rd

Rd
2800

WHITMORE

5

W Pillar Rd
4000

Jennings Rd

E 5 Mile Rd

LAKE

W Pillar Rd

W 5 Mile Rd
7300

RD

42°23'01"

7000

Ryan Rd

6

W NORTH TERRITORIAL RD

N TERRITORIAL RD W

Derek Dr

3700

Memory Ln

3200

Vintage Dr

19

N TERRITORIAL RD W

23

24

1000

42°22'35"

Jennings Rd

Maple Rd

HELLNER RD

48130

48105

7

SOUTH LAKE

26

5600

25

N
5000

30

5500

A   B   C   D   E

42°22'09"

SEE **4330** MAP

83°48'49"   83°48'14"   83°47'38"   83°47'03"   83°46'28"   83°55'28"

RAND McNALLY

MAP
4259

SEE **4187** MAP

1:24,000
1 in. = 2000 ft.

0   0.25   0.5
miles

WHITMORE LAKE DR
E SHORE

Harbor Cove Cir
Hillcrest Dr
Brookside Cir
Whittier St
6
NORTHFIELD TOWNSHIP PK
Whitmore Lake HS
Jennings Rd
A

Lillian Ct
Front St
Phlox Dr
Elizabeth Dr
Ridge Dr
Lakeview Dr
Pine St
Tillman Ct
Lincoln
Garfield
Ash
Forest
Grove
Dr
Butternut
Walnut Dr
Pine
Crestlawn
Cove
Waterlily Dr
Lake
Posey
Pine Dr
Posey Ct
Posey Dr
Maywin
Ivylawn Dr
Cherry Ct
Apple Dr
Sunflower Dr
Garden Ct
Posey Crossing
7 Mile Rd Ct
Blossom Dr
5

A
1 Longfellow St

8

Anna Dr
Westbrook
7
Main St
Westbrook
7 Mile Rd

Donna Ln
7 MILE RD
Soave Ln

9
NOLLAR RD

Pheasant
Spencer
Run
SPENCER RD
10

48178

Schrum Dr
Greenland Av
Lake View
Park Rd
Beach Rd
Winters Ln
Coyle Rd
Shady Beach Dr
Grove Dr
Elm Dr
Beachway
Delaware Rd
Maplegrove Dr
Glenmoor Dr
Shady Ln
Fairmont Dr
Dartmoor Dr
Ideal Pl
Heather Ln
50
6 Mile Rd
17

HORSESHOE LAKE
Lake Shore Dr
Hillsdale Av
Highland Av
Raphael Av
Leonard Av
Edmund Av
Oliver St
S Horseshoe Blvd
Capital Av
Madouse Ct

Mile RD
Plumbery
St Andrew Dr
Turnberry Ct
6
LINKS OF WHITMORE LAKE GOLF COURSE

8000
NOLLAR RD
16

15
SPENCER RD

B
1 Beachway Av
2 Delaware Rd
3 Grove Dr

48189

5 MILE RD
5

E 5 Mile Rd
E 5 Mile Rd
E 5 Mile Rd
Mile Rd
Peninsula Point Dr
7300
NOLLAR RD

42°23'03"

19
Whitmore Mile Rd
NORTH
20
49
TERRITORIAL RD
Jomar
Hoban Wy
21
Spencer Rd
22

7000
E
E NORTH TERRITORIAL RD
NOLLAR RD
1600

23
WHITMORE LAKE RD
6100

30 48105 29
NORTH TERRITORIAL RD
28
NOLLAR RD
27

RAND McNALLY

A   B   C   D   E

SEE **4331** MAP

SEE **4258** MAP
SEE **4260** MAP

MAP
4260

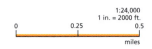

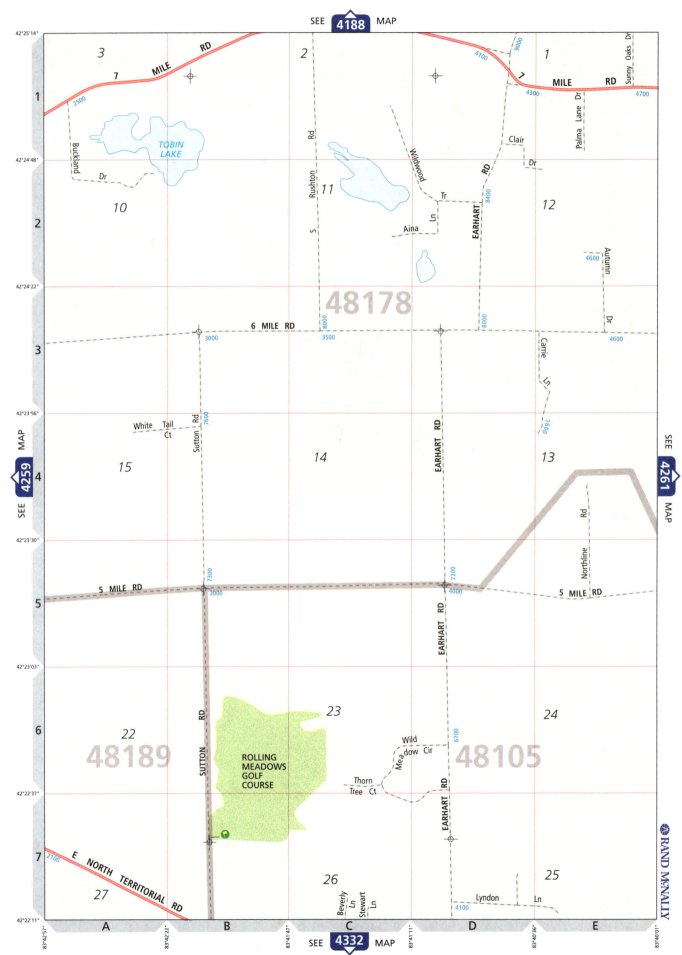

1:24,000
1 in. = 2000 ft.

0   0.25   0.5
miles

MAP
4261

SEE 4189 MAP

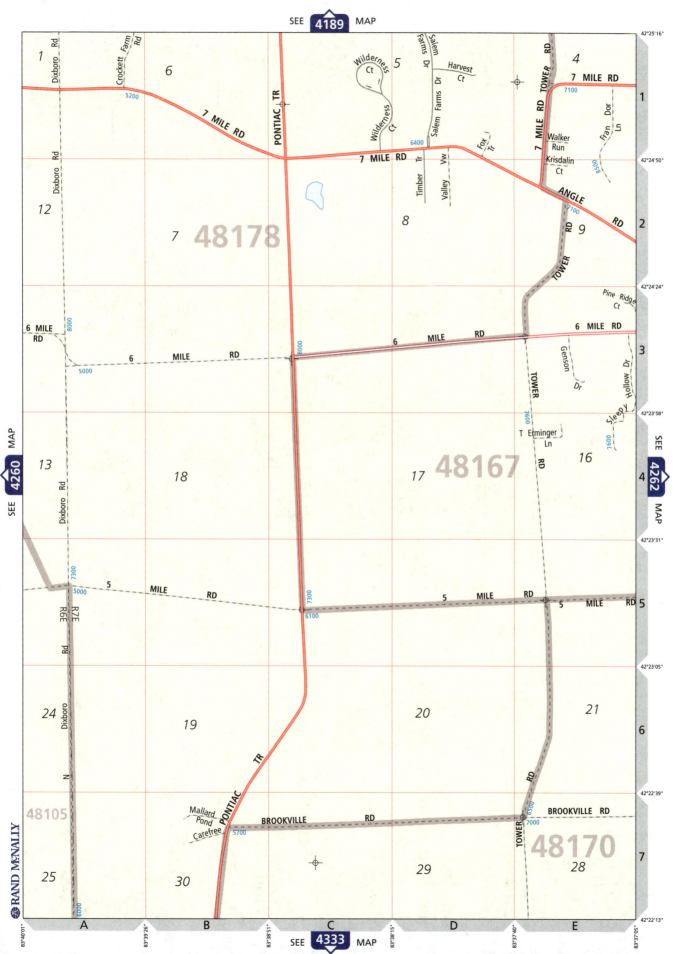

42°25'16"

1   Dixboro Rd   Crockett Farm Rd   6   Wilderness Ct   5   Salem Farms Dr   Harvest Ct   TOWER RD   4   7 MILE RD   1   7100

42°25'16"

5200   7 MILE RD   PONTIAC TR   Wilderness Ct   Salem Farms Dr   7 MILE RD   Fran Dor Ln   8500

42°24'50"

Dixboro Rd   7 MILE RD   6400   7 MILE RD   Timber Tr   Valley Vw   Fox Tr   7 MILE RD   Walker Run   Krisdalin Ct

12   7   48178   8   ANGLE RD   9   7100   ANGLE RD   2

42°24'24"

TOWER RD   Pine Ridge Ct

8000   6 MILE RD   6 MILE RD   Genson Dr   Sleepy Hollow Dr

6 MILE RD   6 MILE RD   3

5000   6 MILE RD   8000   TOWER RD   7600   T Etminger Ln   16   1600   Sleepy

42°23'58"

SEE 4260 MAP   13   18   17   48167   42°23'58"

SEE 4262 MAP

42°23'31"

7300   5000   R6E R7E   5 MILE RD   7300   6100   5 MILE RD   5 MILE RD   5

42°23'05"

24   Dixboro Rd N   19   20   RD   21   6

42°22'39"

48105   Mallard Pond   PONTIAC TR   Carefree   5700   BROOKVILLE RD   6500   7000   BROOKVILLE RD   48170

25   30   29   TOWER RD   28   7

42°22'13"

A   B   C   D   E

83°40'01"   83°39'26"   83°38'51"   83°38'15"   83°37'40"   83°37'05"

SEE 4333 MAP

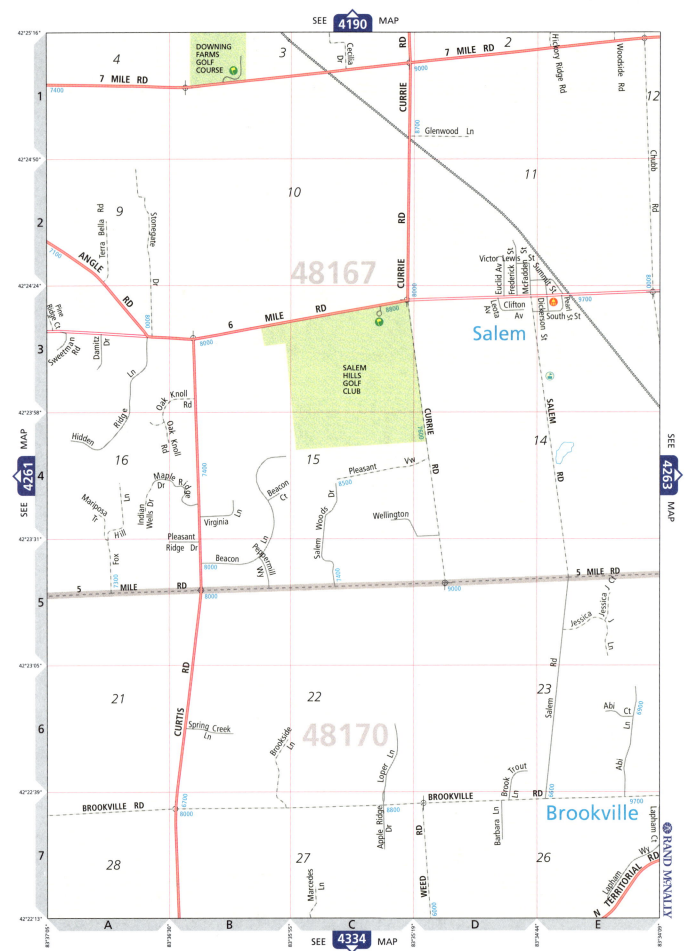

MAP
4262

1:24,000
1 in. = 2000 ft.
0   0.25   0.5
miles

SEE 4190 MAP

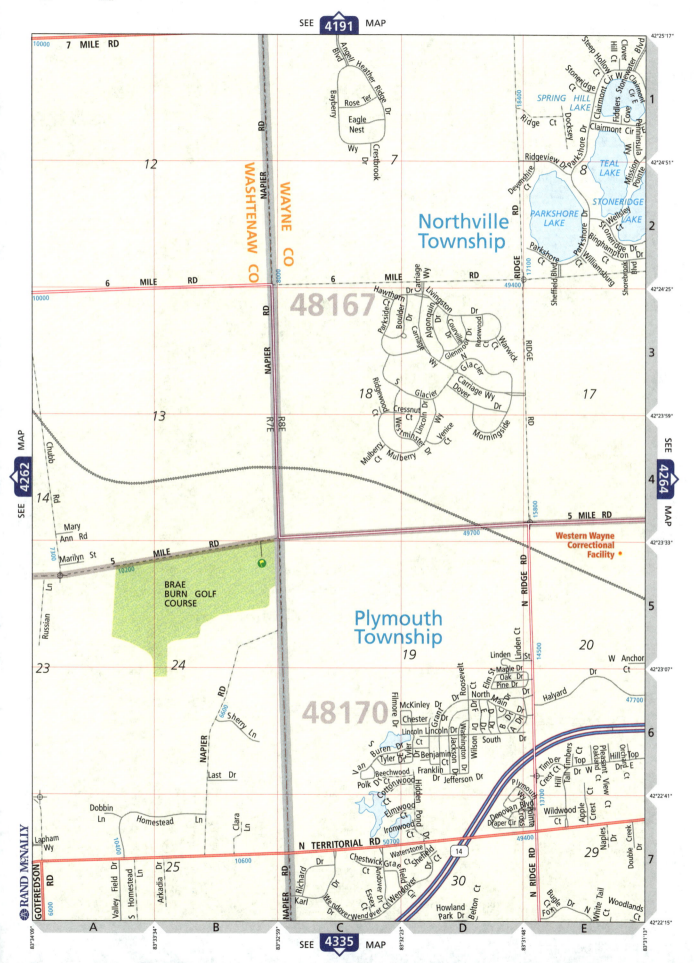

MAP
4263

1:24,000
1 in. = 2000 ft.
0   0.25   0.5
miles

SEE 4191 MAP

7 MILE RD

Angell Blvd
Heather Ridge Dr
Bayberry
Rose Ter
Eagle Nest Wy
Crestbrook Dr

WASHTENAW CO
WAYNE CO
NAPIER RD

12
7

Northville Township

Steep Hollow
Hill Ct
Clover
Stonewater Blvd
Stoneridge Ct
Fiddlers Cove
Clairmont Cir E
Clairmont Cir N
Clairmont Cir
Peninsula
Mission NW
Pointe

SPRING HILL LAKE
TEAL LAKE
STONERIDGE LAKE

Ridge Ct
Docksey
Parkshore
Wellsley Ct
Ridgeview Dr
Devonshire Ct
Binghampton
Williamsburg
Shorebrook Blvd
Stoneridge Dr
Parkshore Dr
Parkshore Ct
Sheffield Blvd

PARKSHORE LAKE

8

1

2

6 MILE RD
6 MILE RD
RIDGE RD

48167

Hawthorn Ct
Papishire Dr
Bowden Dr
Carriage Wy
Livingston Dr
Algonquin Dr
Courville Dr
Rosewood Ct
Glenmore
Warwick Ct
Glacier
Carriage Wy
Dover Dr
Ridgewood Ct
S Glacier
Cressnut Ct
Lincoln Dr
Westminster Dr
Venice Wy
Morningside
Mulberry Ct
Mulberry

18
17

RIDGE RD

3

4

Chubb Rd

SEE 4262 MAP

13

14

Mary Ann Rd
Marilyn St
5 MILE RD
5 MILE RD

Russian Ln

BRAE BURN GOLF COURSE

Plymouth Township

19

Western Wayne Correctional Facility

N RIDGE RD

Linden Ct
Linden St
W Anchor Ct
20

SEE 4264 MAP

5

23

24

NAPIER RD

Sherry Ln

Last Dr

48170

Filmore Dr
McKinley Dr
Chester Ct
Lincoln Lincoln Ct
Grant Dr
Roosevelt
Maple Dr
Oak Dr
Pine Dr
North
Main
A Dr
B Dr
C Dr
D Dr
South
Washington Dr
Wilson
Halyard Dr

19

6

Dobbin Ln
Homestead Ln
Clara Ln

Lapham Wy

Van Buren Dr
Tyler Dr
Beechwood Dr
Polk Ct
Cottonwood Ct
Hidden Pond
Elmwood
Ironwood
Benjamin Ct
Franklin Dr
Jefferson Dr
Timber Crest Hill
Tall Timbers Dr W
Top Dr W
Pleasant View Ct
Oakland Ct
Orchard Top Dr E
Wildwood Ct
Apple Crest
Plymouth Pointe Blvd
Donovan Blvd
Draper Cir
Naples Ct
Double Creek Ct

N TERRITORIAL RD

30
29

7

GOTFREDSON RD
Valley Field Dr
S Homestead Ln
Arkadia Dr
25
Richard Dr
Karl Dr
Wendover Dr
Essex Ct
Wendover Ct
Wendover Cir
Chestwick Ct
Andover Dr
Grae Ct
Sheffield Ct
Waterstone Dr
Howland Park Dr
Belton Ct
Bugle Ct
Fox Dr
White Tail Ct
Woodlands Ct

SEE 4335 MAP

A   B   C   D   E

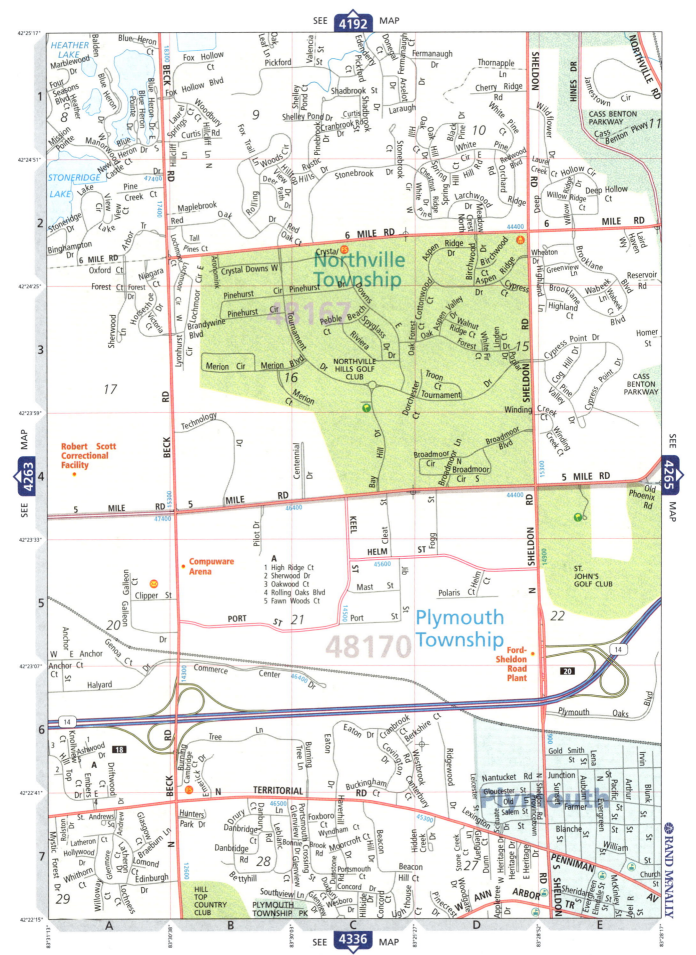

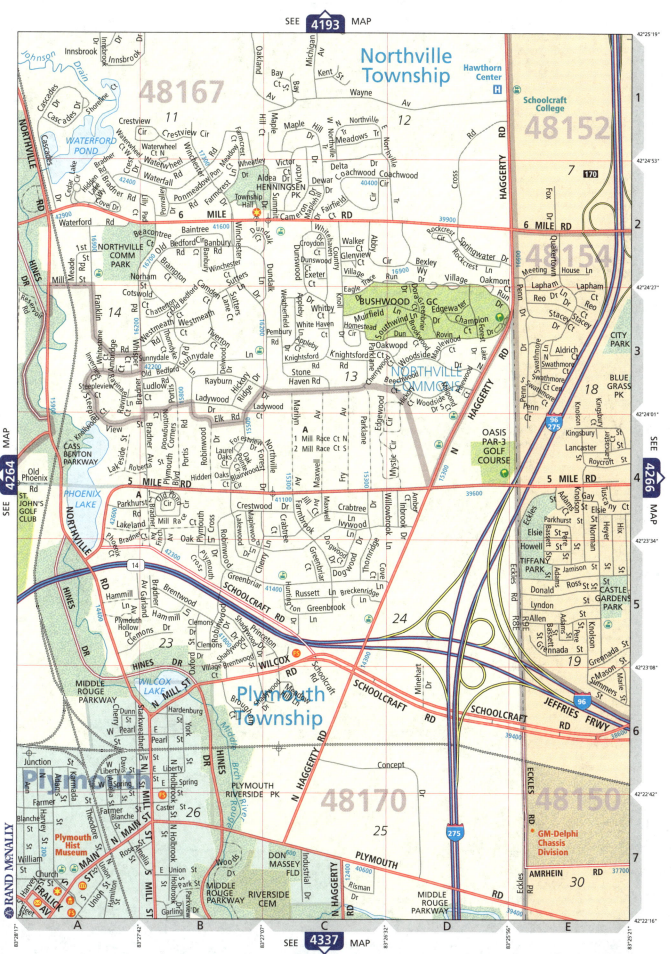

MAP
4265

SEE 4264 MAP

SEE 4266 MAP

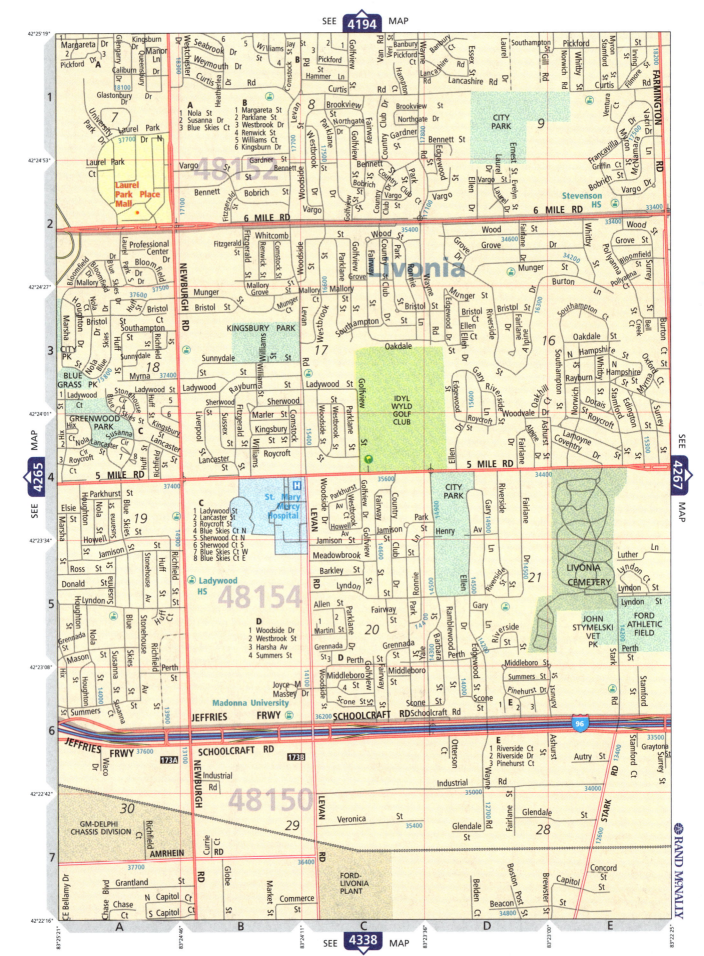

MAP
4266

1:24,000
1 in. = 2000 ft.

0   0.25   0.5
miles

SEE 4194 MAP

SEE 4265 MAP

SEE 4267 MAP

SEE 4338 MAP

RAND MCNALLY

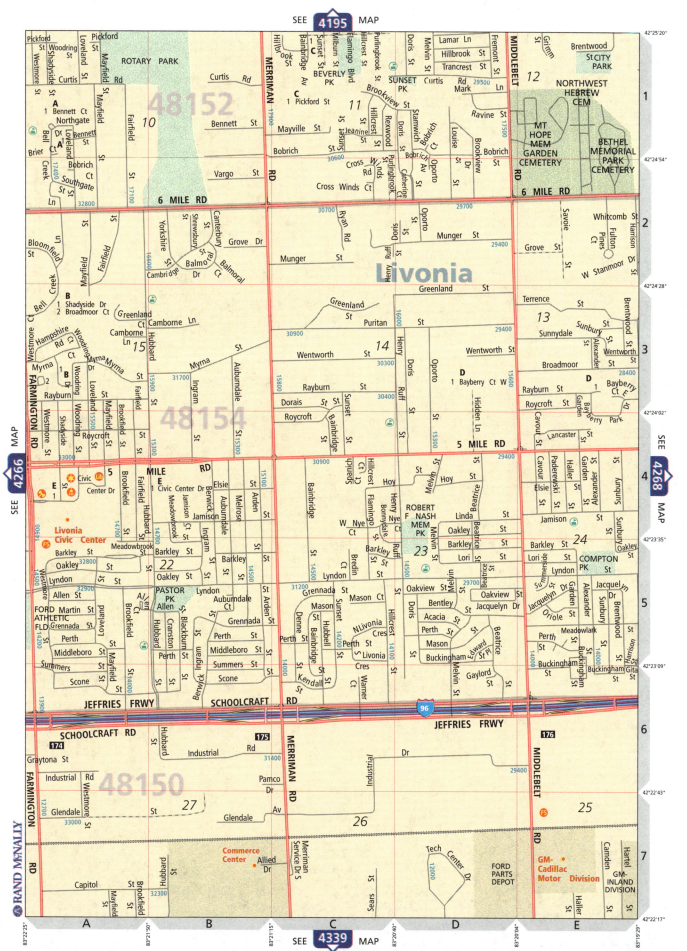

MAP
4267

1:24,000
1 in. = 2000 ft.

0   0.25   0.5
miles

SEE 4195 MAP

SEE 4266 MAP

SEE 4268 MAP

SEE 4339 MAP

48152

48154

48150

Livonia

ROTARY PARK

BEVERLY PK

SUNSET PK

NORTHWEST HEBREW CEM

MT HOPE MEM GARDEN CEMETERY

BETHEL MEMORIAL PARK CEMETERY

Brentwood St CITY PARK

6 MILE RD

5 MILE RD

5 MILE RD

Livonia Civic Center

ROBERT F NASH MEM PK

COMPTON PK

PASTOR PK

FORD ATHLETIC FLD

JEFFRIES FRWY

SCHOOLCRAFT RD

SCHOOLCRAFT RD

JEFFRIES FRWY

Commerce Center

FORD PARTS DEPOT

GM-Cadillac Motor Division

GM-INLAND DIVISION

RAND McNALLY

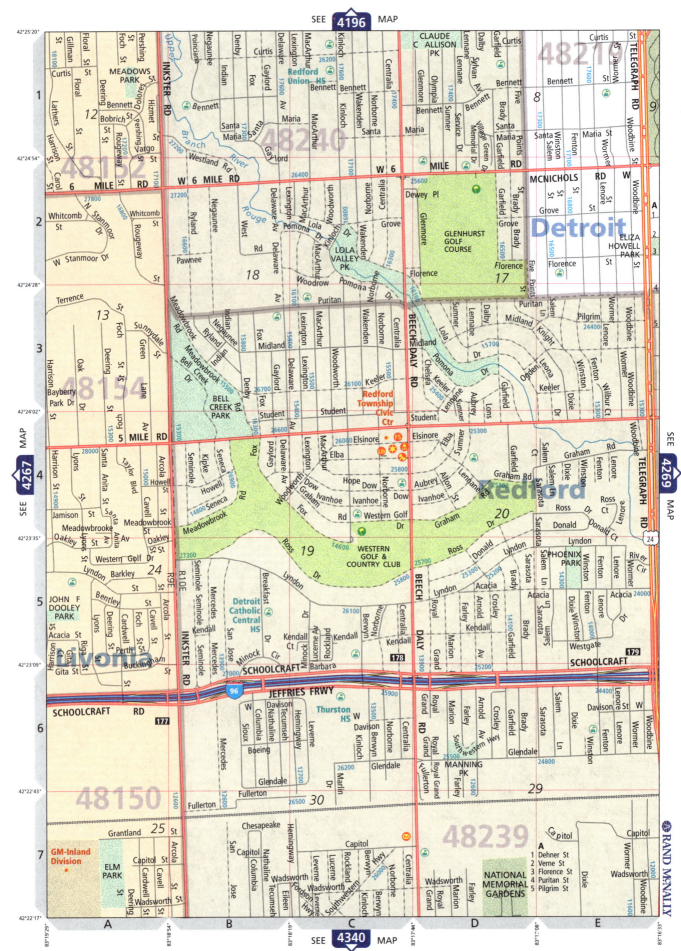

MAP
4268

1:24,000
1 in. = 2000 ft.

0   0.25   0.5
miles

SEE **4196** MAP

SEE **4267** MAP

SEE **4269** MAP

SEE **4340** MAP

RAND M℃NALLY

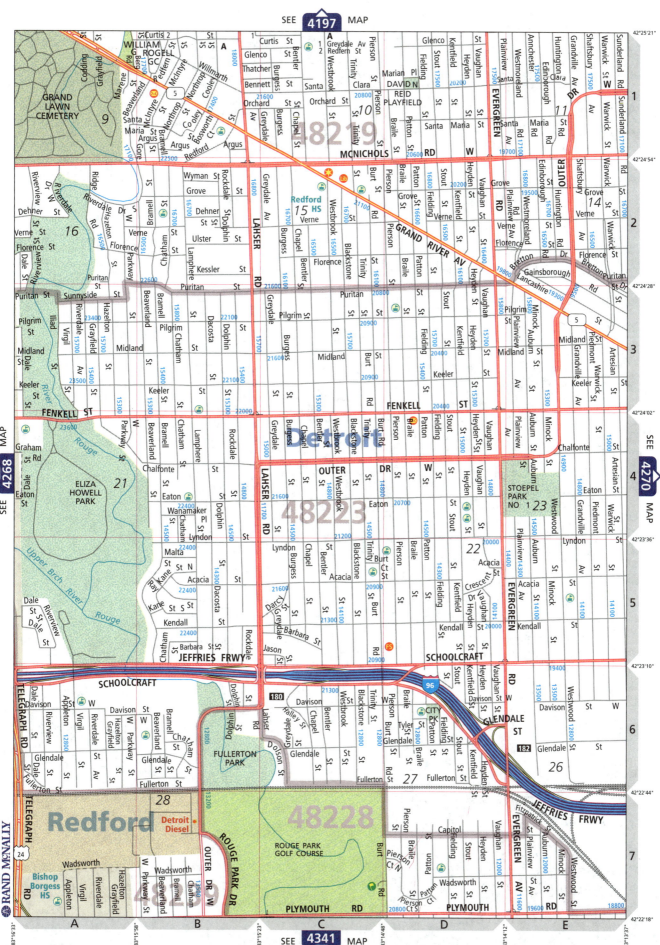

MAP
4269

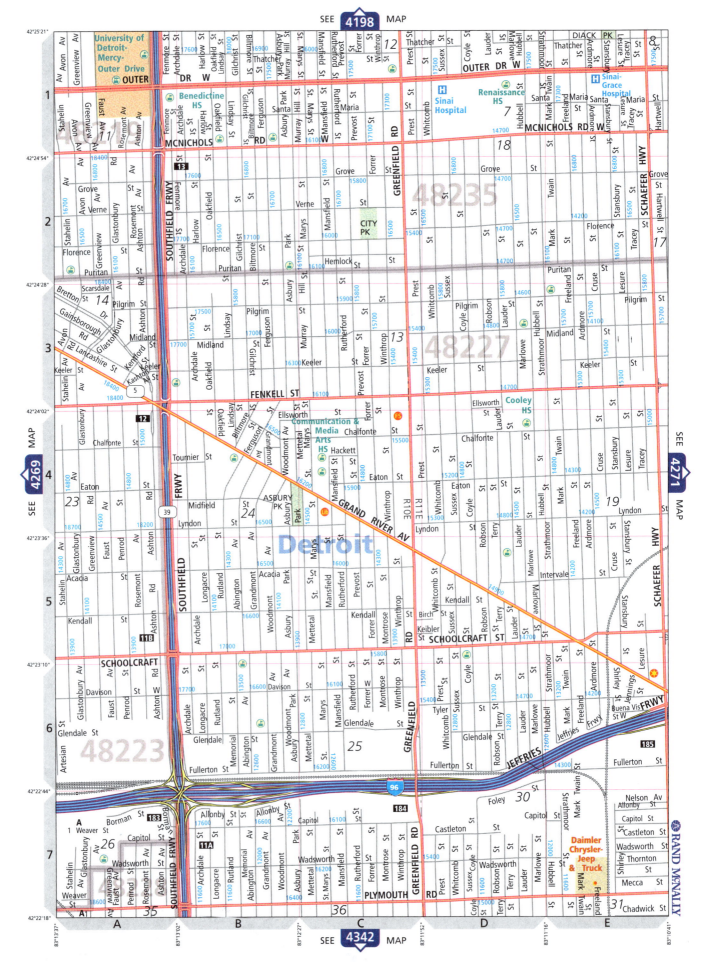

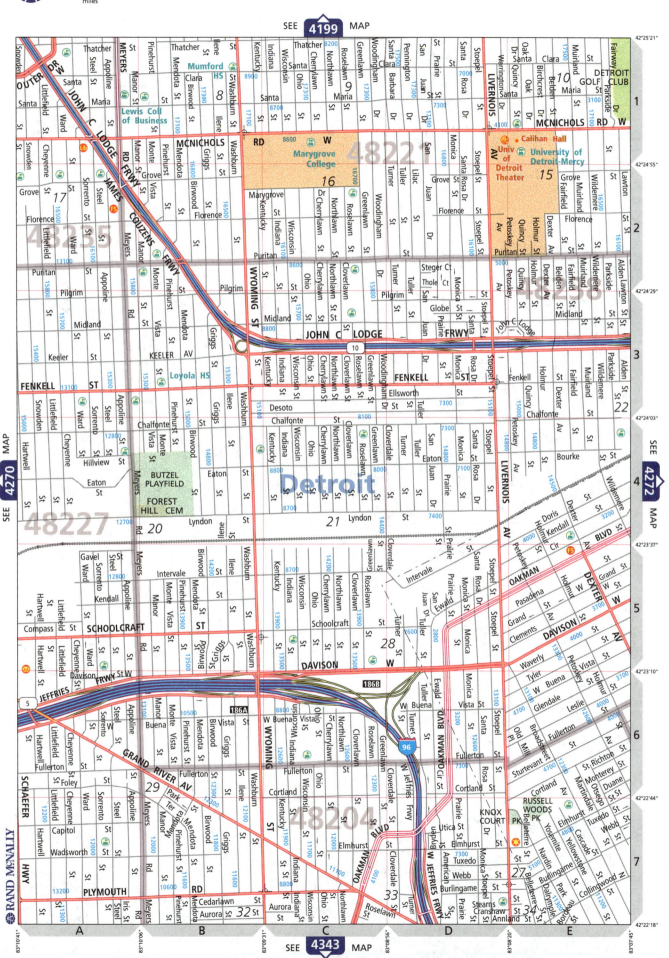

MAP
4271

1:24,000
1 in. = 2000 ft.
0   0.25   0.5
miles

SEE 4199 MAP

SEE 4270 MAP

SEE 4272 MAP

SEE 4343 MAP

RAND McNALLY

MAP
4272

1:24,000
1 in. = 2000 ft.

0   0.25   0.5
miles

SEE **4200** MAP

SEE **4271** MAP

SEE **4273** MAP

SEE **4344** MAP

RAND McNALLY

MAP
4273

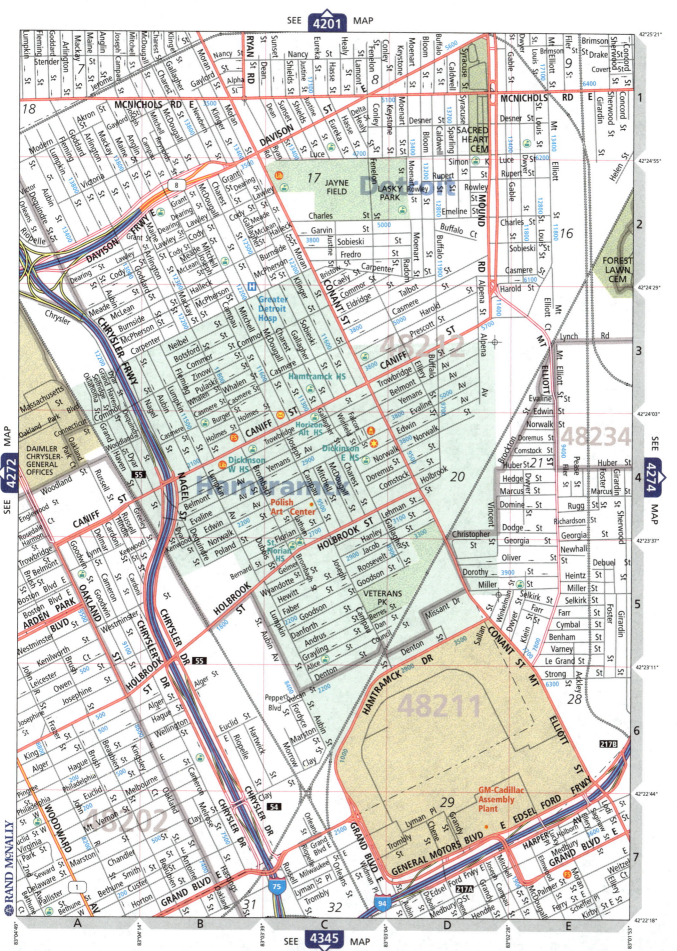

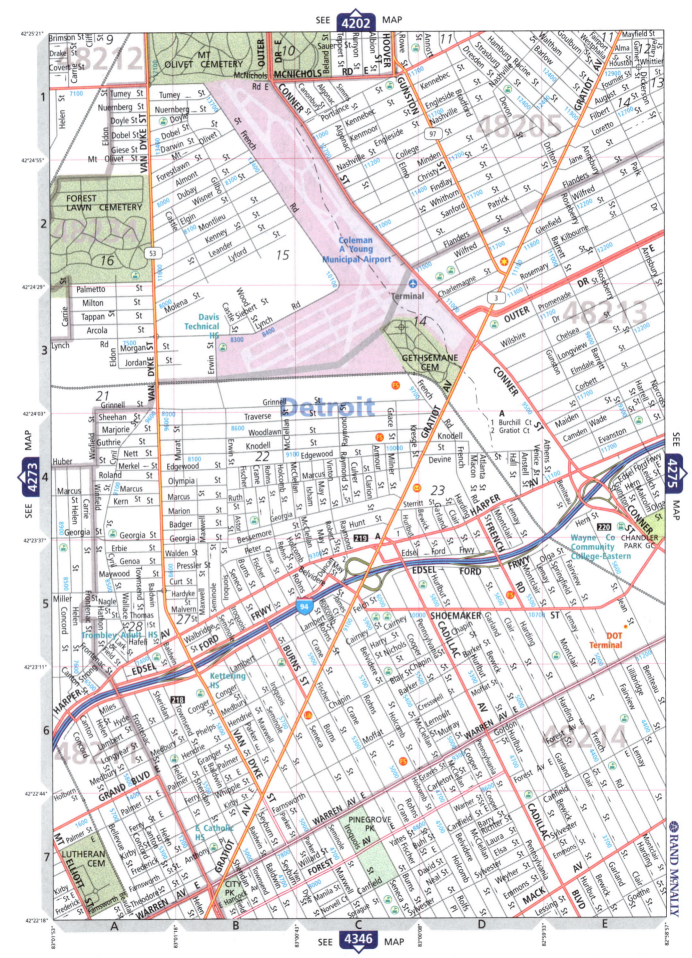

MAP
4274

1:24,000
1 in. = 2000 ft.

0   0.25   0.5
miles

SEE **4202** MAP

SEE **4273** MAP

SEE **4275** MAP

SEE **4346** MAP

RAND McNALLY

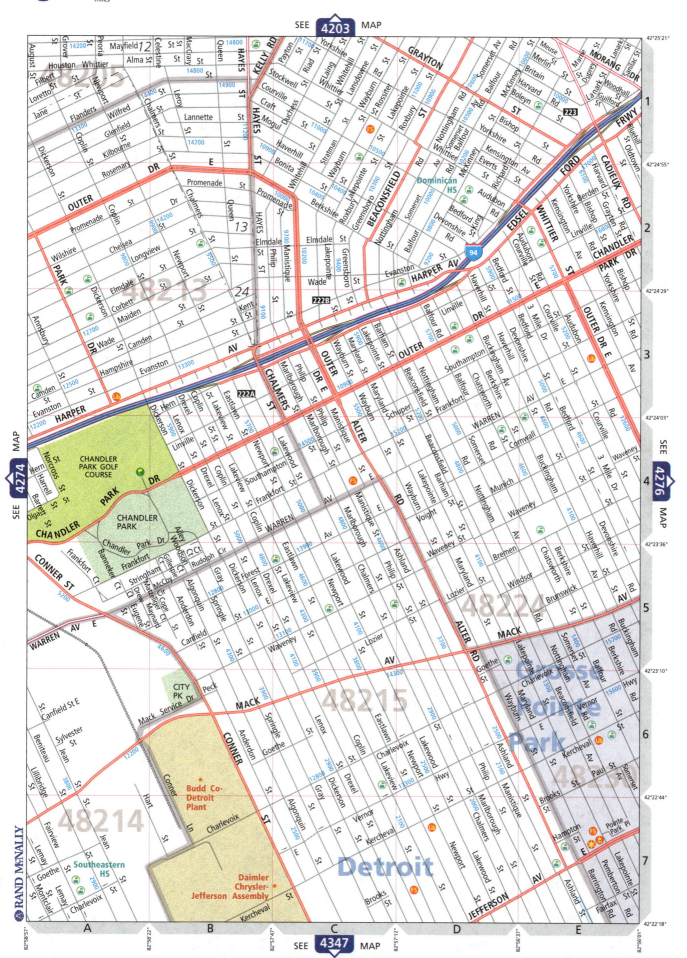

1:24,000
1 in. = 2000 ft.

miles

SEE 4274 MAP

SEE 4276 MAP

RAND M°NALLY

Detroit

CHANDLER PARK GOLF COURSE

CHANDLER PARK

Dominican HS

Southeastern HS

Budd Co- Detroit Plant

Daimler Chrysler- Jefferson Assembly

CITY PK

Grosse Pointe Park

48215

48213

48224

48214

48225

MAP
4276

1:24,000
1 in. = 2000 ft.

0   0.25   0.5
miles

SEE **4204** MAP

LAKE
ST.
CLAIR

SEE **4275** MAP

SEE **4277** MAP

SEE **4348** MAP

RAND McNALLY

MAP
4277

N

1:24,000
1 in. = 2000 ft.

0   0.25   0.5
miles

SEE 4205 MAP

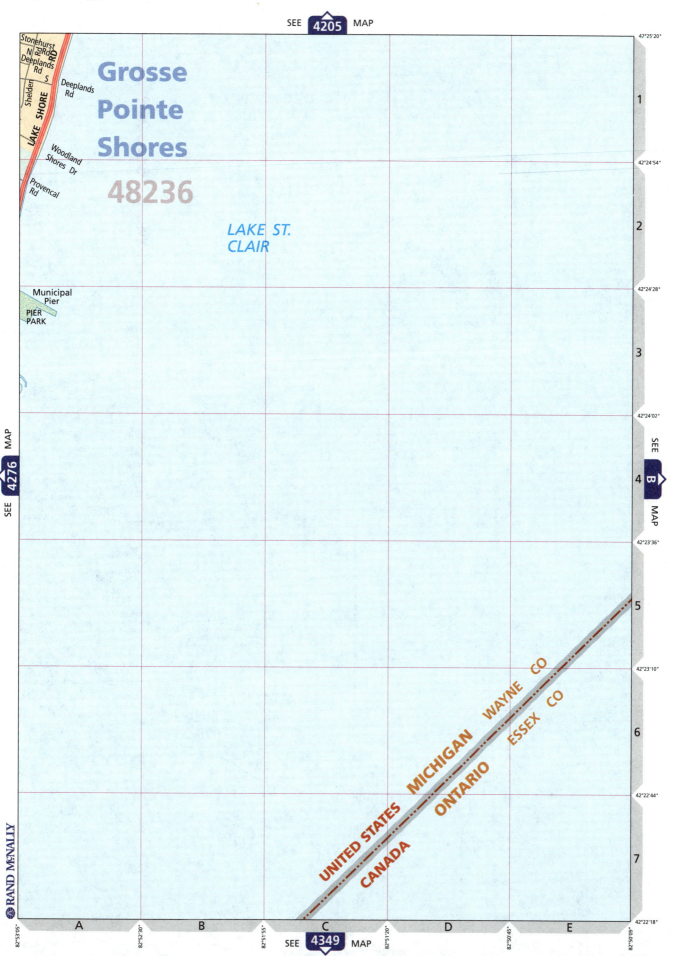

Stonehurst
N 2nd Rd
Deeplands S
Rd
Shelden

LAKE SHORE RD

Deeplands
Rd

Grosse
Pointe
Shores

48236

Woodland
Shores Dr

Provencal
Rd

LAKE ST.
CLAIR

Municipal
Pier

PIER
PARK

42°25'20"

1

42°24'54"

2

42°24'28"

3

42°24'02"

SEE 4276 MAP

SEE B MAP

4

42°23'36"

5

42°23'10"

6

42°22'44"

7

42°22'18"

UNITED STATES
CANADA
MICHIGAN
ONTARIO
WAYNE CO
ESSEX CO

RAND McNALLY

A   B   C   D   E

82°53'05"   82°52'30"   82°51'55"   82°51'20"   82°50'45"   82°50'09"

SEE 4349 MAP

MAP
4329

1:24,000
1 in. = 2000 ft.

0   0.25   0.5
miles

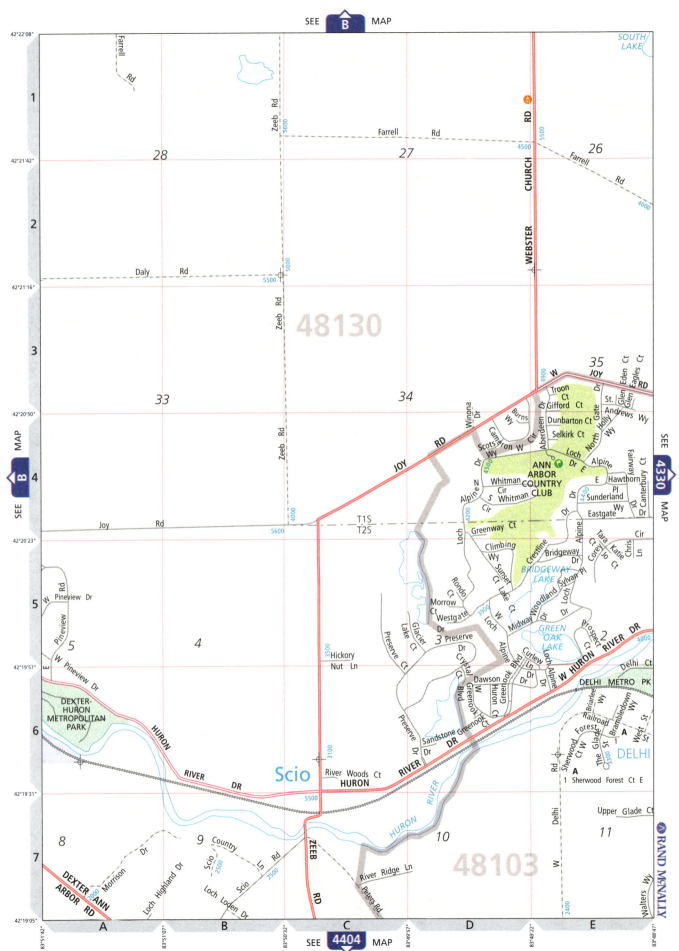

42°22'08"

Farrell Rd

1

Zeeb Rd
5600

Farrell   Rd

28   **27**   4500   5500   **26**

42°21'42"

CHURCH   RD

Farrell   Rd

4000

2

WEBSTER

42°21'16"

Daly   Rd

5000

Zeeb   Rd
5500

48130

3

Zeeb Rd

33   **34**   4900   **35**   Eden Ct   Eagles Ct

W   JOY   RD

Troon Ct

Gifford Ct   St.   Glen   Glen
Andrews   Wy

Winona Dr   Burns Wy   Aberdeen Dr   Dunbarton Ct   North Holly Gate   Wy

42°20'50"

Scotsman Wy   Cameron W   W Cir   Selkirk Ct

JOY   RD   4500

Loch E   Alpine

MAP

B

4

Alpine N   Whitman Cir   **ANN ARBOR COUNTRY CLUB**   Alpine E   Fairway Dr   Hawthorn

SEE

Alpine S   S Whitman Cir   4400   Sunderland Wy   Canterbury Dr

4200   Eastgate Dr

Joy   Rd   4000   T1S   Greenway Ct   Tara Katie Chris
5600   T2S   Loch   Alpine   Corey Jo Ct   Ln   Cir

42°20'23"

Climbing Wy   Crestline Dr   Bridgeway Dr

5

W   Pineview   Rd   Dr   Rondo Ct   Sunset Ct   Lake Ct   *BRIDGEWAY LAKE*   Sylvan Pl   Loch Dr

Pineview   Morrow Ct   Midway   Woodland Dr   *GREEN OAK LAKE*   Prospect

5   **4**   Westgate Dr   3900   Loch   Loch Dr   River Dr   4000

W Pineview Dr   3500   Glacier   **3**   Preserve Dr   Alpine Blvd   Curlew Ln   W   RIVER DR

42°19'57"   E   Hickory   Lake Ct   Crystal   Dawson   Huron Ct   **W HURON**   DELHI METRO PK   Delhi Ct

Nut Ln   Preserve Ct   Dr   Ct Blvd   W   Greenook   Briarlee   Brambledown Wy

DEXTER-HURON METROPOLITAN PARK   Sandstone   Greenook   Railroad   Forest   West St

6

HURON   Preserve Dr   Dr   DR   Sherwood   The Glade   A

3100   Forest Ct W   3900 St   **DELHI**

RIVER   DR   River Woods Ct   **RIVER**   Rd   A

Scio   **HURON**   1 Sherwood Forest Ct E

42°19'31"   5500   *HURON*   Delhi   Upper Glade Ct

8   **9**   Country Dr   Scio   **10**   **11**

7   DEXTER   Morrison   Scio   Ln   Rd   River Ridge Ln   W   2400

ANN   2000   2500   2500   **ZEEB**   Peters Rd   **48103**   Walters Wy

ARBOR RD   Loch Highland Dr   Loch Loden Dr   **RD**

RAND McNALLY

42°19'05"

A   B   C   D   E

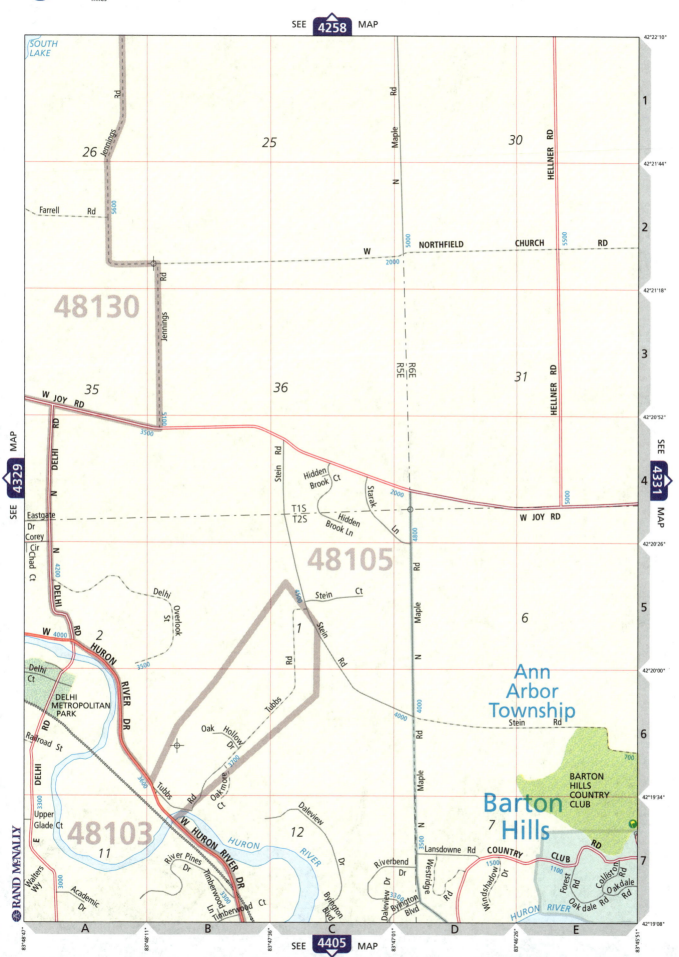

MAP
4330

1:24,000
1 in. = 2000 ft.

0   0.25   0.5
miles

SEE 4258 MAP

SEE 4329 MAP

SEE 4331 MAP

SEE 4405 MAP

SOUTH LAKE

Jennings Rd

26   25   30   HELLNER RD

Farrell Rd

48130   Jennings Rd   NORTHFIELD CHURCH RD

Maple N   W   5000
2000

R6E R5E

HELLNER RD

35   36   31

W JOY RD   DELHI RD N   3500
5100

Stein Rd

Hidden Brook Ct   Starak Ln

2000   5000

Eastgate Dr
Corey Cir
Chad Ct   T1S T2S   Hidden Brook Ln   W JOY RD

48105   Maple Rd N   4800

42°20'26"

Delhi St
Overlook   Stein Ct

Delhi   3500

1   Stein Rd   6

W 4000
HURON RD   2   DELHI RD N   4500   Maple N   4000   Ann Arbor Township

Delhi Ct

DELHI METROPOLITAN PARK   Tubbs   Stein Rd

Railroad St   Oak Hollow Dr   3700   4000

Maple Rd N

DELHI RD E   Oakmore Ct   Tubbs Rd   BARTON HILLS COUNTRY CLUB

3300   Upper Glade Ct   3600   Daleview Dr   Barton Hills

48103   W HURON RIVER DR   HURON RIVER   7   Lansdowne Rd   COUNTRY CLUB RD

11   River Pines Dr   Timberwood Ln   12   Riverbend Dr   Westridge Rd   COUNTRY CLUB   1100   Forest Rd   Colliston Rd

Walters Wy   3000   Academic Dr   Timberwood Ct   Byington Blvd   Daleview Dr   Byington Blvd   3300   3500 N   Windshadow Dr   1500   HURON RIVER   Oak dale Rd   Oakdale Rd

RAND McNALLY

A   B   C   D   E

MAP
4331

1:24,000
1 in. = 2000 ft.

0   0.25   0.5
miles

SEE **4259** MAP

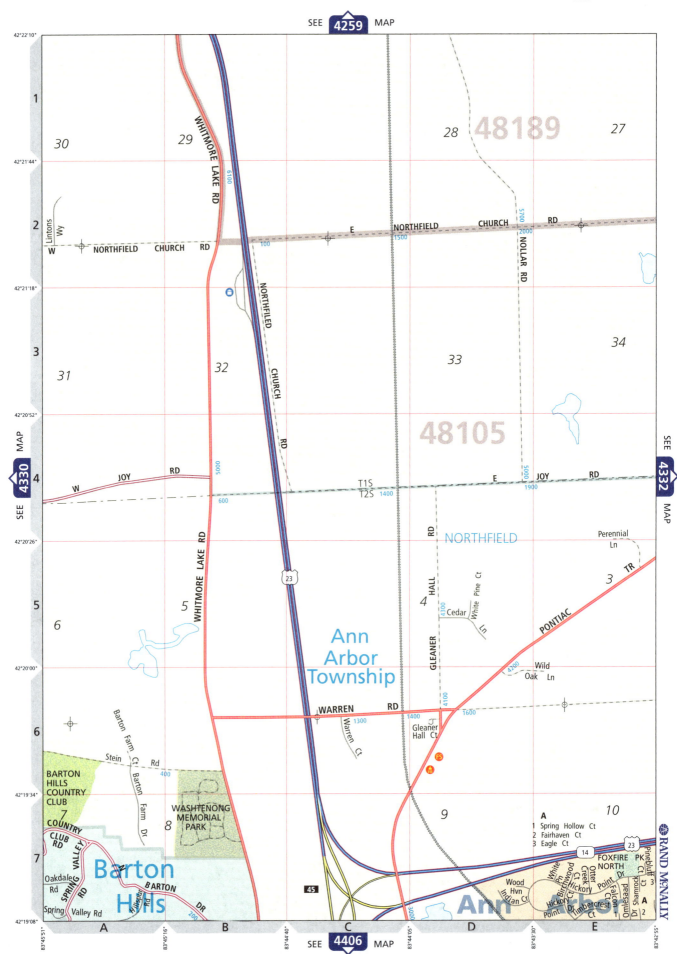

SEE **4330** MAP

SEE **4332** MAP

SEE **4406** MAP

48189

48105

NORTHFIELD

Ann
Arbor
Township

WHITMORE LAKE RD

NORTHFIELD CHURCH RD

NOLLAR RD

JOY RD

WARREN RD

PONTIAC TR

BARTON
HILLS
COUNTRY
CLUB

WASHTENONG
MEMORIAL PARK

Barton
Hills

Ann Arbor

FOXFIRE
NORTH

GLEANER HALL RD

Gleaner
Hall Ct

1 Spring Hollow Ct
2 Fairhaven Ct
3 Eagle Ct

MAP
4332

1:24,000
1 in. = 2000 ft.

0   0.25   0.5
miles

SEE 4260 MAP

SEE 4331 MAP

SEE 4333 MAP

SEE 4407 MAP

48189

27

26

25

N

TERRITORIAL RD   E

42°22'12"
42°21'46"
42°21'20"
42°20'54"
42°20'28"
42°20'02"
42°19'36"
42°19'10"

6200

Beverly Ln

Stewart Ln

Bedford Pl

Glengary Ct Avon
Cir

Dr

Katie Ln   Leland

Trudy Ln

Avon Ct

Tipperary

NORTHFIELD
PARK

SUTTON RD

E   NORTHFIELD

Old Church Ct

CHURCH   RD

PONTIAC   TR

2000   5700   3500   3900   5700   5600

5900

34   35   36

Tepeyac Hill Dr

SUTTON RD

PONTIAC   TR

EARHART   RD

Turtle Point Dr

Tamarack Tr

5100   5500   5000

5100

E   JOY   RD

E JOY RD

3000   4000

T1S
T2S

48105

PONTIAC   TR

Mother Teresa Dr

3   2   1

Ann
Arbor
Township

Hickory Ridge Rd

4000   4000

WARREN   RD   Warren   Rd

2700   4000

NIXON RD

EARHART   RD

10

Trailwood Ln

A
1 Fawnmeadow Ct
2 White Tail Run Ct
3 Foxway Ct
4 Featherstone Ct
5 Mallard Ct

11   12   14   3500

14   23

3 4
Hickory Pt
5
Foxway
Dr
2
A
1

Dunwoodie Ct

Elsinore Ct

Strand

Kilburn

Buckhorn

Aldwych Cir

Park Cir

Bayswater Ln

Dunwoodie Rd

Barclay   Wy

Ashburnam Rd

Ann
Arbor

42

23

DOMINO'S
WORLD
HQS

EARHART

Tower Dr

Frank Lloyd Wright Dr

Barnyard Bnd

RD

A   B   C   D   E

1   2   3   4   5   6   7

83°42'55"   83°42'20"   83°41'45"   83°41'09"   83°40'34"   83°39'59"

MAP
4333

1:24,000
1 in. = 2000 ft.

0   0.25   0.5

miles

SEE **4261** MAP

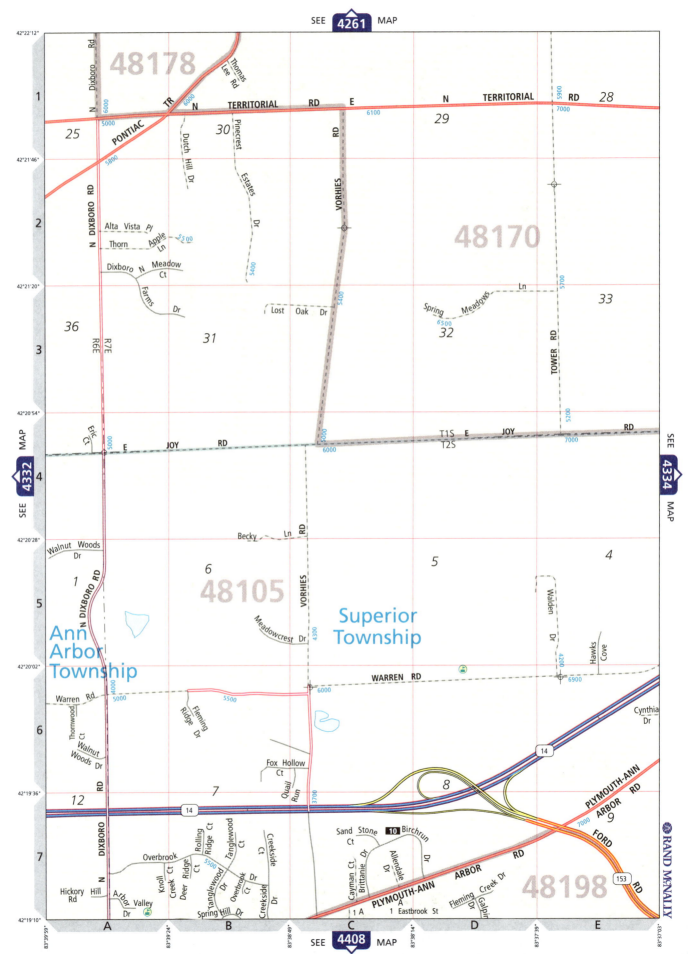

42°22'12"

48178

Dixboro Rd

N

1

6000

TR

N   TERRITORIAL   RD   E   6100   N   TERRITORIAL   RD   28

5000

Thomas Lee Rd

25   PONTIAC   30   Pinecrest   29

5800

42°21'46"

Dutch Hill Dr

Estates

N   DIXBORO   RD

Alta Vista Pl

2   Thorn   Apple   Ln   5500   Dr   VORHIES   RD   **48170**

5400

Dixboro   N   Meadow

Ct

Farms

Dixboro   Dr   5400   Ln   5700   33

Lost   Oak   Dr   Spring   Meadows

36   R7E   31   5400   6500   32   TOWER RD

R6E

3

42°21'20"

42°20'54"

MAP
4332
SEE

Eric Ct   5000   E   JOY   RD   5000   T1S   E   JOY   RD   5200   SEE

6000   T2S   7000   **4334** MAP

4

42°20'28"

Becky   Ln   RD

Walnut Woods Dr

1   6   5   4

48105   VORHIES

Walden Dr

Superior Township   4200

5   Meadowcrest Dr   4300   Hawks Cove

42°20'02"

Ann Arbor Township   4000   WARREN   RD   6900

Warren   Rd   5000   5500   6000   Cynthia Dr

Thornwood Ct   Fleming Ridge Dr

6   Walnut Woods Dr   14

Fox Hollow Ct   8   PLYMOUTH-ANN

12   7   Quail Run   3700   9   ARBOR RD   7000

42°19'36"   14   FORD

Sand Stone Ct   **10** Birchrun   RD

7   Overbrook   Rolling Ridge Ct   Tanglewood Ct   Creekside Ct   Cayman Ct   Brittanie Dr   Allendale Dr   Dr   **48198**   153

Knoll   Deer Ridge Ct   5500   Tanglewood Dr   Overbrook Ct   Creekside Dr   PLYMOUTH-ANN   ARBOR   Fleming Creek Dr

Hickory Rd   Hill   Arbor Valley Dr   Spring Hill Dr   Creekside Dr   1 A   1 Eastbrook St   Fleming Dr   Galpin

42°19'10"

A   B   C   D   E

83°39'59"   83°39'24"   83°38'49"   83°38'14"   83°37'39"   83°37'03"

SEE **4408** MAP

RAND MCNALLY

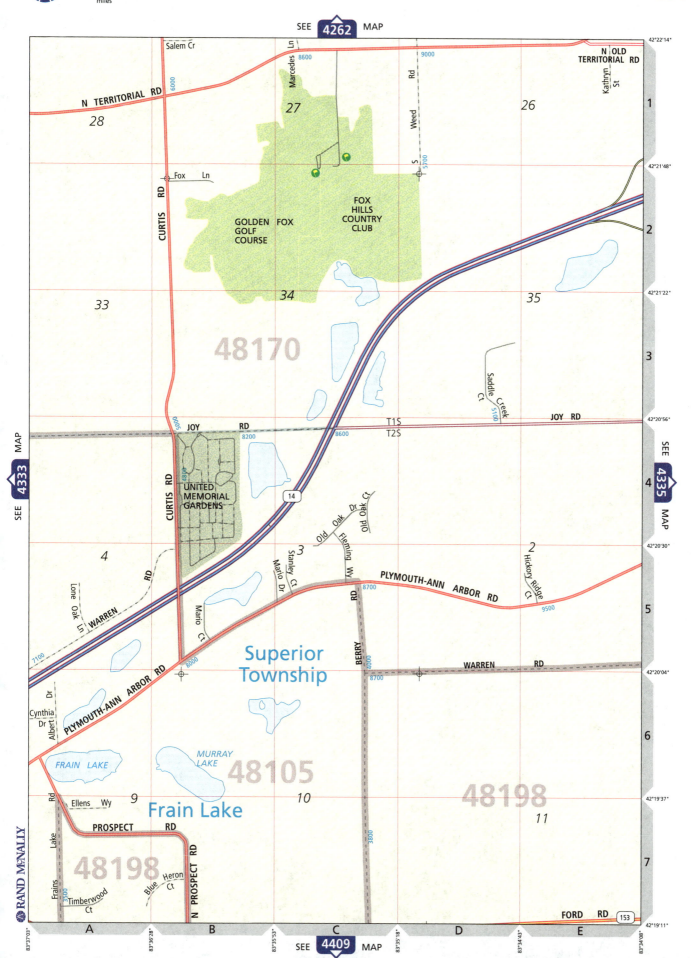

MAP
4334

1:24,000
1 in. = 2000 ft.
0   0.25   0.5
miles

N

SEE **4262** MAP

Salem Cr

Marcedes Ln
8600
9000

N OLD
TERRITORIAL RD

Weed Rd

Kathryn St

N TERRITORIAL RD
6000

28

27

26

1

CURTIS RD

Fox Ln

S
5700

42°22'14"

42°21'48"

GOLDEN FOX
GOLF COURSE

FOX
HILLS
COUNTRY
CLUB

2

33

34

35

42°21'22"

48170

3

SEE **4333** MAP

Saddle Creek Ct
5100

JOY RD
8200

JOY RD
8600

T1S
T2S

42°20'56"

SEE **4335** MAP

CURTIS RD
6000

UNITED
MEMORIAL
GARDENS

Old Oak Dr

Old Oak Ct

14

Fleming Wy

Hickory Ridge Ct
9500

4

42°20'30"

4

WARREN RD

Lone Oak Ln

Stanley Ct

Mario Dr

Mario Ct

3

RD
8700

PLYMOUTH-ANN ARBOR RD

2

5

7100

PLYMOUTH-ANN ARBOR RD
8000

Superior
Township

BERRY RD
4000

WARREN RD
8700

42°20'04"

Cynthia Dr

Albert Dr

FRAIN LAKE

MURRAY
LAKE

48105

6

RD

Ellens Wy

9

Frain Lake

10

48198

11

42°19'37"

PROSPECT RD

Lake Rd

N PROSPECT RD

48198

Blue Heron Ct

Frains

Timberwood Ct

3500

7

FORD RD

153

42°19'11"

A   B   C   D   E

83°37'03"   83°36'28"   83°35'53"   83°35'18"   83°34'43"   83°34'08"

SEE **4409** MAP

RAND MCNALLY

MAP
4335

1:24,000
1 in. = 2000 ft.

0   0.25   0.5
miles

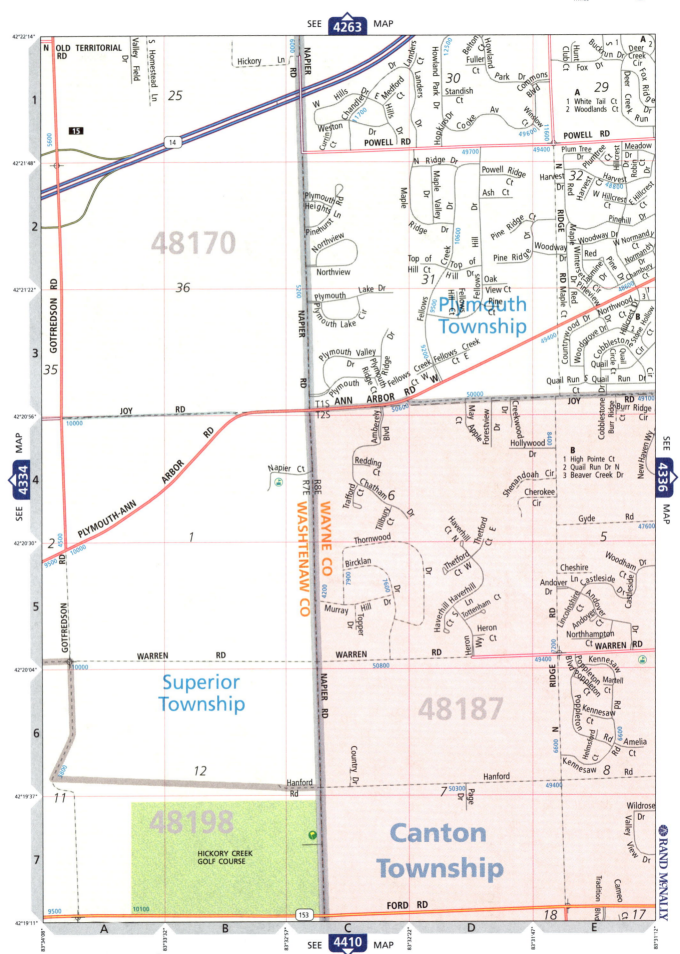

SEE **4263** MAP

OLD TERRITORIAL RD

Valley Field Dr
S Homestead Ln

Hickory Ln

25

15

14

48170

GOTFREDSON RD

36

35

NAPIER RD

Plymouth Heights Ln
Pinehurst
Northview
Northview

Plymouth Lake Dr
Plymouth Lake Cir

Plymouth Valley Dr
Plymouth Ridge
Plymouth Ridge Ct

W Hills Dr
Chandler Dr
Weston Ct
Currituck Ct

Medford Dr
Hills Dr

Landers Dr
Landers Dr

POWELL RD

Hopkins Dr

Howland Park Dr
Standish Ct

30

Cooke Av

Belton Ct
Fuller Ct

Howland Park Dr
Commons Blvd

Window

12500

49600

11600

POWELL RD

Plum Tree Dr
Plumtree Ct

Hillcrest

Meadow

Club Ct
Hunt Ct
Fox

Deer Creek Cir

Buck Run Dr

Deer Creek Run

Fox Ridge Dr

A
1 White Tail Ct
2 Woodlands Ct

29

N Ridge Dr

Powell Ridge Ct
Ash Ct

Maple Valley Rd

Maple Ridge Dr

Top of Hill Ct
Top of Hill Dr

Oak View Ct

Fellows

Fellows

Creek

Pine

Powell Ridge Ct

Pine Ridge Ct

Woodway Dr

Pine Ridge Dr

Harvest Red

32

W Hillcrest Ct

Harvest

Pinehill

Robin

E Hillcrest

Hillcrest

N

RIDGE RD

Maple Red
Maple Ct Red

Jasmine
Pineview

Winterset Dr

W Normand Ct
Normand Ct

Chambury Ct

3

48800

48600

Plymouth Township

Fellows Creek

Fellows Creek Ct E

Fellows Creek W

Country RD

Northwood Dr

Woodgrove Dr

Hillcrest Dr

Cobblestone

Stone Hollow

Quail Cir

B

Quail Run S

Quail Run Dr

Cir

49400

9200

49700

49400

ANN ARBOR RD W

JOY RD

PLYMOUTH-ANN ARBOR RD

Napier Ct

5200

5600

5600

15

5600

T1S
T2S

Amberely Blvd
Redding Ct
Chatham 6
Trafford Dr
Tillbury Ct
Thornwood
Bircklan
Murray Hill

May Apple Ct
Forestview Ct
Creekwood Dr
Hollywood Dr

50000

50600

8400

Burr Ridge Cir

Cobblestone

New Haven Wy

B
1 High Pointe Ct
2 Quail Run Dr N
3 Beaver Creek Dr

JOY RD

49100

SEE **4336** MAP

WAYNE CO
WASHTENAW CO

R7E R8E

1

2

4500

9500

10000

10000

42°20'30"

Thornwood Dr

Topper

Haverhill Ct N

Thetford Ct E
Thetford Ct W

Haverhill Ct S
Haverhill

Heron
Heron Ct
Heron Wy

Tottenham Ct

Shenandoah Cir

Cherokee Cir

Gyde Rd

5

47600

Woodham Dr

Cheshire Ct

Castleside Dr
Castleside Dr

Andover Ln
Andover Dr
Andover Ct

Lincolnshire Ct

Northhampton Ct

RIDGE RD

7200

7900

7600

7200

4200

WARREN RD

WARREN RD

WARREN RD

Superior Township

50800

49400

Kennesaw Ct
Poppleton Blvd
Poppleton Ct
Poppleton Ct
Poppleton Rd
Kennesaw Rd
Kennesaw Ct
Kennesaw Rd

Martell Ct

Amelia Ct

Helmsford Rd

6600

8

N

0099

48187

Country Dr

Hanford Rd

Page

7 50300

Hanford Rd

12

11

8800

10000

Hanford Rd

48198

HICKORY CREEK GOLF COURSE

NAPIER RD

Canton Township

Wildrose Dr

Valley View Dr

Tradition

Cameo Ct

18   17

9500

10100

FORD RD

153

RAND McNALLY

A   B   C   D   E

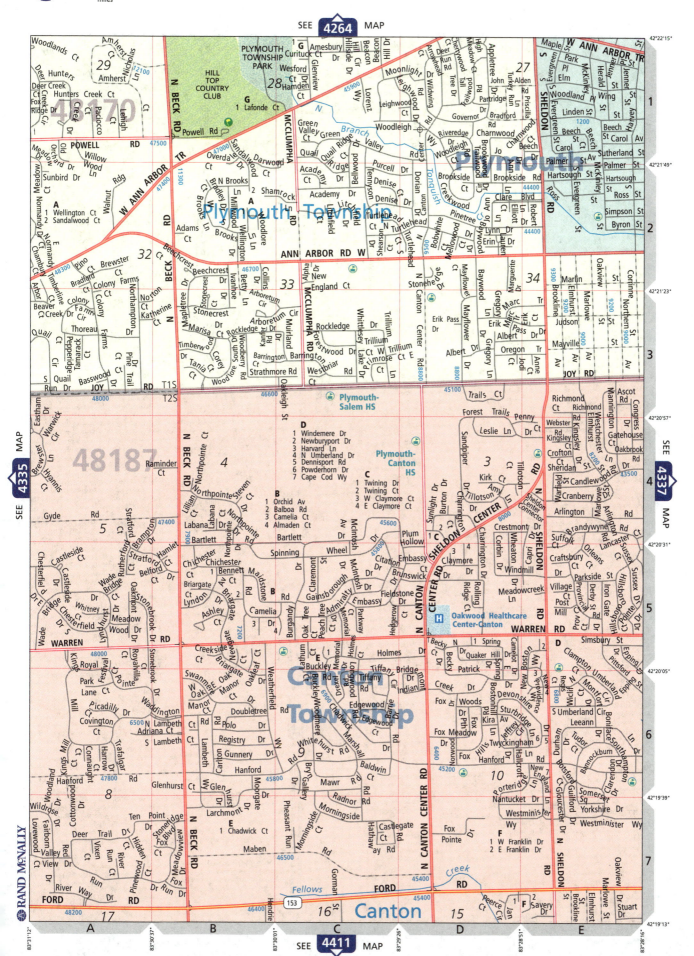

MAP
4336

1:24,000
1 in. = 2000 ft.

miles

SEE 4264 MAP

SEE 4335 MAP

SEE 4337 MAP

SEE 4411 MAP

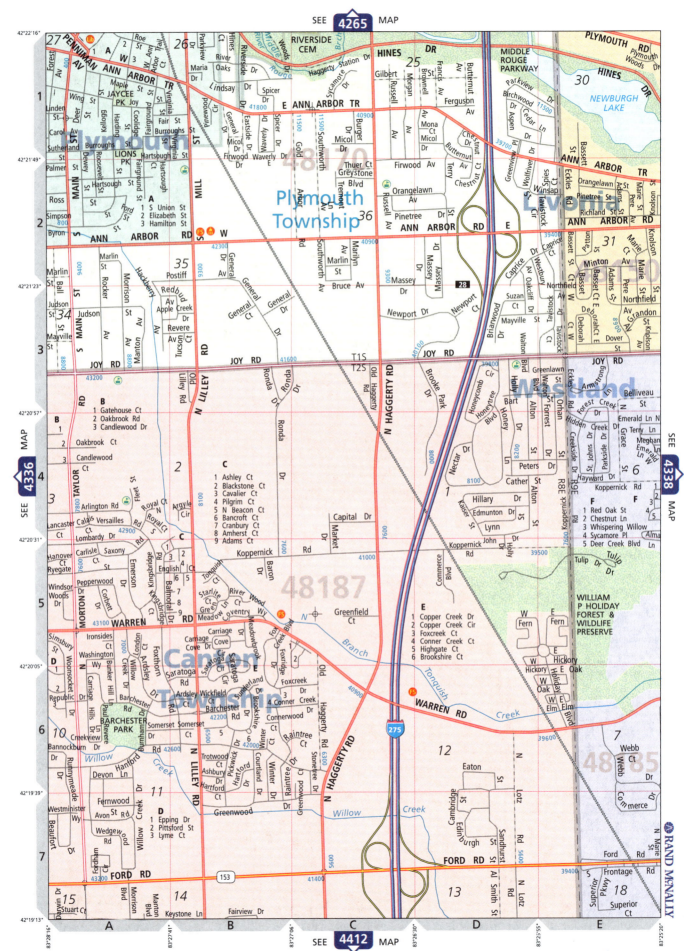

MAP
4337

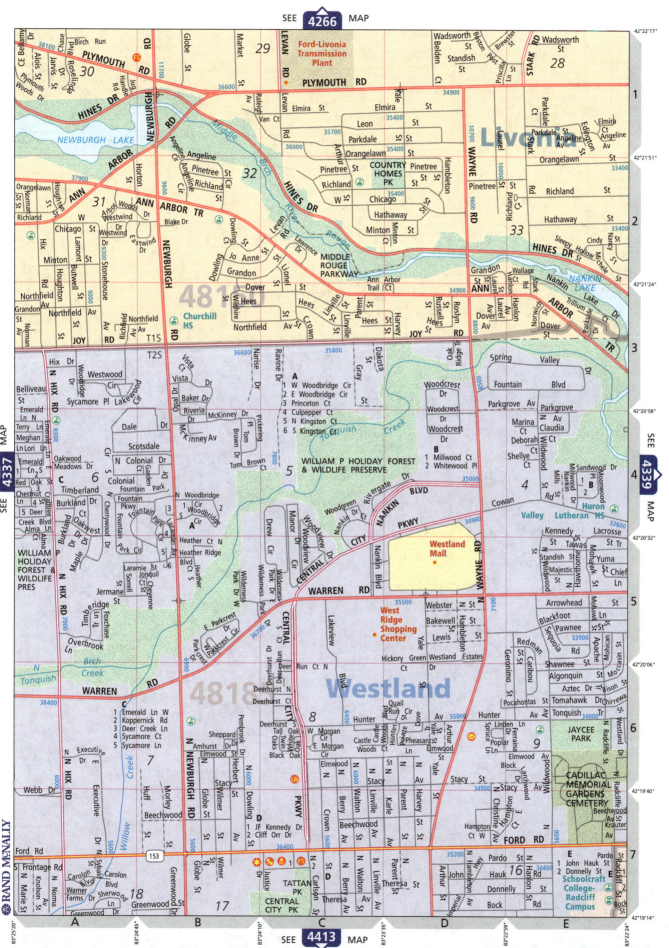

MAP
4338

SEE **4266** MAP

SEE **4337** MAP

SEE **4339** MAP

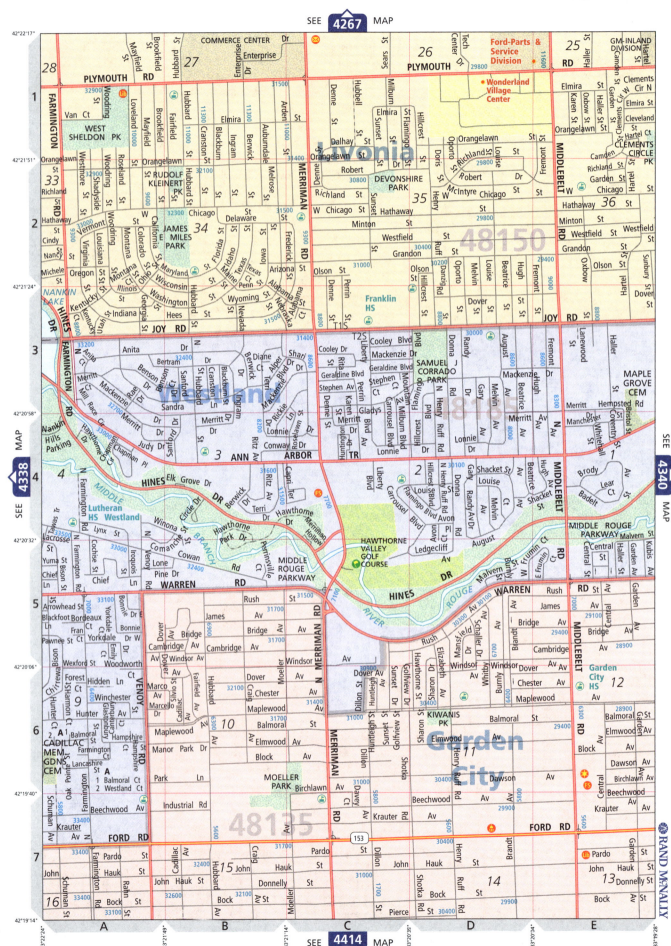

MAP
4339

SEE **4267** MAP

1:24,000
1 in. = 2000 ft.
0   0.25   0.5
miles

48150

Livonia

Westland

48185

Garden City

48135

SEE **4338** MAP

SEE **4340** MAP

RAND M^cNALLY

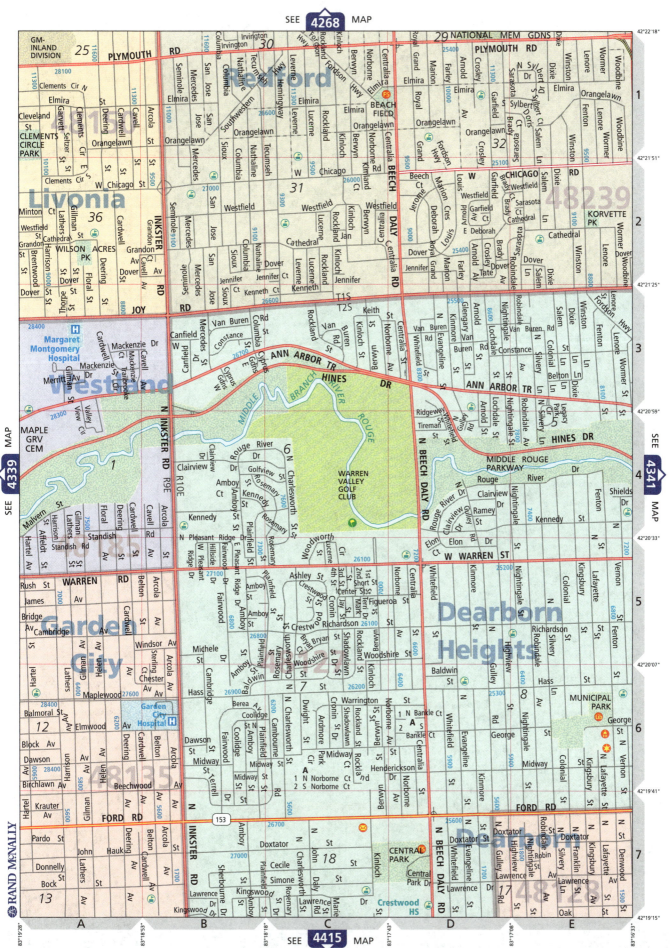

MAP
4340

SEE 4268 MAP

SEE 4339 MAP

SEE 4341 MAP

SEE 4415 MAP

1:24,000
1 in. = 2000 ft.
0   0.25   0.5
miles

RAND McNALLY

MAP
4341

1:24,000
1 in. = 2000 ft.

0   0.25   0.5
miles

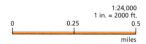

SEE 4269 MAP

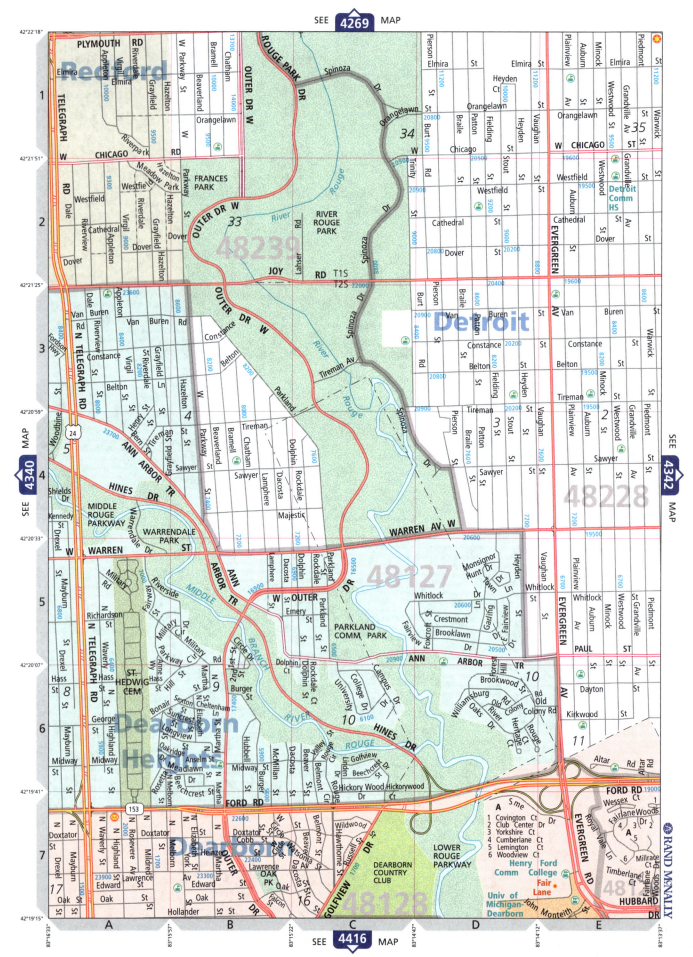

SEE 4340 MAP

SEE 4342 MAP

SEE 4416 MAP

RAND M?NALLY

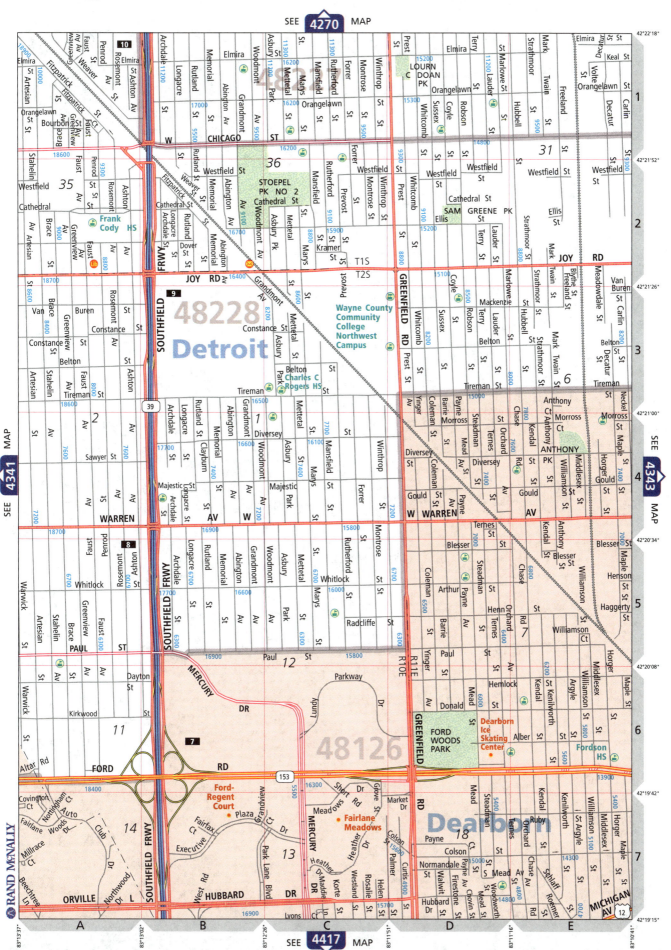

MAP
4342

SEE 4270 MAP

SEE 4341 MAP

SEE 4343 MAP

SEE 4417 MAP

MAP
4343

1:24,000
1 in. = 2000 ft.

0   0.25   0.5
miles

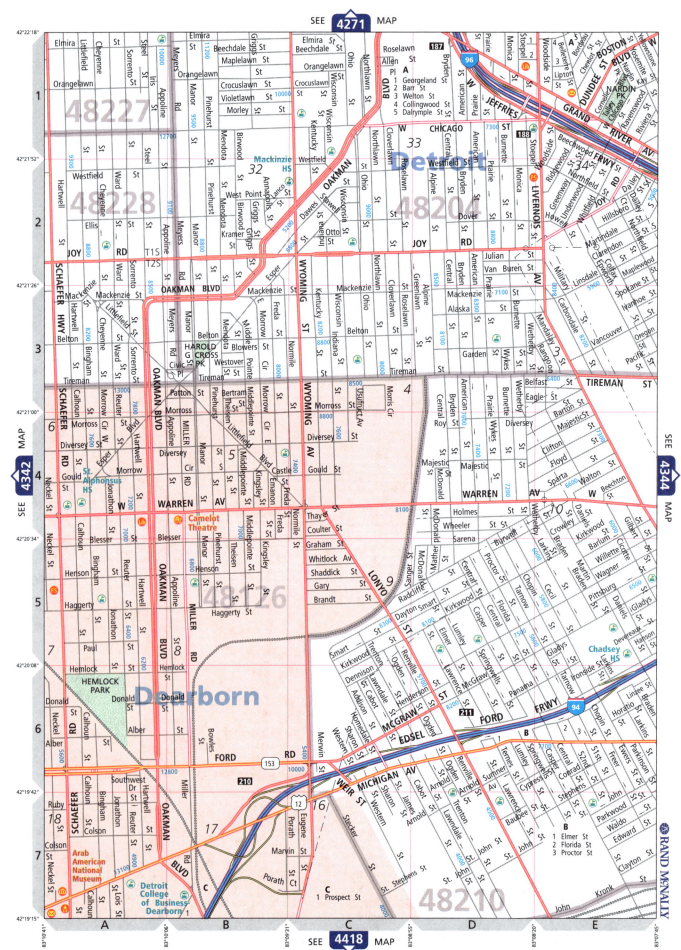

SEE **4342** MAP

SEE **4344** MAP

RAND MCNALLY

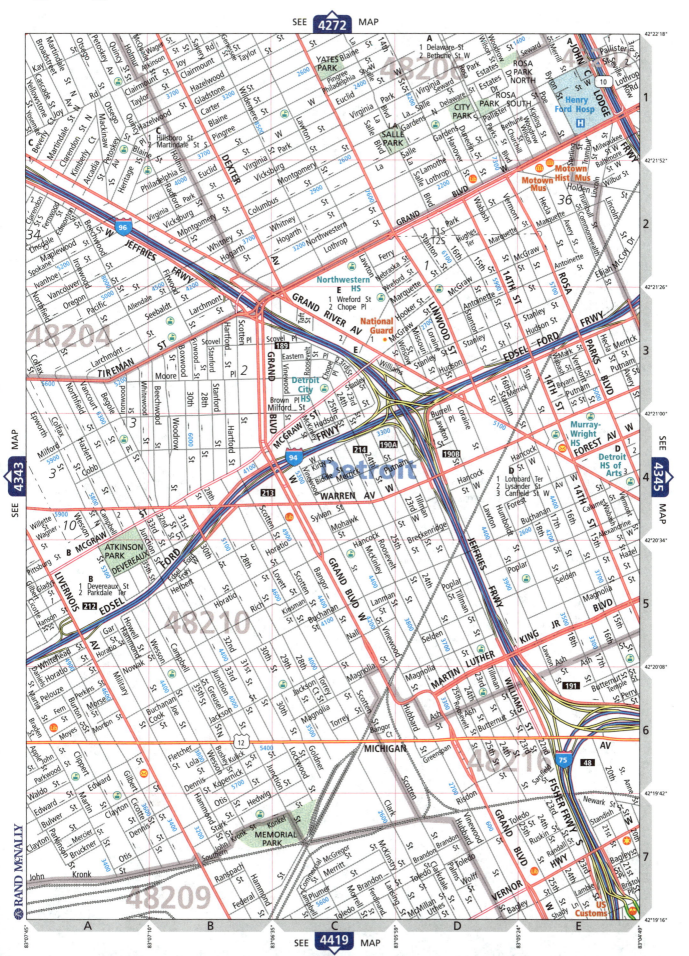

MAP
4344

SEE 4272 MAP

SEE 4343 MAP

SEE 4345 MAP

SEE 4419 MAP

MAP
4345

1:24,000
1 in. = 2000 ft.

0   0.25   0.5
miles

SEE 4273 MAP

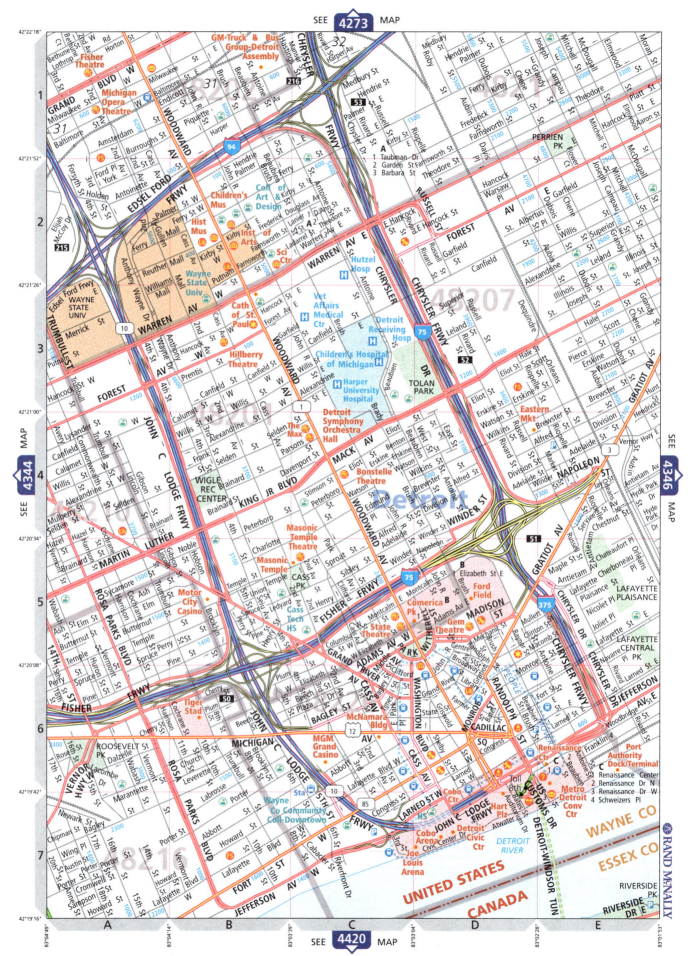

SEE 4344 MAP

SEE 4346 MAP

SEE 4420 MAP

RAND McNALLY

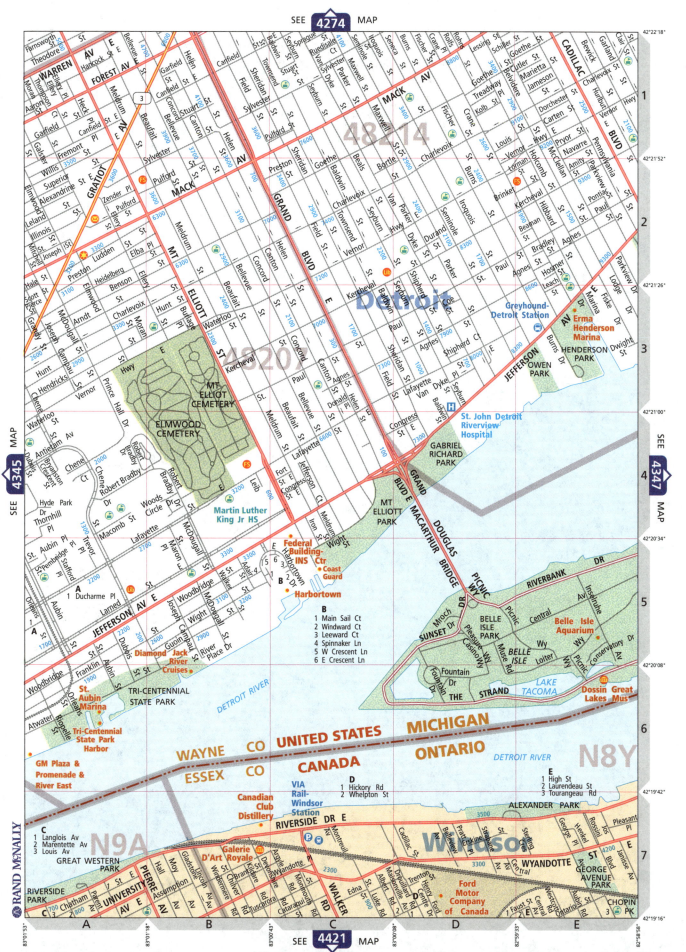

MAP
4346

N

1:24,000
1 in. = 2000 ft.
0   0.25   0.5
miles

SEE 4274 MAP

SEE 4345 MAP

SEE 4347 MAP

SEE 4421 MAP

1
2
3
4
5
6
7

A   B   C   D   E

42°22'18"
42°21'52"
42°21'26"
42°21'00"
42°20'34"
42°20'08"
42°19'42"
42°19'16"

83°01'53"
83°01'18"
83°00'43"
83°00'08"
82°59'33"
82°58'58"

WARREN AV E
FOREST AV E
GRATIOT
MACK AV
MACK
MT ELLIOTT ST
GRAND BLVD E
48214
48207
Detroit

MT ELLIOT CEMETERY
ELMWOOD CEMETERY

Greyhound-Detroit Station
Erma Henderson Marina
HENDERSON PARK
OWEN PARK
JEFFERSON
St. John Detroit Riverview Hospital
GABRIEL RICHARD PARK

Martin Luther King Jr HS
MT ELLIOTT PARK
Federal Building-INS Ctr
Coast Guard
Harbortown

JEFFERSON AV E
BLVD E MACARTHUR BRIDGE
DOUGLAS
PICNIC WY
RIVERBANK DR
SUNSET DR
BELLE ISLE PARK
Belle Isle Aquarium
BELLE ISLE
Dossin Great Lakes Mus
LAKE TACOMA
THE STRAND

Diamond Jack River Cruises
St. Aubin Marina
TRI-CENTENNIAL STATE PARK
Tri-Centennial State Park Harbor
DETROIT RIVER
GM Plaza & Promenade & River East

WAYNE CO   UNITED STATES   MICHIGAN
ESSEX CO   CANADA   ONTARIO
DETROIT RIVER   N8Y

B
1 Main Sail Ct
2 Windward Ct
3 Leeward Ct
4 Spinnaker Ln
5 W Crescent Ln
6 E Crescent Ln

D
1 Hickory Rd
2 Whelpton St

E
1 High St
2 Laurendeau St
3 Tourangeau Rd

Canadian Club Distillery
VIA Rail-Windsor Station
ALEXANDER PARK
RIVERSIDE DR E

C
1 Langlois Av
2 Marentette Av
3 Louis Av

N9A
GREAT WESTERN PARK
RIVERSIDE PARK
Galerie D'Art Royale
Windsor
WYANDOTTE ST
GEORGE AVENUE PARK

PIERRE AV
UNIVERSITY AV E
WALKER RD
Ford Motor Company of Canada
CHOPIN PK

RAND MCNALLY

MAP
4347

1:24,000
1 in. = 2000 ft.

0   0.25   0.5
miles

SEE 4275 MAP

Church of Latter Day Saints Temple

DAIMLER CHRYSLER-JEFFERSON ASSEMBLY

Pewabic Pottery

Fisher Mansion

A
1 Southpark St
2 Northpark St
3 N Eastlawn Ct
4 S Eastlawn Ct
5 S Piper Ct
6 N Piper Ct
7 Coplin St

Harbor Hill Marina

48214

Detroit

WATERWORKS PARK

ALFRED BRUSH FORD PARK

RIVERFRONT-LAKEWOOD PARK

48215

DETROIT RIVER

BELLE ISLE

William Livingstone Memorial Lighthouse

SEE 4346 MAP

BELLE ISLE

LAKE MUSKODAY

BLUE HURON LAGOON

Belle Isle Nature Center

BELLE ISLE

Belle Isle Lighthouse

MICHIGAN
ONTARIO

PECHE ISLAND

PECHE ISLAND PARK

SEE 4348 MAP

LAKE OKONOKA

UNITED STATES
CANADA

48207

BELLE ISLE PARK

US Coast Guard

KIWANIS PARK

DETROIT RIVER

N86

CEDARVIEW PARK

WAYNE CO
ESSEX CO

B
1 Gateside Ct
2 Enfield Ct
3 Gregory Pl
4 Heathfield Ct

COVENTRY GARDENS

RIVERSIDE MEM PARK

Riverside HS

REAUME PARK

N8Y

WYANDOTTE

RIVERSIDE MEM PARK

REALTOR PARK

Windsor

FJ Brennan HS

CHOPIN PK

THOMPSON PARK

RAND McNALLY

B

SEE 4422 MAP

MAP
4348

1:24,000
1 in. = 2000 ft.
0   0.25   0.5
miles

SEE 4276 MAP

42°22'18"
42°21'52"
42°21'26"
42°21'00"
42°20'34"
42°20'07"
42°19'41"
42°19'15"

1
2
3
4
5
6
7

SEE 4347 MAP

SEE 4349 MAP

Grosse Pointe Park

Detroit

WINDMILL POINTE PK

RIVERFRONT-LAKEWOOD PK

Windmill Point Lighthouse

DETROIT RIVER

DETROIT RIVER

WAYNE CO
MICHIGAN
UNITED STATES
ESSEX CO
ONTARIO
CANADA

LAKE ST. CLAIR

PECHE ISLAND PARK

PECHE ISLAND

Riverside Marina

Lakeview Pk Marina

EAST END PARK

RIVERSIDE DR E

Shoreview Cir

Tecumseh

RIVERSIDE RD E

Windsor

N8P

LITTLE RIVER CORRIDOR PK

RIVERDALE PK

LITTLE RIVER ACRES

LESPERANCE RD

A
1 Foxhill Ct
2 Darlington Cres
3 Denby Ct
4 Copperfield Ct
5 Blencarn Ct

A   B   C   D   E

SEE 4423 MAP

82°56'02"
82°54'51"
82°53'41"
82°52'30"

RAND McNALLY

MAP
4349

1:24,000
1 in. = 2000 ft.

0   0.25   0.5
miles

N

SEE **4277** MAP

1

MICHIGAN
ONTARIO

WAYNE CO UNITED STATES

ESSEX CO CANADA

2

LAKE
ST. CLAIR

3

SEE **4348** MAP

SEE **B** MAP

4

5

42°22'18"
42°21'52"
42°21'26"
42°21'00"
42°20'34"
42°20'07"
42°19'41"
42°19'15"

Coronado

6

RIVERSIDE RD E

Dillon Dr
Barry Cres
Burdid
Percy Pl
Coronado
Keith Pl
Kimberly
Lacasse

Dillon
Mason
Michael Dr
James Cres
Simard

Dillon
Simard
Cres
James
Cres
Pl

Shannon Amanda
Cres
Ct
Salich Ct
Jasper Pl

River Dr
Woodridge Dr

13000

2800

Manwell Av Little
Shield
Michael
River
Centennial
Wedgewood
Dr
PIQUA
PK

Meander Cres

Brenda

Brenda Cres

Clapp St

LACASSE
PARK

Revalus
St. Thomas
Woodridge
Donalda Ct
Veronica
Grace
Rd
St

Jelso Pl

MANNING
PK

RD

100

MANNING

13000

LITTLE
RIVER

Tecumseh

LAKEWOOD
GOLF CLUB

13500

Christy David
Cres Cres
Ln

David Cres

Jeffrey Pl
Grant Av

Edgewater Blvd

St. Mark's

Lovelly Rd

A

1 Arlington Blvd
2 Kensington Blvd

A

2

BEACH GROVE GOLF
& CC

7

A   B   C   D   E

82°53'05"
82°52'31"
82°51'55"
82°51'20"
82°50'45"

SEE **4424** MAP

RAND McNALLY

.01.05.28

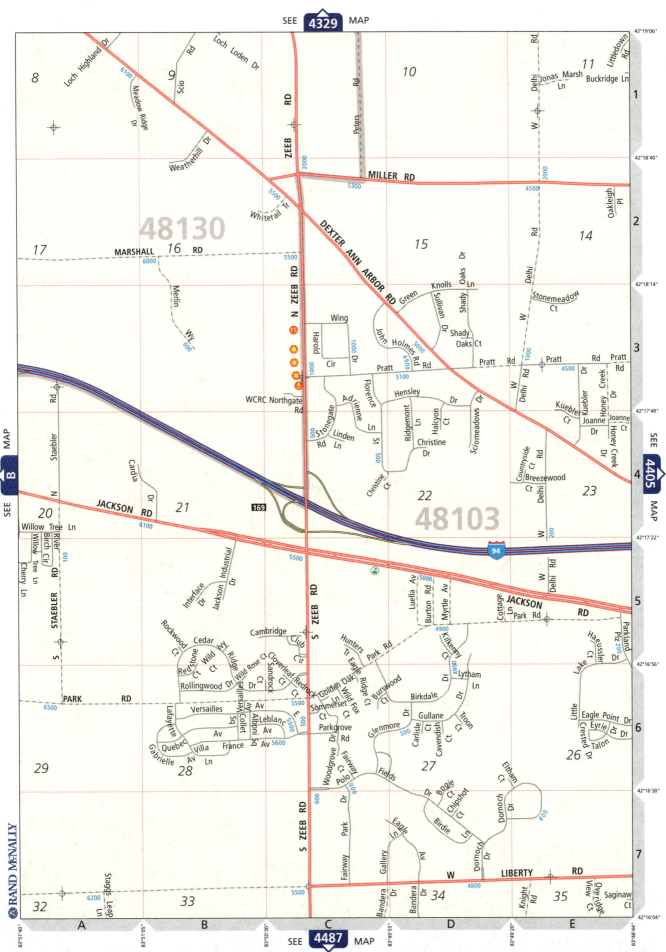

MAP
4404

1:24,000
1 in. = 2000 ft.

0   0.25   0.5
miles

SEE 4329 MAP

SEE B MAP

SEE 4405 MAP

SEE 4487 MAP

48130

48103

RAND McNALLY

MAP
4405

1:24,000
1 in. = 2000 ft.

0   0.25   0.5
miles

N

SEE 4330 MAP

48105

SEE 4404 MAP

SEE 4406 MAP

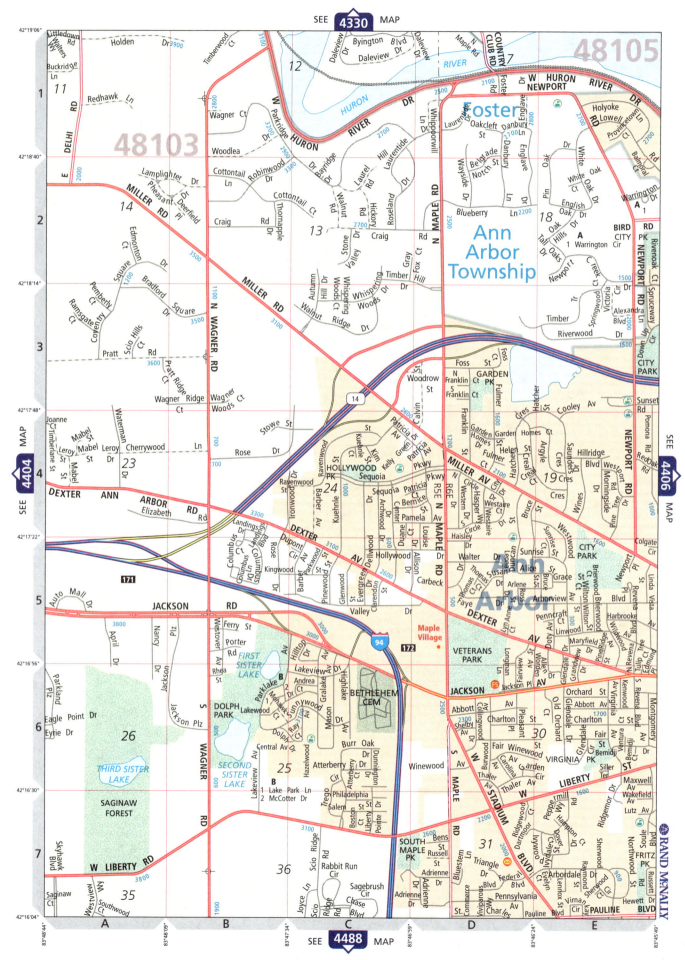

42°19'06"
42°18'40"
42°18'14"
42°17'48"
42°17'22"
42°16'56"
42°16'30"
42°16'04"

48103

Ann
Arbor
Township

Ann
Arbor

Foster

HURON RIVER DR

MILLER RD

N WAGNER RD

WAGNER RD

S MAPLE RD

N MAPLE RD

NEWPORT RD

DEXTER AV

JACKSON RD

W LIBERTY RD

STADIUM BLVD

SAGINAW FOREST

THIRD SISTER LAKE

SECOND SISTER LAKE

FIRST SISTER LAKE

DOLPH PARK

BETHLEHEM CEM

VETERANS PARK

Maple Village

HOLLYWOOD PK

CITY PARK

GARDEN PK

BIRD HILLS CITY PK

SOUTH MAPLE PK

SAGINAW FOREST

11   14   23   26   35

12   13   24   25   36

18   19   30   31

SEE 4488 MAP

RAND MCNALLY

A   B   C   D   E

83°48'44"   83°48'09"   83°47'34"   83°46'59"   83°46'24"   83°45'49"

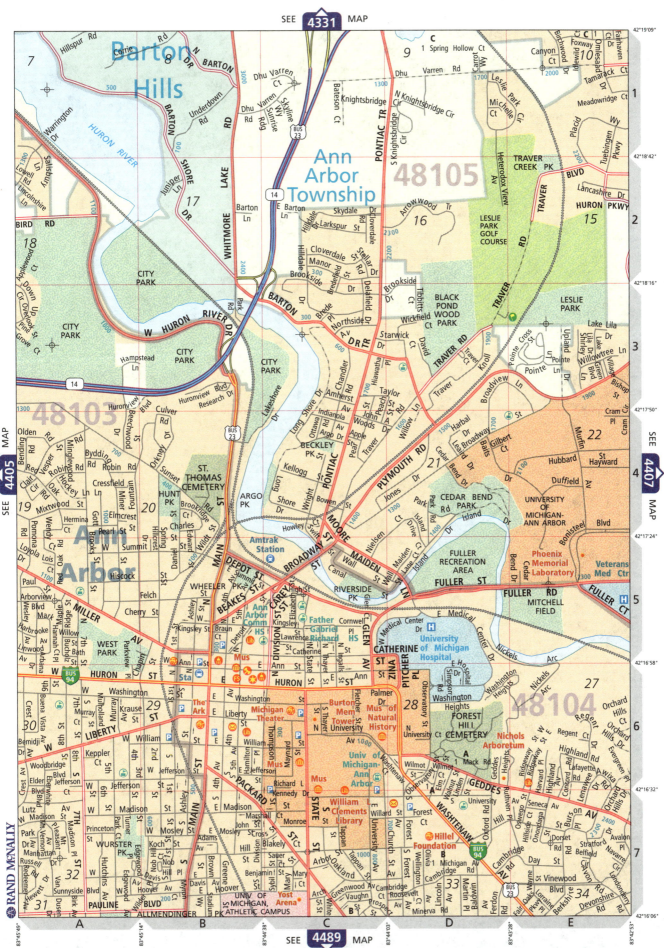

MAP
4406

1:24,000
1 in. = 2000 ft.

0   0.25   0.5
miles

N

Barton
Hills

Ann
Arbor
Township

48105

Barton Hills

HURON RIVER

BARTON DR

N BARTON

LAKE RD

WHITMORE

SHORE DR

JUNIPER LN

Corrie Rd
Hillspur Rd

Warrington Dr

Salisbury Dr
Lowell Rd
Lincolnshire Ln

BIRD RD

Applewood Dr
Down Up Rd
Overlook St
Pine St
Grove Ct

18

CITY PARK

CITY PARK

CITY PARK

Hampstead Ln

CITY PARK

Underdown Rd

Dhu Varren Ct
Dhu Varren Rd
Skyline Rdg
Sunrise

BUS 23

14

Barton Ln
E Barton Ln

3000

500

100

1100

2400

W HURON RIVER DR

BARTON DR

Park Rd

Lakeshore Dr

14

48103

Huronview Blvd
Beechwood Dr
Culver Rd
Orkney Rd
Sunset Rd
Research Dr
Huronview Blvd

BUS 23

Olden Rd
Bending Rd
Red Oak
Clair Cir
Vesper Rd
Minglewood Rd
Robinson Rd
Robin Rd
Hickey Ln
Cressfield Ln
Miner Ln

19

Mixtwood St
Hermina St
Elmcrest St
Pomona Rd
Loyola Ln Lois Rd
Wendy
Red
Paul

1100

20

HUNT PK

Brookridge

Charles St
Spring
Hillcrest
Edward St
Daniel St
Wildt Ct

ST THOMAS CEMETERY

400

ST THOMAS CEMETERY

700

Pearl St
Summit
Brooks

Ann Arbor

MILLER AV

WEST PARK

Arborview Blvd
Wesley
Mark
7th
Willow
Bath
Hannah Ct Pl
Harbrooke Av
Linwood Av
Buchoz
Parkview Dr
Chapin St

W HURON ST

BUS 94

Hiscock

Cherry St

Kingsley St

Felch St

WHEELER St

BEAKES St

DEPOT ST

CAREY ST

Braun Ct
Detroit St

Ann Arbor Comm HS

DIVISION ST

High St
Elizabeth St
Kingsley St
Lawrence St
E Catherine St

Father Gabriel Richard HS

Ann Arbor Comm HS

Amtrak Station

BROADWAY ST

MOORE ST

MAIDEN LN

Wall St
Canal
Glen Ct

Wall St
Maiden Ln

RIVERSIDE PK

CATHERINE ST

ZINA ST

PITCHER PL

W Medical Center Dr

University of Michigan Hospital

H

FULLER ST

FULLER RD

FULLER ST

FULLER RECREATION AREA

MITCHELL FIELD

Nickels Arc

48104

27

Washington Heights
Simpson Dr
Nickels Arc

Phoenix Memorial Laboratory

Veterans Med Ctr

2300

UNIVERSITY OF MICHIGAN-ANN ARBOR

Bonisteel Blvd

CEDAR BEND PARK

Island Dr

Cedar Bend Dr

Murfin
Hubbard
Hayward
Duffield Av

22

Cram Ct
Pl

Gilbert Ct

Baits

Broadway
Leland Dr
Harbal
Willow Ln

1500
1700

Broadview Ln

Pointe Cross St
Pointe Ln
Pointe

Upland Ct

Lila
Lake
Shirley St
Willowtree Ln
Village
Green Blvd
Bishop St

Leslie Park

Lake Lila

2400

1900

TRAVER RD

TRAVER RD

Traver Knoll
Traver

David St
Starwick

Wickfield Ct

BLACK POND WOOD PARK

PLYMOUTH RD

Jones St
Island

Park Rd
Park Rd

Island Dr

Cedar Bend Dr

1400

1300

1400

21

Chandler Rd
Hiawatha
Amherst
Taylor
John Woods
Peach
Cedar
Apple
Pear
Traver

PONTIAC ST

BECKLEY PK

Kellogg St

Long Shore Dr
Long Shore Dr
Ottawa
Indianola Av
Argo Rd

ARGO PK

Shore Dr
Howley St
Bowen St
Wright St

NielSen Ct
Swift St

HURON ST

Ann St
E Ann St
E Huron St
E Washington St
State St
N State St
N Thayer St
S Thayer St
S Ingalls St
Washington Heights

Observatory St

FOREST HILL CEMETERY

Nichols Arboretum

Mack Ave
Geddes

Washtenaw

Wilmot St
Elm St
Walnut St
Linden St

A

GEDDES

University
Church St
Forest Ct
Olivia Av
Michigan

Hillel Foundation

BUS 94

Oswego St
Onondaga St

Oxford Rd
Hill St

Ridgeway Pl
Ridgeway Av
Harvard Rd
Concord Pl
Highland Rd
Lafayette Av
Lenawee Dr
Orchard Hills Dr
Evergreen Dr

27

Regent St
Regent Ct
Highland Rd

Orchard Hills Dr
Regent St
Wixom Ct
Orchard Hills Dr

Dorset Rd
Stratford Pl
Avalon
Belfield Rd
Navarre Pl

Burton Mem Tower
University

Mus of Natural History

Univ of Michigan-Ann Arbor

Mus

William L Clements Library

Michigan Theater

The Ark

29 ST

LIBERTY

W William St
W Liberty St
W Washington St
W Jefferson St
W Madison St

30

Crest Dr
Buena Vista Dr
Bemidji St
Woodbridge Dr
Elder Blvd
Lutz Av
Park
7th St
Mt Vernon Av
Manhattan
Russell St
Redeemer

32

Krause
Mulholland
6th
5th
4th
3rd
2nd
1st
Keppler Ct
Elder Ct
Jefferson
Jefferson Blvd
Madison
Princeton Av
Turner
Koch Av
Edgewood
Davis Av
Hoover Av
Nob
Benjamin
Mary
Hill
Adams
Greene
Brown
Prospect

WURSTER PK

PAULINE

ALLMENDINGER

BLVD

Thompson
Maynard
Hamilton
Forest
Tappan
Church St
S Forest Av
Willard
Monroe
Mosley
Marshall Ct
John St
S Division St
E Jefferson St
Packard

PACKARD

MAIN ST

STATE ST

Richard L Kennedy Dr

Arbor-Oakland
Greenwood Av
Cambridge Rd
Roosevelt Av
Vaughn St
White St
Minerva Av
Lincoln Av
Baldwin Av
Martin Pl
Wells St
Ferdon Rd

33

Michigan Av

S Forest Av
Olivia Av

WASHTENAW AV

Wellington
Cambridge Rd
Day Av
Devonshire Rd
Berkshire Rd
Vinewood Blvd
Fair Oaks Pkwy
Londonderry Rd

34

UNIV OF MICHIGAN, ATHLETIC CAMPUS

Yost Arena

STADIUM

BUS 23

RAND McNALLY

42°19'09"
42°18'42"
42°18'16"
42°17'50"
42°17'24"
42°16'58"
42°16'32"
42°16'06"

83°45'49"
83°45'14"
83°44'38"
83°44'03"
83°43'28"
83°42'53"

7 8 9 10
1
2
3
4
5
6
7

A B C D E

MAP
4407

1:24,000
1 in. = 2000 ft.
0   0.25   0.5
miles

SEE **4332** MAP

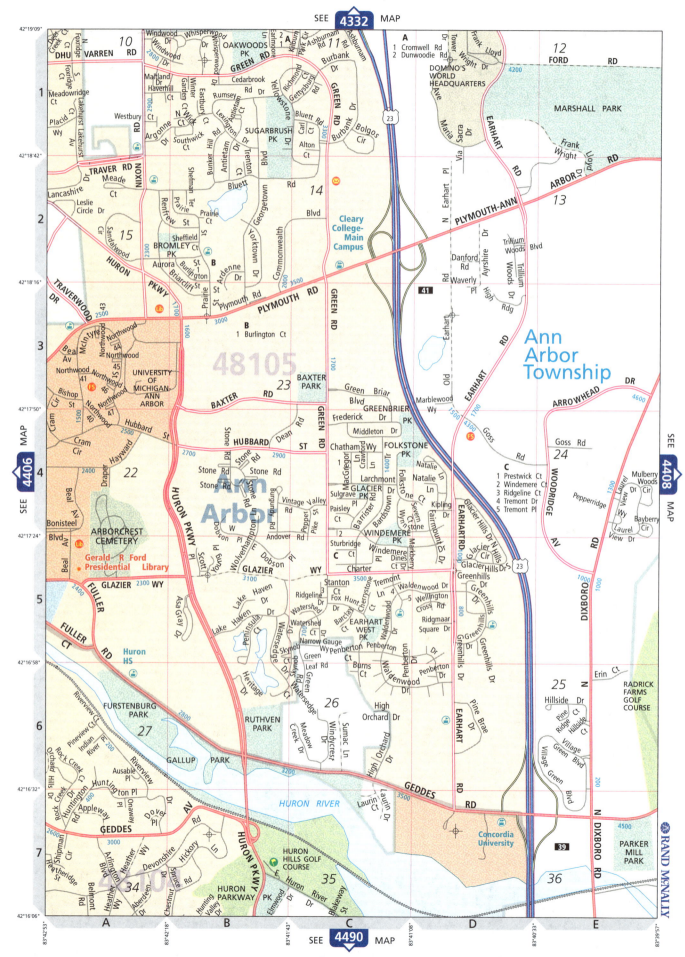

MAP
SEE **4406**

SEE **4408** MAP

Ann Arbor Township

48105

Ann Arbor

UNIVERSITY OF MICHIGAN-ANN ARBOR

Cleary College-Main Campus

Gerald R Ford Presidential Library

ARBORCREST CEMETERY

Huron HS

FURSTENBURG PARK

GALLUP PARK

RUTHVEN PARK

HURON RIVER

HURON HILLS GOLF COURSE

HURON PARKWAY

Concordia University

RADRICK FARMS GOLF COURSE

PARKER MILL PARK

MARSHALL PARK

DOMINO'S WORLD HEADQUARTERS

BAXTER PARK

SEE **4490** MAP

RAND McNALLY

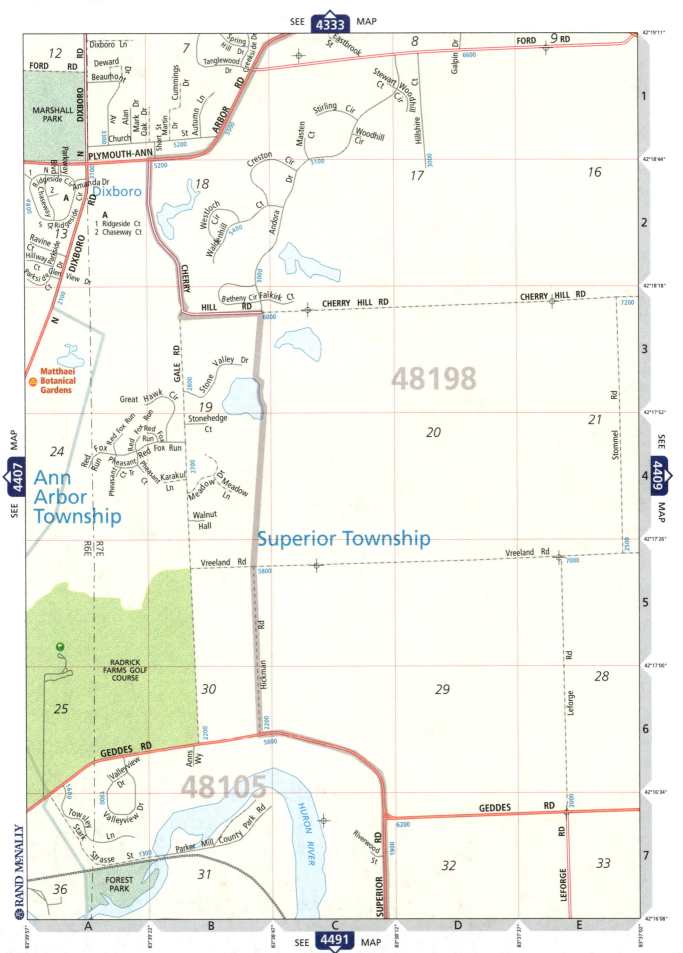

MAP
4408

1:24,000
1 in. = 2000 ft.

0   0.25   0.5
miles

SEE 4333 MAP

FORD 9 RD

12   FORD RD   7   8

Dixboro Ln
Deward Dr
Beaumont Dr
Spring Hill Dr
Tanglewood Dr
Eastbrook St
Creeksjde Dr
Galpin Dr
6600

MARSHALL PARK

Cummings Dr
Autumn Ln
Short St
St Martin Dr
Mark Oak Dr
Alan Av
Church
3000

DIXBORO RD

ARBOR RD
5500
5200

Stewart Ct
Woodhill Ct
Hillshire Dr
3000

Stirling Cir
Masten Ct
Woodhill Cir

PLYMOUTH-ANN
5200

42°18'44"

17   16

Dixboro

18   Creston Dr
Cir
3100

Ridgeside Cir
Chaseway Cir
1
2
A
Amanda Dr
N
4800
S Ridgeside Dr

A
1 Ridgeside Ct
2 Chaseway Ct

13   Westloch Cir
Waldenhill Cir
5400
Andora Ct
3000

Ravine Ct
Hillway Dr
Parkside Dr
Glen View Dr
Parksive Ct
2100

DIXBORO RD
N

CHERRY

Betheny Cir Falkirk Ct
HILL RD
6000

CHERRY HILL RD

CHERRY HILL RD
7200

42°18'18"

Matthaei Botanical Gardens

GALE RD
2800

Stone Valley Dr

48198

Rd

Stommel

3

Great Hawk Cir

19   Stonehedge Ct

20   21   42°17'52"

24   Red Fox Run
Red Fox Run
Red Fox Run
Red Fox Run
Pheasant Ln
Pheasant Ct Tr
Pheasant Ct
Karakul Ln
2700

Ann Arbor Township

SEE 4407 MAP

Meadow Dr
Meadow Ln

Walnut Hall

Superior Township

Vreeland Rd
2500

SEE 4409 MAP

42°17'26"

Vreeland Rd
5800

Vreeland Rd
7000

R7E
R6E

Rd
Hickman

Rd

Leforge

5

42°17'00"

RADRICK FARMS GOLF COURSE

30   29   28

25

Rd

42°16'34"

GEDDES RD
2200
5800

Anns Wy

Valleyview Dr
Valleyview Dr
1600
1900

48105

GEDDES RD
2000

Towsley Ln
Stark
Strasse St
1300

Parker Mill County Park Rd

HURON RIVER

Riverwood St
SUPERIOR RD
6200
1900

GEDDES RD

LEFORGE RD

36   31   32   33

FOREST PARK

7

42°16'08"

A   B   C   D   E

83°39'57"   83°39'22"   83°38'47"   83°38'12"   83°37'37"   83°37'02"

SEE 4491 MAP

RAND McNALLY

MAP
4409

1:24,000
1 in. = 2000 ft.
0   0.25   0.5
miles

SEE 4334 MAP

42°19'11"

FORD RD   153   8000   FORD RD   8800

WESTLAWN WEST MEM GARDENS

Cherokee Tr

N PROSPECT RD

3200

Rolling Acres Ln

Lake Rd

Berry Rd

42°18'44"

16   15   14

Frains Rd

2

3000   3000

42°18'18"

CHERRY   HILL   RD   CHERRY HILL RD

8700   9000

SUPERIOR CENTER PARK

N PROSPECT RD

3

48198

42°17'52"

21   22   23

Superior Township

SEE 4408 MAP

4

2500   2600

Vreeland   Rd

8000

N HARRIS RD

SEE 4410 MAP

42°17'26"

Vreeland   Rd   Vreeland   Rd

7200   9000

5

42°17'00"

28   27   26

Hunters Creek

Paddock Wy   Dr

6

2000

2000

2000

GEDDES   RD

8000   9000   Arlington Dr

N Harris Rd

Barrington Dr   Somerset Ln   Brookside Blvd

Ascot   Dr

Andover Dr

Arbor Woods

Mulberry Ln

Maplelawn Blvd

9500

42°16'34"

Ardmoor Dr   Stamford Dr   Eral Ct   Savannah Rd

Abbey Dr

Ridgeview Dr

Evergreen

Spruce Ln

Aspen Ln

Knollwood Blvd

Forestview Dr

White Oak Dr

Wexford Dr

7

33   34   35

Wiltshire Dr   Sheffield Dr   York Ct   Berkshire Ct   Thames Ct   Norfolk Av   Hamlet Dr   Manchester Dr   MacArthur Ct   MacArthur Blvd

Ashley Ln   Gardner St   Sherwood   Beechlawn Ct   Parklawn Ct   Edgewood Ct

FS

8400   1000

42°16'08"

A   B   C   D   E

83°37'02"   83°36'27"   83°35'51"   83°35'16"   83°34'41"   83°34'38"

SEE 4492 MAP

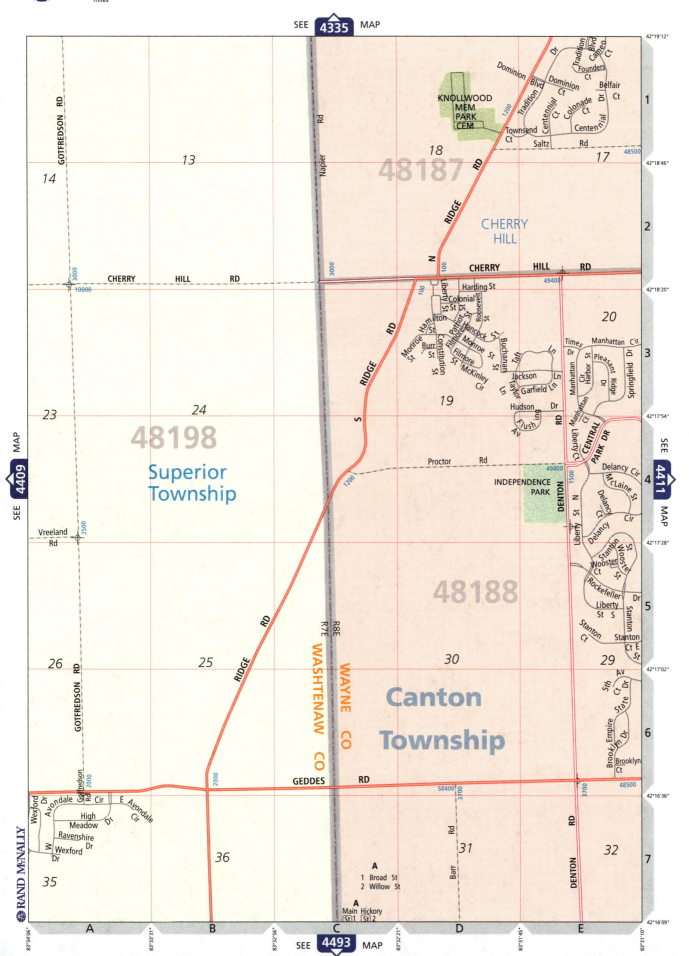

MAP
4410

1:24,000
1 in. = 2000 ft.

0   0.25   0.5
miles

SEE 4335 MAP

SEE 4409 MAP

SEE 4411 MAP

SEE 4493 MAP

48187

CHERRY
HILL

KNOLLWOOD
MEM
PARK
CEM

48198

Superior
Township

48188

Canton
Township

WASHTENAW CO
WAYNE CO

INDEPENDENCE
PARK

RAND McNALLY

GOTFREDSON RD
CHERRY HILL RD
Vreeland Rd
GEDDES RD
RIDGE RD
DENTON RD
Proctor Rd

A   1 Broad St   2 Willow St
A   Main   Hickory   St 1   St 2

MAP
4411

SEE 4336 MAP

1:24,000
1 in. = 2000 ft.
0   0.25   0.5
miles

N

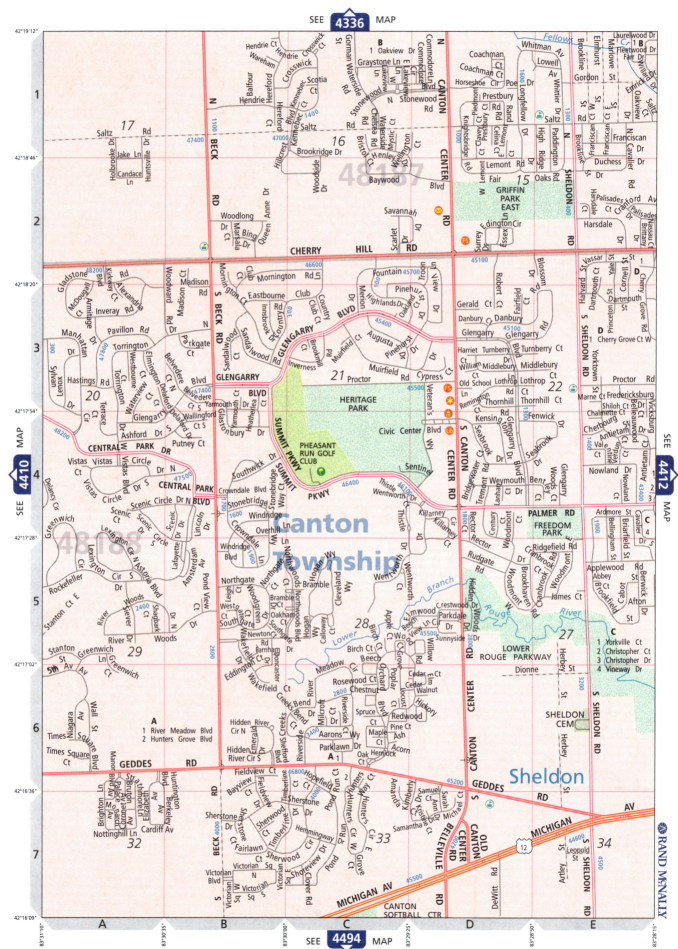

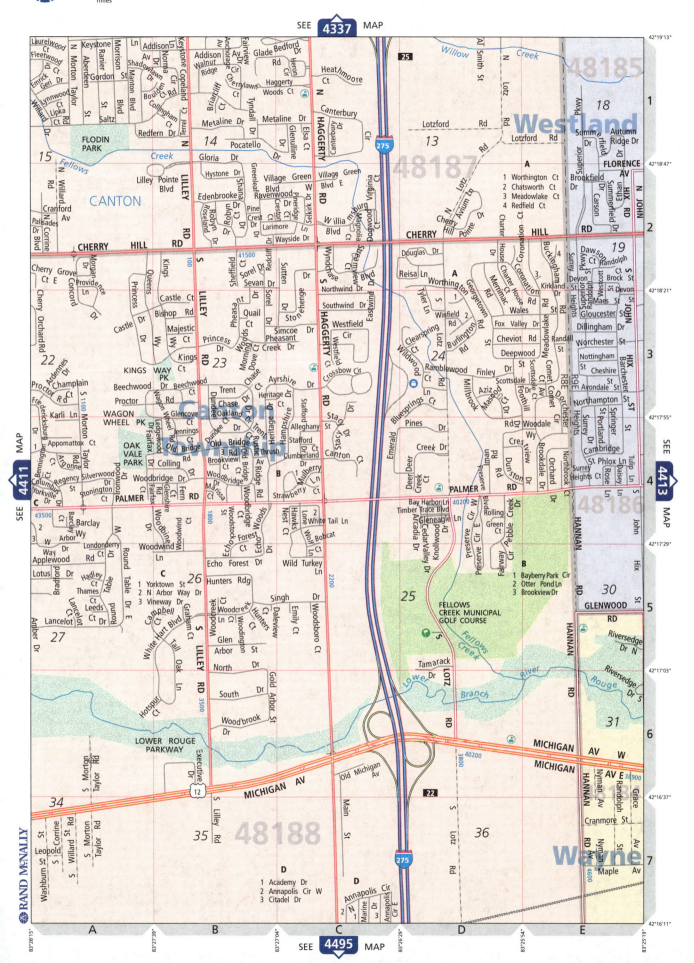

MAP 4412

SEE 4337 MAP

SEE 4411 MAP

SEE 4413 MAP

SEE 4495 MAP

1:24,000
1 in. = 2000 ft.
0   0.25   0.5
miles

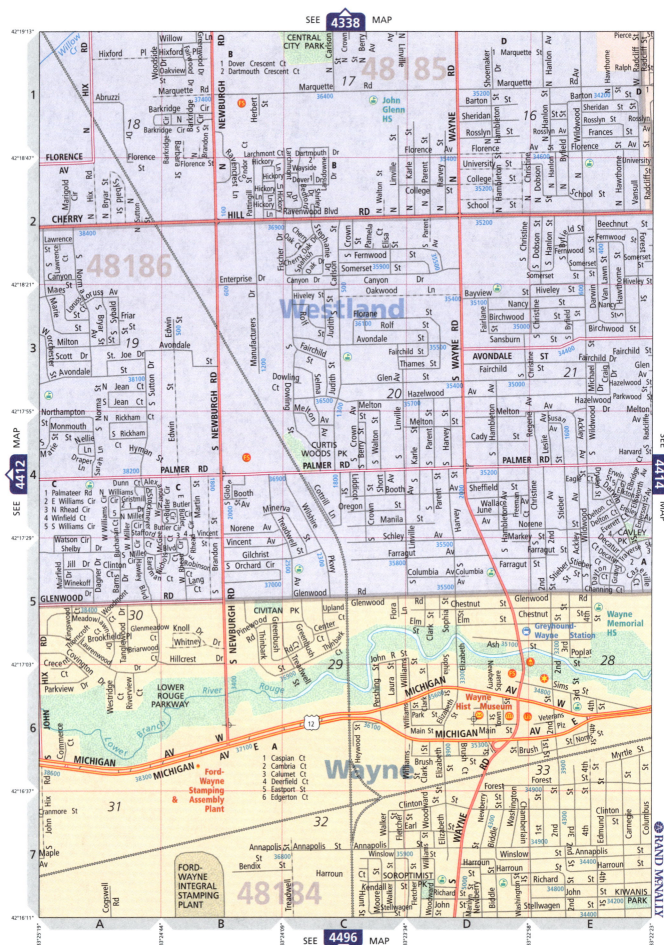

MAP
4413

1:24,000
1 in. = 2000 ft.
0   0.25   0.5
miles

SEE **4338** MAP

SEE **4412** MAP

SEE **4414** MAP

SEE **4496** MAP

RAND M⁹NALLY

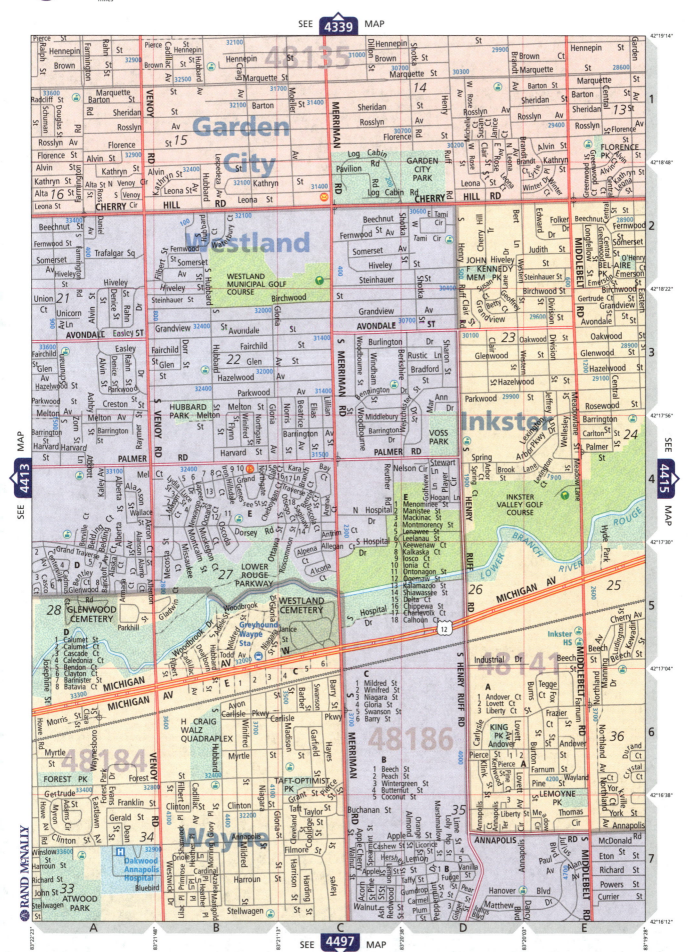

MAP
4414

MAP
4415

1:24,000
1 in. = 2000 ft.
0   0.25   0.5
miles

SEE 4340 MAP

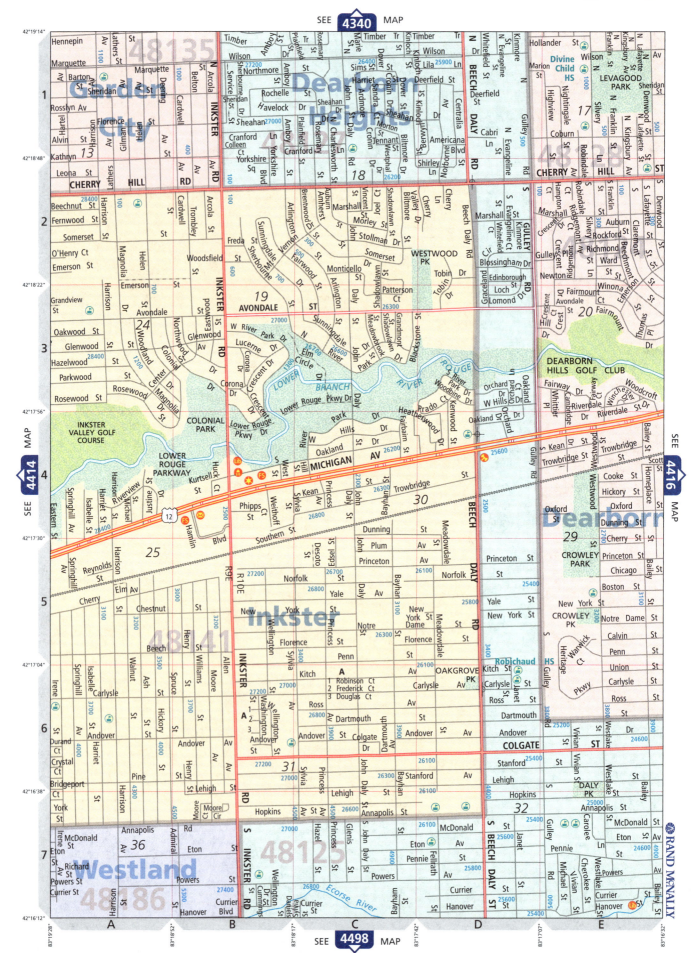

SEE 4414 MAP

SEE 4416 MAP

SEE 4498 MAP

RAND MCNALLY

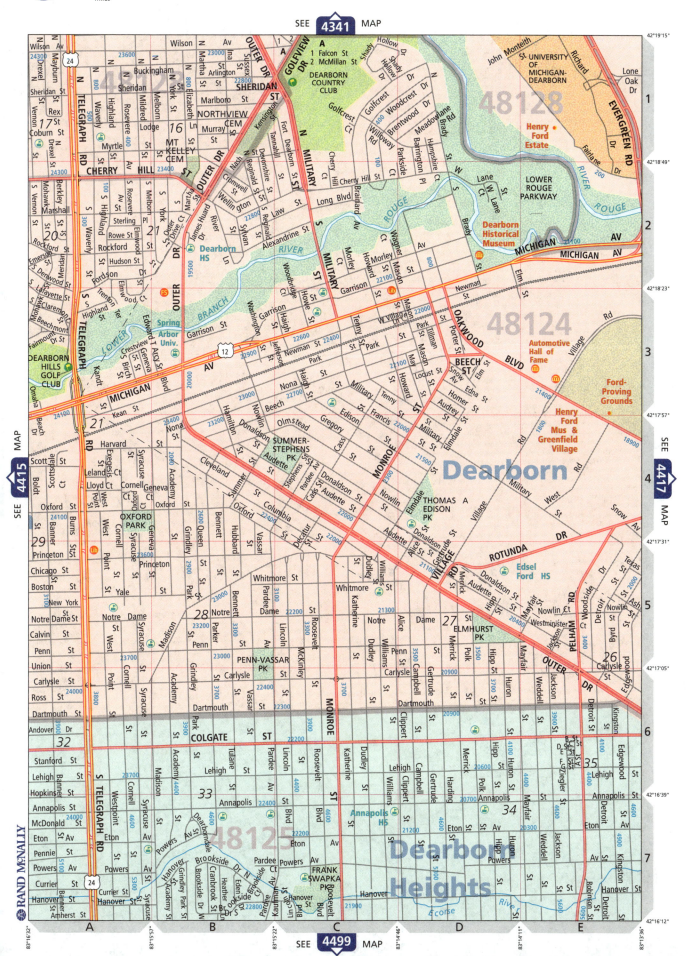

MAP
4416

SEE 4341 MAP
SEE 4415 MAP
SEE 4417 MAP
SEE 4499 MAP

1:24,000
1 in. = 2000 ft.
0   0.25   0.5
miles

48128

Dearborn

Dearborn Heights

48124

48125

RAND McNALLY

MAP
4417

1:24,000
1 in. = 2000 ft.
0   0.25   0.5
miles

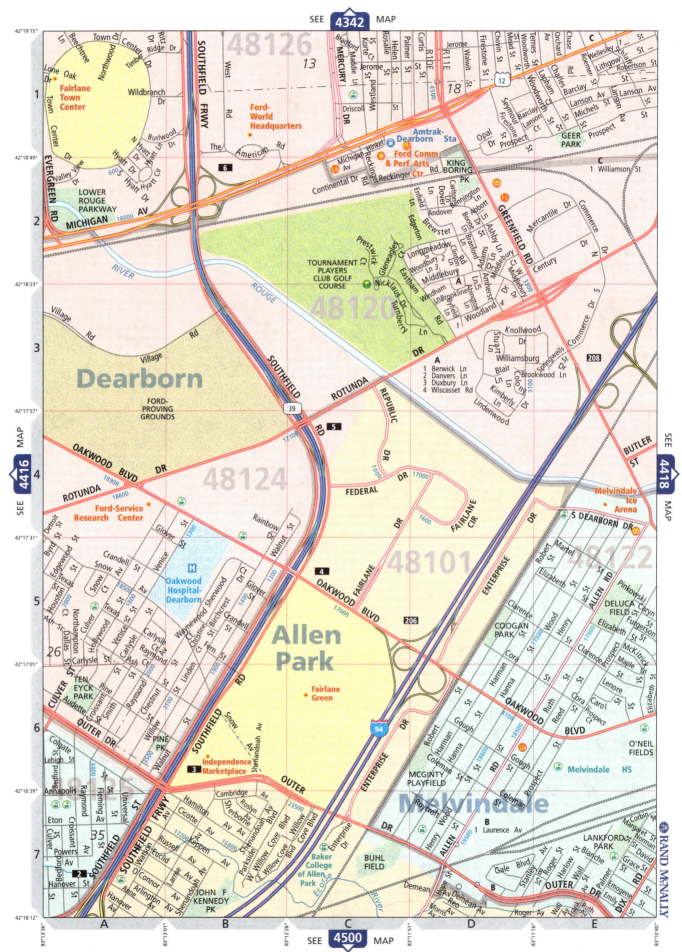

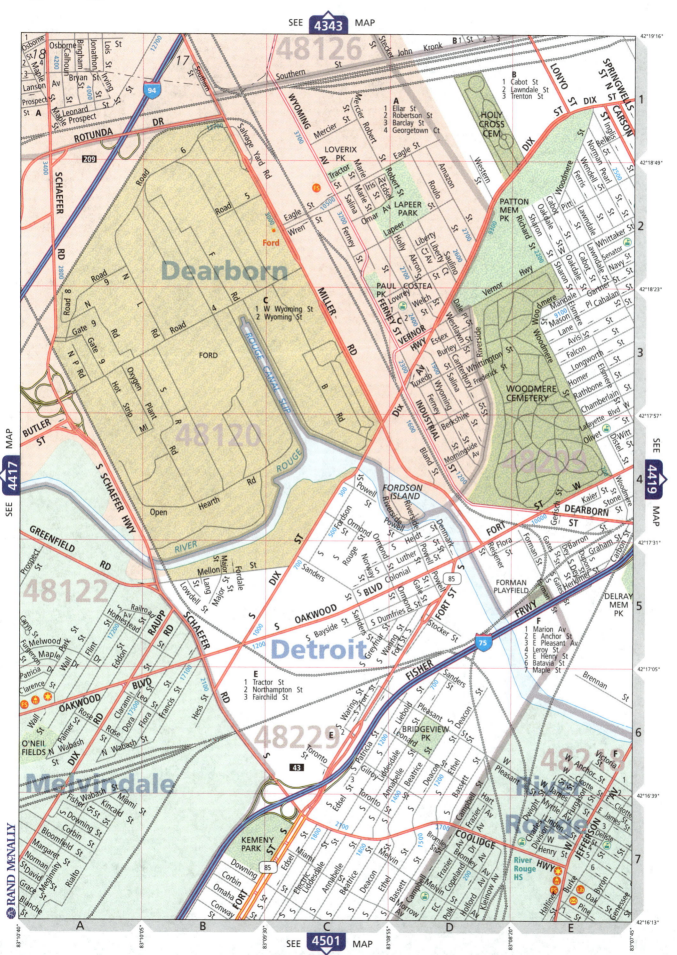

MAP
4418

SEE 4343 MAP

N
1:24,000
1 in. = 2000 ft.
0   0.25   0.5
miles

SEE 4417 MAP

SEE 4419 MAP

SEE 4501 MAP

RAND MCNALLY

Dearborn

Detroit

Melvindale

River Rouge

48126

48120

48122

48229

48209

48217

Ford

ROUGE CANAL SLIP

ROUGE RIVER

FORDSON ISLAND

HOLY CROSS CEM

PATTON MEM PK

WOODMERE CEMETERY

DELRAY MEM PK

LAPEER PARK

PAUL COSTEA PK

FORMAN PLAYFIELD

BRIDGEVIEW PK

O'NEIL FIELDS

KEMENY PARK

River Rouge HS

MAP
4419

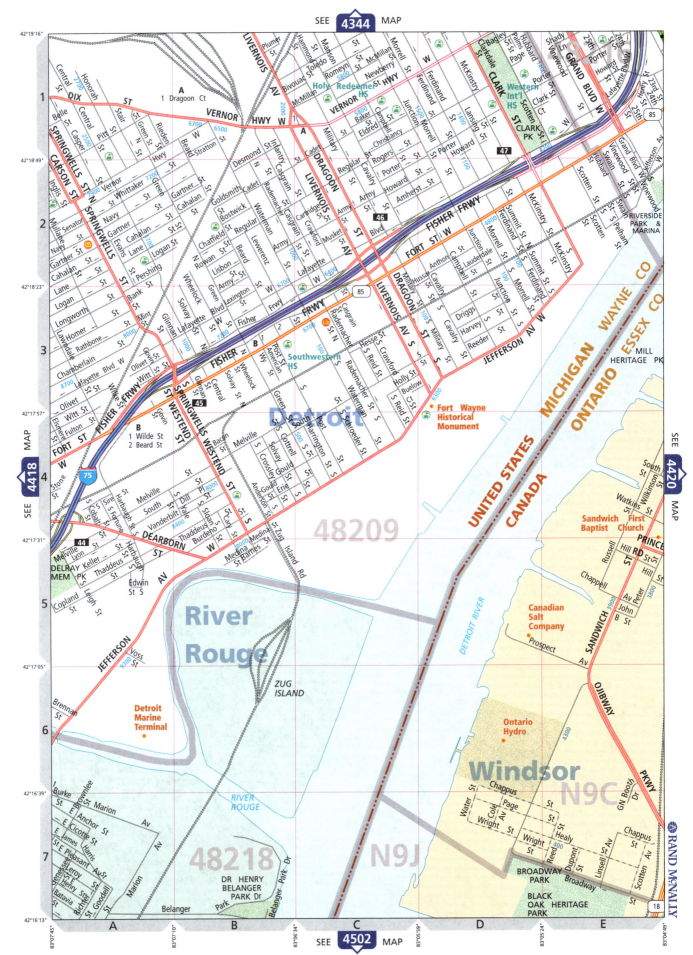

SEE 4344 MAP

1:24,000
1 in. = 2000 ft.

0   0.25   0.5
miles

Detroit

48209

River Rouge

ZUG ISLAND

Detroit Marine Terminal

48218

DR HENRY BELANGER PARK Dr

Windsor

N9C

N9J

Fort Wayne Historical Monument

Holy Redeemer HS

Western Int'l HS

RIVERSIDE PARK & MARINA

Southwestern HS

DELRAY MEM PK

DETROIT RIVER

MILL HERITAGE PK

Sandwich First Baptist Church

Canadian Salt Company

Ontario Hydro

BROADWAY PARK

BLACK OAK HERITAGE PARK

UNITED STATES
CANADA

MICHIGAN WAYNE CO
ONTARIO ESSEX CO

SEE 4418 MAP

SEE 4420 MAP

SEE 4502 MAP

RAND MCNALLY

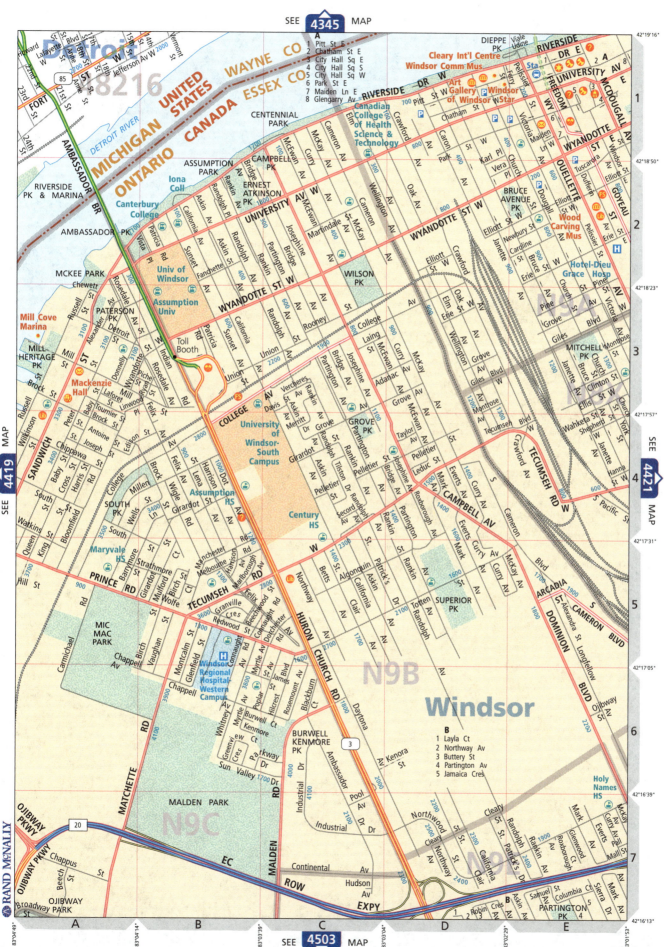

MAP
4420

1:24,000
1 in. = 2000 ft.
0   0.25   0.5
miles

N

A
1 Pitt St E
2 Chatham St E
3 City Hall Sq E
4 City Hall Sq S
5 City Hall Sq W
6 Park St E
7 Maiden Ln E
8 Glengarry Av

DIEPPE PK   Viale Udine
RIVERSIDE DR E
Cleary Int'l Centre
Windsor Comm Mus
Art Gallery of Windsor
UNIVERSITY AV

Detroit
WAYNE CO
ESSEX CO
UNITED STATES
CANADA
MICHIGAN
ONTARIO
Detroit River
AMBASSADOR BR

RIVERSIDE PK & MARINA
CENTENNIAL PARK
Canadian College of Health Science & Technology

ASSUMPTION PARK
CAMPBELL PK
Iona Coll
Canterbury College
ERNEST ATKINSON PK
UNIVERSITY AV W

AMBASSADOR PK
Univ of Windsor
Assumption Univ
WYANDOTTE ST W
WILSON PK
BRUCE AVENUE PK
Wood Carving Mus

MCKEE PARK
PATERSON PK
Toll Booth
Hotel-Dieu Grace Hosp

Mill Cove Marina
MILL HERITAGE PK
Mackenzie Hall

SANDWICH
COLLEGE AV
University of Windsor-South Campus
GROVE PK
MITCHELL PK

SOUTH PK
Assumption HS
Century HS

Maryvale HS
PRINCE RD
TECUMSEH RD
SUPERIOR PK

MIC MAC PARK
Windsor Regional Hospital-Western Campus

N9B
Windsor

BURWELL KENMORE PK

B
1 Layla Ct
2 Northway Av
3 Buttery St
4 Partington Av
5 Jamaica Cres

Holy Names HS

MALDEN PARK
N9C

OJIBWAY PKWY
Chappus St
Beech St
Broadway Park
OJIBWAY PARK
EC ROW EXPY

PARTINGTON PK

RAND McNALLY

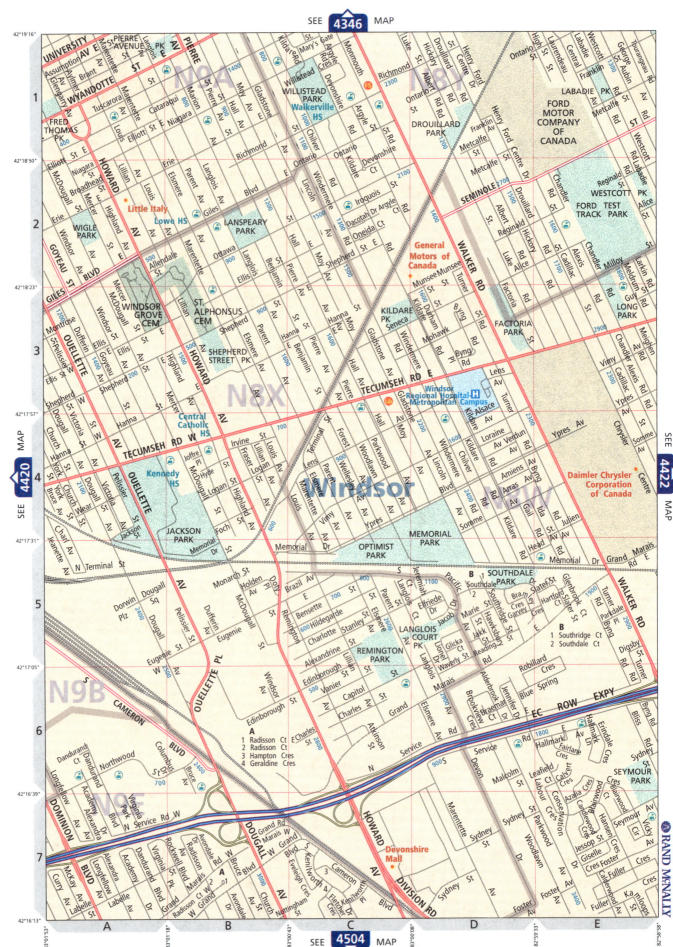

MAP
4421

1:24,000
1 in. = 2000 ft.

0   0.25   0.5
miles

SEE 4346 MAP

SEE 4420 MAP

SEE 4422 MAP

SEE 4504 MAP

RAND M°NALLY

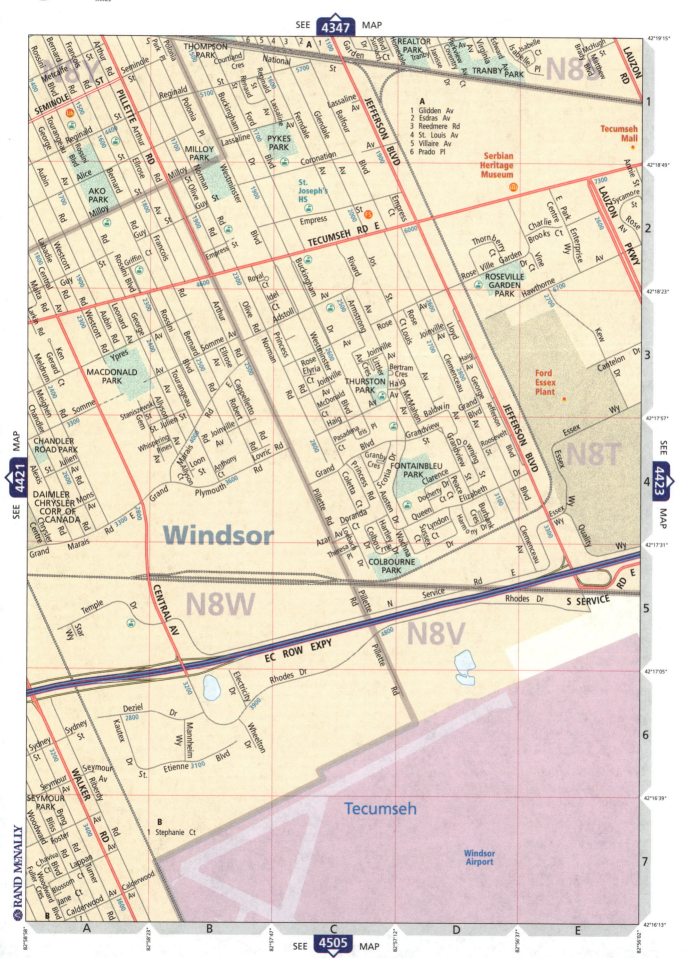

MAP
4422

1:24,000
1 in. = 2000 ft.
0   0.25   0.5
miles

N8Y

N8S

N8T

N8W

N8V

Windsor

Tecumseh

A   1 Glidden Av
     2 Esdras Av
     3 Reedmere Rd
     4 St. Louis Av
     5 Villaire Av
     6 Prado Pl

B   1 Stephanie Ct

Tecumseh Mall

Serbian Heritage Museum

Ford Essex Plant

Windsor Airport

SEMINOLE

PILLETTE RD

JEFFERSON BLVD

LAUZON RD

LAUZON PKWY

TECUMSEH RD E

EC ROW EXPY

CENTRAL AV

WALKER RD

S SERVICE RD E

AKO PARK

PYKES PARK

MILLOY PARK

THOMPSON PARK

REALTOR PARK

TRANBY PARK

ROSEVILLE GARDEN PARK

MACDONALD PARK

THURSTON PARK

FONTAINBLEU PARK

CHANDLER ROAD PARK

COLBOURNE PARK

SEYMOUR PARK

DAIMLER CHRYSLER CORP OF CANADA

St. Joseph's HS

SEE 4421 MAP

SEE 4423 MAP

RAND MCNALLY

MAP
4423

1:24,000
1 in. = 2000 ft.
0   0.25   0.5
miles

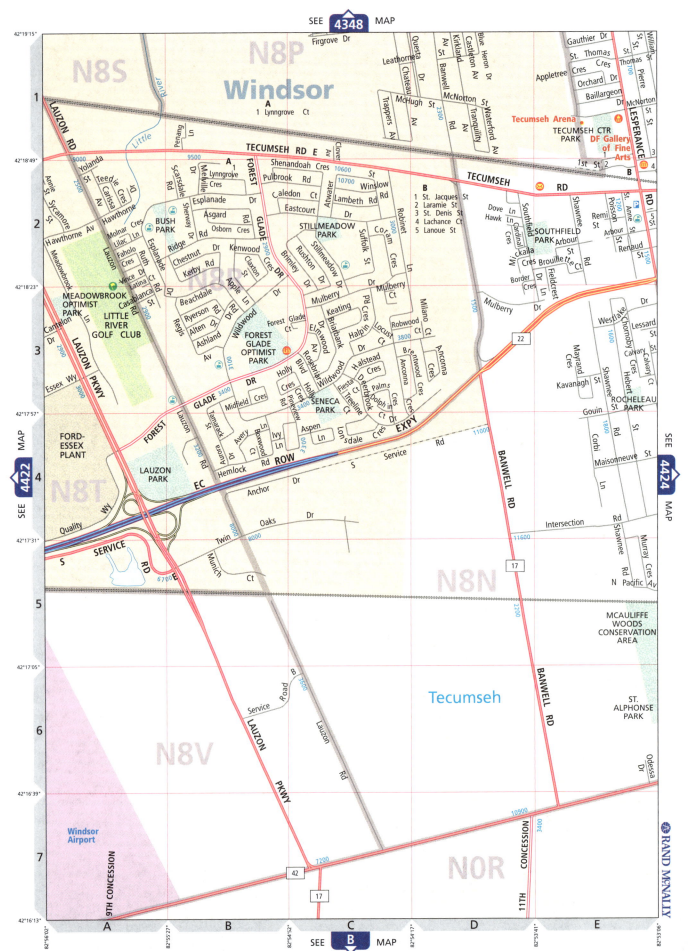

SEE 4348 MAP

N8S

N8P

Windsor

SEE 4422 MAP

SEE 4424 MAP

N8T

N8N

N8V

N0R

Tecumseh

Windsor Airport

MCAULIFFE WOODS CONSERVATION AREA

ST. ALPHONSE PARK

SEE B MAP

RAND McNALLY

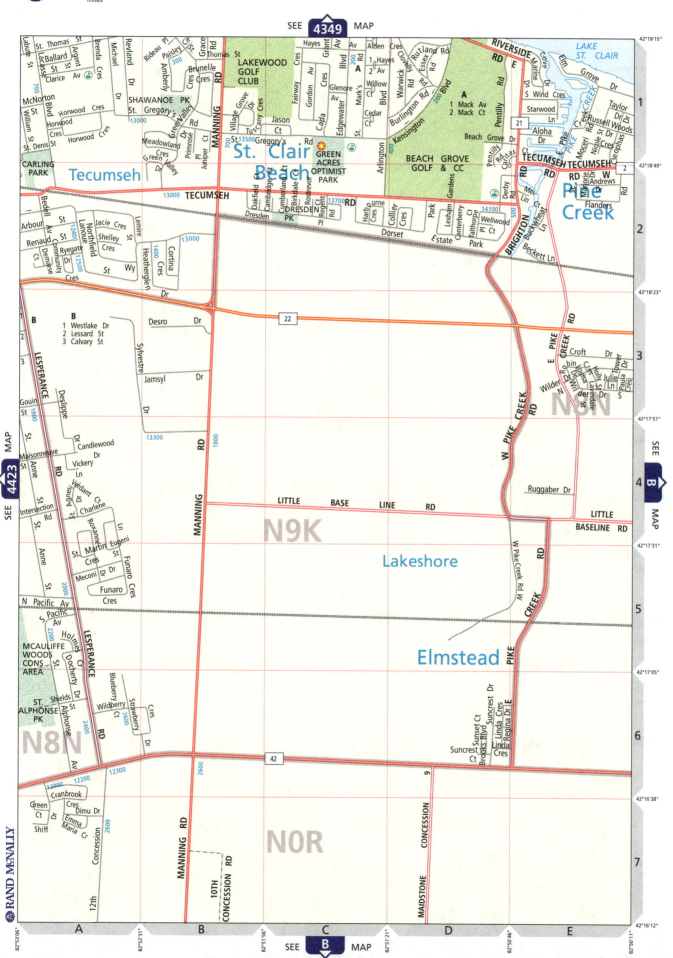

MAP
4424

1:24,000
1 in. = 2000 ft.
0   0.25   0.5
miles

SEE 4349 MAP

RIVERSIDE RD E

LAKE ST. CLAIR

LAKEWOOD GOLF CLUB

SHAWANOE PK

CARLING PARK

Tecumseh

St. Clair Beach

GREEN ACRES OPTIMIST PARK

BEACH GROVE GOLF & CC

TECUMSEH

Pine Creek

N8N

N9K

Lakeshore

Elmstead

MCAULIFFE WOODS CONS AREA

ST. ALPHONSE PK

N8N

N0R

LITTLE BASE LINE RD

LITTLE BASELINE RD

MANNING RD

LESPERANCE RD

10TH CONCESSION RD

MAIDSTONE CONCESSION

W PIKE CREEK RD

SEE 4423 MAP

SEE B MAP

SEE B MAP

RAND McNALLY

MAP
4487

1:24,000
1 in. = 2000 ft.

0   0.25   0.5

miles

SEE **4404** MAP

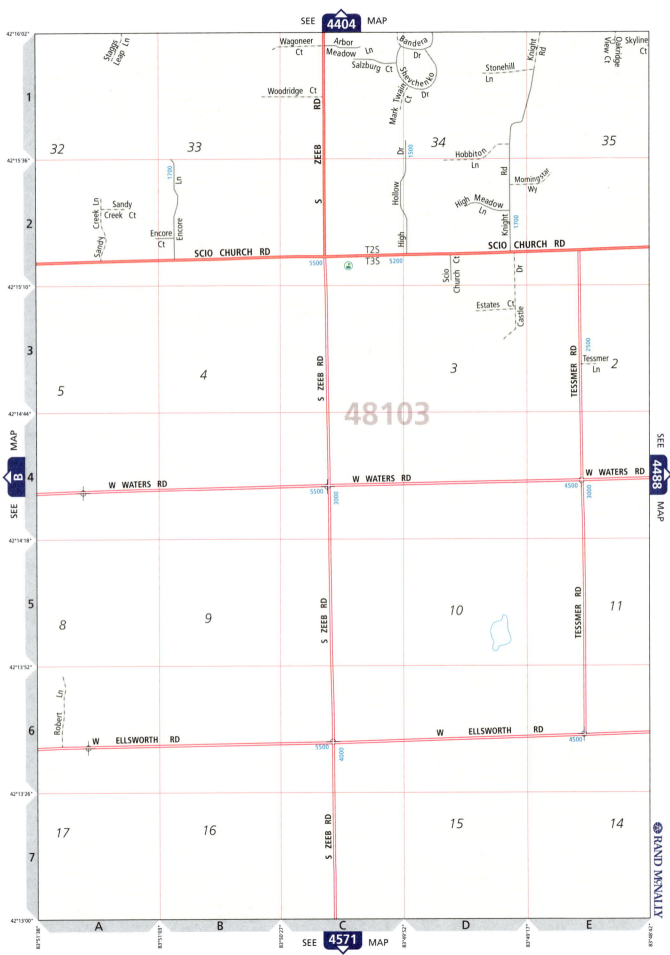

42°16'02"

Staggs Leap Ln

Wagoneer Ct

Arbor Meadow Ln

Bandera Dr

Salzburg Ct

Shevchenko Dr

Knight Rd

Oakridge View Ct

Skyline Ct

Woodridge Ct

Stonehill Ln

Mark Twain Ct

S ZEEB RD

1

32   33   34   35

42°15'36"

Sandy Creek Ln

Sandy Creek Ct

Ln

1700

Encore Ct

Encore

2

Hollow Dr

1500

Hobbiton Ln

Morningstar Wy

High Meadow Ln

Knight Rd

High

S

Sandy

SCIO CHURCH RD

T2S

5500

T3S

5200

SCIO CHURCH RD

Knight

1700

42°15'10"

Scio Church Ct

Estates Ct

Castle Dr

3

5   4   3   Tessmer Ln

2

S ZEEB RD

TESSMER RD

2500

42°14'44"

48103

SEE **4488** MAP

SEE **B** MAP

4

W WATERS RD

5500

3000

W WATERS RD

W WATERS RD

4500

3000

42°14'18"

5

8   9   10   11

S ZEEB RD

TESSMER RD

42°13'52"

Robert Ln

6

W ELLSWORTH RD

5500

4000

W ELLSWORTH RD

4500

S ZEEB RD

42°13'26"

7

17   16   15   14

S ZEEB RD

42°13'00"

A   83°51'38"   83°51'03"   B   83°50'27"   C   83°49'52"   D   83°49'17"   E

83°48'42"

MAP
4488

1:24,000
1 in. = 2000 ft.

0   0.25   0.5
miles

SEE 4405 MAP

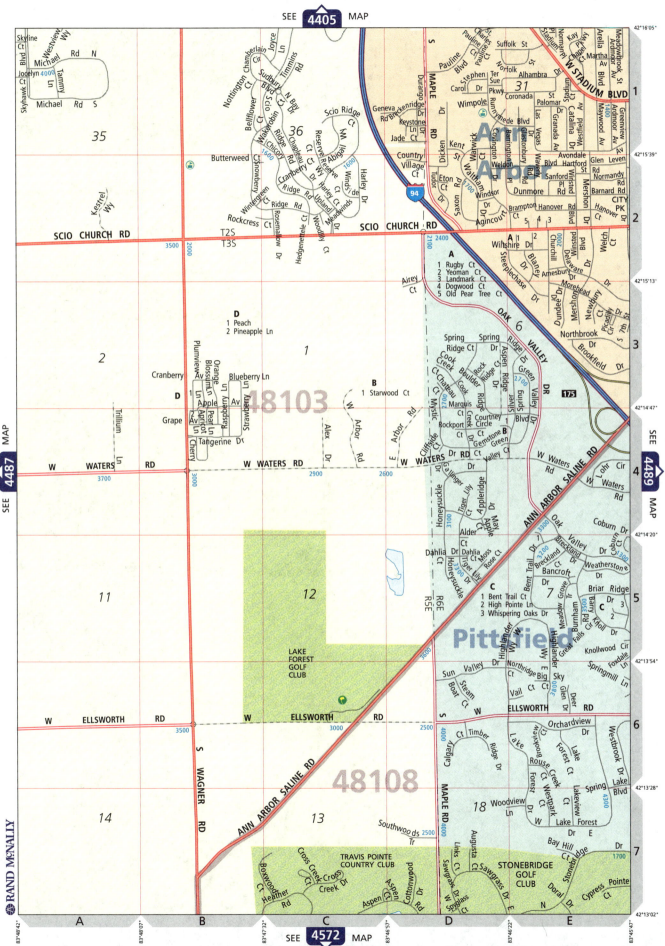

42°16'05"

42°15'39"

42°15'13"

42°14'47"

42°14'20"

42°13'54"

42°13'28"

42°13'02"

SEE 4487 MAP

SEE 4489 MAP

Ann Arbor

CITY PK

Pittsfield

48103

48108

A 6 OAK VALLEY DR

175

LAKE FOREST GOLF CLUB

TRAVIS POINTE COUNTRY CLUB

STONEBRIDGE GOLF CLUB

SCIO CHURCH RD

W WATERS RD

W ELLSWORTH RD

ANN ARBOR SALINE RD

S WAGNER RD

MAPLE RD

A   1   1 Rugby Ct
         2 Yeoman Ct
         3 Landmark Ct
         4 Dogwood Ct
         5 Old Pear Tree Ct

D   1 Peach
     2 Pineapple Ln

B   1 Starwood Ct

C   1 Bent Trail Ct
     2 High Pointe Ln
     3 Whispering Oaks Ct

RAND McNALLY

SEE 4572 MAP

83°48'42"   83°48'07"   83°47'32"   83°46'57"   83°46'22"   83°45'47"

A   B   C   D   E

MAP
4489

1:24,000
1 in. = 2000 ft.

0   0.25   0.5

miles

SEE **4406** MAP

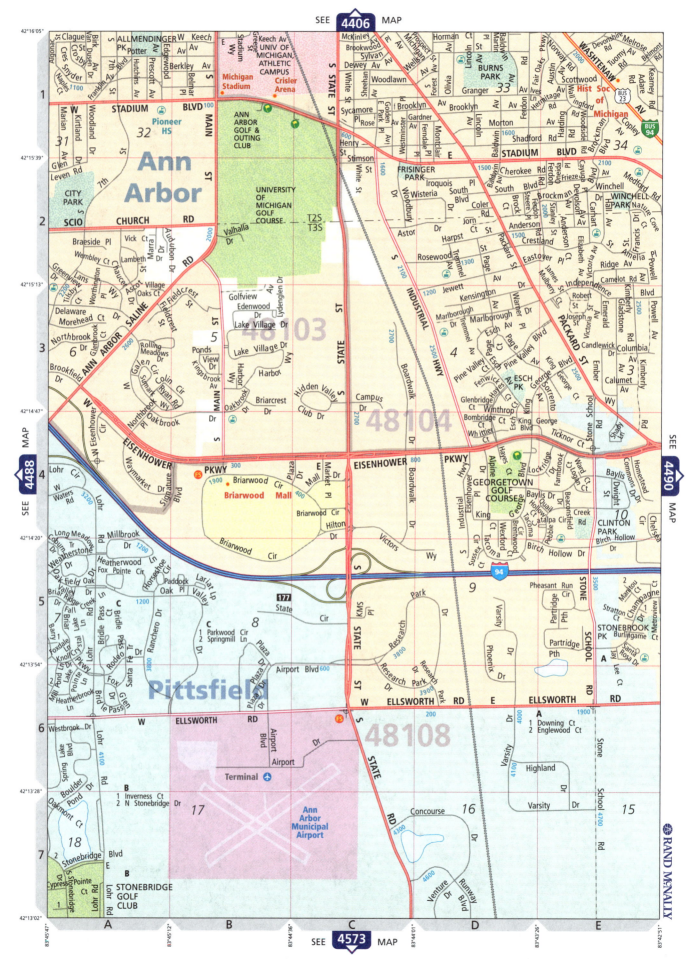

SEE **4488** MAP

SEE **4490** MAP

SEE **4573** MAP

RAND McNALLY

MAP
4490

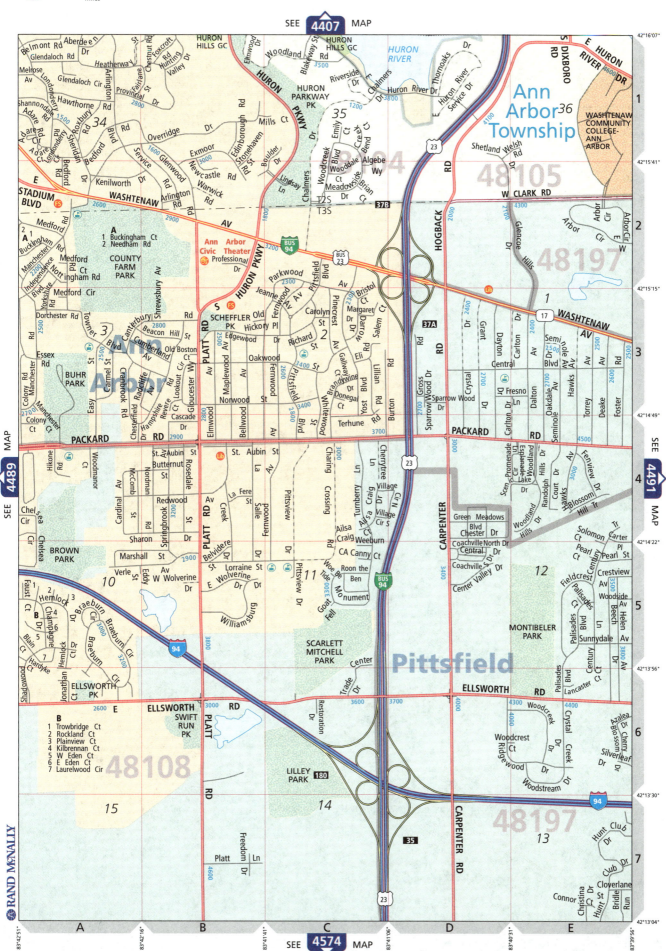

1:24,000
1 in. = 2000 ft.

0   0.25   0.5
miles

N

RAND MCNALLY

MAP
4491

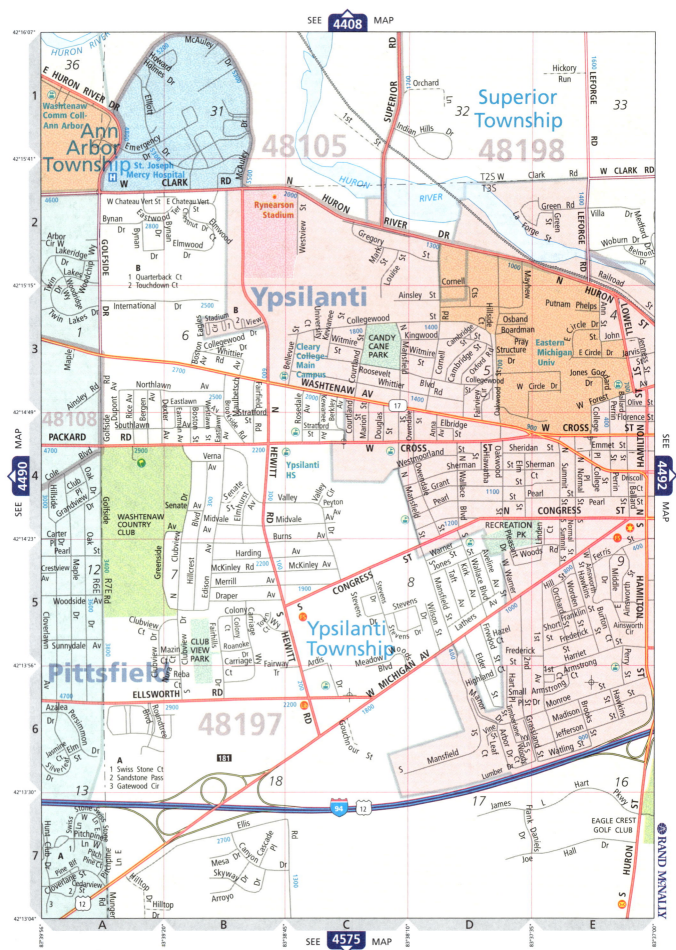

1:24,000
1 in. = 2000 ft.

0   0.25   0.5

miles

SEE **4408** MAP

SEE **4490** MAP

SEE **4492** MAP

SEE **4575** MAP

RAND MCNALLY

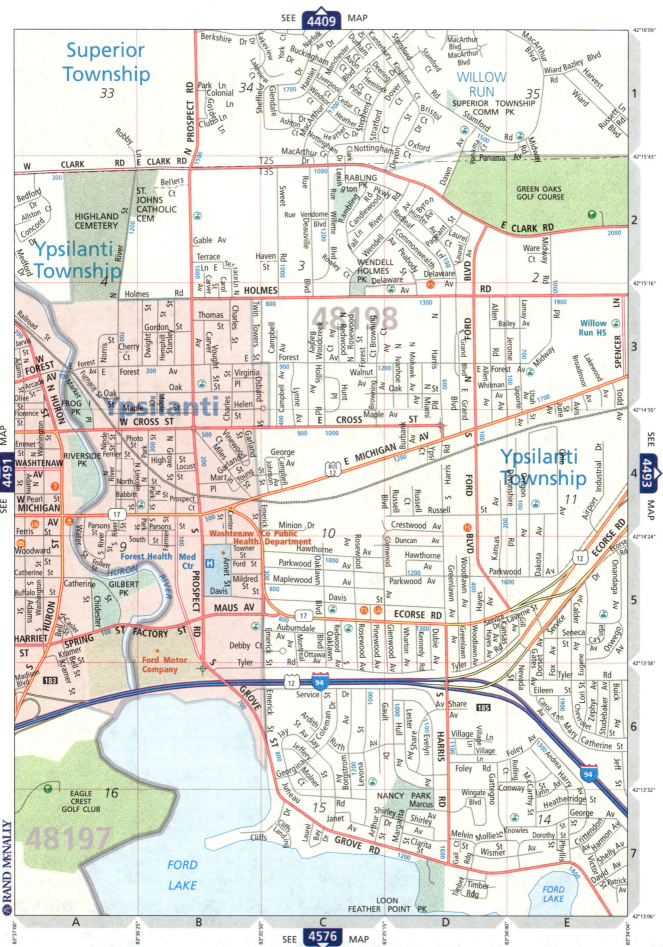

MAP
4493

1:24,000
1 in. = 2000 ft.

0   0.25   0.5
miles

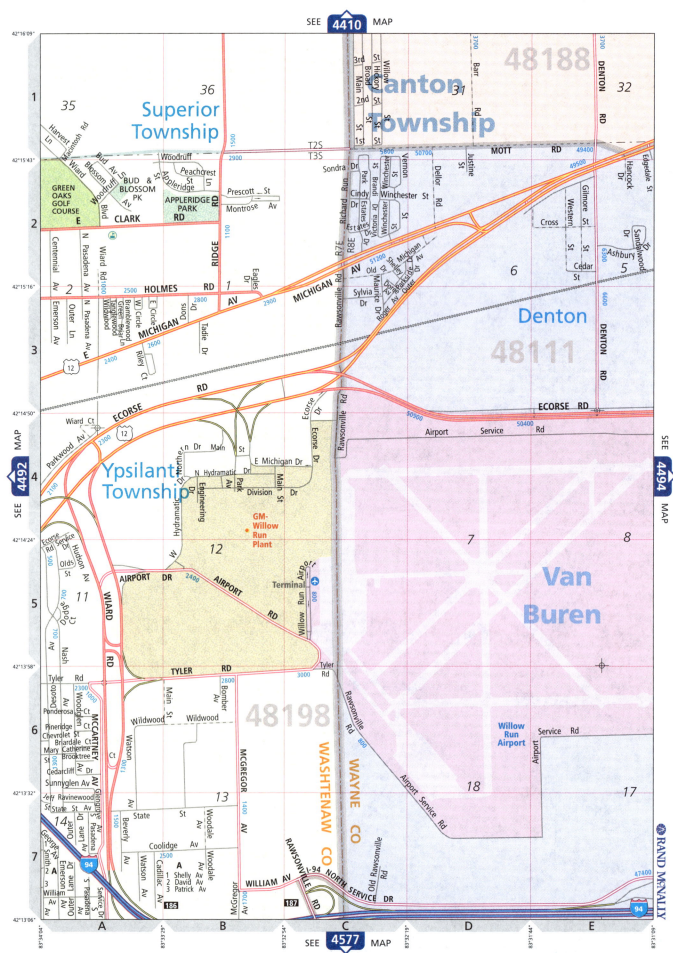

SEE 4410 MAP

42°16'09"

35   36   48188

Superior Township   Canton   31   32   Township

42°15'43"   T2S / T3S

Woodruff   2900   MOTT   RD   49400

GREEN OAKS GOLF COURSE   BUD & BLOSSOM PK   APPLERIDGE PARK   Prescott St   Montrose Av   Sondra Dr   Cindy Dr   Winchester St

Denton

42°15'16"   HOLMES   RD   MICHIGAN   AV   48111

MICHIGAN   Riley Ct   RD   ECORSE

42°14'50"   ECORSE   12   E Michigan Dr   Airport Service Rd   ECORSE RD   50400

SEE 4492 MAP

Ypsilanti Township   GM-Willow Run Plant   Terminal

42°14'24"   11   12   7   8   **Van Buren**

AIRPORT DR   AIRPORT RD

42°13'58"   TYLER   RD   Tyler Rd

Tyler Rd   48198   Willow Run Airport   18   17

42°13'32"   13

14   WASHTENAW CO   WAYNE CO

42°13'06"   William Av   WILLIAM AV   186   187   Rawsonville Rd

SEE 4577 MAP

A   B   C   D   E

SEE 4494 MAP

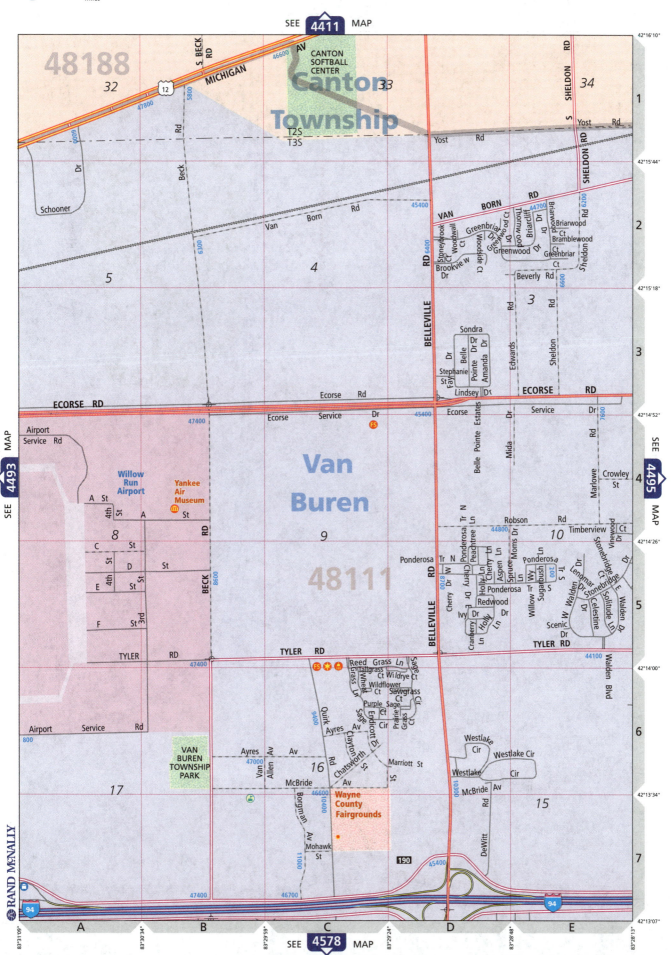

MAP
4494

1:24,000
1 in. = 2000 ft.
0   0.25   0.5
miles

SEE 4411 MAP

48188

32   CANTON SOFTBALL CENTER   33   34

Canton Township

T2S
T3S

S. BECK RD

MICHIGAN AV

12

46600

47800

6000

5800

Schooner

Dr

Beck   Rd

Beck

6300

SHELDON RD

S Yost Rd

Yost   Rd

5   Van   Born   Rd   45400

Van   Born   Rd   4

VAN   BORN   RD

44700

Stoneybrook

Woodwall Ct

Greenbriar

Greenwood Ct

Thornwood Dr

Briarcliff

Brianwood Ct

Briarwood

Bramblewood Ct

Greenwood Dr

Greenbriar Ct

Sheldon Rd

6200

6300

Brookvie w Dr

Beverly Rd

6600

BELLEVILLE

Rd   3   Rd

Sondra Dr

Belle Dr

Edwards

Sheldon

Stephanie
St
Fay Dr

Belle Pointe Dr

Amanda Dr

Lindsey Dr

Ecorse   Rd

ECORSE   RD

ECORSE   RD

47400

Ecorse   Service   Dr   45400

Ecorse

Belle Pointe Estates

Mida   Dr

Service   Dr

Rd   7600

SEE 4493 MAP

SEE 4495 MAP

Airport Service Rd

Willow Run Airport

Yankee Air Museum

Van Buren

Marlowe

Crowley St

A St

4th St

A St

C St

D St

E St

4th St

F St   3rd St

8

BECK   RD

8600

9   48111   10

Tr N

Robson   Rd   Timberview

44800

Tr N Ln

Ponderosa

Peachtree Ln

Aspen Ln

Spruce Ln

Morris Dr

Ponderosa Dr

Ponderosa Tr S

Stonebridge Ct

Lengmar Dr

Promauia Ct

Stonebridge E

Ponderosa
Tr W

Cherry Dr W

Holly Ln

Cherry Ln

Willow Wy

Ponderosa Tr S

Walden Dr

Celestine

Solitude Ln

Walden Dr

BELLEVILLE   RD

Cherry Dr

Redwood

Holly Dr

Scenic Dr

Ivy Ln

Holly Ln

Cranberry Ln

TYLER RD

TYLER RD

TYLER   RD

Reed Grass Ln

44100

Walden Blvd

TYLER   RD

47400

Tallgrass Ct

Grass Ln

Wheat Ct

Wildflower Ct

Purple Sage Ct

Sage Ct

Wildrye Ct

Savgrass Ct

Sage Ln

Prairie Grass Ct

Endicott Dr

Sage Cir

Quirk Rd

9400

Ayres Av

Airport   Service   Rd

800

Ayres Av

47000

Van Allen Av

McBride   Av

16

Claytworth St

Chatsworth St

Marriott St

Westlake Cir

Westlake Cir

Westlake Cir

10300

McBride Av

DeWitt Rd

15

VAN BUREN TOWNSHIP PARK

17

Borgman Av   46600

Wayne County Fairgrounds

10400

11000

Mohawk St

190

45400

94   47400   46700   94

RAND McNALLY

SEE 4578 MAP

A   B   C   D   E

MAP
4495

1:24,000
1 in. = 2000 ft.

0   0.25   0.5
miles

SEE **4412** MAP

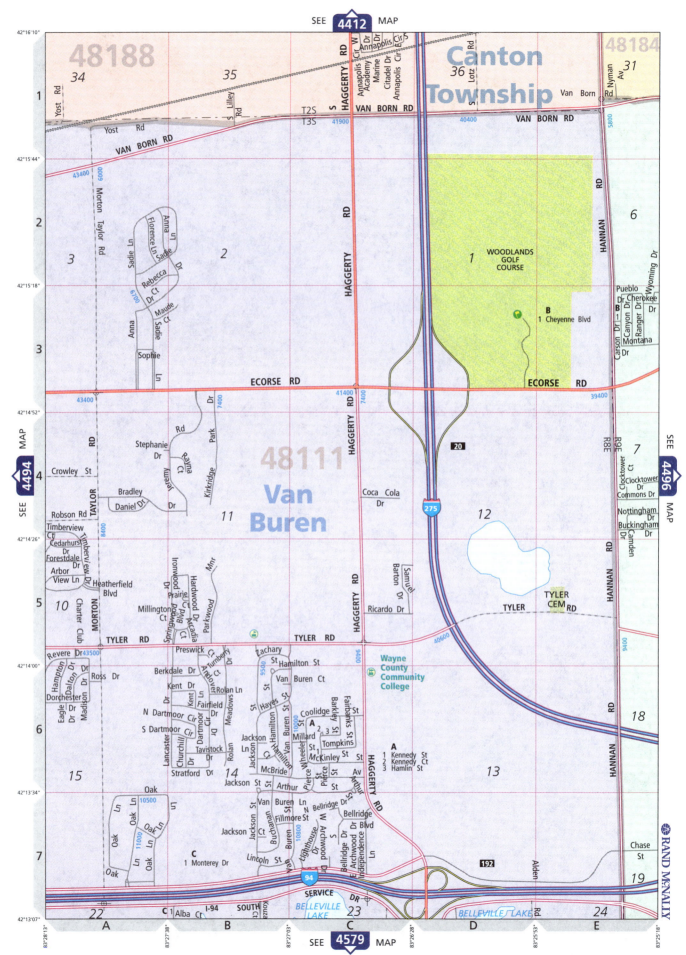

48188

Canton Township

48184

34   35   36   31

Yost Rd   Lilley Rd   HAGGERTY RD   Annapolis Academy   Marine Citadel Dr   Annapolis Cir   Annapolis Cir W   Lotz Rd   Van Born Rd   Nyman Av

1

VAN BORN RD   VAN BORN RD

Yost Rd   T2S T3S   41900   40400   VAN BORN RD   5800

VAN BORN RD

43400   0009   Morton Taylor Rd

2   Anna Ln   Florence Ln   Sadie Ln   Anna Ln   Sadie Dr   6700   Rebecca Ct Dr   Maude Ct   Sadie Ct   Anna   Sadie Ln   Sophie Ln   2   HAGGERTY RD   HAGGERTY   1   WOODLANDS GOLF COURSE   HANNAN RD   6   Wyoming Dr

3

3   Pueblo Dr   Cherokee Dr   B 1 Cheyenne Blvd   Carson Dr   Canyon Dr   Ranger Dr   B 1   Montana Dr   Wyoming Dr

ECORSE RD   ECORSE RD

43400   41400   39400

SEE **4494** MAP

TAYLOR RD   Crowley St   Stephanie Dr   Rd   Rayna Ct   Jeremy   Dr   Park   Kirkridge   7400   41400   7400   HAGGERTY RD   20   RGE   RGE   R8E   7   Clocktower Ct   Clocktower Dr   Commons Dr

48111

Van Buren

Bradley Dr   Daniel Dr   Dr   11   Coca Cola Dr   275   12   Nottingham Dr   Buckingham Dr   Camden Dr

Robson Rd   8400   Timberview Ct   Cedarhurst Dr   Forestdale Dr   Arbor View Ln   Timberview Dr   Heatherfield Blvd   MORTON   Ironwood Dr   Prairie Dr   Hardwood Dr   Spring Blvd   Arcadia Ct   Mnr   Parkwood   Samuel Barton Dr   Ricardo Dr   Samuel   Barton Dr   HAGGERTY RD   TYLER CEM   TYLER   TYLER RD   9400

5   10   Charter Club   Millington Ct   Spring Ct   15   TYLER RD   40600   TYLER RD

Revere Dr   43500   Preswick Dr   Zachary St   Hamilton St   9500   0406   **Wayne County Community College**

Hampton Dr   Dalton Dr   Ross Dr   Berkdale Dr   Andover Ct   Turnberry Dr   Rolan Ln   Van Buren Ct   St

Dorchester Dr   Eagle Dr   Madison Dr   Kent Dr   Kent Dr   Fairfield Dr   Dartmoor Dr   Meadows   Rolan Ln   Hayes St   Hamilton St   Van Buren St   10000   Coolidge   Barkley   Fairbanks   A   1   Kennedy St

6   N Dartmoor Cir   S Dartmoor Cir   Lancaster Dr   Churchill Dr   Tavistock Dr   Jackson Ln   Hamilton Ct   Millard   Tompkins   McKinley St   St   A 1   2 3   A   1 Kennedy St   2 Kennedy Ct   3 Hamlin St   18

15   Stratford Dr   14   McBride   Jackson St   Arthur St   Pierce St   Pierce St   Av   Haggerty Rd   13

Oak Ln   10500   Oak Ln   Oak Ln   11000   Oak Ln   Oak Ln   Jackson St   Van Buren Ln   Buchanan   Fillmore St   Lincoln St   Lighthouse Dr   Independence   Bellridge Dr   Archwood   Bellridge Dr   Bellridge Blvd   Ln   192   Alden   Chase St

7   Oak Ln   C   1 Monterey Dr   Jackson Ct   Van Buren St   10800   Archwood   19

Oak Ln   94   Kouza Ct   SERVICE DR   Dr

22   C 1 Alba Ct   I-94   SOUTH   23   24

BELLEVILLE LAKE   **BELLEVILLE LAKE**

A   B   C   D   E

SEE **4579** MAP

RAND McNALLY

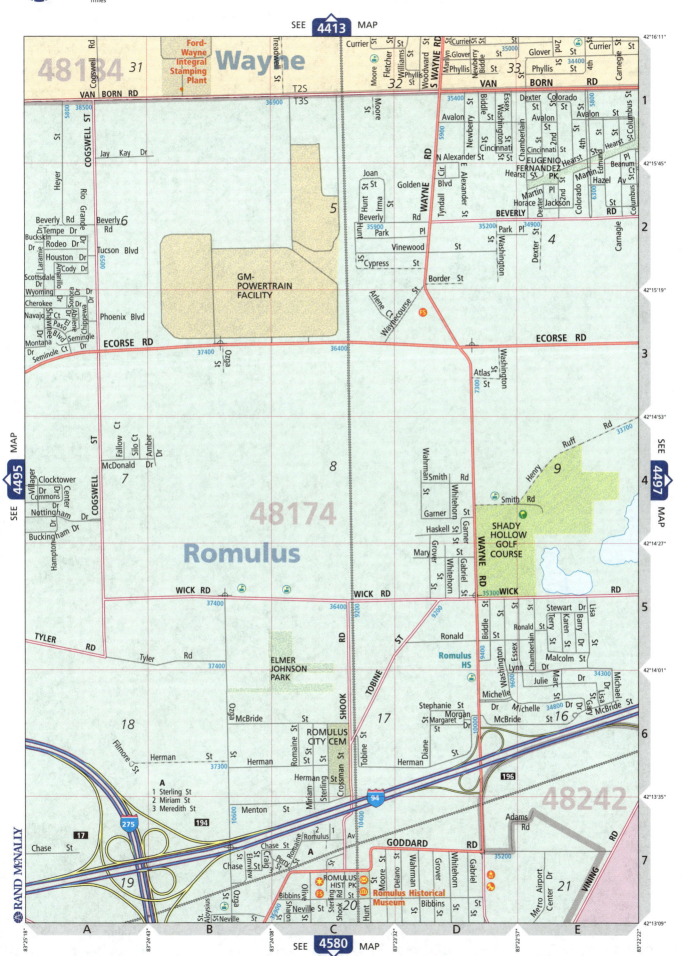

MAP
4496

1:24,000
1 in. = 2000 ft.
0   0.25   0.5
miles

SEE 4413 MAP

48184   31

Ford-Wayne Integral Stamping Plant

Wayne

Cogswell Rd

VAN BORN RD   T2S   T3S

Currier St   St   St   St   Currier   St
Glover   St   Glover   2nd   St
Fletcher   Williams St   Phyllis   Newberry   Biddle   St   34400   4th   St
Moore   Woodward   Phyllis   32   33   Phyllis   St   Carnegie St
Marilyn   VAN   BORN   RD

42°16'11"

Moore St   35400   St   Essex   St   Dexter   Colorado   St   5080   1
Avalon   Biddle   Washington   Chamberlain   Avalon   St   Columbus St
9500   N Alexander St   Cincinnati   2nd   Cincinnati   4th   Hearst   Beanum
WAYNE RD   Avalon St   St   St   St   EUGENIO   Martin   Hazel Av   **42°15'45"**
Joan   E Alexander St   FERNANDEZ   Hearst   Martin Pl   Columbus
Hunt   St   Golden   Tyndall Blvd   PK   Horace   Dexter   Colorado RD
St   Irma   Rd   Pl   Hearst   Jackson   St   St
Beverly   BEVERLY   St   RD
Park   35900   St   35200   Park Pl   34900   4   Carnegie   **42°15'45"**
Vinewood   St   Washington   Dexter St   2
Cypress   St   St

Border   St

Arlene Cir   FS   Atlas   Washington   **42°15'19"**
Waynecourse St   St   St   2301   ECORSE RD
Ozga St   37400   36400   3
ECORSE RD

SHADY HOLLOW GOLF COURSE

SEE 4495 MAP

SEE 4497 MAP

Ruff   Rd   33700   **42°14'53"**
Fallow Ct   Silo Ct   Amber Dr   Henry   9   4
McDonald Dr   8   Wahrman St   Smith   Rd
7   Smith   Rd   **42°14'27"**
Cogswell   Whitehorn   Garner
48174   St   Garner   St   St
Villager   Clocktower   Haskell   St   Garner St
Commons   Center Dr   **Romulus**   Mary   Grover   Gabriel St   WICK RD
Nottingham Dr   35300 WICK   RD   5
Buckingham Dr   WICK RD   37400   36400   9200   Stewart   Lisa   **42°14'01"**
Hampton Dr   Biddle   Dr
Ronald   Terry   Karen   Barry   St
TYLER   RD   TOBINE ST   Ronald   Essex   Chamberlain   Malcolm   Michael
Tyler   Rd   Romulus HS   Washington   Lynn   Marc   Julie   Dr   34300   St
37400   ELMER JOHNSON PARK   9600   Dr   Michelle   St Gary   McBride
18   McBride   SHOOK RD   17   Stephanie   St   Michelle   34800   Dr   Dr   St Lisa   Michael   6
Ozga St   McBride   St   Morgan   Dr   10000   Dr   16   McBride
Filmore St   Romaine St   Romulus CITY CEM   Margaret   Diane   St   Herman   **42°13'35"**
Herman   St   Herman   St   Tobine St   St
37300   Sterling   Crossman   St   Herman   48242
A   Miriam   196
1 Sterling St   Menton   St   10600   94   Adams   Rd
2 Miriam St   275   194   Romulus   1   Av   GODDARD   RD   35200
3 Meredith St   17   Chase St   2   A   Moore   Delano   Wahrman   Grover   Whitehorn   Gabriel   **42°13'35"**
Chase   Romaine   St   St   St   St   St   St   St   Metro Airport   7
19   Craig   Emview   Perry   St   ROMULUS   St   21   Center Dr   VINING RD
Chase St   St   St   HIST PK   Romulus Historical   St
Ozga   Olive   St   FS   Museum   Bibbins   St
Aloysius St   Sharon   Shook   Neville St   20   Hunt   St
Neville   St   Bibbins   St   **42°13'09"**

A   B   C   D   E

RAND MCNALLY

SEE 4580 MAP

83°25'18"   83°24'43"   83°24'08"   83°23'32"   83°22'57"   83°22'22"

MAP
4497

1:24,000
1 in. = 2000 ft.

0   0.25   0.5

miles

N

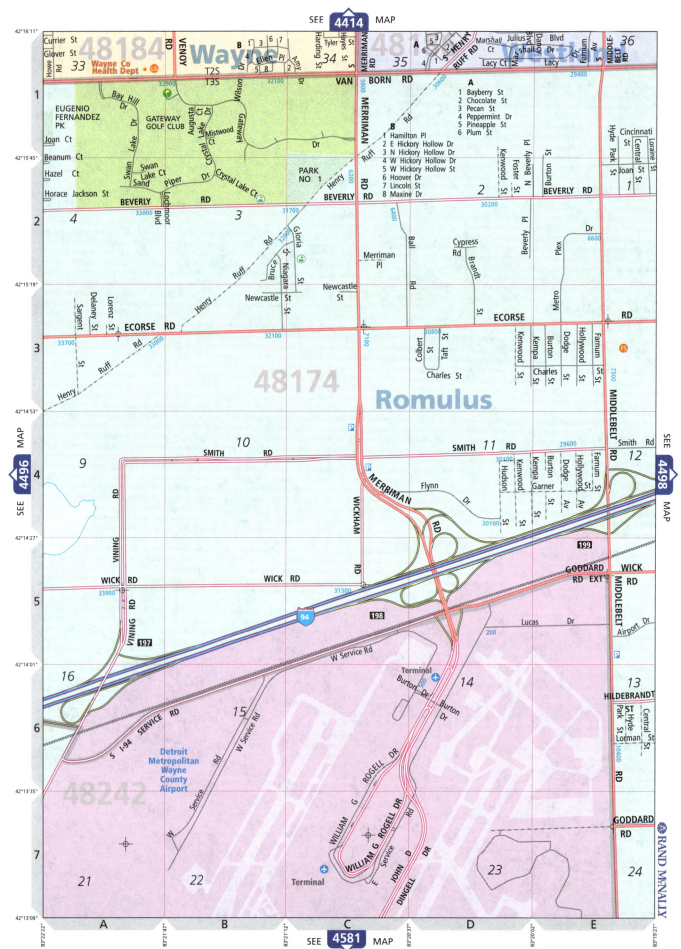

SEE **4414** MAP

48184 VENOY RD **Wayne** B West

Currier St
Glover St
Howe Rd 33
Wayne Co Health Dept ● Lib

T2S
T3S

Bay Hill Dr
Augusta
Wilson Dr

VAN BORN RD

GATEWAY GOLF CLUB

EUGENIO FERNANDEZ PK

Joan Ct

Beanum Ct

Hazel Ct

Horace Jackson St

Swan Lake Dr
Swan Lake Ct
Sand
Piper
Crystal Lake Ct
Mistwood Ct
Gateway

BEVERLY RD

Lochmoor Blvd

4   3

Ruff Rd

MERRIMAN RD

Henry

BEVERLY RD

PARK NO 1

Gloria St

Ruff

Bruce
Niagara St

Newcastle St

Newcastle St

Newcastle St

Merriman Pl

Ball Rd

Cypress Rd

Brandt St

Plex

Metro

A
1 Bayberry St
2 Chocolate St
3 Pecan St
4 Peppermint Dr
5 Pineapple St
6 Plum St

B
1 Hamilton Pl
2 E Hickory Hollow Dr
3 N Hickory Hollow Dr
4 W Hickory Hollow Dr
5 W Hickory Hollow St
6 Hoover Dr
7 Lincoln St
8 Maxine Dr

Foster St
Kenwood St
Beverly Pl N

Beverly Pl

2

Hyde Park
Cincinnati

Joan St

Central St
Loraine St

BEVERLY RD

1

Delaney St
Sargent
Lorenz St
Ruff Rd

ECORSE RD

St
Ruff Rd

Henry

48174

Colbert St
Charles St
Taft St

Kenwood St
Kempa St
Burton St
Dodge St
Hollywood St
Farnum St

Charles St

ECORSE RD

MIDDLEBELT RD

FS

Romulus

9

10

SMITH RD

WICKHAM RD

MERRIMAN RD

SMITH 11 RD
Smith Rd

Flynn Dr

Hudson
Kenwood St
Kempa St
Garner
Burton St
Dodge Av
Hollywood Av
Farnum St

12

SEE **4498** MAP

VINING RD

WICK RD

WICK RD

199

GODDARD RD EXT WICK RD

MIDDLEBELT RD

I-94

198

Lucas Dr

Airport Dr

200

VINING RD

197

W Service Rd

16

S I-94 SERVICE RD

15

Detroit Metropolitan Wayne County Airport

48242

Terminal

Burton Dr

14

WILLIAM G ROGELL DR

Burton Dr

13

HILDEBRANDT ST

Park St
Lorman St
Central St
Hyde

21

22

Terminal

WILLIAM G ROGELL DR

JOHN D DINGELL DR

Service Rd

23

GODDARD RD

24

RAND McNALLY

A   B   C   D   E

SEE **4581** MAP

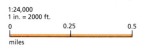

MAP
4498

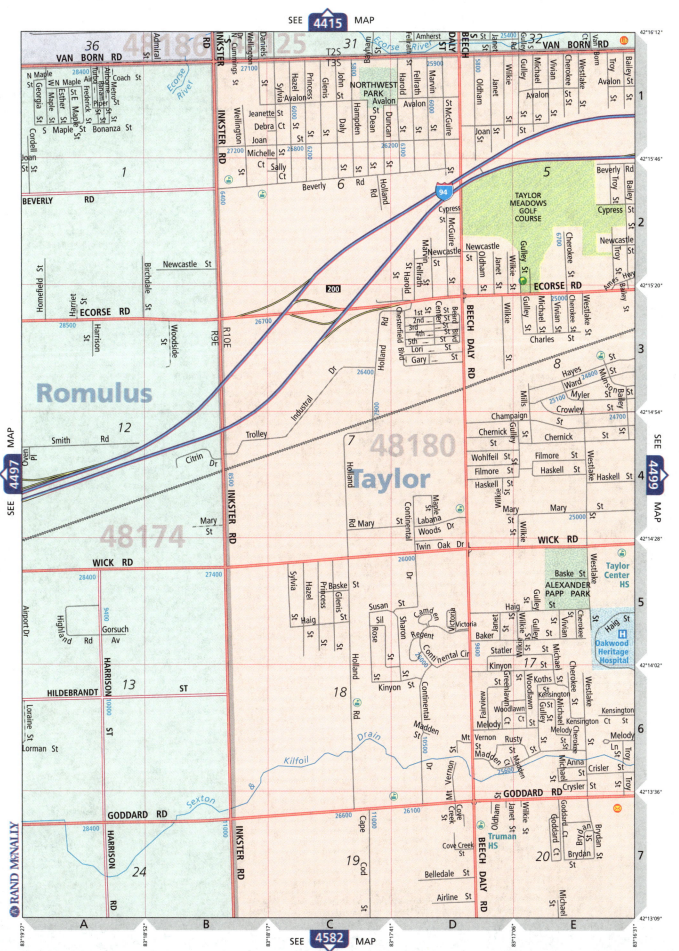

1:24,000
1 in. = 2000 ft.

0   0.25   0.5
miles

SEE **4415** MAP

N

42°16'12"

36

VAN BORN RD

VAN BORN RD

Lib

Northwest Park

Taylor Meadows Golf Course

I-94

200

Romulus

Taylor

48180

48174

Ecorse Rd

Beverly Rd

Ecorse Rd

Wick Rd

Taylor Center HS

Alexander Papp Park

Oakwood Heritage Hospital

Hildebrandt St

Goddard Rd

Truman HS

Rand McNally

42°15'46"
42°15'20"
42°14'54"
42°14'28"
42°14'02"
42°13'36"
42°13'09"

SEE **4497** MAP

SEE **4499** MAP

SEE **4582** MAP

A   B   C   D   E

MAP
4499

1:24,000
1 in. = 2000 ft.
0   0.25   0.5
miles

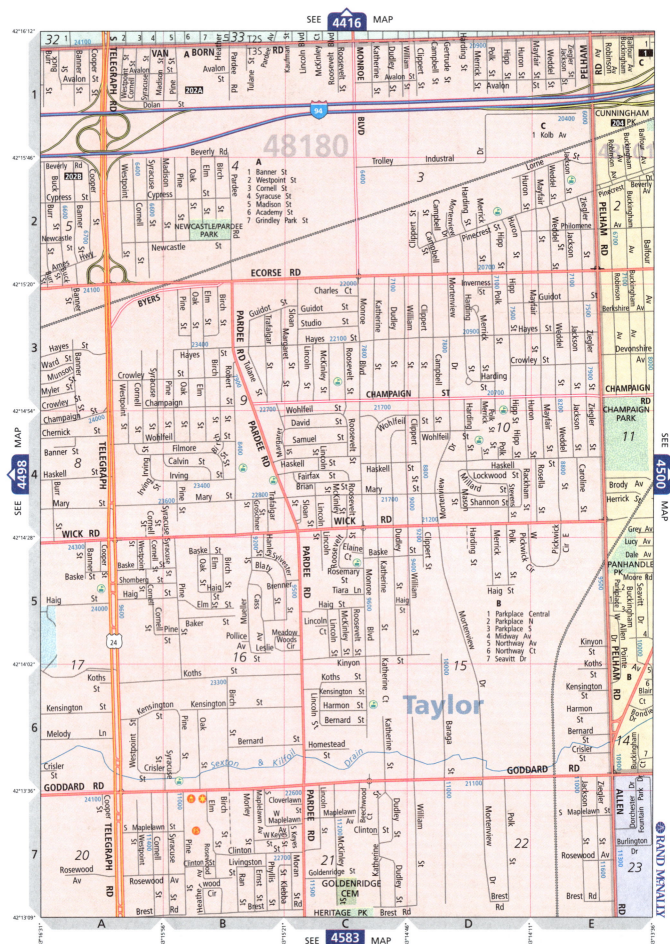

SEE 4416 MAP

48180

MAP 4498

SEE 4500 MAP

Taylor

SEE 4583 MAP

RAND McNALLY

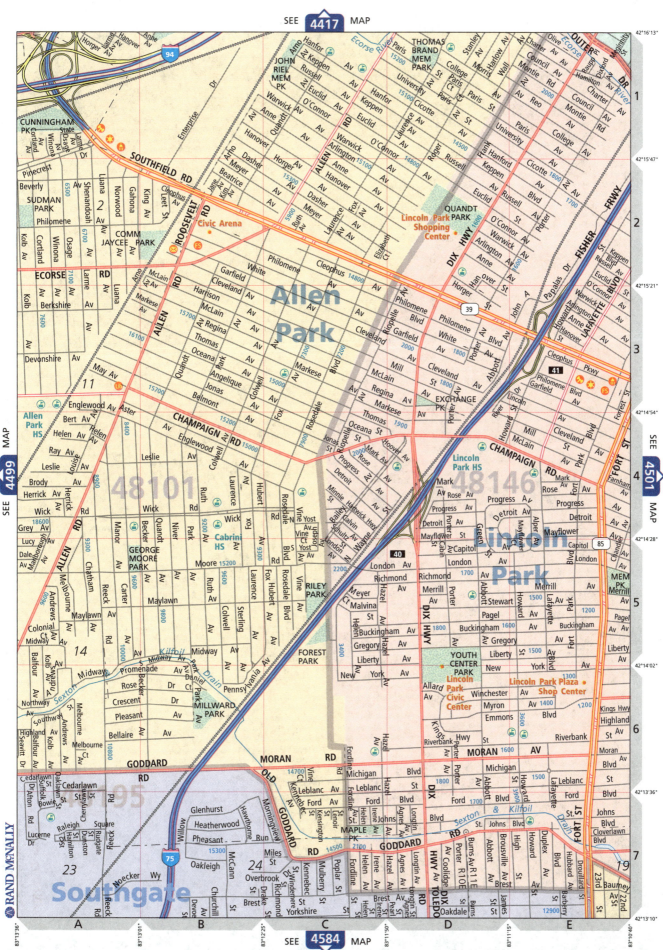

1:24,000
1 in. = 2000 ft.
0   0.25   0.5
miles

SEE 4499 MAP

SEE 4501 MAP

SEE 4584 MAP

Allen Park

Lincoln Park

Southgate

48101

48146

48195

MAP
4501

1:24,000
1 in. = 2000 ft.
0   0.25   0.5
miles

SEE 4418 MAP

SEE 4500 MAP

SEE 4502 MAP

A
1 Charter St
2 Pennsylvania Av
3 Demean Av

B
1 W Great Lakes St

C
1 Warwick Av
2 Arlington Av

D
1 Hilda Av
2 Labadie Ct
3 John II Av

E
1 N Riverbank St
2 S Riverbank St

RAND McNALLY

SEE 4585 MAP

MAP
4502

1:24,000
1 in. = 2000 ft.
0   0.25   0.5
miles

SEE 4419 MAP

42°16'13"

48218
River
Rouge

DR HENRY
BELANGER PARK

BLACK OAK
HERITAGE
PARK

Oak St
Richter St
Coolidge Hwy
Pine St
Maple St
Goodell
Marion
Av

E Great Lakes St

Broadway St

OJIBWAY
PARK

1

42°15'47"

Ironwood   Dr

Maplewood   Rd

Cherry Blossom   Dr

Weaver   Rd

Windsor
Raceway

Weaver
Rd

Marigold St

UNITED STATES
CANADA

Nicholson
Terminal

Ecorse
48229

DETROIT
RIVER

WAYNE CO
ESSEX CO

Windsor

Sprucewood   Av

300   600

SPRUCEWOOD AV

800

OJIBWAY PKWY

2

42°15'21"

DETROIT RIVER

N9J

Morton   Dr

400   600

Morton

Old   Morton   Industrial   Dr   6100

18

Morton
Darlene   Dr   Dr

Michael
Cres

Steven
Dr

Ramblewood   Av

Pope
St

OJIBWAY
OAKS
PARK

Gladwin
St

Wales
Centre
Av

3

42°14'55"

SEE 4501 MAP

MICHIGAN
ONTARIO

Riverrilla Ct

Rivervilla Ct

Front Rd

Antaya St

River   Av

300

Turkey   Creek

Marne   Av

600

TURTLE
CLUB
PARK

SENATOR
PAUL LUCIER
PARK

Turkey

Wales
Ct   Wales
St

Creek

Oakridge
St

Reaume   Av

Smith
Cres   Rd

4

42°14'29"

FIGHTING ISLAND

Park
Haven Marina

Major   Blvd

Riverview Av

Grondin   St

Reaume
St

Vermont   Av

100   200

Riverview   Av

Meleche St

Milford St

Michigan   Av

Turtle
Club Rd

Rene   Av

Grondin   St

Reaume   Av

Smith
Cres   Av

Smith
Cres

Rd

Elsworth   Av

Bouffard
Rd   700

Ulster
St

Superior   St

Bouffard   Av

Merrill   Av

Rene   Av

Dr Menard   Dr

Carnegie   Av

Olcott   St

Schwab   St

Vandernoot   Av

Mayfair   Av

State   Av

Gaylord Av

Gilbert Av

600

Rd

5

42°14'02"

Westport Marina

GIL MAURE
PARK

St Williams St

LA SALLE YOUTH
CENTER PARK

Lasalle

Adams Ln

W Stiers Av

FRONT   RD

LAURIER

Huron   St   100

Lafferty   Av

Kenwood   Av

200

DR

Divine   Av   200

Michigan   St   900

300

Birmingham   Av

400

Superior   Av

Huron St

Lafferty
Av

42°14'02"

Beach Ln

Delaware   St

Sacred   Blvd

Boismier   Av

Heart   Dr

Michigan   Av

Blvd

Hazel   Av

Maple   Av

Kenwood   Av

Alfred   Av

Delaware   Av

500

Mayfair   Av

Gilbert   Av

Marquette

Kenwood
Blvd   St
Golfwood
Cres

6

Sunset
Marina

Senator
Manhattan St

Wahneta

Pinewood Pl

Divine Av   200

Fields   Av

1600

Gignac
Cres

International   Av

Essex   Av

Sunnyside   Av

100

Gary   Av   2000

300

Sacred   Av

500   600

Heard
Dr

Gilbert
Av

Menomine

42°13'36"

Old
Front
Rd

2200

GRASSY
ISLAND

Marcel
Ln

18

7

ESSEX
GOLF &
COUNTRY
CLUB

42°13'10"

A   83°07'45"   83°07'09"   B   83°06'34"   C   83°05'59"   D   83°05'24"   E   83°04'49"

SEE 4586 MAP

MAP
4503

1:24,000
1 in. = 2000 ft.

0   0.25   0.5

miles

N

SEE **4420** MAP

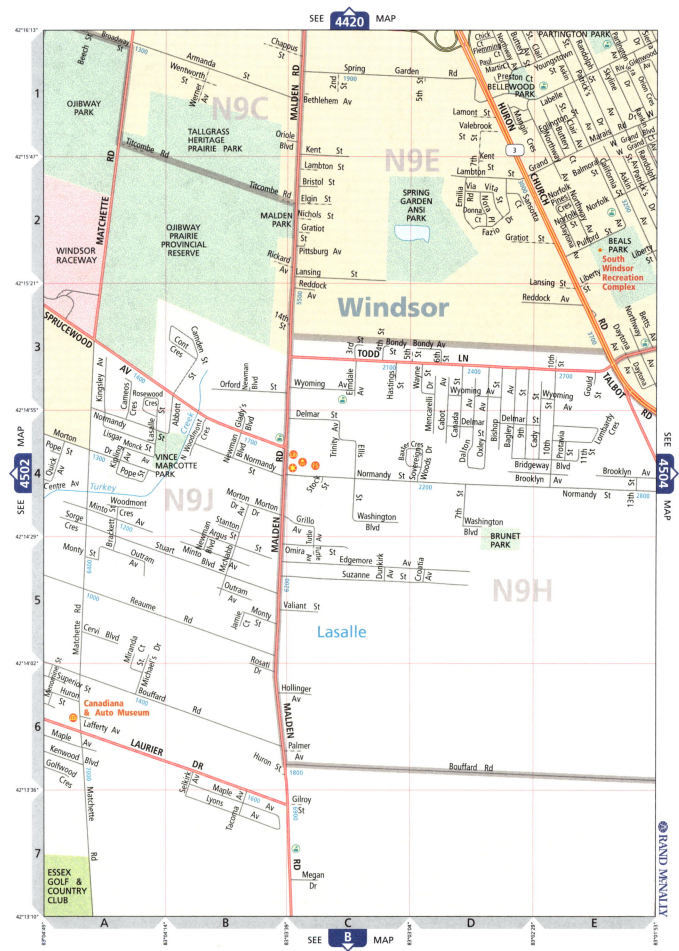

N9C

N9E

N9J

N9H

Windsor

Lasalle

OJIBWAY
PARK

TALLGRASS
HERITAGE
PRAIRIE PARK

OJIBWAY
PRAIRIE
PROVINCIAL
RESERVE

WINDSOR
RACEWAY

MALDEN
PARK

SPRING
GARDEN
ANSI
PARK

BELLEWOOD
PARK

BEALS
PARK

South
Windsor
Recreation
Complex

Canadiana
& Auto Museum

VINCE
MARCOTTE
PARK

BRUNET
PARK

ESSEX
GOLF &
COUNTRY
CLUB

SEE **4502** MAP

SEE **4504** MAP

SEE **B** MAP

RAND McNALLY

1
2
3
4
5
6
7

A   B   C   D   E

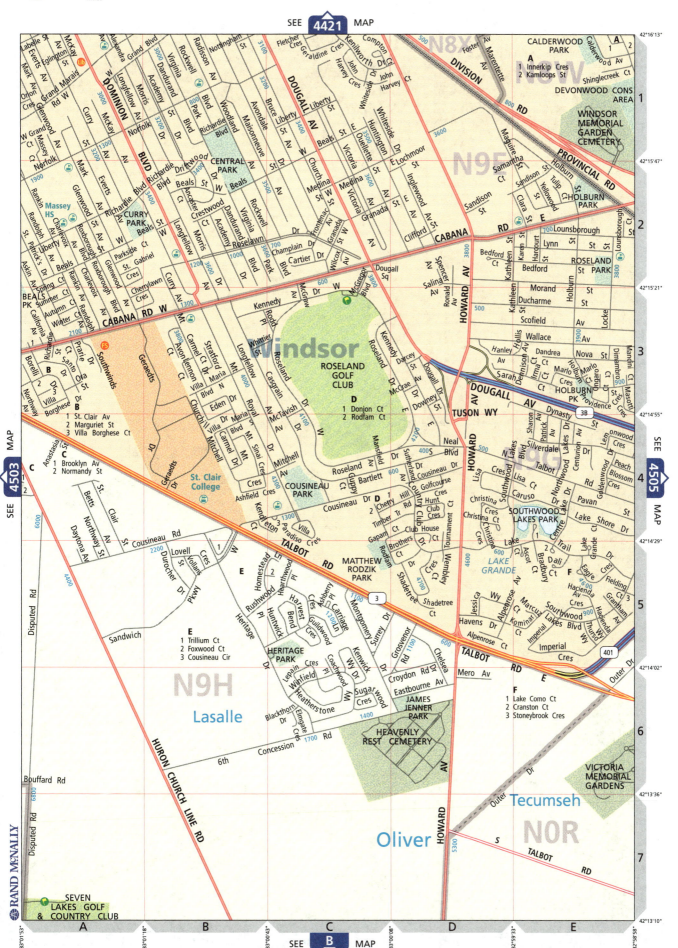

SEE 4503 MAP

SEE 4505 MAP

SEE B MAP

MAP
4505

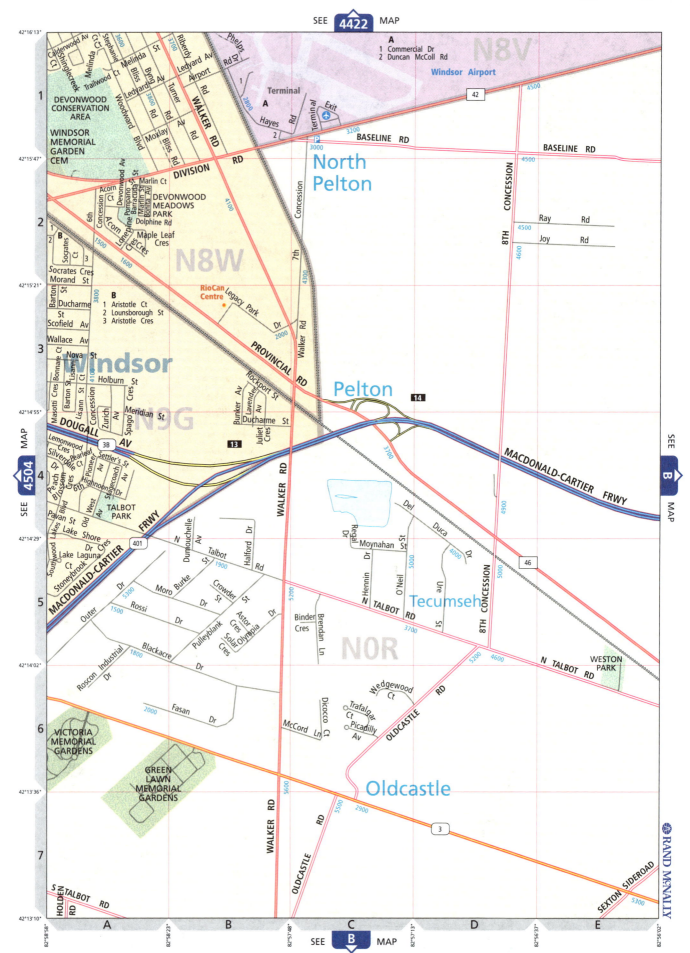

MAP
4505

1:24,000
1 in. = 2000 ft.
0   0.25   0.5
miles

SEE 4422 MAP

A
1 Commercial Dr
2 Duncan McColl Rd

Windsor Airport

N8V

Terminal

42°16'13"

DEVONWOOD
CONSERVATION
AREA

WINDSOR
MEMORIAL
GARDEN
CEM

North
Pelton

42°15'47"

BASELINE RD

BASELINE RD

DIVISION

DEVONWOOD
MEADOWS
PARK

Ray   Rd

Joy   Rd

N8W

42°15'21"

RioCan
Centre

B
1 Aristotle Ct
2 Lounsborough St
3 Aristotle Cres

Legacy Park

Windsor

PROVINCIAL RD

Pelton

14

42°14'55"

N9G

SEE 4504 MAP

TALBOT
PARK

MACDONALD-CARTIER FRWY

MACDONALD-CARTIER

SEE B MAP

42°14'29"

401

Tecumseh

N0R

42°14'02"

WESTON
PARK

OLDCASTLE RD

N TALBOT RD

42°13'36"

VICTORIA
MEMORIAL
GARDENS

GREEN
LAWN
MEMORIAL
GARDENS

Oldcastle

3

42°13'10"

S TALBOT RD

SEXTON SIDEROAD

SEE B MAP

A   B   C   D   E

82°58'58"   82°58'23"   82°57'48"   82°57'13"   82°56'37"   82°95'28"

MAP
4571

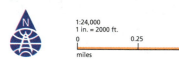

1:24,000
1 in. = 2000 ft.

0   0.25   0.5
miles

SEE **4487** MAP

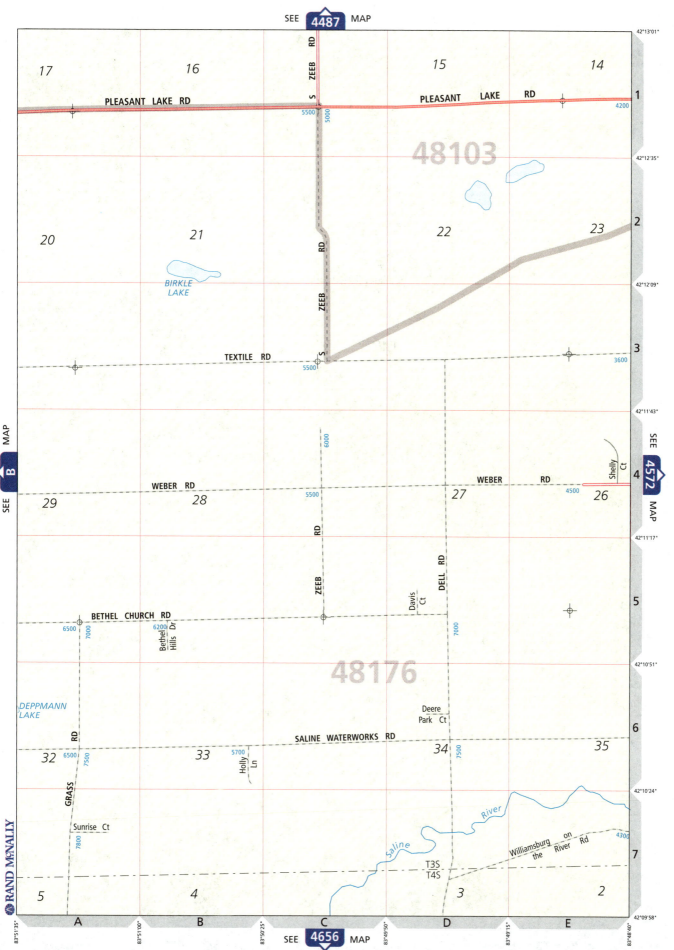

42°13'01"

17   16   15   14

1

PLEASANT LAKE RD   PLEASANT LAKE RD

S ZEEB RD

5500   5000   4200

42°12'35"

48103

20   21   22   23   2

42°12'09"

ZEEB RD

BIRKLE LAKE

ZEEB

TEXTILE RD   3

S 5500   3600

42°11'43"

6000

SEE **4572** MAP

SEE **B** MAP

WEBER RD   WEBER RD   Shelly Ct   4

29   28   27   4500   26

5500

42°11'17"

ZEEB RD   DELL RD

Davis Ct   5

BETHEL CHURCH RD

6500 7000

Bethel Hills Dr
6200   7000

42°10'51"

48176

DEPPMANN LAKE

Deere Park Ct   6

SALINE WATERWORKS RD

RD   32   33   5700   34   7500   35

6500 7500   Holly Ln

42°10'24"

GRASS   River   4300

Sunrise Ct   Saline   Williamsburg on the River Rd   7

7800

5   4   T3S
T4S   3   2

42°09'58"

A   B   C   D   E

83°51'35"   83°51'00"   83°50'25"   83°49'50"   83°49'15"   83°48'40"

SEE **4656** MAP

RAND McNALLY

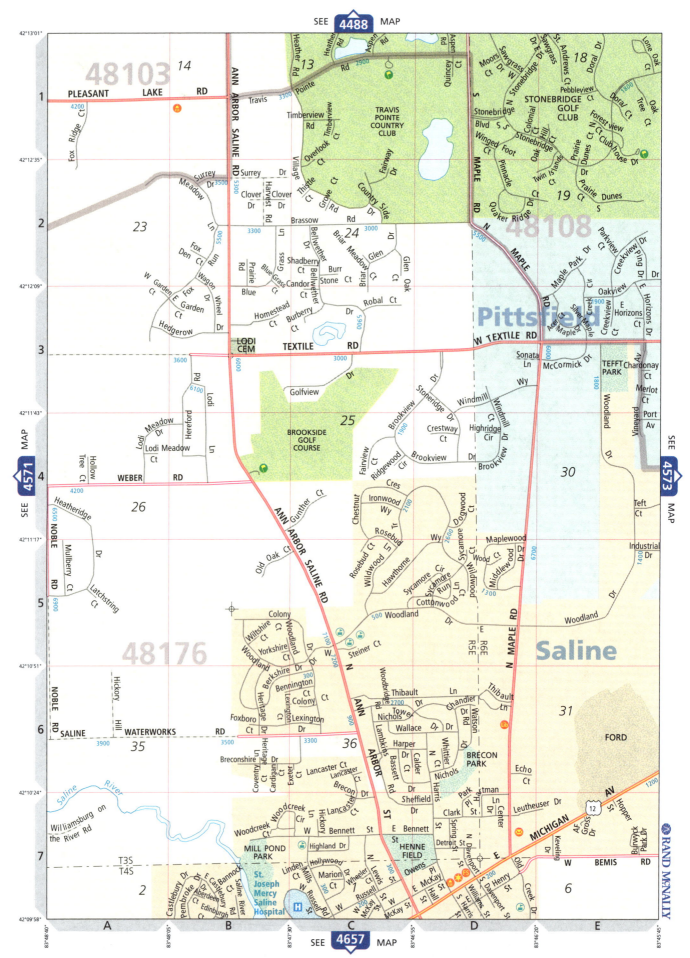

MAP
4572

1:24,000
1 in. = 2000 ft.

0   0.25   0.5
miles

SEE 4488 MAP

SEE 4571 MAP

SEE 4573 MAP

SEE 4657 MAP

48103
48108
48176

Pittsfield

Saline

MAP
4573

1:24,000
1 in. = 2000 ft.
0   0.25   0.5
miles

SEE 4489 MAP

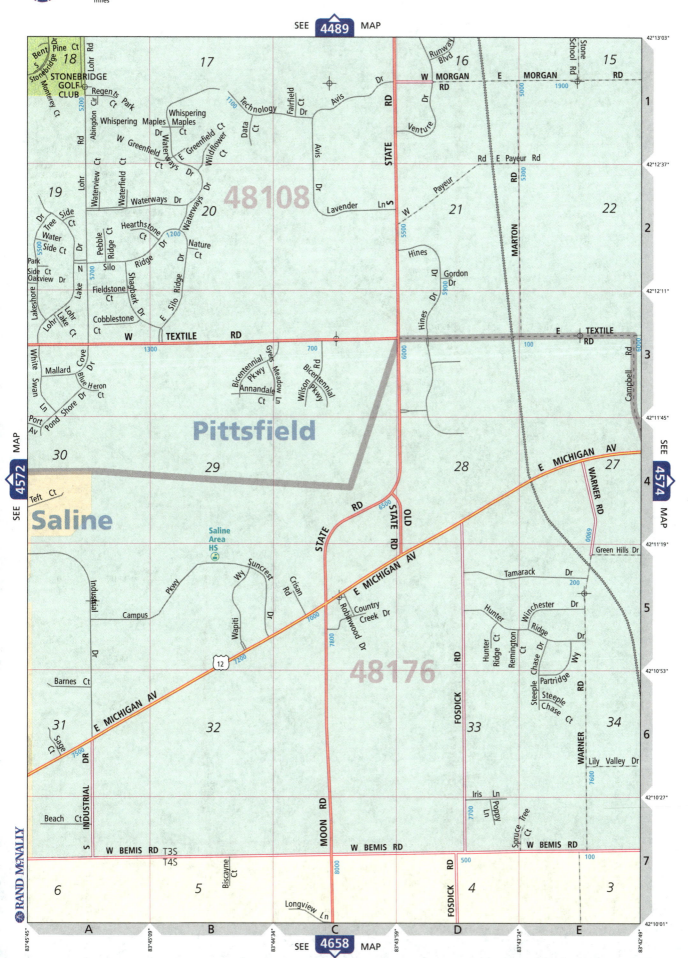

SEE 4572 MAP

SEE 4574 MAP

STONEBRIDGE GOLF CLUB

48108

Pittsfield

Saline

48176

Saline Area HS

RAND MCNALLY

SEE 4658 MAP

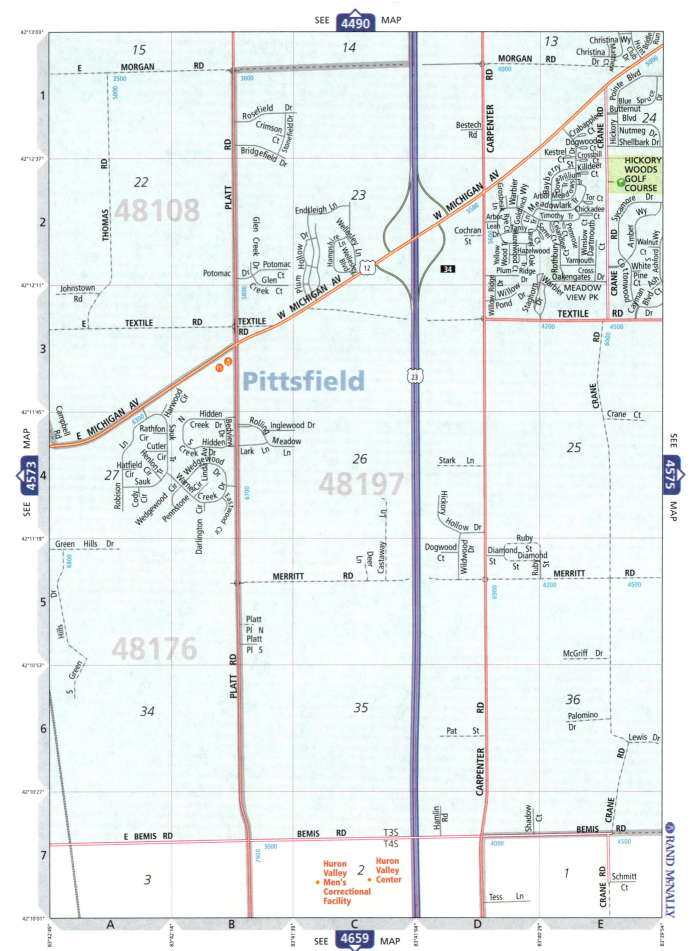

MAP 4575

1:24,000
1 in. = 2000 ft.
0   0.25   0.5
miles

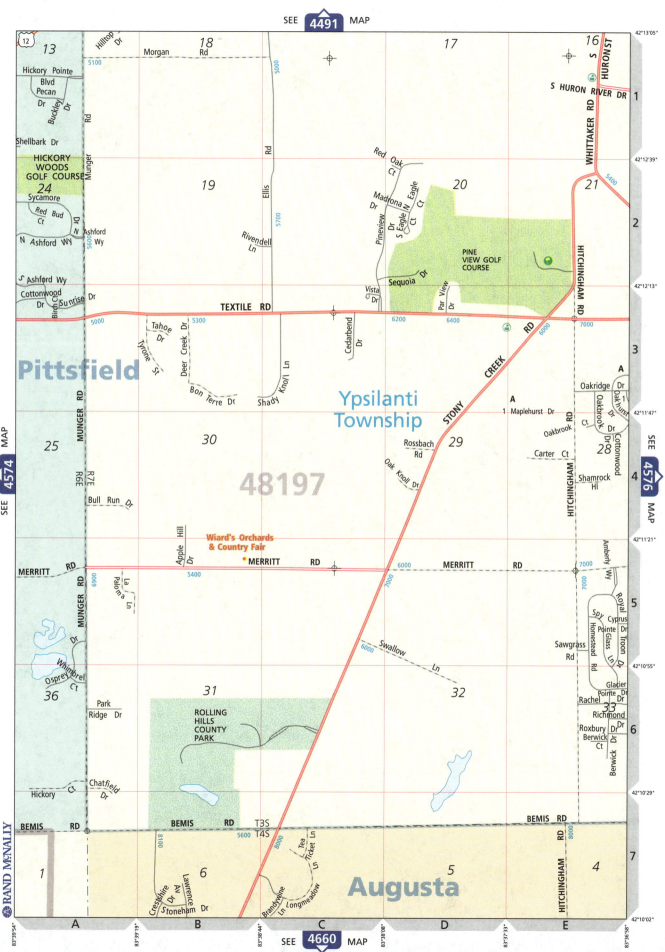

42°13'05"

12
13
Hilltop Dr
Morgan Rd
18
17
16
S HURON ST
1
S HURON RIVER DR
Hickory Pointe
Blvd
Pecan
Dr
Buckley Dr
Munger Rd
5100
5000
WHITTAKER RD
42°12'39"
Shellbark Dr
HICKORY WOODS GOLF COURSE
24
Ellis Rd
19
Red Oak Ct
S Eagle Dr
N Eagle Ct
Madrona Dr
Pineview Dr
20
21
5400
2
Sycamore
Red Bud Ct
Dr N
Ashford Wy
5600
5700
Rivendell Ln
PINE VIEW GOLF COURSE
N Ashford Wy

42°12'13"
S Ashford Wy
Cottonwood Dr
Birch Ct
Sunrise Dr
Sequoia Dr
Par View Dr
HITCHINGHAM RD
Vista Dr
TEXTILE RD
5000
5300
6200
6400
6000
7000
3
Tahoe Dr
Deer Creek Dr
Tyrone St
Cedarbend Dr
STONY CREEK RD

Pittsfield
MUNGER RD
Bon Terre Dr
Shady Knoll Ln
Ypsilanti Township
Oakridge Dr
Oakhurst Dr
A
42°11'47"
SEE 4574 MAP
R6E R7E
25
30
Rossbach Rd
Oak Knoll Dr
29
1 Maplehurst Dr
A
Oakbrook Dr
Ct
Oakbrook Dr
Cottonwood Dr
28
Carter Ct
SEE 4576 MAP
48197
Shamrock Hl
Bull Run Dr
HITCHINGHAM RD
4
Apple Hill Dr
Wiard's Orchards & Country Fair
Amberly Wy
42°11'21"
MERRITT RD
MERRITT RD
6000
MERRITT RD
7000
La Paloma Ln
MUNGER RD
5400
7000
Spy Pointe Dr
Cyprus Dr
Royal Troon Dr
5
6900
Homestead Ln
Pointe Glass Ln
Sawgrass Rd
42°10'55"
Whimbrel Dr
Swallow Ln
6000
Glacier Pointe Dr
Osprey Ct
36
Park Ridge Dr
31
32
Rachel Dr
33
Richmond Dr
Roxbury Dr
Berwick Ct
6
ROLLING HILLS COUNTY PARK
Berwick Dr
42°10'29"
Hickory Ct
Chatfield Dr
BEMIS RD
BEMIS RD
T3S
BEMIS RD
HITCHINGHAM RD
Augusta
1
BEMIS RD
T4S
8100
5600
8000
Crestshire Dr
6
Lawrence Av
Stoneham Dr
Brandywine Ln
Longmeadow Ln
Tea Ticket Ln
5
8000
4
7

42°10'02"

A   B   C   D   E

83°39'54"   83°39'19"   83°38'44"   83°38'08"   83°37'33"   83°36'58"

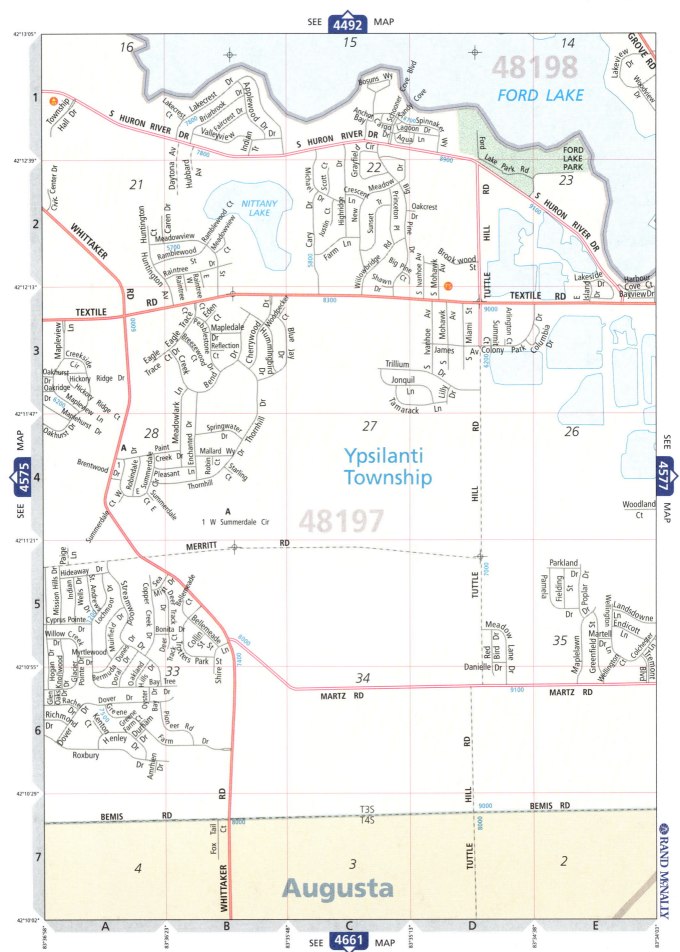

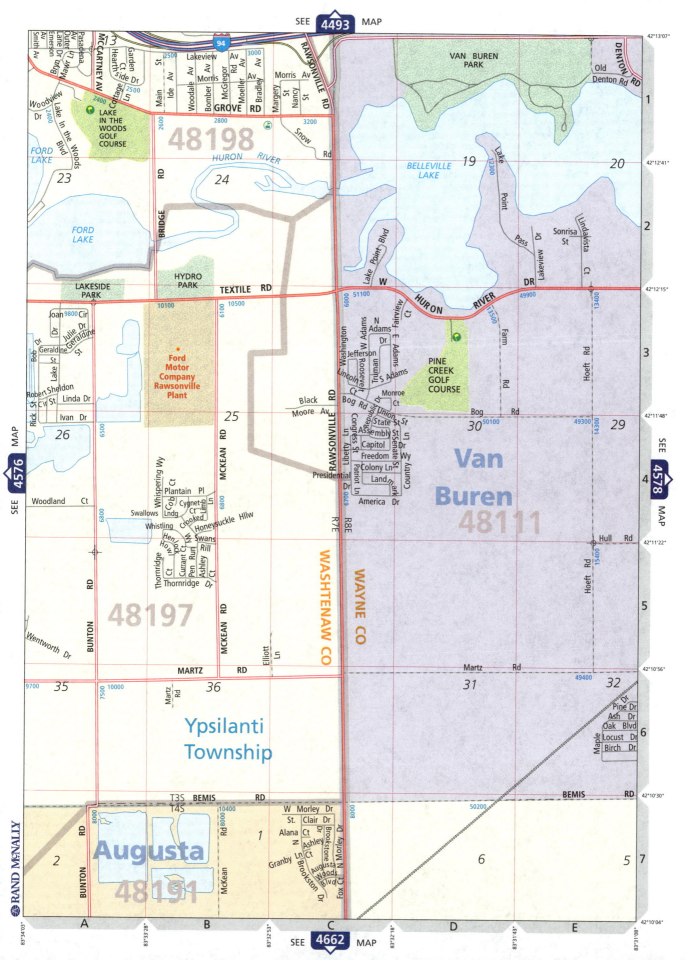

MAP
4577

1:24,000
1 in. = 2000 ft.

0   0.25   0.5
miles

SEE 4493 MAP
SEE 4576 MAP
SEE 4578 MAP
SEE 4662 MAP

VAN BUREN PARK

DENTON RD
Old Denton Rd

BELLEVILLE LAKE

Lake Point Pass

LAKE IN THE WOODS GOLF COURSE

FORD LAKE

HURON RIVER

LAKESIDE PARK

HYDRO PARK

TEXTILE RD

Ford Motor Company Rawsonville Plant

PINE CREEK GOLF COURSE

Sonrisa St
Lindavista Ct
Lakeview Dr

W HURON RIVER DR

Farm Rd
Hoeft Rd
Bog Rd

48198

48197

Van Buren
48111

Ypsilanti Township

Hull Rd

Martz Rd
MARTZ RD

Bunton RD
McKean RD
WASHTENAW CO
WAYNE CO

BEMIS RD
T3S
T4S

Augusta
48191

Pine Dr
Ash Dr
Oak Blvd
Locust Dr
Birch Dr
Maple Dr

W Morley Dr
St. Clair Dr
Alana Ct
Granby Ln
Ashley
Brookstone
Augusta Woods Blvd
Brookston Dr
Fox Ct
N Morley Dr

MAP
4578

1:24,000
1 in. = 2000 ft.
0   0.25   0.5
miles

SEE **4494** MAP

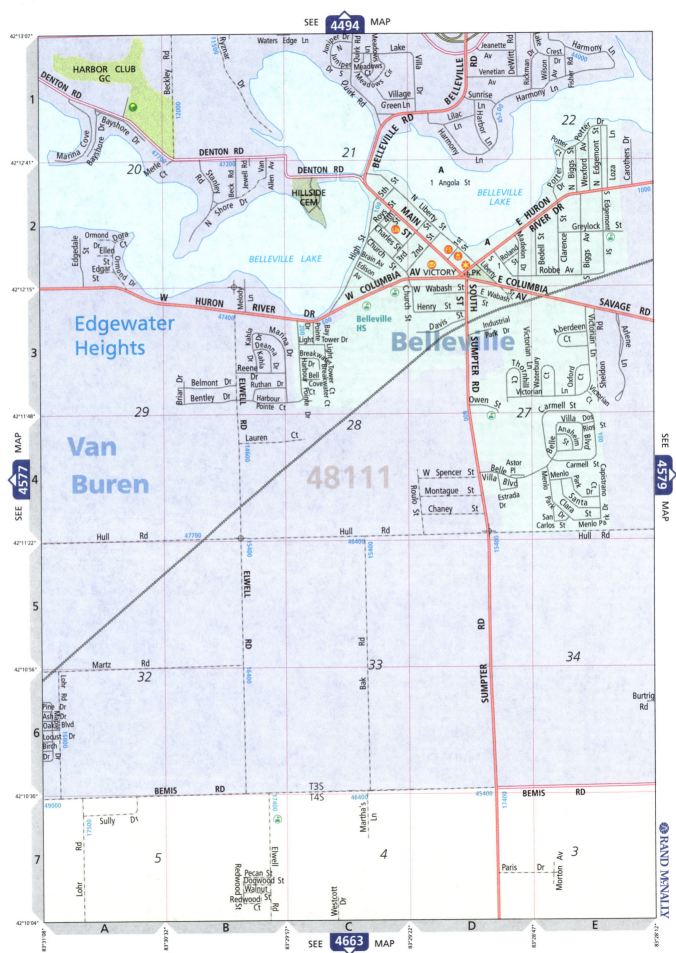

HARBOR CLUB GC

DENTON RD

Beckley Rd

Ryznar Dr

Waters Edge Ln

Juniper Dr

Quirk Rd

Meadows Rd

Lake

Jeanette Av

DeWitt Rd

Rickman

Wilson

Crest Dr

Fisher Rd

Harmony Ln

Juniper S Dr

N Meadows Ct

Meadows Cir

Villa

Venetian Av

Harmony Ln

Bayshore Dr

Bayshore Dr

Marina Cove

Village Green Ln

Sunrise

Lilac Ln

N Harbor Ln

Harmony Ln

22

Potter Dr

Potter St

Edgemont St

Carothers Dr

DENTON RD

Merle Ct

Stanley Rd

Beck Rd

N Shore Dr

Van

Jewell Rd

Allen Av

DENTON RD

HILLSIDE CEM

1 Angola St

A

BELLEVILLE LAKE

Potter Ct

N Biggs St

Wexford Av

N Edgemont St

Loza

20

Edgedale

Ormond Ct

Dora Ct

Ellen St

Edgar St

Ormond Dr

5th St

N Liberty St

A

Potter St

Roland Dr

Madelon Dr

Bedell St

Greylock

Clarence St

Biggs Av

S Edgemont St

E HURON RIVER DR

BELLEVILLE LAKE

MAIN ST

Roys St

4th St

Charles St

3rd St

2nd

Robbe Av

Edgewater Heights

High St

Church

Brain Av

Edison Av

W COLUMBIA AV

VICTORY PK

E COLUMBIA AV

Melody Ln

W HURON RIVER DR

Church St

W Wabash St

Henry St

E Wabash St

SAVAGE RD

Van Buren

Marina Dr

Kaela Dr

Deanna Dr

Kahla Dr

Bay Pointe Dr

Light Tower Dr

Belleville HS

Davis

Industrial Park Dr

Aberdeen Ct

Victorian Rd

Arlene Ln

Belleville

Reene Dr

Ruthan Dr

Breakwater Dr

Bell Harbour Cove Pointe

Victorian Ln

Victorian Ln

Thornhill Ct

Anwater Ln

Oxford Ln

SOUTH ST

SUMPTER RD

Briari Ct

Belmont Dr

Bentley Dr

ELWELL RD

Harbour Pointe Ct

Breakwater Ct

Owen St

Carmell St

27

Villa Dr

Rios Blvd

Dos

Anaheim St

Shelden

Victorian

29

Lauren Ct

28

Belle

Astor Dr

Carmell St

Capistrano Dr

Menlo Park Dr

48111

W Spencer St

Belle Pl

Villa Blvd

Estrada Dr

Menlo Ct

Santa Clara

SEE **4579** MAP

Roulo St

Montague St

Chaney St

San Carlos St

Menlo Park

Menlo Pa

Hull Rd

Hull Rd

Hull Rd

Hull Rd

ELWELL RD

SUMPTER RD

5

Martz Rd

32

Bak Rd

33

34

Lohr Dr

Pine Dr

Ash Dr

Maple Blvd

Oak Dr

Locust Dr

Birch Dr

Burtrig Rd

BEMIS RD

T3S

T4S

BEMIS RD

Lohr Rd

Sully Dr

7

5

Redwood

Redwood St

Pecan St

Dogwood St

Walnut St

Redwood St Ct

Elwell Rd

Westcott Dr

Martha's Ln

4

Paris Dr

Morton Av

3

A   B   C   D   E

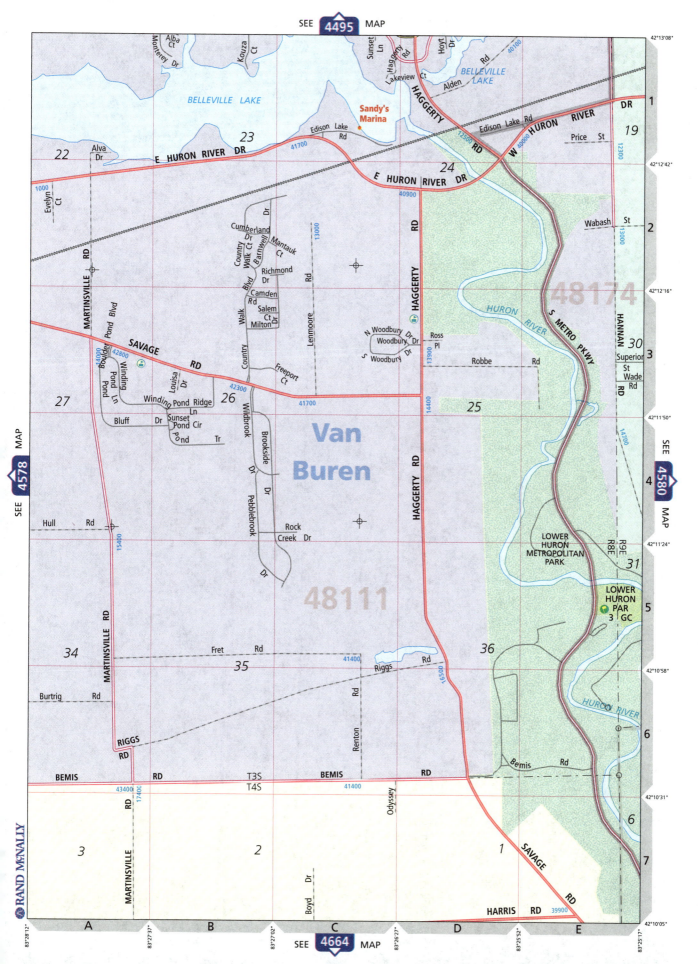

MAP
4579

1:24,000
1 in. = 2000 ft.
0   0.25   0.5
miles

SEE **4495** MAP

SEE **4578** MAP

SEE **4580** MAP

SEE **4664** MAP

RAND M^cNALLY

BELLEVILLE LAKE
BELLEVILLE LAKE
Sandy's Marina
HURON RIVER
HURON RIVER
Van Buren
48174
48111
LOWER HURON METROPOLITAN PARK
LOWER HURON PAR 3 GC

MAP
4580

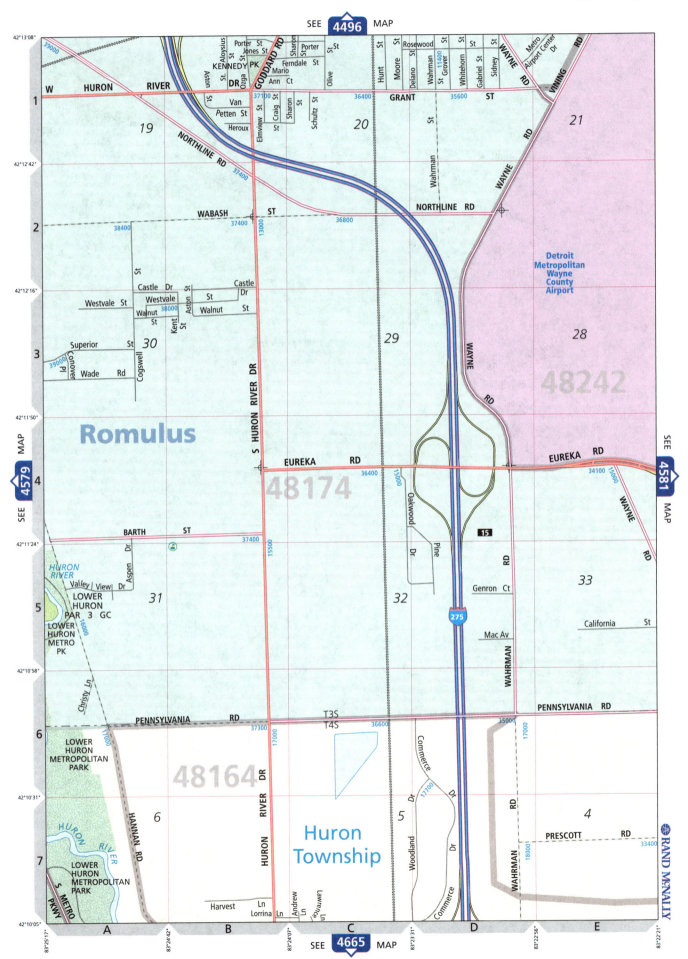

SEE 4496 MAP

42°13'08"

39000

W   HURON   RIVER

1

19

KENNEDY   PK

Aloysius St   Porter St   Jones St   Sharon   Porter

Aston   Ozga   Ferndale   St   St   St

Mario

St   Dr   Ann   Ct   Olive   St

Van   Petten   St   Elmview St   Craig St   Sharon St   Schultz St   St

Heroux

37100   37400

NORTHLINE   RD

Hunt St   Moore   St   Rosewood   St   St   St   St

Delano   Wahram   St   Grover   Whitehorn   Gabriel St   Sidney St

GRANT   ST

Metro   Airport Center   Dr

WAYNE   RD

VINING   RD

21

36400   35600   St

13000

42°12'42"

NORTHLINE RD   37400

WABASH   ST   37400   36800

NORTHLINE   RD

WAYNE   RD

Wahrman

2

38400

42°12'16"

Castle   Dr   Castle   Dr

Westvale   St   Westvale   St   St

JS   Walnut   St   38000   Walnut   St

Aston St   St

Kent St

WAYNE

Detroit Metropolitan Wayne County Airport

28

48242

S HURON RIVER DR

30

Superior   St   *29*

39000   Conover   Pl

Wade   Rd   Cogswell

3

42°11'50"

Romulus

RD

EUREKA   RD   36400   15000   EUREKA   RD   34100   15000

48174

Oakwood   Dr   15

4

SEE 4579 MAP   SEE 4581 MAP

42°11'24"

BARTH   ST   37400

HURON RIVER

Aspen   Dr

HURON RIVER

Valley   View   Dr

LOWER HURON PAR 3 GC

LOWER HURON METRO PK

31

15500

Pine   Dr

32

Genron   Ct

WAHRMAN   RD

WAYNE   RD

33

Mac Av

California   St

5

I-275

42°10'58"

Christy Ln

PENNSYLVANIA   RD   T3S   T4S   37300   17000   36600   PENNSYLVANIA   RD   35000   17000

6

LOWER HURON METROPOLITAN PARK

48164

HURON RIVER   DR

Commerce   Dr   Dr

Woodland   Dr   17700

Dr   RD   18000

WAHRMAN

42°10'31"

6

HANNAN   RD

16000

Huron Township

5

4

PRESCOTT   RD   33400

7

LOWER HURON METROPOLITAN PARK

HURON RIVER

S METRO PKWY

Harvest   Ln   Andrew   Ln   Lawrence Ln

Lorrina Ln

Commerce   Dr

42°10'05"

A   B   C   D   E

83°25'17"   83°24'42"   83°24'07"   83°23'31"   83°22'56"   83°22'21"

SEE 4665 MAP

RAND McNALLY

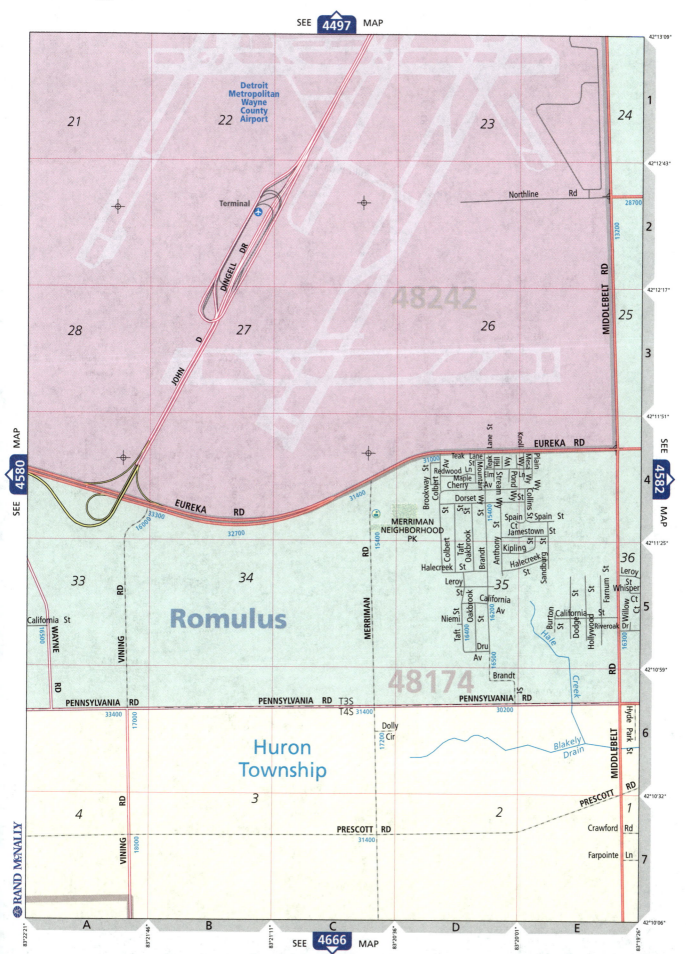

MAP
4581

1:24,000
1 in. = 2000 ft.
0   0.25   0.5
miles

SEE **4497** MAP

42°13'09"

1

**Detroit
Metropolitan
Wayne
County
Airport**

21   22   23   24

Northline   Rd   28700   42°12'43"

Terminal ✈   13200   42°12'17"

DINGELL DR

25

MIDDLEBELT RD

28   27   26

48242

3

JOHN D

42°11'51"

SEE **4580** MAP

EUREKA RD   EUREKA RD

SEE **4582** MAP

Lane St
Knoll St
Teak Lane Ct
Redwood Ln
Colbert Av   Mesa St
Brookway St   Maple Cherry   Tjepk Wy   Plain St
Dorset St   Hill St   Stream Wy
Mountain St   Elm Av   Pond Wy   Collins Wy
31000   Wy
31400   15400   Spain St   Spain St
Ct   Jamestown St
Colbert St   Taft   Oakbrook   Anthony St   Kipling St
Halecreek St   St   Brandt St   Halecreek St
Sandburg St
Leroy St   35   Leroy St
Farnum St   Whisper Ct
California Av   Willow Dr
16200   Burton St   California St   Riveroak Dr
Niemi St   Oakbrook St   Doppo St   Hollywood St
Taft St   Hale Creek
Dru Av
Brandt St

31000   4
31400
15400

33300
160000
33300
EUREKA RD
32700

MERRIMAN RD
15400

MERRIMAN RD

15400

Romulus

33   34

California St
16500
WAYNE RD

VINING RD

42°11'25"

36

5

16300

42°10'59"

16500

48174

Brandt St

PENNSYLVANIA   RD   PENNSYLVANIA RD T3S   PENNSYLVANIA   RD   MIDDLEBELT RD
33400   17000   T4S 31400   30200

Hyde Park St

Dolly Cir
17200

**Huron
Township**

Blakely Drain

6

VINING RD
18000

3

2   PRESCOTT RD   42°10'32"
PRESCOTT   RD   Crawford Rd
31400   Farpointe Ln   7

4   1

A   B   C   D   E

83°22'21"   83°21'46"   83°21'11"   83°20'36"   83°20'02"   83°19'26"   42°10'06"

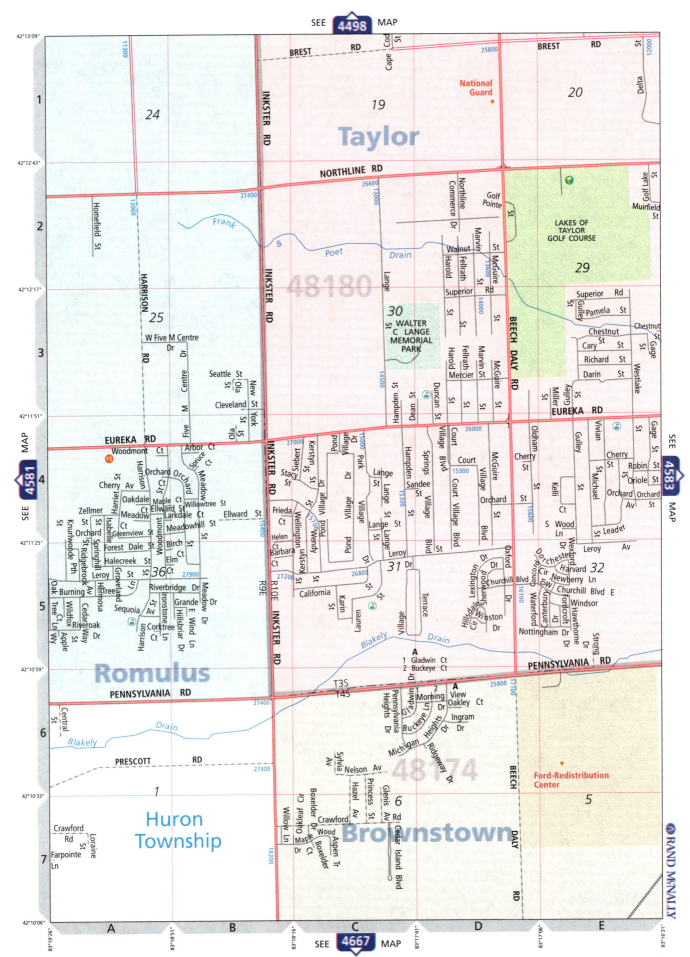

MAP
4582

1:24,000
1 in. = 2000 ft.
0   0.25   0.5
miles

SEE **4498** MAP

BREST   RD
BREST   RD

Cape Cod
25800
12000
Delta
St

National Guard

Taylor

19
20

24

INKSTER RD
HARRISON RD

13300
13000

NORTHLINE RD
27400
26600
13000

Northline Commerce Dr
Golf Pointe

Frank & Poet Drain

Marvin St
McGuire St
Walnut St
Harold St
Fellrath St
Superior St

13000
14000

48180

Lange St

29

LAKES OF TAYLOR GOLF COURSE

Golf Lake St
Muirfield St

Superior Rd
Gulley St
Pamela St
Chestnut St

W Five M Centre Dr
Centre Dr

25

Harrison RD

14500

30
WALTER C LANGE MEMORIAL PARK

Marvin St
McGuire St
Fellrath St
Harold St
Mercier St

Cary St
Richard St
Darin St

Gage St
Westlake

Seattle St
Ola St
New St
Cleveland St
York St
Ola St

Hampden St
Dean St
Duncan St

EUREKA RD

Miller St
Gulley St

EUREKA RD
Five M

Woodmont Ct
Arbor Ct
Spruce Ct

Sieber St
Kerstyn St
Stacy St
Pond Ct
Park Village Dr
Village Dr
Village Dr

15000
26000
Court Village Blvd
15300

Oldham St
Cherry St

Vivian St
Gage St
Cherry St
Robin St
Oriole St

FS
Woodmont
Orchard Ct
Orchard Ct
Meadow St
Willowtree St

Lange St
Springs Village Blvd
McGuire St

Kelli Ct
St Michael St
Orchard Av

Cherry Av
Harriet St
Oakdale Ct
Maple Ct
Ellward St
Larkdale Ct

Hampden St
Sandee St
Court Village Blvd
Orchard Blvd

15600

Zellmer St
Meadow Ct
Greenview St
Meadowhill St

Frieda Ct
Wellington Ln
Village Pond Dr
Lange St
Lange St

S Wood Ln

Leroy

Orchard St
Isabele St
Springhill St
Ridgebrook St
Woodmont St
Birch St
Ellward St

Helen Ct
Wendy St
Lange St
Lange St

Wexford Dr
Harvard St
Newberry Ln

Leroy Av

Knurlwoode Pth
Forest Dale St
Elm Ct
Barbara St

Leroy St
Dorchester Cir
Churchill Blvd
Churchill Blvd E
Windsor Dr

Halecreek St
36
27900
Riverbridge Dr

31 Dr
Lexington Dr
Oxford Dr
Sherwood Dr
Waterford Dr
32
Fordcroft Dr
Nottingham Dr

Leroy St
California St
Karin St

Hillsdale Cir
Winston Dr
Churchill Blvd
Hawthorne Dr

Oak Tree Ln Ct
Wildfox St
Cedar Way
Riveroak Dr
Apple St
Corktree Ln
Treeland
Sequoia Av
Grande Dr
E Wind Ln
Hillsbriar Dr

Burning Av
Hermosa St
Groveland
Ironstone Ln
Meadow Dr

Lauren Ct
Village Dr
Terrace St

Strong St

Blakely Drain

A
1 Gladwin Ct
2 Buckeye Ct

PENNSYLVANIA RD

Romulus

T3S
T4S
27400
25800
27100

A

PENNSYLVANIA RD

Central St

Drain
Blakely

1 2 Morning Dr
Pennsylvania Heights Dr
Buckeye Ln
Oakley Ct
View Ct
Ingram Dr

PRESCOTT RD
27400

Sylvia Av
Michigan Heights Dr
Ridgeway Dr

Ford-Redistribution Center

48174

BEECH DALY RD

1

Nelson Av

6

5

Huron Township

Crawford Rd
Loraine St
Farpointe Ln

Willow Ln
Kelekej Cir
Crawford Dr
Maple Dr
Wood Ct
Boxelder Dr
Aspen Tr
Boxelder Ct

Hazel Av
Princess St
Glenis Av
Cedar Island Blvd

Brownstown

18200

RAND McNALLY

SEE **4581** MAP
SEE **4583** MAP

42°13'09"
42°12'43"
42°12'17"
42°11'51"
42°11'25"
42°10'59"
42°10'33"
42°10'06"

A   B   C   D   E

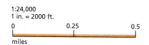

MAP
4583

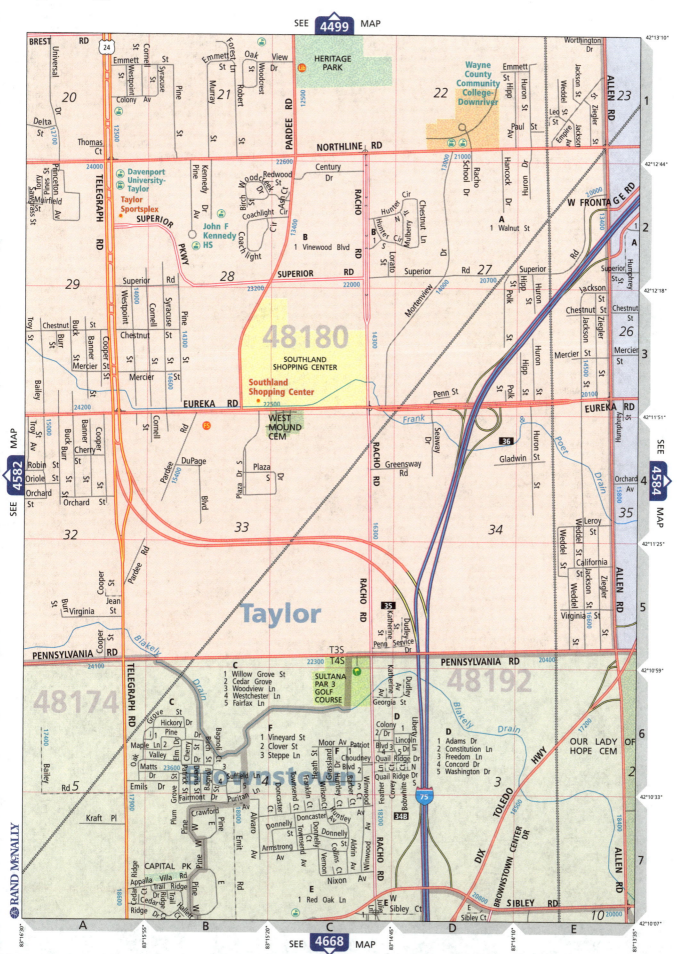

1:24,000
1 in. = 2000 ft.

0   0.25   0.5
miles

SEE 4499 MAP
SEE 4582 MAP
SEE 4584 MAP
SEE 4668 MAP

N

BREST RD

Universal Dr

Emmett St
Cornell St
Westpoint St
Syracuse St
Colony Av
Pine St
Murray St
Robert St

Forest Ln
Emmett St
Oak Dr
View Dr
Woodcrest Dr

HERITAGE PARK

Worthington Dr
Emmett St
St Hipp
Huron St
Paul Av
Weddel St
Jackson St
Ziegler St
Leo St
Empire St
Jackson

Wayne County Community College-Downriver

ALLEN RD

20   21   22   23

1

Delta St

Thomas Ct

Princeton St
Muirfield Av
Sawgrass St

TELEGRAPH RD

Davenport University-Taylor

Taylor Sportsplex

SUPERIOR

Kennedy Pine
Pine Av

John F Kennedy HS

KENNEDY PKWY

Redwood St
WoodCreek Dr
Birch St
Coachlight Cir
Coachlight Cir

Century Dr

RACHO RD

Hunter Cir N
Mulberry Jr Cir
Hunter Cir S
Lorato St

Chestnut Ln

School Dr
Racho Dr
Hancock Dr

1 Walnut St

W FRONTAGE RD

Huron

Superior St
Humphrey St

NORTHLINE RD

B
1 Vinewood Blvd

B

2

A
A

SUPERIOR RD

29   28

Superior Rd
Westpoint
Cornell
Syracuse St
Chestnut
Pine St
Mercier

SUPERIOR RD

48180
SOUTHLAND SHOPPING CENTER

Mortenview Dr

Superior Rd   27

Superior Rd

St Polk
Hipp St
Huron St

Jackson St
Chestnut St
Mercier St
Ziegler St

Chestnut St

Mercier St

26

3

Troy St
Chestnut
Buck St
Burr St
Banner St
Mercier St
Cooper St
Bailey

Southland Shopping Center

Penn St

Hipp St
Huron St
Polk St
Huron St

EUREKA RD

Eureka Rd
Humphrey

EUREKA RD

Cornell Rd

FS

WEST MOUND CEM

Frank

Seaway Dr

Eureka Rd

Orchard Av

4

Troy St
Banner
Buck Burr
Cherry St
Cooper St
Robin St
Oriole St
Orchard St
Orchard St

Pardee Rd

DuPage

Plaza Dr
Plaza S Dr
Plaza Blvd

RACHO RD

Greensway Rd

Gladwin

36

Huron St

Poet Drain

Orchard Av

Leroy St
Weddel St
California
Jackson St
Ziegler St

35

32   33   34

5

Cooper St
Burr
Virginia
Jean St

Pardee Rd

Taylor

RACHO RD

Katherine St
Penn St
Dudley Service Dr

35

Weddel St
Virginia St

ALLEN RD

PENNSYLVANIA RD

Blakely Drain

T3S
T4S

22300

PENNSYLVANIA RD

48192

42°10'59"

48174

Grove St
Hickory Dr
Pine Dr
Maple Ln
Valley St
Matts Dr
Emils Dr

Bagnoli St
Birch St
Cherry St
Patrick St
Dennis St

C
1 Willow Grove St
2 Cedar Grove
3 Woodview Ln
4 Westchester Ln
5 Fairfax Ln

C

SULTANA PAR 3 GOLF COURSE

F
1 Vineyard St
2 Clover St
3 Steppe Ln

Moor Av
Suffield Ln
Townsend Ct
Franklin Ct
Wilson Ct
Barber Ct
Huntley Ct

Patriot Blvd
Choudney Blvd

Katherine Av
Dudley Av
Georgia St
Colony Dr
Blvd Dr
Liberty St
Lincoln St
Quail Ridge Dr
Quail Ridge Dr

Winwood Av
Coventry
Whitewood

Adams Dr

D
1 Adams Dr
2 Constitution Ln
3 Freedom Ln
4 Concord Dr
5 Washington Dr

Blakely Drain

TOLEDO HWY

OUR LADY OF HOPE CEM

D
3

6

Bailey Rd

Brownstown

Kraft Pl

Oak St
Elm
Plum
Pine W
Crawford

Fairmont Dr
Puritan
Alvaro Av
Doncaster Ct
Doncaster
Donnelly Ct
Donnelly
Armstrong Av
Collins Av
Vernon

Townsend Ct
Wilmood Av
Aldrin Av

Federal Ln

75

34B

Blakely Drain

DIX

BROWNSTOWN CENTER DR

ALLEN RD

7

CAPITAL PK

Appalla Villa Rd
Cedar Ridge Dr
Trail Ridge
Pine Ridge Dr
Hallett

E
1 Red Oak Ln

Nixon

Sibley Ct

E   W

E Sibley Ct

SIBLEY RD

10

A   B   C   D   E

SEE 4668 MAP

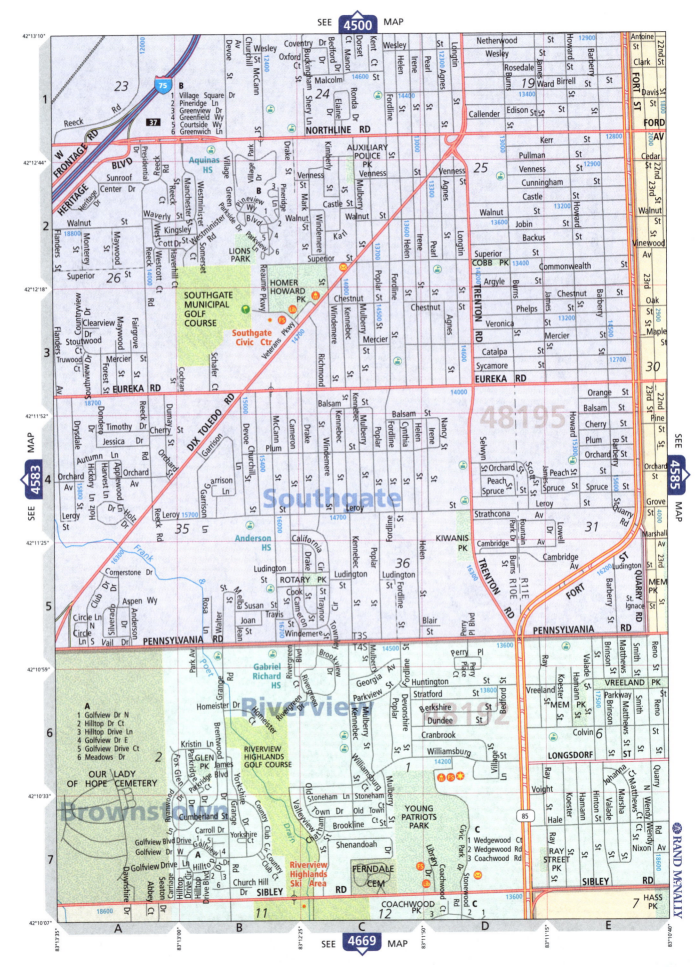

MAP
4584

1:24,000
1 in. = 2000 ft.

0   0.25   0.5
miles

N

SEE **4500** MAP

SEE **4583** MAP

SEE **4585** MAP

SEE **4669** MAP

Southgate

48195

Riverview 48192

Brownstown

RAND McNALLY

1:24,000
1 in. = 2000 ft.
0   0.25   0.5
miles

GRASSY I

Wyandotte

Antoine
20th St 16th St
Clark 19th St 15th St
21st 18th Alkali 13th 1700
Davis 17th 14th St St
FORD AV

Spruce St Glenn Ct FS
Cedar St MT CARMEL CEMETERY
Oxford Ct 9th
PULASKI PARK Mulberry Cora Walnut
St Mollno St 10th Cora Walnut
Poplar Poplar Our Lady of Mt Carmel HS
OAK CLUB Vinewood Av Ct
PK Superior Blvd
Superior Ash St 30 Superior Blvd
Chestnut St Chestnut
Chestnut Oak 11th
Elm St 15th Elm
Maple Maple St
Dee St Sycamore St
Sycamore St
EUREKA AV

20th 17th 15th 9th St
Pine St Orange St
19th 16th Pine
21st 18th Lee Cherry 11th
VFW PK Arch St
Orchard 13th Orchard St
22nd Marshall 14th Av
31 20th 19th Marshall
St. 18th 17th 16th 15th Ludington
Ignace St
MEMORIAL PARK

PENNSYLVANIA RD

Riverview

Vreeland St
VREELAND PK
Parkway St
Clark Colvin St
PENNSALT PARK Grant McKinley
Garfield St
LONGSDORF ST
Riverview Community HS
Hale St 6 Krause
Nixon Av Cleveland St
Washington St
SIBLEY RD
HASS PK 7

BASF

21

Henry Ford Wyandotte Hospital H

29 Mulberry 28
Walnut Van Alstyne Blvd
Ford-McNichol Home/Wyandotte Mus
Superior Blvd BISHOP PARK
Chestnut
Oak St Elm
Maple St
Yack Arena Sycamore St 100

Orange William M Kreger Dr
Pine 33 BASF PARK
Cherry Wyandotte Boat & Rowing Club
Plum
Orchard
Forest Grove
32 Hillsdale WYANDOTTE SHORES GOLF COURSE
Marshall Av BIDDLE AV
Ludington St
Negaunee St
Central

DETROIT RIVER

MICHIGAN ONTARIO

WAYNE CO ESSEX CO

SEE 4586 MAP

DETROIT RIVER

48138

Parke Ln

UNITED STATES CANADA

T3S
T4S

5 JEFFERSON AV
ELECTRIC ST
Payne St
Ford Av
W

Harbor Point
MERIDIAN RD Cardinal Av Annette Av PARKE LN
Annette Av
Paulina Cardinal Heron Av
Av Dr Paulina Av

BRIDGE
Toll Booth
Toll Booth RD
9100 8600 GROSSE ILE
Voigt Heron Av

MERIDIAN RD Thorofare Rd PARKE LN

THOROFARE CANAL

MCLOUTH STEEL PRODUCTS 8

MAP
4586

SEE 4502 MAP

ESSEX GOLF & COUNTRY CLUB

42°13'10"

Holiday Harbour

Jolly   Av

Runstedler   Dr

Victory   St

Island   View Marina

18

100

800

Crystal Harbour   Dr

Pare   Ln

Crystal Harbour   Dr

FRONT RD

OPTIMIST PARK

GRASSY ISLAND

Bechard   Av

FRONT RD

Dossenbach   Dr

Bechard   Av

Willow   Dr

Martin   Ln

2600

200

42°12'44"

Martin   Ln

Riverfront Harbour

3000

1

2

Lasalle

FIGHTING ISLAND

42°12'18"

Mueller's Marina

La Salle River Run Marina

3

42°11'52"

N9J

MAP 4585 SEE

SEE B MAP

4

FRONT RD

42°11'26"

Vista Av

3000

Malden   Rd   MALDEN   RD

5

River Canard

DETROIT RIVER

42°11'00"

N

ST

RIVERVIEW   DR

RD   S

6

Amherstburg

FRONT   ST

18

20

CANARD   RIVER

CONCESSION   RD

42°10'34"

N9V

5

7

2ND

42°10'08"

RAND McNALLY

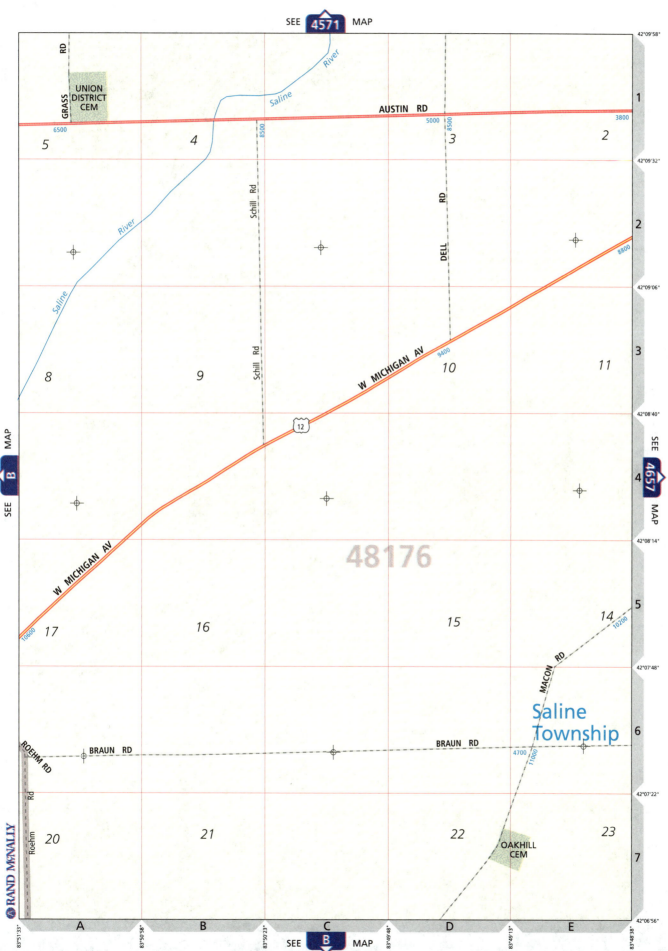

MAP
4656

1:24,000
1 in. = 2000 ft.

0   0.25   0.5

miles

SEE 4571 MAP

SEE B MAP

SEE 4657 MAP

SEE B MAP

42°09'58"
42°09'32"
42°09'06"
42°08'40"
42°08'14"
42°07'48"
42°07'22"
42°06'56"

83°51'33"
83°50'58"
83°50'23"
83°49'48"
83°49'13"
83°48'38"

1 2 3 4 5 6 7

A B C D E

RD
GRASS
UNION
DISTRICT
CEM
6500

AUSTIN RD
5000
8500
3800
8800

5 4 3 2

Schill Rd
Saline River
River
Saline

8500

DELL RD

8 9 10 11

W MICHIGAN AV
9400
12

Schill Rd

48176

W MICHIGAN AV
10600

17 16 15 14
10200

MACON RD

Saline
Township

BRAUN RD
BRAUN RD
4700
11000

ROEHM RD
Rd
Roehm Rd

20 21 22 23

OAKHILL
CEM

RAND McNALLY

MAP
4657

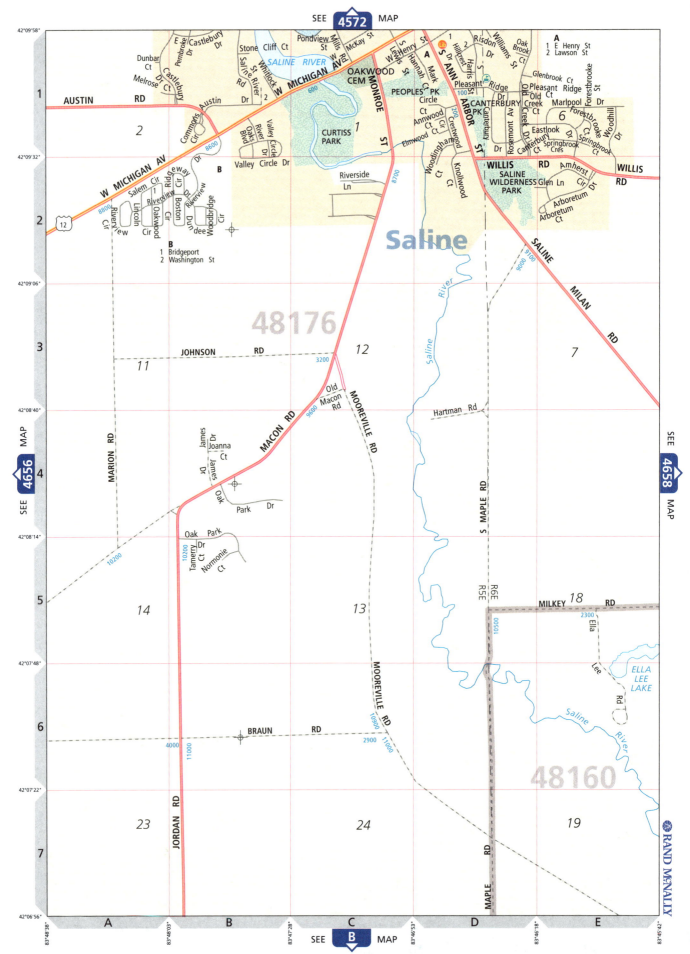
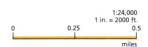

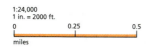

MAP
4658

SEE ⬆ 4573 MAP

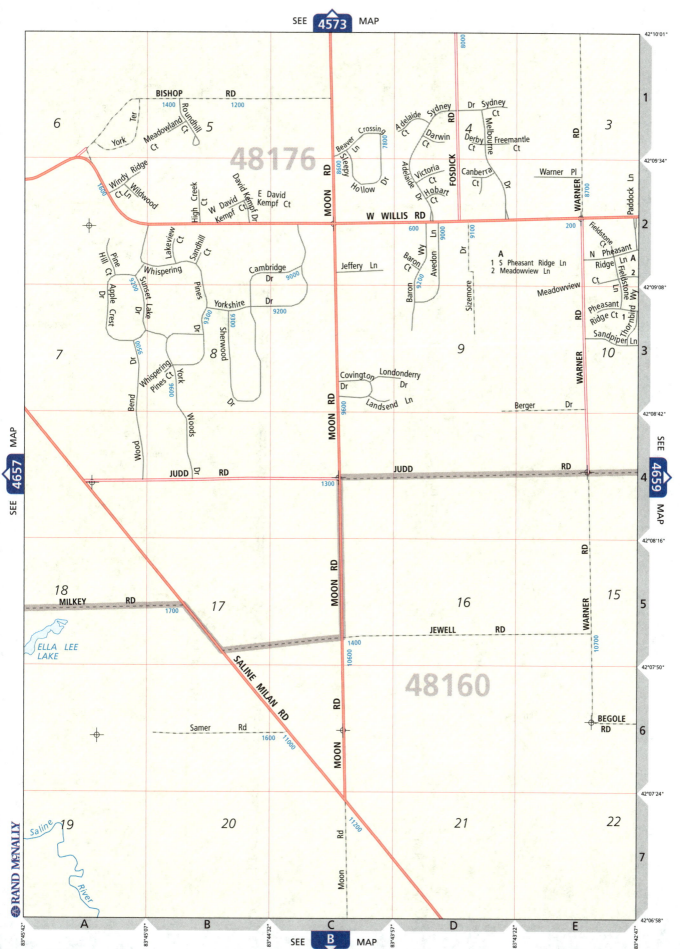

SEE 4657 MAP

SEE 4659 MAP

SEE B MAP

1:24,000
1 in. = 2000 ft.

0   0.25   0.5

miles

48176

48160

BISHOP RD
1400   1200

6   5   York Ter   Roundhill Ct   Meadowland Ct

Windy Ridge Ct Ln   Wildwood   High Creek Ct   W David Kempf Ct   David Kempf Dr   E David Kempf Ct
1600

MOON RD   8600   Sleepy Hollow Dr   Beaver Crossing Ln   Adelaide Ct   Sydney Ct   Darwin Ct   Adelaide Dr   Victoria Ct   Hobart Ct   FOSDICK RD   7800   Dr Sydney   4   Melbourne Dr   Derby Ct   Freemantle Ct   Canberra Ct   Warner Pl   WARNER RD   8700   Paddock Ln   3

W WILLIS RD   600   9000   200   Fieldstone Ct

Lakeview Ct   Sandhill Ct   Pine Hill Ct   Whispering   Apple Crest Dr   Sunset Lake Dr   9200   Cambridge Dr   9000   Pines   Yorkshire   9300   Sherwood Dr   9200   Jeffery Ln   Baron Ct   Baron Wy   9200   Avedon Ln   9000   Sizemore Dr   9100   A 1 S Pheasant Ridge Ln 2 Meadowview Ln   Meadowview   Pheasant Ridge Ln N   Ct   Fieldstone Ln   Pheasant Ridge Ct   Sandpiper Ln   Thornbird Ln   2   A   1   10

7   9500   8   9500   Whispering Pines Ct   9600   York Dr   Woods Dr   Covington Dr   Londonderry Dr   Landsend Ln   9600   MOON RD   9   Berger Dr   WARNER RD

Wood Bend Dr   JUDD RD   1300   JUDD RD   4

18   MILKEY RD   1700   17   MOON RD   16   JEWELL RD   1400   10600   WARNER RD   10700   15   5

ELLA LEE LAKE

SALINE MILAN RD   Samer Rd   1600   11000   BEGOLE RD   6

48160

Saline   19   20   Moon Rd   11200   21   22   7

River

RAND McNALLY

MAP
4659

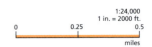

1:24,000
1 in. = 2000 ft.

0   0.25   0.5

miles

SEE 4574 MAP

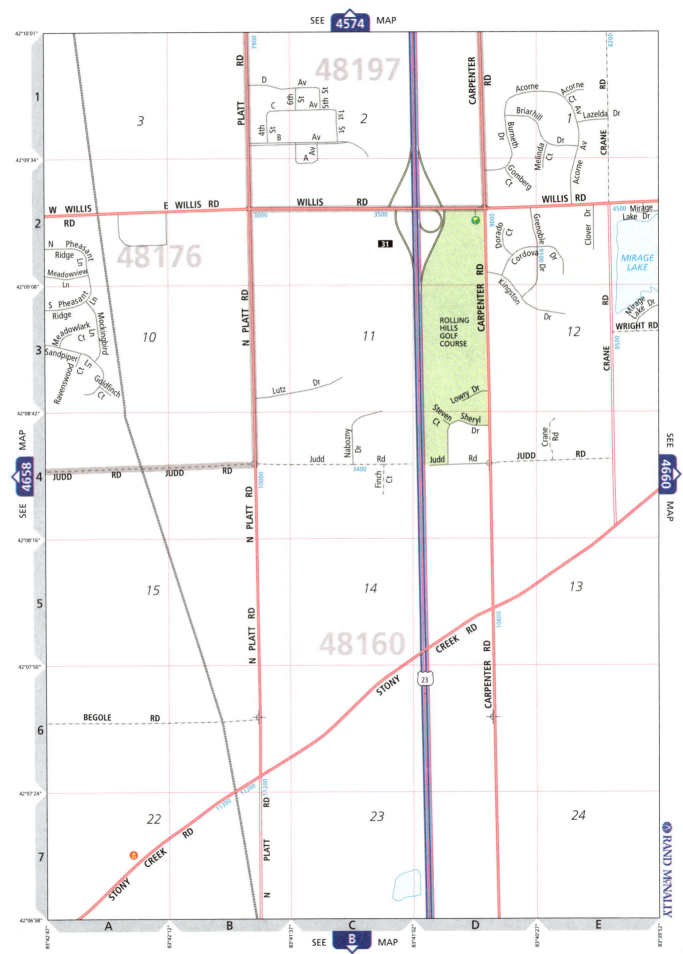

48197

CARPENTER RD

PLATT RD

7900

8200

D

C   6th St   5th St   1st St

Av

St

4th St

B

A Av

Av

Av

3

2

1

Acorne
Acorne Ct
Av   Lazelda Dr
Briarhill
Burneth Dr
Melinda Ct   Dr
Gomberg Ct
Acorne Av

CRANE RD

42°10'01"

42°09'34"

SEE
4658
MAP

W   WILLIS   RD

E   WILLIS   RD

WILLIS   RD

WILLIS   RD

3000

3500

9000

4500 Mirage Lake Dr

N Pheasant
Ridge Ln
Meadowview Ln
S Pheasant Ridge Ln
Meadowlark Ct Ln
Sandpiper Ln
Ravenswood Ct
Goldfinch Ct

Mockingbird

48176

31

CARPENTER RD

Dorado Ct
Cordova Dr
Grenoble Dr
9100
Kingston
Dr
Clover Dr

MIRAGE LAKE

Mirage Lake Dr

CRANE RD
9500

10

11

ROLLING
HILLS
GOLF
COURSE

12

WRIGHT RD

42°09'08"

42°08'42"

Lutz   Dr

Nabozny Dr

Lowry Dr

Steven Ct   Sheryl Dr

JUDD   RD

JUDD   RD

JUDD   Rd

Judd   Rd

Judd   Rd

JUDD   RD

3400

Finch Ct

Crane Rd

N PLATT RD

10000

42°08'16"

15

14

13

N PLATT RD

48160

42°07'50"

STONY   CREEK RD

23

CARPENTER RD

10600

42°07'24"

BEGOLE   RD

6

11300   11200
RD 11200

N PLATT

22

STONY CREEK RD

23

24

7

42°06'58"

A   B   C   D   E

83°42'47"   83°42'12"   83°41'37"   83°41'02"   83°40'27"   25.66.28

SEE
4660
MAP

RAND McNALLY

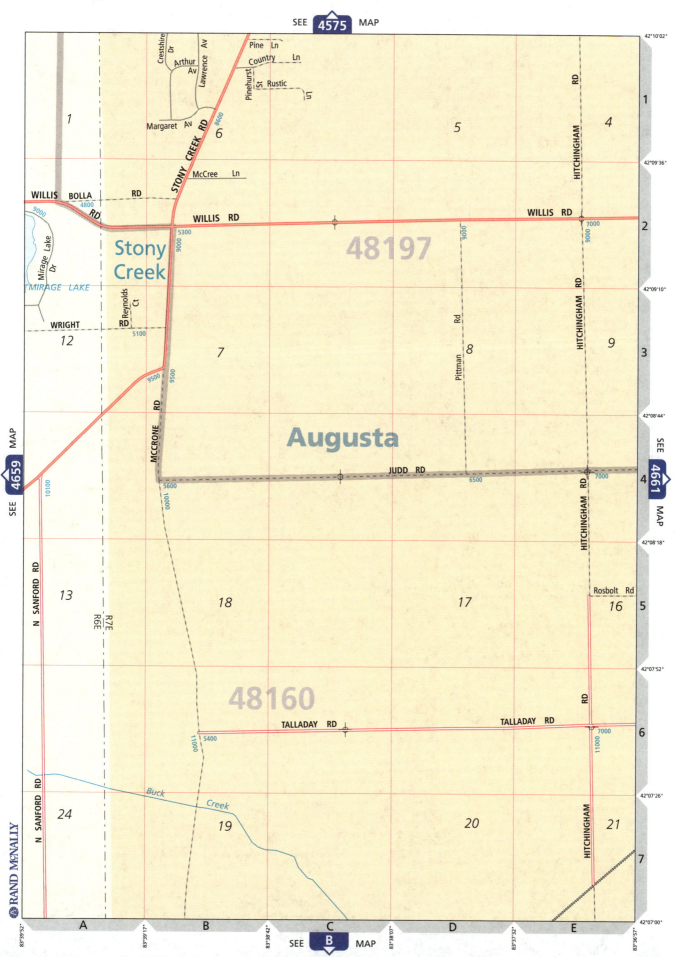

MAP
4660

1:24,000
1 in. = 2000 ft.

0   0.25   0.5

miles

SEE **4575** MAP

Crestshire Dr

Arthur Av

Lawrence Av

Pine Ln

Country Ln

Pinehurst St Rustic Ln

Margaret Av

STONY CREEK RD

8600

McCree Ln

WILLIS BOLLA RD

4800

WILLIS RD

WILLIS RD

7000

9000

9000

Stony Creek

5300

9000

48197

9000

Reynolds Ct

WRIGHT RD

5100

Pittman Rd

9500

9500

MCCRONE RD

Augusta

JUDD RD

6500

7000

5600

10000

SEE **4659** MAP

10100

SEE **4661** MAP

HITCHINGHAM RD

HITCHINGHAM RD

Mirage Lake Dr

MIRAGE LAKE

Rosbolt Rd

N SANFORD RD

R7E
R6E

48160

TALLADAY RD

TALLADAY RD

7000

11000 5400

RD

11000

Buck   Creek

N SANFORD RD

HITCHINGHAM RD

1

6

2

12

7

8

9

3

13

18

17

16

5

24

19

20

21

6

7

RAND MCNALLY

SEE **B** MAP

42°10'02"

42°09'36"

42°09'10"

42°08'44"

42°08'18"

42°07'52"

42°07'26"

42°07'00"

83°39'52"   83°39'17"   83°38'42"   83°38'07"   83°37'32"   83°36'57"

A   B   C   D   E

MAP
4661

SEE 4576 MAP

1:24,000
1 in. = 2000 ft.
0   0.25   0.5
miles

48197

Lincoln

4

WHITTAKER RD

3

RD

HILL

TUTTLE

Winona
Ct
Barton
Ln

Cheri
Ln

8800

Lincoln
HS

WILLIS   RD

9000

8000

9000

7000

9

9000

9500

9600

Rd

Macey

Rd

11

Augusta

10

WHITTAKER   RD

Hill

JUDD   RD

9000

Tuttle

7000

SEE 4660 MAP

SEE 4662 MAP

Rosbolt   Rd

16

7000

Rosbolt   Rd

8400

15

14

Tuttle

48160

48191

Hill

11000

TALLADAY   RD

TALLADAY   RD

7800

8000

11000

Whittaker

Rd

Paint

Red
Oak Ln
Pin Oak Ln
Scarlet Oak
Ln
White
Oak Ln
Burr
Oak Ln
English
Oak Ln
Black
Oak Ln
White Oak
Ln

Laurel Oak Ln

Spanish Oak
Ln

21

Stony

Creek

WHITTAKER   RD

English
Oak Ct

22

Creek

23

McFall

Dr

11000

A   B   C   D   E

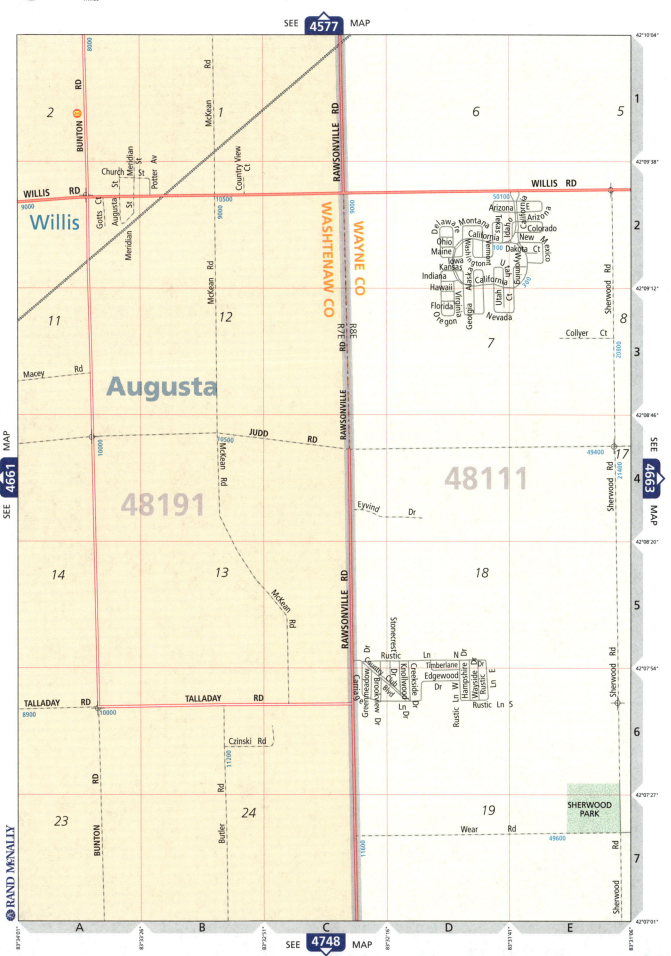

MAP
4662

1:24,000
1 in. = 2000 ft.

0   0.25   0.5
miles

42°10'04"

1

2   BUNTON   1

McKean   Rd

6   5

Country View Ct

Church St   Meridian St   Potter Av

RAWSONVILLE   RD

WILLIS   RD

WILLIS   RD

9000   Willis   Gotts Ct   Augusta St   10500   9000   42°09'38"

Meridian   WASHTENAW CO   WAYNE CO   0006   50100   Arizona   California E   2

Delaware   Montana   Arizona   Colorado

Ohio   California   Idaho   Texas   New   Mexico

Maine   Washington   Vermont   Dakota   Ct   100

Iowa   Kansas   Wyoming   300

11   McKean   Rd   12   Indiana   Alaska   Utah   California   42°09'12"

Hawaii   Georgia   Utah   Ct   Sherwood   Rd   8

Florida   Virginia   Nevada

Oregon   Collyer   Ct   20800   3

Macey   Rd

Augusta

R8E   R7E   42°08'46"

JUDD   RD   10500   RD   10000   McKean   Rd   42°08'20"   49400   17   SEE [4663] MAP

48191   **48111**

Eyvind   Dr   Sherwood   Rd   21400

14   13   18

McKean   Rd

Stonecrest Dr   Ln   N Dr   42°07'54"

Rustic   Timberlane   Wayside Dr   Rustic Ln E

Greenmeadow Dr   County Club Dr   Knollwood Ln Dr   Creekside Dr   Edgewood Dr   Hampshire   Rustic Ln W   Rustic Ln S

Carriage   Brookview Dr

TALLADAY   RD   8900   10000   TALLADAY   RD

BUNTON   RD   Czinski Rd   11200

SHERWOOD PARK   42°07'27"

23   24   19   Wear   Rd   49600

Butler   Rd   11600   Sherwood   Rd   7

Sherwood   42°07'01"

A   83°34'01"   B   83°33'26"   C   83°32'51"   D   83°32'16"   E   83°31'41"   83°31'06"

MAP
4663

1:24,000
1 in. = 2000 ft.

0   0.25   0.5
miles

SEE **4578** MAP

42°10'04"

17500

Harris   Rd

Westcott Dr

Harris   Rd

45400

Harris   Rd

SUMPTER   RD

1

Rd

Lohr

Elwell

Rd

5

4

3

42°09'38"

North

WILLIS   RD

45400

WILLIS RD

48900

19600

47400

19600

Sharon Ct

Crandell   Ct

WILLIS   RD

Branch

2

Karr   Rd

ELWELL   RD

Weimer Dr

19900

Rymut Dr

19900

Claxton   Dr

Rd

42°09'12"

8

Wilmot

20600

Kozma   St

44300

9

10

3

Creek

Swan

42°08'46"

MAP **4662**

JUDD   RD

45400

JUDD   RD

SEE

Karr   Rd

47100

Meri Dr

ELWELL   RD

Bontekos St

Av

48111

Clemmons Ct

SEE **4664** MAP

4

Reed   St

Fenster

Traskos   St

SUMPTER   RD

Ray   Ln

Prince   Rd

42°08'20"

Bohn   Rd

Clay   Rd

15

44800

Rd

17

16

5

Karr   Rd

ELWELL   RD

42°07'54"

Dunn   Rd

45400

23600

43400

Karr   Rd

Bohn   Rd

23600

Victoria St

6

Bohn Rd

GRAHAM PARK

42°07'27"

Thatcham Ln

Wear   Rd

20

21

Wear   Rd

22

Wear   Rd

Karr   Rd

Wear   Rd

47400

46300

SUMPTER   RD

ELWELL   RD

Sumpter

7

METROPOLITAN
MEM   PK
CEM

ELWELL

42°07'01"

83°31'06"

A

83°30'31"

B

83°29'56"

C

83°29'21"

D

83°28'46"

E

83°28'11"

SEE **4749** MAP

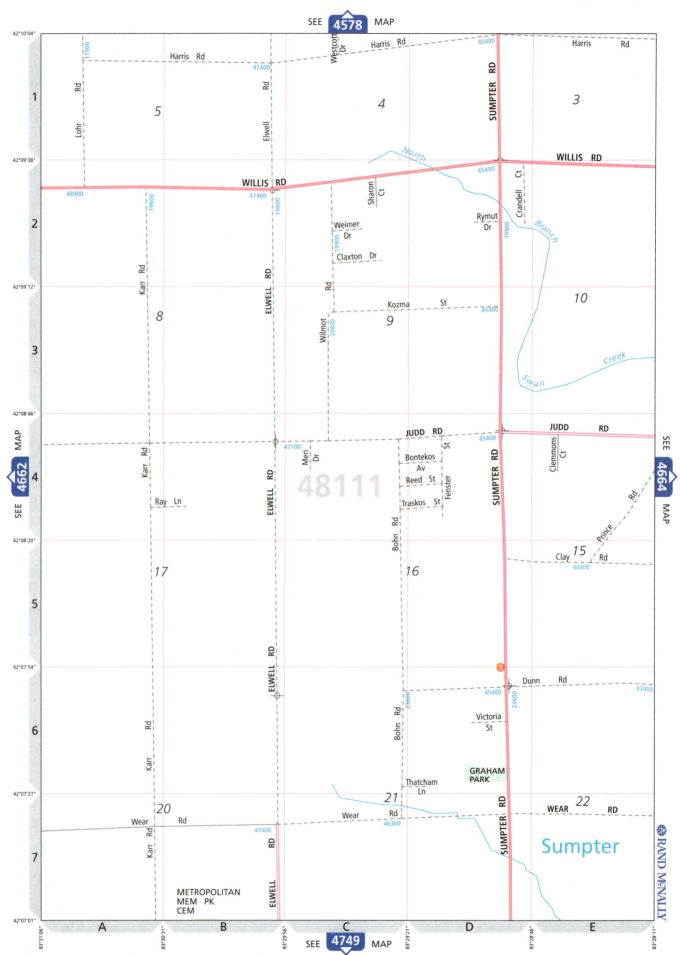

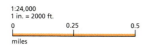

MAP
4664

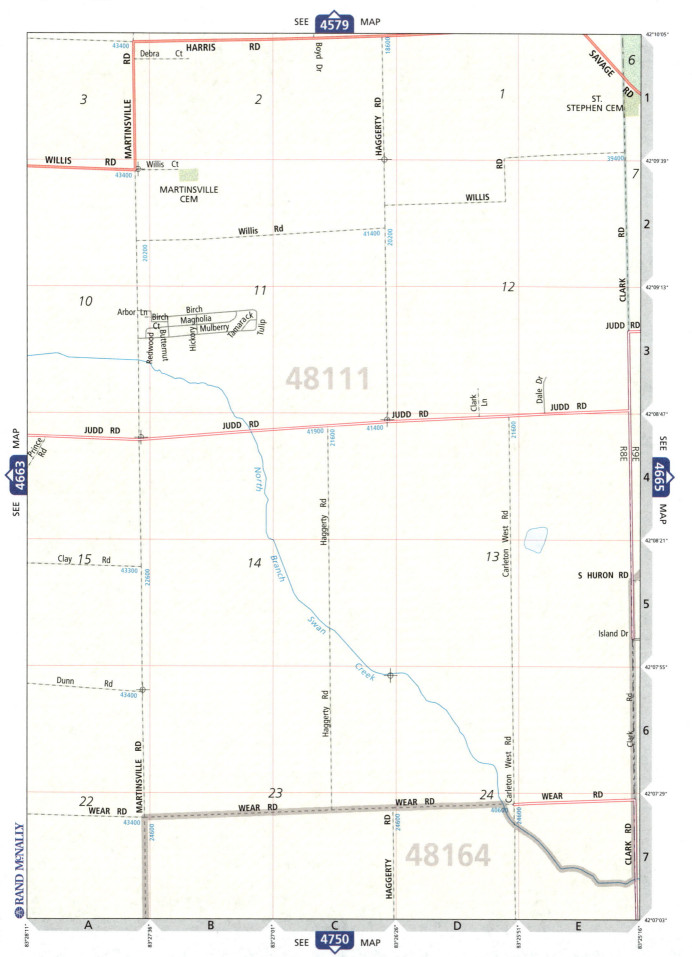

1:24,000
1 in. = 2000 ft.

0   0.25   0.5
miles

42°10'05"

43400 Debra Ct HARRIS RD

Boyd Dr

18600

SAVAGE RD

6

3   MARTINSVILLE   2   HAGGERTY RD   1   ST. STEPHEN CEM   1

WILLIS RD   39400   42°09'39"

Willis Ct   RD   7

43400

MARTINSVILLE CEM   WILLIS

2

CLARK RD

Willis Rd   41400   20200   42°09'13"

20200

10   11   12

Arbor Ln   Birch

Birch   Magnolia   JUDD RD

Redwood Butternut Ct   Mulberry Tamarack Tulip   3

Hickory

48111

Clark Ln   Dale Dr

JUDD RD   JUDD RD   42°08'47"

JUDD RD   JUDD RD   JUDD RD   SEE

Prince Rd   41900 21600   41400   21600   4665 MAP

North   R8E R9E

4

Carleton West Rd   42°08'21"

Clay 15 Rd   14   13   S HURON RD

43300   22600   Branch   5

Island Dr

Swan

42°07'55"

Haggerty Rd   Creek

Dunn Rd   6

43400   Carleton West Rd

Clark Rd

22   23   24   WEAR RD   42°07'29"

WEAR Rd   WEAR RD   WEAR RD

43400 24600   40600   24600

HAGGERTY RD   24600   48164   7

CLARK RD

42°07'03"

A   B   C   D   E

83°28'11"   83°27'36"   83°27'01"   83°26'26"   83°25'51"   83°25'16"

MAP
4665

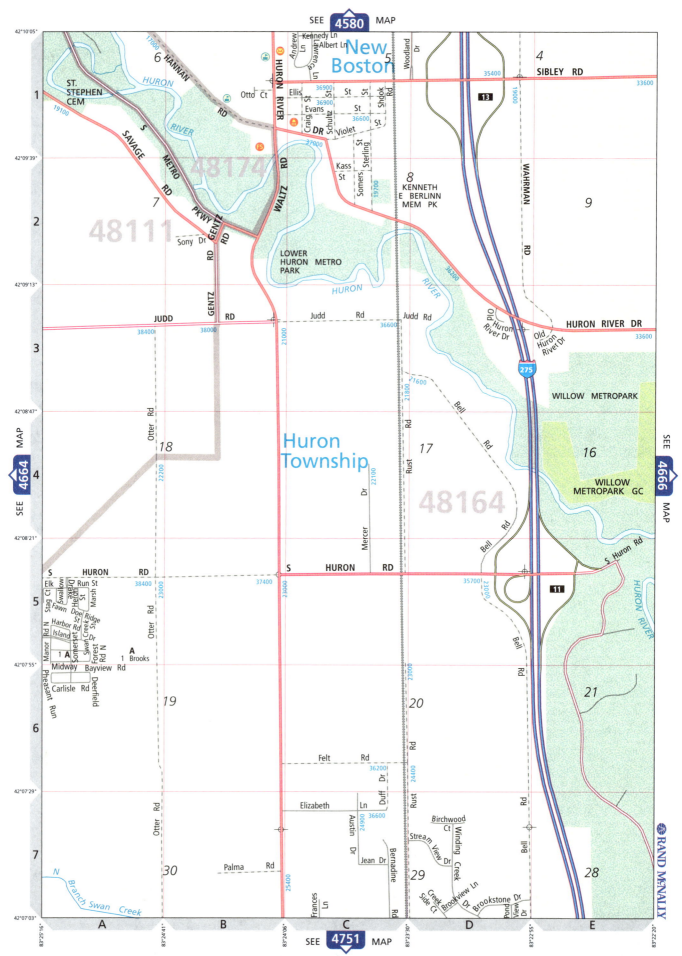

1:24,000
1 in. = 2000 ft.

0   0.25   0.5
miles

SEE 4580 MAP

New Boston

Kennedy Ln
Andrew Ln
Albert Ln
Lawrence Ln

Woodland Dr

SIBLEY RD

5

4

13

35400

33600

19000

Otto Ct

Ellis 36900

Evans

Craig St

Schultz

Violet St

St   St   St

Shook Rd

Kass St

Somers St

Sterling St

48174

WAHRMAN RD

8
KENNETH E BERLINN MEM PK

9

ST. STEPHEN CEM

HANNAN RD

HURON RIVER DR

HURON RIVER

SAVAGE RD

METRO PKWY

GENTZ RD

WALTZ RD

19100

19700

37000

7

48111

Sony Dr

LOWER HURON METRO PARK

HURON RIVER

36400

GENTZ RD

JUDD RD

38400   38000

Judd   Rd

Judd Rd

36600

Old Huron River Dr

Old Huron River Dr

HURON RIVER DR

33600

275

21000

Otter Rd

22200

18

21600

21800

Bell Rd

WILLOW METROPARK

16

17

Rust Rd

Mercer Dr

22100

48164

Bell Rd

Bell Rd

WILLOW METROPARK GC

S   HURON   RD

S   HURON   RD

S. Huron Rd

Elk Ct
Swallow
Run St
Drake St
Marsh
Fawn
Doe St
Ridge
Harbor Rd
Island
Somerset
Swan Creek Dr
Forest Rd
Stag Ct
N Rd
Manor
1 A

Midway
Bayview Rd
Deerfield

Pheasant Run
Carlisle Rd

38400   23000

37400

35700

23000

11

Bell Rd

HURON RIVER

A
1 Brooks

19

20

21

Felt   Rd

36200

Duff Dr

24400

Rust Rd

Bell Rd

Elizabeth Ln

Austin Dr

24900

36600

Birchwood Ct

Stream View Dr

Winding Creek

30

Palma   Rd

25400

29

28

Jean Dr

Bernadine

Frances Ln

Creek Side Ct

Brookview Ln

Brookstone Dr

Pond View Dr

N Branch Swan Creek

Huron Township

SEE 4664 MAP

SEE 4666 MAP

SEE 4751 MAP

42°10'05"
42°09'39"
42°09'13"
42°08'47"
42°08'21"
42°07'55"
42°07'29"
42°07'03"

83°25'16"
83°24'41"
83°24'06"
83°23'30"
83°22'55"

A   B   C   D   E

1   2   3   4   5   6   7

6

RAND MCNALLY

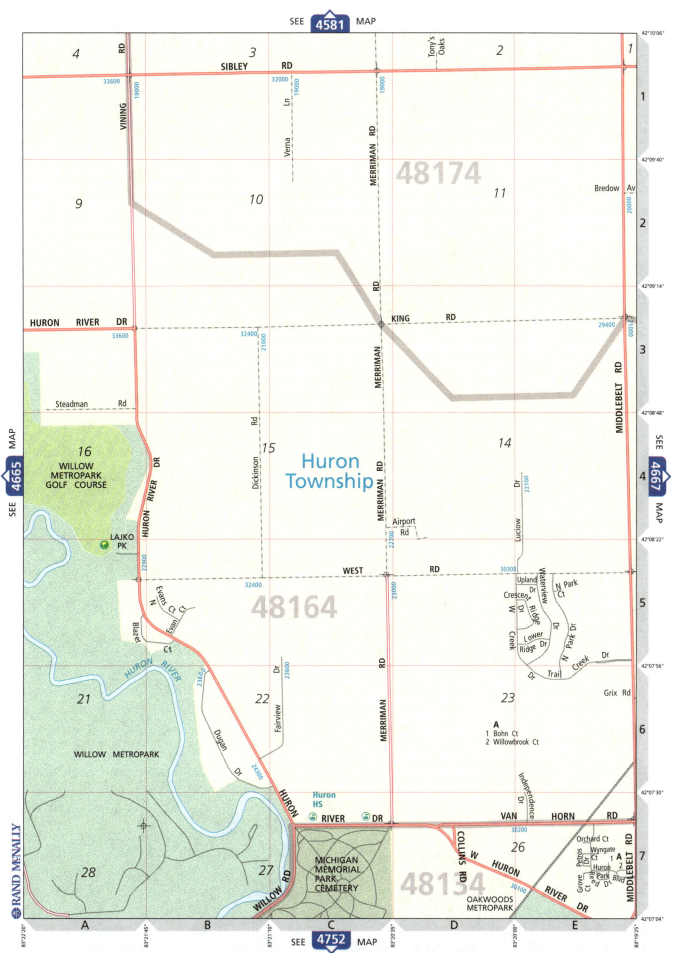

MAP
4666

1:24,000
1 in. = 2000 ft.

0   0.25   0.5
miles

N

SEE 4581 MAP

SEE 4665 MAP

SEE 4667 MAP

SEE 4752 MAP

42°10'06"
42°09'40"
42°09'14"
42°08'48"
42°08'22"
42°07'56"
42°07'30"
42°07'04"

4   3   2   1
1
2
3
4
5
6
7

A   B   C   D   E

83°22'20"   83°21'45"   83°21'10"   83°20'35"   83°20'00"   83°19'25"

SIBLEY   RD
33600   32000   19000
VINING   RD
19000
Verna   Ln
19000
MERRIMAN   RD
Tony's Oaks
48174
Bredow   Av
20000

9   10   11

HURON   RIVER   DR
33600   32400   21000
KING   RD
29400
30000
MERRIMAN   RD

Steadman   Rd
MIDDLEBELT   RD

16
WILLOW
METROPARK
GOLF   COURSE

Dickinson   Rd

15
Huron
Township

14

LAJKO
PK
22900

Luciow   Dr
22100

Airport   Rd
22100

WEST   RD
32400   23000   30300

Upland   Ct
Waterview   Dr
N   Park   Ct
Crescent   Ridge   W   Dr
Lower   Ridge   Dr
N   Park   Dr
Creek   Dr
Trail   Dr

Evans   Ct
N   Ct
Evan   Ct
Blazer   Ct

48164

Grix   Rd

21

Fairview   Dr
23600

22

23

A
1 Bohn Ct
2 Willowbrook Ct

HURON   RIVER
23800

Dugan   Dr
24300

WILLOW   METROPARK

Independence   Dr

MERRIMAN   RD

Huron
HS

RIVER   DR
VAN   HORN   RD
30200

COLLINS   RD
W   HURON

Orchard Ct
Wyngate Ct   1 A
Pettos Ct   2
Huron   Blvd
Reed Dr
Grove
Park
MIDDLEBELT   RD

28   27

MICHIGAN
MEMORIAL
PARK
CEMETERY

48134

WILLOW   RD

26
30200
30100

RIVER   DR

OAKWOODS
METROPARK

RAND McNALLY

MAP
4667

1:24,000
1 in. = 2000 ft.
0   0.25   0.5
miles

SEE 4582 MAP

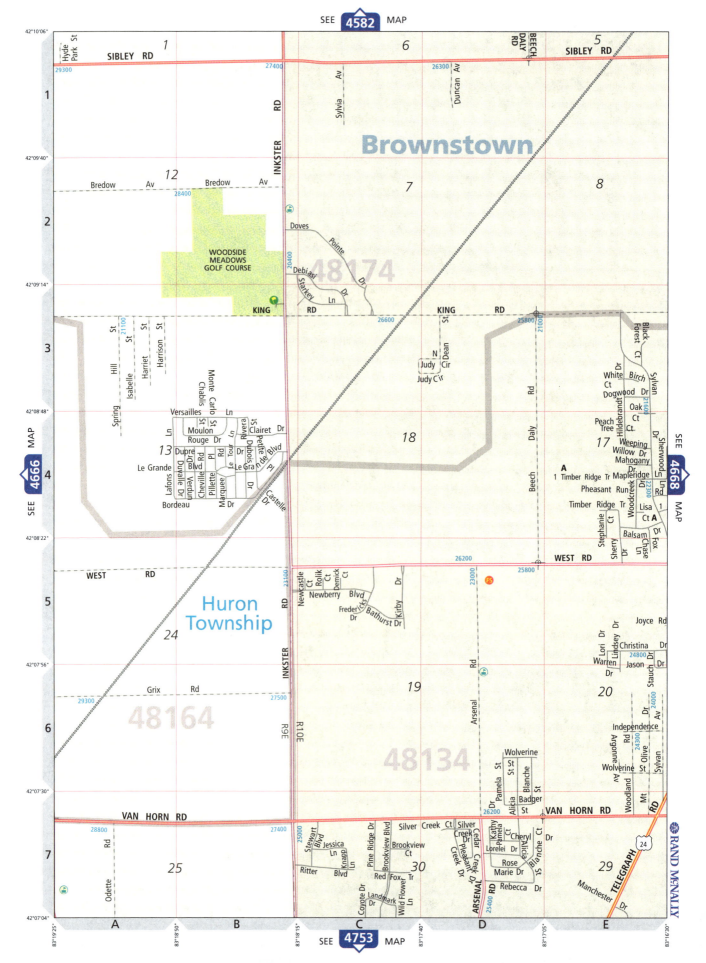

42°10'06"
Hyde Park St
SIBLEY RD
29300
27400
BEECH RD
DALY RD
SIBLEY RD
26300
5
1
6

Brownstown

42°09'40"
Bredow Av
12
Bredow Av
7
8
28400

INKSTER RD

2
Doves
Pointe
Dr
WOODSIDE MEADOWS GOLF COURSE
48174
20400
Debiasi
Starkey Ln
Dr

42°09'14"
KING RD
26600
KING RD
25800
21000
Black Forest Ct
Sylvan

3
Spring
Hill St
Isabelle St
Harriet St
Harrison St
21100
St
Dean
N
Judy Cir
Judy Cir
Rd
White Ct
Dogwood
Birch
Dr
21600
Dr
Oak Ct

42°08'48"
Versailles Ln
Monte Carlo
Chablis
St
St
Ln
Rivera
JS
Clairet
Dr
Peach Tree Ct
Hildebrandt

Moulon
Rouge Dr
Petite
Dubois
Blvd
Dr
18
Daly
Weeping Dr
Willow Dr
Mahogany
17

13
Dupre
Le Grande Blvd
Duyale Dr
Cheville Rd
Pillette Rd
PL
Le Tour
Dr
Le Gra
PL
Beech
A
1 Timber Ridge Tr
Mapleridge
Pheasant Run
22300
Sherwood Dr
Rd

Lafons
Verdun
Marquee
Dr
Castelle Dr
Timber Ridge Tr
Woodcreek
Lisa
1
A

42°08'22"
Bordeau
Stephanie Ct
Sherry
Balsam
Chase Ln
Fox Dr

West Rd
26200
25800
WEST RD

5
WEST RD
Newcastle
Rolik Ct
Demick Ct
Dr
23000
FS
23100
Newberry Blvd
Freder cks
Bathurst Dr
Kirby Dr

Huron Township
24
Arsenal
Lori Dr
Lindsey Dr
Christina Dr
Warren Dr
24800
Jason Dr
Joyce Rd

42°07'56"
Grix Rd
27500
19
Rd
Stauch
20

29300
48164
INKSTER RD
R9E
R10E

6
48134
Independence Rd
Argonne Rd
24300
Olive Av
Wolverine St
Sylvan
24000
Woodland

42°07'30"
Wolverine St
St
Blanche St
Badger St
Pamela St
Alicia St
Mt

VAN HORN RD
26200
VAN HORN RD
TELEGRAPH
24

7
VAN HORN RD
28800
27400
25000
Stewart Blvd
Jessica Ln
Knapp Ln
Pine Ridge Dr
Brookview Blvd
Brookview Ct
Silver Creek Ct
Silver Creek Dr
Cedar Creek Dr
Kathy
Pamela
Lorelei Dr
Cheryl Ct
Alicia
Blanche Ct
Dr
Manchester Dr

Odette Rd
25
Ritter Blvd
Red Fox Tr
Wild Flower Ln
Landmark Dr
Coyote Dr
30
Pleasant
Rose Dr
Marie Dr
Rebecca Dr
29

42°07'04"
A   B   C   D   E
83°19'25"   83°18'50"   83°18'15"   83°17'40"   83°17'05"   83°16'28"

RAND McNALLY

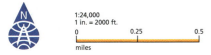
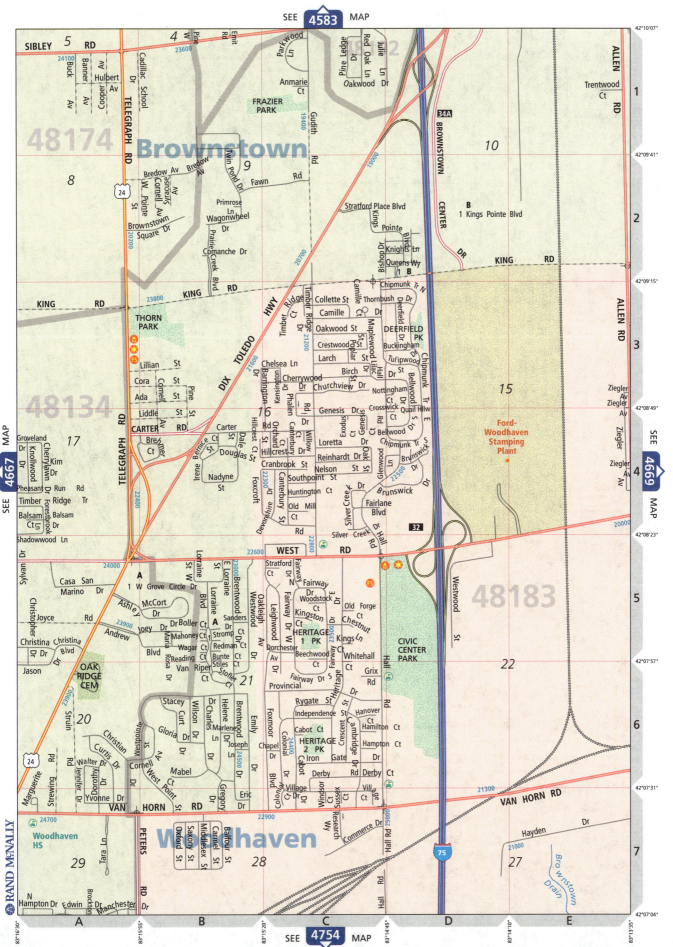

MAP
4669

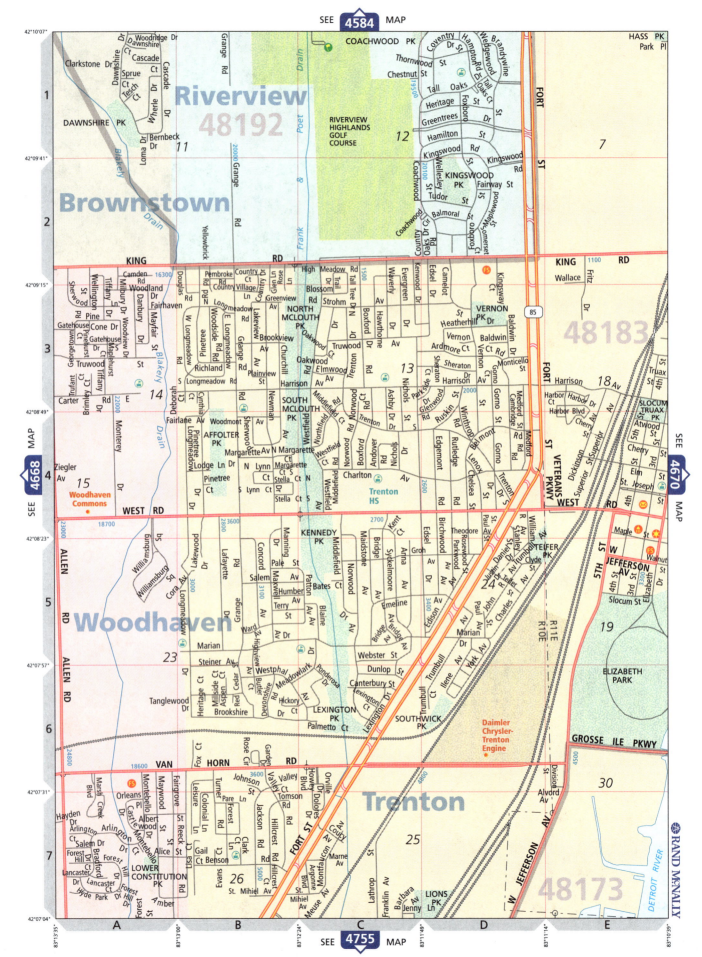

SEE 4584 MAP

1:24,000
1 in. = 2000 ft.
0   0.25   0.5
miles

SEE 4668 MAP

SEE 4670 MAP

SEE 4755 MAP

Riverview 48192

Brownstown

Woodhaven

Trenton

48183

48173

RAND McNALLY

MAP
4670

SEE 4585 MAP

SEE 4669 MAP

SEE 4671 MAP

SEE 4756 MAP

1:24,000
1 in. = 2000 ft.

0   0.25   0.5
miles

CANADA ESSEX CO
UNITED MICHIGAN WAYNE CO
STATES

Grosse Ile N
Channel Front
Range Lighthouse

Trenton

McLouth
Steel
Products

48183

KING RD

MEYER
ELLIAS PARK

Riverside
Osteopathic
Hospital

ROTARY
PARK

DETROIT
RIVER

ELIZABETH
PARK

WEST
SHORE GOLF &
COUNTRY CLUB

GROSSE ILE
48138

DETROIT
RIVER

STONY ISLAND

GROSSE ILE

PKWY

BELLEVUE RD

WATER'S
EDGE
COUNTRY CLUB

GROSSE
ILE
GOLF &
COUNTRY
CLUB

Grosse
Ile HS

Grosse
Ile

RAND McNALLY

MAP
4671

1:24,000
1 in. = 2000 ft.
0   0.25   0.5
miles

SEE **4586** MAP

DETROIT
RIVER

Sari Ln

NORTH   SIDEROAD

5

DETROIT RIVER

FRONT ST N

Amherstburg

2ND CONCESSION RD

Marina

Canal
St

Edgewater
Beach

Lane Cir Golfview Ct
Park Ct   Forest Hill
       Cranbrook   Linwood Old Colony Dr
Park   Forest Dr Track
Lane   Forest
Dr Hill Cir

SEE 4670 MAP

10

CANADA
UNITED STATES

MIDDLE   SIDEROAD

SEE B MAP

Angstrom
Cres Dr
West
Golfwood Dr Wright Av
Pointe Turner Cres
Wyandotte St
Golfwood Dr Fairway Cres Fairway Cres
Golfwood Dr

Ironwood Dr
Dr Links Dr
Ironwood Clubview Fescue Ln
Dr

N9V

ESSEX CO
WAYNE CO

Kingsbridge
Dr
Baker Cambridge
Cres Ct Oxford
Whelan Cres
Dr

FRONT ST N

20

Knob

18

McLellan   Av

DETROIT RIVER

Easy Hill
St

Marsh Marsh
Ct Dr Dr

Texas Rd   Texas Rd

MICHIGAN
ONTARIO

STONY
ISLAND

48138

THOMAS RD

Brumon
Yacht
Club

Brunner Fraser Av Av Girard St

A   B   C   D   E

42°10'08"
42°09'41"
42°09'15"
42°08'49"
42°08'23"
42°07'57"
42°07'31"
42°07'05"

83°07'44"   83°07'09"   83°06'34"   83°05'59"   83°05'24"

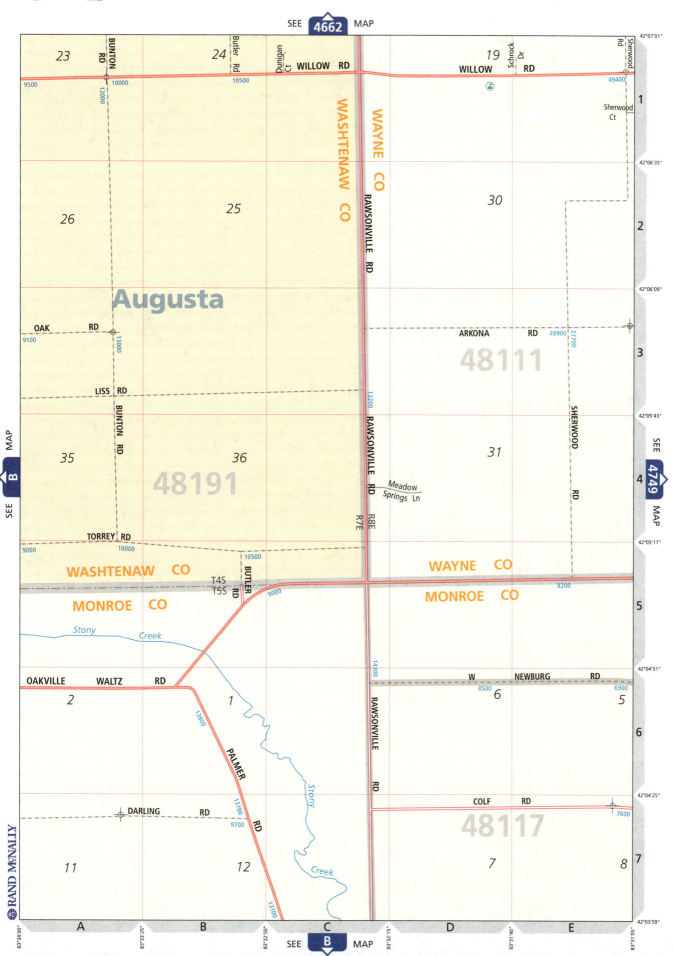

MAP
4748

SEE 4662 MAP

1:24,000
1 in. = 2000 ft.
0   0.25   0.5
miles

23   BUNTON RD   24   Butler Rd   Dunigan Ct   WILLOW RD   19   Schrock Dr   WILLOW   RD   Sherwood Rd   42°07'01"
9500   10000   10500   49400   Sherwood Ct

1

26   25   30   42°06'35"

WASHTENAW CO   WAYNE CO   2

Augusta   42°06'09"

OAK   RD   RAWSONVILLE RD   ARKONA   RD   49900   27700   42°05'43"
9100   13000   48111

LISS   RD   SHERWOOD   RD   3

35   BUNTON RD   36   31   4

SEE 4749 MAP

48191   13200   RAWSONVILLE RD   Meadow Springs Ln   42°05'17"

TORREY   RD   R7E   R8E

9000   10000   10500   42°05'17"

WASHTENAW   CO   Butler RD   WAYNE   CO   8200
T4S T5S   9000

MONROE   CO   MONROE   CO   5

Stony   Creek

OAKVILLE   WALTZ   RD   W   NEWBURG   RD   42°04'51"
2   1   8500   6900
13800   6   5   RAWSONVILLE RD   14300

PALMER   Stony   6

DARLING   RD   COLF   RD   42°04'25"
13700   9700   RD   48117   7600

11   12   Creek   7   8   7

RAND McNALLY

A   83°34'00"   B   83°33'25"   83°33'05"   C   SEE B MAP   83°32'15"   D   83°31'40"   E   83°31'05"   42°03'59"

MAP
4749

1:24,000
1 in. = 2000 ft.

0   0.25   0.5
miles

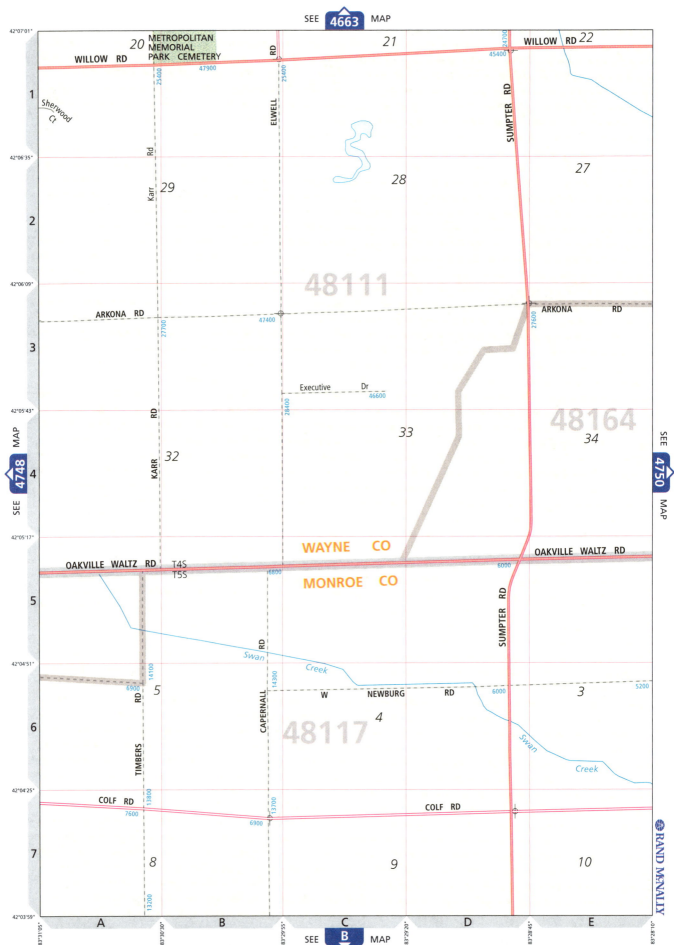

42°07'01"

WILLOW RD   20   METROPOLITAN MEMORIAL PARK CEMETERY   RD   21   WILLOW RD 22   SUMPTER RD

47900   25400   25400   45400   24700

1

Sherwood Ct

42°06'35"

Karr   Rd   29   ELWELL   28   27

2

42°06'09"

48111

Karr   RD   ARKONA RD   47400   ARKONA   RD

27700   27600

3

Executive   Dr   46600

42°05'43"

28400

RD   33   **48164**   34

KARR   32

4

42°05'17"

WAYNE   CO

OAKVILLE WALTZ RD   OAKVILLE WALTZ RD

T4S   6800   6000

T5S   **MONROE   CO**   SUMPTER RD

5

RD

Swan   Creek

42°04'51"

CAPERNALL   14300   6000   5200

14100

RD   5   W   NEWBURG   RD   3

6900

6

TIMBERS   **48117**   4   Swan

13800   Creek

42°04'25"

COLF RD   COLF RD

7600   13700   COLF RD

13200   6900

7

8   9   10

42°03'59"

83°31'05"   83°30'30"   83°29'55"   83°29'20"   83°28'45"   83°28'10"

A   B   C   D   E

RAND M^cNALLY

MAP
4750

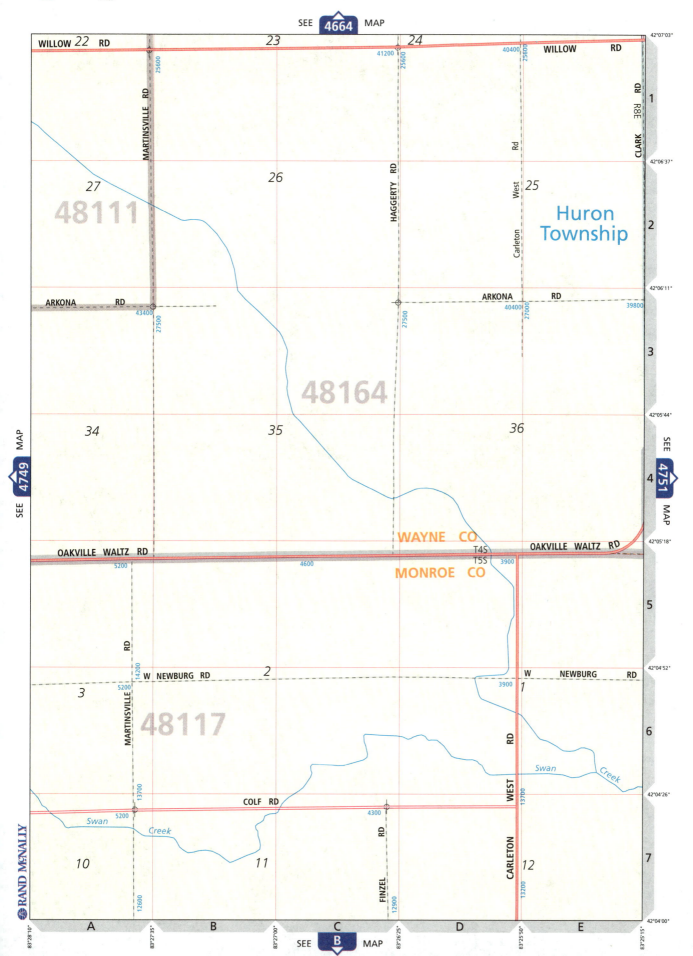

SEE 4664 MAP

1:24,000
1 in. = 2000 ft.

0   0.25   0.5
miles

WILLOW 22 RD   23   24   WILLOW   RD

25600   41200   25600   40400 25600

MARTINSVILLE RD

1

42°07'03"

42°06'37"

Rd

27   26   West 25   Huron
Township

48111

HAGGERTY RD

Carleton

CLARK RD
R8E

2

42°06'11"

ARKONA   RD   43400   27500   27500   ARKONA   RD   40400 27000   39800

3

48164

42°05'44"

34   35   36

SEE 4749 MAP

SEE 4751 MAP

4

42°05'18"

WAYNE   CO
T4S
T5S
MONROE CO

OAKVILLE WALTZ RD   5200   4600   3900   OAKVILLE WALTZ RD

5

42°04'52"

RD
14200

W NEWBURG RD   2   W   NEWBURG   RD

MARTINSVILLE

3   5200   48117   3900   1

WEST   RD

6

42°04'26"

Swan   Creek

COLF RD   5200   4300   13700

Swan   Creek

10   11   FINZEL RD   12900   CARLETON 13200   12

7

42°04'00"

13600

42°28'10"   42°27'35"   42°27'00"   42°26'25"   42°25'50"   42°25'15"

A   B   C   D   E

SEE B MAP

RAND McNALLY

MAP
4751

1:24,000
1 in. = 2000 ft.

0   0.25   0.5
miles

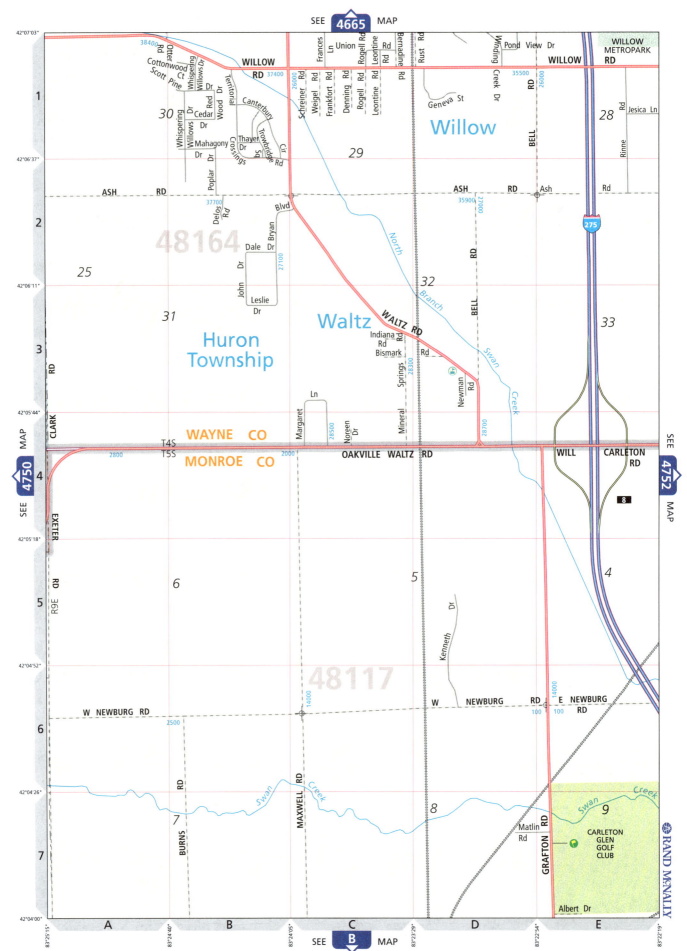

SEE **4665** MAP

WILLOW METROPARK

WILLOW RD

Willow

30

28

29

48164

25

31

Huron Township

Waltz

32

33

WAYNE CO
T4S
T5S
MONROE CO

OAKVILLE WALTZ RD

MAP

SEE **4750**

SEE **4752** MAP

48117

6

5

4

W NEWBURG RD

W NEWBURG RD   E NEWBURG RD

7

8

9

CARLETON GLEN GOLF CLUB

Albert Dr

A   B   C   D   E

SEE **B** MAP

RAND McNALLY

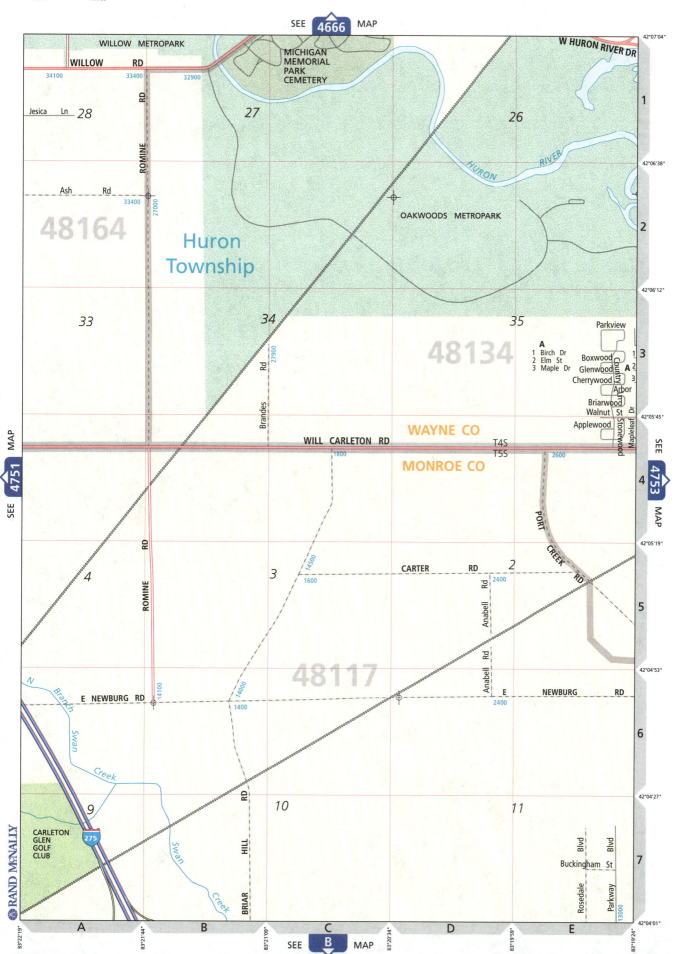

MAP
4752

1:24,000
1 in. = 2000 ft.

0   0.25   0.5
miles

SEE **4666** MAP

WILLOW METROPARK

WILLOW RD

34100   33400   32900

W HURON RIVER DR

Jesica Ln **28**

ROMINE RD

27

MICHIGAN MEMORIAL PARK CEMETERY

26

42°07'04"

1

Ash Rd

27000

33400

48164

Huron Township

HURON RIVER

42°06'38"

OAKWOODS METROPARK

2

42°06'12"

33

27900

34

Brandes Rd

35

48134

Parkview

A
1 Birch Dr
2 Elm St
3 Maple Dr

Boxwood

Glenwood

Cherrywood

Arbor

Briarwood

Walnut St

Applewood

Country Ln

Stonewood

Mapleleaf Dr

A

1

2

3

3

42°05'45"

WILL CARLETON RD

WAYNE CO

T4S

1800

T5S

MONROE CO

2600

SEE **4751** MAP

SEE **4753** MAP

4

42°05'19"

ROMINE RD

4

3

14500

1600

CARTER RD

2

Anabell Rd

2400

PORT CREEK RD

5

42°04'53"

48117

14100

E NEWBURG RD

14000

1400

Anabell Rd

E NEWBURG RD

2400

6

N Branch

Swan

Creek

42°04'27"

9

275

Swan

BRIAR HILL RD

10

11

Buckingham St

Rosedale Blvd

Parkway Blvd

13000

7

CARLETON GLEN GOLF CLUB

Creek

42°04'01"

83°22'19"

A

83°21'44"

B

83°21'09"

C

SEE **B** MAP

83°20'34"

D

83°19'59"

E

83°19'24"

MAP
4753

1:24,000
1 in. = 2000 ft.

0   0.25   0.5

miles

SEE **4667** MAP

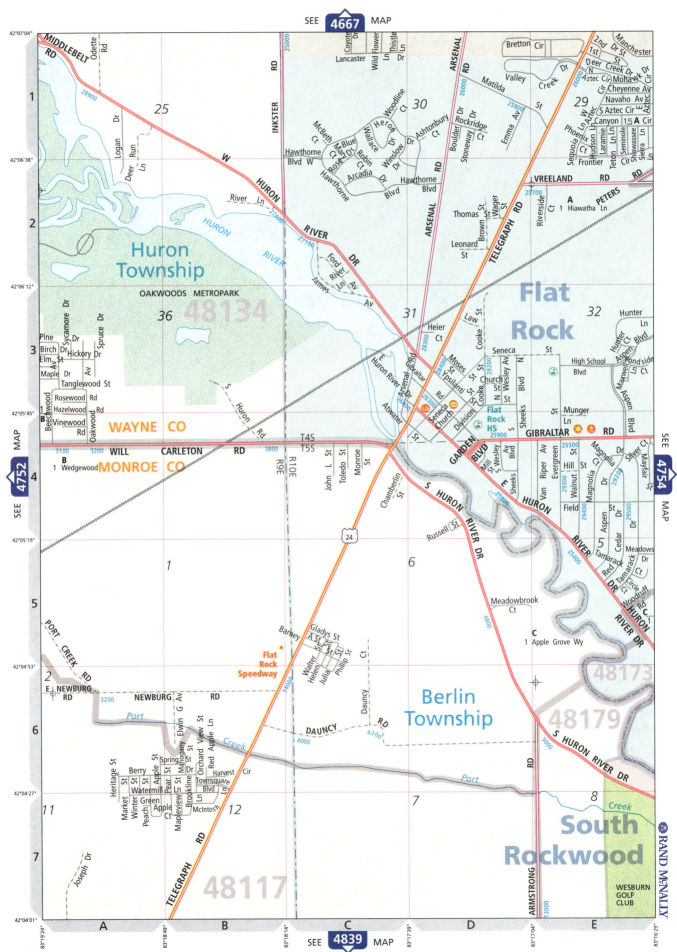

SEE **4752** MAP

SEE **4754** MAP

SEE **4839** MAP

MIDDLEBELT RD
Odette Rd
Logan Dr
Deer Run Ln

25

W HURON RIVER DR

Huron
Township

OAKWOODS METROPARK

48134

36

HURON RIVER

Pine
Sycamore Dr
Birch Dr
Elm St
Hickory Dr
Spruce Dr
Maple Dr
Av
Tanglewood St
Rosewood Rd
Hazelwood Rd
Vinewood Rd
Beechwood Av
Oakwood Rd

WAYNE CO

MONROE CO

1 Wedgewood

WILL CARLETON RD

INKSTER RD

River Ln
Ford River Ln
James Av
Av

S Huron Rd

3100 3200   3800

T4S
T5S

R9E R10E

John St
Toledo St
Monroe St
Chamberlin St

Lancaster
Coyote
Wild Flower Ln
Thistle Ln
Woodline Ct
Heron Ct
McBeth Ct
Wallace
Blue Nan Dr
Rose Ct
Robin Ct
Winslow Dr
Ashtonbury Ct
Hawthorne Blvd W
Hawthorne
Arcadia Dr
Hawthorne Blvd
Hawthorne Blvd

30

ARSENAL RD

ARSENAL RD

Boulder Dr
Stoneway Dr
Rockridge Ct
Emma Av

Matilda St

VREELAND RD

Thomas St
Brown St
Wager St
Leonard St

TELEGRAPH RD

Riverside

25700

31

Heier Ct
Law St
Moses St
Cooke St
Church St
Ipsilanti St
Cooke St
Seneca St
Gibraltar Rd
Huron River Dr
Atwater St
Division St
Garden St

GARDEN BLVD

GIBRALTAR RD

S HURON RIVER DR

Seneca
Church
Lib

Flat Rock HS
25900

Flat
Rock

32

High School Blvd

Hunter Ln
Hunter Ct
Aspen Blvd
Maxwell
Pond side Ct
Munger Ln

Wesley Av
Blvd N
Sheeks St

Will
S Wesley
Aspen Blvd
Van Riper Av
Evergreen
Hill
Field
Walnut St
Aspen Dr
Magnolia
Magnolia
Cedar Dr
Tamarack
Tamarack Ct
Tamarack Circle Ct
Silver Ct
Mayfair St

48173
48179

5

Red Dr
Meadows Dr
Woodruff Rd

C
1 Apple Grove Wy

6

Russell St
Meadowbrook Ct

24

1

Port Creek Rd

NEWBURG RD
E NEWBURG RD
3200

Port Creek

Flat
Rock
Speedway

Barney
Gladys St
A St
B St
C St
Walter
Helen
Julia
Phillip St
Dauncy Ct

DAUNCY RD

Berlin
Township

S HURON RIVER DR

7

8

Creek

South
Rockwood

Heritage St
Market St
Winter St
Peach St
Berry St
Apple St
Pear St
Mahogany Ln
Green
Apple
Mapleview Ln
Spring St
Brookline St
Orchard
Red Apple Ln
Townsquare Blvd
McIntosh St
Harvest Cir
Elwin G Av
View St

11

12

Joseph Dr

TELEGRAPH RD

48117

ARMSTRONG RD

WESBURN GOLF CLUB

A   B   C   D   E

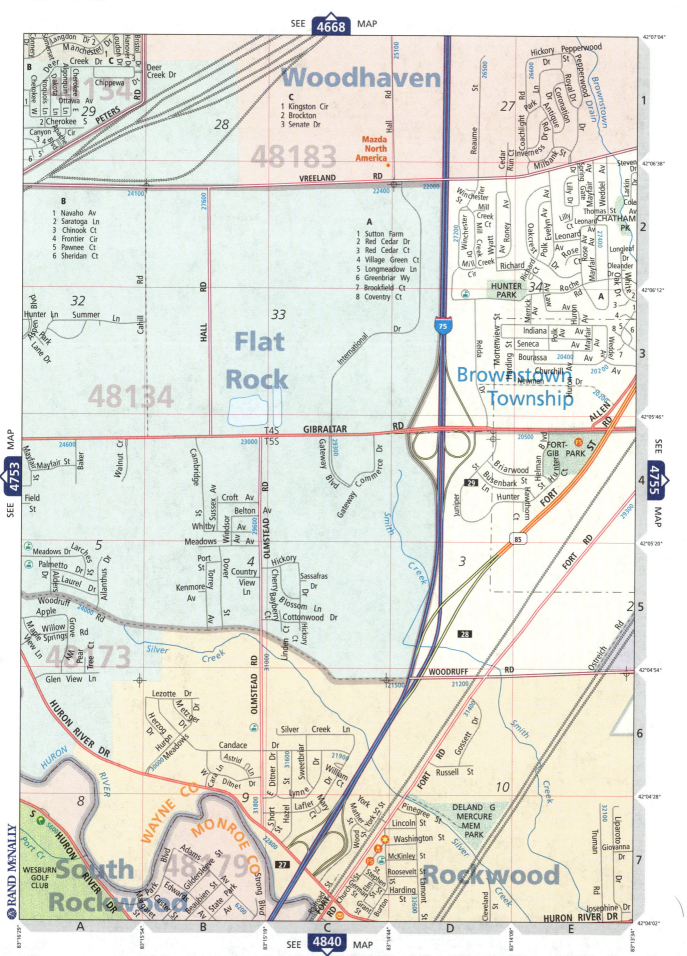

MAP
4754

SEE 4668 MAP

N

1:24,000
1 in. = 2000 ft.
0   0.25   0.5
miles

Woodhaven

42°07'04"

Langdon Dr 2
Manchester Dr 1
Hanover Dr
Bristol Ct
Loudon Dr 1
B
Deer Creek Dr
Chippewa

Conney Ln
Winchester Dr
Deer Creek Dr
Algonquin Creek Dr C
Dakota
Cherokee
Iroquois Dr
Ottawa Av
E S
29
Cherokee
W S
2
Canyon Blvd
Cherokee
Cir
6
5

PETERS RD

28

48183

C
1 Kingston Cir
2 Brockton
3 Senate Dr

Reaume St

26500
Hickory Dr
Pepperwood Dr
Royal Dr
Coronation Dr
Antique Rd
Milbank St
Coachlight Rd
Inverness
Cedar Run Ct
Park

27

Brownstown Drain

26600

42°06'38"

Steven St

Hall Rd

Mazda North America

VREELAND RD
22400   22000

Winchester St
Mill Creek Ct
27700
Winchester Dr
Mill Creek
Cir

Roney Av
Wyatt Av
Richard Av

Oakcrest Av
Polk Av
Evelyn Av
Lilly Dr
Lilly
Leonard Av
Rose Av
Rose Ct
Richard Av
Roche Rd

Spring Gate
Thomas St
Leonard Av
Mayfair Av

CHATHAM PK

27400

Longleaf Av
Oleander Av
Oak Dr
White St

42°06'12"

24100
27600

B
1 Navaho Av
2 Saratoga Ln
3 Chinook Ct
4 Frontier Cir
5 Pawnee Ct
6 Sheridan Ct

A
1 Sutton Farm
2 Red Cedar Dr
3 Red Cedar Ct
4 Village Green Ct
5 Longmeadow Ln
6 Greenbriar Wy
7 Brookfield Ct
8 Coventry Ct

34

A
3
2
4
8
5
6
7
1

HUNTER PARK

Merrick Av
Huron Av
Mayfair Av

32
Hunter Ln
Summer Ln
Aspen Park Ln
Lane Dr

Cahill Rd

HALL RD

33

Flat Rock

48134

International Dr

Mortenview St
Relda Rd
Indiana Av
Seneca Av
Bourassa 20400 Av
Churchill Av

Polk Av
Mayfair Av
Wedde Av
Newman

Harding Av

Brownstown Township

20200

20200

42°06'12"

ALLEN RD

42°05'46"

SEE 4753 MAP

24600
Mayfair St
Baker Rd
Field St

T4S
T5S
23000

GIBRALTAR RD

Walnut Cr

Cambridge St
Sussex St
Croft Av
Whitby Av
Meadows Av
Windsor Av
Belton Av

29300
Gateway Commerce Dr
Gateway Blvd

Smith Creek

20500

Briarwood Blvd
Busenbark Ln
Hunter Ct

29

FORT-GIB PARK FS
Helman St
Hawthorn St

FORT ST

Juniper St

85

42°05'20"

FORT RD

29300

SEE 4755 MAP

4

5
Meadows Dr
Palmetto Dr
Alders Dr
Laurel Dr
Larches St
Ailanthus Dr

Port St
Torrey St
Kenmore Av
Dover St

4
Country View Ln

Hickory
Cherry
Sassafras Dr
Bayberry Ln
Blossom Ln
Cottonwood Dr

3

28

Ostreich Rd

42°05'20"

2

Woodruff Apple Rd
24000
Willow Springs Ct
Maple View Ln
Grove Rd
Pear Tree Ct
Glen View Ln

48173

Silver Creek

Linden Ct

OLMSTEAD RD

30900

WOODRUFF RD
21500   21200

Smith Creek

42°04'54"

HURON RIVER DR

Lezotte Dr
Metzger Dr
Herzog Dr
Hurpn Dr
30000 Meadows

Candace Dr
Astrid
W Cara Ln
Ditner Dr

Silver Creek Ln

Sweetbriar Dr
31600
21900
William Ct

Gossett Dr
31400
Russell St

DELAND G MERCURE MEM PARK

10

32100
Liparoto Dr
Giovanna Dr

8

HURON RIVER DR

WAYNE CO
MONROE CO

9
E Ditner St
Short St
Hazel St
Laflet St
Lynne St
Mary Dr

York St
Mather St
Wood St
York St St
Stephen St
German Elm St

Pinegree St
Lincoln St
Washington St
McKinley St
Roosevelt Av
Harding Av
Grant St
Burton St

FORT RD
Lamont St

Silver Creek
Truman Dr

7

42°04'28"

42°04'02"

South Rockwood

WESBURN GOLF CLUB S
5600
HURON RIVER DR
Port Ct

48179
Park Blvd
Edwards Av
Margaret Dr
Adams St
Custer Av
Gildersleeve St
Beaubien Av
State Park Av

27
Strong Blvd
6200

Railroad St
Church St
Stephen St

Rockwood
FS

RAND McNALLY

SEE 4840 MAP

83°16'29"   83°15'54"   83°15'38"   83°14'44"   83°14'09"   83°13'34"

MAP
4755

1:24,000
1 in. = 2000 ft.
0   0.25   0.5
miles

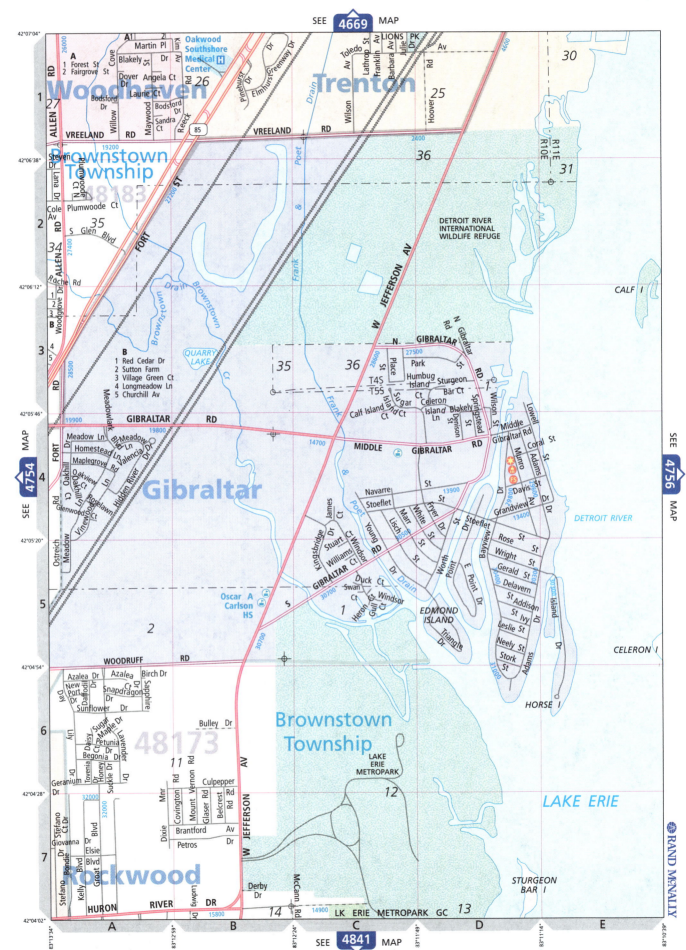

SEE 4669 MAP

Woodhaven

Trenton

Brownstown Township

48183

DETROIT RIVER INTERNATIONAL WILDLIFE REFUGE

CALF I

Gibraltar

SEE 4754 MAP

SEE 4756 MAP

DETROIT RIVER

QUARRY LAKE

B
1 Red Cedar Dr
2 Sutton Farm
3 Village Green Ct
4 Longmeadow Ln
5 Churchill Av

A
1 Forest St
2 Fairgrove St

MIDDLE   GIBRALTAR   RD

EDMOND ISLAND

CELERON I

HORSE I

Oscar A Carlson HS

WOODRUFF   RD

Brownstown Township

48173

LAKE ERIE METROPARK

LAKE ERIE

Rockwood

HURON   RIVER   DR

STURGEON BAR I

LK ERIE METROPARK GC

SEE 4841 MAP

N

1:24,000
1 in. = 2000 ft.

0   0.25   0.5
miles

MAP
4756

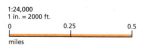

SEE 4670 MAP

Hawthorne
Glen
Hawthorne Pl
Nancy Blvd
Dr
James Dr
Nathan Dr
MERIDIAN
RD
Halcyon Ct
26100
26200

RIVER
RD

9400

9800

RD

Loma N Cir
Loma Cir
Loma S
Loma Cir
Loma Ct

RIVER
Cir

48138

W

RD

Lexington
Yorktown
Hornet Av
4th Av
Hawk St
Kitty St
Intrepid
Saratoga
Midway
Liberty

Rucker   Rd
8300

Lake   Rd
8300

GROH   RD
9600
9400

GROH   RD
8400
27600

E

Elba Dr

42°07'05"
42°06'39"
42°06'13"
42°05'47"
42°05'20"
42°04'54"
42°04'28"
42°04'02"

1

2

3

4

5

6

7

Terminal

Johnson
Reo Rd
Stinson Cir
Brodhead Rd

FRENCHMAN'S

Grosse Ile
Municipal
Airport

River
Rd
E

ELBA
ISLAND

Elba
Dr

28200

DETROIT RIVER

Boucher
Swan Dr
Rd
Swan
28400
Barbara
Chatham
Elbamar
Wilber
28500 Rd
28500
Island Dr
S
Ln
Pointe

SWAN
ISLAND

CREEK

GROSSE
ILE

WAYNE CO
ESSEX CO

SEE 4757 MAP

N9V

Coleman
Brook Cir
Gloccamorra Dr
Rd
Dr
Elbamar

ROUND
ISLAND

Heartside
Dr Rd

MESO ISLAND

River

SUGAR
ISLAND

SEE 4755 MAP

Bayview
Dr
HICKORY
ISLAND
River Rd
E
E

48173

CELERON
ISLAND

Brownstown
Township

LAKE ERIE

MICHIGAN
ONTARIO

UNITED STATES
CANADA

RAND McNALLY

MAP
4757

1:24,000
1 in. = 2000 ft.

0   0.25   0.5
miles

N

SEE 4671 MAP

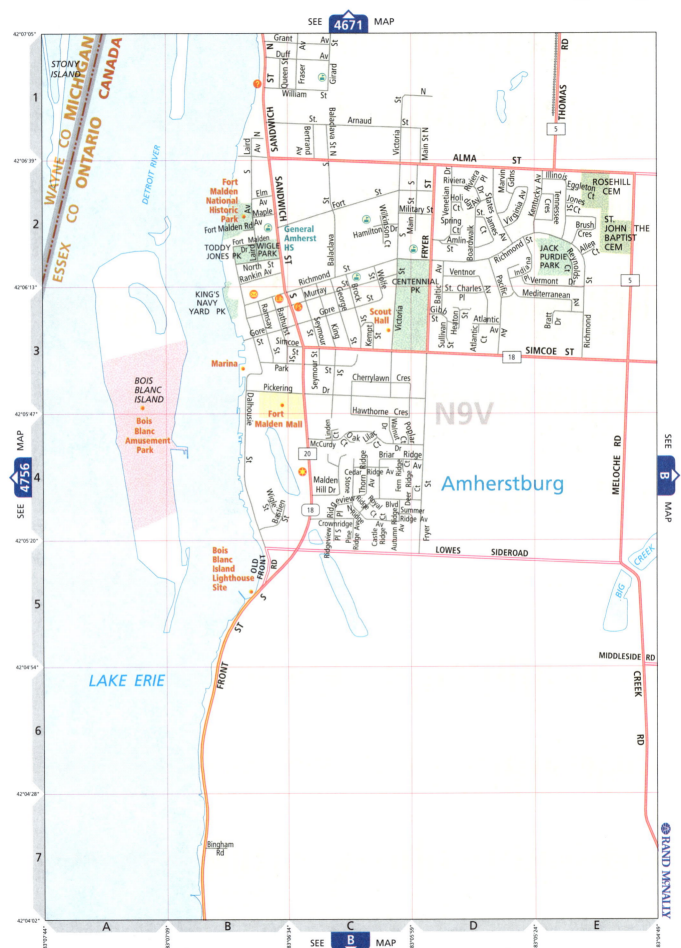

STONY ISLAND

WAYNE CO MICHIGAN

ESSEX CO ONTARIO

CANADA

DETROIT RIVER

Fort Malden National Historic Park

TODDY JONES PK

KING'S NAVY YARD PK

Marina

BOIS BLANC ISLAND

Bois Blanc Amusement Park

SEE MAP 4756

Bois Blanc Island Lighthouse Site

LAKE ERIE

Bingham Rd

FRONT ST S

OLD FRONT RD

Dalhousie St

Wigle St

Bastien St

Grant Av
Duff St
Queen St
Fraser St
Girard St
William St

SANDWICH ST N

Laird Av S

Laird Av S

Elm Av
Maple Av
Fort Malden Rd

Fort Malden Dr

WIGLE PARK

North St
Rankin Av

Ramsay St

Gore St

Bathurst St

Simcoe St

Park St

Pickering St

McCurdy

SANDWICH ST

St. St
Bertrand Av

Fort St

Balaclava St

Murtay St

Gore St

King St

Seymour St

Seymour St

Pickering Dr

Linden St

Oak Ct
Lilac Ct

Crownridge Pl S

Ridgeview Pl S

Pine Ridge Ct

Castle Ridge Ct

N Ridge Ct

Thorn Ridge Av

Stone Ridge Av

Cedar Ridge Av

Briar Ridge Av

Malden Hill Dr

Ridge Av

Royal Blvd

Deer Ridge Ct

Fern Ridge Ct

Autumn Ridge

Summer Ridge Av

Fryer St

Balaclava St N

Arnaud St

Victoria St

N St

Main St N

ALMA ST

Fort St

St

Hamilton

Wilkinson Ct

Military St

Main St S

FRYER ST

Richmond St

George St

Brock St

Wolfe St

Victoria St

CENTENNIAL PK

Scout Hall

Kempt St

Cherrylawn Cres

Hawthorne Cres

Walnut Dr

Poplar Dr

General Amherst HS

Riviera Dr
Riviera Pl
Venetian Ct
Holiday Ct
Spring Ct
Amlin St

Boardwalk

States James Av

Marvin Gdns

Kentucky Av
Tennessee Cres

Virginia Av

Richmond St

Indiana Pl

Ventnor Av

St. Charles Pl

Baltic Av

Gibb St

Sullivan Ct
Heaton St

Atlantic Av
Atlantic Ct

Pacific Av

Vermont

Mediterranean Av

Atlantic Av

Bratt Dr

Richmond St

Illinois St
Eggleton Ct
Jones St Ct

Brush Cres

Reynolds Ct

Allen Ct

ROSEHILL CEM

ST. JOHN THE BAPTIST CEM

JACK PURDIE PARK

N9V

Amherstburg

SIMCOE ST 18

LOWES SIDEROAD

MELOCHE RD

CREEK RD

BIG CREEK

MIDDLESIDE RD

SEE B MAP

THOMAS RD

5

5

Fort Malden Mall

20

18

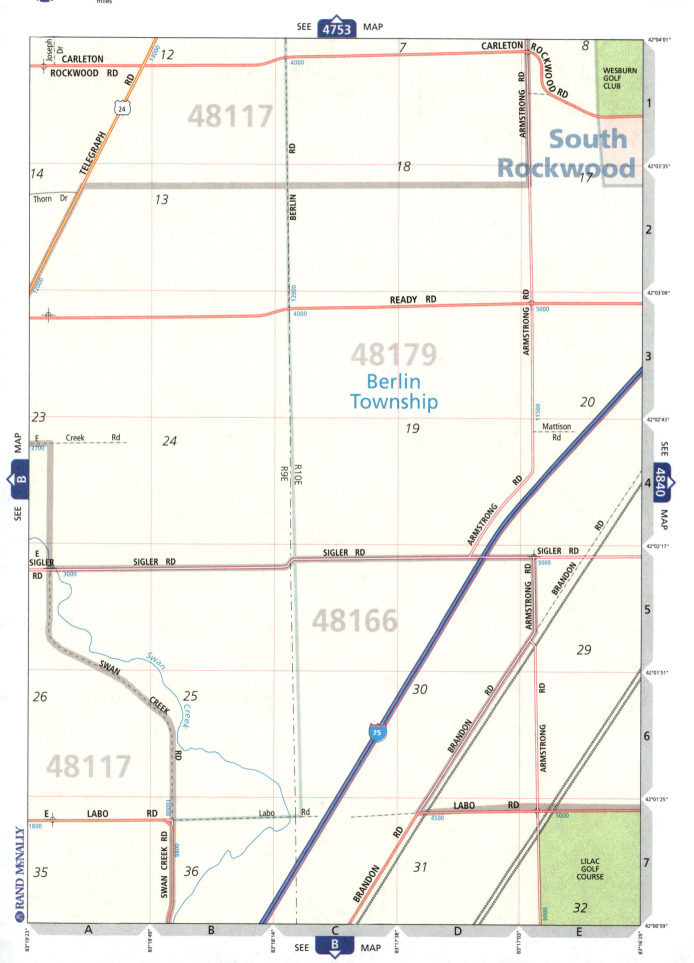

MAP
4840

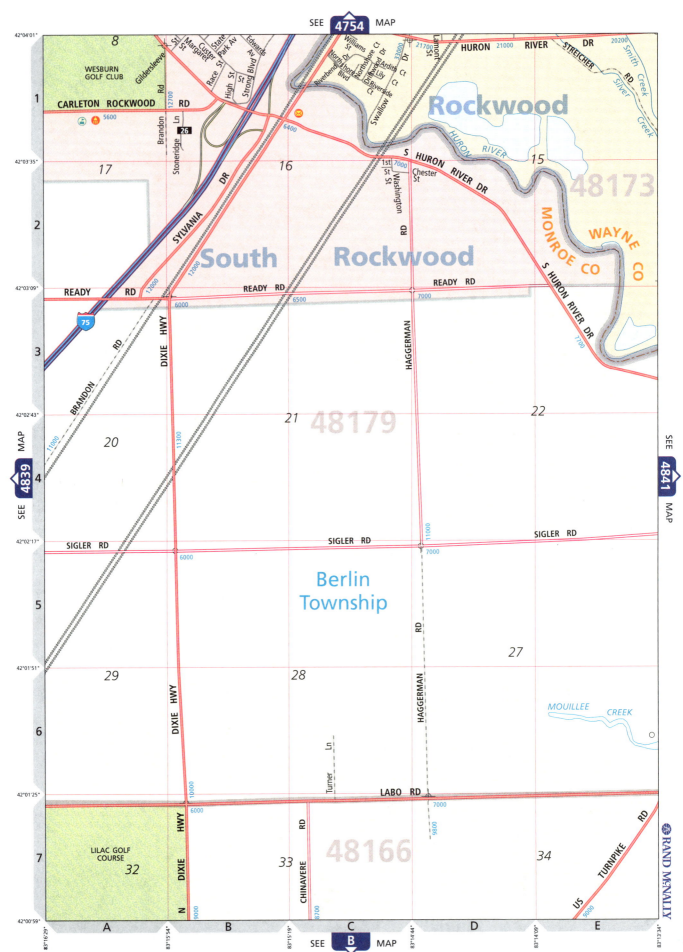

1:24,000
1 in. = 2000 ft.
0   0.25   0.5
miles

WESBURN GOLF CLUB

CARLETON ROCKWOOD RD

Rockwood

HURON RIVER STREICHER DR

Smith Creek

Silver Creek

48173

S HURON RIVER DR

MONROE CO

WAYNE CO

South Rockwood

SYLVANIA DR

READY RD   READY RD   READY RD

75

BRANDON RD

DIXIE HWY

HAGGERMAN

S HURON RIVER DR

48179

21   22

SEE **4839** MAP

SEE **4841** MAP

SIGLER RD   SIGLER RD   SIGLER RD

Berlin Township

HAGGERMAN RD

MOUILLEE CREEK

29   28   27

DIXIE HWY

Turner Ln

LABO RD

DIXIE HWY

LILAC GOLF COURSE

CHINAVERE RD

48166

TURNPIKE RD

US

RAND MCNALLY

MAP
4841

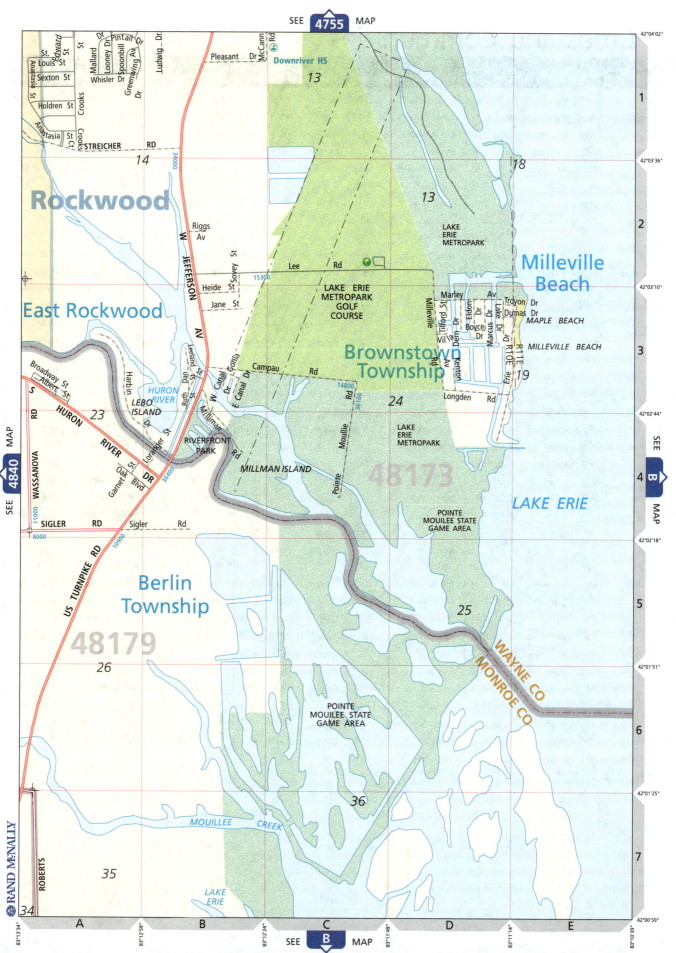

1:24,000
1 in. = 2000 ft.
0   0.25   0.5
miles

SEE 4755 MAP

Downriver HS

13

St. Louis St
Anastasia St
Sexton St
Holdren St
Anastasia St
Edward St
Mallard Dr
Looney Dr
Whisler Dr
Spoonbill Dr
Greenwing Av
Pintail Dr
Ludwig Dr
Crooks Ct
Crooks St

STREICHER RD
14

Pleasant Dr McCann Rd

13

18

LAKE
ERIE
METROPARK

Rockwood

Riggs Av

W JEFFERSON AV

34000

Sovey St
Sexey St
Heide St
Jane St

Lee Rd

15300

LAKE ERIE
METROPARK
GOLF
COURSE

**Milleville
Beach**

Marley St
Milleville Rd
Tilford St
Vil
Eldon Dr
Boyce Dr
Lake Dr
Marcus Dr
Av
Trdyon Dr
Dumas Dr
Erie R10E R11E

MAPLE BEACH

MILLEVILLE BEACH

East Rockwood

Broadway St
Albert St
Harbin St
S
WASSANOVA RD
HURON RIVER DR
Leeland St
Dan
Ruth St
Loranger St
Oak St
Garnet Blvd
HURON
RIVER
LEBO
ISLAND
W Canal Dr
Grotia
E Canal Dr
Milliman Rd

23

Campau Rd

14800

Kenton Av
Longden Rd

**Brownstown
Township**

24

36100

LAKE
ERIE
METROPARK

19

RIVERFRONT
PARK

MILLMAN ISLAND

Moullie

Pointe

48173

POINTE
MOUILEE STATE
GAME AREA

LAKE ERIE

34400

11000
SIGLER RD
8000
Sigler Rd

10900

US TURNPIKE RD

**Berlin
Township**

48179

26

25

SEE 4840 MAP

SEE B MAP

WAYNE CO
MONROE CO

POINTE
MOUILEE STATE
GAME AREA

36

ROBERTS

35

34

MOUILLEE CREEK

*LAKE
ERIE*

42°04'02"
42°03'36"
42°03'10"
42°02'44"
42°02'18"
42°01'51"
42°01'25"
42°00'59"

1
2
3
4
5
6
7

A   B   C   D   E

83°13'34"
83°12'59"
83°12'24"
83°11'49"
83°11'14"
83°10'39"

SEE B MAP

Cities and Communities

Community Name	Abbr.	County	ZIP Code	Map Page	Community Name	Abbr.	County	ZIP Code	Map Page	Community Name	Abbr.	County	ZIP Code	Map Page
* Allen Park	ALPK	Wayne	48101	4500	* Grosse Pointe Park	GPPK	Wayne	48230	4275	* River Rouge	RVRG	Wayne	48218	4418
Amherstburg	Amhg	Essex	N9V	4671	* Grosse Pointe Shores	GSPS	Wayne	48236	4205	* Riverview	RVVW	Wayne	48192	4584
* Ann Arbor	AARB	Washtenaw	48104	4406	* Grosse Pointe Woods	GSPW	Wayne	48236	4204	* Rockwood	RKWD	Wayne	48173	4754
Ann Arbor Township	AATp	Washtenaw	48105	4332	Hamburg		Livingston	48189	4186	* Romulus	RMLS	Wayne	48174	4496
* Augusta	AGST	Washtenaw	48191	4661	Hamburg Township	HbgT	Livingston	48189	4186	Royal Oak Township	ROTp	Oakland	48220	4199
* Barton Hills	BNHL	Washtenaw	48105	4331	* Hamtramck	HMTK	Wayne	48212	4273	St. Clair Beach	Tcmh	Essex	N8N	4424
* Belleville	BLVL	Wayne	48111	4578	* Harper Woods	HRWD	Wayne	48225	4204	* St. Clair Shores	STCS	Macomb	48021	4204
Berlin Township	BrTp	Monroe	48166	4840	* Hazel Park	HZLP	Oakland	48030	4200	Salem		Washtenaw	48167	4262
Brookville		Washtenaw	48170	4262	* Highland Park	HDPK	Wayne	48203	4272	* Saline	SALN	Washtenaw	48176	4572
* Brownstown	BNTN	Wayne	48134	4667	Huron Township	HnTp	Wayne	48134	4666	Saline Township		Washtenaw	48176	4656
Brownstown Township	BwTp	Wayne	48173	4841	* Inkster	INKR	Wayne	48141	4415	Scio		Washtenaw	48130	4329
Canton		Wayne	48187	4336	Lakeshore	Lksr	Essex	N8N	4424	Sheldon		Wayne	48188	4411
* Canton Township	CNTN	Wayne	48188	4411	Lasalle	LSal	Essex	N9J	4586	* Southfield	SFLD	Oakland	48034	4197
* Center Line	CTNL	Macomb	48015	4202	Lincoln		Washtenaw	48197	4661	* Southgate	SOGT	Wayne	48195	4584
* Dearborn	DRBN	Wayne	48126	4343	* Lincoln Park	LNPK	Wayne	48146	4500	* South Lyon	SLYN	Oakland	48178	4189
* Dearborn Heights	DBHT	Wayne	48127	4340	-- Livingston County	LvgC				* South Rockwood	SRKW	Monroe	48179	4840
Denton		Wayne	48111	4493	* Livonia	LVNA	Wayne	48154	4267	Stony Creek		Washtenaw	48197	4660
* Detroit	DET	Wayne	48226	4345	Lyon Township	LyTp	Oakland	48178	4190	Sumpter		Wayne	48111	4663
* Dexter	DXTR	Washtenaw	48130	4329	-- Macomb	McoC				Superior Township	SpTp	Washtenaw	48105	4409
Dixboro		Washtenaw	48198	4408	* Melvindale	MVDL	Wayne	48122	4418	* Taylor	TYLR	Wayne	48180	4499
East Rockwood	BwTp	Wayne	48173	4841	Milleville Beach		Wayne	48173	4841	Tecumseh	Tcmh	Essex	N8N	4349
* Eastpointe	EPTE	Macomb	48021	4203	-- Monroe County	MonC				* Trenton	TNTN	Wayne	48183	4669
* Ecorse	ECRS	Wayne	48229	4501	New Boston		Wayne	48164	4665	* Van Buren	VNBN	Wayne	48111	4494
Edgewater Beach		Essex	N9V	4671	North Pelton		Essex	N0R	4505	Waltz	HnTp	Wayne	48164	4751
Edgewater Heights		Wayne	48111	4578	* Northville	NHVL	Wayne	48167	4192	* Warren	WRRN	Macomb	48015	4201
Elmstead		Essex	N9K	4424	Northville Township	NvlT	Wayne	48167	4264	-- Washtenaw County	WasC			
-- Essex County	EsxC				* Novi	NOVI	Oakland	48375	4192	-- Wayne County	WynC			
* Farmington	FMTN	Oakland	48335	4194	-- Oakland County	OakC				* Wayne	WYNE	Wayne	48184	4413
* Farmington Hills	FNHL	Oakland	48167	4194	* Oak Park	OKPK	Oakland	48237	4198	* Westland	WTLD	Wayne	48185	4338
* Ferndale	FRDL	Oakland	48220	4199	Oldcastle		Essex	N0R	4505	Whitmore Lake		Washtenaw	48189	4187
* Flat Rock	FTRK	Wayne	48134	4753	Oliver		Essex	N9H	4504	Whittaker		Washtenaw	48191	4661
Foster		Washtenaw	48103	4405	Pelton		Essex	N0R	4505	Willis		Washtenaw	48191	4662
Frain Lake		Washtenaw	48105	4334	Pine Creek		Essex	N8N	4424	Willow		Wayne	48164	4751
* Garden City	GDNC	Wayne	48135	4339	* Pittsfield	PTFD	Washtenaw	48176	4574	* Windsor	WIND	Essex	N9A	4420
* Gibraltar	GBTR	Wayne	48173	4755	* Pleasant Ridge	PTRG	Oakland	48069	4199	* Woodhaven	WDHN	Wayne	48183	4668
Green Oak Township	GOTp	Livingston	48116	4187	* Plymouth	PLYM	Wayne	48170	4265	* Wyandotte	WYDT	Wayne	48192	4585
Grosse Ile		Wayne	48138	4670	* Plymouth Township	PyTp	Wayne	48170	4337	* Ypsilanti	YPLT	Washtenaw	48197	4492
* Grosse Pointe	GSPT	Wayne	48230	4276	* Redford	Rdfd	Wayne	48239	4268	Ypsilanti Township	YpTp	Washtenaw	48197	4576
* Grosse Pointe Farms	GSPF	Wayne	48236	4276	River Canard		Essex	N9J	4586					

*Indicates incorporated city or charter township

List of Abbreviations

Admin	Administration	Cr	Creek	Jct	Junction	PO	Post Office
Agri	Agricultural	Cres	Crescent	Knl	Knoll	Pres	Preserve
Ag	Agriculture	Cross	Crossing	Knls	Knolls	Prov	Provincial
AFB	Air Force Base	Curv	Curve	Lk	Lake	Rwy	Railway
Arpt	Airport	Cto	Cut Off	Lndg	Landing	Rec	Recreation
Al	Alley	Dept	Department	Ln	Lane	Reg	Regional
Amer	American	Dev	Development	Lib	Library	Res	Reservoir
Anx	Annex	Diag	Diagonal	Ldg	Lodge	Rst	Rest
Arc	Arcade	Div	Division	Lp	Loop	Rdg	Ridge
Arch	Archaeological	Dr	Drive	Mnr	Manor	Rd	Road
Aud	Auditorium	Drwy	Driveway	Mkt	Market	Rds	Roads
Avd	Avenida	E	East	Mdw	Meadow	St.	Saint
Av	Avenue	El	Elevation	Mdws	Meadows	Ste.	Sainte
Bfld	Battlefield	Env	Environmental	Med	Medical	Sci	Science
Bch	Beach	Est	Estate	Mem	Memorial	Sci	Sciences
Bnd	Bend	Ests	Estates	Metro	Metropolitan	Sci	Scientific
Bio	Biological	Exh	Exhibition	Mw	Mews	Shop Ctr	Shopping Center
Blf	Bluff	Expm	Experimental	Mil	Military	Shr	Shore
Blvd	Boulevard	Expo	Exposition	Ml	Mill	Shrs	Shores
Brch	Branch	Expwy	Expressway	Mls	Mills	Skwy	Skyway
Br	Bridge	Ext	Extension	Mon	Monument	S	South
Brk	Brook	Frgds	Fairgrounds	Mtwy	Motorway	Spr	Spring
Bldg	Building	ft	Feet	Mnd	Mound	Sprs	Springs
Bur	Bureau	Fy	Ferry	Mnds	Mounds	Sq	Square
Byp	Bypass	Fld	Field	Mt	Mount	Stad	Stadium
Bywy	Byway	Flds	Fields	Mtn	Mountain	St For	State Forest
Cl	Calle	Flt	Flat	Mtns	Mountains	St Hist Site	State Historic Site
Cljn	Callejon	Flts	Flats	Mun	Municipal	St Nat Area	State Natural Area
Cmto	Caminito	For	Forest	Mus	Museum	St Pk	State Park
Cm	Camino	Fk	Fork	Nat'l	National	St Rec Area	State Recreation Area
Cap	Capitol	Ft	Fort	Nat'l For	National Forest	Sta	Station
Cath	Cathedral	Found	Foundation	Nat'l Hist Pk	National Historic Park	St	Street
Cswy	Causeway	Frwy	Freeway	Nat'l Hist Site	National Historic Site	Smt	Summit
Cem	Cemetery	Gdn	Garden	Nat'l Mon	National Monument	Sys	Systems
Ctr	Center	Gdns	Gardens	Nat'l Park	National Park	Tech	Technical
Ctr	Centre	Gen Hosp	General Hospital	Nat'l Rec Area	National Recreation Area	Tech	Technological
Cir	Circle	Gln	Glen	Nat'l Wld Ref	National Wildlife Refuge	Tech	Technology
Crlo	Circulo	GC	Golf Course	Nat	Natural	Ter	Terrace
CH	City Hall	Grn	Green	NAS	Naval Air Station	Terr	Territory
Clf	Cliff	Grds	Grounds	Nk	Nook	Theol	Theological
Clfs	Cliffs	Grv	Grove	N	North	Thwy	Throughway
Clb	Club	Hbr	Harbor/Harbour	Orch	Orchard	Toll Fy	Toll Ferry
Cltr	Cluster	Hvn	Haven	Ohwy	Outer Highway	TIC	Tourist Information Center
Col	Coliseum	HQs	Headquarters	Ovl	Oval	Trc	Trace
Coll	College	Ht	Height	Ovlk	Overlook	Trfwy	Trafficway
Com	Common	Hts	Heights	Ovps	Overpass	Tr	Trail
Coms	Commons	HS	High School	Pk	Park	Tun	Tunnel
Comm	Community	Hwy	Highway	Pkwy	Parkway	Tpk	Turnpike
Co.	Company	Hl	Hill	Pas	Paseo	Unps	Underpass
Cons	Conservation	Hls	Hills	Psg	Passage	Univ	University
Conv & Vis Bur	Convention and Visitors Bureau	Hist	Historical	Pass	Passenger	Vly	Valley
Cor	Corner	Hllw	Hollow	Pth	Path	Vet	Veterans
Cors	Corners	Hosp	Hospital	Pn	Pine	Vw	View
Corp	Corporation	Hse	House	Pns	Pines	Vil	Village
Corr	Corridor	Ind Res	Indian Reservation	Pl	Place	Wk	Walk
Cte	Corte	Info	Information	Pln	Plain	Wall	Wall
CC	Country Club	Inst	Institute	Plns	Plains	Wy	Way
Co	County	Int'l	International	Plgnd	Playground	W	West
Ct	Court	I	Island	Plz	Plaza	WMA	Wildlife Management Area
Ct Hse	Court House	Is	Islands	Pt	Point		
Cts	Courts	Isl	Isle	Pnd	Pond		

INDEX 3

Detroit & Wayne County Street Index

SR-102 W 8 Mile Rd

HIGHWAYS

ALT - Alternate Route
BUS - Business Route
CO - County Highway/Road
FM - Farm To Market Road
HIST - Historic Highway
I - Interstate Highway
LP - State Loop
P - Provincial Highway
PK - Park & Recreation Road
RTE - Other Route
SPR - State Spur
SR - State Route/Highway
US - United States Highway

STREET Block	City	ZIP	Map#	Grid
CO-2				
200	Lksr	N8N	4424	E2
CO-2 Tecumseh Rd				
-	Lksr	N8N	4424	E2
CO-2 Tecumseh Rd W				
200	Lksr	N8N	4424	E2
CO-5				
-	Amhg	N9V	4757	E1
200	Amhg	N9V	4586	E7
900	Amhg	N9V	4671	E1
CO-5 2nd Concession Rd				
900	Amhg	N9V	4671	E1
1800	Amhg	N9V	4586	E7
CO-5 Alma St				
500	Amhg	N9V	4757	E1
CO-5 Creek Rd				
3400	Amhg	N9V	4757	E5
CO-5 Meloche Rd				
100	Amhg	N9V	4757	E2
CO-5 S Riverview Dr				
200	Amhg	N9V	4586	E6
CO-5 Thomas Rd				
-	Amhg	N9V	4671	E7
-	Amhg	N9V	4757	E1
CO-10				
2000	Amhg	N9V	4671	B4
CO-10 Middle Sideroad				
2000	Amhg	N9V	4671	E4
CO-17				
-	Tcmh	N0R	4423	C7
1800	Tcmh	N8N	4423	D5
CO-17 Banwell Rd				
1800	Tcmh	N8N	4423	D5
CO-18				
100	Amhg	N9V	4757	D3
CO-18 Pike Rd				
3000	Amhg	N9V	4757	E3
CO-18 Simcoe St				
100	Amhg	N9V	4757	D3
CO-20				
-	WIND	-	4420	A7
10	Amhg	N9V	4757	C4
300	Amhg	N9V	4671	B5
700	EsxC	N9V	4757	C4
1600	Amhg	N9V	4586	C7
2400	Amhg	N9J	4586	C7
CO-20 Front St N				
300	Amhg	N9V	4671	B5
1600	Amhg	N9V	4586	C7
2400	Amhg	N9J	4586	C7
CO-20 Front St S				
600	Amhg	N9V	4757	B5
700	EsxC	N9V	4757	B5
CO-20 Sandwich St N				
10	Amhg	N9V	4757	B1
CO-20 Sandwich St S				
10	Amhg	N9V	4757	C4
CO-21				
100	Lksr	N8N	4424	E1
100	Lksr	N9K	4424	E1
100	Tcmh	N8N	4424	E1
CO-21 Little Baseline Rd				
200	Lksr	N8N	4424	E4
200	Lksr	N9K	4424	E4
CO-21 E Pike Creek Rd				
300	Lksr	N8N	4424	E5
300	Lksr	N9K	4424	E5
CO-21 W Pike Creek Rd				
100	Lksr	N8N	4424	E1
100	Lksr	N9K	4424	E1
100	Tcmh	N8N	4424	E1
CO-22				
-	Lksr	N8N	4424	C3
-	Lksr	N9K	4424	C3
-	Tcmh	N8N	4423	D3
-	Tcmh	N8N	4424	C3
-	Tcmh	N8R	4423	D3
-	Tcmh	N9K	4423	D3
-	Tcmh	N9K	4424	C3
-	WIND	N8N	4423	D3
-	WIND	N8R	4423	D3
CO-42				
-	Lksr	N0R	4424	C6
-	Lksr	N8N	4424	C6
-	Lksr	N9K	4424	C6
-	Tcmh	N0R	4423	C7
-	Tcmh	N0R	4424	C6
-	Tcmh	N0R	4505	D1
-	Tcmh	N8N	4423	C7
-	Tcmh	N8N	4424	C6
-	Tcmh	N8V	4423	C7
-	Tcmh	N8V	4505	D1
-	Tcmh	N9K	4424	C6
CO-46				
-	Tcmh	N0R	4505	D5
I-75				
-	ALPK	-	4500	B7
-	BNTN	-	4583	D7
-	BNTN	-	4668	D7
-	BrTp	-	4839	C6
-	BrTp	-	4840	A3
-	BwTp	-	4754	D3
I-75				
-	DET	-	4200	D5
-	DET	-	4272	E2
-	DET	-	4273	C7
-	DET	-	4344	E6
-	DET	-	4345	D3
-	DET	-	4418	D5
-	DET	-	4419	A4
-	DET	-	4501	A2
-	FTRK	-	4754	D3
-	HMTK	-	4273	C7
-	HZLP	-	4200	D5
-	LNPK	-	4500	B7
-	LNPK	-	4501	A2
-	MVDL	-	4418	D5
-	MVDL	-	4501	A2
-	RKWD	-	4754	D3
-	SOGT	-	4500	B7
-	SOGT	-	4583	D7
-	SOGT	-	4584	A1
-	SRKW	-	4754	D3
-	SRKW	-	4840	A3
-	TYLR	-	4583	D7
-	WDHN	-	4668	D7
-	WDHN	-	4754	D3
I-75 Chrysler Frwy				
-	DET	-	4200	D5
-	DET	-	4272	E2
-	DET	-	4273	C7
-	DET	-	4345	D3
-	HMTK	-	4273	C7
-	HZLP	-	4200	D5
I-75 Fisher Frwy				
-	DET	-	4418	D5
-	DET	-	4501	A2
-	LNPK	-	4500	E2
-	LNPK	-	4501	A2
-	MVDL	-	4418	D5
-	MVDL	-	4501	A2
I-75 Fisher Frwy N				
-	DET	-	4344	E6
-	DET	-	4345	B6
-	DET	-	4418	E5
-	DET	-	4419	E1
I-75 Fisher Frwy S				
-	DET	-	4344	E6
-	DET	-	4345	C5
-	DET	-	4418	E5
-	DET	-	4419	A4
I-94				
-	AARB	-	4405	C5
-	AARB	-	4488	D2
-	AARB	-	4489	D5
-	AARB	-	4490	B5
-	ALPK	-	4417	C6
-	ALPK	-	4499	C1
-	ALPK	-	4500	B1
-	DET	-	4204	A3
-	DET	-	4273	C7
-	DET	-	4274	C5
-	DET	-	4275	D2
-	DET	-	4276	A1
-	DET	-	4343	E6
-	DET	-	4344	C4
-	DET	-	4345	B1
-	DRBN	-	4343	E6
-	DRBN	-	4417	C6
-	DRBN	-	4418	B1
-	EPTE	-	4204	A3
-	HRWD	-	4204	A3
-	PTFD	-	4488	D2
-	PTFD	-	4489	D5
-	PTFD	-	4490	B5
-	PTFD	-	4491	C7
-	RMLS	-	4495	C7
-	RMLS	-	4496	C7
-	RMLS	-	4497	C5
-	RMLS	-	4498	D2
-	STCS	-	4204	A3
-	TYLR	-	4498	D2
-	TYLR	-	4499	C1
-	VNBN	-	4493	E7
-	VNBN	-	4494	E7
-	VNBN	-	4495	C7
-	WasC	-	4404	D5
-	WasC	-	4405	C5
-	WasC	-	4488	D2
-	YPLT	-	4491	C7
-	YPLT	-	4492	C6
-	YpTp	-	4491	C7
-	YpTp	-	4492	C6
-	YpTp	-	4493	A7
-	YpTp	-	4577	B1
I-94 BUS				
-	AARB	-	4490	C2
-	PTFD	-	4490	C5
-	PTFD	48105	4490	C2
100	AARB	48104	4406	D7
200	AARB	48103	4406	A6
1400	AARB	48103	4405	E6
1900	AARB	48104	4489	E1
I-94 Edsel Ford Frwy				
-	DET	-	4204	A7
-	DET	-	4273	C7
-	DET	-	4274	C5
-	DET	-	4275	D2
-	DET	-	4276	A1
-	DET	-	4343	E6
-	DET	-	4344	C4
-	DET	-	4345	B1
I-94 BUS E Huron St				
100	AARB	48104	4406	B6
I-94 BUS W Huron St				
100	AARB	48104	4406	A6
200	AARB	48103	4406	A6
1400	AARB	48103	4405	E6
I-94 BUS Jackson Av				
1500	AARB	48103	4405	E6
I-94 BUS Jackson Rd				
3000	AARB	48103	4405	C5
I-94 BUS Washtenaw Av				
-	PTFD	48104	4490	C2
-	PTFD	48105	4490	C2
-	PTFD	48108	4490	C2
400	AARB	48104	4406	D7
1900	AARB	48104	4489	E1
2100	AARB	48104	4490	C2
I-96				
-	DET	-	4269	D6
-	DET	-	4270	C6
-	DET	-	4271	D6
-	DET	-	4343	D1
-	DET	-	4344	A2
-	LVNA	-	4265	E6
-	LVNA	-	4266	E6
-	LVNA	-	4267	D6
-	LVNA	-	4268	B6
-	RDFD	-	4268	B6
I-96 Jeffries Frwy				
-	DET	-	4269	B6
-	DET	-	4270	B6
-	DET	-	4271	D6
-	DET	-	4343	D1
-	DET	-	4344	A2
-	LVNA	-	4265	E6
-	LVNA	-	4266	E6
-	LVNA	-	4267	D6
-	LVNA	-	4268	B6
-	RDFD	-	4268	B6
I-275				
-	CNTN	-	4337	C6
-	CNTN	-	4412	D7
-	CNTN	-	4495	D4
-	FNHL	-	4193	E4
-	HnTp	-	4580	D5
-	HnTp	-	4665	D3
-	HnTp	-	4751	E2
-	LVNA	-	4193	E4
-	LVNA	-	4265	E4
-	MonC	-	4751	E2
-	MonC	-	4752	A7
-	NvlT	-	4265	E4
-	PyTp	-	4265	D7
-	PyTp	-	4337	C6
-	RMLS	-	4495	D4
-	RMLS	-	4496	A7
-	RMLS	-	4580	D5
-	VNBN	-	4495	D4
I-375				
-	DET	-	4345	E5
I-375 Chrysler Frwy				
-	DET	-	4345	E5
P-2				
-	Lksr	N8N	4424	E3
-	Tcmh	N8N	4423	E3
-	Tcmh	N8N	4424	A3
-	Tcmh	N9K	4423	E2
-	Tcmh	N9K	4424	A3
-	WIND	N8N	4423	D4
-	WIND	N8R	4423	D4
P-3				
-	Tcmh	N0R	4504	C5
-	Tcmh	N0R	4505	D7
-	Tcmh	N9H	4504	C5
500	WIND	N9G	4504	C5
600	WIND	N9B	4420	C6
600	WIND	N9C	4420	C6
1500	LSal	N9H	4504	C5
2200	WIND	N9E	4420	C6
2500	WIND	N9E	4503	D1
2500	WIND	N9G	4503	D1
3700	WIND	N9H	4503	D1
3800	LSal	N9H	4503	D1
P-3 Ambassador Br				
-	WIND	N9B	4420	A2
-	WIND	N9C	4420	B3
P-3 Huron Church Rd				
800	WIND	N9B	4420	C6
800	WIND	N9C	4420	C6
2200	WIND	N9E	4420	C6
2500	WIND	N9E	4503	D1
3700	WIND	N9H	4503	D1
3800	LSal	N9H	4503	D1
3800	WIND	N9G	4503	D1
P-3 Talbot Rd				
600	LSal	N9H	4504	D5
600	WIND	N9G	4504	D5
2500	LSal	N9H	4503	E3
2500	WIND	N9G	4503	E3
P-3 Talbot Rd E				
-	Tcmh	N0R	4504	E6
500	Tcmh	N9H	4504	D5
500	WIND	N9G	4504	D5
P-3B				
-	WIND	-	4504	E4
-	WIND	-	4505	A4
200	WIND	N9A	4420	E1
1500	WIND	N8X	4421	A4
2600	WIND	N9E	4421	B6
P-3B Dougall Av				
-	WIND	-	4504	E4
-	WIND	-	4505	A4
2600	WIND	N8X	4421	B6
2600	WIND	N9E	4421	B6
P-3B Ouellette Av				
200	WIND	N9A	4420	E1
1500	WIND	N8X	4421	A4
P-3B Ouellette Pl				
100	WIND	N8X	4421	B6
P-18				
10	Amhg	N9V	4757	C4
100	LSal	N9J	4502	C7
300	Amhg	N9V	4671	B6
700	EsxC	N9V	4757	C4
1600	Amhg	N9V	4586	C7
2400	Amhg	N9J	4586	C7
2400	LSal	N9J	4586	C1
4700	WIND	N9C	4419	E7
4700	WIND	N9C	4420	A7
4900	WIND	N9C	4502	E3
P-18				
4900	WIND	N9J	4419	E7
4900	WIND	N9J	4502	E3
P-18 Front Rd				
-	LSal	N9J	4502	C7
2400	LSal	N9J	4586	C1
P-18 Front St N				
300	Amhg	N9V	4671	B6
1600	Amhg	N9V	4586	C7
2400	Amhg	N9J	4586	C7
P-18 Front St S				
600	Amhg	N9V	4757	B5
700	EsxC	N9V	4757	B5
P-18 Ojibway Pkwy				
4700	WIND	N9C	4419	E7
4700	WIND	N9C	4420	A7
4900	WIND	N9C	4502	E3
4900	WIND	N9J	4419	E7
4900	WIND	N9J	4502	E3
P-18 Sandwich St N				
10	Amhg	N9V	4757	B1
P-18 Sandwich St S				
10	Amhg	N9V	4757	C4
P-401				
-	Tcmh	-	4504	E5
-	Tcmh	-	4505	A5
-	WIND	-	4504	E5
-	WIND	-	4505	A5
P-401 MacDonald-Cartier Frwy				
-	Tcmh	-	4504	E5
-	Tcmh	-	4505	A5
-	WIND	-	4504	E5
-	WIND	-	4505	A5
SR-1				
-	FRDL	48203	4200	A5
10	DET	48226	4345	C3
2100	DET	48201	4345	C3
5000	DET	48202	4345	C3
7400	DET	48202	4273	A7
8900	DET	48202	4272	C2
11700	DET	48203	4272	C2
11700	HDPK	48203	4272	C2
17900	DET	48203	4200	A5
21400	FRDL	48220	4200	A5
21800	FRDL	48220	4199	E3
23600	FRDL	48069	4199	E3
23600	PTRG	48069	4199	E3
23600	PTRG	48220	4199	E3
SR-1 Woodward Av				
-	FRDL	48203	4200	A5
10	DET	48226	4345	C3
2100	DET	48201	4345	C3
5000	DET	48202	4345	C3
7400	DET	48202	4273	A7
8900	DET	48202	4272	E6
11700	HDPK	48203	4272	E5
17500	DET	48203	4272	C1
17900	DET	48203	4200	A5
21400	FRDL	48220	4200	A5
21800	FRDL	48220	4199	E3
23600	FRDL	48069	4199	E3
23600	PTRG	48069	4199	E3
23600	PTRG	48220	4199	E3
SR-3				
10	DET	48226	4345	E4
1100	DET	48207	4345	E4
2600	DET	48207	4346	A1
2800	DET	48216	4420	A1
7000	DET	48207	4274	D3
7200	DET	48213	4274	D3
7200	DET	48214	4274	D3
11900	DET	48205	4274	D3
13100	DET	48205	4202	E7
13700	DET	48205	4203	A5
15400	EPTE	48205	4203	A5
20700	EPTE	48021	4203	A5
SR-3 Cadillac Sq				
10	DET	48226	4345	D6
SR-3 Fort St W				
800	DET	48226	4345	C7
2800	DET	48216	4420	A1
SR-3 Gratiot Av				
200	DET	48226	4345	E4
1100	DET	48207	4345	E4
2600	DET	48207	4346	A1
7000	DET	48207	4274	D3
7200	DET	48213	4274	D3
7200	DET	48214	4274	D3
11900	DET	48205	4274	D3
13100	DET	48205	4202	E7
13700	DET	48205	4203	A5
15400	EPTE	48205	4203	A5
20700	EPTE	48021	4203	A5
SR-3 Randolph St				
600	DET	48226	4345	D6
SR-5				
-	FMTN	-	4194	B2
-	FMTN	-	4195	D4
-	FNHL	-	4194	B2
13500	DET	48227	4271	A6
13600	DET	48227	4270	A3
18200	DET	48223	4270	A3
19000	DET	48223	4269	E3
19800	DET	48219	4269	B1
23500	DET	48219	4197	A7
23800	DET	48219	4196	D6
24700	RDFD	48219	4196	D6
25000	RDFD	48240	4196	D6
27300	LVNA	48152	4196	D6
27300	RDFD	48152	4196	D6
27500	FNHL	48152	4196	D6
27700	FNHL	48336	4196	D6
28200	FNHL	48336	4195	D4
SR-5 Grand River Av				
13500	DET	48227	4271	A6
13600	DET	48227	4270	A3
18200	DET	48223	4270	A3
19000	DET	48223	4269	E3
19800	DET	48219	4269	B1
SR-5 Grand River Av				
23500	DET	48219	4197	A7
23800	DET	48219	4196	D6
24700	RDFD	48219	4196	D6
25000	RDFD	48240	4196	D6
27300	LVNA	48152	4196	D6
27300	RDFD	48152	4196	D6
27500	FNHL	48152	4196	D6
27700	FNHL	48336	4196	D6
28200	FNHL	48336	4195	D4
SR-8				
-	DET	-	4272	C4
-	DET	-	4273	B2
-	HDPK	-	4272	C4
SR-8 Davison Frwy E				
-	DET	-	4272	E2
-	DET	-	4273	A2
-	HDPK	-	4272	C4
SR-8 Davison Frwy W				
-	DET	-	4272	C4
-	DET	-	4273	B2
-	HDPK	-	4272	C4
SR-10				
-	DET	-	4198	D6
-	DET	-	4199	A7
-	DET	-	4271	C3
-	DET	-	4272	B3
-	DET	-	4344	E1
-	DET	-	4345	A3
-	SFLD	-	4197	E2
-	SFLD	-	4198	A2
SR-10 John C Lodge Frwy				
-	DET	-	4198	D6
-	DET	-	4199	A7
-	DET	-	4271	C3
-	DET	-	4272	B3
-	DET	-	4344	E1
-	DET	-	4345	A3
-	SFLD	-	4197	E2
-	SFLD	-	4198	A2
SR-14				
-	AARB	-	4331	E7
-	AARB	-	4332	B7
-	AARB	-	4405	C3
-	AARB	-	4406	A3
-	AATp	-	4331	E7
-	AATp	-	4332	B7
-	AATp	-	4333	B7
-	AATp	-	4405	C3
-	AATp	-	4406	A3
-	LVNA	-	4265	A5
-	PyTp	-	4263	D7
-	PyTp	-	4264	E5
-	PyTp	-	4265	A5
-	PyTp	-	4335	B1
-	SpTp	-	4333	E6
-	SpTp	-	4334	C4
-	WasC	-	4334	C4
-	WasC	-	4335	B1
-	WasC	-	4405	C3
-	WasC	-	4406	A3
SR-14 Jeffries Frwy				
-	LVNA	-	4265	E6
SR-17				
10	YPLT	48197	4492	A4
10	YPLT	48198	4492	A4
10	YpTp	48198	4492	C5
400	YPLT	48197	4491	C3
1700	YpTp	48197	4491	C3
2700	YpTp	48108	4491	C3
4000	PTFD	48105	4490	E3
4000	PTFD	48108	4490	E3
4300	PTFD	48197	4490	E3
4700	PTFD	48108	4491	C3
4700	PTFD	48197	4491	C3
SR-17 W Cross St				
100	YPLT	48197	4492	A4
400	YPLT	48197	4491	E4
SR-17 Ecorse Rd				
10	YPLT	48198	4492	C5
10	YpTp	48198	4492	C5
SR-17 N Hamilton St				
10	YPLT	48197	4491	E4
SR-17 N Huron St				
10	YPLT	48197	4492	A4
SR-17 E Michigan Av				
10	YPLT	48198	4492	A4
SR-17 W Michigan Av				
10	YPLT	48197	4492	A4
10	YPLT	48198	4492	A4
SR-17 Washtenaw Av				
400	YPLT	48197	4491	C3
1700	YpTp	48197	4491	C3
2700	YpTp	48108	4491	C3
4000	PTFD	48105	4490	E3
4000	PTFD	48108	4490	E3
4300	PTFD	48197	4490	E3
4700	PTFD	48108	4491	C3
4700	PTFD	48197	4491	C3
SR-36				
-	HbgT	48116	4186	B3
-	HbgT	48189	4186	B3
8000	GOTp	48116	4186	B3
8000	GOTp	48189	4186	B3
9200	GOTp	48116	4187	A4
9200	GOTp	48189	4187	A4
SR-36 9 Mile Rd				
8000	GOTp	48116	4186	C3
8000	GOTp	48189	4186	C3
9200	GOTp	48116	4187	A4
9200	GOTp	48189	4187	A4
SR-39				
-	ALPK	-	4417	C4
-	DET	-	4198	A6
-	DET	-	4270	A4
-	DET	-	4342	B3
-	DRBN	-	4342	B3
-	DRBN	-	4417	C4
-	SFLD	-	4198	A6
SR-39				
1200	LNPK	48146	4501	A3
1300	LNPK	48146	4500	D3
2200	LNPK	48101	4500	D3
14500	ALPK	48101	4500	D3
SR-39 Southfield Frwy				
-	ALPK	-	4417	C4
-	ALPK	-	4500	A1
-	DET	-	4198	A6
-	DET	-	4270	A4
-	DET	-	4342	B3
-	DRBN	-	4342	B3
-	DRBN	-	4417	C4
-	SFLD	-	4198	A6
SR-39 Southfield Rd				
1200	LNPK	48146	4500	D3
1200	LNPK	48146	4501	A3
2200	LNPK	48101	4500	D3
14500	ALPK	48101	4500	D3
SR-53				
-	WRRN	48234	4202	A7
5300	DET	48213	4274	A2
9700	DET	48234	4274	A2
17100	DET	48212	4202	A7
17100	DET	48212	4274	A2
17100	DET	48234	4202	A7
20600	WRRN	48089	4202	A7
20600	WRRN	48091	4202	A7
23700	CTNL	48015	4202	A7
23700	WRRN	48015	4202	A7
SR-53 Van Dyke Av				
-	WRRN	48234	4202	A4
20600	WRRN	48089	4202	A4
20600	WRRN	48091	4202	A4
23700	CTNL	48015	4202	A1
23700	WRRN	48015	4202	A1
SR-53 Van Dyke St				
5300	DET	48213	4274	A2
9700	DET	48234	4274	A2
17100	DET	48212	4202	A7
17100	DET	48212	4274	A2
17100	DET	48234	4202	A7
SR-85				
-	BwTp	48173	4754	E4
-	BwTp	48183	4754	E4
-	DET	48209	4418	D5
-	LNPK	48195	4500	E5
-	TNTN	48183	4584	D7
-	TNTN	48192	4584	D7
900	LNPK	48146	4501	B1
900	LNPK	48229	4501	B1
1000	DET	48226	4345	C7
1000	DET	48229	4418	D5
1000	LNPK	48146	4500	E5
1000	LNPK	48192	4500	E5
1000	WYDT	48146	4500	E5
1000	WYDT	48192	4500	E5
1200	SOGT	48192	4500	E5
1200	SOGT	48195	4500	E5
1300	WYDT	48192	4584	D7
1300	WYDT	48195	4584	D7
1400	DET	48216	4345	B7
1400	SOGT	48192	4584	D7
1600	TNTN	48183	4669	D3
1600	TNTN	48192	4669	D3
2100	DET	48216	4420	A1
2700	DET	48229	4501	B1
3500	DET	48216	4419	E1
4000	DET	48209	4419	E1
5200	TNTN	48183	4755	B1
5800	GBTR	48183	4755	B1
5800	WDHN	48183	4755	B1
12200	SOGT	48195	4584	D7
17000	RVVW	48192	4584	D7
17000	RVVW	48195	4584	D7
19500	RVVW	48192	4669	D3
27000	BwTp	48183	4755	B1
27200	BwTp	48173	4755	B1
27200	GBTR	48173	4755	B1
SR-85 Fort St				
-	BwTp	48173	4754	E4
-	BwTp	48183	4754	E4
-	LNPK	48195	4500	E5
-	TNTN	48183	4584	D7
-	TNTN	48192	4584	D7
900	LNPK	48146	4501	B2
900	LNPK	48229	4501	B2
1000	LNPK	48146	4500	E5
1000	LNPK	48192	4500	E5
1000	WYDT	48146	4500	E5
1000	WYDT	48192	4500	E5
1200	SOGT	48192	4500	E5
1200	SOGT	48195	4500	E5
1300	WYDT	48192	4584	D7
1300	WYDT	48195	4584	D7
1400	SOGT	48192	4584	D7
1600	TNTN	48183	4669	D3
1600	TNTN	48192	4669	D3
5200	TNTN	48183	4755	B1
5800	GBTR	48183	4755	B1
5800	WDHN	48183	4755	B1
12200	SOGT	48195	4584	D7
17000	RVVW	48192	4584	D7
17000	RVVW	48195	4584	D7
19500	RVVW	48192	4669	D3
27000	BwTp	48183	4755	B1
27200	BwTp	48173	4755	B1
27200	GBTR	48173	4755	B1
SR-85 Fort St S				
1000	DET	48229	4418	C7
2700	DET	48229	4501	B1
3300	LNPK	48229	4501	B1
SR-85 Fort St W				
-	DET	48209	4418	D5
-	DET	48229	4418	D5
1000	DET	48226	4345	C7
1400	DET	48216	4345	B7
2100	DET	48216	4420	A1
3500	DET	48216	4419	E1
4000	DET	48209	4419	E1
SR-97				
11200	DET	48213	4274	D1
11500	DET	48205	4274	D1
17100	DET	48234	4274	D1
17300	DET	48205	4202	C5
17300	DET	48234	4202	C5
20300	WRRN	48205	4202	C5
20700	WRRN	48089	4202	C5
SR-97 Groesbeck Hwy				
20300	DET	48205	4202	C4
20300	WRRN	48205	4202	C4
20700	WRRN	48089	4202	D4
SR-97 Gunston St				
-	DET	48234	4274	C1
11200	DET	48213	4274	D2
11500	DET	48205	4274	D2
SR-97 Hoover St				
17100	DET	48205	4274	D1
17100	DET	48234	4274	D1
17300	DET	48205	4202	C5
17300	DET	48234	4202	C5
SR-102				
-	DET	48075	4198	A4
-	DET	48203	4200	B4
-	HZLP	48203	4200	B4
-	SFLD	48235	4198	A4
10	HZLP	48030	4200	B4
100	FRDL	48220	4200	B4
400	FRDL	48203	4199	C4
400	FRDL	48220	4199	C4
900	FRDL	48203	4200	B4
1500	DET	48030	4200	B4
1500	FRDL	48030	4200	B4
1700	GSPW	48236	4204	B4
1900	DET	48234	4200	B4
1900	WRRN	48030	4200	B4
1900	WRRN	48091	4200	B4
1900	WRRN	48203	4200	B4
1900	WRRN	48234	4200	B4
2000	DET	48234	4201	D4
2000	WRRN	48234	4201	D4
2100	GSPW	48225	4204	B4
2200	WRRN	48091	4201	D4
2600	DET	48203	4199	C4
3000	DET	48220	4199	C4
3000	DET	48221	4199	C4
4100	FRDL	48221	4199	C4
7000	WRRN	48091	4202	A4
7100	DET	48234	4202	A4
7100	WRRN	48234	4202	A4
8000	WRRN	48089	4202	A4
8100	ROTp	48220	4199	C4
8100	ROTp	48221	4199	C4
11000	ROTp	48235	4199	C4
11000	ROTp	48237	4199	C4
11300	DET	48089	4202	A4
11600	DET	48205	4202	A4
11600	WRRN	48205	4202	A4
12700	DET	48235	4199	C4
12700	OKPK	48235	4199	C4
12700	OKPK	48237	4199	C4
13400	DET	48235	4198	A4
13400	OKPK	48235	4198	A4
13400	OKPK	48237	4198	A4
13800	DET	48205	4203	D4
13800	WRRN	48205	4203	D4
13900	WRRN	48089	4203	D4
14700	WRRN	48021	4203	D4
14800	EPTE	48021	4203	D4
14800	EPTE	48205	4203	D4
16800	SFLD	48075	4198	A4
17300	DET	48225	4203	D4
17700	EPTE	48225	4203	D4
17700	HRWD	48225	4203	D4
18000	HRWD	48225	4204	B4
18100	DET	48219	4198	A4
18100	SFLD	48219	4198	A4
18600	DET	48219	4197	D5
18600	SFLD	48219	4197	D5
18800	SFLD	48075	4197	D5
20200	DET	48075	4197	D5
22000	SFLD	48034	4197	D5
22500	DET	48034	4197	D5
24000	DET	48034	4196	B5
24000	DET	48219	4196	B5
24000	SFLD	48034	4196	B5
24900	SFLD	48240	4196	B5
25000	RDFD	48240	4196	B5
27400	FNHL	48152	4196	B5
27400	FNHL	48336	4196	B5
27400	LVNA	48152	4196	B5
SR-102 E 8 Mile Rd				
-	DET	48030	4200	C4
-	DET	48203	4200	D4
-	HZLP	48030	4200	E4
-	HZLP	48203	4200	D4
100	FRDL	48220	4200	A4
900	FRDL	48203	4200	B4
1500	FRDL	48030	4200	C4
1900	WRRN	48030	4200	E4
1900	WRRN	48091	4200	E4
2200	WRRN	48091	4201	A4
7000	WRRN	48091	4202	A4
8000	WRRN	48089	4202	A4
SR-102 W 8 Mile Rd				
-	DET	48203	4200	A4
-	FRDL	48203	4200	A4
-	FRDL	48220	4200	A4
10	HZLP	48030	4200	C4
18100	DET	48219	4198	A4
18100	DET	48235	4198	A4
18100	SFLD	48219	4198	A4
18100	SFLD	48235	4198	A4
18400	SFLD	48075	4198	A4
18600	DET	48219	4197	D5
18600	SFLD	48219	4197	D5
18800	SFLD	48075	4197	D5
20200	DET	48075	4197	D5
22000	SFLD	48034	4197	D5
22500	DET	48034	4197	D5

INDEX 4

SR-102 W 8 Mile Rd — Detroit & Wayne County Street Index — Alexander Ct

Detroit & Wayne County Street Index

STREET Block City ZIP Map# Grid

SR-102 W 8 Mile Rd
24000 DET 48034 4196 B5
24000 DET 48219 4196 B5
24000 SFLD 48034 4196 B5
25000 RDFD 48240 4196 B5
25000 SFLD 48240 4196 B5
27400 FNHL 48152 4196 B5
27400 FNHL 48336 4196 B5
27400 LVNA 48152 4196 B5
SR-102 8 Mile Rd E
1500 DET 48030 4200 B4
1500 DET 48203 4200 B4
1500 HZLP 48030 4200 B4
1500 HZLP 48203 4200 B4
1900 DET 48234 4200 B4
1900 WRRN 48030 4200 B4
1900 WRRN 48091 4200 B4
1900 WRRN 48203 4200 B4
1900 WRRN 48234 4200 B4
2000 DET 48234 4201 D4
2000 WRRN 48091 4201 D4
2000 WRRN 48234 4201 D4
7100 DET 48234 4202 A4
7100 WRRN 48091 4202 A4
7100 WRRN 48234 4202 A4
11300 DET 48089 4202 A4
11600 DET 48205 4202 A4
11600 WRRN 48205 4202 A4
11800 WRRN 48089 4202 A4
13800 DET 48205 4203 D4
13800 WRRN 48205 4203 D4
13900 WRRN 48089 4203 D4
14700 WRRN 48021 4203 D4
14800 EPTE 48021 4203 D4
14800 EPTE 48205 4203 D4
17300 DET 48225 4203 D4
17300 EPTE 48225 4203 D4
17300 HRWD 48225 4203 D4
SR-102 8 Mile Rd W
- DET 48075 4198 A4
- DET 48219 4197 C5
- SFLD 48075 4197 C5
- SFLD 48219 4197 C5
- SFLD 48235 4198 A4
10 DET 48203 4200 C4
10 HZLP 48030 4200 C4
10 HZLP 48203 4200 C4
400 FRDL 48203 4199 C4
400 FRDL 48220 4199 C4
600 FRDL 48203 4200 B4
600 FRDL 48220 4200 B4
2600 DET 48203 4199 C4
3000 DET 48220 4199 C4
3000 DET 48221 4199 C4
4100 FRDL 48221 4199 C4
8100 ROTp 48220 4199 C4
8100 ROTp 48221 4199 C4
11000 ROTp 48235 4199 C4
11000 ROTp 48237 4199 C4
12700 DET 48235 4199 C4
12700 OKPK 48235 4199 C4
12700 OKPK 48237 4199 C4
13400 DET 48235 4198 A4
13400 OKPK 48235 4198 A4
13400 OKPK 48237 4198 A4
16800 SFLD 48075 4198 A4
23900 SFLD 48034 4197 A5
24300 DET 48034 4196 E5
24300 DET 48219 4196 E5
24300 SFLD 48034 4196 E5
SR-102 Vernier Rd
1700 GSPW 48236 4204 B4
2100 GSPW 48225 4204 B4
17700 EPTE 48021 4203 E4
17700 EPTE 48225 4203 E4
17700 HRWD 48225 4203 E4
18000 HRWD 48225 4204 B4
SR-153
- DET 48126 4342 C6
- DET 48128 4342 C6
- DRBN 48228 4341 A7
- SpTp 48105 4333 D7
- SpTp 48198 4333 E7
- WTLD 48185 4337 B7
7500 SpTp 48198 4409 A1
8000 SpTp 48105 4409 A1
8800 SpTp 48198 4334 E7
9500 SpTp 48198 4335 C7
10000 DRBN 48126 4343 B6
13800 DRBN 48126 4342 C6
18100 DET 48228 4342 C6
19000 DRBN 48128 4342 C6
19000 DRBN 48228 4342 C6
19300 DRBN 48126 4341 A7
19300 DRBN 48128 4341 A7
20000 DRBN 48127 4341 A7
20500 DBHT 48127 4341 A7
20500 DBHT 48128 4341 A7
23400 WynC 48127 4341 A7
23400 WynC 48128 4341 A7
24400 DBHT 48127 4340 B7
24400 DBHT 48128 4340 B7
24400 DRBN 48128 4340 B7
27400 GDNC 48135 4340 B7
28500 GDNC 48135 4339 C7
32900 GDNC 48185 4339 C7
32900 WTLD 48185 4339 C7
33800 WTLD 48135 4338 B7
33800 WTLD 48185 4338 B7
39400 CNTN 48187 4337 B7
43400 CNTN 48187 4336 C7
48200 CNTN 48187 4335 C7
49400 CNTN 48198 4335 C7
SR-153 Ford Rd
- DET 48126 4342 C6
- DET 48128 4342 C6
- DRBN 48228 4341 A7
- SpTp 48105 4333 D7
- SpTp 48198 4333 E7
- WTLD 48185 4337 B7

SR-153 Ford Rd
7500 SpTp 48198 4409 A1
8000 SpTp 48105 4409 A1
8800 SpTp 48198 4334 E7
9500 SpTp 48198 4335 C7
10000 DRBN 48126 4343 B6
13800 DRBN 48126 4342 C6
18100 DET 48228 4342 C6
19000 DRBN 48128 4342 C6
19000 DRBN 48228 4342 C6
19300 DRBN 48126 4341 A7
19300 DRBN 48128 4341 A7
20000 DRBN 48127 4341 A7
20500 DBHT 48127 4341 A7
20500 DBHT 48128 4341 A7
23400 WynC 48127 4341 A7
23400 WynC 48128 4341 A7
24400 DBHT 48127 4340 B7
24400 DBHT 48128 4340 B7
24400 DRBN 48128 4340 B7
27400 GDNC 48135 4340 B7
28500 GDNC 48135 4339 C7
32900 GDNC 48185 4339 C7
32900 WTLD 48185 4339 C7
33800 WTLD 48135 4338 B7
33800 WTLD 48185 4338 B7
39400 CNTN 48187 4337 B7
43400 CNTN 48187 4336 C7
48200 CNTN 48187 4335 C7
49400 CNTN 48198 4335 C7
US-12
- DRBN 48128 4417 D1
- VNBN 48198 4493 A4
- YPLT - 4491 A7
- YPLT - 4492 C6
- YpTp - 4491 C7
- YpTp - 4492 C6
10 DET 48226 4345 C6
100 SALN 48176 4572 E7
100 SALN 48176 4657 A2
1300 DET 48216 4345 C6
1900 YpTp 48198 4492 E5
2100 YpTp 48198 4493 A4
2500 DET 48216 4344 B6
3100 PTFD 48197 4491 A7
4000 DET 48210 4344 B6
4700 PTFD 48197 4574 C2
4700 PTFD 48197 4575 A1
6100 PTFD 48108 4574 C2
6100 PTFD 48176 4574 C2
6400 PTFD 48176 4573 B5
6900 DET 48210 4343 C7
7600 SALN 48176 4573 B5
8600 WasC 48176 4657 A2
8800 WasC 48176 4656 C4
9400 DET 48126 4343 C7
10000 DRBN 48126 4343 C7
13800 DRBN 48126 4342 E7
14200 DRBN 48126 4417 D1
16300 DRBN 48120 4417 D1
19000 DRBN 48124 4417 D1
20000 DRBN 48124 4416 B3
20000 DRBN 48128 4416 B3
24500 DRBN 48124 4415 A4
25400 DBHT 48125 4415 A4
25600 DBHT 48141 4415 A4
25800 INKR 48141 4258 E1
28900 INKR 48141 4414 D5
30400 WTLD 48141 4414 D5
30400 WTLD 48186 4414 D5
31200 WTLD 48184 4414 D5
31400 WYNE 48184 4414 D5
34000 WYNE 48184 4413 C6
38900 WYNE 48184 4412 B6
39200 WYNE 48188 4412 B6
39400 CNTN 48188 4412 B6
43600 CNTN 48188 4411 D7
45900 CNTN 48111 4494 B1
45900 CNTN 48188 4494 B1
47400 VNBN 48111 4494 B1
48800 CNTN 48111 4493 A4
48800 CNTN 48188 4493 A4
49100 VNBN 48111 4493 A4
US-12 BUS
- YPLT 48197 4491 E6
- YpTp 48197 4491 E6
10 YPLT 48197 4492 C4
10 YPLT 48198 4492 C4
800 YpTp 48198 4492 C4
2100 YpTp 48198 4493 A3
50600 VNBN 48111 4493 D2
51200 VNBN 48198 4493 C2
US-12 Ecorse Rd
1900 YpTp 48198 4492 E5
2100 YpTp 48198 4493 A4
US-12 BUS S Hamilton St
- YPLT 48197 4492 A6
10 YPLT 48197 4491 E4
US-12 BUS S Huron St
- YPLT 48197 4491 E6
- YpTp 48197 4491 E6
10 YPLT 48197 4492 A4
US-12 Michigan Av
- DRBN 48128 4417 D1
10 DET 48226 4345 C6
1300 DET 48216 4345 C6
2500 DET 48216 4344 B6
4000 DET 48210 4344 B6
6900 DET 48210 4343 C7
9400 DET 48126 4343 C7
10000 DRBN 48126 4343 C7
13800 DRBN 48126 4342 E7
14200 DRBN 48126 4417 D1
16300 DRBN 48120 4417 D1
19000 DRBN 48124 4417 D1
20000 DRBN 48124 4416 B3
20000 DRBN 48128 4416 B3
24500 DRBN 48124 4415 A4
25400 DBHT 48125 4415 A4

US-12 Michigan Av
25600 DBHT 48141 4415 A4
25800 INKR 48141 4415 A4
28900 INKR 48141 4414 D5
30400 WTLD 48141 4414 D5
30400 WTLD 48186 4414 D5
31200 WTLD 48184 4414 D5
39400 CNTN 48188 4412 B6
43600 CNTN 48188 4411 D7
45900 CNTN 48111 4494 B1
45900 CNTN 48188 4494 B1
47400 VNBN 48111 4494 B1
48800 CNTN 48111 4493 A4
48800 CNTN 48188 4493 A4
49100 VNBN 48111 4493 A4
US-12 BUS Michigan Av
50500 VNBN 48111 4493 D2
51300 VNBN 48198 4493 C2
51300 YpTp 48198 4493 C2
US-12 E Michigan Av
100 SALN 48176 4572 E7
6100 PTFD 48108 4574 C2
6100 PTFD 48176 4574 C2
6100 PTFD 48197 4574 C2
6400 PTFD 48176 4573 B5
7600 SALN 48176 4573 B5
US-12 BUS E Michigan Av
10 YPLT 48198 4492 C4
800 YpTp 48198 4492 C4
2100 YpTp 48198 4493 A3
US-12 W Michigan Av
100 SALN 48176 4657 A2
3100 PTFD 48197 4491 A7
3100 YpTp 48197 4491 A7
4700 PTFD 48197 4574 E1
4700 PTFD 48197 4575 A1
8600 WasC 48176 4657 A2
8800 WasC 48176 4656 C4
US-12 BUS W Michigan Av
10 YPLT 48197 4492 A4
10 YPLT 48198 4492 A4
US-12 Michigan Av E
31400 WYNE 48184 4414 C5
33800 WYNE 48184 4413 C6
38900 WYNE 48184 4412 E6
39200 WYNE 48188 4412 E6
US-12 Michigan Av W
31400 WYNE 48184 4414 C5
34000 WYNE 48184 4413 E6
38900 WYNE 48184 4412 E6
US-23
- AARB - 4331 E7
- AARB - 4332 B7
- AARB - 4407 D5
- AARB - 4490 D1
- AATp - 4331 C5
- AATp - 4332 B7
- AATp - 4407 C1
- AATp - 4490 D1
- GOTp - 4186 E7
- GOTp - 4187 B2
- PTFD - 4490 D4
- PTFD - 4574 C3
- WasC - 4186 E7
- WasC - 4258 E1
- WasC - 4259 A2
- WasC - 4331 C5
- WasC - 4574 C3
- WasC - 4659 D6
US-23 BUS
- AARB 48103 4406 B4
- AARB 48105 4406 B4
- AATp - 4331 C7
- AATp - 4406 C1
- AATp 48103 4406 B4
- PTFD 48104 4490 C2
- PTFD 48105 4490 C2
- PTFD 48108 4490 C2
400 AARB 48104 4406 E7
1900 AARB 48104 4489 E1
2100 AARB 48104 4490 C2
US-23 BUS E Huron St
100 AARB 48104 4406 B6
US-23 BUS N Main St
- AARB 48103 4406 B4
- AARB 48105 4406 B4
- AATp 48103 4406 B4
100 AARB 48103 4406 B4
US-23 BUS Washtenaw Av
- PTFD 48104 4490 C2
- PTFD 48105 4490 C2
- PTFD 48108 4490 C2
400 AARB 48104 4406 D7
1900 AARB 48104 4489 E1
2100 AARB 48104 4490 C2
US-24
- DET 48034 4196 E3
- DET 48223 4268 E5
100 DRBN 48124 4416 A1
100 DRBN 48128 4416 A1
1500 DRBN 48128 4341 A4
2200 DRBN 48127 4341 A4
3800 DRBN 48125 4416 A7
3900 DBHT 48125 4416 A7
5600 DBHT 48127 4341 A4
5700 DBHT 48125 4499 A5
5700 DBHT 48180 4499 A5
5800 TYLR 48180 4499 A5
8700 DBHT 48239 4341 A4
8800 RDFD 48239 4341 A4
11600 RDFD 48239 4269 A7
12000 MonC 48117 4839 A1
12000 MonC 48179 4839 A1
12000 TYLR 48180 4583 A1
12600 DET 48223 4269 A7
12600 DET 48239 4269 A7
12600 RDFD 48223 4269 A7
13000 MonC 48117 4753 C5

US-24
13500 MonC 48134 4753 C5
14000 BrTp 48134 4753 C5
14200 RDFD 48223 4268 E5
14200 RDFD 48239 4268 E5
15000 FTRK 48134 4753 C5
15800 RDFD 48219 4268 E5
16100 DET 48219 4268 E5
16600 TYLR 48174 4583 A1
17000 BNTN 48174 4583 A1
18200 DET 48219 4196 E3
18500 BNTN 48174 4668 A2
20600 BNTN 48183 4668 A2
20700 SFLD 48034 4196 E3
21000 BNTN 48134 4668 A2
24800 BNTN 48134 4667 E7
25800 BNTN 48134 4753 C5
US-24 Telegraph Rd
- DET 48034 4196 E3
- DET 48223 4268 E5
5800 TYLR 48180 4499 A5
8800 RDFD 48239 4341 A2
11600 RDFD 48239 4269 A7
12000 MonC 48117 4839 A1
12000 MonC 48179 4839 A1
12000 TYLR 48180 4583 A1
12600 DET 48223 4269 A7
12600 DET 48239 4269 A7
12600 RDFD 48223 4269 A7
13000 MonC 48117 4753 C5
13500 MonC 48134 4753 C5
14000 BrTp 48134 4753 C5
14200 RDFD 48223 4268 E5
14200 RDFD 48239 4268 E5
15000 FTRK 48134 4753 C5
15800 RDFD 48219 4268 E5
16100 DET 48219 4268 E5
16600 TYLR 48174 4583 A1
17000 BNTN 48174 4583 A1
18200 DET 48219 4196 E3
18500 BNTN 48174 4668 A2
20600 BNTN 48183 4668 A2
20700 SFLD 48034 4196 E3
21000 BNTN 48134 4668 A2
24800 BNTN 48134 4667 E7
25800 BNTN 48134 4753 C5
US-24 N Telegraph Rd
100 DRBN 48124 4416 A1
100 DRBN 48128 4416 A1
1500 DRBN 48128 4341 A4
2200 DRBN 48127 4341 A4
5600 DBHT 48127 4341 A4
8700 DBHT 48239 4341 A4
US-24 S Telegraph Rd
100 DRBN 48124 4416 A2
3800 DRBN 48125 4416 A6
3900 DBHT 48125 4416 A6
5600 DBHT 48125 4499 A1
5600 DBHT 48180 4499 A1

A

A Av
- WasC 48197 4659 C2
A Dr
14100 PyTp 48170 4263 D6
A St
- DBHT 48125 4416 E6
- FNHL 48336 4195 D2
10 BrTp 48134 4753 C5
2000 VNBN 48111 4494 A4
Aaron St
3300 DET 48207 4345 E1
3300 DET 48207 4346 A1
Aarons Wy
46300 CNTN 48188 4411 C6
Abbey Ct
1000 NHVL 48167 4192 B5
1100 WIND N8S 4348 A7
2200 CNTN 48188 4411 E5
19000 BNTN 48192 4584 A7
Abbey Ln
9200 SpTp 48198 4409 D7
Abbott Av
2000 AARB 48103 4405 D6
4000 LNPK 48146 4500 D7
Abbott Ln
- WTLD 48186 4414 A4
10 DRBN 48120 4417 D2
Abbott St
10 RVRG 48218 4501 E1
600 DET 48226 4345 C6
1400 DET 48216 4345 B7
5700 LSal N9J 4503 B4
Abby Cir
16700 NvIT 48167 4265 C2
Abel St
- SLYN 48178 4189 B2
Aberdeen Ct
200 BLVL 48111 4578 E3
300 SALN 48176 4572 B7
Aberdeen Dr
900 AARB 48104 4407 A7
1100 AARB 48104 4490 A1
4700 WasC 48103 4329 E4
4800 WasC 48130 4329 E4
47400 NOVI 48374 4192 A3
Aberdeen St
1300 CNTN 48187 4412 A1
Abi Ct
9700 WasC 48170 4262 E6
Abi Ln
6500 WasC 48170 4262 E6
Abigail Wy
1500 WasC 48103 4488 C1
Abilene Dr
6900 RMLS 48174 4496 A3
Abingdon Cir
5000 PTFD 48108 4573 A1
Abington Av
8800 DET 48228 4342 B2
9500 DET 48227 4342 B1
11600 DET 48227 4270 B7
Abington Ct
35800 FNHL 48335 4194 C3
Abington Dr
22200 FNHL 48335 4194 C3
Abington Ln
10 DRBN 48120 4417 D3
Able St
- SLYN 48178 4189 B2
Abruzzi Dr
38000 WTLD 48185 4413 A1
Acacia
24000 RDFD 48239 4268 E5
Acacia Rd
25000 SFLD 48034 4197 B1
Acacia St
- DET 48223 4269 D5
- DET 48223 4270 A5
- DET 48227 4270 A5
28100 LVNA 48154 4268 A5
30100 LVNA 48154 4267 D5
Academic Dr
2800 WasC 48103 4330 A7
Academy Ct
11100 PyTp 48170 4336 C2
Academy Dr
2300 WIND N9E 4421 A6
3000 WIND N9E 4504 B1
5000 CNTN 48187 4412 B7
5000 CNTN 48188 4495 C1
45900 PyTp 48170 4336 C2
Academy St
100 FRDL 48220 4199 E3
100 FRDL 48220 4200 A3
1500 DRBN 48124 4416 B4
3900 DBHT 48124 4416 B6
3900 DBHT 48125 4416 B6
5400 DBHT 48125 4499 B2
Acer Ct
2100 PTFD 48108 4572 E3
Ackert Ct
24500 NOVI 48375 4193 B1
Ackley Av
1500 WTLD 48186 4413 E4
Ackley St
7600 DET 48211 4273 E6
Acorn
- CNTN 48188 4411 C6
Acorn Cres
3900 WIND N8W 4505 A2
Acorn Ct
3800 WIND N8W 4505 A2
Acorn St
700 WTLD 48186 4414 C7
Acorn Tr
24900 NOVI 48374 4191 D1
Acorne Av
8400 WasC 48160 4659 D1
Acorne Ct
4400 WasC 48160 4659 E1
Ada Av
23800 WRRN 48091 4201 A1
Ada St
400 SLYN 48178 4189 B3
23500 BNTN 48183 4668 B3
Adair Ct
1100 WIND N8S 4347 E7
Adair St
200 DET 48207 4346 B5
E Adams
6100 VNBN 48111 4577 C3
N Adams
6100 VNBN 48111 4577 C3
S Adams
6200 VNBN 48111 4577 C3
W Adams
6100 VNBN 48111 4577 C3
Adams Av
100 AARB 48104 4406 B7
6000 SRKW 48179 4754 B7
Adams Av E
- DET 48201 4345 D5
10 DET 48226 4345 D5
Adams Av W
10 DET 48226 4345 C6
Adams Cir
4200 WYNE 48184 4414 A7
Adams Ct
200 FRDL 48220 4199 E4
200 FRDL 48220 4200 A4
15100 LVNA 48154 4265 E4
24600 FNHL 48335 4194 A1
25700 SLYN 48178 4189 A1
42500 CNTN 48187 4337 B5
47300 PyTp 48170 4336 B2
Adams Dr
21500 BNTN 48192 4583 D6
29000 GBTR 48173 4755 D4
Adams Ln
10 DRBN 48120 4417 D2
10 LSal N9J 4502 C5
Adams Rd
10800 RMLS 48174 4496 D7
10800 RMLS 48242 4496 D7
Adams St
100 PLYM 48170 4265 A6
9000 LVNA 48150 4337 E1
14200 LVNA 48154 4265 E5
33400 FMTN 48335 4194 E1
N Adams St
10 YPLT 48197 4492 A4
S Adams St
10 YPLT 48197 4492 A5
Adanac Av
1400 WIND N9B 4420 C3
Adare Cir
2400 AARB 48104 4490 A1
Adare Ct
2700 AARB 48104 4490 A1
Adare Rd
2300 AARB 48104 4489 E1
2400 AARB 48104 4490 A1
Addington Ln
45400 NOVI 48374 4192 C2
45400 NOVI 48375 4192 C2
Addison Av
42000 CNTN 48187 4412 B1
Addison Ct
15800 SFLD 48075 4198 C1
Addison Dr
18200 SFLD 48075 4198 A1
19000 SFLD 48075 4197 E1
Addison St
5200 DET 48210 4343 C6
13300 GBTR 48173 4755 D5
15500 SFLD 48075 4198 C1
22600 SFLD 48034 4197 A1
Adelaide Av
500 WIND N8P 4348 B5
Adelaide Ct
500 WasC 48176 4658 D1
Adelaide Dr
- WasC 48176 4658 D2
Adelaide St
10 DET 48201 4345 C5
900 WYDT 48192 4585 B4
1300 DET 48207 4345 D4
Adele St
3000 WYNE 48184 4414 B5
Adelein Av
27000 SFLD 48034 4196 A3
Adeline St
400 DET 48203 4200 B5
Admiral St
4600 WTLD 48186 4415 A7
5600 WTLD 48186 4498 B1
Admiralty Dr
7300 CNTN 48187 4336 C5
Adriana Ct
- CNTN 48187 4336 A6
Adrienne Dr
2600 AARB 48103 4405 D7
2700 WasC 48103 4405 D7
Adrienne Ln
400 WasC 48103 4404 C3
Adstoll Av
4700 WIND N8T 4422 C3
Affeldt St
7200 WTLD 48135 4340 A4
7200 WTLD 48185 4340 A4
AF Gross Dr
- SALN 48176 4572 E7
Afton
- CNTN 48188 4411 E5
Afton Rd
11000 SOGT 48195 4500 A7
19200 DET 48203 4200 B6
Agincourt
2100 AARB 48103 4488 D2
Agnes Av
4000 LNPK 48146 4500 D7
14600 EPTE 48021 4203 B3
Agnes St
200 ECRS 48229 4501 C3
6800 DET 48207 4346 C3
8700 DET 48214 4346 E2
12100 SOGT 48195 4500 D7
12100 SOGT 48195 4584 D1
Agnew Pl
15500 SFLD 48075 4198 C1
15500 SFLD 48237 4198 C1
Ahlanthus Dr
29700 FTRK 48134 4754 A5
Ailey Ct
12700 DET 48213 4275 B4
Ailsa Craig Ct
3100 PTFD 48108 4490 C4
Ailsa Craig Dr
3000 PTFD 48108 4490 C4
Aina Ln
3700 WasC 48178 4260 C2
Ainsley Rd
4900 PTFD 48108 4491 A3
4900 YpTp 48108 4491 A3
4900 YpTp 48197 4491 A3
Ainsley St
1300 YPLT 48197 4491 C3
Ainsworth Cir
400 YPLT 48197 4491 E5
E Ainsworth St
100 YPLT 48197 4491 E5
W Ainsworth St
10 YPLT 48197 4491 E5
Airborne St
5800 RMLS 48174 4498 A1
Air Coach St
28000 RMLS 48174 4498 A1
Aire Ct
9300 WIND N8S 4348 A7
Aire Pl
1100 WIND N8S 4348 A7
Airey Ct
2200 PTFD 48103 4488 D3
2200 WasC 48103 4488 D3
Airline Dr
11900 GOTp 48178 4188 B4
Airline St
25800 TYLR 48180 4498 D7
Airport Blvd
- PTFD 48108 4489 B6
Airport Dr
- YpTp 48198 4493 A5
700 PTFD 48108 4489 B6
28200 RMLS 48174 4498 A5
29100 RMLS 48174 4497 E5
Airport Rd
- Tcmh N8V 4505 B1
Airport Rd
2300 WIND N8W 4505 B1
2400 YpTp 48198 4493 B5
22600 HnTp 48164 4666 C4
Airport Industrial Dr
10 YpTp 48198 4492 E4
Airport Service Rd
- VNBN 48111 4493 D4
800 VNBN 48111 4494 A6
Akron Ct
33000 WTLD 48186 4414 A4
Akron St
2400 DRBN 48120 4418 D2
2700 DET 48212 4273 A1
Alabama Ct
31400 LVNA 48150 4339 C3
Alabama St
31400 LVNA 48150 4339 B3
Alameda St
400 DET 48203 4200 C4
Alamo Ct
33000 WTLD 48186 4414 A5
Alan Av
29400 WTLD 48186 4414 E7
Alan Cres
500 WIND N8S 4347 E6
Alana Ct
10800 AGST 48191 4577 C7
Alan Mark Dr
3300 SpTp 48105 4408 A1
Alanson St
33000 WTLD 48186 4414 A4
Alaska
800 WynC 48111 4662 D2
Alaska Ct
33100 WTLD 48186 4414 A5
Alaska St
6300 DET 48204 4343 D3
Alba Ct
42600 VNBN 48111 4495 B7
42600 VNBN 48111 4579 B1
Albany Av
19500 SFLD 48075 4197 D3
20700 WRRN 48091 4201 D3
Albany St
100 FRDL 48220 4199 D3
8700 OKPK 48237 4199 A3
13200 OKPK 48237 4198 E3
18500 SFLD 48075 4198 A3
20200 DET 48234 4201 D4
Alber St
13200 DRBN 48126 4343 A6
13900 DRBN 48126 4342 E6
Albert Dr
100 MonC 48117 4751 E7
3800 SpTp 48105 4334 A6
44900 PyTp 48170 4336 D3
Albert Ln
- HnTp 48164 4665 C1
Albert Rd
800 WIND N8Y 4346 C7
1000 WIND N8Y 4421 D1
1800 WIND N8W 4421 D2
Albert St
10 BrTp 48179 4841 A3
18400 WDHN 48183 4669 A7
18600 DET 48219 4196 D7
18600 DET 48240 4196 D7
18600 RDFD 48240 4196 D7
Alberta Av
33100 WTLD 48186 4414 A4
Alberta St
800 FRDL 48220 4199 D3
1800 WTLD 48186 4414 A4
Albion Av
22500 FNHL 48336 4195 D2
Albion St
4000 WYDT 48192 4585 C4
17100 DET 48234 4274 C1
19100 DET 48234 4202 C5
Alboni Sq
500 WasC 48103 4404 B6
Alcona Ct
31400 WTLD 48186 4414 C5
Alcoy St
18000 DET 48205 4202 E6
Aldea Dr
41200 NvIT 48167 4265 B2
Alden Cres
10 Tcmh N8N 4424 C1
Alden Rd
40100 VNBN 48111 4495 D7
40100 VNBN 48111 4579 D1
Alden St
15400 DET 48238 4271 E2
Alder Ct
2300 PTFD 48103 4488 D5
Alderbrook Dr
2900 WIND N8W 4421 D6
Alders Dr
29700 FTRK 48134 4754 A5
Alderton St
20200 DET 48219 4197 B5
Aldgate Ct
36800 FNHL 48335 4194 B4
Aldrich Ct
16200 LVNA 48154 4265 E3
Aldridge St
11400 WIND N8P 4348 D7
Aldrin Av
18300 BNTN 48192 4583 C7
Aldwych Cir
3200 AARB 48105 4332 C7
Alex Dr
2500 WasC 48103 4488 C4
Alexander Av
3000 WIND N9C 4420 A3
Alexander Ct
4300 ECRS 48229 4501 D4

STREET
Block City ZIP Map# Grid

Alexander Dr
1800 WTLD 48186 4413 A4
Alexander St
- ECRS 48229 4501 E2
- RVRG 48229 4501 E2
10 RVRG 48218 4501 E2
15800 LVNA 48154 4267 E3
E Alexander St
6100 RMLS 48174 4496 D2
N Alexander St
35400 RMLS 48174 4496 D1
Alexandra Av
2600 WIND N9E 4421 A7
2800 WIND N9E 4504 A1
Alexandra Blvd
1500 AATp 48103 4405 E3
Alexandra St
1800 WIND N9B 4420 E5
Alexandria Ct
100 CNTN 48188 4411 A3
Alexandria Towne St
10 SFLD 48075 4198 B2
Alexandrine St
500 WIND N8X 4421 C5
22400 DRBN 48124 4416 B2
Alexandrine St E
10 DET 48201 4345 C3
1500 DET 48207 4345 D2
3100 DET 48207 4346 A2
Alexandrine St W
- DET 48201 4345 A4
1400 DET 48210 4345 A4
2000 DET 48210 4344 E4
Alexis Rd
1500 WIND N8Y 4421 E2
1800 WIND N8W 4421 E2
2500 WIND N8W 4422 A4
E Alexis St
10 ECRS 48229 4501 D3
W Alexis St
10 ECRS 48229 4501 D3
Alfred Av
1200 LSal N9J 4502 E6
Alfred St
10 DET 48201 4345 C4
10 WYDT 48192 4501 C6
1300 DET 48207 4345 E4
Algebe Wy
- AATp 48104 4490 C2
Alger Ln
23100 STCS 48080 4204 E3
Alger Pl
10 GSPT 48230 4276 D6
Alger St
- BwTp 48173 4841 B3
10 DET 48202 4273 A6
1100 DET 48211 4273 B6
19500 STCS 48080 4204 C3
Algonac St
- DET 48205 4274 C1
1300 AARB 48103 4489 A1
19100 DET 48234 4202 C5
Algonquin Dr
16900 NvIT 48167 4263 D3
43400 NOVI 48375 4192 E2
Algonquin Ln
26100 FTRK 48134 4754 A1
Algonquin St
400 DET 48214 4347 C1
1200 DET 48214 4275 C7
1600 WIND N9B 4420 C5
34000 WTLD 48185 4338 E6
Alhambra Dr
1700 AARB 48103 4488 E1
Alice St
500 AARB 48103 4405 D5
2200 HMTK 48212 4273 C6
2400 WIND N8Y 4421 D2
2600 DRBN 48124 4416 D5
3800 WIND N8Y 4422 A2
18400 WDHN 48183 4669 A7
22800 STCS 48080 4204 D2
Alicia St
24600 BNTN 48134 4667 D7
Aline Dr
1100 GSPW 48236 4204 D4
Alkali St
100 WYDT 48192 4585 C1
Allan Av
13600 OKPK 48237 4198 E1
Allard Av
- HRWD 48225 4204 B6
400 GSPF 48236 4276 C1
1600 GSPW 48236 4204 B6
1800 LNPK 48146 4500 D6
2200 GSPW 48225 4204 B6
Allegan Ct
31500 WTLD 48186 4414 C5
Alleghany St
41400 CNTN 48188 4412 C4
Allen Av
10 YpTp 48198 4492 D3
3000 INKR 48141 4415 B5
Allen Ct
10 Amhg N9V 4757 E2
22800 STCS 48080 4205 A3
32400 LVNA 48154 4267 A5
61100 LyTp 48178 4189 B5
Allen Dr
100 AARB 48103 4405 E5
800 NHVL 48167 4192 E5
Allen Pl
- DET 48204 4343 C1
Allen Rd
- BNTN 48180 4583 E5
- BNTN 48195 4583 E5
- MVDL 48101 4417 D7
700 YpTp 48198 4492 D3
4000 ALPK 48101 4417 D7
4000 ALPK 48122 4417 D7
Allen Rd
4300 ALPK 48101 4500 C2
10000 ALPK 48101 4499 E7
10500 TYLR 48101 4499 E7
10500 TYLR 48180 4499 E7
10900 ALPK 48195 4499 E7
10900 TYLR 48195 4499 E7
11000 SOGT 48195 4499 E7
12100 SOGT 48195 4583 E1
12100 TYLR 48180 4583 E1
12100 TYLR 48195 4583 E1
17000 BNTN 48192 4583 E7
17000 MVDL 48122 4417 E5
19000 BNTN 48183 4583 E7
19000 BNTN 48183 4668 E1
21000 WDHN 48183 4668 E3
22100 WDHN 48183 4669 A5
26000 WDHN 48183 4755 A1
27000 BwTp 48183 4755 A1
28500 BwTp 48183 4754 E4
Allen St
200 FRDL 48220 4199 E4
32900 LVNA 48154 4267 A5
35900 LVNA 48154 4266 C5
38700 LVNA 48154 4265 E5
Allendale Dr
3600 SpTp 48105 4333 C7
3600 SpTp 48198 4333 C7
Allendale St
500 WIND N8X 4421 A2
4100 DET 48204 4344 A3
Allen Pointe Dr
- ALPK 48101 4499 E5
Allenton Ct
33000 WTLD 48186 4414 A5
Allied Dr
- LVNA 48150 4267 B7
Allison Dr
500 WasC 48103 4405 D5
Allonby St
13600 DET 48227 4270 E7
Allston Ct
300 YpTp 48198 4492 A2
Allyn Av
- EPTE 48021 4203 A3
14200 WRRN 48089 4203 A3
14700 WRRN 48021 4203 A3
Allyson Av
2500 WIND N8W 4422 B3
Allyson Ct
2600 WIND N8W 4422 B4
Alma Ct
7500 WTLD 48185 4338 A5
Alma Ln
38500 WTLD 48185 4337 E4
38500 WTLD 48185 4338 A5
Alma St
10 Amhg N9V 4757 D2
12900 DET 48205 4274 E1
13900 DET 48205 4275 A1
Alma St CO-5
500 Amhg N9V 4757 D2
Almaden Ct
7200 CNTN 48187 4336 C4
Almira St
23100 SFLD 48034 4196 D2
Almond Av
22700 EPTE 48021 4204 A1
Almond Cir
36600 FNHL 48335 4194 B3
Almond St
600 WTLD 48186 4414 D7
Almont St
1800 FRDL 48220 4200 B2
8000 DET 48234 4274 B2
Aloha Dr
300 Tcmh N8N 4424 E1
Alois St
11400 LVNA 48150 4338 A1
Alpena Av
10200 HMTK 48212 4273 D3
Alpena Ct
31500 WTLD 48186 4414 C5
Alpena St
- DET 48212 4273 D2
Alpenrose Av
4500 WIND N9G 4504 D5
Alpenrose Ct
600 WIND N9G 4504 D5
Alper Av
2900 LNPK 48146 4500 E4
Alper Blvd
8500 WTLD 48185 4339 B3
Alpha Dr
9400 PyTp 48170 4336 C2
Alpha St
3800 DET 48212 4273 B1
Alpine Dr
- AARB 48104 4489 D4
3200 AARB 48108 4489 D4
15900 LVNA 48154 4266 D3
Alpine St
8000 DET 48204 4343 D3
Alsace Av
1900 WIND N8W 4421 D4
Al Smith St
1700 CNTN 48187 4337 D7
1700 CNTN 48187 4412 D1
Alstead St
18900 DET 48236 4204 A7
Alta St
33300 GDNC 48135 4414 A2
Alta Loma St
33400 FMTN 48335 4194 E2
Altar Rd
- DET 48228 4342 A6
- DRBN 48126 4341 E6
- DRBN 48128 4341 E6
- DRBN 48128 4342 A6
- DRBN 48228 4341 E6
Altar Rd
- DRBN 48228 4342 A6
Alta Vista Pl
5600 WasC 48105 4333 A2
Alten Dr
9300 WIND N8R 4423 B3
Alter Rd
10 DET 48214 4348 A2
10 GPPK 48214 4348 A2
400 DET 48214 4347 E1
500 DET 48214 4275 D5
5600 DET 48224 4275 C4
Althea Ct
19400 NvIT 48167 4193 C6
Alton Ct
3300 AARB 48105 4407 C1
22400 NOVI 48375 4192 D3
Alton St
8200 CNTN 48187 4337 D3
14800 RDFD 48239 4268 D4
Alva Dr
43200 VNBN 48111 4579 A1
Alvaro Av
18100 BNTN 48192 4583 B7
Alvin Ct
29000 GDNC 48135 4414 E1
Alvin St
1000 WTLD 48186 4414 A3
28400 GDNC 48135 4415 A1
29400 GDNC 48135 4414 E1
Alvina Av
2900 WRRN 48091 4201 B4
Alvord Av
1500 TNTN 48183 4669 D7
Alwar St
19300 DET 48205 4203 A5
Alwyne Ln
17400 DET 48203 4272 B1
Alyaberry Dr
9800 GOTp 48178 4188 E2
Amalfi Dr
11200 WIND N8P 4348 C6
Amanda Ct
4000 CNTN 48188 4411 C6
13100 Tcmh N8N 4349 B7
Amanda Dr
- AATp 48105 4408 A2
6900 VNBN 48111 4494 D3
Amarillo Dr
6600 RMLS 48174 4496 A2
Amazon St
2700 DRBN 48120 4418 D2
Ambassador Br
- DET 48216 4344 E7
- DET 48216 4419 E1
- DET 48216 4420 A1
- WIND N9B 4420 A1
- WIND N9C 4420 A1
Ambassador Br P-3
- WIND N9B 4420 A1
- WIND N9C 4420 A1
Ambassador Dr
1800 WIND N9C 4420 C6
2300 WIND N9E 4420 C6
Amber
- WDHN 48183 4669 A7
Amber Av
23000 WRRN 48089 4202 D1
Amber Ct
9300 WasC 48189 4186 D7
15100 PyTp 48170 4265 D4
18800 LVNA 48152 4195 D7
43500 CNTN 48188 4412 A5
Amber Dr
2200 CNTN 48188 4411 E5
2400 CNTN 48188 4412 A5
7900 RMLS 48174 4496 B4
Amber Wy
5500 PTFD 48197 4574 E2
Amberely Blvd
- CNTN 48170 4335 C4
- CNTN 48187 4335 C4
Amberlund Ct
22400 NOVI 48374 4192 B3
Amberly Cres
300 Tcmh N8N 4424 B1
Amberly Wy
7000 YpTp 48197 4575 E5
Ambeth St
30400 FNHL 48336 4195 C4
Amboy Ct
- DBHT 48127 4340 B4
42300 NvIT 48167 4193 C6
Amboy St
100 DBHT 48127 4415 B1
100 DBHT 48141 4415 B1
7200 DBHT 48127 4340 B4
Ambridge Ct
42900 NvIT 48170 4265 A3
Amelia Ct
48700 CNTN 48187 4335 E6
Amelia Pl
2100 AARB 48104 4489 E2
Amelia St
300 PLYM 48170 4265 A6
America Dr
51000 VNBN 48111 4577 C4
American St
7200 DET 48210 4343 D3
8800 DET 48204 4343 D1
10300 DET 48204 4271 D7
Americana Blvd
- DBHT 48127 4415 D1
American Wy St
100 DET 48209 4419 B3
Ames Hwy
24000 TYLR 48180 4499 A2
24500 TYLR 48180 4498 E3
Amesburg Dr
- NOVI 48374 4191 C1
Amesbury Dr
2200 AARB 48103 4488 E2
45700 PyTp 48170 4336 C1
Amethyst Cir
500 WasC 48189 4186 D7
Amherst
- FNHL 48167 4194 A4
- FNHL 48335 4194 A4
Amherst Av
700 AARB 48105 4406 C3
Amherst Cir
300 SALN 48176 4657 E2
Amherst Ct
11600 PyTp 48170 4336 A1
42500 CNTN 48187 4337 B4
Amherst Dr
45400 NOVI 48374 4192 C1
Amherst Ln
10 DRBN 48120 4417 D2
Amherst Rd
10 PTRG 48069 4199 D1
Amherst St
100 INKR 48141 4415 C2
5600 DET 48209 4419 C2
24000 DBHT 48125 4416 A7
25400 DBHT 48125 4498 D1
Amhurst Dr
36100 WTLD 48185 4338 B6
Amiens Av
1900 WIND N8W 4421 D4
Amity St
9300 DET 48214 4346 E2
Amlin St
400 Amhg N9V 4757 D2
Amrad St
- DET 48234 4201 D5
Amrhein Rd
36400 LVNA 48150 4266 A7
37700 LVNA 48150 4265 E7
Amrhien Dr
7700 YpTp 48197 4576 A6
Amsterdam Av
2000 CNTN 48188 4411 B5
Amsterdam St
10 DET 48202 4345 A1
Amy Dr
5700 WYNE 48184 4497 C1
41000 NOVI 48375 4193 C4
Amy Ln
8100 CNTN 48187 4336 D4
Anabell Rd
14400 MonC 48117 4752 D5
Anaheim St
200 BLVL 48111 4578 E4
Anastasia St
- BwTp 48173 4841 A1
- LSal N9H 4504 A4
33200 RKWD 48173 4841 A1
Anatole St
4900 DET 48236 4276 B2
Ancaster Ct
3400 WIND N9E 4504 B2
Anchor Ct
42300 NvIT 48167 4193 C5
E Anchor Ct
47600 PyTp 48170 4264 A5
W Anchor Ct
47700 PyTp 48170 4263 E5
47700 PyTp 48170 4264 A6
Anchor Dr
8000 WIND N8N 4423 B4
8000 WIND N8T 4423 B4
Anchor St
- PyTp 48170 4264 A5
E Anchor St
10 RVRG 48218 4418 E5
10 RVRG 48218 4419 A7
W Anchor St
10 RVRG 48218 4418 E6
Anchorage Av
- CNTN 48187 4412 B1
Anchor Bay
8500 YpTp 48197 4576 C1
Anconna Cres
3300 WIND N8R 4423 C3
Anderdon St
4300 DET 48214 4275 B5
5000 DET 48213 4275 B5
Anderson Av
1500 AARB 48104 4489 D2
Anderson Ct
2000 AARB 48104 4489 E2
Anderson Dr
16600 SOGT 48195 4584 A5
Anderson Rd
9100 WynC 48138 4670 C3
S Anderson St
700 DET 48209 4419 B4
Andora Dr
3000 SpTp 48198 4408 C2
Andover Av
27400 INKR 48141 4415 B6
Andover Ct
19300 NvIT 48167 4193 A7
30100 INKR 48141 4414 D6
49100 CNTN 48188 4335 E5
Andover Dr
800 NHVL 48167 4192 B5
1800 SpTp 48198 4409 E7
7200 CNTN 48187 4335 E5
9400 VNBN 48111 4495 B6
13400 PyTp 48170 4263 C7
15600 DRBN 48120 4417 D2
24000 DBHT 48125 4416 A6
24300 DBHT 48125 4415 D6
25400 DBHT 48141 4415 D6
47900 NOVI 48374 4192 A2
48100 NOVI 48374 4191 E2
Andover Rd
2500 TNTN 48183 4669 C4
Andover Rd
3300 AARB 48105 4407 B5
Andover St
19100 DET 48203 4200 D6
28000 INKR 48141 4415 A6
29600 INKR 48141 4414 D6
Andrea Av
1300 YpTp 48198 4492 E6
Andrea Ct
3000 AARB 48103 4405 C6
Andresen Ct
10 HZLP 48030 4200 C1
Andrew Blvd
23900 BNTN 48134 4668 A5
Andrew Dr
- PyTp 48170 4264 A7
Andrew Ln
- HnTp 48164 4580 C7
18500 HnTp 48164 4665 C1
Andrews Av
9600 ALPK 48101 4500 A5
10500 ALPK 48195 4500 A6
Andrus St
2200 HMTK 48212 4273 C5
Angela Ct
26400 WDHN 48183 4755 A1
Angeline Av
34000 LVNA 48150 4338 E1
Angeline Cir
36700 LVNA 48150 4338 B1
Angelique Av
2200 LNPK 48101 4500 B3
2200 LNPK 48146 4500 B3
14500 ALPK 48101 4500 B3
Angell Blvd
- NvIT 48167 4191 C7
- NvIT 48167 4263 C1
Angle Rd
6900 WasC 48167 4261 E2
6900 WasC 48178 4261 E2
7100 WasC 48167 4262 A2
Anglin St
13400 DET 48212 4273 A1
17400 DET 48212 4201 A7
18000 DET 48234 4201 A6
Angling St
19100 LVNA 48152 4196 A6
20300 LVNA 48152 4195 E5
20300 LVNA 48336 4195 E5
Angola St
10 BLVL 48111 4578 D2
Angstrom Cres
- Amhg N9V 4671 C4
Anita Av
500 GSPW 48236 4205 A5
1800 GSPW 48236 4204 C4
2200 HRWD 48225 4204 C4
2200 HRWD 48236 4204 C4
Anita Ct
33200 WTLD 48185 4339 A3
Anita Dr
31900 WTLD 48185 4339 A3
Anita St
19600 HRWD 48225 4204 A4
Anmarie Ct
22000 BNTN 48183 4668 C1
Ann St
200 PLYM 48170 4265 A6
800 YPLT 48197 4491 E3
E Ann St
700 AARB 48104 4406 C6
W Ann St
100 AARB 48104 4406 B6
300 AARB 48103 4406 B6
Anna Av
400 YPLT 48197 4491 D4
2900 TNTN 48183 4669 C5
Anna Dr
10 WasC 48189 4259 A2
6200 VNBN 48111 4495 A2
Anna St
17000 SFLD 48075 4198 B1
25100 TYLR 48180 4498 E6
E Annabelle Av
10 HZLP 48030 4200 C1
W Annabelle Av
10 HZLP 48030 4200 C1
Annabelle Ct
9700 GOTp 48178 4188 C2
Annabelle St
1400 FRDL 48220 4200 A1
S Annabelle St
- LNPK 48229 4501 B2
1800 DET 48229 4418 C7
2400 DET 48229 4501 B2
Anna Maria Ct
22200 NOVI 48374 4192 C3
Annandale Ct
1200 PTFD 48108 4573 B3
Annapolis Cir
30000 INKR 48141 4414 E7
Annapolis Cir E
4900 CNTN 48188 4412 C7
4900 CNTN 48188 4495 C1
Annapolis Cir N
40900 CNTN 48188 4412 C7
Annapolis Cir S
40900 CNTN 48188 4495 C1
Annapolis Cir W
5000 CNTN 48188 4412 B7
5100 CNTN 48188 4495 C1
Annapolis Ct
30200 INKR 48141 4414 D7
Annapolis Rd
27400 INKR 48141 4415 A7
27400 WTLD 48186 4415 A7
28900 INKR 48141 4414 E7
28900 INKR 48186 4414 E7
28900 WTLD 48186 4414 E7
Annapolis St
9000 DET 48204 4343 B2
17600 ALPK 48101 4417 A7
17600 DBHT 48101 4417 A7
17600 DBHT 48125 4417 A7
18600 DBHT 48125 4416 E7
24300 DBHT 48125 4415 E7
25600 DBHT 48141 4415 C7
25800 INKR 48141 4415 C7
27000 DBHT 48186 4415 C7
31400 WYNE 48184 4414 B7
34000 WYNE 48184 4413 E7
Annapolis Ter
30100 INKR 48141 4414 D7
Ann Arbor Rd
37400 LVNA 48150 4338 A2
38400 LVNA 48150 4337 E2
Ann Arbor Rd E
39400 PyTp 48170 4337 C2
Ann Arbor Rd W
100 PLYM 48170 4337 A2
100 PyTp 48170 4337 A2
900 PLYM 48170 4336 C2
900 PyTp 48170 4336 C2
10800 SpTp 48170 4335 C3
10800 WasC 48170 4335 C3
48300 PyTp 48170 4335 C3
50400 CNTN 48187 4335 C3
50400 PyTp 48187 4335 C3
50500 CNTN 48170 4335 C3
N Ann Arbor St
10 SALN 48176 4572 C6
500 WasC 48176 4572 C6
S Ann Arbor St
100 SALN 48176 4657 D1
Ann Arbor Tr
20000 DBHT 48127 4341 C5
20000 DBHT 48228 4341 C5
20000 DET 48127 4341 B5
20000 DET 48228 4341 C5
22700 DET 48239 4341 B5
24300 DBHT 48127 4340 D3
27400 WTLD 48185 4340 C3
28600 WTLD 48185 4339 B4
33500 WTLD 48185 4338 D3
33700 LVNA 48185 4338 D3
34000 LVNA 48150 4338 D3
38400 LVNA 48150 4337 E2
E Ann Arbor Tr
100 PLYM 48170 4337 C1
200 PyTp 48170 4337 C1
W Ann Arbor Tr
100 PLYM 48170 4337 A1
1000 PLYM 48170 4336 E1
1300 PyTp 48170 4264 D7
44400 PyTp 48170 4264 D7
45100 PyTp 48170 4336 A2
Ann Arbor Saline Rd
- AARB 48103 4488 E4
- AARB 48108 4488 E4
- AARB 48108 4489 A3
2000 AARB 48103 4489 A3
2000 WasC 48103 4489 A3
2700 PTFD 48103 4488 E4
2700 PTFD 48108 4488 E4
3400 WasC 48103 4488 E4
3600 WasC 48108 4488 E4
4600 WasC 48103 4572 B1
4600 WasC 48108 4572 B1
5000 WasC 48176 4572 B1
6900 SALN 48176 4572 B4
Ann Arbor Trail Ct
35500 LVNA 48150 4338 C2
W Ann Arbor Trail Ct
300 PLYM 48170 4337 A1
Annchester Rd
17100 DET 48219 4269 E1
20200 DET 48219 4197 E5
Anne Av
1700 LNPK 48146 4500 D2
17000 ALPK 48101 4417 A7
17000 ALPK 48101 4500 B1
Anne Ct
44500 PyTp 48170 4336 E3
Anne Wy
6200 DBHT 48127 4341 A5
Annette Av
8400 WynC 48138 4585 C6
Annewood St
32800 FMTN 48336 4195 A4
Annie St
2500 WIND N8T 4422 E2
2500 WIND N8T 4423 A2
Annin St
400 DET 48203 4200 B6
Annland St
6300 DET 48204 4271 D7
Ann Lynn Dr
9700 GOTp 48178 4188 C2
Annott St
17100 DET 48205 4274 D1
17300 DET 48205 4202 C7
Anns Wy
2100 SpTp 48105 4408 B6
Annsbury St
9000 DET 48213 4275 A3
9900 DET 48213 4274 E2
11500 DET 48205 4274 E1
Annwood Ct
100 SALN 48176 4657 D1
Anselm St
5600 DBHT 48127 4341 B6
Anstell St
6400 DET 48213 4274 D4
Antago St
19100 LVNA 48152 4196 A6
Antaya St
100 LSal N9J 4502 D4
Anthon St
5600 DET 48209 4419 D2
Anthony Ct
10 DRBN 48126 4342 E3
4100 WIND N8W 4422 B4
Anthony St
6800 DRBN 48126 4342 E4
15400 RMLS 48174 4581 D5
Anthony Wayne Dr
4700 DET 48201 4345 A3
5000 DET 48202 4345 A2
Antietam Av
2100 DET 48207 4345 E4
2300 DET 48207 4346 A4
Antietam Ct
2700 AARB 48105 4407 B1
43600 CNTN 48188 4411 E4
Antietam Dr
2400 AARB 48105 4407 B2
43600 CNTN 48188 4411 E4
Antique Ct
20800 SFLD 48075 4197 C2
Antique Ln
23100 SFLD 48075 4197 C2
Antique Rd
26800 WDHN 48183 4754 E1
Antler Dr
22100 NOVI 48375 4193 B3
Antoine St
100 WYDT 48192 4501 B7
700 WYDT 48192 4585 A1
2200 WYDT 48192 4584 E1
Antoinette St
10 DET 48202 4345 A2
1700 DET 48210 4344 E2
Antonio Dr
2600 WasC 48167 4190 B7
Antrim Ct
31600 WTLD 48186 4414 C4
Antwerp St
18800 DET 48234 4202 B6
Anvil St
19300 DET 48205 4203 A4
Apache Blvd
26600 FTRK 48134 4754 A1
Apache Tr
6500 WTLD 48185 4338 E5
Appalla Villa Rd
23600 BNTN 48174 4583 A7
Appaloosa Ln
56500 LyTp 48178 4190 A1
Apple Av
10 WasC 48103 4488 B3
Apple Ct
- CNTN 48188 4411 C5
Apple Ln
2900 WIND N8R 4423 B2
Apple St
400 WTLD 48184 4414 C7
400 WTLD 48186 4414 C7
700 AARB 48105 4406 C4
4300 DET 48210 4344 A6
13400 MonC 48117 4753 A6
Apple Wy
16400 RMLS 48174 4582 A5
Apple Blossom Ct
100 WasC 48189 4259 B2
Apple Blossom Ln
19000 NvIT 48167 4191 D7
Applebrooke Dr
50700 NOVI 48167 4191 C4
Appleby Ct
41100 NvIT 48167 4265 C3
Appleby Ln
16000 NvIT 48167 4265 C3
Apple Creek Dr
42400 PyTp 48170 4337 A3
Apple Crest Ct
13500 PyTp 48170 4263 E7
Apple Crest Dr
9200 WasC 48176 4658 A3
Applecrest Dr
24600 NOVI 48375 4193 A1
Apple Grove Ct
11100 GOTp 48178 4188 B5
Applegrove St
10 ECRS 48229 4501 D4
Apple Grove Wy
30100 FTRK 48173 4754 A5
30200 FTRK 48173 4753 E5
Apple Hill Dr
6800 YpTp 48197 4575 B5
Apple Ridge Dr
6200 WasC 48170 4262 C7
Appleridge Dr
2300 PTFD 48103 4488 D4
Appleridge St
2700 YpTp 48198 4493 B2
Appleton
8800 RDFD 48127 4341 A2
9800 RDFD 48239 4341 A1
11600 RDFD 48239 4269 A7
Appleton St
7900 DBHT 48127 4341 A3
12600 DET 48223 4269 A6
19200 DET 48219 4197 A6
Appletree Cres
12000 Tcmh N8N 4423 E1
Appletree Dr
11700 PyTp 48170 4336 D1
12200 PyTp 48170 4264 D7
Appleview Ct
9100 HbgT 48116 4186 A1
Appleway
2600 AARB 48104 4407 A7
Applewood
18900 NvIT 48167 4192 C7
28900 HnTp 48134 4752 E4
Applewood Av
1200 LNPK 48146 4501 B4
Applewood Ct
2200 AARB 48103 4406 A2

Detroit & Wayne County Street Index

STREET
Block City ZIP Map# Grid

Applewood Dr
5100 YpTp 48197 4576 B1
Applewood Ln
15500 SOGT 48195 4584 A4
Applewood Rd
43100 CNTN 48188 4412 A5
43400 CNTN 48188 4411 E5
Appoline St
5600 DRBN 48126 4343 B5
8000 DET 48228 4343 A2
9500 DET 48227 4343 A1
13500 DET 48227 4271 A5
17100 DET 48235 4271 A1
18000 DET 48235 4199 A7
Appomattox Ct
43600 CNTN 48188 4412 A4
Apricot Ln
10 WasC 48103 4488 B4
April Dr
10 WasC 48103 4405 A5
Aqua Ln
8600 YpTp 48197 4576 C1
10600 GOTp 48178 4188 D4
Aqueduct Ct
19600 NvlT 48167 4193 C6
Arbana Dr
100 AARB 48103 4406 A5
Arbor
28800 HnTp 48134 4752 E3
Arbor Cir
- PTFD 48197 4490 E2
Arbor Cir E
2000 PTFD 48197 4490 E2
Arbor Cir W
- PTFD 48197 4491 A2
2000 PTFD 48197 4490 E2
Arbor Ct
9300 PyTp 48170 4336 A2
27900 RMLS 48174 4582 B4
30100 INKR 48141 4414 D4
Arbor Dr
600 YPLT 48197 4491 D6
Arbor Ln
10 WynC 48111 4664 A3
21700 NOVI 48375 4193 C4
21900 FNHL 48336 4195 E3
Arbor Pl
15500 SFLD 48075 4198 C1
15500 SFLD 48237 4198 C1
E Arbor Rd
2500 WasC 48103 4488 D4
W Arbor Rd
2500 WasC 48103 4488 C4
Arbor St
700 AARB 48104 4406 C7
Arbor Tr
47400 NvlT 48167 4264 A2
Arbor Wy
10 LyTp 48167 4189 E5
Arbordale Dr
900 AARB 48103 4405 E7
Arboretum Cir
46600 PyTp 48170 4336 B3
Arboretum Ct
300 SALN 48176 4657 E2
Arboretum Dr
700 SALN 48176 4657 E2
Arbor Leah Dr
- PTFD 48197 4574 D2
Arbor Meadow Ln
5300 WasC 48103 4487 C1
Arbor Meadows Dr
10 PTFD 48197 4574 D2
Arbor Valley Dr
5000 SpTp 48105 4333 A7
Arborview Blvd
1000 AARB 48103 4406 A5
1300 AARB 48103 4405 E5
Arbor View Ln
- VNBN 48111 4495 A5
Arborway Rd
27200 SFLD 48034 4196 A3
Arbor Woods Blvd
1900 SpTp 48198 4409 E6
Arbor Woods Dr
37500 LVNA 48150 4338 A2
N Arbor Wy Dr
- CNTN 48188 4411 E4
2000 CNTN 48188 4412 B5
W Arbor Wy Dr
43400 CNTN 48188 4412 A4
Arbour St
11900 Tcmh N8N 4423 E2
12300 Tcmh N8N 4424 A2
Arcade St
200 YPLT 48197 4492 A3
Arcadia Ct
8900 VNBN 48111 4495 B5
Arcadia Dr
- CNTN 48188 4412 D4
26600 FTRK 48134 4753 C2
Arcadia St
1200 WIND N9B 4420 E5
8700 DET 48204 4344 A2
Arch St
700 AARB 48104 4406 C7
1000 WYDT 48192 4585 B4
Archdale St
8800 DET 48228 4342 B2
9500 DET 48227 4342 B1
15000 DET 48227 4270 B3
18000 DET 48235 4270 B1
19900 DET 48235 4198 A5
Archer St
20200 DET 48219 4197 A5
Archwood Cir
21300 FNHL 48336 4195 C4
Archwood Dr
- WasC 48103 4405 C4
500 AARB 48103 4405 C4
E Archwood Dr
41400 VNBN 48111 4495 C7
W Archwood Dr
41400 VNBN 48111 4495 C7
Arcola Av
100 GDNC 48135 4415 B1
100 GDNC 48141 4415 B1
6400 GDNC 48135 4340 B5
Arcola St
100 INKR 48141 4415 B2
7000 DET 48234 4274 A3
7200 WTLD 48185 4340 B4
9500 LVNA 48150 4340 B1
12000 LVNA 48150 4268 B7
14700 LVNA 48154 4268 A4
Arden St
9600 LVNA 48150 4339 B1
14500 LVNA 48154 4267 B4
Arden Glen Ct
22500 NOVI 48374 4192 B3
Ardenne Dr
2100 AARB 48105 4407 B2
Ardennes Dr
- CNTN 48188 4412 A3
Arden Park Blvd
10 DET 48202 4272 E5
300 DET 48202 4273 A5
Ardis Dr
- YpTp 48197 4491 C6
Ardith Ct
10 RKWD 48173 4840 C1
Ardith St
- YpTp 48198 4492 C6
Ardmoor Av
1200 AARB 48103 4488 E1
Ardmoor Dr
8400 SpTp 48198 4409 C7
Ardmore Ct
9800 WasC 48167 4190 B6
Ardmore Dr
100 FRDL 48220 4199 E3
100 FRDL 48220 4200 A3
Ardmore Rd
1800 TNTN 48183 4669 D3
Ardmore St
700 DBHT 48127 4415 C1
12600 DET 48227 4270 E6
17100 DET 48235 4270 E1
18900 DET 48235 4198 E6
44000 CNTN 48188 4411 E4
Ardmore Park Cir
6200 DBHT 48127 4340 C6
Ardsley Ct
6600 CNTN 48187 4337 B6
Ardsley Dr
6700 CNTN 48187 4337 A5
Arella Blvd
1100 AARB 48103 4488 E1
Arena Dr
42400 NOVI 48375 4192 E2
42400 NOVI 48375 4193 A2
Arenac Ct
31700 WTLD 48186 4414 C4
Argent St
700 Tcmh N8N 4424 A1
Argo Dr
400 AARB 48105 4406 C4
Argonne Av
24500 BNTN 48134 4667 E6
Argonne Blvd
5000 TNTN 48183 4669 C7
Argonne Ct
43500 CNTN 48188 4412 A4
Argonne Dr
2700 AARB 48105 4407 A1
Argus
22400 DET 48219 4269 B1
Argus St
1500 LSal N9J 4503 B4
Argyle Cir
42500 CNTN 48187 4337 B4
Argyle Cres
- DET 48203 4200 A5
1400 AARB 48103 4405 E4
19300 DET 48203 4199 E6
Argyle Ct
2000 WIND N8Y 4421 C2
Argyle Rd
400 WIND N8Y 4346 C7
1100 WIND N8Y 4421 C1
Argyle St
5600 DRBN 48126 4342 E6
12700 SOGT 48195 4584 D2
23000 NOVI 48374 4192 A2
Ariel Ct
9300 GOTp 48116 4186 E1
Ariel St
24000 SFLD 48075 4198 C1
Aristotle Cres
3800 WIND N9G 4505 A3
Aristotle Ct
3800 WIND N9G 4505 A3
Arizona
10 WynC 48111 4662 D2
E Arizona
10 WynC 48111 4662 E2
Arizona St
31400 LVNA 48150 4339 B2
Arizona St E
10 DET 48203 4272 C1
Arizona St W
10 DET 48203 4272 C1
Arkadia Dr
6100 WasC 48170 4263 B7
Arkona Rd
42900 WynC 48164 4750 A3
43400 WynC 48111 4749 E3
43400 WynC 48111 4750 A3
43400 WynC 48164 4749 E3
48400 WynC 48111 4748 D3
Arleen Ct
18800 LVNA 48152 4195 D7
Arlene Ct
6800 RMLS 48174 4496 C3
Arlene Ln
13500 VNBN 48111 4578 E3
Arlene St
1900 AARB 48103 4405 D5
Arlington Av
1200 LNPK 48146 4501 E4
1700 LNPK 48146 4500 D2
14500 ALPK 48101 4500 C1
17000 ALPK 48101 4417 A7
Arlington Blvd
100 Tcmh N8N 4349 D7
100 Tcmh N8N 4424 C2
700 AARB 48104 4407 A7
1100 AARB 48104 4490 A1
Arlington Cir
9000 GOTp 48178 4188 B3
Arlington Ct
9000 YpTp 48197 4576 D3
19300 WDHN 48183 4669 A7
Arlington Dr
9000 SpTp 48198 4409 D7
19000 WDHN 48183 4669 A7
Arlington Rd
- AARB 48104 4490 B2
42800 CNTN 48187 4337 A4
43900 CNTN 48187 4336 E4
Arlington St
100 INKR 48141 4415 B2
13400 DET 48212 4273 A1
17400 DET 48212 4201 A7
22700 DRBN 48128 4416 B1
Armada Ct
33100 WTLD 48186 4414 A5
Armanda St
1300 WIND N9C 4503 B1
Armitage Dr
200 CNTN 48188 4411 A3
Armour St
8900 DET 48213 4274 C4
Armstrong Av
2500 WIND N8T 4422 C3
22200 BNTN 48192 4583 B7
Armstrong Ct
600 YPLT 48197 4491 E6
Armstrong Dr
500 YPLT 48197 4491 E6
Armstrong Ln
39100 WTLD 48185 4337 E3
Armstrong Rd
10000 BrTp 48179 4839 E6
11000 BrTp 48166 4839 D4
12000 BrTp 48117 4839 E1
13000 BrTp 48117 4753 E7
13000 BrTp 48134 4753 E7
13000 BrTp 48179 4753 E7
Army St
7000 DET 48209 4419 B3
Arndt St
2600 DET 48207 4346 A3
Arnet St
100 YPLT 48198 4492 B5
Arno Av
7300 ALPK 48101 4500 A2
Arnold Av
9500 RDFD 48239 4340 D1
13900 RDFD 48239 4268 D5
Arnold St
- DET 48210 4343 D6
8000 DBHT 48127 4340 D3
8500 DBHT 48239 4340 D3
33400 FNHL 48335 4194 E4
Arnscliffe Ct
9200 WIND N8S 4348 A7
Arnscliffe Pl
1200 WIND N8S 4348 A7
Aronomink
- NvlT 48167 4264 B2
Arras Av
1900 WIND N8W 4421 D4
Arrow Dr
800 SLYN 48178 4189 D1
Arrowhead Ct
12000 PyTp 48170 4336 D1
Arrowhead Dr
4600 AATp 48105 4407 E3
11100 GOTp 48178 4188 E4
Arrowhead St
33600 WTLD 48185 4338 E5
33600 WTLD 48185 4339 A5
Arrowwood Tr
2300 AARB 48105 4406 D2
2300 AATp 48105 4406 D2
Arroyo Dr
1300 YpTp 48197 4491 B7
Arselot Dr
18200 NvlT 48167 4264 C1
Arsenal Rd
23000 BNTN 48134 4667 D6
25600 BNTN 48134 4753 D1
26000 FTRK 48134 4753 D2
Artesian St
- DET 48126 4342 A5
- DET 48128 4342 A5
- DRBN 48126 4342 A5
- DRBN 48128 4342 A5
5600 DET 48228 4342 A5
12600 DET 48223 4270 A6
13500 DET 48223 4269 E4
Arthur Av
8400 AGST 48197 4660 B1
19600 GSPW 48236 4204 B6
19600 HRWD 48236 4204 B6
19700 HRWD 48225 4204 B6
Arthur Ct
23100 STCS 48080 4204 E2
Arthur Rd
800 WIND N8Y 4347 A7
1300 WIND N8Y 4422 A1
1800 WIND N8W 4422 B3
Arthur St
100 PLYM 48170 4264 E6
1500 YpTp 48198 4492 C7
6200 WTLD 48185 4338 D6
9800 LVNA 48150 4338 C1
10500 VNBN 48111 4495 B6
14600 DRBN 48126 4342 D5
Artley St
4400 CNTN 48188 4411 E7
Arundel St
34400 FMTN 48335 4194 D2
Arva Ct
10000 GOTp 48178 4188 D2
Arvilla Dr
3500 WasC 48189 4258 A4
Arvilla Ln
100 WasC 48189 4258 A4
Arvilla St
11400 WIND N8P 4348 D7
Asa Gray Dr
200 AARB 48105 4407 B5
Asbury Pk
8800 DET 48228 4342 C2
9500 DET 48227 4342 C1
15300 DET 48227 4270 B3
16100 DET 48235 4270 B3
18200 DET 48235 4198 B7
Ascension Av
20700 WRRN 48089 4202 A3
Ascot Ct
4600 WIND N9G 4504 E5
Ascot Dr
9000 SpTp 48198 4409 D7
Ascot Rd
43800 CNTN 48187 4336 E3
Ascot St
2000 AARB 48103 4489 A3
Asgard Rd
9600 WIND N8R 4423 B2
Ash
- CNTN 48188 4411 C6
Ash Av
15600 EPTE 48021 4203 C2
18200 EPTE 48021 4204 A2
Ash Ct
200 SLYN 48178 4189 C1
4600 PTFD 48197 4574 E2
22700 TYLR 48180 4583 C2
49500 PyTp 48170 4335 D2
Ash Dr
10 VNBN 48111 4577 E6
10 VNBN 48111 4578 A6
10 WasC 48189 4259 A1
Ash Rd
33400 HnTp 48164 4752 A2
35000 HnTp 48164 4751 D2
Ash St
700 WTLD 48186 4414 C7
1400 DET 48201 4345 A5
1700 WYDT 48192 4585 A2
2000 DET 48210 4345 A5
2000 DET 48216 4345 A5
2900 INKR 48141 4415 A5
3400 DET 48210 4344 D6
3400 DET 48216 4344 D6
17600 DRBN 48101 4417 A5
17600 DRBN 48124 4417 A5
18800 DRBN 48124 4416 E5
34500 WYNE 48184 4413 D5
Ashberry Pl
1200 LSal N9H 4504 C5
Ashburnam Rd
3400 AARB 48105 4332 C7
3400 AARB 48105 4407 C1
Ashbury Dr
42200 CNTN 48187 4337 B6
42800 NOVI 48375 4193 A5
43000 NOVI 48375 4192 E5
48800 VNBN 48111 4493 E2
Ashby Dr
2200 TNTN 48183 4669 C3
Ashby Ln
10 DRBN 48120 4417 D2
Ashby St
1400 WTLD 48186 4414 A3
Ashfield Cres
4300 WIND N9G 4504 B4
Ashford Cir
45800 NOVI 48374 4192 B2
Ashford Dr S
47400 CNTN 48188 4411 A4
N Ashford Wy
4600 PTFD 48197 4575 A2
S Ashford Wy
5600 PTFD 48197 4574 E2
5800 PTFD 48197 4575 A3
Ashland Dr
9300 WIND N8R 4423 B3
Ashland St
10 DET 48214 4348 A2
300 DET 48214 4347 E1
1000 DET 48214 4275 D6
Ashley Blvd
- NOVI 48374 4192 A1
Ashley Ct
200 YpTp 48197 4577 B5
10800 AGST 48191 4577 C7
19600 LVNA 48152 4194 B6
42500 CNTN 48187 4337 B4
47000 CNTN 48187 4336 B5
Ashley Dr
- BNTN 48134 4668 A5
1800 SpTp 48198 4409 D7
Ashley St
- GSPF 48236 4276 B1
4900 DET 48236 4276 B1
5400 DET 48224 4276 B1
22500 FNHL 48336 4195 C2
26500 DBHT 48127 4340 C5
N Ashley St
100 AARB 48104 4406 B5
300 AARB 48103 4406 B5
S Ashley St
100 AARB 48104 4406 B7
400 AARB 48103 4406 B7
Ashover Ct
36900 FNHL 48335 4194 B3
Ashover Dr
36700 FNHL 48335 4194 B3
Ashton Av
6000 DET 48228 4342 A5
11600 DET 48228 4270 A7
16100 DET 48219 4270 A2
19900 DET 48219 4198 A5
Ashton Ct
8500 SpTp 48198 4492 C1
Ashton Rd
14300 DET 48223 4270 A5
Ashtonbury Ct
26500 FTRK 48134 4753 D1
Ashurst St
13500 LVNA 48150 4266 E6
15300 LVNA 48154 4266 D4
Ashwood Dr
47900 PyTp 48170 4264 A6
Askin Av
300 WIND N9B 4420 B2
2500 WIND N9E 4420 E7
2500 WIND N9E 4503 E1
3400 WIND N9E 4504 A2
Aspen Blvd
28000 FTRK 48134 4754 A3
28200 FTRK 48134 4753 E3
Aspen Ct
2700 WasC 48108 4488 D7
3900 TNTN 48183 4669 B6
11000 GOTp 48178 4188 B5
21700 FNHL 48335 4194 A4
Aspen Dr
11300 PyTp 48170 4337 D1
15500 RMLS 48174 4580 A5
18800 LVNA 48152 4194 D7
29100 FTRK 48134 4753 E4
36800 FNHL 48335 4194 A4
Aspen Ln
100 VNBN 48111 4494 D5
9700 SpTp 48198 4409 E7
10000 WIND N8R 4423 C4
Aspen Rd
2600 WasC 48108 4488 C7
2700 WasC 48108 4572 C1
Aspen St
41700 NOVI 48375 4193 B2
Aspen Tr
18200 BNTN 48174 4582 C7
Aspen Wy
100 SLYN 48178 4189 C2
16600 SOGT 48195 4584 A5
Aspen Ridge Dr
- NvlT 48167 4264 D2
2600 PTFD 48103 4488 D3
Aspen Valley Dr
16200 NvlT 48167 4264 D3
Assembly St
51100 VNBN 48111 4577 C4
Assumption St
500 WIND N9A 4421 A1
1500 WIND N9A 4346 B7
1600 WIND N8Y 4346 B7
Aster Av
14800 ALPK 48101 4500 A3
Aston St
12000 RMLS 48174 4580 B1
Astor Cres
2000 Tcmh N0R 4505 B5
Astor Ct
9500 WasC 48167 4190 B6
21400 WynC 48138 4670 B3
Astor Dr
1200 AARB 48104 4489 C2
Astor Pl
100 BLVL 48111 4578 D4
Astor St
8900 DET 48213 4274 B4
30600 FNHL 48336 4195 C3
30800 FMTN 48336 4195 B3
Astoria Blvd
2400 CNTN 48188 4411 A5
Astrid Ln
23200 RKWD 48173 4754 B6
Athens St
6400 DET 48213 4274 E4
Athlone Dr
7200 HbgT 48116 4186 B2
Atkinson St
10 DET 48202 4272 E6
500 WIND N8X 4421 C6
1400 DET 48206 4272 C7
3400 DET 48206 4344 A1
Atlanta St
9100 DET 48213 4274 D4
Atlantic Av
100 Amhg N9V 4757 D3
20700 WRRN 48091 4201 C3
Atlantic Ct
10 Amhg N9V 4757 D3
Atlantic Pointe
22000 FNHL 48336 4195 C3
Atlas St
35200 RMLS 48174 4496 D3
Atterberry Ct
2900 AARB 48103 4405 C6
Atterberry Dr
2800 AARB 48103 4405 C6
Atwater St
10 DET 48226 4345 D7
500 DET 48207 4345 D7
1300 DET 48207 4346 A6
10600 WIND N8R 4423 C2
26200 FTRK 48134 4753 C3
Atwood Dr
- WYNE 48184 4414 A7
9800 GOTp 48178 4188 D2
Atwood St
10 TNTN 48183 4670 A4
300 TNTN 48183 4669 E4
Aubin Rd
1100 WIND N8Y 4346 E7
1200 WIND N8Y 4421 E1
1500 WIND N8Y 4422 A2
1800 WIND N8W 4422 A2
Aubrey
14800 RDFD 48239 4268 D4
Auburn St
100 INKR 48141 4415 C2
200 PLYM 48170 4264 E6
5600 DET 48228 4341 E5
11600 DET 48228 4269 E7
14800 DET 48223 4269 E4
24800 DRBN 48124 4415 E2
E Auburn St
10 ECRS 48229 4501 E2
W Auburn St
10 ECRS 48229 4501 D2
Auburndale Av
800 YpTp 48198 4492 C5
Auburndale Ct
14400 LVNA 48154 4267 B5
Auburndale St
- DET 48238 4272 C4
- HDPK 48238 4272 C4
10 HDPK 48203 4272 C4
9600 LVNA 48150 4339 B1
15300 LVNA 48154 4267 B3
19100 LVNA 48152 4195 B7
Audette St
18000 DRBN 48124 4417 A6
22700 DRBN 48124 4416 B4
Auditorium Dr
- DET 48226 4345 D7
Audobon St
200 SLYN 48178 4189 C3
Audrey Av
23000 WRRN 48091 4201 C1
Audrey Ln
24700 SFLD 48075 4197 D1
Audrey St
20100 DET 48235 4198 C5
21500 DRBN 48124 4416 D3
Audubon Dr
2000 WasC 48103 4489 A2
Audubon Rd
1000 GPPK 48230 4276 A6
3400 DET 48224 4276 A4
3400 DET 48230 4276 A4
9000 DET 48224 4275 D2
August Av
8000 WTLD 48185 4339 D3
8600 WTLD 48150 4339 D3
August St
12600 DET 48205 4274 E1
13100 DET 48205 4275 A1
Augusta Ct
4400 PTFD 48108 4488 D7
19100 LVNA 48152 4194 B7
32700 RMLS 48174 4497 B1
Augusta Dr
19100 LVNA 48152 4194 B7
45400 CNTN 48188 4411 C3
Augusta St
8700 AGST 48191 4662 A2
Augusta Woods Blvd
- AGST 48191 4577 C7
Aurora Av
16100 EPTE 48021 4203 C1
Aurora Dr
3200 WIND N8R 4423 B4
Aurora St
2700 AARB 48105 4407 A2
10000 DET 48204 4271 B7
Ausable Pl
300 AARB 48104 4407 A6
Austen Dr
2900 WIND N8T 4422 C4
Austin Av
1000 LNPK 48146 4501 A3
1000 LNPK 48229 4501 A3
1800 AARB 48104 4489 E1
Austin Dr
700 SALN 48176 4657 B1
24700 HnTp 48164 4665 C7
Austin Rd
- VNBN 48111 4493 D2
3500 SALN 48176 4657 A1
3500 WasC 48176 4657 A1
3800 WasC 48176 4656 D1
Austin St
2600 DET 48216 4345 A7
Austrian Wy
10100 OKPK 48237 4199 B1
Auto Club Dr
- DRBN 48126 4342 A7
Auto Mall Dr
500 WasC 48103 4405 A5
Automobile Blvd
21700 WRRN 48089 4202 A2
24000 CTNL 48015 4202 A1
Autry St
33900 LVNA 48150 4266 E6
Autumn Ct
10 WIND N9E 4504 A3
Autumn Dr
4600 WasC 48178 4260 E2
Autumn Ln
3300 SpTp 48105 4408 B1
16800 SOGT 48195 4584 A4
Autumn Tr
11700 GOTp 48178 4188 C6
Autumn Hill Dr
- WasC 48103 4405 C3
Autumn Park Blvd
22400 NOVI 48374 4192 B3
Autumn Park Ct
47200 NOVI 48374 4192 A3
Autumn Ridge Av
300 Amhg N9V 4757 C5
Autumn Ridge Dr
600 WTLD 48185 4412 E1
19200 NvlT 48167 4192 B7
55200 LyTp 48167 4190 C5
Avalon Pl
2200 AARB 48104 4406 E7
Avalon St
200 HDPK 48203 4272 C4
19500 STCS 48080 4204 B2
24100 TYLR 48180 4499 A1
25000 TYLR 48180 4498 E1
35000 RMLS 48174 4496 D1
Avedon Ln
9000 WasC 48176 4658 D2
Aveline Av
100 YpTp 48197 4491 D5
Ave Maria
4000 AATp 48105 4407 D1
Averhill Ct
13100 DET 48214 4347 D2
Averhill St
22100 FNHL 48336 4195 E3
Avery Ln
9500 WIND N8R 4423 B4
Avery St
3800 DET 48210 4345 A4
5900 DET 48210 4344 E2
Avis Dr
500 PTFD 48108 4573 C1
Avis St
10 YpTp 48198 4492 E3
8700 DET 48209 4418 E3
Avium Ln
200 CNTN 48187 4412 D2
Avon Av
17500 DET 48219 4270 A1
18200 DET 48219 4198 A7
Avon Ct
800 GSPW 48236 4204 E4
3800 WasC 48105 4332 D2
3800 WIND N9G 4504 B3
8500 SpTp 48198 4492 C1
24900 NOVI 48374 4192 C1
30300 WTLD 48185 4339 D4
Avon Ln
3800 WasC 48105 4332 C2
20700 SFLD 48075 4197 E4
22300 SFLD 48075 4198 A3
Avon Pl
30300 WTLD 48185 4339 D4
Avon Rd
700 AARB 48104 4406 E7
15500 DET 48223 4270 A3
15900 DET 48219 4270 A3
21800 OKPK 48237 4198 C2
43000 CNTN 48187 4337 A7
Avon St
31400 WYNE 48184 4414 B6
Avondale Av
1400 AARB 48103 4488 E2
11600 WRRN 48089 4202 C1
E Avondale Cir
- SpTp 48198 4410 A7
W Avondale Cir
- SpTp 48198 4410 A7
Avondale Dr
3000 WIND N9E 4421 B7
3000 WIND N9E 4504 B1
Avondale St
- DET 48214 4348 A1
- GPPK 48230 4348 A1
12500 DET 48214 4347 D2
25200 DRBN 48124 4415 E3
25400 DBHT 48125 4415 B3
25800 INKR 48141 4415 A3
28900 INKR 48141 4414 E3
30400 WTLD 48186 4414 B3
33600 WTLD 48186 4413 D3
38900 WTLD 48186 4412 E3
Awixa Rd
300 AARB 48104 4406 E6
Aylebury Dr
9900 GOTp 48178 4188 E2
Aylmer Av
200 WIND N9A 4421 A1
Ayres Av
46600 VNBN 48111 4494 B6
Ayrshire Dr
2100 AATp 48105 4407 D2
41400 CNTN 48188 4412 B3
Azalea Cir
21800 WynC 48138 4670 B3
Azalea Ct
17100 BwTp 48173 4755 A6
Azalea Dr
4600 PTFD 48197 4490 E6
4600 PTFD 48197 4491 A6
17900 BwTp 48173 4755 A6
Azalea Pl
4900 WYNE 48184 4414 B7
Azalia Cres
1300 WIND N8W 4421 E7
Azar Av
4700 WIND N8T 4422 C5
Aziz Dr
1200 CNTN 48188 4412 D3

INDEX 7

E Aztec Cir — Detroit & Wayne County Street Index — Beechcrest Dr

STREET
Block City ZIP Map# Grid

E Aztec Cir
26200 FTRK 48134 4753 E1
N Aztec Cir
25200 FTRK 48134 4753 E1
S Aztec Cir
25000 FTRK 48134 4753 E1
W Aztec Cir
26100 FTRK 48134 4753 E1
Aztec Dr
34000 WTLD 48185 4338 E6

B

B Av
- WasC 48176 4659 B1
- WasC 48197 4659 B1
B Dr
14100 PyTp 48170 4263 D6
B Rd
- DRBN 48120 4418 C3
B St
- FNHL 48336 4195 D2
- MVDL 48122 4417 E7
10 DBHT 48125 4416 E6
Babbitt St
100 YPLT 48198 4492 A4
Baby St
3400 WIND N9C 4420 A4
Bach Av
20700 WRRN 48091 4201 B4
Bach St
22000 WRRN 48091 4201 B2
Backus St
12700 SOGT 48195 4584 D2
Bacon St
7800 DET 48209 4419 B4
Badelt St
29000 WTLD 48185 4339 E4
Badger St
8000 DET 48213 4274 B4
25800 BNTN 48134 4667 D7
Bagley Av
500 YpTp 48198 4492 C3
5700 LSal N9H 4503 D4
Bagley St
1200 DET 48226 4345 C6
1400 DET 48216 4345 A7
3300 DET 48216 4344 D7
4100 DET 48209 4419 D1
Bagnoli Ct
17500 BNTN 48174 4583 B6
Bagnoli St
17600 BNTN 48174 4583 B6
Bailey Av
1600 YpTp 48198 4492 D3
2600 LNPK 48146 4500 C4
3100 ALPK 48101 4500 C4
3100 ALPK 48146 4500 C4
Bailey Rd
17400 BNTN 48174 4583 A6
Bailey St
1800 DRBN 48124 4415 E4
3900 DBHT 48125 4415 E6
7900 TYLR 48180 4498 E3
14200 TYLR 48180 4583 A3
Baillargeon Dr
12000 Tcmh N8N 4423 E1
Bainbridge Av
18200 LVNA 48152 4267 C1
19100 LVNA 48152 4195 C6
Bainbridge St
14500 LVNA 48154 4267 C4
Baintree Cir
41800 NvlT 48167 4265 B2
Baits Dr
- AARB 48105 4406 D4
Bak Rd
15400 VNBN 48111 4578 C6
Baker
- FTRK 48134 4754 A4
Baker Cres
- Amhg N9V 4671 B5
Baker Dr
- WTLD 48185 4338 B3
Baker Ln
10 GSPF 48236 4276 E4
Baker St
5600 DET 48209 4419 C1
23300 TYLR 48180 4499 B5
25000 TYLR 48180 4498 D5
47200 NOVI 48374 4192 A2
Bakewell St
34900 WTLD 48185 4338 D5
Balaclava St N
10 Amhg N9V 4757 C1
Balaclava St S
10 Amhg N9V 4757 C2
Balboa Rd
46800 CNTN 48187 4336 C4
Balcombe
22800 NOVI 48375 4193 B3
Balden
18900 NvlT 48167 4192 A7
18900 NvlT 48167 4264 A1
Baldwin Av
900 AARB 48104 4406 D7
1400 AARB 48104 4489 D1
5500 WIND N8T 4422 D3
Baldwin Ct
1800 TNTN 48183 4669 D3
45500 CNTN 48187 4336 C6
47500 NOVI 48374 4192 A3
Baldwin Dr
1700 TNTN 48183 4669 D3
Baldwin Pl
1700 AARB 48104 4489 D1
Baldwin St
1000 DET 48214 4346 C3
4400 DET 48214 4274 B7
5000 DET 48213 4274 B7
Baldwin St
25600 DBHT 48127 4340 D6
Balfour
- CNTN 48187 4411 B1
Balfour Av
5800 ALPK 48125 4499 E1
6300 ALPK 48101 4499 E1
10000 ALPK 48101 4500 A5
10800 ALPK 48195 4500 A6
Balfour Blvd
1600 WIND N8T 4422 C1
Balfour Rd
3400 DET 48224 4275 D3
3400 DET 48230 4275 D3
11100 DET 48224 4203 E7
Balfour St
- HRWD 48225 4203 E6
600 GPPK 48230 4348 A1
1000 GPPK 48230 4276 A6
1100 GPPK 48230 4275 E5
20400 HRWD 48225 4204 A4
25000 WDHN 48183 4668 B7
Ball Rd
6400 RMLS 48174 4497 C2
Ball St
8800 PyTp 48170 4337 A3
8800 PyTp 48187 4337 A3
Ballantyne Ct E
20000 GSPW 48236 4204 D7
Ballantyne Ct W
20000 GSPW 48236 4204 D7
Ballantyne Rd
400 GSPS 48236 4276 E1
500 GSPS 48236 4204 E7
700 GSPS 48236 4205 A6
Ballard St
10 YPLT 48197 4491 E4
12500 Tcmh N8N 4424 A1
Balmoral Av
900 DET 48203 4200 B6
Balmoral Ct
2600 AARB 48103 4405 E1
6200 WTLD 48185 4339 A6
31800 LVNA 48154 4267 B2
Balmoral Dr
1200 DET 48203 4200 A6
7200 CNTN 48187 4337 A5
21900 WynC 48138 4670 B4
31700 LVNA 48154 4267 B2
Balmoral St
2300 WIND N9E 4503 E2
14200 RVVW 48192 4669 D2
28400 GDNC 48135 4340 A6
29400 GDNC 48135 4339 D6
33400 WTLD 48185 4339 A6
Balsam Ct
24600 BNTN 48134 4668 A4
Balsam Dr
- BNTN 48134 4668 A4
24900 BNTN 48134 4667 E4
Balsam St
14500 SOGT 48195 4584 C3
Baltic Av
10 Amhg N9V 4757 D3
Baltimore St E
10 DET 48202 4345 A1
Baltimore St W
10 DET 48202 4345 A1
1100 DET 48202 4344 E2
Baltree Ct
20000 GSPW 48236 4204 C6
Banbury Ct
35200 LVNA 48152 4266 D1
41900 NvlT 48167 4265 B2
Banbury Rd
35100 LVNA 48152 4266 C1
41800 NvlT 48167 4265 B2
Bancroft Av
- WTLD 48186 4414 A5
Bancroft Ct
7400 CNTN 48187 4337 B4
Bancroft Dr
1900 PTFD 48108 4488 E5
Bandera Dr
1000 WasC 48103 4404 C7
1000 WasC 48103 4487 C1
Banff St
- WIND N8P 4348 D7
Bangor Ct
- DET 48216 4344 C6
Bangor St
3700 DET 48216 4344 C5
5300 DET 48210 4344 C5
Bank St
7800 DET 48209 4419 A3
N Bankle Ct
6100 DBHT 48127 4340 D6
S Bankle Ct
6000 DBHT 48127 4340 D6
Banneker Ct
12300 DET 48213 4275 A5
Banner Av
19000 BNTN 48174 4668 A1
Banner St
2100 DRBN 48124 4416 A4
3900 DBHT 48125 4416 A6
5700 DBHT 48125 4499 B2
9200 TYLR 48180 4499 A5
14200 TYLR 48180 4583 A1
Bannister St
2500 WTLD 48186 4414 A6
Bannock Ct
600 SALN 48176 4572 B7
Bannockburn Dr
43500 CNTN 48187 4336 E6
43500 CNTN 48187 4337 A6
Banwell Rd
500 WIND N8P 4348 C6
1400 Tcmh N8N 4423 D1
1400 Tcmh N8R 4423 D1
Banwell Rd
1400 WIND N8R 4423 D1
2300 WIND N8P 4423 D1
2700 WIND N8N 4423 D1
Banwell Rd CO-17
1800 Tcmh N8N 4423 D4
Baraga St
10000 TYLR 48180 4499 D6
Barbara
26300 RDFD 48239 4268 C6
Barbara Av
5200 TNTN 48183 4669 C7
5300 TNTN 48183 4755 C1
Barbara Ct
27200 TYLR 48180 4582 B5
Barbara Ln
6100 WasC 48170 4262 D7
11100 GOTp 48178 4187 E3
28200 WynC 48138 4756 A3
Barbara St
600 WTLD 48185 4413 B1
5000 DET 48202 4345 C2
14000 LVNA 48154 4266 D5
22400 DET 48223 4269 B5
Barbara Fritchie St
24700 SFLD 48075 4197 D2
Barber Av
300 WasC 48103 4405 C5
500 AARB 48103 4405 C4
Barber Ct
18100 BNTN 48192 4583 C6
Barber St
3500 WYNE 48184 4414 C6
Barberry St
12000 SOGT 48195 4500 E7
12200 SOGT 48195 4584 E3
Barchester Rd
42200 CNTN 48187 4337 B6
Barchester St
300 WTLD 48186 4412 E3
Barclay Ct
10 DRBN 48126 4417 D1
700 AARB 48105 4407 C5
1800 CNTN 48188 4412 A4
22000 NOVI 48374 4192 A4
22400 STCS 48080 4205 A3
Barclay Dr
7900 WasC 48167 4190 B6
22300 NOVI 48374 4192 A4
Barclay Rd
400 GSPF 48236 4204 C7
400 GSPF 48236 4276 C1
Barclay St
13800 DRBN 48126 4417 E1
13800 DRBN 48126 4418 D1
Barclay Wy
2600 AATp 48105 4332 B7
43400 CNTN 48188 4412 A4
Bardstown Tr
1000 AARB 48105 4407 C4
Barfield St
23300 FNHL 48336 4195 D1
Barham St
6000 DET 48224 4275 C3
Barker Rd
10 WasC 48189 4187 A7
100 WasC 48189 4186 E7
Barker St
9300 DET 48213 4274 C6
Barkley St
9800 VNBN 48111 4495 C6
27500 LVNA 48154 4268 A5
29000 LVNA 48154 4267 E5
35900 LVNA 48154 4266 C5
Barkridge Cir
- WTLD 48185 4413 B1
Barkridge Cir N
37400 WTLD 48185 4413 A1
Barkridge Cir S
37400 WTLD 48185 4413 A1
Barlow St
12000 DET 48205 4274 D1
18600 DET 48205 4202 D6
Barlum St
6300 DET 48210 4343 E5
Barnard Rd
1400 AARB 48103 4488 E2
Barnes Ct
1200 PTFD 48176 4573 A6
Barnes St
7800 DET 48209 4419 B5
Barney St
10 BrTp 48134 4753 B5
Barns Dr
- WTLD 48186 4413 A5
Barnwell Dr
- VNBN 48111 4579 B2
Barnyard Bnd
- AATp 48105 4332 D7
Baron Ct
9100 WasC 48176 4658 D2
Baron Dr
7500 CNTN 48187 4337 B5
Baron Wy
9000 WasC 48176 4658 D3
Barr Rd
3700 CNTN 48188 4410 D7
3700 CNTN 48188 4493 D1
Barr St
6300 DET 48204 4343 C1
Barracuda St
200 WIND N8W 4505 A2
Barrett St
5800 DET 48213 4275 A4
6000 DET 48213 4274 E3
Barrie Dr
6600 CNTN 48187 4336 C6
Barrie St
7600 DRBN 48126 4342 D3
Barrington Av
31400 WTLD 48186 4414 C4
Barrington Ct
46500 PyTp 48170 4336 B3
Barrington Dr
8200 SpTp 48198 4409 C7
21500 WDHN 48183 4668 B3
30700 WTLD 48186 4414 C4
Barrington Pl
100 DRBN 48124 4416 D1
1500 AARB 48103 4488 D1
Barrington Rd
400 DET 48214 4348 A1
400 GPPK 48214 4348 A1
400 GPPK 48230 4348 A1
700 DET 48214 4347 E1
700 DET 48230 4347 E1
700 DET 48230 4348 A1
700 GPPK 48230 4347 E1
800 DET 48214 4275 E7
800 DET 48230 4275 E7
800 GPPK 48230 4275 E7
45900 PyTp 48170 4336 C3
Barrington St
29100 INKR 48141 4414 E4
33600 WTLD 48186 4414 A4
Barrister Rd
1200 AARB 48105 4407 C4
Barron St
9500 DET 48209 4418 E5
Barry Av
300 Tcmh N8N 4349 A6
Barry Dr
9300 RMLS 48174 4496 E5
Barry St
3500 WYNE 48184 4414 C6
9400 DET 48214 4274 D7
Barry Knoll Dr
3500 PTFD 48108 4488 E5
3600 PTFD 48108 4489 A5
Barrymore Ln
3400 WIND N9C 4420 A5
Bart Av
1900 WRRN 48030 4200 E2
1900 WRRN 48091 4200 E2
2200 WRRN 48091 4201 A2
Bart Ct
7900 WasC 48167 4190 C6
Bart St
39400 CNTN 48187 4337 D3
Barth St
37400 RMLS 48174 4580 A4
Bartholomaei Av
20700 WRRN 48091 4201 B4
Bartlett Dr
300 WIND N9G 4504 C4
45600 CNTN 48187 4336 C4
Bartlett Rd
46800 CNTN 48187 4336 B5
Bartlett St
10 HDPK 48203 4272 C2
Barton Dr
10 AATp 48105 4406 C3
200 AARB 48105 4406 C3
N Barton Dr
- AATp 48105 4406 B1
10 BNHL 48105 4406 B1
200 BNHL 48105 4331 A7
Barton Ln
10 AATp 48105 4406 B2
9000 AGST 48197 4661 D1
E Barton Ln
100 AARB 48105 4406 C2
100 AATp 48105 4406 C2
Barton St
4100 WIND N9G 4505 A3
6300 DET 48210 4343 E4
28400 GDNC 48135 4415 A1
28600 GDNC 48135 4414 E1
34900 WTLD 48185 4413 D1
Barton Farm Ct
3800 AATp 48105 4331 A6
Barton Farm Dr
3500 AATp 48105 4331 A6
Barton Shore Dr
10 AATp 48105 4406 B1
10 BNHL 48105 4406 B1
Base Line Rd
39800 NOVI 48167 4193 C5
39800 NvlT 48167 4193 C5
40000 NOVI 48375 4193 C5
40000 NvlT 48375 4193 C5
Baseline Rd
- NOVI 48167 4192 E5
- NOVI 48167 4193 A5
- NvlT 48167 4193 A5
- Tcmh N8V 4505 C1
100 NHVL 48167 4192 D5
700 NvlT 48167 4192 E5
3000 Tcmh N0R 4505 C1
W Baseline Rd
200 NHVL 48167 4192 D5
Bashian Dr
24200 NOVI 48375 4193 C1
Basil St
20000 DET 48235 4198 D5
Basin St
25300 SFLD 48034 4196 D4
Baske St
- TYLR 48180 4498 E5
21300 TYLR 48180 4499 C5
Basset Ct E
9000 LVNA 48150 4337 E2
Basset Ct W
9000 LVNA 48150 4337 E2
Bassett Dr
700 SALN 48176 4572 C6
Bassett St
9700 LVNA 48150 4337 E1
14700 LVNA 48154 4265 E4
S Bassett St
- LNPK 48229 4501 C1
1000 DET 48229 4418 D6
2100 DET 48229 4501 C1
Basswood Ct
48000 PyTp 48170 4336 A3
Bastien St
500 Amhg N9V 4757 B4
Batavia Ct
2800 WTLD 48186 4414 A6
Batavia St
10 RVRG 48218 4418 E5
100 RVRG 48218 4419 A7
Bates Ct
2900 TNTN 48183 4669 C5
Bates St
- ROTp 48220 4199 B3
800 DET 48226 4345 D6
Bateson Ct
2800 AATp 48105 4406 C1
Bath Dr
- CNTN 48187 4337 A5
Bath St
900 AARB 48103 4406 A5
Bathurst Dr
27000 BNTN 48134 4667 C5
Bathurst St
200 Amhg N9V 4757 B3
Battelle Av
23000 HZLP 48030 4200 C1
Battleford Ln
47200 NHVL 48167 4192 A5
Baubee St
- DET 48210 4343 D7
Bauman St
19100 DET 48203 4200 B5
Baumey Av
500 WYDT 48192 4501 B7
2200 WYDT 48192 4500 E7
Baxter Cres
5900 LSal N9H 4503 C4
Baxter Rd
2900 AARB 48105 4407 B3
Bay Ct
- NvlT 48167 4265 C1
31800 WTLD 48186 4414 C4
N Bay Dr
1100 WasC 48103 4488 C1
Bay St
- NvlT 48167 4265 C1
Bayberry Cir
4600 AATp 48105 4407 E4
Bayberry Ct
30400 FTRK 48134 4754 C5
Bayberry Ct E
28600 LVNA 48154 4267 E3
Bayberry Ct W
28700 LVNA 48154 4267 D3
Bayberry St
10 PTFD 48197 4574 E2
10 WTLD 48186 4497 D1
Bayberry Wy
18700 NvlT 48167 4263 C1
Bayberry Park Cir
1400 CNTN 48188 4412 E5
Bayberry Park Dr
28600 LVNA 48154 4267 E3
Bayham St
5300 DBHT 48125 4415 C7
5300 DBHT 48125 4498 C1
5300 DBHT 48180 4498 C1
Bayhan St
2000 INKR 48141 4415 C4
Bay Harbor Ln
40400 CNTN 48188 4412 D4
Bay Hill Ct
1900 PTFD 48108 4488 E7
Bay Hill Dr
15300 NvlT 48167 4264 C4
33100 RMLS 48174 4497 A1
Baylis Dr
2800 AARB 48108 4489 D4
3000 PTFD 48108 4489 E4
Baylis St
15500 DET 48238 4272 A3
16100 DET 48221 4272 A2
Baypoint Dr
23000 FNHL 48335 4194 A2
Bay Pointe Dr
200 BLVL 48111 4578 C3
Bayridge Dr
2800 WasC 48103 4405 C2
Bayshore Dr
48200 VNBN 48111 4578 A1
S Bayside St
200 DET 48229 4418 C5
Bays Water Cres
1300 WIND N8S 4348 A7
Bays Water Ct
9300 WIND N8S 4348 A7
Bayswater Ln
3400 AARB 48105 4332 C7
Bay Tree Dr
7500 YpTp 48197 4576 A6
Bay Valley Dr
- FNHL 48336 4195 D4
Bayview Ct
47000 CNTN 48188 4411 B7
Bayview Dr
9600 YpTp 48197 4576 E3
29200 GBTR 48173 4755 D5
29700 WynC 48138 4756 C5
Bayview Rd
38900 HnTp 48164 4665 A6
Bayview St
34000 WTLD 48186 4413 D3
Baywood Blvd
45400 CNTN 48187 4411 C2
Baywood Dr
9000 PyTp 48170 4336 D2
Baywood Dr
37400 FNHL 48335 4194 A3
Bazley Blvd
1400 SpTp 48198 4492 E1
Beach Ct
1200 PTFD 48176 4573 A7
Beach Ln
10 LSal N9J 4502 C6
Beach St
4200 ECRS 48229 4501 C4
Beachdale Rd
9200 WIND N8R 4423 B3
Beach Grove Dr
400 Tcmh N8N 4424 D1
Beach Park Rd
9500 GOTp 48178 4188 A1
Beachview Dr
- WIND N8P 4348 B5
Beachway Av
10 WasC 48189 4258 E3
200 WasC 48189 4259 A3
Beacon Ct
- WasC 48167 4262 B4
N Beacon Ct
7500 CNTN 48187 4337 B4
Beacon Ln
8000 WasC 48167 4262 B5
Beacon Rd
41100 NOVI 48375 4193 C4
Beacon St
23600 FMTN 48336 4195 B1
33900 LVNA 48150 4266 D7
Beacon Hill Cir
45800 PyTp 48170 4336 C1
Beacon Hill Ct
12600 PyTp 48170 4264 C7
Beacon Hill Dr
11700 PyTp 48170 4336 C1
12400 PyTp 48170 4264 C7
Beacon Hill Rd
10 GSPF 48236 4276 E3
Beacon Hill St
2600 AARB 48104 4490 B3
Beaconsfield Av
800 GPPK 48230 4276 A7
800 GPPK 48230 4348 A1
1000 GPPK 48230 4275 E6
20700 STCS 48021 4204 A3
20700 STCS 48080 4204 A3
22300 EPTE 48080 4204 B1
22700 EPTE 48021 4204 B1
Beaconsfield Dr
- AARB 48108 4489 E4
Beaconsfield St
- DET 48224 4203 E6
10500 DET 48224 4275 C2
19200 HRWD 48225 4203 E6
20600 HRWD 48021 4204 A5
20600 HRWD 48080 4204 A5
20600 HRWD 48225 4204 A5
Beacontree Ct
42300 NvlT 48167 4265 A2
N Beacon Woods Dr
20600 NvlT 48167 4192 A5
Beakes St
100 AARB 48103 4406 B5
100 AARB 48104 4406 B5
Beal Av
1500 AARB 48105 4407 A3
Beal St
400 NHVL 48167 4192 E7
Beals St
2400 DET 48214 4346 C2
Beals St E
10 WIND N9E 4504 C1
Beals St W
1500 WIND N9E 4504 A2
Beaman St
8700 DET 48214 4346 E2
Beanum Ct
6000 RMLS 48174 4496 E2
6100 RMLS 48174 4497 A2
Beard Blvd
- TYLR 48180 4498 D3
Beard St
1800 DET 48209 4419 B1
Beatrice Av
1400 WTLD 48186 4414 C3
8000 WTLD 48185 4339 D3
8600 WTLD 48185 4339 D3
15500 ALPK 48101 4500 B2
Beatrice St
- LVNA 48154 4267 D4
8800 LVNA 48150 4339 D2
13900 LVNA 48154 4267 D5
20200 LVNA 48152 4195 D5
20400 LVNA 48336 4195 D5
S Beatrice St
- LNPK 48229 4501 B2
1700 DET 48229 4418 C7
2400 DET 48229 4501 B2
Beaubien St
400 DET 48226 4345 D6
3700 DET 48201 4345 C3
5300 DET 48202 4345 B2
5800 DET 48211 4345 B1
6500 DET 48202 4273 B7
13000 SRKW 48179 4754 B7
Beaufait Av
1800 GSPW 48236 4204 C5
2100 GSPW 48225 4204 C5
Beaufait St
400 DET 48207 4346 C3
5000 DET 48211 4274 A7
19900 HRWD 48225 4204 A4
Beaufield St
1500 FRDL 48220 4199 D2
Beauford Ct
21500 FNHL 48167 4194 A4
Beauford Ln
21300 FNHL 48167 4193 E4
21300 FNHL 48167 4194 A4
Beaufort Dr
5900 CNTN 48187 4337 A7
Beaumont Av
3300 SpTp 48105 4408 A1
Beaupre Av
10 GSPF 48236 4276 C4
Beaupre Ln
300 GSPF 48236 4276 E3
Beaver St
1300 DRBN 48128 4341 C7
5600 DBHT 48127 4341 C6
5600 DBHT 48128 4341 C7
Beaver Creek Dr
48400 PyTp 48170 4336 A3
48700 PyTp 48170 4335 E4
Beaver Crossing Ln
900 WasC 48176 4658 C1
Beaverland
7200 DET 48127 4341 B4
9500 DET 48239 4341 B1
11600 DET 48239 4269 B7
Beaverland St
14500 DET 48223 4269 B4
17300 DET 48219 4269 A1
20200 DET 48219 4197 B5
Bechard Av
100 LSal N9J 4586 C1
Beck Rd
5800 CNTN 48111 4494 B2
5800 VNBN 48111 4494 B2
12400 VNBN 48111 4578 B2
15300 NvlT 48167 4264 A1
20200 NvlT 48167 4192 A6
21000 NHVL 48167 4192 A6
21000 NHVL 48374 4192 A6
21000 NOVI 48167 4192 A4
21000 NOVI 48374 4192 A4
N Beck Rd
100 CNTN 48187 4411 B1
5600 CNTN 48187 4336 B7
8800 PyTp 48170 4336 B2
12200 PyTp 48170 4264 B6
S Beck Rd
- CNTN 48111 4494 B1
100 CNTN 48188 4411 B3
4800 CNTN 48188 4494 B1
Beckenham Blvd
47400 NOVI 48374 4192 A3
Beckenham Ct
22600 NOVI 48374 4192 A3
Becker Av
8400 ALPK 48101 4500 B4
10800 ALPK 48195 4500 A6
22800 WRRN 48089 4202 D2
Beckett Ln
100 Lksr N8N 4424 E2
Beckley Rd
11500 VNBN 48111 4578 B1
Becky Ct
7100 CNTN 48187 4336 D5
Becky Dr
6900 CNTN 48187 4336 D5
Becky Ln
5600 SpTp 48105 4333 B4
Bedell Av
1200 Tcmh N8N 4424 A2
Bedell St
10 BLVL 48111 4578 E2
Bedford Ct
500 WIND N9G 4504 D2
Bedford Dr
100 WTLD 48185 4413 C2
300 YpTp 48198 4491 E2
300 YpTp 48198 4492 A2
12200 SOGT 48195 4584 C1
21600 NOVI 48167 4192 D4
41500 CNTN 48187 4412 C1
Bedford Ln
600 GPPK 48230 4276 B7
Bedford Pl
5900 WasC 48105 4332 C1
Bedford Rd
700 GPPK 48230 4276 A7
2500 AARB 48104 4490 A2
Bedford St
600 WIND N9G 4504 E2
4100 DBHT 48125 4417 A6
9100 DET 48224 4275 D2
17400 RVVW 48192 4584 D6
Bedford Towne St
10 SFLD 48075 4197 D2
Bedview Dr
6300 PTFD 48176 4574 B4
Beech
- CNTN 48188 4411 C5
Beech Ct
700 PLYM 48170 4336 E1
25700 RDFD 48239 4340 D2
25800 SFLD 48034 4196 C2
Beech Dr
3500 PTFD 48197 4490 E5
44400 PyTp 48170 4336 D1
Beech Rd
8000 WasC 48189 4259 A3
20700 SFLD 48034 4196 D4
Beech St
300 WTLD 48186 4414 C6
1200 DET 48226 4345 B6
1200 PLYM 48170 4336 E1
4700 WIND N9C 4420 A7
21700 DRBN 48124 4416 D3
27400 INKR 48141 4415 A5
29400 INKR 48141 4414 E5
Beechcrest Ct
47200 PyTp 48170 4336 B2
Beechcrest Dr
47000 PyTp 48170 4336 B2

INDEX 8

Beechcrest St — Detroit & Wayne County Street Index — Black Oak Ln

STREET
Block City ZIP Map# Grid

Beechcrest St
23200 DBHT 48127 4341 B6
Beechdale St
10000 DET 48204 4343 B1
Beech Daly Rd
100 DBHT 48141 4415 D2
100 INKR 48141 4415 D2
1400 DBHT 48125 4415 D4
5800 TYLR 48180 4498 D3
8800 RDFD 48239 4340 D2
11600 RDFD 48239 4268 C1
11800 TYLR 48180 4582 D3
16100 RDFD 48240 4268 C1
16100 TYLR 48174 4582 D6
17100 BNTN 48174 4582 D6
18300 RDFD 48240 4196 C7
18600 BNTN 48174 4667 D1
21000 BNTN 48134 4667 D4
N Beech Daly Rd
100 DBHT 48127 4415 D1
100 DBHT 48141 4415 D1
1300 DBHT 48127 4340 D7
8600 DBHT 48239 4340 D4
S Beech Daly St
4600 DBHT 48125 4415 D7
5600 DBHT 48125 4498 D1
5700 DBHT 48180 4498 D1
Beechlawn
1800 SpTp 48198 4409 E7
Beechmont St
100 DRBN 48124 4415 E2
1100 DRBN 48124 4416 A3
Beechnut St
28400 INKR 48141 4414 E2
28400 INKR 48141 4415 A2
33400 WTLD 48186 4414 A2
33900 WTLD 48186 4413 E2
Beechton St
6300 DET 48210 4343 E4
Beechtree Ln
- DRBN 48126 4342 A7
- DRBN 48126 4417 A1
Beech View Ln
45500 CNTN 48188 4411 C5
Beechwood Av
20900 EPTE 48021 4203 B2
27400 GDNC 48135 4340 A6
28300 HnTp 48134 4753 A4
29400 GDNC 48135 4339 D7
32900 WTLD 48185 4339 A7
33600 WTLD 48185 4338 E7
Beechwood Ct
11000 TYLR 48180 4499 C7
22300 WDHN 48183 4668 C5
40300 NvlT 48167 4265 D3
42200 CNTN 48188 4412 B3
50400 PyTp 48170 4263 C6
Beechwood Dr
1300 AARB 48103 4406 A4
1500 WasC 48103 4406 A4
42200 CNTN 48188 4412 A3
Beechwood St
3500 WIND N9C 4420 B5
5700 DET 48210 4344 B3
7400 DET 48204 4344 A2
9500 DET 48204 4343 E1
34400 FNHL 48335 4194 D2
36900 WTLD 48185 4338 B7
Begole Rd
10 WasC 48160 4658 E6
10 WasC 48160 4659 A6
Begole St
5700 DET 48210 4344 A3
6300 DET 48204 4344 A3
Begonia Dr
17500 BwTp 48173 4755 A6
Behrendt Av
20700 WRRN 48091 4201 C3
Beierman Av
23100 WRRN 48091 4201 C1
Bel Air Ln
58600 LyTp 48178 4189 D3
Beland St
17100 DET 48234 4274 C1
19100 DET 48234 4202 C5
Belanger Av
300 GSPF 48236 4276 C2
Belanger Park Dr
10 RVRG 48218 4419 A7
Belcrest Rd
32000 BwTp 48173 4755 B7
Belden Ct
11600 LVNA 48150 4266 D7
11600 LVNA 48150 4338 D1
Belden St
15400 DET 48238 4271 E2
17100 DET 48221 4271 E1
Belding Ct
33300 WTLD 48186 4414 A5
Belfair Ct
49000 CNTN 48187 4410 E1
Belfast St
6300 DET 48210 4343 D3
29400 FNHL 48336 4195 D4
Belfield Cir
800 AARB 48104 4406 E7
Belford Ct
47400 CNTN 48187 4336 A5
Belfore Ct
58000 LyTp 48178 4189 D1
Belgrade Notch St
2300 AATp 48103 4405 D2
Bell Ct
22400 FNHL 48335 4194 D3
Bell Rd
- HnTp 48117 4751 D3
- MonC 48117 4751 D3
21600 HnTp 48164 4665 D3
27000 HnTp 48164 4751 D3
Bell St
10 ECRS 48229 4501 D2
10 YPLT 48197 4492 A5
Belladonna Dr
24800 LyTp 48178 4189 E1
Bellagio Ct
47800 NOVI 48167 4191 E4
47800 NOVI 48167 4192 A4
Bellagio Dr
500 WIND N8P 4348 C6
47300 NOVI 48167 4192 A4
47300 NOVI 48374 4192 A4
Bellaire Av
15500 ALPK 48101 4500 A6
Bell Cove Ct
700 BLVL 48111 4578 C3
Bell Creek Ct
16100 LVNA 48154 4266 E3
Bell Creek Dr
- LVNA 48154 4268 B3
- RDFD 48154 4268 B3
- RDFD 48239 4268 B3
Bell Creek Ln
16300 LVNA 48154 4267 A3
17100 LVNA 48152 4267 A1
Belle St
7800 DET 48209 4419 A1
7900 DET 48209 4418 E1
Belleauwood Ct
43700 CNTN 48188 4411 E3
Belledale St
25800 TYLR 48180 4498 D7
Belle Isle Vw
400 WIND N8S 4347 D7
Bellemeade Ct
7100 YpTp 48197 4576 B5
Belle Meade Rd
10 GSPS 48236 4205 A6
Bellemeade St
7200 YpTp 48197 4576 B5
Belleperche Pl
200 WIND N8S 4347 D6
Belle Pointe Dr
7000 VNBN 48111 4494 D3
Belle Pointe Ests
- VNBN 48111 4494 D4
Bellers Ct
200 YpTp 48198 4492 B2
Belleterre St
9600 DET 48204 4343 E1
11300 DET 48204 4271 E7
Belleview Av
200 WIND N8Y 4346 D7
Belle Villa Blvd
- VNBN 48111 4578 D4
10 BLVL 48111 4578 D4
Belleville Rd
- BLVL 48111 4578 C2
4700 CNTN 48111 4494 D3
4700 CNTN 48188 4411 D7
4700 CNTN 48188 4494 D3
5800 VNBN 48111 4494 D3
12000 VNBN 48111 4578 C2
Bellevue Rd
7800 WynC 48138 4670 C7
Bellevue St
400 DET 48207 4346 C3
600 YPLT 48197 4491 C3
5000 DET 48207 4274 A7
5000 DET 48211 4274 A7
Bellflower Ct
3200 WasC 48103 4488 B1
Bellingham Dr
- NOVI 48374 4191 C1
Bellingham St
1800 CNTN 48188 4411 E4
Belliveau St
38300 WTLD 48185 4337 E3
38300 WTLD 48185 4338 A3
Bellridge Blvd
41400 VNBN 48111 4495 C7
N Bellridge Dr
41600 VNBN 48111 4495 C7
S Bellridge Dr
41500 VNBN 48111 4495 C7
Bellwether Dr
5500 WasC 48176 4572 C2
Bellwood Av
2500 AARB 48104 4490 B4
Bellwood Dr
11100 PyTp 48170 4336 C2
21800 WDHN 48183 4668 D3
Bellwood Dr S
21900 WDHN 48183 4668 C4
Belmar Pl
1100 AARB 48103 4489 B1
Belmont Av
1900 HMTK 48212 4273 B4
11600 WRRN 48089 4202 C1
14500 ALPK 48101 4500 B3
Belmont Dr
400 YpTp 48198 4491 E2
47400 VNBN 48111 4578 B3
Belmont Ln
100 HbgT 48189 4186 A6
Belmont Rd
1000 AARB 48104 4407 A7
1600 TNTN 48183 4669 D4
2100 AARB 48104 4489 E1
2100 AARB 48104 4490 A1
Belmont St
10 DET 48202 4272 E5
500 DET 48202 4273 A5
500 DET 48211 4273 A5
1400 DRBN 48128 4341 D7
5600 DBHT 48127 4341 C6
5600 DBHT 48128 4341 C7
Belton
22500 DET 48239 4341 B3
22700 DBHT 48127 4341 B3
Belton Av
100 GDNC 48135 4415 B1
100 GDNC 48141 4415 B1
1500 GDNC 48135 4340 B7
23000 FTRK 48134 4754 B4
Belton Ct
12500 PyTp 48170 4263 D7
12500 PyTp 48170 4335 D1
Belton Ln
23200 DBHT 48127 4341 A3
24600 DBHT 48127 4340 E3
Belton St
- DET 48228 4341 E3
- DET 48228 4342 E3
6800 GDNC 48135 4340 A5
10300 DET 48204 4343 B3
12900 DET 48228 4343 A3
Belvedere Ct N
300 CNTN 48188 4411 B3
Belvedere Ct S
500 CNTN 48188 4411 B3
Belvidere St
1200 DET 48214 4346 D1
3000 AARB 48108 4490 B5
3700 DET 48214 4274 D7
5000 DET 48213 4274 C5
Bemidji Ct
500 AARB 48103 4405 E6
Bemidji Dr
1300 AARB 48103 4406 A6
1400 AARB 48103 4405 E6
Bemis Rd
3000 PTFD 48197 4574 C7
3000 WasC 48197 4574 C7
4000 WasC 48160 4574 E7
4500 PTFD 48197 4575 A7
4500 WasC 48160 4575 A7
4500 WasC 48197 4575 A7
5000 AGST 48197 4575 B7
5000 YpTp 48197 4575 B7
7000 AGST 48197 4576 A7
7000 YpTp 48197 4576 A7
9000 AGST 48191 4577 B7
9000 AGST 48197 4577 B7
9000 YpTp 48197 4577 B7
10000 YpTp 48191 4577 B7
40600 VNBN 48111 4579 C6
40600 WynC 48111 4579 C6
43400 VNBN 48111 4578 D7
43400 WynC 48111 4578 D7
49000 VNBN 48111 4577 E7
49000 WynC 48111 4577 E7
50200 VNBN 48191 4577 B7
50200 VNBN 48197 4577 B7
50200 WynC 48191 4577 B7
E Bemis Rd
10 PTFD 48176 4574 A7
10 WasC 48176 4574 A7
W Bemis Rd
10 PTFD 48176 4573 E7
10 PTFD 48176 4574 A7
10 WasC 48176 4573 E7
10 WasC 48176 4574 A7
400 SALN 48176 4572 E7
1500 SALN 48176 4573 A7
1500 WasC 48176 4572 E7
Bending Rd
1200 AARB 48103 4406 A4
Bendix St
36900 WYNE 48184 4413 B7
Bendon Ct
33400 WTLD 48186 4414 A6
Benham St
6300 DET 48211 4273 E5
Beniteau St
2100 DET 48214 4347 A1
2500 DET 48214 4275 A6
4400 DET 48214 4274 E6
6000 DET 48213 4274 E4
Benjamin Ct
50200 PyTp 48170 4263 D6
Benjamin St
400 AARB 48104 4406 B7
1300 WIND N8X 4421 B2
1600 WIND N8W 4421 C3
Bennett
26600 RDFD 48240 4268 B1
Bennett Ct
32900 LVNA 48152 4267 A1
46800 CNTN 48187 4336 B5
Bennett Dr
7300 HbgT 48189 4186 B5
Bennett St
100 WYDT 48192 4501 C6
2400 DRBN 48124 4416 B4
21400 DET 48219 4269 B1
24000 DET 48219 4268 E1
27600 LVNA 48152 4268 A1
32800 LVNA 48152 4267 A1
35400 LVNA 48152 4266 D1
E Bennett St
10 SALN 48176 4572 C7
100 FRDL 48220 4200 A4
W Bennett St
100 FRDL 48220 4199 E4
100 FRDL 48220 4200 A4
100 SALN 48176 4572 C7
Bennington Ct
300 SALN 48176 4572 B6
1600 CNTN 48188 4412 A4
Bennington Dr
30700 WTLD 48186 4414 C3
43400 NOVI 48375 4192 E2
Bennington Ln
10 DRBN 48120 4417 D2
Bens St
2500 AARB 48103 4405 D7
Bensette St
500 WIND N8X 4421 C5
800 WIND N8W 4421 C5
Benson Ct
32500 WTLD 48185 4339 A3
Benson Dr
32500 WTLD 48185 4339 A3
Benson Rd
3300 TNTN 48183 4669 B7
Benson St
2800 DET 48207 4346 A3
7000 DET 48214 4346 A3
E Benson St
10 ECRS 48229 4501 D4
W Benson St
10 ECRS 48229 4501 D4
Bentcliffe
1300 WIND N8S 4348 A7
Bentler Ct
20500 DET 48219 4197 C5
Bentler St
13900 DET 48223 4269 C5
17100 DET 48219 4269 C1
18200 DET 48219 4197 C7
21600 SFLD 48075 4197 C3
Bentley Ct
1600 CNTN 48188 4411 E4
33400 WTLD 48186 4414 A5
Bentley Dr
47400 VNBN 48111 4578 B3
Bentley St
27500 LVNA 48154 4268 A5
29400 LVNA 48154 4267 D5
Benton St
600 DET 48201 4345 C4
Bent Pine Ct
1700 PTFD 48108 4573 A1
Bent Trail Ct
2000 PTFD 48108 4488 D5
Bent Trail Dr
3000 PTFD 48108 4488 E5
Benzie Ct
31800 WTLD 48186 4414 C4
Berden St
- DET 48224 4275 E2
- DET 48224 4276 A1
18900 DET 48236 4276 B1
19200 HRWD 48225 4204 B7
Berdeno Av
23000 HZLP 48030 4200 C2
Berea Av
26800 DBHT 48127 4340 B6
Beresford St
10 HDPK 48203 4272 D3
Berg Rd
17800 DET 48219 4269 A1
18200 DET 48219 4197 A7
20300 DET 48034 4197 A6
20700 SFLD 48034 4197 A3
24000 SFLD 48034 4196 E1
Bergen Av
400 YpTp 48197 4491 A4
Berger Dr
600 WasC 48176 4658 E3
Berkdale Dr
42700 VNBN 48111 4495 A6
Berkeley Av
3800 CNTN 48188 4411 B7
Berkeley Rd
19100 DET 48221 4199 E6
Berkley Av
300 AARB 48103 4489 B1
400 YpTp 48197 4491 C4
Berkley St
100 DRBN 48124 4416 A2
24000 OKPK 48237 4198 E1
Berkshire Av
3100 WRRN 48091 4201 A3
16700 ALPK 48101 4500 A3
18700 ALPK 48101 4499 E3
19300 ALPK 48180 4499 E3
Berkshire Ct
9900 WasC 48167 4190 A6
13600 PyTp 48170 4264 C6
Berkshire Dr
300 SALN 48176 4572 B6
1000 WTLD 48186 4414 C3
8000 WynC 48138 4670 D3
8200 SpTp 48198 4492 B1
8400 SpTp 48198 4409 C7
Berkshire Pl
10 GSPF 48236 4276 D5
Berkshire Rd
700 AARB 48104 4406 E7
700 GPPK 48230 4348 A1
1000 GPPK 48230 4276 A6
1200 GPPK 48230 4275 E5
Berkshire St
9000 DET 48224 4275 C2
9800 DRBN 48120 4418 D4
13800 RVVW 48192 4584 D6
Berlin Rd
12000 BrTp 48117 4839 C2
12000 BrTp 48179 4839 C2
12000 MonC 48117 4839 C2
12000 MonC 48179 4839 C2
Bermuda St
- PTRG 48220 4199 E1
10 PTRG 48069 4199 E1
1900 FRDL 48220 4199 E1
3100 FRDL 48069 4199 E1
Bermuda Dunes Dr
7300 YpTp 48197 4576 A6
Bern St
7600 DBHT 48127 4341 A4
Bernadine Rd
25000 HnTp 48164 4665 C7
25200 HnTp 48164 4751 C1
Bernard Rd
1300 WIND N8Y 4422 A1
1800 WIND N8W 4422 A2
Bernard St
2200 HMTK 48212 4273 B5
20000 TYLR 48180 4499 E6
Bernbeck Dr
16600 BNTN 48192 4669 A1
E Bernhard Av
10 HZLP 48030 4200 C4
W Bernhard Av
10 HZLP 48030 4200 C4
Bernice Ct
22900 BNTN 48183 4668 B4
Bernice St
2600 AARB 48103 4405 C4
Berns Ct
20000 GSPW 48236 4204 D6
Berres St
2900 HMTK 48212 4273 C5
Berry Av
24000 WRRN 48089 4203 B1
N Berry Av
1600 WTLD 48185 4338 C7
1600 WTLD 48185 4413 C1
Berry Dr
3300 MonC 48117 4753 A6
Berry Ln
21800 LyTp 48167 4190 B5
21800 LyTp 48178 4190 B5
Berry Rd
3000 SpTp 48198 4409 C2
3500 SpTp 48105 4334 C5
3500 SpTp 48198 4334 C5
4000 SpTp 48170 4334 C5
Berry St
3100 DET 48234 4201 B7
S Berry St
1400 WTLD 48186 4413 C4
Bert Av
17000 ALPK 48101 4500 A4
Bert Ln
100 INKR 48141 4414 D2
Bertha St
400 WIND N8P 4348 A5
1300 FRDL 48220 4199 D4
Bertram Cres
2700 WIND N8T 4422 C3
Bertram Dr
22500 NOVI 48374 4192 C3
32000 WTLD 48185 4339 A3
Bertram St
10400 DRBN 48126 4343 B3
Bertrand Av
10 Amhg N9V 4757 C1
Berville Ct
33500 WTLD 48186 4414 A5
Berwick Ct
- NOVI 48167 4191 C4
7000 YpTp 48197 4575 E6
Berwick Dr
2200 CNTN 48188 4411 E5
7400 YpTp 48197 4575 E6
8500 WTLD 48185 4339 B3
Berwick Ln
10 DRBN 48120 4417 D3
Berwick St
9600 LVNA 48150 4339 B1
13900 LVNA 48150 4267 B6
14500 LVNA 48154 4267 B4
Berwyn
9500 RDFD 48239 4340 C1
13900 RDFD 48239 4268 C5
Berwyn St
400 DBHT 48127 4415 D1
5600 DBHT 48127 4340 C7
8600 DBHT 48239 4340 C3
Bessemore St
8600 DET 48213 4274 B5
Bestech Rd
3900 PTFD 48197 4574 D1
Best Hall
10 YPLT 48197 4491 E3
Bethany St
19100 LVNA 48152 4194 A7
Bethany Wy
24300 NOVI 48375 4193 C1
Bethel Church Rd
5000 WasC 48176 4571 A5
Bethel Hills Dr
7000 WasC 48176 4571 B5
Betheny Cir
5300 SpTp 48198 4408 B3
Bethlawn Blvd
20700 ROTp 48220 4199 C3
Bethlehem Av
1800 WIND N9E 4503 C1
Bethune Ct
- DET 48202 4273 A7
- DET 48202 4345 A1
N Bethune Pl
21200 ROTp 48220 4199 A4
S Bethune Pl
21000 ROTp 48220 4199 B4
Bethune St E
10 DET 48202 4273 A7
Bethune St W
10 DET 48202 4273 A7
10 DET 48202 4345 A1
1100 DET 48202 4344 D1
1500 DET 48206 4344 D1
Betts Av
1400 WIND N9B 4420 C5
3700 WIND N9E 4503 E3
4100 LSal N9H 4504 A4
Betty Dr
300 WIND N8S 4347 E5
Betty Ln
9400 PyTp 48170 4336 B2
Bettyhill
46500 PyTp 48170 4264 B7
Betty Ln Dr
500 INKR 48141 4414 D3
Beverly Av
1500 YpTp 48198 4493 A7
16600 ALPK 48101 4500 A2
18700 ALPK 48101 4499 E2
Beverly Ct
8900 DET 48204 4344 A1
Beverly Ln
6100 WasC 48105 4260 C7
6100 WasC 48105 4332 C1
Beverly Pl
6400 RMLS 48174 4497 D2
N Beverly Pl
6300 RMLS 48174 4497 D2
Beverly Rd
10 GSPF 48236 4276 D5
24100 TYLR 48180 4499 A2
24800 TYLR 48180 4498 C2
27400 RMLS 48174 4498 A2
27400 RMLS 48180 4498 C2
28900 RMLS 48174 4497 E2
38400 RMLS 48174 4496 A2
44400 VNBN 48111 4494 E2
Beverly St
23700 OKPK 48237 4198 C1
Beverly Glen St
11200 WIND N8P 4348 C6
Bewick St
1400 DET 48214 4347 A1
2100 DET 48214 4346 E1
3400 DET 48214 4274 E7
5900 DET 48213 4274 C4
Bexley Wy
40000 NvlT 48167 4265 D2
Bibbins St
35400 RMLS 48174 4496 D7
Bicentennial Dr
- LVNA 48152 4194 C7
Bicentennial Pkwy
1300 PTFD 48108 4573 B3
Bicking Ct
23500 FMTN 48336 4195 A1
Biddle Av
10 WYDT 48192 4501 C7
10 WYDT 48229 4501 C7
1400 WYDT 48192 4585 C1
4500 RVVW 48192 4585 C5
Biddle St
3800 DET 48210 4344 C4
4800 WYNE 48184 4413 D7
5200 WYNE 48184 4496 D1
9200 RMLS 48174 4496 D5
S Biggs Av
10 BLVL 48111 4578 E2
N Biggs St
10 BLVL 48111 4578 E2
Big Pine Ct
5800 YpTp 48197 4576 C2
Big Pine Dr
5400 YpTp 48197 4576 C2
Big Sky Ct
2400 PTFD 48108 4488 E6
Billenca Dr
- NOVI 48374 4191 C1
Biltmore Dr
100 DBHT 48127 4415 C1
100 DBHT 48141 4415 C1
Biltmore St
100 INKR 48141 4415 C2
15300 DET 48227 4270 B4
16100 DET 48235 4270 B2
18200 DET 48235 4198 B7
Binder Cres
2500 Tcmh N0R 4505 C5
Binder St
17800 DET 48212 4201 B7
18000 DET 48234 4201 B7
Bing Dr
47000 CNTN 48187 4411 B2
Bingham Ct
36400 FNHL 48335 4194 B1
Bingham Rd
- Amhg N9V 4757 B7
Bingham St
4200 DRBN 48126 4418 A1
6200 DRBN 48126 4343 A5
8000 DET 48228 4343 A3
Binghampton Ct
48200 NvlT 48167 4263 E2
Binghampton Dr
48200 NvlT 48167 4263 E2
48200 NvlT 48167 4264 A2
Birch
10 WynC 48111 4664 B3
Birch Ct
- CNTN 48188 4411 C5
100 WynC 48111 4664 B3
5800 PTFD 48197 4575 A3
15700 RMLS 48174 4582 A5
Birch Dr
10 VNBN 48111 4577 E6
10 VNBN 48111 4578 A6
16200 BwTp 48173 4755 A6
21600 WDHN 48183 4668 C3
29300 HnTp 48134 4752 E3
29300 HnTp 48134 4753 A3
Birch Ln
600 GSPW 48236 4204 E7
Birch Run
37900 LVNA 48150 4338 A1
Birch St
- TYLR 48180 4583 B2
3500 WIND N9C 4420 B5
6400 TYLR 48180 4499 B2
15300 DET 48227 4270 D5
17500 BNTN 48174 4583 B6
S Birch St
1200 DRBN 48124 4416 A3
Birchcrest Dr
1400 DRBN 48124 4417 B5
17100 DET 48221 4271 E1
18000 DET 48221 4199 E6
Birchdale St
6700 RMLS 48174 4498 B2
Birch Hollow Dr
2800 AARB 48108 4489 D5
3000 PTFD 48108 4489 E5
Birchlawn Av
28400 GDNC 48135 4340 A6
28600 GDNC 48135 4339 E6
Birchridge St
19000 SFLD 48075 4197 E3
Birchrun Dr
3700 SpTp 48105 4333 C7
3700 SpTp 48198 4333 C7
Birchway Ct
1000 SLYN 48178 4189 A4
Birchwood Av
2800 TNTN 48183 4669 D4
21900 EPTE 48021 4203 B2
Birchwood Ct
3100 AARB 48105 4331 E7
35700 HnTp 48164 4665 D7
44400 NvlT 48167 4264 D2
Birchwood Dr
- NvlT 48167 4264 D2
3000 AARB 48105 4406 E1
3100 AARB 48105 4331 E7
39500 PyTp 48170 4337 D1
Birchwood St
20900 FMTN 48336 4195 A4
29400 INKR 48141 4414 E3
30400 WTLD 48186 4414 B3
34400 WTLD 48186 4413 D3
Bircklan Dr
7200 CNTN 48187 4335 C5
Bird Rd
1100 AARB 48103 4406 A2
1200 AATp 48103 4406 A2
1300 AATp 48103 4405 E2
Birdie Ln
4800 WasC 48103 4404 D7
Birk Av
1100 AARB 48103 4406 A7
1100 AARB 48103 4489 A1
Birkdale Ct
500 Tcmh N8N 4424 C2
Birkdale Dr
4800 WasC 48103 4404 D6
Birmingham Av
500 LSal N9J 4502 D5
Birrell St
12800 SOGT 48195 4584 E1
Birwood Ct
- FNHL 48167 4194 A3
36900 FNHL 48335 4194 A3
Birwood St
8800 DET 48204 4343 B1
12300 DET 48204 4271 B7
12600 DET 48238 4271 B6
18000 DET 48221 4271 B1
20200 DET 48221 4199 B5
Biscayne Av
19000 EPTE 48021 4204 B1
Biscayne Ct
8000 WasC 48176 4573 B7
Bishop Dr
20500 BNTN 48183 4668 C2
Bishop Ln
800 GPPK 48230 4276 B6
Bishop Rd
800 GPPK 48230 4276 B5
1000 WasC 48176 4658 B1
42400 CNTN 48188 4412 B3
Bishop St
2300 AARB 48105 4406 E3
2300 AARB 48105 4407 A3
3400 DET 48224 4276 A3
5700 LSal N9H 4503 D4
9100 DET 48224 4275 D1
14500 OKPK 48237 4198 D1
Bismark Rd
26300 HnTp 48164 4751 C3
Bison St
6600 WTLD 48185 4338 E6
6600 WTLD 48185 4339 A5
Bittersweet Ln
11000 HbgT 48189 4186 C6
Bivouac St
6100 DET 48209 4419 B1
Blackacre Dr
1600 Tcmh N0R 4505 A5
Blackburn Ct
3700 WIND N9C 4420 C6
Blackburn St
8500 WTLD 48185 4339 B3
9600 LVNA 48150 4339 B1
13900 LVNA 48154 4267 B5
21500 STCS 48080 4204 D1
22800 STCS 48080 4205 A1
Blackett Av
22200 WRRN 48089 4202 E1
Blackfoot Ln
33600 WTLD 48185 4338 E5
33600 WTLD 48185 4339 A5
Black Forest Ct
21100 BNTN 48134 4667 E3
Blackmar Av
24100 WRRN 48091 4201 D1
Blackmoor St
18000 DET 48234 4202 B6
Black Moore Av
10800 YpTp 48111 4577 C3
Blackmore Dr
22100 WynC 48138 4670 B4
Black Oak
36400 WTLD 48185 4338 C6
Black Oak Ln
300 AGST 48191 4661 C7

STREET
Block City ZIP Map# Grid

Black Pine Dr
17100 NvlT 48167 4264 D1
Blackstone Av
23000 WRRN 48089 4202 D1
Blackstone Ct
20500 DET 48219 4197 C5
42400 CNTN 48187 4337 B4
Blackstone St
1000 INKR 48141 4415 C3
13900 DET 48223 4269 C5
16100 DET 48219 4269 C2
19100 DET 48219 4197 C5
24000 OKPK 48237 4198 E1
Blackthorn Dr
800 LSal N9H 4504 C6
Blain Ct
10 AARB 48108 4490 A5
Blaine Av
3100 TNTN 48183 4669 C5
Blaine St
10 DET 48202 4272 E7
1400 DET 48206 4272 D7
2600 DET 48206 4344 B1
4000 DET 48204 4344 A1
Blair Ct
18900 ALPK 48101 4499 E6
Blair Ln
10 DRBN 48120 4417 D3
Blair St
9300 DET 48213 4274 C6
14300 SOGT 48195 4584 D5
Blairmoor Ct
10 GSPS 48236 4205 A4
500 GSPW 48236 4205 A4
1100 GSPW 48236 4204 D4
Blairwood Cir
41500 NvlT 48170 4265 B4
Blairwood Cres
1400 WIND N8W 4421 E7
Blairwood Ct
3200 WIND N8W 4421 E6
Blake Dr
37200 LVNA 48150 4338 B2
Blake St
19100 DET 48203 4200 C6
Blakely
13700 GBTR 48173 4755 D3
Blakely Ct
400 AARB 48104 4406 C7
Blakely Dr
18500 WDHN 48183 4755 A1
Blakeway St
1100 AATp 48104 4407 C7
1100 AATp 48104 4490 C1
Blanchard Blvd
36800 FMTN 48335 4194 B1
Blanche Ct
25100 BNTN 48134 4667 D7
Blanche St
600 PLYM 48170 4265 A7
1000 PLYM 48170 4264 E7
2500 MVDL 48122 4418 A7
2800 MVDL 48122 4417 E7
24600 BNTN 48134 4667 D6
Bland St
1200 DRBN 48120 4418 D4
Blaney Dr
2100 AARB 48103 4488 E2
Blaty St
9400 TYLR 48180 4499 B5
Blauvelt Dr
9500 WynC 48138 4670 B6
Blazer Ct
23200 HnTp 48164 4666 A5
Blencarn Ct
9100 WIND N8S 4348 B7
Blesser St
10000 DRBN 48126 4343 A5
14700 DRBN 48126 4342 D5
Bliss Rd
3100 WIND N8W 4421 E6
3200 WIND N8W 4422 A7
3600 WIND N8W 4505 A1
Bliss St
7100 DET 48234 4202 A5
Block
34700 WTLD 48185 4338 D6
Block Av
28400 GDNC 48135 4340 A6
28600 GDNC 48135 4339 E6
Bloom St
11900 DET 48212 4273 D1
19100 DET 48234 4201 D5
Bloomcrest Dr
45600 NvlT 48167 4192 C6
Bloomfield Dr
38100 LVNA 48154 4266 A2
Bloomfield Rd
- DET 48221 4199 E5
3200 WIND N9C 4420 A5
Bloomfield St
2300 MVDL 48122 4418 A7
16700 LVNA 48154 4267 A2
33600 LVNA 48154 4266 E2
Bloomsbury Cir
7900 WasC 48167 4190 B6
Blossingham Dr
25400 DBHT 48125 4415 D2
Blossom Av
1300 YpTp 48198 4493 A2
Blossom Ct
1800 WIND N8W 4422 A7
Blossom Dr
100 CNTN 48187 4411 E1
100 CNTN 48188 4411 E2
Blossom Ln
19600 GSPW 48236 4204 C7
26000 WynC 48138 4670 D7
Blossom Pl
19600 GSPW 48236 4204 C7
Blossom Rd
2800 TNTN 48183 4669 C3
Blossom Hill Tr
4500 PTFD 48108 4490 E4
Blowers St
10400 DET 48204 4343 B3
Blue Spr
1500 WIND N8W 4421 D6
Blueberry Ct
2500 Tcmh N9K 4424 A6
Blueberry Ln
200 WasC 48103 4488 B3
2200 AATp 48103 4405 D2
2500 WasC 48103 4405 D2
Bluebird Ln
32400 WYNE 48184 4414 A7
Blue Grass Ct
5600 WasC 48176 4572 B2
Blue Grass Ln
5500 WasC 48176 4572 B3
Blue Heron Ct
1300 WIND N8P 4348 D7
3500 SpTp 48198 4334 B1
6100 PTFD 48108 4573 A3
47600 NvlT 48167 4264 A1
Blue Heron Dr
1100 WasC 48189 4258 C2
1400 WIND N8P 4348 D7
1700 WIND N8P 4423 D1
10600 GOTp 48178 4187 D4
26400 FTRK 48134 4753 C1
Blue Heron Dr E
18400 NvlT 48167 4264 A1
Blue Heron Dr S
47000 NvlT 48167 4264 A1
Blue Heron Dr W
18500 NvlT 48167 4264 A1
Blue Heron Pointe Dr
18000 NvlT 48167 4264 A1
Bluehill St
5500 DET 48224 4276 A2
6100 DET 48224 4275 E1
Blue Jay Dr
8200 YpTp 48197 4576 C3
Blue Skies Ct
18500 LVNA 48152 4266 B1
Blue Skies Ct E
15300 LVNA 48154 4266 B5
Blue Skies Ct N
15500 LVNA 48154 4266 B4
Blue Skies Ct W
15300 LVNA 48154 4266 B5
Blue Skies Dr
16600 LVNA 48154 4266 A2
Blue Skies St
14500 LVNA 48154 4266 A4
18700 LVNA 48152 4194 A7
Bluesprings Ct
40400 CNTN 48188 4412 C4
Blue Spruce Dr
5000 PTFD 48197 4574 E1
35200 FNHL 48335 4194 C3
Bluestem Ln
1000 AARB 48103 4405 D7
Bluett Rd
2800 AARB 48105 4407 B2
Blunk St
100 PLYM 48170 4264 E6
Blythe St
8200 DET 48228 4342 E2
Boardman
- YPLT 48197 4491 D3
Boardwalk Av
- NOVI 48167 4191 C4
10 Amhg N9V 4757 D2
Boardwalk Dr
2700 AARB 48104 4489 C3
2700 AARB 48108 4489 C3
Bob Dr
6100 YpTp 48197 4577 A3
Bobcat Ct
41400 CNTN 48188 4412 C4
Bobrich Ct
29900 LVNA 48152 4267 D1
Bobrich St
27600 LVNA 48152 4268 A1
30200 LVNA 48152 4267 C1
33400 LVNA 48152 4266 E2
Bobwhite Ct
9600 PyTp 48170 4336 D2
17700 BNTN 48192 4583 D7
Bock Rd
34400 WTLD 48185 4338 D7
Bock St
27400 GDNC 48135 4340 A7
28400 GDNC 48135 4339 E7
33600 GDNC 48135 4338 E7
Bodsford Dr
19000 WDHN 48183 4755 A1
Boeing
26500 RDFD 48239 4268 B6
Boening Dr
19400 SFLD 48075 4197 E4
Bog Rd
49300 VNBN 48111 4577 D4
Bogie Ct
700 WasC 48103 4404 D6
Bohn Ct
25400 HnTp 48134 4666 D6
Bohn Rd
21600 WynC 48111 4663 C5
Boismier Av
100 LSal N9J 4502 C6
Bolam Av
23000 WRRN 48089 4203 A1
Boldt St
2100 DRBN 48124 4416 A4
Boleyn St
9100 DET 48224 4275 D1
Bolgos Cir
3000 AARB 48105 4407 C1
Bolla Rd
4800 WasC 48160 4660 A2
4800 WasC 48197 4660 A2
5000 AGST 48197 4660 A2
Boller Ct
23300 BNTN 48183 4668 B5
Bomber Av
1100 YpTp 48198 4493 B6
2000 YpTp 48198 4577 B1
Bombridge Ct
2800 AARB 48104 4489 D4
Bonair St
23200 DBHT 48127 4341 A6
Bonanza St
28000 RMLS 48174 4498 A1
Bonaventure Dr
8600 GOTp 48116 4186 E1
Bondie Dr
18900 ALPK 48101 4499 E6
32000 BwTp 48173 4755 A7
32500 RKWD 48173 4755 A7
Bondie St
10 ECRS 48229 4501 C4
300 WYDT 48192 4501 B6
Bondy Av
2200 LSal N9H 4503 D3
Bondy St
2100 LSal N9H 4503 C3
Boniface Dr
6600 CNTN 48187 4336 E6
Bonisteel Blvd
- AARB 48105 4406 E5
- AARB 48105 4407 A4
Bonita Av
10 WIND N8W 4505 A2
Bonita Dr
7300 YpTp 48197 4576 A5
Bonita St
10300 DET 48224 4275 C2
10800 DET 48213 4275 C2
Bonnare Ct
4100 WIND N9G 4505 A3
Bonner St
2100 FRDL 48220 4200 A1
Bonnie Dr E
7000 WTLD 48185 4339 A5
Bonnie Dr W
7000 WTLD 48185 4339 A5
Bonnie Brook Dr
24400 NOVI 48374 4192 B1
Bonnie Brook Rd
46600 PyTp 48170 4264 B7
Bonnydale St
30400 LVNA 48154 4267 C4
Bonstelle Av
17000 SFLD 48075 4198 A2
Bontekos Av
45900 WynC 48111 4663 C4
Bon Terre Dr
5000 YpTp 48197 4575 B3
Bonzanno St
10 ECRS 48229 4501 D4
Boone Ln
10 DRBN 48120 4417 D2
Booth Av
37200 WTLD 48186 4413 B4
Borchart St
41400 NOVI 48375 4193 B2
Bordeau Dr
27400 HnTp 48164 4667 A4
27400 HnTp 48174 4667 A4
Bordeau St
9900 DET 48204 4343 E1
10000 DET 48204 4271 E7
Bordeaux Ct
33400 WTLD 48185 4339 A5
Borden Lk
10000 GOTp 48178 4188 E2
Border Cres
1400 Tcmh N8N 4423 D2
Border St
35200 RMLS 48174 4496 D2
Borderhill
24300 NOVI 48375 4193 C1
Borelli Dr
3800 WIND N9G 4504 A3
Borgman Av
10400 VNBN 48111 4494 C7
Borgstrom Av
1000 YpTp 48198 4492 C6
Borman St
- DET 48223 4270 A7
- DET 48227 4270 A7
Bortle St
8000 DET 48214 4346 C2
Boston Av
2600 YpTp 48197 4491 B3
Boston Blvd E
100 DET 48202 4272 E5
300 DET 48202 4273 A5
Boston Blvd W
10 DET 48202 4272 D6
2600 DET 48206 4272 A7
4000 DET 48204 4272 A7
4700 DET 48204 4343 E1
Boston Cir
100 WasC 48176 4657 B2
Boston Ct
600 AARB 48103 4405 C7
Boston St
400 YpTp 48197 4491 B4
24000 DRBN 48124 4416 A5
24300 DRBN 48124 4415 E5
Bostonhill Ln
6500 CNTN 48187 4336 D6
Boston Post St
11600 LVNA 48150 4338 D1
12000 LVNA 48150 4266 D7
Bostwick Pl
33400 FNHL 48335 4194 E3
33400 FNHL 48336 4194 E3
Bostwick St
6700 DET 48209 4419 B2
Bosuns Wy
5000 YpTp 48197 4576 C1
Bosworth Ct
17100 DET 48219 4269 B1
Botsford Ct
6200 CNTN 48187 4336 E6
Botsford Dr
20800 FNHL 48336 4196 A4
Botsford St
2300 HMTK 48212 4273 B3
Boucher Rd
10200 WynC 48138 4756 A3
Bouffard Rd
10 LSal N9J 4502 C5
1800 LSal N9H 4503 D6
1800 LSal N9H 4504 A6
1800 LSal N9J 4503 D6
1800 LSal N9J 4504 A6
Boulden Ct
42600 CNTN 48187 4412 A1
Boulder Av
20700 EPTE 48021 4203 C3
Boulder Cir
21000 NHVL 48167 4192 C5
Boulder Ct
43200 NOVI 48375 4192 E1
Boulder Dr
- NvlT 48167 4263 D3
1900 AARB 48104 4490 C2
21900 FNHL 48335 4194 B3
26500 FTRK 48134 4753 D1
Boulder St
19100 DET 48205 4203 C5
Boulder Pond Blvd
- VNBN 48111 4579 A3
Boulder Pond Dr
4000 PTFD 48108 4489 A7
Boulder Ridge Blvd
2200 PTFD 48103 4488 D3
Bourassa Av
20200 BwTp 48183 4754 E3
Bourassa St
10 ECRS 48229 4501 D5
Bourbon St
- DET 48228 4342 A1
Bourke St
3000 DET 48238 4271 E4
Bournemouth Av
7700 WynC 48138 4670 D3
Bournemouth Cir
400 GSPF 48236 4276 D1
Bournemouth Rd
1500 GSPF 48236 4276 C1
1500 GSPW 48236 4276 C1
1700 GSPW 48236 4204 B7
1800 GSPW 48225 4204 B7
1800 HRWD 48225 4204 B7
Bournemouth St
20800 HRWD 48225 4204 B7
Bowen St
700 AARB 48105 4406 C4
Bowery St
10600 HbgT 48189 4186 B4
Bowie St
18600 SOGT 48195 4500 A7
Bowles St
5600 DRBN 48126 4343 B6
Boxelder Ct
18200 BNTN 48174 4582 C7
Boxelder Dr
18200 BNTN 48174 4582 C6
Boxford Rd
1500 TNTN 48183 4669 C3
1500 TNTN 48192 4669 C3
Boxwood
28700 HnTp 48134 4752 E3
Boxwood Ct
3300 WIND N8R 4423 B4
4500 WasC 48108 4488 B7
21300 FNHL 48336 4195 C4
Boxwood St
6500 DET 48210 4344 B3
Boyce Dr
13700 BwTp 48173 4841 D3
Boyd Dr
18100 WynC 48111 4579 C7
18100 WynC 48111 4664 C1
Brace St
9500 DET 48228 4342 A1
Brackett St
- LSal N9J 4503 A5
Bradburn Ct
700 NHVL 48167 4192 C5
Bradbury Ct
4600 WIND N9G 4504 E5
Braden St
4600 DET 48210 4344 A6
5600 DET 48210 4343 E5
Bradford
- CNTN 48188 4412 A5
Bradford Ct
10 DRBN 48126 4417 C1
9400 PyTp 48170 4336 A2
Bradford Ct N
2300 WRRN 48091 4201 A1
Bradford Dr
25500 WDHN 48183 4669 A7
Bradford St
11500 DET 48205 4274 D1
11500 DET 48213 4274 D1
19900 DET 48205 4202 D4
30500 WTLD 48186 4414 D3
Bradford Square Dr
3500 WasC 48103 4405 A2
Bradley Av
2000 YpTp 48198 4577 B1
Bradley Ct
11100 PyTp 48170 4336 B2
37800 FNHL 48335 4194 A2
Bradley Dr
37600 FNHL 48335 4194 A2
42700 VNBN 48111 4495 A4
Bradley St
8700 DET 48214 4346 E2
Bradner Av
15000 PyTp 48170 4265 B4
15300 NvlT 48170 4265 B4
Bradner Ct
42400 PyTp 48170 4265 A5
Bradner Rd
15700 NvlT 48170 4265 B3
42500 NvlT 48167 4265 A2
Bradsford Ct
21900 STCS 48080 4204 E3
Brady
- DET 48201 4345 C3
9500 RDFD 48239 4340 D1
13900 RDFD 48239 4268 D5
16500 RDFD 48240 4268 D2
19200 RDFD 48240 4196 D6
Brady Ct
9200 RDFD 48239 4340 D2
Brady Ln
22500 FNHL 48335 4194 A3
N Brady St
100 DRBN 48124 4416 D1
S Brady St
600 DRBN 48124 4416 D2
Braeburn Cir
2600 AARB 48108 4490 A5
Braeburn Ln
12900 PyTp 48170 4264 A7
49200 NOVI 48374 4191 D1
Braemar Ct
1100 WIND N8W 4421 D6
Braeside Cir
22600 FNHL 48335 4194 E3
Braeside Pl
700 AARB 48103 4489 A2
Braile St
8000 DET 48228 4341 D3
11600 DET 48228 4269 D7
13900 DET 48223 4269 D5
17100 DET 48219 4269 D1
19100 DET 48219 4197 C5
Brain Av
200 BLVL 48111 4578 C2
Brainard Av
100 DRBN 48124 4416 C2
Brainard St
- DET 48201 4345 A4
1400 DET 48210 4345 A4
Bramble
- CNTN 48188 4411 C5
Bramble Ct
2300 CNTN 48188 4411 B5
Brambledown Wy
3600 WasC 48103 4329 E6
Bramblewood Ct
44400 VNBN 48111 4494 E2
47200 NOVI 48374 4192 C2
Bramblewood Dr
24200 NOVI 48374 4192 B1
Bramblewood Ln
- YpTp 48198 4493 A3
Bramcaster Rd
19500 GSPW 48236 4204 B7
Bramell
7200 DET 48127 4341 B4
9500 DET 48239 4341 B1
11600 DET 48239 4269 B7
Bramell St
13900 DET 48223 4269 B4
17100 DET 48219 4269 B1
Bramford St
20100 DET 48234 4202 A4
Bramley Cres
2700 WIND N8W 4421 D5
Brampton Ct
2000 AARB 48103 4488 E2
42100 NvlT 48167 4265 B2
Brampton Dr
7800 CNTN 48187 4336 A5
Branch Ct
31900 WTLD 48186 4414 C4
Brandes Rd
27900 HnTp 48134 4752 B4
Brandi Dr
10 VNBN 48111 4493 C2
S Brandon Av
21700 FNHL 48034 4196 A3
21700 FNHL 48336 4196 A3
Brandon Rd
9200 BrTp 48166 4839 C7
10000 BrTp 48179 4839 D6
11000 BrTp 48179 4840 A3
12600 SRKW 48179 4840 A3
Brandon St
4400 DET 48209 4344 C7
N Brandon St
500 WTLD 48185 4413 B1
22000 FNHL 48336 4196 A3
S Brandon St
1800 WTLD 48186 4413 B5
W Brandon St
22000 FNHL 48336 4196 A3
Brandt Av
100 GDNC 48135 4414 D1
6400 GDNC 48135 4339 D5
Brandt Ct
29700 GDNC 48135 4414 D2
Brandt St
6600 RMLS 48174 4497 D2
8500 DRBN 48126 4343 C5
15000 RMLS 48174 4581 D5
Brandywine Blvd
47300 NvlT 48167 4264 B3
Brandywine Dr
2600 AARB 48104 4490 C3
Brandywine Ln
8200 AGST 48197 4575 C7
Brandywine St
19300 RVVW 48192 4669 D1
Brandywyne Rd
43700 CNTN 48187 4336 E4
Brandywynne St
23000 SFLD 48034 4196 D2
Branford Ln
10 DRBN 48120 4417 D2
Brant St
500 WIND N9A 4421 A1
1800 WIND N8Y 4346 B7
Brantford Av
15600 BwTp 48173 4755 B7
Brassow Rd
2500 WasC 48108 4572 C2
2500 WasC 48176 4572 C2
Bratt Dr
10 Amhg N9V 4757 E3
Braun Ct
300 AARB 48103 4406 B5
300 AARB 48104 4406 B5
Braun Rd
2900 WasC 48176 4657 B6
4000 WasC 48176 4656 D6
Braydon Ct
22800 NOVI 48374 4192 C3
Brazil Av
600 WIND N8X 4421 C5
Breakfast Dr
14000 RDFD 48239 4268 B5
Breakwater Ct
300 BLVL 48111 4578 C3
Breakwater Dr
600 BLVL 48111 4578 C3
W Breckenridge Av
400 HZLP 48030 4200 B2
Breckenridge Dr
2500 AARB 48103 4488 D1
Breckenridge Ln
40400 PyTp 48170 4265 C5
Breckenridge St
- OKPK 48220 4199 C2
- OKPK 48237 4199 C2
3200 DET 48210 4344 D5
E Breckenridge St
100 FRDL 48220 4199 E2
700 FRDL 48220 4200 A2
W Breckenridge St
100 FRDL 48220 4199 D2
Breckland Ct
3300 PTFD 48108 4488 E5
Breckland Dr
1900 PTFD 48108 4488 E5
Brecon Dr
100 SALN 48176 4572 C6
Breconshire Dr
- SALN 48176 4572 B6
- WasC 48176 4572 B6
Brede Pl
2000 AARB 48105 4406 C3
Bredefield St
2100 AARB 48105 4406 C3
Bredin Ct
14500 LVNA 48154 4267 C5
Bredow Av
23400 BNTN 48174 4668 B2
27400 HnTp 48174 4667 B2
28400 HnTp 48174 4666 E2
Breezewood Ct
4500 WasC 48103 4404 E4
7800 YpTp 48197 4576 B3
Breezewood St
400 WIND N8P 4348 B5
Brehmer Ct
22100 BNTN 48183 4668 B4
Bremen St
15300 DET 48224 4275 D5
17200 DET 48224 4276 A4
Brenda
40500 NOVI 48375 4193 C1
Brenda Cres
500 Tcmh N8N 4349 A7
700 Tcmh N8N 4424 A1
Brenda Ln
- NOVI 48375 4193 C1
Brendan Ln
5200 Tcmh N0R 4505 C5
Brennan St
9600 DET 48209 4418 E6
9600 DET 48209 4419 A6
Brenner
22700 TYLR 48180 4499 B5
Brents Ct
21900 STCS 48080 4204 D3
Brentwood Cres
10800 WIND N8R 4423 C3
Brentwood Ct
3400 AARB 48108 4489 D4
24100 NOVI 48374 4192 C2
Brentwood Dr
- YpTp 48197 4576 A4
100 DRBN 48124 4416 C1
17600 RVVW 48192 4584 B6
23000 BNTN 48183 4668 B5
41800 PyTp 48170 4265 B5
Brentwood St
- PyTp 48170 4265 B6
100 INKR 48141 4415 C2
8900 LVNA 48150 4340 A2
15900 LVNA 48154 4267 E3
18200 LVNA 48152 4267 E1
19900 LVNA 48152 4195 E5
Brentwood St E
900 DET 48203 4200 D6
2900 DET 48234 4201 A6
7400 DET 48234 4202 A6
Brentwood St W
10 DET 48203 4200 B6
Brest Av
1300 LNPK 48146 4500 D7
1300 SOGT 48195 4500 D7
1800 SOGT 48146 4500 C7
Brest Rd
20000 TYLR 48180 4499 E7
20000 TYLR 48195 4499 E7
24000 TYLR 48180 4583 A1
24400 TYLR 48180 4582 E1
26500 TYLR 48174 4582 C1
Brest St
14500 SOGT 48195 4500 B7
Bretton Cir
25700 BNTN 48134 4753 D1
25700 FTRK 48134 4753 D1
Bretton Dr
18200 DET 48223 4270 A3
18800 DET 48223 4269 E2
19100 DET 48219 4269 E2
33700 LVNA 48152 4194 E6
Bretton St
29000 LVNA 48152 4195 D6
Brewster Ct
47800 PyTp 48170 4336 A2
Brewster Ln
8200 CNTN 48187 4336 A4
Brewster Rd
3500 DRBN 48120 4417 D2
Brewster St
600 DET 48201 4345 D4
1900 DET 48207 4345 E3
11700 LVNA 48150 4266 E7
11700 LVNA 48150 4338 D1
Brian Ct
1700 AATp 48104 4490 C2
1900 SpTp 48198 4409 E7
Brian St
22000 TYLR 48180 4499 C4
Briar Dr
14100 VNBN 48111 4578 B3
Briar Pkwy
- PTFD 48108 4489 A5
Briar Rdg
46100 NOVI 48374 4192 C1
Briarbank Av
25000 SFLD 48034 4197 B1
Briarbank Dr
3100 WIND N8R 4423 C3
Briarbrook Dr
7800 YpTp 48197 4576 B1
Briarcliff Ct
9900 WasC 48167 4190 A6
42000 CNTN 48187 4412 B1
Briarcliff Dr
500 GSPW 48236 4205 A4
800 GSPW 48236 4204 E4
6200 VNBN 48111 4494 E2
Briarcliff Pl
10 GSPS 48236 4205 A4
Briarcliff Rd
19900 DET 48221 4199 E4
Briarcliff St
2700 AARB 48105 4407 B2
Briarcrest Dr
100 AARB 48103 4489 B3
Briardale Ct
2300 YpTp 48198 4493 A6
Briarfield St
1900 CNTN 48188 4411 E4
Briargate Ct
7400 CNTN 48187 4336 B5
Briargate Dr
7200 CNTN 48187 4336 B5
Briar Glen Dr
5500 WasC 48176 4572 C2
Briar Hill Dr
28000 FNHL 48336 4196 A1
28100 FNHL 48336 4195 E1
Briarhill Dr
4100 WasC 48160 4659 D1
Briar Hill Rd
13000 MonC 48117 4752 B7
14500 MonC 48134 4752 B7
Briarlee Wy
3600 WasC 48103 4329 E6
Briar Meadow Ct
5600 WasC 48176 4572 C2
Briar Meadow Rd
56500 LyTp 48167 4190 A4
56500 LyTp 48178 4190 A4
Briar Ridge Av
300 Amhg N9V 4757 C4
Briar Ridge Dr
1600 PTFD 48108 4489 A5
1700 PTFD 48108 4488 E5
Briar Ridge Ln
35600 FMTN 48335 4194 C1
Briarwood
28900 HnTp 48134 4752 E3
Briarwood Cir
100 AARB 48108 4489 B4
Briarwood Ct
38200 WYNE 48184 4413 A5
44400 VNBN 48111 4494 E2
Briarwood Dr
6200 VNBN 48111 4494 E2
8800 PyTp 48170 4337 D3
Briarwood Pl
10 GSPF 48236 4276 D4
Briarwood St
20400 BwTp 48173 4754 D4
Brick Ln
700 SLYN 48178 4189 C1

Detroit & Wayne County Street Index

STREET
Block City ZIP Map# Grid

Brickscape Dr
21000 NHVL 48167 4192 E5
21000 NOVI 48167 4192 E5
21000 NOVI 48375 4192 E5
Bridge Av
100 WIND N9B 4420 B2
3500 TNTN 48183 4669 C5
28400 GDNC 48135 4340 A5
28600 GDNC 48135 4339 E5
Bridge Rd
- RVVW 48192 4585 B7
- WynC 48192 4585 B7
2600 YpTp 48197 4577 B2
2600 YpTp 48198 4577 B2
8300 WynC 48138 4585 B7
Bridge St
20500 SFLD 48034 4196 E4
27400 LVNA 48152 4196 A7
34600 LVNA 48152 4194 D7
Bridgefield Dr
3000 PTFD 48108 4574 B1
3000 PTFD 48197 4574 B1
Bridgeman St
34400 FNHL 48335 4194 D4
Bridgemont Dr
6800 CNTN 48187 4336 D6
Bridgeport
10 WasC 48176 4657 B2
Bridgeport Ct
4300 INKR 48141 4414 E6
4300 INKR 48141 4415 A6
Bridgewater Ct
1700 CNTN 48188 4411 D4
Bridgewater Ct E
13800 GOTp 48178 4188 E3
13800 GOTp 48178 4189 A3
Bridgewater Ct W
13700 GOTp 48178 4188 E3
Bridgewater Dr
10300 GOTp 48178 4188 E3
Bridgeway Blvd
2500 LSal N9H 4503 D4
Bridgeway Dr
4500 WasC 48103 4329 E5
Bridge Wy Dr
- WasC 48103 4329 E5
Bridle Run
4700 PTFD 48197 4490 E7
4700 PTFD 48197 4574 E1
Bridle Hills Ct
27400 FNHL 48336 4196 A1
Bridle Hills Dr
27400 FNHL 48034 4196 A1
27400 FNHL 48336 4196 A1
S Bridle Hills Dr
27600 FNHL 48336 4196 A2
Bridle Pass
3700 PTFD 48108 4489 A5
Bridle Pass Ct
3700 PTFD 48108 4489 A5
Brier Ct
32900 LVNA 48152 4267 A1
Brierstone St
21200 HRWD 48225 4204 B7
Brierwood Ct
600 AARB 48103 4405 E5
Brierwood St
300 AARB 48103 4405 E5
Brighton Ln
4100 CNTN 48188 4411 A7
Brighton Rd
100 Tcmh N8N 4424 E2
500 Lksr N8N 4424 E2
Brighton St
10 HDPK 48203 4272 A2
100 DET 48203 4272 A2
Brimley Ct
21800 WDHN 48183 4669 A3
Brimley Dr
2900 WIND N8R 4423 B2
Brimson St
- DET 48212 4273 E1
6800 DET 48212 4274 A1
Bringard Dr
- DET 48234 4202 C4
- HRWD 48225 4203 C4
13600 DET 48205 4202 E4
13800 DET 48205 4203 A4
16800 DET 48225 4203 C4
Brinker St
18000 DET 48234 4201 A6
Brinket St
- DET 48214 4346 D2
Brinson St
17000 RVVW 48192 4584 E5
17000 RVVW 48195 4584 E5
Bristlewood Ct
- GOTp 48178 4188 A5
Bristol Ct
10 AARB 48104 4490 C3
800 CNTN 48187 4411 C1
1000 NHVL 48167 4192 C5
8900 SpTp 48198 4492 D1
37400 LVNA 48154 4266 A3
Bristol Dr
25700 BNTN 48134 4754 A1
Bristol Ln
10 HbgT 48189 4186 A5
Bristol Pl
3000 DET 48216 4344 E7
Bristol St
1800 WIND N9E 4503 C2
8000 WTLD 48185 4339 E3
35400 LVNA 48154 4266 C3
Bristow St
3800 DET 48212 4273 C2
Britain St
- DET 48224 4203 C7
10000 DET 48224 4275 E1
Brittanie Dr
3600 SpTp 48105 4333 C7
3600 SpTp 48198 4333 C7
Brittany Av
22700 EPTE 48021 4203 E1
Brittany Ct
47500 NOVI 48374 4192 A3
Brittany Dr
100 CNTN 48187 4411 E2
Brittany Hill Ct
36600 FMTN 48335 4194 B1
Brittany Hill Dr
36600 FMTN 48335 4194 B1
Brixton Pl
21400 SFLD 48075 4198 B4
Broad St
- CNTN 48188 4410 C7
- CNTN 48188 4493 C1
Broadhead St
400 WIND N9A 4421 A2
Broadmoor Av
- YpTp 48198 4492 E3
Broadmoor Blvd
- NvlT 48167 4264 D4
Broadmoor Cir N
44500 NvlT 48167 4264 D4
Broadmoor Cir S
44800 NvlT 48167 4264 D4
Broadmoor Ct
33300 LVNA 48154 4267 A3
Broadmoor Ln
- NvlT 48167 4264 D4
Broadmoor St
28400 LVNA 48154 4267 E3
Broadmoor Park Blvd
24100 NOVI 48374 4192 C2
Broadmoor Park Ln
23400 NOVI 48374 4192 A2
Broadstone Rd
1600 GSPW 48236 4204 B7
Broadstone St
21200 HRWD 48225 4204 B7
Broadstreet Av
9200 DET 48204 4344 A1
9900 DET 48204 4271 E6
12600 DET 48238 4271 E6
Broadview Ln
1700 AARB 48105 4406 D3
Broadview St
24000 FMTN 48336 4195 B1
24200 FNHL 48336 4195 B1
Broadway St
10 BrTp 48179 4841 A3
300 WIND N9C 4419 E7
300 WIND N9J 4419 E7
800 AARB 48104 4406 C5
800 AARB 48105 4406 C5
800 WIND N9C 4420 A7
800 WIND N9C 4502 E1
800 WIND N9C 4503 A1
800 WIND N9J 4420 A7
800 WIND N9J 4502 E1
800 WIND N9J 4503 A1
1200 DET 48226 4345 D5
21400 STCS 48080 4204 C1
W Broadway St
10 ECRS 48229 4501 D3
Brock Av
20700 EPTE 48021 4203 B3
Brock Ct
1900 AARB 48104 4489 D2
Brock St
100 Amhg N9V 4757 C3
200 WIND N9C 4420 A3
12600 DET 48205 4203 C7
39100 WTLD 48186 4412 E2
Brockman Blvd
2100 AARB 48104 4489 E1
Brockshire St
22100 NOVI 48375 4193 B4
Brockton
- BNTN 48134 4668 A7
- BNTN 48134 4754 C1
Brockton St
9300 DET 48211 4273 D4
9300 DET 48212 4273 D4
Brodhead Rd
10300 WynC 48138 4756 A3
Brody Av
17300 ALPK 48101 4500 A4
19000 ALPK 48101 4499 E4
29000 WTLD 48185 4339 E4
Broken Stone Ct
23500 NOVI 48375 4192 E2
Brombach St
9100 HMTK 48212 4273 C5
Bromley Av
- RVRG 48218 4418 D7
Bromley St
- DET 48229 4418 D7
- RVRG 48218 4418 D7
- RVRG 48229 4418 D7
Brook Cir
28700 WynC 48138 4756 A4
Brookdale Ct
10 FMTN 48336 4195 B3
Brookdale Dr
1400 CNTN 48188 4412 E4
Brookdale St
22400 FMTN 48336 4195 A2
Brooke Ct
12000 GOTp 48178 4188 D3
Brooke Park Dr
8000 CNTN 48187 4337 D3
Brookfield Av
19000 LVNA 48152 4195 A7
Brookfield Ct
22000 SLYN 48178 4189 A5
28300 BwTp 48183 4754 C3
Brookfield Dr
- WTLD 48185 4412 E2
1300 AARB 48103 4488 E3
1300 AARB 48103 4489 A3
22300 SLYN 48178 4189 B4
Brookfield Pl
38500 WYNE 48184 4413 A5
Brookfield St
1900 CNTN 48188 4411 E5
9500 LVNA 48150 4339 A1
11800 LVNA 48150 4267 A7
14700 LVNA 48154 4267 A4
Brook Forest
22400 NOVI 48375 4193 C3
Brookhaven Rd
1900 CNTN 48188 4411 D5
Brooklane Blvd
- NvlT 48167 4264 E2
Brooklawn Dr
20400 DBHT 48127 4341 D5
Brookline Av
8800 PyTp 48170 4336 E2
Brookline Ln
10 DRBN 48120 4417 D3
3500 MonC 48117 4753 B7
Brookline St
1100 CNTN 48187 4411 E1
1800 CNTN 48187 4336 E7
14600 RVVW 48192 4584 C7
Brook Ln St
29800 INKR 48141 4414 D4
Brooklyn Av
1100 AARB 48104 4489 C1
2500 LSal N9H 4503 D4
3000 LSal N9H 4504 A4
Brooklyn Ct
48900 CNTN 48188 4410 E6
Brooklyn Dr
3300 CNTN 48188 4410 E6
Brooklyn St
- DET 48201 4345 B5
- DET 48216 4345 B5
1400 DET 48226 4345 B6
Brookmill Ct
600 CNTN 48188 4411 C3
Brookplace Ct
23800 FNHL 48336 4195 D1
Brookridge Ct
200 AARB 48103 4406 B4
Brookridge Dr
46400 CNTN 48187 4411 C1
Brooks
38900 HnTp 48164 4665 A5
Brooks Blvd
10 Lksr N9K 4424 D6
N Brooks Ln
46800 PyTp 48170 4336 B2
S Brooks Ln
46800 PyTp 48170 4336 B2
W Brooks Ln
10300 PyTp 48170 4336 B2
Brooks St
600 AARB 48103 4406 A4
600 YPLT 48197 4491 E6
14700 DET 48214 4275 E7
Brookshire Ct
6600 CNTN 48187 4337 D5
Brookshire Dr
3100 TNTN 48183 4669 B6
6600 CNTN 48187 4337 B6
Brookside Blvd
- SpTp 48198 4409 C7
Brookside Ct
22800 DBHT 48125 4416 B7
45000 PyTp 48170 4336 D2
Brookside Dr
200 AARB 48105 4406 C2
800 AATp 48105 4406 D3
9000 WasC 48189 4259 A1
14500 VNBN 48111 4579 B4
22000 SFLD 48034 4197 B2
22000 SFLD 48075 4197 B2
Brookside Dr N
22800 DBHT 48125 4416 B7
Brookside Dr S
22700 DBHT 48125 4416 B7
Brookside Dr W
5400 DBHT 48125 4416 B7
Brookside Ln
6500 WasC 48170 4262 B6
Brookside Pl
10 LyTp 48167 4189 E6
Brookside Rd
400 YpTp 48197 4491 B3
44400 PyTp 48170 4336 D2
N Brookston Dr
8000 AGST 48191 4577 C7
Brookstone Dr
8000 AGST 48191 4577 C7
35400 HnTp 48164 4665 D7
Brooktree Ct
2300 YpTp 48198 4493 A6
Brook Trout Ln
6700 WasC 48170 4262 D7
Brookview Av
3200 TNTN 48183 4669 B3
Brookview Blvd
25000 BNTN 48134 4667 C7
25700 BNTN 48134 4753 C1
Brookview Cres
1000 WIND N8W 4421 D6
Brookview Ct
4000 PTFD 48108 4488 E6
27000 BNTN 48134 4667 C7
42000 CNTN 48188 4412 B4
Brookview Dr
- RVVW 48195 4584 C5
10 WynC 48138 4662 C6
1500 CNTN 48188 4412 E5
1900 WasC 48176 4572 C4
6200 PTFD 48176 4572 D4
15000 RVVW 48192 4584 C5
17100 LVNA 48152 4267 D1
45400 VNBN 48111 4494 D2
Brookview Ln
35700 HnTp 48164 4665 D7
Brookview St
30000 LVNA 48152 4267 C1
35400 LVNA 48152 4266 C1
Brookville Rd
5600 WasC 48170 4261 B7
5600 WasC 48178 4261 B7
7000 WasC 48170 4262 A7
Brookway Dr
61100 LyTp 48178 4189 B5
Brookway St
15000 RMLS 48174 4581 D4
Brookwood Ct
100 SLYN 48178 4189 C3
16200 NvlT 48167 4265 D3
Brookwood Dr
200 SLYN 48178 4189 C2
10500 PyTp 48170 4336 D1
44000 OakC 48167 4192 D3
Brookwood Ln
10 DRBN 48120 4417 D3
Brookwood Pl
800 AARB 48104 4489 C1
Brookwood St
8800 YpTp 48197 4576 D2
20000 DBHT 48127 4341 D6
Broquet Dr
41400 NOVI 48167 4193 B4
41400 NOVI 48375 4193 B4
Brothers Ct
4500 WIND N9G 4504 D5
Brougham Ct
14000 PyTp 48170 4265 B6
Brouillette Ct
1100 Tcmh N8N 4423 E2
Brousville Av
4000 LNPK 48146 4500 D7
Brown Ct
29400 GDNC 48135 4414 E1
Brown Pl
3700 DET 48210 4344 C3
Brown St
800 AARB 48104 4406 B7
27100 FTRK 48134 4753 D2
30400 GDNC 48135 4414 C1
Brownell Av
11200 PyTp 48170 4337 D1
Browning Av
400 YpTp 48198 4492 C3
E Browning Av
600 HZLP 48030 4200 D1
W Browning Av
10 HZLP 48030 4200 C1
Browning Ct
700 YpTp 48198 4492 C3
Browning Dr
200 SLYN 48178 4189 C3
Browning St
1400 FRDL 48220 4200 A1
Brownlee St
10 RVRG 48218 4419 A7
Brownstown Center Dr
19600 BNTN 48183 4583 D7
19600 BNTN 48183 4668 D1
19600 BNTN 48192 4583 D7
Brownstown Square Dr
23000 BNTN 48174 4668 A2
Bruce Av
100 WIND N9A 4420 E2
1200 WIND N8X 4420 E3
2100 WIND N8X 4421 A4
2400 WIND N9E 4421 B6
3100 WIND N9E 4504 C1
41100 PyTp 48170 4337 C3
Bruce St
700 AARB 48103 4405 D4
21600 WRRN 48091 4201 B2
32000 RMLS 48174 4497 B2
Bruckner St
6600 DET 48210 4344 A7
Brunelle Cres
400 Tcmh N8N 4424 B1
Brunner Av
10 Amhg N9V 4671 B7
Brunswick Dr
- GOTp 48178 4188 C3
21600 WDHN 48183 4668 C4
44900 CNTN 48187 4336 C5
Brunswick St
15500 DET 48224 4275 E5
16300 DET 48224 4276 A5
Brush Cres
10 Amhg N9V 4757 E2
Brush Ct
3900 WYNE 48184 4413 D6
Brush St
500 DET 48226 4345 D6
4800 DET 48201 4345 C3
5100 DET 48202 4345 B2
8900 DET 48202 4273 A5
10300 DET 48202 4272 E4
16000 HDPK 48203 4272 D1
16400 DET 48203 4272 D1
17700 DET 48203 4200 D7
35300 WYNE 48184 4413 D6
Bruton Av
3900 CNTN 48188 4411 A6
Bryan Blvd
27000 HnTp 48164 4751 B2
Bryan Ct
26600 DBHT 48127 4340 C5
Bryan St
13000 DRBN 48126 4418 A1
26500 DBHT 48127 4340 C5
Bryanston Crescent St
2100 DET 48207 4346 A4
Bryant St
1900 DET 48210 4344 E3
N Bryar St
100 WTLD 48185 4413 A2
S Bryar St
300 WTLD 48186 4413 A3
Brydan St
11200 TYLR 48180 4498 E7
Bryden St
7200 DET 48210 4343 D3
9500 DET 48204 4343 D1
12000 DET 48204 4271 D7
Bryn Mawr Ct
20000 NvlT 48167 4193 A6
Bryn Mawr Ln
2200 YpTp 48198 4577 A1
Bryn Mawr Rd
45600 CNTN 48187 4336 C6
Brys Dr
- STCS 48080 4204 B3
1100 GSPW 48236 4204 D4
2100 GSPW 48080 4204 C4
2100 STCS 48236 4204 C4
Brys Dr N
500 GSPW 48236 4205 A4
600 GSPW 48236 4204 E4
Brys Dr S
500 GSPW 48236 4205 A4
800 GSPW 48236 4204 E4
Bryson St
900 DET 48203 4200 B6
Buchanan Ct
2000 WTLD 48186 4413 A5
24200 FNHL 48335 4194 B1
Buchanan St
400 CNTN 48188 4410 D3
2000 DET 48210 4344 E4
10600 VNBN 48111 4495 B7
31400 WYNE 48184 4414 C7
Buchner Hill Dr
300 NHVL 48167 4192 D5
Bucholz Ct
200 AARB 48103 4406 A5
Buck Av
19000 BNTN 48174 4668 A1
Buck St
5800 TYLR 48180 4499 A1
14200 TYLR 48180 4583 A3
Buckeye Ct
17000 BNTN 48174 4582 D6
Buckeye Ln
17100 BNTN 48174 4582 C6
Buckhorn Ct
3200 AARB 48105 4332 B7
Buckingham Av
600 LNPK 48146 4501 A5
1000 LNPK 48146 4500 E5
3400 DET 48224 4275 E4
3400 DET 48230 4275 E4
5800 ALPK 48125 4499 E1
6300 ALPK 48101 4499 E1
Buckingham Ct
10 AARB 48104 4490 A2
10700 ALPK 48101 4499 E6
10900 ALPK 48195 4499 E6
13800 PyTp 48170 4264 C6
25600 LyTp 48178 4189 D1
40100 NOVI 48375 4193 C1
Buckingham Dr
10 HbgT 48189 4186 B6
200 WIND N8S 4347 A6
1500 WIND N8T 4422 B1
2700 WasC 48167 4190 C7
8500 SpTp 48198 4492 C1
21600 WDHN 48183 4668 D3
21900 FNHL 48335 4194 B4
38900 RMLS 48174 4495 E4
38900 RMLS 48174 4496 A4
Buckingham Rd
200 CNTN 48187 4412 E2
200 CNTN 48188 4412 E2
1000 GPPK 48230 4276 A6
1200 GPPK 48230 4275 E5
2300 AARB 48104 4490 A2
Buckingham St
2800 MonC 48117 4752 E7
12100 SOGT 48195 4584 C1
22700 DRBN 48128 4416 A1
27400 LVNA 48154 4268 A6
29600 LVNA 48154 4267 D5
Buckland Dr
8500 WasC 48170 4260 A1
Buckley Ct
6900 CNTN 48187 4336 C6
Buckley Dr
5000 PTFD 48197 4575 A1
Buckley Rd
45700 CNTN 48187 4336 C5
Buckridge Ln
4000 WasC 48103 4404 E1
4000 WasC 48103 4405 A1
Buckrun Dr
48800 PyTp 48170 4335 E1
Buckskin Dr
39000 RMLS 48174 4496 A2
Buckwheat Ln
10 Lksr N8N 4424 E2
10 Tcmh N8N 4424 E2
Bud Av
1400 YpTp 48198 4493 A1
Bud Ln
200 LyTp 48167 4189 E5
Buelow Ct
6300 DET 48209 4419 C3
Buena Vista Av
200 AARB 48103 4406 A6
W Buena Vista St
2200 DET 48238 4272 A5
3700 DET 48238 4271 E6
12700 DET 48227 4271 B6
Buena Vista St E
10 HDPK 48203 4272 D3
Buena Vista St W
- DET 48238 4271 D6
10 HDPK 48203 4272 C4
13600 DET 48227 4270 E6
Buffalo Av
500 TNTN 48183 4670 A1
Buffalo Ct
5500 DET 48212 4273 D2
Buffalo St
100 YPLT 48197 4492 A5
9300 HMTK 48212 4273 D3
17100 DET 48212 4273 D1
20200 DET 48234 4201 D4
Bugle Ct
49200 PyTp 48170 4263 E7
Buhl St
8800 DET 48214 4274 C7
Buhr St
6700 DET 48212 4201 E7
6700 DET 48212 4202 A7
Buick Av
1000 YpTp 48198 4492 E6
Bulley Dr
15700 BwTp 48173 4755 B6
Bull Run Dr
5100 YpTp 48197 4575 A4
Bulwer St
6800 DET 48210 4344 A7
Bunker Av
4600 WIND N9G 4505 B4
Bunker Hill Ln
6800 CNTN 48187 4337 A5
Bunker Hill Rd
2300 AARB 48105 4407 B2
Bunte Ct
23200 BNTN 48183 4668 B5
Bunton Rd
5800 YpTp 48197 4577 A5
7500 YpTp 48191 4577 A7
8000 AGST 48191 4577 A7
8000 AGST 48191 4662 A1
8000 AGST 48197 4577 A7
11000 AGST 48191 4748 A1
Burbank Av
10 YpTp 48198 4492 D4
Burbank Cres
3000 WIND N8T 4422 D4
Burbank Dr
3300 AARB 48105 4407 C1
Burberry Ct
3100 WasC 48176 4572 C3
Burchill Ct
10100 DET 48213 4274 D4
Burdeno St
7900 DET 48209 4419 B5
Burdette St
2000 FRDL 48220 4200 A1
Burdick Cres
200 Tcmh N8N 4349 A6
Burgandy Dr
7200 CNTN 48187 4336 C5
12800 GOTp 48178 4188 C1
Burger Dr
11400 PyTp 48170 4337 C1
Burger St
2000 DRBN 48128 4341 B6
2300 HMTK 48212 4273 B4
5600 DBHT 48127 4341 B6
5600 DBHT 48128 4341 B6
Burgess
17100 DET 48219 4269 C1
19100 DET 48219 4197 C6
Burgess Ct
20500 DET 48219 4197 C5
Burgess St
14000 DET 48223 4269 C5
Burgundy Rd
1400 AARB 48105 4407 B4
Burke St
- RVRG 48218 4419 A6
100 RVRG 48218 4418 E7
200 RVRG 48218 4501 E1
5200 Tcmh N0R 4505 B5
Burkland Ct
38300 WTLD 48185 4338 A4
Burkland Dr
7600 WTLD 48185 4338 A5
Burlage Pl
2500 DET 48207 4346 B3
Burley St
9900 DRBN 48120 4418 D3
Burlingame Ct
10 AARB 48108 4489 E5
Burlingame St
- DET 48202 4272 D5
1900 DET 48206 4272 C6
4000 DET 48204 4272 A7
6300 DET 48204 4271 D7
Burlington Ct
2900 AARB 48105 4407 B3
22600 NOVI 48374 4192 B2
Burlington Dr
11000 SOGT 48195 4499 E7
19100 DET 48203 4200 A6
30500 WTLD 48186 4414 C3
Burlington Rd
200 Tcmh N8N 4424 D1
700 CNTN 48188 4412 D3
Burlington St
2800 AARB 48105 4407 B2
Burlwood Dr
- DRBN 48126 4417 A1
Burneth Dr
8600 WasC 48160 4659 D1
8800 WasC 48197 4659 D1
Burnette St
7200 DET 48210 4343 D3
9500 DET 48204 4343 D1
Burnham Dr
6500 CNTN 48187 4337 A6
Burnham Rd
3400 PTFD 48108 4488 E5
Burning Bush Rd
8000 WynC 48138 4670 C3
Burning Tree Ln
13500 PyTp 48170 4264 B6
28500 RMLS 48174 4582 A5
Burnly Av
6400 GDNC 48135 4339 D6
Burnly St
7200 WTLD 48185 4339 D5
Burns Av
1800 YpTp 48197 4491 B5
4100 LNPK 48146 4500 D7
Burns Ct
3700 AARB 48105 4407 C6
Burns Dr
400 DET 48214 4346 E3
Burns Rd
13000 MonC 48117 4751 B7
Burns St
2600 DRBN 48124 4416 A4
3500 INKR 48141 4414 E6
3700 DET 48214 4346 D1
4100 DET 48214 4274 C7
5000 DET 48213 4274 C6
12000 SOGT 48195 4500 D7
12200 SOGT 48195 4584 D2
Burns Wy
4500 WasC 48130 4329 D4
Burnside St
3300 DET 48212 4273 C2
Burntwood Dr
48200 NOVI 48374 4191 E2
Burr Av
14200 WRRN 48089 4203 A3
Burr St
8800 TYLR 48180 4499 A4
14300 TYLR 48180 4583 A3
50400 CNTN 48188 4410 D3
Burrell Pl
2900 DET 48210 4344 D4
Burr Oak Dr
300 AARB 48103 4405 C6
Burr Oak Ln
300 AGST 48191 4661 B6
Burroughs St
10 DET 48202 4345 A1
300 PLYM 48170 4337 A1
Burr Ridge Cir
- CNTN 48187 4335 E3
Burr Ridge Ct
- CNTN 48187 4335 E4
Burr Stone Ct
3000 WasC 48176 4572 C2
Burson Pl
500 AARB 48104 4406 E7
Burswood Ct
400 WasC 48103 4404 C6
Burt Ct
20900 DET 48223 4269 C5
Burt Rd
8800 DET 48228 4341 D1
11600 DET 48228 4269 C7
12200 DET 48223 4269 C7
16800 DET 48219 4269 C2
18400 DET 48219 4197 C7
Burton Av
10000 OKPK 48237 4199 B1
Burton Ct
400 YPLT 48197 4491 E5
16100 LVNA 48154 4266 E3
39900 NOVI 48375 4193 D1
Burton Dr
- RMLS 48242 4497 C6
8000 CNTN 48187 4336 D4
39400 NOVI 48375 4193 D1
Burton Ln
34000 LVNA 48154 4266 E2
Burton Rd
10 WasC 48103 4404 D5
2400 AARB 48104 4490 D4
Burton St
3700 INKR 48141 4414 E6
4400 DET 48210 4344 A6
6100 RMLS 48174 4497 E2
12700 OKPK 48237 4199 A1
15000 OKPK 48237 4198 D1
16000 RMLS 48174 4581 E5
32300 BwTp 48173 4754 C7
Burtrig Rd
43600 VNBN 48111 4578 E6
43600 VNBN 48111 4579 A6
Burwell Ct
1600 WIND N9C 4420 B6
Burwell St
6800 DET 48210 4343 D5
Burwood Av
100 AARB 48103 4405 D6
Burwyck Park Dr
100 SALN 48176 4572 E7
Busenbark Ln
20600 BwTp 48173 4754 D4
Bush St
23000 SFLD 48034 4196 E3
Bushey St
3700 DET 48210 4344 B6
E Butler Cir
2000 WTLD 48186 4413 B4
N Butler Cir
37600 WTLD 48186 4413 B4
S Butler Cir
37600 WTLD 48186 4413 A4
W Butler Cir
2000 WTLD 48186 4413 B4

STREET
Block City ZIP Map# Grid

Butler Ct
4000 TNTN 48183 4669 B6
Butler Ln
47300 NOVI 48374 4192 A1
Butler Rd
10400 AGST 48191 4662 B7
11200 AGST 48191 4748 B1
13900 MonC 48191 4748 B5
Butler St
400 NHVL 48167 4192 E6
14000 DRBN 48120 4418 A4
15000 DRBN 48120 4417 E4
Buttercrest St
21200 SFLD 48075 4197 E3
Butternut
100 WynC 48111 4664 B3
Butternut Av
11000 PyTp 48170 4337 D1
Butternut Blvd
- PTFD 48197 4574 E1
Butternut Ln
42200 NOVI 48375 4193 A1
Butternut Rd
9100 WasC 48189 4259 B1
Butternut St
100 WTLD 48186 4414 C6
2000 DET 48216 4345 A5
2800 AARB 48108 4490 B4
3000 DET 48216 4344 D6
Butterweed Ct
1600 WasC 48103 4488 B2
Buttery Ct
2800 WIND N9E 4503 E1
Buttery St
2500 WIND N9E 4420 D7
2500 WIND N9E 4503 D1
Butwell St
8800 LVNA 48150 4338 A2
Bydding Rd
1100 AARB 48103 4406 A4
Byers
- TYLR 48180 4499 A3
Byfield Ln
10 DRBN 48120 4417 D3
N Byfield St
200 WTLD 48185 4413 E1
S Byfield St
200 WTLD 48186 4413 E2
Byington Blvd
- WasC 48105 4330 C7
2600 WasC 48105 4405 C1
Bynan Dr
2800 YpTp 48197 4491 B2
Byng Rd
1800 WIND N8W 4421 D3
3100 WIND N8W 4422 A7
3600 WIND N8W 4505 A1
Byrd St
1800 DRBN 48124 4417 A5
2000 DRBN 48124 4416 E5
Byrne Ct
45100 NOVI 48167 4192 C4
Byrne Dr
44800 NOVI 48167 4192 D4
Byromar Ln
9100 WynC 48138 4670 C3
Byron
27400 FNHL 48034 4196 A5
27400 FNHL 48336 4196 A5
Byron Av
1300 YpTp 48198 4492 D2
Byron St
- DET 48203 4272 C5
100 RVRG 48218 4418 E7
200 RVRG 48218 4501 E1
400 PLYM 48170 4337 A2
1000 PLYM 48170 4336 E2
7300 DET 48202 4344 E1
7300 DET 48210 4344 E1
8300 DET 48206 4272 D7
9800 DET 48202 4272 C5
11700 HDPK 48203 4272 C5
27000 SFLD 48034 4196 A5

C

C Av
- WasC 48197 4659 B1
C Dr
14100 PyTp 48170 4263 D6
C St
- FNHL 48336 4195 D2
10 DBHT 48125 4416 E7
2000 VNBN 48111 4494 A5
Cabacier St
500 DET 48226 4345 C7
Cabana Rd E
10 WIND N9E 4504 D2
10 WIND N9G 4504 D2
800 WIND N8W 4504 D2
Cabana Rd W
100 WIND N9E 4504 A3
100 WIND N9G 4504 A3
2500 WIND N9E 4503 E3
2500 WIND N9G 4503 E3
Cabin St
- LNPK 48146 4500 D5
Cabot Av
5700 LSal N9H 4503 D4
Cabot Ct
24300 WDHN 48183 4668 C6
Cabot Dr
24200 WDHN 48183 4668 C6
Cabot St
1900 DET 48209 4418 E2
2200 CNTN 48188 4411 E4
3800 DET 48210 4418 E1
5200 DET 48210 4343 C6
Cabri Ln
10 DBHT 48127 4415 D1
Ca Canny Ct
3600 PTFD 48108 4490 C5
Cada Cres
200 Tcmh N8N 4424 C1
Cadet St
6000 DET 48209 4419 C1
Cadieux Rd
300 GPPK 48230 4276 B5
300 GSPT 48230 4276 B5
3400 DET 48224 4276 A2
3400 DET 48230 4276 B5
5700 DET 48224 4275 E1
Cadillac Av
1100 GDNC 48135 4414 B1
1700 YpTp 48198 4493 A7
3300 WYNE 48184 4414 B5
5000 DET 48213 4274 D5
6400 GDNC 48135 4339 B6
6700 WRRN 48091 4201 E2
7000 WRRN 48091 4202 A2
8000 WRRN 48089 4202 A2
Cadillac Blvd
1300 DET 48214 4347 A2
1400 DET 48214 4346 E1
3400 DET 48214 4274 D7
Cadillac Cir
8500 WynC 48138 4670 C5
Cadillac Ct
23600 WynC 48138 4670 C5
Cadillac Sq
10 DET 48226 4345 D6
Cadillac Sq SR-3
10 DET 48226 4345 D6
Cadillac St
200 WIND N8Y 4346 D7
1500 WIND N8Y 4421 E2
1800 WIND N8W 4421 E2
32400 FNHL 48336 4195 A3
33400 FNHL 48335 4194 E3
33400 FNHL 48336 4194 E3
Cadillac School Dr
19000 BNTN 48174 4668 B1
Cadmus Ct
2800 WTLD 48186 4414 A5
Cady St
5700 LSal N9H 4503 E4
35000 WTLD 48186 4413 D4
E Cady St
100 NHVL 48167 4192 D6
W Cady St
100 NHVL 48167 4192 D6
Caely St
3800 DET 48212 4273 C2
Cahalan St
8000 DET 48209 4419 A2
8300 DET 48209 4418 E3
Cahill Rd
27000 FTRK 48134 4754 A3
27000 FTRK 48183 4754 A3
Cairney St
9100 DET 48213 4274 C5
Calais Ct
43100 CNTN 48187 4337 A4
Calder Av
500 YpTp 48198 4492 E5
Calder Ct
700 SALN 48176 4572 D6
Calderwood Av
1500 WIND N8W 4421 E7
1600 WIND N8W 4504 E1
1700 WIND N8W 4505 A1
1800 WIND N8W 4422 A7
Caldwell St
12800 DET 48212 4273 D1
19800 NvlT 48167 4192 C6
20200 DET 48234 4201 D4
Caledon Ct
10100 WIND N8R 4423 B2
Caledonia Av
20700 HZLP 48030 4200 D3
Caledonia Ct
2600 WTLD 48186 4414 A5
Calf Island Ct
14000 GBTR 48173 4755 C4
Calgary Ct
3900 PTFD 48108 4488 D6
Calhoun Ct
31900 WTLD 48186 4414 D5
Calhoun St
4000 DRBN 48126 4418 A1
6200 DRBN 48126 4343 A4
Caliburn Dr
37400 LVNA 48152 4266 A1
California
300 WynC 48111 4662 D2
California Av
100 WIND N9B 4420 B2
2300 WIND N9E 4420 D7
2500 WIND N9E 4503 E2
3700 WIND N9E 4504 A3
30500 RMLS 48174 4581 D5
California Cir
15000 SOGT 48195 4584 B5
California St
10 HDPK 48203 4272 E4
9200 LVNA 48150 4339 A2
19500 STCS 48080 4204 B2
20000 TYLR 48180 4583 E5
20000 TYLR 48195 4583 E5
26800 TYLR 48180 4582 C5
29400 RMLS 48174 4581 E5
34100 RMLS 48174 4580 E5
Calkins St
100 SLYN 48178 4189 A2
Calla Dr
9900 GOTp 48178 4188 C2
Callender St
12800 SOGT 48195 4584 D1
Calloway Ct
2600 CNTN 48188 4411 C5
Calm Meadow Ct
23500 WynC 48138 4670 B5
Calumet Av
2000 AARB 48104 4489 E3
Calumet Ct
33800 WTLD 48186 4413 B6
33800 WTLD 48186 4414 A5
Calumet Rd
10600 GOTp 48189 4187 C4
Calumet St
- DET 48201 4345 A4
1400 DET 48210 4345 A4
1900 DET 48210 4344 E4
33600 WTLD 48186 4414 A5
Calvary Ct
1600 Tcmh N8N 4423 E3
Calvary St
1700 Tcmh N8N 4423 E3
1700 Tcmh N8N 4424 A3
Calvert Cres
1300 WIND N8W 4421 E6
Calvert St
10 DET 48202 4272 D5
1400 DET 48206 4272 B7
Calvin Av
400 GSPF 48236 4276 C2
2100 LNPK 48146 4500 C4
Calvin St
1600 WasC 48103 4405 D4
23400 TYLR 48180 4499 B4
24000 DRBN 48124 4416 A5
24300 DRBN 48124 4415 E5
Camborne Ln
32400 LVNA 48154 4267 A3
40600 NOVI 48375 4193 C1
Cambourne Rd
5600 DBHT 48127 4340 C6
E Cambourne St
100 FRDL 48220 4199 E2
400 FRDL 48220 4200 A2
W Cambourne St
100 FRDL 48220 4199 D2
Cambria Ct
34000 WTLD 48186 4413 B6
Cambridge Av
300 SLYN 48178 4189 A3
2800 DET 48221 4199 E6
12700 DET 48235 4199 A6
13300 SOGT 48195 4584 D5
14500 DET 48235 4198 D6
16900 ALPK 48101 4417 B7
18100 DET 48219 4198 A6
18800 DET 48219 4197 E6
27100 RDFD 48240 4196 B6
27400 GDNC 48135 4340 A5
28600 GDNC 48135 4339 E5
S Cambridge Av
8400 DET 48221 4199 C6
Cambridge Av N
8200 DET 48221 4199 C6
Cambridge Blvd
100 PTRG 48069 4199 C1
11800 GOTp 48178 4188 B2
Cambridge Ct
- Amhg N9V 4671 C5
500 Tcmh N8N 4424 C2
1200 AARB 48104 4406 C7
9700 GOTp 48178 4188 B2
13200 PyTp 48170 4264 B6
19700 NvlT 48167 4193 D6
Cambridge Dr
1300 DRBN 48124 4415 E3
9000 WasC 48176 4658 B2
20700 NOVI 48167 4193 C5
20700 NOVI 48375 4193 C5
24200 WDHN 48183 4668 C6
Cambridge Rd
10 GSPF 48236 4276 E2
1300 AARB 48104 4406 D7
2200 TNTN 48183 4669 D3
Cambridge St
700 YPLT 48197 4491 D3
6100 DBHT 48127 4340 B6
24800 WDHN 48183 4668 C6
29000 FTRK 48134 4754 B4
31700 LVNA 48154 4267 B2
39200 WTLD 48186 4412 E4
40000 CNTN 48187 4337 D7
Cambridge Club Cir
5500 WasC 48103 4404 B5
Camden
- TYLR 48180 4498 D5
Camden Av
15000 EPTE 48021 4203 B1
Camden Ct
41700 NvlT 48167 4265 B3
Camden Dr
8400 RMLS 48174 4495 E4
Camden Rd
- VNBN 48111 4579 B3
16200 WDHN 48183 4669 A2
Camden St
400 FRDL 48220 4200 A4
5700 LSal N9J 4503 B3
11300 DET 48213 4274 E4
11600 LVNA 48150 4267 E7
11600 LVNA 48150 4339 E1
12200 DET 48213 4275 A3
14400 DET 48224 4275 A3
Camelia Ct
7200 CNTN 48187 4336 C4
Camelia Dr
46600 CNTN 48187 4336 B5
Camelot Dr
6900 CNTN 48187 4336 D5
Camelot Rd
1900 AARB 48104 4489 E2
Camelot St
1500 TNTN 48183 4669 D2
1500 TNTN 48192 4669 D2
Cameo Ct
2000 CNTN 48187 4335 E7
2000 CNTN 48187 4410 E1
Cameos Cres
5900 LSal N9J 4503 A3
Cameron Av
100 WIND N9B 4420 C1
S Cameron Blvd
1500 WIND N9B 4420 D4
1900 WIND N9B 4421 A6
1900 WIND N9E 4421 A6
Cameron Cir
4500 WasC 48130 4329 D4
Cameron Dr
17100 NvlT 48167 4265 C2
Cameron Pl
10 GSPT 48230 4276 D6
Cameron St
8900 DET 48211 4273 A5
15000 SOGT 48195 4584 B4
17100 DET 48203 4272 D1
19100 DET 48203 4200 D5
Camille Ct
21900 WDHN 48183 4668 C3
22600 FNHL 48335 4194 A3
Camille Dr
21800 WDHN 48183 4668 C3
Camley St
9200 DET 48224 4275 E1
9400 DET 48224 4276 A1
9700 DET 48224 4204 A7
Campau Rd
14800 BwTp 48173 4841 B3
Campbell Av
100 WIND N9B 4420 D4
400 YpTp 48198 4492 C3
21700 WRRN 48089 4202 B2
Campbell Ct
2400 CNTN 48188 4412 A5
Campbell Dr
10000 HbgT 48116 4186 B3
10000 HbgT 48189 4186 B3
Campbell Rd
6000 PTFD 48108 4573 E3
6000 PTFD 48108 4574 A3
6000 PTFD 48176 4573 E3
6000 PTFD 48176 4574 A3
Campbell St
100 DET 48229 4418 D7
100 RVRG 48218 4418 D7
100 RVRG 48229 4418 D7
300 RVRG 48218 4501 C1
1000 DET 48209 4419 C1
2400 DET 48209 4344 C7
3000 DRBN 48124 4416 D6
3900 DBHT 48124 4416 D6
3900 DBHT 48125 4416 D6
5600 DBHT 48125 4499 D1
6800 TYLR 48180 4499 D2
Campbell St N
5600 DET 48210 4344 A4
Campbell St S
100 DET 48209 4419 D2
Campus Dr
1000 AARB 48103 4489 C3
1000 AARB 48104 4489 C3
5900 DBHT 48127 4341 C6
Campus Pkwy
- PTFD 48176 4573 A5
Canada St
5700 LSal N9H 4503 D4
Canal Dr
20000 WynC 48138 4670 C2
W Canal Dr
35900 BwTp 48173 4841 B3
Canal Dr E
35900 BwTp 48173 4841 B3
Canal St
- Amhg N9V 4671 B3
900 AARB 48104 4406 C5
900 AARB 48105 4406 C5
10100 GOTp 48189 4187 B5
Canberra Ct
400 WasC 48176 4658 D2
Candace Dr
20000 RKWD 48173 4754 B6
Candace Ln
47800 CNTN 48187 4411 A2
Candler St
10 HDPK 48203 4272 D1
Candlewick Dr
1900 AARB 48104 4489 E3
Candlewood Cres
3200 WIND N8W 4421 E7
Candlewood Ct
43200 CNTN 48187 4337 A4
Candlewood Dr
12300 Tcmh N9K 4424 A4
43500 CNTN 48187 4336 E4
43500 CNTN 48187 4337 A4
Candlewood Ln
1200 YpTp 48198 4492 C2
Candor Ct
3100 WasC 48176 4572 B3
Canfield Av
22900 FNHL 48336 4195 E2
Canfield Dr
8500 DBHT 48127 4340 B3
Canfield Dr W
27200 DBHT 48127 4340 B3
Canfield St E
10 DET 48201 4345 C3
900 DET 48207 4345 D2
3300 DET 48207 4346 A1
7400 DET 48214 4346 B1
9900 DET 48214 4274 E7
11200 DET 48214 4275 A6
Canfield St W
- DET 48210 4344 D4
1100 DET 48201 4345 A4
Canfield St W
1300 DET 48210 4345 A4
Caniff St
1200 DET 48211 4273 A4
1600 HMTK 48212 4273 A4
5500 DET 48212 4273 C3
Canonbury St
13000 DET 48205 4274 C1
Cantaberry Ct
13600 GOTp 48178 4188 E3
Cantelon Dr
6700 WIND N8T 4422 E3
6900 WIND N8T 4423 A3
Canterberry Ct
500 Tcmh N8N 4424 D2
Canterbury Av
21300 WynC 48138 4670 D3
Canterbury Cir
400 CNTN 48187 4412 C1
26700 HnTp 48164 4751 B1
Canterbury Ct
600 SALN 48176 4657 D1
700 GSPW 48236 4205 A4
4400 WasC 48103 4329 E4
6300 WTLD 48185 4339 A6
8500 SpTp 48198 4492 C1
13500 PyTp 48170 4264 C6
22000 WDHN 48183 4668 C4
Canterbury Dr
- TYLR 48180 4582 E5
400 SALN 48176 4657 D1
800 CNTN 48187 4412 C1
19000 LVNA 48152 4195 B7
Canterbury Ln
7800 WasC 48167 4190 C6
Canterbury Rd
500 GSPW 48236 4205 A4
800 GSPW 48236 4204 E4
2400 AARB 48104 4490 A3
19900 DET 48221 4199 D5
Canterbury St
1000 NHVL 48167 4192 E4
1400 DRBN 48120 4418 D3
2500 TNTN 48183 4669 C6
16800 LVNA 48152 4267 B2
16800 LVNA 48154 4267 B2
22100 WDHN 48183 4668 C4
22800 STCS 48080 4204 E2
Canton Ct
41000 CNTN 48188 4412 C4
Canton St
400 DET 48207 4346 C3
4800 DET 48207 4274 A7
6500 DET 48211 4274 A6
19900 HRWD 48225 4204 B5
20700 HRWD 48236 4204 C4
N Canton Center Rd
100 CNTN 48187 4411 D1
1600 CNTN 48187 4336 D7
8800 PyTp 48170 4336 D3
S Canton Center Rd
100 CNTN 48187 4411 D4
100 CNTN 48188 4411 D4
Canyon Cir
24400 FTRK 48134 4754 A1
24900 FTRK 48134 4753 E1
Canyon Ct
2200 AARB 48105 4406 E1
Canyon Dr
2400 YpTp 48197 4491 B7
6900 RMLS 48174 4495 E3
36600 WTLD 48186 4413 C2
Canyon St
4800 DET 48224 4276 B1
4800 DET 48236 4276 B1
4800 GSPF 48236 4276 B1
8800 DET 48224 4204 A7
8800 DET 48236 4204 A7
38400 WTLD 48186 4413 A2
Cape Cod
700 SLYN 48178 4189 B3
Cape Cod St
11000 TYLR 48180 4498 C7
11000 TYLR 48180 4582 C1
Cape Cod Wy
22000 FNHL 48336 4195 C3
44400 CNTN 48187 4336 C4
Capernall Rd
13300 MonC 48117 4749 B6
14300 MonC 48111 4749 B6
Capistrano Ct
10 BLVL 48111 4578 E4
Capital Av
7600 WasC 48189 4259 B4
Capital Dr
41000 CNTN 48187 4337 C4
Capital St
8500 OKPK 48220 4199 B3
10000 OKPK 48237 4199 A3
13100 OKPK 48237 4198 E3
Capitol
24700 RDFD 48239 4268 E7
Capitol Av
400 LNPK 48146 4501 A5
1300 LNPK 48146 4500 D5
1900 WRRN 48091 4200 E2
2200 WRRN 48091 4201 A2
N Capitol Ct
37500 LVNA 48150 4266 A7
S Capitol Ct
37500 LVNA 48150 4266 A7
Capitol Dr
18500 SFLD 48075 4197 E1
18500 SFLD 48075 4198 A1
51000 VNBN 48111 4577 C4
Capitol St
- LVNA 48150 4268 A7
- LVNA 48239 4268 A7
500 WIND N8X 4421 C6
13000 DET 48227 4271 A7
Capitol St
15800 DET 48227 4270 C7
18400 DET 48223 4270 A7
18400 DET 48228 4270 A7
19600 DET 48228 4269 D7
19800 DET 48223 4269 D7
32300 LVNA 48150 4267 A7
33500 LVNA 48150 4266 E7
Cappelletto Rd
2500 WIND N8W 4422 B3
Capri Ct
47400 NOVI 48167 4192 A4
Capri Dr
7500 CNTN 48187 4336 E5
Capri Ter
31400 WTLD 48185 4339 C4
Caprice Ct
9300 PyTp 48170 4337 E2
Caprice Dr
9200 PyTp 48170 4337 D2
Cara Ln
31700 RKWD 48173 4754 B6
Carbeck Dr
600 AARB 48103 4405 D5
Carbon St
9400 DET 48209 4418 E5
Carbondale St
8000 DET 48204 4343 E3
8000 DET 48210 4343 E3
Cardene Ct
19400 NvlT 48167 4193 B7
Cardene Wy
19300 NvlT 48167 4193 B7
Cardia Dr
400 WasC 48103 4404 A4
Cardiff Av
47800 CNTN 48188 4411 A7
Cardigan Ct
- SALN 48176 4572 B6
Cardigan Ct N
2300 WRRN 48091 4201 A1
Cardinal Av
3100 AARB 48108 4490 A4
17800 WynC 48138 4585 D6
Cardinal Cres
1200 Tcmh N8N 4423 D2
Cardinal Dr
18000 WynC 48138 4585 C7
Cardinal Ln
32400 WYNE 48184 4414 B7
Cardoni St
10200 DET 48211 4273 A4
17100 DET 48203 4272 D1
19600 DET 48203 4200 D5
Cardwell Av
100 GDNC 48135 4415 B1
100 GDNC 48141 4415 B1
6400 GDNC 48135 4340 A5
Cardwell St
- LVNA 48150 4268 A5
100 INKR 48141 4415 B2
8500 WTLD 48185 4340 A3
9500 LVNA 48150 4340 A1
13900 LVNA 48154 4268 A5
Carefree
6500 WasC 48178 4261 B7
Caren Dr
5600 YpTp 48197 4576 B2
Carey St
10 AARB 48104 4406 C5
Cargo Dr
8500 YpTp 48197 4576 C1
Carhart Av
2000 AARB 48104 4489 E2
Caribou St
6500 WTLD 48185 4338 E5
Carissa Av
2500 WIND N8R 4423 A2
Caritas Ct
400 Tcmh N8N 4424 D2
Carl Ct
3300 AARB 48105 4407 C1
Carl Dr
33800 LVNA 48152 4194 E6
Carl St
33300 LVNA 48152 4194 E6
Carla Ct
36900 FNHL 48335 4194 B3
Carleton Av
21700 SFLD 48034 4196 D4
Carleton St
9300 DET 48214 4274 D6
Carleton Rockwood Rd
2900 MonC 48117 4839 A1
4000 BrTp 48117 4839 D1
5000 BrTp 48179 4839 D1
5200 SRKW 48179 4839 D1
5300 SRKW 48179 4840 A1
Carleton West Rd
12800 MonC 48117 4750 D7
21600 WynC 48111 4664 D5
24600 WynC 48164 4664 D7
25600 WynC 48164 4750 D2
Carlin St
8800 DET 48228 4342 E1
9500 DET 48227 4342 E1
Carling Cres
300 WIND N8S 4347 E5
Carlisle Av
23000 HZLP 48030 4200 C1
Carlisle Ct
5000 WasC 48103 4404 D6
22300 NOVI 48374 4192 B4
43100 CNTN 48187 4337 A5
Carlisle Pkwy
32000 WYNE 48184 4414 B6
Carlisle Rd
38900 HnTp 48164 4665 A6
Carlisle St
- DET 48225 4203 C4
Carlisle St
- HRWD 48225 4203 C4
13600 DET 48205 4202 E4
13800 DET 48205 4203 A4
N Carlson St
1100 WTLD 48185 4413 C1
5800 WTLD 48185 4338 C7
S Carlson St
100 WTLD 48185 4413 C2
100 WTLD 48186 4413 C2
Carlston St
400 RVRG 48218 4501 D1
Carlton Dr
2700 PTFD 48108 4490 D4
Carlton Ln
10 DRBN 48120 4417 D2
Carlton Rd
6400 CNTN 48187 4336 B6
Carlton St
29100 INKR 48141 4414 E4
Carlyle Av
25800 INKR 48141 4415 D6
Carlysle Ct
10 DRBN 48124 4417 A5
Carlysle St
1800 DRBN 48124 4417 A5
18900 DRBN 48124 4416 E6
24300 DRBN 48124 4415 E6
25400 DBHT 48125 4415 D6
25600 DBHT 48141 4415 D6
27800 INKR 48141 4415 A6
28800 INKR 48141 4414 D6
Carman St
19100 DET 48203 4200 C6
Carmel Ln
10 GSPF 48236 4276 E3
Carmel St
10 WTLD 48186 4414 D7
900 DET 48203 4200 B6
2500 AARB 48104 4490 A3
25100 WDHN 48183 4668 B7
Carmell St
10 BLVL 48111 4578 E4
Carmichael Rd
- WIND N9C 4420 A6
Carnagie St
6000 RMLS 48174 4496 E2
Carnegie Av
300 LSal N9J 4502 D5
Carnegie St
4000 WYNE 48184 4413 E7
5200 WYNE 48184 4496 E1
Carol Av
900 PLYM 48170 4337 A1
1200 PLYM 48170 4336 E1
Carol Dr
2100 AARB 48103 4488 D1
Carol St
900 YpTp 48198 4492 B2
3500 MVDL 48122 4417 E6
17200 LVNA 48152 4268 A2
20400 DET 48235 4198 D4
Carol Ann Av
1800 YpTp 48198 4492 E6
Carolee Ln
4600 DBHT 48125 4415 E7
Carolina Av
500 AARB 48103 4405 D6
Carolina St
22300 STCS 48080 4204 D3
N Carolina St
24300 SFLD 48075 4197 D2
24300 SFLD 48075 4198 A1
Caroline St
300 WIND N9A 4420 E2
8800 TYLR 48180 4499 E4
Carolon Blvd
38300 WTLD 48185 4338 A7
Carolyn St
3500 AARB 48104 4490 C3
Caron Av
100 WIND N9A 4420 D1
Carothers Dr
- VNBN 48111 4578 E2
Carpenter Rd
2300 PTFD 48108 4490 D5
3000 PTFD 48197 4490 D5
4000 PTFD 48197 4574 D1
8000 WasC 48160 4574 D6
8000 WasC 48197 4574 D6
8200 WasC 48160 4659 D1
8200 WasC 48197 4659 D1
Carpenter St
700 NHVL 48167 4192 E5
1900 HMTK 48212 4273 A3
3800 DET 48212 4273 C2
Carriage Ct
2400 YpTp 48197 4491 B5
Carriage Ln
10 WynC 48111 4662 C6
1200 LSal N9H 4504 C5
18400 RVVW 48192 4584 A7
Carriage Wy
- NvlT 48167 4263 D2
10 YpTp 48197 4491 B5
Carriage Cove Cir
42000 CNTN 48187 4337 B5
Carriage Cove Dr
42000 CNTN 48187 4337 B5
Carriage Hill Ct
23800 SFLD 48075 4198 C4
Carriage Hill Dr
- NOVI 48167 4193 C4
- NOVI 48375 4193 C4
Carriage Hill Rd
23600 SFLD 48075 4198 C4
Carriage Hills Dr
6500 CNTN 48187 4337 A6
Carriage Lamp Ct
16200 SFLD 48075 4198 B2

INDEX 12

Carriage Lamp Dr — Detroit & Wayne County Street Index — Cherokee St

Detroit & Wayne County Street Index

STREET
Block City ZIP Map# Grid

Carriage Lamp Dr
16000 SFLD 48075 4198 C4
Carriage Trade Ln
16000 SFLD 48075 4198 C4
Carrie Ln
7600 WasC 48178 4260 E3
Carrie St
- DET 48212 4274 A3
- DET 48234 4274 A3
6500 DET 48211 4274 A4
8300 DET 48213 4274 A4
17500 DET 48212 4202 A7
19900 DET 48234 4202 A4
Carrington Dr
900 NHVL 48167 4192 D5
Carrington Pl
10 GSPF 48236 4276 E2
Carroll Dr
15600 RVVW 48192 4584 B7
Carrot Wy
10 AATp 48105 4406 D1
Carrousel Blvd
8100 WTLD 48185 4339 C3
Carson Dr
100 WTLD 48185 4412 E2
6900 RMLS 48174 4495 E3
Carson St
2300 DET 48209 4419 A2
2500 DET 48209 4418 E1
Carten St
9300 DET 48214 4346 E1
Carter Av
8400 ALPK 48101 4500 A5
Carter Ct
6700 YpTp 48197 4575 E4
Carter Pl
4000 PTFD 48197 4490 E4
4000 PTFD 48197 4491 A4
Carter Rd
1600 MonC 48117 4752 D5
2400 MonC 48134 4752 D5
22000 WDHN 48183 4668 B4
22700 BNTN 48183 4668 B4
Carter Rd E
16400 WDHN 48183 4669 A3
Carter St
2600 DET 48206 4344 B1
4000 DET 48204 4344 B1
Cartier Dr
600 WIND N9E 4504 C2
Cartridge St
6300 DET 48209 4419 C2
Caruso Dr
600 WIND N9G 4504 E4
Carver Av
700 YPLT 48198 4492 B3
900 YpTp 48198 4492 B2
Carver St
300 GSPF 48236 4276 E2
Cary Dr
5500 YpTp 48197 4576 C2
Cary St
25000 TYLR 48180 4582 E3
Cary St S
700 DET 48209 4419 B4
Caryn St
3500 MVDL 48122 4418 A5
3600 MVDL 48122 4417 E5
Casablanca St
7900 WIND N8R 4423 A3
Casa San Marino Dr
24500 BNTN 48134 4668 A5
Cascade Ct
2600 WTLD 48186 4414 A5
16500 BNTN 48192 4669 A1
Cascade Dr
2800 AARB 48104 4490 B4
8000 GOTp 48178 4187 D1
19000 BNTN 48192 4669 A1
22000 NOVI 48375 4193 C3
Cascade Pl
1200 YpTp 48197 4491 B7
Cascade St
9200 DET 48204 4344 A1
9600 DET 48204 4343 E1
9900 DET 48204 4271 E7
Cascades Dr
17100 NvlT 48167 4265 A1
Casco Ct
33800 WTLD 48186 4414 A5
Caseville Ct
34000 WTLD 48186 4413 E5
Casgrain Dr
3800 WIND N9G 4504 C3
Casgrain St
800 DET 48209 4419 B2
Cashew St
500 WTLD 48186 4414 C7
Casino St
8900 DET 48224 4276 A1
9400 DET 48224 4275 E1
10300 DET 48224 4203 E7
12700 DET 48205 4203 D7
Casino Wy
- DET 48207 4346 D5
Casler St
10 YPLT 48197 4492 A5
Casmere St
2600 HMTK 48212 4273 B3
3800 DET 48212 4273 D3
Casper St
2300 DET 48209 4419 A1
5100 DET 48210 4343 D5
Caspian Ct
34100 WTLD 48186 4413 B6
Cass Av
- NvlT 48167 4193 C7
- NvlT 48167 4265 C1
500 DET 48226 4345 C6
2100 DET 48201 4345 C5
Cass Av
5000 DET 48202 4345 B2
9500 TYLR 48180 4499 B5
Cass Ct
- NvlT 48167 4193 C7
34100 FMTN 48335 4194 D2
Cass St
2500 DRBN 48124 4416 C4
21400 FNHL 48335 4194 E3
23800 FMTN 48335 4194 E1
Cass Benton Pkwy
- NvlT 48167 4264 E1
Castaway Ln
6500 PTFD 48197 4574 C5
Castelle Dr
22000 HnTp 48174 4667 B4
Caster St
100 PLYM 48170 4265 B7
Castle Ct
42400 CNTN 48188 4412 B3
Castle Dr
2000 WasC 48103 4487 D3
38000 RMLS 48174 4580 A3
42600 CNTN 48188 4412 A3
Castle St
10000 DRBN 48126 4343 B4
11300 DET 48234 4274 A2
14600 SOGT 48195 4584 C2
Castlebury Dr
200 SALN 48176 4657 A1
500 SALN 48176 4572 B7
E Castlebury Dr
300 SALN 48176 4657 B1
400 SALN 48176 4572 B7
Castlegate Ct
5800 CNTN 48187 4336 C7
Castle Hill Rd
1600 WIND N8P 4348 D6
Castlemeadow Dr
35600 FNHL 48335 4194 C3
Castle Ridge Ct
500 Amhg N9V 4757 C5
Castleside Ct
48300 CNTN 48187 4336 A5
Castleside Dr
48300 CNTN 48187 4336 A5
48600 CNTN 48187 4335 E5
Castleton Av
1700 WIND N8P 4348 D7
1700 WIND N8P 4423 D1
Castleton St
14600 DET 48227 4270 D7
Castlewood
43400 NOVI 48375 4192 E2
Castlewood Dr
25200 WDHN 48183 4669 A7
Castle Woods Blvd
- WTLD 48185 4338 C6
Castle Woods Ct
35600 WTLD 48185 4338 C6
Catalina Dr
1400 AARB 48103 4488 E1
Catalina Cove
100 Tcmh N8P 4348 D6
Catalpa Cir
2800 AARB 48108 4489 D4
Catalpa Ct
1800 FRDL 48220 4199 C2
Catalpa St
12700 SOGT 48195 4584 D3
Cataraqui St
400 WIND N9A 4421 A1
1600 WIND N8Y 4421 A1
2000 WIND N8Y 4346 C7
Cathedral
23600 RDFD 48239 4341 A2
24200 RDFD 48239 4340 E2
27300 RDFD 48150 4340 C2
Cathedral St
- DET 48228 4342 D2
20500 DET 48228 4341 D2
28000 LVNA 48150 4340 A2
Cather St
39400 CNTN 48187 4337 D4
Catherine Ct
17100 LVNA 48152 4267 D2
Catherine St
10 RVRG 48218 4501 E1
10 YPLT 48197 4492 A5
100 AARB 48103 4406 C5
100 AARB 48104 4406 C5
Catherine Industrial Dr
24200 NOVI 48375 4193 A1
Cavalier Ct
42500 CNTN 48187 4337 B4
Cavalier Dr
23000 STCS 48080 4204 D2
S Cavalier Dr
1900 CNTN 48188 4411 E4
N Cavalier Rd
1100 CNTN 48187 4411 E1
Cavalry St
1000 DET 48209 4419 C2
S Cavalry St
100 DET 48209 4419 D3
Cavell Av
8400 WTLD 48185 4340 A3
8900 LVNA 48150 4340 B2
Cavell St
9500 LVNA 48150 4340 A1
12000 LVNA 48150 4268 A7
14500 LVNA 48154 4268 A4
Cavendish Av E
24700 NOVI 48375 4192 D1
Cavendish Av W
24300 NOVI 48375 4192 D1
Cavendish Ct
4900 WasC 48103 4404 D6
24300 NOVI 48375 4192 D1
Cavour St
14900 LVNA 48154 4267 E4
Cayman Blvd
5900 PTFD 48197 4574 E3
Cayman Ct
3600 SpTp 48105 4333 C7
3600 SpTp 48198 4333 C7
Cayuga Av
600 YpTp 48198 4492 E5
23000 HZLP 48030 4200 D2
Cayuga Pl
1800 AARB 48104 4489 E2
CE Bellamy Dr
- LVNA 48150 4266 A7
- LVNA 48150 4338 A1
Cecil St
4700 DET 48210 4343 E5
Cecile St
7800 WIND N8S 4347 D5
26200 DBHT 48127 4340 C7
Cecilia Dr
- WasC 48167 4190 C7
- WasC 48167 4262 C1
Cedar
- CNTN 48188 4411 D6
Cedar Ct
- CNTN 48188 4411 D6
300 Tcmh N8N 4424 C1
8600 SpTp 48198 4492 C1
19800 HRWD 48225 4203 E5
22600 HZLP 48030 4200 E2
Cedar Dr
37800 HnTp 48164 4751 B1
Cedar Grv
17500 BNTN 48174 4583 B6
Cedar Ln
1600 AATp 48105 4331 D5
11300 PyTp 48170 4337 D1
Cedar Rd
600 WasC 48189 4187 B6
Cedar St
1200 WYDT 48192 4585 A1
2100 WYDT 48192 4584 E2
2300 WYDT 48195 4584 E2
49400 VNBN 48111 4493 E2
Cedar Bend Dr
1100 AARB 48105 4406 D4
Cedarbend Dr
6000 YpTp 48197 4575 C3
Cedarbrook Ct
- GOTp 48178 4188 A5
Cedarbrook Dr
- GOTp 48178 4188 A5
Cedarbrook Rd
3000 AARB 48105 4407 B1
Cedarcliff Dr
2300 YpTp 48198 4493 A6
Cedar Creek Dr
25100 BNTN 48134 4667 D7
Cedarcrest Rd
10200 GOTp 48189 4187 B4
Cedargrove St
13500 DET 48205 4202 E7
13500 DET 48205 4203 A7
Cedarhurst Dr
43500 VNBN 48111 4495 A5
Cedarhurst Pl
10 DET 48203 4272 C1
Cedar Island Blvd
18000 BNTN 48174 4582 C7
Cedar Lake Cir
17400 NvlT 48167 4265 A2
Cedarlawn St
10000 DET 48204 4271 B7
17000 SOGT 48195 4500 A6
Cedar Ridge Av
300 Amhg N9V 4757 C4
Cedar Ridge Ct
23900 BNTN 48174 4583 A7
Cedar Ridge Dr
5500 WasC 48103 4404 B5
23600 BNTN 48174 4583 B7
Cedar Run Ct
26800 WDHN 48183 4754 D2
Cedar Valley Dr
1900 CNTN 48188 4412 D4
Cedarview Av
7400 WIND N8S 4347 D6
8900 WIND N8S 4348 A5
Cedar View Ln
12500 GOTp 48178 4188 C1
Cedarview St
4800 PTFD 48197 4491 A7
Cedarwood
47900 NOVI 48374 4192 A2
48100 NOVI 48374 4191 E2
Cedarwood Dr
12000 Tcmh N8N 4348 E7
Cedar Wy St
16100 RMLS 48174 4582 A5
Celandine Ct
200 PTFD 48197 4574 E2
Celeron Island Ln
13900 GBTR 48173 4755 D3
Celestine Dr
9000 VNBN 48111 4494 E5
Celestine St
12300 DET 48205 4275 B1
12600 DET 48205 4203 A7
Celina Ct
1000 CNTN 48187 4411 D1
Centennial Av
900 YpTp 48198 4493 A2
Centennial Ct
1300 CNTN 48187 4410 E1
Centennial Dr
100 Tcmh N8N 4349 B7
1100 CNTN 48187 4410 E1
15300 NvlT 48167 4264 C4
Center Ct
36400 WYNE 48184 4413 C5
Center Dr
300 SALN 48176 4572 D7
500 AARB 48103 4405 C4
500 WasC 48103 4405 C4
8000 RMLS 48174 4496 A4
Center Rdg
400 SLYN 48178 4189 B1
Center St
- TYLR 48180 4498 D3
10 DBHT 48127 4340 C5
10 YPLT 48198 4492 B4
1000 INKR 48141 4415 A3
N Center St
- NOVI 48167 4192 D4
- NOVI 48375 4192 D4
700 NHVL 48167 4192 D6
S Center St
100 NHVL 48167 4192 D7
Centerbrook Ct
21600 GSPW 48236 4204 E4
Centerfarm Ln
21100 FNHL 48167 4194 A5
Centerhill Rd
7300 HbgT 48116 4186 B1
Center Valley Dr
4000 PTFD 48197 4490 D5
Centerville Av
- WTLD 48186 4414 A5
Centerwood Dr
2000 WRRN 48030 4200 E1
2000 WRRN 48091 4200 E1
Central Av
- AARB 48103 4405 B6
- DET 48207 4346 E5
- DET 48207 4347 B4
400 WYDT 48192 4585 B5
800 WIND N8Y 4346 D7
1100 WIND N8Y 4421 E1
1800 WIND N8W 4422 A2
6800 GDNC 48135 4339 E5
Central Blvd
4000 PTFD 48108 4490 D3
Central Ct
100 GDNC 48135 4414 E2
Central Dr
- PTFD 48197 4490 D5
Central St
- WTLD 48185 4339 E5
200 INKR 48141 4414 E2
600 GDNC 48135 4414 E1
800 DET 48209 4419 A1
1700 FRDL 48220 4199 C2
2800 DET 48209 4418 E1
3200 DET 48209 4343 E6
6500 DET 48210 4343 D3
8800 DET 48204 4343 D1
10000 RMLS 48174 4497 E6
17000 HnTp 48174 4582 A6
Central City Pkwy
6100 WTLD 48185 4338 C5
Centralia
9500 RDFD 48239 4340 C1
13900 RDFD 48239 4268 C5
16300 RDFD 48240 4268 C2
19900 RDFD 48240 4196 C6
Centralia St
100 DBHT 48127 4415 D1
8300 DBHT 48127 4340 D3
Central Park Blvd
- CNTN 48188 4411 A4
Central Park Dr
- DBHT 48127 4340 D7
48000 CNTN 48188 4411 A4
48200 CNTN 48188 4410 E4
Centre Av
1100 LSal N9J 4502 E4
1100 LSal N9J 4503 A4
Centre St
1400 DET 48226 4345 D5
Centre Lake Dr
4500 WIND N9G 4504 E4
Centurion Av
4200 WIND N9G 4504 E4
Century Ct
1800 CNTN 48188 4411 D4
3800 PTFD 48197 4490 E5
Century Dr
15000 DRBN 48120 4417 E2
22000 TYLR 48180 4583 C2
Century Tr
3300 PTFD 48197 4490 E5
Cervi Blvd
1000 LSal N9J 4503 A5
Chablis St
21600 HnTp 48174 4667 B3
Chad Ct
4300 WasC 48103 4330 A5
Chadwick Ct
7100 CNTN 48187 4336 B7
Chadwick Dr
6500 CNTN 48187 4336 C6
Chadwick St
13600 DET 48227 4270 E7
Chalfonte Av
10 GSPF 48236 4276 C3
10 GSPF 48230 4276 C3
400 GSPF 48236 4204 D7
400 GSPW 48236 4204 D7
Chalfonte St
- DET 48223 4269 E4
- DET 48223 4270 A4
- DET 48227 4270 A4
- DET 48227 4271 B4
- DET 48238 4271 E3
- GSPT 48230 4276 B3
Chalk Farm Rd W
24600 WRRN 48091 4201 A1
Chalmers Av
6700 WRRN 48091 4201 E3
7000 WRRN 48091 4202 A3
8000 WRRN 48089 4202 B3
Chalmers Dr
1000 AATp 48104 4490 C1
2000 AARB 48104 4490 C2
Chalmers St
200 DET 48214 4347 E1
1000 DET 48214 4275 D7
5000 DET 48213 4275 C5
5000 DET 48224 4275 C5
11500 DET 48205 4275 A1
17100 DET 48205 4203 A7
Chalmette Ct
43800 CNTN 48188 4411 E4
Chalon St
19500 STCS 48080 4204 B3
Chamberlain Cir
3100 WasC 48103 4488 B1
Chamberlain Dr
11400 GOTp 48178 4187 E3
Chamberlain St
4100 WYNE 48184 4413 D7
5400 WYNE 48184 4496 E1
5700 WYNE 48174 4496 E1
8000 DET 48209 4419 A3
8700 DET 48209 4418 E3
9200 RMLS 48174 4496 E5
Chamberlin St
14600 BrTp 48134 4753 C4
Chambury Ct
48600 PyTp 48170 4335 E2
48600 PyTp 48170 4336 A2
Champagne Dr
2000 AARB 48108 4489 E5
2000 PTFD 48108 4489 E5
2100 AARB 48108 4490 A5
Champaign Rd
400 LNPK 48146 4501 A4
1200 LNPK 48146 4500 D4
2200 ALPK 48146 4500 B4
2200 LNPK 48101 4500 B4
16100 ALPK 48101 4500 A3
18700 ALPK 48101 4499 E3
19300 ALPK 48180 4499 E3
Champaign St
20000 TYLR 48180 4499 C3
24700 TYLR 48180 4498 D4
Champine Pl
400 GSPF 48236 4276 C1
Champion Ct
39400 NvlT 48167 4265 D3
Champlain Ct
43500 CNTN 48188 4412 A3
Champlain Dr
600 WIND N9E 4504 C2
Chandler Av
1000 LNPK 48229 4501 B2
1200 LNPK 48146 4501 A3
2900 LNPK 48146 4500 E5
Chandler Dr
300 SALN 48176 4572 D6
11600 PyTp 48170 4335 C1
Chandler Rd
1500 AARB 48105 4406 C3
1700 WIND N8Y 4421 E2
1800 WIND N8W 4421 E3
2400 WIND N8W 4422 A3
Chandler St
10 DET 48202 4273 A7
Chandler Park Dr
12800 DET 48213 4275 A4
16500 DET 48224 4275 E2
17100 DET 48224 4276 A2
18600 DET 48236 4276 A2
Chaney St
10 VNBN 48111 4578 D4
Channing Ct
34200 WTLD 48186 4413 E5
Channing St
100 FRDL 48220 4200 A3
Chapel Ct
1200 AARB 48103 4488 E1
Chapel Dr
- WDHN 48183 4668 B6
Chapel St
14000 DET 48223 4269 C5
17100 DET 48219 4269 C1
19200 DET 48219 4197 C6
Chapin St
100 AARB 48103 4406 A6
8500 DET 48213 4274 C6
Chapleau Dr
1300 WasC 48103 4488 C1
Chapman Cir
32700 WTLD 48185 4339 A4
Chapman Pl
32800 WTLD 48185 4339 A4
Chapman St
8400 OKPK 48237 4199 B1
Chapoton St
22500 STCS 48080 4204 D2
Chapp Av
8000 WRRN 48015 4202 B1
8000 WRRN 48089 4202 B1
Chappell Av
200 WIND N9C 4419 E5
1100 WIND N9C 4420 A5
Chappus St
100 WIND N9C 4419 D6
900 WIND N9C 4420 A7
1600 WIND N9C 4503 B1
Chardonay Ct
2000 PTFD 48108 4572 E3
Charest St
11300 HMTK 48212 4273 C3
13400 DET 48212 4273 B1
17200 DET 48212 4201 B7
19100 DET 48234 4201 A5
Charing Cross
2900 WasC 48167 4190 C6
Charing Crossing Rd
3000 AARB 48108 4490 C4
Charl Av
2100 WIND N8X 4421 A4
Charlemagne St
11000 DET 48213 4274 D3
Charlene Ln
2000 Tcmh N9K 4424 A4
Charles Av
3000 TNTN 48183 4669 D5
Charles Ct
22000 TYLR 48180 4499 C3
Charles Dr
24200 BNTN 48183 4668 B6
Charles St
100 RVRG 48218 4418 E7
200 AARB 48103 4406 B4
200 BLVL 48111 4578 C2
300 WIND N8X 4421 C6
700 YPLT 48198 4492 B3
3700 DRBN 48126 4417 E1
3800 DET 48212 4273 C2
17500 GSPT 48230 4276 C5
25000 TYLR 48180 4498 E3
30900 RMLS 48174 4497 D3
Charles R Av
14600 EPTE 48021 4203 B1
Charleston Ct
1200 NHVL 48167 4192 A5
Charleston St
20000 DET 48203 4200 C4
N Charlesworth St
100 DBHT 48127 4415 C1
100 DBHT 48141 4415 C1
7200 DBHT 48127 4340 C4
Charlevoix Av
10 GSPF 48236 4276 D3
3500 WIND N9E 4504 A2
20700 GSPW 48236 4204 D4
Charlevoix Ct
31900 WTLD 48186 4414 D5
Charlevoix St
- GSPT 48230 4276 A5
2600 DET 48207 4346 A3
7000 DET 48214 4346 C2
10600 DET 48214 4347 A1
10800 DET 48214 4275 A7
15000 GPPK 48230 4275 E6
15900 GPPK 48230 4276 A5
Charlie Brooks Ct
6700 WIND N8T 4422 E2
Charlotte Av
13300 WRRN 48089 4202 E3
Charlotte St
10 DET 48201 4345 B5
500 WIND N8X 4421 C5
E Charlotte St
10 ECRS 48229 4501 D3
W Charlotte St
10 ECRS 48229 4501 D3
Charlton Av
1600 TNTN 48183 4669 C4
Charlton St
2000 AARB 48103 4405 D6
Charnwood Ct
44500 PyTp 48170 4336 D1
Charnwood Dr
44400 PyTp 48170 4336 D1
Charring Crossing Blvd
- GOTp 48189 4187 B4
E Charring Crossing Cir
10700 GOTp 48189 4187 B4
W Charring Crossing Cir
10700 GOTp 48189 4187 B4
Charrington Ct
7700 CNTN 48187 4336 D4
Charrington Dr
7300 CNTN 48187 4336 D4
Charter Av
- ALPK 48101 4500 E1
1700 LNPK 48146 4500 E1
2200 LNPK 48101 4500 E1
Charter Clb
- VNBN 48111 4495 A5
Charter Pl
3500 AARB 48105 4407 C5
Charter St
1300 LNPK 48146 4501 E3
Charter House Ct
300 CNTN 48188 4412 D2
Charter House Dr
200 CNTN 48187 4412 D2
200 CNTN 48188 4412 D2
Chase Blvd
- WasC 48103 4405 C7
11800 LVNA 48150 4338 A1
11900 LVNA 48150 4266 A7
Chase Ct
37700 LVNA 48150 4266 A7
42100 CNTN 48188 4412 B3
Chase Dr
20800 NOVI 48375 4193 A4
42200 CNTN 48188 4412 B3
Chase Rd
4500 DRBN 48126 4342 E7
4500 DRBN 48126 4417 E1
Chase Run
200 LyTp 48167 4189 E5
Chase St
38800 RMLS 48174 4495 E7
38800 RMLS 48174 4496 A7
Chaseway Ct
2800 AATp 48105 4408 A2
Chaseway Dr
2800 AATp 48105 4408 A2
Chateau Av
1200 WIND N8P 4348 C7
1700 WIND N8P 4423 C1
Chateau Ct
2600 PTFD 48103 4488 D3
Chateaufort Pl
1500 DET 48207 4345 E5
E Chateau Vert St
1400 YpTp 48197 4491 B2
W Chateau Vert St
1400 YpTp 48197 4491 A2
Chatfield Dr
5000 YpTp 48197 4575 A6
Chatfield St
7000 DET 48209 4419 B2
Chatham
7200 DET 48127 4341 B4
9500 DET 48239 4341 B1
11600 DET 48239 4269 B7
Chatham Av
9200 ALPK 48101 4500 A5
Chatham Dr
8200 CNTN 48187 4335 C4
Chatham Rd
28200 WynC 48138 4756 A3
Chatham St
14500 DET 48223 4269 B4
16100 DET 48219 4269 B2
18400 RVVW 48192 4584 C7
Chatham St E
10 WIND N9A 4420 C1
600 WIND N9A 4421 A1
700 WIND N9A 4346 A7
Chatham St W
10 WIND N9A 4420 D1
Chatham Wy
3500 AARB 48105 4407 C4
Chatham Hills Dr
36000 FMTN 48335 4194 B1
Chatsworth Ct
40200 CNTN 48188 4412 D2
Chatsworth Dr
45800 VNBN 48111 4494 C6
Chatsworth St
3400 DET 48230 4275 E5
5700 DET 48224 4275 D3
Chatterton Ct
42200 NvlT 48167 4265 B3
Chattman Dr
41400 NOVI 48375 4193 B2
Chaucer Dr
2000 AARB 48103 4489 A2
Chaviva Ct
1800 WIND N8W 4422 A7
Cheboygan Ct
32000 WTLD 48186 4414 B4
Chedworth Ct
44500 OakC 48167 4192 D2
Chedworth Dr
44200 OakC 48167 4192 D3
Chelsea
15400 RDFD 48239 4268 D3
Chelsea Cir
3000 AARB 48108 4489 E4
3200 AARB 48108 4490 A4
3200 PTFD 48108 4490 A4
Chelsea Dr
4700 LSal N9H 4504 D5
Chelsea Ln
22000 WDHN 48183 4668 C3
22300 NOVI 48167 4192 E4
Chelsea Rd
800 CNTN 48187 4411 C1
Chelsea St
2400 TNTN 48183 4669 D4
10700 DET 48213 4274 E3
12500 DET 48213 4275 A2
14900 DET 48224 4275 A2
Cheltenham Dr
47400 NOVI 48374 4192 A3
Cheltenham Ln
23200 DBHT 48127 4341 B6
Chene Ct
200 Tcmh N8N 4348 E7
1900 DET 48207 4346 A4
Chene St
100 Tcmh N8N 4348 E6
100 Tcmh N8P 4348 E6
400 DET 48207 4346 A3
2900 DET 48207 4345 E3
5000 DET 48211 4345 D1
5800 DET 48211 4273 D7
Chenlot St
9700 DET 48204 4343 E1
Cherboneau Pl
1500 DET 48207 4345 E5
Cherbourg St
44200 CNTN 48188 4411 E4
Cheri Ln
9000 AGST 48197 4661 D2
Cherimoor Ln
23500 SFLD 48034 4196 B2
Chernick St
24000 TYLR 48180 4499 A4
25400 TYLR 48180 4498 D4
Cherokee E
26100 FTRK 48134 4754 A1
Cherokee S
24500 FTRK 48134 4754 A1
Cherokee W
26200 FTRK 48134 4754 A1
Cherokee Cir
49400 CNTN 48187 4335 D4
Cherokee Dr
38600 RMLS 48174 4496 A3
39000 RMLS 48174 4495 E3
Cherokee Rd
1600 AARB 48104 4489 D2
Cherokee St
5000 DBHT 48125 4415 E7

Block	City	ZIP	Map#	Grid
Cherokee St				
9600	TYLR	48180	4498	E5
19900	DET	48219	4197	A5
Cherokee Tr				
3000	SpTp	48198	4409	A1
Cherry				
100	WasC	48103	4488	B4
500	WTLD	48186	4414	C7
1000	PLYM	48170	4265	A6
Cherry Av				
27500	INKR	48141	4415	A5
28400	RMLS	48174	4582	A4
28800	INKR	48141	4414	E5
30100	RMLS	48174	4581	D4
Cherry Ct				
100	YPLT	48198	4492	A3
300	WasC	48189	4259	B2
Cherry Dr E				
10	VNBN	48111	4494	D5
Cherry Dr W				
10	VNBN	48111	4494	D5
Cherry Ln				
100	INKR	48141	4415	D2
100	VNBN	48111	4494	D5
100	WasC	48103	4404	A5
12000	GOTp	48178	4188	B4
14700	PyTp	48170	4265	B5
Cherry St				
10	TNTN	48183	4670	A4
200	WYDT	48192	4585	C4
300	TNTN	48183	4669	E4
500	AARB	48103	4406	A5
1300	DET	48201	4345	B6
1700	DET	48216	4345	A6
12700	SOGT	48195	4584	E4
17500	BNTN	48174	4583	B6
24000	TYLR	48180	4583	A4
24600	DRBN	48124	4415	E5
25700	TYLR	48180	4582	D4
Cherry Blossom Dr				
4000	PTFD	48197	4490	E6
5500	WIND	N9J	4502	D2
Cherry Blossom Ln				
30100	FTRK	48134	4754	C5
Cherry Grove Ct E				
43700	CNTN	48188	4412	A2
Cherry Grove Ct W				
43800	CNTN	48188	4411	E3
Cherry Grove Rd				
100	CNTN	48187	4411	E2
100	CNTN	48188	4411	E2
Cherrygrove St				
10	ECRS	48229	4501	D3
Cherry Hill Ct				
10	DRBN	48124	4416	C1
Cherry Hill Rd				
3000	SpTp	48105	4408	B2
3000	SpTp	48198	4408	B2
4400	WIND	N9G	4504	C4
7200	SpTp	48198	4409	A3
9000	SpTp	48198	4410	A2
25400	DBHT	48125	4415	A2
25400	DBHT	48127	4415	A2
25600	DBHT	48141	4415	A2
25800	INKR	48141	4415	A2
27400	GDNC	48135	4415	A2
27400	GDNC	48141	4415	A2
28600	GDNC	48135	4414	D2
28600	GDNC	48141	4414	D2
28600	INKR	48141	4414	D2
29000	INKR	48135	4414	D2
30400	WTLD	48135	4414	D2
30400	WTLD	48186	4414	D2
32300	GDNC	48186	4414	A2
33700	GDNC	48185	4413	A2
33700	GDNC	48186	4413	A2
33700	WTLD	48186	4413	A2
33800	WTLD	48185	4413	A2
38900	WTLD	48185	4412	D2
38900	WTLD	48186	4412	D2
39400	CNTN	48187	4412	D2
39400	CNTN	48188	4412	D2
43700	CNTN	48187	4411	C2
43700	CNTN	48188	4411	C2
48200	CNTN	48187	4410	D2
48200	CNTN	48188	4410	D2
50600	CNTN	48198	4410	D2
Cherry Hill St				
21500	DRBN	48124	4416	C2
23000	DRBN	48128	4416	A2
24400	DRBN	48124	4415	E2
24400	DRBN	48128	4415	E2
Cherry Hill Tr				
200	INKR	48141	4414	D2
Cherry Hill Pointe Dr				
-	CNTN	48187	4412	D2
Cherrylawn Cres				
200	Amhg	N9V	4757	C3
1500	WIND	N9E	4504	A3
Cherrylawn Ct				
42000	CNTN	48187	4412	B1
Cherrylawn Dr				
22000	BNTN	48134	4668	A4
Cherrylawn St				
11100	SOGT	48195	4500	A7
11700	DET	48204	4271	C6
12600	DET	48238	4271	C6
17100	DET	48221	4271	C1
19300	DET	48221	4199	C5
Cherry Oak Ct				
100	WTLD	48186	4413	C2
Cherry Oak Dr				
36600	WTLD	48186	4413	C2
Cherry Orchard Rd				
400	CNTN	48188	4412	A3
Cherry Ridge Rd				
44400	NvlT	48167	4264	D1
Cherrystone Ct				
800	AARB	48105	4407	C5

Block	City	ZIP	Map#	Grid
Cherrytree Ln				
3000	PTFD	48104	4490	C4
3000	PTFD	48108	4490	C4
Cherry Valley Dr				
100	INKR	48141	4415	D2
Cherrywood				
28800	HnTp	48134	4752	E3
Cherrywood Ct				
12200	PyTp	48170	4336	D1
16100	NvlT	48167	4265	C3
Cherrywood Dr				
6000	YpTp	48197	4576	B3
7400	WTLD	48185	4338	A4
22000	WDHN	48183	4668	C3
Cherrywood Ln				
3500	WasC	48103	4405	A4
Cheryl Dr				
26000	BNTN	48134	4667	D7
Chesapeake				
26800	RDFD	48239	4268	B7
Cheshire Ct				
2600	WRRN	48091	4201	A1
22600	NOVI	48374	4192	B2
26000	WynC	48138	4670	C7
Cheshire Dr				
38600	FNHL	48167	4193	E4
Cheshire Ln				
49100	CNTN	48187	4335	E5
Cheshire St				
19100	DET	48236	4204	A7
39200	WTLD	48186	4412	E3
Chesley Dr				
20700	FMTN	48336	4195	A5
32700	FMTN	48335	4194	E5
32700	FMTN	48336	4194	E5
Chester Av				
19600	GSPW	48236	4204	B7
19600	HRWD	48225	4204	B7
19600	HRWD	48236	4204	B7
27500	GDNC	48135	4340	B6
29400	GDNC	48135	4339	D6
Chester Ct				
300	SLYN	48178	4189	A2
22400	FNHL	48335	4194	E3
Chester Dr				
4000	PTFD	48197	4490	D4
50200	PyTp	48170	4263	D6
Chester St				
500	SLYN	48178	4189	A1
3100	FRDL	48220	4200	B1
6900	SRKW	48179	4840	D2
17400	DET	48224	4276	A1
18000	DET	48236	4276	A1
19100	DET	48236	4204	B7
19200	HRWD	48225	4204	B7
Chesterfield Blvd				
7200	TYLR	48180	4498	D3
Chesterfield Ct				
41600	NOVI	48375	4193	A4
Chesterfield Dr				
2900	AARB	48104	4490	A4
Chesterfield Dr E				
7200	CNTN	48187	4336	A5
Chesterfield Dr S				
48000	CNTN	48187	4336	A5
Chesterfield Rd				
-	DET	48221	4199	D6
E Chesterfield St				
100	FRDL	48220	4200	A4
W Chesterfield St				
100	FRDL	48220	4199	E4
100	FRDL	48220	4200	A4
Chestnut				
-	CNTN	48188	4411	C6
Chestnut Av				
10	HZLP	48030	4200	B1
15500	EPTE	48021	4203	C2
Chestnut Cres				
2000	SALN	48176	4572	C4
Chestnut Ct				
10300	PyTp	48170	4337	D2
Chestnut Dr				
1300	YpTp	48197	4491	B2
9400	WIND	N8R	4423	B2
10700	PyTp	48170	4337	D1
Chestnut Ln				
13100	TYLR	48180	4583	D2
21400	FMTN	48336	4195	A4
22100	WDHN	48183	4668	C5
38400	WTLD	48185	4338	A4
38500	WTLD	48185	4337	E4
Chestnut Rd				
1000	AARB	48104	4407	B7
Chestnut St				
-	DET	48207	4345	E4
-	RVVW	48192	4669	C1
10	RVRG	48218	4501	E1
10	WYDT	48192	4585	C2
1900	DRBN	48124	4417	A6
2100	FRDL	48220	4200	B1
2600	WRRN	48091	4201	A2
12700	SOGT	48195	4584	E3
19200	SOGT	48195	4583	E3
20000	TYLR	48180	4583	E3
20000	TYLR	48195	4583	E3
25000	TYLR	48180	4582	E3
27400	INKR	48141	4415	A5
34500	WYNE	48184	4413	D5
Chestnut Ridge Dr				
18000	NvlT	48167	4264	D2
Chestnut Run Ct				
11100	GOTp	48178	4188	B5
Chestnut Tree				
22400	NOVI	48375	4193	B3
Chestwick Ct				
50600	PyTp	48170	4263	C7
Cheville Rd				
22000	HnTp	48174	4667	B4
Cheviot Rd				
39700	CNTN	48188	4412	D3

Block	City	ZIP	Map#	Grid
Chevrolet St				
1900	YpTp	48198	4492	E6
2100	YpTp	48198	4493	A6
Chewett St				
-	WIND	N9C	4420	A3
Cheyenne Av				
25000	FTRK	48134	4753	E1
Cheyenne Blvd				
-	RMLS	48174	4495	E3
Cheyenne St				
7200	WTLD	48185	4338	B5
8500	DET	48228	4343	A2
9500	DET	48227	4343	A1
11300	DET	48227	4271	A6
16100	DET	48235	4271	A4
20400	DET	48235	4199	A4
Chicago Av				
400	TNTN	48183	4670	A1
Chicago Blvd				
10	DET	48202	4272	D6
1200	DET	48206	4272	C7
W Chicago Blvd				
3900	DET	48206	4272	A7
4000	DET	48204	4272	A7
W Chicago Rd				
22400	DET	48239	4341	A1
23200	RDFD	48239	4341	A1
24200	RDFD	48239	4340	E2
27300	RDFD	48150	4340	C2
Chicago St				
24000	DRBN	48124	4416	A5
24300	DRBN	48124	4415	E5
W Chicago St				
-	DET	48239	4341	D1
6300	DET	48204	4343	D1
12700	DET	48227	4343	D1
12700	DET	48228	4343	D1
13700	DET	48227	4342	B1
13700	DET	48228	4342	B1
19000	DET	48228	4341	E1
27400	LVNA	48150	4340	A2
28400	LVNA	48150	4339	E2
37900	LVNA	48150	4338	A2
Chicago St W				
-	DET	48204	4343	D1
Chichester Ct				
7700	CNTN	48187	4336	B5
Chichester Rd				
7200	CNTN	48187	4336	B5
Chick Ct				
2600	WIND	N9E	4503	D1
Chickadee Ct				
100	PTFD	48197	4574	E2
Chickadee Ln				
37000	FNHL	48335	4194	B4
Chicory				
24900	WynC	48138	4670	A6
Chicory Rd				
23200	WynC	48138	4670	A5
Chicory Ridge Rd				
1600	WasC	48103	4488	C1
Chidester St				
300	YPLT	48197	4492	A5
Chief Ln				
33500	WTLD	48185	4338	E5
33500	WTLD	48185	4339	A5
S Chigwidden Dr				
46800	NHVL	48167	4192	A5
E Chigwidden St				
20800	NHVL	48167	4192	B5
Chilver Rd				
200	WIND	N8Y	4346	B7
800	WIND	N8Y	4421	C1
1700	WIND	N8W	4421	D4
Chinavere Rd				
8700	BrTp	48166	4840	C7
Chinook Ct				
24700	FTRK	48134	4754	A3
Chipman St				
2600	DET	48216	4345	A7
Chipmunk Tr				
23600	NOVI	48375	4193	A2
Chipmunk Tr E				
21200	WDHN	48183	4668	D3
Chipmunk Tr N				
21600	WDHN	48183	4668	C3
Chipmunk Tr S				
22000	WDHN	48183	4668	C4
Chippawa St				
200	WIND	N9C	4420	A4
Chippewa				
24300	FNHL	48335	4194	D1
Chippewa Ct				
24300	FNHL	48335	4194	B1
Chippewa Dr				
6900	RMLS	48174	4496	A3
24000	FTRK	48134	4754	A1
Chippewa St				
3700	DET	48221	4199	D5
12700	DET	48235	4199	A5
13300	DET	48235	4198	E5
22400	DET	48219	4197	A5
24200	DET	48219	4196	E5
32000	WTLD	48186	4414	D5
Chipshot Ct				
800	WasC	48103	4404	D7
Chirrewa St				
6500	WTLD	48185	4338	E6
6500	WTLD	48185	4339	A6
Chocolate St				
10	WTLD	48186	4497	D1
Chope Pl				
3300	DET	48210	4344	C3
Chopin St				
5200	DET	48210	4343	D5
Chornoby Cres				
1600	Tcmh	N8N	4423	E3
Choudney Blvd				
-	BNTN	48192	4583	C6

Block	City	ZIP	Map#	Grid
Chovin St				
4500	DRBN	48126	4417	D1
4700	DRBN	48126	4342	D7
Chris Ln				
4300	WasC	48103	4329	E5
Christ Church Ln				
10	GSPF	48236	4276	D5
Christian Dr				
24300	BNTN	48134	4668	A6
24500	BNTN	48183	4668	A6
Christiancy St				
4400	DET	48209	4419	C1
Christina Blvd				
-	BNTN	48134	4668	A5
Christina Cres				
500	WIND	N9G	4504	D4
Christina Ct				
600	WIND	N9G	4504	D4
Christina Dr				
4400	PTFD	48197	4574	E1
4500	PTFD	48197	4490	E7
24500	BNTN	48134	4668	A5
24700	BNTN	48134	4667	E5
Christina Ln				
24400	NOVI	48375	4192	D1
Christina Wy				
-	PTFD	48197	4574	E1
N Christine				
100	WTLD	48185	4413	D2
100	WTLD	48186	4413	D2
S Christine				
100	WTLD	48186	4413	D2
N Christine Av				
5600	WTLD	48185	4338	D7
Christine Ct				
10	DRBN	48124	4417	B5
5100	WasC	48103	4404	C4
20700	GSPW	48236	4204	E5
Christine Dr				
10	GSPF	48236	4276	E3
5000	WasC	48103	4404	D4
Christopher Av				
21600	WRRN	48091	4200	E2
Christopher Ct				
43600	CNTN	48188	4411	E5
Christopher Dr				
400	WIND	N8S	4347	E5
1600	CNTN	48188	4412	A4
1700	CNTN	48188	4411	E5
23500	BNTN	48134	4668	A5
Christopher St				
3800	HMTK	48211	4273	D4
Christy Ln				
100	Tcmh	N8N	4349	C7
16600	RMLS	48174	4580	A6
Christy St				
11000	DET	48205	4274	D2
Chrysler				
-	DET	48203	4273	A3
-	DET	48212	4273	A3
Chrysler Ctr				
2200	WIND	N8W	4421	E4
2500	WIND	N8W	4422	A4
Chrysler Dr				
-	DET	48212	4273	B5
-	HMTK	48212	4273	B5
400	DET	48207	4345	E5
600	DET	48226	4345	E5
2600	DET	48201	4345	C2
5000	DET	48202	4345	C2
5000	DET	48211	4345	C2
7400	DET	48211	4273	B7
11700	DET	48203	4273	A5
11700	HDPK	48203	4273	A5
12000	HDPK	48203	4272	E3
N Chrysler Dr				
20700	HZLP	48030	4200	D3
S Chrysler Dr				
20700	HZLP	48030	4200	D3
Chrysler Frwy				
-	DET	-	4200	D6
-	DET	-	4272	E1
-	DET	-	4273	A3
-	DET	-	4345	C1
-	DET	48207	4345	E5
-	DET	48226	4345	E5
-	HMTK	-	4273	A3
-	HZLP	-	4200	D6
Chrysler Frwy I-75				
-	DET	-	4200	D6
-	DET	-	4272	E1
-	DET	-	4273	A3
-	DET	-	4345	C2
-	HMTK	-	4273	A3
-	HZLP	-	4200	D6
Chrysler Frwy I-375				
-	DET	-	4345	E5
Chubb Rd				
7300	WasC	48167	4263	A4
7700	WasC	48167	4262	E1
9000	WasC	48167	4190	E7
21100	LyTp	48167	4190	E7
22400	LyTp	48178	4190	E3
Church Ct				
20100	HRWD	48225	4204	A5
Church Pl				
1900	TNTN	48183	4670	A3
Church Rd				
7600	WynC	48138	4670	D3
Church St				
10	BLVL	48111	4578	C2
10	HDPK	48203	4272	C1
100	DET	48203	4272	C1
100	NHVL	48167	4192	E6
400	AARB	48104	4406	D7
600	PLYM	48170	4265	A7
800	PLYM	48170	4264	E7
900	WIND	N9A	4420	E2
1400	DET	48216	4345	B6
1400	WIND	N8X	4420	E3

Block	City	ZIP	Map#	Grid
Church St				
1500	WIND	N8X	4421	A4
3000	WIND	N9E	4421	B7
3000	WIND	N9E	4504	C2
5000	SpTp	48105	4408	A1
10000	AGST	48191	4662	A2
23500	OKPK	48237	4198	D1
25900	FTRK	48134	4753	D3
32200	RKWD	48173	4754	C7
Churches St				
23000	SFLD	48034	4196	E2
Church Hill Dr				
18700	RVVW	48192	4584	B7
Churchill Av				
1700	TNTN	48183	4669	B3
12000	SOGT	48195	4500	B7
12000	SOGT	48195	4584	B1
20000	BwTp	48183	4754	E3
20000	BwTp	48183	4755	A3
Churchill Blvd				
-	NOVI	48375	4192	D1
Churchill Blvd E				
-	TYLR	48180	4582	E5
Churchill Blvd W				
-	TYLR	48180	4582	D5
Churchill Ct				
7900	WasC	48167	4190	C7
Churchill Dr				
10	HbgT	48189	4186	B6
2000	AARB	48103	4488	E2
4000	WIND	N9G	4504	B3
9900	VNBN	48111	4495	B6
Churchill St				
7300	DET	48206	4344	D1
7300	DET	48210	4344	D1
8000	WasC	48167	4190	B6
15000	SOGT	48195	4584	B4
Churchview Dr				
22000	WDHN	48183	4668	C3
Cicotte Av				
500	LNPK	48146	4501	A3
1500	LNPK	48146	4500	E2
2200	LNPK	48101	4500	D1
14500	ALPK	48101	4500	D1
16800	ALPK	48101	4417	B7
Cicotte St				
-	DET	48210	4344	A5
-	ECRS	48229	4501	C3
6000	DET	48210	4343	E5
E Cicotte St				
10	RVRG	48218	4418	E7
10	RVRG	48218	4419	A7
W Cicotte St				
10	RVRG	48218	4418	E6
Cider Mill Blvd				
47400	NOVI	48374	4192	A1
Cider Mill Dr				
47000	NOVI	48374	4192	A1
Cincinnati St				
-	RMLS	48174	4496	D1
-	RMLS	48174	4497	E1
17100	DET	48224	4276	A3
Cindy Dr				
-	VNBN	48111	4493	C2
Cindy St				
33400	LVNA	48150	4339	A2
33500	LVNA	48150	4338	E2
E Circle				
-	YpTp	48198	4493	A3
W Circle				
-	YpTp	48198	4493	A3
Circle Ct				
100	SALN	48176	4657	D1
29900	FTRK	48134	4753	E5
Circle Dr				
-	DET	48219	4198	A5
-	DET	48235	4198	A5
-	SFLD	48075	4198	A5
-	SFLD	48235	4198	A5
-	WTLD	48185	4339	B4
10	DBHT	48127	4341	B5
25000	SFLD	48075	4197	C1
E Circle Dr				
-	YPLT	48197	4491	E3
N Circle Dr				
2100	AARB	48103	4405	D4
S Circle Dr				
2100	AARB	48103	4405	D4
W Circle Dr				
2500	YPLT	48197	4491	E3
Circle Ln N				
18800	SOGT	48195	4584	A5
Circle Ln S				
18800	SOGT	48195	4584	A5
W Circle St				
1800	DRBN	48128	4341	B7
Citadel Dr				
4900	CNTN	48188	4412	B7
4900	CNTN	48188	4495	C1
Citation				
43100	NOVI	48375	4193	A3
43400	NOVI	48375	4192	E3
Citation Dr				
-	CNTN	48187	4336	C5
Citrin Dr				
28000	RMLS	48174	4498	B4
City Dr				
1200	AARB	48103	4405	D4
City Hall Sq E				
300	WIND	N9A	4420	C1
City Hall Sq S				
100	WIND	N9A	4420	C1
City Hall Sq W				
300	WIND	N9A	4420	C1
Civic Pl				
10800	DET	48204	4343	B3
10800	DET	48228	4343	B3
Civic Center Blvd				
-	CNTN	48188	4411	C4

Block	City	ZIP	Map#	Grid
Civic Center Dr				
-	DET	48226	4345	D7
-	YpTp	48197	4576	A2
33000	LVNA	48154	4267	A4
Civic Park Dr				
14100	RVVW	48192	4584	D7
Clague St				
1100	AARB	48103	4489	A1
Clair Cir				
1100	AARB	48103	4406	A4
Clair Dr				
4200	WasC	48178	4260	D1
Clair St				
100	GDNC	48135	4414	D1
1000	INKR	48141	4414	D3
Clairet Dr				
27400	HnTp	48174	4667	B4
Clairmont Cir E				
18200	NvlT	48167	4263	E1
18400	NvlT	48167	4264	A1
Clairmont Cir W				
18200	NvlT	48167	4263	E1
Clairmount St				
10	DET	48202	4272	E6
2600	DET	48206	4272	B7
2900	DET	48206	4344	B1
4000	DET	48204	4344	A1
Clairpointe St				
100	DET	48214	4347	C1
Clairpointe Woods Dr				
500	DET	48214	4347	C2
Clairview Av				
7600	WIND	N8S	4347	D5
10300	WIND	N8P	4348	B5
E Clairview Ct				
19900	GSPW	48236	4204	C6
W Clairview Ct				
19900	GSPW	48236	4204	C6
Clairview Dr				
27100	DBHT	48127	4340	B4
Clairview Rd				
10	GSPS	48236	4204	E7
10	GSPS	48236	4205	A7
Clairview St				
17400	DET	48224	4276	B3
Clairwood St				
22300	STCS	48080	4204	D2
23100	McoC	48080	4205	A2
23100	STCS	48080	4205	A2
Clampton Ct				
7000	CNTN	48187	4336	E5
Clapp St				
12300	Tcmh	N8N	4348	E7
12400	Tcmh	N8N	4349	A7
Clara Ln				
6300	WasC	48170	4263	B7
Clara St				
-	WYNE	48184	4414	A6
3800	WIND	N9E	4504	E2
Clarann St				
17000	MVDL	48122	4418	A6
17000	MVDL	48229	4418	A6
Clare Blvd				
44400	PyTp	48170	4336	D2
Clare Ct				
32000	WTLD	48186	4414	B4
Claremont St				
7400	CNTN	48187	4336	C5
S Claremont St				
100	DRBN	48124	4415	E2
1000	DRBN	48124	4416	A3
Clarence Dr				
5300	WIND	N8T	4422	D4
Clarence St				
10	BLVL	48111	4578	E2
3100	MVDL	48122	4418	A6
3400	MVDL	48122	4417	E5
Clarendon Dr				
6300	CNTN	48187	4336	E6
Clarendon St				
400	WasC	48103	4405	C5
Clarendon St N				
8800	DET	48204	4344	A2
Clarendon St S				
4800	DET	48204	4344	A2
5000	DET	48204	4343	E2
Clarice Av				
12500	Tcmh	N8N	4424	A1
Clarion Ct				
8600	GOTp	48116	4186	E1
Clarion St				
8900	DET	48213	4274	C4
Clarita				
26200	RDFD	48240	4196	C7
Clarita St				
-	DET	48219	4196	E7
-	DET	48219	4198	B7
-	DET	48221	4199	D7
-	DET	48235	4198	B7
1200	YpTp	48198	4492	D7
12700	DET	48235	4198	A7
23600	DET	48219	4197	A7
27600	LVNA	48152	4196	A7
30500	LVNA	48152	4195	C7
36600	LVNA	48152	4194	B7
Clark Ct				
4000	DET	48209	4419	D1
4800	TNTN	48183	4669	B7
Clark Dr				
1100	SpTp	48198	4492	C1
Clark Ln				
21400	WynC	48111	4664	D3
Clark Rd				
-	MonC	48117	4751	A4
-	MonC	48164	4751	A4
19000	HnTp	48111	4664	E3
19000	WynC	48111	4664	E3
21600	HnTp	48164	4664	E6
23100	WynC	48164	4664	E6
25600	HnTp	48164	4750	E1

Block	City	ZIP	Map#	Grid
Clark Rd				
25600	WynC	48164	4750	E1
27000	HnTp	48164	4751	A4
E Clark Rd				
10	SpTp	48198	4492	B2
10	YpTp	48198	4492	B2
2200	YpTp	48198	4493	A2
W Clark Rd				
10	SpTp	48198	4492	A2
10	YPLT	48198	4492	A2
300	SpTp	48198	4491	E2
300	YpTp	48198	4491	E2
300	YpTp	48198	4492	A2
700	YPLT	48198	4491	E2
2900	SpTp	48197	4491	B2
2900	YPLT	48197	4491	B2
2900	YpTp	48197	4491	B2
3000	SpTp	48105	4491	B2
4000	AATp	48105	4490	E2
4000	PTFD	48105	4490	E2
4300	AATp	48197	4490	E2
4300	PTFD	48197	4490	E2
4600	AATp	48105	4491	B2
4600	AATp	48197	4491	B2
4600	PTFD	48197	4491	B2
Clark St				
-	DET	48216	4344	C7
100	DET	48209	4419	D1
100	WYDT	48192	4585	C1
200	SALN	48176	4572	D7
2000	DET	48209	4344	C7
2100	WYDT	48192	4584	E1
2300	WYDT	48195	4584	E1
2600	DET	48210	4344	C7
2900	WYNE	48184	4413	D5
17000	RVVW	48192	4585	A6
Clarkdale St				
1900	DET	48209	4344	D7
1900	DET	48209	4419	D1
Clarkshire Dr				
22300	LyTp	48178	4190	A4
Clarkstone Dr				
-	BNTN	48192	4669	A1
Claudia Ct				
34000	WTLD	48185	4338	E4
Clavey Ct				
1300	CNTN	48187	4411	D1
Claxton Dr				
46300	WynC	48111	4663	C2
Claxton St				
3000	WIND	N8R	4423	B2
Clay Rd				
43300	WynC	48111	4663	E5
43300	WynC	48111	4664	A5
Clay St				
900	DET	48211	4273	B7
1900	HMTK	48211	4273	C6
Clayburn St				
7200	DET	48228	4342	B4
E Claymore Ct				
7600	CNTN	48187	4336	C4
W Claymore Ct				
7600	CNTN	48187	4336	C4
Claymore Dr				
44900	CNTN	48187	4336	D5
Clayton Ct				
2800	WTLD	48186	4414	A6
Clayton St				
6800	DET	48210	4344	A7
7100	DET	48210	4343	E7
10000	VNBN	48111	4494	C6
Clear Lake Dr				
22400	FNHL	48335	4194	B2
Clearspring Ct				
40500	CNTN	48188	4412	D3
Clearview Dr				
18400	SOGT	48195	4584	A3
Clearwater Ct				
22700	NOVI	48375	4193	D3
Cleary St				
2300	WIND	N9B	4420	D7
2300	WIND	N9E	4420	D7
Cleat St				
14900	PyTp	48167	4264	C4
14900	PyTp	48170	4264	C4
Clemenceau Av				
2400	WIND	N8T	4422	D3
Clement Ct				
45700	NHVL	48167	4192	C6
Clement Ln				
600	SLYN	48178	4189	B3
Clement Rd				
19100	NvlT	48167	4192	C7
19800	NHVL	48167	4192	C7
Clements Cir E				
9800	LVNA	48150	4340	A1
Clements Cir N				
28000	LVNA	48150	4340	A1
28400	LVNA	48150	4339	E1
Clements Cir S				
28000	LVNA	48150	4340	A2
Clements Cir W				
11000	LVNA	48150	4339	E1
Clements St				
1900	DET	48238	4272	B4
3200	DET	48238	4271	E5
Clemmons Ct				
21600	WynC	48111	4663	E4
Clemons Dr				
42100	PyTp	48170	4265	A5
Cleophas Dr				
10	Lksr	N8N	4424	E1
Cleophus Av				
16200	ALPK	48101	4500	B2
Cleophus Pkwy				
400	LNPK	48146	4501	A4
2100	LNPK	48146	4500	E3
2200	LNPK	48101	4500	E3
Clermont Av				
41000	NOVI	48375	4193	C1

INDEX 15

Cooper St — Detroit & Wayne County Street Index — Cumberland St

STREET
Block City ZIP Map# Grid

Cooper St
4500 DET 48214 4274 D7
5000 DET 48213 4274 C5
9200 TYLR 48180 4499 A5
14300 TYLR 48180 4583 A3
Cope St
4600 DET 48214 4275 B5
Copeland Cir
1300 CNTN 48187 4412 B1
Copland St
9400 DET 48209 4419 A5
Copley Av
2100 AARB 48104 4489 E1
Coplin St
- DET 48214 4347 D3
1000 DET 48214 4275 C6
9000 DET 48213 4275 A2
11500 DET 48205 4275 A1
Copper Creek Cir
- CNTN 48187 4337 D5
Copper Creek Ct
7000 YpTp 48197 4576 A5
Copper Creek Dr
7200 YpTp 48197 4576 A5
41400 CNTN 48187 4337 D5
Copperfield Ct
9000 WIND N8S 4348 B7
Copperfield Pl
1200 WIND N8S 4348 A7
Cora Av
3800 TNTN 48183 4669 A5
3900 WDHN 48183 4669 A5
22100 FNHL 48336 4195 C3
Cora St
10 RVRG 48218 4501 D1
600 WYDT 48192 4501 B6
1400 WYDT 48192 4585 B1
3700 MVDL 48122 4417 E6
23500 BNTN 48183 4668 A3
Cora Greenwood Dr
500 WIND N8P 4348 D6
Coral Ln
24200 NOVI 48375 4193 C1
Coral St
13200 GBTR 48173 4755 D4
Coram Cres
3000 WIND N8R 4423 C2
Coram St
15200 DET 48205 4203 B5
16400 DET 48225 4203 C5
Corbett Dr
7300 CNTN 48187 4337 A5
Corbett St
11100 DET 48213 4274 E3
12200 DET 48213 4275 A3
Corbi Ln
1800 Tcmh N8N 4423 E4
Corbin Dr
7500 CNTN 48187 4336 D4
Corbin St
2300 MVDL 48122 4418 A7
2700 MVDL 48122 4417 E7
12700 DET 48229 4418 B7
Cordell St
6100 RMLS 48174 4498 A1
19400 DET 48205 4203 D5
Cordova Dr
4000 WasC 48160 4659 D2
Cordova St
- DET 48234 4201 B5
Corey Cir
4000 WasC 48103 4330 A4
4100 WasC 48103 4329 E5
Corey Ct
9000 PyTp 48170 4336 B3
Corey Pl
- DET 48214 4347 B1
Corktree Ct
16300 RMLS 48174 4582 A5
Cormorant St
11400 WIND N8P 4348 D7
Cornell Av
20000 BNTN 48174 4668 B2
21300 BNTN 48183 4668 B3
24200 BNTN 48134 4668 A6
Cornell Ct
10 DRBN 48124 4416 A4
Cornell Cts
100 YpTp 48197 4491 D2
200 YPLT 48197 4491 D2
Cornell Rd
500 YPLT 48197 4491 D3
1000 YpTp 48197 4491 D3
18100 SFLD 48075 4198 A3
Cornell St
100 CNTN 48188 4411 E3
2000 DRBN 48124 4416 A4
3900 DBHT 48124 4416 A6
3900 DBHT 48125 4416 A6
5600 DBHT 48125 4499 B2
5600 DBHT 48180 4499 B2
7800 TYLR 48180 4499 A3
13800 TYLR 48180 4583 B3
Cornelle Talley Blvd
5100 DET 48204 4343 E1
Cornerstone Dr
16300 SOGT 48195 4584 A5
Corning St
10000 OKPK 48237 4199 A2
Cornwall Ct
38800 FNHL 48167 4193 E3
Cornwall St
15300 DET 48224 4275 D4
16700 DET 48224 4276 A3
Cornwell Pl
900 AARB 48104 4406 C5
Corona Dr
1300 INKR 48141 4415 B3
Coronada St
1700 AARB 48103 4488 E1
Coronado Dr
100 Tcmh N8N 4349 A6
Coronation Av
6000 WIND N8T 4422 C2
Coronation Ct
200 CNTN 48188 4412 E2
Coronation Dr
26700 WDHN 48183 4754 E1
Coronation Rd
39700 CNTN 48188 4412 D2
Coronet Av
4000 CNTN 48188 4411 A7
Corrie Rd
200 BNHL 48105 4406 A1
N Corrine Blvd
100 CNTN 48187 4412 A2
S Corrine St
4200 CNTN 48188 4412 A7
Corrinne St
8800 PyTp 48170 4336 E2
8800 PyTp 48187 4336 E2
Cortes St
22700 NOVI 48375 4193 D3
Cortina Cres
1400 Tcmh N8N 4424 B2
Cortland Av
6300 ALPK 48101 4500 A1
Cortland Blvd
24100 NOVI 48375 4192 D1
Cortland St
- DET 48204 4271 C6
10 HDPK 48203 4272 D4
1500 DET 48206 4272 C5
34100 FMTN 48335 4194 D2
Costly Ln
58500 LyTp 48178 4189 D2
Cote Dnel Dr
24300 FNHL 48336 4195 C1
Cotswold Ct
42300 NvlT 48167 4265 A3
Cottage Ct
22700 NOVI 48375 4193 D4
Cottage Dr
22700 SFLD 48034 4197 A4
Cottage Ln
10 WasC 48103 4404 D5
2000 YpTp 48198 4577 A1
24200 WRRN 48089 4203 A1
Cottage Pl
1200 WIND N8S 4348 A7
Cottage Grove St
10 HDPK 48203 4272 D3
Cottisford Ct
44100 OakC 48167 4192 E2
Cottisford Rd
43400 NOVI 48167 4192 E3
43400 NOVI 48375 4192 E3
43700 OakC 48167 4192 E3
43700 OakC 48375 4192 E3
Cottontail Ct
2500 WasC 48103 4405 B2
Cottontail Ln
3400 WasC 48103 4405 B2
Cottonwood Ct
16500 NvlT 48167 4264 D3
37800 HnTp 48164 4751 A1
50400 PyTp 48170 4263 C7
Cottonwood Dr
- YpTp 48197 4575 E4
4500 WasC 48108 4488 D7
5700 PTFD 48197 4574 E2
5900 PTFD 48197 4575 A3
6200 CNTN 48187 4336 A7
22700 FTRK 48134 4754 C5
Cottonwood Ln
300 SALN 48176 4572 D5
42200 NOVI 48375 4193 A2
Cottonwood St
26600 WDHN 48183 4754 E1
S Cottrell St
400 DET 48209 4419 B4
Cottrill Ln
1800 WTLD 48186 4413 C4
Coucy Av
3100 TNTN 48183 4669 C7
Coulter St
8800 DRBN 48126 4343 C4
Council Av
- ALPK 48101 4500 E1
1300 LNPK 48146 4501 A2
1700 LNPK 48146 4500 E1
2200 LNPK 48101 4500 E1
Council St
2900 HMTK 48212 4273 C5
Country Ct
3300 TNTN 48183 4669 B2
Country Dr
1500 TNTN 48183 4669 B3
3700 CNTN 48187 4335 C6
Country Ln
5600 AGST 48197 4660 B1
6500 VNBN 48111 4577 D4
28700 HnTp 48134 4752 E3
39400 NOVI 48375 4193 D2
44400 NvlT 48167 4192 D7
Country Club Blvd
100 WynC 48111 4662 C5
Country Club Cir
17900 RVVW 48192 4584 B7
Country Club Ct
300 CNTN 48188 4411 C3
17400 LVNA 48152 4266 C2
18400 RVVW 48192 4584 B7
Country Club Dr
100 GSPF 48236 4276 E2
400 WIND N9G 4504 D4
1800 GSPW 48236 4204 B5
16100 LVNA 48154 4266 C2
17600 LVNA 48152 4266 C1
19600 HRWD 48225 4204 A5
Country Club Dr
21100 HRWD 48236 4204 B5
22900 LyTp 48178 4190 D2
Country Club Ln
100 CNTN 48187 4411 B3
100 CNTN 48188 4411 B3
300 GSPF 48236 4276 D2
23200 WynC 48138 4670 A5
Country Club Rd
700 AATp 48105 4331 A7
700 BNHL 48105 4330 D7
700 BNHL 48105 4331 A7
1100 AATp 48105 4330 D7
1700 AATp 48105 4405 D1
1700 WasC 48105 4405 D1
Country Creek Dr
800 PTFD 48176 4573 C5
Country Knoll Dr
16100 NvlT 48167 4265 C2
Country Oaks Dr
20700 RVVW 48192 4669 C2
Countryside Ct
4500 WasC 48103 4404 E4
Country Side Dr
5400 WasC 48176 4572 C2
Country View Ct
- AGST 48191 4662 B2
Countryview Dr
14300 SOGT 48195 4584 A3
Country View Ln
23000 FTRK 48134 4754 B5
Country Village Ct
2500 AARB 48103 4488 D2
Country Village Ln
3300 TNTN 48183 4669 B3
Country Walk Blvd
13500 VNBN 48111 4579 B3
Country Walk Ct
- VNBN 48111 4579 B2
Countrywood Dr
9000 PyTp 48170 4335 E3
Cour Louis St
500 WRRN 48091 4201 A4
Cour Marie St
800 WRRN 48091 4201 A4
Cour Renee St
600 WRRN 48091 4201 A3
Cour Retta St
900 WRRN 48091 4201 A4
Courtland Av
22700 EPTE 48021 4204 A1
Courtland Cres
1600 WIND N8T 4422 B1
Courtland Dr
6100 CNTN 48187 4337 B6
Courtland St
400 YPLT 48197 4491 C4
13700 OKPK 48237 4198 E3
Courtney Ct
200 LyTp 48167 4189 E5
Courtney Cir Ct
2200 PTFD 48103 4488 D4
Court Ridge Ct
35500 FNHL 48335 4194 C3
Courtside Wy
13500 SOGT 48195 4584 B1
Courtview Dr
45500 CNTN 48188 4411 D5
Courtview Tr
45000 NOVI 48375 4192 C3
Court Village Blvd
15300 TYLR 48180 4582 D4
Courville Dr
16900 NvlT 48167 4263 D3
Cour Ville St
700 WRRN 48091 4201 A4
Courville St
3400 DET 48224 4276 A4
9100 DET 48224 4275 B1
Cousineau Cir
- WIND N9G 4504 B5
Cousineau Dr
800 WIND N9G 4504 C4
Cousineau Rd
- WIND N9G 4504 A5
2000 LSal N9H 4504 A5
Couwlier Av
12300 WRRN 48089 4202 D3
13600 WRRN 48089 4203 A3
Couzens Av
15200 EPTE 48021 4203 B2
24000 HZLP 48030 4200 D1
Cove Ct
40400 PyTp 48170 4265 C5
Cove Dr
100 Tcmh N8N 4424 E1
17200 NvlT 48167 4265 A2
Cove Creek St
- TYLR 48180 4498 D7
Coventry Av
7700 WynC 48138 4670 D3
Coventry Ct
- SALN 48176 4572 B6
1000 WIND N8S 4347 D7
1300 WIND N8S 4348 A7
9500 WasC 48167 4190 B7
28300 BwTp 48183 4754 C3
Coventry Dr
14800 SOGT 48195 4584 B1
19200 RVVW 48192 4669 D1
33900 LVNA 48154 4266 E4
Coventry Ln
400 GSPW 48236 4204 E6
Coventry Rd
40800 NOVI 48375 4193 C5
Coventry St
8000 WTLD 48185 4339 E4
19100 DET 48203 4200 C6
Coventry Wy
41700 CNTN 48187 4337 B5
Coventry Square Dr
1000 WasC 48103 4405 A3
Cove Ridge Dr
13000 GOTp 48178 4188 D4
Covert St
6700 DET 48212 4273 E1
6800 DET 48212 4274 A1
Coveside Cir
43000 NOVI 48375 4193 A2
43100 NOVI 48375 4192 E2
Covey Ct
17700 BNTN 48192 4583 D6
Covington Ct
400 NHVL 48167 4192 D7
5500 DRBN 48126 4341 D7
5500 DRBN 48126 4342 A7
47900 CNTN 48187 4336 A6
Covington Dr
200 DET 48203 4272 B1
800 DET 48203 4200 A7
1200 WasC 48176 4658 C3
1400 AARB 48103 4488 D1
13800 PyTp 48170 4264 C6
38400 WYNE 48184 4413 A5
Covington Rd
32000 BwTp 48173 4755 B7
Covington St
500 SLYN 48178 4189 C1
Cowan Rd
31600 WTLD 48185 4339 B5
33600 WTLD 48185 4338 D4
Coyle Rd
7800 WasC 48189 4258 E4
7800 WasC 48189 4259 A3
Coyle St
9100 DET 48228 4342 D1
9500 DET 48227 4342 D1
14200 DET 48227 4270 D4
16100 DET 48235 4270 D3
18000 DET 48235 4198 D5
23600 OKPK 48237 4198 D1
Coyote Dr
25600 BNTN 48134 4667 C7
25600 BNTN 48134 4753 C1
Crabapple Ct
10 PTFD 48197 4574 E1
Crabtree Ct
41200 PyTp 48170 4265 C4
Crabtree Ln
40600 PyTp 48170 4265 C4
Crabtree St
7800 WTLD 48185 4338 A4
Craft St
10900 DET 48224 4275 B1
11100 DET 48213 4275 B1
Craftsbury Ct
44200 CNTN 48187 4336 E5
Craig Av
100 GDNC 48135 4414 B1
6100 GDNC 48135 4339 B6
Craig Dr
1100 WTLD 48186 4413 E3
Craig Rd
3000 WasC 48103 4405 B2
Craig St
11000 RMLS 48174 4496 B7
12000 RMLS 48174 4580 B1
19000 HnTp 48164 4665 C1
19300 HRWD 48225 4204 B7
19400 GSPW 48236 4204 B7
Cram Cir
1500 AARB 48105 4407 A4
1600 AARB 48105 4406 E4
Cram Pl
2100 AARB 48105 4406 E4
Cranberry Av
10 WasC 48103 4488 B3
Cranberry Ct
1700 WasC 48103 4488 C2
Cranberry Dr
43900 CNTN 48187 4336 E4
Cranberry Ln
300 VNBN 48111 4494 D5
Cranbrook Cres
12000 Tcmh N0R 4424 A7
Cranbrook Ct
- Amhg N9V 4671 C4
13600 PyTp 48170 4264 C6
44600 CNTN 48188 4411 D5
Cranbrook Dr
17500 NvlT 48167 4264 C1
19400 DET 48221 4199 B5
27400 FNHL 48034 4196 A1
27400 FNHL 48336 4196 A1
Cranbrook Rd
2200 CNTN 48188 4411 E5
2600 AARB 48104 4490 A3
Cranbrook St
5400 DBHT 48125 4416 B7
13900 RVVW 48192 4584 D6
22000 WDHN 48183 4668 C4
Cranbrooke Dr
22400 NOVI 48375 4193 D1
Cranbrooke Ln
23000 NOVI 48375 4193 D2
Cranbury Ct
42500 CNTN 48187 4337 B4
Crandell Ct
19600 WynC 48111 4663 D2
Crandell St
17600 DRBN 48101 4417 B5
18300 DRBN 48124 4417 A5
Crane Ct
6300 PTFD 48197 4574 E4
Crane Rd
6000 PTFD 48197 4574 E3
8000 WasC 48160 4574 E7
8200 WasC 48160 4659 E1
Crane St
900 DET 48214 4346 D1
Crane St
3700 DET 48214 4274 D7
5000 DET 48213 4274 C6
Cranford Av
43700 CNTN 48187 4411 E2
43700 CNTN 48187 4412 A2
Cranford Ln
10 GSPT 48230 4276 B6
26600 DBHT 48127 4415 B1
Cranmore St
38900 WYNE 48184 4413 A7
39200 WYNE 48184 4412 E7
Cranshaw St
5500 DET 48204 4271 D7
Cranston Ct
4600 WIND N9G 4504 E6
Cranston St
8500 WTLD 48185 4339 B3
9600 LVNA 48150 4339 B1
13900 LVNA 48154 4267 B5
Crawford Av
100 WIND N9A 4420 D1
1200 WIND N8X 4420 E4
23100 BNTN 48192 4583 B7
23200 BNTN 48174 4583 B7
Crawford Ln
1400 AARB 48105 4407 C4
Crawford Rd
26000 BNTN 48174 4582 C7
29000 HnTp 48174 4581 E7
29000 HnTp 48174 4582 A7
Crawford St
800 DET 48209 4419 C2
S Crawford St
100 DET 48209 4419 C3
Creal Cres
1200 AARB 48103 4405 D4
Creal Ct
1300 AARB 48103 4405 D4
Crecent Ct
38500 WYNE 48184 4413 A6
Creek Dr
- AARB 48104 4490 B4
3000 AARB 48108 4490 B4
W Creek Dr
23000 HnTp 48164 4666 E5
Creek Rd
3400 Amhg N9V 4757 E6
Creek Rd CO-5
3400 Amhg N9V 4757 E6
E Creek Rd
2700 MonC 48117 4839 A4
2700 MonC 48179 4839 A4
Creek Bend Ct
1300 AATp 48104 4490 C1
Creek Bend Dr
7800 YpTp 48197 4576 B3
Creek Dale Ct
23500 FNHL 48336 4196 A2
Creeks Bend Ct
3300 CNTN 48188 4411 B6
Creeks Bend Dr
46700 CNTN 48188 4411 B6
Creekside Cir
6100 YpTp 48197 4576 A3
Creek Side Ct
25500 HnTp 48164 4665 D7
25800 HnTp 48164 4751 D1
Creekside Ct
3600 SpTp 48105 4333 B7
46400 CNTN 48187 4336 B5
Creekside Dr
200 WynC 48111 4662 D6
3400 SpTp 48105 4408 B1
3500 SpTp 48105 4333 B7
8100 WTLD 48185 4337 E4
23900 FNHL 48336 4195 D1
Creekview Ct
5800 PTFD 48108 4572 E3
Creekview Dr
5500 PTFD 48108 4572 E2
43200 CNTN 48187 4337 A6
61300 SLYN 48178 4189 A4
Creekwood Cir
10000 PyTp 48170 4336 D2
Creekwood Dr
8600 CNTN 48170 4335 D3
8600 CNTN 48187 4335 D3
Crescent Ct
10 DRBN 48124 4415 E2
21900 FNHL 48335 4194 B3
Crescent Dr
300 DRBN 48124 4415 E2
1500 INKR 48141 4415 B3
14100 DET 48223 4269 D5
15500 ALPK 48101 4500 A6
Crescent Ln
8400 YpTp 48197 4576 C2
E Crescent Ln
300 DET 48207 4346 C5
700 GSPW 48236 4276 D1
W Crescent Ln
300 DET 48207 4346 C5
800 GSPW 48236 4204 D7
Crescent St
24100 WDHN 48183 4668 C6
Crescent Ridge Dr
23200 HnTp 48164 4666 D5
Crescentwood Av
14500 EPTE 48021 4203 B2
Cressfield Ln
600 AARB 48103 4406 A4
Cressnut Ct
- NvlT 48167 4263 C3
Cresswell St
9300 DET 48213 4274 D6
Crest Av
100 AARB 48103 4406 A6
Crest Dr
17600 NvlT 48167 4265 A2
E Crest Ln
600 SLYN 48178 4189 A1
N Crest Ln
600 SLYN 48178 4189 A1
W Crest Ln
600 SLYN 48178 4189 A1
Crestbrook Dr
- NvlT 48167 4263 C1
Crested Dr
400 WasC 48103 4404 E6
Crestland St
1500 AARB 48104 4489 D2
19500 HRWD 48225 4203 E6
Crestlawn Dr
200 WasC 48189 4259 B1
Crestline Dr
4200 WasC 48103 4329 E5
Crestmont Dr
44600 CNTN 48187 4336 D4
Crestmont Ln
20600 DBHT 48127 4341 D5
Creston Cir
3200 SpTp 48198 4408 B2
Creston Ct
41700 CNTN 48187 4412 B2
Creston St
32900 WTLD 48186 4414 A3
Crestshire Dr
8400 AGST 48197 4575 B7
8400 AGST 48197 4660 B1
Crestview Av
- PTFD 48197 4490 E5
4700 PTFD 48197 4491 A5
Crestview Cir
42000 NvlT 48167 4265 B1
Crestview Ct
24400 FNHL 48335 4193 E1
Crestview Dr
1600 CNTN 48188 4412 D4
45800 NOVI 48374 4192 B1
Crestview Rd
11700 GOTp 48189 4187 A6
Crestview St
23500 DRBN 48124 4416 A3
Crestway Ct
200 WasC 48176 4572 D4
Crestwood Av
1200 YpTp 48198 4492 D4
Crestwood Cir
400 SALN 48176 4657 D1
Crestwood Ct
1000 SLYN 48178 4189 A4
1000 WIND N9E 4504 B2
Crestwood Dr
10 GSPS 48236 4205 A4
41100 PyTp 48170 4265 B4
45400 CNTN 48188 4411 D5
Crestwood St
6800 DBHT 48127 4340 C5
22000 WDHN 48183 4668 C3
Crimson Ct
3000 PTFD 48197 4574 B1
Crisan Rd
- PTFD 48176 4573 C5
Crisler St
20000 TYLR 48180 4499 E6
24600 TYLR 48180 4498 E6
Crittendon Av
1800 YpTp 48198 4492 E7
Croatia Av
- LSal N9H 4503 D5
Crockett Farm Rd
9000 WasC 48178 4261 A1
Crocuslawn St
8700 DET 48204 4343 C1
Croft Av
23000 FTRK 48134 4754 B4
Croft Dr
300 Lksr N8N 4424 E3
Crofton Ct
44100 CNTN 48187 4336 E4
Croissant St
- DRBN 48125 4417 A7
3200 DRBN 48124 4417 A6
4200 DBHT 48125 4417 A7
Cromwell Rd
3300 AARB 48105 4407 C1
Cromwell St
2600 DET 48216 4345 A7
3100 WasC 48167 4190 A7
22800 DRBN 48124 4416 B2
23100 DRBN 48128 4416 B2
Cronin Dr
400 DBHT 48127 4415 C1
6500 DBHT 48127 4340 C5
Crooked Ln
11600 GOTp 48178 4188 A2
Crooked Limb Ln
10 YpTp 48197 4577 B4
Crooks Ct
33900 BwTp 48173 4841 A1
Crooks St
33100 BwTp 48173 4841 A1
Crosby Cres
1200 AARB 48103 4489 A1
Crosley
9500 RDFD 48239 4340 D1
13900 RDFD 48239 4268 D5
Cross Rd
- NvlT 48167 4265 D2
Cross St
400 AARB 48104 4406 B7
3400 WIND N9C 4420 A4
49400 VNBN 48111 4493 E2
E Cross St
10 YPLT 48197 4492 C4
10 YPLT 48198 4492 C4
800 YpTp 48198 4492 C4
W Cross St
10 YPLT 48197 4492 B4
W Cross St
400 YPLT 48197 4491 E4
W Cross St SR-17
100 YPLT 48197 4492 A4
400 YPLT 48197 4491 E4
Crossbill Ct
10 PTFD 48197 4574 E1
Crossbow Cir
40000 CNTN 48188 4412 C3
Cross Creek Ct
3000 WasC 48108 4488 C7
Cross Creek Dr
4500 WasC 48108 4488 C7
9500 GOTp 48178 4187 C2
Crossing Ct
100 WasC 48189 4259 B2
Crossley Av
23000 HZLP 48030 4200 E2
S Crossley St
400 DET 48209 4419 B4
Crossman St
10300 RMLS 48174 4496 C6
Crosswick
46500 CNTN 48187 4411 C1
Crosswick Ct
1800 CNTN 48187 4411 C1
21900 WDHN 48183 4668 C4
Cross Winds Ct
17100 LVNA 48152 4267 C2
Crosswinds Dr
39800 NOVI 48375 4193 C3
Cross Winds Rd
17100 LVNA 48152 4267 C2
17100 LVNA 48154 4267 C2
Crosswinds Rd
- NOVI 48375 4193 D3
Crowder St
1900 Tcmh N0R 4505 B5
Crowley St
6600 DET 48210 4343 E4
20000 TYLR 48180 4499 D3
24700 TYLR 48180 4498 E4
43400 VNBN 48111 4494 E4
43400 VNBN 48111 4495 A4
S Crown Av
1300 WTLD 48186 4413 C4
Crown St
8800 LVNA 48150 4338 C3
N Crown St
1600 WTLD 48185 4338 C7
1600 WTLD 48185 4413 C1
S Crown St
100 WTLD 48185 4413 C2
100 WTLD 48186 4413 C2
Crowndale Blvd
- CNTN 48188 4411 B4
Crowndale Ln
1200 CNTN 48188 4411 B4
Crownridge Blvd
200 Amhg N9V 4757 C4
Croydon Ct
41100 NvlT 48167 4265 C2
Croydon Rd
1000 LSal N9H 4504 D6
Crusade Av
20700 EPTE 48021 4203 C3
Crusade St
19600 DET 48205 4203 C5
Cruse St
14500 DET 48227 4270 E4
16100 DET 48235 4270 E3
Crysler St
25100 TYLR 48180 4498 E6
Crystal Ct
3700 WasC 48103 4329 D5
3700 WasC 48130 4329 D5
4100 INKR 48141 4414 E6
4100 INKR 48141 4415 A6
Crystal Dr
2400 PTFD 48108 4490 D3
Crystal Creek Dr
4000 PTFD 48197 4490 E6
Crystal Downs E
15500 NvlT 48167 4264 C2
Crystal Downs W
46400 NvlT 48167 4264 B2
Crystal Harbour Dr
100 LSal N9J 4586 C1
Crystal Lake Ct
32500 RMLS 48174 4497 B2
Crystal Lake Dr
5800 RMLS 48174 4497 B2
19300 NvlT 48167 4193 A7
Crystal Lake Ln
3600 PTFD 48108 4489 A5
Culpepper Ct
7500 WTLD 48185 4338 C4
Culpepper Rd
15700 BwTp 48173 4755 B6
Culver Av
- DRBN 48125 4417 A5
1300 DRBN 48124 4417 A5
Culver Rd
1300 AARB 48103 4406 B4
Culver St
4000 DBHT 48125 4417 A6
8900 DET 48213 4274 C4
Cumberland Av
2700 AARB 48104 4490 A3
Cumberland Ct
500 Tcmh N8N 4424 C2
Cumberland Dr
- VNBN 48111 4579 B2
21700 NOVI 48375 4192 D4
41400 CNTN 48188 4412 C4
Cumberland Rd
16000 SFLD 48075 4198 B2
Cumberland St
15600 RVVW 48192 4584 B7

STREET
Block City ZIP Map# Grid

Cumberland Wy
19300 DET 48203 4200 A6
Cumberlane Ct
10 DRBN 48126 4341 D7
Cummings Dr
3300 SpTp 48105 4408 B1
Cummings St
5300 DBHT 48125 4415 B7
N Cummings St
5500 DBHT 48125 4498 B1
5500 DBHT 48180 4498 B1
Cunningham Av
23000 WRRN 48091 4201 C1
Cunningham St
12700 SOGT 48195 4584 D2
Curie Av
20700 WRRN 48091 4201 C2
Curie St
24100 WRRN 48091 4201 C1
Curituck Ct
46300 PyTp 48170 4336 C1
Curlew Ln
3700 WasC 48103 4329 D5
Currant Ct
200 YpTp 48197 4577 B5
Currie Ct
12600 LVNA 48150 4266 B7
20900 LyTp 48167 4190 C5
Currie Rd
7300 WasC 48167 4262 D4
9000 WasC 48167 4190 C7
20800 LyTp 48167 4190 C7
22400 LyTp 48178 4190 C4
Currier St
- DBHT 48125 4416 A7
- WTLD 48186 4414 E7
- WTLD 48186 4415 A7
25400 DBHT 48125 4415 D7
27300 DBHT 48186 4415 B7
33900 WYNE 48184 4496 E1
33900 WYNE 48184 4497 A1
Currin Ct
11600 PyTp 48170 4335 C1
Curry Av
100 WIND N9B 4420 C1
2400 WIND N9E 4420 E7
2600 WIND N9E 4421 A7
2800 WIND N9E 4504 A1
Curt Dr
24100 BNTN 48183 4668 B6
Curt St
8000 DET 48213 4274 B5
Curtain Av
18000 EPTE 48021 4203 E2
18200 EPTE 48021 4204 A2
Curtis
25800 RDFD 48240 4268 B1
Curtis Dr
24300 BNTN 48134 4668 A6
Curtis Rd
4100 SpTp 48105 4334 B4
4100 SpTp 48170 4334 B4
5000 WasC 48170 4334 B2
6300 WasC 48170 4262 B6
7300 WasC 48167 4262 B6
29400 LVNA 48152 4267 D1
33400 LVNA 48152 4266 E1
46900 NvlT 48167 4264 B1
Curtis St
- DET 48235 4199 A7
4500 DRBN 48126 4417 D1
4700 DRBN 48126 4342 D7
6300 DET 48221 4199 D7
13700 DET 48235 4198 D7
18100 DET 48219 4198 A7
18900 DET 48219 4197 E7
22000 DET 48219 4269 B1
24000 DET 48219 4268 E1
27800 LVNA 48152 4268 A1
Curwood St
16000 HDPK 48203 4272 B2
Cushing Av
21700 EPTE 48021 4203 D2
Cushing St
19900 DET 48205 4203 D4
19900 DET 48225 4203 D4
19900 HRWD 48225 4203 D4
Custer St
10 DET 48202 4273 A7
1100 DET 48211 4273 A7
6000 SRKW 48179 4754 B7
6000 SRKW 48179 4840 B1
Custis St
24300 SFLD 48075 4197 E1
24300 SFLD 48075 4198 A1
Cutler Cir
1000 PTFD 48176 4574 A4
Cutler St
9300 DET 48214 4346 E1
Cygnet Ct
10 YpTp 48197 4577 B4
Cyman Av
20700 WRRN 48091 4201 D2
Cymbal St
6300 DET 48211 4273 E5
Cynthia Ct
2200 TNTN 48183 4669 B3
Cynthia Dr
7300 SpTp 48105 4333 E6
7300 SpTp 48105 4334 A6
Cynthia St
15200 SOGT 48195 4584 C4
Cypress Ct
16400 NvlT 48167 4264 D3
45400 CNTN 48188 4411 D3
Cypress Rd
30100 RMLS 48174 4497 D2
Cypress St
7700 DET 48210 4343 D6
24000 TYLR 48180 4499 A2
25800 TYLR 48180 4498 D2
35600 RMLS 48174 4496 C2
Cypress Point Dr
44200 NvlT 48167 4264 E3
Cypress Pointe Ct
1600 PTFD 48108 4488 E7
1600 PTFD 48108 4489 A7
Cyprus Gdns E
26700 DBHT 48127 4340 B3
Cyprus Gdns W
26900 DBHT 48127 4340 B3
Cyprus Pointe Dr
- YpTp 48197 4575 E5
7200 YpTp 48197 4576 A5
Czinski Rd
10500 AGST 48191 4662 B6

D

D Av
- WasC 48176 4659 B1
- WasC 48197 4659 B1
D Dr
14000 PyTp 48170 4263 D6
D St
- FNHL 48336 4195 D2
10 DBHT 48125 4416 E6
2000 VNBN 48111 4494 A5
Dacosta
7200 DET 48127 4341 B4
7200 DET 48239 4341 B4
Dacosta St
1200 DRBN 48128 4341 C7
5600 DBHT 48128 4341 B6
6700 DBHT 48127 4341 B5
13900 DET 48223 4269 B5
Dacotah Dr
1700 WIND N8Y 4421 C2
Daffodil Dr
31100 BwTp 48173 4755 A6
Dagner Dr
2600 WTLD 48186 4413 A5
Dahlia Ct
2300 PTFD 48103 4488 D5
21300 WynC 48138 4670 C3
Dahlia Dr
- PTFD 48103 4488 D5
Dailey Ct
8900 DET 48204 4343 E2
Dailey St
- DET 48204 4343 E2
Daisey Ln
1600 WTLD 48186 4412 E4
Daisy Ct
31400 BwTp 48173 4755 A6
Daisy Ln
21800 SFLD 48034 4196 D4
Dakota W
10 DET 48203 4272 C1
Dakota Av
200 YpTp 48198 4492 E5
Dakota Ct
200 WynC 48111 4662 E2
Dakota Ln
26100 FTRK 48134 4754 A1
Dakota St
8400 WTLD 48185 4338 C3
Dalby
15900 RDFD 48239 4268 D3
18200 RDFD 48240 4268 D1
20400 RDFD 48240 4196 D5
Dale
8800 RDFD 48239 4341 A2
Dale Av
18600 ALPK 48101 4499 E5
18600 ALPK 48101 4500 A5
22700 EPTE 48021 4203 B1
Dale Dr
21500 WynC 48111 4664 E3
37400 WTLD 48185 4338 A4
37500 HnTp 48164 4751 B2
Dale Pl
- DRBN 48120 4418 D3
- DRBN 48209 4418 D3
Dale St
- RDFD 48239 4269 A5
8000 DBHT 48127 4341 A3
8600 DBHT 48239 4341 A3
14700 RDFD 48223 4269 A4
15300 DET 48223 4269 A3
16100 DET 48219 4269 A2
19200 DET 48219 4196 E6
22000 BNTN 48183 4668 B4
Daleview Ct
2600 CNTN 48188 4412 B5
13200 GOTp 48178 4188 D1
Daleview Dr
- WasC 48105 4330 C7
2600 WasC 48105 4405 C1
9200 GOTp 48178 4188 D1
21700 NOVI 48374 4192 C4
Dalhay St
30800 LVNA 48150 4339 C1
Dalhousie St
100 Amhg N9V 4757 B3
Dali Ct
4600 WIND N9G 4504 E5
Dallas Av
3100 WRRN 48091 4201 A2
Dallas Ct
9100 WynC 48138 4670 C7
Dallas Dr
25000 WynC 48138 4670 C6
Dallas St
3100 DRBN 48124 4417 A5
Dalrymple St
10000 DET 48204 4271 E7
10000 DET 48204 4343 C1
Dalton Av
2400 PTFD 48108 4490 E3
5700 LSal N9H 4503 D4
Dalton Dr
9400 VNBN 48111 4495 A6
Daly Rd
5500 WasC 48130 4329 A2
Dalzelle St
1900 DET 48216 4345 A6
Damitz Dr
7500 WasC 48167 4262 A3
Damman St
19600 HRWD 48225 4204 A5
Dan St
2900 HMTK 48212 4273 C5
35600 BwTp 48173 4841 B3
Danbridge Ct
46600 PyTp 48170 4264 B7
Danbridge Rd
46600 PyTp 48170 4264 B7
Danbury Ct
13100 PyTp 48170 4264 B7
45200 CNTN 48188 4411 D3
Danbury Dr
21200 WDHN 48183 4669 A3
Danbury Ln
2600 AATp 48103 4405 D1
19900 HRWD 48225 4204 B4
23400 NOVI 48375 4193 D2
Danbury Rd
44400 CNTN 48188 4411 D3
Danbury St
20000 DET 48203 4200 C4
Dancy Blvd
4800 WTLD 48186 4414 E7
5500 WTLD 48186 4497 E1
Dandrea Ct
700 WIND N9G 4504 E3
Dandurand Blvd
2300 WIND N9E 4421 A6
3000 WIND N9E 4504 B1
Dandurand Ct
1000 WIND N9E 4421 A6
Danford Rd
4000 AATp 48105 4407 D2
Danforth St
2200 HMTK 48212 4273 C5
Daniel Av
100 WTLD 48186 4414 A2
Daniel Ct
15400 ALPK 48101 4500 B6
Daniel Dr
3100 TNTN 48183 4669 D5
43000 VNBN 48111 4495 A4
Daniel St
700 AARB 48103 4406 B5
Danielle Dr
- YpTp 48197 4576 D6
12300 GOTp 48178 4188 B3
39400 NvlT 48167 4193 D6
Daniels St
4900 DET 48210 4344 A6
5500 DBHT 48125 4415 B7
5500 DBHT 48125 4498 B1
5500 DBHT 48180 4498 B1
5800 TYLR 48180 4498 B1
6100 DET 48210 4343 E4
D Ann St
500 DET 48202 4345 C2
Dante St
24000 OKPK 48237 4198 E1
Danvers Ln
10 DRBN 48120 4417 D3
Danzig St
8800 LVNA 48150 4339 D2
Darcey Ct
22400 NOVI 48374 4192 B3
Darcey St
- WIND N9G 4504 D3
Darcy Av
- ECRS 48229 4501 B3
Darcy St
14100 DET 48223 4269 C5
Dardanella St
29000 LVNA 48152 4195 E7
37700 LVNA 48152 4194 A7
Darfield Rd
- WIND N8S 4348 A7
Darin St
25000 TYLR 48180 4582 E3
Darlene Dr
400 LSal N9J 4502 E4
Darling Rd
9700 MonC 48191 4748 A7
Darlington Cir
1300 PTFD 48176 4574 B5
Darlington Cres
8400 WIND N8S 4347 E7
8400 WIND N8S 4348 A7
Darlington Ct
1300 WIND N8S 4347 E7
Darrow Dr
2300 AARB 48104 4490 C3
Dartmoor Cir
9800 VNBN 48111 4495 B6
N Dartmoor Cir
42700 VNBN 48111 4495 A6
S Dartmoor Cir
42700 VNBN 48111 4495 A6
Dartmoor Dr
200 WasC 48189 4259 A4
22400 NOVI 48374 4192 B4
Dartmoor Rd
500 AARB 48103 4405 D7
Dartmouth Av
10100 OKPK 48237 4199 B1
26300 INKR 48141 4415 C6
Dartmouth Ct
200 CNTN 48188 4411 E3
5600 PTFD 48197 4574 E2
Dartmouth Dr
36700 WTLD 48185 4413 C1
Dartmouth Pl
19500 NvlT 48167 4193 A7
Dartmouth St
- DRBN 48125 4416 D6
12700 OKPK 48237 4199 A1
13600 OKPK 48237 4198 D1
19000 DBHT 48124 4416 D6
19000 DBHT 48125 4416 D6
24000 DRBN 48124 4416 A6
24300 DBHT 48125 4415 D6
24300 DRBN 48124 4415 D6
25400 DBHT 48141 4415 D6
25800 INKR 48141 4415 C6
43900 CNTN 48188 4411 E3
S Dartmouth St
- LNPK 48146 4501 B1
- LNPK 48229 4501 B1
2900 DET 48229 4501 B1
3300 DET 48146 4501 B1
Dartmouth Crescent Ct
500 WTLD 48185 4413 B1
Darwin Ct
500 WasC 48176 4658 D1
Darwin Dr
1900 CNTN 48187 4337 A7
Darwin St
100 WTLD 48186 4413 E3
8000 DET 48234 4274 A1
Darwood Ct
46400 PyTp 48170 4336 B1
Dasher Av
15500 ALPK 48101 4500 B2
Data Ct
5400 PTFD 48108 4573 B1
Dauncy Ct
13600 BrTp 48134 4753 C6
Dauncy Rd
3800 MonC 48134 4753 C6
4000 BrTp 48134 4753 C6
Davenport Av
24700 NOVI 48374 4192 C1
Davenport St
10 DET 48201 4345 B4
N Davenport St
100 SALN 48176 4572 D7
S Davenport St
100 SALN 48176 4572 D7
Davey Av
23000 HZLP 48030 4200 E2
Davey Ct
5800 GDNC 48135 4339 C6
David Av
2100 YpTp 48198 4492 E7
2100 YpTp 48198 4493 B7
22700 EPTE 48021 4203 D1
David Cres
100 Tcmh N8N 4349 C7
David Ct
1700 AARB 48105 4406 D3
David St
2500 MVDL 48122 4418 A7
2700 MVDL 48122 4417 E7
8800 DET 48214 4274 D7
22100 TYLR 48180 4499 C4
E David Kempf Ct
1100 WasC 48176 4658 C2
W David Kempf Ct
1200 WasC 48176 4658 B2
David Kempf Dr
- WasC 48176 4658 B2
E Davis Av
100 AARB 48103 4406 B7
100 AARB 48104 4406 B7
W Davis Av
200 AARB 48103 4406 B7
Davis Ct
6800 WasC 48176 4571 D5
Davis Pl
5000 DET 48211 4345 D1
Davis St
10 BLVL 48111 4578 D3
100 WYDT 48192 4585 C1
500 PLYM 48170 4265 A6
500 YPLT 48198 4492 B5
800 YpTp 48198 4492 C5
2100 WYDT 48192 4584 E1
2300 WIND N9B 4420 C3
2300 WYDT 48195 4584 E1
13200 GBTR 48173 4755 D4
E Davison
- DET 48203 4272 E3
- DET 48203 4273 A2
- HDPK 48203 4272 E3
W Davison
- HDPK 48203 4272 D3
26500 RDFD 48239 4268 B6
Davison E
- HDPK 48203 4272 E3
Davison W
10 HDPK 48203 4272 A4
1600 DET 48238 4272 A4
3200 DET 48238 4271 E5
Davison Frwy E
- DET - 4272 E2
- DET - 4273 A2
- HDPK - 4272 C4
Davison Frwy E SR-8
- DET - 4272 B4
- DET - 4273 A2
- HDPK - 4272 C4
Davison Frwy W
- DET - 4272 D3
- DET - 4273 A2
- HDPK - 4272 D3
Davison Frwy W SR-8
- DET - 4272 D3
- DET - 4273 A2
- HDPK - 4272 D3
Davison St E
1900 DET 48212 4273 C1
5900 DET 48212 4201 E7
6700 DET 48212 4202 A7
Davison St W
- DET 48227 4270 A6
- DET 48227 4271 A6
- DET 48238 4271 A6
- RDFD 48223 4269 A6
- RDFD 48239 4269 A6
18200 DET 48223 4270 A6
19000 DET 48223 4269 E6
24000 RDFD 48239 4268 E6
Dawes St
8800 DET 48204 4343 C2
Dawn Av
1500 SpTp 48198 4492 D2
1500 YpTp 48198 4492 D2
Dawnshire Ct
16900 BNTN 48192 4669 A1
Dawnshire Dr
19000 BNTN 48192 4584 A7
19100 BNTN 48192 4669 A1
Dawson Av
27400 GDNC 48135 4340 A6
29400 GDNC 48135 4339 D6
Dawson Ct
100 WTLD 48186 4412 E2
Dawson Dr
3600 WasC 48103 4329 D6
Dawson Rd
800 WIND N8Y 4347 A7
Dawson St
27300 DBHT 48127 4340 B6
Day St
1900 AARB 48104 4406 E7
Day Lily Dr
31000 BwTp 48173 4755 A6
31000 RKWD 48173 4755 A6
Dayton Ct
34200 WTLD 48186 4413 E5
Dayton Dr
2300 PTFD 48108 4490 D3
Dayton St
7700 DET 48210 4343 C5
18100 DET 48228 4342 A6
19100 DET 48228 4341 E6
Daytona Av
1600 WIND N9B 4420 C6
2200 WIND N9E 4420 C6
3200 WIND N9E 4503 E2
3800 WIND N9G 4503 E3
4300 LSal N9H 4504 A4
5400 YpTp 48197 4576 B2
S Deacon St
- LNPK 48229 4501 B2
1600 DET 48229 4418 C7
3500 DET 48229 4501 B2
Deake Av
2500 PTFD 48108 4490 E3
Dean Ct
22300 SLYN 48178 4189 A4
Dean Dr
61300 SLYN 48178 4189 B4
Dean Ln
200 GSPF 48236 4276 C4
Dean Rd
1600 AARB 48105 4407 B4
Dean St
4400 WYNE 48184 4414 A7
6000 TYLR 48180 4498 C1
13400 DET 48212 4273 C1
14600 TYLR 48180 4582 D4
18000 DET 48234 4201 B6
20700 WRRN 48091 4201 C2
21000 BNTN 48174 4667 D3
Deanna Dr
13800 VNBN 48111 4578 B3
Dearborn Ct
19700 NvlT 48167 4193 C6
S Dearborn Dr
4000 MVDL 48122 4417 E4
4500 ALPK 48101 4417 E4
4500 MVDL 48101 4417 E4
Dearborn St
- DRBN 48209 4418 E4
3200 WYNE 48184 4414 B5
8400 DET 48209 4419 A4
9300 DET 48209 4418 E4
Dearborndale St
4600 DBHT 48125 4416 B7
Dearing St
1900 DET 48212 4273 A2
Deaton Dr
22500 LyTp 48178 4189 C4
Debby Ct
800 YpTp 48198 4492 B5
Debiasi Dr
26900 BNTN 48174 4667 B2
Deborah
25500 RDFD 48239 4340 D2
E Deborah
25200 RDFD 48239 4340 D2
Deborah Ct
2200 TNTN 48183 4669 A3
34400 WTLD 48185 4338 E4
Deborah Ct E
8800 LVNA 48150 4337 E3
Deborah Ct W
8800 LVNA 48150 4337 E3
Debra Ct
27000 TYLR 48180 4498 B1
43000 WynC 48111 4664 A1
Debra Ln
200 NHVL 48167 4192 D5
Debuel St
6400 DET 48211 4273 E5
Decatur Ct
34100 WTLD 48186 4413 E5
Decatur St
2800 DRBN 48124 4416 C5
8800 DET 48228 4342 E1
9500 DET 48227 4342 E1
Dee St
1400 WYDT 48192 4585 A3
Deep Hollow Cir
44000 NvlT 48167 4264 E2
Deep Hollow Ct
44000 NvlT 48167 4264 E2
Deeplands Ct
10 GSPS 48236 4276 E1
Deeplands Rd
400 GSPS 48236 4276 E1
500 GSPW 48236 4276 E1
N Deeplands Rd
10 GSPS 48236 4276 E1
10 GSPS 48236 4277 A1
S Deeplands Rd
10 GSPS 48236 4276 E1
10 GSPS 48236 4277 A1
Deepwood St
39700 CNTN 48188 4412 D3
Deer Ln
6500 PTFD 48197 4574 C5
Deer St
400 PLYM 48170 4337 A1
Deerbrook Dr
3300 WIND N8R 4423 C3
Deer Creek Blvd
38400 WTLD 48185 4338 A4
38500 WTLD 48185 4337 E5
Deer Creek Cir
11600 PyTp 48170 4336 A1
12200 PyTp 48170 4335 E1
Deer Creek Ct
3000 AARB 48105 4407 A1
11900 PyTp 48170 4336 A1
40600 CNTN 48188 4412 D4
Deer Creek Dr
- FTRK 48134 4753 E1
6000 YpTp 48197 4575 B3
24000 FTRK 48134 4754 B1
40400 CNTN 48188 4412 D4
Deer Creek Ln
7800 WTLD 48185 4338 A6
Deer Creek Run
11700 PyTp 48170 4335 E1
Deere Park Ct
5000 WasC 48176 4571 D6
Deerfield
23600 HnTp 48164 4665 A6
Deerfield Av
15100 EPTE 48021 4203 C1
Deerfield Ct
2300 WTLD 48186 4413 B6
Deerfield Dr
21300 WDHN 48183 4668 D3
Deerfield Pl
- WasC 48103 4405 B2
Deerfield Rd
22500 NOVI 48375 4193 C3
Deerfield St
25800 DBHT 48127 4415 D1
Deer Glen Dr
3800 PTFD 48108 4488 E6
Deer Haven Dr
59200 LyTp 48178 4189 D5
Deerhurst N
36500 WTLD 48185 4338 B6
Deerhurst S
36500 WTLD 48185 4338 C6
Deerhurst Ct
36500 WTLD 48185 4338 B6
Deerhurst Dr
6800 WTLD 48185 4338 C6
Deering Av
100 GDNC 48135 4415 A1
100 GDNC 48141 4415 A1
1500 GDNC 48135 4340 A7
Deering St
7200 WTLD 48185 4340 A4
8600 SpTp 48198 4492 C1
9500 LVNA 48150 4340 A1
11600 LVNA 48150 4267 A7
15300 LVNA 48154 4268 A3
17100 LVNA 48152 4268 A1
19400 LVNA 48152 4196 A5
Deer Path Dr
17300 NvlT 48167 4264 B2
Deer Pines Dr
40700 CNTN 48188 4412 D4
Deer Ridge Ct
400 Amhg N9V 4757 C4
3600 SpTp 48105 4333 B7
Deer Run Ct N
36500 WTLD 48185 4338 C6
Deer Run Ct S
6800 WTLD 48185 4338 C6
Deer Run Ln
28200 HnTp 48134 4753 A2
Deer Run Rd
44800 PyTp 48170 4336 D1
49400 NOVI 48167 4191 C4
Deer Track Ct
7300 YpTp 48197 4576 A5
Deer Track Dr
7100 YpTp 48197 4576 B5
Deer Trail Dr
47800 CNTN 48187 4336 A7
Deerwood Ct
38600 FNHL 48167 4193 E4
Defer Pl
1600 DET 48214 4347 A1
Defer St
23700 STCS 48080 4204 E1
Dehner St
23500 DET 48219 4269 A2
23800 DET 48219 4268 E7
Dejarol St
10600 GOTp 48178 4188 C4
Delafield Dr
2000 AARB 48105 4406 C3
Delaford Ct
400 CNTN 48188 4411 A3
Delaford Dr
500 CNTN 48188 4411 B4
Delancy Cir
1600 CNTN 48188 4410 E4
1600 CNTN 48188 4411 A4
Delancy Ct
1600 CNTN 48188 4410 E4
Delaney St
6800 RMLS 48174 4497 A3
Delano St
11000 RMLS 48174 4496 D7
11200 RMLS 48174 4580 D1
Delavern St
13200 GBTR 48173 4755 D5
Delaware
500 WynC 48111 4662 D2
Delaware Av
300 LSal N9J 4502 D6
1300 YpTp 48198 4492 C3
14900 RDFD 48239 4268 B4
16100 RDFD 48240 4268 B2
20000 RDFD 48240 4196 B5
Delaware Blvd
100 LSal N9J 4502 C6
Delaware Dr
2000 AARB 48103 4488 E2
2200 AARB 48103 4489 A3
Delaware Rd
10 WasC 48189 4258 E3
200 WasC 48189 4259 A4
Delaware St
10 DET 48202 4273 A7
600 DET 48202 4272 E7
800 DET 48202 4344 D1
1900 DET 48206 4344 D1
20700 SFLD 48034 4196 B4
20700 SFLD 48240 4196 B4
31500 LVNA 48150 4339 B2
Del Duca Dr
3600 Tcmh N0R 4505 C4
Delhi Ct
3700 WasC 48103 4329 E6
3700 WasC 48103 4330 A6
E Delhi Rd
2000 WasC 48103 4405 A1
2700 WasC 48103 4330 A6
3900 WasC 48105 4330 A6
N Delhi Rd
4000 WasC 48103 4330 A5
4000 WasC 48105 4330 A5
W Delhi Rd
800 WasC 48103 4404 E3
2400 WasC 48103 4329 E7
Delhi Overlook St
3500 WasC 48105 4330 B5
Delisle St
10 RVRG 48218 4418 E7
Dell Rd
6000 WasC 48176 4571 D5
8000 WasC 48176 4656 D2
Dellor Rd
5800 VNBN 48111 4493 D2
Dellwood Dr
500 AARB 48103 4405 C5
Delmar St
1800 LSal N9H 4503 C4
8900 DET 48211 4273 A4
Delmont Dr
24800 NOVI 48374 4191 D1
Delos Rd
27000 HnTp 48164 4751 B2
Delta Ct
32100 WTLD 48186 4414 D5
Delta Dr
40400 NvlT 48167 4265 C2
Delta St
4800 DET 48212 4273 C1
12000 TYLR 48180 4582 E1
12000 TYLR 48180 4583 A1
Delton Ct
2200 WTLD 48186 4413 E4
Delwood Dr
- NvlT 48167 4265 B3
Demarse Ct
12300 Tcmh N8N 4424 A2
Demean Av
- ALPK 48101 4417 C7
- ALPK 48122 4417 C7
1500 LNPK 48146 4501 E3
15000 MVDL 48122 4417 D7
Demick Ct
23100 BNTN 48134 4667 C5
Deming Ln
10 GSPF 48236 4276 D5
Denby
15500 RDFD 48239 4268 B3
17300 RDFD 48240 4268 B1
20400 RDFD 48240 4196 B5
Denby Ct
1300 WIND N8S 4348 B7
22600 NOVI 48374 4192 B2
Denice St
1000 WTLD 48186 4414 A3
Denise Ct
45500 PyTp 48170 4336 C2
Denise Dr
45500 PyTp 48170 4336 C2
Denison St
29000 GBTR 48173 4755 D4
Denmark St
12700 DET 48229 4418 D4
Denne St
8300 WTLD 48185 4339 C3
10900 LVNA 48150 4339 C1

INDEX 17
Denne St
Detroit & Wayne County Street Index
Drexel St

STREET Block City ZIP Map# Grid

Denne St
14000 LVNA 48154 4267 C5
Denning Rd
26000 HnTp 48164 4751 C1
Dennis St
6300 DET 48210 4344 A7
17800 BNTN 48174 4583 B6
Dennison Ct
4200 WIND N9G 4504 E3
Dennison St
8600 DET 48210 4343 C6
Dennisport Rd
44400 CNTN 48187 4336 C4
Denton Rd
- BLVL 48111 4578 C2
100 CNTN 48188 4410 E7
3700 CNTN 48111 4493 E1
3700 CNTN 48188 4493 E1
5800 VNBN 48111 4493 E3
46600 VNBN 48111 4578 B1
49000 VNBN 48111 4577 E1
Denton St
2000 HMTK 48211 4273 C6
2000 HMTK 48212 4273 C6
Denver St
17100 DET 48224 4276 B4
N Denwood St
100 DRBN 48128 4415 E1
1100 DRBN 48128 4340 E7
S Denwood St
100 DRBN 48124 4415 E2
700 DRBN 48124 4416 A2
De Petris Wy
10 GSPF 48236 4276 D3
Depot St
100 AARB 48103 4406 B5
100 AARB 48104 4406 B5
100 AARB 48105 4406 B5
Dequindre
- DET 48207 4345 D3
Dequindre Rd
- HZLP 48203 4200 E1
- WRRN 48203 4200 E1
- WRRN 48234 4200 E1
20700 HZLP 48030 4200 E1
20700 WRRN 48030 4200 E1
20700 WRRN 48091 4200 E1
22600 HZLP 48091 4200 E1
Dequindre St
10000 HMTK 48212 4273 A4
12200 DET 48212 4273 A2
12800 DET 48203 4273 A2
14000 DET 48203 4272 E1
14000 DET 48212 4272 E1
17500 DET 48203 4200 E7
17500 DET 48212 4200 E7
18000 DET 48234 4200 E7
Derby Ct
400 WasC 48176 4658 D1
22000 WDHN 48183 4668 C6
23300 FNHL 48336 4196 A2
Derby Dr
15400 BwTp 48173 4755 B7
Derby Ln
23300 FNHL 48336 4196 A2
Derby Rd
400 Tcmh N8N 4424 D2
22100 WDHN 48183 4668 C6
Derby St
7300 CNTN 48187 4336 E5
19900 DET 48203 4200 C4
Derek Dr
6700 WasC 48130 4258 A6
6700 WasC 48189 4258 A6
Derek St
1100 WIND N8P 4348 D7
Dern Dr
35100 BwTp 48173 4841 D3
Deslippe Dr
1700 Tcmh N9K 4424 A3
Desmond St
6500 DET 48209 4419 B2
Desner St
5000 DET 48212 4273 D1
Desoto Av
500 YpTp 48198 4493 A6
Desoto St
- INKR 48141 4415 C5
6300 DET 48238 4271 C3
Desro Dr
13300 Tcmh N9K 4424 B3
Detroit Av
10 TNTN 48183 4585 A7
10 TNTN 48192 4585 A7
100 TNTN 48183 4670 A1
400 LNPK 48146 4501 B5
2100 LNPK 48146 4500 C4
2200 ALPK 48146 4500 C4
Detroit Ct
700 LNPK 48146 4501 A5
Detroit St
100 SLYN 48178 4189 B2
200 SALN 48176 4572 D7
200 WIND N9C 4420 A3
400 AARB 48104 4406 B5
1800 DRBN 48124 4416 E5
1800 DRBN 48124 4417 A4
3900 DBHT 48124 4416 E6
5400 DBHT 48125 4416 E7
17100 DET 48224 4276 A3
Detroit-Windsor Tun
- DET 48226 4345 D7
- WIND N9A 4345 D7
- WIND N9A 4420 E1
Devere Ct
500 RVRG 48218 4501 D1
Devereaux St
6300 DET 48210 4344 A5
6500 DET 48210 4343 E5
Devine St
10300 DET 48213 4274 D4
Devoe St
12000 SOGT 48195 4500 B7
12000 SOGT 48195 4584 B1
Devolson Av
2000 AARB 48104 4489 E2
Devon Ct
900 SLYN 48178 4189 C4
Devon Dr
3000 WIND N8W 4421 D6
3000 WIND N8X 4421 D6
Devon Ln
43000 CNTN 48187 4337 A6
Devon St
1500 SpTp 48198 4492 D2
1500 YpTp 48198 4492 D2
12400 DET 48205 4274 D1
39300 WTLD 48186 4412 E2
Devonshire Av
17100 ALPK 48101 4500 A3
18700 ALPK 48101 4499 E3
19300 ALPK 48180 4499 E3
Devonshire Ct
2000 WIND N8Y 4421 C2
17700 NvlT 48167 4263 D2
Devonshire Dr
6600 CNTN 48187 4336 D6
10000 GOTp 48178 4188 E2
22300 WDHN 48183 4668 B4
23800 NOVI 48374 4192 C2
Devonshire Rd
10 YpTp 48198 4492 E4
300 WIND N8Y 4346 B7
900 WIND N8Y 4421 C1
1000 GPPK 48230 4276 A6
1400 GPPK 48230 4275 E4
2000 AARB 48104 4489 E1
2100 AARB 48104 4406 E7
2200 AARB 48104 4407 A7
4000 TNTN 48183 4669 B6
9100 DET 48224 4275 D2
Devonshire St
100 DRBN 48124 4416 B1
17400 RVVW 48192 4584 C6
Devonwood Av
3800 WIND N8W 4505 A2
Devron Ct
22500 NOVI 48374 4192 C3
Dewar Dr
41000 NvlT 48167 4265 C2
Deward Dr
3400 SpTp 48105 4408 A1
Dewey Av
700 AARB 48104 4489 C1
Dewey Pl
- RDFD 48240 4268 C2
Dewey St
900 PLYM 48170 4337 A1
DeWitt Rd
4800 CNTN 48188 4411 D7
10400 VNBN 48111 4494 D7
11400 VNBN 48111 4578 D1
Dexter Av
400 YpTp 48197 4491 A3
1500 AARB 48103 4405 D5
2600 WasC 48103 4405 C4
7300 DET 48206 4344 B2
7300 DET 48210 4344 B2
9500 DET 48206 4272 A6
12600 DET 48238 4272 A6
15400 DET 48238 4271 E2
16100 DET 48221 4271 E2
Dexter Blvd
20700 WRRN 48089 4203 A3
Dexter Ct
21700 WRRN 48089 4203 A2
Dexter St
5800 RMLS 48174 4496 E1
Dexter Ann Arbor Rd
3500 WasC 48103 4405 A4
4100 WasC 48103 4404 C2
5100 WasC 48130 4404 C2
6300 WasC 48130 4329 A7
Dey St
100 DET 48209 4418 E5
S Dey St
100 DET 48209 4418 E5
Deziel Dr
2700 WIND N8W 4422 A6
Dhu Varren Ct
3000 AATp 48105 4406 B1
Dhu Varren Rd
600 AATp 48105 4406 D1
1700 AARB 48105 4406 D1
2200 AARB 48105 4407 A1
2500 AATp 48105 4407 A1
Diamond Cir
200 WasC 48189 4186 E7
Diamond St
4000 PTFD 48197 4574 D5
Diane Ct
8600 WTLD 48185 4339 B3
Diane St
9900 RMLS 48174 4496 D6
Dicken Dr
1400 AARB 48103 4488 D2
Dickerson Dr
9700 GOTp 48178 4188 C2
Dickerson St
- DET 48205 4275 A1
1000 DET 48214 4275 C6
1000 DET 48214 4347 D1
5000 DET 48213 4275 B5
7900 WasC 48167 4262 E3
12000 DET 48205 4274 E1
Dickinson Av
2300 TNTN 48183 4669 E4
Dickinson Rd
21000 HnTp 48164 4666 B4
Dicocco Ct
5400 Tcmh N0R 4505 C6
Dieppe St
200 WIND N8S 4347 E5
Digsby St
2200 WIND N8W 4421 E5
Dijon Av
19000 EPTE 48021 4204 B1
Dill Pl
8000 DET 48209 4419 B4
Dillingham Dr
39200 WTLD 48186 4412 E3
Dillon Av
5600 GDNC 48135 4339 C6
Dillon Dr
12000 Tcmh N8N 4348 E6
12000 Tcmh N8P 4348 E6
12600 Tcmh N8N 4349 A6
Dillon Rd
11800 WIND N8P 4348 D6
Dillon St
1100 GDNC 48135 4414 C1
6400 GDNC 48135 4339 C6
6400 WTLD 48185 4339 C6
Dimambro Ct
4100 WIND N9G 4504 E3
Dimu Dr
12100 Tcmh N0R 4424 A7
Dina Ct
36700 FNHL 48335 4194 B3
Dines Ct
3700 AARB 48105 4407 C5
Dinky St
- LyTp 48167 4189 E5
Dinser Dr
24500 NOVI 48374 4191 E1
Dionne St
44500 CNTN 48188 4411 D6
Disputed Rd
6000 LSal N9H 4504 A5
6800 LSal N9J 4504 A7
Distel St
700 DET 48209 4418 E4
E Ditner Dr
31600 RKWD 48173 4754 C6
W Ditner Dr
23100 RKWD 48173 4754 B6
Diversey St
- DET 48126 4342 B4
- DET 48228 4342 B4
6300 DET 48210 4343 D4
8700 DRBN 48126 4343 C4
15200 DRBN 48126 4342 D4
Divine St
800 LSal N9J 4502 D5
Division Dr
- YpTp 48198 4493 B4
Division Rd
400 WIND N8X 4421 C7
500 WIND N8W 4504 D1
500 WIND N8X 4504 D1
1300 WIND N8W 4505 B2
Division St
10 RVRG 48218 4418 E7
200 PLYM 48170 4265 B6
400 DET 48201 4345 D4
800 INKR 48141 4414 E3
1300 DET 48207 4345 D4
4500 TNTN 48183 4669 E6
25800 FTRK 48134 4753 D4
N Division St
100 AARB 48104 4406 C5
S Division St
100 AARB 48104 4406 B7
Dix Av
- DRBN 48229 4418 D3
9300 DET 48120 4418 D3
9300 DET 48209 4418 D3
9300 DRBN 48120 4418 D3
9300 DRBN 48209 4418 D3
Dix Hwy
800 LNPK 48146 4500 D2
Dix Rd
17400 MVDL 48122 4418 A6
18800 MVDL 48122 4417 E7
Dix St
6700 DET 48209 4419 A1
8300 DET 48209 4418 E1
9300 DRBN 48209 4418 E1
S Dix St
100 DET 48229 4418 C5
1000 DET 48122 4418 C5
1000 MVDL 48122 4418 C5
Dixboro Ln
3500 SpTp 48105 4408 A1
Dixboro Rd
7300 WasC 48178 4261 A4
9000 WasC 48178 4189 A7
20700 GOTp 48178 4189 A5
20700 LyTp 48178 4189 A5
21500 SLYN 48178 4189 A2
N Dixboro Rd
10 AATp 48105 4407 E7
1700 AATp 48105 4408 A2
2100 SpTp 48105 4408 A2
3500 AATp 48105 4333 A7
3500 SpTp 48105 4333 A7
5000 WasC 48105 4333 A2
6000 WasC 48105 4261 A6
6000 WasC 48178 4261 A6
6000 WasC 48178 4333 A1
S Dixboro Rd
10 AATp 48105 4407 E7
10 AATp 48105 4490 E1
Dixboro Farms Dr
5000 WasC 48105 4333 A2
Dixford Av
800 LNPK 48146 4500 E1
Dixie
10000 RDFD 48239 4340 E1
11900 RDFD 48239 4268 E7
Dixie Hwy
10000 BrTp 48166 4840 B6
10000 BrTp 48179 4840 B6
11900 SRKW 48179 4840 B3
12700 RKWD 48173 4840 B3
12700 RKWD 48179 4840 B3
N Dixie Hwy
9000 BrTp 48166 4840 B7
Dixie Ln
8200 DBHT 48127 4340 E3
8400 DBHT 48239 4340 E3
Dixie Mnr
32000 BwTp 48173 4755 A7
Dix Toledo Hwy
- BNTN 48134 4668 B3
- BNTN 48183 4583 D7
- BNTN 48192 4668 B3
17000 BNTN 48192 4583 D7
19000 BNTN 48183 4668 B3
20700 WDHN 48183 4668 B3
Dix Toledo Rd
- BNTN 48192 4583 E5
- BNTN 48195 4583 E5
- SOGT 48195 4583 E5
12000 SOGT 48146 4500 D7
12000 SOGT 48195 4500 D7
12200 SOGT 48195 4584 B4
Doane Rd
11600 GOTp 48178 4188 A1
Dobbin Ln
10300 WasC 48170 4263 A7
Dobel St
8000 DET 48234 4274 A1
E Dobson Pl
3300 AARB 48105 4407 B5
W Dobson Pl
3100 AARB 48105 4407 B4
N Dobson St
200 WTLD 48185 4413 E2
S Dobson St
100 WTLD 48186 4413 E2
Docherty Ct
5400 WIND N8T 4422 D4
Docherty Dr
2200 Tcmh N8N 4424 A5
Docksey
18000 NvlT 48167 4263 E1
Dodge Av
6700 WRRN 48091 4201 E2
7000 WRRN 48091 4202 A2
8200 RMLS 48174 4497 E4
11300 WRRN 48089 4202 C2
Dodge Ct
700 YpTp 48198 4493 A5
Dodge Pl
10 GSPT 48230 4276 D6
Dodge St
4000 DET 48211 4273 D4
7100 RMLS 48174 4497 E3
16000 RMLS 48174 4581 E5
Doepfer Rd
20700 WRRN 48091 4201 C3
Doe Ridge St
38700 HnTp 48164 4665 A5
Dogwood Ct
100 CNTN 48187 4412 C2
300 SALN 48176 4572 D4
1900 AARB 48103 4488 D3
3600 PTFD 48197 4574 D5
14700 PyTp 48170 4265 C5
Dogwood Dr
14700 PyTp 48170 4265 C5
24900 BNTN 48134 4667 E3
Dogwood St
10 WynC 48111 4578 B7
Dohany Dr
32100 FNHL 48336 4195 A1
Doheny Dr
600 NHVL 48167 4192 E6
700 NvlT 48167 4192 E6
900 NvlT 48167 4193 A6
Dolan St
23500 TYLR 48180 4499 A1
Dolly Cir
31000 HnTp 48174 4581 C6
Dolores Av
3100 WRRN 48091 4201 A1
Dolores Dr
4500 TNTN 48183 4669 C7
Dolores St
17100 LVNA 48152 4268 A1
Dolph Dr
3100 AARB 48103 4405 B6
Dolphin
7200 DET 48127 4341 B4
7200 DET 48239 4341 B4
Dolphin Av
23600 SFLD 48034 4197 A2
Dolphin Ct
3300 WIND N8R 4423 C3
22200 DBHT 48127 4341 B5
Dolphin St
6500 DBHT 48127 4341 C6
12800 DET 48228 4269 B6
13900 DET 48223 4269 B4
16700 DET 48219 4269 B2
Dolphine Rd
10 WIND N8W 4505 A2
Dolson St
12600 DET 48223 4269 C6
12600 DET 48228 4269 C6
Domine St
5800 DET 48211 4273 D4
Dominion Blvd
- CNTN 48187 4410 D1
1700 WIND N9B 4420 E5
2200 WIND N9C 4420 E5
2400 WIND N9E 4421 A7
2800 WIND N9E 4504 A1
Dominion Ct
49100 CNTN 48187 4410 E1
Donald
25000 RDFD 48239 4268 D5
Donald Av
21700 EPTE 48021 4203 D1
Donald Ct
24300 RDFD 48239 4268 E4
Donald Pl
6900 DET 48207 4346 C3
Donald St
- DRBN 48126 4342 D6
- DRBN 48126 4343 A6
37900 LVNA 48154 4266 A5
38700 LVNA 48154 4265 E5
Donalda Ct
200 Tcmh N8N 4349 B7
Donaldson St
23000 DRBN 48124 4416 B4
Doncaster Av
22100 BNTN 48192 4583 C7
Doncaster Ct
18100 BNTN 48192 4583 C6
Doncaster Dr
2800 CNTN 48188 4411 B5
Dondero Dr
15200 SOGT 48195 4584 A3
Donegal Ct
10 AARB 48104 4490 C3
18400 NvlT 48167 4264 C1
Donjon Ct
700 WIND N9G 4504 C3
Donna Ct
2300 WIND N9E 4503 D2
Donna Ln
1000 WasC 48189 4259 C2
Donna Rd
8000 WTLD 48185 4339 D3
8600 WTLD 48150 4339 D3
Donna St
19400 LVNA 48152 4195 B6
Donnelly Ct
22300 BNTN 48192 4583 C7
Donnelly St
2800 WIND N9C 4420 A3
22200 BNTN 48192 4583 C7
28400 GDNC 48135 4340 A7
28600 GDNC 48135 4339 E7
33600 GDNC 48135 4338 E7
34400 WTLD 48185 4338 D7
Donovan Blvd
49500 PyTp 48170 4263 D7
Donovan Ct
21200 SFLD 48075 4197 C3
Donovan Pl
10 GSPT 48230 4276 C6
Donovan St
200 SLYN 48178 4189 C2
Dons Dr
200 YpTp 48198 4493 B3
Dora Ct
48300 VNBN 48111 4578 A2
Dora Dr
16600 NvlT 48167 4265 D3
Dora St
17000 MVDL 48122 4418 A6
17000 MVDL 48229 4418 A6
Dorado Ct
9000 WasC 48160 4659 D2
Dorais St
30900 LVNA 48154 4267 C3
33900 LVNA 48154 4266 E3
Doral Ct
5100 PTFD 48108 4572 E1
Doral Dr
- LyTp 48178 4190 C2
4800 PTFD 48108 4488 E7
4800 PTFD 48108 4572 E1
7400 YpTp 48197 4576 A6
Doranda Ct
4700 WIND N8T 4422 C4
Dorchester Av
22500 WDHN 48183 4668 C5
Dorchester Cir
- TYLR 48180 4582 E5
39400 CNTN 48188 4412 E3
Dorchester Ct
15500 NvlT 48167 4264 C3
Dorchester Dr
11000 SOGT 48195 4499 E7
43400 VNBN 48111 4495 A6
Dorchester Rd
2400 AARB 48104 4490 A3
3400 WIND N9C 4420 C5
Dorchester St
9300 DET 48214 4346 E1
Doree Av
6600 VNBN 48111 4493 C3
Doreen St
27400 FNHL 48034 4196 A3
27400 FNHL 48336 4196 A3
Doremus Ln
100 STCS 48080 4204 E2
Doremus St
3300 HMTK 48212 4273 C4
6100 DET 48211 4273 E4
6100 DET 48212 4273 E4
22400 STCS 48080 4204 E2
23000 STCS 48080 4205 A2
Dorian Dr
9800 PyTp 48170 4336 D2
Doris Ct
24900 RDFD 48239 4340 E1
Doris St
10 HDPK 48203 4272 B3
2600 DET 48238 4272 A4
2900 DET 48238 4271 E4
9700 LVNA 48150 4339 D1
16900 LVNA 48154 4267 D2
17200 LVNA 48152 4267 D1
19800 LVNA 48152 4195 D6
Dorisa Ct
43700 NHVL 48167 4192 E5
Dormar Dr
400 WIND N8S 4348 A5
Dormont Av
23800 WRRN 48091 4200 E1
Dornoch Dr
800 WasC 48103 4404 D7
Dorothy Dr
24500 BNTN 48134 4668 A7
Dorothy St
100 SLYN 48178 4189 B3
1600 YpTp 48198 4492 E7
3800 HMTK 48211 4273 D5
3800 HMTK 48212 4273 D5
3900 DET 48211 4273 D5
Dorr St
1000 WTLD 48186 4414 B3
Dorset Av
600 YpTp 48198 4492 E6
18100 SFLD 48075 4198 A4
19000 SFLD 48075 4197 E4
Dorset Ct
12100 SOGT 48195 4584 C1
Dorset Pk
500 Tcmh N8N 4424 C2
Dorset Rd
2100 AARB 48104 4406 E7
Dorset St
30200 RMLS 48174 4581 D4
Dorsey Rd
31400 WTLD 48186 4414 B4
Dort Dr
9900 GOTp 48189 4187 A5
Dorthen Av
1400 GSPW 48236 4204 C7
Dorwin Plz
- WIND N8X 4421 A5
Dos Rios St
100 BLVL 48111 4578 E4
Dossenbach Dr
300 LSal N9J 4586 D1
Dot Av
1000 WIND N9C 4420 B4
Doty Av
200 AARB 48103 4405 E5
Doty Pl
2500 WIND N8X 4421 B5
Double Creek Dr
12700 PyTp 48170 4263 E7
Doubletree Rd
46100 CNTN 48187 4336 B6
Dougall Av
- WIND - 4505 A4
100 WIND N9A 4420 E2
1200 WIND N8X 4420 E2
1500 WIND N8X 4421 A4
2600 WIND N8X 4421 B7
3100 WIND N9E 4504 C1
3800 WIND N9G 4504 C1
Dougall Av P-3B
- WIND - 4504 D3
- WIND - 4505 A4
2600 WIND N8X 4421 B6
2600 WIND N9E 4421 B6
Dougall Dr
4100 WIND N9G 4504 D3
Dougall Sq
- WIND N8X 4421 A5
- WIND N9G 4504 C2
Douglas Ct
3900 INKR 48141 4415 C6
Douglas Dr
24100 LyTp 48178 4189 E2
40300 CNTN 48188 4412 D2
Douglas Rd
1500 TNTN 48183 4669 B2
1500 TNTN 48192 4669 B2
Douglas St
400 YPLT 48197 4491 C4
800 GDNC 48135 4414 A1
22800 BNTN 48183 4668 B4
Douglas MacArthur Bridge
- DET 48207 4346 D4
Dove Av
- HbgT 48189 4186 A6
Dove Ln
11800 Tcmh N8N 4423 D2
Dove Tr
100 PTFD 48197 4574 E2
35400 WTLD 48185 4338 D6
Dover
- DET 48239 4341 B2
23700 RDFD 48239 4341 A2
24800 RDFD 48239 4340 E2
Dover Av
27400 LVNA 48150 4340 A2
32500 GDNC 48135 4339 A5
34500 LVNA 48150 4338 D3
Dover Blvd
25400 NOVI 48374 4192 C1
Dover Ct
10 AARB 48103 4405 E7
1700 SpTp 48198 4492 D1
10000 GOTp 48178 4188 E2
Dover Dr
7300 YpTp 48197 4576 A6
16600 NvlT 48167 4263 D3
18900 WDHN 48183 4755 A1
36700 WTLD 48185 4413 C2
Dover Hl
22500 FNHL 48335 4194 D3
Dover Ln
10 DRBN 48120 4417 D2
Dover Pl
3000 AARB 48104 4407 A7
Dover St
- DET 48228 4341 E2
- DET 48228 4342 B2
600 DBHT 48127 4415 C1
1500 FRDL 48220 4199 D2
7100 DET 48204 4343 D2
28300 LVNA 48150 4340 A2
29400 LVNA 48150 4339 D3
30100 FTRK 48134 4754 B5
34100 LVNA 48185 4338 E3
35500 LVNA 48150 4338 B3
38900 LVNA 48150 4337 E3
Dover Crescent Ct
300 WTLD 48185 4413 B1
Dover Hill Ct
22500 FNHL 48335 4194 E3
Doves Pointe Dr
20200 BNTN 48174 4667 B2
Dow
25800 RDFD 48239 4268 C4
Dowling Ct
1200 WTLD 48186 4413 B3
36500 LVNA 48150 4338 B2
Dowling St
36400 LVNA 48150 4338 B2
N Dowling St
5600 WTLD 48185 4338 B7
S Dowling St
500 WTLD 48186 4413 C3
Downey St
- WIND N9G 4504 D3
Downing Ct
10 AARB 48108 4489 E6
9800 WasC 48167 4190 B6
Downing St
- DET 48229 4501 C1
2300 MVDL 48122 4418 A7
3000 WIND N8T 4422 D4
12700 DET 48229 4418 B7
21500 STCS 48080 4204 D1
Down Up Cir
2000 AARB 48103 4405 E3
2100 AARB 48103 4406 A3
2200 AATp 48103 4405 E3
Downy Nest
800 SLYN 48178 4189 C2
Doxtator St
24100 DRBN 48128 4341 A7
25000 DRBN 48128 4340 D7
25400 DBHT 48127 4340 D7
Doyle Av
13600 WRRN 48089 4202 E1
13900 WRRN 48089 4203 A1
14400 WRRN 48021 4203 A1
Doyle Ct
20000 GSPW 48236 4204 E7
Doyle Pl E
19800 GSPW 48236 4204 E7
Doyle Pl W
19800 GSPW 48236 4204 D7
Doyle St
7500 DET 48234 4274 A1
Dragoon Ct
2000 DET 48209 4419 B1
Dragoon St
100 DET 48209 4419 C2
Dragoon St S
100 DET 48209 4419 C2
Drake
- HnTp 48164 4665 A5
Drake Rd
22400 FNHL 48335 4194 C1
23300 FMTN 48335 4194 C1
Drake St
6700 DET 48212 4273 E1
6800 DET 48212 4274 A1
11800 SOGT 48195 4500 B7
13000 SOGT 48195 4584 B1
Drake Heights Dr
34900 FMTN 48335 4194 C2
Drakeshire Ln
35000 FMTN 48335 4194 C1
Drakeshire Pl
35000 FMTN 48335 4194 D1
Draper
- AARB 48105 4407 A4
Draper Av
2200 YpTp 48197 4491 B5
Draper Cir
49600 PyTp 48170 4263 D7
Draper Ln
38400 WTLD 48186 4413 A4
E Drayton St
100 FRDL 48220 4199 E1
700 FRDL 48220 4200 A1
W Drayton St
700 FRDL 48220 4199 C1
1000 FRDL 48069 4199 C1
Drennan St
4000 ECRS 48229 4501 D3
Dreschfeld Av
25800 WynC 48138 4670 A7
Dresden Pl
500 Tcmh N8N 4424 B2
Dresden St
11900 DET 48205 4274 D1
18600 DET 48205 4202 D6
29200 FNHL 48336 4195 D4
Drew Cir
7400 WTLD 48185 4338 C4
Drew Ct
12300 DET 48213 4275 A5
Drexel Rd
45600 CNTN 48187 4336 C6
Drexel St
1000 DET 48214 4275 D7
1000 DET 48214 4347 D1
5000 DET 48213 4275 B5

INDEX 18
Drexel St — Detroit & Wayne County Street Index — E Eisenhower Pkwy

STREET Block	City	ZIP	Map#	Grid
Drexel St				
5600	DBHT	48127	4341	A5
N Drexel St				
100	DRBN	48124	4416	A1
100	DRBN	48128	4416	A1
1500	DRBN	48128	4341	A7
2000	DRBN	48127	4341	A7
Drifton St				
11700	DET	48205	4274	E1
Driftwood Ct				
13600	PyTp	48170	4264	A6
Driftwood Dr				
10	RKWD	48173	4840	C1
3400	WIND	N9E	4504	B2
Driggs St				
5600	DFT	48209	4419	D3
Driscoll Ct				
10	YPLT	48197	4491	E4
Driscoll St				
15800	DRBN	48126	4417	C1
Drocton Ct				
45000	NOVI	48375	4192	D3
Drouillard Rd				
200	WIND	N8Y	4346	D7
1000	WIND	N8Y	4421	D1
1800	WIND	N8W	4421	D2
Drouillard St				
4100	LNPK	48146	4500	E7
Dru Av				
30500	RMLS	48174	4581	D5
Drury Ln				
12800	PyTp	48170	4264	B7
Dryden St				
2000	WTLD	48186	4413	E4
Drysdale St				
15000	SOGT	48195	4584	A4
Duane Ct				
600	AARB	48103	4405	C5
Duane St				
3700	DET	48206	4272	A6
4000	DET	48204	4271	E6
4000	DET	48204	4272	A6
Dubay St				
8000	DET	48234	4274	B2
Dube Dr				
12300	Tcmh	N8N	4348	E7
Dubie Av				
500	YpTp	48198	4492	D5
Dubois Dr				
22000	HnTp	48174	4667	B4
Dubois St				
2300	DET	48207	4346	A4
4100	DET	48207	4345	E2
5000	DET	48211	4345	D1
5800	DET	48211	4273	D7
9200	HMTK	48212	4273	B5
Dubuar St				
400	NHVL	48167	4192	C6
Ducharme Pl				
-	DET	48207	4346	A5
Ducharme St				
500	WIND	N9G	4504	E3
900	WIND	N9G	4505	A3
Duchess Ct				
23300	NOVI	48375	4192	E2
Duchess Dr				
44100	CNTN	48187	4411	E2
Duchess St				
11500	DET	48224	4275	C1
11700	DET	48224	4203	C7
Duck Ct				
30300	GBTR	48173	4755	C5
Dudley Av				
17100	BNTN	48192	4583	D6
Dudley St				
3300	DRBN	48124	4416	C5
3900	DBHT	48124	4416	C6
3900	DBHT	48125	4416	C6
5800	TYLR	48125	4499	C1
5800	TYLR	48180	4499	C1
16700	TYLR	48180	4583	D5
Duff Av				
10	Amhg	N9V	4757	B1
Duff Dr				
24500	HnTp	48164	4665	C7
Dufferin Av				
700	WIND	N9A	4420	E2
1100	WIND	N9A	4421	A3
2500	WIND	N8X	4421	B5
Duffield				
-	AARB	48105	4406	E4
Dugan Dr				
23800	HnTp	48164	4666	B6
Dukebury Ct				
41600	NOVI	48375	4193	B3
Dumas Dr				
13600	BwTp	48173	4841	D3
Dumay St				
15000	SOGT	48195	4584	A3
S Dumfries St				
300	DET	48229	4418	C5
Dumouchelle Av				
5100	Tcmh	N0R	4505	B5
Dunbar Ct				
1000	SALN	48176	4657	A1
Dunbar St				
25000	SFLD	48034	4197	B1
Dunbarton Ct				
4700	WasC	48103	4329	E4
44700	NOVI	48375	4192	D3
Dunbarton Dr				
44500	NOVI	48375	4192	C3
45400	NOVI	48374	4192	C3
Duncan				
-	DET	48213	4274	C5
Duncan Av				
1100	YpTp	48198	4492	D5
19000	BNTN	48174	4667	D1
S Duncan Cir				
24000	FNHL	48336	4195	C1
Duncan St				
600	AARB	48103	4405	D5
6000	TYLR	48180	4498	C1
14600	TYLR	48180	4582	D3
Duncan McColl Rd				
2800	Tcmh	N0R	4505	C1
2800	Tcmh	N8V	4505	C1
Dundalk Ct				
16700	NvlT	48167	4265	B2
Dundalk Ln				
16500	NvlT	48167	4265	C2
Dundee Cir				
200	WasC	48176	4657	B2
Dundee Ct				
1100	CNTN	48188	4412	B4
Dundee Dr				
1000	CNTN	48188	4412	B3
2300	AARB	48103	4488	E3
20700	NOVI	48375	4193	A5
Dundee St				
9600	DET	48204	4343	E1
13900	RVVW	48192	4584	D6
Dunedin St				
7300	DET	48206	4344	D1
7300	DET	48210	4344	D1
Dungarran Ct				
37500	FNHL	48167	4194	A5
Dunhill Dr				
10	HbgT	48189	4186	B6
Dunigan Ct				
11800	AGST	48191	4748	C1
Dunkirk Av				
-	LSal	N9H	4503	C5
Dunkirk St				
20900	FNHL	48336	4195	C5
E Dunlap St				
100	NHVL	48167	4192	D6
W Dunlap St				
100	NHVL	48167	4192	D6
Dunlop St				
2500	TNTN	48183	4669	C6
Dunmore Rd				
1700	AARB	48103	4488	E2
Dunn Ct				
1800	WTLD	48186	4413	A4
12600	PyTp	48170	4264	D7
Dunn Rd				
43400	WynC	48111	4663	D6
43400	WynC	48111	4664	A6
Dunn St				
200	PLYM	48170	4265	A6
Dunnabeck Ct				
21800	NOVI	48374	4192	A4
Dunning St				
24600	DRBN	48124	4415	E4
26100	INKR	48141	4415	C4
Dunnington Dr				
400	AARB	48103	4405	C6
Dun Rovin Dr				
39400	LVNA	48167	4265	D3
39400	NvlT	48167	4265	D3
39400	NvlT	48170	4265	D3
Dunsany Ct				
47100	NHVL	48167	4192	A5
Dunsany Rd				
46800	NHVL	48167	4192	A5
Duns Scotus St				
20800	SFLD	48075	4197	B2
Dunstable Ct				
36900	FNHL	48335	4194	B4
Dunston Rd				
1500	CNTN	48188	4412	D4
Dunston St				
16200	SOGT	48195	4500	A7
Dunstone Rd				
12500	PyTp	48170	4264	C7
Dunswood Ct				
41100	NvlT	48167	4265	C2
Dunswood Dr				
16500	NvlT	48167	4265	C2
Dunwoodie Ct				
3200	AARB	48105	4332	B7
Dunwoodie Rd				
3100	AARB	48105	4407	C1
3200	AARB	48105	4332	B7
DuPage Blvd				
15300	TYLR	48180	4583	B4
Duplex Av				
4000	LNPK	48146	4500	E7
Dupont Av				
400	YpTp	48197	4491	A4
Dupont Cir				
400	WasC	48103	4405	B5
Dupont St				
4800	WIND	N9C	4419	E7
S Dupont St				
100	DET	48209	4418	E5
Dupre Dr				
27500	HnTp	48174	4667	B4
Duprey St				
10400	DET	48224	4275	E1
10600	DET	48224	4203	E7
19100	DET	48224	4204	A7
19100	DET	48225	4204	A7
20300	HRWD	48225	4204	A5
Durand Ct				
4000	INKR	48141	4414	E6
4000	INKR	48141	4415	A6
Durand St				
8000	DET	48214	4346	D2
Durango Dr				
1400	AARB	48103	4488	D1
Durham				
-	DET	48203	4199	E4
Durham Ct				
8500	SpTp	48198	4492	C1
Durham Dr				
-	YpTp	48197	4576	A6
6400	CNTN	48187	4336	E6
Durham Pl				
1600	WIND	N8W	4421	D3
Durocher Dr				
1500	LSal	N9H	4504	B5
Dutch Hill Dr				
5700	WasC	48105	4333	B1
N Duval Ct				
10	GSPS	48236	4205	A4
S Duval Ct				
10	GSPS	48236	4205	A4
N Duval Rd				
-	GSPS	48236	4205	B4
Duvalle Dr				
22000	HnTp	48174	4667	B4
Duxbury Ct				
12300	PyTp	48170	4264	C7
Duxbury Ln				
10	DRBN	48120	4417	D3
Dwight St				
100	RVRG	48218	4418	E7
200	TNTN	48183	4670	A3
700	YPLT	48198	4492	B3
3100	PTFD	48108	4489	E4
6000	DBHT	48127	4340	C6
9000	DET	48214	4346	E3
9300	DET	48214	4347	A3
Dwyer St				
-	DET	48211	4273	E4
11500	DET	48212	4273	E1
17600	DET	48212	4201	E7
20500	DET	48234	4201	D4
Dyar Ln				
10	GSPF	48236	4276	D5
Dyar St				
12000	HMTK	48212	4273	A3
Dynasty St				
600	WIND	N9G	4504	E3
E				
E Dr				
14100	PyTp	48170	4263	D6
E St				
-	FNHL	48336	4195	D3
10	DBHT	48125	4416	E6
2000	VNBN	48111	4494	A5
Eagle Av				
700	WasC	48103	4404	D7
Eagle Cres				
4600	WIND	N9G	4504	E5
Eagle Ct				
1900	WTLD	48186	4413	E4
3100	AARB	48105	4331	E7
13000	GOTp	48178	4188	D4
N Eagle Ct				
5500	YpTp	48197	4575	D2
S Eagle Ct				
5500	YpTp	48197	4575	D2
Eagle Dr				
-	VNBN	48111	4495	A6
Eagle St				
10	HbgT	48189	4186	A6
6400	DET	48210	4343	D3
9300	DRBN	48120	4418	D1
Eagle Wy				
100	SLYN	48178	4189	C2
Eagle Cove Dr				
10700	GOTp	48178	4188	D4
Eagle Crest Dr				
100	SLYN	48178	4189	C2
Eagle Heights Dr				
600	SLYN	48178	4189	C1
Eagle Nest				
-	NvlT	48167	4263	C1
Eagle Point Dr				
-	WasC	48103	4404	E6
-	WasC	48103	4405	A6
Eagle Ridge Ct				
300	WasC	48103	4404	C5
Eagle Run Dr				
9000	HbgT	48116	4186	A1
Eagles Cir				
2400	YPLT	48197	4491	B3
Eagles Dr				
2700	YpTp	48198	4493	B2
Eagle Trace Ct				
6100	YpTp	48197	4576	A3
Eagle Trace Dr				
6000	YpTp	48197	4576	B3
39500	NvlT	48167	4265	C3
Eardman Ct				
2500	WTLD	48186	4413	A5
N Earhart Pl				
2500	AATp	48105	4407	D2
Earhart Rd				
10	AARB	48104	4407	D6
10	AARB	48105	4407	D6
1400	AATp	48105	4407	D3
2400	AATp	48105	4332	D7
5000	WasC	48105	4332	D3
6000	WasC	48105	4260	D7
8000	WasC	48178	4260	D2
9000	WasC	48178	4188	D7
Earl Blvd				
1000	FRDL	48220	4199	C2
Earl Ct				
100	GSPF	48236	4276	E2
23900	FMTN	48335	4194	D1
Earl St				
35500	WYNE	48184	4413	D7
Earlmoore Ln				
3100	AARB	48105	4332	B7
3100	AARB	48105	4407	B1
Easley Dr				
600	WTLD	48186	4414	A3
Eason St				
200	HDPK	48203	4272	B2
300	DET	48203	4272	B2
East St				
400	NHVL	48167	4192	D6
600	DET	48201	4345	D4
20700	SFLD	48034	4196	C4
Eastborne Rd				
19400	GSPW	48236	4204	C7
Eastborne St				
19200	HRWD	48225	4204	B7
19200	HRWD	48225	4276	B1
Eastbourne Av				
1000	LSal	N9H	4504	D6
Eastbourne Rd				
46800	CNTN	48188	4411	B3
Eastbrook Ct				
21500	GSPW	48236	4204	E4
Eastbrook St				
3500	SpTp	48198	4333	C7
3500	SpTp	48198	4408	C1
Eastburn St				
-	HRWD	48225	4203	C4
13800	DET	48205	4203	A4
16800	DET	48225	4203	C4
Eastbury Ct				
10	AARB	48105	4407	B1
Eastcourt Dr				
10100	WIND	N8R	4423	C2
Eastcreek Dr				
500	SLYN	48178	4189	C3
Easterling Av				
23000	HZLP	48030	4200	C1
Eastern Pl				
3400	DET	48210	4344	C3
Eastern St				
100	INKR	48141	4414	E3
2300	INKR	48141	4415	A4
Eastfarm Ln				
20900	FNHL	48167	4194	A5
Eastfarm Ln Ct				
21000	FNHL	48167	4194	A5
Eastgate Dr				
4000	WasC	48103	4329	E4
4000	WasC	48103	4330	A4
Eastham Dr				
8600	CNTN	48187	4336	A4
Eastham Rd				
3300	DRBN	48120	4417	C2
Eastland Ct				
21700	EPTE	48021	4204	A3
Eastland Dr				
18500	HRWD	48225	4203	E4
19300	HRWD	48225	4204	A4
Eastland Village Dr				
19600	HRWD	48225	4204	A4
Eastlawn Av				
200	WIND	N8S	4347	D6
2500	YpTp	48197	4491	B3
4100	WYNE	48184	4414	A7
N Eastlawn Ct				
500	DET	48214	4347	D2
S Eastlawn Ct				
500	DET	48214	4347	D2
Eastlawn St				
-	DET	48213	4275	B3
700	DET	48214	4347	D1
1000	DET	48214	4275	C6
22100	STCS	48080	4204	B2
Eastlook Dr				
300	SALN	48176	4657	D1
Eastman Av				
400	YpTp	48197	4491	B4
Easton Dr				
100	SLYN	48178	4189	C3
Eastover Pl				
1500	AARB	48104	4489	D2
Eastport St				
2000	WTLD	48186	4413	B7
Eastside Dr				
11300	PyTp	48170	4337	B1
East Valley Dr				
-	FNHL	48336	4195	D5
Eastwind Dr				
700	CNTN	48188	4412	C3
9300	LVNA	48150	4338	A2
East Wind Ln				
16200	RMLS	48174	4582	B5
Eastwood Av				
22000	WRRN	48021	4203	B2
22000	WRRN	48089	4203	B2
Eastwood Blvd				
20700	WRRN	48021	4203	B3
20700	WRRN	48089	4203	B3
Eastwood Cir				
1300	PTFD	48176	4574	B4
Eastwood Ct				
21700	WRRN	48021	4203	B2
21700	WRRN	48089	4203	B2
Eastwood Dr				
18500	HRWD	48225	4203	D5
19600	HRWD	48225	4204	A6
Eastwood St				
-	DET	48234	4202	C6
1000	INKR	48141	4415	B3
13600	DET	48205	4202	E6
15500	DET	48205	4203	C6
21900	OKPK	48237	4199	A3
Eastwood Ter				
2900	YpTp	48197	4491	A2
Easy St				
-	Amhg	N9V	4671	C6
2300	AARB	48104	4490	A3
Eaton Av				
500	RVRG	48218	4501	C1
Eaton Ct				
800	SLYN	48178	4189	C3
22400	NOVI	48375	4192	C3
Eaton Dr				
300	NHVL	48167	4192	D7
8100	WasC	48167	4190	B6
13500	PyTp	48170	4264	C6
Eaton St				
-	DET	48223	4269	E4
-	DET	48223	4270	A4
7000	DET	48238	4271	D4
12700	DET	48227	4271	A4
15300	DET	48227	4270	D4
23900	RDFD	48223	4269	A4
40000	CNTN	48187	4337	D6
Eberwhite Blvd				
400	AARB	48103	4406	A6
EC Copeland Dr				
200	RVRG	48218	4418	D7
300	RVRG	48218	4501	C1
Echo Ct				
500	SALN	48176	4572	D6
Echo Ln				
36500	FNHL	48335	4194	B2
Echo Forest Ct				
41800	CNTN	48188	4412	B5
Echo Forest Dr				
41700	CNTN	48188	4412	B5
Echo Woods Dr				
1900	CNTN	48188	4412	B5
Eckles Rd				
-	CNTN	48187	4337	E3
-	WTLD	48185	4337	E3
-	WTLD	48187	4337	E3
9600	LVNA	48150	4337	E2
12200	LVNA	48150	4265	E7
12200	PyTp	48150	4265	E7
14400	LVNA	48154	4265	E5
14400	PyTp	48170	4265	E5
14600	LVNA	48170	4265	E5
14600	PyTp	48154	4265	E5
Eckles St				
15100	LVNA	48154	4265	E4
15100	LVNA	48170	4265	E4
15100	PyTp	48170	4265	E4
Ecorse Av				
-	ECRS	48229	4501	D3
Ecorse Dr				
-	YpTp	48198	4493	C4
Ecorse Rd				
-	YpTp	48111	4493	A4
10	YPLT	48198	4492	D5
10	YpTp	48198	4492	D5
2100	YpTp	48198	4493	A4
16100	ALPK	48101	4500	A2
19000	ALPK	48101	4499	B2
20000	TYLR	48180	4499	B2
26700	TYLR	48180	4498	A3
27300	TYLR	48174	4498	A3
27400	RMLS	48174	4498	A3
28900	RMLS	48174	4497	D3
33700	RMLS	48174	4496	E3
38600	RMLS	48174	4495	D3
39400	VNBN	48111	4495	D3
39400	VNBN	48174	4495	D3
43400	VNBN	48111	4494	E3
47400	VNBN	48111	4493	E3
51000	VNBN	48198	4493	E3
Ecorse Rd SR-17				
10	YPLT	48198	4492	D5
10	YpTp	48198	4492	D5
Ecorse Rd US-12				
1900	YpTp	48198	4492	E5
2100	YpTp	48198	4493	A4
Ecorse Service Dr				
43900	VNBN	48111	4494	D4
EC Row Expwy				
-	WIND	-	4420	B7
-	WIND	-	4421	E6
-	WIND	-	4422	B5
-	WIND	-	4423	B4
Edcliff Ct				
200	WYDT	48192	4501	C6
Eddington Ct				
2800	CNTN	48188	4411	B6
Eddington Pl				
19400	NvlT	48167	4193	A7
Eddon St				
17100	MVDL	48122	4418	A5
Eddy St				
3400	AARB	48108	4490	B5
Eden Ct				
7900	YpTp	48197	4576	B3
E Eden Ct				
2100	AARB	48108	4490	A6
W Eden Ct				
10	AARB	48108	4490	A6
Eden Dr				
-	NOVI	48375	4193	B4
4000	WIND	N9G	4504	B3
5200	DBHT	48125	4416	B7
Edenbrooke Dr				
41900	CNTN	48187	4412	B2
Edenderry Dr				
-	GOTp	48178	4189	A2
13700	GOTp	48178	4188	E2
18100	NvlT	48167	4264	C1
18400	NvlT	48167	4192	C7
Edenwood Dr				
100	WasC	48103	4489	B3
Edgar St				
6800	WIND	N8S	4347	D7
48400	VNBN	48111	4578	A2
Edgedale St				
-	CNTN	48111	4493	E1
-	CNTN	48188	4493	E1
5800	VNBN	48111	4493	E1
13000	VNBN	48111	4578	A2
Edgefield St				
18900	DET	48236	4204	A7
18900	DET	48236	4276	B2
19200	HRWD	48225	4204	A7
Edgemere Rd				
10	GSPF	48236	4276	D5
Edgemont Dr				
24100	SFLD	48034	4196	B1
Edgemont Pk				
800	GPPK	48230	4276	B6
Edgemont Rd				
2400	TNTN	48183	4669	D4
N Edgemont St				
10	BLVL	48111	4578	E2
S Edgemont St				
10	BLVL	48111	4578	E2
Edgemore Av				
1800	LSal	N9H	4503	C5
Edgerton Ct				
2000	WTLD	48186	4413	B7
Edgerton Ln				
10	DRBN	48120	4417	C2
Edgeton St				
6700	DET	48212	4201	E7
6800	DET	48212	4202	A7
Edgevale St				
10	DET	48203	4272	C1
Edgewater				
22000	NOVI	48375	4193	D3
Edgewater Blvd				
100	Tcmh	N8N	4349	C7
200	Tcmh	N8N	4424	C1
Edgewater Dr				
39400	NvlT	48167	4265	D3
Edgewood Av				
-	AARB	48103	4406	A7
1000	AARB	48103	4489	A1
19800	LVNA	48152	4194	D5
Edgewood Cir				
15500	NvlT	48170	4265	C4
Edgewood Ct				
9700	SpTp	48198	4409	E7
45500	CNTN	48187	4336	C6
Edgewood Ct N				
24600	NOVI	48374	4192	C2
Edgewood Ct S				
24500	NOVI	48374	4192	C2
Edgewood Dr				
200	WynC	48111	4662	D6
3000	AARB	48104	4490	B3
16100	LVNA	48154	4266	D3
24500	NOVI	48374	4192	A1
N Edgewood Dr				
10	GSPS	48236	4205	A5
S Edgewood Dr				
10	GSPS	48236	4205	A5
Edgewood Pl				
100	FRDL	48203	4199	E4
100	FRDL	48220	4199	E4
800	AARB	48103	4406	A7
Edgewood Rd				
6400	CNTN	48187	4336	C6
Edgewood St				
1800	DRBN	48124	4417	A5
3100	DRBN	48124	4416	E6
3900	DBHT	48125	4416	E6
3900	DRBN	48125	4416	E6
8600	DET	48213	4274	C4
15600	LVNA	48154	4266	D3
17400	LVNA	48152	4266	D1
20700	STCS	48080	4204	C2
Edinborough Ct				
36400	FNHL	48335	4194	B4
Edinborough Ln				
47300	NOVI	48374	4192	A2
Edinborough Rd				
-	DET	48223	4269	E2
1500	AARB	48104	4490	B1
17100	DET	48219	4269	E1
18400	DET	48219	4197	E6
Edinborough St				
10	WIND	N8X	4421	B6
25500	DBHT	48125	4415	D2
Edinburgh Ct				
400	SALN	48176	4572	B7
Edinburgh Dr				
47400	PyTp	48170	4264	A7
Edinburgh St				
5900	CNTN	48187	4337	D7
23200	SFLD	48034	4196	D2
Edington Cir				
100	CNTN	48187	4411	D2
Edington St				
10700	LVNA	48150	4338	E1
15300	LVNA	48154	4266	E3
Edison Av				
10	YpTp	48197	4491	B5
200	BLVL	48111	4578	C2
3100	TNTN	48183	4669	D5
Edison St				
10	DET	48202	4272	E6
3200	WIND	N9C	4420	A4
3400	DET	48206	4272	B7
12800	SOGT	48195	4584	D1
21500	DRBN	48124	4416	C4
Edison Lake Rd				
40000	VNBN	48174	4579	D1
41200	VNBN	48111	4579	C1
Edlie Ct				
-	DET	48214	4347	B2
Edlie St				
10800	DET	48214	4347	B1
Edmonton Ct				
3900	WasC	48103	4405	A2
Edmonton St				
-	DET	48204	4344	A2
33500	FNHL	48335	4194	E5
Edmore Dr				
13600	DET	48205	4202	E4
13800	DET	48205	4203	A4
16800	DET	48225	4203	C4
Edmund Av				
7500	WasC	48189	4259	A4
Edmund Pl				
10	AARB	48103	4405	E6
10	DET	48201	4345	C4
Edmund St				
4000	WYNE	48184	4413	E7
6000	RMLS	48174	4496	E2
Edmunton Dr				
1100	GSPW	48236	4204	D4
39600	CNTN	48187	4337	D4
Edmunton St				
20200	STCS	48080	4204	B3
Edna St				
2500	WIND	N8Y	4346	C7
21500	DRBN	48124	4416	D3
33800	FNHL	48335	4194	E4
Edom Av				
21600	WRRN	48089	4202	D3
Edsel Dr				
1500	TNTN	48183	4669	D2
1500	TNTN	48192	4669	D2
Edsel St				
2700	INKR	48141	4415	C5
3200	DRBN	48120	4418	C2
S Edsel St				
-	LNPK	48146	4501	B1
1800	DET	48229	4418	C7
2400	DET	48229	4501	B1
3500	LNPK	48229	4501	B1
Edsel Ford Ct				
23100	STCS	48080	4204	E3
23200	STCS	48080	4205	A3
Edsel Ford Frwy				
-	DET	-	4204	A7
-	DET	-	4273	E6
-	DET	-	4274	C5
-	DET	-	4275	D2
-	DET	-	4276	A1
-	DET	-	4343	C6
-	DET	-	4344	D3
-	DET	-	4345	A2
Edsel Ford Frwy I-94				
-	DET	-	4204	A7
-	DET	-	4273	E6
-	DET	-	4274	C5
-	DET	-	4275	D2
-	DET	-	4276	A1
-	DET	-	4343	C6
-	DET	-	4344	A5
-	DET	-	4345	A2
E Edsel Ford Frwy				
-	DET	48211	4273	E7
-	DET	48224	4204	B6
-	DET	48224	4276	A1
-	DET	48236	4204	B6
19200	HRWD	48225	4204	B6
19600	GSPW	48225	4204	B6
19600	GSPW	48236	4204	B6
19600	HRWD	48236	4204	B6
Edsel Ford Frwy E				
-	DET	48211	4273	D7
-	DET	48211	4274	A6
-	DET	48213	4274	C5
-	DET	48213	4275	B3
-	DET	48224	4275	C3
200	DET	48202	4345	A3
400	DET	48211	4345	A3
Edsel Ford Frwy W				
-	DET	48210	4343	E6
-	DET	48210	4344	B5
1400	DET	48202	4344	B5
Edshire Ln				
19700	GSPW	48236	4204	E7
19700	GSPW	48236	4276	E1
Edward Av				
800	WIND	N8S	4347	D6
1300	WIND	N8S	4422	D1
Edward Dr				
29400	INKR	48141	4414	E2
Edward Pl				
29600	LVNA	48154	4267	D5
Edward St				
800	AARB	48103	4406	B4
6300	DET	48210	4344	A6
7100	DET	48210	4343	E7
16000	HDPK	48203	4272	B2
23600	DRBN	48128	4341	A7
33000	BwTp	48173	4841	A1
Edward N Hines Dr				
-	WTLD	48185	4339	C4
Edwards Av				
6000	SRKW	48179	4754	B7
6200	SRKW	48179	4840	B1
Edwards Rd				
6600	VNBN	48111	4494	E3
Edward T Arcy Sr Blvd				
-	DRBN	48124	4416	A3
Edwin Av				
3300	HMTK	48212	4273	D4
Edwin Dr				
24100	BNTN	48134	4668	A7
Edwin St				
500	WTLD	48186	4413	B3
6200	DET	48211	4273	E4
6200	DET	48212	4273	E4
Edwin St S				
800	DET	48209	4419	A5
Eecloo Av				
21400	WRRN	48089	4203	A3
Eggleton Ct				
10	Amhg	N9V	4757	E2
Eglington St				
1300	WIND	N9E	4504	A1
2400	WIND	N9E	4503	E1
Ego Av				
16000	EPTE	48021	4203	D3
Ehlert Av				
21700	WRRN	48089	4203	A2
Eileen				
11700	RDFD	48239	4268	B7
Eileen St				
1700	YpTp	48198	4492	E6
W Eisenhower Cir				
900	AARB	48103	4489	A4
E Eisenhower Pkwy				
300	AARB	48103	4489	C4
300	AARB	48108	4489	C4

STREET Block City ZIP Map# Grid

E Eisenhower Pkwy
600 AARB 48104 4489 C4
3000 PTFD 48104 4489 C4
3000 PTFD 48108 4489 C4
W Eisenhower Pkwy
100 AARB 48103 4489 A4
100 AARB 48108 4489 A4
200 WasC 48103 4489 A4
Eisenhower Pl
1100 AARB 48108 4489 D4
Elaine Ct
9300 TYLR 48180 4499 C5
23400 OKPK 48237 4198 E2
Elaine Dr
12600 SOGT 48195 4584 C1
Elaine St
23000 STCS 48080 4204 C1
Elba
25500 RDFD 48239 4268 D4
Elba Dr
27500 WynC 48138 4756 C2
Elba Pl
3600 DET 48207 4346 A2
Elbamar Dr
28200 WynC 48138 4756 A3
Elbridge Ct
2000 WTLD 48186 4413 E4
Elbridge St
1200 YPLT 48197 4491 D4
Elder Blvd
1000 AARB 48103 4406 A6
Elder Ct
21300 WynC 48138 4670 C3
Elder St
10 YpTp 48197 4491 D5
400 YPLT 48197 4491 D5
Eldon Dr
35200 BwTp 48173 4841 D3
Eldon St
13300 DET 48212 4274 A1
13300 DET 48234 4274 A1
29100 FNHL 48336 4195 D2
Eldred St
5600 DET 48209 4419 C1
29500 FNHL 48336 4195 D4
Eldridge St
3800 DET 48212 4273 C3
Eleanor Av
24200 WRRN 48089 4203 B1
Electric Av
1200 LNPK 48146 4501 A3
Electric St
1000 WYDT 48192 4501 B7
2000 WYDT 48192 4585 B1
17000 RVVW 48192 4585 A6
S Electric St
1800 DET 48229 4418 C7
2600 DET 48229 4501 B1
3500 LNPK 48229 4501 B1
Electricity Dr
3200 WIND N8W 4422 B6
Elena Dr
22400 FNHL 48335 4194 B3
Elford Ct
1100 GSPW 48236 4204 D7
Elfriede Dr
1100 WIND N8X 4421 D5
Elgin St
1800 WIND N9E 4503 C2
8000 DET 48234 4274 B2
Eli Rd
3600 AARB 48104 4490 C3
Elia Ct
36800 FNHL 48335 4194 B3
Elias St
1400 WTLD 48186 4414 C3
Elijah McCoy Dr
- DET 48210 4344 E2
1100 DET 48202 4345 A2
1200 DET 48202 4344 E2
Elinor St
400 WIND N8P 4348 B6
Eliot St
10 DET 48201 4345 C4
900 DET 48207 4345 D3
Elisa St
200 WTLD 48186 4413 C2
Eliza St
10 ECRS 48229 4501 E3
Elizabeth Av
2400 AARB 48104 4489 E2
3800 CNTN 48188 4411 A7
3600 GDNC 48135 4339 D5
Elizabeth Ct
400 GSPF 48236 4276 C1
5800 ALPK 48101 4500 C2
24100 FMTN 48336 4195 A1
Elizabeth Dr
3300 TNTN 48183 4669 E5
Elizabeth Ln
23900 NOVI 48374 4192 C2
36600 HnTp 48164 4665 C7
Elizabeth Rd
3500 WasC 48103 4405 A4
10700 GOTp 48189 4187 C4
Elizabeth St
10 RVRG 48218 4501 D1
200 PLYM 48170 4337 A2
500 AARB 48104 4406 C5
2900 WYNE 48184 4413 D6
3300 MVDL 48122 4418 A6
3800 MVDL 48122 4417 E5
9100 WasC 48189 4259 A1
19600 STCS 48080 4204 C2
N Elizabeth St
- DRBN 48127 4341 B7
100 DRBN 48124 4416 B1
100 DRBN 48128 4416 B1
1700 DRBN 48128 4341 B7
6000 DBHT 48127 4341 B6
W Elizabeth St
10 DET 48201 4345 C5
10 DET 48226 4345 C5
1300 DET 48216 4345 C6
Elizabeth St E
- DET 48201 4345 D5
- DET 48226 4345 D5
Elk Rd
41600 NvlT 48167 4265 B4
41600 NvlT 48170 4265 B4
Elk St
10 HbgT 48189 4186 A6
Elk Grove Dr
- WTLD 48185 4339 B4
Elkhart St
18500 HRWD 48225 4203 D6
19900 HRWD 48225 4204 A6
Elk Run St
38700 HnTp 48164 4665 A5
Elkton St
34000 WTLD 48186 4413 E4
Ellair Pl
800 GPPK 48230 4276 B6
Ella Lee Rd
10600 WasC 48160 4657 E5
Ellar St
13600 DRBN 48126 4418 D1
Ellen Ct
20500 LVNA 48152 4194 C5
35000 LVNA 48154 4266 D3
Ellen Dr
13900 LVNA 48150 4266 D5
15300 LVNA 48154 4266 D4
17100 LVNA 48152 4266 D2
20500 LVNA 48152 4194 C5
20600 LVNA 48335 4194 C5
Ellen Pl
32000 WYNE 48184 4497 B1
Ellen St
12800 DET 48238 4272 B5
48400 VNBN 48111 4578 A2
Ellens Wy
7500 SpTp 48105 4334 A7
Ellery Pl
4700 DET 48207 4346 A1
Ellery St
- DET 48211 4273 E7
- DET 48211 4346 A1
4400 DET 48207 4346 A1
9800 HMTK 48212 4273 D3
Elliott Av
2000 LNPK 48146 4501 B4
Elliott Ct
10400 PyTp 48170 4336 D2
Elliott Dr
5200 SpTp 48197 4491 A1
Elliott Ln
7200 YpTp 48197 4577 B5
Elliott St E
10 WIND N9A 4420 E2
400 WIND N9A 4421 A2
Elliott St W
900 WIND N9A 4420 D2
Ellis Rd
1100 YpTp 48197 4491 B7
1300 YpTp 48197 4575 C2
Ellis St
- DET 48228 4343 A2
5900 LSal N9H 4503 C4
10400 DET 48204 4343 A2
15500 DET 48228 4342 D2
36500 HnTp 48164 4665 C1
Ellis St E
10 WIND N8X 4421 A3
Ellis St W
10 WIND N8X 4421 A3
300 WIND N8X 4420 E3
Ellrose Av
800 WIND N8Y 4347 A7
1300 WIND N8Y 4422 A2
1800 WIND N8W 4422 A2
Ellsworth Av
2000 WTLD 48186 4413 E4
Ellsworth Rd
1900 YpTp 48197 4491 A6
3700 PTFD 48197 4490 D6
4600 PTFD 48197 4491 A6
E Ellsworth Rd
10 AARB 48108 4489 D6
10 PTFD 48108 4489 D6
2300 AARB 48108 4490 B6
2900 PTFD 48108 4490 B6
3600 PTFD 48197 4490 B6
W Ellsworth Rd
10 AARB 48108 4489 C6
10 PTFD 48108 4489 C6
1600 PTFD 48108 4488 E6
2500 WasC 48103 4488 C6
2500 WasC 48108 4488 C6
3500 WasC 48103 4487 D6
Ellsworth St
6300 DET 48238 4271 D3
15900 DET 48227 4270 B4
Ellward St
- RMLS 48174 4582 A4
27400 RMLS 48180 4582 B4
Elm
- CNTN 48188 4411 D6
- INKR 48141 4415 A5
E Elm
- CNTN 48187 4337 E6
W Elm
- CNTN 48187 4337 E6
Elm Av
10 Amhg N9V 4757 B2
800 WIND N9A 4420 D3
1200 WIND N8X 4420 D3
Elm Ct
10 GSPF 48236 4276 D5
15700 RMLS 48174 4582 B5
19800 HRWD 48225 4203 E5
22600 HZLP 48030 4200 E3
Elm Dr
10 WasC 48189 4259 A3
17500 BNTN 48174 4583 B6
Elm Ln
30100 RMLS 48174 4581 D4
Elm Pl
100 SLYN 48178 4189 B2
Elm St
- DRBN 48124 4416 D2
- PTFD 48197 4491 A6
10 RVRG 48218 4501 E1
10 TNTN 48183 4670 A4
10 YPLT 48197 4491 D4
200 NHVL 48167 4192 D6
300 TNTN 48183 4669 E4
500 AARB 48104 4406 D6
1300 DET 48216 4345 A5
1300 PLYM 48170 4336 E1
1400 WYDT 48192 4585 A3
6400 TYLR 48180 4499 B2
14300 PyTp 48170 4263 D6
14400 OKPK 48237 4198 D2
29300 HnTp 48134 4752 E3
29300 HnTp 48134 4753 A3
32700 RKWD 48173 4754 C7
35700 WYNE 48184 4413 D5
El Marco Dr
24200 FNHL 48336 4195 C1
Elm Cir Dr
- INKR 48141 4415 C3
Elm Crest Rd
10000 GOTp 48189 4187 B5
Elmcrest St
600 AARB 48103 4406 A4
Elmdale Av
5700 LSal N9H 4503 C3
Elmdale Rd
11400 GOTp 48189 4187 A6
Elmdale St
1300 PLYM 48170 4264 E7
2100 DRBN 48124 4416 D4
11100 DET 48213 4274 E3
12500 DET 48213 4275 A3
14900 DET 48224 4275 B2
Elmer St
5200 DET 48210 4343 D5
Elmgate Cres
900 LSal N9H 4504 C6
Elm Grove Dr
200 Lksr N8N 4424 E1
Elm Grove St
22700 FNHL 48336 4195 E2
Elmhurst Av
200 YpTp 48197 4491 B4
8800 PyTp 48170 4336 E3
8800 PyTp 48187 4336 E3
24200 FNHL 48336 4195 C1
Elmhurst Dr
5400 TNTN 48183 4755 B1
Elmhurst St
10 HDPK 48203 4272 D5
1300 CNTN 48187 4411 E1
1500 DET 48206 4272 C5
4000 DET 48204 4272 A6
4200 DET 48204 4271 E7
8000 CNTN 48187 4336 E3
Elmington Ct
300 CNTN 48188 4411 A3
Elmira
22400 DET 48239 4341 A1
23700 RDFD 48239 4341 A1
24100 RDFD 48239 4340 E1
Elmira Ct
33500 LVNA 48150 4338 E1
Elmira St
- DET 48228 4341 D1
10000 DET 48204 4343 B1
12700 DET 48227 4343 A1
13600 DET 48227 4342 E1
18900 DET 48228 4342 A1
27400 LVNA 48150 4340 A1
28400 LVNA 48150 4339 E1
35800 LVNA 48150 4338 C1
Elmo St
11500 DET 48205 4274 C2
Elm Park Av
10 PTRG 48069 4199 C1
Elm Park Blvd
10 PTRG 48069 4199 D1
Elmsleigh Ln
10 GSPT 48230 4276 C6
Elmsmere Dr
900 NHVL 48167 4192 B4
900 NHVL 48374 4192 B4
Elmview St
11000 RMLS 48174 4496 B7
12000 RMLS 48174 4580 B1
Elmwood Av
2500 AARB 48104 4490 B4
2900 TNTN 48183 4669 C3
3100 WIND N8R 4423 C3
21700 EPTE 48021 4203 B2
27400 GDNC 48135 4340 A6
29400 GDNC 48135 4339 D6
34400 WTLD 48185 4338 E6
Elmwood Cir
45400 CNTN 48188 4411 D5
Elmwood Ct
100 SALN 48176 4657 C1
1300 YpTp 48197 4491 B2
23500 DRBN 48124 4416 A2
50400 PyTp 48170 4263 C7
Elmwood Dr
1000 AATp 48104 4407 B7
1000 AARB 48104 4490 B1
1200 YpTp 48197 4491 B2
Elmwood St
- WTLD 48185 4338 B6
100 DRBN 48124 4416 A2
100 DRBN 48128 4416 A2
3600 DET 48207 4346 A2
4400 DET 48207 4345 E1
5000 DET 48211 4345 E1
5500 DET 48211 4273 E7
Elon Ct
25500 DBHT 48127 4340 D5
Elon Dr
25300 DBHT 48127 4340 D5
El Paso Blvd
7000 RMLS 48174 4496 A3
Elroy Av
21700 WRRN 48089 4203 A2
Elsa Ct
41400 CNTN 48187 4412 C1
Elsa St
9300 DET 48214 4274 D7
Elsie Blvd
- BwTp 48173 4755 A7
Elsie St
28900 LVNA 48154 4267 E4
38100 LVNA 48154 4266 A4
39000 LVNA 48154 4265 E4
Elsinore
25500 RDFD 48239 4268 D4
Elsinore Ct
3300 AARB 48105 4332 B7
Elsmere Av
800 WIND N9A 4421 B2
1200 WIND N8X 4421 B2
2100 WIND N8W 4421 C4
19000 EPTE 48021 4204 B1
Elsmere St
700 DET 48209 4419 A4
1000 DET 48209 4418 E3
Elsworth Av
100 LSal N9J 4502 C5
Eltham Ct
700 WasC 48103 4404 D6
Elton St
10 ECRS 48229 4501 D3
Elwell Rd
13700 VNBN 48111 4578 B3
17400 WynC 48111 4578 B7
18100 WynC 48111 4663 B1
24600 WynC 48111 4749 B1
Elwin G Av
13700 MonC 48134 4753 B6
Ely Ct
900 NHVL 48167 4192 D5
23700 FMTN 48336 4195 A1
N Ely Dr
100 NHVL 48167 4192 D4
Ely Dr S
100 NHVL 48167 4192 D5
Elyria Ct
5000 WIND N8T 4422 C3
E Elza Av
1100 HZLP 48030 4200 E3
W Elza Av
10 HZLP 48030 4200 C3
Elza St
4400 WRRN 48091 4201 C3
Emanon St
7200 DRBN 48126 4343 B4
Embassy Ct
45400 CNTN 48187 4336 C5
Embassy Dr
7400 CNTN 48187 4336 C5
Ember Ct
21900 WynC 48138 4670 D4
Ember Wy
2700 AARB 48104 4489 E3
Embers Ct
13700 PyTp 48170 4264 A6
Emeline Av
2200 TNTN 48183 4669 C5
Emeline St
5800 DET 48212 4273 D2
Emerald Av
2500 AARB 48104 4489 E3
Emerald Cir
10 WasC 48189 4186 D6
Emerald Cir E
10 WasC 48189 4186 E7
Emerald Cir S
10 WasC 48189 4186 D7
Emerald Dr
3600 CNTN 48188 4411 B6
Emerald Ln E
8100 WTLD 48185 4338 A4
Emerald Ln N
38400 WTLD 48185 4337 E4
38400 WTLD 48185 4338 A4
Emerald Ln S
38400 WTLD 48185 4338 A4
Emerald Ln W
8000 WTLD 48185 4338 A6
8200 WTLD 48185 4337 E4
Emerald Pines Dr
1400 CNTN 48188 4412 C4
Emergency Dr
- SpTp 48105 4491 A1
- SpTp 48197 4491 A1
Emerick Dr
13000 PyTp 48170 4264 B6
Emerick St
10 YpTp 48198 4492 C4
700 YPLT 48198 4492 C6
Emerson Av
100 YpTp 48198 4493 A3
1800 YpTp 48198 4577 A1
2100 WTLD 48186 4413 E4
Emerson Dr
7200 CNTN 48187 4337 A5
Emerson St
700 DET 48214 4347 D1
24300 DRBN 48124 4416 A2
24500 DRBN 48124 4415 E2
28600 INKR 48141 4415 A2
29000 INKR 48141 4414 E2
Emery Dr
45100 NOVI 48167 4192 D4
Emery St
- DET 48203 4200 E6
- DET 48234 4200 E6
- DET 48234 4202 A6
3800 DET 48234 4201 A6
22000 DBHT 48127 4341 B5
Emilia Rd
3000 WIND N9E 4503 D2
Emilie Av
20700 EPTE 48021 4203 E3
Emiline St
10 RVRG 48218 4501 D1
Emils Dr
23600 BNTN 48174 4583 A6
Emily Ct
1300 AATp 48104 4490 C1
2600 CNTN 48188 4412 C5
6700 WTLD 48185 4339 A5
20700 NOVI 48375 4193 A5
Emily Dr
24100 BNTN 48183 4668 B6
Emily St
2500 MVDL 48122 4500 E1
2700 MVDL 48122 4417 E7
7300 DET 48234 4202 A7
Emit Rd
18000 BNTN 48192 4583 B7
18000 BNTN 48192 4668 B1
Emma Av
26400 FTRK 48134 4753 D1
Emma Maria Cres
12100 Tcmh N0R 4424 A7
Emmet St
100 YPLT 48197 4492 A4
300 YPLT 48197 4491 E4
Emmett Av
27100 SFLD 48034 4196 B4
27400 FNHL 48034 4196 A4
27400 FNHL 48336 4196 A4
Emmett St
23600 TYLR 48180 4583 A1
27000 SFLD 48034 4196 B4
Emmons Av
1900 WRRN 48030 4200 E4
1900 WRRN 48091 4200 E4
1900 WRRN 48091 4201 A4
Emmons Blvd
10 WYDT 48192 4501 A6
300 LNPK 48146 4501 A6
300 LNPK 48192 4501 A6
1000 LNPK 48146 4500 D6
Emmons Ct
10 WYDT 48192 4501 C6
Emmons St
9300 DET 48214 4274 D7
Emogene St
2500 MVDL 48122 4417 E7
E Emory Ct
19900 GSPW 48236 4204 D7
W Emory Ct
19900 GSPW 48236 4204 D7
Empire Av
- ECRS 48229 4501 B3
1100 LNPK 48229 4501 B3
1200 LNPK 48146 4501 B3
18000 EPTE 48021 4203 E2
18200 EPTE 48021 4204 A2
Empire St
20000 TYLR 48180 4583 E1
20000 TYLR 48195 4583 E1
Empire State Dr
3100 CNTN 48188 4410 E6
Empress Ct
2000 WIND N8T 4422 C2
Empress St
4900 WIND N8T 4422 B2
Emrick Dr
43500 CNTN 48187 4411 E1
43500 CNTN 48187 4412 A1
Emwill St
900 FRDL 48220 4199 D3
Enchanted Dr
6300 YpTp 48197 4576 B4
24500 NOVI 48374 4192 C2
Encore Ct
1900 WasC 48103 4487 A2
Encore Ln
1700 WasC 48103 4487 B2
Endicott Ln
9500 YpTp 48197 4576 E5
Endicott St
10 DET 48202 4345 A1
10300 VNBN 48111 4494 C6
Endsleigh Ln
3300 PTFD 48197 4574 C2
Enfield Ct
1200 WIND N8S 4347 C6
Enfield Ln
10 DRBN 48120 4417 D2
Enfield Pl
8200 WIND N8S 4347 E7
Engel
- DET 48214 4347 B2
Engineering Dr
- YpTp 48198 4493 B4
Englave Dr
2600 AATp 48103 4405 D1
Engle St
500 DET 48214 4347 B2
Englehardt St
21500 STCS 48080 4204 C2
Engleside St
11000 DET 48205 4274 C1
11000 DET 48234 4274 C1
Englewood Av
14700 ALPK 48101 4500 B4
Englewood Ct
10 AARB 48108 4489 E6
Englewood St
- DET 48211 4273 A4
10 DET 48202 4272 E5
500 DET 48202 4273 A4
English Ct
42400 CNTN 48187 4337 A5
English Oak Ct
500 AGST 48191 4661 B7
English Oak Dr
2600 AATp 48103 4405 E2
English Oak Ln
300 AGST 48191 4661 C7
Ennishore Dr
22400 NOVI 48375 4193 B3
Ensley Av
2100 WTLD 48186 4413 E4
Enterprise Dr
- LVNA 48150 4339 B1
500 MVDL 48101 4417 D5
3000 ALPK 48101 4417 C6
8000 ALPK 48101 4500 B1
37100 WTLD 48186 4413 B2
Enterprise Wy
6900 WIND N8T 4422 E2
Epping Ct
6900 CNTN 48187 4336 E6
Epping Dr
6900 CNTN 48187 4337 A6
7000 CNTN 48187 4336 E5
Epworth St
5900 DET 48210 4344 A4
7500 DET 48204 4343 E2
7500 DET 48210 4343 E2
Equestrian Tr
- NOVI 48167 4191 E5
- NOVI 48167 4192 A5
Eral Ct
8500 SpTp 48198 4409 C7
Erbie St
7200 DET 48213 4274 A5
Eric Ct
5000 WasC 48105 4333 A4
38000 FNHL 48335 4194 A2
Eric Dr
23000 BNTN 48183 4668 B7
Erie Dr
35100 BwTp 48173 4841 D3
Erie St
7200 DET 48209 4419 B4
Erie St E
10 WIND N9A 4420 E2
200 WIND N9A 4421 A2
Erie St W
900 WIND N9A 4420 D3
Erik Ct
44400 PyTp 48170 4336 E3
Erik Pass Dr
- PyTp 48170 4336 D3
Erin Cir
22200 NOVI 48374 4192 C4
Erin Ct
4600 AATp 48105 4407 E6
Erin Dr
44700 PyTp 48170 4336 D2
Erindale Cres
3000 WIND N8W 4421 E6
Erle St
400 DET 48203 4200 C7
Ernest St
34800 LVNA 48152 4266 D1
Ernst St
11500 TYLR 48180 4499 B7
Erskine St
10 DET 48201 4345 C4
1400 DET 48207 4345 D3
3400 WIND N8Y 4346 D7
Erwin St
9700 DET 48213 4274 B3
9900 DET 48234 4274 B3
34200 WTLD 48186 4413 E4
Esch Av
2500 AARB 48104 4489 D3
Esch Ct
1300 AARB 48104 4489 D4
Esdras Av
200 WIND N8S 4347 B6
1100 WIND N8S 4422 D1
Esper Blvd
7400 DRBN 48126 4343 A4
7900 DET 48228 4343 A4
Esper St
8000 DET 48204 4343 B2
8000 DET 48228 4343 B2
8000 DRBN 48126 4343 B2
Esplanade Dr
9200 WIND N8R 4423 A2
Esplanade Ln
- PTFD 48108 4490 E4
Essex Av
- GPPK 48230 4347 E1
8000 WRRN 48089 4202 A1
8000 WRRN 48091 4202 A1
12300 DET 48214 4347 C2
14900 DET 48230 4347 E1
15200 GPPK 48230 4348 A1
15300 GPPK 48230 4276 A7
Essex Ct
12500 PyTp 48170 4263 C7
Essex Ln
100 CNTN 48187 4411 D2
Essex Rd
100 Tcmh N8N 4424 D1
2400 AARB 48104 4490 A3
Essex St
- LSal N9J 4502 D6
- LVNA 48152 4266 D1
9200 RMLS 48174 4496 D5
9800 DRBN 48120 4418 D3
Essex Wy
- WIND N8T 4422 E4
- WIND N8T 4423 A3
Essex Wy Ct
22300 SFLD 48034 4197 A2
Essex Wy St
22500 SFLD 48034 4197 A2
Estate Pk
500 Tcmh N8N 4424 D2
Estates Ct
2200 WasC 48103 4487 D3
Estates Dr
100 VNBN 48111 4493 C2
1600 DET 48206 4344 D1
Estelle St
24000 SFLD 48075 4198 C1
Esther St
5900 RMLS 48174 4498 A1
Estrada Dr
300 BLVL 48111 4578 D4
Etch Ct
8200 WasC 48167 4190 B6
Ethan Dr
200 WTLD 48185 4412 E2
Ethel Av
1200 LNPK 48146 4501 B3
S Ethel St
- LNPK 48146 4501 B2
1500 DET 48229 4418 C7
2100 DET 48229 4501 B2
3700 LNPK 48229 4501 B2
Ethelyn Ct
15900 EPTE 48021 4203 C2
Eton Av
17800 DBHT 48101 4417 A7
17800 DBHT 48125 4417 A7
18600 DBHT 48125 4416 E7
24300 DBHT 48125 4415 E7
Eton Ct
2300 AARB 48103 4488 D2
Eton St
28900 WTLD 48186 4414 E7
28900 WTLD 48186 4415 A7
Euclid Av
8000 WasC 48167 4262 D3
14500 ALPK 48101 4500 C1
17000 ALPK 48101 4417 A7
Euclid St
1300 LNPK 48146 4501 A3
1700 LNPK 48146 4500 D2
2200 LNPK 48101 4500 D2
Euclid St E
10 DET 48202 4273 A7
1500 DET 48211 4273 B6
Euclid St W
10 DET 48202 4272 E7
10 DET 48202 4273 A7
1400 DET 48206 4272 D7
2600 DET 48206 4344 B2
4000 DET 48204 4344 B2
Eugene Av
500 YpTp 48198 4492 E6
Eugene St
4800 DET 48214 4275 A5
4800 DRBN 48126 4343 C7
Eugeni St
2000 Tcmh N9K 4424 A5
Eugenie St E
10 WIND N8X 4421 B5
700 WIND N8W 4421 B5
Eugenie St W
100 WIND N8X 4421 A5
Eureka Av
10 WYDT 48192 4585 A3
2200 WYDT 48192 4584 E3
2300 WYDT 48195 4584 E3
23000 WRRN 48091 4201 B1
Eureka Rd
900 WYDT 48192 4585 B3
12700 SOGT 48195 4584 D3
19200 SOGT 48195 4583 E3
20000 TYLR 48180 4583 E3
24800 TYLR 48180 4582 E4
27400 RMLS 48174 4582 A4
27400 RMLS 48180 4582 A4
29400 RMLS 48242 4581 E4
32700 RMLS 48174 4581 B4
34000 RMLS 48174 4580 E4
34000 RMLS 48242 4580 E4
Eureka St
13400 DET 48212 4273 C1
18600 DET 48234 4201 C6
Evaline Av
1900 HMTK 48212 4273 B4
Evaline St
5900 DET 48211 4273 E3
5900 DET 48212 4273 E3
Evan Ct
23200 HnTp 48164 4666 B5
N Evangeline St
100 DBHT 48125 4415 D1
100 DBHT 48127 4415 D1
8200 DBHT 48127 4340 D3
8600 DBHT 48239 4340 D3
S Evangeline St
100 DBHT 48125 4415 D2
Evans Ct
4800 TNTN 48183 4669 B7
Evans Ct N
23000 HnTp 48164 4666 B5
Evans St
1500 DET 48209 4419 A2
4300 WYNE 48184 4414 A6
36500 HnTp 48164 4665 C1

INDEX 20
Evanston St
Detroit & Wayne County Street Index
Fisher Frwy E

STREET Block City ZIP Map# Grid

Evanston St
11200 DET 48213 4274 E4
12200 DET 48213 4275 A4
14400 DET 48224 4275 A3
Eveleigh Cres
100 WIND N9E 4421 C7
Evelyn Av
1000 YpTp 48198 4492 D6
27000 BwTp 48183 4754 E2
E Evelyn Av
1100 HZLP 48030 4200 E3
W Evelyn Av
10 HZLP 48030 4200 C3
Evelyn Ct
900 AARB 48103 4405 E7
12700 VNBN 48111 4579 A2
Evelyn St
34800 LVNA 48152 4266 D2
Everett Ct
- WTLD 48186 4413 E4
Evergreen Av
5600 DBHT 48127 4341 E5
5600 DBHT 48228 4341 E5
5600 DET 48228 4341 E5
11600 DET 48228 4269 E7
12200 DET 48223 4269 E7
16100 EPTE 48021 4203 C1
Evergreen Dr
400 AARB 48103 4405 C5
400 WasC 48103 4405 C5
1500 TNTN 48183 4669 C2
12000 Tcmh N8N 4348 E7
Evergreen Ln
1700 SpTp 48198 4409 E7
Evergreen Pl
300 AARB 48104 4406 E6
Evergreen Rd
- DRBN 48124 4416 E1
- DRBN 48124 4417 A2
- DRBN 48126 4341 E7
- DRBN 48126 4417 A2
- DRBN 48128 4417 A2
- DRBN 48228 4341 E7
- SFLD 48219 4197 D5
4800 DRBN 48126 4416 E1
4800 DRBN 48128 4341 E7
4800 DRBN 48128 4416 E1
5600 DBHT 48127 4341 E7
5600 DBHT 48128 4341 E7
5600 DBHT 48228 4341 E7
5600 DET 48228 4341 E7
8200 GOTp 48116 4187 C1
12800 DET 48223 4269 E5
16100 DET 48219 4269 E5
18200 DET 48219 4197 D7
20700 SFLD 48075 4197 D5
Evergreen St
28200 FTRK 48134 4753 E4
N Evergreen St
100 PLYM 48170 4264 E7
S Evergreen St
100 PLYM 48170 4264 E7
600 PLYM 48170 4336 E1
N Evers Pl
21200 ROTp 48220 4199 A4
S Evers Pl
21000 ROTp 48220 4199 B4
Everts Av
1400 WIND N9B 4420 D4
2300 WIND N9E 4420 E7
2600 WIND N9E 4421 A7
2600 WIND N9E 4504 A1
Everts St
9100 DET 48224 4275 D1
Ewald Cir
1800 DET 48238 4271 E4
1800 DET 48238 4272 A4
3400 DET 48204 4271 D6
Ewers St
4300 DET 48210 4343 E6
Executive Dr
42500 CNTN 48188 4412 B6
46600 WynC 48111 4749 C3
E Executive Dr
5600 WTLD 48185 4338 A7
N Executive Dr
37900 WTLD 48185 4338 A6
Executive Plaza Dr
16800 DRBN 48126 4342 B7
Exegesis St
2000 DRBN 48124 4416 A4
Exeter Ct
- SALN 48176 4572 C6
41100 NvlT 48167 4265 C2
44800 NOVI 48375 4192 D3
Exeter Rd
13000 MonC 48117 4751 A4
14700 MonC 48164 4751 A4
Exeter St
19900 DET 48203 4200 C5
Exmoor Rd
2900 AARB 48104 4490 B1
Exodus Ct
21900 WDHN 48183 4668 C4
Eyrie Dr
4100 WasC 48103 4404 E6
4100 WasC 48103 4405 A6
Eyvind Dr
50900 WynC 48111 4662 C4

F

F Dr
14100 PyTp 48170 4263 D6
F Rd
- DRBN 48120 4418 B2
F St
10 DBHT 48125 4416 E6
2000 VNBN 48111 4494 A5
Faber St
1900 HMTK 48212 4273 C5
Factoria St
1600 WIND N8Y 4421 D3
1800 WIND N8W 4421 D3
Factory St
10 YPLT 48197 4492 B5
10 YPLT 48198 4492 B5
Faholo Cres
7900 WIND N8R 4423 A2
Fair St
100 PLYM 48170 4337 A1
200 FRDL 48220 4200 B4
1900 AARB 48103 4405 D6
Fair Acres Dr
10 GSPF 48236 4276 E3
Fairbairn St
1600 INKR 48141 4415 C4
Fairbanks St
9800 VNBN 48111 4495 C6
Fairborn Dr
5600 CNTN 48187 4336 A7
Fairbrook Ct
300 NHVL 48167 4192 D7
Fairbrook St
100 NHVL 48167 4192 D7
Fairchild Dr
34200 WTLD 48186 4413 E3
Fairchild St
- DET 48229 4418 B6
29400 FNHL 48336 4195 D3
33600 WTLD 48186 4413 E3
33600 WTLD 48186 4414 A3
Faircourt St
1500 GSPW 48236 4204 C6
Faircrest Dr
7900 YpTp 48197 4576 B1
Faircrest St
14000 DET 48205 4203 B6
Fairfax Ct
10 DRBN 48126 4342 B7
1000 NHVL 48167 4192 C5
1600 CNTN 48188 4412 A4
34100 LVNA 48152 4194 D6
Fairfax Dr
1400 CNTN 48188 4412 A4
34500 LVNA 48152 4194 D6
Fairfax Ln
17700 BNTN 48174 4583 B6
Fairfax St
- DET 48214 4275 E7
- DET 48230 4275 E7
14900 GPPK 48230 4275 E7
15300 GPPK 48230 4276 A7
16200 SFLD 48075 4198 B1
22100 TYLR 48180 4499 C4
31400 LVNA 48152 4195 B6
Fairfax Towne St
10 SFLD 48075 4198 B2
Fairfield Av
6400 GDNC 48135 4339 B6
21900 WRRN 48089 4202 D2
Fairfield Ct
300 CNTN 48188 4411 D3
600 PTFD 48108 4573 C1
800 SLYN 48178 4189 C3
17100 NvlT 48167 4265 C2
Fairfield Dr
42700 VNBN 48111 4495 B6
Fairfield Rd
400 YpTp 48197 4491 B3
Fairfield St
600 FRDL 48220 4199 E4
9600 LVNA 48150 4339 B1
15400 DET 48238 4271 E2
16100 DET 48221 4271 E2
16700 LVNA 48154 4267 A2
17100 LVNA 48152 4267 A1
18000 DET 48221 4199 E6
Fairford Rd
- GSPS 48236 4204 E7
10 GSPS 48236 4205 A7
600 GSPW 48236 4204 D7
Fairground St
200 PLYM 48170 4337 A1
Fairgrove St
14700 SOGT 48195 4584 A3
25000 WDHN 48183 4669 A6
26000 WDHN 48183 4755 A1
Fairhaven
- WDHN 48183 4669 A3
Fairhaven Ct
3100 AARB 48105 4331 E7
3100 AARB 48105 4406 E1
Fairhaven Dr
800 SLYN 48178 4189 C2
Fairhills Dr
10 YpTp 48197 4491 B5
Fairholme Rd
1000 GSPW 48236 4204 C6
Fairlake Ln
10 McoC 48236 4205 B3
Fairlane Av
2200 TNTN 48183 4669 A4
Fairlane Blvd
21900 WDHN 48183 4668 C4
Fairlane Cir
1300 ALPK 48101 4417 D4
Fairlane Cres
3000 WIND N8W 4421 E6
Fairlane Ct
19000 LVNA 48152 4194 D7
21700 EPTE 48021 4204 A3
Fairlane Dr
- LVNA 48154 4266 D2
200 DRBN 48128 4416 E1
1500 ALPK 48101 4417 C5
N Fairlane Dr
11100 GOTp 48178 4187 E2
S Fairlane Dr
11000 GOTp 48178 4187 E3
Fairlane Rd
10000 GOTp 48178 4187 B3
10000 GOTp 48189 4187 B3
Fairlane St
700 WTLD 48186 4413 D3
1300 AARB 48104 4490 A1
12600 LVNA 48150 4266 D7
Fairlane Woods Dr
- DRBN 48126 4341 E7
5500 DRBN 48126 4342 A7
Fairlawn Ct
47000 CNTN 48188 4411 B7
Fairmont Dr
- BNTN 48192 4583 B7
200 WasC 48189 4259 A4
22500 FNHL 48335 4194 D3
23400 BNTN 48174 4583 B7
Fairmont St
100 RVRG 48218 4501 D1
Fairmount Ct
10 DRBN 48124 4415 E3
Fairmount Dr
1000 AARB 48105 4407 D4
11600 DET 48205 4202 D5
11600 DET 48234 4202 D5
13800 DET 48205 4203 A4
24200 DRBN 48124 4415 E3
24200 DRBN 48124 4416 A3
Fair Oaks Dr
7000 GOTp 48189 4186 C5
7000 HbgT 48189 4186 C5
44100 CNTN 48187 4411 D2
Fair Oaks Pkwy
10 AARB 48104 4406 E7
10 AARB 48104 4489 E1
Fairport St
12300 DET 48205 4274 E1
18000 DET 48205 4202 E6
Fairview Av
900 WIND N8S 4347 D6
Fairview Cir
500 YPLT 48197 4491 D4
Fairview Ct
1700 WasC 48176 4572 C4
13400 VNBN 48111 4577 D3
Fairview Dr
9200 WasC 48167 4190 B6
20500 DBHT 48127 4341 C5
23600 HnTp 48164 4666 C6
24300 LyTp 48178 4189 E1
42000 CNTN 48187 4337 B7
42000 CNTN 48187 4412 B1
E Fairview Dr
20300 DBHT 48127 4341 D5
Fairview St
100 AARB 48103 4405 D6
400 DET 48214 4347 A1
2500 DET 48214 4275 A7
3800 DET 48214 4274 E6
5500 DET 48213 4274 E5
10000 TYLR 48180 4498 D6
23800 FMTN 48335 4194 C1
Fairway Cir
2000 CNTN 48188 4412 D5
Fairway Cres
- Amhg N9V 4671 C4
200 Tcmh N8N 4424 C1
Fairway Ct
500 WasC 48103 4404 C6
1300 DRBN 48124 4415 E3
Fairway Dr
2800 WasC 48176 4572 C2
4200 WasC 48103 4329 E4
17100 DET 48221 4199 E6
17100 DET 48221 4271 E1
20400 GSPW 48236 4204 D7
21600 SFLD 48034 4197 A3
23000 WDHN 48183 4668 C5
23200 WynC 48138 4670 B5
25000 DRBN 48124 4415 E3
N Fairway Dr
22100 WDHN 48183 4668 C5
S Fairway Dr
11800 GOTp 48178 4188 A4
Fairway Dr E
23000 WDHN 48183 4668 C6
Fairway Dr S
22300 WDHN 48183 4668 C6
Fairway Dr W
23100 WDHN 48183 4668 C5
Fairway Ln
20500 GSPW 48236 4204 E5
Fairway St
6900 DBHT 48127 4341 A5
13800 RVVW 48192 4669 D2
13900 LVNA 48150 4266 C6
14500 LVNA 48154 4266 C4
17200 LVNA 48152 4266 C1
18500 LVNA 48152 4194 C7
Fairway Tr
200 YpTp 48197 4491 B6
Fairway Hills Dr
24400 NOVI 48374 4192 B1
Fairway III Rd
40100 NvlT 48167 4193 C6
Fairway Park Dr
600 WasC 48103 4404 C7
Fairwood Blvd
10 PTRG 48069 4199 D1
Fairwood Dr
1200 WTLD 48185 4413 B1
6400 DBHT 48127 4340 B5
Fairwood St
300 INKR 48141 4415 C2
500 FRDL 48069 4199 E1
Falcon Ct
3100 AARB 48105 4331 E7
Falcon St
1100 DRBN 48128 4416 C1
1300 DRBN 48128 4341 B7
8700 DET 48209 4418 E3
9800 HMTK 48212 4273 C4
Falkirk Ct
5300 SpTp 48198 4408 B3
Fallbrook Ct
41500 NvlT 48167 4193 B6
Fallbrook Rd
41500 NvlT 48167 4193 B6
Fall Creek Ln
1500 PTFD 48108 4489 A5
Fallow Ct
7900 RMLS 48174 4496 A4
Fall River Dr
12500 GOTp 48178 4188 C3
Fall River Rd
1100 YpTp 48198 4492 C2
Falmouth Av
45500 NOVI 48374 4192 C1
Falstaff Cir
1000 WasC 48167 4190 B7
Fanchette St
2200 WIND N9B 4420 B2
Fargo
25800 RDFD 48240 4196 C5
27300 RDFD 48152 4196 A6
Fargo Av
33400 LVNA 48152 4194 E6
Fargo St
18100 DET 48219 4198 A5
18100 DET 48235 4198 A5
20000 DET 48219 4197 D5
24200 DET 48219 4196 E5
27400 LVNA 48152 4196 A6
28600 LVNA 48152 4195 E6
34600 LVNA 48152 4194 D6
Fargo St S
32800 LVNA 48152 4195 A6
33000 LVNA 48152 4194 E6
Farley
9900 RDFD 48239 4340 D1
13900 RDFD 48239 4268 D5
Farm Ln
10 YpTp 48197 4576 C2
Farm Rd
13500 VNBN 48111 4577 D3
Farmbrook Ct
3200 AARB 48108 4489 E4
Farmbrook Dr
14500 PyTp 48170 4265 C4
Farmbrook St
4500 DET 48224 4276 B2
Farmcrest Ct
17600 NvlT 48167 4265 B1
Farmcrest Ln
17400 NvlT 48167 4265 B2
Farmdale St
100 FRDL 48220 4199 D3
Farmer St
100 PLYM 48170 4265 A7
100 YPLT 48198 4492 B5
1000 PLYM 48170 4264 E7
1400 DET 48226 4345 D6
Farmington Ct
33400 WTLD 48185 4339 A6
Farmington Rd
100 GDNC 48186 4414 A2
1100 GDNC 48135 4414 A1
1700 GDNC 48135 4339 A7
2200 GDNC 48185 4339 A7
8800 LVNA 48150 4339 A1
11700 LVNA 48150 4267 A6
14500 LVNA 48154 4267 A3
15900 LVNA 48154 4266 E1
17100 LVNA 48152 4266 E1
18500 LVNA 48152 4194 E6
20200 LVNA 48335 4194 E6
20200 LVNA 48336 4194 E6
20700 FMTN 48336 4194 E6
20700 FNHL 48336 4194 E6
20700 FNHL 48336 4194 E6
23900 FMTN 48335 4195 A1
23900 FMTN 48336 4195 A1
24100 FMTN 48335 4194 E1
N Farmington Rd
8300 WTLD 48185 4339 A3
8600 WTLD 48150 4339 A3
S Farmington Rd
100 WTLD 48186 4414 A2
Farm View Ct
24000 LyTp 48178 4189 E2
Farnham Av
400 LNPK 48146 4501 A4
1100 LNPK 48146 4500 E4
Farnham Dr
- CNTN 48188 4411 B5
Farnsworth St
10 DET 48202 4345 B2
1400 DET 48211 4345 D2
3600 DET 48211 4346 A1
6500 DET 48211 4274 A7
8000 DET 48213 4274 B7
Farnum Av
5500 WTLD 48186 4497 E1
Farnum St
3900 INKR 48141 4414 E6
7100 RMLS 48174 4497 E3
16000 RMLS 48174 4581 E5
Farpointe Ln
29000 HnTp 48174 4581 E7
29000 HnTp 48174 4582 A7
Farr Dr
- CNTN 48187 4411 E1
Farr St
6300 DET 48211 4273 E5
Farragut Av
35300 WTLD 48186 4413 C5
Farragut Ct
42100 NvlT 48167 4193 B5
Farragut St
34800 WTLD 48186 4413 D5
Farrand Pk
10 HDPK 48203 4272 D4
Farrell Rd
3800 WasC 48130 4330 A2
5500 WasC 48130 4329 A1
Farrow St
1200 FRDL 48220 4200 B2
Fasan Dr
2000 Tcmh N0R 4505 B6
Faust Av
5600 DET 48228 4342 A5
11600 DET 48228 4270 A7
12800 DET 48223 4270 A6
17100 DET 48219 4270 A1
18200 DET 48219 4198 A7
Faust Ct
10 AARB 48108 4490 A5
Faust St
3400 WIND N8Y 4346 D7
Fawn
10 HbgT 48189 4186 A5
38900 HnTp 48164 4665 A5
Fawn Rd
22400 BNTN 48183 4668 B2
Fawn Tr
41400 NOVI 48375 4193 B4
Fawnmeadow Ct
3100 AARB 48105 4332 A6
Fawn Woods Ct
13800 PyTp 48170 4264 B5
Fay Dr
6900 VNBN 48111 4494 D3
Faye Dr
2200 AARB 48103 4405 D5
Fayette St
20200 DET 48203 4200 B4
Fazio Dr
3000 WIND N9E 4503 D2
Feather Ct
700 SLYN 48178 4189 C2
Feather Ln
17700 BNTN 48192 4583 C7
Featherly Dr
- HbgT 48189 4186 A4
Featherstone Ct
3200 AARB 48105 4332 A7
Federal Av
20700 WRRN 48089 4202 B3
Federal Blvd
1900 AARB 48103 4405 D7
Federal Dr
17000 ALPK 48101 4417 C4
Federal St
5600 DET 48209 4344 B7
24000 CTNL 48015 4202 A1
Felch St
100 AARB 48103 4406 B5
9300 DET 48213 4274 C5
Felice St
200 WYDT 48192 4501 C7
Felix Av
600 WIND N9C 4420 B3
E Felker Av
10 HZLP 48030 4200 C2
N Felker Av
400 HZLP 48030 4200 C2
S Felker Av
400 HZLP 48030 4200 C2
Fellows Creek Ct E
50000 PyTp 48170 4335 D3
Fellows Creek Ct W
50400 PyTp 48170 4335 C3
Fellows Creek Dr
9000 PyTp 48170 4335 D3
Fellows Hill Ct
9600 PyTp 48170 4335 D3
Fellows Hill Dr
9700 PyTp 48170 4335 D3
Fellrath St
4600 DBHT 48125 4415 D7
5600 DBHT 48125 4498 D1
5800 TYLR 48180 4498 D1
13400 TYLR 48180 4582 D2
Felt Rd
36100 HnTp 48164 4665 C6
Fendt St
34500 FNHL 48335 4194 D5
Fenelon St
11400 DET 48212 4273 C2
11400 HMTK 48212 4273 C2
19900 DET 48234 4201 C4
Fenkell St
2000 DET 48238 4272 A3
2900 DET 48238 4271 E3
12700 DET 48227 4271 A3
13500 DET 48227 4270 B3
18100 DET 48223 4270 B3
19000 DET 48223 4269 D3
Fenmore St
18000 DET 48235 4270 A1
18200 DET 48235 4198 A7
Fenmore Wy
41000 NOVI 48375 4193 C3
Fenster St
21700 WynC 48111 4663 D4
Fenton
8800 RDFD 48239 4340 E1
14300 RDFD 48239 4268 E5
Fenton St
5600 DBHT 48128 4340 E5
8000 DBHT 48127 4340 E3
16100 DET 48219 4268 E1
19900 DET 48219 4196 E5
Fenview Dr
3000 PTFD 48108 4490 E4
Fenway Dr
21600 NOVI 48167 4192 E4
Fenwick Ct
2600 AARB 48104 4489 D3
Fenwick Dr
44400 CNTN 48188 4411 D4
Ferdinand St
800 DET 48209 4419 D1
1900 DET 48209 4344 C7
S Ferdinand St
100 DET 48209 4419 D2
Ferdon Rd
1000 AARB 48104 4406 D7
1000 AARB 48104 4489 D1
Ferguson Av
40100 PyTp 48170 4337 D1
Ferguson St
15300 DET 48227 4270 B3
16100 DET 48235 4270 B3
18200 DET 48235 4198 B7
Fermanaugh Ct
18400 NvlT 48167 4264 C1
Fermanaugh Dr
45700 NvlT 48167 4264 D1
E Fern
- CNTN 48187 4337 E5
W Fern
- CNTN 48187 4337 D5
Fern Av
24200 EPTE 48021 4203 C1
Fern Ct
1600 CNTN 48188 4412 B4
Fern St
- ALPK 48101 4417 B5
600 FRDL 48220 4200 B4
6600 DET 48210 4344 A6
17600 DRBN 48101 4417 B5
17600 DRBN 48124 4417 B5
21600 OKPK 48237 4199 A3
Fernbrooke Dr
10000 GOTp 48116 4187 B1
Ferndale Av
1500 WIND N8T 4422 C1
Ferndale Pl
1600 AARB 48104 4489 D1
Ferndale St
36700 RMLS 48174 4580 C1
Ferney St
2800 DRBN 48120 4418 C2
Fernhill St
400 DET 48203 4200 B5
Fern Ridge Ct
400 Amhg N9V 4757 C4
Fernwood Av
2500 AARB 48104 4490 C3
3000 AARB 48108 4490 C4
30700 WTLD 48186 4414 C2
Fernwood St
- DET 48204 4344 A2
28400 INKR 48141 4414 E2
28400 INKR 48141 4415 A2
33400 WTLD 48186 4414 A2
34500 WTLD 48186 4413 E2
43000 CNTN 48187 4337 A7
Ferraina Dr
6200 WTLD 48185 4338 E6
Ferrier St
100 YPLT 48198 4492 A4
Ferris Av
1200 LNPK 48146 4501 A3
4200 LNPK 48192 4501 A7
Ferris St
10 HDPK 48203 4272 D2
100 YPLT 48197 4492 A4
400 YPLT 48197 4491 E5
2300 DET 48209 4418 E2
Ferry Rd
7500 WynC 48138 4670 D5
Ferry St
100 WIND N9A 4420 D1
3400 WasC 48103 4405 B5
Ferry St E
10 DET 48202 4345 B2
1000 DET 48211 4345 D1
3100 DET 48211 4273 E7
3600 DET 48211 4274 A7
7700 DET 48213 4274 B7
Ferry St W
10 DET 48202 4345 B2
Ferry Mall
400 DET 48202 4345 A2
Ferry Park St
1400 DET 48202 4344 C2
1400 DET 48210 4344 C2
Fescue Ln
- Amhg N9V 4671 D4
Festival Ct
7000 CNTN 48187 4336 A6
Fiddlers Cove
18300 NvlT 48167 4263 E1
Field St
3600 DET 48214 4346 B1
4700 DET 48214 4274 B7
6600 DET 48213 4274 A5
24900 FTRK 48134 4753 E4
24900 FTRK 48134 4754 A4
Fieldcrest Dr
9000 GOTp 48116 4187 B1
9500 GOTp 48178 4187 B2
10200 GOTp 48189 4187 B3
Fieldcrest Ln
1600 Tcmh N8N 4423 E2
3500 PTFD 48197 4490 E5
Fieldcrest St
200 AARB 48103 4489 A3
Fielding Ct
900 WIND N9G 4504 E5
Fielding St
100 FRDL 48220 4200 A4
1100 FRDL 48220 4199 D4
Fielding St
7000 YpTp 48197 4576 E5
7200 DET 48228 4341 D3
11600 DET 48228 4269 D7
12200 DET 48223 4269 D7
17100 DET 48219 4269 D1
18100 DET 48219 4197 D7
Fields Av
200 LSal N9J 4502 D6
Fieldstone Ct
1300 PTFD 48108 4573 A3
9200 WasC 48176 4658 E2
Fieldstone Dr
45400 CNTN 48187 4336 C5
Fieldstone Ln
9200 WasC 48176 4658 E2
Fieldview Ct
46900 CNTN 48188 4411 B6
Fieldview Dr
3900 CNTN 48188 4411 B6
Fiesta Ct
10300 WIND N8R 4423 C3
Figueroa St
25800 DBHT 48127 4340 C5
Filbert St
400 WTLD 48186 4414 B2
3300 WYNE 48184 4414 B5
12500 DET 48205 4274 E1
13000 DET 48205 4275 A1
Filer St
9100 DET 48211 4273 E4
17100 DET 48212 4273 E1
17600 DET 48212 4201 E7
19600 DET 48234 4201 E5
Fillmore St
42000 VNBN 48111 4495 B7
Filmore Dr
14100 PyTp 48170 4263 C6
Filmore St
- RMLS 48174 4496 A6
300 CNTN 48188 4410 D3
18200 LVNA 48152 4266 E1
18500 LVNA 48152 4194 E7
23300 TYLR 48180 4499 B4
25500 TYLR 48180 4498 D4
31500 WYNE 48184 4414 C7
Finch Av
15000 PyTp 48170 4265 B5
Finch Ct
10100 WasC 48160 4659 C4
Findlay St
11000 DET 48205 4274 D2
Fink Av
30700 FMTN 48336 4195 B2
31100 FNHL 48336 4195 B2
Finlan St
21500 STCS 48080 4204 C1
Finley Dr
39900 CNTN 48188 4412 D3
Finnegan Dr
9800 HbgT 48116 4186 C2
Finneren Ct
33000 FNHL 48336 4195 A1
Finzel Rd
12900 MonC 48117 4750 C7
Fireside Ct
22600 NOVI 48375 4193 D3
Firestone St
4000 DRBN 48126 4417 D1
4700 DRBN 48126 4342 D7
Firgrove Dr
- WIND N8P 4348 C7
- WIND N8P 4423 C1
Firwood Av
21700 EPTE 48021 4203 B2
40500 PyTp 48170 4337 C2
Firwood Dr
42000 PyTp 48170 4337 B2
Firwood Rd
9200 GOTp 48178 4187 E1
Firwood St
10 YpTp 48197 4491 D5
7300 DET 48204 4344 B2
7300 DET 48210 4344 B3
Fischer Dr
100 WTLD 48185 4413 B2
100 WTLD 48186 4413 B2
Fischer St
900 DET 48214 4346 D1
4100 DET 48214 4274 C7
5000 DET 48213 4274 C6
Fisher Av
6700 WRRN 48091 4201 E4
7000 WRRN 48091 4202 A4
11300 WRRN 48089 4202 C4
Fisher Frwy
- DET - 4418 D6
- DET - 4501 A1
- LNPK - 4500 E2
- LNPK - 4501 A1
- MVDL - 4418 D6
- MVDL - 4501 A1
Fisher Frwy I-75
- DET - 4418 D6
- DET - 4501 A1
- LNPK - 4500 E2
- LNPK - 4501 A1
- MVDL - 4418 D6
- MVDL - 4501 A1
W Fisher Frwy
- DET 48201 4345 B6
- DET 48216 4345 B6
- DET 48216 4419 E1
2600 DET 48216 4344 E7
4100 DET 48209 4419 E1
Fisher Frwy E
- DET 48226 4345 E4
10 DET 48201 4345 E4
1400 DET 48207 4345 E4

Block	City	ZIP	Map#	Grid
Fisher Frwy N				
-	DET	-	4344	E6
-	DET	-	4345	C5
-	DET	-	4418	E5
-	DET	-	4419	D2
Fisher Frwy N I-75				
-	DET	-	4344	E6
-	DET	-	4345	C5
-	DET	-	4418	E5
-	DET	-	4419	D2
Fisher Frwy S				
-	DET	-	4344	A7
-	DET	-	4345	A6
-	DET	-	4418	E5
-	DET	-	4419	B3
Fisher Frwy S I-75				
-	DET	-	4344	A7
-	DET	-	4345	A6
-	DET	-	4418	E5
-	DET	-	4419	B3
Fisher Frwy W				
-	DET	48209	4419	A4
-	DET	48218	4418	B7
1400	DET	48201	4345	C5
1400	DET	48216	4345	C5
3000	DET	48216	4344	E6
Fisher Rd				
10	GSPF	48230	4276	C3
10	GSPT	48236	4276	C5
10	GSPT	48230	4276	C5
200	GSPT	48236	4276	C3
400	DET	48224	4276	C3
400	GSPT	48224	4276	C3
11400	VNBN	48111	4578	E1
Fisher St				
2300	MVDL	48122	4418	A7
Fisk Av				
12800	WRRN	48089	4202	E2
Fiske Dr				
300	DET	48214	4346	E3
S Fitzgerald				
-	ROTp	48220	4199	A4
Fitzgerald Blvd				
10400	ROTp	48220	4199	A4
Fitzgerald St				
16600	LVNA	48154	4266	B2
17000	LVNA	48152	4266	B2
19000	LVNA	48152	4194	B7
Fitzpatrick Ct				
18400	DET	48228	4342	A1
Fitzpatrick St				
18300	DET	48228	4342	A1
18900	DET	48228	4341	E1
19400	DET	48223	4269	E7
19400	DET	48228	4269	E7
Five M Centre Dr				
14200	RMLS	48174	4582	B4
W Five M Centre Dr				
28000	RMLS	48174	4582	A3
Five Points St				
16100	DET	48219	4268	D2
16100	RDFD	48240	4268	D2
16800	RDFD	48240	4268	D2
18200	DET	48240	4196	D7
18200	DET	48240	4268	D1
18200	RDFD	48240	4196	D7
19100	DET	48219	4196	D5
19100	RDFD	48240	4196	D5
19300	WynC	48219	4196	D5
20100	WynC	48240	4196	D5
Flamingo Blvd				
-	WTLD	48150	4339	D3
7600	WTLD	48185	4339	C4
18500	LVNA	48152	4195	C7
18500	LVNA	48152	4267	C1
Flamingo St				
9800	LVNA	48150	4339	C1
14500	LVNA	48154	4267	C4
Flanders Av				
14300	SOGT	48195	4583	E3
14300	SOGT	48195	4584	A3
Flanders Rd				
200	Lksr	N8N	4424	E2
Flanders St				
11000	DET	48205	4274	D2
11000	DET	48213	4274	D2
13000	DET	48205	4275	A1
13000	DET	48213	4275	A1
13700	SOGT	48195	4584	A2
15200	DET	48224	4275	A1
21400	FNHL	48335	4194	E3
32600	FMTN	48335	4195	A4
33100	FMTN	48336	4194	E4
33100	FMTN	48336	4194	E4
Fleet St				
300	PLYM	48170	4265	A7
2600	DET	48238	4272	A4
7900	CNTN	48187	4337	A4
Fleetwood Ct				
43400	CNTN	48187	4412	A1
Fleetwood Dr				
1800	GSPW	48236	4204	B5
19600	HRWD	48225	4204	A4
43500	CNTN	48187	4411	E1
Fleming St				
4500	DBHT	48125	4417	A7
11300	HMTK	48212	4273	B3
13400	DET	48212	4201	A7
17400	DET	48212	4201	A7
19900	DET	-	4201	A4
22900	FMTN	48335	4194	E3
Fleming Wy				
4200	SpTp	48105	4334	C4
4200	SpTp	48170	4334	C4
Fleming Creek Dr				
6500	SpTp	48198	4333	D7
Fleming Ridge Dr				
3900	SpTp	48105	4333	B6
Flemming Ct				
2600	WIND	N9E	4503	D1

Block	City	ZIP	Map#	Grid
Fletcher Cres				
3100	WIND	N9E	4421	C7
3100	WIND	N9E	4504	C1
Fletcher St				
-	DET	48210	4344	B6
200	AARB	48104	4406	C6
4300	WYNE	48184	4413	C7
4800	WYNE	48184	4496	C1
Flint St				
17100	MVDL	48122	4418	A5
Flo St				
23500	WRRN	48091	4201	A1
Flora Av				
400	WIND	N8P	4348	A5
Flora Ln				
2900	WYNE	48184	4413	C5
Flora St				
10200	DET	48209	4418	D5
17000	DET	48122	4418	B6
17000	MVDL	48122	4418	B6
Floral Av				
7200	WTLD	48135	4340	A4
7200	WTLD	48185	4340	A4
Floral St				
8800	LVNA	48150	4340	A2
17400	LVNA	48152	4268	A1
19900	LVNA	48152	4196	A5
22400	FMTN	48336	4195	C2
Florane St				
35400	WTLD	48186	4413	C3
Florence				
25700	RDFD	48240	4268	D2
Florence Av				
400	WIND	N8P	4348	B6
38400	WTLD	48185	4412	E2
38400	WTLD	48185	4413	E2
Florence Dr				
47600	NOVI	48167	4192	A4
Florence Ln				
6200	VNBN	48111	4495	A2
Florence St				
-	DET	48219	4269	E2
-	DET	48219	4269	E2
-	DET	48221	4272	A2
-	DET	48235	4270	A2
200	HDPK	48203	4272	B2
300	YPLT	48197	4491	E4
300	YPLT	48197	4492	A4
500	WasC	48103	4404	C3
1900	DET	48203	4272	A2
6300	DET	48221	4270	D2
14300	DET	48235	4270	E2
24600	DFT	48219	4268	E2
26600	INKR	48141	4415	B5
28400	GDNC	48135	4415	A1
28600	GDNC	48135	4414	E1
37700	WTLD	48185	4413	A2
Florian St				
2200	HMTK	48212	4273	C5
Florida				
600	WynC	48111	4662	D3
Florida St				
4900	DET	48210	4343	E7
9200	LVNA	48150	4339	E2
Floros Ln				
-	GOTp	48178	4189	A2
Flower Av				
24200	EPTE	48021	4203	C1
Flower Ct				
4700	DET	48207	4345	E1
Flowerdale St				
200	FRDL	48220	4199	D3
Floyd St				
6300	DET	48210	4343	E4
Flushing Av				
-	DET	48188	4410	D4
Flynn Dr				
-	RMLS	48174	4497	D4
Flynn St				
1500	WTLD	48185	4414	B4
Foch St				
300	WIND	N8X	4421	B4
15300	LVNA	48154	4268	A4
18000	LVNA	48152	4268	A1
18400	LVNA	48152	4196	A7
Fogg St				
14900	PyTp	48167	4264	D5
14900	PyTp	48170	4264	D5
Foley St				
1600	YpTp	48198	4492	E6
Foley Rd				
1400	YpTp	48198	4492	D6
Foley St				
-	DET	48227	4270	D7
10500	DET	48204	4271	A6
10800	DET	48227	4271	A6
Folker Dr				
30400	INKR	48141	4414	E2
Folkstone Ct				
1300	AARB	48105	4407	A2
31700	FMTN	48336	4195	B1
Folkstone Dr				
31600	FMTN	48336	4195	B1
Follett St				
10	YPLT	48198	4492	A5
Folsom Rd				
30400	FMTN	48335	4195	A3
32400	FMTN	48335	4195	A3
Fonner Ct E				
46000	NvIT	48167	4192	C6
Fonner Ct W				
46000	NvIT	48167	4192	C6
Fonner Rd				
46000	NvIT	48167	4192	C6
Fontana Ln				
10	GSPS	48236	4205	A6

Block	City	ZIP	Map#	Grid
Fonville Ct				
34100	LVNA	48152	4194	E6
Fonville Dr				
33800	LVNA	48152	4194	E6
Fonville St				
31500	LVNA	48152	4195	B6
Foothill Dr				
600	CNTN	48188	4412	D3
Foot Hills Ct				
43900	NOVI	48167	4192	E4
Ford Av				
10	WYDT	48192	4585	A1
2100	WYDT	48192	4584	E1
2300	WYDT	48195	4584	E1
6700	WRRN	48091	4201	E2
7000	WRRN	48091	4202	A2
8000	WRRN	48089	4202	A2
11200	RVVW	48192	4585	A2
14500	ALPK	48101	4500	C7
20700	HZLP	48030	4200	C3
26800	FTRK	48134	4753	C2
Ford Blvd				
200	WIND	N8S	4347	A7
400	LNPK	48146	4501	A7
1000	LNPK	48146	4501	A7
1500	WIND	N8T	4422	B1
N Ford Blvd				
100	YpTp	48198	4492	D3
S Ford Blvd				
100	YpTp	48198	4492	D4
Ford Ct				
1500	GSPW	48236	4204	C6
Ford Pl				
10	DET	48202	4345	A2
Ford Rd				
-	DET	48126	4342	A6
-	DET	48128	4342	A6
-	SpTp	48105	4408	A1
-	SpTp	48105	4408	A1
-	SpTp	48198	4408	E1
-	WTLD	48185	4337	D7
4200	AATp	48105	4407	E1
4200	AATp	48105	4489	D1
6000	SpTp	48198	4408	E1
7500	SpTp	48198	4409	C1
8000	SpTp	48198	4409	C1
8800	SpTp	48198	4335	C7
9500	SpTp	48198	4335	C7
10000	DRBN	48126	4343	B6
14800	DRBN	48126	4342	A6
18100	DET	48228	4342	A6
19000	DRBN	48228	4341	E7
19000	DRBN	48228	4341	E7
19300	DRBN	48126	4341	E7
20500	DBHI	48127	4341	B7
20500	DBHT	48127	4341	B7
23300	DRBN	48127	4341	B7
23400	WynC	48127	4341	B7
23400	WynC	48128	4341	B7
24400	DBHT	48128	4340	E7
24400	DRBN	48128	4340	E7
27400	GDNC	48135	4340	A7
28500	GDNC	48135	4339	E7
32900	GDNC	48135	4339	A7
32900	WTLD	48135	4339	A7
33800	WTLD	48135	4338	E7
33800	WTLD	48185	4338	E7
39400	CNTN	48187	4337	E7
43400	CNTN	48187	4336	C7
48200	CNTN	48187	4335	C7
49400	CNTN	48187	4335	C7
Ford Rd SR-153				
-	DET	48126	4342	A6
-	DET	48126	4342	A6
-	SpTp	48105	4333	E7
-	WTLD	48185	4337	D7
7500	SpTp	48198	4409	A1
8000	SpTp	48198	4409	C1
8800	SpTp	48198	4334	C7
9500	SpTp	48198	4335	C7
10000	DRBN	48126	4343	B6
13800	DRBN	48126	4342	A6
18100	DET	48228	4342	A6
19000	DRBN	48228	4341	E7
19300	DRBN	48126	4341	E7
20000	DRBN	48127	4341	E7
20500	DBHT	48127	4341	B7
20500	DBHT	48128	4341	B7
23400	WynC	48127	4341	B7
24400	DBHT	48128	4340	E7
24400	DRBN	48128	4340	E7
27400	GDNC	48135	4340	A7
28500	GDNC	48135	4339	E7
32900	WTLD	48135	4339	A7
33800	WTLD	48135	4338	E7
39400	CNTN	48187	4337	D7
43400	CNTN	48187	4336	C7
48200	CNTN	48187	4335	C7
49400	CNTN	48187	4335	C7
Ford St				
300	HDPK	48203	4272	C3
500	PLYM	48170	4337	A7
700	YPLT	48197	4492	A4
1600	DET	48238	4272	A4
Fordale St				
-	DET	48229	4418	B5
Fordcroft				
-	TYLR	48180	4582	E5

Block	City	ZIP	Map#	Grid
Fordcroft St				
10	DET	48236	4276	E1
Fordham Cir				
5600	CNTN	48187	4337	A7
Fordham St				
14100	DET	48205	4203	C6
Ford Lake Park Rd				
-	YpTp	48197	4576	D1
Fordline Rd				
3800	ALPK	48101	4500	C6
3800	LNPK	48146	4500	C6
Fordline St				
11200	ALPK	48101	4500	C7
8500	CNTN	48170	4335	D4
8500	CNTN	48170	4335	D4
11600	SOGT	48101	4500	C7
11600	SOGT	48146	4500	C7
11600	SOGT	48195	4500	C7
16500	SOGT	48195	4584	C5
17000	RVVW	48192	4584	C6
17000	RVVW	48195	4584	C6
Fordson Dr				
23400	DRBN	48124	4416	A2
Fordson Hwy				
24000	DBHT	48127	4341	A3
24200	DBHT	48127	4340	E3
24400	DBHT	48239	4340	E3
25800	RDFD	48239	4340	C1
26400	RDFD	48239	4268	C7
S Fordson St				
300	DET	48229	4418	C4
Fordway Dr				
44600	NOVI	48375	4192	D3
Fordyce St				
-	DET	48211	4273	C6
Forest Av				
400	PLYM	48170	4337	A1
2100	WIND	N8W	4421	C4
E Forest Av				
10	YPLT	48198	4492	A3
800	YpTp	48198	4492	C3
S Forest Av				
800	AARB	48104	4406	D7
W Forest Av				
10	YPLT	48197	4492	A3
400	YPLT	48197	4491	E3
Forest Av E				
10	DET	48201	4345	B3
900	DET	48207	4345	D2
3400	DET	48207	4346	A1
7200	DET	48214	4346	A1
10400	DET	48214	4274	E6
12300	DET	48214	4275	B5
Forest Av W				
10	DET	48201	4345	A3
1400	DET	48201	4345	A3
2200	DET	48210	4344	D4
Forest Ct				
700	YpTp	48198	4492	C3
1300	AARB	48104	4406	D7
1000	WYDT	48146	4500	E7
33400	WTLD	48185	4339	A6
37000	FNHL	48335	4194	B4
47800	NvIT	48264	4264	A3
Forest Dr				
600	SLYN	48178	4189	B1
9000	WasC	48189	4259	A1
16600	NvIT	48264	4264	A3
22100	WynC	48138	4670	B4
Forest Hl				
-	DBHT	48127	4341	D6
Forest Ln				
4600	TNTN	48183	4669	B7
23000	TYLR	48180	4583	B1
24400	LyTp	48178	4189	A2
Forest Rd				
900	BNHL	48105	4330	E7
Forest Rd N				
23400	HnTp	48164	4665	A5
Forest St				
10	RVRG	48218	4501	E2
200	WTLD	48186	4413	E2
400	WYDT	48192	4585	B4
14700	SOGT	48195	4584	A3
23400	OKPK	48220	4199	C1
23800	OKPK	48069	4199	C1
26100	WYDT	48146	4755	A1
32000	WYNE	48184	4414	A6
35300	WYNE	48184	4413	D6
Forestbrook Ct				
22500	BNTN	48134	4668	A4
Forestbrooke Ct				
500	SALN	48176	4657	E1
Forestbrooke St				
500	SALN	48176	4657	E1
Forest Creek Ct				
7800	HbgT	48189	4186	C4
Forest Creek Dr				
39100	WTLD	48185	4337	E3
Forestdale Dr				
43500	VNBN	48111	4495	A5
Forest Dale St				
28400	RMLS	48174	4582	A5
Forest Edge Dr				
9200	GOTp	48173	4188	B1
Forest Glade Ct				
9900	WIND	N8R	4423	B3
Forest Glade St				
2700	WIND	N8R	4423	B2
3500	WIND	N8T	4423	A4
Forest Hill Cir				
-	Amhg	N9V	4671	C4
Forest Hill Ct				
19300	WDHN	48183	4669	A7
Forest Hill Dr				
18900	WDHN	48183	4669	A7
Forest Lake Dr				
16100	NvIT	48167	4265	D4

Block	City	ZIP	Map#	Grid
Forestlawn St				
8000	DET	48234	4274	A2
Forest Park Dr				
-	WYNE	48184	4414	A7
Forest Park Dr E				
23700	NOVI	48374	4192	A2
Forest Trails Dr				
44400	CNTN	48187	4336	D3
Forestview Ct				
5100	PTFD	48108	4572	E1
Forestview Dr				
1800	SpTp	48198	4409	E7
8500	CNTN	48170	4335	D4
8500	CNTN	48170	4335	D4
15500	NvIT	48170	4265	B4
25500	GBTR	48034	4196	C1
Forestwood Dr				
46000	PyTp	48170	4336	C3
Forman St				
100	DET	48209	4418	E4
S Forman St				
100	DET	48209	4418	E5
Forrer St				
9100	DET	48228	4342	C1
9500	DET	48227	4342	C1
14500	DET	48227	4270	C4
18000	DET	48235	4198	C7
18000	DET	48235	4270	C1
Forrest Dr				
2000	LNPK	48146	4500	E4
Forrest St				
2000	LNPK	48146	4500	E4
Foss Ct				
2100	AARB	48103	4405	D3
Foss St				
2200	AARB	48103	4405	D3
Fossil Hill Ct				
10500	CNTN	48189	4187	D4
Fossil Hill Dr				
10400	CNTN	48187	4187	C4
Foster Av				
800	WIND	N8W	4421	D7
800	WIND	N8W	4504	D1
800	WIND	N8X	4421	D7
800	WIND	N8X	4422	A7
1900	WIND	N8W	4422	A7
Foster Rd				
-	WasC	48105	4405	D1
Foster St				
-	DET	48211	4273	E4
6300	RMLS	48174	4497	D2
Foster Winter Dr				
22000	SFLD	48075	4198	C3
Founders Ct				
49000	CNTN	48187	4410	E1
Fountain Blvd				
33800	WTLD	48185	4338	D3
Fountain Dr				
-	DET	48207	4346	D6
N Fountain Pk				
7800	WTLD	48185	4338	A4
Fountain Pkwy				
37400	WTLD	48185	4338	A4
Fountain St				
400	AARB	48103	4406	A4
Fountain Park Cir				
37500	WTLD	48185	4338	A4
Fountain Park Dr				
19500	RVVW	48192	4669	D1
Fountain View Dr				
45400	CNTN	48188	4411	C2
Four Lakes Dr				
10800	GOTp	48178	4188	A4
Fournier St				
12600	DET	48205	4274	A1
Four Seasons Blvd				
-	NvIT	48167	4264	A1
Fox				
14600	RDFD	48239	4268	C4
17300	RDFD	48240	4268	B1
20300	RDFD	48240	4196	B5
Fox Av				
600	YpTp	48198	4492	E6
1300	FRDL	48220	4199	D4
6300	ALPK	48101	4500	C4
Fox Cr				
22600	FNHL	48335	4194	A2
Fox Ct				
4300	TNTN	48183	4669	B6
8300	AGST	48191	4577	C7
47500	CNTN	48187	4336	B7
Fox Dr N				
49000	PyTp	48170	4263	E7
Fox Dr S				
48000	PyTp	48170	4335	E1
Fox Ln				
7600	WasC	48189	4258	C4
8000	WasC	48170	4334	B2
Fox Pth				
6600	CNTN	48187	4336	D6
Fox Run				
5500	WasC	48176	4572	B4
Fox Tr				
8800	WasC	48176	4261	D1
Foxboro Ct				
700	SALN	48176	4572	B6
13200	PyTp	48170	4264	C7
Foxboro Dr				
20100	RVVW	48192	4669	D1

Block	City	ZIP	Map#	Grid
Fox Chase Ln				
22700	BNTN	48134	4667	A5
Foxchase Ln				
7000	WTLD	48185	4338	A5
Fox Creek Blvd				
7100	CNTN	48187	4337	B5
Foxcreek Ct				
6900	CNTN	48187	4337	D5
Foxcreek Dr				
6700	CNTN	48187	4337	B6
Foxcroft Rd				
3000	AARB	48104	4490	B1
22300	WDHN	48183	4668	B4
Foxcroft St				
6400	DBHT	48127	4341	D5
Foxdale Ln				
1700	PTFD	48108	4488	E6
1700	PTFD	48108	4489	A5
Fox Den Ct				
3600	WasC	48176	4572	B2
Fox Glen Dr				
3800	PTFD	48108	4489	A6
17500	RVVW	48192	4584	A6
Foxhill Ct				
1200	WIND	N8S	4348	B7
Fox Hill Ln				
7300	WasC	48167	4262	A5
Foxhill Pl				
8500	WIND	N8S	4348	A7
Fox Hills Rd				
6400	CNTN	48187	4336	D6
Fox Hollow Blvd				
-	NvIT	48167	4264	B1
Fox Hollow Ct				
5700	SpTp	48105	4333	B6
18400	NvIT	48167	4264	B1
Fox Hunt Dr				
3500	AARB	48105	4407	C5
Fox Meadow Dr				
-	CNTN	48187	4336	D6
Foxmoor Blvd				
23700	WDHN	48183	4668	C6
Foxmoor Dr				
22600	NOVI	48374	4192	A2
Fox Pointe Cir				
1300	PTFD	48108	4489	A5
Fox Pointe Ct				
44800	CNTN	48187	4336	D7
Fox Pointe Ln				
59400	LyTp	48178	4189	D6
Fox Ridge Ct				
5000	WasC	48103	4572	A1
N Foxridge Ct				
3000	AARB	48105	4407	A1
S Foxridge Ct				
2900	AARB	48105	4407	A1
Fox Ridge Dr				
11800	PyTp	48170	4335	E1
11800	PyTp	48170	4336	A1
Foxridge Dr				
7000	CNTN	48187	4337	D5
Fox Run Dr				
47400	CNTN	48187	4336	B7
Fox Tail St				
8000	AGST	48197	4576	B7
Foxthorn Rd				
6500	CNTN	48187	4337	A5
Foxton Dr				
22400	NOVI	48375	4192	D3
Fox Trail Ln				
17500	NvIT	48167	4264	B1
Fox Valley Dr				
39700	CNTN	48188	4412	D3
Foxway Ct				
3200	AARB	48105	4332	A5
39700	NvIT	48167	4193	D7
Foxway Dr				
2300	AARB	48105	4406	C1
2800	AARB	48105	4332	A7
Foxwood Dr				
1800	LSal	N9H	4504	B5
Fox Woods Dr				
7100	CNTN	48187	4336	D6
Frains Lake Rd				
3000	SpTp	48198	4409	A2
3500	SpTp	48105	4334	A3
3500	SpTp	48105	4409	A2
3500	SpTp	48198	4334	A3
Fralick Av				
800	PLYM	48170	4265	A7
Fran Ct				
33400	WTLD	48185	4339	A2
Francavilla Dr				
-	LVNA	48154	4266	E2
17100	LVNA	48152	4266	E2
Frances Ln				
25800	HnTp	48164	4665	C7
25800	HnTp	48164	4751	C1
Frances St				
34000	WTLD	48185	4413	E1
Francis Av				
11600	PyTp	48170	4337	D1
Francis St				
-	DET	48229	4501	B1
200	ECRS	48229	4501	C2
17000	DET	48122	4418	B6
17000	MVDL	48122	4418	B6
21500	DRBN	48124	4416	C2
Franciscan Ct E				
1200	CNTN	48187	4411	E1
Franciscan Ct W				
1200	CNTN	48187	4411	E1
Franciscan Dr				
44100	CNTN	48187	4411	E1
Francois Rd				
1200	WIND	N8Y	4347	A5
1300	WIND	N8Y	4422	A1
1800	WIND	N8W	4422	B2
Fran Dor Ln				
8500	WasC	48167	4261	D1

STREET
Block City ZIP Map# Grid

Frank Av
300 WIND N8S 4347 E6
800 LNPK 48101 4417 E7
800 LNPK 48101 4500 D1
800 LNPK 48122 4417 E7
800 LNPK 48146 4417 E7
800 LNPK 48146 4500 D1
Frank St
- DET 48201 4345 B4
Frank Daniels Dr
1200 YpTp 48197 4491 D7
Frankfort Ct
5200 DET 48213 4275 A5
Frankfort Rd
26000 HnTp 48164 4751 C1
Frankfort St
12000 DET 48213 4275 A5
14300 DET 48224 4275 B4
16900 DET 48224 4276 A3
18500 DET 48236 4276 B2
Franklin Av
2800 WIND N8Y 4421 D1
5300 TNTN 48183 4755 C1
Franklin Blvd
1200 AARB 48103 4489 A1
Franklin Ct
18100 BNTN 48192 4583 C6
N Franklin Ct
1800 AARB 48103 4405 D3
S Franklin Ct
1700 AARB 48103 4405 D3
Franklin Dr
14100 PyTp 48170 4263 D6
E Franklin Dr
1900 CNTN 48187 4336 D7
W Franklin Dr
2000 CNTN 48187 4336 D7
Franklin Rd
16100 NvlT 48167 4265 A3
16100 NvlT 48170 4265 A3
Franklin St
500 DET 48226 4345 E6
500 YPLT 48197 4491 E5
800 DET 48207 4345 E6
1300 DET 48207 4346 A6
1500 AARB 48103 4405 D4
3600 WIND N8Y 4421 E1
4200 WIND N8Y 4347 A7
4200 WIND N8Y 4422 A1
32900 WYNE 48184 4414 A7
N Franklin St
100 DRBN 48128 4415 E1
1100 DRBN 48128 4340 E7
S Franklin St
100 DRBN 48124 4415 E2
Franklin Ter
25100 SLYN 48178 4189 B1
Franklin Mill St
40300 NOVI 48375 4193 C2
Frank Lloyd Wright Dr
10 AATp 48105 4332 D7
10 AATp 48105 4407 D1
Fraser Av
- Amhg N9V 4671 C7
100 Amhg N9V 4757 C1
2200 WIND N8X 4421 B4
Frazer Av
21100 SFLD 48075 4197 C3
21900 SFLD 48034 4197 C3
Frazer St
9000 DET 48202 4273 A6
Frazier Av
200 RVRG 48218 4418 D7
300 RVRG 48218 4501 C1
Frazier Ct
3700 INKR 48141 4414 E6
Freda St
7400 DRBN 48126 4343 B3
8000 DET 48204 4343 B3
27300 INKR 48141 4415 B2
Frederick Ct
3800 INKR 48141 4415 C6
Frederick Dr
3500 AARB 48105 4407 C4
Frederick St
- DET 48213 4274 A7
1000 YPLT 48197 4491 D5
1400 DET 48211 4345 D1
3500 DET 48211 4274 A7
5900 RMLS 48174 4498 A1
8000 WasC 48167 4262 D3
8900 LVNA 48150 4339 C2
9900 DRBN 48120 4418 D3
22600 FMTN 48336 4195 A2
46000 NvlT 48167 4192 B7
Frederick Douglass Av
200 DET 48202 4345 B2
Fredericks Dr
23000 BNTN 48134 4667 C5
Fredericksburg Dr
43400 CNTN 48188 4412 A3
43800 CNTN 48188 4411 E3
Fredrick St
24500 SFLD 48034 4196 D4
Fredricksburg Towne St
10 SFLD 48075 4198 A2
Fredro St
3800 DET 48212 4273 C2
Freedom Dr
4600 PTFD 48108 4490 B7
Freedom Ln
17500 BNTN 48192 4583 D6
Freedom Rd
30500 FNHL 48336 4195 C3
32500 FMTN 48336 4195 C3
32600 FMTN 48336 4194 C2
33400 FMTN 48335 4194 C2
34400 FNHL 48335 4194 C2
Freedom Wy
300 WIND N9A 4420 E1
51000 VNBN 48111 4577 C4
Freeland St
8800 DET 48228 4342 E1
9500 DET 48227 4270 E7
9500 DET 48227 4342 E1
16100 DET 48235 4270 E3
19100 DET 48235 4198 E5
Freeman Ct
2000 WTLD 48186 4413 D4
Freeman St
14000 WRRN 48089 4203 A3
Freemantle Ct
300 WasC 48176 4658 D1
Freemont
45500 NOVI 48374 4192 C1
Freeport Ct
42000 VNBN 48111 4579 C3
Freer St
4300 DET 48210 4343 E6
Freeway Park Dr
23800 FNHL 48335 4194 A1
Fremont Av
8000 WTLD 48185 4339 E3
8600 WTLD 48150 4339 E3
Fremont Pl
3300 DET 48207 4346 A1
Fremont St
8800 LVNA 48150 4339 E2
18200 LVNA 48152 4267 D1
20200 LVNA 48152 4195 D5
20400 LVNA 48336 4195 D5
French Dr
13300 GOTp 48178 4188 D5
French Rd
3700 DET 48214 4274 E6
5000 DET 48213 4274 D4
10100 DET 48234 4274 B1
Fresard St
22300 STCS 48080 4204 E1
Fresno Ln
4200 PTFD 48108 4490 E3
Fret Rd
41400 VNBN 48111 4579 B5
Freud St
10400 DET 48214 4347 A2
Frey Ct
7000 HbgT 48189 4186 B5
Friar Ln
25000 SFLD 48034 4197 B1
Friar St
38200 WTLD 48186 4413 A3
Frieda Ct
27200 TYLR 48180 4582 B4
Frieze Av
1800 AARB 48104 4489 E2
Frisbee St
23600 DET 48219 4197 A6
23800 DET 48219 4196 E6
Fritz Dr
1600 TNTN 48183 4669 E2
Front Rd
- LSal N9J 4502 C5
2400 LSal N9J 4586 C1
Front Rd P-18
- LSal N9J 4502 C5
2400 LSal N9J 4586 C1
Front St
100 WasC 48189 4259 B1
Front St N
300 Amhg N9V 4671 B6
1600 Amhg N9V 4586 C6
2400 Amhg N9J 4586 C6
Front St N CO-20
300 Amhg N9V 4671 B6
1600 Amhg N9V 4586 C6
2400 Amhg N9J 4586 C6
Front St N P-18
300 Amhg N9V 4671 B6
1600 Amhg N9V 4586 C6
2400 Amhg N9J 4586 C6
Front St S
600 Amhg N9V 4757 B6
700 EsxC N9V 4757 B6
Front St S CO-20
600 Amhg N9V 4757 B6
700 EsxC N9V 4757 B6
Front St S P-18
600 Amhg N9V 4757 B6
700 EsxC N9V 4757 B6
S Frontage Rd
- WTLD 48185 4337 E7
- WTLD 48185 4338 A7
W Frontage Rd
- SOGT 48195 4583 E2
- SOGT 48195 4584 A2
Frontenac Av
400 WIND N9E 4504 C2
Frontenac St
6500 DET 48211 4274 A5
6500 DET 48213 4274 A5
Frontier Cir
24500 FTRK 48134 4754 A2
24800 FTRK 48134 4753 E2
E Frumin Ct
7200 WTLD 48185 4339 E5
W Frumin Ct
7200 WTLD 48185 4339 D5
Fry Av
15300 NvlT 48170 4265 C4
Fry Rd
19100 NvlT 48167 4193 C7
Fryer Dr
29200 GBTR 48173 4755 D4
Fryer St
10 Amhg N9V 4757 D2
Fudge St
100 WTLD 48186 4414 D7
Fuller Cres
1300 WIND N8W 4421 E7
1500 WIND N8W 4422 A7
Fuller Ct
2200 AARB 48104 4406 E5
2200 AARB 48105 4406 E5
2200 AARB 48105 4407 A5
2300 AARB 48104 4407 A5
49900 PyTp 48170 4335 D1
Fuller Dr
22400 NOVI 48374 4192 C3
Fuller Rd
1500 AARB 48104 4406 E5
1500 AARB 48105 4406 E5
2300 AARB 48105 4407 A5
2400 AARB 48104 4407 A5
Fuller St
1500 AARB 48104 4406 D5
1500 AARB 48105 4406 D5
Fullerton
- RDFD 48239 4268 D6
Fullerton St
- DET 48223 4270 B6
2600 DET 48206 4272 A6
2600 DET 48238 4272 A6
3700 DET 48206 4271 E6
6300 DET 48204 4271 D6
6300 DET 48238 4271 D6
12700 DET 48227 4271 A6
13600 DET 48227 4270 E6
20900 DET 48228 4269 C6
23800 DET 48223 4269 A6
23900 RDFD 48223 4269 A6
Fulmer Ct
2100 AARB 48103 4405 D4
Fulmer St
1400 AARB 48103 4405 D3
Fulton Dr
9300 GOTp 48189 4187 A6
Fulton St
8700 DET 48209 4419 A4
Fulton Pines Ct
16700 LVNA 48152 4267 E2
16700 LVNA 48154 4267 E2
Funaro Cres
2000 Tcmh N9K 4424 A5
Furgason St
100 RVRG 48218 4418 E7
Furgerson St
3500 MVDL 48122 4417 E5
3500 MVDL 48122 4418 A5
Furnace St
- YPLT 48198 4492 A3

G

G St
10 DBHT 48125 4416 E6
Gable Av
500 YpTp 48198 4492 B2
Gable Dr
33800 LVNA 48152 4194 E7
Gable St
17100 DET 48212 4273 D1
17400 DET 48212 4201 D7
18000 DET 48234 4201 D7
30500 LVNA 48152 4195 C7
33300 LVNA 48152 4194 E7
Gabriel St
8900 RMLS 48174 4496 D5
11200 RMLS 48174 4580 D1
Gabrielle Av
5900 WasC 48103 4404 B6
Gage Av
22100 WynC 48138 4670 C4
Gage St
14200 TYLR 48180 4582 E3
Gahona Av
6500 ALPK 48101 4500 A2
Gail Ct
1400 YpTp 48198 4492 D7
4800 TNTN 48183 4669 B7
Gail Rd
2500 WIND N8W 4421 D4
Gainsboro Av
10 PTRG 48069 4199 E1
Gainsboro St
- PTRG 48069 4199 E1
2200 FRDL 48220 4200 A1
2300 FRDL 48220 4199 E1
2600 FRDL 48069 4199 E1
Gainsborough Dr
45700 CNTN 48187 4336 C5
Gainsborough Rd
18600 DET 48223 4270 A3
18800 DET 48223 4269 E2
Galaxie Av
- ROTp 48237 4199 A3
10500 ROTp 48220 4199 A3
Gale Blvd
10 MVDL 48122 4417 D7
Gale Rd
2200 SpTp 48105 4408 B3
2800 SpTp 48198 4408 B3
Gale St
- DET 48229 4418 D5
Galen Cir
500 AARB 48103 4489 A3
Gallagher St
9300 HMTK 48212 4273 C4
13400 DET 48212 4273 B1
17200 DET 48212 4201 B7
19100 DET 48234 4201 A4
Galleon Ct
14800 PyTp 48170 4264 A5
Galleon Dr
47400 PyTp 48170 4264 A5
Gallery Dr
6300 CNTN 48187 4336 C6
Gallery Ln
800 WasC 48103 4404 C7
Gallinger Dr
3000 PTFD 48103 4488 D4
Gallway Ct
10 AARB 48104 4490 C3
Galpin Dr
3500 SpTp 48198 4333 D7
3500 SpTp 48198 4408 D1
Galster St
4400 DET 48207 4346 A1
4600 DET 48207 4345 E1
Galway Ct
13100 GOTp 48178 4188 E2
Galway Dr
- NOVI 48374 4192 B4
43400 NOVI 48167 4192 C4
Gamewood Dr
10600 GOTp 48178 4188 B4
Gandy Ct
8000 WynC 48138 4670 D6
Gapam Ct
4500 WIND N9G 4504 C5
Gar St
6100 DET 48210 4344 A5
Garden Av
100 GDNC 48135 4414 E1
100 GDNC 48141 4414 E1
6800 GDNC 48135 4339 E5
7200 WTLD 48185 4339 E5
Garden Blvd
29000 FTRK 48134 4753 D4
Garden Cir
2000 AARB 48103 4405 D6
Garden Ct
100 WasC 48189 4259 B2
1100 WIND N8S 4347 C7
1100 WIND N8S 4422 C1
2000 YpTp 48198 4577 A1
37500 WTLD 48185 4338 B4
E Garden Ct
3600 WasC 48176 4572 B3
W Garden Ct
3800 WasC 48176 4572 A2
Garden Dr
3500 TNTN 48183 4669 B6
Garden Ln
21300 ROTp 48220 4199 C3
Garden St
5100 DET 48202 4345 C2
6300 DET 48204 4343 D3
11000 LVNA 48150 4339 E1
15500 LVNA 48154 4267 E3
Gardendale St
200 FRDL 48220 4199 D3
20100 DET 48221 4199 E4
Garden Homes Ct
2100 AARB 48103 4405 D4
Garden Homes Dr
2200 AARB 48103 4405 D4
Gardner Av
1200 AARB 48104 4489 C1
Gardner St
400 NHVL 48167 4192 E7
9700 SpTp 48198 4409 E7
20800 OKPK 48237 4198 D4
36400 LVNA 48152 4266 B2
Garfield
9500 RDFD 48239 4340 D1
15300 RDFD 48239 4268 D3
18200 RDFD 48240 4268 D1
19900 RDFD 48240 4196 D5
Garfield Av
300 LNPK 48146 4501 A4
1800 LNPK 48146 4500 D3
2200 LNPK 48101 4500 D3
14500 ALPK 48101 4500 B2
E Garfield Av
600 HZLP 48030 4200 D1
W Garfield Av
10 HZLP 48030 4200 C1
Garfield Ct
9100 RDFD 48239 4340 D2
Garfield Dr
8700 WasC 48189 4259 A1
Garfield Ln
49400 CNTN 48188 4410 E3
Garfield Rd
- NOVI 48374 4191 D3
21500 NOVI 48167 4191 D5
Garfield St
10 DET 48201 4345 B3
600 WYDT 48192 4501 C6
1400 DET 48207 4345 D2
1500 FRDL 48220 4200 A1
3400 DET 48207 4346 A1
3800 WYNE 48184 4414 C6
11500 RVVW 48192 4585 A6
Garland Av
14600 PyTp 48170 4265 B5
Garland St
200 YPLT 48198 4492 B4
1400 DET 48214 4347 A1
2500 DET 48214 4346 E1
2900 DET 48214 4274 E6
5800 DET 48213 4274 D4
Garling Dr
100 PLYM 48170 4265 B7
6400 DBHT 48127 4341 D5
Garner St
- RMLS 48174 4497 E4
24000 SFLD 48034 4196 E2
35400 RMLS 48174 4496 D4
Garnet Cir
500 WasC 48189 4186 D7
Garnet St
8200 BrTp 48179 4841 A4
12300 DET 48205 4274 E1
Garrick Av
1900 WRRN 48030 4200 E3
1900 WRRN 48091 4200 E3
2100 WRRN 48091 4201 A3
Garrison Ct
9300 GOTp 48178 4187 D1
Garrison Ln
15400 SOGT 48195 4584 B4
Garrison St
22900 DRBN 48124 4416 B3
Garson St
13000 WRRN 48089 4202 E2
Gartner St
7200 DET 48209 4419 A2
8300 DET 48209 4418 E3
Garvett St
9800 LVNA 48150 4340 A1
Garvey Cres
2700 WIND N8W 4421 D5
Garvin St
3800 DET 48212 4273 C2
Gary Av
100 LSal N9J 4502 D7
8100 WTLD 48185 4339 D3
Gary Ct
60500 LyTp 48178 4189 D5
Gary Dr
9800 RMLS 48174 4496 E6
Gary Ln
15600 LVNA 48154 4266 D3
19900 LVNA 48152 4194 D5
22800 STCS 48080 4205 A3
23000 STCS 48080 4204 E3
Gary St
8500 DRBN 48126 4343 C5
20500 DET 48203 4200 B4
26000 TYLR 48180 4498 D3
Gascony Av
21700 EPTE 48021 4203 E2
Gate 9
- DRBN 48120 4418 A3
Gatehouse
- WDHN 48183 4669 A3
Gatehouse Ct
43500 CNTN 48187 4336 E4
43500 CNTN 48187 4337 A4
Gatehouse Dr S
16400 WDHN 48183 4669 A3
Gates Av
700 YpTp 48198 4492 E5
Gates St
100 DET 48209 4418 E4
S Gates St
100 DET 48209 4418 E5
Gateshead St
4900 DET 48236 4276 B1
5600 DET 48224 4276 B1
Gateside Ct
1100 WIND N8S 4347 C6
Gateside Pl
8200 WIND N8S 4347 E7
Gateway Blvd
29300 FTRK 48134 4754 C4
Gateway Cir
17300 SFLD 48075 4198 A2
Gateway Dr
32300 RMLS 48174 4497 B1
Gateway Commerce Dr
29100 FTRK 48134 4754 C4
Gatewood Cir
4700 PTFD 48197 4491 A6
Gattegno St
1300 YpTp 48198 4492 D6
Gaukler St
19500 STCS 48080 4204 B2
Gault Dr
1000 YpTp 48198 4492 C6
Gauthier Dr
200 Tcmh N8N 4348 D6
200 Tcmh N8P 4348 D6
500 Tcmh N8N 4423 E1
500 Tcmh N8P 4423 E1
Gavel St
12700 DET 48227 4271 A5
Gay St
38700 LVNA 48154 4265 E4
Gaylord
15300 RDFD 48239 4268 B3
17100 RDFD 48240 4268 B1
20300 RDFD 48240 4196 B5
Gaylord Av
400 LSal N9J 4502 E5
Gaylord St
2900 DET 48212 4273 A1
29600 LVNA 48154 4267 D6
G DiMaso MD Dr
- DET 48236 4276 B1
- GSPW 48236 4276 B1
Geddes Av
1100 AARB 48104 4406 D6
2600 AARB 48104 4407 A7
Geddes Hts
10 AARB 48104 4406 D6
Geddes Rd
- SpTp 48105 4408 D7
3100 AARB 48104 4407 C6
3100 AARB 48105 4407 C6
3200 AATp 48104 4407 C6
3200 AATp 48105 4407 C6
4700 AATp 48105 4408 A6
5800 SpTp 48105 4408 D7
6800 SpTp 48198 4409 C7
9700 SpTp 48198 4410 C6
44600 CNTN 48188 4411 D6
48400 CNTN 48188 4410 C6
Geimer St
2200 HMTK 48212 4273 C5
Geitzen St
- DET 48234 4202 C7
11600 DET 48205 4202 C7
Gem Av
2500 WIND N8W 4422 A4
Gemstone Ct
2200 PTFD 48103 4488 D4
General Ct
9100 PyTp 48170 4337 B3
General Dr
11300 PyTp 48170 4337 B1
General Motors Blvd
2500 DET 48211 4273 D7
Genesis Ct
21900 WDHN 48183 4668 C4
Genesis Dr
22000 WDHN 48183 4668 C4
Genessee St
100 RVRG 48218 4418 E7
100 RVRG 48218 4419 A7
200 RVRG 48218 4501 E1
9200 DET 48206 4272 B7
9200 DET 48206 4344 B1
32100 WTLD 48186 4414 B4
Geneva Ct
10 DRBN 48124 4416 A4
Geneva Rd
1400 AARB 48103 4488 C1
Geneva St
200 HDPK 48203 4272 A2
300 DET 48203 4272 A2
1200 DRBN 48124 4416 A3
24000 OKPK 48237 4199 A1
26000 HnTp 48164 4751 D1
Genevieve
200 WIND N8S 4347 E5
Genoa Ct
14300 PyTp 48170 4264 A5
Genoa St
7200 DET 48213 4274 A5
Genron Ct
35300 RMLS 48174 4580 D5
Genson Dr
7800 WasC 48167 4261 E3
Gentner St
20700 WRRN 48089 4203 A3
Gentz Rd
20200 HnTp 48111 4665 B2
20200 HnTp 48164 4665 B2
Geoffrey Ct
600 INKR 48141 4414 D3
23400 OKPK 48237 4198 E2
George Av
200 WIND N8Y 4346 E7
800 YpTp 48198 4492 C4
1200 WIND N8Y 4421 E1
1500 WIND N8Y 4422 A1
1800 WIND N8W 4422 A1
2300 YpTp 48198 4493 A7
E George Av
900 HZLP 48030 4200 C4
W George Av
10 HZLP 48030 4200 C4
George St
100 TNTN 48183 4670 A3
200 Amhg N9V 4757 C3
300 TNTN 48183 4669 E3
16000 HDPK 48203 4272 B2
23800 DBHT 48127 4341 A6
25000 DBHT 48127 4340 D6
Georgeland St
6300 DET 48204 4343 C1
Georgetown Blvd
2000 AARB 48105 4407 B2
Georgetown Ct
- DRBN 48126 4418 D1
Georgetown Rd
21300 WDHN 48183 4669 A3
Georgetown St
400 CNTN 48188 4412 D2
George Washington Dr
15500 SFLD 48075 4198 C1
18600 SFLD 48075 4197 D2
Georgia
700 WynC 48111 4662 D3
Georgia Av
14500 RVVW 48192 4584 C6
Georgia St
- BNTN 48192 4583 C6
4000 DET 48211 4273 D5
5800 RMLS 48174 4498 A1
6800 DET 48211 4274 A4
7200 DET 48213 4274 A4
8800 LVNA 48150 4339 A3
Georgiana Av
12300 WRRN 48089 4202 D4
Georgina Dr
1000 YpTp 48198 4492 C6
Geraedts Dr
- WIND N9G 4504 A3
Gerald Av
19100 NvlT 48167 4192 E7
19100 NvlT 48167 4193 A7
19300 NHVL 48167 4192 E7
Gerald Ct
45100 CNTN 48188 4411 D3
Gerald St
10 HDPK 48203 4272 D3
13300 GBTR 48173 4755 D5
33100 WYNE 48184 4414 A7
Geraldine Blvd
31000 WTLD 48185 4339 C3
Geraldine Cres
200 WIND N9E 4421 B6
200 WIND N9E 4504 C1
Geraldine St
9800 YpTp 48197 4577 A3
Geranium Dr
17100 BwTp 48173 4755 A6
Geri Dr
43400 CNTN 48187 4412 A1
Gerisch St
- DET 48209 4418 E4
German St
22300 RKWD 48173 4754 C7
Geronimo St
6400 WTLD 48185 4338 D5
Gertrude Ct
29100 INKR 48141 4414 E3
Gertrude St
2600 DRBN 48124 4416 D5
3900 DBHT 48124 4416 D6
3900 DBHT 48125 4416 D6
5600 DBHT 48125 4499 D1
33500 WYNE 48184 4414 A7
Gettysburg Rd
3400 AARB 48105 4407 C1
Ghesquiere Ct
20000 GSPW 48236 4204 D6
Gibb St
400 Amhg N9V 4757 D3
Gibraltar Rd
- BwTp 48134 4754 C4
- FTRK 48134 4754 C4
14700 GBTR 48173 4755 A4
19800 GBTR 48183 4755 A4
19900 BwTp 48173 4754 C4
19900 BwTp 48173 4755 A4
19900 BwTp 48183 4754 C4
19900 BwTp 48183 4755 A4
25000 FTRK 48134 4753 E4
N Gibraltar Rd
27000 GBTR 48173 4755 D3
S Gibraltar Rd
29200 GBTR 48173 4755 C5
Gibson Av
23200 WRRN 48089 4202 C1
Gibson Dr
24000 WRRN 48089 4202 C1
Gibson St
- DET 48210 4345 A5
200 SLYN 48178 4189 A2
3500 DET 48201 4345 A5
Giese St
7500 DET 48234 4274 A1
Gifford Ct
4800 WasC 48103 4329 E3
Giftos Dr
- DET 48236 4276 C1
Gignac Cres
200 LSal N9J 4502 D6
Gilbar St
22800 NOVI 48375 4193 B3
Gilbert Av
400 LSal N9J 4502 E5
Gilbert Ct
1500 AARB 48105 4406 D4
Gilbert St
5400 DET 48210 4344 A5
5700 DET 48210 4343 E5
40100 PyTp 48170 4337 C1
Gilbo St
11300 DET 48234 4274 B2
Gilchrist St
15000 DET 48227 4270 B3
16100 DET 48235 4270 B2
18200 DET 48235 4198 B5
36600 WTLD 48186 4413 B5
Gildersleeve St
13000 SRKW 48179 4754 B7
13000 SRKW 48179 4840 A1
Giles Blvd E
10 WIND N8X 4421 A3
10 WIND N9A 4421 A3
Giles Blvd W
900 WIND N8X 4420 D3
900 WIND N9A 4420 D3
Gill Av
500 YpTp 48198 4492 E5
Gill Rd
18200 LVNA 48152 4266 D1
18500 LVNA 48152 4194 D7
22900 FMTN 48335 4194 D1
22900 FNHL 48335 4194 D3
Gillespie Ct
12600 DET 48213 4275 B5
Gillman St
9000 LVNA 48150 4340 A2
18200 LVNA 48152 4268 A1
20200 LVNA 48152 4196 A5
Gilman Av
100 GDNC 48135 4415 A1
100 GDNC 48141 4415 A1
1500 GDNC 48135 4340 A7
Gilman St
8400 WTLD 48185 4340 A3
Gilmore St
6000 VNBN 48111 4493 E2
Gilroy St
1900 LSal N9J 4503 C7
12000 DET 48229 4418 C6
Ginger St
10 WTLD 48186 4414 D7
10 WTLD 48186 4497 D1
Giovanna Dr
- RKWD 48173 4754 E7
- RKWD 48173 4755 A7
Girard St
100 Amhg N9V 4671 C7
100 Amhg N9V 4757 C1
Girardin St
- DET 48211 4273 E4
13300 DET 48212 4273 E1
19100 DET 48234 4201 E6
Girardot St
2100 WIND N9B 4420 C4
2800 WIND N9C 4420 B4
Giselle Cres
1300 WIND N8W 4421 E7
Gita Ct
28200 LVNA 48154 4268 A5
Gita St
28100 LVNA 48154 4268 A6
28500 LVNA 48154 4267 E6
Gitre St
12500 DET 48205 4202 E7

STREET Block City ZIP Map# Grid

N Glacier
49400 NvlT 48167 4263 D3
S Glacier
- NvlT 48167 4263 D3
Glacier Hills Cir
4000 AARB 48105 4407 D5
Glacier Hills Dr N
- AARB 48105 4407 D4
Glacier Hills Dr S
4000 AARB 48105 4407 D5
Glacier Lake Ct
3800 WasC 48130 4329 D5
Glacier Pointe Dr
7100 YpTp 48197 4575 E6
7100 YpTp 48197 4576 A6
Glade Rd
41400 CNTN 48187 4412 B1
Gladhill Ln
23100 STCS 48080 4204 E3
Gladstone Av
200 WIND N9A 4346 B7
600 WIND N9A 4421 B1
1200 WIND N8X 4421 B1
1600 WIND N8W 4421 C3
2000 AARB 48104 4489 E3
2800 PTFD 48104 4489 E3
Gladstone Rd
47800 CNTN 48188 4411 A3
Gladstone St
10 DET 48202 4272 E7
1600 DET 48206 4272 C7
2600 DET 48206 4344 B1
4000 DET 48204 4344 B1
Gladwin Ct
2900 WYNE 48184 4414 B5
17000 BNTN 48174 4582 D5
Gladwin Dr
17100 BNTN 48174 4582 C6
42100 NOVI 48167 4193 A5
Gladwin St
1100 LSal N9J 4502 E4
20400 TYLR 48180 4583 D4
Gladys Av
29800 WTLD 48185 4339 C4
Glady's Blvd
5800 LSal N9J 4503 B4
Gladys St
- DET 48210 4343 E5
10 BrTp 48134 4753 C5
6300 DET 48210 4344 A5
Glander Av
15500 EPTE 48021 4203 C3
Glaser Rd
32000 BwTp 48173 4755 B7
Glasgow Ct
13000 PyTp 48170 4264 A7
Glastonbury Av
11600 DET 48228 4270 A7
15500 DET 48223 4270 A3
15900 DET 48219 4270 A3
Glastonbury Dr
18100 LVNA 48152 4266 A1
46900 CNTN 48188 4411 B4
Glastonbury Rd
1400 AARB 48103 4488 E1
17100 DET 48219 4270 A2
18200 DET 48219 4198 A7
Glastonbury St
6200 WTLD 48185 4339 A6
Glazier Wy
2300 AARB 48105 4407 A5
Gleaner Hall Ct
1500 AATp 48105 4331 D6
Gleaner Hall Rd
3900 AATp 48105 4331 D5
Gleason St
11900 DET 48229 4501 B1
Glen Av
100 AARB 48104 4406 C5
33600 WTLD 48186 4413 E3
33600 WTLD 48186 4414 A3
S Glen Blvd
19400 BwTp 48183 4755 A2
Glen Ct
300 AARB 48104 4406 C5
22300 STCS 48080 4204 D1
22600 FNHL 48335 4194 D3
Glen Ln
300 SALN 48176 4657 E2
1500 TNTN 48183 4669 B3
1500 TNTN 48192 4669 B3
Glen St
32600 WTLD 48186 4414 B3
34400 WTLD 48186 4413 C3
Glen Arbor Ln
500 GSPW 48236 4204 D5
Glen Arbor St
41800 CNTN 48188 4412 B5
Glenbridge Ct
2700 AARB 48104 4489 D3
Glenbrook Ct
400 SALN 48176 4657 D1
1900 WIND N8W 4421 E5
2600 AARB 48103 4489 A3
Glenco St
20000 DET 48219 4269 D1
Glencoe Hills Dr
2100 PTFD 48105 4490 E2
2100 PTFD 48197 4490 E2
Glencove Ct
42300 CNTN 48188 4412 B3
Glen Creek Ct
5700 PTFD 48197 4574 B2
Glencreek Ct
23400 FNHL 48336 4195 E2
Glen Creek Dr
5700 PTFD 48197 4574 B2
Glencreek Dr
23300 FNHL 48336 4195 E2
23400 FNHL 48336 4196 A1
Glencroft Ln
23400 FNHL 48336 4195 E2
Glenda St
24200 NOVI 48375 4192 C1
Glendale
10200 GOTp 48189 4187 B5
26500 RDFD 48239 4268 B6
Glendale Av
1500 WIND N8T 4422 C1
31400 LVNA 48150 4267 B7
Glendale Cir
500 AARB 48103 4405 E6
500 WasC 48103 4405 E6
Glendale Dr
200 AARB 48103 4405 E6
8300 SpTp 48198 4492 C1
Glendale St
- RDFD 48223 4269 A6
- RDFD 48239 4269 A6
10 HDPK 48203 4272 C4
1500 DET 48238 4272 B5
3700 DET 48238 4271 E6
16600 DET 48227 4270 B6
19000 DET 48223 4269 E6
32000 LVNA 48150 4267 A7
35000 LVNA 48150 4266 D7
Glendaloch Cir
1300 AARB 48104 4490 A1
Glendaloch Rd
2200 AARB 48104 4490 A1
Gleneagle Ln
- CNTN 48188 4412 D4
Glen Eagles Ct
4100 WasC 48103 4329 E3
Gleneagles Ct
10 DRBN 48120 4417 C2
Glen Eagles Dr
19100 LVNA 48152 4194 B7
Glen Eden Ct
4100 WasC 48103 4329 E3
Gleneyrie Dr
24000 SFLD 48034 4196 B1
Glenfield St
3700 WIND N9C 4420 B6
11000 DET 48213 4274 D2
12700 DET 48213 4275 A1
Glengarry Av
100 WIND N9A 4420 C1
400 WIND N9A 4421 A1
Glengarry Blvd
1300 CNTN 48188 4411 D4
Glengarry Dr
18100 LVNA 48152 4266 A1
18500 LVNA 48152 4194 A7
Glengarry Rd
8300 WynC 48138 4670 C4
44400 CNTN 48188 4411 D3
Glengarry Woods Ct
1500 CNTN 48188 4411 E4
Glengary Ct
3800 WasC 48105 4332 C1
10700 GOTp 48189 4187 B4
Glengary Ln
12900 PyTp 48170 4264 D7
Glengary St
8200 DBHT 48127 4340 D3
8500 DBHT 48239 4340 D3
Glengrove Av
1400 YpTp 48198 4493 A7
E Glen Haven Cir
20800 NOVI 48167 4193 B5
21300 NOVI 48375 4193 B4
W Glen Haven Cir
20800 NOVI 48167 4193 B5
21000 NOVI 48375 4193 B5
Glenhill Dr
900 NHVL 48167 4192 B5
Glenhurst
15000 SOGT 48195 4500 B7
Glenhurst Ct
47300 CNTN 48187 4336 B6
Glenhurst Dr
46900 CNTN 48187 4336 B6
Glenhurst St
18600 DET 48219 4197 A7
Glenis Av
17400 BNTN 48174 4582 C6
Glenis St
4600 DBHT 48125 4415 C7
5800 TYLR 48180 4498 C1
Glenita St
23500 WRRN 48091 4201 A1
Glen Leven Rd
1100 AARB 48103 4489 A2
1400 AARB 48103 4488 E2
Glen Lodge Rd
20700 ROTp 48220 4199 B3
Glenmeadow Ct
38100 WYNE 48184 4413 A5
Glen Meadows Dr
700 SLYN 48178 4189 C1
Glenmoor Dr
200 WasC 48189 4259 A4
16900 NvlT 48167 4263 D3
Glenmoor Hts
22500 FNHL 48336 4195 D2
Glenmore
17300 RDFD 48240 4268 D1
20100 RDFD 48240 4196 C5
Glenmore Ct
12600 PyTp 48170 4264 A7
Glenmore Dr
500 WasC 48103 4404 C6
Glenn Ct
1100 WYDT 48192 4585 A1
Glen Oak Ct
5600 WasC 48176 4572 C2
Glen Oaks Dr
- YpTp 48197 4576 A6
Glen Orchard Dr
24400 FNHL 48336 4195 A1
Glenore Av
100 Tcmh N8N 4424 C1
Glen Ridge Ct
23900 NOVI 48375 4193 C1
Glenshire Rd
1600 CNTN 48188 4412 B4
Glenside St
24800 SFLD 48034 4196 D1
Glenulline Dr
800 CNTN 48187 4412 C1
Glen Valley Dr
33000 FNHL 48336 4195 A1
33100 FNHL 48335 4194 E1
33100 FNHL 48336 4194 E1
Glenview Ct
12500 PyTp 48170 4264 C7
33700 FMTN 48335 4194 E1
39600 NvlT 48167 4265 C2
Glen View Dr
- AATp 48105 4408 A2
Glenview Dr
11900 PyTp 48170 4336 C1
12500 PyTp 48170 4264 B7
33700 FMTN 48335 4194 E1
Glen View Ln
31300 FTRK 48173 4754 A6
Glenwild Dr
21600 FNHL 48167 4194 A4
Glenwood
28700 HnTp 48134 4752 E3
Glenwood Av
100 YpTp 48198 4492 D5
2800 WIND N9E 4503 E1
3100 WIND N9E 4504 A1
27400 INKR 48141 4415 B3
Glenwood Ct
2400 WIND N9E 4420 E7
19500 GBTR 48173 4755 A4
Glenwood Ln
9000 WasC 48167 4262 D1
21900 WDHN 48183 4668 C4
Glenwood Rd
1600 AARB 48104 4490 B2
2200 TNTN 48183 4669 D3
32900 WTLD 48186 4414 A5
32900 WYNE 48184 4414 A5
32900 WYNE 48186 4414 A5
34000 WTLD 48186 4413 D5
34000 WYNE 48184 4413 D5
35000 WTLD 48184 4413 C5
38900 WTLD 48186 4412 E5
38900 WYNE 48184 4412 E5
Glenwood St
300 AARB 48103 4405 C5
300 WasC 48103 4405 C5
13600 DET 48205 4202 E6
13800 DET 48205 4203 A6
27700 INKR 48141 4415 A3
28400 INKR 48141 4414 E3
E Glenwood St
10 ECRS 48229 4501 E2
W Glenwood St
10 ECRS 48229 4501 D2
Glicka Ct
1100 WIND N8X 4421 D5
Glidden Av
800 WIND N8S 4347 B7
1100 WIND N8S 4422 D1
Glinnan St
800 DET 48209 4419 A3
Globe Av
22700 WRRN 48089 4202 C2
Globe St
6300 DET 48238 4271 D3
11700 LVNA 48150 4266 B7
11700 LVNA 48150 4338 B1
N Globe St
2000 WTLD 48185 4338 B7
S Globe St
1800 WTLD 48186 4413 B4
Gloccamorra Dr
10300 WynC 48138 4756 A4
Gloria Av
1400 WTLD 48186 4414 B3
Gloria Dr
23400 BNTN 48183 4668 B6
41900 CNTN 48187 4412 B1
Gloria St
3000 WYNE 48184 4414 B5
6400 RMLS 48174 4497 C2
Gloryland Wy
52900 LyTp 48178 4190 E2
Gloucester Ct
3000 WasC 48167 4190 C6
Gloucester Dr
6100 CNTN 48187 4336 E6
19100 DET 48203 4200 A6
Gloucester St
1500 PLYM 48170 4264 D7
39200 WTLD 48186 4412 E3
Gloucester Wy
2600 AARB 48104 4490 B3
Glover St
600 DET 48214 4347 B1
17600 DRBN 48101 4417 B5
18300 DRBN 48124 4417 A4
33900 WYNE 48184 4497 A1
35000 WYNE 48184 4496 D1
Glyme Dr
41400 NOVI 48375 4193 B3
Glynn Ct
10 DET 48202 4272 D6
1400 DET 48206 4272 D6
GN Booth Dr
4600 WIND N9C 4419 E7
Goat Fell
3300 PTFD 48108 4490 C5
Goddard Ct
11000 TYLR 48180 4498 E7
Goddard Rd
10 WYDT 48192 4501 B7
700 LNPK 48146 4501 B7
700 LNPK 48192 4501 B7
700 WYDT 48146 4501 B7
1000 LNPK 48146 4500 C7
1000 WYDT 48146 4500 C7
1000 WYDT 48192 4500 C7
1200 LNPK 48192 4500 C7
14500 ALPK 48146 4500 C7
14500 SOGT 48101 4500 C7
14500 SOGT 48146 4500 C7
15000 ALPK 48101 4500 A6
15000 ALPK 48195 4500 A6
15000 SOGT 48195 4500 A6
19000 ALPK 48101 4499 D6
19000 ALPK 48195 4499 D6
19000 SOGT 48195 4499 D6
20000 TYLR 48180 4499 D6
24100 TYLR 48180 4498 D7
26500 TYLR 48174 4498 A7
27400 RMLS 48174 4498 B7
28400 RMLS 48174 4497 E7
33800 RMLS 48174 4496 C7
33800 RMLS 48242 4496 C7
37000 RMLS 48174 4580 B1
Goddard St
12200 DET 48212 4273 A2
17400 DET 48212 4201 A7
19100 DET 48234 4201 A5
Goddard Rd Ext
- RMLS 48174 4497 E5
- RMLS 48242 4497 E5
Goddell St
10 WYDT 48192 4501 C7
Godfrey St
300 SLYN 48178 4189 B2
Goethe Av
20700 GSPW 48236 4204 D4
21400 STCS 48080 4204 D4
Goethe St
- GSPT 48230 4276 C4
- GSPT 48236 4276 C4
7200 DET 48214 4346 C2
10400 DET 48214 4274 E7
14800 DET 48214 4275 D6
15000 GPPK 48230 4275 D6
Goff St
27500 LVNA 48152 4196 A7
Gohl Rd
3500 LNPK 48146 4501 A5
Gold Arbor Rd
9500 PyTp 48170 4337 C1
Gold Arbor St
3400 CNTN 48188 4412 B6
Golden Av
1400 AARB 48104 4489 C1
Golden Blvd
35400 RMLS 48174 4496 D2
Golden Ln
1500 SpTp 48198 4492 B1
Golden Gate E
10 DET 48203 4200 D7
Golden Gate W
10 DET 48203 4200 C7
Golden Oak Ln
5400 WasC 48103 4404 C6
Goldenridge St
22000 TYLR 48180 4499 C7
Goldenwood Dr
4200 WIND N9G 4504 E4
Goldfinch Ct
9800 WasC 48176 4659 A3
Goldfinch Ln
300 PTFD 48197 4574 D2
Goldner St
3200 DET 48210 4344 C6
Gold Smith St
1200 PLYM 48170 4264 E6
Goldsmith St
6700 DET 48209 4419 B2
20700 FNHL 48335 4194 B4
Golfcourse Cres
4300 WIND N9G 4504 D4
Golfcrest Ct
10 DRBN 48124 4416 C1
Golfcrest Dr
100 DRBN 48124 4416 C1
Golf Lake St
- TYLR 48180 4582 E2
Golf Pointe Cir
23200 WynC 48138 4670 B5
Golf Pointe St
- TYLR 48180 4582 D2
Golfside Dr
2000 PTFD 48197 4491 A2
2000 YpTp 48197 4491 A2
2500 PTFD 48108 4491 A2
2500 YpTp 48108 4491 A2
Golfside Rd
2600 PTFD 48108 4491 A4
2600 YpTp 48108 4491 A4
2600 YpTp 48197 4491 A4
3000 PTFD 48197 4491 A4
Golfview Av
10 AARB 48103 4489 B3
10 WasC 48103 4489 B3
Golf View Dr
- NvlT 48167 4193 D6
Golfview Dr
- Amhg N9V 4671 C4
1000 DRBN 48124 4416 C1
1000 DRBN 48128 4416 C1
1100 DRBN 48128 4341 C7
3000 WasC 48176 4572 C3
5600 DBHT 48127 4341 C6
5600 DBHT 48128 4341 C6
6400 GDNC 48135 4339 C6
Golfview Dr
15000 LVNA 48154 4266 C4
15600 RVVW 48192 4584 B7
22700 SFLD 48034 4197 A4
23200 WynC 48138 4670 B5
Golfview Dr E
15600 RVVW 48192 4584 A6
Golfview Dr N
15700 RVVW 48192 4584 A6
Golfview Dr W
15800 RVVW 48192 4584 A7
Golfview Ln
- WTLD 48186 4414 D4
Golfview St
- LVNA 48150 4266 C5
16100 LVNA 48154 4266 C2
17300 LVNA 48152 4266 C1
18500 LVNA 48152 4194 C7
26600 DBHT 48127 4340 B4
Golfview Dr Blvd
15700 RVVW 48192 4584 A7
Golfview Dr Ct
15600 RVVW 48192 4584 A6
Golfview Dr Ln
15800 RVVW 48192 4584 A7
Golfwood Cres
800 LSal N9J 4502 E6
900 LSal N9J 4503 A6
Golfwood Dr
- Amhg N9V 4671 C5
Gomberg Ct
8800 WasC 48160 4659 D2
Gonia
- BwTp 48173 4841 B3
Goodell St
100 RVRG 48218 4419 A7
100 RVRG 48218 4502 A1
200 RVRG 48218 4501 E1
E Goodell St
10 ECRS 48229 4501 D4
W Goodell St
10 ECRS 48229 4501 D4
Goodrich St
2300 FRDL 48220 4200 A1
Goodson St
2200 HMTK 48212 4273 C5
Goodwin St
8900 DET 48211 4273 A5
Gordon Av
200 Tcmh N8N 4424 C1
Gordon Dr
300 PTFD 48108 4573 D2
Gordon St
- CNTN 48187 4412 A1
200 YPLT 48198 4492 B3
10100 DET 48214 4274 D6
43900 CNTN 48187 4411 E1
Gore
17100 DET 48219 4269 B1
Gore St
10 Amhg N9V 4757 B3
Gorget Dr
13200 GOTp 48178 4188 D4
Gorman St
900 LNPK 48146 4501 A2
1700 CNTN 48187 4336 C7
1700 CNTN 48187 4411 C1
Gorno Ct
2100 TNTN 48183 4669 D3
Gorno Dr
2400 TNTN 48183 4669 D4
Gorno St
2200 TNTN 48183 4669 D3
Gorsuch Av
28100 RMLS 48174 4498 A5
Goss Rd
4200 AATp 48105 4407 D4
Gossett Dr
31500 RKWD 48173 4754 D6
Gotfredson Rd
2000 SpTp 48198 4410 A6
3500 SpTp 48198 4335 A5
3800 SpTp 48170 4335 A5
5000 WasC 48170 4335 A3
6000 WasC 48170 4263 A7
Gott St
500 AARB 48103 4406 A4
Gotts Ct
9000 AGST 48191 4662 A2
Gouchnour St
700 YpTp 48197 4491 C6
Gough St
3700 MVDL 48122 4417 D6
Gouin St
11900 Tcmh N8N 4423 E4
12200 Tcmh N8N 4424 A3
12300 Tcmh N9K 4424 A3
Goulburn St
12200 DET 48205 4274 E1
12600 DET 48205 4202 D7
Gould St
- DET 48209 4419 B4
5700 LSal N9H 4503 E3
8700 DRBN 48126 4343 C4
15000 DRBN 48126 4342 D4
Goulson Av
1900 WRRN 48091 4201 A2
2100 WRRN 48091 4201 A2
E Goulson Av
1100 HZLP 48030 4200 E2
1700 HZLP 48091 4200 E2
W Goulson Av
200 HZLP 48030 4200 B2
Governor Bradford Rd
44400 PyTp 48170 4336 D1
Govin St
900 DET 48209 4419 A3
Goyeau St
10 WIND N9A 4420 E2
1000 WIND N9A 4421 A2
Goyeau St
1200 WIND N8X 4421 A3
Grabar Sq
23100 WRRN 48089 4203 A1
Grace Av
3800 WYNE 48184 4412 E6
Grace Ct
1000 NHVL 48167 4192 D4
Grace Rd
100 Tcmh N8N 4349 B7
300 Tcmh N8N 4424 B1
Grace St
700 NHVL 48167 4192 D5
1900 AARB 48103 4405 E5
2500 MVDL 48122 4417 E7
2500 MVDL 48122 4418 A7
8900 DET 48213 4274 C4
23900 FMTN 48335 4194 E1
N Grace St
8100 WTLD 48185 4337 E4
Graceland Cir
25400 DBHT 48125 4415 D3
Graefield Cir
12900 PyTp 48170 4263 C7
Graefield Dr
500 SLYN 48178 4189 C3
Grafton Rd
13200 MonC 48117 4751 E7
Graham Ct
2200 CNTN 48188 4412 B5
Graham Ln
- NOVI 48374 4192 A1
Graham Rd
- DET 48223 4269 A4
23900 RDFD 48223 4269 A4
24000 RDFD 48239 4268 E4
Graham St
8700 DRBN 48126 4343 C5
9400 DET 48209 4418 E5
Gralake Av
100 AARB 48103 4405 C6
Granada Av
1400 AARB 48103 4488 E1
Granada St E
10 WIND N9E 4504 C2
Granada St W
100 WIND N9E 4504 C2
Granby Cres
2900 WIND N8T 4422 C4
Granby Ln
- AGST 48191 4577 C7
Grand E
10 HDPK 48203 4272 E3
Grand W
10 HDPK 48203 4272 C3
Grand Blvd
4800 WIND N8T 4422 C4
E Grand Blvd
- DET 48207 4346 D4
400 YpTp 48198 4492 D3
W Grand Blvd
100 WIND N9E 4421 B7
800 WIND N9E 4504 A1
2000 WIND N9E 4503 E1
Grand Blvd E
10 DET 48214 4346 D4
700 DET 48207 4346 C2
1000 DET 48207 4274 A7
1000 DET 48214 4274 A7
1100 DET 48211 4274 A7
1100 DET 48213 4274 A7
1900 DET 48211 4273 B7
2800 DET 48202 4273 B7
2900 DET 48202 4345 B1
Grand Blvd W
10 DET 48216 4419 E1
1100 DET 48216 4344 C5
2000 DET 48204 4344 B3
2000 DET 48206 4344 B3
2600 DET 48202 4344 D2
2600 DET 48210 4344 D2
2800 DET 48202 4345 A1
Grand Ct
600 SLYN 48178 4189 C1
W Grand Ct
1800 WIND N9E 4503 E1
1800 WIND N9E 4504 A1
Grand St W
1500 DET 48238 4272 A4
3200 DET 48238 4271 E5
Grande Dr
28100 RMLS 48174 4582 B5
Grand Haven St
12000 HMTK 48212 4273 A3
Grand Lake St
21500 STCS 48080 4204 C1
Grand Marais Rd E
500 WIND N8X 4421 C6
2300 WIND N8W 4421 E5
2300 WIND N8W 4422 A5
Grand Marais Rd W
400 WIND N9E 4421 B7
1100 WIND N9E 4504 A1
1900 WIND N9E 4503 E2
Grand Marais St
700 GPPK 48230 4276 B7
Grandmont Av
8800 DET 48228 4342 B1
9500 DET 48227 4342 B1
14800 DET 48227 4270 B4
Grandmont St
1000 INKR 48141 4415 C3
Grandon Av
27400 LVNA 48150 4340 A2
Grandon Ct
27400 LVNA 48150 4340 B2
Grandon St
28600 LVNA 48150 4339 E2
28600 LVNA 48150 4340 A2
34500 LVNA 48150 4338 D2
Grandon St
38400 LVNA 48150 4337 E3
Grand River Av
10 DET 48226 4345 D6
1900 DET 48201 4345 C5
3100 DET 48216 4345 C5
3300 DET 48210 4345 C5
4200 DET 48210 4344 C3
7300 DET 48204 4344 C3
7300 DET 48206 4344 C3
9100 DET 48204 4343 E1
10500 DET 48204 4271 A6
12500 DET 48227 4271 A6
12500 DET 48238 4271 A6
13600 DET 48227 4270 C4
18200 DET 48223 4270 A2
19000 DET 48223 4269 D2
19800 DET 48219 4269 D2
23500 DET 48219 4197 A7
23800 DET 48219 4196 C6
24700 RDFD 48219 4196 C6
25000 RDFD 48240 4196 C6
27300 LVNA 48152 4196 C6
27300 RDFD 48152 4196 C6
27500 FNHL 48152 4196 C6
27700 FNHL 48336 4196 C6
30200 FNHL 48336 4195 C3
30700 FMTN 48336 4195 A2
33200 FMTN 48335 4194 D1
33200 FMTN 48336 4194 D1
34200 FNHL 48335 4194 D1
38100 FNHL 48335 4193 D1
38800 FNHL 48375 4193 D1
39400 NOVI 48375 4193 D1
Grand River Av SR-5
13500 DET 48227 4271 A6
13600 DET 48227 4270 C4
18200 DET 48223 4270 C4
19000 DET 48223 4269 D2
19800 DET 48219 4269 D2
23500 DET 48219 4197 A7
23800 DET 48219 4196 C6
24700 RDFD 48219 4196 C6
25000 RDFD 48240 4196 C6
27300 LVNA 48152 4196 C6
27300 RDFD 48152 4196 C6
27500 FNHL 48152 4196 C6
27700 FNHL 48336 4196 C6
28200 FNHL 48336 4195 D4
E Grand River Av
10 DET 48226 4345 D6
Grand Traverse St
31400 WTLD 48186 4414 B4
33900 WTLD 48186 4413 E5
Grand Valley Dr
- FNHL 48336 4195 D4
Grandview Av
30400 WTLD 48186 4414 C3
Grandview Ct
10 DRBN 48126 4342 B7
Grandview Dr
100 AARB 48103 4405 E6
4700 PTFD 48197 4491 A4
4900 YpTp 48197 4491 A4
13200 GBTR 48173 4755 D4
Grandview St
- DET 48219 4196 E6
700 NHVL 48167 4192 C7
2900 WIND N8T 4422 D4
28500 INKR 48141 4415 A3
29400 INKR 48141 4414 D3
31400 WTLD 48186 4414 B3
Grandville Av
5800 DET 48228 4341 E5
13500 DET 48223 4269 E4
17300 DET 48219 4269 E1
20200 DET 48219 4197 E5
Grandy St
3400 DET 48207 4346 A3
3500 DET 48207 4345 E3
5000 DET 48211 4345 D1
5700 DET 48211 4273 D7
E Granet Av
900 HZLP 48030 4200 E3
W Granet Av
10 HZLP 48030 4200 C3
Grange Rd
- RVVW 48192 4669 B1
1500 TNTN 48183 4669 B3
1500 TNTN 48192 4669 B3
10500 GOTp 48189 4187 C5
17000 RVVW 48192 4584 B6
17000 RVVW 48195 4584 B6
Granger Av
700 AARB 48104 4489 D1
Granger St
7700 DET 48213 4274 B6
Granite Ct
19300 NvlT 48167 4193 B7
Grant Av
10 Amhg N9V 4757 B1
100 Tcmh N8N 4349 C7
100 Tcmh N8N 4424 C1
1200 LNPK 48146 4501 B3
Grant Dr
2300 PTFD 48108 4490 D3
13900 PyTp 48170 4263 D6
Grant St
- ROTp 48220 4199 C4
900 YPLT 48197 4491 D4
2400 DET 48212 4273 A2
11500 RVVW 48192 4585 A6
22100 RKWD 48173 4754 C7
31400 WYNE 48184 4414 C7
34700 RMLS 48174 4580 C1
34700 RMLS 48242 4580 C1
Grantham Av
900 WIND N9G 4504 E5
Grantland St
27400 LVNA 48150 4268 A7

INDEX 24

Grantland St — Detroit & Wayne County Street Index — Hamilton Rd

STREET Block City ZIP Map# Grid

Grantland St
37400 LVNA 48150 4266 A7
Granville Cres
1300 WIND N9C 4420 B5
Granzon St
- OKPK 48237 4198 E3
Grape Av
10 WasC 48103 4488 B4
Grasmere Rd
46700 NHVL 48167 4192 B5
Grass Rd
7000 WasC 48176 4571 A7
7600 WasC 48176 4656 A1
Grassland Dr
17600 BNTN 48192 4583 C6
Grassland St
600 YPLT 48197 4491 D6
Gratiot Av
10 DET 48226 4345 D6
1100 DET 48207 4345 E5
2600 DET 48207 4346 A2
7000 DET 48207 4274 B7
7200 DET 48213 4274 B7
7200 DET 48214 4274 B7
11900 DET 48205 4274 E1
13100 DET 48205 4202 E7
13700 DET 48205 4203 A6
15400 EPTE 48205 4203 B3
20700 EPTE 48021 4203 B3
Gratiot Av SR-3
200 DET 48226 4345 E5
1100 DET 48207 4345 E5
2600 DET 48207 4346 A2
7000 DET 48207 4274 B7
7200 DET 48213 4274 B7
7200 DET 48214 4274 B7
11900 DET 48205 4274 E1
13100 DET 48205 4202 E7
13700 DET 48205 4203 A6
15400 EPTE 48205 4203 B3
20700 EPTE 48021 4203 B3
Gratiot Ct
- DET 48213 4274 D4
Gratiot St
1800 WIND N9E 4503 C2
Graves Av
24600 WynC 48138 4670 B6
Graves St
9100 DET 48214 4274 D6
Gravier St
17100 DET 48224 4276 B4
Gray St
1100 DET 48214 4275 C6
1100 DET 48214 4347 C1
5000 DET 48213 4275 B5
8200 WTLD 48185 4338 C3
Grayfield
8800 RDFD 48127 4341 A2
9500 RDFD 48239 4341 A1
11600 RDFD 48239 4269 A7
Grayfield Cir
5400 YpTp 48197 4576 C2
Grayfield Dr
28500 FNHL 48336 4195 D2
Grayfield St
8000 DBHT 48127 4341 A3
14900 DET 48223 4269 A3
18200 DET 48219 4197 A7
18200 DET 48219 4269 A1
Gray Fox Ct
2100 WasC 48103 4405 C2
Grayling Av
28500 FNHL 48336 4195 E4
Grayling St
2200 HMTK 48212 4273 C5
Grays Dr
7600 WynC 48138 4670 C6
Grayson St
2300 FRDL 48220 4200 A1
Graystone Ln
45500 CNTN 48187 4411 C1
Grayton St
1000 GPPK 48230 4276 B5
3400 DET 48224 4276 A4
9100 DET 48224 4275 D1
11700 DET 48224 4203 C7
Graytona St
33400 LVNA 48150 4266 E6
33400 LVNA 48150 4267 A6
Greater Mack Av
21400 STCS 48080 4204 C3
Great Falls Cir
3500 PTFD 48108 4488 E5
Great Hawk Cir
5300 SpTp 48105 4408 A3
E Great Lakes St
10 RVRG 48218 4501 E1
200 ECRS 48229 4502 A1
200 RVRG 48218 4502 A1
W Great Lakes St
10 RVRG 48218 4501 E3
Greeley St
- HZLP 48030 4200 E5
- HZLP 48203 4200 E5
9500 DET 48211 4273 A4
17100 DET 48203 4272 E1
17500 DET 48203 4200 E6
Green Ct
11900 Tcmh N0R 4424 A7
20700 GSPW 48236 4204 D5
Green Rd
500 AATp 48105 4407 C6
700 AARB 48105 4407 C4
700 YPLT 48198 4491 E2
Green St
400 YPLT 48198 4491 E2
2900 LNPK 48146 4500 D4
Green St N
2300 DET 48209 4419 A1
Green St S
100 DET 48209 4419 B3
Green Apple Ct
3400 MonC 48117 4753 A7
Green Briar
- YpTp 48198 4493 A3
Green Briar Blvd
- AARB 48105 4407 C3
Greenbriar Cir
20800 LyTp 48178 4189 C6
Greenbriar Ct
14700 PyTp 48170 4265 C5
44400 VNBN 48111 4494 E2
Greenbriar Dr
6400 VNBN 48111 4494 D2
Greenbriar Ln
20900 LyTp 48178 4189 C5
40300 PyTp 48170 4265 B5
Greenbriar St
10 GSPS 48236 4205 A6
13900 OKPK 48237 4198 D4
Greenbriar Wy
28300 BwTp 48183 4754 C2
Greenbrier Ct
39500 NvlT 48167 4265 D3
Greenbrook Ln
41000 PyTp 48170 4265 C5
Greenbrooke Dr
25100 SFLD 48034 4196 D1
Greenbush Ct
36700 WYNE 48184 4413 C5
Greenbush Rd
36700 WYNE 48184 4413 B5
Greencrest St
23100 STCS 48080 4204 E3
23100 STCS 48080 4205 A3
Greendale E
10 DET 48203 4200 C7
Greendale W
10 DET 48203 4200 B7
Greendale Dr
500 WIND N8S 4348 A5
Greene St
800 AARB 48104 4406 B7
Greene Farm Ct
7600 YpTp 48197 4576 A6
Greene Farm Dr
7500 YpTp 48197 4576 A6
Greenfield Ct
- CNTN 48187 4337 C5
E Greenfield Ct
1300 PTFD 48108 4573 B1
W Greenfield Ct
1400 PTFD 48108 4573 A1
Greenfield Rd
- OKPK 48235 4198 C4
- SFLD 48235 4198 C4
2500 DRBN 48120 4417 D2
2500 DRBN 48122 4417 D2
2800 MVDL 48122 4418 A4
3900 DRBN 48126 4417 D2
4700 DRBN 48126 4342 D6
6300 DET 48126 4342 D2
6300 DET 48228 4342 D2
9500 DET 48227 4342 D2
12600 DET 48227 4270 C6
16100 DET 48235 4270 C2
16500 MVDL 48122 4417 D2
18200 DET 48235 4198 C7
20400 DET 48075 4198 C7
20700 OKPK 48075 4198 C4
20700 OKPK 48237 4198 C4
20700 SFLD 48075 4198 C4
20700 SFLD 48237 4198 C4
Greenfield St
7200 YpTp 48197 4576 E6
Greenfield Wy
13600 SOGT 48195 4584 B1
Green Hill Rd
21000 FNHL 48335 4194 C4
Greenhill Rd
24000 WRRN 48091 4201 A1
Green Hills Dr
10 PTFD 48176 4573 E5
10 PTFD 48176 4574 A5
Greenhills Dr
600 AARB 48105 4407 D5
S Green Hills Dr
6800 PTFD 48176 4574 A6
Greening Ct
23600 NOVI 48375 4192 E2
Greening Dr
23400 NOVI 48375 4192 E2
Green Knolls Ln
4900 WasC 48103 4404 D3
Greenland Av
10 WasC 48189 4259 A3
Greenland Ct
32500 LVNA 48154 4267 A3
Greenland St
30400 LVNA 48154 4267 C3
Greenlawn Av
300 YpTp 48198 4492 D5
Greenlawn Ct
25400 TYLR 48180 4498 D6
Greenlawn St
8000 DET 48204 4343 D2
12000 DET 48204 4271 C6
14200 DET 48238 4271 C5
16100 DET 48221 4271 C2
18000 DET 48221 4199 C6
39400 CNTN 48187 4337 D3
Greenleaf Dr
200 CNTN 48187 4412 B2
Green Leaf Rd
3400 AATp 48105 4407 C5
Green Ln Av
15300 LVNA 48154 4268 A3
Green Lodge Dr
- DET 48235 4198 C5
Greenmeadow Dr
10 WynC 48111 4662 C6
Green Meadow Ln
7200 CNTN 48187 4337 B5
Green Meadows Blvd
4000 PTFD 48108 4490 D4
4000 PTFD 48197 4490 D4
Greenmont Ct
11100 GOTp 48178 4188 B5
Green Oak Industrial Dr
- GOTp 48189 4186 D6
Green Oaks Dr
10900 GOTp 48178 4188 A4
Greenook Blvd
3600 WasC 48103 4329 D6
W Greenook Blvd
3600 WasC 48103 4329 D6
Greenook Ct
4800 WasC 48103 4329 D6
Greenpark Blvd
500 WIND N8P 4348 C6
Greenridge Ct
46700 NvlT 48167 4192 B6
Greenridge Dr
45600 NvlT 48167 4192 B6
Greensboro
22200 NOVI 48375 4193 D3
Greensboro Tr
9000 DET 48224 4275 C2
Greenside Av
10 YpTp 48197 4491 A5
Greenspan
- DET 48216 4344 D6
Greensway Rd
21800 TYLR 48180 4583 C4
Greentree Ln
21800 NOVI 48375 4193 C4
Greentree Tr
12500 GOTp 48178 4188 C2
Greentrees Dr
13700 RVVW 48192 4669 D1
Green Valley Ct
2100 PTFD 48103 4488 D4
46100 PyTp 48170 4336 C1
Green Valley Dr
800 Tcmh N8N 4424 B1
2700 PTFD 48103 4488 E3
Green Valley Rd
45400 PyTp 48170 4336 C1
Green Valley St
24300 SFLD 48034 4197 A1
Greenview Av
- DET 48219 4198 A7
3200 TNTN 48183 4669 B3
9500 DET 48228 4342 A1
11500 DET 48228 4270 A7
16100 DET 48219 4270 A2
Greenview Cres
1600 WIND N9C 4420 B6
Greenview Dr
1400 AARB 48103 4488 E1
2000 AARB 48103 4489 A2
13300 SOGT 48195 4584 B1
Greenview Ln
44000 NvlT 48167 4264 E2
Greenview Pl
39800 PyTp 48170 4337 D2
Greenview Rd
12800 DET 48223 4270 A5
20700 SFLD 48075 4198 A4
Greenview St
28400 RMLS 48174 4582 A4
Greenwald Dr
18100 SFLD 48075 4198 A3
18600 SFLD 48075 4197 D3
Greenway Cir
11800 GOTp 48178 4188 B4
Greenway Ct
4200 WasC 48103 4329 D4
Greenway Dr
5400 TNTN 48183 4755 B1
Greenway St
- DET 48204 4343 E2
Greenwich Cir
48500 CNTN 48188 4411 A4
Greenwich Ct
3000 CNTN 48188 4411 A5
Greenwich Dr
47400 NOVI 48374 4192 A1
Greenwich Ln
13800 SOGT 48195 4584 B1
48300 CNTN 48188 4411 A5
Greenwing Dr
33000 BwTp 48173 4841 A1
Greenwood Av
900 AARB 48104 4406 C7
Greenwood Ct
100 GDNC 48135 4414 E2
6300 VNBN 48111 4494 D2
41500 CNTN 48187 4337 C7
Greenwood Dr
- WTLD 48185 4413 B1
38000 WTLD 48185 4338 A7
41400 CNTN 48187 4337 B7
44600 VNBN 48111 4494 D2
E Greenwood Dr
37500 FNHL 48167 4194 A4
W Greenwood Dr
37600 FNHL 48167 4194 A4
Greenwood Rd
10200 GOTp 48189 4187 B5
Greenwood St
200 GDNC 48135 4414 E1
300 INKR 48141 4414 E2
37400 WTLD 48185 4338 A7
Gregory Av
1300 LNPK 48146 4500 D5
Gregory Dr
10100 WynC 48138 4670 A6
24800 BNTN 48183 4668 B7
Gregory Ln
8800 PyTp 48170 4336 D3
Gregory Pl
8300 WIND N8S 4347 C6
Gregory St
1300 YPLT 48197 4491 C2
21500 DRBN 48124 4416 C4
Greig Ct
400 RVRG 48218 4501 D1
Greiner St
11000 DET 48234 4202 B7
11600 DET 48205 4202 D7
Grenelefe Cir E
54700 LyTp 48178 4190 D2
Grenelefe Cir W
54800 LyTp 48178 4190 D2
Grennada St
31000 LVNA 48154 4267 C5
35900 LVNA 48154 4266 C5
38400 LVNA 48154 4265 E5
Grenoble Dr
9000 WasC 48160 4659 D2
Greusel St
3400 DET 48210 4344 B6
Grey Av
18600 ALPK 48101 4499 E4
18600 ALPK 48101 4500 A4
Greydale Av
17200 DET 48219 4269 C1
19200 DET 48219 4197 B6
Greydale Ct
21600 DET 48219 4197 B6
Greydale St
12800 DET 48223 4269 C6
S Greyfriar St
- LNPK 48229 4501 B1
500 DET 48229 4418 C5
2900 DET 48229 4501 B1
Greylock St
500 BLVL 48111 4578 E2
Greystone Blvd
40900 PyTp 48170 4337 C2
GR Fink
10 ECRS 48229 4501 E2
Griffin Av
20700 WRRN 48089 4202 C4
Griffin Ct
4100 WIND N8W 4422 A2
33400 LVNA 48152 4266 E2
Griggs St
10200 DET 48204 4343 B1
12200 DET 48204 4271 B6
13500 DET 48238 4271 B5
16100 DET 48221 4271 B1
19900 DET 48221 4199 B5
Grillo Av
1800 LSal N9H 4503 C4
Grimm St
18300 LVNA 48152 4267 E1
18900 LVNA 48152 4195 E7
Grindley Park St
1800 DRBN 48124 4416 B4
3900 DBHT 48124 4416 B6
3900 DBHT 48125 4416 B6
5100 DBHT 48125 4499 B2
Grinnell St
7200 DET 48213 4274 A3
7200 DET 48234 4274 A3
Gristmill Dr
- WTLD 48186 4413 A4
Griswold Rd
21400 LyTp 48167 4189 D5
21400 LyTp 48178 4189 D5
Griswold St
- NOVI 48167 4193 A5
- NvlT 48167 4193 A5
10 DET 48226 4345 D6
100 NHVL 48167 4192 E6
600 NvlT 48167 4192 E6
Grix Rd
22000 WDHN 48183 4668 C6
27500 HnTp 48164 4667 A6
29300 HnTp 48164 4666 E6
Grixdale E
900 DET 48203 4200 E7
Grixdale W
10 DET 48203 4200 C7
Grixdale St E
- DET 48234 4200 E7
2900 DET 48234 4201 B7
7500 DET 48234 4202 A7
Groat Blvd
31900 BwTp 48173 4755 A7
Grodan Dr
25000 SFLD 48034 4196 E1
Groesbeck Hwy
20300 DET 48205 4202 C4
20300 WRRN 48205 4202 C4
20700 WRRN 48089 4202 E2
Groesbeck Hwy SR-97
20300 DET 48205 4202 C4
20300 WRRN 48205 4202 C4
20700 WRRN 48089 4202 E2
Groh Av
2000 TNTN 48183 4669 C5
Groh Rd
8400 WynC 48138 4756 C2
Grondin St
100 LSal N9J 4502 D4
Groomes Dr
10500 GOTp 48189 4187 C5
Grosbeak Ln
300 PTFD 48197 4574 D2
Groschner St
9000 TYLR 48180 4499 B4
Gross Rd
2400 PTFD 48108 4490 D3
Grosse Ile Pkwy
- WynC 48173 4670 A6
- WynC 48183 4670 A6
10 TNTN 48173 4669 E6
10 TNTN 48183 4669 E6
7700 WynC 48138 4670 A6
Grosse Pointe Blvd
10 GSPF 48230 4276 D5
10 GSPF 48236 4276 D5
Grosse Pointe Ct
700 DET 48224 4276 B4
700 DET 48230 4276 B4
700 GSPT 48230 4276 B4
Grosvenor Rd
- WIND N9G 4504 D5
1100 LSal N9H 4504 D5
Grotto Ct
18000 DET 48205 4202 E7
Grove
- CNTN 48188 4411 C5
25800 RDFD 48240 4268 C2
Grove Av
900 WIND N9A 4420 D3
1400 WIND N9B 4420 D3
22700 EPTE 48021 4203 C1
Grove Ct
3000 WasC 48176 4572 C2
4700 CNTN 48188 4411 C7
22500 NOVI 48375 4193 D5
25400 HnTp 48134 4666 E7
Grove Dr
9100 WasC 48189 4259 A1
10200 GOTp 48189 4187 B5
31400 LVNA 48154 4267 B2
35000 LVNA 48154 4266 D2
Grove Rd
800 YpTp 48198 4492 C7
1900 YpTp 48198 4576 E1
2100 YpTp 48198 4577 B1
Grove St
- DET 48219 4270 A2
- DRBN 48126 4342 C6
10 HDPK 48203 4272 B1
300 DET 48203 4272 A2
1100 WYDT 48192 4585 A4
2200 WYDT 48192 4584 E4
2300 WYDT 48195 4584 E4
2500 DET 48221 4272 A2
6300 DET 48221 4271 D2
13100 DET 48235 4271 A2
15500 DET 48235 4270 C2
20100 DET 48219 4269 D2
23000 STCS 48080 4204 C1
23300 FMTN 48336 4195 A2
24300 DET 48219 4268 E2
29100 LVNA 48154 4267 E2
33600 LVNA 48154 4266 E2
N Grove St
10 YPLT 48198 4492 B4
S Grove St
10 YPLT 48198 4492 B6
700 YpTp 48198 4492 B6
W Grove Cir Dr
- BNTN 48183 4668 B5
Groveland
15800 RMLS 48174 4582 A5
Groveland Dr
24600 BNTN 48134 4668 A4
Grover St
8700 RMLS 48174 4496 D5
11400 RMLS 48174 4580 D1
12300 DET 48205 4275 A1
12600 DET 48205 4203 A7
Groveview Av
8200 RDTp 48220 4199 C4
Gruebner St
19100 DET 48234 4202 B5
Grunalt Av
23800 WRRN 48091 4201 B1
Gudith Rd
20800 BNTN 48183 4668 C1
21000 WDHN 48183 4668 C1
Guidot St
- TYLR 48180 4499 E3
Guildwood Cres
1400 LSal N9H 4504 C5
Guilford
- NOVI 48375 4193 D2
Guilford Dr
6200 CNTN 48187 4336 E6
Guilford Rd
40300 NOVI 48375 4193 C2
Guilford St
3500 DET 48224 4276 A2
9100 DET 48224 4275 E1
Gull Ct
30400 GBTR 48173 4755 C5
Gullane Dr
4800 WasC 48103 4404 D6
Gullen Mall
5000 DET 48201 4345 A2
5000 DET 48202 4345 A2
Gulley Pl
10 DRBN 48124 4415 D2
N Gulley Rd
100 DBHT 48125 4415 D1
100 DBHT 48127 4415 D1
100 DRBN 48124 4415 D1
100 DRBN 48128 4415 D1
1300 DRBN 48128 4340 D7
5600 DBHT 48128 4340 D7
8000 DBHT 48127 4340 D4
S Gulley Rd
100 DBHT 48125 4415 D4
100 DRBN 48124 4415 D4
1400 DRBN 48125 4415 D4
5500 DBHT 48125 4498 E1
Gulley St
8200 TYLR 48180 4498 D4
14400 TYLR 48180 4582 E3
Gumdrop St
300 WTLD 48186 4414 D7
Gunnery Dr
45900 CNTN 48187 4336 B6
Gunston St
- DET 48234 4274 C1
11200 DET 48213 4274 E3
11500 DET 48205 4274 C1
Gunston St SR-97
- DET 48234 4274 C1
11200 DET 48213 4274 C1
11500 DET 48205 4274 C1
Gunther Ct
10 WasC 48176 4572 C4
Guoin St
2600 DET 48207 4346 B5
Guppy Ct
4300 WIND N9G 4504 C4
Guthrie St
7200 DET 48213 4274 A4
Guy St
3300 WIND N8W 4421 E3
3500 WIND N8W 4422 A2
4700 WIND N8T 4422 B2
Gyde Rd
47400 CNTN 48187 4336 A4
47600 CNTN 48187 4335 E4
Gyers Meadow Ln
6100 PTFD 48108 4573 B3

H

Hacienda Av
800 WIND N9G 4504 E5
Hacienda Wy
1000 WIND N9G 4504 E5
Hackberry Av
8900 PyTp 48170 4337 A2
Hackett St
15900 DET 48227 4270 C4
Hadley Ct
43100 CNTN 48188 4412 A5
Haeussler Ct
100 WasC 48103 4404 E5
Hafeli
7500 DET 48213 4274 A5
N Hagadorn Ct
700 SLYN 48178 4189 A1
N Hagadorn St
100 SLYN 48178 4189 A1
S Hagadorn St
100 SLYN 48178 4189 A2
Haggerman Rd
9800 BrTp 48166 4840 D6
10000 BrTp 48179 4840 D6
11900 SRKW 48179 4840 C3
Haggerty Rd
5800 VNBN 48111 4495 C3
12500 VNBN 48174 4579 D1
12600 VNBN 48111 4579 D3
16900 LVNA 48167 4265 D2
16900 NvlT 48167 4265 D2
18100 LVNA 48167 4193 D7
18100 NvlT 48167 4193 D7
18600 WynC 48111 4664 C1
19100 LVNA 48152 4193 D5
20000 NvlT 48152 4193 D5
20800 NOVI 48167 4193 D3
21000 FNHL 48167 4193 D3
21200 FNHL 48375 4193 D5
21200 NOVI 48375 4193 D5
21800 FNHL 48335 4193 D3
24600 WynC 48164 4664 C7
25600 WynC 48164 4750 C2
N Haggerty Rd
100 CNTN 48187 4412 C1
100 PLYM 48170 4265 C7
2100 CNTN 48187 4337 C6
8800 PyTp 48170 4337 C4
13000 PyTp 48170 4265 C6
15100 NvlT 48170 4265 C6
15300 NvlT 48167 4265 D4
16000 LVNA 48167 4265 D4
16000 LVNA 48170 4265 D4
S Haggerty Rd
100 CNTN 48187 4412 C3
100 CNTN 48188 4412 C3
5000 CNTN 48188 4495 C1
5300 CNTN 48111 4495 C1
Haggerty St
10300 DRBN 48126 4343 B5
13700 DRBN 48126 4342 E5
Haggerty Station Dr
41100 PyTp 48170 4337 C1
Haggerty Woods Ct
- CNTN 48187 4412 B1
Hague St
- DET 48211 4273 B6
10 DET 48202 4273 A6
Haig Av
5400 WIND N8T 4422 C3
Haig St
24000 TYLR 48180 4499 A5
26600 TYLR 48180 4498 C5
Haigh St
1200 DRBN 48124 4416 C3
Haisley Dr
2300 AARB 48103 4405 D5
Halcyon Ct
600 WasC 48103 4404 D4
8100 WynC 48138 4756 D1
Haldane Dr
34100 LVNA 48152 4194 D6
Haldane St
30400 LVNA 48152 4195 C6
33300 LVNA 48152 4194 E7
Hale St
1500 DET 48207 4345 D3
2900 DET 48207 4346 A3
12000 RVVW 48192 4584 E7
12000 RVVW 48192 4585 A7
Halecreek St
28400 RMLS 48174 4582 A5
30500 RMLS 48174 4581 D5
Haley Ln
10200 GOTp 48189 4187 C6
Halford Dr
1900 Tcmh N0R 4505 B5
Halifax Ln
22500 NOVI 48374 4192 A3
Hall Av
- RVRG 48218 4501 C1
- RVRG 48229 4501 C1
200 WIND N9A 4346 B7
600 WIND N9A 4421 B1
1200 WIND N8X 4421 C2
1600 WIND N8W 4421 C3
2000 AARB 48104 4489 E2
Hall Ct
400 RVRG 48218 4501 D1
Hall Pl
10 GSPF 48236 4276 D4
Hall Rd
10400 HbgT 48189 4186 C4
11700 WasC 48189 4186 C6
21200 WDHN 48183 4668 C3
25100 WDHN 48183 4754 C1
27000 FTRK 48134 4754 B3
Hall St
100 SALN 48176 4572 D7
9100 DET 48213 4274 D4
Hallcroft Dr
6400 CNTN 48187 4336 D6
Halleck St
1900 DET 48212 4273 B3
Haller St
8300 WTLD 48150 4339 E3
8300 WTLD 48185 4339 E3
11000 LVNA 48150 4339 E1
11600 LVNA 48150 4267 E7
14900 LVNA 48154 4267 E4
Hallett Ct
18900 BNTN 48174 4583 B7
Halley St
12900 DET 48223 4269 C6
Halley Crescent Dr
24000 WynC 48138 4670 B6
Hallmark Av
1300 WIND N8W 4421 E6
Hallmark Ln
- WIND N8W 4421 E6
Hallwood Ct
24400 FNHL 48335 4194 A1
Hally Pl
- GPPK 48230 4276 A7
Halpin Rd
3100 WIND N8R 4423 C3
Halstead Cres
10500 WIND N8R 4423 C3
Halsted Rd
- FMTN 48335 4194 A1
20700 FNHL 48167 4194 A4
20700 FNHL 48335 4194 A4
Halston Ct
45400 NOVI 48374 4192 C2
Haltiner St
10 RVRG 48218 4418 E7
10 RVRG 48218 4501 D1
300 RVRG 48229 4501 D1
Halyard Dr
47400 PyTp 48170 4264 A6
47700 PyTp 48170 4263 E6
Hamann St
17100 RVVW 48192 4584 E6
Hamata Av
10 HZLP 48030 4200 B1
Hamata St
2100 FRDL 48220 4200 B1
N Hambleton Av
1800 WTLD 48185 4338 D7
S Hambleton Av
1200 WTLD 48186 4413 D4
Hambleton St
9900 LVNA 48150 4338 D2
N Hambleton St
800 WTLD 48185 4413 D1
6900 WTLD 48185 4338 D5
Hamburg Ct
9500 HbgT 48116 4186 B2
Hamburg Rd
9000 HbgT 48116 4186 B1
11400 HbgT 48189 4186 B5
S Hamburg Rd
9500 WasC 48189 4186 B7
Hamburg St
11900 DET 48205 4274 D1
18600 DET 48205 4202 D6
Hamden Ct
46300 PyTp 48170 4336 C1
Hamilton Av
1800 LNPK 48146 4500 E1
9400 DET 48202 4272 D5
11700 DET 48203 4272 D5
11700 HDPK 48203 4272 D5
16800 ALPK 48101 4417 B7
21200 FNHL 48336 4195 E3
Hamilton Ct
200 GSPF 48236 4276 D2
9900 VNBN 48111 4495 B6
22000 WDHN 48183 4668 C6
25100 SLYN 48178 4189 B1
Hamilton Dr
200 Amhg N9V 4757 C2
Hamilton Pl
400 AARB 48104 4406 B6
5600 WYNE 48184 4497 C1
Hamilton Rd
17400 DET 48203 4200 A7
17400 DET 48203 4272 A1

STREET
Block City ZIP Map# Grid

Hamilton Rd
17400 DET 48221 4200 A7
17400 DET 48221 4272 A1
Hamilton St
100 PLYM 48170 4265 A7
200 PLYM 48170 4337 A2
300 CNTN 48188 4410 D3
1300 DRBN 48124 4416 B3
9500 VNBN 48111 4495 B6
13700 RVVW 48192 4669 D1
16200 SOGT 48195 4500 A7
N Hamilton St
10 YPLT 48197 4491 E4
N Hamilton St SR-17
10 YPLT 48197 4491 E4
S Hamilton St
- YPLT 48197 4492 A6
10 YPLT 48197 4491 E5
S Hamilton St US-12 BUS
- YPLT 48197 4492 A6
10 YPLT 48197 4491 E5
Hamlet Ct
7800 CNTN 48187 4336 B5
Hamlet Dr
1700 SpTp 48198 4409 C7
1700 SpTp 48198 4492 C1
Hamlet St
5000 DET 48234 4201 D4
Hamlin Blvd
2500 INKR 48141 4415 B4
Hamlin Ct
33700 FMTN 48335 4194 E2
Hamlin Rd
7600 PTFD 48197 4574 D7
Hamlin St
41500 VNBN 48111 4495 C6
Hammer Ln
36200 LVNA 48152 4266 C1
Hammerstone Dr
11000 GOTp 48178 4188 D5
Hammill Ln
42400 PyTp 48170 4265 A5
Hammond St
2300 DET 48209 4419 C1
2500 DET 48209 4344 B7
4400 DET 48210 4344 A5
Hampden St
5800 TYLR 48180 4498 C1
15000 TYLR 48180 4582 C4
Hampshire Ct
100 DRBN 48124 4416 D1
6300 WTLD 48185 4339 A6
Hampshire Dr
400 WynC 48111 4662 D6
1100 CNTN 48188 4412 C4
Hampshire Ln
5500 PTFD 48197 4574 C2
Hampshire Rd
2500 AARB 48104 4490 B4
33000 LVNA 48154 4267 A3
Hampshire St
12500 DET 48213 4275 A3
32900 WTLD 48185 4339 A6
N Hampshire St
33500 LVNA 48154 4266 E3
S Hampshire St
33500 LVNA 48154 4266 E3
Hampstead Ln
600 WasC 48103 4406 A3
Hampton Cres
100 WIND N9E 4421 B6
Hampton Ct
10 DRBN 48124 4415 E2
10 NHVL 48167 4192 D7
300 SLYN 48178 4189 B3
1900 AARB 48103 4405 E7
18200 LVNA 48152 4266 C1
22000 WDHN 48183 4668 C6
22400 FNHL 48335 4194 C3
24500 NOVI 48375 4193 A1
Hampton Ct E
5600 WTLD 48185 4338 E7
Hampton Ct W
5600 WTLD 48185 4338 D7
Hampton Dr
300 SLYN 48178 4189 C4
8700 RMLS 48174 4496 A5
9400 VNBN 48111 4495 A6
N Hampton Dr
24700 BNTN 48134 4668 A7
Hampton Rd
- HRWD 48080 4204 B4
10 GSPS 48236 4205 A5
500 GSPW 48236 4205 A5
600 GSPW 48236 4204 E4
2200 HRWD 48236 4204 B4
8200 WynC 48138 4670 C3
20800 HRWD 48225 4204 B4
Hampton St
14900 DET 48214 4275 E7
15000 GPPK 48230 4275 E7
19200 RVVW 48192 4669 D1
Hampton Hill St
24200 NOVI 48375 4193 B1
Hampton Towne St
10 SFLD 48075 4198 B2
Hamtramck Dr
1000 DET 48211 4273 C6
1000 HMTK 48211 4273 C6
E Hancock Av
- DET 48214 4274 B7
Hancock Ct
600 FRDL 48220 4199 E3
Hancock Dr
- CNTN 48111 4493 E2
- CNTN 48188 4493 E2
5900 VNBN 48111 4493 E2
10700 GOTp 48189 4187 C4
13000 TYLR 48180 4583 D1
Hancock St
21500 FNHL 48336 4195 E3
49900 CNTN 48188 4410 D3
E Hancock St
1300 DET 48207 4345 D2
W Hancock St
- DET 48210 4344 E4
Hancock St E
10 DET 48201 4345 B3
3000 DET 48207 4345 E1
3500 DET 48207 4346 A1
Hancock St W
10 DET 48201 4345 B3
1500 DET 48210 4345 A3
3300 DET 48210 4344 C5
Handy Rd
10 GSPF 48236 4276 D5
Handy St
8000 WIND N8S 4347 D5
Hanfor Av
14500 ALPK 48101 4500 C1
Hanford Av
1300 LNPK 48146 4501 A2
1700 LNPK 48146 4500 D1
2200 LNPK 48101 4500 D1
Hanford Rd
- SpTp 48170 4335 C6
- SpTp 48198 4335 C6
41400 CNTN 48187 4337 A6
43700 CNTN 48187 4336 D6
48300 CNTN 48187 4335 D6
51100 CNTN 48170 4335 C6
51100 CNTN 48198 4335 C6
Hanley Av
500 WIND N9G 4504 D3
Hanley St
2900 HMTK 48212 4273 C5
9200 TYLR 48180 4499 B5
Hanlon Av
8800 LVNA 48150 4338 E3
N Hanlon Av
1100 WTLD 48185 4413 E1
Hanlon St
9000 LVNA 48150 4338 E2
N Hanlon St
600 WTLD 48185 4413 E1
1700 WTLD 48185 4338 E7
S Hanlon St
100 WTLD 48186 4413 E2
Hanna St
17100 MVDL 48122 4417 D6
19100 DET 48203 4200 E4
Hanna St E
1100 WIND N8X 4421 C3
Hanna St W
10 WIND N8X 4421 A4
400 WIND N8X 4420 E4
Hannah Ct
20700 NOVI 48375 4193 A5
Hannan Rd
1800 CNTN 48186 4412 E4
1800 CNTN 48188 4412 E4
1800 WTLD 48186 4412 E4
2700 WYNE 48184 4412 E5
3400 WYNE 48188 4412 E5
4900 CNTN 48188 4495 E2
4900 WYNE 48184 4495 E2
5700 RMLS 48174 4495 E2
5800 VNBN 48111 4495 E5
5800 VNBN 48174 4495 E5
5800 VNBN 48188 4495 E2
11000 RMLS 48111 4495 E6
11300 RMLS 48174 4579 E3
11300 VNBN 48111 4579 E3
11900 VNBN 48174 4579 E3
14700 RMLS 48174 4580 A7
17000 HnTp 48164 4580 A7
17000 HnTp 48164 4665 B1
17000 HnTp 48174 4665 B1
17000 HnTp 48174 4580 A7
17000 HnTp 48174 4665 B1
Hanover Av
14500 ALPK 48101 4500 C2
17200 ALPK 48101 4417 A7
Hanover Blvd
27400 WTLD 48186 4415 B7
28000 WTLD 48186 4498 A1
29400 WTLD 48186 4414 D7
Hanover Ct
1500 AARB 48103 4488 E2
22000 WDHN 48183 4668 C6
43600 CNTN 48187 4337 A5
Hanover Dr
25700 BNTN 48134 4754 A1
Hanover Rd
10 PTRG 48069 4199 C1
1600 AARB 48103 4488 E2
Hanover St
1700 LNPK 48146 4500 D2
7300 DET 48206 4344 D1
7300 DET 48210 4344 D1
18100 DBHT 48101 4417 A7
18100 DBHT 48125 4417 A7
18600 DBHT 48125 4416 E7
25100 DBHT 48125 4415 D7
Hansen Cres
1300 WIND N8W 4421 E7
Hanson Ct
22300 STCS 48080 4204 D1
Hanson St
6300 DET 48210 4344 A5
6500 DET 48210 4343 E5
Harbal Dr
1600 AARB 48105 4406 D4
Harbaugh St S
200 DET 48209 4419 A4
Harbert Dr
39800 NvlT 48167 4193 D6
Harbin Dr
17400 BwTp 48173 4841 A3
Harbor Blvd
1300 TNTN 48183 4669 E4
Harbor Ct
10 GSPF 48236 4276 E2
1500 TNTN 48183 4669 E3
Harbor Dr
1200 TNTN 48183 4669 E3
Harbor Ln
11700 VNBN 48111 4578 D1
Harbor Pt
8100 WynC 48138 4585 D6
Harbor Rd
39100 HnTp 48164 4665 A5
Harbor St
300 CNTN 48188 4410 E3
Harbor Wy
100 AARB 48103 4489 B3
9000 GOTp 48178 4187 E1
Harbor Cove Cir
9300 WasC 48189 4187 A7
9300 WasC 48189 4259 A1
Harbor Hill Rd
10 GSPF 48236 4276 E4
Harbor Island
14300 DET 48214 4347 E2
14300 DET 48214 4348 A2
Harbor Place Dr
3000 STCS 48080 4205 A2
E Harbortown Dr
200 DET 48207 4346 C5
Harbour Cove Ct
9500 YpTp 48197 4576 E2
Harbourne Cres
500 Tcmh N8N 4424 C2
Harbour Pointe Ct
700 BLVL 48111 4578 B3
46900 VNBN 48111 4578 B3
Harbour Pointe Dr
200 BLVL 48111 4578 C3
Harbour Village Dr
- NvlT 48167 4193 B7
E Harbour Village Dr
19200 NvlT 48167 4193 B7
W Harbour Village Dr
19300 NvlT 48167 4193 B7
Harbrooke Av
1200 AARB 48103 4406 A5
1300 AARB 48103 4405 E5
Harcourt Rd
700 GPPK 48230 4276 A7
Harcourt St
3800 WIND N9G 4504 E2
Harden Av
24500 SFLD 48075 4198 B1
Harden Cir
15700 SFLD 48075 4198 B1
Hardenburg St
100 PLYM 48170 4265 B6
Harding Av
1900 YpTp 48197 4491 B5
23000 HZLP 48030 4200 D1
Harding Rd
1500 AARB 48104 4489 E1
Harding St
- CNTN 48188 4410 D3
500 PLYM 48170 4337 A1
1400 DET 48214 4347 A1
2900 DET 48214 4275 A7
3200 DRBN 48124 4416 D6
3700 DET 48214 4274 E6
3900 DBHT 48124 4416 D6
3900 DBHT 48125 4416 D6
4900 WYNE 48184 4414 C7
5200 WYNE 48184 4497 C1
5600 DBHT 48125 4499 D1
5800 DET 48213 4274 D4
6600 TYLR 48180 4499 D2
21600 RKWD 48173 4754 D7
23600 OKPK 48237 4198 C1
28400 BwTp 48183 4754 D3
Hardwood Dr
8700 VNBN 48111 4495 B5
Hardy St
19200 LVNA 48152 4195 B6
Hardyke Ct
2200 AARB 48108 4490 A5
Hardyke St
8000 DET 48213 4274 B5
Harlan Dr
22100 WynC 48138 4670 B4
Harley Ct
1900 WasC 48103 4488 C2
Harley Dr
1700 WasC 48103 4488 C2
Harlow Av
3600 ALPK 48101 4500 D1
Harlow St
18000 DET 48235 4270 B1
18200 DET 48235 4198 B7
19100 MVDL 48122 4417 E7
Harlowshire St
33500 FNHL 48335 4194 E4
Harman St
17100 MVDL 48122 4417 D6
Harmon Av
1900 YpTp 48198 4492 E7
Harmon Ct
6400 WTLD 48185 4339 A6
Harmon Ln
10000 GOTp 48178 4187 C3
Harmon St
- DET 48211 4273 A5
10 DET 48202 4272 E5
500 DET 48202 4273 A5
20000 TYLR 48101 4499 E6
22000 TYLR 48180 4499 C6
23000 STCS 48080 4204 C1
Harmony Dr
3100 WIND N8I 4422 D4
Harmony Ln
40200 NvlT 48167 4193 C7
44000 VNBN 48111 4578 E1
Harned St
19100 DET 48234 4201 A5
Harnor Ct
8600 DET 48206 4272 D7
Harold Cir
1000 WasC 48103 4404 C3
Harold St
3800 DET 48212 4273 D3
3800 HMTK 48212 4273 D3
5800 TYLR 48180 4498 D1
13400 TYLR 48180 4582 D2
Harper Av
- DET 48224 4204 A7
- HRWD 48080 4204 C3
10 DET 48202 4345 B1
500 DET 48211 4345 B1
2200 DET 48211 4273 E7
7100 DET 48211 4274 A6
7200 DET 48213 4274 A6
12200 DET 48213 4275 A4
14400 DET 48224 4275 D2
17300 DET 48224 4276 A1
19200 HRWD 48224 4204 A7
20700 HRWD 48225 4204 B5
21000 STCS 48080 4204 C3
21000 STCS 48225 4204 C3
Harper Ct
19800 HRWD 48225 4203 E5
Harper Dr
10 SALN 48176 4572 C6
Harper Lake Av
21500 STCS 48080 4204 D1
Harpers Ferry Ct
10200 GOTp 48189 4187 B4
Harpst St
1200 AARB 48104 4489 D2
Harrell St
5800 DET 48213 4275 A4
9000 DET 48213 4274 E3
Harriet Ct
23400 OKPK 48237 4198 C2
45300 CNTN 48188 4411 D3
Harriet St
100 YPLT 48197 4492 A5
400 YPLT 48197 4491 E5
2100 INKR 48141 4415 A4
7000 RMLS 48174 4498 A3
15300 RMLS 48174 4582 A4
21100 HnTp 48174 4667 A3
26200 DBHT 48127 4415 C1
Harrington St S
500 DET 48209 4419 C4
Harris Rd
39900 WynC 48111 4579 D7
39900 WynC 48111 4664 B1
43400 WynC 48111 4663 E1
N Harris Rd
200 YpTp 48198 4492 D3
1800 SpTp 48198 4409 D7
S Harris Rd
10 YpTp 48198 4492 D4
Harris St
- RVRG 48218 4419 A7
2300 FRDL 48220 4200 A1
3400 WIND N9C 4420 A4
N Harris St
100 SALN 48176 4572 D6
S Harris St
100 SALN 48176 4572 D7
200 SALN 48176 4657 D1
Harrison Av
- WTLD 48186 4415 A6
10 TNTN 48183 4670 A3
100 GDNC 48135 4415 A1
100 GDNC 48141 4415 A1
300 TNTN 48183 4669 E3
1000 WIND N9C 4420 B4
1500 GDNC 48135 4340 A6
4000 INKR 48141 4415 A6
14500 ALPK 48101 4500 B3
18900 LVNA 48152 4195 E7
Harrison Blvd
- LNPK 48192 4501 A7
- WYDT 48146 4501 A7
- WYDT 48192 4501 A7
500 LNPK 48146 4501 A7
1000 LNPK 48146 4500 E7
Harrison Rd
11000 RMLS 48174 4498 A7
11300 RMLS 48174 4582 A2
Harrison St
- WTLD 48186 4415 A7
100 INKR 48141 4415 A2
2500 DET 48216 4345 A6
3300 DET 48210 4345 A5
4800 WYNE 48184 4414 C7
7100 RMLS 48174 4498 A3
7400 WTLD 48185 4340 A4
8800 LVNA 48150 4340 A3
14500 LVNA 48154 4268 A4
15000 RMLS 48174 4582 A4
16200 LVNA 48154 4267 E2
16900 LVNA 48152 4267 E2
17500 LVNA 48152 4268 A1
21100 HnTp 48174 4667 A3
Harroun Ct
36200 WYNE 48184 4413 C7
Harroun St
33900 WYNE 48184 4414 A7
34800 WYNE 48184 4413 D7
Harrow Ct
6400 CNTN 48187 4336 A6
8200 WasC 48167 4190 B6
E Harry Av
900 HZLP 48030 4200 E3
W Harry Av
10 HZLP 48030 4200 C3
Harry St
1300 YpTp 48198 4492 E6
9300 DET 48213 4274 C5
Harry Stahl Blvd
22700 STCS 48080 4204 E1
22700 STCS 48080 4205 A1
Harsdale Ct
22000 FNHL 48335 4194 B3
44200 CNTN 48187 4411 E2
Harsdale Dr
22000 FNHL 48335 4194 B3
43900 CNTN 48187 4411 E2
Harsha Av
- LVNA 48154 4266 B5
Hart Av
- RVRG 48218 4418 D7
Hart Pl
500 YPLT 48197 4491 D6
N Hart Pl
21200 ROTp 48220 4199 A4
S Hart Pl
21000 ROTp 48220 4199 B4
Hart St
- DET 48214 4347 B1
3000 DET 48214 4275 A7
Hartel Av
100 GDNC 48135 4415 A1
100 GDNC 48141 4415 A1
1900 GDNC 48135 4340 A7
7200 WTLD 48185 4340 A5
Hartel Ct
9800 LVNA 48150 4339 E1
Hartel St
6400 GDNC 48135 4340 A6
8800 LVNA 48150 4339 E3
11600 LVNA 48150 4267 E7
Hartford Ct
1800 WIND N8W 4421 E5
42200 CNTN 48187 4337 B6
Hartford Dr
42000 CNTN 48187 4337 B6
Hartford St
1600 AARB 48103 4488 E2
6500 DET 48210 4344 B3
Hartley Dr
3100 WIND N8T 4422 C4
Hartman Ln
300 SALN 48176 4572 D7
Hartman Rd
- WasC 48176 4657 D4
Hartsough Ct
900 PLYM 48170 4337 A2
Hartsough St
100 PLYM 48170 4337 A1
800 PLYM 48170 4336 E2
Hartwell St
5600 DRBN 48126 4343 A5
8000 DET 48228 4343 A3
9500 DET 48227 4343 A2
12600 DET 48227 4271 A6
15700 DET 48227 4270 E2
17100 DET 48235 4270 E1
18200 DET 48235 4198 E7
Hartwick Hwy
2200 LNPK 48146 4500 C4
Hartwick St
7800 DET 48211 4273 B6
Harvard
- TYLR 48180 4582 E5
- WTLD 48186 4414 A4
Harvard Av
100 SLYN 48178 4189 B3
Harvard Ct
38700 FNHL 48167 4193 E4
Harvard Ln
6900 CNTN 48187 4336 C4
Harvard Pl
10 AARB 48104 4406 E6
Harvard Rd
1000 GPPK 48230 4276 B5
3400 DET 48224 4276 A4
9100 DET 48224 4275 E1
Harvard St
100 CNTN 48188 4411 E3
23400 DRBN 48124 4416 A4
33600 WTLD 48186 4414 A4
Harvest Bnd
1300 LSal N9H 4504 C5
Harvest Cir
3600 MonC 48117 4753 B6
Harvest Ct
6600 WasC 48178 4261 D1
10600 PyTp 48170 4335 E2
23700 NOVI 48375 4192 D2
Harvest Dr
23700 NOVI 48375 4192 D2
48500 PyTp 48170 4335 E2
Harvest Ln
1500 SpTp 48198 4492 E1
1500 SpTp 48198 4493 A1
15500 SOGT 48195 4584 A4
37400 HnTp 48164 4580 B7
Harvest Rd
5300 WasC 48176 4572 B2
Harvey St
5500 DET 48209 4419 D3
8800 LVNA 48150 4338 D3
N Harvey St
100 PLYM 48170 4265 A7
100 WTLD 48185 4413 D2
5600 WTLD 48185 4338 D7
S Harvey St
100 PLYM 48170 4265 A7
400 PLYM 48170 4336 E1
1800 WTLD 48186 4413 D4
Harwood Cir
1200 PTFD 48176 4574 A4
Haskell
35400 RMLS 48174 4496 D4
Haskell St
20000 TYLR 48101 4499 D4
21300 TYLR 48180 4499 C4
25400 TYLR 48180 4498 D4
Hasper Dr
1000 AARB 48103 4405 D4
Hass St
- DBHT 48127 4341 A6
27200 DBHT 48127 4340 B6
Hasse St
13400 DET 48212 4273 C1
19100 DET 48234 4201 C5
Hastings Rd
47800 CNTN 48188 4411 A3
Hastings St
5700 LSal N9H 4503 C3
6000 DET 48211 4345 B1
6100 DET 48202 4345 B1
6200 DET 48202 4273 B7
6200 DET 48211 4273 B7
Hatcher Av
21300 ROTp 48220 4199 A3
Hatcher Cres
1400 AARB 48103 4405 D4
Hatcher St
1800 AARB 48103 4405 E3
Hatfield Cir
800 PTFD 48176 4574 A4
Hathaway Dr
7800 WasC 48167 4190 A6
Hathaway Rd
5700 CNTN 48187 4336 C7
Hathaway St
24400 FNHL 48335 4194 A1
28800 LVNA 48150 4339 E2
35200 LVNA 48150 4338 C2
Hathon St
7900 DET 48213 4274 A5
Havana St
19100 DET 48203 4200 B6
Havelock Dr
26800 DBHT 48127 4415 B1
Haven Dr
12300 GOTp 48178 4188 C1
Haven St
800 YpTp 48198 4492 B2
Havens Dr
500 WIND N9G 4504 D5
Haverfor Ct
2600 WRRN 48091 4201 A1
Havergale St
22400 NOVI 48374 4192 C3
Haverhill Ct
10 AARB 48105 4407 A1
13800 SOGT 48195 4584 A2
Haverhill Ct N
7800 CNTN 48187 4335 D4
Haverhill Ct S
7200 CNTN 48187 4335 D5
Haverhill Dr
12700 PyTp 48170 4264 C7
Haverhill Ln
7300 CNTN 48187 4335 D5
Haverhill St
3400 DET 48230 4275 E4
9100 DET 48224 4275 C1
10900 DET 48213 4275 C1
Hawaii
600 WynC 48111 4662 D3
Hawk Ln
11800 Tcmh N8N 4423 D2
Hawkins St
100 YPLT 48197 4491 E5
Hawks Av
2400 PTFD 48108 4490 E3
Hawksbury St
2800 WIND N8W 4421 D5
Hawks Cove
4000 SpTp 48105 4333 E5
Hawks Nest Ct
1900 CNTN 48188 4412 C4
Hawley Blvd
2400 WTLD 48186 4413 A5
Hawthorn Ct
- NvlT 48167 4263 C3
29500 BwTp 48173 4754 E4
Hawthorn Ln
200 SLYN 48178 4189 C3
Hawthorn Pl
4200 WasC 48103 4329 E4
Hawthorne
11200 SOGT 48195 4500 B7
Hawthorne Av
800 YpTp 48198 4492 C5
6200 WIND N8T 4422 E3
7600 WIND N8T 4423 A2
Hawthorne Blvd
26500 FTRK 48134 4753 C2
Hawthorne Blvd W
- FTRK 48134 4753 C1
Hawthorne Cres
200 Amhg N9V 4757 C4
Hawthorne Dr
- TYLR 48180 4582 E5
- WTLD 48185 4339 A4
1500 TNTN 48183 4669 C3
7900 WIND N8R 4423 A2
Hawthorne Ln
42200 NOVI 48375 4193 A2
Hawthorne Pl
9800 WynC 48138 4670 A7
9800 WynC 48138 4756 A1
Hawthorne Rd
10 GSPS 48236 4205 A5
500 GSPW 48236 4205 A5
1900 GSPW 48236 4204 D4
2200 HRWD 48236 4204 B4
2500 AARB 48104 4490 A1
Hawthorne St
1500 DRBN 48128 4341 C7
6400 GDNC 48135 4339 D5
17100 DET 48203 4272 D1
17800 DET 48203 4200 D5
20800 HRWD 48225 4204 B4
20800 HRWD 48236 4204 B4
22100 FMTN 48336 4195 C2
22100 FNHL 48336 4195 C2
N Hawthorne St
- WTLD 48185 4413 E1
100 WTLD 48185 4413 E2
7200 WTLD 48185 4338 E5
S Hawthorne St
300 WTLD 48186 4413 E3
Hawthorne Wy
2200 SALN 48176 4572 C5
Hawthorne Glen Dr
9400 WynC 48138 4756 A1
Hawthorne Park Dr
- WTLD 48185 4339 B4
Hayden Dr
- WDHN 48183 4669 A7
21000 WDHN 48183 4668 E7
Hayden St
4400 WRRN 48091 4201 C4
22700 FMTN 48336 4195 A2
Hayes
- AARB 48104 4489 D3
Hayes Av
- Tcmh N8N 4424 C1
400 YpTp 48198 4492 D5
21900 EPTE 48021 4203 B3
23100 EPTE 48089 4203 B1
23200 WRRN 48089 4203 B1
E Hayes Av
900 HZLP 48030 4200 D4
W Hayes Av
10 HZLP 48030 4200 C4
Hayes Ct
3200 AARB 48108 4489 D4
19700 NvlT 48167 4193 A6
Hayes Rd
2700 Tcmh N8V 4505 B1
Hayes St
- EPTE 48021 4203 B4
- EPTE 48205 4203 B4
3700 WYNE 48184 4414 C6
4700 WYNE 48184 4497 C1
9000 DET 48213 4275 B2
9000 DET 48224 4275 B2
11300 DET 48205 4275 B1
12600 DET 48205 4203 B5
20000 TYLR 48180 4499 D3
24300 TYLR 48180 4498 E3
42000 VNBN 48111 4495 B6
Haynes Av
22000 FNHL 48336 4195 C3
Haynes St
23300 FNHL 48336 4195 C1
Hayward
10 AARB 48105 4406 E4
10 AARB 48105 4407 A4
Hayward Dr
39000 WTLD 48185 4337 E4
Hazel Av
3300 LNPK 48146 4500 C5
17000 BNTN 48174 4582 C6
34200 RMLS 48174 4496 E2
Hazel Ct
1100 YpTp 48197 4491 D5
6000 RMLS 48174 4497 A2
Hazel St
800 LSal N9J 4502 D6
1000 WYDT 48192 4501 B7
2000 DET 48210 4344 E5
2000 DET 48210 4345 A5
4600 DBHT 48125 4415 C7
5800 TYLR 48180 4498 C1
31600 RKWD 48173 4754 C7
S Hazel St
9700 WasC 48178 4189 B6
Hazelcrest Pl
10 HZLP 48030 4200 C2
Hazelhurst St
19500 SFLD 48075 4197 D3
23200 SFLD 48034 4197 A3
24200 SFLD 48034 4196 E3
E Hazelhurst St
100 FRDL 48220 4199 C4
100 FRDL 48220 4200 A3
W Hazelhurst St
100 FRDL 48220 4199 E3
Hazelnut Ct
25000 WynC 48138 4670 C7
Hazel Park Race Track
- HZLP 48030 4200 D1
Hazelridge St
13400 DET 48205 4202 E7
13900 DET 48205 4203 A7
Hazelton
8800 RDFD 48127 4341 A2
8800 RDFD 48239 4341 A2
11600 RDFD 48239 4269 A7
Hazelton Ct
22100 NOVI 48374 4192 B4
Hazelton St
7400 DBHT 48127 4341 B3
15300 DET 48223 4269 A3
16100 DET 48219 4269 A2
Hazelwood
300 PTFD 48197 4574 D2
Hazelwood Av
300 AARB 48103 4405 C6
23000 HZLP 48030 4200 D1
31400 WTLD 48186 4414 B3
34400 WTLD 48186 4413 D3
Hazelwood Ct
300 PTFD 48197 4574 D2
Hazelwood Dr
34200 WTLD 48186 4413 E3

Detroit & Wayne County Street Index

Detroit & Wayne County Street Index

STREET	Block	City	ZIP	Map#	Grid
Hillsdale Ct					
	32200	WTLD	48186	4414	B4
Hillsdale St					
	500	WYDT	48192	4585	B4
Hillshire Ct					
	3000	SpTp	48198	4408	D1
Hillside Ct					
	10	AARB	48104	4406	E7
	900	YPLT	48197	4491	D3
	4400	AATp	48105	4407	E6
	22200	NOVI	48167	4191	C4
Hillside Dr					
	3000	PTFD	48108	4491	A4
	3000	PTFD	48197	4491	A4
	4200	AATp	48105	4407	E6
	7200	DBHT	48127	4340	B5
	12200	PyTp	48170	4336	C1
	12400	PyTp	48170	4264	C7
	22100	NOVI	48167	4191	C4
Hillspur Rd					
	300	BNHL	48105	4331	A7
	300	BNHL	48105	4406	A1
Hilltop Dr					
	1300	YpTp	48197	4491	A7
	1500	YpTp	48197	4575	A1
	2900	AARB	48103	4405	C5
	18600	RVVW	48192	4584	B7
Hill Top Dr E					
	47800	PyTp	48170	4264	A6
	48300	PyTp	48170	4263	E6
Hill Top Dr W					
	13500	PyTp	48170	4263	E6
Hilltop St					
	21000	SFLD	48034	4196	E4
Hilltop Dr Blvd					
	18600	RVVW	48192	4584	B7
Hilltop Dr Cir					
	18700	RVVW	48192	4584	B7
Hilltop Dr Ct					
	18600	RVVW	48192	4584	A6
Hilltop Dr Ln					
	18600	RVVW	48192	4584	A6
Hilltop View Dr					
	17100	NvlT	48167	4264	B2
Hillview Ct					
	23300	FMTN	48335	4194	B2
	23300	FNHL	48335	4194	B2
Hillview St					
	12700	DET	48227	4271	A4
Hillway Ct					
	4800	AATp	48105	4408	A2
Hilton Dr					
	600	AARB	48108	4489	C4
Hilton Rd					
	-	DET	48203	4200	A3
	-	FRDL	48203	4200	A3
	100	FRDL	48220	4200	A3
Hindle St					
	9500	DET	48211	4273	A4
Hines Ct					
	12000	PyTp	48170	4337	B1
Hines Dr					
	-	LVNA	48150	4337	E1
	-	LVNA	48150	4339	A3
	-	NHVL	48167	4192	E7
	-	NvlT	48167	4192	E7
	-	NvlT	48167	4264	E1
	-	NvlT	48167	4265	A2
	-	NvlT	48170	4265	A2
	-	PLYM	48170	4265	B6
	-	PLYM	48170	4337	C1
	-	PyTp	48170	4265	A6
	-	PyTp	48170	4337	C1
	-	WTLD	48150	4339	A3
	-	WTLD	48185	4339	A4
	-	WTLD	48185	4340	C3
	10	DBHT	48127	4341	A4
	5600	PTFD	48108	4573	D2
	24500	DBHT	48127	4340	E4
	37400	LVNA	48150	4338	A1
Hinkel					
	-	DRBN	48126	4417	C1
Hinton St					
	18000	RVVW	48192	4584	E7
Hipp Av					
	12300	TYLR	48180	4583	D1
Hipp St					
	3500	DRBN	48124	4416	D5
	3900	DBHT	48124	4416	D6
	3900	DBHT	48125	4416	D6
	5800	TYLR	48125	4499	D1
	8700	TYLR	48180	4499	D2
	14000	TYLR	48180	4583	E2
Hiscock St					
	100	AARB	48103	4406	A5
Hitchingham Rd					
	5800	YpTp	48197	4575	E2
	8000	AGST	48197	4575	E7
	8000	AGST	48197	4660	E2
	10000	AGST	48160	4660	E7
Hi Tech Dr					
	9000	GOTp	48116	4186	E4
Hiveley St					
	29400	INKR	48141	4414	D2
	30400	WTLD	48186	4414	C2
	33600	WTLD	48186	4413	E2
Hix Ct					
	15500	LVNA	48154	4266	A4
Hix Dr					
	8500	WTLD	48185	4338	A3
Hix Rd					
	8800	LVNA	48150	4338	A2
N Hix Rd					
	100	WTLD	48185	4413	A2
	1800	WTLD	48185	4338	A6
Hix St					
	14600	LVNA	48154	4265	E4
	15300	LVNA	48154	4266	A4
Hixford Pl					
	38000	WTLD	48185	4413	A1
Hizmet St					
	17400	LVNA	48152	4268	A1
Hoban Wy					
	1400	WasC	48189	4259	D6
Hobart Av					
	13600	WRRN	48089	4202	E2
	13700	WRRN	48089	4203	A2
Hobart Ct					
	500	WasC	48176	4658	D2
Hobbiton Ln					
	4800	WasC	48103	4487	D1
Hobson St					
	3100	DET	48201	4345	B5
Hockey Ln					
	900	AARB	48103	4406	A4
Hoeft Rd					
	13400	VNBN	48111	4577	E3
Hofer Av					
	22800	EPTE	48021	4203	D1
Hogan Dr					
	7000	YpTp	48197	4576	A6
Hogan Ln					
	-	WTLD	48186	4414	D4
Hogan Wy					
	2600	CNTN	48188	4411	C5
Hogarth St					
	2600	DET	48206	4344	C2
	4000	DET	48204	4344	B2
Hogback Rd					
	1100	AATp	48105	4490	D2
	1100	PTFD	48105	4490	D2
	2100	PTFD	48108	4490	D4
Holborn St					
	-	DET	48211	4274	A7
	3500	DET	48211	4273	E7
Holbrook Av					
	18800	EPTE	48021	4204	A1
Holbrook St					
	10	DET	48202	4273	A6
	900	DET	48211	4273	A6
	1800	DET	48212	4273	B5
	2100	HMTK	48212	4273	C5
N Holbrook St					
	100	PLYM	48170	4265	B7
S Holbrook St					
	100	PLYM	48170	4265	B7
Holbrooke Dr					
	600	CNTN	48187	4411	A2
Holburn St					
	800	WIND	N9G	4504	E3
	900	WIND	N9G	4505	A3
	3600	WIND	N9E	4504	E2
Holcomb St					
	1100	DET	48214	4346	E1
	3700	DET	48214	4274	D7
	5000	DET	48213	4274	C6
Holden Av					
	300	WIND	N8X	4421	B5
Holden Dr					
	3900	WasC	48103	4405	A1
Holden Rd					
	5700	Tcmh	N0R	4505	A7
Holden St					
	1000	DET	48202	4344	E2
	1000	DET	48202	4345	A2
	1400	DET	48210	4344	E2
Holdren St					
	18800	BwTp	48173	4841	A1
	19500	RKWD	48173	4841	A1
Holford Av					
	200	RVRG	48218	4418	D7
	300	RVRG	48218	4501	D1
Holiday Blvd					
	-	CNTN	48187	4337	E6
Holiday Ct					
	10	Amhg	N9V	4757	D2
	9200	WasC	48189	4258	E1
Holiday Dr					
	9000	WasC	48189	4258	E1
	9300	WasC	48189	4186	E7
Holiday Rd					
	19700	GSPW	48236	4204	C6
Holland Av					
	18000	EPTE	48021	4203	E2
	18700	EPTE	48021	4204	A2
Holland Rd					
	6400	TYLR	48180	4498	C2
Hollander St					
	22700	DRBN	48128	4341	B7
	23800	DRBN	48128	4416	A1
	25000	DRBN	48128	4415	D1
Hollinger Av					
	1800	LSal	N9H	4503	B6
Hollis Av					
	-	WIND	N9G	4504	E3
Hollis Rd					
	400	YpTp	48198	4492	C3
Hollow Tree Ct					
	6300	WasC	48176	4572	A4
Holly Cres					
	9800	WIND	N8R	4423	B3
Holly Dr					
	8000	CNTN	48187	4337	D3
Holly Ln					
	200	VNBN	48111	4494	D5
	7600	WasC	48176	4571	B6
Holly St					
	10	Lksr	N8N	4424	E3
	2400	DRBN	48120	4418	D2
	6300	DET	48209	4419	C3
Holly Wy					
	4700	WasC	48103	4329	E4
Hollydale					
	40900	NOVI	48375	4193	C2
Hollywood E					
	400	DET	48203	4200	D6
Hollywood W					
	400	DET	48203	4200	B6
Hollywood Av					
	500	GSPW	48236	4205	A5
	600	GSPW	48236	4204	C4
	2200	HRWD	48236	4204	C4
	8200	RMLS	48174	4497	E4
Hollywood Dr					
	300	SALN	48176	4572	C7
	2500	AARB	48103	4405	C5
	2500	WasC	48103	4405	C5
	12800	PyTp	48170	4264	A7
	20700	SFLD	48075	4198	A4
	49500	CNTN	48187	4335	D4
Hollywood St					
	1300	DRBN	48124	4417	A5
	7100	RMLS	48174	4497	E3
	16000	RMLS	48174	4581	E5
	20000	HRWD	48080	4204	B4
	20000	HRWD	48225	4204	B4
	20800	HRWD	48236	4204	B4
Hollywood Ct					
	8000	DET	48234	4202	A6
Holmbury Ct					
	21400	NHVL	48167	4192	A4
Holmbury Rd					
	21400	NHVL	48167	4192	A5
Holmes Cres					
	2200	Tcmh	N8N	4424	A5
Holmes Ct					
	7100	CNTN	48187	4336	C5
Holmes Dr					
	45400	CNTN	48187	4336	C5
Holmes Rd					
	100	YPLT	48198	4492	A3
	100	YpTp	48198	4492	A3
	2200	YpTp	48198	4493	A3
Holmes St					
	2300	HMTK	48212	4273	B4
	7000	DET	48210	4343	D4
Holmur St					
	9200	DET	48204	4344	A1
	9200	DET	48206	4344	A1
	9700	DET	48204	4272	A7
	9700	DET	48206	4272	A7
	12600	DET	48204	4271	E6
	12600	DET	48206	4271	E6
	15400	DET	48238	4271	E2
	16100	DET	48221	4271	E2
Holyoke Ct					
	24400	NOVI	48374	4192	A1
Holyoke Ln					
	2700	AARB	48103	4405	E1
	24300	NOVI	48374	4192	A1
Holz Dr					
	-	SOGT	48195	4584	A4
Homedale Blvd					
	800	WIND	N8S	4347	C7
	1300	WIND	N8S	4422	C1
Homedale St					
	5200	DET	48210	4343	C6
Homefield St					
	6700	RMLS	48174	4498	A3
	13000	RMLS	48174	4582	A2
Homeister Ct					
	15400	RVVW	48192	4584	B6
Homeister Dr					
	15500	RVVW	48192	4584	B6
Homeplace St					
	2100	DRBN	48124	4415	E4
Homer St					
	-	NvlT	48167	4264	E3
	8000	DET	48209	4419	A3
	8700	DET	48209	4418	E3
	16200	NvlT	48167	4265	A3
	21500	DRBN	48124	4416	D3
Homestead Cir					
	16000	NvlT	48167	4265	C3
Homestead Ct					
	-	NOVI	48374	4192	B1
	3200	WasC	48176	4572	B3
Homestead Ln					
	1700	LSal	N9H	4504	B5
	10400	WasC	48170	4263	A7
	19400	GBTR	48173	4755	A4
S Homestead Ln					
	10400	WasC	48170	4263	A7
	10400	WasC	48170	4335	A1
Homestead Rd					
	7000	YpTp	48197	4575	E5
Homestead St					
	2600	MVDL	48122	4418	A5
	22200	TYLR	48180	4499	C6
Homestead Commons Dr					
	3000	AARB	48108	4489	E4
	3000	PTFD	48108	4489	E4
Honey Ln					
	8100	CNTN	48187	4337	D4
Honeycomb Cir					
	8500	CNTN	48187	4337	D3
Honey Creek Dr					
	700	WasC	48103	4404	E4
Honeysuckle Ct					
	3300	PTFD	48103	4488	D5
Honey Suckle Dr					
	31700	BwTp	48173	4755	A6
Honeysuckle Dr					
	3000	PTFD	48103	4488	D4
Honeysuckle Hllw					
	10	YpTp	48197	4577	B4
Honeytree Blvd					
	8100	CNTN	48187	4337	D4
Hong Ct					
	1100	WIND	N8P	4348	D7
Honorah St					
	2300	DET	48209	4419	A1
Hooker St					
	2600	DET	48210	4344	D3
Hoover Av					
	2200	LNPK	48146	4500	C4
	23000	HZLP	48030	4200	D1
W Hoover Av					
	100	AARB	48103	4406	B7
Hoover Ct					
	24300	FNHL	48335	4194	B1
Hoover Dr					
	5600	WYNE	48184	4497	C2
Hoover Rd					
	-	DET	48089	4202	C2
	5400	TNTN	48183	4755	D1
	20700	WRRN	48089	4202	C2
Hoover St					
	17100	DET	48205	4274	C1
	17100	DET	48234	4274	C1
	17300	DET	48205	4202	C6
	17300	DET	48234	4202	C6
Hoover St SR-97					
	17100	DET	48205	4274	C1
	17100	DET	48234	4274	C1
	17300	DET	48205	4202	C6
	17300	DET	48234	4202	C6
E Hoover St					
	100	AARB	48103	4406	B7
	100	AARB	48104	4406	B7
Hope					
	25800	RDFD	48239	4268	C4
Hope St					
	4100	ALPK	48101	4417	D7
	4100	ALPK	48122	4417	D7
Hopecrest Ct					
	33100	FNHL	48336	4194	E1
Hopefield Ct					
	3900	CNTN	48188	4411	C6
Hopkins Dr					
	11600	PyTp	48170	4335	D1
Hopkins St					
	24000	DBHT	48125	4416	A7
	24300	DBHT	48125	4415	D7
	25400	DBHT	48141	4415	D7
	26100	INKR	48141	4415	B7
Hopper St					
	-	SALN	48176	4572	E7
Horace Jackson St					
	34200	RMLS	48174	4497	A2
	34300	RMLS	48174	4496	E2
Horatio St					
	6100	DET	48210	4344	A5
	6800	DET	48210	4343	E6
Horger Av					
	14500	ALPK	48101	4500	C2
Horger St					
	1700	LNPK	48146	4500	D3
	7200	DRBN	48126	4342	E4
E Horizons Ct					
	5800	PTFD	48108	4572	E3
E Horizons Dr					
	5700	PTFD	48108	4572	E3
Horman Ct					
	1300	AARB	48104	4489	D1
Hornet Av					
	-	WynC	48138	4756	B1
Horsemill Rd					
	7500	WynC	48138	4670	C1
S Horseshoe Blvd					
	7600	WasC	48189	4259	B4
Horseshoe Cir					
	1200	PTFD	48108	4489	A5
	45000	CNTN	48187	4411	D1
Horseshoe Dr					
	-	NvlT	48167	4264	A3
Horseshoe Creek Ct					
	7800	HbgT	48189	4186	C4
Horton St					
	10	DET	48202	4273	A7
	10	DET	48202	4345	A1
	400	NHVL	48167	4192	E5
	2700	FRDL	48069	4199	E1
	2700	FRDL	48220	4199	E1
	9700	LVNA	48150	4338	A2
Horwood Cres					
	12500	Tcmh	N8N	4424	A1
Hosmer St					
	8700	DET	48214	4346	E2
E Hospital Dr					
	-	AARB	48104	4406	D6
N Hospital Dr					
	-	WTLD	48186	4414	C4
S Hospital Dr					
	-	WTLD	48184	4414	C5
	-	WTLD	48186	4414	C5
Hotspur Ct					
	42600	CNTN	48188	4412	A6
Hot Strip Ml					
	-	DRBN	48120	4418	A3
Houghton Dr					
	15900	LVNA	48154	4266	A3
Houghton Rd					
	10800	GOTp	48189	4187	C4
Houghton St					
	8800	LVNA	48150	4338	A2
	14900	LVNA	48154	4266	A4
	20000	DET	48219	4197	B5
House St					
	8000	DET	48234	4202	A6
Houston Dr					
	38600	RMLS	48174	4496	A2
Houston St					
	1800	DRBN	48124	4417	A5
Houston Whittier St					
	12900	DET	48205	4274	E1
	13900	DET	48205	4275	A1
	15200	DET	48224	4275	A1
Howard Av					
	800	WIND	N9A	4421	A2
	1200	WIND	N8X	4421	A2
	3200	WIND	N9E	4421	C7
	3300	WIND	N9E	4504	D3
	3800	WIND	N9G	4504	D3
	4800	LSal	N9H	4504	D7
	4800	Tcmh	N9H	4504	D7
	5200	Tcmh	N0R	4504	D7
Howard St					
	400	DET	48226	4345	B7
	800	DRBN	48124	4416	C2
	1000	LNPK	48146	4501	A2
	2000	LNPK	48146	4500	D4
	2600	DET	48216	4345	A7
	2700	DET	48216	4420	A1
	3500	DET	48216	4419	E1
	5600	DET	48209	4419	C2
	7800	HbgT	48189	4186	C4
	12000	SOGT	48195	4500	E7
	12200	SOGT	48195	4584	E2
Howard Holmes Dr					
	-	SpTp	48197	4491	A1
Howe Rd					
	3600	WYNE	48184	4414	A6
	5300	WYNE	48184	4497	A1
	5500	WYNE	48174	4497	A1
Howe St					
	800	DRBN	48124	4416	C3
Howell					
	27000	RDFD	48239	4268	B4
	27300	RDFD	48154	4268	B4
Howell Av					
	36000	LVNA	48154	4266	C4
Howell St					
	-	LVNA	48154	4268	A4
	4700	DET	48210	4344	A5
	8800	DET	48204	4343	E2
	37500	LVNA	48154	4266	A5
	38900	LVNA	48154	4265	E5
Howey Blvd					
	-	TNTN	48183	4669	C6
Howland Park Dr					
	11900	PyTp	48170	4335	D1
	12500	PyTp	48170	4263	D7
Howley Ct					
	600	AARB	48105	4406	C4
Hoy St					
	30100	LVNA	48154	4267	C4
Hoyt Dr					
	11600	VNBN	48111	4579	D1
Hoyt St					
	19100	DET	48205	4203	A4
Hubbard Av					
	1100	GDNC	48135	4414	B1
	1700	GDNC	48135	4339	B7
	4100	LNPK	48146	4500	E7
	5400	YpTp	48197	4576	B2
S Hubbard Ct					
	100	WTLD	48186	4414	B2
Hubbard Dr					
	16300	DRBN	48126	4342	D7
	19300	DRBN	48126	4341	E7
	19300	DRBN	48128	4341	E7
Hubbard St					
	-	LVNA	48150	4267	B6
	1000	DET	48209	4419	D1
	1000	DET	48216	4419	D1
	1600	DET	48209	4344	D7
	2100	AARB	48105	4406	E4
	2100	AARB	48105	4407	A4
	2600	DRBN	48124	4416	B4
	3100	DET	48216	4344	D6
	8800	LVNA	48150	4339	B3
	13900	LVNA	48154	4267	B5
	16600	LVNA	48152	4267	B3
	19800	LVNA	48152	4195	A5
	20200	LVNA	48336	4195	A5
N Hubbard St					
	8000	WTLD	48185	4339	B3
S Hubbard St					
	400	WTLD	48186	4414	B2
	2900	WYNE	48184	4414	B5
Hubbell St					
	-	OKPK	48235	4198	D4
	2000	DRBN	48128	4341	B6
	5600	DBHT	48127	4341	B6
	5600	DBHT	48128	4341	B6
	8000	DET	48228	4342	E3
	9500	DET	48227	4342	E1
	10900	LVNA	48150	4339	C1
	13900	DET	48227	4270	D4
	13900	LVNA	48154	4267	C5
	16100	DET	48235	4270	D3
	18000	DET	48235	4198	D7
	20700	OKPK	48237	4198	D4
Huber St					
	5900	DET	48211	4273	D4
	5900	DET	48212	4273	D4
	6300	DET	48234	4273	E4
	7000	DET	48211	4274	A4
	7000	DET	48234	4274	A4
	7200	DET	48213	4274	A4
Hubert Av					
	8900	ALPK	48101	4500	B4
Huck Ct					
	-	INKR	48141	4415	B4
Hudson Av					
	500	YpTp	48198	4493	A5
	2000	WIND	N9E	4420	C7
	7000	WRRN	48091	4201	E3
	7000	WRRN	48091	4202	A3
	8000	WRRN	48089	4202	A3
Hudson Dr					
	49400	CNTN	48188	4410	D3
Hudson Ln					
	26500	FTRK	48134	4753	E1
Hudson St					
	500	WYDT	48192	4585	B1
	2100	DET	48210	4344	C5
	8200	RMLS	48174	4497	D4
	23600	DRBN	48124	4416	A2
Huff Ct					
	14400	LVNA	48154	4266	A5
Huff St					
	5600	WTLD	48185	4338	B7
	15500	LVNA	48154	4266	A3
Hugh Av					
	8000	WTLD	48185	4339	E3
	8600	WTLD	48150	4339	E3
Hugh St					
	8800	LVNA	48150	4339	D2
	20200	LVNA	48152	4195	D5
	20400	LVNA	48336	4195	D5
Hughes Av					
	20700	HZLP	48030	4200	D2
Hughes St					
	1900	DET	48238	4272	A3
Hughes Ter					
	2200	DET	48210	4344	D2
Hugo St					
	20700	FNHL	48336	4195	A4
Hulbert Av					
	24000	BNTN	48174	4668	A1
Hull Av					
	1000	YpTp	48198	4492	D6
Hull Rd					
	43400	VNBN	48111	4578	E5
	43400	VNBN	48111	4579	A4
	44800	BLVL	48111	4578	E5
	47700	VNBN	48111	4577	E4
Hull St					
	17100	DET	48203	4272	E1
	19100	DET	48203	4200	E4
	20400	DET	48030	4200	E4
Humber Av					
	3200	TNTN	48183	4669	B5
Humboldt St					
	3700	DET	48210	4344	D4
Humbug Island Ct					
	13900	GBTR	48173	4755	C3
Hummingbird Ct					
	8000	YpTp	48197	4576	B3
Hummingbird Dr					
	8100	YpTp	48197	4576	B3
Humphrey Rd					
	11000	HbgT	48189	4186	A6
Humphrey St					
	3700	DET	48206	4272	A7
	4000	DET	48204	4272	A7
	15000	SOGT	48195	4583	E4
Hunt Pl					
	500	YpTp	48198	4492	C3
Hunt St					
	2200	DET	48207	4345	E3
	2600	DET	48207	4346	A3
	4600	WYNE	48184	4413	C7
	6400	RMLS	48174	4496	C2
	11200	RMLS	48174	4580	C1
Hunt Club Cres					
	4400	WIND	N9G	4504	D4
Hunt Club Ct					
	49200	PyTp	48170	4335	E1
Hunt Club Dr					
	1700	GSPW	48236	4204	B5
	4400	PTFD	48197	4490	E7
	4600	PTFD	48197	4491	A7
	4800	PTFD	48197	4574	E1
	20400	HRWD	48225	4204	A5
	21100	HRWD	48236	4204	B5
Hunter Av					
	900	YpTp	48198	4492	D2
	32900	WTLD	48185	4339	A6
	35600	WTLD	48185	4338	C6
Hunter Cir N					
	21400	TYLR	48180	4583	C2
Hunter Cir S					
	21400	TYLR	48180	4583	C2
Hunter Ct					
	6400	WTLD	48185	4339	A6
	28300	FTRK	48134	4753	E3
	29200	BwTp	48173	4754	E4
Hunter Ln					
	24900	FTRK	48134	4753	E3
	24900	FTRK	48134	4754	A3
Hunter St					
	29300	BwTp	48173	4754	D4
Hunter Pointe St					
	6200	WTLD	48185	4338	D6
Hunter Ridge Ct					
	7100	PTFD	48176	4573	D5
Hunter Ridge Dr					
	100	PTFD	48176	4573	D5
Hunters Cir E					
	3900	CNTN	48188	4411	C7
Hunters Cir W					
	3900	CNTN	48188	4411	C7
Hunters Ct					
	2600	CNTN	48188	4412	B5
Hunters Ln					
	23000	SFLD	48034	4197	A2
Hunters Rdg					
	42000	CNTN	48188	4412	B5
Hunters Tr					
	200	WasC	48103	4404	C5
Hunters Creek Ct					
	11800	PyTp	48170	4336	A1
Hunters Creek Dr					
	2000	SpTp	48198	4409	A6
	11600	PyTp	48170	4336	A1
Hunters Grove Blvd					
	3800	CNTN	48188	4411	A6
Hunters Park Dr					
	-	PyTp	48170	4264	B7
Hunters Ridge Dr					
	20800	LyTp	48167	4191	A5
Hunters Wy Ct					
	3800	CNTN	48188	4411	C6
Huntingcross Dr					
	44700	NOVI	48375	4192	D3
Huntington Av					
	3400	WIND	N9E	4504	C1
	5700	YpTp	48197	4576	A2
	18500	HRWD	48225	4203	E5
	19600	HRWD	48225	4204	A5
Huntington Blvd					
	-	CNTN	48188	4411	B6
	1400	GSPW	48236	4204	B6
Huntington Ct					
	5600	YpTp	48197	4576	A2
	22400	WDHN	48183	4668	C4
Huntington Dr					
	700	SLYN	48178	4189	A3
	8000	WTLD	48185	4339	C4
	14400	PyTp	48170	4265	C5
	44600	NOVI	48375	4192	D1
Huntington Pl					
	400	AARB	48104	4407	A6
Huntington Rd					
	-	DET	48223	4269	E2
	300	AARB	48104	4407	A7
	16100	DET	48219	4269	E2
	20200	DET	48219	4197	E5
Huntington St					
	13700	RVVW	48192	4584	C6
Hunting Valley Dr					
	3000	AARB	48104	4407	B7
	3000	AARB	48104	4490	B1
Huntleigh Av					
	6400	GDNC	48135	4339	C6
Huntley Av					
	18200	BNTN	48192	4583	C7
Huntley Ct					
	13500	GOTp	48178	4188	E2
	18100	BNTN	48192	4583	C6
Huntsville Dr					
	600	CNTN	48187	4411	A2
Huntwick Pl					
	1200	LSal	N9H	4504	C5
Hupp Av					
	7000	WRRN	48091	4201	E2
	7000	WRRN	48091	4202	A2
	8000	WRRN	48089	4202	A2
Hurlbut St					
	1400	DET	48214	4346	E1
	1400	DET	48214	4347	A2
	3700	DET	48214	4274	D6
	6000	DET	48213	4274	C4
Huron Av					
	-	BwTp	48183	4754	E3
Huron Cir					
	21800	WynC	48138	4670	B3
Huron Ct					
	3600	WasC	48103	4329	D6
Huron Dr					
	13000	TYLR	48180	4583	E2
Huron Pkwy					
	-	AARB	48104	4407	B7
	-	AATp	48104	4407	B7
	-	AATp	48104	4490	B1
	1600	AARB	48105	4407	A2
	1800	AARB	48104	4490	B1
	1800	AATp	48105	4407	A2
	2700	AARB	48105	4406	E2
	2700	AATp	48105	4406	E2
S Huron Pkwy					
	2100	AARB	48104	4490	B2
S Huron Rd					
	27600	HnTp	48134	4753	B3
	27600	MonC	48134	4753	B3
	35700	HnTp	48164	4665	C5
	39000	HnTp	48111	4664	E5
	39000	HnTp	48164	4664	E5
Huron St					
	-	FRDL	48220	4200	B1
	100	LSal	N9J	4502	D5
	800	LSal	N9J	4503	A6
	2600	DET	48216	4345	A5
	3500	DRBN	48124	4416	D6
	3900	DBHT	48124	4416	D6
	3900	DBHT	48125	4416	D6
	5800	TYLR	48125	4499	D1
	5800	TYLR	48180	4499	D1
	14300	TYLR	48180	4583	E3
E Huron St					
	100	AARB	48104	4406	C6
E Huron St I-94 BUS					
	100	AARB	48104	4406	C6
E Huron St US-23 BUS					
	100	AARB	48104	4406	C6
N Huron St					
	10	YPLT	48197	4492	A3
	700	YPLT	48197	4491	E2
	900	YPLT	48198	4491	E2
N Huron St SR-17					
	10	YPLT	48197	4492	A4
S Huron St					
	-	YPLT	48197	4491	E7
	10	YPLT	48197	4492	A5
	900	YpTp	48197	4491	E7
	1500	YpTp	48197	4575	E1
S Huron St US-12 BUS					
	-	YPLT	48197	4491	E6
	-	YpTp	48197	4491	E6
	10	YPLT	48197	4492	A5
W Huron St					
	100	AARB	48104	4406	A6
	200	AARB	48103	4406	A6
	1400	AARB	48103	4405	E6
W Huron St I-94 BUS					
	100	AARB	48104	4406	A6
	200	AARB	48103	4406	A6
	1400	AARB	48103	4405	E6
Huron Church Rd					
	100	WIND	N9B	4420	C5
	100	WIND	N9C	4420	C5
	2200	WIND	N9E	4420	C5
	2500	WIND	N9E	4503	D1
	3700	WIND	N9H	4503	D1
	3800	LSal	N9H	4503	D1
	3800	WIND	N9G	4503	D1
Huron Church Rd P-3					
	800	WIND	N9B	4420	C5
	800	WIND	N9C	4420	C5
	2200	WIND	N9E	4420	C5
	2500	WIND	N9E	4503	D1
	3700	WIND	N9H	4503	D1
	3800	LSal	N9H	4503	D1
	3800	WIND	N9G	4503	D1

INDEX 28
Huron Church Line Rd
Detroit & Wayne County Street Index
James Ct

STREET Block City ZIP Map# Grid

Huron Church Line Rd
- WIND N9G 4503 E3
3900 LSal N9H 4503 E4
3900 LSal N9H 4504 B6
Huron Meadows Dr
30000 RKWD 48173 4754 B6
Huron Oaks Ct
8900 HbgT 48116 4186 C1
Huron Oaks Dr
7800 HbgT 48116 4186 C1
Huron Park Blvd
- HnTp 48134 4666 E7
Huron Park Ct
7000 HbgT 48116 4186 A1
Huron Park Dr
9300 HbgT 48116 4186 A1
Huron River Dr
5000 WasC 48103 4329 C6
5000 WasC 48130 4329 C6
14800 BwTp 48173 4755 A7
17000 HnTp 48164 4580 B7
17000 HnTp 48174 4580 B7
18600 HnTp 48164 4665 B1
20000 RKWD 48173 4755 A7
20000 RKWD 48173 4840 E1
21000 HnTp 48164 4666 A3
22100 RKWD 48173 4754 E7
23900 FTRK 48173 4754 A6
24700 FTRK 48134 4753 E5
24700 FTRK 48173 4753 E5
30800 HnTp 48134 4666 C7
E Huron River Dr
- VNBN 48174 4579 C2
10 BLVL 48111 4578 E2
700 VNBN 48111 4578 E2
800 VNBN 48111 4579 B2
3200 AARB 48104 4407 C7
3200 AATp 48104 4407 C7
3500 AARB 48104 4490 D1
3500 AATp 48104 4490 D1
4100 AATp 48105 4490 E1
4800 AATp 48105 4491 A1
4800 SpTp 48105 4491 A1
4800 SpTp 48197 4491 A1
25100 FTRK 48134 4753 D4
N Huron River Dr
1000 YPLT 48197 4491 C2
1000 YPLT 48198 4491 C2
1200 SpTp 48197 4491 C2
1200 SpTp 48198 4491 C2
1200 YpTp 48197 4491 C2
1500 YPLT 48105 4491 C2
1700 SpTp 48105 4491 C2
S Huron River Dr
4400 BrTp 48134 4753 D4
4800 BrTp 48179 4753 E6
5100 SRKW 48179 4753 E6
5300 SRKW 48179 4754 A7
5900 SRKW 48179 4840 D1
7000 YpTp 48197 4575 E1
7000 YpTp 48197 4576 A1
7500 BrTp 48179 4840 E2
7900 BrTp 48179 4841 A4
12000 RMLS 48174 4580 B4
W Huron River Dr
600 BLVL 48111 4578 B3
600 VNBN 48111 4578 B3
1000 AARB 48103 4406 B3
1000 AARB 48105 4406 B3
1000 AATp 48103 4406 B3
1000 AATp 48105 4406 B3
1600 AARB 48103 4405 E1
1600 AARB 48105 4405 E1
1600 AATp 48103 4405 E1
1600 AATp 48105 4405 E1
2100 WasC 48103 4405 E1
2100 WasC 48105 4405 E1
3100 WasC 48103 4330 B7
3100 WasC 48105 4330 B7
4000 WasC 48103 4329 E5
26400 FTRK 48134 4753 B2
27100 HnTp 48134 4753 B2
29400 HnTp 48134 4752 E1
29500 HnTp 48134 4666 E7
37400 RMLS 48174 4580 A1
38400 RMLS 48174 4579 E1
39400 VNBN 48111 4579 E1
39400 VNBN 48174 4579 E1
48700 VNBN 48111 4577 D3
E Huron River Service Dr
4000 AATp 48104 4490 D1
Huronview Blvd
500 AARB 48103 4406 A3
600 WasC 48103 4406 A3
Hussar St
6000 DET 48209 4419 D2
Hutchins Av
700 AARB 48103 4406 A7
1100 AARB 48103 4489 A1
Hutton St
100 NHVL 48167 4192 E6
Hyacinth St
- DET 48229 4501 C2
Hyacinthe St
200 ECRS 48229 4501 D3
Hyannis Ct
8100 CNTN 48187 4336 A4
Hyatt Cir
- DRBN 48126 4417 A2
Hyatt Dr
- DRBN 48126 4417 A1
N Hyatt Dr
- DRBN 48126 4417 A1
S Hyatt Dr
- DRBN 48126 4417 A2
Hyatt Ln
- DRBN 48126 4417 A2
Hyde Pk
2500 INKR 48141 4414 E4
Hyde St
300 WIND N8X 4421 B4
7000 DET 48211 4274 A6
Hyde Park Ct
19100 WDHN 48183 4669 A7
Hyde Park Dr
1900 DET 48207 4345 E4
1900 DET 48207 4346 A4
18900 WDHN 48183 4669 A7
Hyde Park St
6100 RMLS 48174 4497 E1
17000 HnTp 48174 4581 E6
18900 HnTp 48174 4667 A1
N Hydramatic Dr
- YpTp 48198 4493 B4
W Hydramatic Dr
- YpTp 48198 4493 B4
Hyland St
- PTRG 48069 4199 C1
2100 FRDL 48220 4199 C1
2500 FRDL 48069 4199 C1
Hyman St
38100 WTLD 48186 4413 A4
Hystone Dr
41900 CNTN 48187 4412 B2

I

I-75
- ALPK - 4500 B7
- BNTN - 4583 D7
- BNTN - 4668 D7
- BrTp - 4839 C6
- BrTp - 4840 A3
- BwTp - 4754 D3
- FTRK - 4754 D3
- LNPK - 4500 B7
- RKWD - 4754 D3
- SRKW - 4754 D3
- SRKW - 4840 A3
- TYLR - 4583 D7
- WDHN - 4668 D7
- WDHN - 4754 D3
I-75 Chrysler Frwy
- DET - 4200 D5
- DET - 4272 E2
- DET - 4273 C7
- DET - 4345 D3
- HMTK - 4273 C7
- HZLP - 4200 D5
I-75 Fisher Frwy
- DET - 4418 D5
- DET - 4501 A2
- LNPK - 4500 E2
- LNPK - 4501 A2
- MVDL - 4418 D5
- MVDL - 4501 A2
I-75 Fisher Frwy N
- DET - 4344 E6
- DET - 4345 B6
- DET - 4418 E5
- DET - 4419 E1
I-75 Fisher Frwy S
- DET - 4344 E6
- DET - 4345 C5
- DET - 4418 E5
- DET - 4419 A4
I-94
- AARB - 4405 C5
- AARB - 4488 D2
- AARB - 4489 D5
- AARB - 4490 B5
- ALPK - 4417 C6
- ALPK - 4499 C1
- ALPK - 4500 B1
- DRBN - 4343 B7
- DRBN - 4417 C6
- DRBN - 4418 B1
- EPTE - 4204 A3
- HRWD - 4204 A3
- PTFD - 4488 D2
- PTFD - 4489 D5
- PTFD - 4490 B5
- PTFD - 4491 C7
- RMLS - 4495 C7
- RMLS - 4496 C7
- RMLS - 4497 C5
- RMLS - 4498 D2
- STCS - 4204 A3
- TYLR - 4498 D2
- TYLR - 4499 C1
- VNBN - 4493 E7
- VNBN - 4494 E7
- VNBN - 4495 C7
- WasC - 4404 D5
- WasC - 4405 C5
- WasC - 4488 D2
- YPLT - 4491 C7
- YPLT - 4492 C6
- YpTp - 4491 C7
- YpTp - 4492 C6
- YpTp - 4493 A7
- YpTp - 4577 B1
I-94 BUS
- PTFD - 4490 C5
I-94 Edsel Ford Frwy
- DET - 4204 A7
- DET - 4273 C7
- DET - 4274 C5
- DET - 4275 D2
- DET - 4276 A1
- DET - 4343 E6
- DET - 4344 C4
- DET - 4345 B1
I-94 BUS E Huron St
100 AARB 48104 4406 B6
I-94 BUS W Huron St
100 AARB 48104 4406 A6
200 AARB 48103 4406 A6
1400 AARB 48103 4405 E6
I-94 BUS Jackson Av
1500 AARB 48103 4405 E6
I-94 BUS Jackson Rd
3000 AARB 48103 4405 C5
I-94 North Service Dr
- VNBN 48111 4493 C7
- YpTp 48111 4493 C7
- YpTp 48198 4493 C7
S I-94 Service Rd
- RMLS 48174 4497 A6
- RMLS 48242 4497 A6
I-94 South Service Dr
41100 VNBN 48111 4495 B7
I-94 BUS Washtenaw Av
- PTFD 48104 4490 C2
- PTFD 48105 4490 C2
- PTFD 48108 4490 C2
400 AARB 48104 4406 D7
1900 AARB 48104 4489 E1
2100 AARB 48104 4490 C2
I-96
- DET - 4269 D6
- DET - 4270 C6
- DET - 4271 A6
I-96 Jeffries Frwy
- DET - 4269 B6
- DET - 4270 A7
- DET - 4271 D6
- DET - 4343 D1
- DET - 4344 A2
- LVNA - 4265 E6
- LVNA - 4266 E6
- LVNA - 4267 D6
- LVNA - 4268 B6
- RDFD - 4268 B6
I-275
- CNTN - 4337 C6
- CNTN - 4412 C1
- CNTN - 4495 D4
- FNHL - 4193 E4
- HnTp - 4580 D5
- HnTp - 4665 D3
- HnTp - 4751 E2
- LVNA - 4193 E4
- LVNA - 4265 E4
- MonC - 4752 A7
- NvIT - 4265 E4
- PyTp - 4265 D7
- PyTp - 4337 C6
- RMLS - 4495 D4
- RMLS - 4496 A7
- RMLS - 4580 D5
- VNBN - 4495 D4
I-375 Chrysler Frwy
- DET - 4345 E5
Ida Av
13600 WRRN 48089 4202 E3
13600 WRRN 48089 4203 A3
Ida Ln E
19700 GSPW 48236 4204 D7
Ida Ln W
19800 GSPW 48236 4204 C7
Ida Rd
2500 WIND N8W 4421 E4
Idaho
100 WynC 48111 4662 E2
Idaho Av
900 FRDL 48220 4200 A3
Idaho St
9100 LVNA 48150 4339 B2
15700 DET 48238 4272 B2
Ide Av
2000 YpTp 48198 4577 B1
Ideal Pl
200 WasC 48189 4259 A4
Idel Ct
5000 WIND N8T 4422 B3
Idlewild Ct
3000 AARB 48105 4406 E1
Ilene Av
1900 TNTN 48183 4669 D6
Ilene St
11600 DET 48204 4271 B6
13500 DET 48238 4271 B5
16100 DET 48221 4271 B1
19900 DET 48221 4199 B5
Iliad St
15300 DET 48223 4269 A3
15900 DET 48219 4269 A3
Illinois St
10 Amhg N9V 4757 E2
2800 DET 48207 4345 E2
3100 DET 48207 4346 A2
32800 LVNA 48150 4339 A3
Iman Rd
1700 CNTN 48188 4412 D4
Imperial Cres
900 WIND N9G 4504 E5
Imperial Hwy
1700 WTLD 48185 4338 D7
19400 RDFD 48240 4196 D6
19900 DET 48219 4196 D6
19900 DET 48240 4196 D6
Ina St
400 DRBN 48128 4416 B1
Inbrook Dr
15000 PyTp 48170 4265 D4
Independence
25000 BNTN 48134 4667 E6
Independence Blvd
1800 AARB 48104 4489 E2
2100 AARB 48104 4490 A3
Independence Ct
24300 FNHL 48335 4194 A1
Independence Dr
24200 FMTN 48335 4194 A1
24300 FNHL 48335 4194 A1
24400 HnTp 48134 4666 E6
24400 HnTp 48164 4666 E6
Independence Ln
- VNBN 48111 4495 C7
Independence St
22300 WDHN 48183 4668 C6
27600 FNHL 48336 4196 A4
27900 FNHL 48336 4195 E4
Indian
15700 RDFD 48239 4268 B3
17300 RDFD 48240 4268 B1
20400 RDFD 48240 4196 B5
Indian Cr
2200 AARB 48105 4331 D7
Indian Rd
300 WIND N9C 4420 B3
Indian St
21500 SFLD 48034 4196 B3
Indian Tr
5300 YpTp 48197 4576 B1
Indiana
600 WynC 48111 4662 D2
Indiana Av
10 PTRG 48069 4199 E1
20200 BwTp 48183 4754 E3
Indiana Pl
10 Amhg N9V 4757 D2
Indiana Rd
36500 HnTp 48164 4751 C3
Indiana St
7200 DRBN 48126 4343 C3
8000 DET 48204 4343 C2
11400 DET 48204 4271 C7
13500 DET 48238 4271 C5
17100 DET 48221 4271 C1
19900 DET 48221 4199 B4
32600 LVNA 48150 4339 A3
Indian Creek Dr
20700 FNHL 48335 4194 D3
45000 CNTN 48187 4336 D6
Indiandale St
2200 DET 48238 4272 B4
Indian Hills Dr
6200 SpTp 48198 4491 C1
Indianola Av
500 AARB 48105 4406 C4
Indian River Pl
200 AARB 48104 4407 A6
Indian Wells Dr
7000 YpTp 48197 4576 A5
7400 WasC 48167 4262 A4
Indianwood Dr
22700 LyTp 48178 4190 D3
Indoplex Cir
24200 FNHL 48335 4194 C1
Industrial Dr
100 PLYM 48170 4265 C7
1100 PTFD 48176 4573 A5
1400 SALN 48176 4572 E5
1400 SALN 48176 4573 A5
4000 WIND N9C 4420 C7
10000 HbgT 48116 4186 C3
29400 LVNA 48150 4267 C6
29800 INKR 48141 4414 D5
N Industrial Dr
24500 FNHL 48335 4193 E1
S Industrial Dr
100 PTFD 48176 4573 A7
Industrial Dr E
22900 STCS 48080 4204 B1
Industrial Dr W
22900 STCS 48080 4204 B1
S Industrial Hwy
1100 AARB 48108 4489 D4
1600 AARB 48104 4489 C3
Industrial Rd
32400 GDNC 48135 4339 B7
32900 LVNA 48150 4267 A6
34000 LVNA 48150 4266 D6
Industrial St
- DET 48209 4418 D3
- DRBN 48209 4418 D3
1000 DRBN 48120 4418 D3
Industrial Park Ct
23400 FNHL 48335 4194 A1
Industrial Park Dr
300 BLVL 48111 4578 D3
23200 FNHL 48335 4194 A2
23600 FNHL 48335 4193 E2
Infantry St
1500 DET 48209 4419 B1
N Ingalls St
100 AARB 48104 4406 C5
Ingleside Dr
- SFLD 48034 4196 D1
Inglewood Av
3600 WIND N9E 4504 D2
3800 WIND N9G 4504 D2
Inglewood Dr
4100 PTFD 48197 4574 B4
Inglis St
2300 DET 48209 4418 E2
2300 DET 48209 4419 A2
Ingram Dr
8300 WTLD 48185 4339 B3
8700 WTLD 48150 4339 B3
26200 BNTN 48174 4582 D6
Ingram Rd
21500 NOVI 48375 4193 B4
Ingram St
9600 LVNA 48150 4339 B1
14000 LVNA 48154 4267 B6
19300 LVNA 48152 4195 B6
Inkster Rd
- FNHL 48152 4196 A6
- SFLD 48152 4196 A6
- SFLD 48240 4196 A6
100 INKR 48141 4415 B2
5800 RMLS 48174 4498 B1
5800 TYLR 48174 4498 B1
5800 TYLR 48180 4498 B1
6200 RMLS 48180 4498 B1
Inkster Rd
8800 LVNA 48150 4340 B2
8800 RDFD 48150 4340 B2
8800 RDFD 48239 4340 B2
11000 RMLS 48174 4582 B1
11000 TYLR 48174 4582 B1
11000 TYLR 48180 4582 B1
11300 LVNA 48239 4340 B2
11600 LVNA 48150 4268 B5
11600 LVNA 48239 4268 B5
11600 RDFD 48239 4268 B5
12500 RDFD 48150 4268 B5
13000 RMLS 48180 4582 B2
13900 LVNA 48154 4268 B5
13900 RDFD 48154 4268 B5
15800 RDFD 48240 4268 A1
16900 LVNA 48152 4268 A1
16900 RDFD 48152 4268 A1
17000 BNTN 48174 4582 B5
17000 HnTp 48174 4582 B5
18200 BNTN 48174 4667 B2
18200 HnTp 48174 4667 B2
18400 LVNA 48152 4196 A7
18400 RDFD 48152 4196 A7
18400 RDFD 48240 4196 A7
18600 LVNA 48240 4196 A7
20700 FNHL 48034 4196 A1
20700 FNHL 48336 4196 A1
20700 SFLD 48034 4196 A1
20700 SFLD 48336 4196 A6
22100 BNTN 48134 4667 B6
22100 HnTp 48134 4667 B6
22100 HnTp 48164 4667 B6
25200 BNTN 48134 4753 B1
25200 HnTp 48134 4753 B1
25900 FTRK 48134 4753 B1
N Inkster Rd
100 DBHT 48127 4415 B1
100 GDNC 48135 4415 B1
1500 DBHT 48127 4340 B7
1500 GDNC 48135 4340 B7
6800 GDNC 48127 4340 B4
7200 WTLD 48185 4340 B4
8700 DBHT 48185 4340 B4
S Inkster Rd
4600 DBHT 48125 4415 B7
4600 DBHT 48186 4415 B7
4600 WTLD 48186 4415 B7
5600 DBHT 48125 4498 B1
5600 DBHT 48186 4498 B1
5600 WTLD 48186 4498 B1
Inlet Ct
19400 NvIT 48167 4193 A7
Inman St
2700 FRDL 48220 4200 A1
Innerkip Cres
3500 WIND N8W 4421 E7
3500 WIND N8W 4504 E1
Innsbrook Dr
300 CNTN 48188 4411 B3
18500 NvIT 48167 4193 A7
18500 NvIT 48167 4265 A1
22200 FNHL 48167 4194 A3
22300 FNHL 48335 4194 A3
Insbrook Dr N
22300 FNHL 48167 4194 A3
Inselruhe Av
- DET 48207 4346 E5
Interface Dr
5700 WasC 48103 4404 B5
International Av
100 LSal N9J 4502 C6
International Dr
10 FTRK 48134 4754 C3
10 FTRK 48183 4754 C3
2500 YpTp 48197 4491 A3
Intersection Rd
11600 Tcmh N8N 4423 E4
12000 Tcmh N8N 4424 A4
Intervale St
7000 DET 48238 4271 D5
13100 DET 48227 4271 B5
13800 DET 48227 4270 E5
Intrepid St
9300 WynC 48138 4756 B2
Inveray Rd
47800 CNTN 48188 4411 A3
Inverness Ct
1600 PTFD 48108 4489 A7
23100 NOVI 48374 4192 A2
42800 NvIT 48170 4265 A3
Inverness Dr
26800 WDHN 48183 4754 E1
Inverness Rd
46400 CNTN 48188 4411 C3
Inverness St
- TYLR 48180 4499 D3
15300 DET 48238 4272 A3
16100 DET 48221 4272 A3
Ionia Ct
32100 WTLD 48186 4414 D5
Iosco Ct
32200 WTLD 48186 4414 D5
Iowa
500 WynC 48111 4662 D2
Iowa St
5900 DET 48212 4201 D7
6700 DET 48212 4202 A7
9000 LVNA 48150 4339 B2
Ira Blvd
21700 WRRN 48091 4201 C3
Irene Av
- WTLD 48186 4415 A7
4000 LNPK 48146 4500 C7
Irene St
3200 INKR 48141 4415 A6
12100 SOGT 48195 4500 C7
12100 SOGT 48195 4584 C1
22000 BNTN 48183 4668 B4
Iris Av
- DRBN 48120 4418 C2
Iris Ln
200 PTFD 48176 4573 D7
Iris Pl
5100 WIND N8T 4422 C4
Iris St
9500 DET 48227 4343 A1
11300 DET 48227 4271 A7
Irma Ct
4200 WIND N9G 4504 E3
Irma St
6200 RMLS 48174 4496 C2
Iron Ct
32200 WTLD 48186 4414 B4
Iron St
200 DET 48207 4346 C4
Irongate Ct
19800 NvIT 48167 4193 C6
Iron Gate Dr
7200 CNTN 48187 4336 E5
22000 WDHN 48183 4668 C6
Ironside Ct
21900 NOVI 48167 4192 D4
Ironside St
6900 DET 48210 4343 E6
Ironsides Ct
43100 CNTN 48187 4337 A5
Ironstone Ln
16100 RMLS 48174 4582 A5
Ironton St
200 RVRG 48218 4501 E2
300 ECRS 48218 4501 E2
3400 ECRS 48229 4501 E2
Ironwood Ct
19600 NvIT 48167 4193 A6
50400 PyTp 48170 4263 C7
Ironwood Dr
- Amhg N9V 4671 D4
300 WIND N9J 4502 D1
600 AARB 48103 4405 B4
600 WasC 48103 4405 B4
1500 CNTN 48188 4412 A4
8700 VNBN 48111 4495 B5
Ironwood St
6100 DET 48210 4344 A3
7300 DET 48204 4344 A3
Ironwood Wy
500 SALN 48176 4572 C4
Iroquois Ct
47400 NOVI 48374 4192 A2
Iroquois Ln
26200 FTRK 48134 4754 A1
Iroquois Pl
1200 AARB 48104 4489 D2
Iroquois St
1700 WIND N8Y 4421 C2
3700 DET 48214 4346 C1
4100 DET 48214 4274 C7
6400 DET 48213 4274 B5
7300 WTLD 48185 4339 A5
Irvin St
200 PLYM 48170 4264 E6
Irvine Blvd
13100 OKPK 48237 4199 A2
13200 OKPK 48237 4198 E2
Irvine Ct
45400 NOVI 48374 4192 C3
Irvine Dr
45400 NOVI 48374 4192 C3
Irvine Ln
100 GSPF 48236 4276 E2
Irvine St
500 WIND N8X 4421 B4
Irving Dr
19800 LVNA 48152 4194 E6
Irving St
3800 DRBN 48126 4418 A1
18200 LVNA 48152 4266 E1
18500 LVNA 48152 4194 E7
23600 TYLR 48180 4499 A4
Irvington
26900 RDFD 48239 4340 B1
Irvington St
19100 DET 48203 4200 D5
Isabelle Ct
7100 WIND N8S 4422 E1
Isabelle Pl
200 WIND N8S 4347 D6
1300 WIND N8S 4422 D1
Isabelle St
2100 INKR 48141 4415 A4
15600 RMLS 48174 4582 A4
21000 HnTp 48174 4667 A3
Isack Dr
300 WIND N8S 4347 E5
Isham
9100 DET 48213 4274 C4
Island Blvd
7600 WynC 48138 4670 C4
Island Ct
10 GSPT 48230 4276 D6
Island Dr
- WynC 48173 4755 E5
900 AARB 48104 4406 D5
900 AARB 48105 4406 D5
2900 WynC 48138 4670 B4
23300 HnTp 48164 4665 A5
30300 GBTR 48173 4755 E5
39300 HnTp 48164 4664 E5
E Island Dr
5900 YpTp 48197 4576 E3
Island Dr Ct
900 AARB 48105 4406 D4
Island Estate Dr
20100 WynC 48138 4670 B2
Ithaca Av
21000 ROTp 48220 4199 B3
Ithaca St
23800 OKPK 48237 4199 B1
Itham Ct
42800 NvIT 48167 4193 A6
Ivan Dr
9700 YpTp 48197 4577 A4
Ivanhoe
26000 RDFD 48239 4268 C4
N Ivanhoe Av
500 YpTp 48198 4492 D3
S Ivanhoe Av
5800 YpTp 48197 4576 D2
Ivanhoe Dr
9300 PyTp 48170 4336 B2
Ivanhoe St
4700 DET 48204 4344 A3
5500 DET 48204 4343 E3
Ives Av
7700 WynC 48138 4670 D1
Ives Ln
1700 AARB 48104 4489 D1
Ivy Dr
300 VNBN 48111 4494 D5
Ivy Ln
- WIND N8R 4423 B4
1100 YPLT 48197 4491 D6
Ivy St
13200 GBTR 48173 4755 D5
Ivydale St
800 AARB 48103 4405 E7
Ivylawn Ct
300 WasC 48189 4259 B1
Ivylawn Dr
300 WasC 48189 4259 B1
Ivywood Dr
1700 AARB 48103 4405 D7
Ivywood Ln
40200 PyTp 48170 4265 C4

J

Jacie Cres
12700 Tcmh N8N 4424 A2
Jackson Av
1500 AARB 48103 4405 D6
6700 WRRN 48091 4201 E4
7000 WRRN 48091 4202 A4
11200 WRRN 48089 4202 C4
12500 TYLR 48180 4583 E1
20000 GSPW 48236 4204 C5
Jackson Av I-94 BUS
1500 AARB 48103 4405 D6
Jackson Ct
10900 VNBN 48111 4495 B7
Jackson Dr
13900 PyTp 48170 4263 D6
Jackson Ln
9900 VNBN 48111 4495 B6
49600 CNTN 48188 4410 D3
Jackson Pl
1900 AARB 48103 4405 D6
Jackson Plz
10 WasC 48103 4405 B6
Jackson Rd
3000 AARB 48103 4405 A5
3000 WasC 48103 4405 A5
4200 WasC 48103 4404 E5
4600 TNTN 48183 4669 B7
Jackson Rd I-94 BUS
3000 AARB 48103 4405 C5
Jackson St
- DET 48210 4344 B6
100 WIND N8X 4421 A4
3300 DRBN 48124 4416 E5
3900 DBHT 48124 4416 E6
3900 DBHT 48125 4416 E7
5800 TYLR 48125 4499 E1
6400 TYLR 48180 4499 E1
10600 VNBN 48111 4495 B6
14000 TYLR 48180 4583 E3
14000 TYLR 48195 4583 E3
Jackson Industrial Dr
10 WasC 48103 4404 B5
Jacksonville St
21300 FNHL 48336 4195 E3
Jacob Av
14600 EPTE 48021 4203 B3
Jacob Dr
2600 WIND N8X 4421 D5
Jacob St
2900 HMTK 48212 4273 C5
Jacquelyn Dr
29400 LVNA 48154 4267 D5
Jade Ct
2500 AARB 48103 4488 D1
2500 WasC 48103 4488 D1
5200 WRRN 48091 4201 D2
Jade Ln
100 WasC 48189 4186 D7
Jahn St
38400 LVNA 48152 4193 E6
Jake Ln
47800 CNTN 48187 4411 A1
Jakk St
- WIND N8W 4421 D5
Jamaica Cres
2600 WIND N9E 4420 D6
2600 WIND N9E 4503 E1
James Av
8700 YpTp 48197 4576 D3
26800 FTRK 48134 4753 C2
27400 GDNC 48135 4340 A5
28600 GDNC 48135 4339 E5
James Blvd
15600 RVVW 48192 4584 B6
James Cres
12800 Tcmh N8N 4349 A7
James Ct
6100 DET 48213 4274 C5
29800 GBTR 48173 4755 C4
33700 FMTN 48335 4194 E3
44400 CNTN 48188 4411 E5

INDEX 30
Karen Ct
Detroit & Wayne County Street Index
Kominar Ct

STREET
Block City ZIP Map# Grid

Karen Ct
22400 FNHL 48336 4195 E3
Karen St
3800 WIND N9G 4504 E2
8300 WTLD 48185 4339 C3
9300 RMLS 48174 4496 E5
11000 LVNA 48150 4339 E1
Karim Blvd
24200 NOVI 48375 4193 D1
Karin St
16100 TYLR 48180 4582 C5
Karl Dr
- PyTp 48170 4263 C7
23500 BNTN 48134 4667 E5
Karl Pl
400 WIND N9A 4420 D2
Karl St
13200 SOGT 48195 4584 C2
22000 DET 48219 4197 B7
N Karle Av
5600 WTLD 48185 4338 D7
N Karle St
100 WTLD 48185 4413 D2
S Karle St
1300 WTLD 48186 4413 D4
Karli Ln
43500 CNTN 48188 4412 A4
Karmada St
500 PLYM 48170 4265 A6
Karr Rd
19600 WynC 48111 4663 A3
25300 WynC 48111 4749 A2
Kartar Ln
39500 NOVI 48375 4193 D2
Kashton Av
- DET 48223 4270 A3
Kass St
36600 HnTp 48164 4665 C2
Kate Av
23800 WRRN 48091 4201 A1
Katherine Av
17100 BNTN 48192 4583 C6
Katherine Ct
10100 TYLR 48180 4499 C5
47500 PyTp 48170 4336 A3
Katherine St
2900 DRBN 48124 4416 C5
3900 DBHT 48124 4416 C6
3900 DBHT 48125 4416 C6
5800 TYLR 48125 4499 C1
7100 TYLR 48180 4499 C3
16700 TYLR 48180 4583 C5
Kathleen Av
23800 WRRN 48091 4200 E1
Kathleen St
3800 WIND N9G 4504 D2
Kathron Ct
19500 WynC 48138 4670 D1
Kathryn St
5800 WasC 48170 4334 E1
28400 GDNC 48135 4415 A2
28600 GDNC 48135 4414 E2
Kathy Dr
1900 HbgT 48189 4186 C3
25100 BNTN 48134 4667 D7
Katie Dr
40700 NOVI 48375 4193 C4
Katie Ln
5800 WasC 48105 4332 C2
Katie Jo Ct
4200 WasC 48103 4329 E5
Kaufman St
5500 DBHT 48125 4416 C7
5500 DBHT 48125 4499 C1
Kautex Dr
2700 WIND N8W 4422 A6
Kavanagh St
1700 Tcmh N8N 4423 E3
Kay Pkwy
1100 AARB 48103 4488 E1
Kay St
4200 DET 48204 4344 A1
4800 DET 48204 4343 E1
22600 LyTp 48178 4189 B3
Keal St
13600 DET 48227 4342 E1
Kean St
23400 DRBN 48124 4416 A4
24600 DRBN 48124 4415 E4
26300 INKR 48141 4415 C4
Keane St
26100 SFLD 48034 4196 C5
Kearney Rd
1400 AARB 48104 4489 E1
Kearny Rd
7000 WasC 48189 4258 D4
8800 WasC 48189 4186 C7
S Kearny Rd
7400 WasC 48189 4258 D5
Keating Cres
10500 WIND N8R 4423 C3
Keating St
19100 DET 48203 4200 C5
20400 DET 48030 4200 C5
E Keech Av
100 AARB 48103 4489 B1
100 AARB 48104 4489 B1
W Keech Av
300 AARB 48103 4489 B1
Keefer St
22000 SFLD 48034 4196 E3
Keel St
14500 PyTp 48170 4264 C4
14900 PyTp 48167 4264 C4
Keeler
25000 RDFD 48239 4268 D3
Keeler Av
10000 DET 48238 4271 B3
Keeler St
- DET 48223 4270 A3
- DET 48227 4271 A3
18100 DET 48227 4270 A3
20900 DET 48223 4269 D3
Keelson Dr
100 DET 48214 4347 D2
Keewenaw Ct
32300 WTLD 48186 4414 D5
Keibler St
15300 DET 48227 4270 D5
Keith Av
12500 Tcmh N8N 4349 A7
19400 WynC 48138 4670 B1
Keith St
25900 DBHT 48127 4340 C3
Keller St
8900 DET 48209 4419 A5
Kelli Ct
25300 TYLR 48180 4582 E4
Kellogg St
300 AARB 48105 4406 C4
500 PLYM 48170 4337 A1
Kelly Blvd
19000 BwTp 48173 4755 A7
Kelly Rd
- EPTE 48225 4203 E3
11300 DET 48205 4275 B1
11300 DET 48213 4275 B1
11300 DET 48224 4275 B1
19000 DET 48205 4203 C7
19000 DET 48224 4203 C7
19100 DET 48225 4203 C7
19100 HRWD 48225 4203 C7
20700 EPTE 48021 4203 E3
21800 EPTE 48021 4204 A1
Kelly Green Dr
1300 WasC 48103 4405 C4
Kempa St
- DET 48234 4202 B5
7100 RMLS 48174 4497 D3
Kemper Dr
9000 GOTp 48178 4187 E1
Kempt St
200 Amhg N9V 4757 C3
Kenberton Ct
10000 OKPK 48237 4199 B1
Kenberton Dr
10 PTRG 48069 4199 C1
8600 OKPK 48237 4199 B1
Kenberton St
8400 OKPK 48237 4199 C1
Kendal St
5600 DRBN 48126 4342 E6
Kendall
25200 RDFD 48239 4268 D5
Kendall Ct
26500 RDFD 48239 4268 B5
Kendall Rd
4100 WRRN 48091 4201 B1
Kendall St
- DET 48223 4270 A5
- DET 48227 4271 A5
10 HDPK 48203 4272 B3
10 HDPK 48238 4272 B3
2700 DET 48238 4272 A4
10000 DET 48238 4271 A5
17700 DET 48227 4270 C5
22400 DET 48223 4269 B5
31200 LVNA 48154 4267 C6
35700 WYNE 48184 4413 C7
Kendleton Ct
4400 WIND N9G 4504 B4
Ken Gerard Ct
- WIND N8W 4422 A3
Kenilworth Dr
2600 AARB 48104 4490 A2
3000 WIND N9E 4421 C7
3100 WIND N9E 4504 C1
Kenilworth Pl
10 WIND N9E 4421 C7
Kenilworth St
10 DET 48202 4272 E6
200 DET 48202 4273 A6
5600 DRBN 48126 4342 E6
Kenmoor St
11000 DET 48205 4274 C1
11000 DET 48234 4274 C1
Kenmore Av
20300 HRWD 48225 4204 A5
21200 HRWD 48236 4204 B6
23400 FTRK 48134 4754 B5
Kenmore Ct
1600 WIND N9C 4420 B6
Kenmore Dr
1700 GSPW 48236 4204 C6
36700 FNHL 48335 4194 B4
Kennebec
1200 CNTN 48187 4411 C1
Kennebec Av
11100 ALPK 48101 4500 C6
Kennebec Ct
1200 CNTN 48187 4411 C1
Kennebec St
11000 DET 48205 4274 C1
11600 SOGT 48101 4500 C7
11600 SOGT 48195 4500 C7
16000 SOGT 48195 4584 C5
17000 RVVW 48192 4584 C6
17000 RVVW 48195 4584 C6
Kennebee Dr
- NOVI 48374 4191 C1
Kennedy Ct
9900 VNBN 48111 4495 C6
Kennedy Dr
13400 TYLR 48180 4583 B2
Kennedy Dr E
3800 WIND N9G 4504 C3
Kennedy Dr W
400 WIND N9G 4504 B3
Kennedy Ln
36900 HnTp 48164 4665 C1
Kennedy Rd
500 YpTp 48198 4492 D5
Kennedy St
9900 VNBN 48111 4495 C6
24100 DBHT 48127 4341 A4
27000 DBHT 48127 4340 B4
34000 WTLD 48185 4338 E4
Kennesaw Ct
48900 CNTN 48187 4335 E6
Kennesaw Rd
6400 CNTN 48187 4335 E6
Kenneth
26200 RDFD 48239 4340 C3
Kenneth Ct
26600 RDFD 48239 4340 B3
Kenneth Dr
14000 MonC 48117 4751 D5
Kenneth St
- DET 48203 4200 A4
Kenney Ct
100 Tcmh N8N 4348 E6
100 Tcmh N8P 4348 E6
Kenney St
8000 DET 48234 4274 B2
Kenora St
2500 WIND N9B 4420 D6
Kenosha St
18500 HRWD 48225 4203 E6
19900 HRWD 48225 4204 A6
24200 OKPK 48237 4198 D1
Kensington
22400 NOVI 48374 4192 A3
24300 FNHL 48335 4194 B1
Kensington Av
100 FRDL 48220 4199 D3
1000 GPPK 48230 4276 B6
1400 GPPK 48224 4276 B6
3400 DET 48224 4276 A3
9100 DET 48224 4275 D1
Kensington Blvd
100 Tcmh N8N 4349 D7
100 Tcmh N8N 4424 D1
Kensington Ct
9900 WasC 48167 4190 B6
24600 TYLR 48180 4498 E6
Kensington Dr
1200 AARB 48104 4489 D3
1200 CNTN 48188 4411 D4
22000 WDHN 48183 4668 C3
Kensington St
600 DRBN 48124 4416 B1
600 DRBN 48128 4416 B1
11300 ALPK 48101 4500 C7
20000 TYLR 48101 4499 E6
20000 TYLR 48180 4499 E6
24000 TYLR 48180 4498 E6
Kent Ct
2900 TNTN 48183 4669 C4
4000 WasC 48167 4190 A6
12300 SOGT 48195 4584 C1
48700 NOVI 48374 4191 E1
Kent Dr
42700 VNBN 48111 4495 B6
Kent Ln
9700 VNBN 48111 4495 B6
Kent St
- NvlT 48167 4265 C1
1800 WIND N9E 4503 C1
2300 AARB 48103 4488 D1
13500 RMLS 48174 4580 B3
14400 DET 48213 4275 B3
Kentfield St
12600 DET 48223 4269 D6
15800 DET 48219 4269 D3
19900 DET 48219 4197 D5
Kentford St
15400 DET 48223 4270 A3
Kentland St
- NvlT 48167 4192 B5
Kenton Av
35400 BwTp 48173 4841 D3
Kenton Ct
7500 YpTp 48197 4576 A6
Kenton Dr
- GOTp 48189 4187 A6
Kenton St
1500 FRDL 48220 4199 D2
15000 OKPK 48237 4198 C1
Kentucky Av
10 Amhg N9V 4757 E2
Kentucky Ct
33300 LVNA 48150 4339 A3
Kentucky St
7200 DRBN 48126 4343 C3
9200 DET 48204 4343 C1
11600 DET 48204 4271 C7
15400 DET 48238 4271 B3
17100 DET 48221 4271 B1
19900 DET 48221 4199 B4
33100 LVNA 48150 4339 A3
Kenwick Wy
1200 LSal N9H 4504 C5
Kenwood Av
100 AARB 48103 4405 E6
Kenwood Blvd
100 LSal N9J 4502 C5
900 LSal N9J 4503 A6
Kenwood Cres
9800 WIND N8R 4423 B2
Kenwood Ct
200 GSPF 48236 4276 C3
30800 LVNA 48152 4195 C5
Kenwood Dr
1400 TNTN 48183 4669 C2
1400 TNTN 48192 4669 C2
Kenwood Rd
10 GSPF 48236 4276 D4
Kenwood St
1400 DET 48211 4273 A5
1500 INKR 48141 4415 D3
1700 HMTK 48212 4273 B5
4000 INKR 48141 4414 D6
7100 RMLS 48174 4497 D3
8100 FRDL 48220 4199 B2
8100 OKPK 48220 4199 B2
13200 OKPK 48237 4199 A2
15300 OKPK 48237 4198 C2
20800 FNHL 48336 4195 D5
Kenyon Ct
- NvlT 48167 4193 A6
Keppen Av
14500 ALPK 48101 4500 C1
16800 ALPK 48101 4417 B7
Keppen Blvd
1300 LNPK 48146 4501 A2
1700 LNPK 48146 4500 D2
2200 LNPK 48101 4500 D2
Keppler Ct
10 AARB 48103 4406 A6
Kerby Ct
10 GSPF 48236 4276 E3
Kerby Ln
100 GSPF 48236 4276 E3
Kerby Rd
10 GSPF 48236 4276 E3
9400 WIND N8R 4423 B2
Kercheval Av
10 GSPF 48236 4276 D4
Kercheval Pl
16800 GSPT 48230 4276 B5
Kercheval St
- GPPK 48230 4276 A6
6300 DET 48207 4346 B3
7000 DET 48214 4346 C3
10300 DET 48214 4347 A1
12000 DET 48214 4275 B7
15000 GPPK 48230 4275 E6
16800 GSPT 48230 4276 C5
Kern St
7200 DET 48213 4274 A4
Kerr St
12700 SOGT 48195 4584 E1
Kerry Ln
300 LyTp 48167 4189 E5
Kerstyn St
15000 TYLR 48180 4582 C4
Kessler St
22000 DET 48219 4269 B2
Kestrel Ct
10 PTFD 48197 4574 E1
600 SLYN 48178 4189 C1
6700 HbgT 48116 4186 A1
Kestrel Rdg
6700 HbgT 48116 4186 A1
S Kestrel Rdg
9100 HbgT 48116 4186 A1
Kestrel Wy
1700 WasC 48103 4488 A2
Kestrel Ridge Dr
500 SLYN 48178 4189 C1
Keveling Dr
100 SALN 48176 4572 E7
100 WasC 48176 4572 E7
Kew Dr
2700 WIND N8T 4422 E3
Kewadin St
3200 INKR 48141 4414 E5
Kewanee Av
400 YpTp 48197 4491 C3
Kewanee St
700 YPLT 48197 4491 C3
S Keyes St
22700 TYLR 48180 4499 C7
W Keyes St
22700 TYLR 48180 4499 B7
Keynes Ct
9600 WasC 48167 4190 A6
Keystone Ln
2500 AARB 48103 4488 D1
42500 CNTN 48187 4337 A7
42500 CNTN 48187 4412 B1
Keystone St
13400 DET 48212 4273 C1
19900 DET 48234 4201 C4
K Hill Ct
11200 GOTp 48178 4188 A6
Kilbourne St
11700 DET 48213 4274 E2
12700 DET 48213 4275 A1
Kilbrennan Ct
10 AARB 48108 4490 A6
Kilburn Park Cir
3100 AARB 48105 4332 B7
3100 AARB 48105 4407 C1
Kildare Rd
400 WIND N8Y 4346 B7
700 WIND N8Y 4421 B1
1500 WIND N8W 4421 D3
Kilkenny Ct
100 WasC 48103 4404 D5
9800 HbgT 48116 4186 C2
Kilkenny Dr
7200 HbgT 48116 4186 B2
E Kilkenny Dr
9700 HbgT 48116 4186 C2
N Kilkenny Dr
7800 HbgT 48116 4186 C2
S Kilkenny Dr
7600 HbgT 48116 4186 C2
Killarney Cir
46400 CNTN 48188 4411 D4
Killarney Ct
46400 CNTN 48188 4411 D4
Killdeer Ct
10 PTFD 48197 4574 E2
Kilrush Dr
21600 NOVI 48167 4192 C4
Kim Av
6000 ALPK 48101 4500 B2
26300 WDHN 48183 4755 B1
Kim Dr
- BNTN 48134 4668 A4
Kim St
1100 AARB 48103 4405 C4
Kimberly Ct
8700 DET 48204 4344 A2
45400 NOVI 48374 4192 C2
Kimberly Dr
4000 CNTN 48188 4411 C7
12500 Tcmh N8N 4349 A7
Kimberly Ln
10 DRBN 48120 4417 D3
Kimberly Rd
2300 AARB 48104 4489 E3
Kimberly St
13100 SOGT 48195 4584 C1
Kimland Ct
9300 RDFD 48239 4340 C2
Kincaid St
2300 MVDL 48122 4418 A7
King Av
6300 ALPK 48101 4500 B2
N King Pl
21200 ROTp 48220 4199 A4
S King Pl
21000 ROTp 48220 4199 B4
King Rd
- TNTN 48183 4669 A2
10 TNTN 48183 4670 A2
1200 TNTN 48192 4669 A2
1600 RVVW 48192 4669 A2
17000 BNTN 48183 4669 A2
17000 WDHN 48183 4669 A2
20000 BNTN 48183 4668 D2
20000 WDHN 48183 4668 D2
24000 BNTN 48134 4667 D3
24000 BNTN 48134 4668 A3
24000 BNTN 48174 4667 D3
24000 BNTN 48174 4668 A3
27400 HnTp 48174 4667 B3
29400 HnTp 48164 4666 D3
29400 HnTp 48174 4666 D3
King St
10 DET 48202 4273 A6
200 Amhg N9V 4757 C3
900 DET 48211 4273 A6
3500 WIND N9C 4420 A5
King George Blvd
1200 AARB 48108 4489 D4
1300 AARB 48104 4489 D4
King George Ct
1500 AARB 48104 4489 E3
King Richard St
9100 DET 48224 4275 D2
Kings Ct
1000 CNTN 48188 4412 B3
22100 WDHN 48183 4668 C5
Kings Ct E
19600 GSPW 48236 4204 C7
Kings Ct W
19600 GSPW 48236 4204 C7
Kings Hwy
200 WYDT 48192 4501 B6
300 LNPK 48146 4501 A5
1700 LNPK 48146 4500 D6
Kings Wy
100 CNTN 48187 4412 B2
100 CNTN 48188 4412 B2
Kingsbridge Ct
7200 CNTN 48187 4337 A5
Kingsbridge Dr
- Amhg N9V 4671 B5
29800 GBTR 48173 4755 C5
Kingsbridge Rd
7300 CNTN 48187 4337 A5
Kingsbrook Av
100 AARB 48103 4489 B3
Kingsburn Ct
37100 LVNA 48152 4194 B7
Kingsburn Dr
36800 LVNA 48152 4194 A7
37400 LVNA 48152 4266 A1
N Kingsbury Av
100 DRBN 48128 4415 E1
1100 DRBN 48128 4340 E7
Kingsbury Ct
38700 LVNA 48154 4265 E3
Kingsbury St
5600 DBHT 48128 4340 E6
6000 DBHT 48127 4340 E5
37400 LVNA 48154 4266 A4
38400 LVNA 48154 4265 E4
Kingslane Ct
33200 FMTN 48336 4194 E3
Kingsley Av
5900 LSal N9J 4503 A3
Kingsley Ct
8200 DET 48202 4273 A6
44200 CNTN 48187 4336 E4
Kingsley Dr
8300 CNTN 48187 4336 E4
Kingsley St
7200 DRBN 48126 4343 B4
15600 SOGT 48195 4584 A2
E Kingsley St
100 AARB 48103 4406 C5
100 AARB 48104 4406 C5
W Kingsley St
100 AARB 48103 4406 B5
Kings Mill Ct
6400 CNTN 48187 4336 A6
Kings Mill Dr
- CNTN 48187 4336 A5
Kings Pointe
24200 NOVI 48375 4193 B1
Kings Pointe Blvd
21500 BNTN 48183 4668 C2
Kings Pointe Dr
24600 NOVI 48375 4193 B1
Kingston Cir
24300 BNTN 48134 4754 C1
Kingston Cres
8200 WIND N8S 4347 E6
Kingston Ct
8600 SpTp 48198 4492 D1
22300 WDHN 48183 4668 C5
31500 FNHL 48336 4195 B3
N Kingston Ct
7400 WTLD 48185 4338 C4
S Kingston Ct
7300 WTLD 48185 4338 C4
Kingston Dr
4000 WasC 48160 4659 D3
Kingston Rd
19100 DET 48221 4199 E6
Kingston St
3900 DBHT 48124 4416 E6
3900 DBHT 48125 4416 E6
Kingsville St
18500 DET 48224 4203 D6
18500 HRWD 48224 4203 D6
18500 HRWD 48225 4203 D6
20200 DET 48224 4204 A7
20200 DET 48225 4204 A7
20600 HRWD 48224 4204 A7
20900 DET 48236 4204 A7
20900 HRWD 48225 4204 A7
20900 HRWD 48236 4204 A7
21600 DET 48225 4276 B1
21600 DET 48236 4276 B1
21600 HRWD 48225 4276 B1
21900 GSPW 48236 4276 B1
Kingsway Ct
1500 TNTN 48183 4669 D2
1500 TNTN 48192 4669 D2
Kingswood Ct
38700 WYNE 48184 4413 A5
Kingswood Dr
27000 DBHT 48127 4415 B1
27200 DBHT 48127 4340 B7
Kingswood Rd
13700 RVVW 48192 4669 D2
Kingswood St
8700 DET 48221 4199 B6
Kingwood St
1100 YPLT 48197 4491 D3
3100 WasC 48103 4405 B5
Kinloch
9500 RDFD 48239 4340 C1
14600 RDFD 48239 4268 C6
16100 RDFD 48240 4268 C2
19700 RDFD 48240 4196 C5
Kinloch St
100 DBHT 48127 4415 C1
8300 DBHT 48127 4340 C3
20700 SFLD 48034 4196 C4
Kinmore Ct
300 DBHT 48125 4415 D2
Kinmore St
1100 DBHT 48127 4415 D1
8000 DBHT 48127 4340 D3
8600 DBHT 48239 4340 D3
Kinsel St
24200 SFLD 48034 4196 E1
Kinsman St
4200 DET 48210 4344 C5
Kinyon St
20000 TYLR 48101 4499 E5
20000 TYLR 48180 4499 E5
26100 TYLR 48180 4498 C6
Kipke
15000 RDFD 48239 4268 B4
Kipling Av
6000 LSal N9J 4503 A4
Kipling Dr
3900 AARB 48105 4407 D4
Kipling St
7300 DET 48206 4344 E1
7300 DET 48210 4344 E1
21800 OKPK 48237 4198 E3
22500 STCS 48080 4204 E2
30100 RMLS 48174 4581 D5
Kira Av
- CNTN 48187 4336 D6
Kirby Dr
- BNTN 48134 4667 C5
11600 GOTp 48178 4188 B3
Kirby St
33100 FMTN 48335 4194 E4
33100 FMTN 48336 4194 E4
33100 FMTN 48336 4195 A4
33400 FNHL 48335 4194 E4
W Kirby St
3800 DET 48210 4344 C4
Kirby St E
10 DET 48202 4345 B2
600 DET 48211 4345 B2
3300 DET 48211 4273 E7
3500 DET 48211 4274 A7
7700 DET 48213 4274 B7
Kirby St W
10 DET 48202 4345 B2
Kirk Av
200 YpTp 48197 4491 D5
Kirk Ct
44700 CNTN 48187 4336 D4
Kirkland Av
1700 WIND N8P 4423 D1
Kirkland Dr
39500 CNTN 48188 4412 E2
Kirkridge Park Dr
7400 VNBN 48111 4495 B4
Kirkway Blvd
- CNTN 48188 4411 A2
Kirkwood St
7600 DET 48210 4343 D5
18100 DET 48228 4342 A6
19300 DET 48228 4341 E6
Kirtland Dr
1400 AARB 48103 4489 A1
Kitch Av
26100 INKR 48141 4415 C6
Kitch St
25600 DBHT 48125 4415 D6
25600 DBHT 48141 4415 D6
Kitchener St
400 DET 48214 4347 D1
Kitty Hawk St
26900 WynC 48138 4756 B2
Klages Rd
9300 HbgT 48116 4186 B1
Klarr Dr
38000 FNHL 48167 4194 A4
38200 FNHL 48167 4193 E4
Klebba St
11400 TYLR 48180 4499 B7
Klein St
7800 DET 48211 4273 E5
Kleinow Av
200 RVRG 48218 4418 D7
300 RVRG 48218 4501 D1
Klenk St
14600 DET 48214 4348 A2
Klinger St
11300 HMTK 48212 4273 C2
13400 DET 48212 4273 B1
17300 DET 48212 4201 B7
19100 DET 48234 4201 B5
Klink St
4100 INKR 48141 4414 D6
KMS Pl
600 AARB 48108 4489 C5
Knapp Ln
25400 BNTN 48134 4667 C7
Knight
15800 RDFD 48239 4268 E3
Knight Rd
1000 WasC 48103 4404 E7
1000 WasC 48103 4487 E1
Knights Ln
21600 BNTN 48183 4668 D2
Knightsbridge Cir
- AATp 48105 4406 C1
N Knightsbridge Cir
2800 AATp 48105 4406 D1
S Knightsbridge Cir
2600 AATp 48105 4406 D1
Knightsbridge Rd
800 CNTN 48187 4411 D1
Knightsford Rd
41100 NvlT 48167 4265 C3
Knob Hill Dr
- Amhg N9V 4671 C5
Knodell St
8000 DET 48213 4274 B4
Knoll Dr
37400 WYNE 48184 4413 B5
Knoll Wy
15000 RMLS 48174 4581 D4
Knoll Creek Ct
3600 SpTp 48105 4333 A7
Knollview Ct
13900 PyTp 48170 4264 A6
Knollwood Bnd
1600 SpTp 48198 4409 E7
Knollwood Cir
3600 PTFD 48108 4488 E5
Knollwood Ct
700 SALN 48176 4657 D2
42500 NvlT 48167 4265 A4
Knollwood Dr
100 WynC 48111 4662 D6
1800 CNTN 48188 4412 D5
7200 YpTp 48197 4576 A6
15500 DRBN 48120 4417 D3
22000 BNTN 48134 4668 A4
Knollwood Ln
35000 FNHL 48335 4194 C4
Knollwood St
24300 NOVI 48375 4193 A1
Knolson Av
8800 LVNA 48150 4337 E3
Knolson St
1400 WTLD 48185 4338 A7
9000 LVNA 48150 4337 E2
14900 LVNA 48154 4265 E4
Knowles St
1600 YpTp 48198 4492 E7
Knox Av
13600 WRRN 48089 4202 E2
13700 WRRN 48089 4203 A2
14400 WRRN 48021 4203 A2
Knox St
10 ECRS 48229 4501 D3
Knudsen Ct
21300 WynC 48138 4670 C3
Knudsen Dr
21600 WynC 48138 4670 C4
Knudsen Rd
21000 WynC 48138 4670 C2
Knurlwoode St
15600 RMLS 48174 4582 A4
Koch St
100 AARB 48103 4406 B7
Koester St
17100 RVVW 48192 4584 E6
Kolb Av
5800 ALPK 48101 4499 E1
5800 ALPK 48125 4499 E1
6500 ALPK 48101 4500 A2
10500 ALPK 48195 4500 A6
Kolb St
8800 DET 48214 4346 D1
Kominar Ct
4600 WIND N9G 4504 E5

INDEX 31

Koneta Dr — Detroit & Wayne County Street Index — Laura Av

STREET Block City ZIP Map# Grid

Koneta Dr
10000 GOTp 48116 4187 A3
Konkel St
4800 DET 48210 4344 C7
5600 DET 48209 4344 C7
Kopernick St
4800 DET 48210 4344 B6
Koppernick Rd
7600 CNTN 48187 4337 E4
7600 WTLD 48185 4337 E4
7600 WTLD 48187 4337 E4
38400 WTLD 48185 4338 A6
Korte St
\- GPPK 48214 4348 A1
\- GPPK 48230 4348 A1
4400 DRBN 48126 4417 C1
4700 DRBN 48126 4342 C7
13100 DET 48214 4347 E2
14800 DET 48214 4348 A1
Koteh St
9800 WIND N8P 4348 A6
Koths St
20000 TYLR 48101 4499 E6
22000 TYLR 48180 4499 C6
25100 TYLR 48180 4498 E6
Kouza Ct
42100 VNBN 48111 4495 B7
42100 VNBN 48111 4579 B1
Kozma St
44300 WynC 48111 4663 C3
Kraft Pl
24000 BNTN 48174 4583 A7
Kramer St
10 YPLT 48197 4492 A5
10200 DET 48204 4343 B2
15800 DET 48228 4342 C2
Krause St
500 AARB 48103 4406 A6
17700 RVVW 48192 4585 A7
Krauter Av
28400 GDNC 48135 4340 A7
28600 GDNC 48135 4339 E7
33400 WTLD 48185 4339 A7
33600 WTLD 48185 4338 E7
Kresge St
9100 DET 48213 4274 C4
Kress St
23500 DET 48219 4197 A7
Krisdalin Ct
7000 WasC 48167 4261 E2
7000 WasC 48178 4261 E2
Kristin Ln
15600 RVVW 48192 4584 B6
Kristin Chicoine Dr
\- GSPF 48236 4276 E4
Kristine Ct
4100 CNTN 48188 4411 D7
Kristy Ln
23000 SFLD 48034 4196 D3
Kruger Av
23200 SFLD 48034 4197 A4
Kubis Av
7200 WTLD 48185 4339 E5
Kuebler Ct
4400 WasC 48103 4404 E3
Kuebler Dr
800 WasC 48103 4404 E3
Kuehnle Ct
1200 AARB 48103 4405 C4
Kuehnle St
500 AARB 48103 4405 C4
1500 WasC 48103 4405 C4
Kulick St
5600 DET 48210 4344 B6
Kurtsell St
27400 INKR 48141 4415 B4

L

N L Rd
\- DRBN 48120 4418 A3
Labadie Ct
300 ECRS 48229 4501 E4
Labadie Rd
1200 WIND N8Y 4421 E1
1700 WIND N8Y 4422 A2
1800 WIND N8W 4422 A2
Labadie St
100 WYDT 48192 4501 C6
200 ECRS 48229 4501 C4
Labana Ct
7900 CNTN 48187 4336 B4
Labana Dr
47100 CNTN 48187 4336 B4
Labana Woods Dr
25800 TYLR 48180 4498 D4
La Belle Rd
400 GSPF 48236 4276 C1
La Belle St
1500 DET 48238 4272 A4
Labelle St
10 HDPK 48203 4272 D3
300 HDPK 48238 4272 B3
800 WIND N9E 4421 A7
1500 WIND N9E 4504 A1
1600 WIND N9E 4503 E1
Labo Rd
3500 BrTp 48117 4839 B7
3500 BrTp 48166 4839 B7
3500 MonC 48117 4839 B7
3500 MonC 48166 4839 B7
4500 BrTp 48179 4839 C4
5200 BrTp 48166 4840 C7
5200 BrTp 48179 4840 C7
E Labo Rd
\- BrTp 48117 4839 A7
\- BrTp 48166 4839 A7
1800 MonC 48117 4839 A7
Labour Cres
1200 WIND N8W 4421 E6

Labrosse St
1200 DET 48226 4345 B7
1400 DET 48216 4345 B7
Labute St
600 Tcmh N8N 4348 E7
600 Tcmh N8N 4424 A1
Lacasse Blvd
100 Tcmh N8N 4348 E6
400 Tcmh N8N 4349 A7
600 Tcmh N8N 4424 A1
Lachance Ct
12300 Tcmh N8N 4423 D2
Laclede St
3100 LNPK 48146 4501 B5
Lacombe Dr
\- DET 48216 4345 A6
Lacrosse St
33600 WTLD 48185 4338 E4
Lacy Ct
30200 WTLD 48186 4497 D1
Lacy Dr
29600 WTLD 48186 4497 E1
Ladarrel St
400 DET 48202 4345 C2
Ladene Ln
40000 NOVI 48375 4193 C4
Ladywood Ct
38100 LVNA 48154 4266 A3
41500 NvlT 48167 4265 B3
41500 NvlT 48170 4265 B3
Ladywood Dr
41600 NvlT 48167 4265 B3
41900 NvlT 48170 4265 B3
Ladywood St
36400 LVNA 48154 4266 B3
Laetham Av
24200 EPTE 48021 4203 B1
Lafayette Blvd
\- WRRN 48091 4201 A4
800 LNPK 48146 4501 A2
1400 LNPK 48146 4500 E3
4000 DET 48209 4419 E1
N Lafayette Blvd
100 WRRN 48091 4201 A3
S Lafayette Blvd
\- WRRN 48091 4201 A4
Lafayette Blvd E
500 DET 48226 4345 D6
Lafayette Blvd W
100 DET 48226 4345 C6
1400 DET 48216 4345 B7
2300 DET 48216 4420 A1
3300 DET 48216 4419 E1
5800 DET 48209 4419 C2
8700 DET 48209 4418 E4
Lafayette Cir
24300 SFLD 48075 4197 E1
Lafayette Dr
\- CNTN 48188 4411 B5
2800 TNTN 48183 4669 B5
24600 WynC 48138 4670 B6
Lafayette Ln
5800 WasC 48103 4404 B6
Lafayette Rd
2100 AARB 48104 4406 E6
N Lafayette St
100 DRBN 48124 4415 E1
100 DRBN 48128 4415 E1
100 SLYN 48178 4189 B1
1100 DRBN 48128 4340 E7
5600 DBHT 48128 4340 E6
6400 DBHT 48127 4340 E5
S Lafayette St
100 DRBN 48124 4415 E2
100 SLYN 48178 4189 B3
700 DRBN 48124 4416 A3
Lafayette St E
900 DET 48207 4345 E5
1900 DET 48207 4346 C4
7000 DET 48214 4346 D3
Lafayette Plaisance St
10 DET 48207 4345 E5
La Fere St
3100 AARB 48108 4490 B4
Lafferty Av
100 LSal N9J 4502 C5
900 LSal N9J 4503 A6
Lafler Dr
31500 RKWD 48173 4754 C7
Lafonde Ct
46300 PyTp 48170 4336 B1
Lafons Ln
21900 HnTp 48174 4667 A4
Lafontaine St
\- GSPF 48236 4276 B2
4900 DET 48236 4276 B2
5100 DET 48224 4276 B2
Laforet St
500 WIND N9C 4420 A3
La Forge St
800 YPLT 48198 4491 D2
La Garonne St
22000 SFLD 48075 4198 A3
Lagoon Ct
41300 NvlT 48167 4193 A6
Lagoon Dr
8500 YpTp 48197 4576 C1
Lahser Rd
\- SFLD 48219 4197 B6
8800 DET 48239 4341 C2
12800 DET 48228 4269 C6
15000 DET 48223 4269 C4
16100 DET 48219 4269 B2
18200 DET 48219 4197 B6
20700 SFLD 48034 4197 B6
20700 SFLD 48075 4197 B2
Laing St
1500 WIND N9B 4420 C3
11400 DET 48224 4275 C1
11600 DET 48224 4203 C7

Laing St
19200 HRWD 48225 4203 D6
Laird Av N
10 Amhg N9V 4757 B1
Laird Av S
10 Amhg N9V 4757 B2
Laird Haven Wy
16100 NvlT 48167 4264 E2
Lake Ct
10 GPPK 48230 4348 B1
10 GSPT 48230 4276 C6
4700 WasC 48103 4329 D5
Lake Dr
6000 YpTp 48197 4577 A3
10200 GOTp 48189 4187 B5
35200 BwTp 48173 4841 D3
Lake Rd
8300 WynC 48138 4756 C2
Lake St
100 NHVL 48167 4192 D6
E Lake St
100 SLYN 48178 4189 C2
W Lake St
100 SLYN 48178 4189 A2
700 LyTp 48178 4189 A2
Lake Como Ct
4500 WIND N9G 4504 E6
Lakecrest Ct
7800 YpTp 48197 4576 A1
Lake Crest Dr
44500 VNBN 48111 4578 E1
Lakecrest Dr
7700 YpTp 48197 4576 B1
Lakecrest Ln
10 GSPF 48236 4276 D5
Lake Forest Ct
4000 PTFD 48108 4488 E6
Lake Forest Dr E
4000 PTFD 48108 4488 E7
Lake Forest Dr W
4000 PTFD 48108 4488 D6
Lake Grande Ct
4500 WIND N9G 4504 E5
Lake Haven Dr
1000 AARB 48105 4407 B5
Lakehaven Dr
\- AARB 48105 4407 B5
Lakehurst Av
2700 AARB 48105 4407 A1
Lakehurst Ct
2900 AARB 48105 4407 A1
Lake In the Woods Blvd
2100 YpTp 48198 4577 A1
Lake Laguna Ct
1000 WIND N9G 4505 A5
Lakeland Av
200 GSPT 48230 4276 C6
800 DET 48230 4276 C5
Lakeland Ct
800 GSPT 48230 4276 B4
41900 PyTp 48170 4265 A4
Lakeland St
24300 FNHL 48336 4195 C1
Lake Lila Dr
1800 AARB 48105 4406 E3
Lake Park Ln
300 AARB 48103 4405 B7
Lake Pine Dr
8800 WasC 48189 4259 B1
Lake Point Blvd
13100 VNBN 48111 4577 C2
Lakepointe Dr
9400 WasC 48189 4187 B7
Lake Pointe Ln
3800 PTFD 48108 4489 A6
Lakepointe St
500 GPPK 48230 4348 A1
800 GPPK 48230 4275 E7
800 GPPK 48230 4276 A7
3500 DET 48230 4275 D5
10800 DET 48224 4275 C1
11400 DET 48224 4203 D7
Lake Point Pass
12300 VNBN 48111 4577 D1
Lake Ravine Dr
22500 SFLD 48034 4196 A2
Lake Ravines Dr
22400 SFLD 48034 4196 B3
Lakeridge Dr
4800 PTFD 48197 4491 A2
Lakeshore Ct
9500 GOTp 48178 4188 A2
Lake Shore Dr
800 WIND N9G 4504 E4
7800 WasC 48189 4259 A3
11600 GOTp 48189 4187 A6
Lakeshore Dr
\- STCS 48080 4205 A3
\- STCS 48236 4205 A3
10 GSPF 48230 4276 D5
400 GSPF 48236 4276 E2
400 GSPF 48236 4277 A2
1300 AARB 48103 4406 C4
1300 AARB 48105 4406 C4
5500 PTFD 48108 4573 A3
Lake Shore Ln
700 NHVL 48167 4192 E6
Lakeshore Ln
10 GSPS 48236 4204 E7
10 GSPS 48236 4205 A7
400 GSPW 48236 4204 E7
Lake Shore Rd
300 GSPF 48236 4276 E4
400 GSPF 48236 4277 A1
400 GSPS 48236 4277 A1
500 GSPS 48236 4205 B5
900 McoC 48236 4205 B5
Lakeside Ct
10 GSPT 48230 4276 C6

Lakeside Dr
\- DET 48207 4347 B4
9400 YpTp 48197 4576 E2
Lakeside St
15300 NvlT 48170 4265 A4
Lake Success Dr
42500 NvlT 48167 4193 A6
Lake Trail Dr
500 WIND N9G 4504 D5
Lake View Av
10 WasC 48189 4259 A3
Lakeview Av
100 GSPF 48236 4276 E2
500 WasC 48103 4405 B7
1700 TNTN 48183 4669 B3
2100 YpTp 48198 4577 B1
Lakeview Blvd
6400 WTLD 48185 4338 C5
Lake View Cir
17200 NvlT 48167 4264 A2
Lake View Ct
47700 NvlT 48167 4264 A2
Lakeview Ct
4300 PTFD 48108 4488 E6
8300 SpTp 48198 4492 B1
9100 WasC 48176 4658 B2
10400 GOTp 48189 4187 C5
15800 GPPK 48230 4348 B1
23700 STCS 48080 4204 C1
41100 VNBN 48111 4579 C1
N Lakeview Ct
24600 FNHL 48335 4194 C1
S Lakeview Ct
24600 FNHL 48335 4194 C1
Lakeview Dr
500 WIND N8P 4348 D6
2100 YpTp 48198 4576 E1
2100 YpTp 48198 4577 E2
2900 AARB 48103 4405 C6
8300 SpTp 48198 4492 B1
9200 WasC 48189 4259 A1
10300 GOTp 48189 4187 C5
13000 VNBN 48111 4577 E2
E Lakeview Ln
1500 CNTN 48187 4411 C1
W Lakeview Ln
1500 CNTN 48187 4411 C1
Lakeview St
10 GSPF 48236 4276 E2
1000 DET 48214 4275 C6
6100 DET 48213 4275 B3
20600 STCS 48080 4204 C1
Lake Villa Dr
46000 VNBN 48111 4578 C1
Lake Village Dr
\- AARB 48103 4489 B3
200 WasC 48103 4489 B3
Lakeway St
22700 FMTN 48336 4195 B2
Lakewood Av
10 YpTp 48198 4492 E3
Lakewood Cir
37700 WTLD 48185 4338 A3
Lakewood Ct
9300 WasC 48189 4186 D7
Lakewood Dr
500 SLYN 48178 4189 B1
2800 TNTN 48183 4669 B5
3000 AARB 48103 4405 B6
9100 WasC 48189 4186 D7
9300 WynC 48138 4670 B4
14800 PyTp 48170 4265 B4
Lakewood St
10 DET 48214 4347 E1
1000 DET 48214 4275 D6
6100 DET 48213 4275 C4
La Loire St
22300 SFLD 48075 4198 A3
Lamar Ln
29500 LVNA 48152 4267 D1
Lamar St
30300 FNHL 48336 4195 C2
31400 FMTN 48336 4195 B1
Lamay Av
10 YpTp 48198 4492 E3
Lamb Ct
33600 FMTN 48335 4194 B1
Lamb St
10 HbgT 48189 4186 A6
Lambert St
7000 DET 48211 4274 A6
7200 DET 48213 4274 A6
N Lambeth Ct
6600 CNTN 48187 4336 B6
S Lambeth Ct
6400 CNTN 48187 4336 B6
Lambeth Dr
500 AARB 48103 4489 A2
Lambeth Rd
10600 WIND N8R 4423 C2
Lambeth Wy
6200 CNTN 48187 4336 B6
Lambie Pl
3000 DET 48216 4344 E7
Lambkins Rd
500 SALN 48176 4572 C6
600 WasC 48176 4572 C6
Lambrecht Av
22700 EPTE 48021 4203 E1
Lambton St
1800 WIND N9E 4503 C2
Lamont St
2300 WIND N9E 4503 D1
8800 LVNA 48150 4338 A2
17100 DET 48212 4273 C1
19100 DET 48234 4201 C5
32600 RKWD 48173 4754 D7
32600 RKWD 48173 4840 D1
Lamothe St
1900 DET 48206 4344 D2

Lamoyne St
33900 LVNA 48154 4266 E4
Lamphere
7200 DET 48127 4341 B4
7200 DET 48239 4341 B4
Lamphere St
6700 DBHT 48127 4341 B5
13900 DET 48223 4269 B4
16100 DET 48219 4269 B2
Lamplighter Ct
16200 SFLD 48075 4198 B2
Lamplighter Dr
3500 WasC 48103 4405 A2
Lamplighter Ln
23600 SFLD 48075 4198 B2
Lana Ct
38200 FNHL 48335 4193 E3
38200 FNHL 48335 4194 A3
Lana Dr
27000 BwTp 48183 4755 A2
38200 FNHL 48335 4193 E3
38200 FNHL 48335 4194 A3
Lanark St
10000 DET 48224 4275 E1
10500 DET 48224 4203 E7
10600 DET 48224 4204 A7
Lancashire Ct
35200 LVNA 48152 4266 D1
Lancashire Dr
2300 AARB 48105 4406 E2
2300 AARB 48105 4407 A2
Lancashire Ln
26000 WynC 48138 4670 C7
Lancashire Rd
35100 LVNA 48152 4266 D1
Lancashire St
18200 DET 48223 4270 A3
18800 DET 48223 4269 E2
33000 WTLD 48185 4339 A6
Lancaster Av
1800 GSPW 48236 4204 C5
2100 GSPW 48225 4204 C5
Lancaster Ct
500 SALN 48176 4572 C6
3900 PTFD 48197 4490 E6
19200 WDHN 48183 4669 A7
22300 NOVI 48374 4192 B4
38500 LVNA 48154 4265 E4
43600 CNTN 48187 4336 E4
43600 CNTN 48187 4337 A4
Lancaster Dr
9500 VNBN 48111 4495 B6
19100 WDHN 48183 4669 A7
27000 BNTN 48134 4753 C1
Lancaster Ln
3200 WasC 48167 4190 A7
Lancaster St
19600 HRWD 48225 4204 A5
28800 LVNA 48154 4267 E4
38100 LVNA 48154 4266 A4
38300 LVNA 48154 4265 E4
Lancelot Ct
2400 CNTN 48188 4412 A5
Lancelot Dr
43000 CNTN 48188 4412 A5
Lanco St
9000 DET 48204 4343 B2
Lancrest Ct
21900 FNHL 48335 4194 C3
Landau St
24100 CTNL 48015 4202 A1
Landers Ct
12200 PyTp 48170 4335 D1
Landers Dr
11600 PyTp 48170 4335 D1
Landings Blvd
500 WasC 48103 4405 B5
Landings Dr
3300 WasC 48103 4405 B4
Landmark
51000 VNBN 48111 4577 C4
Landmark Ct
1900 AARB 48103 4488 D3
Landmark Dr
27000 BNTN 48134 4667 C7
Landsdowne Ln
9500 YpTp 48197 4576 E5
9500 YpTp 48197 4577 A5
Landsend Ln
1100 WasC 48176 4658 C3
W Lane Ct
10 DRBN 48124 4416 D2
Lane St
7200 DET 48209 4419 A2
8700 DET 48209 4418 E3
W Lane St
10 DRBN 48124 4416 D2
Lanewood St
8300 WTLD 48150 4339 E3
8300 WTLD 48185 4339 E3
Lang Ct
37400 WTLD 48186 4413 B5
Lang St
\- DET 48229 4418 B5
Langdon Dr
24600 BNTN 48134 4668 A7
24700 BNTN 48134 4754 A1
Lange St
15600 TYLR 48180 4582 C4
Langfield St
500 NHVL 48167 4192 E5
Langholm St
19100 DET 48234 4202 C6
Langley Dr
\- NOVI 48374 4191 C1
Langlois Av
100 WIND N9A 4346 A7
400 WIND N9A 4421 A1
2700 WIND N8X 4421 D5
2900 WIND N8W 4421 D5

Langlois Ct
2600 WIND N8X 4421 C5
Lanhan Ct
1700 CNTN 48188 4411 D4
Lanier Ln
500 SLYN 48178 4189 C2
Lanier St
400 DET 48202 4345 B2
Lanman St
3800 DET 48210 4344 C5
Lannette St
14500 DET 48213 4275 B1
Lannoo St
\- GSPF 48236 4276 B1
4900 DET 48236 4276 B1
5800 DET 48224 4276 B1
Lanoue St
12300 Tcmh N8N 4423 D2
12300 Tcmh N8N 4424 A2
Lans Wy
500 AARB 48103 4489 A2
Lansbury Ln
36500 FMTN 48335 4194 B2
Lansdowne Dr
300 WTLD 48185 4413 C2
Lansdowne Rd
1600 AATp 48105 4330 D7
Lansdowne St
11200 DET 48224 4275 C1
11600 DET 48224 4203 D7
19200 HRWD 48225 4203 D6
Lansing St
1000 DET 48209 4419 D1
1800 WIND N9E 4503 C2
2000 DET 48209 4344 C7
Lanson Av
13800 DRBN 48126 4418 A1
14400 DRBN 48126 4417 E1
Lanson Ct
10 DRBN 48126 4417 D1
Lanthorn Ln
\- NHVL 48167 4192 B5
Lantz St E
\- DET 48234 4200 E5
\- DET 48234 4201 D5
10 DET 48203 4200 C5
8000 DET 48234 4202 A5
Lantz St W
10 DET 48203 4200 B5
La Paloma Ln
7100 YpTp 48197 4575 A5
Lapeer Dr
32400 WTLD 48186 4414 B4
Lapeer St
9500 DRBN 48120 4418 C2
Lapham Ct
6400 WasC 48170 4262 E7
38400 LVNA 48154 4265 E3
Lapham Dr
38900 LVNA 48154 4265 E3
Lapham St
3900 DRBN 48126 4417 E1
Lapham Wy
\- WasC 48170 4263 A7
9700 WasC 48170 4262 E7
Laporte Av
10 YpTp 48198 4492 E3
300 WIND N8S 4347 D5
Lappan Av
1800 WIND N8W 4422 A7
Lappin St
11600 DET 48205 4202 E6
11600 DET 48234 4202 B6
15600 DET 48205 4203 C5
16200 DET 48225 4203 C5
Laprairie St
100 FRDL 48220 4199 E3
Laramie Av
\- WTLD 48185 4338 B4
Laramie Dr
6400 RMLS 48174 4496 A2
Laramie Ln
26500 FTRK 48134 4753 E1
Laramie St
\- Tcmh N8N 4423 D2
\- Tcmh N8P 4423 D2
37500 WTLD 48185 4338 A5
Laraugh Dr
18200 NvlT 48167 4264 C1
Larch Ln
9500 GOTp 48178 4188 D1
Larch St
22000 WDHN 48183 4668 C3
Larches St
29700 FTRK 48134 4754 A5
Larchmont Ct
600 WTLD 48185 4413 B1
Larchmont Dr
100 WTLD 48185 4413 C1
3500 AARB 48105 4407 C4
45600 CNTN 48187 4336 B7
Larchmont St
5000 DET 48204 4344 A3
5200 DET 48210 4344 A3
Larchwood Dr
\- WTLD 48185 4338 E6
44400 NvlT 48167 4264 D2
Larchwood St
900 DET 48203 4200 B6
Larges Dr
24600 SFLD 48034 4197 A1
Lariat Av
16000 EPTE 48021 4203 C1
Lariat Lp
1100 PTFD 48108 4489 B5
Larimore Ln
41400 CNTN 48187 4412 B2
Lark Av
4100 WRRN 48091 4201 B4

Lark Ct
5200 WRRN 48091 4201 D1
Lark Hbr
35500 FMTN 48335 4194 C2
Lark Ln
4000 PTFD 48197 4574 B4
Lark St
6600 DET 48213 4274 A5
Larkdale Ct
15500 RMLS 48174 4582 A4
Larkin Dr
27000 BwTp 48183 4754 E2
Larkin Rd
1800 WIND N8W 4421 E2
2200 WIND N8W 4422 A3
Larkins Ct
24800 SFLD 48034 4196 D1
Larkins St
5200 DET 48210 4343 E5
24500 SFLD 48034 4196 D2
Larkshire St
23300 FNHL 48336 4195 D1
Larkspur Av
10300 WynC 48138 4670 A7
Larkspur St
200 AARB 48105 4406 C2
200 AATp 48105 4406 C2
20900 FMTN 48336 4195 A4
Larme Av
4400 ALPK 48101 4417 B7
6300 ALPK 48101 4500 A1
Larned St E
\- DET 48226 4345 E6
900 DET 48207 4345 E6
1400 DET 48207 4346 A5
Larned St W
10 DET 48226 4345 D6
Larry Dr
400 NHVL 48167 4192 D5
La Salle Av
16100 DET 48221 4272 A2
21700 WRRN 48089 4203 A2
La Salle Blvd
7300 DET 48210 4344 D2
7700 DET 48206 4344 C1
8800 DET 48206 4272 C7
12600 DET 48238 4272 B5
20700 WRRN 48089 4203 A3
La Salle Ct
\- DET 48238 4272 A3
Lasalle Ct
8300 WynC 48138 4670 C5
La Salle Dr
\- AARB 48104 4490 B4
3000 AARB 48108 4490 B4
La Salle Gdns N
2200 DET 48206 4344 D1
La Salle Gdns S
1900 DET 48206 4344 C2
La Salle Pl
200 GSPF 48236 4276 E3
Lasalle St
5900 LSal N9J 4503 A4
La Seine St
22300 SFLD 48075 4198 A3
Laser Ln
20900 LyTp 48178 4189 B6
Lassaline Av
5100 WIND N8T 4422 B1
Last Dr
10700 WasC 48170 4263 B6
Las Vegas Dr
1400 AARB 48103 4488 E1
Latchstring Ct
4000 WasC 48176 4572 A5
Latham St
9300 HMTK 48212 4273 C4
Latheron Ct
13100 PyTp 48170 4264 A7
Latheron Dr
12500 PyTp 48170 4264 A7
Lathers Av
100 GDNC 48141 4415 A2
1000 YpTp 48197 4491 D5
1100 GDNC 48135 4415 A1
1500 GDNC 48135 4340 A7
Lathers St
7200 WTLD 48185 4340 A4
8900 LVNA 48150 4340 A2
17200 LVNA 48152 4268 A1
18600 LVNA 48152 4196 A7
19900 LVNA 48152 4195 E6
Lathrop St
4800 TNTN 48183 4669 C7
4800 TNTN 48183 4755 C1
Lathrup Blvd
24300 SFLD 48075 4198 A1
Lathrup St
21500 SFLD 48075 4198 B3
Lathum Ct
7100 CNTN 48187 4336 C5
Lathum Dr
45800 NOVI 48374 4192 B2
Latina Ct
7900 WIND N8R 4423 A3
Lauder St
\- OKPK 48235 4198 D4
\- OKPK 48237 4198 D4
9300 DET 48228 4342 D1
9500 DET 48227 4342 D1
15100 DET 48227 4270 D4
16100 DET 48235 4270 D3
20400 DET 48235 4198 D4
Lauderdale St
\- DET 48209 4419 D2
Laukel St
21500 STCS 48080 4204 D1
Laura Av
\- SFLD 48075 4198 A2

INDEX 32
Laura St

Detroit & Wayne County Street Index

Lindsey Dr

STREET
Block City ZIP Map# Grid

Laura St
3200 WYNE 48184 4413 C6
9300 DET 48214 4274 D7
Laurel Av
1100 YpTp 48198 4492 D2
8800 LVNA 48150 4338 D3
Laurel Ct
1100 YpTp 48198 4492 D2
Laurel Dr
17100 LVNA 48154 4266 D2
18200 LVNA 48152 4266 D1
19100 LVNA 48152 4194 D6
24400 FTRK 48134 4754 A5
Laurel Pk S
16600 LVNA 48154 4266 A2
16900 LVNA 48152 4266 A2
Laurel St
9500 LVNA 48150 4338 D1
12300 DET 48205 4274 E1
12600 DET 48205 4202 E7
Laurel Bay
1200 WIND N8P 4348 D7
Laurel Bay Dr
1600 YpTp 48198 4492 C7
Laurel Creek Ct
17500 NvlT 48167 4264 D2
Laurel Hill Rd
2700 WasC 48103 4405 C2
Laurel Oak Ln
200 AGST 48191 4661 B7
Laurel Oak Tr
300 PTFD 48197 4574 D2
Laurel Oaks Ct
41600 NvlT 48170 4265 B4
Laurel Park Ct
- LVNA 48152 4266 A2
Laurel Park Dr N
17100 LVNA 48152 4266 A1
Laurel Springs Ct
18100 NvlT 48167 4264 B1
Laurel View Dr
- AATp 48105 4407 E4
Laurelwood Cir
2400 AARB 48108 4490 A6
Laurelwood Ct
43400 CNTN 48187 4412 A1
Laurelwood Dr
43600 CNTN 48187 4411 E1
Laurelwood St
20900 FMTN 48336 4195 A4
Lauren
- PyTp 48170 4336 D2
Lauren Av
23000 WRRN 48089 4203 A1
Lauren Ct
46900 VNBN 48111 4578 B4
Lauren Ln
21200 FNHL 48335 4194 B4
Lauren St
16000 TYLR 48180 4582 C5
Laurence Av
- MVDL 48101 4417 D7
- MVDL 48122 4417 D7
5700 ALPK 48101 4500 C2
Laurendeau St
1100 WIND N8Y 4346 E6
1100 WIND N8Y 4421 E1
Laurentide Dr
2600 AATp 48103 4405 D1
2700 WasC 48103 4405 C2
Laurenwood Dr
38000 WYNE 48184 4413 A5
Laurie Ct
26500 WDHN 48183 4755 A1
Laurier Dr
100 LSal N9J 4502 C5
800 LSal N9J 4503 A6
Laurin Ct
10 AATp 48104 4407 C7
Laurin Dr
10 AATp 48104 4407 C7
Lauzon Pkwy
- Tcmh N8V 4423 B6
2600 WIND N8T 4422 E2
2700 WIND N8T 4423 A3
Lauzon Rd
200 WIND N8S 4347 D5
1500 WIND N8S 4422 E1
1800 WIND N8R 4423 A2
1800 WIND N8S 4423 A1
1800 WIND N8T 4423 A2
3600 Tcmh N8N 4423 C6
3600 Tcmh N8V 4423 C6
Lavender Av
4600 WIND N9G 4505 B3
Lavender Dr
- BwTp 48173 4755 A6
Lavender Ln
800 PTFD 48108 4573 C2
Laverne St
500 YpTp 48198 4492 E5
Lavindale St
10 Lksr N8N 4424 E3
Law
- FTRK 48134 4753 D3
Law Av
20400 BwTp 48183 4754 E3
Law St
22400 DRBN 48124 4416 C2
Lawley St
1900 DET 48212 4273 A2
Lawn Rd
23800 SFLD 48034 4196 E1
Lawndale St
800 DET 48209 4419 A3
1600 DET 48209 4418 E2
3800 DET 48210 4418 E1
5100 DET 48210 4343 C6
20200 STCS 48080 4204 C1
Lawrence Av
8100 AGST 48197 4575 B7
8400 AGST 48197 4660 B1
23300 WRRN 48091 4202 A1
23400 WRRN 48015 4202 A1
24100 DRBN 48128 4341 A7
25000 DRBN 48128 4340 D7
Lawrence Ct
38500 WTLD 48186 4413 A2
Lawrence Dr
25400 DBHT 48127 4340 D7
36200 LVNA 48150 4338 C2
Lawrence Ln
18400 HnTp 48164 4580 C7
18400 HnTp 48164 4665 C1
Lawrence Rd
800 WIND N8Y 4347 A7
Lawrence St
10 DET 48202 4272 D5
700 AARB 48104 4406 C5
1500 DET 48206 4272 C6
4000 DET 48204 4272 A7
23800 CTNL 48015 4202 A1
24000 CTNL 48015 4201 E1
38500 WTLD 48186 4413 A2
Lawson Av
23000 WRRN 48089 4203 A1
Lawson St
200 SALN 48176 4657 E1
Lawton St
3000 DET 48216 4344 E5
7300 DET 48206 4344 C1
7300 DET 48210 4344 C2
9100 DET 48206 4272 B7
15300 DET 48238 4272 A3
15700 DET 48238 4271 E2
16100 DET 48221 4271 E2
Layla Ct
2600 WIND N9E 4420 D6
Lazelda Dr
4400 WasC 48160 4659 E1
Lazy K
22700 LyTp 48178 4190 B4
Leach St
8700 DET 48214 4346 E3
Leader St
15300 TYLR 48180 4582 E4
Leaf Ct
600 YPLT 48197 4491 D6
Leafield Ct
3100 WIND N8W 4421 E6
Leaird Dr
1600 AARB 48105 4406 D4
Leander St
8000 DET 48234 4274 B2
Lear Ct
7700 WTLD 48185 4339 E4
Learning Ln
10400 HbgT 48116 4186 B3
10400 HbgT 48189 4186 B3
Leathorne St
11500 WIND N8P 4423 C1
Leblanc Av
5500 WasC 48103 4404 B6
14500 ALPK 48101 4500 C7
Leblanc Rd
12800 PyTp 48170 4264 B7
Le Blanc St
- DET 48229 4501 B2
10 ECRS 48229 4501 C5
10 RVRG 48218 4501 D1
Leblanc St
400 LNPK 48146 4501 A6
1200 LNPK 48146 4500 C6
E Le Bost
23500 NOVI 48375 4193 C2
W Le Bost
23100 NOVI 48375 4193 B2
Lebost Ct
24500 NOVI 48375 4193 B1
N Lebost Dr
24400 NOVI 48375 4193 B1
Ledgecliff Av
30300 WTLD 48185 4339 D5
Ledgewood Dr
1400 CNTN 48188 4412 B4
Leduc St
1600 WIND N9B 4420 D4
Ledyard Av
1900 WIND N8W 4505 A1
Ledyard St
400 DET 48201 4345 B5
Lee Ct
20700 GSPW 48236 4204 E5
22900 STCS 48080 4204 E2
Lee Ln
23500 SFLD 48034 4197 A1
Lee Pl
1400 DET 48206 4272 D7
Lee Rd
14300 BwTp 48173 4841 C2
Lee St
1100 WYDT 48192 4585 B4
17100 SFLD 48075 4198 B1
Leeann Ln
43700 CNTN 48187 4336 E6
Lee Baker Dr
- SFLD 48075 4198 A2
24400 SFLD 48075 4197 E1
Leeds Ct
9800 WasC 48167 4190 A6
43100 CNTN 48188 4412 A5
Leeds St
22900 NOVI 48375 4192 D3
Lee Gate Ln
10 GSPF 48236 4276 D4
Lee Heights St
23400 SFLD 48034 4197 A1
Leelanau St
32400 WTLD 48186 4414 D4
Leeland St
35500 BwTp 48173 4841 B3
Leelane St
30800 FNHL 48336 4195 B1
31400 FMTN 48336 4195 A1
Leet St
6300 ALPK 48101 4500 B2
Leeward Ct
200 DET 48207 4346 C5
Leewin St
22400 DET 48219 4197 A5
24200 DET 48219 4196 E5
Leewright Av
22200 SFLD 48034 4196 D3
Le Fever Av
21700 WRRN 48091 4201 C2
Leforge Rd
1200 YPLT 48197 4491 E2
1200 YPLT 48198 4491 E2
1200 YpTp 48198 4491 E2
1500 SpTp 48198 4491 E1
1600 SpTp 48198 4408 E7
Legacy Park Cir
- DBHT 48127 4340 E3
Legacy Park Dr
2000 WIND N8W 4505 B3
Legend Ct
39400 NvlT 48167 4193 D6
Le Grand St
6300 DET 48211 4273 E5
Le Grande Blvd
27400 HnTp 48174 4667 A4
Lehigh Ct
11600 PyTp 48170 4336 A1
41200 NvlT 48167 4193 B6
Lehigh Ln
41200 NvlT 48167 4193 A6
Lehigh St
18200 DBHT 48125 4417 A6
18600 DBHT 48125 4416 E6
24300 DBHT 48125 4415 D6
25400 DBHT 48141 4415 D6
27400 INKR 48141 4415 B7
Lehman St
2900 HMTK 48212 4273 D4
Leib
- DET 48207 4346 B4
Leicester Ct
10 DET 48202 4272 E6
10 DET 48202 4273 A6
Leicester St
400 PLYM 48170 4264 D6
Leidel Ct
41300 NvlT 48167 4193 C6
Leidich St
5800 DET 48213 4274 E4
Leigh Ct
2300 CNTN 48188 4411 B5
S Leigh St
400 DET 48209 4419 A5
Leighwood Ct
45500 PyTp 48170 4336 C1
Leighwood Dr
11700 PyTp 48170 4336 C1
23000 WDHN 48183 4668 C5
Leisure Ln
4500 TNTN 48183 4669 B6
Leitch Rd
1800 FRDL 48220 4200 B2
Lejeune Av
1200 LNPK 48146 4501 B4
Leland Ct
23800 DRBN 48124 4416 A4
Leland Dr
5700 WasC 48105 4332 C2
Leland St
900 DET 48207 4345 D3
1800 FRDL 48220 4199 E2
3100 DET 48207 4346 A2
Lelo Ct
23600 SFLD 48075 4198 B2
Lemay St
400 DET 48214 4347 A1
2500 DET 48214 4275 A7
5000 DET 48214 4274 E5
6000 DET 48213 4274 D4
Lemen Rd
11000 GOTp 48116 4186 D5
11000 GOTp 48189 4186 D5
Lemington Ct
10 DRBN 48126 4341 D7
Lemire St
12600 Tcmh N8N 4424 A2
Lemon St
- WTLD 48186 4414 C7
E Lemont Ct
1000 CNTN 48187 4411 D1
W Lemont Ct
1000 CNTN 48187 4411 D2
Lemont Rd
44800 CNTN 48187 4411 D2
Lemonwood Cres
900 WIND N9G 4504 E4
1000 WIND N9G 4505 A4
Lena Av
900 WIND N9C 4420 B4
Lena St
800 PLYM 48170 4264 E6
Lenawee Dr
400 AARB 48104 4406 E7
Lenawee St
32400 WTLD 48186 4414 D4
Lenmoore Rd
13000 VNBN 48111 4579 C3
Lennane
15300 RDFD 48239 4268 D3
17100 RDFD 48240 4268 D1
19900 RDFD 48240 4196 D5
Lennon Av
1800 GSPW 48236 4204 C5
Lennon Av
2100 GSPW 48225 4204 C5
Lennon Ct
3900 WIND N9G 4504 B3
Lennon St
19000 HRWD 48225 4204 A4
Lennox St
300 SLYN 48178 4189 B2
900 AARB 48103 4405 E7
2700 FRDL 48220 4200 B1
2700 HZLP 48030 4200 B1
Lenoir Av
400 RVRG 48218 4501 D2
Lenoir Ct
400 RVRG 48218 4501 D1
Lenoir St
11300 ALPK 48101 4500 C7
Lenore
9500 RDFD 48239 4340 E1
15500 RDFD 48239 4268 E3
16100 DET 48219 4268 E2
19100 DET 48219 4196 E6
Lenore St
3500 MVDL 48122 4417 E6
8000 DBHT 48127 4340 E3
8600 DBHT 48239 4340 E3
Lenox Dr
300 CNTN 48188 4411 A3
Lenox St
1000 DET 48214 4275 C7
1000 DET 48214 4347 D1
2500 TNTN 48183 4669 D4
5000 DET 48213 4275 B4
Lens Av
600 WIND N8X 4421 C4
700 WIND N8W 4421 C4
Leo St
2400 MVDL 48122 4418 A6
20300 TYLR 48180 4583 E1
Leon St
35100 LVNA 48150 4338 C1
N Leona Av
300 GDNC 48135 4414 D1
Leona Ct
29900 GDNC 48135 4414 D2
Leona Dr
500 AARB 48103 4405 D5
15300 RDFD 48239 4268 E3
15900 RDFD 48240 4268 E3
Leona St
28400 GDNC 48135 4415 A2
28900 GDNC 48141 4414 E2
28900 INKR 48141 4414 E2
29900 GDNC 48135 4414 D2
Leonard Av
2300 WIND N8W 4422 A3
7700 WasC 48189 4259 B4
13600 WRRN 48089 4202 E2
13600 WRRN 48089 4203 A2
20400 BwTp 48183 4754 E2
Leonard St
- DET 48229 4418 D6
13100 DRBN 48126 4418 A1
26000 FTRK 48134 4753 D2
Leontine Rd
25900 HnTp 48164 4751 C1
Leopold St
43600 CNTN 48188 4412 A7
44400 CNTN 48188 4411 E7
Leota Av
7900 WasC 48167 4262 D3
Lepain Cres
1900 LSal N9H 4504 C6
Le Quinne Ct
24000 FMTN 48335 4195 A1
24000 FMTN 48336 4195 A1
Le Rhone St
22000 SFLD 48075 4198 A3
Lernoult St
9300 DET 48213 4274 D6
Leroy Av
25000 TYLR 48180 4582 E5
Leroy Dr
3800 WasC 48103 4405 A4
Leroy St
10 RVRG 48218 4418 E5
10 RVRG 48218 4419 A7
1200 FRDL 48220 4199 C3
3500 WasC 48103 4405 A4
8500 OKPK 48237 4199 B3
11000 DET 48213 4275 B1
11500 DET 48205 4275 B1
12800 SOGT 48195 4584 D4
20000 TYLR 48180 4583 E4
20000 TYLR 48195 4583 E4
25800 TYLR 48180 4582 C5
27900 RMLS 48174 4582 A5
30000 RMLS 48174 4581 D5
Lesia Dr
11700 GOTp 48189 4187 C6
Leslie
13200 GBTR 48173 4755 D5
Leslie Av
1500 WTLD 48186 4413 E4
17100 ALPK 48101 4500 A4
19300 GSPW 48236 4204 B7
19300 HRWD 48225 4204 B7
Leslie Dr
37500 HnTp 48164 4751 B3
Leslie Ln
44700 CNTN 48187 4336 D4
Leslie St
10 HDPK 48203 4272 C4
2300 DET 48238 4272 B5
3700 DET 48238 4271 E6
14500 OKPK 48237 4198 C1
22900 TYLR 48180 4499 B5
Leslie Cir Dr
2300 AARB 48105 4407 A2
Leslie Park Cir
2800 AARB 48105 4406 D1
Lespedeza Av
32300 GDNC 48135 4414 B1
Lesperance Rd
100 Tcmh N8N 4348 E6
600 Tcmh N8N 4423 E1
1600 Tcmh N8N 4424 A3
1600 Tcmh N9K 4424 A3
Lessard St
12200 Tcmh N8N 4423 E3
12200 Tcmh N8N 4424 A3
Lessing St
9300 DET 48214 4274 D7
9300 DET 48214 4346 D1
Lester Av
1000 YpTp 48198 4492 D6
Lesure St
15300 DET 48227 4270 E3
16100 DET 48235 4270 E3
18600 DET 48235 4198 E5
Le Tour Ln
21800 HnTp 48174 4667 B4
Leutheuser Dr
- SALN 48176 4572 D7
Levan Ct
19100 LVNA 48152 4194 B7
Levan Rd
9800 LVNA 48150 4338 C1
11600 LVNA 48150 4266 C7
13900 LVNA 48154 4266 C4
17100 LVNA 48152 4266 B1
18500 LVNA 48152 4194 B7
Leverette St
1300 DET 48226 4345 B6
1400 DET 48216 4345 B6
Leverne
9500 RDFD 48239 4340 C1
12700 RDFD 48239 4268 C6
Levona St
1000 YpTp 48198 4492 C6
Lewerenz St
800 DET 48209 4419 B2
Lewis Dr
4600 PTFD 48197 4574 E6
Lewis St
34900 WTLD 48185 4338 D5
N Lewis St
200 SALN 48176 4572 C7
S Lewis St
100 SALN 48176 4657 C1
Lewiston Rd
10 GSPF 48236 4276 C4
E Lewiston St
100 FRDL 48220 4199 E2
700 FRDL 48220 4200 A2
W Lewiston St
800 FRDL 48220 4199 C2
Lexham Gdns
500 Tcmh N8N 4424 D2
Lexington
- WynC 48138 4756 B2
15000 RDFD 48239 4268 C4
16800 RDFD 48240 4268 B2
19900 RDFD 48240 4196 B5
Lexington Av
22700 EPTE 48021 4203 E1
Lexington Blvd
20300 NHVL 48167 4192 C6
20600 NvlT 48167 4192 C6
N Lexington Blvd
- NHVL 48167 4192 A5
Lexington Cir
1000 WIND N8S 4347 E6
Lexington Cir N
2200 CNTN 48188 4411 A4
Lexington Cir S
2200 CNTN 48188 4411 A5
Lexington Ct
400 SALN 48176 4572 B6
1800 INKR 48141 4414 E4
2700 TNTN 48183 4669 C6
20600 NHVL 48167 4192 C5
20600 NvlT 48167 4192 C5
Lexington Dr
- TYLR 48180 4582 D5
300 SALN 48176 4572 C6
3000 AARB 48105 4407 B1
4000 TNTN 48183 4669 C6
11800 GOTp 48178 4188 B2
25600 SLYN 48178 4189 A1
Lexington Pkwy
1000 YpTp 48198 4492 C2
1500 INKR 48141 4414 E4
Lexington Rd
400 GSPF 48236 4204 C7
400 GSPF 48236 4276 C1
Lexington St
1500 PLYM 48170 4264 D7
7000 DET 48209 4419 B3
Leyte St
21800 FNHL 48336 4196 A3
Lezotte Dr
20000 RKWD 48173 4754 B6
Liberal St
13600 DET 48205 4202 E5
15600 DET 48205 4203 C5
16400 DET 48225 4203 C5
Liberty
- WynC 48138 4756 B2
Liberty Av
600 LNPK 48146 4501 A5
1000 LNPK 48146 4500 E5
2700 DRBN 48120 4418 D2
Liberty Blvd
8100 WTLD 48185 4339 C3
8700 WTLD 48150 4339 C3
Liberty Ct
1200 CNTN 48188 4410 E4
9900 DRBN 48120 4418 D2
Liberty Ct
30000 INKR 48141 4414 D6
Liberty Ln
6600 VNBN 48111 4577 C4
17500 BNTN 48192 4583 D6
W Liberty Rd
2700 AARB 48103 4405 A7
2700 WasC 48103 4405 A7
4200 WasC 48103 4404 D7
Liberty St
200 CNTN 48188 4410 D2
1600 WIND N9E 4504 A2
2700 WIND N9E 4503 E2
22500 STCS 48080 4204 E2
23000 McoC 48080 4205 A2
23000 STCS 48080 4205 A2
23300 FMTN 48335 4194 E2
29400 FNHL 48336 4195 D3
29900 INKR 48141 4414 D7
E Liberty St
100 AARB 48104 4406 B6
100 PLYM 48170 4265 B6
100 SLYN 48178 4189 B2
N Liberty St
10 BLVL 48111 4578 D2
S Liberty St
10 BLVL 48111 4578 D2
W Liberty St
100 AARB 48104 4406 A6
100 PLYM 48170 4265 A6
100 SLYN 48178 4189 B2
200 AARB 48103 4406 A6
1200 AARB 48103 4405 E6
1400 WasC 48103 4405 E6
Liberty St N
1300 CNTN 48188 4410 E4
Liberty St S
2000 CNTN 48188 4410 E5
Liberty Pointe Dr
400 AARB 48103 4405 C7
Library Dr
- RVVW 48192 4584 D7
Library St
1200 DET 48226 4345 D6
Lichfield Rd
19900 DET 48203 4199 E4
19900 DET 48221 4199 E4
Licorice St
200 WTLD 48186 4414 D7
S Liddesdale St
- LNPK 48229 4501 B1
700 DET 48229 4418 C6
2900 DET 48229 4501 B1
Liddicot St
1800 WTLD 48186 4413 C4
Liddle St
23600 BNTN 48183 4668 B4
S Liebold St
700 DET 48229 4418 D6
Lighthouse Ct
12400 PyTp 48170 4264 C7
12400 PyTp 48170 4336 C1
Lighthouse Dr
10800 VNBN 48111 4495 C7
Lighthouse Pt
19400 WynC 48138 4670 D1
Lightsway Dr
44800 NOVI 48375 4192 D3
Light Tower Ct
300 BLVL 48111 4578 C3
Light Tower Dr
600 BLVL 48111 4578 C3
Lila Ln
25800 DBHT 48127 4415 D1
Lilac Ct
- NvlT 48167 4193 A7
400 Amhg N9V 4757 C4
Lilac Dr
21500 WDHN 48183 4668 C3
Lilac Ln
7900 WIND N8R 4423 A2
21600 SFLD 48034 4196 D4
45400 VNBN 48111 4578 D1
Lilac Pl
5100 WYNE 48184 4414 B7
Lilac St
16100 DET 48221 4271 D2
22400 FMTN 48336 4195 B2
N Lilley Rd
100 CNTN 48187 4412 B2
1800 CNTN 48187 4337 B6
8800 PyTp 48170 4337 B3
S Lilley Rd
100 CNTN 48187 4412 B3
100 CNTN 48188 4412 B3
5100 CNTN 48111 4495 B1
5100 CNTN 48188 4495 B1
Lilley Pointe Blvd
42400 CNTN 48187 4412 A2
Lillian Av
900 WIND N9A 4421 A2
1200 WIND N8X 4421 B3
2400 WIND N8W 4421 C5
Lillian Ct
300 WasC 48189 4259 B1
8000 CNTN 48187 4336 B4
Lillian Rd
2600 AARB 48104 4490 C3
Lillian St
1400 WTLD 48186 4414 C3
23600 BNTN 48183 4668 B3
60400 LyTp 48178 4189 B4
Lillibridge St
400 DET 48214 4347 B2
3800 DET 48214 4274 E6
3800 DET 48214 4275 A6
5000 DET 48213 4274 E6
Lilly Ct
27300 BwTp 48183 4754 E2
Lilly Dr
8600 YpTp 48197 4576 D3
27100 BwTp 48183 4754 E2
Lilly Pad Ct
17200 NvlT 48167 4265 B2
Lily Ct
10 RKWD 48173 4840 C1
Lily Valley Dr
100 PTFD 48176 4573 E6
Lime St
100 WTLD 48186 4414 D7
Lime Kiln Dr
12000 GOTp 48178 4188 B3
Lincoln Av
200 WIND N8Y 4346 B7
200 WIND N9A 4346 B7
300 LNPK 48146 4501 A4
600 WIND N8Y 4421 C2
600 WIND N9A 4421 C2
800 AARB 48104 4406 D7
1200 WIND N8X 4421 C2
1300 LNPK 48146 4500 E3
1400 AARB 48104 4489 D1
1500 WIND N8W 4421 D4
16000 EPTE 48021 4203 D3
Lincoln Blvd
3900 DBHT 48124 4416 C6
3900 DBHT 48125 4416 C6
5500 DBHT 48125 4499 C1
Lincoln Cir
100 WasC 48176 4657 A2
Lincoln Ct
6200 VNBN 48111 4577 C3
9700 TYLR 48180 4499 C5
24500 FNHL 48335 4194 A1
50200 PyTp 48170 4263 D6
Lincoln Dr
1600 CNTN 48188 4411 B4
8700 WasC 48189 4259 A1
16300 NvlT 48167 4263 D4
21600 BNTN 48192 4583 D6
49700 PyTp 48170 4263 D6
Lincoln Rd
200 GSPT 48230 4276 C5
900 DET 48224 4276 C3
900 GSPT 48224 4276 C3
Lincoln St
- DET 48210 4344 E2
- DRBN 48124 4416 C5
600 WYDT 48192 4501 C6
3400 DET 48201 4345 A5
3400 DET 48210 4345 A5
5600 WYNE 48184 4497 C2
5700 DET 48202 4344 E2
7800 TYLR 48180 4499 C3
13600 HDPK 48203 4272 C3
21700 RKWD 48173 4754 D7
42000 VNBN 48111 4495 B7
N Lincoln St
10 YPLT 48198 4492 A4
Lincolnshire Ct
49200 CNTN 48187 4335 E5
Lincolnshire Dr
1400 DET 48203 4200 A6
1800 DET 48221 4200 A6
Lincolnshire Ln
1200 AARB 48103 4406 A2
Linda Av
6400 PTFD 48176 4574 B4
Linda Cres
- Lksr N8N 4424 D6
- Lksr N9K 4424 D6
Linda Dr
9900 YpTp 48197 4577 A3
Linda St
29400 LVNA 48154 4267 D4
Lindavista Ct
12000 VNBN 48111 4577 E2
Linda Vista St
600 AARB 48103 4405 E5
Lindbergh St
600 WYDT 48192 4501 B6
1400 WYDT 48192 4585 B1
Linden Ct
100 YPLT 48197 4491 E5
400 Amhg N9V 4757 C4
400 SALN 48176 4572 B7
500 NHVL 48167 4192 D6
14400 PyTp 48170 4263 D5
16200 NvlT 48167 4264 D3
30500 FTRK 48134 4754 C5
Linden Dr
5600 DBHT 48127 4341 C6
Linden Ln
500 WasC 48103 4404 C4
34800 WTLD 48185 4338 D6
Linden St
10 RVRG 48218 4418 E7
100 NHVL 48167 4192 D6
500 AARB 48104 4406 D7
800 PLYM 48170 4337 A1
900 PLYM 48170 4336 E1
1000 DRBN 48124 4417 B6
29400 FNHL 48336 4195 D2
49400 PyTp 48170 4263 D5
Lindenwood Dr
3000 DRBN 48120 4417 D3
Lindenwood Ln
25000 SFLD 48034 4196 B1
Lindsay Dr
200 PLYM 48170 4337 B1
41400 PyTp 48170 4337 B1
Lindsay Ln
1800 AATp 48104 4490 C2
Lindsay St
14800 DET 48227 4270 B4
16100 DET 48235 4270 B3
18200 DET 48235 4198 B7
Lindsey Dr
23500 BNTN 48134 4667 E5

INDEX 33

Lindsey Dr — Detroit & Wayne County Street Index — Lynne Av

STREET Block City ZIP Map# Grid

Lindsey Dr
44800 VNBN 48111 4494 D3
Lingemann St
22700 STCS 48080 4204 E2
Link Rd
20900 SFLD 48034 4196 E4
Links Ct
4400 PTFD 48108 4488 D7
Links Dr
- Amhg N9V 4671 D4
Linnhurst St
11000 DET 48234 4202 C6
12300 DET 48205 4202 D6
15700 DET 48205 4203 C6
Linsdale St
- DET 48204 4344 A2
5200 DET 48204 4343 E2
Linsell Av
4700 WIND N9C 4419 E7
Lintons Wy
6300 WasC 48105 4331 A2
Linville Av
18900 DET 48225 4276 B1
18900 DET 48236 4276 B1
19000 GSPW 48225 4204 B7
19000 GSPW 48225 4276 B1
19000 GSPW 48236 4204 B7
19000 GSPW 48236 4276 B1
19000 HRWD 48225 4276 B1
N Linville Av
1700 WTLD 48185 4338 C7
1700 WTLD 48185 4413 C1
S Linville Av
1100 WTLD 48186 4413 C4
Linville St
- DET 48224 4276 A1
8800 LVNA 48150 4338 C3
13000 DET 48213 4275 B4
14300 DET 48224 4275 B4
18600 DET 48236 4276 B1
N Linville St
100 WTLD 48185 4413 C2
Linwood Av
1200 AARB 48103 4406 A5
1300 AARB 48103 4405 E5
22700 EPTE 48021 4203 B1
Linwood Dr
- Amhg N9V 4671 C4
Linwood Pl
3200 WIND N9C 4420 A3
Linwood St
5200 DET 48210 4344 D3
7300 DET 48206 4344 D3
9000 DET 48206 4272 B6
12600 DET 48238 4272 A3
16100 DET 48221 4272 A3
Linzee St
6800 DET 48210 4343 E6
Lionel Dr
2700 WIND N8X 4421 D5
Lionel St
9000 LVNA 48150 4338 C2
Liparoto Dr
32000 RKWD 48173 4754 E7
Lipka Ct
43400 CNTN 48187 4412 A1
Lipton St
5500 DET 48204 4343 E1
Lisa Cres
500 WIND N9G 4504 D4
Lisa Ct
600 WIND N9G 4504 E4
4700 TNTN 48183 4669 B7
22800 FNHL 48335 4194 B2
25000 BNTN 48134 4667 E4
Lisa St
9200 RMLS 48174 4496 E5
Lisa Lori Ln
11200 GOTp 48178 4188 A5
Lisann Ct
4100 WIND N9G 4505 A3
Lisann St
4200 WIND N9G 4505 A4
Lisbon St
7000 DET 48209 4419 B2
Lisch St
29900 GBTR 48173 4755 C4
Liscomb Av
22700 EPTE 48021 4203 C2
Lisette
- DET 48214 4347 A2
Lisgar St
1300 LSal N9J 4503 A4
Liss Rd
9000 AGST 48191 4748 A3
10000 AGST 48111 4748 A3
List St
28900 FNHL 48336 4195 D5
Lister Av
18000 EPTE 48021 4203 E2
18300 EPTE 48021 4204 A2
Litchfield Ct
46100 PyTp 48170 4336 C2
Litchfield Dr
45800 PyTp 48170 4336 C2
Lithgow St
13800 DRBN 48126 4417 E1
Little Base Line Rd
10 Lksr N8N 4424 C4
10 Lksr N9K 4424 C4
Little Baseline Rd
200 Lksr N8N 4424 E4
200 Lksr N9K 4424 E4
Little Baseline Rd CO-21
200 Lksr N8N 4424 E4
200 Lksr N9K 4424 E4
Littledown Rd
4000 WasC 48103 4405 A1
4100 WasC 48103 4404 E1
Little Falls Blvd
43300 NOVI 48375 4192 E1
Littlefield Blvd
- DET 48228 4343 B4
7200 DRBN 48126 4343 B4
Littlefield St
- DRBN 48126 4343 A3
8400 DET 48228 4343 A1
9500 DET 48227 4343 A1
13200 DET 48227 4271 A5
17100 DET 48235 4271 A1
19100 DET 48235 4199 A5
Little Lake Dr
100 WasC 48103 4404 E6
Little Mack Av
23500 STCS 48080 4204 C1
Littler Cres
2700 WIND N8T 4422 C3
Little Rapids Ct
23400 NOVI 48375 4193 A2
Little River Blvd
- WIND N8P 4348 C7
Little River Dr
11100 WIND N8P 4348 C7
Little River Rd
- Tcmh N8P 4348 E7
7900 WIND N8S 4347 E7
8400 WIND N8S 4348 A7
12400 Tcmh N8N 4348 E7
12500 Tcmh N8N 4349 A7
Littlestone Rd
- GSPF 48236 4204 B6
1600 GSPW 48236 4204 B6
19500 HRWD 48225 4204 B6
19500 HRWD 48236 4204 B6
Little Stones Ct
23600 NOVI 48375 4193 A2
Little Valley Dr
- FNHL 48336 4195 D4
Livernois Av
- DET 48209 4419 B1
2700 DET 48209 4344 A5
3100 DET 48210 4344 A5
6000 DET 48210 4343 D2
8000 DET 48204 4343 D2
10600 DET 48204 4271 D4
12500 DET 48238 4271 D4
16100 DET 48221 4271 D1
18000 DET 48221 4199 D6
Livernois Av S
100 DET 48209 4419 C3
Livernois St
1900 FRDL 48220 4199 D2
Liverpool Av
19600 LVNA 48152 4194 B6
Liverpool Ct
8500 SpTp 48198 4492 C1
Liverpool St
15400 LVNA 48154 4266 B4
Livingston Dr
50600 NvlT 48167 4263 D3
Livingston St
10400 HbgT 48189 4186 B4
22900 TYLR 48180 4499 B7
N Livonia Cres
14200 LVNA 48154 4267 C5
S Livonia Cres
14100 LVNA 48154 4267 C5
Llewelyn Ct
41200 NOVI 48167 4193 C5
41200 NOVI 48375 4193 C5
Llewelyn Dr
41300 NOVI 48167 4193 B5
41300 NOVI 48375 4193 B5
Llorac Ln
41300 NOVI 48167 4193 B5
Lloyd Ct
23800 DRBN 48124 4416 A4
Lloyd George Blvd
2400 WIND N8T 4422 D3
Loch Alpine Dr
- WasC 48103 4329 E5
Loch Alpine Dr E
3700 WasC 48103 4329 E5
Loch Alpine Dr W
3700 WasC 48103 4329 D5
Lochdale
36400 FNHL 48335 4194 B1
Lochdale St
8000 DBHT 48127 4340 D3
8600 DBHT 48239 4340 D3
Loch Highland Dr
2100 WasC 48130 4329 A7
2100 WasC 48130 4404 A1
Loch Loden Dr
5000 WasC 48130 4329 B7
5000 WasC 48130 4404 B1
Loch Lomond Dr
25500 DBHT 48125 4415 D3
Lochmoor Blvd
- RMLS 48174 4497 A2
10 GSPS 48236 4205 A6
1400 GSPW 48236 4204 C6
Lochmoor Cir E
16700 NvlT 48167 4264 B3
Lochmoor Cir W
16700 NvlT 48167 4264 B2
Lochmoor Ct
17000 NvlT 48167 4264 B2
Lochmoor Dr
1800 GSPW 48236 4204 C5
7000 YpTp 48197 4576 A5
Lochmoor Pl
900 GSPW 48236 4204 E5
Lochmoor St
100 WIND N9E 4504 D2
19600 HRWD 48225 4204 A5
21100 HRWD 48236 4204 B5
Lochness Ct
12300 PyTp 48170 4264 A7
Lochrisen Wy
43100 NOVI 48375 4193 A2
43200 NOVI 48375 4192 E1
Locke St
3800 WIND N9G 4504 E3
Lockridge Dr
3200 AARB 48108 4489 D4
Lockwood St
3100 DET 48210 4344 C6
20500 TYLR 48180 4499 D4
Locust Ct
- CNTN 48188 4411 C6
3100 WIND N8R 4423 C3
Locust Dr
10 VNBN 48111 4577 E6
10 VNBN 48111 4578 A6
Locust St
400 YPLT 48198 4492 B4
22100 DRBN 48124 4416 D3
24100 FMTN 48335 4194 D1
24100 FNHL 48335 4194 D1
Lodewyck St
4500 DET 48224 4276 B2
Lodge Ct
22800 NOVI 48375 4193 D3
Lodge Dr
300 DET 48214 4346 E2
300 DET 48214 4347 A3
Lodge Ln
3700 TNTN 48183 4669 B4
22800 DRBN 48128 4416 A1
Lodi Ln
6100 WasC 48176 4572 B3
Lodi St
- DET 48211 4273 E7
Lodi Meadow Ct
3700 WasC 48176 4572 A4
Lodi Meadow Dr
6300 WasC 48176 4572 A4
Loebach Dr
3000 WIND N8T 4422 C4
Logan Ct
2900 AARB 48108 4489 E4
Logan Dr
27100 HnTp 48134 4753 A1
Logan St
300 WIND N8X 4421 B4
7200 DET 48209 4419 A2
Loganberry Rdg N
42000 NOVI 48375 4193 A1
Loganberry Rdg S
42000 NOVI 48375 4193 A1
Log Cabin Rd
- WTLD 48135 4414 C2
200 GDNC 48135 4414 C2
Log Cabin St
15400 DET 48238 4272 A3
16100 DET 48203 4272 A2
16100 DET 48221 4272 A2
17000 HDPK 48203 4272 A2
Logue Av
21700 WRRN 48091 4201 B2
Lohr Cir
3000 PTFD 48108 4488 E4
3000 PTFD 48108 4489 A4
Lohr Rd
3200 PTFD 48108 4489 A4
4700 PTFD 48108 4573 A1
16400 VNBN 48111 4578 A6
17400 WynC 48111 4578 A7
17500 WynC 48111 4663 A1
Lohr Lake Ct
5900 PTFD 48108 4573 A3
Lohr Lake Dr
5900 PTFD 48108 4573 A3
Lois Ct
10 AARB 48103 4406 A5
Lois St
4200 DRBN 48126 4418 A1
4400 DRBN 48126 4343 A7
Lois Ln Dr
24200 SFLD 48075 4197 B1
Loiter Wy
- DET 48207 4347 A5
10 DET 48207 4346 E5
Lola Dr
15300 RDFD 48239 4268 D3
15900 RDFD 48240 4268 D3
Lola St
5900 DET 48210 4344 B6
Lolly Pop St
200 WTLD 48186 4414 D7
Loma Cir
- WynC 48138 4756 A1
N Loma Cir
10100 WynC 48138 4756 A1
S Loma Cir
10100 WynC 48138 4756 A1
Loma Ct
27100 WynC 48138 4756 A1
Loma Dr
- BNTN 48192 4669 A2
Lombard Ter
1700 DET 48210 4344 D4
Lombardy Cres
2700 LSal N9H 4503 E4
Lombardy Dr
42800 CNTN 48187 4337 A5
Lomond Ct
12600 PyTp 48170 4264 A7
London Av
700 LNPK 48146 4501 A5
1000 LNPK 48146 4500 E5
2100 ALPK 48101 4500 C5
2100 LNPK 48101 4500 C5
London Ct
7000 CNTN 48187 4337 A5
22800 SFLD 48034 4197 A2
39700 NvlT 48167 4193 D6
London St
6300 DET 48221 4199 D7
E London St
3000 WRRN 48091 4201 B4
Londonderry
23500 NOVI 48375 4193 C2
Londonderry Cir
10 AARB 48104 4490 A1
Londonderry Ct
43100 CNTN 48188 4412 A5
Londonderry Dr
1100 WasC 48176 4658 C3
10300 GOTp 48178 4188 E3
10300 GOTp 48178 4189 A3
Londonderry Rd
2100 AARB 48104 4406 E7
2100 AARB 48104 4490 A1
Lone Oak Ct
4800 PTFD 48108 4572 E1
Lone Oak Dr
- DRBN 48126 4416 E1
- DRBN 48126 4417 A1
Lone Oak Ln
4000 SpTp 48105 4334 A5
Lonepine Cres
1600 WIND N8W 4505 A2
Lone Pine Dr
32500 WTLD 48185 4339 A5
Lone Pine Ln
35200 FNHL 48335 4194 C3
Lone Wolf Ln
1800 CNTN 48188 4412 C4
Long Blvd
22100 DRBN 48124 4416 C2
Long St
27400 LVNA 48152 4196 A5
Longacre Ct
23200 FMTN 48335 4194 D2
23200 FNHL 48335 4194 D2
Longacre St
9400 DET 48228 4342 B2
9500 DET 48227 4342 B1
13900 DET 48227 4270 B5
22500 FNHL 48335 4194 D3
23500 FMTN 48335 4194 D1
Longden Rd
14100 BwTp 48173 4841 D3
Longfellow Av
1700 WIND N9B 4420 E5
2200 WIND N9B 4421 A6
2200 WIND N9E 4420 E5
2200 WIND N9E 4421 A6
3000 WIND N9E 4504 A1
3800 WIND N9G 4504 B3
Longfellow Dr
200 SLYN 48178 4189 B3
900 CNTN 48187 4411 D1
Longfellow St
10 WasC 48189 4259 A2
300 INKR 48141 4414 E2
1100 DET 48202 4272 C7
1400 DET 48206 4272 D6
Longford Ct
10000 GOTp 48178 4189 A2
Longford Dr
10100 GOTp 48178 4188 E3
10100 GOTp 48178 4189 A2
Longleaf Dr
20200 BwTp 48183 4754 E2
Longman Ln
100 AARB 48103 4405 D5
Longmeadow Dr
2300 TNTN 48183 4669 B4
2800 WDHN 48183 4669 B5
Longmeadow Ln
8000 AGST 48197 4575 C7
28300 BwTp 48183 4754 C2
28300 BwTp 48183 4755 A3
E Longmeadow Rd
1700 TNTN 48183 4669 B3
N Longmeadow Rd
3600 TNTN 48183 4669 B3
S Longmeadow Rd
3600 TNTN 48183 4669 B3
W Longmeadow Rd
1700 TNTN 48183 4669 B3
Longmeadow St
15500 DRBN 48120 4417 D2
Long Meadow Tr
1500 PTFD 48108 4489 A4
Long Point Wy
23400 NOVI 48375 4193 A2
23500 NOVI 48375 4192 E1
Longridge Ct
20000 NvlT 48167 4193 B6
Longridge Rd
20200 NvlT 48167 4193 B6
Longsdorf St
11500 RVVW 48192 4585 A6
12500 RVVW 48192 4584 E6
Long Shore Dr
400 AARB 48105 4406 C4
Longtin Av
4100 LNPK 48146 4500 D7
Longtin St
12100 SOGT 48195 4500 D7
12100 SOGT 48195 4584 D1
Longview Ln
1000 WasC 48176 4573 C7
Longview St
10900 DET 48213 4274 E3
12500 DET 48213 4275 A2
14900 DET 48224 4275 A2
23200 DBHT 48127 4341 A6
Longwood Av E
10 DET 48203 4272 C1
Long Wood Ct
20200 NvlT 48167 4193 A6
Longwood Dr
33400 FNHL 48335 4194 E3
Longwood Pl W
10 DET 48203 4272 C1
Longwood Rd
6700 CNTN 48187 4336 C5
Longworth St
8000 DET 48209 4419 A3
8700 DET 48209 4418 E3
Longyear St
7000 DET 48211 4274 A6
Lonnie Dr
31400 WTLD 48185 4339 B4
Lons
15300 RDFD 48239 4268 D3
Lonsdale Cres
10300 WIND N8R 4423 C4
Lonyo St
2900 DET 48209 4418 E1
3800 DET 48210 4343 C5
6500 DRBN 48126 4343 C5
Lookout Cir
2600 AARB 48104 4490 B3
Loomis Ct
23500 FMTN 48336 4195 A2
Loomis Dr
32100 FMTN 48336 4195 A1
Loon St
- WIND N8W 4422 B4
Looney Dr
33100 BwTp 48173 4841 A1
Loper Ln
6600 WasC 48170 4262 C6
Loraine Av
1900 WIND N8W 4421 D4
Loraine St
700 GSPT 48230 4276 B4
800 DET 48230 4276 B4
5000 DET 48210 4344 D3
6100 RMLS 48174 4497 E1
10100 RMLS 48174 4498 A6
18000 HnTp 48174 4582 A7
Lorals Wy
55600 LyTp 48167 4190 C4
Loranger St
11000 BrTp 48179 4841 B4
Lorato St
13900 TYLR 48180 4583 C2
Lorelei Dr
26000 BNTN 48134 4667 D7
Loren St
22900 STCS 48080 4204 E2
Lorenz St
6800 RMLS 48174 4497 A3
Lorenz Wy
11600 PyTp 48170 4336 C1
Loretta Av
24100 WRRN 48091 4201 C1
Loretta Dr
22000 WDHN 48183 4668 C4
Loretto St
12300 DET 48205 4274 E1
13000 DET 48205 4275 A1
Lori Ct
24000 FNHL 48336 4195 E1
Lori Dr
400 WIND N8S 4347 E5
400 WIND N8S 4348 A5
23500 BNTN 48134 4667 E5
Lori Ln
38400 WTLD 48185 4338 A4
Lori St
1000 YpTp 48198 4492 E6
26000 TYLR 48180 4498 D3
29400 LVNA 48154 4267 D5
Lorman St
8800 DET 48214 4346 D2
28900 RMLS 48174 4497 E6
Lorne St
20000 TYLR 48180 4499 E2
Lorraine Av
24000 CTNL 48015 4202 B1
24300 WRRN 48089 4202 B1
Lorraine Blvd
23100 BNTN 48183 4668 B5
Lorraine Dr
28400 FNHL 48336 4195 E2
Lorraine Pl
1900 AARB 48104 4406 E7
Lorraine St
3000 AARB 48108 4490 B5
E Lorraine St
23000 BNTN 48183 4668 B5
Lorraine St W
23000 BNTN 48183 4668 B5
Lorrina Ln
37100 HnTp 48164 4580 B7
Loruss Av
38400 WTLD 48186 4413 A3
Loruss Ct
400 WTLD 48186 4413 A3
Los Angeles Av
1900 WRRN 48091 4200 E2
2200 WRRN 48091 4201 A2
Lost Oak Dr
5500 WasC 48105 4333 B3
Lothrop Ct
45000 CNTN 48188 4411 D3
Lothrop Rd
10 DET 48202 4345 A1
200 GSPF 48236 4276 C3
800 DET 48202 4344 E1
45100 CNTN 48188 4411 D3
Lothrop St
2600 DET 48206 4344 C2
Lottie St
100 SLYN 48178 4189 B1
Lotus Dr
43500 CNTN 48188 4412 A5
N Lotz Rd
100 CNTN 48187 4412 D2
1700 CNTN 48187 4337 D7
S Lotz Rd
100 CNTN 48187 4412 D3
100 CNTN 48188 4412 D3
5400 CNTN 48188 4495 D1
Lotzford Rd
39500 CNTN 48187 4412 D1
Loudon Dr
25700 BNTN 48134 4754 A1
Louis
22100 HnTp 48164 4666 E4
Louis
9200 RDFD 48239 4340 D2
Louis Av
100 WIND N9A 4346 A7
200 WIND N9A 4421 A1
1200 WIND N8X 4421 A2
2300 WIND N8W 4421 C4
Louis St
10 RVRG 48218 4501 E1
9100 DET 48214 4346 D1
Louisa Dr
10 Lksr N8N 4424 E3
14300 VNBN 48111 4579 B3
Louise Av
8300 ALPK 48101 4500 A4
Louise Ct
7600 WTLD 48185 4339 D4
Louise Dr
600 AARB 48103 4405 D4
Louise St
- LVNA 48150 4339 D1
200 HDPK 48203 4272 B2
1000 YPLT 48197 4491 C2
1700 DET 48203 4272 B2
17100 LVNA 48152 4267 D1
17200 SFLD 48075 4198 A2
20300 LVNA 48152 4195 D5
20400 LVNA 48336 4195 D5
30300 WTLD 48185 4339 D4
Louisiana St
10 DET 48203 4200 D7
8900 LVNA 48150 4339 A2
Lounsborough Ct
3800 WIND N9G 4504 E2
Lounsborough St
700 WIND N9G 4504 E2
900 WIND N9G 4505 A3
Louvert Ct
44500 NOVI 48375 4192 D3
Loveland St
9600 LVNA 48150 4339 A1
17100 LVNA 48152 4267 A1
17100 LVNA 48154 4267 A1
18200 LVNA 48152 4195 A7
Lovell Cres
1500 LSal N9H 4504 B5
Lovett Av
4100 INKR 48141 4414 D6
Lovett Ct
4000 INKR 48141 4414 D6
Lovett St
3400 DET 48210 4344 C5
Lovewood Ct
5800 CNTN 48187 4336 A7
Lovric Rd
4400 WIND N8W 4422 B4
Lowdell St
14000 DET 48229 4418 B5
Lowell Av
44500 CNTN 48187 4411 E1
Lowell Dr
16100 SOGT 48195 4584 E4
19400 DET 48203 4200 A6
Lowell Rd
2600 AARB 48103 4405 E2
2600 AARB 48103 4406 A2
Lowell St
700 YPLT 48197 4491 E3
28800 GBTR 48173 4755 D3
Lower Ridge Dr
30600 HnTp 48164 4666 E5
Lower Rouge Pkwy Dr
- INKR 48141 4415 B4
Lowes Sideroad
100 Amhg N9V 4757 D5
Lowrey St
9700 DRBN 48120 4418 D3
Lowrie Dr
23300 WynC 48138 4670 C5
Lowry Dr
- WasC 48160 4659 D3
Loyola Dr
800 AARB 48103 4406 A5
900 AARB 48103 4405 E5
Loza Ln
10 BLVL 48111 4578 E2
Lozier Av
6700 WRRN 48015 4201 E2
6700 WRRN 48091 4201 E2
6900 WRRN 48015 4202 A1
8000 WRRN 48089 4202 A2
8000 WRRN 48091 4202 A1
Lozier St
- DET 48224 4275 D5
14300 DET 48214 4275 C5
Luana Av
6300 ALPK 48101 4500 A2
Lucas Dr
200 RMLS 48174 4497 D5
200 RMLS 48242 4497 D5
Luce St
3800 DET 48212 4273 C1
32500 WTLD 48186 4414 B4
Lucerne
9500 RDFD 48239 4340 C1
11700 RDFD 48239 4268 C7
Lucerne Av
14000 RDFD 48239 4268 C5
Lucerne Ct
10 AARB 48108 4489 E5
Lucerne Dr
18800 SOGT 48195 4500 A7
Lucerne Dr
19200 DET 48203 4200 A6
19400 DET 48203 4199 E6
22000 SFLD 48075 4198 B3
27000 INKR 48141 4415 B3
Lucerne St
7200 DBHT 48127 4340 C5
Luciow Dr
22100 HnTp 48164 4666 E4
Lucky Pl
5900 DET 48211 4273 E7
Lucy Av
18600 ALPK 48101 4499 E5
18600 ALPK 48101 4500 A5
Ludden St
3100 DET 48207 4346 A2
Ludington St
1300 WYDT 48192 4585 A5
2200 WYDT 48192 4584 E5
3200 INKR 48141 4414 E5
14900 SOGT 48195 4584 B5
Ludlow Ct
42200 NvlT 48167 4265 B3
Ludwig Dr
33100 BwTp 48173 4755 B7
33100 BwTp 48173 4841 B1
Luella Av
10 WasC 48103 4404 D5
Lujon Ct
21400 FNHL 48167 4193 E4
Lujon Dr
20700 FNHL 48167 4193 E5
Lumber Dr
1100 YPLT 48197 4491 D6
Lumley St
5100 DET 48210 4343 D5
Lumpkin Av
9500 HMTK 48212 4273 B4
Lumpkin St
11300 HMTK 48212 4273 B3
13400 DET 48212 4273 A1
17400 DET 48212 4201 A7
17800 DET 48212 4200 E6
19100 DET 48234 4200 E6
20100 DET 48234 4201 A4
Lundy Dr
21300 FNHL 48336 4195 B3
Lundy Parkway Dr
- DRBN 48126 4342 C6
Luther Ln
33400 LVNA 48154 4266 E5
S Luther St
200 DET 48229 4418 D5
Lutz Av
900 AARB 48103 4406 A7
1300 AARB 48103 4405 E7
Lutz Dr
3000 WasC 48160 4659 B3
Lycaste St
1500 DET 48214 4347 B1
Lydenglen Dr
100 WasC 48103 4489 B3
Lydgate Ct
22400 NOVI 48375 4192 D3
Lydia Av
14600 EPTE 48021 4203 B3
Lydia St
32500 WTLD 48186 4414 B4
Lyford St
8000 DET 48234 4274 B2
Lyman Pl
- DET 48211 4273 C7
Lyme Ct
43500 CNTN 48187 4337 A7
Lyn Anne Ct
200 AARB 48103 4405 D5
Lynch Rd
- DET 48211 4273 E3
6300 DET 48212 4273 E3
6300 DET 48234 4273 E3
6500 DET 48212 4274 A3
6500 DET 48234 4274 A3
Lyndhurst Dr
7200 CNTN 48187 4336 A5
Lyndon
24300 RDFD 48239 4268 E5
27300 RDFD 48154 4268 B5
Lyndon Av
46700 CNTN 48187 4336 B5
Lyndon Ct
5400 WIND N8T 4422 D4
33600 LVNA 48154 4266 E5
Lyndon Ln
4100 WasC 48105 4260 D7
Lyndon St
- DET 48223 4270 B4
6300 DET 48238 4271 C4
12700 DET 48227 4271 B4
13500 DET 48227 4270 E4
19200 DET 48223 4269 E5
27400 LVNA 48154 4268 A5
32400 LVNA 48154 4267 B5
34600 LVNA 48154 4266 C5
38700 LVNA 48154 4265 E5
Lynn Av
1700 YpTp 48198 4492 E7
N Lynn Ct
3300 TNTN 48183 4669 B4
S Lynn Ct
3300 TNTN 48183 4669 B4
Lynn Dr
34300 RMLS 48174 4496 D6
44700 PyTp 48170 4336 D2
Lynn St
600 WIND N9G 4504 E2
900 DET 48211 4273 A5
39600 CNTN 48187 4337 D4
Lynne Av
500 YpTp 48198 4492 C3

STREET
Block City ZIP Map# Grid

Lynne Dr
31600 RKWD 48173 4754 C7
Lynngrove Cres
9600 WIND N8R 4423 B2
Lynngrove Ct
2700 WIND N8R 4423 B1
Lynnwood Ct
43400 CNTN 48187 4412 A1
Lynwood Dr
24300 NOVI 48374 4191 E1
24300 NOVI 48374 4192 A1
Lynx St
33000 WTLD 48185 4339 A4
Lyon Blvd
100 SLYN 48178 4189 C1
Lyon Ct
400 SLYN 48178 4189 C2
Lyon St
9000 DET 48209 4419 A5
N Lyon Tr
21700 LyTp 48178 4189 C5
S Lyon Tr
60600 LyTp 48178 4189 C5
Lyonhurst Cir
16500 NvlT 48167 4264 B3
Lyon Meadow Ct
21800 LyTp 48178 4189 B4
Lyons Av
1400 LSal N9J 4503 B7
Lyons Ct
10 DRBN 48126 4342 C7
Lyons Rd
24100 WynC 48138 4670 D6
Lyons St
13200 OKPK 48237 4198 E3
13200 OKPK 48237 4199 A3
14600 LVNA 48154 4268 A4
S Lyon Woods Dr
- SLYN 48178 4189 B3
Lyric Ct
42700 NvlT 48167 4193 A6
Lysander St
1500 DET 48210 4345 A4
1700 DET 48210 4344 D4
Lytham Ln
4800 WasC 48103 4404 D6
Lytle Pl
300 GDNC 48135 4414 E2
Lytle St
34400 FNHL 48335 4194 D3

M

Mabel Ct
23400 BNTN 48183 4668 B6
Mabel St
- HDPK 48203 4272 B3
600 WasC 48103 4405 A4
Maben Rd
45400 CNTN 48187 4336 B7
Mac Av
35500 RMLS 48174 4580 D5
Mac St
20700 WRRN 48091 4201 A4
MacArthur
15100 RDFD 48239 4268 C4
18200 RDFD 48240 4268 C1
19900 RDFD 48240 4196 C5
MacArthur Blvd
- WRRN 48234 4202 B3
1500 SpTp 48198 4492 C1
9000 SpTp 48198 4409 D7
20700 WRRN 48089 4202 B3
MacArthur Dr
1000 SpTp 48198 4492 C1
MacArthur St
24000 CTNL 48015 4202 B1
Macauley St
20700 SFLD 48075 4197 D4
Maccrary St
12300 DET 48205 4275 B1
12600 DET 48205 4203 B7
MacDonald-Cartier Frwy
- Tcmh - 4504 E5
- Tcmh - 4505 D4
- WIND - 4504 E5
- WIND - 4505 A5
MacDonald-Cartier Frwy P-401
- Tcmh - 4504 E5
- Tcmh - 4505 D4
- WIND - 4504 E5
- WIND - 4505 A5
Macey Rd
9000 AGST 48191 4661 E3
9500 AGST 48191 4662 A3
MacGregor Ln
1400 AARB 48105 4407 C4
Macintosh Rd
1400 SpTp 48198 4493 A1
1400 YpTp 48198 4493 A1
Mack Av
10 DET 48201 4345 C4
100 Tcmh N8N 4424 D1
900 DET 48207 4345 C4
3000 DET 48207 4346 B2
7000 DET 48214 4346 B2
9300 DET 48214 4274 D7
11000 DET 48214 4275 B6
14900 DET 48224 4275 D5
15000 DET 48230 4275 D5
15000 GPPK 48214 4275 D5
15000 GPPK 48230 4275 D5
16000 GPPK 48230 4276 A5
16300 GPPK 48224 4276 A5
17100 DET 48224 4276 A5
17100 DET 48230 4276 A5
17100 GSPT 48230 4276 A5
17900 GSPT 48224 4276 B3
18100 DET 48236 4276 B3

Mack Av
18100 GSPF 48236 4276 B3
19200 GSPW 48236 4276 B3
19400 GSPF 48236 4204 C7
19400 GSPW 48236 4204 C7
Mack Ct
100 Tcmh N8N 4424 D1
Mack Rd
500 AARB 48104 4406 D6
Mackay St
11300 HMTK 48212 4273 B3
13400 DET 48212 4273 A1
17400 DET 48212 4201 A7
18000 DET 48234 4201 A6
Mackenzie Ct
27600 WTLD 48185 4340 A3
Mackenzie Dr
28000 WTLD 48185 4340 A3
30600 WTLD 48185 4339 C3
Mackenzie St
6300 DET 48204 4343 D3
12900 DET 48228 4343 A3
15000 DET 48228 4342 D3
Mackinac St
32500 WTLD 48186 4414 D4
Mackinaw St
8600 DET 48204 4344 A1
Mack Plaza Dr
20000 GSPW 48236 4204 C6
Mack Service Dr
12000 DET 48214 4275 A6
Macomb Rd
7500 WynC 48138 4670 C6
Macomb St
300 DET 48226 4345 D5
2600 DET 48207 4346 A4
33700 FMTN 48335 4194 E2
Macon Rd
8700 WasC 48176 4657 B4
8800 SALN 48176 4657 B4
10200 WasC 48176 4656 E6
Macon St
9100 DET 48213 4274 D4
Mada Av
20900 SFLD 48075 4197 B3
21300 SFLD 48034 4197 B3
Maddelein St
14000 DET 48205 4203 A6
16200 DET 48224 4203 C6
16200 DET 48225 4203 C6
Madden Ct
25600 TYLR 48180 4498 E6
Madden St
25100 TYLR 48180 4498 D6
Maddie Ln
4700 DRBN 48126 4417 C1
4800 DRBN 48126 4342 C7
Madeira St
1300 DET 48203 4272 E1
Madelon Dr
10 BLVL 48111 4578 D2
E Madge Av
10 HZLP 48030 4200 C3
W Madge Av
10 HZLP 48030 4200 C3
Madison Av
400 GSPF 48236 4276 C2
Madison Blvd
- YPLT 48197 4492 A6
Madison Ct
- NvlT 48167 4193 C6
100 CNTN 48188 4411 B3
Madison Dr
9400 VNBN 48111 4495 A6
Madison Pl
600 AARB 48103 4406 A7
Madison Rd
47400 CNTN 48188 4411 B3
Madison St
- DET 48226 4345 D5
400 YPLT 48197 4491 E6
3300 DRBN 48124 4416 B5
3900 DBHT 48124 4416 B6
3900 DBHT 48125 4416 B6
5600 DBHT 48125 4499 B2
5600 DBHT 48180 4499 B2
5800 TYLR 48180 4499 A1
31600 WYNE 48184 4414 C6
E Madison St
100 AARB 48104 4406 B7
W Madison St
1000 AARB 48103 4406 A7
1200 AARB 48103 4405 E7
Madouse Ct
600 WasC 48189 4259 B4
Madrona Dr
6200 YpTp 48197 4575 C2
Mae Ln
6000 WasC 48178 4189 C7
Maes St
38300 WTLD 48186 4413 A3
39200 WTLD 48186 4412 E3
Magnolia
100 WynC 48111 4664 B3
Magnolia Ct
100 CNTN 48187 4412 C2
21300 FNHL 48336 4195 C4
29100 FTRK 48134 4753 E4
Magnolia Dr
100 INKR 48141 4415 A2
29100 FTRK 48134 4753 E4
Magnolia Pkwy
18100 SFLD 48075 4198 A4
19000 SFLD 48075 4197 D4
Magnolia St
- DET 48210 4345 A5
2100 DET 48210 4344 E5
3900 DET 48216 4344 C6
Maguire St
3600 WIND N9E 4504 D1

Mahagony Dr
37800 HnTp 48164 4751 B1
Mahogany Dr
24900 BNTN 48134 4667 E4
Mahogany St
13500 MonC 48117 4753 B6
Mahon Av
19500 SFLD 48075 4197 D3
Mahon Dr
21000 SFLD 48075 4197 B3
Mahoney Ct
23400 BNTN 48183 4668 B5
Maiden Ln
- AARB 48104 4406 C5
900 AARB 48105 4406 C5
Maiden Ln E
- WIND N9A 4420 C1
Maiden Ln W
- WIND N9A 4420 E1
Maiden St
11100 DET 48213 4274 E4
12200 DET 48213 4275 A3
Maiden Ln Ct
900 AARB 48105 4406 D5
Maidstone Av
2900 TNTN 48183 4669 C4
Maidstone Rd
46400 CNTN 48187 4336 B5
Maidstone Concession 9
600 Lksr N0R 4424 D7
600 Lksr N9K 4424 D7
Main Dr
49500 PyTp 48170 4263 D6
Main St
- CNTN 48188 4410 C7
- CNTN 48188 4412 C7
- CNTN 48188 4493 C1
- YpTp 48198 4493 B4
10 BLVL 48111 4578 C2
2400 YpTp 48198 4577 B1
2900 WRRN 48091 4201 A4
7600 WasC 48189 4259 A2
9400 WasC 48189 4187 A7
35600 WYNE 48184 4413 D6
E Main St
100 NHVL 48167 4192 E6
N Main St
- AARB 48103 4406 B5
- AARB 48105 4406 B5
- AATp 48103 4406 B5
100 AARB 48104 4406 B5
100 PLYM 48170 4265 A7
11000 GOTp 48189 4187 A6
11900 WasC 48189 4187 A6
N Main St US-23 BUS
- AARB 48103 4406 B5
- AARB 48105 4406 B5
- AATp 48103 4406 B5
100 AARB 48104 4406 B5
S Main St
- AARB 48108 4489 B3
100 AARB 48104 4406 B7
100 NHVL 48167 4192 E7
100 PLYM 48170 4265 A7
200 PLYM 48170 4337 A2
500 AARB 48103 4406 B7
500 NvlT 48167 4192 E7
1000 AARB 48104 4489 B1
2100 AARB 48103 4489 B3
2200 WasC 48103 4489 B3
8800 PyTp 48170 4337 A3
8800 PyTp 48187 4337 A3
W Main St
100 NHVL 48167 4192 C6
700 NvlT 48167 4192 C6
Main St N
10 Amhg N9V 4757 D1
Main St S
10 Amhg N9V 4757 D2
Maine
500 WynC 48111 4662 D2
Maine St
13400 DET 48212 4273 A1
17400 DET 48212 4201 A7
18000 DET 48234 4201 A6
31800 LVNA 48150 4339 B2
Main Sail Ct
200 DET 48207 4346 C5
Maison Rd
400 GSPF 48236 4276 C1
Maisonneuve Av
3200 WIND N9E 4504 B1
Maisonneuve St
11900 Tcmh N8N 4423 E4
12100 Tcmh N8N 4424 A4
Maisonville Av
900 WIND N8Y 4346 C7
Maitland Dr
2700 AARB 48105 4407 A1
Majestic
22000 DET 48239 4341 B4
Majestic Av
21000 ROTp 48220 4199 B3
Majestic Ct
42400 CNTN 48188 4412 B3
Majestic St
- DET 48126 4342 C4
- DET 48228 4342 B4
7700 DET 48210 4343 D4
23000 OKPK 48237 4199 B1
34000 WTLD 48185 4338 E5
Major Blvd
10 LSal N9J 4502 C4
Major St
1000 DET 48229 4418 B5
Malcolm St
- DET 48213 4274 E4
1100 WIND N8W 4421 D6
14500 SOGT 48195 4584 C1
34500 RMLS 48174 4496 E5

Malden Rd
- WIND N9B 4420 C7
3800 WIND N9C 4420 C7
4500 WIND N9C 4503 C1
4500 WIND N9E 4420 C7
4500 WIND N9E 4503 C1
5200 WIND N9H 4503 C1
5600 LSal N9H 4503 B5
5700 LSal N9J 4503 B5
9400 Amhg N9J 4586 D5
9400 Amhg N9V 4586 D5
9400 LSal N9J 4586 D5
Malden St
21700 FNHL 48336 4196 A3
Malden Hill Dr
10 Amhg N9V 4757 C4
Mall Dr
- AARB 48108 4489 C4
Mallard Ct
2500 AARB 48105 4332 A7
Mallard Dr
33000 BwTp 48173 4841 A1
Mallard Wy
7900 YpTp 48197 4576 B4
Mallard Cove Dr
1500 PTFD 48108 4573 A3
Mallard Pond
6500 WasC 48178 4261 B7
Mallina St
18900 DET 48236 4276 B1
19100 DET 48236 4204 B7
Mallory Ct
36200 LVNA 48154 4266 C3
Mallory Dr
37400 LVNA 48154 4266 A2
Mallory St
36400 LVNA 48154 4266 B3
Malott
41100 NOVI 48375 4193 B2
Malta Rd
1800 WIND N8W 4421 E2
1800 WIND N8W 4422 A2
Malta St
22400 DET 48223 4269 B5
Malvern Ct
19300 NvlT 48167 4193 A7
Malvern St
8000 DET 48213 4274 B5
21900 STCS 48080 4204 D3
28200 WTLD 48185 4340 A4
29800 WTLD 48185 4339 D5
Malvina St
2000 LNPK 48146 4500 C5
Manatee Av
10 HZLP 48030 4200 B1
Manatee St
2100 FRDL 48220 4200 B1
Manchester Blvd
1600 GSPW 48236 4204 B6
7800 WynC 48138 4670 C7
20800 HRWD 48225 4204 B6
Manchester Ct
10 AARB 48104 4490 A3
21500 FNHL 48335 4194 B4
39700 NvlT 48167 4193 D7
Manchester Dr
- BNTN 48134 4667 E7
- BNTN 48134 4668 A7
- BNTN 48134 4753 E1
- FTRK 48134 4753 E1
- FTRK 48134 4754 A1
1700 SpTp 48198 4492 C1
1800 SpTp 48198 4409 C7
24200 BNTN 48134 4754 A1
Manchester Ln
21700 FNHL 48335 4194 B3
Manchester Pkwy
10 HDPK 48203 4272 C3
Manchester Rd
1800 AARB 48104 4490 A2
2800 WIND N9C 4420 B5
Manchester St
10 HDPK 48203 4272 D3
13100 SOGT 48195 4584 B2
28900 WTLD 48185 4339 E4
Mancini Ct
4100 WIND N9G 4504 E3
Mandalay Ct
8700 GOTp 48116 4186 E1
Mandalay St
8000 DET 48204 4343 E3
Mandale St
8700 DET 48209 4418 E3
Manderson Rd
17400 DET 48203 4272 B1
Mangin Cres
2800 WIND N9E 4503 D1
Manhattan Cir
48000 CNTN 48188 4411 A3
49300 CNTN 48188 4410 E3
Manhattan Ct
500 CNTN 48188 4410 E4
Manhattan Dr
1200 AARB 48103 4406 A7
Manhattan St
10 LSal N9J 4502 C6
Manila St
8000 DET 48214 4274 C7
35500 WTLD 48186 4413 C4
Manistee St
23000 OKPK 48237 4199 B1
32600 WTLD 48186 4414 D4
Manistique St
200 DET 48214 4347 E2
200 DET 48214 4348 A2
500 DET 48214 4275 D6
9100 DET 48224 4275 C2
Manitou Cres
9500 WIND N8P 4348 A6

Manitou Ct
10 AARB 48108 4489 E5
500 WIND N8P 4348 A6
Mann Ct
19500 NvlT 48167 4193 A7
Mannheim Wy
3300 WIND N8W 4422 B6
Manning Dr
2800 TNTN 48183 4669 B4
3200 INKR 48141 4414 E6
Manning Rd
- Lksr N8N 4424 B1
200 Tcmh N8N 4349 B7
300 Tcmh N8N 4424 B1
1100 Lksr N9K 4424 B1
1700 Tcmh N9K 4424 B4
2600 Lksr N0R 4424 B7
2600 Tcmh N0R 4424 B7
Manning St
11100 DET 48234 4202 C5
13200 DET 48205 4202 E5
15600 DET 48205 4203 C5
16400 DET 48225 4203 C5
22700 FMTN 48336 4195 A2
Mannington Rd
8200 CNTN 48187 4336 E3
Manor Av
400 GSPF 48236 4276 C2
8600 ALPK 48101 4500 A4
Manor Blvd
- CNTN 48188 4411 A6
Manor Cir
7300 WTLD 48185 4338 C4
Manor Ct
21800 FMTN 48336 4195 A3
Manor Dr
300 AARB 48105 4406 C2
700 YPLT 48197 4491 D6
12100 SOGT 48195 4584 C1
N Manor Dr
33100 FMTN 48336 4194 E3
33100 FMTN 48336 4195 A3
S Manor Dr
33100 FMTN 48336 4194 E3
33100 FMTN 48336 4195 A3
Manor Ln
18100 LVNA 48152 4266 A1
Manor Rd N
23300 HnTp 48164 4665 A5
Manor St
6500 DRBN 48126 4343 B5
8000 DET 48204 4343 B2
8000 DET 48228 4343 B3
11300 DET 48204 4271 B7
14800 DET 48238 4271 B3
16600 DET 48221 4271 A1
19900 DET 48221 4199 A5
Manor Park Dr
32400 GDNC 48135 4339 A6
41600 NOVI 48375 4193 B1
Manorwood Dr
47400 NvlT 48167 4264 A1
Mansfield Av
- WIND N9G 4504 C4
Mansfield Dr
6600 GDNC 48135 4339 D5
44500 NOVI 48375 4192 D1
Mansfield St
6300 DET 48228 4342 C4
9500 DET 48227 4342 C1
15300 DET 48227 4270 C4
16100 DET 48235 4270 C2
18200 DET 48235 4198 C7
20500 DET 48075 4198 C5
N Mansfield St
10 YPLT 48197 4491 C4
10 YpTp 48197 4491 C4
S Mansfield St
10 YPLT 48197 4491 D5
10 YpTp 48197 4491 D5
Mansion Ct
22400 NOVI 48375 4193 D3
Manson St
2300 DET 48209 4419 C1
Mansur St
6100 DET 48211 4345 B1
Mantauk Ct
- VNBN 48111 4579 B2
Manton Av
8800 PyTp 48170 4337 A3
8800 PyTp 48187 4337 A3
Manton Blvd
1300 CNTN 48187 4412 A1
1900 CNTN 48187 4337 A7
Manufacturers Dr
100 WTLD 48185 4413 B3
100 WTLD 48186 4413 B3
Maple
- RMLS 48174 4581 D4
2600 PTFD 48108 4491 A3
Maple Av
10 Amhg N9V 4757 B2
100 LSal N9J 4502 D6
800 LSal N9J 4503 A6
1100 YpTp 48198 4492 C4
38900 WYNE 48184 4412 E7
38900 WYNE 48184 4413 A7
Maple Ct
- CNTN 48188 4411 C6
500 YPLT 48198 4492 B3
15400 RMLS 48174 4582 A4
22600 HZLP 48030 4200 D3
Maple Dr
10 VNBN 48111 4577 E6
10 VNBN 48111 4578 A6
300 SLYN 48178 4189 B1
3000 PTFD 48108 4491 A5
3000 PTFD 48197 4491 A5
3200 MVDL 48122 4418 A5
3500 MVDL 48122 4417 E5

Maple Dr
7600 WTLD 48185 4338 A5
29300 HnTp 48134 4753 A3
49400 PyTp 48170 4263 D6
Maple Ln
23600 BNTN 48174 4583 A6
N Maple Ln
20600 GSPW 48236 4204 D5
S Maple Ln
20600 GSPW 48236 4204 D5
Maple Rd
11400 WasC 48160 4657 D7
11400 WasC 48176 4657 D7
N Maple Rd
10 SALN 48176 4572 D5
100 AARB 48103 4405 D4
800 WasC 48103 4405 D4
3000 AATp 48103 4405 D1
3000 WasC 48105 4405 D1
3100 AATp 48105 4330 D6
3100 AATp 48105 4405 D1
5000 WasC 48105 4258 C7
5000 WasC 48105 4330 D1
5500 PTFD 48108 4572 D2
5500 PTFD 48176 4572 D2
5500 WasC 48108 4572 D2
5500 WasC 48176 4572 D2
S Maple Rd
200 AARB 48103 4405 D6
400 WasC 48103 4405 D6
1100 AARB 48103 4488 D1
1100 WasC 48103 4488 D1
3500 PTFD 48103 4488 D7
3500 PTFD 48108 4488 D7
3500 WasC 48108 4488 D7
4400 PTFD 48108 4572 D2
4400 WasC 48108 4572 D2
4900 PTFD 48176 4572 D2
4900 WasC 48176 4572 D2
9000 WasC 48176 4657 D4
10500 WasC 48160 4657 D4
Maple St
- TYLR 48180 4498 D4
10 RVRG 48218 4418 E6
10 RVRG 48218 4501 E1
10 WYDT 48192 4585 C3
100 RVRG 48218 4502 A1
100 TNTN 48183 4670 A5
100 YPLT 48198 4492 A4
200 PLYM 48170 4337 A1
200 TNTN 48183 4669 E4
900 DET 48207 4345 E5
1000 PLYM 48170 4336 E1
2300 WYDT 48192 4584 E3
2300 WYDT 48195 4584 E3
3000 WRRN 48091 4201 B4
3800 DRBN 48126 4418 A1
6400 DRBN 48126 4342 E5
22400 FMTN 48336 4195 A2
E Maple St
5900 RMLS 48174 4498 A1
N Maple St
28500 RMLS 48174 4498 A1
S Maple St
28500 RMLS 48174 4498 A1
W Maple St
5800 RMLS 48174 4498 A1
Maplebrook
47100 NvlT 48167 4264 B2
Maple Creek Cir
2000 PTFD 48108 4572 E3
Maple Creek Ct
12200 GOTp 48178 4188 B4
E Mapledale Av
10 HZLP 48030 4200 C1
W Mapledale Av
600 HZLP 48030 4200 C1
Mapledale Dr
8000 YpTp 48197 4576 B3
Mapledale Rd
11500 GOTp 48189 4187 A6
Mapledale St
- FRDL 48069 4199 E1
- FRDL 48220 4199 E1
1500 FRDL 48220 4200 A1
Maplefield Rd
10 PTRG 48069 4199 C1
10 PTRG 48237 4199 C1
Maplegrove Dr
200 WasC 48189 4259 A4
Maplegrove Rd
19400 GBTR 48173 4755 A4
Maple Hill Ct
17900 NvlT 48167 4265 C1
Maple Hill Dr
17300 NvlT 48167 4265 C1
Maplehill Dr
17100 NvlT 48167 4265 C2
Maplehurst Ct
21500 WDHN 48183 4669 A3
Maplehurst Dr
6200 YpTp 48197 4575 E4
6200 YpTp 48197 4576 A4
E Maplehurst St
100 FRDL 48220 4199 E2
400 FRDL 48220 4200 A2
W Maplehurst St
700 FRDL 48220 4199 C2
Maplelawn
9700 SpTp 48198 4409 E7
Maplelawn Av
22000 TYLR 48180 4499 C7
S Maplelawn Av
11000 TYLR 48180 4499 B7
W Maplelawn Av
22600 TYLR 48180 4499 B7
Maplelawn Dr
6700 YpTp 48197 4576 E6
Maplelawn St
10000 DET 48204 4343 B1

S Maplelawn St
20000 TYLR 48195 4499 E7
23600 TYLR 48180 4499 A7
Maple Leaf Cres
3900 WIND N8W 4505 A2
Mapleleaf Dr
28500 HnTp 48134 4753 A3
28700 HnTp 48134 4752 E4
Maple Ln Av
1300 HZLP 48030 4200 E1
Maplenut St
33000 FMTN 48336 4195 A3
33100 FMTN 48336 4194 E4
Maple Park Dr
2000 PTFD 48108 4572 E2
Mapleridge Av
20700 SFLD 48075 4197 E4
Maple Ridge Dr
7800 WasC 48167 4262 A4
11100 PyTp 48170 4335 C2
Mapleridge Ln
24800 BNTN 48134 4667 E4
Maple Ridge St
300 AARB 48103 4406 A5
Mapleridge St
13600 DET 48205 4202 E7
13900 DET 48205 4203 A7
22000 SFLD 48075 4197 E2
Mapleton Rd
10 GSPF 48236 4276 D4
Mapletree Dr
9200 PyTp 48170 4336 B3
Maple Valley Dr
11200 PyTp 48170 4335 D2
Maple View Ln
30500 FTRK 48173 4754 A5
Mapleview Ln
6000 YpTp 48197 4576 A3
Mapleview St
13400 MonC 48117 4753 B7
18900 DET 48205 4202 E6
Maplewood Av
- WTLD 48185 4339 B6
800 YpTp 48198 4492 C5
2500 AARB 48104 4490 B3
15100 EPTE 48021 4203 B2
27400 DBHT 48127 4340 A6
27400 GDNC 48135 4340 A6
28600 GDNC 48135 4339 D6
Maplewood Ct
100 SLYN 48178 4189 C2
16000 NvlT 48167 4265 D3
20600 RVVW 48192 4669 D2
Maple Wood Dr
27200 BNTN 48174 4582 C7
Maplewood Dr
1300 SALN 48176 4572 D5
21700 SFLD 48034 4196 C3
Maplewood Ln
14900 PyTp 48170 4265 B4
Maplewood Rd
5500 WIND N9J 4502 D2
Maplewood St
100 NHVL 48167 4192 D5
4900 DET 48204 4344 A2
5200 DET 48204 4343 E2
19700 LVNA 48152 4195 E6
20200 RVVW 48192 4669 D2
21300 WDHN 48183 4668 C3
Mar Ann Dr
1300 WTLD 48186 4414 D3
Marantette St
1900 DET 48216 4345 A7
Marblehead St
31500 FMTN 48336 4195 A1
Marblewood Dr
- NvlT 48167 4264 A1
Marblewood Wy
3900 AATp 48105 4407 D3
Marbud St
20000 DET 48205 4203 A4
Marc Dr
28400 FNHL 48336 4195 E2
Marc St
9600 RMLS 48174 4496 E6
Marc Tr
9100 PyTp 48170 4336 D3
Marcedes Ln
6100 WasC 48170 4262 C7
6100 WasC 48170 4334 C1
Marcel Ln
10 LSal N9J 4502 C7
Marcella Av
- GOTp 48178 4188 C4
Marcello Dr
32500 GDNC 48135 4339 A6
Marcello Ln
10800 GOTp 48178 4187 D4
10800 GOTp 48189 4187 D4
Marcia Ln
10400 GOTp 48178 4187 E3
Marco Av
32500 GDNC 48135 4339 A6
Marcus Av
1200 YpTp 48198 4492 D7
Marcus Dr
35100 BwTp 48173 4841 D3
Marcus St
- DET 48211 4274 A4
5900 DET 48211 4273 D4
8600 DET 48213 4274 C4
Marcuz Ct
800 WIND N9G 4504 E5
Marcy St
5000 WRRN 48091 4201 B1
Marene St
17400 DET 48219 4269 A1
Marentette Av
100 WIND N9A 4346 A7
200 WIND N9A 4421 A1

STREET
Block City ZIP Map# Grid

Marentette Av
2200 WIND N8W 4421 C4
3000 WIND N8X 4421 D7
3400 WIND N8W 4504 D1
3400 WIND N8X 4504 D1
Marford Ct
20000 GSPW 48236 4204 C6
Margaret Av
5200 AGST 48197 4660 B1
Margaret Dr
3600 AARB 48104 4490 C3
Margaret Ln
28500 HnTp 48117 4751 C4
28500 HnTp 48164 4751 C4
Margaret St
10 WasC 48189 4187 A7
2500 MVDL 48122 4418 A7
2700 MVDL 48122 4417 E7
6000 SRKW 48179 4754 A7
6000 SRKW 48179 4840 B1
7400 TYLR 48180 4499 B3
35500 RMLS 48174 4496 D6
Margaret St E
10 DET 48203 4200 C7
Margaret St W
10 DET 48203 4200 C7
Margareta
25000 RDFD 48240 4196 D7
Margareta Dr
37600 LVNA 48152 4266 A1
Margareta St
3800 DET 48221 4199 E7
12700 DET 48235 4199 A7
14000 DET 48235 4198 D7
18300 DET 48219 4198 A7
19300 DET 48219 4197 E7
24400 DET 48219 4196 D7
24800 DET 48240 4196 D7
24800 RDFD 48240 4196 D7
27400 LVNA 48152 4196 A7
36200 LVNA 48152 4266 B1
36700 LVNA 48152 4194 B7
N Margarette Ct
3200 TNTN 48183 4669 B4
Margarette Ct S
3200 TNTN 48183 4669 B4
Margarette Dr
3300 TNTN 48183 4669 B4
Margarita St
1500 YpTp 48198 4492 D7
Margery St
2100 YpTp 48198 4577 C1
Marguerite
24800 BNTN 48134 4668 A7
Marguerite Dr
9400 PyTp 48170 4336 D2
Marguriet St
2500 WIND N9G 4504 A4
2600 WIND N9G 4503 E3
Maria Dr
400 PLYM 48170 4337 B1
Marian Av
1400 AARB 48103 4489 A1
Marian Ct
1000 GSPW 48236 4204 E4
Marian Dr
2300 TNTN 48183 4669 B5
Marian Pl
20500 DET 48219 4269 D1
Maria Rosa Dr
- BNTN 48134 4668 B5
Marie Av
20700 WRRN 48089 4202 D3
Marie Ct
9300 LVNA 48150 4337 E2
Marie St
10 ECRS 48229 4501 D2
1200 DBHT 48127 4340 C7
1200 DBHT 48127 4415 C1
1200 WIND N8W 4421 D5
1300 FRDL 48220 4199 D4
3200 DRBN 48120 4418 C2
9100 LVNA 48150 4337 E2
14000 LVNA 48154 4265 E6
N Marie St
- WTLD 48185 4337 E7
1700 WTLD 48185 4338 A7
S Marie St
100 WTLD 48185 4413 A3
100 WTLD 48186 4413 A3
Marietta St
9300 DET 48214 4346 E1
Marigold Cir
200 WTLD 48185 4413 A2
Marigold Pl
5100 WYNE 48184 4414 B7
Marigold St
- WIND N9J 4502 E2
Marilyn Av
9300 PyTp 48170 4337 C2
15300 NvlT 48170 4265 C3
Marilyn St
- WYNE 48184 4413 D7
- WYNE 48184 4496 D1
10000 WasC 48167 4263 A5
19100 NvlT 48167 4193 B7
Marina Ct
34400 WTLD 48185 4338 E4
Marina Dr
- DET 48214 4346 E3
13800 VNBN 48111 4578 B3
Marina Rd
9500 GOTp 48178 4188 A1
Marina Cove
48500 VNBN 48111 4578 A1
Marine Av
23000 EPTE 48021 4204 A1
Marine Dr
100 Tcmh N8N 4424 E1
4900 CNTN 48188 4412 C7
4900 CNTN 48188 4495 C1
Mariner Ct
19500 NvlT 48167 4193 C6
Mario Ct
4100 SpTp 48170 4334 B5
Mario Dr
4100 SpTp 48105 4334 B5
4100 SpTp 48170 4334 B5
Mario Ann Ct
36800 RMLS 48174 4580 B1
Marion
9900 RDFD 48239 4340 D1
13900 RDFD 48239 4268 D5
Marion Av
10 RVRG 48218 4418 E5
10 RVRG 48218 4419 A7
400 RVRG 48218 4502 A1
600 RVRG 48218 4501 E1
600 WIND N9A 4421 B1
1200 LNPK 48146 4501 A3
Marion Cres
9000 RDFD 48239 4340 D2
Marion Ct
300 SALN 48176 4572 C7
Marion Dr
9000 HbgT 48116 4186 A1
Marion Rd
8900 WasC 48176 4657 A4
Marion St
400 YPLT 48197 4491 C4
8600 DET 48213 4274 A4
25300 DRBN 48128 4415 D1
Mariposa Tr
7500 WasC 48167 4262 A4
Marisa Ct
46800 PyTp 48170 4336 B3
Marissa Ct
42100 CNTN 48188 4412 B4
Marjorie Dr
200 Lksr N8N 4424 E2
1000 WIND N8S 4348 A6
Marjorie St
7200 DET 48213 4274 A4
Marjorie Ann St
60500 LyTp 48178 4189 B3
Mark Av
1400 WIND N9B 4420 D4
2200 LNPK 48146 4500 C4
2600 WIND N9E 4420 E7
2800 WIND N9E 4503 E1
2800 WIND N9E 4504 A1
Mark Ln
29400 LVNA 48152 4267 D1
Mark St
- DET 48210 4344 E3
100 DBHT 48127 4340 C5
1000 YPLT 48197 4491 C2
13300 SOGT 48195 4584 C2
Markberry Dr
1000 AARB 48105 4407 C5
Markese Av
2200 LNPK 48101 4500 C3
2200 LNPK 48146 4500 C3
16100 ALPK 48101 4500 A3
Market Dr
- DRBN 48126 4342 D7
7600 CNTN 48187 4337 C4
Market Pl
400 AARB 48108 4489 C4
400 YPLT 48198 4492 A3
Market St
2400 DET 48207 4345 E4
11700 LVNA 48150 4266 B7
11700 LVNA 48150 4338 B1
13400 MonC 48117 4753 A7
Markey St
35000 WTLD 48186 4413 D5
Mark Hannah Ct
200 SALN 48176 4657 D1
Mark Hannah Pl
200 AARB 48103 4406 A5
Marks Ct
21900 STCS 48080 4204 D3
Marks Dr
41000 NOVI 48375 4193 B4
Mark Twain Ct
1400 WasC 48103 4487 C1
Mark Twain St
8200 DET 48228 4342 E2
9500 DET 48227 4342 E1
13900 DET 48227 4270 E4
16100 DET 48235 4270 E2
19200 DET 48235 4198 E5
Marlboro St
22500 DRBN 48124 4416 B1
22500 DRBN 48128 4416 B1
Marlborough Av
1300 WIND N9C 4420 B5
9200 ALPK 48101 4500 A5
Marlborough Dr
1200 AARB 48104 4489 D3
10000 WynC 48138 4670 A6
Marlborough St
- DET 48224 4275 C3
200 DET 48214 4347 E1
900 DET 48214 4275 D7
Marlene Ln
- BNTN 48183 4668 B6
Marler St
36500 LVNA 48154 4266 B4
Marley Av
13600 BwTp 48173 4841 D3
Marlin Av
23800 WRRN 48091 4201 A1
Marlin Ct
10 WIND N8W 4505 A2
Marlin Dr
12600 RDFD 48239 4268 C6
Marlin St
- PyTp 48170 4336 E2
100 WIND N8W 4505 A2
41000 PyTp 48170 4337 C2
Marlo Cres
4200 WIND N9G 4504 E3
Marlo Ct
4100 WIND N9G 4504 E3
Marlow Ct
24100 OKPK 48237 4198 D1
Marlow St
14500 OKPK 48237 4198 D1
Marlowe Av
8800 PyTp 48170 4336 E3
8800 PyTp 48187 4336 E3
Marlowe Rd
7400 VNBN 48111 4494 E4
Marlowe St
- CNTN 48187 4336 E4
1300 CNTN 48187 4411 E1
9300 DET 48228 4342 D1
9500 DET 48227 4342 D1
11300 DET 48227 4270 D7
16100 DET 48235 4270 D3
18000 DET 48235 4198 D6
Marlpool Dr
400 SALN 48176 4657 E1
Marmon Av
23000 WRRN 48089 4202 C1
Marne Av
100 LSal N9J 4502 C4
3100 TNTN 48183 4669 C7
Marne Ct
43900 CNTN 48188 4411 E3
Marne St
10500 DET 48224 4203 E7
10500 DET 48224 4275 E1
Marquee Rd
22000 HnTp 48174 4667 B4
Marquette Dr
100 DET 48214 4347 A2
8500 WynC 48138 4670 C5
Marquette Rd
33900 WTLD 48185 4413 D1
Marquette St
1400 DET 48202 4344 E2
1900 DET 48210 4344 D2
6700 LSal N9J 4502 E6
27400 GDNC 48135 4415 A1
28600 GDNC 48135 4414 E1
33700 GDNC 48135 4413 D1
Marquis Ct
2300 PTFD 48103 4488 D3
Marr St
30000 GBTR 48173 4755 C4
Marra Dr
2000 WasC 48103 4489 A2
Marriott St
10200 VNBN 48111 4494 D6
Marsala Ct
100 CNTN 48187 4411 B2
Marseilles St
4200 DET 48224 4276 B2
Marsh
23100 HnTp 48164 4665 A5
Marsh Ct
- Amhg N9V 4671 C6
Marsh Dr
- Amhg N9V 4671 C6
Marsha St
15700 LVNA 48154 4266 A3
18000 RVVW 48192 4584 E7
Marshall Av
- WYDT 48192 4584 E4
- WYDT 48192 4585 A4
1100 LNPK 48146 4501 A2
13600 WRRN 48089 4202 E2
13700 WRRN 48089 4203 A2
Marshall Ct
10 AARB 48104 4406 B7
30200 WTLD 48186 4497 D1
Marshall Dr
29600 WTLD 48186 4497 D1
Marshall Rd
5500 WasC 48130 4404 A2
6000 CNTN 48187 4336 C6
9400 GOTp 48178 4187 D2
11000 GOTp 48189 4187 E6
Marshall St
2800 AARB 48108 4490 A5
23200 DRBN 48124 4416 E2
24400 DRBN 48124 4415 E2
25400 DBHT 48125 4415 D2
25700 DBHT 48141 4415 D2
26400 INKR 48141 4415 C2
E Marshall St
100 FRDL 48220 4199 C4
100 FRDL 48220 4200 A3
W Marshall St
100 FRDL 48220 4199 E3
Marsh Creek Blvd
- WDHN 48183 4669 A6
Marshfield St
800 FRDL 48220 4199 D3
Marshmallow St
200 WTLD 48186 4414 D7
Marston St
10 DET 48202 4273 A7
1900 DET 48211 4273 C6
Mart Ct
5200 WRRN 48091 4201 D2
Mart St
11300 GOTp 48189 4187 C5
Martel Ct
36500 FNHL 48335 4194 B1
Martel Dr
24400 FNHL 48335 4194 B1
Martel St
4000 MVDL 48122 4417 E5
Martell Ct
48900 CNTN 48187 4335 E6
Martell Dr
9500 YpTp 48197 4576 E5
Marter Rd
20700 GSPW 48236 4204 D5
21600 STCS 48236 4204 D5
21700 STCS 48080 4204 D5
23100 STCS 48080 4205 A2
Martha Av
1500 AARB 48103 4488 E1
Martha Ln
53200 LyTp 48167 4190 E5
N Martha St
100 DRBN 48124 4416 B1
100 DRBN 48128 4416 B1
1300 DRBN 48128 4341 B7
5600 DBHT 48127 4341 B6
5600 DBHT 48128 4341 B6
S Martha St
100 DRBN 48124 4416 B2
Martha's Ln
17400 WynC 48111 4578 C7
Martha Washington Dr
24000 SFLD 48075 4198 A1
24600 SFLD 48075 4197 D2
Martin Dr
3300 SpTp 48105 4408 B1
Martin Ln
10 LSal N9J 4586 C2
26000 WynC 48138 4670 C7
Martin Pl
10 GSPT 48230 4276 D6
600 YPLT 48198 4492 B4
1000 AARB 48104 4406 D7
1000 AARB 48104 4489 D1
18500 WDHN 48183 4755 A1
34800 RMLS 48174 4496 E2
Martin Rd
1800 FRDL 48220 4200 B1
Martin St
1800 WTLD 48186 4413 B4
4600 DET 48210 4344 A6
4900 DET 48210 4343 E5
32900 LVNA 48154 4267 A5
35900 LVNA 48154 4266 C5
Martindale Rd
24200 LyTp 48178 4189 D1
24200 SLYN 48178 4189 D1
Martindale St
1300 WIND N9B 4420 C2
Martindale St N
8800 DET 48204 4344 A1
9600 DET 48204 4272 A7
11300 DET 48204 4271 E6
Martindale St S
4800 DET 48204 4344 B1
5000 DET 48204 4343 E2
Martinique Av
400 WIND N8P 4348 A5
Martinique Pl
9700 WIND N8P 4348 A6
Martin Luther King Jr Blvd
400 DET 48201 4345 A5
1500 DET 48210 4345 A5
2100 DET 48210 4344 D6
Martinsville Rd
12400 VNBN 48111 4579 A3
12600 MonC 48117 4750 A6
14200 MonC 48164 4750 A6
17400 WynC 48111 4579 A7
18500 WynC 48111 4664 A1
24600 WynC 48111 4750 A1
24600 WynC 48164 4664 A7
Marton Rd
5000 PTFD 48108 4573 D2
Martz Rd
8000 YpTp 48197 4576 C6
10200 YpTp 48197 4577 B6
47400 VNBN 48111 4578 A5
49000 VNBN 48111 4577 D6
49400 VNBN 48197 4577 D6
Marvin Gdns
10 Amhg N9V 4757 D2
Marvin St
5800 TYLR 48180 4498 D1
10000 DRBN 48126 4343 B7
13400 TYLR 48180 4582 D2
Marx St
17100 DET 48203 4272 E1
17500 DET 48203 4200 E6
Mary Ct
600 AARB 48104 4406 C7
3600 WasC 48189 4258 A3
27000 FTRK 48134 4753 C1
31700 RKWD 48173 4754 C7
Mary Ln
60600 LyTp 48178 4189 C4
Mary St
300 GSPF 48236 4276 E2
800 AARB 48104 4406 C7
20700 TYLR 48180 4499 C4
24500 TYLR 48180 4498 E4
27400 RMLS 48174 4498 B4
35400 RMLS 48174 4496 D5
Mary Alexander Ct
100 NHVL 48167 4192 D6
Mary Ann Rd
10000 WasC 48167 4263 A4
Mary Catherine St
1900 YpTp 48198 4492 E6
2200 YpTp 48198 4493 A6
Maryfield Dr
1700 AARB 48103 4405 E5
Marygrove Dr
8100 DET 48221 4271 B2
Maryland Dr
18100 SFLD 48075 4198 A1
Maryland St
1000 GPPK 48230 4275 E6
3500 DET 48224 4275 D5
3500 DET 48230 4275 E6
16000 SFLD 48075 4198 B1
32200 LVNA 48150 4339 B2
Masch Av
23000 WRRN 48091 4201 C1
Masi Ct
21300 WynC 48138 4670 D3
Mason Av
100 AARB 48103 4405 C6
Mason Ct
30600 LVNA 48154 4267 C5
32500 WTLD 48186 4414 B4
Mason Ln
7000 WasC 48189 4258 E3
Mason Pl
8700 DET 48209 4418 E3
12700 Tcmh N8N 4349 A7
Mason St
800 DRBN 48124 4416 C2
8800 TYLR 48180 4499 D4
31000 LVNA 48154 4267 C5
37700 LVNA 48154 4266 A5
38400 LVNA 48154 4265 E6
Masood Ct
1300 CNTN 48188 4412 D3
Masotti Cres
4200 WIND N9G 4504 E3
4200 WIND N9G 4505 A4
Massachusetts St
10 HDPK 48203 4272 E4
200 HDPK 48203 4273 A4
Massey Ct
3100 WIND N9E 4504 A1
Massey Dr
9300 PyTp 48170 4337 D2
Mast St
45500 PyTp 48170 4264 C5
Masten Ct
3300 SpTp 48198 4408 C1
Matchette Rd
3700 WIND N9C 4420 A7
4700 WIND N9C 4503 A2
4900 WIND N9J 4503 A5
5900 LSal N9J 4503 A5
Mather St
6500 DET 48210 4343 D5
22400 RKWD 48173 4754 C7
Mathias Dr
8300 WynC 48138 4670 C6
Matilda St
25700 FTRK 48134 4753 D1
Matlin Rd
200 MonC 48117 4751 D7
Matthew Ct
4800 PTFD 48197 4574 E1
Matthew Dr
4700 WTLD 48186 4414 D7
Matthew Brady Blvd
300 WIND N8S 4347 D7
1300 WIND N8S 4422 E1
Matthews St
17000 RVVW 48192 4584 E5
17000 RVVW 48195 4584 E5
Mattison Rd
5100 BrTp 48179 4839 E4
Matts Dr
23400 BNTN 48174 4583 A6
Matzeliger Ct
12400 DET 48213 4275 A5
Maude Ct
42500 VNBN 48111 4495 A3
Maude Lea St
23600 NOVI 48375 4193 C2
Mauer St
20000 STCS 48080 4204 B3
Maulbetsch Av
500 YpTp 48197 4491 B3
Maumee St
16600 GPPK 48230 4276 B6
16800 GSPT 48230 4276 B6
Maurice Dr
6500 VNBN 48111 4493 C2
Maus Av
400 YPLT 48198 4492 B5
800 YpTp 48198 4492 B5
Maxine Dr
5700 WYNE 48184 4497 C2
Maxine St
19600 STCS 48080 4204 B2
E Maxlow Av
10 HZLP 48030 4200 D3
W Maxlow Av
10 HZLP 48030 4200 C3
Maxwell Av
1400 AARB 48103 4405 E6
2800 TNTN 48183 4669 B5
6700 WRRN 48091 4201 E2
7000 WRRN 48091 4202 A2
11300 WRRN 48089 4202 C2
15200 PyTp 48170 4265 C4
15300 NvlT 48170 4265 C4
Maxwell Ln
25100 FTRK 48134 4753 E3
Maxwell Rd
13000 MonC 48117 4751 C7
Maxwell St
2100 DET 48214 4346 C1
4200 DET 48214 4274 C7
5000 DET 48213 4274 B6
19100 NvlT 48167 4193 C7
May Av
16100 ALPK 48101 4500 A3
May St
1300 DRBN 48124 4416 D3
6500 DET 48213 4274 C4
May Apple Ct
3100 PTFD 48103 4488 D4
8300 CNTN 48170 4335 D3
8300 CNTN 48187 4335 D3
Mayburn St
6100 DBHT 48127 4341 A5
N Mayburn St
600 DRBN 48128 4416 A1
1500 DRBN 48128 4341 A7
Maybury Dr
- NOVI 48167 4191 E5
- NOVI 48167 4192 A5
Maybury Ln
19100 NvlT 48167 4191 D7
Maybury Grand St
5600 DET 48210 4344 D3
Mayfair
600 SLYN 48178 4189 C1
Mayfair Av
300 LSal N9J 4502 E5
27000 BwTp 48183 4754 E2
Mayfair Dr
16100 SFLD 48075 4198 B3
Mayfair St
3500 DRBN 48124 4416 D5
3900 DBHT 48124 4416 D5
3900 DBHT 48125 4416 E7
5800 TYLR 48125 4499 E1
5800 TYLR 48180 4499 E1
21200 WDHN 48183 4669 A3
24800 FTRK 48134 4754 A4
24900 FTRK 48134 4753 E4
Mayfield Av
19400 LVNA 48152 4195 A7
Mayfield St
9600 LVNA 48150 4339 A1
11800 LVNA 48150 4267 A7
13100 DET 48205 4274 E1
13900 DET 48205 4275 A1
16600 LVNA 48154 4267 A2
17200 LVNA 48154 4267 A1
19800 LVNA 48152 4195 A5
20100 LVNA 48336 4195 A5
21400 FNHL 48336 4195 A3
22700 FMTN 48336 4195 A2
Mayflower Av
400 LNPK 48146 4501 A5
1300 LNPK 48146 4500 E4
Mayflower Ct
1500 LNPK 48146 4500 E4
9200 PyTp 48170 4336 D2
Mayflower Dr
8800 PyTp 48170 4336 D3
Mayflower St
- LNPK 48146 4500 D5
Mayhew
- YPLT 48197 4491 D2
- YPLT 48198 4491 D2
Maylawn Av
16100 ALPK 48101 4500 A5
Maynard St
300 AARB 48104 4406 C6
4700 DET 48214 4275 A5
Mayo Ct
45000 NOVI 48167 4192 D4
Mayo Dr
45000 NOVI 48167 4192 D4
45000 NOVI 48375 4192 D4
Mayrand Cres
1700 Tcmh N8N 4423 E3
Mayville St
30600 LVNA 48152 4267 C1
39500 PyTp 48170 4337 D3
43600 PyTp 48170 4336 E3
Maywood Av
10 PTRG 48069 4199 D1
1400 AARB 48103 4488 E1
Maywood Ct
22500 FNHL 48335 4194 E3
Maywood Dr
22500 FNHL 48335 4194 D3
Maywood St
7400 DET 48213 4274 A5
13700 SOGT 48195 4584 A2
25000 WDHN 48183 4669 A6
26300 WDHN 48183 4755 A1
Mazin Ct
2900 YpTp 48197 4491 B5
McAllister St
25000 SFLD 48034 4196 D1
McAuley Dr
5200 SpTp 48105 4491 B1
5200 SpTp 48197 4491 B1
McBeth Ct
26600 FTRK 48134 4753 C1
McBride Av
41400 VNBN 48111 4495 B6
45900 VNBN 48111 4494 C6
McBride St
36400 RMLS 48174 4496 B6
McCann Rd
33000 BwTp 48173 4755 B7
33000 BwTp 48173 4841 B1
McCann St
12000 SOGT 48195 4500 B7
12000 SOGT 48195 4584 B1
McCarthy St
1300 YpTp 48198 4492 E6
McCartney Av
1000 YpTp 48198 4493 A6
1700 YpTp 48198 4577 A1
McClain Dr
23000 OKPK 48237 4198 E2
McClatchey Dr
3700 WasC 48189 4258 A2
McClellan St
1200 DET 48214 4346 E1
3700 DET 48214 4274 D7
5000 DET 48213 4274 C6
McClumpha Rd
8800 PyTp 48170 4336 C3
McClung Av
17900 SFLD 48075 4198 A2
20800 SFLD 48075 4197 B2
McComb St
3100 AARB 48108 4490 A4
McCord Ln
- Tcmh N0R 4505 B6
McCormick Dr
2000 PTFD 48176 4572 E3
McCormick St
18500 DET 48224 4203 D6
20400 DET 48224 4204 A7
21700 DET 48236 4276 B1
McCort Dr
23500 BNTN 48134 4668 B5
McCotter Dr
200 AARB 48103 4405 B7
McCoy Cir
12400 DET 48213 4275 B5
12500 DET 48214 4275 B5
McCrae Av
- WIND N9G 4504 D3
McCree Ln
5500 AGST 48197 4660 B2
McCrone Rd
9500 AGST 48160 4660 B4
9500 AGST 48197 4660 B4
McCrory Ln
25600 LyTp 48178 4189 D1
McCurdy Dr
200 Amhg N9V 4757 C4
McDonald Ct
5000 WIND N8T 4422 C3
McDonald Dr
800 NHVL 48167 4192 C5
38000 RMLS 48174 4496 A4
McDonald St
6900 DET 48210 4343 D4
24000 DBHT 48125 4416 A7
25400 DBHT 48125 4415 D7
28900 WTLD 48186 4414 E7
28900 WTLD 48186 4415 A7
McDougal Av
26200 WynC 48138 4670 A7
McDougall Av
10 WIND N9A 4420 E1
800 WIND N9A 4421 A2
1200 WIND N8X 4421 A3
McDougall Ct
100 CNTN 48188 4411 A3
McDougall St
- DET 48211 4273 E7
2100 WIND N8X 4421 B4
2500 DET 48207 4346 A3
4100 DET 48207 4345 E1
5000 DET 48211 4345 E1
11300 HMTK 48212 4273 B3
17200 DET 48212 4273 A1
17400 DET 48212 4201 A7
18000 DET 48234 4201 A7
McDowell St
2300 FRDL 48220 4200 A1
McEwan Av
100 WIND N9B 4420 C1
McFadden St
8000 WasC 48167 4262 D3
McFall Dr
11500 AGST 48191 4661 E7
McGee Ct
2200 WTLD 48186 4413 B5
McGraw Av
- WIND N9G 4504 C3
McGraw St
1900 DET 48210 4344 E2
6500 DET 48210 4343 D6
9400 DET 48126 4343 C6
McGregor Av
1100 YpTp 48198 4493 B6
McGregor Blvd
3800 WIND N9G 4504 C3
McGregor Rd
2000 YpTp 48198 4577 B1
McGregor St
4800 DET 48209 4344 C7
McGriff Dr
4200 PTFD 48197 4574 E5
McGuire St
5800 TYLR 48180 4498 D1
15000 TYLR 48180 4582 D4
E McHattie St
100 SLYN 48178 4189 B2
W McHattie St
100 SLYN 48178 4189 B2
McHugh St
7700 WIND N8S 4422 E1
11100 WIND N8P 4423 C1
McIntosh Av
- CNTN 48187 4336 C4
McIntosh Dr
- CNTN 48187 4336 C5
McIntosh Ln
3600 MonC 48117 4753 B7
McIntyre St
1000 AARB 48105 4407 A3
17300 DET 48219 4269 B1
19900 DET 48219 4197 B5
29500 LVNA 48150 4339 D2
McKay Av
1700 WIND N9B 4420 D5
2400 WIND N9E 4420 E7
2600 WIND N9E 4421 A7
3000 WIND N9E 4504 A1
E McKay St
10 SALN 48176 4572 D7
W McKay St
200 SALN 48176 4572 C7
200 SALN 48176 4657 C1
McKean Rd
6100 YpTp 48197 4577 B4
8000 AGST 48191 4577 B7

INDEX 36
McKean Rd
Detroit & Wayne County Street Index
Michigan Av US-12

STREET Block City ZIP Map# Grid

McKean Rd
8000 AGST 48191 4662 B1
McKenzi Ln
56600 LyTp 48178 4190 A1
McKeon Ct
9800 WasC 48178 4188 B6
McKinley Av
100 GSPF 48236 4276 C4
400 DET 48236 4276 C4
700 AARB 48104 4489 C1
1900 YpTp 48197 4491 C5
McKinley Cir
500 CNTN 48188 4410 D3
McKinley Ct
5600 DBHT 48125 4499 C1
McKinley Dr
50400 PyTp 48170 4263 D6
McKinley Pl
10 GSPF 48236 4276 D5
McKinley Rd
2200 YpTp 48197 4491 B5
McKinley St
- RVVW 48192 4585 A6
300 PLYM 48170 4264 E7
400 PLYM 48170 4336 E1
1100 WYDT 48192 4501 C7
1400 WYDT 48192 4585 C1
2000 LNPK 48146 4501 A4
2900 DRBN 48124 4416 D5
3900 DBHT 48124 4416 D5
3900 DBHT 48125 4416 D5
5500 DET 48210 4344 C4
7800 TYLR 48180 4499 C3
21700 RKWD 48173 4754 D7
41400 VNBN 48111 4495 C6
McKinney Av
36800 WTLD 48185 4338 B4
McKinney Dr
36500 WTLD 48185 4338 B4
McKinney St
9200 DET 48224 4275 D2
11000 DET 48224 4203 E7
McKinstry St
1000 DET 48209 4419 D1
2300 DET 48209 4344 C7
S McKinstry St
100 DET 48209 4419 E2
McKitrick St
3200 MVDL 48122 4417 E5
McLain Av
2200 LNPK 48101 4500 C3
2200 LNPK 48146 4500 C3
14500 ALPK 48101 4500 B3
McLaine St
1400 CNTN 48188 4410 E4
McLean St
10 HDPK 48203 4272 D4
1900 DET 48212 4273 A3
McLellan Av
- Amhg N9V 4671 D6
McMahon Av
2800 WIND N8T 4422 D3
N McMahon Cir
41000 NOVI 48375 4193 B2
S McMahon Cir
41000 NOVI 48375 4193 C2
McMillan Av
23800 WRRN 48091 4201 B1
McMillan Rd
200 GSPF 48236 4276 C3
McMillan St
- DET 48209 4344 D7
1100 DRBN 48128 4341 B6
1100 DRBN 48128 4416 C1
5600 DBHT 48127 4341 B6
5600 DBHT 48128 4341 B6
5600 DET 48209 4419 C1
McMunn St
100 SLYN 48178 4189 B3
McNabb Av
- LSal N9J 4503 B5
McNally Rd
10400 GOTp 48189 4187 C6
10700 GOTp 48178 4187 D6
McNamara Dr
17200 LVNA 48152 4266 E2
McNichols Rd E
10 DET 48203 4272 D1
10 HDPK 48203 4272 D1
1900 DET 48212 4272 D1
2200 DET 48212 4273 A1
6900 DET 48212 4274 B1
7500 DET 48234 4274 B1
11000 DET 48205 4274 B1
12500 DET 48205 4202 D7
McNichols Rd W
10 DET 48203 4272 A1
10 HDPK 48203 4272 A1
800 DET 48221 4272 A1
2700 DET 48221 4271 E1
12700 DET 48235 4271 B1
13400 DET 48235 4270 D1
18100 DET 48219 4270 A1
19000 DET 48219 4269 C1
24000 DET 48219 4268 D2
McNorton St
- Tcmh N8P 4423 E1
- WIND N8P 4423 D1
12000 Tcmh N8N 4423 E1
12400 Tcmh N8N 4424 A1
McPherson St
1900 DET 48212 4273 A3
McQuade St
9200 DET 48206 4344 A1
9500 DET 48206 4272 A7
McTague Ct
500 WIND N8P 4348 D6
McTavish Av
1100 WIND N9G 4504 C4
S Mead Av
- DRBN 48126 4342 D7
Mead St
4500 DRBN 48126 4417 D1
5000 DRBN 48126 4342 D6
Meade Ct
2500 AARB 48105 4407 A2
Meade Rd
16600 NvlT 48167 4265 A2
Meade St
- DET 48203 4273 A3
1900 DET 48212 4273 A3
Meadlawn Dr
23200 DBHT 48127 4341 B6
Meadow Av
6700 WRRN 48091 4201 E3
7000 WRRN 48091 4202 A3
8000 WRRN 48089 4202 A3
Meadow Cir
4400 INKR 48141 4414 E7
Meadow Ct
28400 RMLS 48174 4582 A4
48400 PyTp 48170 4336 A2
N Meadow Ct
5000 WasC 48105 4333 A2
Meadow Dr
5600 SpTp 48105 4408 B4
16000 RMLS 48174 4582 B5
48600 PyTp 48170 4335 E1
48600 PyTp 48170 4336 A1
Meadow Ln
10 GSPF 48236 4276 D5
3300 WasC 48189 4258 B4
3500 WasC 48176 4572 B2
3600 WasC 48103 4572 B2
5600 SpTp 48105 4408 B4
9900 GOTp 48178 4187 D2
29000 GBTR 48173 4755 A4
Meadow Pk
23200 RDFD 48239 4341 A2
Meadow St
15000 RMLS 48174 4582 B4
Meadowbrook Ct
4800 BrTp 48134 4753 D5
Meadowbrook Dr
7000 CNTN 48187 4337 B5
Meadowbrook Ln
10 LyTp 48167 4189 E6
2600 WIND N8T 4423 A2
Meadowbrook Rd
15300 RDFD 48239 4268 B3
16100 LVNA 48154 4268 B3
16100 RDFD 48154 4268 B3
16100 RDFD 48240 4268 B3
19100 NvlT 48167 4193 D6
20700 NOVI 48167 4193 B5
21000 NOVI 48375 4193 B1
Meadowbrook St
100 DET 48214 4347 A2
1000 INKR 48141 4415 C3
1100 AARB 48103 4488 E1
27400 LVNA 48154 4268 A4
32400 LVNA 48154 4267 A5
35500 LVNA 48154 4266 C5
Meadowbrooke Av
27800 LVNA 48154 4268 A4
Meadow Creek Dr
200 AATp 48105 4407 C6
Meadowcreek Ln
44400 CNTN 48187 4336 D5
Meadowcrest Dr
5300 SpTp 48105 4333 B5
Meadow Crest North
- NvlT 48167 4264 D2
Meadowdale St
500 FRDL 48220 4199 E3
2800 INKR 48141 4415 D4
8600 DET 48228 4342 E2
Meadow Grove Tr
3500 PTFD 48108 4488 E5
W Meadowhill Dr
- FNHL 48167 4194 A3
Meadowhill Dr E
37400 FNHL 48167 4194 A4
Meadowhill Dr W
37600 FNHL 48167 4194 A3
Meadow Hill Ln
14100 PyTp 48170 4265 C6
Meadowhill St
28100 RMLS 48174 4582 B4
Meadowlake Ct
300 CNTN 48188 4412 D2
Meadowlake Rd
200 CNTN 48187 4412 E3
200 CNTN 48188 4412 E3
Meadowland Cres
13000 Tcmh N8N 4424 B1
Meadowland Ct
8600 WasC 48176 4658 B1
Meadowlane Rd
400 DRBN 48124 4416 D1
Meadowlane St
1400 INKR 48141 4414 E3
Meadowlark Blvd
- GBTR 48173 4755 A3
Meadowlark Ct
9600 WasC 48176 4659 A3
32600 FMTN 48336 4195 A5
Meadowlark Dr
3100 TNTN 48183 4669 B6
Meadowlark Ln
6300 YpTp 48197 4576 B4
Meadowlark St
20900 FMTN 48336 4195 A5
22800 OKPK 48237 4199 B2
28400 LVNA 48154 4267 E5
33100 FMTN 48335 4194 E5
33100 FMTN 48336 4194 E5
Meadowlark Tr
100 PTFD 48197 4574 D2
Meadowlawn Dr
38400 WYNE 48184 4413 A5
Meadow Ln Dr
7300 YpTp 48197 4576 D5
Meadow Ln St
1900 INKR 48141 4414 E4
Meadowridge Ct
2400 AARB 48105 4406 E1
2400 AARB 48105 4407 A1
Meadow Ridge Dr
1700 WasC 48130 4404 A1
Meadowridge Dr
19100 LVNA 48152 4196 A6
Meadows Av
23000 FTRK 48134 4754 B5
Meadows Cir
11500 VNBN 48111 4578 C1
Meadows Ct
11500 VNBN 48111 4578 C1
Meadows Dr
- DRBN 48126 4342 C7
15600 RVVW 48192 4584 A6
24500 FTRK 48134 4754 A5
24600 FTRK 48134 4753 E5
Meadows Ln
11600 VNBN 48111 4578 C1
Meadows Tr
40400 NvlT 48167 4265 C1
Meadowside Dr
1500 AATp 48104 4490 C2
Meadow Springs Ln
8400 WynC 48111 4748 D4
Meadowview Ct
4500 PTFD 48197 4491 A7
7800 YpTp 48197 4576 B2
9000 WasC 48176 4658 E3
Meadowview Dr
5800 CNTN 48187 4336 B7
Meadowview Ln
9100 WasC 48176 4658 D2
9100 WasC 48176 4659 A2
Meadowview St
5700 YpTp 48197 4576 A2
20300 LVNA 48152 4193 E6
20500 LVNA 48167 4193 E6
Meadow Wood Dr
47900 CNTN 48187 4336 A5
Meadow Woods Blvd
1600 YpTp 48197 4491 C6
Meadow Woods Cir
22400 TYLR 48180 4499 B5
Meadwinds
- WasC 48103 4488 C2
Meander Cres
12400 Tcmh N8N 4348 E7
12400 Tcmh N8N 4349 A7
Mecca St
13600 DET 48227 4270 E7
Mechanic St
400 DET 48226 4345 D5
Meconi Dr
12300 Tcmh N9K 4424 A5
Mecosta St
32800 WTLD 48186 4414 B5
Medbury St
- DET 48211 4345 C1
- DET 48213 4274 A6
2100 DET 48211 4273 D7
6800 DET 48211 4274 A6
Medford Cir
10 AARB 48104 4490 A3
Medford Ct
10 AARB 48104 4490 A2
11900 PyTp 48170 4335 C1
Medford Dr
1200 YpTp 48198 4491 E2
1200 YpTp 48198 4492 A2
Medford Rd
2000 AARB 48104 4489 E2
2000 AARB 48104 4490 A2
2400 TNTN 48183 4669 D4
Medford St
2200 TNTN 48183 4669 D3
E Medical Center Dr
1500 AARB 48104 4406 D5
W Medical Center Dr
1100 AARB 48104 4406 C5
Medina St
8000 DET 48209 4419 B5
Medina St E
10 WIND N9E 4504 C2
Medina St W
100 WIND N9E 4504 C2
Mediterranean Av
10 Amhg N9V 4757 D3
Meeting Hall Ln
23500 NOVI 48375 4193 D2
Meeting House Ln
38500 LVNA 48154 4265 E2
Megan Dr
1800 LSal N9J 4503 C7
Meghan Ln
38400 WTLD 48185 4337 E4
38400 WTLD 48185 4338 A4
Meginnity St
- LNPK 48122 4500 E1
- LNPK 48146 4500 E1
18200 MVDL 48122 4418 A7
19200 MVDL 48122 4500 E1
Meighen Rd
2200 WIND N8W 4421 E3
2300 WIND N8W 4422 A3
Mei-Lin Ct
400 Tcmh N8N 4424 E2
Mel Ct
1900 WTLD 48186 4414 A4
Melba Jean St
16400 SOGT 48195 4584 B5
N Melborn St
100 DRBN 48128 4416 B1
1700 DRBN 48128 4341 A7
5600 DBHT 48127 4341 A6
S Melborn St
100 DRBN 48124 4416 A2
100 DRBN 48128 4416 A2
Melbourne Av
9200 ALPK 48101 4500 A5
10800 ALPK 48195 4500 A6
Melbourne Ct
10800 ALPK 48101 4500 A6
Melbourne Dr
8700 WasC 48176 4658 D1
Melbourne Rd
2800 WIND N9C 4420 B5
Melbourne St
10 DET 48202 4273 A7
900 DET 48211 4273 A7
Meldrum Rd
1800 WIND N8W 4421 E2
2300 WIND N8W 4422 A3
Meldrum St
400 DET 48207 4346 B4
Melinda Ct
1800 WIND N8W 4505 A1
8800 WasC 48160 4659 E2
Melinda St
1900 WIND N8W 4505 A1
Mellon St
13700 DET 48229 4418 B5
Mellowood Ct
9600 PyTp 48170 4336 D2
Meloche Rd
100 Amhg N9V 4757 E4
Meloche Rd CO-5
100 Amhg N9V 4757 E4
Meloche St
- LSal N9J 4502 D4
Melody Ln
100 VNBN 48111 4578 B3
24000 TYLR 48180 4498 E6
24000 TYLR 48180 4499 A6
Melody Rd
24000 WRRN 48089 4203 A1
Melody St
25400 TYLR 48180 4498 D6
Melrose Av
2100 AARB 48104 4489 E1
2200 AARB 48104 4490 A1
6600 WIND N8S 4348 A7
18100 SFLD 48075 4198 A4
18700 SFLD 48075 4197 E4
22700 EPTE 48021 4203 D1
Melrose Ct
1000 SALN 48176 4657 A1
22000 EPTE 48021 4203 D2
Melrose St
7300 DET 48211 4273 B7
8900 LVNA 48150 4339 B2
14300 LVNA 48154 4267 B4
Melton Av
33000 WTLD 48186 4414 A4
36600 WTLD 48186 4413 C3
Melton St
32100 WTLD 48186 4414 B3
36100 WTLD 48186 4413 C3
Melville Av
23000 HZLP 48030 4200 E2
Melville Dr
9600 WIND N8R 4423 B2
Melville St
8900 DET 48209 4419 A4
Melvin Av
- RVRG 48229 4418 D7
300 RVRG 48218 4418 D7
8000 WTLD 48185 4339 D3
Melvin St
- DET 48229 4418 C7
1400 YpTp 48198 4492 D7
8800 LVNA 48150 4339 D2
13900 LVNA 48154 4267 D6
14600 LVNA 48154 4267 D4
18100 LVNA 48152 4267 D1
18600 LVNA 48152 4195 D7
20400 LVNA 48336 4195 D5
Melwood Dr
3200 MVDL 48122 4418 A5
Memorial Dr
- HZLP 48030 4200 C2
- WIND N8X 4421 B5
1500 WIND N8W 4421 E5
7100 CNTN 48187 4336 C5
17100 RDFD 48240 4268 D1
Memorial St
8800 DET 48228 4342 B2
9500 DET 48227 4342 B1
12600 DET 48227 4270 B6
Memory Ln
6000 WasC 48105 4258 B6
6000 WasC 48189 4258 B6
Memphis Av
23000 WRRN 48091 4201 E2
Menard Ln
300 LSal N9J 4502 D5
Menard St
8200 WIND N8S 4347 E6
8900 WIND N8S 4348 A5
9500 WIND N8P 4348 A5
Mencarelli Dr
5700 LSal N9H 4503 D4
Mendota Av
- ROTp 48220 4199 B3
Mendota Dr
10200 GOTp 48178 4188 C3
Mendota St
8000 DET 48204 4343 B3
11400 DET 48204 4271 B7
14800 DET 48238 4271 B3
16200 DET 48221 4271 B1
19900 DET 48221 4199 B5
Menlo Park Dr
10 BLVL 48111 4578 E4
Menomine St
- LSal N9J 4502 E7
- LSal N9J 4503 A6
Menominee St
32600 WTLD 48186 4414 D4
Menton St
36400 RMLS 48174 4496 B7
Mercantile Dr
15100 DRBN 48120 4417 D2
Mercedes
9500 RDFD 48239 4340 B1
13900 RDFD 48239 4268 B5
Mercedes St
8400 DBHT 48127 4340 B3
8700 DBHT 48239 4340 B3
Mercer Dr
22100 HnTp 48164 4665 C5
Mercer St
600 WIND N9A 4421 A2
1200 WIND N8X 4421 A2
Mercier St
- TYLR 48195 4583 E3
6600 DET 48210 4344 A7
9600 DRBN 48120 4418 C1
16100 SOGT 48195 4584 A3
19200 SOGT 48195 4583 E3
24000 TYLR 48180 4583 A3
25800 TYLR 48180 4582 D3
Mercury Dr
- DET 48228 4342 B6
- DRBN 48228 4342 B6
4500 DRBN 48126 4417 C1
5700 DRBN 48126 4342 B6
Meredith St
11000 RMLS 48174 4496 B7
Meri Dr
21700 WynC 48111 4663 C4
Meridan St
100 DRBN 48124 4416 A2
Meridian Ln
21700 NOVI 48375 4193 B3
Meridian Rd
17500 WynC 48138 4585 C6
18700 WynC 48138 4670 C2
25900 WynC 48138 4756 B1
Meridian St
1300 WIND N9G 4505 A4
8800 AGST 48191 4662 A2
Merion Blvd
- NvlT 48167 4264 B3
Merion Cir
46600 NvlT 48167 4264 B3
Merion Ct
15700 NvlT 48167 4264 C3
Merion Dr
100 CNTN 48188 4411 C3
Merkel St
7300 DET 48213 4274 A4
Merle Ct
47900 VNBN 48111 4578 A2
Merlin St
10300 DET 48224 4275 E1
Merlin Wy
600 WasC 48130 4404 B3
Merlot Ct
2000 PTFD 48108 4572 E3
Mero Av
500 Tcmh N9H 4504 D6
Merrick Av
28000 BwTp 48183 4754 E3
Merrick St
1100 DET 48202 4345 A3
1400 DET 48210 4344 E3
1400 DET 48210 4345 A3
2700 DRBN 48124 4416 D5
3900 DBHT 48124 4416 D6
3900 DBHT 48125 4416 D6
5800 TYLR 48125 4499 D1
8200 TYLR 48180 4499 D3
Merrill Av
- DET 48203 4200 E3
- HZLP 48203 4200 E3
400 LSal N9J 4502 D5
700 LNPK 48146 4501 A5
1800 LNPK 48146 4500 D5
1900 YpTp 48197 4491 B5
20700 HZLP 48030 4200 E3
23600 SFLD 48075 4198 B2
Merrill St
8200 DET 48202 4272 E7
8200 DET 48202 4273 A7
8200 DET 48206 4272 E7
8200 DET 48206 4344 E1
Merrill Plaisance St
10 DET 48203 4272 B1
800 DET 48203 4200 A7
Merrilyn Ct
24000 FMTN 48336 4195 A1
Merrimac Rd
400 CNTN 48188 4412 D2
Merriman Ct
19100 LVNA 48152 4195 C6
Merriman Hllw
- WTLD 48185 4339 C4
Merriman Pl
31000 RMLS 48174 4497 C2
Merriman Rd
- RMLS 48242 4497 C4
100 GDNC 48135 4414 C1
1600 GDNC 48135 4339 C6
5800 RMLS 48174 4497 C1
5800 RMLS 48184 4497 C1
5800 RMLS 48242 4497 C1
8800 LVNA 48150 4339 C2
11800 LVNA 48150 4267 C6
13900 LVNA 48154 4267 C6
15000 RMLS 48174 4581 C5
15000 RMLS 48242 4581 C5
17000 HnTp 48174 4581 C5
17100 LVNA 48152 4267 B1
18000 HnTp 48174 4666 C2
18100 LVNA 48152 4195 B6
19000 HnTp 48164 4666 C3
N Merriman Rd
6400 GDNC 48135 4339 C5
6400 WTLD 48185 4339 C5
7000 WTLD 48135 4339 C5
8700 WTLD 48150 4339 C5
S Merriman Rd
100 WTLD 48135 4414 C3
100 WTLD 48186 4414 C3
2900 WYNE 48186 4414 C6
3000 WTLD 48184 4414 C6
3000 WYNE 48184 4414 C6
5600 WTLD 48184 4497 C1
5600 WTLD 48186 4497 C1
5600 WYNE 48184 4497 C1
Merriman Service Dr S
12100 LVNA 48150 4267 C7
Merritt Av
28100 WTLD 48185 4340 A3
29400 WTLD 48185 4339 D4
Merritt Ct
33000 WTLD 48185 4339 A3
Merritt Dr
900 WIND N9B 4420 C4
32500 WTLD 48185 4339 A4
Merritt Rd
3000 PTFD 48176 4574 B5
3700 PTFD 48197 4574 E5
4500 PTFD 48197 4575 A5
5000 YpTp 48197 4575 B5
7300 YpTp 48197 4576 B5
Merritt St
4600 DET 48209 4344 C7
Merriweather Pl
14200 WRRN 48089 4203 A1
Merriweather Rd
200 GSPF 48236 4276 C3
Merriwood Park Dr
31400 LVNA 48152 4195 B5
Merriwood Park Ln
31400 LVNA 48152 4195 B5
Mershon Dr
1600 AARB 48103 4488 E2
Merton Rd
200 DET 48203 4272 B1
1000 DET 48221 4272 B1
Merwin St
5200 DET 48210 4343 C6
Mesa Dr
1300 YpTp 48197 4491 B7
Mesa Wy
15000 RMLS 48174 4581 E4
Metaline Dr
41800 CNTN 48187 4412 B1
Metcalfe St
2500 WIND N8Y 4421 D1
4200 WIND N8Y 4422 A1
Methuen Av
23800 WRRN 48091 4200 E1
S Metro Pkwy
- HnTp 48111 4579 E3
- HnTp 48111 4580 A7
- HnTp 48111 4665 A2
- HnTp 48164 4665 A2
- HnTp 48174 4579 E3
- HnTp 48174 4580 A7
- HnTp 48174 4665 A2
- VNBN 48111 4579 E3
- VNBN 48174 4579 E3
- WynC 48111 4579 E3
- WynC 48174 4579 E3
Metro St
5800 RMLS 48174 4498 A1
Metro Airport Center Dr
11100 RMLS 48174 4496 E7
11100 RMLS 48174 4580 D1
Metro Plex Dr
6600 RMLS 48174 4497 E3
Metroview Ct
10 AARB 48108 4489 E5
Metroview Rd
20700 FNHL 48335 4194 B4
Mettetal St
8800 DET 48228 4342 C2
9500 DET 48227 4342 C1
14700 DET 48227 4270 C4
Metzger Dr
20100 RKWD 48173 4754 B6
Meuse Av
5100 TNTN 48183 4669 C7
Meuse St
10400 DET 48224 4275 E1
Meyer Av
15500 ALPK 48101 4500 B2
Meyer Ct
2000 LNPK 48146 4500 C5
E Meyers Av
10 HZLP 48030 4200 C3
W Meyers Av
10 HZLP 48030 4200 C3
Meyers Rd
- OKPK 48221 4199 A5
- OKPK 48235 4199 A5
- ROTp 48221 4199 A5
- ROTp 48235 4199 A5
8000 DET 48204 4343 B3
8000 DET 48228 4343 B3
9500 DET 48227 4343 B1
11300 DET 48204 4271 B7
11300 DET 48227 4271 B7
12600 DET 48238 4271 A5
16100 DET 48221 4271 A2
16100 DET 48235 4271 A2
18000 DET 48221 4199 A6
18000 DET 48235 4199 A6
20700 OKPK 48237 4199 A5
20700 ROTp 48220 4199 A5
20900 ROTp 48237 4199 A3
21800 OKPK 48220 4199 A3
N Miami Av
500 YpTp 48198 4492 D3
Miami Dr
22100 WynC 48138 4670 B4
Miami St
2300 MVDL 48122 4418 A7
11700 DET 48229 4418 C7
S Miami St
6000 YpTp 48197 4576 D3
Michael Av
1900 WRRN 48030 4200 E3
1900 WRRN 48091 4200 E3
2000 WRRN 48091 4201 A3
Michael Cres
500 LSal N9J 4502 E4
Michael Ct
45400 CNTN 48188 4411 D7
Michael Dr
400 Tcmh N8N 4349 A7
700 Tcmh N8N 4424 A1
1100 WTLD 48186 4413 E3
5300 YpTp 48197 4576 C2
9500 RMLS 48174 4496 E6
Michael Rd N
3700 WasC 48103 4488 A1
Michael Rd S
3700 WasC 48103 4488 A1
Michael St
5100 DBHT 48125 4415 E7
10000 TYLR 48180 4498 E5
15000 TYLR 48180 4582 E4
Michaux Ct
10 GSPS 48236 4205 A5
Michaux Ln
700 GSPS 48236 4205 A5
Michelaks Ln
13000 GOTp 48178 4188 D1
Michele Av
- ECRS 48229 4501 C4
Michele St
27200 DBHT 48127 4340 B5
33400 LVNA 48150 4338 E2
33400 LVNA 48150 4339 A2
Michelle Ct
600 GDNC 48135 4414 D1
1800 AARB 48105 4406 D1
27000 TYLR 48180 4498 B1
Michelle Dr
34600 RMLS 48174 4496 D6
Michels St
14600 DRBN 48126 4417 E1
Michigan Av
- DRBN 48128 4417 A2
- LNPK 48146 4501 A6
- NvlT 48167 4193 C7
- NvlT 48167 4265 C1
10 DET 48226 4345 B6
400 LSal N9J 4502 D5
1000 AARB 48104 4406 C7
1000 AARB 48104 4489 C1
1300 DET 48216 4345 B6
2500 DET 48216 4344 C6
4000 DET 48210 4344 C6
6900 DET 48210 4343 C6
9400 DET 48126 4343 C6
10000 DRBN 48126 4343 C6
13800 DRBN 48126 4342 E7
14200 DRBN 48126 4417 A2
16300 DRBN 48120 4417 C2
19000 DRBN 48124 4417 A2
20000 DRBN 48124 4416 E2
20000 DRBN 48128 4416 E2
24500 DRBN 48124 4415 C4
25400 DBHT 48125 4415 C4
25600 DBHT 48141 4415 C4
25800 INKR 48141 4415 C4
28900 INKR 48141 4414 D5
30400 WTLD 48141 4414 D5
30400 WTLD 48186 4414 D5
31200 WTLD 48184 4414 D5
39400 CNTN 48188 4412 B7
43600 CNTN 48188 4411 E7
45900 CNTN 48111 4494 B1
45900 CNTN 48188 4494 B1
47400 VNBN 48111 4494 B1
48800 CNTN 48111 4493 C3
48800 CNTN 48188 4493 C3
49100 VNBN 48111 4493 C3
51300 VNBN 48198 4493 C3
51300 YpTp 48198 4493 C3
Michigan Av US-12
- DRBN 48128 4417 A2
10 DET 48226 4345 B6
1300 DET 48216 4345 B6
2500 DET 48216 4344 C6
4000 DET 48210 4344 C6
6900 DET 48210 4343 C6
9400 DET 48126 4343 C6
10000 DRBN 48126 4343 C6
13800 DRBN 48126 4342 E7
14200 DRBN 48126 4417 A2
16300 DRBN 48120 4417 A2
19000 DRBN 48124 4417 A2
20000 DRBN 48124 4416 E2
20000 DRBN 48128 4416 E2
24500 DRBN 48124 4415 C4
25400 DBHT 48125 4415 C4
25600 DBHT 48141 4415 C4
25800 INKR 48141 4415 C4
28900 INKR 48141 4414 D5
30400 WTLD 48141 4414 D5
30400 WTLD 48186 4414 D5
31200 WTLD 48184 4414 D5
39400 CNTN 48188 4412 B7

Block	City	ZIP	Map#	Grid
Michigan Av US-12				
43600	CNTN	48188	4411	E7
45900	CNTN	48111	4494	B1
45900	CNTN	48188	4494	B1
47400	VNBN	48111	4494	B1
48800	CNTN	48111	4493	C3
48800	CNTN	48188	4493	C3
49100	VNBN	48111	4493	C3
Michigan Av US-12 BUS				
50500	VNBN	48111	4493	C2
51300	VNBN	48198	4493	C2
51300	YpTp	48198	4493	C2
E Michigan Av				
10	YPLT	48198	4492	C4
100	SALN	48176	4572	E7
700	PTFD	48176	4573	A6
700	SALN	48176	4573	A6
700	WasC	48176	4573	A6
800	YpTp	48198	4492	C4
2100	YpTp	48198	4493	A3
6100	PTFD	48108	4574	A4
6100	PTFD	48176	4574	A4
6100	PTFD	48197	4574	A4
E Michigan Av SR-17				
10	YPLT	48198	4492	B4
E Michigan Av US-12				
100	SALN	48176	4572	E7
700	PTFD	48176	4573	A6
700	SALN	48176	4573	A6
700	WasC	48176	4573	A6
6100	PTFD	48108	4574	A4
6100	PTFD	48176	4574	A4
6100	PTFD	48197	4574	A4
E Michigan Av US-12 BUS				
10	YPLT	48198	4492	C4
800	YpTp	48198	4492	C4
2100	YpTp	48198	4493	A3
W Michigan Av				
10	YPLT	48197	4492	A4
10	YPLT	48198	4492	A4
100	SALN	48176	4657	C1
400	YPLT	48197	4491	C6
1000	YpTp	48197	4491	C6
3100	PTFD	48197	4491	C6
4700	PTFD	48197	4574	D2
4700	PTFD	48197	4575	A1
8600	WasC	48176	4657	A2
8800	WasC	48176	4656	C3
W Michigan Av SR-17				
10	YPLT	48197	4492	A4
10	YPLT	48198	4492	A4
W Michigan Av US-12				
100	SALN	48176	4657	C1
3100	PTFD	48197	4491	A7
3100	YpTp	48197	4491	A7
4700	PTFD	48197	4574	D2
4700	PTFD	48197	4575	A1
8600	WasC	48176	4657	A2
8800	WasC	48176	4656	C3
W Michigan Av US-12 BUS				
10	YPLT	48197	4492	A4
10	YPLT	48198	4492	A4
Michigan Av E				
31400	WYNE	48184	4414	A6
33800	WYNE	48184	4413	A6
38900	WYNE	48184	4412	E6
39200	WYNE	48188	4412	E6
Michigan Av E US-12				
31400	WYNE	48184	4414	A6
33800	WYNE	48184	4413	A6
38900	WYNE	48184	4412	E6
39200	WYNE	48188	4412	E6
Michigan Av W				
31400	WYNE	48184	4414	A6
34000	WYNE	48184	4413	D6
38900	WYNE	48184	4412	E6
Michigan Av W US-12				
31400	WYNE	48184	4414	A6
34000	WYNE	48184	4413	D6
38900	WYNE	48184	4412	E6
Michigan Blvd				
700	LNPK	48146	4501	A6
1000	LNPK	48146	4500	D6
14500	ALPK	48101	4500	C6
E Michigan Dr				
-	YpTp	48198	4493	B4
Michigan Heights Dr				
17000	BNTN	48174	4582	C6
Mickaila Cres				
1400	Tcmh	N8N	4423	D2
Micol Dr				
42000	PyTp	48170	4337	B1
Mida Dr				
7400	VNBN	48111	4494	E4
Middle Dr				
100	YPLT	48197	4491	E5
Middle St				
200	DET	48226	4345	C6
Middlebelt Rd				
100	GDNC	48135	4414	E2
100	INKR	48135	4414	E2
100	INKR	48141	4414	E5
1500	GDNC	48135	4339	A5
5800	RMLS	48174	4497	E3
8800	LVNA	48150	4339	E1
9200	RMLS	48242	4497	E5
11000	RMLS	48174	4581	E3
11600	LVNA	48150	4267	E6
13000	RMLS	48242	4581	E3
13900	LVNA	48154	4267	E6
16700	LVNA	48152	4267	D1
17000	HnTp	48174	4581	E6
18200	HnTp	48174	4666	E4
18500	LVNA	48152	4195	D6
20700	FNHL	48336	4195	D4
21000	HnTp	48164	4666	E4
24400	HnTp	48134	4666	E7
25600	HnTp	48134	4667	A7
Middlebelt Rd				
25600	HnTp	48134	4752	E1
25600	HnTp	48134	4753	A1
N Middlebelt Rd				
7200	WTLD	48135	4339	E4
7200	WTLD	48185	4339	E4
8600	WTLD	48150	4339	E4
S Middlebelt Rd				
4600	WTLD	48186	4414	E7
5500	WTLD	48186	4497	E1
Middleboro St				
32800	LVNA	48154	4267	A5
35900	LVNA	48154	4266	C6
Middlebury Ct				
10	DRBN	48120	4417	D2
44900	CNTN	48188	4411	D3
Middlebury Dr				
15500	DRBN	48120	4417	D2
W Middlebury Dr				
3300	DRBN	48120	4417	D2
Middlebury Ln				
45100	CNTN	48188	4411	D3
Middlebury St				
30700	WTLD	48186	4414	C4
Middlefield Ct				
2300	TNTN	48183	4669	C3
Middlefield Dr				
2800	TNTN	48183	4669	C5
Middlefield Rd				
2300	TNTN	48183	4669	C4
Middle Gibraltar Rd				
13300	GBTR	48173	4755	D4
Middle Pointe St				
8000	DET	48204	4343	B3
Middlepointe St				
7600	DRBN	48126	4343	B3
Middlesex Rd				
500	GPPK	48230	4348	A1
Middlesex St				
5600	DRBN	48126	4342	E6
23100	STCS	48080	4204	E3
23100	STCS	48080	4205	A3
25000	WDHN	48183	4668	B7
Middleside Rd				
3000	Amhg	N9V	4757	E5
Middle Sideroad				
2000	Amhg	N9V	4671	E4
Middle Sideroad CO-10				
2000	Amhg	N9V	4671	E4
Middleton Ct				
8700	WynC	48138	4670	C2
Middleton Dr				
3600	AARB	48105	4407	C4
Middlewood Dr				
1300	SALN	48176	4572	D5
Midfield Cres				
9500	WIND	N8R	4423	B3
Midfield St				
17700	DET	48227	4270	B4
Midland				
25700	RDFD	48239	4268	D3
Midland St				
-	DET	48223	4269	E3
-	DET	48227	4271	A3
-	DET	48238	4272	A3
200	HDPK	48203	4272	B3
1600	DET	48203	4272	B3
3000	DET	48238	4271	C3
13800	DET	48227	4270	E3
18200	DET	48223	4270	A3
23900	RDFD	48223	4268	E3
23900	RDFD	48239	4268	E3
Midsummer Ln				
3500	WasC	48167	4190	C7
Midvale Av				
1800	YpTp	48197	4491	B4
Midway				
27200	WynC	48138	4756	B2
38900	HnTp	48164	4665	A5
Midway Av				
-	ALPK	48101	4499	D5
17400	ALPK	48101	4500	A5
18600	SFLD	48075	4198	A3
18700	SFLD	48075	4197	E3
21500	SFLD	48034	4197	B3
S Midway Av				
15500	ALPK	48101	4500	B5
Midway Dr				
4600	WasC	48103	4329	D5
44400	NOVI	48375	4192	D3
Midway Rd				
1000	YpTp	48198	4492	E2
1400	SpTp	48198	4492	E1
Midway St				
24000	DBHT	48127	4341	A6
24400	DBHT	48127	4340	E6
Mihelich Ct				
22000	EPTE	48021	4203	B2
Milan Ct				
-	NOVI	48167	4192	A4
Milano Ct				
3200	WIND	N8R	4423	D3
Milbank St				
-	DET	48234	4201	E5
-	DET	48234	4202	A5
20400	WDHN	48183	4754	E2
Milburn Blvd				
8100	WTLD	48185	4339	C3
Milburn St				
9800	LVNA	48150	4339	C1
18500	LVNA	48152	4267	C1
19100	LVNA	48152	4195	C6
Milbury Dr				
21000	WDHN	48183	4669	A2
Milcroft Ct				
3300	CNTN	48188	4411	C6
Mildred Ct				
9700	GOTp	48178	4188	C2
Mildred St				
700	YPLT	48198	4492	B5
Mildred St				
3000	WYNE	48184	4414	B5
N Mildred St				
100	DRBN	48128	4416	A1
1300	DRBN	48128	4341	A7
Miles St				
100	YPLT	48198	4492	B4
7000	DET	48211	4274	A6
14900	ALPK	48101	4500	C7
14900	SOGT	48101	4500	C7
14900	SOGT	48195	4500	C7
Milford Av				
-	LSal	N9J	4502	D4
Milford Ct				
57100	LyTp	48178	4190	A1
Milford Rd				
24200	LyTp	48178	4190	A1
Milford St				
3700	DET	48210	4344	C3
Military Cir				
6700	DBHT	48127	4341	A5
Military Rd				
23700	DBHT	48127	4341	A5
Military St				
-	DRBN	48124	4416	D4
300	Amhg	N9V	4757	C2
800	DET	48209	4419	C1
2500	DET	48209	4344	A6
3000	DET	48210	4344	A6
8000	DET	48204	4343	E2
8000	DET	48210	4343	E2
N Military St				
100	DRBN	48124	4416	C1
700	DRBN	48128	4416	C1
S Military St				
100	DET	48209	4419	D3
100	DRBN	48124	4416	C2
Milkey Rd				
1700	WasC	48160	4657	E5
1700	WasC	48160	4658	A5
1700	WasC	48176	4657	E5
1700	WasC	48176	4658	A5
Mill Rd				
22300	NOVI	48375	4193	C3
Mill St				
10	ECRS	48229	4501	C5
10	WIND	N9C	4420	A3
400	LNPK	48146	4501	A4
2200	LNPK	48101	4500	D3
2200	LNPK	48146	4500	D3
29000	FTRK	48134	4753	D4
42800	NvlT	48167	4265	A2
42800	NvlT	48170	4265	A2
N Mill St				
100	SLYN	48178	4189	C1
1100	PLYM	48170	4265	B6
S Mill St				
100	PLYM	48170	4265	B7
100	SLYN	48178	4189	C2
200	PLYM	48170	4337	B2
800	PyTp	48170	4337	B2
Millard St				
10	VNBN	48111	4495	C6
20700	TYLR	48180	4499	D4
23200	SFLD	48034	4197	A4
Millbrook Dr				
1200	PTFD	48108	4489	A4
Millbrook Rd				
1000	CNTN	48188	4412	D3
Millbrooke Wy				
12800	GOTp	48178	4188	D3
Mill Creek Cir				
21200	BwTp	48183	4754	D2
Mill Creek Ct				
21200	BwTp	48183	4754	D2
Millcreek Ct				
24300	FNHL	48336	4195	E1
Mill Creek Dr				
27300	BwTp	48183	4754	D2
Millcreek Dr				
24300	FNHL	48336	4195	E1
Millen St				
2800	WIND	N9C	4420	A4
Miller Av				
100	AARB	48103	4406	A5
100	AARB	48104	4406	A5
1400	AARB	48103	4405	D4
2500	WasC	48103	4405	D4
N Miller Cir				
38100	WTLD	48186	4413	A4
S Miller Cir				
38100	WTLD	48186	4413	A5
W Miller Cir				
2100	WTLD	48186	4413	A4
Miller Rd				
-	DET	48120	4418	C3
-	DET	48209	4418	C3
2800	DRBN	48120	4418	C3
3000	AARB	48103	4405	B3
3000	WasC	48103	4405	B3
4000	WasC	48103	4404	C2
4200	DRBN	48126	4343	B6
4200	DRBN	48126	4418	C3
4500	WasC	48130	4404	C2
Miller St				
100	WYDT	48192	4585	C1
3800	HMTK	48211	4273	D5
3900	DET	48211	4273	D5
6800	DET	48211	4274	A5
7100	DET	48213	4274	A5
14600	TYLR	48180	4582	E3
15100	OKPK	48237	4198	C4
Milleville Rd				
35100	BwTp	48173	4841	D3
Milliman Rd				
15400	BwTp	48173	4841	B4
Millington Ct				
8800	VNBN	48111	4495	A5
Milloy St				
2400	WIND	N0W	4421	E2
Milloy St				
2400	WIND	N8Y	4421	E2
3700	WIND	N8W	4422	A2
3700	WIND	N8Y	4422	A2
4700	WIND	N8T	4422	B2
Millpond Ct				
900	NHVL	48374	4192	C4
40000	NvlT	48167	4265	D3
Mill Pond Ln				
3800	PTFD	48108	4489	A6
Mill Race Cir				
33200	WTLD	48185	4339	A3
42100	PyTp	48170	4265	B4
Millrace Ct				
10	DRBN	48126	4341	E7
10	DRBN	48126	4342	A7
Mill Race Ct N				
42200	PyTp	48170	4265	C4
Mill Race Ct S				
42200	PyTp	48170	4265	C4
Mill Rd Ct E				
40400	NOVI	48375	4193	C3
Mill Rd Ct W				
40700	NOVI	48375	4193	C3
Mills Ct				
3100	AARB	48104	4490	B1
Mills Rd				
100	SALN	48176	4657	C1
300	SALN	48176	4572	C7
Mills St				
7900	TYLR	48180	4498	E3
Millside Ct				
4100	TNTN	48183	4669	B6
Millstream				
24400	NOVI	48375	4193	C1
Millwood Ct				
33900	WTLD	48185	4338	D4
Millwood Dr				
7700	WTLD	48185	4338	E4
10300	PyTp	48170	4336	B2
Milner St				
8900	DET	48213	4274	C4
Milo St				
3600	DET	48212	4201	B7
Milton Av				
-	LSal	N9J	4502	D4
E Milton Av				
10	HZLP	48030	4200	D4
W Milton Av				
10	HZLP	48030	4200	C4
Milton Dr				
-	VNBN	48111	4579	B3
Milton St				
7000	DET	48234	4274	A3
38400	WTLD	48186	4413	A3
Milwaukee St E				
10	DET	48202	4345	A1
600	DET	48202	4273	C7
900	DET	48211	4273	C7
Milwaukee St W				
10	DET	48202	4345	A1
1100	DET	48202	4344	E1
Minden St				
11000	DET	48205	4274	D2
11000	DET	48234	4274	D2
Minehart Dr				
14100	PyTp	48170	4265	D6
Miner St				
500	AARB	48103	4406	A4
Mineral Springs Rd				
28100	HnTp	48164	4751	C4
28300	HnTp	48117	4751	C4
Minerva Rd				
1300	AARB	48104	4406	D7
1300	AARB	48104	4489	D1
Minerva St				
-	DET	48224	4276	A1
2000	WTLD	48186	4413	B4
2600	WRRN	48091	4201	A1
3000	FRDL	48069	4199	E1
3000	FRDL	48220	4199	E1
Minglewood St				
1200	AARB	48103	4406	A4
Minion Dr				
700	YpTp	48198	4492	C4
Minneapolis St				
17100	DET	48224	4276	A4
Minnesota St				
-	DET	48212	4200	E7
10	DET	48203	4200	C7
3600	DET	48212	4201	A7
Minnie St				
2200	ALPK	48146	4500	C4
2200	LNPK	48146	4500	C4
Minock Cir				
26700	RDFD	48239	4268	B5
Minock Dr				
13900	RDFD	48239	4268	C5
Minock St				
5600	DET	48228	4341	E5
11600	DET	48228	4269	E7
14900	DET	48223	4269	E4
Mint St				
7800	DET	48209	4419	A3
Minto Av				
800	LSal	N9J	4503	A4
Minton Av				
38800	LVNA	48150	4337	E2
Minton Ct				
28600	LVNA	48150	4340	A2
35500	LVNA	48150	4338	D2
Minton St				
29400	LVNA	48150	4339	C2
35300	LVNA	48150	4338	C2
Mirabeau Pl				
200	GSPF	48236	4276	D3
Mirage Lake Dr				
-	WasC	48160	4659	E2
9000	WasC	48160	4660	A2
Miranda Ct				
1300	LSal	N9J	4503	A5
Miriam St				
10500	RMLS	48174	4496	B7
Missant Dr				
-	HMTK	48211	4273	D5
-	HMTK	48212	4273	D5
Missaukee Ct				
32700	WTLD	48186	4414	B5
Mission Ct				
36100	FMTN	48335	4194	C2
Mission Ln				
23100	FMTN	48335	4194	C2
23100	FNHL	48335	4194	C2
41400	NOVI	48167	4193	B5
Mission Hills Dr				
7000	YpTp	48197	4576	A5
Mission Pointe				
17800	NvlT	48167	4263	E2
18000	NvlT	48167	4264	A1
Missouri St				
5400	DET	48210	4344	D3
Mistwood Ct				
5900	RMLS	48174	4497	B1
Mitchell Av				
-	WIND	N9G	4504	C4
Mitchell Cres				
3100	WIND	N9G	4504	B4
Mitchell Ct				
500	RVRG	48218	4501	D1
Mitchell St				
3400	DET	48207	4346	A2
3800	DET	48207	4345	E2
5000	DET	48211	4345	E1
5500	DET	48211	4273	D7
11300	HMTK	48212	4273	B3
17100	DET	48212	4273	A1
17400	DET	48212	4201	A7
19100	DET	48234	4201	A5
Mitchelldale Av				
20700	ROTp	48220	4199	C4
20700	ROTp	48221	4199	C4
Mixtwood St				
900	AARB	48103	4406	A4
Moccasin St				
6700	WTLD	48185	4338	E6
Moceri Cres				
200	Lksr	N8N	4424	E1
Mocking Bird Ct				
47600	NOVI	48374	4191	E1
Mockingbird Ln				
9300	WasC	48176	4659	A3
Modern St				
1600	DET	48203	4272	E2
1900	DET	48212	4273	A1
Moeller Av				
100	GDNC	48135	4414	B1
2000	YpTp	48198	4577	B1
6400	GDNC	48135	4339	B6
Moenart St				
13400	DET	48212	4273	D1
18000	DET	48234	4201	D6
Moffat St				
8200	DET	48213	4274	C6
Mogul St				
10800	DET	48224	4275	B1
11000	DET	48213	4275	B1
N Mohawk Av				
500	YpTp	48198	4492	D3
S Mohawk Av				
5800	YpTp	48197	4576	D2
Mohawk Ct				
-	AARB	48103	4405	B6
Mohawk Dr				
25000	FTRK	48134	4753	E1
Mohawk St				
100	DRBN	48124	4416	A2
1600	WIND	N8W	4421	D3
3800	DET	48210	4344	C4
6900	WTLD	48185	4338	E5
46500	VNBN	48111	4494	C7
Mohican St				
6800	WTLD	48185	4338	E5
20100	DET	48205	4203	B4
Mok Av				
15600	EPTE	48021	4203	C2
Molena St				
8000	DET	48234	4274	A3
Mollie St				
1400	YpTp	48198	4492	D7
Mollno St				
1000	WYDT	48192	4585	B2
Molnar Cres				
7900	WIND	N8R	4423	A2
Molner Ct				
1300	YpTp	48198	4492	C6
Moms Dr				
8400	VNBN	48111	4494	D5
Mona Ct				
11400	PyTp	48170	4337	D1
Monarch Av				
4000	CNTN	48188	4411	A7
Monarch Dr				
13600	GOTp	48178	4188	E2
13700	GOTp	48178	4189	A2
Monarch St				
300	WIND	N8X	4421	B5
19100	DET	48205	4203	B5
Monarda Dr				
9300	GOTp	48116	4186	E1
Monck Av				
1400	LSal	N9J	4503	A4
Monica St				
10000	DET	48204	4271	D7
10000	DET	48204	4343	D1
15800	DET	48221	4271	D1
15800	DET	48238	4271	D2
18200	DET	48221	4199	D7
Monitor St				
20100	DET	48234	4202	B5
Monmouth Rd				
600	WIND	N8Y	4346	C7
900	WIND	N8Y	4421	C1
Monmouth St				
38400	WTLD	48186	4413	A4
Monroe Av				
4200	ECRS	48229	4501	D4
Monroe Blvd				
5800	TYLR	48125	4499	C1
5800	TYLR	48180	4499	C1
Monroe Ct				
6200	VNBN	48111	4577	C3
Monroe St				
10	DET	48226	4345	D6
100	SALN	48176	4657	C1
100	YPLT	48197	4491	E6
500	AARB	48104	4406	C7
600	DET	48207	4345	D6
700	DRBN	48124	4416	C4
3900	DBHT	48124	4416	C6
3900	DBHT	48125	4416	C6
4300	ECRS	48229	4501	D4
14800	BrTp	48134	4753	C4
50000	CNTN	48188	4410	D3
Mons Av				
3000	WIND	N8W	4422	A4
Monsignor Hunt Dr				
6800	DBHT	48127	4341	D5
Montague Ln				
20600	GSPW	48236	4204	E5
Montague St				
10	VNBN	48111	4578	D4
Montana				
400	WynC	48111	4662	D2
Montana Ct				
9100	LVNA	48150	4339	A2
Montana Dr				
39000	RMLS	48174	4495	E3
39000	RMLS	48174	4496	A3
Montana St				
9000	LVNA	48150	4339	A2
Montana St E				
10	DET	48203	4200	C7
Montana St W				
10	DET	48203	4200	C7
Montcalm St				
3700	WIND	N9C	4420	B6
32600	WTLD	48186	4414	B4
E Montcalm St				
-	DET	48201	4345	C5
-	DET	48226	4345	C5
W Montcalm St				
10	DET	48201	4345	C5
Montclair Dr				
22700	FNHL	48336	4195	D2
Montclair Pl				
1500	AARB	48104	4489	D1
Montclair St				
1400	DET	48214	4347	A1
2900	DET	48214	4275	A7
3700	DET	48214	4274	E7
5700	DET	48213	4274	D4
Montebello Ct				
25400	WDHN	48183	4669	A7
Montebello Dr				
25000	WDHN	48183	4669	A6
Monte Carlo St				
21600	HnTp	48174	4667	B3
Monterey Ct				
1700	PTFD	48108	4573	A1
Monterey Dr				
11400	VNBN	48111	4495	B7
11400	VNBN	48111	4579	A1
22000	WDHN	48183	4669	A4
Monterey St				
10	HDPK	48203	4272	D5
3700	DET	48206	4272	A6
4000	DET	48204	4271	E6
13700	SOGT	48195	4584	A2
Monte Vista St				
12600	DET	48238	4271	B6
16500	DET	48221	4271	B1
19900	DET	48221	4199	A5
Montfaucon Av				
4700	TNTN	48183	4669	C7
Montfort Dr				
6800	CNTN	48187	4336	E6
Montgomery Av				
200	AARB	48103	4405	E6
Montgomery Dr				
-	WIND	N9G	4504	C5
4600	LSal	N9H	4504	C5
Montgomery St				
2600	DET	48206	4344	C2
4000	DET	48204	4344	B2
Monticello St				
1600	TNTN	48183	4669	D3
26400	INKR	48141	4415	C2
Montie Rd				
-	ALPK	48101	4500	E1
500	LNPK	48146	4501	B2
1700	LNPK	48146	4500	E1
2200	LNPK	48101	4500	E1
Montlieu St				
8000	DET	48234	4274	B2
Montmorency St				
32600	WTLD	48186	4414	D4
Montreal Av				
500	YpTp	48198	4492	C5
Montreuil Av				
200	WIND	N8Y	4346	C7
Montrose Av				
1000	WIND	N8X	4420	D3
3000	YpTp	48198	4493	B2
20700	WRRN	48089	4203	A3
Montrose St				
10	WIND	N8X	4421	A3
200	WIND	N8X	4420	E3
6300	DET	48228	4342	C4
9500	DET	48227	4342	C1
Montrose St				
13900	DET	48227	4270	C5
19100	DET	48235	4198	C6
Montville Pl				
-	DET	48238	4272	B5
Monty St				
1100	LSal	N9J	4503	A5
Monument				
3200	PTFD	48108	4490	C5
Moon Rd				
7800	PTFD	48176	4573	C7
8000	WasC	48176	4573	C7
8200	WasC	48176	4658	C2
9600	WasC	48160	4658	C5
Moon St				
18900	DET	48236	4276	A1
Mooney St				
22800	FMTN	48336	4195	B2
Moonlight Dr				
45400	PyTp	48170	4336	C1
Moonwood Pl				
7400	WTLD	48185	4338	E4
Moor Av				
22100	BNTN	48192	4583	C6
E Moor Ct				
8300	WIND	N8S	4347	E7
Moorcroft Ct				
12800	PyTp	48170	4264	C7
Moore Av				
3000	INKR	48141	4415	B6
Moore Cir				
27400	INKR	48141	4415	B7
Moore Ct				
4500	INKR	48141	4415	B7
Moore Pl				
3500	DET	48210	4344	B3
Moore Rd				
2200	LNPK	48101	4500	B5
2200	LNPK	48146	4500	B5
14500	ALPK	48101	4500	B5
18700	ALPK	48101	4499	E5
Moore St				
700	AARB	48105	4406	C4
4600	WYNE	48184	4413	C7
5300	WYNE	48184	4496	C1
11000	RMLS	48174	4496	C7
11200	RMLS	48174	4580	C1
33900	FMTN	48335	4194	D2
Mooreville Rd				
2000	WasC	48160	4657	C6
2000	WasC	48176	4657	C6
Moorgate Dr				
-	CNTN	48187	4336	B6
Moorgate St				
22400	NOVI	48374	4192	B3
Moorhouse St				
1400	FRDL	48220	4200	B1
Mooringside				
40900	NOVI	48375	4193	B1
Moorland Dr				
-	GSPS	48236	4205	A4
500	GSPW	48236	4205	A4
800	GSPW	48236	4204	E4
Moors Ct				
2400	PTFD	48108	4572	D1
Moran Av				
400	LNPK	48146	4501	A6
1000	LNPK	48146	4500	E6
Moran Rd				
10	GSPF	48236	4276	D4
400	DET	48236	4276	C3
14500	ALPK	48101	4500	C6
14700	SOGT	48101	4500	C6
Moran St				
3800	DET	48207	4346	A1
4900	DET	48207	4345	E1
5000	DET	48211	4345	E1
5400	DET	48211	4273	E7
11300	HMTK	48212	4273	C2
11400	TYLR	48180	4499	C7
12200	DET	48212	4273	C2
17300	DET	48212	4201	B7
30400	FNHL	48336	4195	C1
Morand St				
500	WIND	N9G	4504	E3
900	WIND	N9G	4505	A2
Morang Dr				
-	DET	48224	4276	A1
9100	DET	48224	4275	E1
11000	DET	48224	4203	D7
12500	DET	48205	4203	C6
Morehead Ct				
1100	AARB	48103	4489	A3
Morehead Dr				
1300	AARB	48103	4488	E3
E Morehouse Av				
600	HZLP	48030	4200	D1
W Morehouse Av				
10	HZLP	48030	4200	C1
Morgan Av				
11200	PyTp	48170	4337	C1
Morgan Blvd				
-	NHVL	48167	4192	C5
-	NHVL	48374	4192	C5
Morgan Cir				
400	NHVL	48167	4192	D4
400	RVRG	48218	4501	D1
E Morgan Cir				
6200	WTLD	48185	4338	C6
W Morgan Cir				
6300	WTLD	48185	4338	C6
Morgan Ct				
500	NHVL	48167	4192	D5
Morgan Dr				
-	CNTN	48187	4412	A2
-	CNTN	48188	4412	A2
35500	RMLS	48174	4496	D6
Morgan Rd				
3700	PTFD	48197	4574	D1
5100	YpTp	48197	4575	B1

INDEX 38
E Morgan Rd — Detroit & Wayne County Street Index — Niagara Ct

STREET Block City ZIP Map# Grid

E Morgan Rd
10 PTFD 48108 4573 E1
2000 PTFD 48108 4574 A1
3000 PTFD 48197 4574 A1
W Morgan Rd
10 PTFD 48108 4573 D1
Morgan St
7500 DET 48234 4274 A3
Morissey Ln
59100 LyTp 48178 4189 D4
Moritz St
23500 OKPK 48237 4199 A1
Morkland Av
- WynC 48138 4670 C1
Morley Av
21500 DRBN 48124 4416 C2
Morley Ct
600 DRBN 48124 4416 C2
N Morley Dr
8000 AGST 48191 4577 C7
W Morley Dr
10700 AGST 48191 4577 C7
Morley St
5600 WTLD 48185 4338 B7
10000 DET 48204 4343 B1
11000 TYLR 48180 4499 B7
26400 INKR 48141 4415 C2
Morlock Av
35000 LVNA 48152 4194 D5
Morlock St
28800 LVNA 48152 4195 D5
Morning Dove Ct
800 CNTN 48188 4412 B3
Morning Dove Ln
10600 GOTp 48178 4187 D5
Morning Glory Pl
4700 WYNE 48184 4414 B7
Morningside
- NvlT 48167 4263 D4
Morningside Av
- DRBN 48120 4418 D4
18400 EPTE 48021 4204 A2
Morningside Ct
45700 CNTN 48187 4336 C7
Morningside Dr
1000 AARB 48103 4405 E4
19000 GSPW 48236 4276 E1
20700 GSPW 48236 4204 E5
20800 GSPW 48236 4205 A5
Morningside Ln
600 GSPW 48236 4204 D5
Morningside Rd
45400 CNTN 48187 4336 C7
Morningside St
22000 STCS 48080 4205 A4
22000 STCS 48236 4205 A4
Morning Star St
38500 LVNA 48152 4193 E5
Morningstar Wy
4500 WasC 48103 4487 D2
Mornington Ct
100 CNTN 48188 4411 B2
Mornington Rd
46400 CNTN 48188 4411 B2
Morningview
11100 SOGT 48195 4500 C7
Morning View Dr
26300 BNTN 48174 4582 D6
Moro Dr
1500 Tcmh N0R 4505 A5
Moross Pl
300 GSPF 48236 4276 D2
Moross Rd
400 GSPF 48236 4276 D2
16000 DET 48205 4203 D6
16100 DET 48224 4203 D6
20400 DET 48224 4204 A7
20800 DET 48236 4204 A7
21300 DET 48236 4276 B1
Morrell St
1000 DET 48209 4419 D1
2000 DET 48209 4344 C7
S Morrell St
100 DET 48209 4419 D3
Morris Av
1300 LNPK 48146 4501 A2
1700 LNPK 48146 4500 D1
2200 LNPK 48101 4500 D1
2600 YpTp 48198 4577 B1
14600 ALPK 48101 4500 D1
15200 ALPK 48101 4417 D7
Morris Cir
- DRBN 48126 4343 C3
Morris Dr
3000 WIND N9E 4504 A1
Morris St
33200 WYNE 48184 4414 A6
Morrison Av
8800 PyTp 48170 4337 A2
8800 PyTp 48187 4337 A2
Morrison Blvd
1300 CNTN 48187 4412 A1
1900 CNTN 48187 4337 A7
Morrison Dr
2000 WasC 48130 4329 A7
Morrissey Av
1900 WRRN 48030 4200 E1
1900 WRRN 48091 4200 E1
2200 WRRN 48091 4201 A1
Morross Ct
10 DRBN 48126 4342 E4
Morross St
8700 DRBN 48126 4343 C3
14400 DRBN 48126 4342 D4
Morrow
- DET 48211 4273 C6
Morrow Av
- RVRG 48218 4418 D7
- RVRG 48229 4418 D7
400 RVRG 48218 4501 D1

E Morrow Cir
8000 DET 48204 4343 B3
Morrow Cir E
7500 DRBN 48126 4343 B3
Morrow Cir S
10300 DRBN 48126 4343 A4
Morrow Cir W
7500 DRBN 48126 4343 A3
Morrow Ct
4600 WasC 48103 4329 D5
Morse St
6300 DET 48210 4344 A6
Mortenview Dr
7100 TYLR 48180 4499 D2
13000 TYLR 48180 4583 D3
Mortenview Rd
6700 TYLR 48180 4499 D2
Mortenview St
28300 BwTp 48183 4754 D3
Morton Av
1400 AARB 48104 4489 D1
18000 WynC 48111 4578 E7
Morton Dr
300 LSal N9J 4502 D3
300 WIND N9J 4502 D3
1000 LSal N9J 4503 A4
1000 WIND N9J 4503 A4
Morton St
6300 DET 48210 4344 A6
23400 OKPK 48237 4199 A1
26200 DBHT 48127 4415 C1
Morton Industrial Dr
6100 LSal N9J 4502 D3
Morton Taylor Rd
5800 VNBN 48111 4495 A2
N Morton Taylor Rd
1300 CNTN 48187 4412 A1
1900 CNTN 48187 4337 A5
S Morton Taylor Rd
400 CNTN 48188 4412 A4
Moselle Pl
300 GSPF 48236 4276 C2
Moses St
26300 FTRK 48134 4753 D3
E Mosley St
100 AARB 48104 4406 B7
W Mosley St
100 AARB 48103 4406 B7
100 AARB 48104 4406 B7
Moss St
200 HDPK 48203 4272 B2
Moss Rose Ct
2200 PTFD 48103 4488 D5
Mother Teresa Dr
- AATp 48105 4332 C4
Motor Dr
- DET 48075 4198 C5
- DET 48235 4198 C5
- SFLD 48075 4198 C5
Mott Av
18000 EPTE 48021 4203 E3
18200 EPTE 48021 4204 A2
Mott Rd
2900 SpTp 48198 4493 D1
2900 YpTp 48198 4493 D1
49400 CNTN 48188 4493 D1
49400 VNBN 48111 4493 D1
Moulon Rouge Dr
27500 HnTp 48174 4667 B4
Mound Rd
- WRRN 48234 4201 D4
11400 DET 48212 4273 D2
17400 DET 48212 4201 D6
18000 DET 48234 4201 D6
20700 WRRN 48091 4201 D4
Mountain Ct
30600 WTLD 48185 4339 C3
Mountain Wy
15000 RMLS 48174 4581 D4
Mountainview Dr
400 NHVL 48167 4192 D5
Mt Carmel Dr
3800 WIND N9G 4504 B3
Mt Elliott Ct
11200 DET 48212 4273 E3
Mt Elliott St
- WRRN 48091 4201 E4
- WRRN 48234 4201 E4
400 DET 48207 4346 B2
5000 DET 48211 4346 B2
5100 DET 48211 4274 A7
9700 DET 48211 4273 E3
9700 DET 48234 4273 E3
11600 DET 48212 4273 E1
17600 DET 48212 4201 E6
18000 DET 48234 4201 E6
Mt Olive Dr
24000 BNTN 48134 4667 E7
Mt Olive Grv
7800 WIND N8S 4347 E6
Mt Olivet St
7500 DET 48234 4274 A2
Mt Pleasant Av
700 AARB 48103 4406 A7
Mt Royal Dr
3800 WIND N9G 4504 B3
Mt Sinai Cres
4100 WIND N9G 4504 B4
Mt Vernon Av
200 GSPF 48236 4276 C3
700 AARB 48103 4406 A7
Mt Vernon Dr
26800 INKR 48141 4415 B2
Mt Vernon Rd
32000 BwTp 48173 4755 B6
Mt Vernon St
10 DET 48202 4273 A7
900 DET 48211 4273 A7
10600 TYLR 48180 4498 D6
18200 SFLD 48075 4198 A1

Mt Vernon St
18600 SFLD 48075 4197 E1
Moxlay Av
1900 WIND N8W 4505 A1
Moy Av
200 WIND N9A 4346 B7
600 WIND N9A 4421 B1
1200 WIND N8X 4421 C2
1700 WIND N8W 4421 C4
Moyes St
6600 DET 48210 4344 A6
Moynahan St
3100 Tcmh N0R 4505 C5
Mroch Dr
- DET 48207 4346 D5
Mueller St
9200 TYLR 48180 4499 B5
E Muir Av
1100 HZLP 48030 4200 E4
W Muir Av
10 HZLP 48030 4200 C4
Muir Rd
10 GSPF 48236 4276 C4
Muirfield Ct
45500 CNTN 48188 4411 C3
Muirfield Dr
2500 WTLD 48186 4413 A5
7200 YpTp 48197 4576 A5
37100 LVNA 48152 4194 B7
45400 CNTN 48188 4411 C3
Muirfield Ln
39500 NvlT 48167 4265 C3
Muirfield St
- TYLR 48180 4582 E2
- TYLR 48180 4583 A2
Muirland Dr
8900 PyTp 48170 4336 C3
Muirland St
15400 DET 48238 4271 E2
16100 DET 48221 4271 E2
18000 DET 48221 4199 E6
Muirwood Ct
35400 FNHL 48335 4194 D1
Muirwood Dr
24600 FNHL 48335 4194 C1
Mulberry
10 WynC 48111 4664 B3
9700 SpTp 48198 4409 E7
Mulberry Ct
- NvlT 48167 4263 C4
2400 AARB 48104 4489 E2
3100 WIND N8R 4423 C3
9900 WasC 48167 4190 B6
21300 FNHL 48336 4195 C4
24300 SFLD 48034 4197 A1
Mulberry Dr
- Tcmh N8N 4423 D3
10400 WIND N8R 4423 C3
25000 SFLD 48034 4197 A1
Mulberry Ln
1500 CNTN 48188 4412 C4
59800 LyTp 48178 4189 C5
Mulberry St
1000 WYDT 48192 4585 B2
1900 DET 48210 4345 A4
11600 SOGT 48101 4500 C7
11600 SOGT 48195 4500 C7
13000 SOGT 48195 4584 C2
17000 RVVW 48192 4584 C5
17000 RVVW 48195 4584 C5
Mulberry Tr
13300 TYLR 48180 4583 D2
Mulberry Wy
16300 NvlT 48167 4263 C4
Mulberry Woods Cir
4600 AATp 48105 4407 E4
Mulford Ct
3400 WIND N9C 4420 B5
Mulford Pl
10 HDPK 48203 4272 D4
Mulholland St
200 AARB 48103 4406 A6
Mullane St
1400 DET 48209 4419 A2
2200 DET 48209 4418 E2
Mullberry Ct
6700 WasC 48176 4572 A5
Mullett St
600 DET 48207 4345 D5
600 DET 48226 4345 D5
Mullin Av
20700 WRRN 48089 4202 C3
Mullins Dr
9100 HbgT 48116 4186 A1
Muncey St
17400 DET 48224 4276 B4
Munger Ct
36400 LVNA 48154 4266 B3
Munger Ln
- FTRK 48134 4753 E4
Munger Rd
4700 PTFD 48197 4491 A7
4700 PTFD 48197 4575 A1
4700 YpTp 48197 4491 A7
4700 YpTp 48197 4575 A1
Munger St
30600 LVNA 48154 4267 C2
34200 LVNA 48154 4266 D2
Munich Ct
- WIND N8N 4423 B5
- WIND N8T 4423 B5
Munich St
15300 DET 48224 4275 D4
17300 DET 48224 4276 A3
Munro Av
29200 GBTR 48173 4755 D4
Munsee St
2200 WIND N8W 4421 D2
Munson St
24300 TYLR 48180 4498 E3

Munson St
24300 TYLR 48180 4499 A3
Murat St
9200 DET 48213 4274 B4
Murfin Av
1200 AARB 48105 4406 E4
Murray Av
200 AARB 48103 4406 A6
Murray Cres
2000 Tcmh N8N 4423 E5
Murray Ct
800 AARB 48103 4406 A6
Murray St
10 Amhg N9V 4757 C3
9300 DET 48213 4274 D6
12300 TYLR 48180 4583 B1
22900 DRBN 48128 4416 B1
Murray Hill Dr
50800 CNTN 48187 4335 C5
51200 CNTN 48170 4335 C5
Murray Hill St
15300 DET 48227 4270 C3
16100 DET 48235 4270 C3
18000 DET 48235 4198 B7
20500 DET 48075 4198 B5
Musch Rd
9500 GOTp 48116 4186 D2
Muse Rd
- DET 48207 4346 D5
Muskegon Ct
32400 WTLD 48186 4414 B4
Musket St
6300 DET 48209 4419 C2
Muskoka Rd
10 GSPF 48236 4276 E2
Myler St
24300 TYLR 48180 4498 E3
24300 TYLR 48180 4499 A3
Myrand St
14400 WRRN 48089 4203 A3
Myrna Ct
32900 LVNA 48154 4267 A3
Myrna Dr
32900 LVNA 48154 4267 A3
Myrna St
32400 LVNA 48154 4267 A3
33400 LVNA 48154 4266 E3
Myron Av
1400 LNPK 48146 4500 D6
4300 WYNE 48184 4414 A7
Myron Ct
1000 AARB 48103 4406 B7
Myron Dr
19800 LVNA 48152 4194 E6
Myron St
17200 LVNA 48152 4266 E1
18500 LVNA 48152 4194 E7
Myrtle Av
10 RVRG 48218 4418 E7
10 WasC 48103 4404 D5
3900 WIND N9C 4420 B6
Myrtle Ct
24200 NOVI 48375 4193 A1
Myrtle St
700 FRDL 48220 4200 A1
23000 DRBN 48128 4416 A1
33300 WYNE 48184 4414 A6
34000 WYNE 48184 4413 E6
Myrtlewood Dr
- YpTp 48197 4576 A5
Mystic Blvd
- NOVI 48375 4192 E3
Mystic Cir
15300 NvlT 48170 4265 D4
Mystic Ct
800 CNTN 48187 4411 C1
Mystic Dr
2400 PTFD 48103 4488 D3
Mystic Wy
9700 WasC 48167 4190 C6
Mystic Forest Dr
12700 PyTp 48170 4264 A7
23100 NOVI 48375 4192 E2
Mystic View Dr
10900 GOTp 48178 4187 D2

N

N Rd
- DRBN 48120 4418 A3
Nabozny Dr
9000 WasC 48160 4659 C4
Nadol Dr
18000 SFLD 48075 4198 A3
18600 SFLD 48075 4197 E3
Nadyne St
22800 BNTN 48183 4668 B4
Nagel St
11300 HMTK 48212 4273 B4
22500 WRRN 48089 4202 C2
Nagle St
7100 DET 48211 4274 A5
7100 DET 48213 4274 A5
Nall St
3800 DET 48210 4344 C5
Nancy Av
22200 SFLD 48034 4196 D3
Nancy Blvd
9900 WynC 48138 4756 A1
Nancy Dr
10 WasC 48103 4405 A5
Nancy St
2100 YpTp 48198 4577 C1
3800 DET 48212 4273 B1
15200 SOGT 48195 4584 D4
33400 LVNA 48150 4338 E2
33400 LVNA 48150 4339 A2
34400 WTLD 48186 4413 D3
Nankin Blvd
7200 WTLD 48185 4338 C5

Nankin Ct
7600 WTLD 48185 4338 C4
Nankin Hills Parking
- WTLD 48185 4339 A4
Nankin Lake Dr
- LVNA 48150 4338 E2
- LVNA 48185 4338 E2
- WTLD 48150 4338 E2
- WTLD 48185 4338 E2
Nankin Mills St
7800 WTLD 48185 4338 E4
Nantucket Dr
- FNHL 48336 4195 C3
12200 GOTp 48178 4188 B2
24300 NOVI 48374 4191 E1
24300 NOVI 48374 4192 A1
44500 CNTN 48187 4336 D7
Nantucket Rd
1500 PLYM 48170 4264 D6
Napier Ct
4200 SpTp 48170 4335 B4
Napier Rd
3000 CNTN 48187 4410 C2
3000 CNTN 48198 4410 C2
3000 SpTp 48198 4410 C2
3500 CNTN 48187 4335 C6
3500 CNTN 48198 4335 C6
3500 SpTp 48198 4335 C6
3700 CNTN 48170 4335 C6
3700 SpTp 48170 4335 C6
4700 SpTp 48187 4335 C6
5000 PyTp 48170 4335 C3
5000 PyTp 48187 4335 C3
5000 WasC 48170 4335 C3
5000 WasC 48187 4335 C3
6300 WasC 48170 4263 B6
6600 PyTp 48170 4263 B6
7300 NvlT 48167 4263 B3
7300 WasC 48167 4263 B3
9000 NvlT 48167 4191 B7
9000 WasC 48167 4191 B7
20800 LyTp 48167 4191 B4
20800 NOVI 48167 4191 B4
22400 LyTp 48178 4191 B3
22400 LyTp 48374 4191 B3
22400 NOVI 48374 4191 B3
Naples Ct
1200 AARB 48103 4489 A1
Naples Dr
12700 PyTp 48170 4263 E7
24500 NOVI 48374 4192 B1
Napoleon St
- DET 48207 4345 E4
400 DET 48201 4345 D5
Nardin Pk
9600 DET 48204 4343 E1
10200 DET 48204 4271 E7
Narise Dr
8200 WTLD 48185 4338 B3
Narrow Gauge Wy
3400 AARB 48105 4407 C5
3400 AATp 48105 4407 C5
Nash Av
500 YpTp 48198 4493 A5
Nash St
100 DRBN 48124 4416 B2
300 DRBN 48128 4416 B2
Nashville St
11000 DET 48205 4274 C2
12800 DET 48205 4202 E7
Nassau Ct
100 CNTN 48187 4411 E2
Natalie Ln
1500 AARB 48105 4407 D4
Natasha Ln
21700 LyTp 48167 4190 C4
21700 LyTp 48178 4190 C4
Nathaline
9100 RDFD 48239 4340 B1
12700 RDFD 48239 4268 B6
Nathan Ct
21500 LyTp 48178 4189 C4
Nathan Dr
26200 WynC 48138 4756 B1
S National St
4700 WIND N8Y 4347 A7
5000 WIND N8T 4422 B1
5000 WIND N8Y 4422 B1
Nature Ct
5600 PTFD 48108 4573 B2
Nature Cove Ct
2100 AARB 48104 4489 E2
Naturelle Dr
10700 GOTp 48178 4188 A4
Naumann St
3800 DET 48212 4201 B7
Navaho Av
24800 FTRK 48134 4754 A2
25000 FTRK 48134 4753 E1
Navahoe St
400 DET 48214 4347 C1
Navajo Ct
38600 RMLS 48174 4496 A3
Navarre Cir
2200 AARB 48104 4406 E7
Navarre Pl
1200 DET 48207 4345 E5
Navarre St
9300 DET 48214 4346 E1
13900 GBTR 48173 4755 C4
Navin Av
34000 LVNA 48152 4194 E6
Navin Ct
33300 LVNA 48152 4195 A6
34500 LVNA 48152 4194 D6
Navin St
30200 LVNA 48152 4195 C6
Navy St
8300 DET 48209 4418 E2
8300 DET 48209 4419 A2

Neal Blvd
300 WIND N9G 4504 D4
Neal St
8800 DET 48214 4274 D7
Nearbrook Ct
22200 FNHL 48335 4194 B3
Nebraska St
2600 DET 48210 4344 C2
8800 LVNA 48150 4339 B3
Neckel St
6400 DRBN 48126 4343 A4
7200 DRBN 48126 4342 E4
Nectar Dr
8100 CNTN 48187 4337 D4
Needham Rd
2100 AARB 48104 4490 A2
Neely St
13300 GBTR 48173 4755 D5
Neeson St
46000 NvlT 48167 4192 C7
Neff Av
- GSPT 48230 4276 A2
3800 DET 48224 4276 A2
3800 DET 48230 4276 A2
Neff Ln
500 GSPT 48230 4276 C5
Neff Rd
300 GSPT 48230 4276 C5
700 DET 48230 4276 B4
Negaunee
15800 RDFD 48239 4268 B3
18200 RDFD 48240 4268 B1
20400 RDFD 48240 4196 B5
Negaunee St
500 WYDT 48192 4585 B5
20700 SFLD 48034 4196 B3
Nehls Av
- WRRN 48021 4203 B2
14500 EPTE 48021 4203 B2
Neibel St
2300 HMTK 48212 4273 B3
Nellie Ln
38400 WTLD 48186 4413 A4
Nelson Av
13600 DET 48227 4270 E7
26600 BNTN 48174 4582 C6
Nelson Cir
- WTLD 48186 4414 C4
Nelson St
22000 WDHN 48183 4668 C4
Nepavine Dr
- NOVI 48374 4191 C1
Neptune Ct
19600 NvlT 48167 4193 C6
Nesquali
23400 HZLP 48030 4200 C1
Netherwood St
12800 SOGT 48195 4584 D1
Nett St
7300 DET 48213 4274 A4
Nevada
300 WynC 48111 4662 D3
Nevada Av
21700 EPTE 48021 4203 C2
Nevada St
800 YpTp 48198 4492 E6
8800 LVNA 48150 4339 B3
Nevada St E
- DET 48212 4200 D7
- DET 48234 4200 D7
10 DET 48203 4200 C7
2200 DET 48212 4201 A7
2200 DET 48234 4201 A7
6800 DET 48212 4202 A7
6800 DET 48234 4202 A7
Nevada St W
10 DET 48203 4200 C7
Neveux St
17100 DET 48224 4276 B4
Neville St
37000 RMLS 48174 4496 B7
New St
10 WYDT 48192 4501 C6
Newark St
2400 DET 48216 4345 A7
2700 DET 48216 4344 E7
Newaygo St
32500 WTLD 48186 4414 B4
Newbern St
13400 DET 48212 4273 B1
Newberry Blvd
27100 BNTN 48134 4667 C5
Newberry Dr
24900 NOVI 48375 4192 D1
Newberry Ln
- TYLR 48180 4582 E5
Newberry Pl
10 GSPF 48236 4276 D4
Newberry St
3700 WYNE 48184 4413 D6
5300 WYNE 48184 4496 D1
5600 DET 48209 4419 C1
5800 RMLS 48174 4496 D1
22800 STCS 48080 4204 E2
New Boston Wy
6900 CNTN 48187 4336 E6
Newburg Rd
3200 MonC 48134 4753 A6
E Newburg Rd
100 MonC 48117 4751 E6
300 MonC 48117 4752 A6
2400 MonC 48117 4753 A6
2400 MonC 48134 4753 A6
W Newburg Rd
100 MonC 48117 4751 D6
3000 MonC 48117 4750 E6
6900 MonC 48111 4748 E6
6900 MonC 48111 4749 C6
6900 MonC 48117 4748 E6
6900 MonC 48117 4749 C6

Newburgh Rd
8800 LVNA 48150 4338 B2
11700 LVNA 48150 4266 B6
13900 LVNA 48154 4266 B6
17200 LVNA 48152 4266 B2
18600 LVNA 48152 4194 A6
20500 LVNA 48167 4194 A6
20500 LVNA 48335 4194 A6
N Newburgh Rd
100 WTLD 48185 4413 B1
1600 WTLD 48185 4338 B6
S Newburgh Rd
100 WTLD 48185 4413 B4
100 WTLD 48186 4413 B4
2900 WYNE 48184 4413 B5
Newbury Ct
2400 AARB 48103 4488 E3
Newbury St
300 WIND N9A 4420 D2
Newburyport Dr
44400 CNTN 48187 4336 C4
New Castle Ct
47700 NvlT 48167 4264 A2
Newcastle Ct
23100 BNTN 48134 4667 C5
Newcastle Ln
10 HbgT 48189 4186 A5
Newcastle Rd
1500 GSPW 48236 4204 B7
1500 GSPW 48236 4276 D1
3000 AARB 48104 4490 B2
21200 HRWD 48225 4204 B7
Newcastle St
- TYLR 48180 4498 D2
- TYLR 48180 4499 A2
27400 RMLS 48174 4498 B2
31900 RMLS 48174 4497 B3
E Newell Cir
23500 FNHL 48336 4196 A1
W Newell Cir
23500 FNHL 48336 4195 E1
23500 FNHL 48336 4196 A1
New England Ct
46300 PyTp 48170 4336 C2
New England Ln
6100 CNTN 48187 4336 E6
Newgate Ct
7000 CNTN 48187 4336 B5
Newhall St
6300 DET 48211 4273 E5
New Hampshire Dr
17300 SFLD 48075 4198 A1
New Hampshire St
15600 SFLD 48075 4198 C1
New Haven Ct
900 NHVL 48167 4192 A5
New Haven Wy
8100 CNTN 48187 4335 E4
New Jersey Dr
18100 SFLD 48075 4198 A1
New Jersey St
16000 SFLD 48075 4198 B1
Newman Blvd
5700 LSal N9J 4503 B3
Newman Dr
1700 TNTN 48183 4669 B3
20200 BwTp 48183 4754 E3
Newman Rd
28400 HnTp 48164 4751 D3
Newman St
22200 DRBN 48124 4416 C3
New Meadow Dr
5400 YpTp 48197 4576 C2
New Mexico
200 WynC 48111 4662 E2
Newport Ct
9800 WasC 48167 4190 A6
40500 PyTp 48170 4337 D3
New Port Dr
18300 BwTp 48173 4755 A6
Newport Dr
40100 PyTp 48170 4337 C3
Newport Pl
700 AARB 48103 4405 E5
Newport Rd
800 AARB 48103 4405 E4
2000 AATp 48103 4405 E2
2800 WasC 48103 4405 D1
Newport St
- DET 48213 4275 B4
500 DET 48214 4347 D1
1000 DET 48214 4275 D6
11500 DET 48205 4275 A1
22900 SFLD 48075 4197 E3
Newport Creek Dr
1500 AATp 48103 4405 E2
New Providence Wy
6800 CNTN 48187 4336 E6
Newton Rd
46400 CNTN 48188 4411 B5
Newton St
24700 DRBN 48124 4415 E2
New Town St W
400 DET 48214 4347 D1
New York Av
400 LNPK 48146 4501 A5
400 TNTN 48183 4585 A7
1900 LNPK 48146 4500 C6
New York St
14500 RMLS 48174 4582 B3
17100 DET 48224 4276 A3
24000 DRBN 48124 4416 A5
24300 DRBN 48124 4415 E5
25400 DBHT 48125 4415 D5
25400 DBHT 48141 4415 D5
26600 INKR 48141 4415 B5
Niagara Av
3200 CNTN 48188 4411 A6
Niagara Ct
16900 NvlT 48167 4264 A2

INDEX 39

Niagara St — Detroit & Wayne County Street Index — E Oakridge St

STREET
Block City ZIP Map# Grid

Niagara St
400 WIND N9A 4421 A2
1600 WIND N8Y 4421 B1
3000 WYNE 48184 4414 B5
6600 RMLS 48174 4497 B2
Nicholas Ln
12000 PyTp 48170 4336 A1
Nichols Ct
2500 WTLD 48186 4413 B5
Nichols Dr
10 SALN 48176 4572 C6
2400 TNTN 48183 4669 C4
Nichols St
1800 WIND N9E 4503 C2
2200 TNTN 48183 4669 C3
9300 DET 48213 4274 C5
Nickels Arc
10 AARB 48104 4406 E6
Nicklaus Dr
- DRBN 48120 4417 C3
Nicolai Av
16200 EPTE 48021 4203 C1
Nicole St
10 Lksr N8N 4424 E1
Nicolet Pl
1300 DET 48207 4345 E5
Nielsen Ct
1000 AARB 48105 4406 C5
Nieman St
10 RVRG 48218 4501 E1
Niemi
- RMLS 48174 4581 D5
Nightingale St
100 DRBN 48124 4415 E1
100 DRBN 48128 4415 E1
1300 DRBN 48128 4340 E7
5600 DBHT 48128 4340 E7
7800 DBHT 48127 4340 D3
8600 DBHT 48239 4340 D3
Nilan Dr
23500 NOVI 48375 4193 D2
Ninde St
300 YPLT 48198 4492 A4
Nine Mack Dr
23000 STCS 48080 4204 D2
Nita St
2400 WRRN 48091 4201 A2
Niver Av
8400 ALPK 48101 4500 B4
Nixon Av
12000 RVVW 48192 4584 E7
12000 RVVW 48192 4585 A7
22000 BNTN 48192 4583 C7
Nixon Rd
2000 AARB 48105 4407 A2
2700 AATp 48105 4407 A2
3200 AATp 48105 4332 A6
Nob Hill Ct
300 AARB 48103 4406 B7
Nob Hill Pl
300 AARB 48103 4406 B7
Noble Rd
6500 WasC 48176 4572 A4
Noble St
- DET 48201 4345 B5
Noecker Wy
15500 SOGT 48195 4500 A7
Noel Dr
23400 SFLD 48075 4197 D2
Nola Cir
15500 LVNA 48154 4266 A4
Nola Ct
16500 LVNA 48154 4266 A3
Nola Dr
15900 LVNA 48154 4266 A3
Nola St
15000 LVNA 48154 4266 A4
18700 LVNA 48152 4194 A7
18700 LVNA 48152 4266 B1
Noling Woods Dr
12800 GOTp 48178 4188 C1
Nollar Rd
5000 WasC 48105 4331 D2
5700 WasC 48189 4259 D7
5700 WasC 48189 4331 D2
Nona St
22100 DRBN 48124 4416 C3
Nora Pl
3000 WIND N9E 4503 D2
Norbert Av
4100 WRRN 48091 4201 B1
Norbert St
11800 WIND N8P 4348 D7
Norborne
9500 RDFD 48239 4340 C1
14700 RDFD 48239 4268 C4
16500 RDFD 48240 4268 C2
20400 RDFD 48240 4196 C5
Norborne Av
100 DBHT 48127 4415 D2
100 DBHT 48141 4415 D2
8300 DBHT 48127 4340 C3
N Norborne Ct
6100 DBHT 48127 4340 C6
S Norborne Ct
6000 DBHT 48127 4340 C6
Norchester St
600 SLYN 48178 4189 C1
Norcrest Dr
22400 STCS 48080 4204 E3
22500 STCS 48080 4205 A3
23500 SFLD 48034 4196 E3
23500 SFLD 48034 4197 A3
Norcross St
5800 DET 48213 4275 A4
9100 DET 48213 4274 E3
Nordman Rd
3000 AARB 48108 4490 B4
Noreen Dr
28700 HnTp 48117 4751 C4

Noreen Dr
28700 HnTp 48164 4751 C4
Norene Av
37000 WTLD 48186 4413 B4
Norene Ct
7300 HbgT 48189 4186 B5
Norene Dr
7300 HbgT 48189 4186 B5
Norene St
34500 WTLD 48186 4413 D4
Norfolk
25000 RDFD 48240 4196 C5
27200 RDFD 48152 4196 A5
Norfolk N
13200 DET 48235 4198 E5
13200 DET 48235 4199 A5
Norfolk S
13200 DET 48235 4198 E5
13200 DET 48235 4199 A5
Norfolk Av
1700 SpTp 48198 4409 C7
1700 SpTp 48198 4492 C1
Norfolk Ct
22400 NOVI 48374 4192 B4
Norfolk Dr
4600 WasC 48167 4190 A6
Norfolk St
- DET 48221 4199 D5
- DET 48235 4199 A5
300 WIND N9E 4504 A1
2000 AARB 48103 4488 D1
2500 WIND N9E 4503 E2
13500 DET 48235 4198 D5
22900 DET 48219 4197 A5
24200 DET 48219 4196 E5
25400 DBHT 48125 4415 D5
25400 DBHT 48141 4415 D5
25800 INKR 48141 4415 D5
27400 LVNA 48152 4196 A5
29400 LVNA 48152 4195 D5
34400 LVNA 48152 4194 D5
Norfolk Pines Cres
2600 WIND N9E 4503 E2
Norfolk Towne St
10 SFLD 48075 4198 B2
Norham St
42300 NvlT 48167 4265 A2
N Norma Av
1800 WTLD 48185 4338 A7
S Norma Av
100 WTLD 48185 4413 A2
100 WTLD 48186 4413 A2
Norma Dr
- CNTN 48187 4412 B1
S Norma St
1300 WTLD 48186 4413 A4
N Normal St
10 YPLT 48197 4491 E4
S Normal St
10 YPLT 48197 4491 E4
Norman Av
8800 LVNA 48150 4338 A3
Norman Pl
1100 AARB 48103 4488 E1
Norman Rd
1400 WIND N8Y 4422 B2
1800 WIND N8T 4422 B3
Norman St
2300 DET 48209 4418 E1
2500 MVDL 48122 4418 A7
2700 MVDL 48122 4417 E7
9700 LVNA 48150 4338 A2
14200 LVNA 48154 4265 E4
Normandale St
15100 DRBN 48126 4342 D7
Normandy Av
22700 EPTE 48021 4203 E1
E Normandy Ct
48400 PyTp 48170 4336 A2
W Normandy Ct
48600 PyTp 48170 4335 E2
Normandy Dr
9500 PyTp 48170 4335 E2
10000 PyTp 48170 4336 A2
Normandy Rd
1400 AARB 48103 4488 E2
Normandy St
1300 LSal N9J 4503 A4
1800 LSal N9H 4503 C4
2800 LSal N9H 4504 A4
15300 DET 48238 4272 A3
16100 DET 48221 4272 A2
Normile St
7400 DRBN 48126 4343 C3
8000 DET 48204 4343 C3
Normonie Ct
10200 WasC 48176 4657 B5
Norris St
600 YPLT 48198 4492 A3
1400 WTLD 48186 4414 C3
34500 WYNE 48184 4413 E6
North Dr
100 WYDT 48192 4501 C6
41800 CNTN 48188 4412 B6
49400 PyTp 48170 4263 D6
North St
10 Amhg N9V 4757 B2
10 DET 48203 4272 A1
10 HDPK 48203 4272 A1
10 YPLT 48198 4492 A4
Northampton Ct
3100 DRBN 48124 4417 A5
Northampton Dr
8800 PyTp 48170 4336 A2
Northampton St
- DET 48229 4418 B6
38400 WTLD 48186 4413 A4
39200 WTLD 48186 4412 E3
Northboro Rd
9300 GOTp 48116 4187 C1

Northbrook Ct
1600 CNTN 48188 4412 E4
Northbrook Dr
1300 AARB 48103 4488 E3
1400 AARB 48103 4489 A3
Northbrook Pl
2900 AARB 48103 4489 A4
Northend Av
- FRDL 48220 4199 C3
8500 OKPK 48237 4199 B3
8500 ROTp 48220 4199 C3
8900 OKPK 48220 4199 C3
8900 ROTp 48237 4199 A3
13200 OKPK 48237 4198 E3
Northern Av
8800 PyTp 48170 4336 E3
8800 PyTp 48187 4336 E3
Northern Dr
- YpTp 48198 4493 B4
Northfarm Dr
38500 FNHL 48167 4193 E4
Northfield Av
37500 LVNA 48150 4338 A3
38400 LVNA 48150 4337 E3
39400 PyTp 48170 4337 E3
Northfield Blvd
10000 OKPK 48237 4199 A1
15000 OKPK 48237 4198 C1
Northfield Rd
2200 TNTN 48183 4669 C4
Northfield St
5800 DET 48210 4344 A3
7400 DET 48204 4344 A3
8400 DET 48204 4343 E2
Northfield Wy
12400 Tcmh N8N 4424 A2
E Northfield Church Rd
100 WasC 48105 4331 C2
100 WasC 48189 4331 C2
2000 WasC 48105 4332 B2
2000 WasC 48189 4332 B2
W Northfield Church Rd
10 WasC 48105 4331 A2
600 WasC 48105 4330 D2
3500 WasC 48130 4330 D2
Northfiled Church Rd
- WasC 48105 4331 B3
Northgate Ct
47200 CNTN 48188 4411 B5
North Gate Dr
4700 WasC 48105 4329 E4
Northgate Dr
32900 LVNA 48152 4267 A1
35900 LVNA 48152 4266 C1
47100 CNTN 48188 4411 B5
Northgate St
1600 WTLD 48186 4414 B4
Northhampton Ct
48800 CNTN 48187 4335 E5
North Hills Ct
- NOVI 48167 4192 D3
Northland Av
3200 INKR 48141 4414 E6
4500 INKR 48186 4414 E6
Northland Dr
- OKPK 48237 4198 B4
- SFLD 48237 4198 B4
15500 SFLD 48075 4198 B4
34400 LVNA 48152 4194 D6
Northland St
37400 LVNA 48152 4194 A7
Northland Park Ct
17300 SFLD 48075 4198 B4
Northlawn Av
2500 YpTp 48197 4491 A3
Northlawn St
8800 DET 48204 4343 C1
10000 DET 48204 4271 C7
12600 DET 48238 4271 C6
17100 DET 48221 4271 C1
19400 DET 48221 4199 C5
Northline Rd
7400 WasC 48105 4260 E5
12800 SOGT 48195 4584 C1
18900 SOGT 48195 4583 C1
20000 TYLR 48180 4583 C1
20000 TYLR 48195 4583 C1
24500 TYLR 48180 4582 C2
26600 TYLR 48174 4582 C2
27400 RMLS 48174 4582 C2
28700 RMLS 48174 4581 D2
29900 RMLS 48242 4581 D2
35400 RMLS 48174 4580 D2
38600 RMLS 48174 4580 B1
39000 RMLS 48174 4495 E7
Northline Commerce Dr
25800 TYLR 48180 4582 D2
Northmore St
26800 DBHT 48127 4415 B1
Northpark St
500 DET 48214 4347 D2
Northpointe Ct
8100 CNTN 48187 4336 B4
Northpointe Dr
47000 CNTN 48187 4336 B4
Northridge Ct
2500 PTFD 48108 4488 E6
Northridge Dr
19700 NvlT 48167 4193 B6
Northrop St
17200 DET 48219 4269 B1
19900 DET 48219 4197 B5
Northshore Blvd
10 RKWD 48173 4840 C1
Northshore Ct
10 RKWD 48173 4840 C1
Northshore Dr
100 STCS 48080 4204 E1
Northside Av
600 AARB 48105 4406 C3

North Sideroad
1000 Amhg N9V 4671 D1
North Star
10800 HbgT 48189 4186 A4
E North Territorial Rd
10 WasC 48105 4259 B6
10 WasC 48189 4259 B6
2100 WasC 48189 4260 A7
W North Territorial Rd
3600 WasC 48105 4258 A6
3600 WasC 48130 4258 A6
3600 WasC 48189 4258 A6
Northumberland St
47000 NOVI 48374 4192 B2
Northview
- PyTp 48170 4335 C2
Northview Rd
45800 NvlT 48167 4192 C6
Northville Blvd
- WasC 48167 4190 A6
Northville Rd
- NHVL 48167 4192 E7
- NvlT 48167 4192 E7
14100 PLYM 48170 4265 A4
14100 PyTp 48170 4265 A4
15800 NvlT 48167 4265 A4
15800 NvlT 48170 4265 A4
18400 NvlT 48167 4264 E1
E Northville Tr
17200 NvlT 48167 4265 C1
N Northville Tr
40400 NvlT 48167 4265 C1
W Northville Tr
17900 NvlT 48167 4265 C1
Northville Forest Dr
15300 NvlT 48170 4265 C4
Northville Place Dr
- NvlT 48167 4192 E5
- NvlT 48375 4193 A5
20400 NvlT 48167 4193 A5
Northway Av
- ALPK 48101 4500 A6
1400 WIND N9B 4420 C5
2500 WIND N9B 4420 D6
3700 WIND N9E 4503 E3
3800 WIND N9G 4503 E3
3900 WIND N9G 4504 A3
10000 ALPK 48101 4499 D5
Northway Ct
10000 ALPK 48101 4499 D5
Northway St
1300 FRDL 48220 4199 D4
4300 LSal N9H 4504 A4
Northwestern Hwy
- DET 48075 4198 B3
- DET 48235 4198 B3
23000 SFLD 48075 4197 E1
23000 SFLD 48075 4198 A2
Northwestern St
2600 DET 48206 4344 C2
3700 DET 48204 4344 C2
Northwind Ct
39400 NvlT 48167 4193 D7
Northwind Dr
41000 CNTN 48188 4412 C3
Northwood Ct
9000 PyTp 48170 4335 E3
Northwood Dr
- DRBN 48126 4342 A7
- DRBN 48126 4417 A1
1000 INKR 48141 4415 B3
Northwood St
500 WIND N9E 4421 A6
900 AARB 48103 4405 E7
1200 WIND N9B 4421 A6
1300 WIND N9E 4420 D7
2500 WIND N9B 4420 D7
Northwood 40
1100 AARB 48105 4407 A3
Northwood 41
1400 AARB 48105 4407 A3
Northwood 43
- AARB 48105 4407 A3
Northwood 44
- AARB 48105 4407 A3
Northwood 45
- AARB 48105 4407 A3
Northwood 46
- AARB 48105 4407 A3
Northwood 47
- AARB 48105 4407 A3
Northwood Lakes Dr
4200 WIND N9G 4504 E4
Northwoods Blvd
2400 CNTN 48188 4411 C5
Northwoods Ct
2000 CNTN 48188 4411 B5
Norton Av
16400 EPTE 48021 4203 D1
18200 EPTE 48021 4204 A1
Norton Ct
19900 GSPW 48236 4204 C6
46000 NvlT 48167 4192 C7
47500 PyTp 48170 4336 A3
Norvell Ct
8000 DET 48214 4274 C7
Norwalk St
1900 HMTK 48212 4273 B5
5900 DET 48211 4273 E4
5900 DET 48212 4273 E4
Norway Rd
1800 AARB 48104 4489 E1
Norway St
- DET 48229 4418 C5
Norwich Rd
10 PTRG 48069 4199 C1
18200 LVNA 48152 4266 E1
18500 LVNA 48152 4194 E7
Norwich St
8800 LVNA 48150 4338 E3

Norwich St
15300 LVNA 48154 4266 E3
N Norwood
20100 SFLD 48075 4197 D1
S Norwood
20100 SFLD 48075 4197 D1
W Norwood
24100 SFLD 48075 4197 D1
Norwood Av
2900 TNTN 48183 4669 C5
6300 ALPK 48101 4500 A2
Norwood Ct
2300 TNTN 48183 4669 C4
42200 NvlT 48167 4193 C5
Norwood Dr
- HRWD 48236 4204 B5
1700 GSPW 48236 4204 B5
6400 CNTN 48187 4336 D6
20800 HRWD 48225 4204 B5
Norwood Rd
2400 TNTN 48183 4669 C4
Norwood St
2900 AARB 48104 4490 B3
17800 DET 48212 4201 B7
19100 DET 48234 4201 B5
23000 OKPK 48237 4199 B2
Nothdurft Blvd
- DET 48236 4276 B1
Notre Dame St
300 GSPT 48230 4276 B4
800 DET 48230 4276 B4
20700 DRBN 48124 4416 C5
24300 DRBN 48124 4415 E5
25400 DBHT 48125 4415 E5
25400 DBHT 48141 4415 C5
25800 INKR 48141 4415 C5
Nottingham Ct
5500 DRBN 48126 4342 A7
8600 SpTp 48198 4492 C1
21800 WDHN 48183 4668 C3
23600 SFLD 48034 4197 B2
Nottingham Dr
- TYLR 48180 4582 D5
1100 WasC 48167 4190 A7
8600 SpTp 48198 4492 C1
24400 NOVI 48374 4191 E1
38400 RMLS 48174 4496 A4
39000 RMLS 48174 4495 E4
Nottingham Ln
22500 SFLD 48034 4197 B2
Nottingham Rd
800 GPPK 48230 4276 A7
1000 GPPK 48230 4275 E5
2400 AARB 48104 4490 A2
10400 DET 48224 4275 D1
11300 DET 48224 4203 D7
Nottingham St
300 WIND N9E 4421 B7
300 WIND N9E 4504 B1
39200 WTLD 48186 4412 E3
Nottinghill Ln
48100 CNTN 48188 4411 A7
Nottington Ct
1300 WasC 48103 4488 B1
Nottingwood Ct
42200 NvlT 48170 4265 B4
Nova St
800 WIND N9G 4504 E3
900 WIND N9G 4505 A3
Novara St
14400 DET 48205 4203 A5
16400 DET 48225 4203 C5
Novi Rd
800 NHVL 48167 4192 E4
1000 NOVI 48167 4192 E4
1000 NOVI 48375 4192 E4
Novi St
700 NHVL 48167 4192 E5
Nowak St
5900 DET 48210 4344 A6
Nowland Ct
1600 CNTN 48188 4411 E4
Nowland Dr
43400 CNTN 48188 4411 E4
Nowlin Ct
10 DRBN 48124 4416 E5
Nowlin St
1000 DRBN 48124 4416 B3
Nuernberg St
8000 DET 48234 4274 A1
Nummer Av
21700 WRRN 48089 4203 A2
Nummer St
20700 WRRN 48089 4203 A3
Nura Ct
200 YpTp 48197 4491 B6
Nutmeg Dr
4500 PTFD 48197 4574 E1
Nye Ct
30400 LVNA 48154 4267 C4
W Nye Ct
30800 LVNA 48154 4267 C4
Nyman Av
3800 WYNE 48184 4412 E6
5600 WYNE 48184 4495 E1

O

Oak
- FNHL 48034 4196 B4
- FNHL 48336 4196 B4
E Oak
- CNTN 48187 4337 E6
W Oak
- CNTN 48187 4337 E6
Oak Av
100 WIND N9A 4420 D2
1200 WIND N8X 4420 D3
15800 EPTE 48021 4203 C2
18400 EPTE 48021 4204 A2

Oak Blvd
10 VNBN 48111 4577 E6
10 VNBN 48111 4578 A6
8100 BrTp 48179 4841 A4
Oak Ct
- CNTN 48188 4411 C6
400 Amhg N9V 4757 C4
22600 HZLP 48030 4200 E2
25000 BNTN 48134 4667 E3
Oak Dr
3200 PTFD 48197 4491 A4
3300 SpTp 48105 4408 B1
15300 LVNA 48154 4268 A3
17100 DET 48221 4271 E1
18600 DET 48221 4199 D6
49400 PyTp 48170 4263 D6
N Oak Dr
10300 ROTp 48220 4199 B3
Oak Ln
11100 VNBN 48111 4495 A7
41900 PyTp 48170 4265 B5
Oak Rd
9100 AGST 48191 4748 A3
Oak St
10 RVRG 48218 4418 E7
10 WYDT 48192 4585 D3
10 YPLT 48198 4492 A3
100 RVRG 48218 4501 E1
100 RVRG 48218 4502 A1
1100 YpTp 48198 4492 D3
2200 WYDT 48192 4584 E3
2300 WYDT 48195 4584 E3
2900 WRRN 48091 4201 B4
9300 TYLR 48180 4499 B5
21100 WDHN 48183 4668 C4
24100 DRBN 48128 4341 A7
24400 DRBN 48128 4340 E7
Oak Brook Ct
300 SALN 48176 4657 D1
Oakbrook Ct
6300 YpTp 48197 4575 E4
43200 CNTN 48187 4337 A4
Oakbrook Dr
100 AARB 48103 4489 B3
6300 YpTp 48197 4575 E3
W Oakbrook Dr
10 WasC 48103 4489 A4
200 AARB 48103 4489 A4
Oakbrook Rd
43500 CNTN 48187 4337 A4
43700 CNTN 48187 4336 E4
Oakbrook St
16200 RMLS 48174 4581 D5
Oakbrooke Dr
200 SLYN 48178 4189 C2
Oakcleft St
2700 AATp 48103 4405 D1
Oakcliff Dr
9100 PyTp 48170 4337 D2
Oak Creek Dr
800 SLYN 48178 4189 C4
Oak Crest Ct
13300 OKPK 48237 4198 E2
Oakcrest Dr
- YpTp 48197 4576 D2
27100 BwTp 48183 4754 E2
Oak Crest St
23000 OKPK 48237 4198 E2
23000 OKPK 48237 4199 A2
Oakdale Blvd
10 PTRG 48069 4199 C1
Oakdale Ct
28400 RMLS 48174 4582 A4
Oakdale Dr
2400 PTFD 48108 4490 E3
Oakdale Rd
700 BNHL 48105 4330 E7
700 BNHL 48105 4331 A7
Oakdale St
1900 DET 48209 4418 E2
12700 SOGT 48195 4500 D7
35200 LVNA 48154 4266 C3
Oakengates Dr
4200 PTFD 48197 4574 E2
Oakfield Ct
500 Tcmh N8N 4424 B2
Oakfield Dr
1500 PTFD 48108 4489 A5
Oakfield St
14900 DET 48227 4270 B4
18000 DET 48235 4270 B1
19900 DET 48235 4198 B5
Oak Forest Ct
16200 NvlT 48167 4264 C3
Oak Forest Dr
44400 NvlT 48167 4264 D3
Oak Glen Dr
23000 SFLD 48034 4196 C2
Oak Grove Av
1700 HZLP 48030 4200 E1
Oak Grove St
17200 BNTN 48174 4583 A6
Oakham Ct
2500 CNTN 48188 4411 B5
Oak Hill Ct
5100 PTFD 48108 4572 E1
17300 NvlT 48167 4264 D1
Oakhill Ct
15600 LVNA 48154 4266 D3
29300 GBTR 48173 4755 A4
Oak Hill Dr
17300 NvlT 48167 4264 D1
Oakhill Dr
29000 GBTR 48173 4755 A4
Oak Hills Dr
2500 AATp 48103 4405 E2
Oak Hollow Dr
3200 WasC 48103 4330 B6
Oakhurst Dr
6100 YpTp 48197 4575 E3

Oakhurst Dr
6100 YpTp 48197 4576 A3
Oak Knoll Dr
6000 YpTp 48197 4575 D4
Oak Knoll Rd
7900 WasC 48167 4262 A3
Oakland Av
- NvlT 48167 4193 B7
- NvlT 48167 4265 B1
700 AARB 48104 4406 C7
33200 FMTN 48335 4194 E1
33200 FMTN 48336 4194 E1
33200 FMTN 48336 4195 A1
Oakland Ct
1400 DBHT 48125 4415 D3
13900 PyTp 48170 4263 E6
45400 CNTN 48188 4411 C3
Oakland Dr
25400 DBHT 48125 4415 D4
25600 DBHT 48141 4415 D4
26200 INKR 48141 4415 C4
42200 CNTN 48188 4412 B3
Oakland St
600 NHVL 48167 4192 E5
6200 DET 48202 4273 B7
11300 DET 48211 4273 A5
13700 HDPK 48203 4272 D2
17100 DET 48203 4272 D1
17700 DET 48203 4200 D7
33400 FMTN 48335 4194 E1
Oakland Hills Dr
7400 YpTp 48197 4576 A6
Oakland Park Blvd
- HDPK 48203 4272 E4
- HDPK 48203 4273 A4
10 PTRG 48069 4199 D1
Oakland Park Ct
- DET 48203 4273 A4
- DET 48212 4273 A4
- HDPK 48203 4273 A4
- HDPK 48212 4273 A4
Oaklane St
22400 WRRN 48089 4202 E2
Oaklawn Blvd
10 YpTp 48198 4492 C5
Oaklawn St
11000 SOGT 48195 4500 A6
Oakleaf Cir
18200 BNTN 48174 4582 C7
Oak Leaf Ct
18800 NvlT 48167 4192 B7
Oakleaf Ct
7000 CNTN 48187 4336 B6
Oak Leaf Ln
18700 NvlT 48167 4264 B1
19000 NvlT 48167 4192 B7
Oakleigh
15300 SOGT 48195 4500 B7
Oakleigh Av
23100 WDHN 48183 4668 B5
Oakleigh Pl
1800 WasC 48103 4404 E2
Oakleigh St
8800 PyTp 48170 4336 C3
Oakley Ct
26100 BNTN 48174 4582 D6
Oakley St
27800 LVNA 48154 4268 A5
29400 LVNA 48154 4267 D4
Oakman Blvd
10 HDPK 48203 4272 A4
10 HDPK 48238 4272 A4
800 DET 48238 4272 A4
1900 DET 48238 4271 E5
3400 DET 48204 4271 D6
4300 DET 48204 4343 C2
5600 DRBN 48126 4343 A5
5900 DET 48228 4343 A3
6700 DET 48126 4343 A3
Oakman Ct
2600 DET 48238 4272 A4
E Oak Manor Ct
46400 CNTN 48187 4336 B6
W Oak Manor Ct
46500 CNTN 48187 4336 B6
Oakmont Ct
1700 PTFD 48108 4489 A7
16600 NvlT 48167 4265 D2
Oakmont Dr
7200 CNTN 48187 4336 A5
Oakmore Ct
3600 WasC 48103 4330 B7
3600 WasC 48105 4330 B7
Oak Park Blvd
8100 OKPK 48069 4199 B1
8100 OKPK 48220 4199 B1
8200 OKPK 48237 4199 A1
14400 OKPK 48237 4198 D2
Oak Park Dr
3300 WasC 48176 4657 B4
Oakpark Dr
300 Tcmh N8N 4348 E7
Oak Pointe Cir
15400 NvlT 48170 4265 B4
Oak Pointe Ln
9500 WasC 48167 4190 B6
Oak Pointe St
6000 WTLD 48185 4339 A7
Oakridge Cir
- GOTp 48178 4188 B4
Oakridge Dr
7000 YpTp 48197 4575 E3
7200 YpTp 48197 4576 A3
23400 DBHT 48127 4341 A6
Oakridge St
6400 LSal N9J 4502 E5
E Oakridge St
100 FRDL 48220 4199 E1
800 FRDL 48220 4200 A1

STREET
Block City ZIP Map# Grid

W Oakridge St
700 FRDL 48069 4199 C1
700 FRDL 48220 4199 C1
Oak Ridge Tr
- WTLD 48185 4338 D3
Oak River Dr
7700 WynC 48138 4670 D4
Oak Tree
40100 NOVI 48375 4193 C2
Oak Tree Ct
4900 PTFD 48108 4572 E1
7200 CNTN 48187 4336 C5
Oak Tree Dr
20800 LyTp 48178 4189 D6
Oak Tree Ln
16100 RMLS 48174 4582 A5
Oak Valley Dr
1100 PTFD 48108 4489 A5
1300 PTFD 48108 4488 E4
2100 PTFD 48103 4488 D3
2100 WasC 48103 4488 D3
Oak View Ct
50000 PyTp 48170 4335 D2
Oakview Ct
19700 GBTR 48173 4755 A4
Oak View Dr
22600 TYLR 48180 4583 B1
Oakview Dr
1600 CNTN 48187 4411 C1
1700 PTFD 48108 4572 E3
1700 PTFD 48108 4573 A2
1900 CNTN 48187 4336 E7
Oakview St
8800 PyTp 48170 4336 E2
8800 PyTp 48187 4336 E2
30100 LVNA 48154 4267 D5
37400 WTLD 48185 4413 B1
Oakville Waltz Rd
- MonC 48164 4751 C4
10 HnTp 48117 4751 C4
10 HnTp 48164 4751 C4
10 MonC 48117 4751 C4
3000 MonC 48117 4750 E5
3000 MonC 48164 4750 E5
5200 MonC 48117 4749 E5
5200 MonC 48164 4749 E5
6000 MonC 48111 4749 E5
7700 MonC 48111 4748 A6
8800 AGST 48191 4748 A6
8800 MonC 48191 4748 A6
Oakway Dr
- DET 48207 4347 A4
Oakwest Dr
38200 WTLD 48185 4338 A4
Oakwood
100 WasC 48176 4657 A2
Oakwood Av
22700 EPTE 48021 4203 B1
23000 EPTE 48089 4203 B1
28200 HnTp 48134 4753 A4
Oakwood Blvd
- ALPK 48122 4417 D6
800 DRBN 48124 4416 D3
2300 MVDL 48122 4418 A6
3200 MVDL 48122 4417 D6
16500 ALPK 48101 4417 D6
17600 DRBN 48101 4417 C5
17600 DRBN 48124 4417 C5
S Oakwood Blvd
100 DET 48229 4418 C5
1300 DET 48122 4418 C5
Oakwood Ct
2000 TNTN 48183 4669 C3
13900 PyTp 48170 4264 B5
16100 NvlT 48167 4265 C3
Oakwood Dr
1700 TNTN 48183 4669 C3
15000 RMLS 48174 4580 C4
15200 OKPK 48237 4198 C2
22000 BNTN 48192 4668 C1
40400 NOVI 48375 4193 C3
Oakwood Ln
35400 WTLD 48186 4413 C3
Oakwood St
- YPLT 48198 4491 D3
500 YPLT 48197 4491 D3
3000 AARB 48104 4490 B3
22000 WDHN 48183 4668 C3
28400 INKR 48141 4414 E3
28400 INKR 48141 4415 A3
Oakwood Meadows Dr
37700 WTLD 48185 4338 A4
Observatory St
100 AARB 48104 4406 D6
Ocalla Dr
11000 WRRN 48089 4202 B1
Oceana Av
14500 ALPK 48101 4500 B3
Oceana Ct
32400 WTLD 48186 4414 B4
Oceana St
2200 LNPK 48101 4500 C4
2200 LNPK 48146 4500 C4
O'Connor Av
500 LNPK 48146 4501 A3
1700 LNPK 48146 4500 D2
14500 ALPK 48101 4500 C1
17000 ALPK 48101 4417 A7
O'Connor St
21500 STCS 48080 4204 C2
Odessa Dr
3200 Tcmh N8N 4423 E6
Odette Rd
25200 HnTp 48134 4667 A7
25200 HnTp 48134 4753 A1
O'Donnell Dr
8000 WynC 48138 4670 D2
Odyssey
17000 WynC 48111 4579 C7
Ogden
15400 RDFD 48239 4268 D3
Ogden St
4800 DET 48210 4343 D6
Ogemaw St
32300 WTLD 48186 4414 D5
O'Henry Ct
28600 INKR 48141 4414 E2
28600 INKR 48141 4415 A2
Ohio
500 WynC 48111 4662 D2
Ohio Av
10 YpTp 48198 4492 E4
Ohio St
9500 DET 48204 4343 C1
11700 DET 48204 4271 C6
15400 DET 48238 4271 C3
17100 DET 48221 4271 C1
20400 DET 48221 4199 C4
32600 LVNA 48150 4339 A2
Ojibway Pkwy
- WIND N9C 4419 E6
4700 WIND N9C 4420 A7
4900 WIND N9C 4502 E3
4900 WIND N9J 4419 E6
4900 WIND N9J 4502 E3
Ojibway Pkwy P-18
4700 WIND N9C 4419 E7
4700 WIND N9C 4420 A7
4900 WIND N9C 4502 E3
4900 WIND N9J 4419 E7
4900 WIND N9J 4502 E3
Ojibway St
1200 WIND N9B 4420 E6
Oklahoma St
12000 HMTK 48212 4273 A3
Ola St
14500 RMLS 48174 4582 B3
Olcott Av
400 LSal N9J 4502 D5
Old Bedford Ct
16300 NvlT 48167 4265 B3
Old Bedford Rd
16100 NvlT 48167 4265 B2
Old Boston Ct
2500 AARB 48104 4490 B3
Old Bridge Ct
1500 CNTN 48188 4412 B4
19300 NvlT 48167 4193 A7
Old Bridge Rd
41800 CNTN 48188 4412 B4
Oldbrook Ln
10 GSPF 48236 4276 E3
Old Canton Center Rd
4000 CNTN 48188 4411 D7
Oldcastle Rd
5200 Tcmh N0R 4505 C6
Old Church Ct
5700 WasC 48105 4332 B2
Old Colony Rd
20000 DBHT 48228 4341 E6
20200 DBHT 48127 4341 D6
Old Colony Track
- Amhg N9V 4671 C4
Old Creek Ct
400 SALN 48176 4657 D1
Old Creek Dr
200 SALN 48176 4572 D7
200 SALN 48176 4657 D1
Old Denton Rd
49100 VNBN 48111 4577 E1
Old Depot Ct
25100 WynC 48138 4670 D7
Old Depot Dr
24900 WynC 48138 4670 D7
Old Earhart Rd
1500 AATp 48105 4407 D3
Olden Rd
1100 AARB 48103 4406 A4
Olde Orchard St
24200 NOVI 48375 4193 D1
Old Forge Ct
22100 WDHN 48183 4668 C5
Old Front Rd
- Amhg N9V 4757 B5
2000 LSal N9J 4502 C6
Old Goddard Rd
11000 ALPK 48101 4500 C6
11000 SOGT 48101 4500 C6
11000 SOGT 48195 4500 C6
Old Haggerty Rd
- CNTN 48187 4337 C3
Oldham St
11000 TYLR 48180 4498 D7
14600 TYLR 48180 4582 D4
Old Hamburg Rd
9500 HbgT 48189 4186 B5
Old Hickory Pl
3200 AARB 48104 4490 B3
Old Homestead Dr
18500 HRWD 48225 4203 D5
19600 HRWD 48225 4204 A6
Old Huron River Dr
35400 HnTp 48164 4665 D3
Old Kent Rd N
24000 WRRN 48091 4201 A1
Old Kent Rd S
2300 WRRN 48091 4201 A1
Old Lilley Rd
- CNTN 48187 4337 B3
Old Macon Rd
- WasC 48176 4657 C3
Old Michigan Av
41000 CNTN 48188 4412 C6
50600 VNBN 48111 4493 C2
51100 VNBN 48198 4493 C2
Old Mill Ct
22400 WDHN 48183 4668 C4
Old Mill Pl
12600 DET 48238 4271 E6
Old Novi Rd
700 NHVL 48167 4192 E5
700 NOVI 48167 4192 E5
700 NvlT 48167 4192 E5
Old Oak Ct
3400 WasC 48176 4572 B5
4300 SpTp 48170 4334 C4
20800 SFLD 48075 4197 C2
Old Oak Dr
8500 SpTp 48170 4334 C4
Old Orchard Ct
1900 AARB 48103 4405 E6
Old Orchard Dr
11400 PyTp 48170 4336 A1
Old Pear Tree Ct
1900 AARB 48103 4488 D3
Old Phoenix Rd
- NvlT 48167 4264 E4
- NvlT 48170 4264 E4
- NvlT 48170 4265 A4
- PyTp 48167 4264 E4
- PyTp 48170 4264 E4
- PyTp 48170 4265 A4
Old Pond Cir
42100 PyTp 48170 4265 B4
Old Pond Ln
500 SLYN 48178 4189 B1
Old Rawsonville Rd
1700 VNBN 48111 4493 C7
Olds St
500 YpTp 48198 4493 A5
Old Salem St
1500 PLYM 48170 4264 D7
Old School Ln
45300 CNTN 48188 4411 D3
Old State Rd
6500 PTFD 48176 4573 D4
N Old Territorial Rd
9600 WasC 48170 4334 E1
9600 WasC 48170 4335 A1
Old Town Ct
14700 RVVW 48192 4584 C7
Old Town Dr
14800 RVVW 48192 4584 C6
Oldtown St
5500 DET 48224 4276 A2
9100 DET 48224 4275 E1
Old West Av
4200 WIND N9G 4505 A4
Oleander Dr
20200 BwTp 48183 4754 E2
Olga St
11700 DET 48213 4274 E4
11900 DET 48213 4275 A4
Olive Av
2000 LNPK 48146 4500 E1
2200 LNPK 48101 4500 E1
Olive Rd
1300 WIND N8Y 4422 B2
1800 WIND N8T 4422 B2
Olive St
200 YPLT 48197 4492 A3
300 YPLT 48197 4491 E3
11100 RMLS 48174 4496 C7
11200 RMLS 48174 4580 C1
Oliver Ct
- ECRS 48229 4501 C2
23500 SFLD 48034 4196 E1
23500 SFLD 48034 4197 A1
Oliver Dr
12000 Tcmh N8N 4348 E7
Oliver St
3800 HMTK 48211 4273 D5
3900 DET 48211 4273 D5
7500 WasC 48189 4259 A4
Olivet St
8500 DET 48209 4419 A3
9000 DET 48209 4418 E4
Olivia Av
900 AARB 48104 4406 D7
1100 AARB 48104 4489 D1
Olmstead Rd
29100 FTRK 48134 4754 C5
31000 RKWD 48134 4754 B6
31000 RKWD 48173 4754 B6
Olmstead St
21500 DRBN 48124 4416 C4
Olson St
28800 LVNA 48150 4339 E2
Olympia
17100 RDFD 48240 4268 D1
20000 RDFD 48240 4196 D5
Olympia Dr
2200 Tcmh N0R 4505 B5
Olympia St
8000 DET 48213 4274 A4
Omaha St
- DET 48229 4501 C1
12700 DET 48229 4418 B7
Omaha Beach Dr
- DRBN 48124 4416 A3
Omar Av
9900 DRBN 48120 4418 C2
O'Mara Ct
19900 GSPW 48236 4204 E7
Omega Dr
10700 GOTp 48178 4188 D4
Omenwood Av
29400 FNHL 48336 4195 D1
Omira St
1800 LSal N9H 4503 C5
17100 DET 48203 4272 D1
18400 DET 48203 4200 D6
Omlesaad Dr
- AARB 48105 4331 E7
2900 AARB 48105 4406 E1
Onandaga Av
500 YpTp 48198 4492 E5
Onaway Ct
41600 NOVI 48167 4193 B5
Onaway Dr
41700 NOVI 48167 4193 B5
Onaway Pl
400 AARB 48104 4407 A7
Oneida Blvd
24500 OKPK 48237 4199 B1
Oneida Ct
1700 WIND N8Y 4421 C2
Oneida Pl
1800 AARB 48104 4489 E2
Oneida St
23000 OKPK 48237 4199 B1
O'Neil St
5000 Tcmh N0R 4505 C5
Ongaro Ct
4100 WIND N9G 4504 E3
Onondaga St
500 AARB 48104 4406 E7
Ontaga Ct
22100 FNHL 48336 4196 A3
Ontaga St
21800 FNHL 48336 4196 A3
Ontario St
1500 WIND N8X 4421 C2
1500 WIND N9A 4421 C2
1600 WIND N8Y 4421 C1
3700 WIND N8Y 4346 E7
4700 WIND N8Y 4347 A7
6900 WIND N8S 4347 C6
17100 DET 48224 4276 A3
Ontonagon St
32200 WTLD 48186 4414 D5
Onyx Cir
400 WasC 48189 4186 D7
Opal Dr
10 DRBN 48126 4417 D1
8400 WTLD 48185 4338 B3
Opal Ln
200 WasC 48189 4186 E7
Opal St
4800 DET 48236 4276 B2
4900 DET 48224 4276 B2
Open Hearth Rd
- DRBN 48120 4418 B4
Oporto Av
17100 LVNA 48152 4267 D2
19800 LVNA 48152 4195 D6
Oporto St
9800 LVNA 48150 4339 D1
16900 LVNA 48152 4267 D2
16900 LVNA 48154 4267 D2
Oppollo St
40700 NvlT 48167 4193 C7
Ora St
2200 WIND N9G 4504 A3
Orange St
100 WTLD 48186 4414 D7
900 WYDT 48192 4585 B3
12700 SOGT 48195 4584 E3
Orange Blossom Ln
200 WasC 48103 4404 A4
Orange Blossom Ln
10 WasC 48103 4488 B3
Orangelawn
22400 DET 48239 4341 B1
23200 RDFD 48239 4341 B1
25400 RDFD 48239 4340 D1
27300 RDFD 48150 4340 B1
Orangelawn Av
40400 PyTp 48170 4337 C2
Orangelawn St
- DET 48227 4343 A1
10000 DET 48204 4343 B1
14400 DET 48227 4342 D1
18700 DET 48228 4342 A1
20800 DET 48228 4341 C1
20800 DET 48239 4341 C1
27400 LVNA 48150 4340 A1
29000 LVNA 48150 4339 E1
35100 LVNA 48150 4338 C2
38800 LVNA 48150 4337 E2
Orchard
- RMLS 48174 4582 A4
Orchard Av
400 HZLP 48030 4200 B2
4500 DRBN 48126 4417 E1
6700 WRRN 48091 4201 E3
7000 WRRN 48091 4202 A3
7200 DRBN 48126 4342 D4
8000 WRRN 48089 4202 A3
17500 SOGT 48195 4584 A4
19200 SOGT 48195 4583 E4
25000 TYLR 48180 4582 E4
Orchard Blvd
- CNTN 48188 4411 C6
S Orchard Cir
37000 WTLD 48186 4413 B5
Orchard Ct
13900 PyTp 48170 4263 E6
15000 RMLS 48174 4582 A4
23200 FMTN 48336 4195 A2
25400 HnTp 48134 4666 E7
Orchard Dr
100 NHVL 48167 4192 C6
1600 CNTN 48188 4412 E4
12000 Tcmh N8N 4423 E1
25600 DBHT 48125 4415 D3
25600 DBHT 48141 4415 D3
Orchard Grv
200 WIND N8S 4347 B6
Orchard Ln
10 GSPF 48236 4276 E4
1400 DBHT 48125 4415 D3
6200 SpTp 48105 4491 D1
6200 SpTp 48198 4491 D1
Orchard Rdg
300 SLYN 48178 4189 A1
Orchard St
10 ECRS 48229 4501 E2
10 RVRG 48218 4501 E2
Orchard St
10 RVRG 48229 4501 E2
300 YPLT 48197 4491 E5
700 FRDL 48220 4200 A2
1100 WYDT 48192 4585 A4
1700 AARB 48103 4405 E6
2200 WYDT 48192 4584 E4
2300 WYDT 48195 4584 E4
13600 SOGT 48195 4584 D4
15300 RMLS 48174 4582 B4
21400 DET 48219 4269 B1
22000 WDHN 48183 4668 C4
24600 TYLR 48180 4583 A4
25700 TYLR 48180 4582 D4
33100 FMTN 48335 4194 E2
33100 FMTN 48336 4194 E2
33100 FMTN 48336 4195 A2
Orchard Hill Pl
39500 NOVI 48167 4193 D5
39500 NOVI 48375 4193 D5
Orchard Hills Ct
100 AARB 48104 4406 E6
Orchard Hills Dr
200 AARB 48104 4406 E6
200 AARB 48104 4407 A6
Orchard Lake Rd
22400 FMTN 48336 4195 B2
23300 FNHL 48336 4195 B2
Orchard Ridge Rd
17100 NvlT 48167 4264 D2
Orchardview Dr
1800 PTFD 48108 4488 E6
Orchard View St
13500 MonC 48117 4753 B6
Orchid Av
- CNTN 48187 4336 C4
Oregon
600 WynC 48111 4662 D3
Oregon Av
10 YpTp 48198 4492 E4
Oregon St
- DET 48204 4344 A3
5500 DET 48204 4343 E3
33100 LVNA 48150 4339 A2
35800 WTLD 48186 4413 C4
Oregon Tr
44400 PyTp 48170 4336 D3
Orford St
1600 LSal N9J 4503 B3
Orhan St
8100 CNTN 48187 4337 E3
Oriole Blvd
1700 WIND N9C 4503 B1
Oriole Ln
32400 WYNE 48184 4414 B7
Oriole St
24500 TYLR 48180 4583 A4
24600 TYLR 48180 4582 E4
29100 LVNA 48154 4267 E5
Orion Cres
2800 WIND N9E 4503 E1
2900 WIND N9E 4504 A1
Orion St
8000 DET 48234 4202 A7
Orkney Dr
1200 AARB 48103 4406 B4
Orleans Ct
43900 CNTN 48187 4336 E5
Orleans Pl
18900 WDHN 48183 4669 A7
23000 SFLD 48034 4197 B2
Orleans St
- DET 48211 4273 C7
- HZLP 48030 4200 E4
- HZLP 48203 4200 E4
500 DET 48207 4346 A5
2400 DET 48207 4345 E3
13400 DET 48203 4273 A2
17100 DET 48203 4272 E1
17500 DET 48203 4200 E6
Ormond Dr
13000 VNBN 48111 4578 A2
25000 SFLD 48034 4196 B1
Ormond St
13200 DET 48229 4418 C4
Orville Dr
4500 TNTN 48183 4669 C6
Orville L Hubbard Dr
15500 DRBN 48126 4342 A7
Osage Av
6300 ALPK 48101 4500 A1
Osband
- YPLT 48197 4491 D3
Osband St
400 YPLT 48198 4492 B3
Osborn Cres
9700 WIND N8R 4423 B2
Osborne St
12900 DRBN 48126 4418 A1
Oscoda Ct
32200 WTLD 48186 4414 B4
Osmus St
19100 LVNA 48152 4195 B6
20200 LVNA 48336 4195 B5
21100 FNHL 48336 4195 B4
Osprey Dr
2000 PTFD 48197 4575 A6
Ostreich Rd
29400 BwTp 48173 4755 A5
29400 GBTR 48173 4755 A5
30000 BwTp 48173 4754 E5
30000 GBTR 48173 4754 E5
30000 RKWD 48173 4754 E6
Oswego Av
600 YpTp 48198 4492 E5
Oswego St
500 AARB 48104 4406 E7
Othello Ln
4800 WasC 48167 4190 A6
Otis Av
1900 WRRN 48091 4200 E2
3000 WRRN 48091 4201 A2
E Otis Av
300 HZLP 48030 4200 D2
W Otis Av
10 HZLP 48030 4200 C2
Otis St
6300 DET 48210 4344 A7
Otsego St
8700 DET 48204 4344 A1
9600 DET 48204 4272 A7
11400 DET 48204 4271 E6
32000 WTLD 48186 4414 C4
Ottawa Av
900 YpTp 48198 4492 C5
24500 FTRK 48134 4754 A1
Ottawa Cir
21800 WynC 48138 4670 B3
Ottawa Rd
1500 AARB 48105 4406 C4
Ottawa St
500 WIND N8X 4421 B2
1600 WIND N8Y 4421 B2
32000 WTLD 48186 4414 B5
Otter Dr
10000 GOTp 48178 4188 C3
Otter Rd
21100 HnTp 48111 4665 A4
22100 HnTp 48164 4665 A4
23000 HnTp 48164 4751 A1
Otter Creek Ct
3100 AARB 48105 4331 E7
Otter Pond Ln
1800 CNTN 48188 4412 E5
Otterson Ct
13500 LVNA 48150 4266 D6
Otto Ct
19000 HnTp 48164 4665 B1
Otto St
8500 DET 48204 4343 C2
Ouellette Av
- WIND N9A 4421 A3
10 WIND N9A 4420 E2
1200 WIND N8X 4421 A3
3400 WIND N9E 4504 C1
Ouellette Av P-3B
200 WIND N9A 4420 E1
1500 WIND N8X 4421 A3
Ouellette Pl
100 WIND N8X 4421 B6
Ouellette Pl P-3B
100 WIND N8X 4421 B6
Outback Dr
23300 LyTp 48178 4190 A3
Outer Dr
- DET 48229 4501 A1
- LNPK 48229 4501 A1
- MVDL 48229 4501 A1
- Tcmh N9H 4504 D7
5200 Tcmh N0R 4505 A5
5400 Tcmh N0R 4504 E6
6500 VNBN 48111 4493 D3
18000 DRBN 48128 4341 B7
18400 DRBN 48128 4416 B1
19100 DRBN 48124 4416 B2
22300 DRBN 48125 4416 E5
22500 DRBN 48124 4417 A6
22500 DRBN 48125 4417 A6
22900 DRBN 48101 4417 A6
23000 ALPK 48101 4417 A6
23800 MVDL 48101 4417 B6
23800 MVDL 48122 4417 B6
24800 LNPK 48101 4417 E7
24800 LNPK 48122 4417 E7
24800 LNPK 48146 4417 E7
25000 LNPK 48122 4500 E1
25000 LNPK 48146 4500 E1
25000 MVDL 48122 4500 E1
25300 LNPK 48122 4501 A1
25300 LNPK 48146 4501 A1
25300 MVDL 48122 4501 A1
25400 MVDL 48146 4501 A1
W Outer Dr
16500 DBHT 48127 4341 C5
17700 DBHT 48128 4341 C5
Outer Dr E
- DET 48205 4274 B1
1400 DET 48234 4200 E5
1500 DET 48234 4201 C5
4100 DET 48234 4202 B5
6000 DET 48234 4274 B1
7800 DET 48213 4274 D3
8800 DET 48213 4275 A2
9800 DET 48224 4275 A2
12500 DET 48224 4276 A4
13300 GPPK 48224 4276 A4
13300 GPPK 48230 4276 A4
Outer Dr W
- DET 48127 4341 B3
2900 DET 48221 4199 B6
4400 DET 48235 4199 B6
5600 DET 48235 4271 A1
5800 DET 48235 4270 D1
8000 DET 48219 4270 A1
8500 DET 48219 4269 E2
12400 DET 48228 4269 B7
12600 DET 48223 4269 B7
13200 DET 48239 4269 B7
13700 DET 48239 4341 B1
25600 DET 48146 4501 B2
25600 DET 48229 4501 B2
25600 LNPK 48146 4501 B2
25700 LNPK 48229 4501 B2
26600 ECRS 48146 4501 B2
26600 ECRS 48229 4501 B2
Outer Ln
100 YpTp 48198 4493 A3
Outer Dr Ct
19300 DRBN 48124 4416 B2
Outer Ln Dr
1700 YpTp 48198 4493 A7
1800 YpTp 48198 4577 A1
Outram Av
1100 LSal N9J 4503 A5
Outwood Dr
23000 SFLD 48034 4196 C2
Oven Pl
10 RMLS 48174 4498 A4
Overbrook Ct
5600 SpTp 48105 4333 B7
Overbrook Dr
5200 SpTp 48105 4333 A7
14900 ALPK 48101 4500 B7
14900 SOGT 48101 4500 B7
14900 SOGT 48195 4500 B7
Overbrook Ln
38100 WTLD 48185 4338 A5
Overdale Ct
11300 PyTp 48170 4336 B1
Overhill Ln
45900 CNTN 48188 4411 B4
Overidge View Ct
1000 WasC 48103 4404 E7
1000 WasC 48103 4487 E1
Over Lake St
22400 STCS 48080 4204 D3
Overland Rd
11000 GOTp 48189 4187 C5
Overlook Ct
3100 WasC 48176 4572 C1
Overlook St
2100 AARB 48103 4406 A3
Overridge Dr
2500 AARB 48104 4490 B1
Owen Av
16200 EPTE 48021 4203 D1
Owen Rd
9300 WynC 48138 4670 C1
Owen St
10 BLVL 48111 4578 D3
10 DET 48202 4272 E6
10 DET 48202 4273 A6
900 DET 48211 4273 A6
Owendale St
10 YPLT 48197 4491 D4
Owens Pl
100 SALN 48176 4572 C7
Oxbow St
8600 WTLD 48150 4339 E2
8600 WTLD 48185 4339 E2
11000 LVNA 48150 4339 E1
Oxford Av
- SLYN 48178 4189 B3
20900 FNHL 48336 4195 E4
Oxford Blvd
10 PTRG 48069 4199 D1
Oxford Cres
- Amhg N9V 4671 C5
Oxford Ct
10 DRBN 48124 4416 A4
300 BLVL 48111 4578 E3
1200 WYDT 48192 4585 A2
2500 WRRN 48091 4201 A1
8800 SpTp 48198 4492 D1
14900 SOGT 48195 4584 B1
33400 LVNA 48154 4266 E3
43000 NOVI 48375 4193 A5
47800 NvlT 48167 4264 A2
Oxford Dr
- TYLR 48180 4582 D5
Oxford Rd
- HRWD 48225 4204 C6
- HRWD 48236 4204 C6
10 GSPS 48236 4204 E7
10 GSPS 48236 4205 A7
500 AARB 48104 4406 D7
700 YPLT 48197 4491 D3
1300 GSPW 48236 4204 C6
N Oxford Rd
600 GSPW 48236 4204 E6
S Oxford Rd
600 GSPW 48236 4204 D6
Oxford St
14400 PyTp 48170 4265 B6
22100 DRBN 48124 4416 B4
25000 DRBN 48124 4415 E4
25000 WDHN 48183 4668 B7
Oxford Manor Ct
1200 SLYN 48178 4189 B4
Oxley Av
5700 LSal N9H 4503 D4
Oxley Rd
16000 SFLD 48075 4198 B2
Oxley St
19900 DET 48235 4198 C5
Oxygen Plant
- DRBN 48120 4418 A3
Oyster Bay Dr
7600 YpTp 48197 4576 A6
Ozga St
7100 RMLS 48174 4496 B3
11300 RMLS 48174 4580 B1

P

N P Rd
- DRBN 48120 4418 A3
P-2
- Lksr N8N 4424 E3
- Tcmh N8N 4423 E3
- Tcmh N9K 4423 E2
P-3
- WIND N9B 4420 B3
- WIND N9C 4420 B3
P-3 Ambassador Br
- WIND N9B 4420 A2
- WIND N9C 4420 B3
P-3 Huron Church Rd
800 WIND N9B 4420 C6

STREET Block City ZIP Map# Grid

P-3 Huron Church Rd
800 WIND N9C 4420 C6
2200 WIND N9E 4420 C6
2500 WIND N9E 4503 D1
3700 WIND N9H 4503 D1
3800 LSal N9H 4503 D1
3800 WIND N9G 4503 D1
P-3 Talbot Rd
600 LSal N9H 4504 D5
600 WIND N9G 4504 D5
2500 LSal N9H 4503 E3
2500 WIND N9G 4503 E3
P-3 Talbot Rd E
- Tcmh N0R 4504 E6
500 Tcmh N9H 4504 D5
500 WIND N9G 4504 D5
P-3B Dougall Av
- WIND - 4504 E4
- WIND - 4505 A4
2600 WIND N8X 4421 B6
2600 WIND N9E 4421 B6
P-3B Ouellette Av
200 WIND N9A 4420 E1
1500 WIND N8X 4421 A4
P-3B Ouellette Pl
100 WIND N8X 4421 B6
P-18
- WIND - 4420 A7
P-18 Front Rd
- LSal N9J 4502 C7
2400 LSal N9J 4586 C1
P-18 Front St N
300 Amhg N9V 4671 B6
1600 Amhg N9V 4586 C7
2400 Amhg N9J 4586 C7
P-18 Front St S
600 Amhg N9V 4757 B5
700 EsxC N9V 4757 B5
P-18 Ojibway Pkwy
4700 WIND N9C 4419 E7
4700 WIND N9C 4420 A7
4900 WIND N9C 4502 E3
4900 WIND N9J 4419 E7
4900 WIND N9J 4502 E3
P-18 Sandwich St N
10 Amhg N9V 4757 B1
P-18 Sandwich St S
10 Amhg N9V 4757 C4
P-401
MacDonald-Cartier Frwy
- Tcmh - 4504 E5
- Tcmh - 4505 A5
- WIND - 4504 E5
- WIND - 4505 A5
Pacific Av
100 Amhg N9V 4757 D2
N Pacific Av
12000 Tcmh N8N 4423 E5
12000 Tcmh N8N 4424 A5
S Pacific Av
- Tcmh N8N 4424 A5
600 WIND N8X 4421 D5
700 WIND N8W 4421 D5
Pacific Pl
10500 GOTp 48189 4187 C5
Pacific St
- DET 48204 4344 A3
200 PLYM 48170 4264 E6
5800 DET 48204 4343 E3
S Pacific St
2100 WIND N8X 4420 E4
2100 WIND N8X 4421 A4
Paciocco Ct
11600 PyTp 48170 4336 A1
Packard Av
7000 WRRN 48091 4201 E3
7000 WRRN 48091 4202 A3
8000 WRRN 48089 4202 A2
Packard Rd
- AARB 48108 4489 E4
1800 YPLT 48197 4491 A4
1800 YpTp 48197 4491 A4
2600 AARB 48104 4489 E4
2600 PTFD 48104 4489 E4
2700 AARB 48104 4490 A4
2700 AARB 48108 4490 A4
2800 PTFD 48104 4490 A4
2800 PTFD 48108 4490 A4
4700 PTFD 48108 4491 A4
Packard St
100 AARB 48104 4406 B6
2100 AARB 48104 4489 D2
2600 PTFD 48104 4489 E3
18000 DET 48234 4202 A6
Paddington Ct
22400 NOVI 48374 4192 B4
Paddington Rd
800 CNTN 48187 4411 E1
Paddock Dr
23500 FNHL 48336 4196 A1
Paddock Ln
- WasC 48176 4658 E2
Paddock Pl
1100 PTFD 48108 4489 A5
Paddock Wy
2000 SpTp 48198 4409 A6
Paderewski St
14900 LVNA 48154 4267 E4
Page
- DET 48209 4419 D1
Page Av
2200 AARB 48104 4489 D2
Page Ct
2600 AARB 48104 4489 D3
Page Dr
6100 CNTN 48187 4335 D6
Page St
100 WIND N9C 4419 D7
Pageant St
1200 YpTp 48198 4492 D2
Pagel Av
400 LNPK 48146 4501 A5
1200 LNPK 48146 4500 D5
Paget Ct
1100 GSPW 48236 4204 D7
Paige Av
6700 WRRN 48091 4201 E2
7000 WRRN 48091 4202 A2
8000 WRRN 48089 4202 A2
Paige Ln
6900 YpTp 48197 4576 A5
Paint Creek Dr
7600 YpTp 48197 4576 A4
Paisley Cir
300 Tcmh N8N 4424 B1
Paisley Ct
3500 AARB 48105 4407 C4
Palace Av
3900 CNTN 48188 4411 A6
Palace Ct
22500 NOVI 48375 4193 D5
Pale St
3200 TNTN 48183 4669 B5
Palisades Blvd
3700 PTFD 48197 4490 E5
Palisades Ct
4500 PTFD 48197 4490 E5
43900 CNTN 48187 4411 E2
Palisades Dr
43700 CNTN 48187 4411 E2
43700 CNTN 48187 4412 A2
Pallister St
10 DET 48202 4273 A7
800 DET 48202 4344 E1
1600 DET 48206 4344 D1
21200 STCS 48080 4204 B3
Pall Mall St
1400 WIND N9E 4420 E7
1400 WIND N9E 4421 A7
Palma Rd
37500 HnTp 48164 4665 B7
Palma Ln Dr
8600 WasC 48178 4260 E1
Palmateer Rd
38100 WTLD 48186 4413 A4
Palmer Av
1800 LSal N9H 4503 C6
Palmer Dr
- AARB 48104 4406 C6
Palmer Rd
13100 MonC 48191 4748 B6
30400 WTLD 48186 4414 C4
33600 WTLD 48186 4413 D4
38800 WTLD 48186 4412 D4
39100 CNTN 48186 4412 D4
39400 CNTN 48188 4412 D4
43800 CNTN 48188 4411 E4
Palmer St
- LNPK 48122 4417 E7
- LNPK 48146 4417 E7
800 PLYM 48170 4337 A2
1200 PLYM 48170 4336 E1
4400 DRBN 48126 4417 C1
4700 DRBN 48126 4342 D7
17100 MVDL 48122 4418 A6
18600 MVDL 48122 4417 E7
24000 HZLP 48030 4200 C1
29100 INKR 48141 4414 E4
Palmer St E
10 DET 48202 4345 B2
1000 DET 48211 4345 C1
2900 DET 48211 4273 E7
6300 DET 48211 4274 A7
7200 DET 48213 4274 A6
Palmer St W
10 DET 48202 4345 A2
Palmerston St
300 RVRG 48218 4501 D1
Palmetto Ct
3100 TNTN 48183 4669 C6
Palmetto Dr
24400 FTRK 48134 4754 A5
Palmetto St
7000 DET 48234 4274 A3
Palms Cres
10500 WIND N8R 4423 C3
Palms St
- DET 48209 4419 D1
1900 DET 48209 4344 D7
Palomar Dr
1700 AARB 48103 4488 E1
Palomino Dr
4400 PTFD 48197 4574 E6
Pamco Dr
31500 LVNA 48150 4267 B6
Pamela Av
2500 AARB 48103 4405 C4
Pamela Ct
25100 BNTN 48134 4667 D7
36000 WTLD 48186 4413 C2
Pamela Dr
7000 YpTp 48197 4576 E5
Pamela St
24600 BNTN 48134 4667 D7
25000 TYLR 48180 4582 E3
Panam St
5800 RMLS 48174 4498 A1
Panama Av
9100 SpTp 48198 4492 D2
9100 YpTp 48198 4492 D2
21700 WRRN 48091 4201 D1
Panama Ct
9100 SpTp 48198 4492 D2
Panama St
7100 DET 48210 4343 D6
20700 WRRN 48091 4201 D2
Papineau Ct
12000 Tcmh N8N 4348 E7
Pardee Av
2500 DRBN 48124 4416 C4
Pardee Av
3900 DBHT 48124 4416 C6
3900 DBHT 48125 4416 C6
5600 DBHT 48125 4499 B1
Pardee Ct
22400 DBHT 48125 4416 B7
Pardee Rd
5800 TYLR 48125 4499 B1
5800 TYLR 48180 4499 B1
12000 TYLR 48180 4583 C1
Pardo St
28400 GDNC 48135 4340 A7
32400 GDNC 48135 4339 A7
33600 GDNC 48135 4338 E7
34400 WTLD 48185 4338 D7
Pare Ln
10 LSal N9J 4586 C1
3800 TNTN 48183 4669 B7
Pare St
23100 STCS 48080 4204 D1
Parent Av
100 WIND N9A 4346 A7
400 WIND N9A 4421 B2
2100 WIND N8X 4421 C4
2600 WIND N8X 4421 C5
S Parent Av
100 WTLD 48185 4413 D2
100 WTLD 48186 4413 D2
Parent St
8900 LVNA 48150 4338 C3
N Parent St
100 WTLD 48185 4413 D2
1800 WTLD 48185 4338 D7
S Parent St
1800 WTLD 48186 4413 D4
Paris Av
1300 LNPK 48146 4501 A2
1700 LNPK 48146 4500 E1
2200 LNPK 48101 4500 E1
Paris Ct
14800 ALPK 48101 4500 D1
Paris Dr
45000 WynC 48111 4578 D7
Paris St
14500 ALPK 48101 4500 D1
Park Av
- GSPF 48236 4276 D4
- YpTp 48198 4493 B4
10 DET 48226 4345 C5
1000 LNPK 48146 4501 A4
2100 DET 48201 4345 C5
6500 ALPK 48101 4500 B3
17000 RVVW 48192 4584 B5
17000 RVVW 48195 4584 B5
N Park Av
15100 EPTE 48021 4203 C1
S Park Av
15300 EPTE 48021 4203 C2
Park Blvd
5900 SRKW 48179 4754 B7
Park Cir
13400 WRRN 48089 4202 E2
N Park Ct
29900 HnTp 48164 4666 E5
E Park Ctr
2500 WIND N8T 4422 E2
Park Dr
- AARB 48103 4406 A7
9000 DET 48213 4275 A2
11000 DET 48213 4274 E2
11500 DET 48205 4274 E2
N Park Dr
300 LyTp 48167 4189 E5
16100 SFLD 48075 4198 B3
23000 HnTp 48164 4666 E5
Park Ln
800 GPPK 48230 4276 B6
8000 SpTp 48198 4492 B1
22400 STCS 48080 4205 A3
26500 WDHN 48183 4754 E1
32400 GDNC 48135 4339 A6
Park Pl
400 SALN 48176 4572 D7
700 TNTN 48183 4669 E1
700 TNTN 48183 4670 A1
1300 PLYM 48170 4336 E1
35600 RMLS 48174 4496 C2
E Park Pl
1100 DET 48226 4345 C6
1400 AARB 48104 4489 C1
N Park Pl
- SFLD 48075 4198 B3
Park Rd
1200 AARB 48105 4406 D4
4200 WasC 48103 4404 E5
7800 WasC 48189 4259 A3
Park St
- WYNE 48184 4413 D6
10 Amhg N9V 4757 B3
100 PLYM 48170 4265 B7
14100 GBTR 48173 4755 D3
15100 OKPK 48237 4198 C2
16200 LVNA 48154 4266 C2
17300 LVNA 48152 4266 C2
17400 MVDL 48122 4418 A5
22400 DRBN 48124 4416 C3
N Park St
10 YPLT 48198 4492 B4
S Park St
10 YPLT 48198 4492 B4
Park St E
10 WIND N9A 4420 C1
Park St W
10 WIND N9A 4420 D2
Park Ter
10500 DET 48204 4271 B6
Parkcreek Rd
22300 FNHL 48335 4194 B3
Parkcrest Cir
36700 WTLD 48185 4338 B5
Parkcrest Dr
20800 HRWD 48225 4204 B6
E Parkcrest Dr
7000 WTLD 48185 4338 B5
W Parkcrest Dr
6900 WTLD 48185 4338 B5
Parkdale Ct
34200 LVNA 48150 4338 E1
Parkdale Dr
45400 CNTN 48188 4411 D5
Parkdale Pl
2100 WIND N8W 4421 E5
Parkdale St
34900 LVNA 48150 4338 C1
Parkdale Ter
5600 DET 48210 4344 A5
Parke Ln
17200 WynC 48138 4585 D5
19300 WynC 48138 4670 D2
Parker Ct
10600 GOTp 48178 4187 D1
Parker St
600 DET 48214 4346 D2
2000 DRBN 48124 4416 B5
3900 DBHT 48124 4416 B5
3900 DBHT 48125 4416 B5
4800 DET 48214 4274 C7
5400 DET 48213 4274 B6
19900 LVNA 48152 4195 B5
20200 LVNA 48336 4195 B5
20700 FNHL 48336 4195 B4
Parker Mill County Park Rd
- SpTp 48105 4408 B7
Park Estates Dr
10 VNBN 48111 4493 C2
Park Forest Ct
41100 NOVI 48375 4193 B3
Park Forest St
11700 GOTp 48178 4188 A5
Parkgate Ct
47400 CNTN 48188 4411 B3
Parkgrove Av
34400 WTLD 48185 4338 D3
Park Grove Ct
43700 NHVL 48167 4192 E5
Parkgrove Rd
5300 WasC 48103 4404 C6
Parkgrove St
- DET 48234 4202 C7
11600 DET 48205 4202 C7
13800 DET 48205 4203 A6
Parkhill St
32900 WYNE 48184 4414 A5
Parkhurst Av
36000 LVNA 48154 4266 C4
Parkhurst Pl E
10 DET 48203 4272 C1
Parkhurst Pl W
10 DET 48203 4272 C1
Parkhurst Rd
42400 PyTp 48170 4265 A4
Parkhurst St
37800 LVNA 48154 4266 A4
38900 LVNA 48154 4265 E4
Parkinson St
- DET 48210 4344 A7
4200 DET 48210 4343 E6
Parklake Av
10 AARB 48103 4405 B6
Parkland
7200 DET 48127 4341 B3
7200 DET 48239 4341 B3
Parkland Dr
9200 YpTp 48197 4576 E5
Parkland Plz
10 WasC 48103 4404 E5
300 WasC 48103 4405 A6
Parkland St
6500 DBHT 48127 4341 C5
Parklane
15300 NvlT 48170 4265 C4
15900 NvlT 48167 4265 C3
Park Lane Cir
- Amhg N9V 4671 B4
Parklane Cir
36000 FNHL 48335 4194 C4
Park Lane Ct
- Amhg N9V 4671 C4
Parklane Ct
21800 FNHL 48335 4194 B4
Parklane Dr
14400 LVNA 48154 4266 C5
17200 LVNA 48152 4266 C1
Parklane St
100 WYDT 48192 4501 C6
16100 LVNA 48154 4266 C2
18400 LVNA 48152 4194 C7
18400 LVNA 48152 4266 B1
21100 FNHL 48335 4194 C4
Parklawn
1800 SpTp 48198 4409 E7
Parklawn Dr
3400 CNTN 48188 4411 C6
Parklawn St
24200 OKPK 48237 4198 E1
Park Ln Blvd
10 DRBN 48126 4342 B7
Park Ln Ct
47900 CNTN 48187 4336 A6
Park Ln Dr
24800 FTRK 48134 4754 A3
Parkplace N
10 ALPK 48101 4499 D5
Parkplace S
10 ALPK 48101 4499 D5
Parkplace W
10 ALPK 48101 4499 E5
Park Place Ct
- NOVI 48167 4191 C5
Park Place Dr
50900 NOVI 48167 4191 C4
Parkplace Central
10 ALPK 48101 4499 D5
Park Ridge Ct
24500 NOVI 48375 4193 A1
Parkridge Ct
18000 RVVW 48192 4584 B6
Park Ridge Dr
- YpTp 48197 4575 A6
Parkridge Dr
2600 WasC 48103 4405 B1
17700 RVVW 48192 4584 B6
Park Ridge Rd
41800 NOVI 48375 4193 A1
Parkshore Ct
49100 NvlT 48167 4263 E2
Parkshore Dr
17300 NvlT 48167 4263 E2
Parkside Blvd
4300 ALPK 48101 4417 B7
21300 ROTp 48220 4199 C3
Park Side Ct
1600 PTFD 48108 4573 A2
Parkside Ct
10 DRBN 48124 4416 D1
1500 WIND N9E 4504 A2
4700 AATp 48105 4408 A2
Parkside Dr
- NvlT 48167 4263 C3
2200 TNTN 48183 4669 C3
2400 AATp 48105 4408 A2
6500 VNBN 48111 4493 C3
8100 WTLD 48185 4337 E4
8800 LVNA 48150 4338 E3
8800 LVNA 48185 4338 E3
13400 SOGT 48195 4584 B2
Parkside St
15400 DET 48238 4271 E2
16100 DET 48221 4271 E1
18000 DET 48221 4199 E6
19500 STCS 48080 4204 A3
43900 CNTN 48187 4336 E5
Parkview
28500 HnTp 48134 4752 E3
Parkview Av
900 WIND N8S 4347 D7
1200 WIND N8S 4422 D1
Parkview Ct
5600 PTFD 48108 4572 E2
Parkview Dr
200 DET 48214 4347 A3
300 DET 48214 4346 E2
300 PLYM 48170 4337 B1
700 PLYM 48170 4265 B7
11200 PyTp 48170 4337 D1
38500 WYNE 48184 4413 A6
Parkview Ln
13800 SOGT 48195 4584 B2
Parkview Pl
10 AARB 48103 4406 A5
Parkview St
2100 DET 48214 4346 E2
14500 RVVW 48192 4584 C6
Park Village Dr
15000 TYLR 48180 4582 C4
Parkville St
19100 LVNA 48152 4195 E6
Parkway Blvd
- AATp 48105 4408 A1
13000 MonC 48117 4752 E7
Parkway Cir
6500 DBHT 48127 4341 A5
Parkway Ct
7200 CNTN 48187 4336 C5
Parkway Dr
- WynC 48138 4670 C6
1100 GSPW 48236 4204 E4
1700 WIND N9C 4420 B6
Parkway St
12500 RVVW 48192 4584 E6
12500 RVVW 48192 4585 A6
W Parkway St
7300 DBHT 48127 4341 B4
8800 DET 48127 4341 B2
8800 DET 48239 4341 B2
8800 RDFD 48127 4341 B2
8800 RDFD 48239 4341 B2
11600 DET 48239 4269 B7
12600 DET 48223 4269 A6
15900 DET 48219 4269 A2
Parkwood Av
- YpTp 48198 4493 A4
800 YpTp 48198 4492 C5
2100 WIND N8W 4421 C4
2200 AARB 48104 4490 C2
2800 TNTN 48183 4669 D5
30700 WTLD 48186 4414 B3
Parkwood Cir
3500 PTFD 48108 4489 B5
Parkwood Ct
38800 FNHL 48167 4193 E4
S Parkwood Dr
800 SLYN 48178 4189 C3
Parkwood Ln
19000 BNTN 48183 4668 C1
21400 FNHL 48167 4193 E4
Parkwood Mnr
8800 VNBN 48111 4495 B5
Parkwood St
400 AARB 48103 4405 C5
400 WasC 48103 4405 C5
6800 DET 48210 4344 A6
7100 DET 48210 4343 E7
28200 INKR 48141 4415 A3
28900 INKR 48141 4414 D3
33600 WTLD 48186 4414 A3
Parkwoods Dr
20800 LyTp 48178 4189 C6
Parsons St
10 DET 48201 4345 B4
10 YPLT 48198 4492 A4
Partington Av
300 WIND N9B 4420 C2
2600 WIND N9E 4420 D6
2600 WIND N9E 4503 E1
Partridge Dr
44800 PyTp 48170 4336 D1
Partridge Pth
3600 AARB 48108 4489 E5
Partridge Wy
7100 PTFD 48176 4573 E6
Par View Dr
5800 YpTp 48197 4575 D3
Pasadena Av
- ROTp 48237 4199 B4
8000 ROTp 48220 4199 B4
N Pasadena Av
100 YpTp 48198 4493 A3
S Pasadena Av
1700 YpTp 48198 4493 A7
1800 YpTp 48198 4577 A1
Pasadena Ct
5000 WIND N8T 4422 C4
10100 ROTp 48220 4199 B4
Pasadena St
300 HDPK 48203 4272 C3
1500 DET 48238 4272 C3
3200 DET 48238 4271 E5
13600 OKPK 48237 4198 E4
Pat St
3800 PTFD 48197 4574 D6
Patrice Dr
200 WIND N8S 4347 B6
Patricia Av
1200 WasC 48103 4405 D4
1400 AARB 48103 4405 C4
24100 WRRN 48091 4201 C1
Patricia Ct
2600 AARB 48103 4405 C4
7000 CTNL 48015 4201 E1
Patricia Dr
3100 MVDL 48122 4418 A6
Patricia Ln
11200 GOTp 48178 4187 E3
Patricia Rd
100 WIND N9B 4420 B2
S Patricia St
700 DET 48229 4418 C6
Patrick Av
1700 YpTp 48198 4492 E7
1700 YpTp 48198 4493 A7
4200 WIND N9G 4504 E4
Patrick Dr
44700 CNTN 48187 4336 D6
Patrick St
17800 BNTN 48174 4583 B6
Patriot Blvd
21700 BNTN 48192 4583 C6
Patriot Ln
6700 VNBN 48111 4577 C4
Patriot St
- CNTN 48188 4410 D3
Patterson Ct
600 INKR 48141 4415 C3
Pattingill St
100 WTLD 48185 4413 B2
Patton Av
3000 TNTN 48183 4669 C5
Patton Ct
20600 DET 48228 4269 D7
Patton St
8000 DET 48228 4341 D3
9300 LVNA 48150 4337 E2
10800 DRBN 48126 4343 B3
11600 DET 48228 4269 D7
13900 DET 48223 4269 D5
17100 DET 48219 4269 D1
19900 DET 48219 4197 D5
Paul Av
29700 WTLD 48186 4414 E7
Paul St
- DET 48126 4342 D5
- DRBN 48126 4342 A5
- DRBN 48228 4342 C5
1100 AARB 48103 4406 A5
13000 DRBN 48126 4343 A5
18400 DET 48228 4342 A5
19100 DET 48228 4341 E5
20400 TYLR 48180 4583 D1
Paula Cres
100 Lksr N8N 4424 E3
Paulina Av
8400 WynC 48138 4585 C7
Paulina Ct
10200 WIND N8P 4348 B6
Pauline Blvd
300 AARB 48103 4406 A7
1400 AARB 48103 4405 E7
1900 AARB 48103 4488 D1
Pauline Ct
2100 AARB 48103 4488 D1
Paul Martin Ct
2600 WIND N9E 4503 D1
Paul Revere Ln
6500 CNTN 48187 4337 A6
Pavan St
800 WIND N9G 4504 E4
800 WIND N9G 4505 A4
Pavilion Dr
22400 NOVI 48375 4193 D3
Pavilion Rd
- GDNC 48135 4414 C2
Pavillon Rd
47600 CNTN 48188 4411 A3
Pawnee
27100 RDFD 48240 4268 B2
27200 RDFD 48154 4268 B2
Pawnee Ct
26700 FTRK 48134 4754 A2
Pawnee St
33600 WTLD 48185 4338 E5
33600 WTLD 48185 4339 A5
Paxton St
2400 FRDL 48220 4200 A1
E Payeur Rd
10 PTFD 48108 4573 D1
W Payeur Rd
10 PTFD 48108 4573 D2
Payne Av
7500 DRBN 48126 4342 D3
Payne Ct
15000 DRBN 48126 4342 D7
Payne St
18000 RVVW 48192 4585 A6
Payton St
11700 DET 48224 4275 C1
11900 DET 48224 4203 C7
Peabody St
900 YpTp 48198 4492 D2
Peace Ct
3000 WIND N8T 4422 D4
Peach
10 WasC 48103 4488 B3
Peach St
300 WTLD 48186 4414 C6
1600 AARB 48105 4406 C4
13400 MonC 48117 4753 A7
13600 SOGT 48195 4584 D4
Peach Blossom Cres
1000 WIND N9G 4504 E4
1000 WIND N9G 4505 A4
Peachcrest St
2600 YpTp 48198 4493 B2
Peachtree
22300 NOVI 48375 4193 D4
Peach Tree Ct
7200 CNTN 48187 4336 C5
25000 BNTN 48134 4667 E4
Peach Tree Ln
600 GSPW 48236 4276 E1
Peachtree Ln
100 VNBN 48111 4494 D5
Pear Ln
10 WasC 48103 4488 B4
Pear St
10 WTLD 48186 4414 D7
1300 AARB 48105 4406 C4
1800 DET 48238 4272 B3
13400 MonC 48117 4753 B6
Pearl Av
1900 WRRN 48030 4200 E3
1900 WRRN 48091 4200 E3
3000 WRRN 48091 4201 A3
E Pearl Av
600 HZLP 48030 4200 D3
W Pearl Av
10 HZLP 48030 4200 C3
Pearl Ct
4500 PTFD 48197 4490 E5
Pearl Dr
100 WasC 48189 4186 D7
Pearl St
- HbgT 48189 4186 B3
100 YPLT 48197 4492 A4
700 AARB 48103 4406 A4
1000 YPLT 48197 4491 D4
2300 DET 48209 4418 E2
4600 PTFD 48197 4490 E5
4600 PTFD 48197 4491 A5
7800 WasC 48167 4262 E3
12100 SOGT 48195 4500 D7
12100 SOGT 48195 4584 D1
20700 FNHL 48336 4195 E5
E Pearl St
100 PLYM 48170 4265 B6
W Pearl St
100 PLYM 48170 4265 A6
Pearleaf Ct
4200 WIND N9G 4505 A4
Pearson St
100 FRDL 48220 4199 E3
13600 OKPK 48237 4198 E3
Pear Tree Ct
30700 FTRK 48173 4754 A5
Pear Tree Ln
500 GSPW 48236 4276 E1
600 GSPW 48236 4204 E7
Pease St
9100 DET 48211 4273 E4
Pebble Ln
48700 NOVI 48374 4191 E1
Pebble Beach Ct
45300 NvlT 48167 4264 C3
Pebblebrook Dr
15000 VNBN 48111 4579 B4
Pebble Creek Dr
1800 CNTN 48188 4412 D4
Pebble Creek Rd
2700 AARB 48108 4489 E4
Pebble Ridge Ct
5500 PTFD 48108 4573 A2
Pebblestone Dr
7900 YpTp 48197 4576 B3
Pebbleview Ct
2000 PTFD 48108 4572 E1
Pecan Dr
5000 PTFD 48197 4575 A1
Pecan St
10 WynC 48111 4578 B7
400 WTLD 48186 4497 D1
Peck
- DET 48214 4275 B6
Peekskill
- SFLD 48034 4196 B1
Peer Rd
9100 GOTp 48178 4188 D1

INDEX 42
Peerce Ct
Detroit & Wayne County Street Index
Plantain Pl

STREET
Block City ZIP Map# Grid

Peerce Ct
1900 CNTN 48187 4336 D7
Peerless St
10600 DET 48224 4203 E7
19200 HRWD 48225 4203 E7
19900 HRWD 48225 4204 A5
Pelham Rd
1800 DRBN 48124 4416 E5
3900 DBHT 48124 4416 E5
3900 DBHT 48125 4416 E5
5800 ALPK 48101 4499 E1
5800 ALPK 48125 4499 E1
5800 TYLR 48101 4499 E1
5800 TYLR 48125 4499 E1
5800 TYLR 48180 4499 E1
6500 ALPK 48180 4499 E2
S Pelham St
100 DET 48209 4419 E2
Pelissier St
200 WIND N9A 4420 E1
1200 WIND N8X 4420 E2
2500 WIND N8X 4421 B5
Pelkey St
12900 DET 48205 4202 E6
Pelletier St
2300 WIND N9B 4420 C4
Pellett Dr
8000 WasC 48189 4258 A2
Pellston Dr
42100 NOVI 48375 4193 A4
Pelouze St
6300 DET 48210 4344 A6
Pemberly Ct
3900 WasC 48103 4405 A3
Pemberton Rd
500 GPPK 48230 4348 A1
700 GPPK 48230 4275 E7
700 GPPK 48230 4347 E1
Pembridge Pl
1900 DET 48207 4346 A5
Pembroke Av
- DET 48203 4199 D5
3200 DET 48221 4199 D5
12700 DET 48235 4199 A5
13300 DET 48235 4198 E5
18100 DET 48219 4198 A6
19800 DET 48219 4197 D5
24700 DET 48219 4196 D6
25000 RDFD 48240 4196 D6
27300 RDFD 48152 4196 A6
34500 LVNA 48152 4194 D6
Pembroke Ct
10 DRBN 48126 4341 E7
Pembroke Dr
300 SALN 48176 4657 B1
500 SALN 48176 4572 B7
Pembroke Rd
3600 TNTN 48183 4669 B2
Pembroke St
27400 LVNA 48152 4196 A6
28300 LVNA 48152 4195 E6
Pembrook Dr
6300 WTLD 48185 4338 B6
Pembrooke Cir
10000 GOTp 48178 4188 D3
Pembury Rd
- NvlT 48167 4265 C3
Pen Run
10 YpTp 48197 4577 B5
Penang Ln
2000 WIND N8R 4423 B1
Penberton Ct
3800 AARB 48105 4407 C5
Penberton Dr
3800 AARB 48105 4407 C5
Peninsula Ct
600 AARB 48105 4407 B5
Peninsula Point Dr
7000 WasC 48189 4259 C5
Penn Ct
15500 LVNA 48154 4265 E3
Penn Dr
15500 LVNA 48154 4265 E3
16800 LVNA 48167 4265 E3
Penn St
20300 DRBN 48124 4416 C5
21000 TYLR 48180 4583 D3
24300 DRBN 48124 4415 E5
25600 DBHT 48125 4415 E5
25600 DBHT 48141 4415 C5
25800 INKR 48141 4415 C5
31700 LVNA 48150 4339 B3
Penncraft Ct
2000 AARB 48103 4405 E5
Pennell St
300 NHVL 48167 4192 E6
Pennie St
24000 DBHT 48125 4416 A7
24600 DBHT 48125 4415 E7
Penniman Av
600 PLYM 48170 4337 A1
800 PLYM 48170 4265 A7
900 PLYM 48170 4264 E7
Pennington Dr
17100 DET 48221 4271 D1
18000 DET 48221 4199 D7
Penninsula Wy
18000 NvlT 48167 4263 E1
Penn Service Dr
21600 TYLR 48180 4583 C5
Pennstone Cir
6500 PTFD 48176 4574 A4
Pennsylvania Av
1000 AARB 48103 4405 D7
1000 LNPK 48146 4501 E3
15000 ALPK 48101 4500 B6
Pennsylvania Rd
- BNTN 48192 4584 A5
- BNTN 48195 4584 A5
- SOGT 48195 4583 D5
1300 RVVW 48192 4585 A5
1300 WYDT 48192 4585 A5
2300 RVVW 48192 4584 D5
2300 WYDT 48192 4584 D5
12700 RVVW 48195 4584 D5
12700 SOGT 48195 4584 D5
20000 BNTN 48180 4583 D5
20000 BNTN 48192 4583 D5
20000 BNTN 48195 4583 D5
20000 TYLR 48180 4583 D5
20000 TYLR 48195 4583 D5
23500 BNTN 48174 4583 A5
23500 TYLR 48174 4583 A5
24800 BNTN 48174 4582 D6
24800 TYLR 48174 4582 D6
24800 TYLR 48180 4582 D6
27400 HnTp 48174 4582 A6
27400 RMLS 48174 4582 A6
29200 HnTp 48174 4581 D6
29200 RMLS 48174 4581 D6
33500 HnTp 48164 4580 E6
33500 HnTp 48174 4580 E6
33500 RMLS 48174 4580 E6
35000 RMLS 48164 4580 E6
Pennsylvania St
1200 DET 48214 4346 E1
3400 DET 48214 4274 D7
5000 DET 48213 4274 C5
15500 SFLD 48237 4198 B1
24000 SFLD 48075 4198 A1
Pennsylvania Heights Dr
17000 BNTN 48174 4582 C6
Penny Ct
44400 CNTN 48187 4336 D4
Penrod St
6000 DET 48228 4342 A5
11600 DET 48228 4270 A7
12800 DET 48223 4270 A6
Penrose St
900 DET 48203 4200 B6
Pentilly Rd
400 Tcmh N8N 4424 D1
Penton Rise Ct
22600 NOVI 48375 4193 B3
Peoria St
12300 DET 48205 4275 A1
12600 DET 48205 4203 A7
Pepper Dr
700 SLYN 48178 4189 C1
Pepper Rd
4200 ECRS 48229 4501 C4
Pepperidge Ct
8900 PyTp 48170 4336 A3
Peppermill Ct
22500 NOVI 48375 4193 C3
Peppermill Wy
1900 AARB 48103 4405 E7
7300 WasC 48167 4262 B5
Peppermint Dr
- WTLD 48174 4497 D1
- WTLD 48186 4497 D1
100 WTLD 48186 4414 D7
Pepper Pike St
1200 AARB 48105 4407 C4
Pepperridge Wy
1200 AATp 48105 4407 E4
Peppers Blvd
1800 DET 48211 4273 C6
Pepperwood Dr
26500 WDHN 48183 4754 E1
43100 CNTN 48187 4337 A5
Pepperwood St
20500 WDHN 48183 4754 E1
Perceval Ln
- NOVI 48375 4192 D1
Percy Pl
- Tcmh N8N 4348 E6
12500 Tcmh N8N 4349 A6
Pere Av
8800 LVNA 48150 4337 E2
Pere St
14900 LVNA 48154 4265 E4
Perennial Ln
2200 AATp 48105 4331 E4
Perkins St
6300 DET 48210 4344 A6
Perrien Pl
500 GSPW 48236 4205 A4
Perrin Av
8000 WTLD 48185 4339 C3
Perrin St
10 RVRG 48218 4501 E1
100 YPLT 48197 4491 E4
8800 LVNA 48150 4339 C2
Perrinsville Ct
7300 WTLD 48185 4339 B5
Perry Dr
11000 HbgT 48189 4186 B5
Perry Pl
1000 RVVW 48192 4584 D5
1000 WYDT 48192 4501 B7
Perry St
- DET 48201 4345 A5
500 YPLT 48197 4491 E5
1400 DET 48216 4345 A5
2400 DET 48216 4344 E6
36800 RMLS 48174 4496 C7
Perry Pl Blvd
- RVVW 48192 4584 D5
- RVVW 48195 4584 D5
Perry Place Ct
- RVVW 48192 4584 D5
Pershing St
3300 WYNE 48184 4413 C6
7700 DET 48209 4419 A2
17300 LVNA 48152 4268 A1
18400 LVNA 48152 4196 A7
Persimmon Dr
4000 PTFD 48197 4491 A6
Perth Ct
22000 NOVI 48374 4192 B4
Perth St
27600 LVNA 48154 4268 A5
29100 LVNA 48154 4267 E5
33800 LVNA 48154 4266 E5
Peter St
2800 WIND N9C 4420 A4
3700 WIND N9C 4419 E5
Peterboro St
400 DET 48201 4345 B4
Peter Hunt St
8500 DET 48213 4274 B5
Peters Av
21400 WRRN 48091 4202 A2
Peters Dr
39500 CNTN 48187 4337 D4
Peters Rd
2000 WasC 48103 4329 C7
2000 WasC 48103 4404 C1
2000 WasC 48130 4329 C7
2000 WasC 48130 4404 C1
24400 FTRK 48134 4753 E2
24400 FTRK 48134 4754 A2
24400 FTRK 48183 4753 E2
24400 FTRK 48183 4754 A2
26000 BNTN 48134 4754 A1
26000 WDHN 48183 4754 A1
26100 BNTN 48134 4668 B7
26100 BNTN 48183 4668 B7
26100 WDHN 48134 4668 B7
26100 WDHN 48183 4668 B7
Peters St
- DET 48229 4501 B1
Petersburg Av
22800 EPTE 48021 4204 A1
Petite Pl
22000 HnTp 48174 4667 B4
Petoskey Av
9200 DET 48204 4344 A1
9600 DET 48204 4272 A7
12100 DET 48204 4271 E5
14600 DET 48238 4271 E4
16100 DET 48221 4271 D2
Petros Dr
15800 BwTp 48173 4755 B7
25300 HnTp 48134 4666 E7
Pettibone St
400 SLYN 48178 4189 B1
Petunia Dr
17500 BwTp 48173 4755 A6
Peyton Av
1800 YpTp 48197 4491 C4
Pfent St
13600 DET 48205 4202 E5
13900 DET 48205 4203 A5
Phalen Dr
- WDHN 48183 4668 C3
Pheasant Ct
5100 SpTp 48105 4408 A4
Pheasant Dr
3500 WasC 48103 4405 A2
Pheasant Ln
35400 WTLD 48185 4338 D6
Pheasant Run
1800 WasC 48189 4259 D2
5900 CNTN 48187 4336 C7
14900 SOGT 48101 4500 B7
14900 SOGT 48195 4500 B7
23600 HnTp 48164 4665 A6
23700 NOVI 48375 4193 A2
Pheasant Tr
5100 SpTp 48105 4408 A4
Pheasant Creek Dr
41400 CNTN 48188 4412 B3
Pheasant Lake Rd
10000 GOTp 48178 4188 D2
Pheasant Ridge Ct
9000 WasC 48176 4658 E3
N Pheasant Ridge Ln
9000 WasC 48176 4658 E2
9000 WasC 48176 4659 A2
S Pheasant Ridge Ln
9000 WasC 48176 4658 D2
9000 WasC 48176 4659 A3
Pheasant Run Cir
3500 AARB 48108 4489 D5
Pheasant Run Rd
24600 BNTN 48134 4668 A4
24700 BNTN 48134 4667 E4
Pheasant Woods Dr
600 CNTN 48188 4412 B3
Phelps
- DET 48213 4274 B6
Phelps Dr
- Tcmh N8V 4505 B1
Phelps St
12700 SOGT 48195 4584 D3
Philadelphia St
2900 AARB 48103 4405 C7
Philadelphia St E
10 DET 48202 4273 A7
900 DET 48211 4273 A7
Philadelphia St W
10 DET 48202 4273 A7
1100 DET 48202 4272 D7
1400 DET 48206 4272 D7
2600 DET 48206 4344 A2
4000 DET 48204 4344 A2
Philip Dr
23500 SFLD 48075 4197 E2
Philip St
200 DET 48214 4347 E1
700 DET 48214 4275 D6
9100 DET 48224 4275 B2
Phillip Dr
21500 NOVI 48375 4193 C4
Phillip St
10 BrTp 48134 4753 C6
Phillips Dr
39700 NvlT 48167 4193 D6
Philomene
20000 TYLR 48180 4499 E2
Philomene Av
14500 ALPK 48101 4500 C2
18700 ALPK 48101 4499 E2
Philomene Blvd
1700 LNPK 48146 4500 D3
2200 LNPK 48101 4500 D3
Phipps St
27200 INKR 48141 4415 B4
Phlox Av
24200 EPTE 48021 4203 C1
Phlox Dr
10 WasC 48189 4259 A1
Phlox Ln
39200 WTLD 48186 4412 E4
Phoenix Blvd
- RMLS 48174 4496 A3
Phoenix Ct
22100 FNHL 48336 4195 E3
25300 FTRK 48134 4753 E1
42700 PyTp 48170 4265 A5
Phoenix Dr
100 AARB 48108 4489 D5
Photo St
10 YPLT 48198 4492 A4
Phyllis St
1500 YpTp 48198 4492 E7
11400 TYLR 48180 4499 B7
35200 WYNE 48184 4496 D1
Picadilly Av
2800 Tcmh N0R 4505 C6
Picadilly Cir
2400 AARB 48103 4488 E3
21700 NOVI 48375 4193 B4
Picadilly Ct
47800 CNTN 48187 4336 A6
Picadilly Dr
22100 NOVI 48375 4193 B4
Picadilly Rd
19900 DET 48221 4199 E4
Picara Dr
24500 NOVI 48374 4192 B1
Piche Av
300 GSPF 48236 4276 C2
Piche St
600 WIND N9C 4420 B3
Pickering Dr
100 Amhg N9V 4757 B3
Pickering Pl
8000 WTLD 48185 4338 B4
Pickett St
23800 FMTN 48335 4194 D1
Pickford
25000 RDFD 48240 4196 D7
Pickford Av
31100 LVNA 48152 4195 B7
Pickford Ct
35400 LVNA 48152 4266 C1
46000 NvlT 48167 4264 C1
Pickford Dr
37700 LVNA 48152 4266 A1
Pickford St
- DET 48219 4196 E7
- DET 48219 4197 D7
- DET 48219 4198 A7
- DET 48240 4196 E7
- RDFD 48240 4196 E7
3800 DET 48221 4199 E7
12700 DET 48235 4199 A7
13700 DET 48235 4198 D7
27400 LVNA 48152 4196 A7
30400 LVNA 48152 4267 C1
31400 LVNA 48152 4195 B7
33400 LVNA 48152 4266 E1
45900 NvlT 48167 4264 B1
W Pickwick Cir
9200 TYLR 48180 4499 D5
Pickwick Cir E
9200 TYLR 48180 4499 E5
Pickwick Dr
6100 CNTN 48187 4337 B6
Picnic Ct
22800 NOVI 48375 4193 D3
Picnic Wy
- DET 48207 4346 D5
Piedmont
- CNTN 48187 4411 D1
Piedmont St
6000 DET 48228 4341 E5
13500 DET 48223 4269 E4
Pierce Av
21400 SFLD 48075 4198 B4
Pierce St
1900 DET 48207 4345 E3
2800 DET 48207 4346 A3
24000 SFLD 48075 4198 B1
29900 INKR 48141 4414 D6
30400 GDNC 48135 4339 C7
31400 WYNE 48184 4414 C6
33600 GDNC 48135 4413 E1
33600 GDNC 48135 4414 A1
41800 VNBN 48111 4495 C6
Pierre Av
100 WIND N9A 4346 A7
500 WIND N9A 4421 B1
1200 WIND N8X 4421 C2
1700 WIND N8W 4421 C3
Pierson Ct N
11700 DET 48228 4269 D7
Pierson Ct S
20700 DET 48228 4269 D7
Pierson Dr
19300 NvlT 48167 4193 C7
Pierson St
7200 DET 48127 4341 D4
7200 DET 48239 4341 D4
8000 DET 48228 4341 D3
11800 DET 48228 4269 D7
12200 DET 48223 4269 D7
17100 DET 48219 4269 C1
19900 DET 48219 4197 C5
Pike Rd
3000 Amhg N9V 4757 E3
Pike Rd CO-18
3000 Amhg N9V 4757 E3
E Pike Creek Rd
10 Tcmh N8N 4424 E1
300 Lksr N8N 4424 E5
300 Lksr N9K 4424 E5
E Pike Creek Rd CO-21
300 Lksr N8N 4424 E5
300 Lksr N9K 4424 E5
W Pike Creek Rd
100 Lksr N8N 4424 E4
100 Lksr N9K 4424 E4
100 Tcmh N8N 4424 E4
W Pike Creek Rd CO-21
100 Lksr N8N 4424 E4
100 Lksr N9K 4424 E4
100 Tcmh N8N 4424 E4
W Pike Creek Rd W
300 Lksr N8N 4424 E5
300 Lksr N9K 4424 E5
Pilgrim
24200 RDFD 48239 4268 E3
Pilgrim Av
23000 FRDL 48220 4200 B2
23000 HZLP 48030 4200 B2
23000 HZLP 48220 4200 B2
Pilgrim Ct
7500 CNTN 48187 4337 B4
Pilgrim St
- DET 48223 4270 A3
- DET 48227 4270 A3
- DET 48227 4271 A3
- DET 48238 4271 A3
200 HDPK 48203 4272 A3
1600 DET 48203 4272 A3
2200 DET 48238 4272 A3
20700 DET 48223 4269 C3
24000 RDFD 48223 4268 E7
24000 RDFD 48239 4268 E7
E Pillar Rd
2800 WasC 48189 4258 B4
W Pillar Rd
3800 WasC 48189 4258 A5
Pillette Pl
22000 HnTp 48174 4667 B4
Pillette Rd
200 WIND N8Y 4347 A7
1300 WIND N8Y 4422 A1
1800 WIND N8T 4422 C4
1800 WIND N8W 4422 C4
3400 WIND N8W 4422 C5
Pilot Dr
- PyTp 48167 4264 B5
- PyTp 48170 4264 B5
Pine
- FNHL 48034 4196 A4
- FNHL 48336 4196 A4
15300 RMLS 48174 4580 D5
Pine E
18000 BNTN 48192 4583 B7
Pine W
18000 BNTN 48174 4583 B7
18000 BNTN 48192 4583 B7
18500 BNTN 48174 4668 B1
18500 BNTN 48192 4668 B1
Pine Av
13000 TYLR 48180 4583 B2
Pine Blf
4700 PTFD 48197 4491 A7
Pine Ct
- CNTN 48188 4411 C6
10 GSPF 48236 4276 D5
8600 SpTp 48198 4492 C1
30000 INKR 48141 4414 D6
50100 PyTp 48170 4335 D3
Pine Dr
10 VNBN 48111 4577 E6
10 VNBN 48111 4578 A6
10 WasC 48189 4259 A1
22500 LyTp 48178 4189 C4
23500 BNTN 48174 4583 B6
29300 HnTp 48134 4752 E3
29300 HnTp 48134 4753 A3
49400 PyTp 48170 4263 D6
Pine Ln
5700 AGST 48197 4660 B1
Pine St
10 RVRG 48218 4418 E7
10 RVRG 48218 4501 E1
10 WIND N9A 4420 E2
100 RVRG 48218 4502 A1
700 WTLD 48186 4414 C7
1200 DET 48201 4345 B5
1300 DET 48216 4345 B5
1300 WYDT 48192 4585 A4
2200 WYDT 48192 4584 E4
2300 WYDT 48195 4584 E4
7800 TYLR 48180 4499 B3
13800 TYLR 48180 4583 B3
17600 DRBN 48101 4417 A6
17600 DRBN 48124 4417 A6
21800 BNTN 48183 4668 B3
27400 INKR 48141 4415 A6
29400 INKR 48141 4414 E6
Pineapple Ln
10 WasC 48103 4488 B3
Pineapple St
400 WTLD 48186 4497 D1
Pinebluff Ct
3200 AARB 48105 4331 E7
Pine Brae Dr
400 AARB 48105 4407 D6
Pinebrook Dr
18100 NvlT 48167 4264 C1
Pine Cone Dr
16400 WDHN 48183 4669 A3
Pine Cove Dr
9000 WasC 48189 4259 B1
Pine Creek Ct
47400 NvlT 48167 4264 A2
Pinecrest Av
2300 AARB 48104 4490 C3
Pine Crest Dr
- CNTN 48187 4412 B2
Pinecrest Dr
- DET 48220 4199 D3
- DET 48221 4199 D3
100 FRDL 48220 4199 D3
2600 FRDL 48069 4199 D2
12000 PyTp 48170 4264 D7
12000 PyTp 48170 4336 D1
17000 ALPK 48101 4500 A2
18700 ALPK 48101 4499 E2
Pinecrest St
20000 TYLR 48101 4499 D2
20000 TYLR 48180 4499 D2
24200 NOVI 48375 4193 A1
Pinecrest Estates Dr
5400 WasC 48105 4333 B1
Pinegree St
21600 RKWD 48173 4754 D7
Pine Grove Ct
2200 AARB 48103 4406 A3
24300 FNHL 48335 4194 C1
Pine Hill Ct
9100 WasC 48176 4658 A2
Pinehill Dr
48600 PyTp 48170 4335 E2
Pinehollow Ln
18600 NvlT 48167 4192 B7
Pinehurst Cir
46300 NvlT 48167 4264 B3
Pinehurst Ct
21400 WDHN 48183 4669 A3
34500 LVNA 48154 4266 D6
Pinehurst Dr
- TNTN 48183 4755 B1
100 CNTN 48188 4411 C3
34400 LVNA 48154 4266 D6
46200 NvlT 48167 4264 C3
Pinehurst Rd
11100 PyTp 48170 4335 C2
Pinehurst St
6500 DRBN 48126 4343 B4
8000 DET 48204 4343 B2
8400 AGST 48197 4660 B1
12500 DET 48204 4271 B6
13500 DET 48238 4271 B5
16500 DET 48221 4271 B1
18000 DET 48221 4199 B7
Pine Ledge Dr
19000 BNTN 48192 4668 C1
Pine Ridge Av
600 Amhg N9V 4757 C4
Pine Ridge Ct
4200 AATp 48105 4407 E6
8000 WasC 48167 4261 E3
8000 WasC 48167 4262 A3
49400 PyTp 48170 4335 D2
Pineridge Ct
2300 YpTp 48198 4493 A6
41500 CNTN 48187 4412 C2
Pine Ridge Dr
25000 BNTN 48134 4667 C7
49300 PyTp 48170 4335 D2
Pineridge Ln
- SOGT 48195 4584 B1
Pine Ridge St
200 AARB 48103 4405 E5
Pine Trail Ct
8800 PyTp 48170 4336 A3
Pinetree Ct
3700 TNTN 48183 4669 B4
Pine Tree Dr
900 AARB 48103 4405 E4
Pinetree Dr
2300 TNTN 48183 4669 B4
40200 PyTp 48170 4337 C2
44400 PyTp 48170 4336 D2
Pinetree Rd
1500 TNTN 48183 4669 B3
1500 TNTN 48192 4669 B3
Pinetree St
34400 LVNA 48150 4338 D2
39000 LVNA 48150 4337 E2
Pine Valley Blvd
1500 AARB 48104 4489 D3
Pine Valley Ct
1300 AARB 48104 4489 D3
Pine Valley Dr
15900 NvlT 48167 4264 E3
Pineview Ct
100 AARB 48104 4407 A6
Pineview Dr
5400 YpTp 48197 4575 C2
9000 PyTp 48170 4335 E3
W Pineview Dr
3200 WasC 48130 4329 A5
Pineview Rd
3300 WIND N8R 4423 C3
E Pineview Rd
3200 WasC 48130 4329 A5
Pineview Wy
13300 SOGT 48195 4584 B2
Pinewood Av
400 YpTp 48198 4492 C5
Pinewood Cir
100 PLYM 48170 4337 B1
Pinewood Cres
100 Tcmh N8N 4348 E6
Pinewood Ct
5800 CNTN 48187 4336 A7
39700 NvlT 48167 4265 D3
Pinewood Pl
1800 LSal N9J 4502 C6
Pinewood Rd
36700 WYNE 48184 4413 B5
Pinewood St
300 WasC 48103 4405 C5
400 AARB 48103 4405 C5
11600 DET 48205 4202 E5
11600 DET 48234 4202 E5
13800 DET 48205 4203 A5
23000 WRRN 48091 4201 D1
Ping Dr
5600 PTFD 48108 4572 E2
Pingree Av
2100 LNPK 48146 4501 A5
24000 WRRN 48089 4203 B1
Pingree Ct
1200 DET 48202 4272 D7
Pingree St
10 DET 48202 4273 A7
1100 DET 48202 4272 D7
1400 DET 48206 4272 D7
2600 DET 48206 4344 B1
4000 DET 48204 4344 B1
Pinkowski
- MVDL 48122 4417 E5
Pinnacle Ct
5100 PTFD 48108 4572 D2
Pino Ct
9500 PyTp 48170 4336 A2
Pin Oak Dr
2600 AATp 48103 4405 E2
Pin Oak Ln
200 AGST 48191 4661 B7
Pintail Dr
16800 BwTp 48173 4841 A1
Pintail Ln
7800 HbgT 48189 4186 C4
Pinyon Tr
10700 GOTp 48178 4187 D1
Pioneer Av
4200 WIND N9G 4505 A4
Pioneer Rd
7600 YpTp 48197 4576 A6
Piper Av
21700 EPTE 48021 4203 D1
Piper Blvd
400 DET 48214 4347 D1
N Piper Ct
500 DET 48214 4347 D3
S Piper Ct
400 DET 48214 4347 D2
Piper St
28200 RMLS 48174 4498 A1
Piquette St
10 DET 48202 4345 B1
1100 DET 48211 4345 B1
Pitch Pine Ct
4900 PTFD 48197 4491 A7
Pitchpine Ln E
4900 PTFD 48197 4491 A7
4900 YpTp 48197 4491 A7
Pitchpine Ln W
4400 PTFD 48197 4491 A7
Pitkin St
10 HDPK 48203 4272 C3
Pitt St
4200 ECRS 48229 4501 D4
7200 DET 48209 4419 A1
8000 DET 48209 4418 E2
Pitt St E
10 WIND N9A 4420 C1
Pitt St W
10 WIND N9A 4420 D1
Pittman Rd
9000 AGST 48197 4660 D3
Pittsburg Av
1800 WIND N9E 4503 C2
Pittsburg St
6300 DET 48210 4344 A5
6400 DET 48210 4343 E5
Pittsfield Blvd
2200 AARB 48104 4490 C2
Pittsford St
6800 CNTN 48187 4336 E5
6800 CNTN 48187 4337 A7
Pittsview Dr
3000 AARB 48108 4490 C4
Place St
28400 GBTR 48173 4755 C3
Placid Wy
2200 AARB 48105 4406 E1
2400 AARB 48105 4407 A1
Plain Wy
15000 RMLS 48174 4581 E4
Plainfield St
100 DBHT 48141 4415 C1
1300 DBHT 48127 4415 B1
7200 DBHT 48127 4340 B4
Plainview Av
6000 DET 48228 4341 E5
11600 DET 48228 4269 E7
13900 DET 48223 4269 E4
16500 DET 48219 4269 E2
20200 DET 48219 4197 D5
Plainview Ct
- DET 48219 4197 D6
10 AARB 48108 4490 A6
Plainview St
3300 TNTN 48183 4669 B3
Plaisance Blvd
22400 NOVI 48375 4192 D3
Planavon St
1800 FRDL 48220 4199 E2
Plantain Pl
10 YpTp 48197 4577 B4

INDEX 43

Platt Ln — Detroit & Wayne County Street Index — Quail Hollow Ct

STREET / Block City ZIP Map# Grid

Platt Ln
4600 PTFD 48108 4490 B7
Platt Pl N
3100 PTFD 48176 4574 B5
3100 PTFD 48197 4574 B5
Platt Pl S
3100 PTFD 48176 4574 B5
3100 PTFD 48197 4574 B5
Platt Rd
2100 AARB 48104 4490 B3
3000 AARB 48108 4490 B5
3800 PTFD 48108 4490 B6
4600 PTFD 48108 4574 B2
5000 PTFD 48197 4574 B2
6100 PTFD 48176 4574 B6
7900 WasC 48176 4574 B6
7900 WasC 48176 4659 B1
7900 WasC 48197 4574 B6
7900 WasC 48197 4659 B1
N Platt Rd
9000 WasC 48160 4659 B3
9000 WasC 48176 4659 B3
9000 WasC 48197 4659 B3
Platt St
3300 DET 48207 4345 E1
Plattsburg St
21200 SFLD 48034 4197 B4
Player Cir
- WTLD 48186 4414 D4
Playview Dr
25900 WynC 48138 4670 A7
Plaza Dr
- AARB 48108 4489 C4
400 DET 48226 4345 C6
3600 PTFD 48108 4489 B5
10500 GOTp 48116 4187 A4
Plaza Dr S
15700 TYLR 48180 4583 B4
Pleasant Av
15500 ALPK 48101 4500 A6
21700 EPTE 48021 4203 D2
E Pleasant Av
10 RVRG 48218 4418 E5
10 RVRG 48218 4419 A7
Pleasant Dr
900 YPLT 48197 4491 D4
15000 BwTp 48173 4841 B1
Pleasant Ln
7700 YpTp 48197 4576 A4
Pleasant Pl
100 AARB 48103 4405 D6
4300 WIND N8Y 4346 E7
4300 WIND N8Y 4347 A7
Pleasant St
500 FRDL 48220 4200 A1
11800 DET 48229 4418 D6
19600 STCS 48080 4204 B1
W Pleasant St
10 RVRG 48218 4418 D6
1700 RVRG 48229 4418 D6
Pleasant Vw
8500 WasC 48167 4262 C4
Pleasant Creek Dr
- BNTN 48134 4667 D7
Pleasant Lake Rd
3500 WasC 48103 4572 A1
4200 WasC 48103 4571 D1
4200 WasC 48176 4571 D1
Pleasant Ridge Ct
300 SALN 48176 4657 D1
Pleasant Ridge Dr
100 SALN 48176 4657 D1
300 CNTN 48188 4410 E3
7800 WasC 48167 4262 B5
E Pleasant Ridge Dr
27000 DBHT 48127 4340 B5
N Pleasant Ridge Dr
27100 DBHT 48127 4340 B5
W Pleasant Ridge Dr
27200 DBHT 48127 4340 B5
Pleasant View Ct
13900 PyTp 48170 4263 E6
Pleasure Wy
- DET 48207 4346 D5
Plum Av
26100 INKR 48141 4415 C5
Plum Hllw
45400 CNTN 48187 4336 D4
Plum St
- DET 48226 4345 B6
300 WYDT 48192 4585 B4
400 WTLD 48186 4414 D7
400 WTLD 48186 4497 D1
600 DET 48201 4345 B6
1400 DET 48216 4345 B6
12700 SOGT 48195 4584 E4
Plumbrooke Dr
23200 SFLD 48075 4197 C2
Plumer St
4600 DET 48209 4344 C7
6200 DET 48209 4419 B1
Plum Grove St
17800 BNTN 48174 4583 B7
Plumhoff Av
20700 WRRN 48091 4201 B4
Plum Hollow Dr
5800 PTFD 48197 4574 C3
Plum Hollow St
23000 SFLD 48034 4197 B2
Plum Ridge Dr
4000 PTFD 48197 4574 D2
Plumridge Ln
24700 SFLD 48034 4196 D2
Plumrose Dr
9600 GOTp 48178 4188 E1
Plumtree Ct
48900 PyTp 48170 4335 E2
Plum Tree Dr
48900 PyTp 48170 4335 E1
Plumview Ln
10 WasC 48103 4488 B3
Plumwoode Ct
19200 BwTp 48183 4755 A2
Plumwoode Ct N
19600 BwTp 48183 4755 A1
Plymouth Cross
15000 PyTp 48170 4265 B4
Plymouth Ct
21500 WynC 48138 4670 B3
Plymouth Rd
100 PLYM 48170 4265 C7
500 PyTp 48170 4265 C7
1400 AARB 48105 4406 C4
1500 AATp 48105 4406 C4
2000 AARB 48105 4407 B3
2000 AATp 48105 4407 B3
3500 WIND N8W 4422 B4
8300 DET 48204 4271 A7
12700 DET 48227 4271 A7
13600 DET 48227 4270 C7
18100 DET 48228 4270 C7
18700 DET 48223 4270 C7
18800 DET 48223 4269 D7
18800 DET 48228 4269 D7
22200 DET 48239 4269 C7
22600 DET 48239 4341 B1
23200 RDFD 48239 4341 A1
24000 RDFD 48239 4340 D1
27400 LVNA 48150 4340 A1
27400 LVNA 48239 4340 A1
28700 LVNA 48150 4339 D1
33400 LVNA 48150 4338 C1
38600 LVNA 48150 4265 E7
38600 LVNA 48150 4337 E1
Plymouth Wy
49400 PyTp 48170 4263 D6
Plymouth-Ann Arbor Rd
4000 AATp 48105 4407 D2
4300 AATp 48105 4408 A1
5000 SpTp 48105 4408 A1
5000 SpTp 48198 4408 A1
6000 SpTp 48105 4333 C7
6000 SpTp 48198 4333 C7
7400 SpTp 48105 4334 A6
8000 SpTp 48170 4334 A6
9500 SpTp 48170 4335 A4
Plymouth Corners Blvd
- PyTp 48170 4265 B4
Plymouth Heights Ln
51300 PyTp 48170 4335 C2
Plymouth Hollow Dr
42400 PyTp 48170 4265 A5
Plymouth Lake Cir
51100 PyTp 48170 4335 C3
Plymouth Lake Dr
51000 PyTp 48170 4335 C3
Plymouth Oaks Blvd
43800 PyTp 48170 4264 E6
Plymouth Ridge Ct
51100 PyTp 48170 4335 C3
Plymouth Ridge Dr
51000 PyTp 48170 4335 C3
Plymouth Valley Dr
51000 PyTp 48170 4335 C3
Plymouth Woods Dr
11400 LVNA 48150 4338 A1
11600 LVNA 48150 4337 E1
Pocahontas Dr
11000 GOTp 48178 4187 E4
Pocahontas St
6800 WTLD 48185 4338 E6
Pocatello Dr
41600 CNTN 48187 4412 B1
Poe Dr
- CNTN 48187 4411 D1
Poe Ln
600 SLYN 48178 4189 C3
Poe St
7300 DET 48202 4344 E1
7300 DET 48206 4344 E1
7300 DET 48210 4344 E1
Poinciana
18200 RDFD 48240 4268 B1
20400 RDFD 48240 4196 B5
Poinciana St
20700 SFLD 48034 4196 B4
Point Dr
29700 GBTR 48173 4755 D5
E Point Dr
30300 GBTR 48173 4755 D5
N Point Dr
300 WasC 48189 4186 E7
Pointe Cross
49400 PyTp 48170 4263 E7
Pointe Dr
7300 CNTN 48187 4336 E5
Pointe Ln
- AARB 48105 4406 E3
1900 AATp 48105 4406 E3
S Pointe Rd
27600 WynC 48138 4756 A3
W Pointe St
17900 BNTN 48174 4668 B2
Pointe Crossing St
1800 AATp 48105 4406 E3
Pointe Moullie Rd
35900 BwTp 48173 4841 C4
Pointe O Woods Ct
23700 LyTp 48178 4190 C2
Pointe Park Pl
10 GPPK 48230 4275 E7
Pointer St
2000 DET 48234 4200 E5
Pointe West Dr
- Amhg N9V 4671 B4
Poisson St
1200 Tcmh N8N 4423 E2
Poland St
- DET 48212 4273 B5
2200 HMTK 48212 4273 B5
Polaris Ct
45100 PyTp 48170 4264 D5
Polk Av
200 RVRG 48218 4418 D7
300 RVRG 48218 4501 D1
27200 BwTp 48183 4754 E2
Polk Dr
50800 PyTp 48170 4263 C6
Polk St
- DRBN 48124 4416 D5
4100 DBHT 48125 4416 D6
5800 TYLR 48125 4499 D1
6700 TYLR 48180 4499 D3
14500 TYLR 48180 4583 D3
Pollice Av
- TYLR 48180 4499 B5
Pollyanna Ct
16600 LVNA 48154 4266 E2
19500 LVNA 48152 4194 E6
Pollyanna Dr
19300 LVNA 48152 4194 E7
Pollyanna St
16300 LVNA 48154 4266 E2
Polo Dr
46100 CNTN 48187 4336 B6
Polo Club Dr
38800 FNHL 48335 4193 E3
Polo Fields Dr
4800 WasC 48103 4404 C6
Polonia Pl
1500 WIND N8Y 4422 B1
Polonia Park Pl
1400 WIND N8Y 4422 B1
Pomona Dr
16100 RDFD 48239 4268 C3
16400 RDFD 48240 4268 B2
Pomona Rd
700 AARB 48103 4406 A4
1000 AARB 48103 4405 E4
Pomona St
17400 DET 48224 4276 B3
Pompano St
300 WIND N8W 4505 A2
Ponchartrain Blvd
- DET 48203 4200 A6
17100 DET 48203 4272 B1
17100 DET 48221 4272 B1
Pond Ct
42900 NvlT 48167 4193 A6
Pond Rd
23600 SFLD 48034 4196 E1
23600 SFLD 48034 4197 A1
Pond Run
4000 CNTN 48188 4411 C7
Pond Wy
15000 RMLS 48174 4581 D4
Pond Bluff Dr
13600 VNBN 48111 4579 A3
Ponderosa Ct
2300 YpTp 48198 4493 A6
Ponderosa Dr
4000 TNTN 48183 4669 C6
9700 GOTp 48178 4188 D2
Ponderosa Tr N
10 VNBN 48111 4494 D5
Ponderosa Tr S
10 VNBN 48111 4494 D5
Pond Island Ct
800 NHVL 48167 4192 C5
Pond Ridge Ln
42400 VNBN 48111 4579 B3
Pond Run Ct
3900 CNTN 48188 4411 C7
Pond Shore Dr
1600 PTFD 48108 4573 A4
Pondside Ct
25000 FTRK 48134 4753 E3
Ponds View Dr
100 AARB 48103 4489 B3
Pondview
22100 NOVI 48375 4193 D4
Pond View Ct
2400 CNTN 48188 4411 B5
Pond View Dr
13000 GOTp 48178 4188 D2
25600 HnTp 48164 4665 D7
25600 HnTp 48164 4751 D1
Pondview St
300 SALN 48176 4657 C1
Pond Village Dr
15000 TYLR 48180 4582 C4
Pon Meadow Ct
41600 NvlT 48167 4265 B2
Ponmeadow Rd
41800 NvlT 48167 4265 B2
Pontchartrain Blvd
- DET 48203 4200 A7
17300 DET 48203 4272 B1
17300 DET 48221 4272 B1
Pontiac St
9300 DET 48214 4346 E2
Pontiac Tr
1000 AARB 48105 4406 C4
1900 AATp 48105 4406 C1
3000 AATp 48105 4331 E5
4500 AATp 48105 4332 A5
4900 WasC 48105 4332 B3
5600 WasC 48105 4333 A1
6000 WasC 48170 4333 A1
6000 WasC 48178 4333 A1
6300 WasC 48170 4261 B7
6300 WasC 48178 4261 B7
6600 WasC 48167 4261 B7
8700 WasC 48178 4189 B6
20700 LyTp 48178 4189 B6
21600 SLYN 48178 4189 B6
Ponvalley Dr
17100 NvlT 48167 4265 B2
Pool Av
2000 WIND N9C 4420 C7
Pope St
1000 LSal N9J 4502 E4
1400 LSal N9J 4503 A4
Poplar
- CNTN 48188 4411 C6
Poplar Av
3100 WRRN 48091 4201 A3
3700 WIND N9C 4420 B6
Poplar Ct
400 Amhg N9V 4757 C4
1000 WYDT 48192 4585 B2
22600 HZLP 48030 4200 D3
Poplar Dr
- NvlT 48167 4264 D3
6600 HbgT 48116 4186 A2
6700 YpTp 48197 4576 E5
26700 HnTp 48164 4751 B2
Poplar Ln
34800 WTLD 48185 4338 D6
Poplar St
1000 WYDT 48192 4585 A2
3200 DET 48210 4344 D5
11600 SOGT 48101 4500 C7
11600 SOGT 48195 4500 C7
13000 SOGT 48195 4584 C2
17400 RVVW 48192 4584 C6
21700 WDHN 48183 4668 C3
34500 WYNE 48184 4413 E5
Poplar Park Blvd
10 PTRG 48069 4199 C1
Poppleton Blvd
- CNTN 48187 4335 E5
Poppleton Ct
49000 CNTN 48187 4335 E6
Poppleton Rd
6500 CNTN 48187 4335 E6
Poppy Ln
7800 PTFD 48176 4573 D7
Porath Ct
- DRBN 48126 4343 B7
Porath St
4800 DRBN 48126 4343 C7
Port Av
2000 PTFD 48108 4572 E4
2000 PTFD 48108 4573 A4
Port St
23300 FTRK 48134 4754 B5
45500 PyTp 48170 4264 C5
Portage St
10 DET 48203 4272 B1
10 HDPK 48203 4272 B1
Portage Wy
- DET 48207 4347 A5
23300 NOVI 48375 4192 E1
23300 NOVI 48375 4193 A3
Port Creek Rd
14000 MonC 48117 4752 E4
14000 MonC 48117 4753 A5
14000 MonC 48134 4752 E4
14000 MonC 48134 4753 A5
Porter Av
- LNPK 48122 4500 E2
2000 LNPK 48146 4500 D3
Porter Rd
3300 WasC 48103 4405 B5
Porter St
1000 DET 48226 4345 B7
1200 DRBN 48124 4416 D3
2600 DET 48216 4345 A7
3000 DET 48216 4344 E7
3900 DET 48216 4419 D1
5600 DET 48209 4419 B1
22500 NOVI 48374 4192 C3
36700 RMLS 48174 4580 C1
Porteridge Ln
6000 CNTN 48187 4336 D6
Portis Rd
15300 NvlT 48170 4265 B4
15800 NvlT 48167 4265 B3
Portlance St
11000 DET 48205 4274 C1
Portland Dr
1200 WTLD 48186 4412 E3
Portsmere Ct
1000 NHVL 48167 4192 B5
Portsmouth Av
24700 NOVI 48374 4192 C1
Portsmouth Ct
12600 PyTp 48170 4264 C7
Portsmouth Crossing St
12800 PyTp 48170 4264 C7
Portsmouth Towne St
10 SFLD 48075 4198 B2
Posey Ct
9000 WasC 48189 4259 B1
Posey Dr
10 WasC 48189 4259 B2
9200 WasC 48189 4187 B7
Post Ln
11300 GOTp 48178 4188 D6
Post St
100 DET 48209 4419 B3
S Post St
100 DET 48209 4419 C4
Postiff Av
42100 PyTp 48170 4337 B2
Post Mill Ct
44200 CNTN 48187 4336 E5
Potomac Cir
23000 FNHL 48335 4194 D2
Potomac Ct
3100 PTFD 48197 4574 B2
25000 SLYN 48178 4189 B1
Potomac Dr
3000 PTFD 48197 4574 B2
25100 SLYN 48178 4189 B1
Potomac Rd
600 NHVL 48167 4192 C6
Potter Av
300 AARB 48103 4489 A1
8900 AGST 48191 4662 B2
Potter Ct
10 BLVL 48111 4578 E1
Potter Dr
10 BLVL 48111 4578 E2
Powderhorn Dr
6500 CNTN 48187 4336 C4
Powell Av
2400 AARB 48104 4489 E2
23000 HZLP 48030 4200 C2
Powell Rd
47000 PyTp 48170 4336 B1
48400 PyTp 48170 4335 E1
Powell St
13100 DET 48229 4418 C4
Powell Ridge Ct
49500 PyTp 48170 4335 D2
Power Rd
21400 FNHL 48336 4195 A4
23600 FMTN 48336 4195 A1
Powers Av
18000 DBHT 48125 4417 A7
20900 DBHT 48125 4416 C7
24300 DBHT 48125 4415 E7
27300 DBHT 48186 4415 C7
Powers St
28900 WTLD 48186 4414 E7
28900 WTLD 48186 4415 A7
Powhatan Ct
11000 GOTp 48178 4187 E5
Prado Ct
26000 INKR 48141 4415 D4
Prado Pl
200 WIND N8S 4347 B6
1100 WIND N8S 4422 D1
Prairie Ct
2400 AARB 48105 4407 B2
8700 VNBN 48111 4495 B5
Prairie Ln
24200 WRRN 48089 4203 A1
Prairie Rd
5600 WasC 48176 4572 B2
Prairie St
2000 AARB 48105 4407 B3
7200 DET 48210 4343 D3
9500 DET 48204 4343 D1
10200 DET 48204 4271 D7
15800 DET 48238 4271 D3
16100 DET 48221 4271 D1
18200 DET 48221 4199 D7
20400 DET 48220 4199 D5
Prairie Creek Blvd
20400 BNTN 48183 4668 B2
Prairie Dunes Ct N
5200 PTFD 48108 4572 E1
Prairie Dunes Ct S
1700 PTFD 48108 4572 E2
Prairie Grass Ct
45700 VNBN 48111 4494 D6
Prarie Ct
3700 WIND N9G 4504 A3
Pratt Pl
200 WIND N8Y 4346 D7
Pratt Rd
3500 WasC 48103 4405 A3
3900 WasC 48103 4404 E3
Pratt Ridge Ct
900 WasC 48103 4405 A3
Pray
- YPLT 48197 4491 D3
Prentis St
400 DET 48201 4345 B3
Prescott Av
1200 AARB 48103 4489 A1
20700 WRRN 48091 4201 B4
Prescott Rd
27400 HnTp 48174 4581 E7
27400 HnTp 48174 4582 A6
33400 HnTp 48174 4580 E7
Prescott St
2900 YpTp 48198 4493 B2
3800 DET 48212 4273 D3
3800 HMTK 48212 4273 D3
21100 SFLD 48075 4197 C3
Preserve Blvd
1800 CNTN 48188 4412 D4
Preserve Cir E
1800 CNTN 48188 4412 D5
Preserve Cir W
1800 CNTN 48188 4412 D5
Preserve Ct
3800 WasC 48130 4329 C5
Preserve Dr
3500 WasC 48130 4329 C6
Presidential Dr
- SOGT 48195 4584 A1
- VNBN 48111 4577 C4
- VNBN 48197 4577 C4
Pressler St
8000 DET 48213 4274 B5
Prest St
8000 DET 48228 4342 D3
11300 DET 48227 4342 D1
14500 DET 48227 4270 D4
16100 DET 48235 4270 C3
20400 DET 48235 4198 C4
Prestbury Ct
1400 CNTN 48187 4411 D1
Prestbury Rd
44900 CNTN 48187 4411 D1
Preston Ct
2600 WIND N9E 4503 D1
Preston Pl
10 GSPF 48236 4276 E1
Preston St
3100 DET 48207 4346 A2
7200 DET 48214 4346 C2
Prestwick
21000 FNHL 48335 4194 B4
Prestwick Av
21200 HRWD 48225 4204 B7
Prestwick Ct
10 DRBN 48120 4417 C2
3500 AARB 48105 4407 D4
40200 NOVI 48167 4193 C5
Prestwick Rd
1500 GSPW 48236 4204 B7
1800 HRWD 48225 4204 B7
Preswick Ct
42600 VNBN 48111 4495 B5
Preswyck Dr
23200 WynC 48138 4670 C5
Prevost St
8800 DET 48228 4342 C2
13900 DET 48227 4270 C5
16100 DET 48235 4270 C3
18200 DET 48235 4198 C7
Price St
39400 VNBN 48174 4579 E1
Primrose Ct
200 PTFD 48197 4574 E2
45600 PyTp 48170 4336 C3
Primrose Ln
23100 BNTN 48183 4668 B2
Primrose Pl
600 Tcmh N8N 4424 B1
4900 WYNE 48184 4414 B7
Prince Rd
300 WIND N9C 4419 E5
500 WIND N9C 4420 A5
21600 WynC 48111 4663 E4
21600 WynC 48111 4664 A4
Prince Hall Dr
2000 DET 48207 4346 A3
Princess Av
2300 INKR 48141 4415 C4
Princess Ct
2300 WRRN 48091 4201 A1
Princess Dr
200 CNTN 48188 4412 A2
Princess Rd
2300 WIND N8T 4422 C3
Princess St
4700 DBHT 48125 4415 C7
5800 TYLR 48180 4498 C1
17600 BNTN 48174 4582 C6
Princeton Av
13000 TYLR 48180 4583 A2
25800 INKR 48141 4415 C5
Princeton Blvd
21900 NOVI 48167 4192 C4
21900 NOVI 48374 4192 C4
Princeton Ct
7700 WTLD 48185 4338 C3
Princeton Dr
- SLYN 48178 4189 A3
14200 PyTp 48170 4265 B5
Princeton Pl
5600 YpTp 48197 4576 C2
Princeton St
200 CNTN 48188 4411 E3
700 AARB 48103 4406 A7
15700 DET 48238 4272 A3
16100 DET 48221 4272 A2
24000 DRBN 48124 4416 A5
24300 DRBN 48124 4415 E5
25400 DBHT 48125 4415 D5
25400 DBHT 48141 4415 D5
Priscilla Ln
- LVNA 48150 4338 D1
11700 PyTp 48170 4336 E1
Pristine Dr
9900 GOTp 48178 4188 E2
Proctor Rd
42300 CNTN 48188 4412 A3
45400 CNTN 48188 4411 C3
49400 CNTN 48188 4410 D4
Proctor St
5200 DET 48210 4343 D5
Professional Dr
3000 AARB 48104 4490 B2
Professional Center Dr
37400 LVNA 48154 4266 A2
Progress Av
800 LNPK 48146 4501 A4
2100 LNPK 48146 4500 C4
Promenade Av
15500 ALPK 48101 4500 A6
Promenade Cir
3000 PTFD 48108 4490 D4
Promenade St
11000 DET 48213 4274 E3
12500 DET 48213 4275 A2
15200 DET 48224 4275 B2
Prospect Av
10 WIND N9C 4419 D5
6700 WRRN 48091 4201 E3
7200 WRRN 48091 4202 A3
12200 WRRN 48089 4202 D3
Prospect Ct
10 YPLT 48198 4492 B4
3900 WasC 48103 4329 E5
18000 MVDL 48122 4417 E6
Prospect Rd
3600 SpTp 48105 4334 A7
3600 SpTp 48198 4334 A7
N Prospect Rd
10 YPLT 48198 4492 B1
900 YpTp 48198 4492 B1
1500 SpTp 48198 4492 B1
1800 SpTp 48198 4409 B7
3300 SpTp 48105 4334 B7
3300 SpTp 48105 4409 B1
3300 SpTp 48198 4334 B7
S Prospect Rd
10 YPLT 48198 4492 B5
Prospect St
1100 AARB 48104 4406 C7
1200 AARB 48104 4489 C1
12700 DRBN 48126 4343 C7
12700 DRBN 48126 4418 A1
14700 DRBN 48126 4417 D1
16000 HDPK 48203 4272 B2
17000 MVDL 48122 4417 E5
17000 MVDL 48122 4418 A5
23200 FMTN 48336 4195 B2
Prosper Av
18000 EPTE 48021 4203 E2
Prosper Dr
22200 SFLD 48034 4196 E3
Protavia St
5900 LSal N9H 4503 E4
Provencal Rd
10 GSPF 48236 4204 D7
10 GSPF 48236 4276 E1
10 GSPF 48236 4277 A2
Providence Cres
4200 WIND N9G 4504 E3
Providence Dr
15500 SFLD 48075 4198 C2
15500 SFLD 48237 4198 C2
Providence Ln
43000 CNTN 48188 4412 A2
Provincetown Ct
2700 AARB 48103 4405 E1
Provincetown Ln
400 PLYM 48170 4264 D7
Provincial Ct
7200 CNTN 48187 4336 E5
Provincial Dr
2700 AARB 48104 4490 A1
22000 WDHN 48183 4668 C6
Provincial Rd
- Tcmh N0R 4505 B3
1000 WIND N8W 4504 E1
1200 WIND N8W 4505 B3
7300 CNTN 48187 4336 E5
Pryor St
9300 DET 48214 4346 E1
Pueblo Dr
39200 RMLS 48174 4495 E3
Pulaski St
2300 HMTK 48212 4273 B3
Pulbrook Rd
10100 WIND N8R 4423 B2
Pulford St
- DET 48214 4346 C1
2400 WIND N9E 4503 E2
3400 DET 48207 4346 A2
Pulleyblank St
5200 Tcmh N0R 4505 B5
Pullman St
12700 SOGT 48195 4584 D1
Purcell Dr
45500 PyTp 48170 4336 C2
Purdue Av
22500 FNHL 48336 4195 D2
Puritan
24000 DET 48219 4268 D3
24000 RDFD 48219 4268 D3
25800 RDFD 48239 4268 C3
25800 RDFD 48240 4268 C3
Puritan Ln
23000 BNTN 48174 4583 B7
Puritan St
10 HDPK 48203 4272 C2
400 DET 48238 4272 A2
400 HDPK 48238 4272 A2
1700 DET 48203 4272 A2
2200 DET 48221 4272 A2
2700 DET 48221 4271 D2
2700 DET 48238 4271 D2
12700 DET 48227 4271 A2
12700 DET 48235 4271 A2
13500 DET 48227 4270 E2
13500 DET 48235 4270 E2
18400 DET 48219 4270 A2
18400 DET 48223 4270 A2
18900 DET 48219 4269 E2
23700 DET 48223 4269 A3
23800 DET 48219 4268 E7
23800 DET 48223 4268 E7
29400 LVNA 48154 4267 C3
Purlingbrook Rd
21500 NOVI 48375 4193 C4
Purlingbrook St
17200 LVNA 48152 4267 C2
19600 LVNA 48152 4195 C5
Purple Sage Ct
45800 VNBN 48111 4494 C6
Putnam Pl
10 GSPS 48236 4205 A4
Putnam St
10 DET 48202 4345 B2
1500 DET 48210 4345 A3
3200 DET 48210 4344 C4
Putnam Phelps
- YPLT 48197 4491 E3
Putney Ct
47400 CNTN 48188 4411 B4

Q

Quail Cir
8800 PyTp 48170 4336 A3
8900 PyTp 48170 4335 E3
Quail Ct
41600 CNTN 48188 4412 B3
Quail Hllw
21000 WDHN 48183 4668 D4
Quail Run
3700 SpTp 48105 4333 B7
Quail Cir Ct
8900 PyTp 48170 4335 E3
Quail Hollow Ct
2800 AARB 48108 4489 E4

STREET Block City ZIP Map# Grid

Quail Hollow Ct
11000 GOTp 48178 4188 B4
Quail Ridge Ct
46100 PyTp 48170 4336 C1
Quail Ridge Dr
46000 PyTp 48170 4336 C1
Quail Ridge Dr N
21500 BNTN 48192 4583 C6
Quail Ridge Dr S
21500 BNTN 48192 4583 C6
Quail Run Cir
6500 WTLD 48185 4338 D6
22100 SLYN 48178 4189 B5
Quail Run Ct
49200 PyTp 48170 4335 E3
S Quail Run Dr
48400 PyTp 48170 4335 E3
48400 PyTp 48170 4336 A3
Quail Run Dr N
9000 PyTp 48170 4335 E4
Quaker Hill Dr
44900 CNTN 48187 4336 D5
Quaker Ridge Dr
2300 PTFD 48108 4572 D2
Quakertown Ln
16100 LVNA 48154 4265 E2
17000 LVNA 48152 4265 E2
Quality Dr
10 ECRS 48229 4501 E2
Quality Wy
- WIND N8T 4422 E4
- WIND N8T 4423 A4
Quandt Av
4700 ALPK 48101 4500 C1
Quarry Rd
- SOGT 48195 4584 E4
- WYDT 48192 4584 E4
- WYDT 48195 4584 E4
17000 RVVW 48192 4584 E6
17000 RVVW 48195 4584 E6
Quarterback Ct
2300 YPLT 48197 4491 A2
Quebec Av
5700 WasC 48103 4404 B6
Queen St
100 Amhg N9V 4757 C1
2200 DRBN 48124 4416 B4
3500 WIND N9C 4420 A5
9400 DET 48213 4275 B2
11500 DET 48205 4275 B1
12600 DET 48205 4203 B7
Queen Anne Ct
42000 NvlT 48167 4193 B5
Queen Anne Dr
100 CNTN 48187 4411 B2
Queen Elizabeth Dr
5200 WIND N8T 4422 D4
Queens Wy
100 CNTN 48187 4412 A2
100 CNTN 48188 4412 A2
21600 BNTN 48183 4668 D2
Queensbury Dr
18100 LVNA 48152 4266 A1
Queens Pointe
24500 NOVI 48375 4193 B1
Queenston Pl
20500 DET 48203 4200 A4
Questa Dr
1700 WIND N8P 4348 C7
1700 WIND N8P 4423 D1
Quick Av
6100 LSal N9J 4503 A4
Quince St
41800 NOVI 48375 4193 B1
Quincey Ct
4900 WasC 48176 4572 D1
Quincy St
8500 DET 48204 4344 A1
9500 DET 48204 4272 A7
15400 DET 48238 4271 E6
17100 DET 48221 4271 E1
Quinn St
8000 DET 48234 4202 A6
Quirk Rd
9400 VNBN 48111 4494 C6
11400 VNBN 48111 4578 C1

R

S R Rd
- DRBN 48120 4418 B4
Rabbit Run Cir
900 WasC 48103 4405 C7
Race St
13000 SRKW 48179 4840 B1
Rachel Dr
7000 YpTp 48197 4575 E6
7100 YpTp 48197 4576 A6
Racho Rd
13000 TYLR 48180 4583 C2
17000 BNTN 48192 4583 C7
Racho School Dr
13000 TYLR 48180 4583 D2
Racine St
11900 DET 48205 4274 D1
Rackham St
8800 TYLR 48180 4499 D4
Radcliff Av
1200 WIND N8P 4348 D7
Radcliff St
100 GDNC 48185 4413 E2
100 GDNC 48186 4413 E2
800 GDNC 48135 4414 A1
1100 GDNC 48135 4413 E1
1700 GDNC 48135 4338 E7
1700 GDNC 48185 4338 E7
1800 WTLD 48185 4338 E7
2000 WTLD 48135 4338 E7
W Radcliff St
- GDNC 48135 4413 E1
W Radcliff St
- GDNC 48185 4413 E1
- WTLD 48185 4413 E1
Radcliffe Av
2700 AARB 48104 4490 A3
Radcliffe St
- DET 48126 4342 C5
- DET 48228 4342 C5
7500 DET 48210 4343 C5
20700 FNHL 48336 4195 D5
N Radcliffe St
5600 WTLD 48185 4338 E6
S Radcliffe St
1100 WTLD 48186 4413 E4
Radclift St
24200 OKPK 48237 4198 D1
N Rademacher St
800 DET 48209 4419 B2
Rademacher St N
100 DET 48209 4419 C3
Rademacher St S
100 DET 48209 4419 C3
Radford St
- DET 48204 4344 B2
Radio Plaza St
10 ROTp 48220 4199 B3
Radisson Av
2700 WIND N9E 4421 B7
3000 WIND N9E 4504 B1
Radisson Ct
2900 WIND N9E 4421 B6
Radisson Ct E
600 WIND N9E 4421 B6
Radisson Ct W
700 WIND N9E 4421 B7
Radnor Cir
10 GSPF 48236 4276 D4
Radnor Rd
45600 CNTN 48187 4336 C7
Radnor St
4400 DET 48224 4276 B2
Radom St
11900 DET 48212 4273 D2
Rae Dr
8300 WTLD 48185 4339 A3
Rafting Wy Ct
43200 NOVI 48375 4192 E1
Rahn St
1100 GDNC 48135 4414 A1
1100 WTLD 48186 4414 A3
1700 GDNC 48135 4339 A7
2200 GDNC 48185 4339 A7
Raid St
19200 HRWD 48225 4203 D6
S Railroad Av
- MVDL 48122 4418 A5
Railroad St
100 NHVL 48167 4192 E6
700 YPLT 48197 4491 E2
700 YPLT 48197 4492 A3
4000 WasC 48103 4330 A6
4100 WasC 48103 4329 E6
32700 RKWD 48173 4754 C7
Rainbow Dr
- DRBN 48124 4417 B4
Raintree Ct
6400 CNTN 48187 4337 B6
E Raintree Ct
5900 YpTp 48197 4576 B2
W Raintree Ct
5900 YpTp 48197 4576 B2
Raintree Dr
6100 CNTN 48187 4337 B6
7800 YpTp 48197 4576 B2
Raleigh Av
- LVNA 48150 4338 B1
Raleigh Square Dr
16200 SOGT 48195 4500 A7
Ralph St
1200 GDNC 48135 4413 E1
1200 GDNC 48135 4414 A1
Ralston St
- DET 48203 4200 B4
Ramblewood Ct
7900 YpTp 48197 4576 B2
40400 CNTN 48188 4412 D3
Ramblewood Dr
100 LSal N9J 4502 E4
Ramblewood St
7800 YpTp 48197 4576 A2
14000 LVNA 48154 4266 D5
Rambling Rd
1000 YpTp 48198 4492 C2
Ramey St
25300 DBHT 48127 4340 D4
Raminder Ct
47400 CNTN 48187 4336 A4
Rampart Cir
20800 SFLD 48034 4196 D4
Ramsay St
200 Amhg N9V 4757 B3
Ramsgate Ct
3900 WasC 48103 4405 A3
Ran St
11500 TYLR 48180 4499 B7
Ranchero Dr
3600 PTFD 48108 4489 A5
E Ranch Hill Dr
23100 SFLD 48034 4197 A1
W Ranch Hill Dr
23300 SFLD 48034 4197 A1
Rand Rd
1300 CNTN 48187 4411 D1
Randall Ct
400 RVRG 48218 4501 D1
22700 NOVI 48374 4192 C3
Randall St
3200 DET 48216 4344 E7
20700 FNHL 48336 4195 C4
39500 CNTN 48188 4412 E3
Randolph Av
1300 WIND N9B 4420 C4
2300 WIND N9E 4420 E7
3100 WIND N9E 4503 E1
3200 WIND N9E 4504 A2
Randolph Ct
39100 WTLD 48186 4412 E2
Randolph Pl
100 WIND N9B 4420 B2
Randolph St
300 WTLD 48186 4412 E3
500 NHVL 48167 4192 D6
1400 DET 48226 4345 D5
4000 WYNE 48184 4412 E6
Randolph St SR-3
600 DET 48226 4345 D6
Randolph Ct Dr
3000 PTFD 48108 4490 E4
Randy Dr
8000 WTLD 48185 4339 D3
8600 WTLD 48150 4339 D3
Raney Ln
24000 LyTp 48178 4189 E2
Rangemore St
26000 SFLD 48034 4196 C2
Ranger Dr
6900 RMLS 48174 4495 E3
Rangoon St
7700 DET 48210 4343 E3
8000 DET 48204 4343 E3
Ranier St
1300 CNTN 48187 4412 A1
Rankin Av
10 Amhg N9V 4757 B2
400 WIND N9B 4420 B2
2300 WIND N9E 4420 E7
3000 WIND N9E 4503 E1
3500 WIND N9E 4504 A2
Ranspach St
6100 DET 48209 4344 B7
Raphael Av
700 WasC 48189 4259 B4
Raphael Rd
32500 FNHL 48336 4195 A1
Raphael St
23000 FMTN 48336 4195 A1
Raspberry Ln
100 WasC 48103 4488 B4
Rathbone Pl
10 GSPT 48230 4276 C6
Rathbone St
8000 DET 48209 4419 A3
8700 DET 48209 4418 E3
Rathfon Cir
1000 PTFD 48176 4574 A4
Rathlone Dr
21600 NOVI 48167 4192 D4
Raupp Pl
800 LNPK 48146 4500 E1
Raupp Rd
17000 MVDL 48122 4418 B5
17000 MVDL 48229 4418 B5
Rausch Av
21700 EPTE 48021 4203 D1
Ravello Ct
47800 NOVI 48167 4191 E4
47800 NOVI 48167 4192 A4
Raven Av
21200 EPTE 48021 4204 A2
Ravencrest Ln
300 WTLD 48185 4413 B1
Ravenshire Dr
- SpTp 48198 4410 A7
Ravenswood Ct
9700 WasC 48176 4659 A3
Ravenswood St
9300 DET 48204 4343 E1
Ravenwood Blvd
36800 WTLD 48185 4413 C2
Ravenwood Dr
41600 CNTN 48187 4412 B2
Ravenwood St
1000 AARB 48103 4405 B4
Ravina Ct
42400 NvlT 48167 4265 A3
Ravina Ln
42400 NvlT 48167 4265 A3
Ravine Cir
24600 FNHL 48335 4194 D1
Ravine Ct
4900 AATp 48105 4408 A2
Ravine Dr
7800 WTLD 48185 4338 C3
Ravine St
25000 SFLD 48034 4196 B1
29400 LVNA 48152 4267 D1
Ravinewood Av
2300 YpTp 48198 4493 A7
Ravinewood Ln
9000 GOTp 48178 4187 D1
Rawsonville Rd
10 VNBN 48198 4493 C3
400 YpTp 48111 4493 C4
1000 VNBN 48111 4493 C6
1000 YpTp 48198 4493 C6
2000 YpTp 48111 4577 C1
2000 YpTp 48198 4577 C1
2100 VNBN 48111 4577 C4
2100 VNBN 48198 4577 C1
6500 VNBN 48197 4577 C4
6500 YpTp 48197 4577 C4
8000 AGST 48191 4577 C4
8000 WynC 48111 4577 C4
8000 WynC 48191 4577 C4
8500 AGST 48191 4662 C2
8500 WynC 48111 4662 C2
8500 WynC 48191 4662 C4
10200 AGST 48111 4662 C5
11600 AGST 48111 4748 C2
11600 AGST 48191 4748 C2
Rawsonville Rd
13000 MonC 48117 4748 C6
13000 MonC 48191 4748 C6
14300 MonC 48111 4748 C6
Ray Av
17300 ALPK 48101 4500 A4
Ray Ct
- AARB 48103 4405 C6
Ray Ln
48100 WynC 48111 4663 A4
Ray Rd
4500 Tcmh N0R 4505 E2
Ray St
17000 RVVW 48192 4584 D5
17000 RVVW 48195 4584 D5
22400 DET 48223 4269 B5
Rayburn Dr
40700 NvlT 48167 4265 B3
40700 NvlT 48170 4265 B3
Rayburn St
28800 LVNA 48154 4267 E3
33400 LVNA 48154 4266 E3
Raymer St
1400 WTLD 48186 4414 A4
Raymo Rd
800 WIND N8Y 4347 A7
Raymond Av
- DRBN 48125 4417 A6
1900 DRBN 48124 4417 A6
4300 DBHT 48125 4417 A6
5100 WIND N8S 4347 B7
5300 ALPK 48101 4417 A6
5300 DBHT 48101 4417 A6
Raymond Ct
10 DRBN 48124 4417 A5
Raymond Rd
19200 GSPW 48236 4276 B1
Raymond St
900 AARB 48103 4405 E7
6600 DET 48213 4274 C4
Rayna Ct
7900 VNBN 48111 4495 B4
Raynor St
1400 DET 48226 4345 D5
Rayson St
100 NHVL 48167 4192 D6
Reading Ct
23400 BNTN 48183 4668 B5
Reading Rd
23900 SFLD 48034 4196 E1
Reading St
1400 WIND N8W 4421 D5
Ready Av
6900 WRRN 48091 4202 A1
Ready Rd
3000 MonC 48179 4839 C3
4000 BrTp 48179 4839 C3
5000 BrTp 48179 4840 A3
5000 SRKW 48179 4840 A3
Reaume Pkwy
14600 SOGT 48195 4584 B2
Reaume Rd
100 LSal N9J 4502 D4
700 LSal N9J 4503 A5
Reaume St
26500 WDHN 48183 4754 D1
Reba Av
2200 WRRN 48091 4201 A2
Reba Ct
3000 YpTp 48197 4491 B6
Rebecca Ct
42600 VNBN 48111 4495 A3
Rebecca Dr
25900 BNTN 48134 4667 D7
Reckinger Rd
- DRBN 48120 4417 C2
- DRBN 48126 4417 C2
Recreation Dr
- NvlT 48167 4192 E7
Rector Ct
1800 CNTN 48188 4411 D4
Rector Dr
44400 CNTN 48188 4411 D5
Red Apple Ln
13500 MonC 48117 4753 B6
Red Bird Dr
7300 YpTp 48197 4576 D5
Redbud Av
9100 PyTp 48170 4337 A3
Red Bud Ct
5500 PTFD 48197 4575 A2
Red Cedar Ct
28100 BwTp 48183 4754 C2
Red Cedar Dr
20000 BwTp 48183 4754 C2
20000 BwTp 48183 4755 A3
29200 FTRK 48134 4753 E5
Red Cedar St
4100 TNTN 48183 4669 B6
Redcliff Dr
- CNTN 48187 4412 B2
Redding Ct
- CNTN 48187 4335 C4
Reddock Av
1800 WIND N9E 4503 C3
Redeemer Av
800 AARB 48103 4406 A7
Redfern Dr
42400 CNTN 48187 4412 A1
Redfern St
17700 DET 48219 4269 B1
18200 DET 48219 4197 B7
Redfield Ct
200 CNTN 48188 4412 D2
Redford St
17100 DET 48219 4269 B2
Red Fox Run
4900 SpTp 48105 4408 A4
Red Fox Tr
27000 BNTN 48134 4667 C7
Redhawk Ln
3900 WasC 48103 4405 A1
Redleaf Ln
1000 YpTp 48198 4492 D2
Redman Ct
23200 BNTN 48183 4668 B5
Redman St
6600 WTLD 48185 4338 E5
Red Maple Ct
9200 PyTp 48170 4335 E3
Red Maple Dr
9400 PyTp 48170 4335 E2
Red Maple Ln
22300 STCS 48080 4204 D2
Redmond Av
20700 EPTE 48021 4203 C3
Redmond St
18700 DET 48205 4203 C4
Red Oak Ct
200 AGST 48191 4661 B6
5400 YpTp 48197 4575 C1
46400 NvlT 48167 4264 B2
Red Oak Dr
46500 NvlT 48167 4264 B2
Red Oak Ln
19000 BNTN 48192 4583 C7
19000 BNTN 48192 4668 C1
Red Oak Rd
800 AARB 48103 4406 A4
1400 AARB 48103 4405 E4
Red Oak St
38500 WTLD 48185 4337 E4
38500 WTLD 48185 4338 A4
Red Pine Ct
47600 NOVI 48374 4191 E1
Red Pine Dr
9500 PyTp 48170 4335 E2
35000 FNHL 48335 4194 D4
Red River Dr
25000 SFLD 48075 4197 E1
Redrock Ct
300 WasC 48103 4404 C6
Red Run Dr
47400 CNTN 48187 4336 A7
Redstone Ct
5000 WasC 48103 4404 B6
Redwing Dr
24400 NOVI 48374 4192 A1
Redwood
- CNTN 48188 4411 C6
100 WynC 48111 4664 B3
Redwood Av
2800 AARB 48108 4490 B4
N Redwood Av
700 YpTp 48198 4492 C3
S Redwood Av
500 YpTp 48198 4492 C5
Redwood Blvd
- NvlT 48167 4264 D2
Redwood Ct
10 WynC 48111 4578 B7
Red Wood Dr
26000 HnTp 48164 4751 B1
Redwood Dr
300 VNBN 48111 4494 D5
Redwood Ln
30500 RMLS 48174 4581 D4
Redwood St
- TYLR 48180 4583 B2
100 WynC 48111 4578 B7
700 WTLD 48186 4414 C7
1300 WIND N9C 4420 B5
Reeck Ct
- SOGT 48195 4584 A2
Reeck Rd
8900 ALPK 48101 4500 A5
10800 ALPK 48195 4500 A7
11000 SOGT 48195 4500 A7
12000 SOGT 48195 4584 A1
25000 TNTN 48183 4669 B7
25000 WDHN 48183 4669 B7
26500 TNTN 48183 4755 B1
26500 WDHN 48183 4755 B1
Reed Ct
500 NHVL 48167 4192 E4
Reed Dr
29600 HnTp 48134 4666 E7
Reed St
500 NHVL 48167 4192 E4
4700 WIND N9C 4419 E7
17300 MVDL 48122 4417 E6
46000 WynC 48111 4663 D4
Reeder St
5600 DET 48209 4419 D3
Reed Grass Ln
45700 VNBN 48111 4494 C5
Reedmere Rd
200 WIND N8S 4347 B6
1100 WIND N8S 4422 D1
Reene Dr
47000 VNBN 48111 4578 B3
N Reese St
100 SLYN 48178 4189 B1
S Reese St
100 SLYN 48178 4189 B2
Reflection Ct
8000 YpTp 48197 4576 B3
Regal Ct
12300 Tcmh N8N 4348 E7
Regal Dr
5000 Tcmh N0R 4505 C4
Regal Pl
10 GSPS 48236 4205 A5
Regency St
1700 CNTN 48188 4412 A4
Regency Park Dr
23300 WRRN 48089 4202 D1
Regene Av
1500 WTLD 48186 4413 E4
Regent
- TYLR 48180 4498 D5
Regent Ct
10 AARB 48104 4406 E6
Regent Dr
10 AARB 48104 4406 E6
19600 DET 48205 4203 A4
Regent Rd
500 Tcmh N8N 4424 C2
Regents Park Ct
1300 PTFD 48108 4573 A1
Regina Av
2200 LNPK 48101 4500 C3
2200 LNPK 48146 4500 C3
14500 ALPK 48101 4500 B3
Regina Dr
10 Lksr N9K 4424 D6
Reginald St
2500 WIND N8Y 4421 D2
3900 WIND N8Y 4422 A1
5100 WIND N8T 4422 B1
N Reginald St
100 DRBN 48124 4416 B2
200 DRBN 48128 4416 B2
S Reginald St
100 DRBN 48124 4416 B2
Regis Av
2900 WIND N8R 4423 B3
Regis Ct
44300 CNTN 48187 4336 E6
Registry Dr
46000 CNTN 48187 4336 B6
Regular St
6000 DET 48209 4419 C2
S Reid St
600 DET 48209 4419 C3
Reimanville Av
20700 ROTp 48220 4199 C3
Rein Av
21700 EPTE 48021 4203 D1
Reindeer Dr
41400 NOVI 48375 4193 B4
Reinhardt Dr
22000 WDHN 48183 4668 C4
Reisa Ln
40600 CNTN 48188 4412 D2
Reisener St
- DET 48209 4418 D5
Relda Dr
28200 BwTp 48183 4754 D3
Remi St
12000 Tcmh N8N 4423 E2
Remington Av
2500 WIND N8X 4421 B5
Remington Ct
7100 PTFD 48176 4573 D5
45300 CNTN 48188 4411 D3
Remington Ln
45700 NOVI 48374 4192 C2
Remington St E
- DET 48203 4200 C5
- DET 48234 4200 D5
2200 DET 48234 4201 A5
Remington St W
10 DET 48203 4200 C5
Renaissance Center
10 DET 48226 4345 E6
Renaissance Dr N
- DET 48226 4345 E6
Renaissance Dr W
- DET 48226 4345 E7
Renaud Rd
10 GSPS 48236 4205 A7
400 GSPW 48236 4204 E6
N Renaud Rd
600 GSPW 48236 4204 D6
S Renaud Rd
900 GSPW 48236 4204 D6
Renaud St
5400 WIND N8T 4422 B1
12200 Tcmh N8N 4423 E2
12300 Tcmh N8N 4424 A2
Rendezvous Dr
500 WIND N8P 4348 D6
Rene Dr
400 LSal N9J 4502 D5
Renford St
22700 NOVI 48375 4193 D3
Renfrew Rd
- DET 48220 4199 E5
19300 DET 48221 4199 E6
Renfrew St
2800 AARB 48105 4407 A2
Reno Ln
300 GSPF 48236 4276 E3
Reno St
100 ECRS 48229 4501 C4
17000 RVVW 48192 4584 E5
18400 DET 48205 4203 A6
19100 DET 48205 4202 E4
Rensellor St
19100 LVNA 48152 4196 A6
Rensselaer St
20700 FNHL 48336 4196 A4
23000 OKPK 48237 4199 A2
Renton Rd
16400 VNBN 48111 4579 C6
Renville St
5000 DET 48210 4343 C5
Renwick St
16600 LVNA 48154 4266 B2
18400 LVNA 48152 4266 B1
18500 LVNA 48152 4194 B7
Reo Av
- ALPK 48101 4500 E1
1300 LNPK 48146 4501 A2
1700 LNPK 48146 4500 E1
2200 LNPK 48101 4500 E1
15100 ALPK 48101 4417 D7
Reo Ct
38500 LVNA 48154 4265 E3
Reo Dr
38800 LVNA 48154 4265 E3
Reo Rd
27000 WynC 48138 4756 A2
Republic Av
- ROTp 48220 4199 C3
6700 WRRN 48091 4201 E2
7000 WRRN 48091 4202 A2
8000 WRRN 48089 4202 A2
21600 FRDL 48220 4199 C3
21600 OKPK 48237 4199 C3
21800 FRDL 48237 4199 C3
22800 OKPK 48220 4199 C3
Republic Dr
- CNTN 48187 4337 A6
100 ALPK 48101 4417 C3
6400 VNBN 48111 4577 C4
Research Dr
10 AARB 48103 4406 B3
23500 FNHL 48335 4193 E2
Research Wy
25000 WDHN 48183 4668 C7
Research Park Dr
3800 AARB 48108 4489 C6
Reserve Ct
1600 WasC 48103 4488 C1
Reserve Dr
6500 HbgT 48116 4186 A2
Reserve Wy
1700 WasC 48103 4488 C2
Reservoir Rd
- NvlT 48170 4265 A3
43200 NvlT 48167 4265 A3
43400 NvlT 48167 4264 E2
Restoration Dr
- PTFD 48108 4490 C6
Reuter St
7600 DRBN 48126 4343 A3
Reuther Rd
- WTLD 48186 4414 C4
Reuther Mall
400 DET 48202 4345 A2
N Revena Blvd
100 AARB 48103 4405 E5
S Revena Blvd
100 AARB 48103 4405 E6
Revena Pl
600 AARB 48103 4405 E5
Revere Av
42400 PyTp 48170 4337 B3
Revere Ct
10 AARB 48104 4490 B4
800 NHVL 48167 4192 C5
Revere Dr
9400 VNBN 48111 4495 A5
Revere St
19100 DET 48234 4201 B4
Revland Dr
400 Tcmh N8N 4349 A7
700 Tcmh N8N 4424 A1
Rex St
18600 DET 48205 4203 C6
24200 DRBN 48128 4416 A1
Rexwood St
17400 LVNA 48152 4267 C1
Reynolds Av
20700 WRRN 48091 4201 A4
23000 HZLP 48030 4200 D1
Reynolds Ct
10 Amhg N9V 4757 E2
9200 AGST 48160 4660 A3
Reynolds St
14000 DET 48212 4273 B1
28400 INKR 48141 4415 A5
Reynold Sweet Pkwy
- SLYN 48178 4189 B3
Rhea St
200 AARB 48103 4405 B6
200 WasC 48103 4405 B6
E Rhead Cir
2400 WTLD 48186 4413 B5
N Rhead Cir
37600 WTLD 48186 4413 A4
W Rhead Cir
2300 WTLD 48186 4413 B5
Rhode Island St
10 HDPK 48203 4272 D4
Rhodes Av
22200 HZLP 48030 4200 C3
Rhodes Ct
9500 WasC 48167 4190 B7
Rhodes Dr
3400 WIND N8W 4422 C6
4800 Tcmh N8V 4422 D5
4800 WIND N8V 4422 D5
Rhododendron Cir
21800 WynC 48138 4670 B3
Rholaine Dr
500 WIND N8S 4348 A6
Rhonswood Ct
38600 FNHL 48167 4193 E5
Rhonswood Dr
37400 FNHL 48167 4194 A5
37400 FNHL 48335 4194 A5
38000 FNHL 48167 4193 E5
Rhonswood St
33500 FNHL 48335 4194 E4
Riad St
11600 DET 48224 4275 C1
11800 DET 48224 4203 C7
Rialto St
17800 MVDL 48122 4418 A7
18600 MVDL 48122 4501 A1
Riberdy Rd
3100 WIND N8W 4422 A6
3700 WIND N8W 4505 B1
Ricardo Dr
40000 VNBN 48111 4495 C5

Detroit & Wayne County Street Index

STREET
Block City ZIP Map# Grid

Rollingwood Dr
5700 WasC 48103 4404 B6
Rolling Woods Cir
17300 NvlT 48167 4264 B2
Rolston Dr
12700 PyTp 48170 4264 A7
Rolyat St
8000 DET 48234 4202 B5
Romaine St
10000 RMLS 48174 4496 C6
Romano St
23800 WRRN 48091 4201 B1
Roma Ridge Dr
24200 NOVI 48374 4192 B1
Rome Av
1900 WRRN 48030 4200 E2
1900 WRRN 48091 4200 E2
2100 WRRN 48091 4201 A2
Romeo Ln
4600 WasC 48167 4190 A6
Romeo St
1800 FRDL 48220 4200 B2
Romeyn St
5600 DET 48209 4419 C1
Romine Rd
14100 MonC 48117 4752 B5
26000 HnTp 48134 4752 A2
26000 HnTp 48164 4752 A2
Romulus Av
36500 RMLS 48174 4496 C7
Ronald Av
3800 WIND N9G 4504 D3
Ronald St
35400 RMLS 48174 4496 D5
Ronda Dr
8600 CNTN 48187 4337 B3
12600 SOGT 48195 4584 C1
Rondeau Pl
- WIND N8P 4348 A5
Rondo Ct
4000 WasC 48103 4329 D5
Rondo St
19000 DET 48205 4203 A6
Roney Av
27000 BwTp 48183 4754 D2
Ronnie Ln
16100 LVNA 48154 4266 C2
Rooney St
1300 WIND N9B 4420 C3
Roon the Ben
3200 PTFD 48108 4490 C5
Roosevelt
6200 VNBN 48111 4577 C3
Roosevelt Av
1200 AARB 48104 4406 D7
21400 FNHL 48336 4195 E3
Roosevelt Blvd
500 YPLT 48197 4491 C3
3900 DBHT 48124 4416 C6
3900 DBHT 48125 4416 C6
5400 DBHT 48125 4499 C1
Roosevelt Ct
14200 PyTp 48170 4263 D6
Roosevelt Pl
200 GSPT 48230 4276 C5
Roosevelt Rd
6500 ALPK 48101 4500 B2
Roosevelt St
- DET 48210 4344 C3
400 CNTN 48188 4410 D3
900 PLYM 48170 4337 A1
2700 DET 48216 4344 D6
2900 DRBN 48124 4416 C5
2900 HMTK 48212 4273 C5
5800 TYLR 48125 4499 C1
5900 WIND N8T 4422 D4
7800 TYLR 48180 4499 C3
21700 RKWD 48173 4754 D7
Rosa Ln
16500 SOGT 48195 4584 B5
Rosalie St
4400 DRBN 48126 4417 C1
4700 DRBN 48126 4342 C7
Rosalind Av
22700 EPTE 48021 4204 A1
Rosaltha Dr
10300 GOTp 48189 4187 B5
Rosa Parks Blvd
- DET 48210 4344 D1
100 DET 48216 4345 B6
3300 DET 48210 4345 A5
7400 DET 48206 4344 D1
8600 DET 48206 4272 D7
15700 DET 48238 4272 B2
16100 DET 48203 4272 B2
16400 HDPK 48203 4272 B2
Rosati Dr
1500 LSal N9J 4503 B5
Rosbolt Rd
7000 AGST 48160 4660 E5
7000 AGST 48160 4661 A5
8400 AGST 48191 4661 C5
Roscommon St
18500 HRWD 48225 4203 E6
19900 HRWD 48225 4204 A6
31900 WTLD 48186 4414 C5
42100 NOVI 48167 4193 A5
42100 NOVI 48375 4193 A5
Roscon Industrial Dr
- Tcmh N0R 4505 A6
Rose Av
600 AARB 48104 4489 C1
2100 LNPK 48146 4500 C4
2600 WIND N8T 4422 E2
27400 BwTp 48183 4754 E2
W Rose Av
800 GDNC 48135 4414 D1
Rose Cir
3400 TNTN 48183 4669 B6
Rose Ct
2600 WIND N8T 4422 D3
19800 HRWD 48225 4203 E5
20400 BwTp 48183 4754 E2
Rose Dr
400 AARB 48103 4405 B5
700 WasC 48103 4405 B4
15500 ALPK 48101 4500 A6
26600 FTRK 48134 4753 C2
Rose Ln
1500 TNTN 48183 4669 B2
1500 TNTN 48192 4669 B2
1600 WTLD 48186 4412 E4
Rose St
100 PLYM 48170 4265 A7
2400 MVDL 48122 4418 A6
2600 DET 48216 4345 A6
9600 TYLR 48180 4498 C5
13100 GBTR 48173 4755 D5
E Rose St
300 GDNC 48135 4414 D1
W Rose St
300 GDNC 48135 4414 D1
Rose Ter
50400 NvlT 48167 4263 C1
Roseberry Av
23000 WRRN 48089 4202 E1
Roseberry St
9400 DET 48213 4274 E2
Rosebriar Blvd
3200 WIND N8R 4423 C3
Rosebud Av
24200 EPTE 48021 4203 C1
Rosebud Ct
500 SALN 48176 4572 C5
Rosebud Ln
200 SALN 48176 4572 C4
Rosedale Av
300 WIND N9C 4420 A2
400 YpTp 48197 4491 C4
Rosedale Blvd
6400 ALPK 48101 4500 C4
13000 MonC 48117 4752 E7
Rosedale Ct
- DET 48211 4273 A5
10 DET 48202 4272 E5
500 DET 48202 4273 A5
N Rosedale Ct
600 GSPW 48236 4205 A4
600 STCS 48080 4205 A4
600 STCS 48236 4205 A4
S Rosedale Ct
600 GSPW 48236 4205 A4
600 STCS 48080 4205 A4
600 STCS 48236 4205 A4
Rosedale Ct N
500 GSPW 48236 4205 A3
500 STCS 48236 4205 A3
23100 STCS 48080 4204 E3
23200 STCS 48236 4205 A3
Rosedale Ct S
500 GSPW 48236 4205 A4
23100 STCS 48080 4204 E3
23200 STCS 48080 4205 A4
23200 STCS 48236 4205 A4
Rosedale St
- AARB 48104 4490 B4
3000 AARB 48108 4490 B4
12700 SOGT 48195 4584 D1
19500 STCS 48080 4204 B2
Rosefield Dr
3000 PTFD 48108 4574 B1
3000 PTFD 48197 4574 B1
Rose Hollow Dr
21600 SFLD 48034 4197 B4
21600 SFLD 48075 4197 B4
Roseland Ct
8400 OKPK 48237 4199 C1
Roseland Dr
100 CNTN 48187 4412 B2
2500 WasC 48103 4405 C2
Roseland Dr E
3900 WIND N9G 4504 C3
Roseland Dr S
400 WIND N9G 4504 C4
Roseland Dr W
3900 WIND N9G 4504 C3
Roseland St
9600 LVNA 48150 4339 A1
Roselawn
19500 GBTR 48173 4755 A4
Roselawn Dr
300 WIND N9E 4504 B2
Roselawn St
8000 DET 48204 4343 C3
8100 WTLD 48185 4339 C4
10100 DET 48204 4271 C7
15400 DET 48238 4271 C3
17100 DET 48221 4271 C1
19900 DET 48221 4199 C4
Roselinda Dr
11600 LVNA 48150 4338 A1
Rosella St
8800 TYLR 48180 4499 E4
Rosemallow Dr
- WasC 48103 4488 C2
Rosemarie Av
24100 WRRN 48089 4202 B1
Rose Marie Dr
26000 BNTN 48134 4667 D7
Rosemary Blvd
12700 OKPK 48237 4199 A2
14000 OKPK 48237 4198 D2
Rosemary St
100 DBHT 48127 4415 C1
100 DBHT 48141 4415 C1
7400 DBHT 48127 4340 B4
11000 DET 48213 4274 D2
12700 DET 48213 4275 A2
22000 TYLR 48180 4499 C5
Rosemont Av
400 SALN 48176 4657 D1
6000 DET 48228 4342 A5
11600 DET 48228 4270 A7
15700 DET 48223 4270 A2
16100 DET 48219 4270 A2
18200 DET 48219 4198 A7
Rosemount Av
3700 WIND N9C 4420 C6
Rose Terrace St
10 GSPF 48236 4276 D6
Rosetta Av
18000 EPTE 48021 4203 E2
18300 EPTE 48021 4204 A2
Rosetta St
5600 DBHT 48127 4341 A6
5600 DBHT 48128 4341 A6
N Rosevere Av
100 DRBN 48128 4416 A1
1700 DRBN 48128 4341 A7
S Rosevere Av
100 DRBN 48124 4416 A2
100 DRBN 48128 4416 A2
Rose Ville Garden Dr
2500 WIND N8T 4422 D2
Rosewood Av
100 YpTp 48198 4492 C5
20000 TYLR 48180 4499 E7
20000 TYLR 48195 4499 E7
Rosewood Cres
5900 LSal N9J 4503 A3
Rosewood Ct
- CNTN 48188 4411 C6
- NOVI 48167 4192 A5
10000 OKPK 48237 4199 B1
17000 NvlT 48167 4263 D3
Rosewood Rd
29100 HnTp 48134 4753 A3
Rosewood St
- RMLS 48174 4580 C1
500 FRDL 48220 4200 A2
1000 AARB 48104 4489 D2
2800 TNTN 48183 4669 D5
16500 DET 48224 4276 A4
22600 OKPK 48237 4199 B2
28400 INKR 48141 4415 A3
28500 INKR 48141 4414 E3
N Rosewood St
700 YpTp 48198 4492 C3
Roslyn Av
16900 ALPK 48101 4417 B7
Roslyn Rd
10 GSPS 48236 4205 A5
500 GSPW 48236 4205 A5
600 GSPW 48236 4204 D4
2200 HRWD 48236 4204 C4
19500 DET 48221 4199 E5
21700 HRWD 48225 4204 C4
Roslyn St
8800 LVNA 48150 4338 D3
Ross Av
25800 INKR 48141 4415 C6
Ross Ct
24300 RDFD 48239 4268 E4
Ross Dr
24500 RDFD 48239 4268 E4
43500 VNBN 48111 4495 A6
Ross Pl
40000 VNBN 48111 4579 D3
Ross St
100 GDNC 48135 4414 A2
100 GDNC 48186 4414 A2
600 AARB 48103 4405 D5
800 PLYM 48170 4336 E2
800 PLYM 48170 4337 A2
24000 DRBN 48124 4416 A6
24300 DRBN 48124 4415 E6
25400 DBHT 48125 4415 D6
25400 DBHT 48141 4415 D6
37900 LVNA 48154 4266 A5
38200 LVNA 48154 4265 E5
Rossbach Rd
6300 YpTp 48197 4575 D4
Rossdale Ct
21900 NOVI 48167 4192 D4
Rossi Dr
1500 Tcmh N0R 4505 A5
Rossini Blvd
200 WIND N8Y 4346 E7
1300 WIND N8Y 4422 A1
1900 WIND N8W 4422 A2
Rossini Dr
- HRWD 48225 4203 B5
13800 DET 48205 4203 A5
16600 DET 48225 4203 B5
Rossiter St
10900 DET 48224 4275 C1
11300 DET 48224 4203 D7
19200 HRWD 48224 4203 D6
19200 HRWD 48225 4203 D6
Rosslyn Av
- GDNC 48135 4413 E1
- GDNC 48185 4413 E1
28400 GDNC 48135 4415 A1
33400 GDNC 48135 4414 A1
34500 WTLD 48185 4413 E1
Rosslyn St
34900 WTLD 48185 4413 D1
Rostrevor Ct
500 Tcmh N8N 4424 C2
Rothbury Ct
5600 PTFD 48197 4574 E2
Rotunda Ct
22600 NOVI 48375 4193 D4
Rotunda Dr
12700 DRBN 48120 4418 A1
12700 DRBN 48126 4418 A1
15000 DRBN 48120 4417 C3
16400 ALPK 48101 4417 C3
16400 DRBN 48101 4417 C3
Rotunda Dr
17100 DRBN 48124 4417 A4
18600 DRBN 48124 4416 D5
Rouge Cir
5600 DBHT 48127 4341 C6
5600 DBHT 48128 4341 C6
Rouge Ct
5700 DBHT 48127 4341 D6
25900 SFLD 48034 4196 C4
Rouge St
500 NHVL 48167 4192 E6
S Rouge St
300 DET 48229 4418 C5
Rougecrest Rd
24000 SFLD 48034 4196 C1
Rougemont Dr
22000 SFLD 48034 4196 B3
Rouge Park Dr
- DET 48228 4269 B7
- DET 48228 4341 B1
- DET 48239 4269 B7
- DET 48239 4341 B1
Rouge River Dr
26600 DBHT 48127 4340 B4
Rougeway St
16200 LVNA 48154 4268 A2
17100 LVNA 48152 4268 A1
Rougewood Dr
21600 SFLD 48034 4196 C3
Roulo St
900 VNBN 48111 4578 D4
2600 DRBN 48120 4418 D2
Roundhill Ct
8500 WasC 48176 4658 B1
Round Table Dr E
1900 CNTN 48188 4412 A5
Round Table Dr W
1800 CNTN 48188 4412 A5
Roundtree Blvd
2900 YpTp 48197 4491 A6
Roundview Dr
44700 NOVI 48375 4192 C2
Rouse Creek Ct
2000 PTFD 48108 4488 E6
Rowan St
7000 DET 48209 4419 B2
Rowe St
17100 DET 48205 4274 C1
19100 DET 48205 4202 C5
23600 DRBN 48124 4416 A2
Rowley Ct
1000 YpTp 48198 4492 C2
Rowley St
5300 DET 48212 4273 D2
Roxana Av
22700 EPTE 48021 4204 A1
Roxanne Dr
2000 Tcmh N9K 4424 A4
Roxborough Av
1400 WIND N9B 4420 D4
2400 WIND N9E 4420 E7
Roxborough Blvd
3500 WIND N9E 4504 A2
Roxbury Av
17200 SFLD 48075 4198 A3
Roxbury Dr
7100 YpTp 48197 4575 E6
7100 YpTp 48197 4576 A6
21800 NOVI 48374 4192 C4
Roxbury Rd
1400 AARB 48104 4490 A1
Roxbury St
10100 DET 48224 4275 C2
11300 DET 48224 4203 D7
Roxford St
23400 DET 48219 4197 A7
Roy St
- DET 48210 4343 D4
Royal Ct
5600 WIND N8T 4422 B2
Royal Ct N
7700 CNTN 48187 4337 A4
Royal Ct S
7700 CNTN 48187 4337 A4
Royal Dr
26700 WDHN 48183 4754 E1
Royal Grand
9500 RDFD 48239 4340 D1
13900 RDFD 48239 4268 D5
Royal Pointe Dr
47600 CNTN 48187 4336 A5
Royal Ridge Ct
500 Amhg N9V 4757 C4
Royal Troon Dr
7000 YpTp 48197 4575 E5
54200 LyTp 48178 4190 D2
Royal Vale Ln
5300 DRBN 48126 4341 E7
5300 DRBN 48128 4341 E7
Royalvilla Ct
7000 CNTN 48187 4336 A5
Royce Dr
10000 GOTp 48178 4188 E3
Roycroft Ct
38200 LVNA 48154 4266 A4
Roycroft St
4000 MVDL 48122 4417 D7
32400 LVNA 48154 4267 A4
34900 LVNA 48154 4266 D4
38400 LVNA 48154 4265 E4
Roys St
100 BLVL 48111 4578 C2
Ruby Ln
300 WasC 48189 4186 E7
Ruby St
4000 PTFD 48197 4574 D5
12900 DRBN 48126 4343 A7
13700 DRBN 48126 4342 E7
Rucker Rd
8300 WynC 48138 4756 C2
Rudgate Rd
44900 CNTN 48188 4411 D5
Rudgate St
16200 SOGT 48195 4500 A7
Rudolph Cir
12700 DET 48213 4275 B5
12700 DET 48214 4275 B5
Rue Deauville Blvd
900 YpTp 48198 4492 C2
Ruedisale Ct
8000 DET 48214 4346 C1
Rue Vendome Blvd
900 YpTp 48198 4492 C2
Rue Willette Blvd
900 YpTp 48198 4492 C2
Rugby Ct
2000 AARB 48103 4488 D2
Rugg St
6300 DET 48211 4273 E4
Ruggaber Dr
200 Lksr N8N 4424 E4
Rumsey Dr
3000 AARB 48105 4407 B1
Runnymeade Dr
5900 CNTN 48187 4337 A6
Runnymede Blvd
1900 AARB 48103 4488 D1
Runstedler Dr
100 LSal N9J 4586 D1
Runway Blvd
4600 PTFD 48108 4489 D7
4600 PTFD 48108 4573 D1
Runyon St
17100 DET 48234 4274 C1
19100 DET 48234 4202 C5
Rupert St
5400 DET 48212 4273 D2
Rural Hill St
100 NHVL 48167 4192 D7
Rush Av
29900 GDNC 48135 4339 D5
Rush St
28400 GDNC 48135 4340 A5
28600 GDNC 48135 4339 E5
Rushton Dr
2900 WIND N8R 4423 C2
N Rushton Rd
8800 GOTp 48178 4188 C2
S Rushton Rd
8000 WasC 48178 4260 C2
9200 WasC 48178 4188 C7
10000 GOTp 48178 4188 C3
Rushwood
48000 NOVI 48374 4192 A2
48100 NOVI 48374 4191 E2
Rushwood Cres
1400 LSal N9H 4504 B5
Ruskin St
2200 TNTN 48183 4669 D4
3200 DET 48216 4344 E7
Russell Av
500 LNPK 48146 4501 A3
1700 LNPK 48146 4500 D2
2200 LNPK 48101 4500 D2
11200 PyTp 48170 4337 C1
15500 ALPK 48101 4500 C1
17000 ALPK 48101 4417 A7
20700 HZLP 48030 4200 D4
Russell Blvd
10 YpTp 48198 4492 D4
Russell Ct
10 YpTp 48198 4492 D4
9500 WasC 48167 4190 B6
Russell Ln
60600 LyTp 48178 4189 C4
Russell Rd
1200 AARB 48103 4406 A7
Russell St
- BrTp 48134 4753 D5
1200 YpTp 48198 4492 D4
1800 DRBN 48128 4341 C7
2000 DET 48207 4345 E4
2500 AARB 48103 4405 D7
3000 WIND N9C 4420 A3
3400 WIND N9C 4419 E4
5000 DET 48211 4345 C1
6100 DET 48211 4273 C7
8800 LVNA 48150 4338 D3
9600 WasC 48167 4190 B6
17300 DET 48203 4272 E1
19100 DET 48203 4200 D5
21200 RKWD 48173 4754 D6
23000 SFLD 48075 4197 C5
W Russell St
10 SALN 48176 4572 C7
300 SALN 48176 4657 C1
Russell Woods Dr
200 Lksr N8N 4424 E1
Russet Ln
44300 NOVI 48375 4192 D2
Russett Ln
41000 PyTp 48170 4265 C5
Russett Rd
800 AARB 48103 4405 E7
1400 SpTp 48198 4492 E1
Russian Ln
9900 WasC 48170 4263 A5
Rust Rd
23000 HnTp 48164 4665 D7
25000 HnTp 48164 4751 D1
Rustic Ln
5600 AGST 48197 4660 C1
30500 WTLD 48186 4414 D3
Rustic Ln E
100 WynC 48111 4662 D6
Rustic Ln N
100 WynC 48111 4662 C5
Rustic Ln S
200 WynC 48111 4662 D6
Rustic Ln W
200 WynC 48111 4662 D6
Rustic Hills Dr
46300 NvlT 48167 4264 C2
Rustic Ridge Rd
1500 CNTN 48188 4412 B4
Rusty St
25500 TYLR 48180 4498 D6
Rutgers Dr
38600 FNHL 48167 4193 E3
Ruth Av
- ALPK 48101 4500 C2
1000 YpTp 48198 4492 C6
2000 LNPK 48146 4417 E7
2000 LNPK 48146 4500 C2
2200 LNPK 48101 4417 E7
22300 FNHL 48336 4195 B3
Ruth Rd
2800 WIND N8R 4423 A2
Ruth St
10 ECRS 48229 4501 D2
8600 DET 48213 4274 B4
11900 GOTp 48178 4188 E6
17600 MVDL 48122 4417 E6
21300 FNHL 48336 4195 B3
36000 BwTp 48173 4841 B3
Ruthan Dr
14200 VNBN 48111 4578 B3
Rutherford Ct
7600 CNTN 48187 4336 A5
36400 FNHL 48335 4194 B1
Rutherford St
8800 DET 48228 4342 C2
9500 DET 48227 4342 C1
15300 DET 48227 4270 C3
16100 DET 48235 4270 C3
18200 DET 48235 4198 C7
20500 DET 48075 4198 C5
Ruthmere Av
10300 WynC 48138 4670 A7
Ruthven Pl
10 AARB 48104 4406 D7
Rutland Av
24000 SFLD 48075 4198 B1
Rutland Rd
100 Tcmh N8N 4424 D1
Rutland St
9200 DET 48228 4342 B1
9500 DET 48227 4342 B1
13900 DET 48227 4270 B5
20700 SFLD 48075 4198 B3
Rutledge Rd
2400 TNTN 48183 4669 D4
Ryan Dr
28500 FNHL 48336 4195 E1
Ryan Rd
- WRRN 48234 4201 B2
400 AARB 48103 4489 A3
7000 WasC 48189 4258 A6
13400 DET 48212 4273 C1
16700 LVNA 48152 4267 C2
16700 LVNA 48154 4267 C2
17700 DET 48212 4201 B6
18000 DET 48234 4201 B6
20700 WRRN 48091 4201 B2
Ryan St
3100 WIND N9C 4420 B3
Ryanwood Dr
17800 RVVW 48192 4584 A7
Rye Ct
200 PTFD 48197 4574 D2
Ryegate Dr
12400 Tcmh N8N 4424 A2
Ryegate St
42900 CNTN 48187 4337 A5
Ryerson Rd
9300 WIND N8R 4423 B3
Rygate St
22300 WDHN 48183 4668 C6
Ryland
15600 RDFD 48239 4268 B3
16100 RDFD 48240 4268 B2
Rymut Dr
45400 WynC 48111 4663 D2
Ryznar Dr
11500 VNBN 48111 4578 B1

S

Sacred Heard Dr
500 LSal N9J 4502 D6
Sacred Heart Dr
100 LSal N9J 4502 C6
Saddle Ln
400 GSPW 48236 4276 E1
Saddle Creek Ct
5100 WasC 48170 4334 D3
Sadie Ln
6100 VNBN 48111 4495 A2
Sage Cir
- VNBN 48111 4494 C6
Sage Ct
100 PTFD 48176 4573 A6
Sagebrush
22800 NOVI 48375 4192 E3
22800 NOVI 48375 4193 A3
Sagebrush Cir
2700 WasC 48103 4405 C7
2800 WasC 48103 4488 C1
Saginaw Ct
4100 WasC 48103 4404 E7
4100 WasC 48103 4405 A7
31900 WTLD 48186 4414 C4
Saginaw St
6300 DET 48211 4273 E7
St. Agnes Dr
1900 Tcmh N9K 4424 A4
St. Albertus Pl
1900 DET 48207 4345 D2
St. Aloysius St
11300 RMLS 48174 4496 B7
11300 RMLS 48174 4580 B1
St. Alphonse Av
2200 Tcmh N8N 4424 A5
St. Andrew
1000 WasC 48189 4259 C3
St. Andrews Av
13000 WRRN 48089 4202 E2
St. Andrews Ct
4700 PTFD 48108 4572 E1
St. Andrews Dr
200 Lksr N8N 4424 E2
7000 YpTp 48197 4576 A5
22800 LyTp 48178 4190 E2
St. Andrews Sq
48000 PyTp 48170 4264 A7
St. Andrews Wy
4100 WasC 48103 4329 E3
St. Anne St
100 DET 48216 4420 A1
1200 DET 48216 4345 A7
1400 Tcmh N8N 4423 E2
1900 DET 48216 4344 E6
2000 Tcmh N8N 4424 A4
St. Anthony Pl
7300 DET 48213 4274 B7
St. Antoine St
400 WIND N9C 4420 A4
600 DET 48226 4345 D5
3500 DET 48201 4345 D4
5900 DET 48211 4345 B1
6000 DET 48202 4345 B1
6500 DET 48202 4273 B7
St. Arnaud St
100 Amhg N9V 4757 C1
St. Aubin Av
8400 DET 48211 4273 B5
8400 HMTK 48212 4273 B5
8800 DET 48212 4273 B5
8800 HMTK 48211 4273 B5
St. Aubin Pl
1100 DET 48207 4346 A5
St. Aubin St
400 DET 48207 4346 A5
2500 DET 48207 4345 E3
2900 AARB 48108 4490 B4
5000 DET 48211 4345 D1
7800 DET 48211 4273 C6
7800 HMTK 48211 4273 C6
11300 HMTK 48212 4273 B3
13000 DET 48212 4273 A2
17100 DET 48212 4272 E1
17400 DET 48212 4200 E6
18000 DET 48234 4200 E6
St. Charles
2000 AARB 48103 4405 D7
2000 AARB 48103 4488 D1
St. Charles Pl
10 Amhg N9V 4757 D3
St. Clair Av
2200 WIND N9B 4420 D7
2300 WIND N9E 4420 D7
2500 WIND N9E 4503 D1
3700 WIND N9E 4504 A4
St. Clair Dr
10800 AGST 48191 4577 C7
St. Clair St
100 DET 48214 4347 A1
300 GSPT 48230 4276 B4
800 DET 48230 4276 B4
2500 DET 48214 4346 E1
2900 DET 48214 4274 E7
4100 LSal N9H 4504 A4
4700 DET 48213 4274 E6
St. Cyril St
6600 DET 48213 4274 A4
9600 DET 48234 4274 A4
St. Denis St
12300 Tcmh N8N 4423 D2
12300 Tcmh N8N 4424 A1
St. Etienne Blvd
2700 WIND N8W 4422 A6
St. Francis Dr
2000 AARB 48104 4489 E2
St. Francis St
19200 LVNA 48152 4196 A5
20700 FNHL 48336 4196 A4
St. Gabriel Cres
1500 WIND N9E 4504 A2
St. George Cir
22800 LyTp 48178 4190 D3
St. Gregory's Rd
12800 Tcmh N8N 4424 A1
St. Hedwig St
4800 DET 48210 4344 B7
St. Ignace St
1500 WYDT 48192 4585 A5
2300 WYDT 48192 4584 E5
St. Jacques St
12100 Tcmh N8N 4423 D2
St. James Ct
10 Amhg N9V 4757 D2
St. James Dr
8000 WynC 48138 4670 D7
St. James St
1500 WIND N9C 4420 C6
4300 DET 48210 4343 C6
St. Jean St
1200 DET 48214 4347 B1
2500 DET 48214 4275 A7
4400 DET 48214 4274 E5
5000 DET 48213 4274 E5
St. Joan St
22300 STCS 48080 4204 D3
St. Joe Dr
38100 WTLD 48186 4413 A3
St. John
500 YPLT 48197 4491 E3

STREET Block City ZIP Map# Grid

St. John St
10 WYDT 48192 4501 B7
300 WIND N8S 4347 E5
6800 DET 48210 4344 A6
8700 DET 48210 4343 D7
St. Johns Blvd
700 LNPK 48146 4501 A7
1000 LNPK 48146 4500 E7
St. Johns Dr
8100 WTLD 48185 4337 E4
St. Joseph St
100 TNTN 48183 4670 A4
200 TNTN 48183 4669 E4
400 WIND N9C 4420 A4
2800 DET 48207 4345 E2
2900 DET 48207 4346 A2
St. Julien Av
2100 WIND N8W 4421 E4
3000 WIND N8W 4422 A4
St. Julien St
3900 WIND N8W 4422 B4
St. Lawrence Blvd
200 NHVL 48167 4192 D7
St. Lawrence St
5100 DET 48210 4343 D5
St. Louis Av
200 WIND N8S 4347 B7
1100 WIND N8S 4422 D1
St. Louis St
100 FRDL 48203 4199 E3
100 FRDL 48220 4199 E3
13400 DET 48212 4273 E1
17600 DET 48212 4201 E6
18000 DET 48234 4201 E6
18900 BwTp 48173 4841 A1
19600 RKWD 48173 4841 A1
St. Luke Rd
600 WIND N8Y 4346 C7
900 WIND N8Y 4421 D1
1800 WIND N8W 4421 D2
St. Mark's Rd
100 Tcmh N8N 4349 C7
100 Tcmh N8N 4424 C1
St. Maron Pl
500 DET 48207 4346 B5
St. Martin Cres
2000 Tcmh N9K 4424 A5
St. Martins Av
- DET 48219 4197 E6
- DET 48219 4198 A6
- DET 48221 4199 D6
12700 DET 48235 4199 A6
15500 DET 48235 4198 C6
25500 RDFD 48240 4196 D6
St. Martins St
27400 LVNA 48152 4196 A6
28800 LVNA 48152 4195 D6
34500 LVNA 48152 4194 D6
St. Martins St N
8200 DET 48221 4199 C5
St. Martins St S
8200 DET 48221 4199 C6
St. Mary Ct
24100 FMTN 48336 4195 A1
St. Mary's Blvd
800 WIND N8S 4347 C6
St. Marys St
8600 DET 48228 4342 C2
9500 DET 48227 4342 C1
15300 DET 48227 4270 C4
16100 DET 48235 4270 C2
18200 DET 48235 4198 B5
20500 DET 48075 4198 B5
St. Mary's Gate
1900 WIND N8Y 4421 C1
St. Michael
2200 INKR 48141 4415 A4
St. Michael's Dr
6600 LSal N9J 4503 A5
St. Mihiel Av
3400 TNTN 48183 4669 B7
St. Patrick St
11000 DET 48205 4274 D2
St. Patrick's Dr
1400 WIND N9B 4420 C5
2300 WIND N9E 4420 D7
2500 WIND N9E 4503 E1
3200 WIND N9E 4504 A2
St. Paul Av
200 WIND N8S 4347 D5
3300 TNTN 48183 4669 D5
St. Paul St
2800 TNTN 48183 4669 D4
6300 DET 48207 4346 B3
8000 DET 48214 4346 D2
15000 GPPK 48230 4275 E6
15600 GPPK 48230 4276 B5
16800 GSPT 48230 4276 B5
St. Pierre St
100 Tcmh N8N 4348 E6
600 Tcmh N8N 4423 E1
St. Rose St
200 WIND N8S 4347 C6
8900 WIND N8S 4348 A6
St. Stephen St
22100 RKWD 48173 4754 C7
St. Stephens St
7900 DET 48210 4343 E7
9300 DRBN 48210 4343 C7
St. Thomas Cres
12000 Tcmh N8N 4423 E1
12000 Tcmh N8P 4423 E1
St. Thomas St
7100 DET 48211 4274 A5
7100 DET 48213 4274 A5
12300 Tcmh N8N 4423 B1
12400 Tcmh N8N 4424 A1
12900 Tcmh N8N 4349 A7
St. Williams St
- LSal N9J 4502 C5

Salem Av
3200 TNTN 48183 4669 B5
Salem Cir
10 WasC 48176 4657 A2
Salem Cr
6100 WasC 48170 4334 B1
Salem Ct
- VNBN 48111 4579 B3
10 AARB 48104 4490 C3
15100 RDFD 48239 4268 E4
24300 NOVI 48374 4192 A1
Salem Dr
19300 WDHN 48183 4669 A7
Salem Ln
8300 DBHT 48127 4340 E3
8400 DBHT 48239 4340 E3
9500 RDFD 48239 4340 E1
15900 RDFD 48239 4268 E3
Salem Rd
6600 WasC 48170 4262 E6
7100 WasC 48167 4262 E6
Salem St
2900 AARB 48103 4405 C7
16100 DET 48219 4268 E1
19900 DET 48219 4196 D5
Salem Farms Dr
8700 WasC 48178 4261 D1
9000 WasC 48178 4189 D7
Salem Woods Dr
7100 WasC 48167 4262 C5
Salich Ct
13100 Tcmh N8N 4349 B7
Salina Av
10 WIND N9G 4504 D2
Salina St
2400 DRBN 48120 4418 C2
Saline Milan Rd
8700 SALN 48176 4657 D2
8900 WasC 48176 4657 D2
9300 WasC 48176 4658 C6
10000 WasC 48160 4658 C6
Saline River Rd
100 SALN 48176 4657 B1
200 SALN 48176 4572 B7
Saline Waterworks Rd
3200 SALN 48176 4572 A6
3200 WasC 48176 4572 A6
4300 WasC 48176 4571 C6
Salisbury Av
21300 WynC 48138 4670 D3
Salisbury Ln
2600 AARB 48103 4406 A2
Salisbury St
19500 STCS 48080 4204 A3
30400 FNHL 48336 4195 C4
Sallan St
8200 DET 48211 4273 D5
Salliotte Rd
10 ECRS 48229 4501 C3
Salliotte St
11700 DET 48229 4501 B2
Sally Ct
27000 TYLR 48180 4498 C2
Salter Av
100 WIND N9A 4420 D1
Salter St
13000 DET 48205 4203 C7
Saltz Ct
1300 CNTN 48187 4411 E1
Saltz Rd
41900 CNTN 48187 4412 A1
43600 CNTN 48187 4411 E1
48000 CNTN 48187 4410 E1
Salvador St
- FMTN 48336 4195 A4
31700 FNHL 48336 4195 A4
Salvage Yard Rd
- DRBN 48120 4418 B1
Salzburg Ct
5200 WasC 48103 4487 C1
Samantha Ct
700 WIND N9E 4504 D2
Samantha Dr
45600 CNTN 48188 4411 C7
Samer Rd
1600 WasC 48160 4658 B6
Samoset Ct
24900 NOVI 48374 4191 D1
Samoset Tr
23500 SFLD 48034 4196 C2
Sampson St
2600 DET 48216 4345 A7
Samuel Ct
45600 CNTN 48188 4411 D7
Samuel St
- WIND N9E 4420 E7
22100 TYLR 48180 4499 C4
Samuel Barton Dr
8000 VNBN 48111 4495 C5
San Carlos St
10 BLVL 48111 4578 E4
Sandalwood Cir
2300 AARB 48105 4407 A2
Sandalwood Ct
500 CNTN 48188 4411 B3
10900 PyTp 48170 4336 A2
Sandalwood Dr
6200 VNBN 48111 4493 E2
11000 PyTp 48170 4336 B1
Sandalwood Rd
400 CNTN 48188 4411 B3
Sandburg St
15500 RMLS 48174 4581 E5
Sand Crane Wy
11000 GOTp 48178 4187 D5
Sandee St
26400 TYLR 48180 4582 C4
Sanders Dr
- BNTN 48183 4668 B5

Sanders St
12800 DET 48229 4418 C5
22500 STCS 48080 4204 E3
Sandhill Ct
9200 WasC 48176 4658 B2
Sandhurst St
5900 CNTN 48187 4337 D7
Sandison St
500 WIND N9E 4504 D2
Sandlewood Ct
9400 WasC 48189 4258 D1
Sandlewood Dr
9400 WasC 48189 4186 D7
9400 WasC 48189 4258 D1
Sandpiper Ct
24500 NOVI 48374 4191 E1
Sand Piper Dr
32600 RMLS 48174 4497 A2
Sandpiper Dr
8100 CNTN 48187 4336 D4
Sandpiper Ln
9400 WasC 48176 4658 E3
9500 WasC 48176 4659 A3
Sand Point Dr
9000 WasC 48189 4186 E7
9000 WasC 48189 4258 E1
Sandpoint Wy
39800 NOVI 48375 4193 D4
Sandra Ct
700 DBHT 48127 4415 C1
26700 WDHN 48183 4755 A1
36600 FNHL 48335 4194 B2
Sandra Ln
31800 WTLD 48185 4339 B3
33000 WTLD 48185 4339 B3
Sandra St
22500 LyTp 48178 4189 C3
Sandrock Ct
200 WasC 48103 4404 C6
Sand Stone Ct
3600 SpTp 48105 4333 C7
Sandstone Dr
5000 WasC 48130 4329 D6
Sandstone Pass
4700 PTFD 48197 4491 A6
Sandwich Pkwy W
- LSal N9H 4504 A5
- WIND N9G 4504 A5
Sandwich St
3000 WIND N9C 4420 A4
3500 WIND N9C 4419 E5
Sandwich St N
10 Amhg N9V 4757 B1
Sandwich St N CO-20
10 Amhg N9V 4757 B1
Sandwich St N P-18
10 Amhg N9V 4757 B1
Sandwich St S
10 Amhg N9V 4757 B2
Sandwich St S CO-20
10 Amhg N9V 4757 B2
Sandwich St S P-18
10 Amhg N9V 4757 B2
Sandwood Dr
33700 WTLD 48185 4338 E4
Sandy Ct
- NvlT 48167 4193 A7
Sandy Bottom Lake Rd
11600 GOTp 48178 4188 A3
Sandy Cove
8600 YpTp 48197 4576 C1
Sandy Creek Ct
6000 WasC 48103 4487 A2
11200 GOTp 48178 4187 E4
Sandy Creek Dr
11000 GOTp 48178 4187 E4
Sandy Creek Ln
1700 WasC 48103 4487 A2
11000 GOTp 48178 4187 E3
Sanford Dr
8500 WTLD 48185 4339 B3
Sanford Pl
1700 AARB 48103 4488 E2
N Sanford Rd
10100 WasC 48160 4660 A5
Sanford St
11000 DET 48205 4274 D2
Sanger St
6500 DET 48210 4343 D5
Sanilac St
9300 DET 48224 4275 E1
9600 DET 48224 4204 A7
19200 HRWD 48225 4204 A6
San Jose
9900 RDFD 48239 4340 B1
13900 RDFD 48239 4268 B5
San Juan Dr
14000 DET 48238 4271 D5
17100 DET 48221 4271 D1
18000 DET 48221 4199 D6
Sansburn St
34500 WTLD 48186 4413 D3
Sansotta Ct
2500 WIND N9E 4503 D2
San Souci St
23400 FNHL 48336 4195 D1
Santa Anita Av
14600 LVNA 48154 4268 A4
Santa Anita St
14900 LVNA 48154 4268 A4
Santa Barbara Dr
17100 DET 48221 4271 D1
19900 DET 48221 4199 C4
20400 DET 48220 4199 C4
Santa Barbara St
24700 SFLD 48075 4197 D2
Santa Clara
19300 DET 48219 4269 D1
Santa Clara St
10 BLVL 48111 4578 E4

Santa Clara St
4000 DET 48221 4271 E1
12700 DET 48235 4271 A1
Santa Fe Tr
3600 PTFD 48108 4489 A6
Santa Maria
25000 RDFD 48240 4268 D1
Santa Maria St
3400 DET 48221 4271 D1
12700 DET 48235 4271 A1
14200 DET 48235 4270 D1
22400 DET 48219 4269 A1
24000 DET 48219 4268 E1
Santa Rosa Dr
10 AARB 48108 4489 E5
12000 DET 48204 4271 D6
15800 DET 48221 4271 D1
15800 DET 48238 4271 D3
18200 DET 48221 4199 D6
Santo Dr
2300 WIND N9G 4504 A3
Sapphire Dr
31000 BwTp 48173 4755 A6
Sarah Ct
500 WIND N9G 4504 D3
8100 WynC 48138 4670 D5
Sarah Ln
1500 WTLD 48186 4413 A4
8300 WynC 48138 4670 C5
Sarah Ann Dr
4000 CNTN 48188 4411 D7
Sarah Flynn Ct
24400 NOVI 48374 4192 B1
Sarah Flynn Dr
24600 NOVI 48374 4192 B1
Sarasota
11300 RDFD 48239 4340 D1
14900 RDFD 48239 4268 D4
Sarasota Ct
9100 RDFD 48239 4340 E2
Saratoga
- WynC 48138 4756 B2
Saratoga Cir
41900 CNTN 48187 4337 B5
Saratoga Ct
1000 NHVL 48167 4192 A5
Saratoga Dr
22300 SFLD 48075 4198 B2
Saratoga Ln
26500 FTRK 48134 4754 A3
Saratoga Rd
42400 CNTN 48187 4337 B6
Saratoga St
8500 OKPK 48237 4199 B3
13600 DET 48205 4202 E6
15600 DET 48205 4203 C6
E Saratoga St
200 FRDL 48220 4199 E2
200 FRDL 48220 4200 A2
W Saratoga St
1200 FRDL 48220 4199 C3
Sarena St
6800 DET 48210 4343 D5
Sargent Av
23500 SFLD 48034 4197 A3
24000 SFLD 48034 4196 E3
Sargent St
6800 RMLS 48174 4497 A3
Sari Ln
- Amhg N9V 4671 D1
Sarina Dr
- NOVI 48374 4192 A3
Sarsfield Av
12300 WRRN 48089 4202 D3
Sarsfield St
- DET 48216 4344 E6
Sassafras Dr
- FTRK 48134 4754 C5
Sauer Ct
500 AARB 48104 4406 C7
Sauer St
- DET 48234 4274 C1
11600 DET 48205 4202 D7
Sauk Tr
6000 PTFD 48108 4574 A4
6000 PTFD 48176 4574 A4
Saulino Ct
2600 DRBN 48120 4418 D2
Saunders Cres
1100 AARB 48103 4405 E4
Savage Rd
500 BLVL 48111 4578 E3
500 VNBN 48111 4578 E3
17400 VNBN 48111 4579 E7
17400 WynC 48111 4579 E7
18600 HnTp 48111 4664 E1
18600 WynC 48111 4664 E1
19100 HnTp 48111 4665 A1
Savage St
- DET 48234 4201 E4
- DET 48234 4202 A4
Savanna St
- WIND N8P 4348 D7
Savannah Dr
100 CNTN 48187 4411 C2
Savannah Ln
1800 SpTp 48198 4409 C7
Savannah St E
10 DET 48203 4200 C7
Savannah St W
10 DET 48203 4200 C7
Savery Dr
44400 CNTN 48187 4336 E7
Savery St
9200 DET 48206 4344 B1
9400 DET 48206 4272 B7
Savoie St
16400 LVNA 48154 4267 E2
16600 LVNA 48152 4267 E2

Savoie Wy
21600 NOVI 48375 4193 D4
Savoy Ct
42600 NvlT 48167 4193 A6
Sawgrass Ct
9500 VNBN 48111 4494 D6
Sawgrass Ct N
23500 LyTp 48178 4190 D2
Sawgrass Ct S
23300 LyTp 48178 4190 C2
Sawgrass Dr E
4500 PTFD 48108 4488 D7
4500 PTFD 48108 4572 E1
Sawgrass Dr W
4500 PTFD 48108 4488 D7
4700 PTFD 48108 4572 D1
Sawgrass Rd
- YpTp 48197 4575 E5
Sawgrass St
- TYLR 48180 4583 A2
Sawyer
22000 DET 48239 4341 B4
22700 DBHT 48127 4341 B4
Sawyer St
- DET 48239 4341 D4
18500 DET 48228 4342 A4
19000 DET 48228 4341 E4
23200 DBHT 48127 4341 B4
Saxon Rd
1700 AARB 48103 4488 D2
Saxony Av
22700 EPTE 48021 4203 E1
Saxony Rd
36400 FMTN 48335 4194 B2
42700 CNTN 48187 4337 A5
Saxony St
25100 WDHN 48183 4668 B7
Saxton Av
19500 SFLD 48075 4197 D3
Scarborough Ln
- NOVI 48375 4193 B1
10 HbgT 48189 4186 A6
Scarlet Ct
24200 NOVI 48374 4192 A1
Scarlet Dr
100 CNTN 48187 4411 C2
Scarlet Dr N
47200 NOVI 48374 4192 A1
Scarlet Dr S
47000 NOVI 48374 4192 A1
Scarlet Oak Ln
300 AGST 48191 4661 B7
Scarsdale Rd
2700 WIND N8R 4423 B2
Scarsdale St
18400 DET 48223 4270 A3
Scenic Ct
47700 CNTN 48188 4411 A4
Scenic Dr
1600 CNTN 48188 4411 B4
44300 VNBN 48111 4494 E5
Scenic Ln
- NOVI 48167 4192 E4
41900 NvlT 48167 4193 A6
Scenic Cir Dr N
47400 CNTN 48188 4411 A4
Scenic Cir Dr S
47500 CNTN 48188 4411 A4
Scenic Harbour Dr
19800 NvlT 48167 4193 A6
Scenic Lake Dr
3100 PTFD 48108 4490 D4
Schaefer Hwy
8000 DET 48228 4343 A2
9500 DET 48227 4343 A2
11300 DET 48227 4271 A7
12200 DET 48227 4270 E5
16100 DET 48235 4270 E2
18000 DET 48235 4198 E6
S Schaefer Hwy
- DRBN 48120 4418 A4
- DRBN 48122 4418 A4
- DRBN 48229 4418 A4
Schaefer Hwy S
900 DET 48122 4418 C7
900 DET 48229 4418 C7
900 MVDL 48122 4418 C7
Schaefer Rd
2800 DRBN 48120 4418 A2
3400 DRBN 48126 4418 A2
4500 DRBN 48126 4343 A7
Schaefer Rd S
2100 DET 48122 4418 B5
2100 DET 48229 4418 B5
2100 MVDL 48122 4418 B5
2200 MVDL 48229 4418 B5
Schafer Ct
14700 SOGT 48195 4584 B3
Schaller Dr
6600 GDNC 48135 4339 D5
Scheffer Pl
- DET 48211 4273 E7
Scherer Pl
10 GSPF 48236 4276 E4
Schill Rd
8500 WasC 48176 4656 B2
Schiller St
9300 DET 48214 4346 D1
Schlaff St
- DRBN 48126 4417 E1
4700 DRBN 48126 4342 E7
Schley Av
35300 WTLD 48186 4413 C5
Schmeman Av
21700 WRRN 48089 4202 D2
Schmitt Ct
4000 WasC 48160 4574 E7
Schoenherr Rd
20700 WRRN 48089 4202 E1

Schoenherr St
17100 DET 48205 4202 E3
School St
300 SLYN 48178 4189 B2
17600 DET 48212 4202 A7
23600 FMTN 48336 4195 A2
34900 WTLD 48185 4413 D2
Schoolcraft
- RDFD 48223 4269 A6
- RDFD 48239 4269 A6
18100 DET 48223 4270 A6
18100 DET 48227 4270 A6
19000 DET 48223 4269 D5
24000 RDFD 48239 4268 E6
27300 RDFD 48150 4268 B6
27300 RDFD 48154 4268 B6
Schoolcraft Rd
27400 LVNA 48150 4268 A6
27400 LVNA 48154 4268 A6
27900 LVNA 48150 4267 A6
27900 LVNA 48154 4267 B6
33400 LVNA 48154 4266 C6
33500 LVNA 48150 4266 B6
38500 LVNA 48150 4265 D6
39400 PyTp 48170 4265 C6
Schoolcraft St
8000 DET 48238 4271 C5
12900 DET 48227 4271 A5
13600 DET 48227 4270 D5
Schoolhouse Ct
19900 NvlT 48167 4193 C6
Schooner Dr
5900 VNBN 48111 4494 A2
Schooner Cove Blvd
5000 YpTp 48197 4576 C1
Schreiner Rd
26000 HnTp 48164 4751 C1
Schrock Dr
25300 WynC 48111 4748 E1
Schroeder Av
22700 EPTE 48021 4203 E1
S Schroeder St
500 DET 48209 4419 C4
Schrum Dr
10 WasC 48189 4259 A3
Schulte St
33700 FMTN 48335 4194 D2
Schultes Av
20700 WRRN 48091 4201 A4
Schultz St
2100 LNPK 48146 4500 C4
12000 RMLS 48174 4580 C1
19000 HnTp 48164 4665 C1
Schuman Av
5600 WTLD 48185 4339 A7
S Schuman Av
100 WTLD 48186 4414 A3
Schuman St
800 GDNC 48135 4414 A1
1700 GDNC 48135 4339 A7
Schuper St
- DET 48224 4275 C4
Schwab St
500 LSal N9J 4502 E5
Schweizers Pl
200 DET 48207 4345 E7
200 DET 48226 4345 E7
Scio Rd
2000 WasC 48130 4404 B1
2400 WasC 48130 4329 B7
Scio Church Ct
2000 WasC 48103 4487 D2
Scio Church Rd
10 AARB 48103 4489 A2
10 WasC 48103 4489 A2
1000 AARB 48103 4488 C2
2400 PTFD 48103 4488 C2
2400 WasC 48103 4488 C2
3700 WasC 48103 4487 D2
Scio Country Ln
2500 WasC 48130 4329 B7
Scio Hills Ct
1000 WasC 48103 4405 A3
Sciomeadows Dr
500 WasC 48103 4404 D4
Scio Ridge Ct
1400 WasC 48103 4488 C1
Scio Ridge Rd
- WasC 48103 4405 C7
1500 WasC 48103 4488 C1
Scituate Dr
300 PLYM 48170 4264 D7
Scofield Av
500 WIND N9G 4504 E3
900 WIND N9G 4505 A3
Scone St
32200 LVNA 48154 4267 A6
35900 LVNA 48154 4266 C6
Scotia Ct
46500 CNTN 48187 4411 C1
Scotia Dr
2900 WIND N8T 4422 C4
Scotia Ln
21400 ROTp 48220 4199 A3
Scotia Rd
21800 OKPK 48237 4199 A2
Scots Wy
4600 WasC 48130 4329 D4
Scotsdale Cir
37400 WTLD 48185 4338 A4
Scott Ct
900 NHVL 48167 4192 C7
5300 YpTp 48197 4576 C2
Scott Dr
23300 FNHL 48336 4195 E1
38500 WTLD 48186 4413 A3
Scott Pl
1000 AARB 48105 4407 B5
Scott St
- DET 48207 4345 D3

Scott St
300 SLYN 48178 4189 C3
800 NHVL 48167 4192 C7
2800 DET 48207 4346 A3
15600 SOGT 48195 4584 D4
24000 DRBN 48124 4416 A4
24400 DRBN 48124 4415 E4
Scotten Av
4700 WIND N9C 4419 E7
Scotten St
1000 DET 48209 4419 D1
1900 DET 48209 4344 D6
2400 DET 48216 4344 D6
5600 DET 48210 4344 B3
7300 DET 48204 4344 B3
28900 FNHL 48336 4195 D4
S Scotten St
100 DET 48209 4419 E2
Scott Pine Dr
37800 HnTp 48164 4751 A1
Scottsdale Ct
10 DRBN 48124 4416 A4
700 CNTN 48188 4412 E3
Scottsdale Dr
39000 RMLS 48174 4496 A2
39600 CNTN 48188 4412 D3
Scottwood Av
1900 AARB 48104 4489 E1
Scovel Pl
3700 DET 48210 4344 B3
Scripps St
13100 DET 48214 4347 E2
14700 DET 48214 4348 A2
Seabrook Ct
19900 NvlT 48167 4193 C6
Seabrook Dr
37100 LVNA 48152 4266 B1
45000 CNTN 48188 4411 D4
Sea Mist Dr
7200 YpTp 48197 4576 A5
Sears St
100 HDPK 48203 4272 C2
11600 LVNA 48150 4267 C7
11600 LVNA 48150 4339 C1
Seaton Dr
19000 BNTN 48192 4584 A7
Seaton Circuit S
2600 WRRN 48091 4201 A1
Seattle St
- RMLS 48174 4582 B3
Seavitt Dr
10700 ALPK 48101 4500 A6
18900 ALPK 48101 4499 D5
Seaway Dr
15000 TYLR 48180 4583 D4
18600 MVDL 48122 4501 A1
Secluded Ln
20000 SFLD 48075 4197 C4
Secord Av
2100 WIND N9B 4420 C4
Sedalia Av
27000 SFLD 48034 4196 A4
27400 FNHL 48034 4196 A4
27400 FNHL 48336 4196 A4
Seebaldt St
- DET 48206 4344 B3
4200 DET 48204 4344 B3
5500 DET 48210 4344 B3
Seeley Rd
- WasC 48103 4405 C7
Seiu Av
2500 DET 48201 4345 B5
Selden St
1100 DET 48201 4345 A4
1900 DET 48210 4345 A4
3200 DET 48210 4344 D5
Selfridge St
12000 HMTK 48212 4273 A3
Selkirk Av
6900 LSal N9J 4503 B6
Selkirk Ct
4700 WasC 48103 4329 E4
Selkirk Dr
200 CNTN 48187 4412 C2
Selkirk St
6100 DET 48211 4273 E5
Selma Av
1100 WTLD 48186 4413 C3
Seltzer St
9800 LVNA 48150 4340 A1
Selwyn St
15600 SOGT 48195 4584 D4
Seminole
9500 RDFD 48239 4340 B1
14700 RDFD 48239 4268 B4
20500 RDFD 48240 4196 A5
Seminole Av
2500 PTFD 48108 4490 E3
Seminole Ct
38600 RMLS 48174 4496 A3
Seminole Dr
38400 RMLS 48174 4496 A3
Seminole Ln
26500 FTRK 48134 4753 E1
Seminole St
2300 WIND N8W 4421 D2
2300 WIND N8Y 4421 D2
3600 DET 48214 4346 C1
4000 WIND N8Y 4422 A1
4100 DET 48214 4274 C7
6400 DET 48213 4274 B5
20700 SFLD 48034 4196 A3
20700 SFLD 48240 4196 A3
Semrau Av
16200 EPTE 48021 4203 C1
18200 EPTE 48021 4204 A1
Senate Av
2600 YpTp 48197 4491 B4
Senate Dr
24000 BNTN 48134 4754 C1

INDEX 48
Senate St — Detroit & Wayne County Street Index — Slocum St

STREET
Block City ZIP Map# Grid

Senate St
300 YpTp 48197 4491 B4
6500 VNBN 48111 4577 C4
Senator St
10 LSal N9J 4502 C6
7000 DET 48209 4419 A2
8300 DET 48209 4418 E2
Seneca
14800 RDFD 48239 4268 B4
Seneca Av
2000 AARB 48104 4406 E7
20200 BwTp 48183 4754 E3
Seneca St
1400 WIND N8W 4421 C3
1800 YpTp 48198 4492 E5
3700 DET 48214 4346 C1
5000 DET 48214 4274 C6
6400 DET 48213 4274 B5
24400 OKPK 48237 4199 A1
25600 FTRK 48134 4753 D3
Sentinel
- CNTN 48188 4411 D4
Sequoia Av
28300 RMLS 48174 4582 A5
Sequoia Dr
6100 YpTp 48197 4575 D3
Sequoia Ln
13300 GOTp 48178 4188 D2
26500 FTRK 48134 4753 E2
Sequoia Pkwy
2500 AARB 48103 4405 C4
Sequoia Rd
33900 WTLD 48185 4338 E5
Serenity Dr
43400 NOVI 48167 4192 E4
Service Dr
- RDFD 48240 4268 D1
- YPLT 48198 4492 C6
1700 YpTp 48198 4493 A7
1800 YpTp 48198 4577 A1
2000 YpTp 48198 4492 E5
W Service Dr
- SFLD 48034 4196 D1
Service Rd
1600 AARB 48104 4490 A1
E Service Rd
- RMLS 48174 4497 C7
- RMLS 48242 4497 C7
N Service Rd E
600 WIND N8X 4421 C6
900 WIND N8W 4421 C6
3500 WIND N8W 4422 D5
4700 WIND N8T 4422 D5
4700 WIND N8V 4422 D5
N Service Rd W
- WIND N9E 4421 A7
S Service Rd
11000 Tcmh N8N 4423 C4
11000 WIND N8N 4423 C4
S Service Rd E
900 WIND N8X 4421 D6
1000 WIND N8W 4421 D6
6700 WIND N8T 4422 E5
6700 WIND N8T 4423 A5
W Service Rd
500 RMLS 48242 4497 C5
Service St
- DBHT 48127 4415 B1
1400 DET 48207 4345 E4
Service Road B
3700 Tcmh N8V 4423 B6
Settler's St
1100 WIND N9G 4505 A4
Sevan Dr
41600 CNTN 48188 4412 B2
Severn Ct
1200 AARB 48105 4407 C4
Severn Rd
- GSPF 48236 4204 B7
1500 GSPW 48236 4204 A7
21200 HRWD 48225 4204 B7
Seville Row
800 DET 48202 4344 E1
Seward St
- DET 48202 4273 A7
600 DET 48202 4272 E7
1100 DET 48202 4344 E1
1900 DET 48206 4344 D1
Sexton St
18800 BwTp 48173 4841 A1
19600 RKWD 48173 4841 A1
23300 DBHT 48127 4341 B6
Sexton Sideroad
5400 Tcmh N0R 4505 E7
Seyburn St
3600 DET 48214 4346 C1
4400 DET 48214 4274 B7
5000 DET 48213 4274 B7
Seymour Av
1500 WIND N8W 4421 E7
1900 WIND N8W 4422 A6
Seymour St
200 Amhg N9V 4757 C3
4000 DRBN 48126 4417 D1
13700 DET 48205 4203 B7
Shacket St
29800 WTLD 48185 4339 D4
Shadberry Ct
3100 WasC 48176 4572 B2
Shadbrook St
18000 NvlT 48167 4264 C1
Shaddick St
8500 DRBN 48126 4343 C5
Shadetree Cres
4600 WIND N9G 4504 D5
Shadetree Ct
4700 WIND N9G 4504 D5
Shadford Rd
1400 AARB 48104 4489 D1
Shadow Ct
7800 PTFD 48197 4574 D7
Shadowglen Dr
22400 FNHL 48335 4194 A3
Shadowlawn Dr
42700 CNTN 48187 4412 A1
Shadowlawn St
100 INKR 48141 4415 C2
6400 DBHT 48127 4340 C5
Shadownook St
- DET 48207 4347 A5
Shadowood Dr
1900 AARB 48108 4490 A6
Shadowpine Wy
22600 NOVI 48375 4193 C3
Shadow Valley Ct
10600 GOTp 48178 4188 C4
Shadowwood Ln
24600 BNTN 48134 4668 A5
Shadow Woods Ln
11000 HbgT 48189 4186 A5
Shady Dr
600 WasC 48189 4187 B6
Shady Ln
2900 PTFD 48104 4489 E4
3600 DET 48216 4344 E7
3600 DET 48216 4419 E1
7800 WasC 48189 4259 A4
Shady Beach Dr
7600 WasC 48189 4259 A3
Shadybrook Dr
21500 NOVI 48375 4193 C4
Shady Hollow Dr
- DRBN 48124 4416 C1
Shady Knoll Ln
5700 YpTp 48197 4575 C3
Shady Ln Av
19500 STCS 48080 4204 B3
Shady Oak Dr
12200 GOTp 48178 4188 B1
Shady Oaks Ct
1100 WasC 48103 4404 D3
Shady Oaks Dr
1000 WasC 48103 4404 D3
Shadyside Dr
15700 LVNA 48154 4267 A3
Shadyside St
9600 LVNA 48150 4339 A2
15300 LVNA 48154 4267 A4
18200 LVNA 48152 4267 A1
18500 LVNA 48152 4195 A7
20100 LVNA 48336 4195 A5
Shadywood Ct
14400 PyTp 48170 4265 B5
Shadywood Dr
14000 PyTp 48170 4265 B5
Shaftsbury Av
16100 DET 48223 4269 E2
17100 DET 48219 4269 E1
19700 DET 48219 4197 E5
Shagbark Ct
2500 CNTN 48188 4411 A5
Shagbark Dr
5700 PTFD 48108 4573 A2
Shakespeare Av
22700 EPTE 48021 4203 D1
Shakespeare Ln
2500 WasC 48167 4190 A7
Shakespeare St
19900 DET 48205 4203 D4
Shamrock Ct
3100 AARB 48105 4331 E7
Shamrock Hl
7100 YpTp 48197 4575 E4
Shamrock Ln
46400 PyTp 48170 4336 B2
Shamrock Pl
4700 WYNE 48184 4414 B7
Shana Dr
200 CNTN 48187 4412 B2
Shannon Ct
900 NHVL 48167 4192 A4
Shannon Dr
9200 HbgT 48116 4186 B1
Shannon Pl
100 Tcmh N8N 4349 B7
Shannon St
20500 TYLR 48180 4499 D4
Shannondale Rd
2400 AARB 48104 4489 E1
2400 AARB 48104 4490 A1
Share Av
1100 YpTp 48198 4492 D6
Shari Dr
8200 WTLD 48185 4339 C3
8700 WTLD 48150 4339 C3
Sharon Av
4200 WIND N9G 4504 E4
Sharon Ct
19700 WynC 48111 4663 C2
Sharon Dr
2800 AARB 48108 4490 A5
6400 GDNC 48135 4339 D6
Sharon St
1100 WTLD 48186 4414 D3
1900 DET 48209 4418 E2
5200 DET 48210 4343 C6
9600 TYLR 48180 4498 D5
11200 RMLS 48174 4496 C7
12000 RMLS 48174 4580 C1
Sharrow Av
21700 WRRN 48089 4202 E2
Shasta Pl
600 FRDL 48220 4199 D3
Shaw
- GOTp 48189 4187 A6
Shaw St
31600 FMTN 48336 4195 B3
Shawcross Pl
10 HDPK 48203 4272 E2
Shawn Av
400 Tcmh N8N 4349 A7
Shawn Dr
8600 YpTp 48197 4576 C2
Shawnee Dr
6900 RMLS 48174 4496 A3
Shawnee Rd
1200 Tcmh N8N 4423 E2
Shawnee St
33000 WTLD 48185 4338 E6
Sheahan Dr
26700 DBHT 48127 4415 B1
Shearson Ct
9600 YpTp 48170 4336 C2
Sheehan Av
1300 AARB 48104 4489 C1
Sheehan St
7200 DET 48213 4274 A4
Sheeks Blvd N
28100 FTRK 48134 4753 D4
Sheeks Blvd S
29000 FTRK 48134 4753 D4
Sheffield Blvd
- NvlT 48167 4263 E3
Sheffield Ct
100 CNTN 48187 4412 B2
100 CNTN 48188 4412 B2
2900 AARB 48105 4407 B2
22200 FNHL 48335 4194 A3
Sheffield Dr
100 SALN 48176 4572 C7
1500 SpTp 48198 4492 C1
1800 SpTp 48198 4409 B7
21500 FNHL 48335 4194 B4
45600 NOVI 48374 4192 C4
Sheffield Rd
20100 DET 48221 4199 D4
Sheffield St
34900 WTLD 48186 4413 D4
Shefford Blvd
3700 CNTN 48188 4411 B6
Shefield Ct
50000 PyTp 48170 4263 D7
Shefman Ter
2600 AARB 48105 4407 B2
Shelbourne Ct
400 GSPF 48236 4204 C7
Shelbourne Rd
400 GSPF 48236 4204 C7
Shelby Av
2300 AARB 48103 4405 D6
Shelby Dr
- WTLD 48186 4413 A5
Shelby St
500 DET 48226 4345 D6
Shelden Rd
500 GSPS 48236 4277 A1
700 GSPS 48236 4205 A6
Sheldon Rd
- NHVL 48167 4192 D7
5800 VNBN 48111 4494 E2
6500 HbgT 48189 4186 A6
13900 BLVL 48111 4578 E3
13900 VNBN 48111 4578 E3
15300 NvlT 48167 4264 D3
18700 NvlT 48167 4192 D7
N Sheldon Rd
100 CNTN 48187 4411 E2
400 PLYM 48170 4264 D6
2000 CNTN 48187 4336 E7
8800 PyTp 48170 4336 E4
8800 PyTp 48187 4336 E4
10400 PyTp 48170 4264 D5
15200 PyTp 48167 4264 D5
S Sheldon Rd
100 CNTN 48187 4411 E3
100 CNTN 48188 4411 E3
100 PLYM 48170 4264 E7
100 PyTp 48170 4264 E7
400 PLYM 48170 4336 E1
400 PyTp 48170 4336 E1
4500 CNTN 48111 4494 E1
4500 CNTN 48188 4494 E1
Sheldon St
6200 YpTp 48197 4577 A3
Sheldon Center Rd
8000 CNTN 48187 4336 D5
Sheldon Center Connector
- CNTN 48187 4336 E4
Shellbark Dr
4500 PTFD 48197 4574 E1
4600 PTFD 48197 4575 A1
Shelley Cres
12700 Tcmh N8N 4424 A2
Shelley Dr
6500 VNBN 48111 4493 C2
Shelley St
15500 SFLD 48075 4198 C1
15500 SFLD 48237 4198 C1
Shelley Pond Ct
18100 NvlT 48167 4264 C1
Shelley Pond Dr
46400 NvlT 48167 4264 B1
Shelly Av
2100 YpTp 48198 4492 E7
2100 YpTp 48198 4493 B7
Shelly Ct
5600 WasC 48176 4571 E4
Shellye Ct
34400 WTLD 48185 4338 E4
Shenandoah Av
4300 ALPK 48101 4417 B6
6300 ALPK 48101 4500 A2
Shenandoah Cir
49400 CNTN 48187 4335 D4
Shenandoah Cres
10100 WIND N8R 4423 B2
Shenandoah Dr
9800 GOTp 48178 4188 A2
14500 RVVW 48192 4584 C7
Shepherd St E
1400 WIND N8X 4421 C2
1600 WIND N8Y 4421 C2
Shepherd St W
10 WIND N8X 4421 A3
400 WIND N8X 4420 E4
Sheppard Dr
6300 WTLD 48185 4338 B6
Sheraton Ct
2200 TNTN 48183 4669 D3
Sheraton Dr
2000 TNTN 48183 4669 D3
Sherborne Av
16900 ALPK 48101 4417 B7
Sherbourne Dr
600 DBHT 48127 4415 B1
1200 DBHT 48127 4340 B7
Sherbourne Rd
3200 DET 48221 4199 D6
Sherbourne St
300 INKR 48141 4415 B2
Sheridan Ct
26700 FTRK 48134 4754 A2
Sheridan Dr
1500 AARB 48104 4490 A1
Sheridan Rd
22500 NOVI 48375 4193 C3
Sheridan St
- DBHT 48127 4415 B1
900 YPLT 48197 4491 D4
1300 PLYM 48170 4264 E7
3600 DET 48214 4346 B1
4700 DET 48214 4274 B7
5900 DET 48213 4274 A6
24000 DRBN 48128 4416 A1
24400 DRBN 48128 4415 E1
27400 GDNC 48135 4415 A1
28600 GDNC 48135 4414 E1
34900 WTLD 48185 4413 D1
44000 CNTN 48187 4336 E4
Sherman Av
12400 WRRN 48089 4202 D3
13600 WRRN 48089 4203 A3
20700 SFLD 48034 4197 A4
Sherman Ct
900 YPLT 48197 4491 D4
Sherman St
900 YPLT 48197 4491 D4
23400 OKPK 48237 4199 C1
Sherrie Ln
200 NHVL 48167 4192 D4
Sherry Dr
22600 BNTN 48134 4667 E5
Sherry Ln
10700 WasC 48170 4263 B6
Sherstone Ct
4700 CNTN 48188 4411 B7
Sherstone Dr
46800 CNTN 48188 4411 C7
Sherway Dr
2800 WIND N8R 4423 B2
Sherwood
9600 SpTp 48198 4409 E7
Sherwood Av
- WRRN 48234 4201 E4
2300 TNTN 48183 4669 B4
20700 WRRN 48091 4201 E4
23400 WRRN 48015 4201 E1
23800 CTNL 48015 4201 E1
23800 CTNL 48091 4201 E1
Sherwood Cir
900 AARB 48103 4405 E7
3900 CNTN 48188 4411 B7
Sherwood Ct
900 AARB 48103 4405 E7
1400 DRBN 48124 4417 B5
46900 CNTN 48188 4411 B7
48900 WynC 48111 4748 E1
48900 WynC 48111 4749 A1
Sherwood Ct N
37400 LVNA 48154 4266 B5
Sherwood Ct S
37400 LVNA 48154 4266 B5
Sherwood Dr
- TYLR 48180 4582 D5
8300 WynC 48138 4670 C4
9300 WasC 48176 4658 B3
48200 PyTp 48170 4264 B5
Sherwood Ln
16400 WDHN 48183 4669 A3
16700 NvlT 48167 4264 A3
22000 BNTN 48134 4667 E4
38000 WTLD 48185 4338 A7
Sherwood Rd
19600 WynC 48111 4662 E3
24600 WynC 48111 4748 E1
Sherwood St
6400 DET 48211 4273 E4
13700 DET 48212 4273 E1
17500 DET 48212 4201 E7
17800 DET 48234 4201 E5
22400 FMTN 48336 4195 B3
37100 LVNA 48154 4266 B3
Sherwood Forest Ct E
4100 WasC 48103 4329 E6
Sherwood Forest Ct W
4300 WasC 48103 4329 E6
Shery Ln
12500 SOGT 48195 4584 C1
Sheryl Dr
3800 WasC 48160 4659 D4
Shetland Dr
4100 AATp 48105 4490 D1
4200 AATp 48197 4490 D1
Shevchenko Dr
1200 WasC 48103 4487 C1
W Shevlin Av
10 HZLP 48030 4200 B1
Shevlin St
1500 FRDL 48220 4200 A1
Shiawassee Cir
25300 SFLD 48034 4196 D4
Shiawassee Dr
18300 DET 48219 4197 A7
24500 DET 48219 4196 D5
24800 DET 48034 4196 D5
24800 DET 48240 4196 D5
24800 SFLD 48034 4196 D5
Shiawassee Ln
26500 FTRK 48134 4753 E1
Shiawassee Rd
- SFLD 48240 4196 C4
25100 SFLD 48034 4196 C4
27400 FNHL 48034 4196 A3
27400 FNHL 48336 4196 A3
29700 FNHL 48336 4195 C2
30700 FMTN 48336 4195 B2
32500 FMTN 48335 4195 B2
33300 FMTN 48335 4194 E1
33300 FNHL 48335 4194 E1
Shiawassee St
31800 WTLD 48186 4414 D5
33400 FMTN 48335 4194 E1
Shields Dr
- DBHT 48127 4340 E4
- DBHT 48127 4341 A4
Shields St
12200 Tcmh N8N 4424 A6
13400 DET 48212 4273 C1
19100 DET 48234 4201 B5
Shiff Dr
11900 Tcmh N0R 4424 A7
Shilo Ct
23000 NOVI 48374 4192 A3
Shilo Dr
23000 NOVI 48374 4192 A3
Shiloh Ct
43800 CNTN 48188 4411 E3
Shinglecreek Ct
3600 WIND N8W 4505 A1
3700 WIND N8W 4504 E1
Shinnecock Dr
23100 LyTp 48178 4190 D2
Shipherd Ct
1000 DET 48214 4346 D3
Shipherd St
1000 DET 48214 4346 D2
Shipman Cir
10 AARB 48104 4407 A7
Shire Ln
7800 YpTp 48197 4576 B6
Shirley Av
1200 YpTp 48198 4492 D7
Shirley Dr
- WTLD 48185 4413 C2
1100 YpTp 48198 4492 C7
Shirley Ln
1800 AARB 48105 4406 E3
25800 DBHT 48127 4415 D2
Shirley St
- DET 48227 4270 E6
Shoal Creek Rd
53300 LyTp 48178 4190 D2
Shoemaker Dr
1100 WTLD 48185 4413 D1
Shoemaker St
9300 DET 48213 4274 D5
Shomberg St
23600 TYLR 48180 4499 A5
Shook Rd
9200 RMLS 48174 4496 C6
19100 HnTp 48164 4665 C1
Shore Dr
300 LNPK 48146 4501 B6
E Shore Dr
10 WasC 48189 4259 A1
200 WasC 48189 4187 C6
11000 GOTp 48189 4187 C6
N Shore Dr
300 LNPK 48146 4501 B6
47100 VNBN 48111 4578 B2
N Shore Rd
11100 GOTp 48189 4187 B5
Shorebrook Blvd
- NvlT 48167 4263 E3
Shoreclub Dr
200 STCS 48080 4205 A2
Shorecrest Cir
10 GSPS 48236 4205 B4
10 McoC 48236 4205 B4
N Shorecrest Cir
10 McoC 48236 4205 A3
S Shorecrest Cir
10 McoC 48236 4205 A3
Shorecrest Ct
11500 GOTp 48178 4188 A1
Shoreham Rd
10 GSPS 48236 4204 E7
10 GSPS 48236 4205 A7
600 GSPW 48236 4204 D7
Shorehaven Wynd
200 WIND N8S 4347 D5
Shoreline Ct
18100 NvlT 48167 4265 A1
Shorepointe Ln
1900 GSPW 48080 4204 C4
1900 GSPW 48236 4204 C4
1900 STCS 48080 •4204 C4
2000 STCS 48236 4204 C4
Shores St
20200 STCS 48080 4204 C1
Shoreview Cir
300 WIND N8P 4348 D5
Shoreview Ct
200 WIND N8P 4348 D5
Shoreview Dr
4500 CNTN 48188 4411 C7
Short Av
1800 WTLD 48186 4413 C4
Short Rd
- DRBN 48126 4342 C6
Short St
- SpTp 48105 4408 B1
- SpTp 48198 4408 B1
10 DBHT 48127 4340 C5
800 YPLT 48197 4491 E5
18200 DET 48219 4196 E7
32000 RKWD 48173 4754 C7
Shotka Rd
500 GDNC 48135 4414 D1
1600 GDNC 48135 4339 D7
Shotka St
100 WTLD 48135 4414 C2
100 WTLD 48186 4414 C2
Shrewsbury Av
- AARB 48104 4490 B3
Shrewsbury Dr
18600 LVNA 48152 4195 B7
Shrewsbury Rd
19400 DET 48221 4199 D5
Shrewsbury St
16800 LVNA 48154 4267 B2
Shurley Dr
21100 WynC 48138 4670 D3
E Sibley Ct
21000 BNTN 48183 4583 D7
21000 BNTN 48192 4583 D7
W Sibley Ct
21600 BNTN 48192 4583 D7
Sibley Rd
11200 RVVW 48192 4585 A7
11200 TNTN 48183 4585 A7
11200 TNTN 48192 4585 A7
12500 RVVW 48192 4584 E7
12500 TNTN 48183 4584 E7
12500 TNTN 48192 4584 E7
16000 BNTN 48192 4584 B7
20000 BNTN 48183 4583 D7
20000 BNTN 48192 4583 D7
22500 BNTN 48183 4668 A1
22500 BNTN 48192 4668 A1
23600 BNTN 48174 4668 A1
24100 BNTN 48174 4667 E1
27400 HnTp 48174 4667 A1
29300 HnTp 48174 4666 B1
33600 HnTp 48164 4665 E1
33600 HnTp 48164 4666 B1
Sibley St
10 DET 48201 4345 C5
Siding Ct
7800 WynC 48138 4670 D6
Sidney St
11300 RMLS 48174 4580 D1
Sidonie Av
12300 WRRN 48089 4202 D3
13600 WRRN 48089 4203 A3
Siebert St
8400 DET 48234 4274 B3
15000 TYLR 48180 4582 C4
Siegal Ct
22000 NOVI 48375 4193 C3
Siegal Dr
21600 NOVI 48375 4193 C4
Sierra Dr
2600 WIND N9E 4420 E7
2600 WIND N9E 4503 E1
Sierra Ln
26500 FTRK 48134 4753 E1
Siever Dr
2500 CNTN 48188 4411 A5
Sigler Rd
3000 MonC 48166 4839 A5
3000 MonC 48179 4839 A5
3400 BrTp 48166 4839 C5
3400 BrTp 48179 4839 C5
5300 BrTp 48179 4840 A5
8000 BrTp 48179 4841 A4
E Sigler Rd
2300 MonC 48117 4839 A5
2300 MonC 48166 4839 A5
Signature Blvd
- AARB 48103 4489 A4
- AARB 48108 4489 A4
Sil St
9600 TYLR 48180 4498 C5
Silken Glen Dr
38500 FNHL 48167 4193 E5
Siller Ter
- AARB 48103 4405 E6
Silman St
200 FRDL 48220 4200 A3
Silo Ct
7900 RMLS 48174 4496 A4
E Silo Ridge Dr
5500 PTFD 48108 4573 B3
N Silo Ridge Dr
1200 PTFD 48108 4573 A2
Silver Ct
29200 FTRK 48134 4753 E4
Silver Dr
11000 HbgT 48189 4186 B5
Silverado Dr
16400 SOGT 48195 4584 A5
Silver Creek Ct
26700 BNTN 48134 4667 C7
Silver Creek Dr
22300 WDHN 48183 4668 C4
26300 BNTN 48134 4667 D7
Silver Creek Ln
21900 RKWD 48173 4754 C6
Silvercrest St
18900 SFLD 48075 4197 E3
Silverdale Dr
600 WIND N9G 4504 E4
1000 WIND N9G 4505 A4
Silver Lake Rd
10000 GOTp 48116 4187 C1
10600 GOTp 48178 4187 C1
Silverleaf Dr
- PTFD 48197 4491 A6
4300 PTFD 48197 4490 E6
Silver Maple Dr
5900 PTFD 48108 4572 E3
Silver Maple St
17300 SFLD 48075 4198 A1
Silver Pine Dr
9000 GOTp 48116 4187 D1
9000 GOTp 48178 4187 D1
Silver Ridge Ct
35000 FNHL 48335 4194 D3
Silverside Dr
9000 GOTp 48178 4187 E1
Silver Spring Dr
2700 PTFD 48103 4488 E3
Silver Springs Dr
19100 NvlT 48167 4193 A6
Silverton Dr
8000 GOTp 48116 4186 C4
8000 GOTp 48189 4186 C4
Silverwood Dr
43200 CNTN 48188 4412 A4
Silvery Ln
23500 NOVI 48375 4193 B2
N Silvery Ln
100 DRBN 48128 4415 E1
1500 DRBN 48128 4340 E7
5600 DBHT 48127 4340 E5
5600 DBHT 48128 4340 E7
8500 DBHT 48239 4340 E3
S Silvery Ln
100 DRBN 48124 4415 E2
Silvio St
6400 GDNC 48135 4339 B6
Simard Cres
12800 Tcmh N8N 4349 A7
Simcheck Dr
22400 LyTp 48178 4191 B3
Simcoe Dr
41400 CNTN 48188 4412 C3
Simcoe St
100 Amhg N9V 4757 B3
Simcoe St CO-18
100 Amhg N9V 4757 D3
Simmons Dr
24200 NOVI 48374 4192 B1
Simms St
13000 DET 48205 4274 C1
13000 DET 48234 4274 C1
Simone St
26200 DBHT 48127 4340 C7
Simon K
5800 DET 48212 4273 D2
Simpson Rd
500 AARB 48104 4406 D6
Simpson St
800 PLYM 48170 4336 E2
800 PLYM 48170 4337 A2
Sims St
26200 DBHT 48127 4415 C1
34200 WYNE 48184 4413 E6
Simsbury St
43500 CNTN 48187 4337 A5
43600 CNTN 48187 4336 E5
Sinacola Ct
24200 FNHL 48335 4194 A1
Singh Blvd
41300 NOVI 48375 4193 B4
Singh Dr
41400 CNTN 48188 4412 B5
Sioux
9100 RDFD 48239 4340 B1
12700 RDFD 48239 4268 B6
Sioux St
17100 DET 48224 4276 A3
S Sire St
8900 DET 48209 4419 A4
Sirron St
8000 DET 48234 4202 A5
Sizemore Dr
9100 WasC 48176 4658 D3
Skydale Dr
600 AARB 48105 4406 C2
Skyhawk Blvd
1000 WasC 48103 4405 A7
1100 WasC 48103 4488 A1
Skyline Ct
4100 WasC 48103 4488 A1
Skyline Dr
2800 WIND N9E 4503 E1
Skyline Wy
2800 AATp 48105 4406 C1
Skynob Ct
600 AARB 48105 4407 B5
Skynob Dr
600 AARB 48105 4407 C6
Skyway Dr
1300 YpTp 48197 4491 B7
Slater St
1800 WIND N8W 4421 E5
Sleepy Hollow Dr
7600 WasC 48176 4261 E4
7800 WasC 48176 4658 C2
Sleepy Hollow St
33800 LVNA 48150 4338 E2
Sloan Dr
21200 HRWD 48225 4204 B7
Sloan St
7100 TYLR 48180 4499 C3
S Sloan St
700 DET 48209 4419 B4
Slocum St
200 TNTN 48183 4669 E5
32800 FMTN 48336 4195 A2
33100 FMTN 48336 4194 E2
33200 FMTN 48335 4194 E2

INDEX 49

Sloman St — Detroit & Wayne County Street Index — SR-102 8 Mile Rd W

STREET
Block City ZIP Map# Grid

Sloman St
21900 OKPK 48237 4199 A3
Slyvan St
- FRDL 48220 4200 A1
Small Pl
1100 YPLT 48197 4491 D6
Smart St
7700 DET 48210 4343 D5
Sme Dr
10 DRBN 48128 4341 D7
Smeeton Dr
800 WIND N8S 4347 E6
800 WIND N8S 4348 A6
Smith Av
1600 YpTp 48198 4493 A7
1800 YpTp 48198 4577 A1
Smith Cres
600 LSal N9J 4502 E5
Smith Rd
28200 RMLS 48174 4498 A4
31800 RMLS 48174 4497 B4
34700 RMLS 48174 4496 D4
Smith St
10 DET 48202 4273 A7
3100 DRBN 48124 4417 A6
17000 RVVW 48192 4584 E5
17000 RVVW 48195 4584 E5
Smithfield Ct
35800 FMTN 48335 4194 C1
Smithfield St
35600 FMTN 48335 4194 C2
Smock St
19100 NvIT 48167 4193 C7
Snapdragon Dr
16700 BwTp 48173 4755 A6
Snapfinger Al
3000 WRRN 48091 4201 A4
Snow Av
17600 ALPK 48101 4417 B6
17600 DRBN 48101 4417 B6
17600 DRBN 48124 4417 A5
21500 DRBN 48124 4416 D3
Snow Ct
10 DRBN 48124 4417 A5
Snow Rd
3100 YpTp 48198 4577 C1
Snowberry Ridge Rd
1500 WasC 48103 4488 B2
Snowden St
14500 DET 48227 4271 A3
16800 DET 48235 4271 A1
18100 DET 48235 4199 A7
19100 DET 48235 4198 E5
Snyder Av
300 AARB 48103 4489 A1
Soave Ln
8500 WasC 48178 4259 E1
Sobieski St
5900 DET 48212 4273 E2
11300 HMTK 48212 4273 C3
Socrates Cres
1000 WIND N9G 4505 A2
Socrates Ct
3800 WIND N9G 4505 A2
Sokol Camp Dr
- GOTp 48178 4187 E4
- GOTp 48178 4188 A4
Solar Cres
2100 Tcmh N0R 4505 B5
Solitude Ln
8900 VNBN 48111 4494 E5
Soloman St
11800 WIND N8P 4348 D7
Solomon Blvd
22000 NOVI 48375 4193 D4
Solomon Ct
4500 PTFD 48197 4490 E4
Solvay St N
700 DET 48209 4419 B3
Solvay St S
400 DET 48209 4419 B4
Somers St
19200 HnTp 48164 4665 C2
Somerset
- BNTN 48134 4754 A1
23300 HnTp 48164 4665 A5
Somerset Av
1000 GPPK 48230 4276 A6
1300 GPPK 48230 4275 E5
10300 DET 48224 4275 D1
11200 DET 48224 4203 D7
30700 WTLD 48186 4414 C2
33600 WTLD 48186 4413 E2
Somerset Ct
13700 SOGT 48195 4584 B2
20600 RVVW 48192 4669 D2
42400 CNTN 48187 4337 B6
47200 NOVI 48374 4192 A3
Somerset Dr
26200 INKR 48141 4415 C2
42600 CNTN 48187 4337 A6
Somerset Ln
8500 SpTp 48198 4409 C7
Somerset Sq
43800 CNTN 48187 4336 E6
Somerset St
27400 INKR 48141 4415 A2
28400 INKR 48141 4414 E2
35600 WTLD 48186 4413 C2
Somme Av
1500 WIND N8W 4421 D4
3000 WIND N8W 4422 A4
Sommerset Ct
400 WasC 48103 4404 C6
Sonata Ln
2300 PTFD 48176 4572 D3
Sondra Dr
- VNBN 48111 4493 C2
44800 VNBN 48111 4494 D3
W Sonoma Av
10 HZLP 48030 4200 B2
Sonoma St
2000 FRDL 48220 4200 B2
Sonora Dr
6900 RMLS 48174 4496 A3
Sonrisa St
49400 VNBN 48111 4577 E2
Sony Dr
19700 HnTp 48111 4665 B2
Sophia St
3200 WYNE 48184 4413 D5
Sophie
- VNBN 48111 4495 A3
Sorel Dr
500 CNTN 48188 4412 B2
Sorge Cres
800 LSal N9J 4503 A4
Sorrel Ct
200 PTFD 48197 4574 D2
Sorrell St
7200 WTLD 48185 4338 A5
Sorrento Av
2800 AARB 48104 4489 E3
Sorrento St
- DET 48235 4271 A2
8200 DET 48228 4343 A2
9500 DET 48227 4343 A1
14700 DET 48227 4271 A3
18000 DET 48235 4199 A6
Soule Blvd
400 AARB 48103 4405 E7
South Blvd
1400 AARB 48104 4489 D2
South Dr
41700 CNTN 48188 4412 B6
49400 PyTp 48170 4263 D6
South St
10 BLVL 48111 4578 D3
200 WIND N9C 4419 E4
300 YPLT 48198 4492 A5
400 SLYN 48178 4189 C2
900 WIND N9C 4420 A4
6300 DET 48209 4419 C4
9500 WasC 48167 4262 E3
Southampton Ct
16200 LVNA 48154 4266 E3
Southampton Dr
19800 LVNA 48152 4194 D6
43900 CNTN 48187 4336 E6
Southampton St
13000 DET 48213 4275 B4
14300 DET 48224 4275 B4
18400 LVNA 48152 4266 D1
18500 LVNA 48152 4194 E7
18600 DET 48224 4276 A2
18600 DET 48236 4276 A2
35400 LVNA 48154 4266 C3
Southdale Ct
2700 WIND N8W 4421 E5
Southdale Dr
1400 WIND N8W 4421 D5
Southern
- DET 48209 4344 B7
- DET 48210 4344 B7
Southern St
9800 DRBN 48120 4418 C1
9800 DRBN 48209 4418 C1
9800 DRBN 48210 4418 C1
9900 DRBN 48126 4418 C1
27000 INKR 48141 4415 B5
Southfarm Ct
38100 FNHL 48167 4194 A5
Southfarm Ln
38000 FNHL 48167 4194 A5
38500 FNHL 48167 4193 E5
Southfield Dr
1200 Tcmh N8N 4423 D2
Southfield Frwy
- ALPK - 4417 A7
- ALPK - 4500 A1
- DET - 4198 A7
- DET - 4270 A2
- DET - 4342 B3
- DRBN - 4417 B1
- DRBN 48126 4342 B7
- DRBN 48228 4342 B7
- SFLD - 4198 A7
3700 DRBN 48125 4417 A7
5600 DET 48228 4342 B5
12000 DET 48228 4270 A7
16700 DET 48219 4270 A2
17500 DET 48219 4198 A7
Southfield Frwy SR-39
- ALPK - 4417 A7
- ALPK - 4500 A1
- DET - 4198 A7
- DET - 4270 B5
- DET - 4342 B3
- DRBN - 4342 B5
- DRBN - 4417 B1
- SFLD - 4198 A7
Southfield Rd
- DRBN 48101 4417 B3
10 ECRS 48229 4501 B4
100 DRBN 48120 4417 B3
100 DRBN 48124 4417 B3
1200 LNPK 48146 4500 A2
1200 LNPK 48146 4501 B4
2200 LNPK 48101 4500 A2
3400 ALPK 48101 4417 B6
14500 ALPK 48101 4500 A2
23000 SFLD 48075 4198 A2
Southfield Rd SR-39
1200 LNPK 48146 4500 A2
1200 LNPK 48146 4501 A3
2200 LNPK 48101 4500 A2
14500 ALPK 48101 4500 A2
Southfield St
4500 ALPK 48101 4417 A7
4500 DBHT 48101 4417 A7
4500 DBHT 48125 4417 A7
5600 ALPK 48125 4417 A7
Southgate Ct
47000 CNTN 48188 4411 B5
Southgate Dr
46900 CNTN 48188 4411 B5
Southgate St
32900 LVNA 48152 4267 A2
Southlawn Av
2500 YpTp 48197 4491 A4
Southpark St
400 DET 48214 4347 D2
Southpoint St
22400 WDHN 48183 4668 C4
Southridge Ct
2600 WIND N8W 4421 E5
Southridge St
2700 WIND N8W 4421 D5
Southview Dr
14800 SOGT 48195 4584 A3
Southview Ln
46400 PyTp 48170 4264 B7
Southway St
- ALPK 48101 4500 A6
Southwest Dr
- DRBN 48126 4343 A6
Southwestern Hwy
25900 RDFD 48239 4268 C7
26500 RDFD 48239 4340 B1
Southwick
25400 RDFD 48240 4196 D6
Southwick Ct
10 AARB 48105 4407 B1
Southwick Dr
45400 CNTN 48188 4411 B4
Southwind Dr
41000 CNTN 48188 4412 C3
Southwind Ln
39600 NvIT 48167 4265 C3
Southwinds Dr
3700 WIND N9G 4504 A3
Southwood Ct
1100 WasC 48103 4405 A7
Southwood Lakes Blvd
4400 WIND N9G 4504 D4
5000 WIND N9G 4505 A5
Southwoods Tr
2500 WasC 48108 4488 C7
Southworth Av
9500 PyTp 48170 4337 C1
Southwyck Ct
22400 NOVI 48374 4192 B3
Sovereign Woods Dr
- LSal N9H 4503 D4
Sovey St
34900 BwTp 48173 4841 B2
Spago Cres
4100 WIND N9G 4505 A4
Spain Ct
30200 RMLS 48174 4581 D4
Spain St
29900 RMLS 48174 4581 E4
Spangler Dr
22400 LyTp 48178 4189 C4
Spanich Ct
15100 LVNA 48154 4267 C4
Spanish Oak Dr
36600 WTLD 48186 4413 C2
Spanish Oak Ln
400 AGST 48191 4661 C7
Sparling St
12800 DET 48212 4273 D1
Sparrow Wood Dr
- PTFD 48108 4490 D3
Sparta St
6300 DET 48210 4343 E4
Spearmint St
500 WTLD 48186 4414 C7
Spencer Av
3800 WIND N9G 4504 D2
Spencer Ln
100 YpTp 48198 4492 E3
Spencer Rd
6400 WasC 48189 4259 E6
7300 WasC 48178 4259 E4
8800 WasC 48178 4187 E7
8800 WasC 48189 4187 E7
Spencer St
100 FRDL 48220 4200 A4
19900 DET 48234 4202 A4
W Spencer St
10 VNBN 48111 4578 D4
Spicer Dr
11300 PyTp 48170 4337 B1
Spicer Rd
- GOTp 48189 4186 D3
8200 GOTp 48116 4186 D3
8700 GOTp 48116 4187 A3
Spies Ct
10000 PyTp 48170 4337 E2
Spindler Av
18700 EPTE 48021 4204 A1
Spinnaker Ln
3300 DET 48207 4346 C5
Spinnaker Wy
8500 YpTp 48197 4576 D1
Spinning Wheel Dr
45600 CNTN 48187 4336 B5
Spinoza Dr
- DET 48228 4341 C4
8800 DET 48239 4341 C2
Spokane St
- DET 48204 4344 A2
5200 DET 48204 4343 E3
Spoonbill Av
33100 BwTp 48173 4841 A1
Sports Park Dr
- NOVI 48167 4191 C5
Sprague St
8000 DET 48214 4274 C7
8000 DET 48214 4346 C1
Sprenger Av
16000 EPTE 48021 4203 D3
Spring Ct
10 Amhg N9V 4757 D2
10 WIND N9E 4504 A3
30200 INKR 48141 4414 D4
Spring Dr
700 NHVL 48167 4192 C7
E Spring Dr
6900 CNTN 48187 4336 D5
N Spring Dr
44800 CNTN 48187 4336 D5
Spring Ln
20200 NvIT 48167 4193 D6
20200 NvIT 48375 4193 D6
Spring St
10 YPLT 48197 4492 A5
300 AARB 48103 4406 B4
300 SALN 48176 4572 D7
3300 MonC 48117 4753 B6
E Spring St
100 PLYM 48170 4265 B6
W Spring St
100 PLYM 48170 4265 A6
Spring Arbor Dr
29600 INKR 48141 4414 D4
Springbrook Av
3000 AARB 48108 4490 B5
22000 FNHL 48336 4195 C3
Springbrook Cres
400 SALN 48176 4657 E1
Springbrook Ct
600 SALN 48176 4657 E1
Springbrook Dr
23000 FNHL 48336 4195 C2
Springbrooke Tr
12800 GOTp 48178 4188 D3
Spring Creek Ln
6700 WasC 48170 4262 B6
Springer St
1200 WTLD 48186 4412 E3
Springfield Ct
900 NHVL 48167 4192 C5
Springfield Dr
300 CNTN 48188 4410 E3
700 NHVL 48167 4192 C4
700 NHVL 48374 4192 C4
Springfield St
5500 DET 48213 4274 E5
Spring Garden Rd
1800 WIND N9E 4503 C1
Spring Garden St
14100 DET 48205 4203 A7
Spring Gate Dr
27100 BwTp 48183 4754 E2
Springhill Av
2100 INKR 48141 4415 A4
Spring Hill Ct
17100 NvIT 48167 4264 D2
Spring Hill Dr
5500 SpTp 48105 4333 B7
5500 SpTp 48105 4408 B1
Spring Hill Rd
44500 NvIT 48167 4264 D2
Spring Hill St
21000 HnTp 48174 4667 A4
Springhill St
15600 RMLS 48174 4582 A5
Spring Hollow Ct
3100 AARB 48105 4331 E7
3100 AARB 48105 4406 D1
Spring Lake Blvd
4000 PTFD 48108 4489 A6
4300 PTFD 48108 4488 E7
Springle St
2100 DET 48214 4275 B6
Spring Meadows Ln
6500 WasC 48170 4333 D3
Springmill Ln
1700 PTFD 48108 4488 E6
1700 PTFD 48108 4489 B5
Spring Ridge Ct
2100 PTFD 48103 4488 D3
Spring Ridge Dr
2100 PTFD 48103 4488 D3
Springstead St
29000 GBTR 48173 4755 D3
Springs Village Blvd
15000 TYLR 48180 4582 D4
Springvale Ct
11900 GOTp 48178 4188 B4
Spring Valley Dr
8600 WTLD 48185 4338 D3
22500 FNHL 48304 4196 A2
22500 FNHL 48336 4196 A2
Spring Valley Rd
- BNHL 48105 4331 A7
Springwater Dr
7900 YpTp 48197 4576 B4
39400 LVNA 48167 4265 D2
39400 NvIT 48167 4265 D2
Springwell Ct
22900 NOVI 48375 4193 D3
Springwells St
900 DET 48209 4419 A2
5000 DET 48210 4343 D5
15700 DRBN 48120 4417 E3
S Springwells St
700 DET 48209 4419 B3
Springwells St N
2300 DET 48209 4419 A2
2700 DET 48209 4418 E1
Springwood Blvd
8900 VNBN 48111 4495 B5
Springwood Ct
1800 AATp 48103 4405 E3
Springwood St
20000 NvIT 48167 4192 B6
Sproat St
100 DET 48201 4345 C5
Spruce Ct
- CNTN 48188 4411 C6
15200 RMLS 48174 4582 B4
Spruce Dr
1000 AARB 48104 4407 B7
28200 HnTp 48134 4753 A3
Spruce Ln
100 VNBN 48111 4494 E5
1900 SpTp 48198 4409 E7
6200 WTLD 48185 4338 D6
Spruce St
1200 DET 48201 4345 A5
1200 WYDT 48192 4585 A1
1400 DET 48216 4345 A5
3000 INKR 48141 4415 A6
13500 SOGT 48195 4584 D4
Spruce Tree Ct
7800 PTFD 48176 4573 D7
Spruceway Ln
2100 AARB 48103 4405 E3
Sprucewood Av
300 WIND N9J 4502 D2
900 WIND N9J 4503 A3
1300 LSal N9J 4503 A3
Sprue Ct
17500 BNTN 48192 4669 A1
Spur Dr
25000 WynC 48138 4670 D7
Spyglass Ct
2400 PTFD 48108 4488 D7
Spyglass Dr
15600 NvIT 48167 4264 C3
Spy Glass Ln
7100 YpTp 48197 4575 E5
Spy Glass Hill Dr
22500 LyTp 48178 4190 D3
Spy Glass Hill Dr N
23300 LyTp 48178 4190 C2
Squire Rd
39400 NOVI 48375 4193 D1
SR-1
- HDPK 48203 4272 C2
- PTRG 48069 4199 D1
SR-1 Woodward Av
- FRDL 48203 4200 A5
10 DET 48226 4345 C3
2100 DET 48201 4345 C3
5000 DET 48202 4345 C3
7400 DET 48202 4273 A7
8900 DET 48202 4272 E6
11700 HDPK 48203 4272 E5
17500 DET 48203 4272 C1
17900 DET 48203 4200 A5
21400 FRDL 48220 4200 A5
21800 FRDL 48220 4199 E3
23600 FRDL 48069 4199 E3
23600 PTRG 48069 4199 E3
23600 PTRG 48220 4199 E3
SR-3
- DET 48226 4345 D6
SR-3 Cadillac Sq
10 DET 48226 4345 D6
SR-3 Fort St W
800 DET 48226 4345 C7
2800 DET 48216 4420 A1
SR-3 Gratiot Av
200 DET 48226 4345 E4
1100 DET 48207 4345 E4
2600 DET 48207 4346 A1
7000 DET 48207 4274 D3
7200 DET 48213 4274 D3
7200 DET 48214 4274 D3
11900 DET 48205 4274 D3
13100 DET 48205 4202 E7
13700 DET 48205 4203 A5
15400 EPTE 48205 4203 A5
20700 EPTE 48021 4203 A5
SR-3 Randolph St
600 DET 48226 4345 D6
SR-5
- FMTN - 4194 B2
- FMTN - 4195 A3
- FNHL - 4194 B2
- FNHL - 4195 A3
SR-5 Grand River Av
13500 DET 48227 4271 A6
13600 DET 48227 4270 A3
18200 DET 48223 4270 A3
19000 DET 48223 4269 E3
19800 DET 48219 4269 B1
23500 DET 48219 4197 A7
23800 DET 48219 4196 D6
24700 RDFD 48219 4196 D6
25000 RDFD 48240 4196 D6
27300 LVNA 48152 4196 D6
27300 RDFD 48152 4196 D6
27500 FNHL 48152 4196 D6
27700 FNHL 48336 4196 D6
28200 FNHL 48336 4195 D4
SR-8 Davison Frwy E
- DET - 4272 E2
- DET - 4273 A2
- HDPK - 4272 C4
SR-8 Davison Frwy W
- DET - 4272 C4
- DET - 4273 B2
- HDPK - 4272 C4
SR-10 John C Lodge Frwy
- DET - 4198 D6
- DET - 4199 A7
- DET - 4271 C3
- DET - 4272 B3
- DET - 4344 E1
- DET - 4345 A3
- SFLD - 4197 E2
SR-10 John C Lodge Frwy
- SFLD - 4198 A2
SR-14
- AARB - 4331 E7
- AARB - 4332 B7
- AARB - 4405 C3
- AARB - 4406 A3
- AATp - 4331 E7
- AATp - 4332 B7
- AATp - 4333 B7
- AATp - 4405 C3
- AATp - 4406 A3
- LVNA - 4265 A5
- PyTp - 4263 D7
- PyTp - 4264 A6
- PyTp - 4265 A5
- PyTp - 4335 B1
- SpTp - 4333 E6
- SpTp - 4334 C4
- WasC - 4334 C4
- WasC - 4335 B1
- WasC - 4405 C3
- WasC - 4406 A3
SR-14 Jeffries Frwy
- LVNA - 4265 E6
SR-17
- YPLT 48197 4491 E4
SR-17 W Cross St
100 YPLT 48197 4492 A4
400 YPLT 48197 4491 E4
SR-17 Ecorse Rd
10 YPLT 48198 4492 C5
10 YpTp 48198 4492 C5
SR-17 N Hamilton St
10 YPLT 48197 4491 E4
SR-17 N Huron St
10 YPLT 48197 4492 A4
SR-17 E Michigan Av
10 YPLT 48198 4492 A4
SR-17 W Michigan Av
10 YPLT 48197 4492 A4
10 YPLT 48198 4492 A4
SR-17 Washtenaw Av
400 YPLT 48197 4491 C3
1700 YpTp 48197 4491 C3
2700 YpTp 48108 4491 C3
4000 PTFD 48105 4490 E3
4000 PTFD 48108 4490 E3
4300 PTFD 48197 4490 E3
4700 PTFD 48108 4491 C3
4700 PTFD 48197 4491 C3
SR-36
- GOTp 48116 4186 B3
- GOTp 48189 4186 B3
- HbgT 48116 4186 B3
- HbgT 48189 4186 B3
SR-36 9 Mile Rd
8000 GOTp 48116 4186 C3
8000 GOTp 48189 4186 C3
9200 GOTp 48116 4187 A4
9200 GOTp 48189 4187 A4
SR-39 Southfield Frwy
- ALPK - 4417 C4
- ALPK - 4500 A1
- DET - 4198 A6
- DET - 4270 A4
- DET - 4342 B3
- DRBN - 4342 B3
- DRBN - 4417 C4
- SFLD - 4198 A6
SR-39 Southfield Rd
1200 LNPK 48146 4500 D3
1200 LNPK 48146 4501 A3
2200 LNPK 48101 4500 D3
14500 ALPK 48101 4500 D3
SR-53 Van Dyke Av
- WRRN 48234 4202 A4
20600 WRRN 48089 4202 A4
20600 WRRN 48091 4202 A4
23700 CTNL 48015 4202 A1
23700 WRRN 48015 4202 A1
SR-53 Van Dyke St
5300 DET 48213 4274 A2
9700 DET 48234 4274 A2
17100 DET 48212 4202 A7
17100 DET 48212 4274 A2
17100 DET 48234 4202 A7
SR-85
- DET 48229 4501 B2
- LNPK 48146 4501 B2
- LNPK 48229 4501 B2
SR-85 Fort St
- BwTp 48173 4754 E4
- BwTp 48183 4754 E4
- LNPK 48195 4500 E5
- TNTN 48183 4584 D7
- TNTN 48192 4584 D7
900 LNPK 48146 4501 B2
900 LNPK 48229 4501 B2
1000 LNPK 48146 4500 E5
1000 LNPK 48192 4500 E5
1000 WYDT 48146 4500 E5
1000 WYDT 48192 4500 E5
1200 SOGT 48192 4500 E5
1200 SOGT 48195 4500 E5
1300 WYDT 48192 4584 D7
1300 WYDT 48195 4584 D7
1400 SOGT 48192 4584 D7
1600 TNTN 48183 4669 D3
1600 TNTN 48192 4669 D3
5200 TNTN 48183 4755 B1
5800 GBTR 48183 4755 B1
5800 WDHN 48183 4755 B1
12200 SOGT 48195 4584 D7
17000 RVVW 48192 4584 D7
17000 RVVW 48195 4584 D7
19500 RVVW 48192 4669 D3
27000 BwTp 48183 4755 B1
27200 BwTp 48173 4755 B1
27200 GBTR 48173 4755 B1
SR-85 Fort St S
1000 DET 48229 4418 C7
2700 DET 48229 4501 B1
3300 LNPK 48229 4501 B1
SR-85 Fort St W
- DET 48209 4418 D5
- DET 48229 4418 D5
1000 DET 48226 4345 C7
1400 DET 48216 4345 B7
2100 DET 48216 4420 A1
3500 DET 48216 4419 E1
4000 DET 48209 4419 E1
SR-97 Groesbeck Hwy
20300 DET 48205 4202 C4
20300 WRRN 48205 4202 C4
20700 WRRN 48089 4202 D4
SR-97 Gunston St
- DET 48234 4274 C1
11200 DET 48213 4274 D2
11500 DET 48205 4274 D2
SR-97 Hoover St
17100 DET 48205 4274 D1
17100 DET 48234 4274 D1
17300 DET 48205 4202 C5
17300 DET 48234 4202 C5
SR-102 E 8 Mile Rd
- DET 48030 4200 C4
- DET 48203 4200 D4
- HZLP 48030 4200 E4
- HZLP 48203 4200 D4
100 FRDL 48220 4200 A4
900 FRDL 48203 4200 B4
1500 FRDL 48030 4200 C4
1900 WRRN 48030 4200 E4
1900 WRRN 48091 4200 E4
2200 WRRN 48091 4201 A4
7000 WRRN 48091 4202 A4
8000 WRRN 48089 4202 A4
SR-102 W 8 Mile Rd
- DET 48203 4200 A4
- FRDL 48203 4200 A4
- FRDL 48220 4200 A4
10 HZLP 48030 4200 C4
18100 DET 48219 4198 A4
18100 DET 48235 4198 A4
18100 SFLD 48219 4198 A4
18100 SFLD 48235 4198 A4
18400 SFLD 48075 4198 A4
18600 DET 48219 4197 D5
18600 SFLD 48219 4197 D5
18800 SFLD 48075 4197 D5
20200 DET 48075 4197 D5
22000 SFLD 48034 4197 D5
22500 DET 48034 4197 D5
24000 DET 48034 4196 B5
24000 DET 48219 4196 B5
24000 SFLD 48034 4196 B5
25000 RDFD 48240 4196 B5
25000 SFLD 48240 4196 B5
27400 FNHL 48152 4196 B5
27400 FNHL 48336 4196 B5
27400 LVNA 48152 4196 B5
SR-102 8 Mile Rd E
1500 DET 48030 4200 B4
1500 DET 48203 4200 B4
1500 HZLP 48030 4200 B4
1500 HZLP 48203 4200 B4
1900 DET 48234 4200 B4
1900 WRRN 48030 4200 B4
1900 WRRN 48091 4200 B4
1900 WRRN 48203 4200 B4
1900 WRRN 48234 4200 B4
2000 DET 48234 4201 D4
2000 WRRN 48091 4201 D4
2000 WRRN 48234 4201 D4
7100 DET 48234 4202 A4
7100 WRRN 48091 4202 A4
7100 WRRN 48234 4202 A4
11300 DET 48089 4202 A4
11600 DET 48205 4202 A4
11600 WRRN 48205 4202 A4
11800 WRRN 48089 4202 A4
13800 DET 48205 4203 D4
13800 WRRN 48205 4203 D4
13900 WRRN 48089 4203 D4
14700 WRRN 48021 4203 D4
14800 EPTE 48021 4203 D4
14800 EPTE 48205 4203 D4
17300 DET 48225 4203 D4
17300 EPTE 48225 4203 D4
17300 HRWD 48225 4203 D4
SR-102 8 Mile Rd W
- DET 48075 4198 A4
- DET 48219 4197 C5
- SFLD 48075 4197 C5
- SFLD 48219 4197 C5
- SFLD 48235 4198 A4
10 DET 48203 4200 C4
10 HZLP 48030 4200 C4
10 HZLP 48203 4200 C4
400 FRDL 48203 4199 C4
400 FRDL 48220 4199 C4
600 FRDL 48203 4200 B4
600 FRDL 48220 4200 B4
2600 DET 48203 4199 C4
3000 DET 48220 4199 C4
3000 DET 48221 4199 C4
4100 FRDL 48221 4199 C4
8100 ROTp 48220 4199 C4
8100 ROTp 48221 4199 C4
11000 ROTp 48235 4199 C4
11000 ROTp 48237 4199 C4
12700 DET 48235 4199 C4
12700 OKPK 48235 4199 C4
12700 OKPK 48237 4199 C4
13400 DET 48235 4198 A4
13400 OKPK 48235 4198 A4
13400 OKPK 48237 4198 A4

INDEX 50
SR-102 8 Mile Rd W
Detroit & Wayne County Street Index
Suffolk Dr

STREET
Block City ZIP Map# Grid

SR-102 8 Mile Rd W
16800 SFLD 48075 4198 A4
23900 SFLD 48034 4197 A5
24300 DET 48034 4196 E5
24300 DET 48219 4196 E5
24300 SFLD 48034 4196 E5
SR-102 Vernier Rd
1700 GSPW 48236 4204 B4
2100 GSPW 48225 4204 B4
17700 EPTE 48021 4203 E4
17700 EPTE 48225 4203 E4
17700 HRWD 48225 4203 E4
18000 HRWD 48225 4204 B4
SR-153 Ford Rd
- DET 48126 4342 C6
- DET 48128 4342 C6
- DRBN 48228 4341 A7
- SpTp 48105 4333 D7
- SpTp 48198 4333 E7
- WTLD 48185 4337 B7
7500 SpTp 48198 4409 A1
8000 SpTp 48105 4409 A1
8800 SpTp 48198 4334 E7
9500 SpTp 48198 4335 C7
10000 DRBN 48126 4343 B6
13800 DRBN 48126 4342 C6
18100 DET 48228 4342 C6
19000 DRBN 48128 4342 C6
19000 DRBN 48228 4342 C6
19300 DRBN 48126 4341 A7
19300 DRBN 48128 4341 A7
20000 DRBN 48127 4341 A7
20500 DBHT 48127 4341 A7
20500 DBHT 48128 4341 A7
23400 WynC 48127 4341 A7
23400 WynC 48128 4341 A7
24400 DBHT 48127 4340 B7
24400 DBHT 48128 4340 B7
24400 DRBN 48128 4340 B7
27400 GDNC 48135 4340 B7
28500 GDNC 48135 4339 C7
32900 GDNC 48185 4339 C7
32900 WTLD 48185 4339 C7
33800 WTLD 48135 4338 B7
33800 WTLD 48185 4338 B7
39400 CNTN 48187 4337 B7
43400 CNTN 48187 4336 C7
48200 CNTN 48187 4335 C7
49400 CNTN 48198 4335 C7
Stacey Ct
38500 LVNA 48154 4265 E3
Stacey Dr
23000 BNTN 48183 4668 B6
23400 BNTN 48134 4668 B6
38800 LVNA 48154 4265 E3
Stacy Av
35400 WTLD 48185 4338 C6
Stacy Dr
1400 CNTN 48188 4412 C4
Stacy St
27000 TYLR 48180 4582 B4
36900 WTLD 48185 4338 B6
Stadium Blvd
22900 STCS 48080 4204 B1
E Stadium Blvd
10 AARB 48103 4489 D1
10 AARB 48104 4489 D1
2300 AARB 48104 4490 A2
W Stadium Blvd
100 AARB 48103 4489 A1
1400 AARB 48103 4488 E1
1800 AARB 48103 4405 D7
Stadium Ct
1600 AARB 48103 4488 E1
Stadium Pl
1800 AARB 48103 4488 E1
Stadium Wy
- AARB 48104 4406 B7
- AARB 48104 4489 B1
Stadium View Dr
- YpTp 48197 4491 B3
2600 YPLT 48197 4491 B3
N Staebler Rd
10 WasC 48103 4404 A4
S Staebler Rd
10 WasC 48103 4404 A5
Stafford Ct
37900 WTLD 48186 4413 A4
41400 CNTN 48188 4412 C4
Stafford Dr
1400 CNTN 48188 4412 C3
Stafford Pl
1000 DET 48207 4346 A5
Stag Ct
23100 HnTp 48164 4665 A5
Stagecoach Av
4200 WIND N9G 4505 A4
Staggs Leap Ln
1100 WasC 48103 4404 A7
1100 WasC 48103 4487 A1
Staghorn Dr
5700 PTFD 48197 4574 D3
Stahelin Av
5600 DET 48228 4342 A5
15300 DET 48223 4270 A3
16100 DET 48219 4270 A2
17500 DET 48219 4269 E1
19100 DET 48219 4197 E5
Stahelin St
20700 SFLD 48075 4197 E4
Stair St
2300 DET 48209 4419 A1
Stamford Ct
1200 SpTp 48198 4492 D1
13400 LVNA 48150 4266 E6
Stamford Dr
20000 LVNA 48152 4194 E5
Stamford Rd
900 SpTp 48198 4409 C7
1200 SpTp 48198 4492 D1

Stamford St
15300 LVNA 48154 4266 E3
18200 LVNA 48152 4266 E1
10500 LVNA 48152 4194 E7
Stamwich St
17100 LVNA 48152 4267 D1
Standard Av
8000 CTNL 48015 4202 A1
Standish Ct
49900 PyTp 48170 4335 D1
Standish Rd
28300 WTLD 48185 4340 A5
Standish St
2800 DET 48216 4344 E7
34000 WTLD 48185 4338 E5
34700 LVNA 48150 4338 D1
Stanford Av
300 SLYN 48178 4189 A3
25800 INKR 48141 4415 C6
Stanford St
5600 DET 48210 4344 B3
24000 DBHT 48125 4416 A6
24300 DBHT 48125 4415 D6
25400 DBHT 48141 4415 D6
Stanhope Rd
1600 GSPW 48236 4204 B7
2200 GSPW 48225 4204 B7
Staniszewski St
3900 WIND N8W 4422 A4
Stanley Av
3700 ALPK 48101 4417 D7
3700 ALPK 48101 4500 D1
19100 MVDL 48122 4417 D7
19600 MVDL 48101 4417 D7
Stanley Ct
4300 SpTp 48105 4334 C5
4300 SpTp 48170 4334 C5
Stanley Rd
12400 VNBN 48111 4578 B2
Stanley St
500 WIND N8X 4421 C5
700 YPLT 48198 4492 B3
1900 DET 48210 4344 E3
2000 AARB 48104 4489 E2
2800 TNTN 48183 4669 D4
N Stanmoor Dr
16300 LVNA 48154 4268 A2
16900 LVNA 48152 4268 A2
W Stanmoor Dr
27800 LVNA 48154 4268 A2
Stansbury St
14200 DET 48227 4270 E4
17100 DET 48235 4270 E1
18900 DET 48235 4198 E6
Stanstead Rd
21000 NHVL 48167 4192 B5
Stanton Ct
3500 AARB 48105 4407 C5
49000 CNTN 48188 4410 E5
Stanton Ct E
48800 CNTN 48188 4410 E5
48800 CNTN 48188 4411 A5
Stanton Dr
21800 WynC 48138 4670 B4
Stanton Ln
10 GSPF 48236 4276 D4
Stanton St
1600 LSal N9J 4503 B4
2500 CNTN 48188 4410 E5
2800 CNTN 48188 4411 A5
6100 DET 48210 4344 D2
Star Wy
- WIND N8W 4422 A5
Starak Ln
4800 WasC 48105 4330 C4
Stark Ln
3800 PTFD 48197 4574 D4
Stark Rd
9200 LVNA 48150 4338 E1
12000 LVNA 48150 4266 E7
13900 LVNA 48154 4266 E5
Stark St
- DET 48210 4344 B7
Starkey Ln
27000 BNTN 48174 4667 C2
Stark Strasse St
- AATp 48105 4408 A7
1300 SpTp 48105 4408 A7
Starkweather St
300 PLYM 48170 4265 A6
Starlane St
19100 SFLD 48075 4197 E3
Starling Ct
8100 YpTp 48197 4576 B4
Starlite Ct
42000 CNTN 48187 4337 B5
Starwick Dr
800 AARB 48105 4406 C3
Starwood Ct
2100 PTFD 48103 4488 C3
Starwood Ln
200 Tcmh N8N 4424 E1
State
- ALPK 48101 4500 A1
State Av
- NvlT 48167 4193 B7
State Cir
500 PTFD 48108 4489 B5
State Rd
6000 PTFD 48108 4573 C5
6000 PTFD 48176 4573 C5
S State Rd
3700 AARB 48108 4489 C6
3700 PTFD 48108 4489 C6
4600 PTFD 48108 4573 C1
State St
10 DET 48226 4345 D6
300 LSal N9J 4502 E5
2100 YpTp 48198 4493 A7
34000 FMTN 48335 4194 D2

State St
51000 VNBN 48111 4577 C4
N State St
100 AARB 48104 4406 C5
S State St
100 AARB 48104 4406 C7
1200 AARB 48104 4489 C1
1500 AARB 48103 4489 C1
1600 WasC 48103 4489 C1
1600 WasC 48104 4489 C1
3000 AARB 48108 4489 C3
3600 PTFD 48108 4489 C5
State Fair Av E
10 DET 48203 4200 C5
State Fair Av W
10 DET 48203 4200 B5
State Fair St E
8600 DET 48234 4202 B5
11600 DET 48205 4202 C5
13800 DET 48205 4203 A5
16600 DET 48225 4203 B5
16600 HRWD 48225 4203 B5
State Park Av
13000 SRKW 48179 4754 B7
13000 SRKW 48179 4840 B1
State Park St
8000 CTNL 48015 4202 A1
States Av
10 Amhg N9V 4757 D2
Statler St
25300 TYLR 48180 4498 D5
Stauber Av
23000 HZLP 48030 4200 B2
Stauch Dr
23500 BNTN 48134 4667 E6
Staunton St
22500 SFLD 48034 4196 A2
Stawell St
8300 DET 48204 4343 C2
Steadman Rd
33600 HnTp 48164 4666 A3
Steadman St
7300 DRBN 48126 4342 D4
Steam Boat Ct
3800 PTFD 48108 4488 D6
Stearns St
5500 DET 48204 4271 D7
Stecker St
- DET 48126 4343 C7
- DET 48210 4343 C7
4000 DRBN 48126 4343 C7
4000 DRBN 48126 4418 C1
4000 DRBN 48210 4343 C7
4000 DRBN 48210 4418 C1
Stedman Dr
- LyTp 48178 4189 D6
Steel St
8500 DET 48228 4343 A1
11300 DET 48227 4343 A1
13200 DET 48227 4271 A5
17100 DET 48235 4271 A1
19100 DET 48235 4199 A6
Steep Hollow Ct
18500 NvlT 48167 4263 E1
Steeple Pth
44600 NOVI 48375 4192 D3
Steeple Chase Ct
7300 PTFD 48176 4573 E6
Steeple Chase Dr
7100 PTFD 48176 4573 E6
Steeplechase Dr
2100 AARB 48103 4488 D2
Steepleview Ct
42700 NvlT 48167 4265 A3
42700 NvlT 48170 4265 A3
Steeple View St
42400 NvlT 48167 4265 A3
42400 NvlT 48170 4265 A3
Steere Pl
1900 AARB 48104 4489 D2
Stefano Ct
32100 RKWD 48173 4755 A7
Stefano Dr
32400 RKWD 48173 4755 A7
Steger Ct
7400 DET 48238 4271 D2
Stein Ct
2700 WasC 48105 4330 C5
Stein Rd
10 AATp 48105 4331 A6
600 AATp 48105 4330 D6
4000 WasC 48103 4330 C5
4000 WasC 48105 4330 C5
Steiner Av
3600 TNTN 48183 4669 B5
Steiner Ct
10 SALN 48176 4572 C5
Steinhauer St
29400 INKR 48141 4414 E2
32400 WTLD 48186 4414 B3
Stella Ct N
3200 TNTN 48183 4669 B4
Stella Ct S
3200 TNTN 48183 4669 B4
Stellar Rd
2200 AARB 48105 4406 C2
Stellwagen St
33900 WYNE 48184 4413 E7
33900 WYNE 48184 4414 A7
Stender St
1400 DET 48203 4272 E1
1900 DET 48212 4272 E1
2200 DET 48212 4273 A1
Stephanie Ct
3600 WIND N8W 4422 B7
3600 WIND N8W 4505 A1
22500 BNTN 48134 4667 E5
Stephanie Dr
100 WTLD 48185 4413 C2
100 WTLD 48186 4413 C2

Stephanie Dr
42800 VNBN 48111 4495 A4
Stephanie St
- VNBN 48111 4494 D3
35500 RMLS 48174 4496 D6
Stephen Av
31000 WTLD 48185 4339 C3
Stephen Ct
30800 WTLD 48185 4339 C3
Stephen Ter
2100 AARB 48103 4488 D1
Stephens Dr
1500 SpTp 48198 4492 C1
14500 EPTE 48021 4203 B1
14500 WRRN 48089 4203 B1
14600 EPTE 48089 4203 B1
14600 WRRN 48021 4203 B1
18200 EPTE 48021 4204 A1
Stephens Rd
10 GSPF 48236 4276 C3
1900 WRRN 48030 4200 E1
1900 WRRN 48091 4200 E1
2300 WRRN 48091 4201 A1
7200 CTNL 48015 4202 A1
8000 WRRN 48015 4202 A1
13600 WRRN 48089 4202 E1
14000 WRRN 48089 4203 A1
14500 WRRN 48021 4203 A1
Stephens St
2500 DRBN 48124 4416 C4
19700 STCS 48021 4204 B1
19700 STCS 48080 4204 B1
Steppe Ln
22000 BNTN 48192 4583 C6
Sterling Av
9600 ALPK 48101 4500 B5
Sterling Cres
200 WIND N8Y 4346 E7
Sterling Ct
6500 GDNC 48135 4340 B5
12700 OKPK 48237 4199 A2
Sterling Pl
23600 DRBN 48124 4416 A2
Sterling St
6400 DET 48202 4344 E2
6400 DET 48210 4344 E2
8000 CTNL 48015 4202 A1
11000 RMLS 48174 4496 B6
19000 HnTp 48164 4665 C2
Sterritt St
10000 DET 48213 4274 C4
Steven Ct
3800 WasC 48160 4659 D3
8100 CNTN 48187 4336 B4
Steven Dr
600 LSal N9J 4502 E4
20000 BwTp 48183 4754 E2
20000 BwTp 48183 4755 A1
Stevens Dr
200 YpTp 48197 4491 C5
Stevens St
10 HDPK 48203 4272 C1
100 DET 48203 4272 C1
8900 TYLR 48180 4499 D4
Stewart Av
700 LNPK 48146 4501 A5
1200 LNPK 48146 4500 D5
23000 WRRN 48021 4203 A1
23000 WRRN 48089 4203 A1
Stewart Blvd
- BNTN 48134 4667 C7
Stewart Ct
3300 SpTp 48198 4408 C1
Stewart Dr
34500 RMLS 48174 4496 E5
Stewart Ln
- WTLD 48186 4414 D4
6100 WasC 48105 4260 C7
6100 WasC 48105 4332 C1
Stieber St
1600 WTLD 48186 4413 E4
W Stiers Av
- LSal N9J 4502 C5
Stiles Ct
23200 BNTN 48183 4668 B6
Still Creek Ct
43200 NOVI 48375 4192 E1
43200 NOVI 48375 4193 A2
Stillmeadow Dr
2800 WIND N8R 4423 C2
Stillmeadow Ln
10 GSPS 48236 4205 A4
Stimson St
10 DET 48201 4345 C4
700 AARB 48103 4489 C2
700 AARB 48104 4489 C2
Stinson Cir
10300 WynC 48138 4756 A2
Stirling Cir
3300 SpTp 48198 4408 C1
Stock St
1900 LSal N9H 4503 C4
Stocker St
12400 DET 48229 4418 D5
33400 FNHL 48335 4194 E3
Stockmeyer Blvd
1800 WTLD 48186 4413 A4
Stockton Av
29400 FNHL 48336 4195 D1
N Stockton Av
23300 FNHL 48336 4195 C1
S Stockton Dr
29900 FNHL 48336 4195 C2
Stockton St
5900 DET 48234 4201 D7
7400 DET 48234 4202 A7
Stockwell St
11100 DET 48224 4275 B1
Stoeflet St
13300 GBTR 48173 4755 D4

Stoepel St
- DET 48238 4271 D3
8800 DET 48204 4343 D1
12000 DET 48204 4271 D7
16100 DET 48221 4271 D2
19900 DET 48221 4199 D5
Stoflet Ct
23200 BNTN 48183 4668 B6
Stoll St
200 WYDT 48192 4501 C7
Stollman Dr
26100 INKR 48141 4415 C2
Stolzenfeld Av
3000 WRRN 48091 4201 B1
Stommel Rd
2500 SpTp 48198 4408 E4
Stone Rd
- AARB 48105 4407 B4
Stone St
7100 HbgT 48189 4186 B3
9200 DET 48209 4418 E4
9200 DET 48209 4419 A4
Stonebridge Blvd E
- PTFD 48108 4489 A7
Stonebridge Blvd S
5300 PTFD 48108 4572 D1
5300 PTFD 48176 4572 D1
Stonebridge Ct
8800 VNBN 48111 4494 E5
Stonebridge Dr
43800 VNBN 48111 4495 A4
43900 VNBN 48111 4494 E5
N Stonebridge Dr
1700 PTFD 48108 4488 E7
1700 PTFD 48108 4489 A7
2100 PTFD 48108 4572 D1
S Stonebridge Dr
1600 PTFD 48108 4489 A7
1700 PTFD 48108 4572 D1
1700 PTFD 48108 4573 A1
Stonebridge Wy
1600 CNTN 48188 4411 B4
Stonebridge Wy Ct
1700 CNTN 48188 4411 B4
Stonebrook Ct
7000 CNTN 48187 4336 A5
17900 NvlT 48167 4264 C1
Stonebrook Dr
7200 CNTN 48187 4336 A5
17100 NvlT 48167 4264 C2
Stone Cliff Ct
200 SALN 48176 4657 B1
Stone Creek Ct
13000 PyTp 48170 4264 D7
Stonecrest Ct
47100 PyTp 48170 4336 B3
Stonecrest Dr
100 WynC 48111 4662 D5
46900 PyTp 48170 4336 B3
Stonecroft Ct
41400 NvlT 48167 4193 B6
Stonecroft Rd
41400 NvlT 48167 4193 B6
Stonefield Dr
5200 PTFD 48197 4574 B1
Stonegate Dr
8000 WasC 48167 4262 A2
Stonegate Rd
400 WasC 48103 4404 C4
Stoneham Ct
14700 RVVW 48192 4584 C7
Stoneham Dr
8100 AGST 48197 4575 B7
Stoneham Ln
14800 RVVW 48192 4584 C7
Stone Haven Rd
41000 NvlT 48167 4265 C3
Stonehaven St
1500 AARB 48104 4490 B2
Stonehedge Blvd
- NOVI 48375 4193 D2
Stonehedge Ct
5500 SpTp 48105 4408 B4
Stonehedge Dr
45300 PyTp 48170 4336 D2
Stonehenge Blvd
23400 NOVI 48375 4193 D2
Stonehenge Dr
300 CNTN 48188 4412 C3
Stone Hill Ln
21100 LyTp 48167 4190 C5
Stonehill Ln
4700 WasC 48103 4487 D1
Stone Hollow Ct
9000 PyTp 48170 4335 E3
Stonehouse Av
8800 LVNA 48150 4338 A2
14000 LVNA 48154 4266 A5
Stonehouse Cir
15500 LVNA 48154 4266 A3
Stonehouse Ct
23500 FMTN 48335 4194 B2
Stonehurst Rd
10 GSPS 48236 4204 E7
10 GSPS 48236 4276 E1
10 GSPS 48236 4277 A1
Stoneleigh St
40700 NvlT 48167 4193 C7
Stonemeadow Ct
4000 WasC 48103 4404 E3
Stoner St
10 RVRG 48218 4501 E1
Stone Ridge Av
200 Amhg N9V 4757 C4
Stoneridge Blvd
47400 CNTN 48187 4336 B7
Stoneridge Ct
18400 NvlT 48167 4263 E1
Stoneridge Dr
1700 WasC 48176 4572 D3

Stoneridge Dr
48500 NvlT 48167 4263 E2
48500 NvlT 48167 4264 A2
Stoneridge Ln
12600 SRKW 48179 4840 B2
Stone School Rd
- AARB 48104 4489 E4
2800 PTFD 48104 4489 E4
3000 AARB 48108 4489 E5
3000 PTFD 48108 4489 E5
4700 PTFD 48108 4573 E1
Stonetree Dr
6100 CNTN 48187 4337 C6
Stone Valley Dr
2100 WasC 48103 4405 C2
5500 SpTp 48105 4408 B3
Stonewater Blvd
18700 NvlT 48167 4192 A7
18700 NvlT 48167 4263 E1
18700 NvlT 48167 4264 A1
Stoneway Dr
26500 FTRK 48134 4753 D1
Stonewood
28900 FTRK 48134 4752 E4
Stonewood Blvd
- CNTN 48187 4411 C1
Stonewood Rd
19000 RVVW 48192 4584 D7
N Stonewood Rd
45500 CNTN 48187 4411 C1
Stoney Dr
700 SLYN 48178 4189 D1
Stoney Wy
57300 LyTp 48178 4190 A1
Stoneybrook Cres
1000 WIND N9G 4505 A5
1200 WIND N9G 4504 E6
Stoneybrook Ct
6400 VNBN 48111 4494 D2
Stoneybrooke Ct
12800 GOTp 48178 4188 D3
Stoney Creek Dr
8900 GOTp 48178 4187 D1
Stoneycroft Dr
25000 SFLD 48034 4197 B1
Stoney River Ct
- GOTp 48178 4188 B4
Stonington Ct
43200 CNTN 48188 4412 A4
Stony Creek Dr
23700 FNHL 48336 4196 A1
Stony Creek Rd
5500 YpTp 48197 4575 D4
7700 AGST 48197 4575 D4
8200 AGST 48197 4660 B2
9000 AGST 48160 4660 B2
9500 WasC 48160 4660 B2
10000 WasC 48160 4659 C6
Stork St
13300 GBTR 48173 4755 D5
Stotter St
19900 DET 48234 4202 A4
Stout Av
7500 WynC 48138 4670 D4
Stout St
7200 DET 48228 4341 D4
11600 DET 48228 4269 D7
12600 DET 48223 4269 D6
15800 DET 48219 4269 D3
19900 DET 48219 4197 D5
Stoutwood Ct
14400 SOGT 48195 4584 A3
Stowe St
3200 WasC 48103 4405 B4
Strabane Av
200 WIND N8Y 4346 D7
Strand Ct
3200 AARB 48105 4332 C7
Strasburg St
11900 DET 48205 4274 D1
17100 DET 48205 4202 D7
Stratford Ct
1500 SpTp 48198 4492 C1
1500 WIND N9G 4504 B3
21600 OKPK 48237 4198 C3
22800 WDHN 48183 4668 C5
23300 SFLD 48034 4197 B2
46600 NvlT 48167 4192 B7
47800 CNTN 48187 4336 A4
Stratford Dr
10 HbgT 48189 4186 A6
600 AARB 48104 4406 E7
900 SLYN 48178 4189 C4
15500 SFLD 48075 4198 C1
15500 SFLD 48237 4198 C1
42700 VNBN 48111 4495 B6
47400 CNTN 48187 4336 A5
Stratford Ln
47100 NOVI 48374 4192 B4
Stratford Pl
10 GSPT 48230 4276 C6
Stratford Rd
100 FRDL 48220 4199 D3
19900 DET 48221 4199 E4
Stratford St
- YPLT 48197 4491 C4
2200 YpTp 48197 4491 B4
13800 RVVW 48192 4584 C6
23600 OKPK 48237 4198 C1
Stratford Place Blvd
21900 BNTN 48183 4668 C2
Strathcona Av
13400 SOGT 48195 4584 D4
Strathcona Dr
- DET 48221 4200 A6
1200 DET 48203 4200 A5
1800 DET 48203 4199 E6
19100 DET 48221 4199 E6
Strathmoor St
8200 DET 48228 4342 E2

Strathmoor St
9500 DET 48227 4342 E1
14000 DET 48227 4270 E5
16100 DET 48235 4270 D3
18000 DET 48235 4198 D7
Strathmore Ln
3800 CNTN 48188 4411 A6
Strathmore Rd
46400 PyTp 48170 4336 B3
Strathmore St
1000 WIND N9C 4420 B5
Stratman St
10600 DET 48224 4275 C1
Stratton Ct
10 GSPS 48236 4205 A6
2000 AARB 48108 4489 E5
Stratton Pl
10 GSPS 48236 4205 A6
Stratton St
6700 DET 48209 4419 B1
Strawberry Ct
22600 NOVI 48375 4193 D4
41400 CNTN 48188 4412 C4
Strawberry Dr
2300 Tcmh N9K 4424 A6
Strawberry Ln
200 WasC 48103 4488 B4
Strawberry Lake Rd
6500 HbgT 48189 4186 A4
Stream Wy
15000 RMLS 48174 4581 D4
Streamview Ct
100 CNTN 48188 4412 C2
Stream View Dr
35800 HnTp 48164 4665 D7
Streamwood Dr
7000 YpTp 48197 4576 A5
Streicher Rd
15900 BwTp 48173 4841 A1
18200 RKWD 48173 4840 E1
18200 RKWD 48173 4841 A1
Strewing Rd
24700 BNTN 48134 4668 A7
Stricker Av
15300 EPTE 48021 4203 C4
Stringham Ct
5000 DET 48213 4275 A5
Strohm Av
2100 TNTN 48183 4669 C3
Stromp Ct
23200 BNTN 48183 4668 B5
Strong Blvd
13000 SRKW 48179 4840 B1
13400 SRKW 48179 4754 B7
Strong Dr
16800 TYLR 48174 4582 E5
16800 TYLR 48180 4582 E5
Strong St
6300 DET 48211 4273 E6
6800 DET 48211 4274 A6
7200 DET 48213 4274 A6
Structure Dr
100 YPLT 48197 4491 D3
Struin Rd
24000 BNTN 48134 4668 A6
Stryker St
300 SLYN 48178 4189 C3
Stuart Blvd
1100 LSal N9J 4503 A5
Stuart Ct
14800 GBTR 48173 4755 C5
43400 CNTN 48187 4337 A7
Stuart Dr
43600 CNTN 48187 4336 E7
Stuart Ln
3200 DRBN 48120 4417 D3
Stuart St
- DET 48214 4346 C1
6600 DET 48207 4346 B1
Studebaker Av
1000 YpTp 48198 4492 E6
6700 WRRN 48091 4201 E3
7000 WRRN 48091 4202 A3
8000 WRRN 48089 4202 A3
Student
25500 RDFD 48239 4268 D4
Studio St
22000 TYLR 48180 4499 C3
Sturbridge Ct
3500 AARB 48105 4407 C5
Sturbridge Ln
6500 CNTN 48187 4336 D6
Sturgeon Bar Ct
13900 GBTR 48173 4755 D3
Sturgis St
11100 DET 48234 4202 B5
Sturtevant St
10 DET 48203 4272 C5
10 HDPK 48203 4272 C5
3700 DET 48206 4271 E6
3700 DET 48206 4272 A6
4000 DET 48204 4271 E6
Suburban St
100 ECRS 48229 4501 C5
Sudbury Blvd
- WasC 48103 4488 C1
Sudbury Ct
41600 NOVI 48375 4193 B4
Sue Pkwy
2000 AARB 48103 4488 D1
Sue St
60600 LyTp 48178 4189 B3
Sue Dee Ln
12800 GOTp 48178 4188 C1
Suffield Ln
23000 BNTN 48174 4583 B6
Suffolk Ct
44200 CNTN 48187 4336 E4
Suffolk Dr
11000 SOGT 48195 4500 A6

STREET Block	City	ZIP	Map#	Grid
N Telegraph Rd				
100	DRBN	48124	4416	A1
100	DRBN	48128	4416	A1
1500	DRBN	48128	4341	A5
2200	DRBN	48127	4341	A5
5600	DBHT	48127	4341	A5
8700	DBHT	48239	4341	A3
N Telegraph Rd US-24				
100	DRBN	48124	4416	A1
100	DRBN	48128	4416	A1
1500	DRBN	48128	4341	A5
2200	DRBN	48127	4341	A5
5600	DBHT	48127	4341	A5
8700	DBHT	48239	4341	A3
S Telegraph Rd				
100	DRBN	48124	4416	A3
3800	DRBN	48125	4416	A6
3900	DBHT	48125	4416	A6
5600	DBHT	48125	4499	A1
5600	DBHT	48180	4499	A1
S Telegraph Rd US-24				
100	DRBN	48124	4416	A3
3800	DRBN	48125	4416	A6
3900	DBHT	48125	4416	A6
5600	DBHT	48125	4499	A1
5600	DBHT	48180	4499	A1
Tempe Dr				
38600	RMLS	48174	4496	A2
Tempest Dr				
4700	WasC	48167	4190	C7
Templar Av				
24500	SFLD	48075	4198	B1
Templar Cir				
16000	SFLD	48075	4198	B1
Temple Dr				
2600	WIND	N8W	4422	A5
Temple St				
-	DET	48201	4345	A5
1400	DET	48216	4345	A5
2300	DET	48216	4344	E6
Tennant St				
26200	DBHT	48127	4415	C1
Tennessee Cres				
10	Amhg	N9V	4757	E2
Tennessee St				
400	DET	48214	4347	C1
Tenny St				
1200	DRBN	48124	4416	C3
Tennyson Dr				
9600	PyTp	48170	4336	C2
Tennyson St				
10	HDPK	48203	4272	E4
Ten Point Dr				
47400	CNTN	48187	4336	A7
Tepeyac Hill Dr				
2800	WasC	48105	4332	B3
Teppert Av				
22700	EPTE	48021	4204	A1
Teppert St				
17100	DET	48234	4274	C1
19100	DET	48234	4202	C5
Terhune Rd				
3500	AARB	48104	4490	C4
Terminal St				
700	DET	48214	4347	B1
900	WIND	N8W	4421	C4
N Terminal St				
-	WIND	N8X	4421	A5
Terminal Exit				
-	Tcmh	N8V	4505	C1
T Erminger Ln				
7000	WasC	48167	4261	E4
Ternes St				
4300	DET	48210	4343	D6
4500	DRBN	48126	4417	D1
7100	DRBN	48126	4342	D4
Terra Bella Rd				
8200	WasC	48167	4262	A2
Terrace Ct				
500	CNTN	48188	4411	A3
22500	NOVI	48375	4193	D3
Terrace Ln E				
500	YpTp	48198	4492	B2
Terrace Ln N				
900	YpTp	48198	4492	B2
Terrace Rd				
10	LyTp	48167	4189	E6
Terrace View Dr				
11000	HbgT	48189	4186	A4
Terrace Village Dr				
16000	TYLR	48180	4582	D5
Terra Del Mar Dr				
-	NOVI	48374	4191	C1
Terrel Ct				
1000	CNTN	48187	4412	B1
Terrell St				
20100	DET	48234	4202	A4
27000	DBHT	48127	4340	B6
Terrence St				
27500	LVNA	48154	4267	E3
27500	LVNA	48154	4268	A3
Terri Dr				
100	DBHT	48127	4340	C5
8200	WTLD	48185	4339	B3
N Territorial Rd				
6100	WasC	48170	4333	D1
7000	WasC	48170	4334	A1
9600	WasC	48170	4262	E7
9600	WasC	48170	4263	C7
44400	PLYM	48170	4264	B7
44400	PyTp	48170	4264	B7
48600	PyTp	48170	4263	C7
N Territorial Rd E				
2900	WasC	48189	4260	B7
2900	WasC	48189	4332	D1
3000	WasC	48105	4332	D1
4000	WasC	48105	4333	B1
5000	WasC	48178	4333	B1
5200	WasC	48170	4333	B1
N Territorial Rd W				
10	WasC	48105	4258	D6
10	WasC	48105	4259	A6
10	WasC	48189	4258	D6
10	WasC	48189	4259	A6
Territorial Crossings Rd				
26200	HnTp	48164	4751	B1
Terry Ln				
38400	WTLD	48185	4337	E4
38400	WTLD	48185	4338	A4
Terry St				
3200	TNTN	48183	4669	B5
9300	DET	48228	4342	D1
9300	RMLS	48174	4496	E5
9500	DET	48227	4342	D1
9500	PyTp	48170	4337	D2
14100	DET	48227	4270	D4
Tesch Ct				
17200	BNTN	48192	4669	A1
Tess Ln				
4000	WasC	48160	4574	D7
4000	WasC	48197	4574	D7
Tessmer Ln				
-	WasC	48103	4487	E3
Tessmer Rd				
2100	WasC	48103	4487	E5
Teton Ln				
26500	FTRK	48134	4753	E2
Texas				
100	WynC	48111	4662	D2
Texas Ct				
9100	LVNA	48150	4339	B2
Texas Rd				
10	Amhg	N9V	4671	D6
Texas St				
9000	LVNA	48150	4339	B2
18300	DRBN	48124	4417	A5
19000	DRBN	48124	4416	E5
Textile Rd				
2500	WasC	48176	4572	B3
3400	PTFD	48197	4574	B3
3600	WasC	48176	4571	B3
4500	PTFD	48197	4575	B3
5000	WasC	48103	4571	B3
5000	YpTp	48197	4575	B3
7000	YpTp	48197	4576	A3
9700	YpTp	48197	4577	B3
10600	YpTp	48111	4577	B3
E Textile Rd				
100	PTFD	48108	4573	E3
100	PTFD	48176	4573	E3
2200	PTFD	48108	4574	A3
2400	PTFD	48197	4574	A3
W Textile Rd				
100	PTFD	48108	4573	B3
100	PTFD	48176	4573	B3
1600	PTFD	48108	4572	D3
1700	PTFD	48176	4572	D3
1700	SALN	48108	4572	D3
1700	SALN	48176	4572	D3
1700	WasC	48176	4572	D3
Thaddeus St				
8000	DET	48209	4419	B5
Thaler Av				
-	AARB	48103	4405	D6
Thames Ct				
8400	SpTp	48198	4492	C1
43100	CNTN	48188	4412	A5
Thames St				
35400	WTLD	48186	4413	C3
Tharp Dr				
7600	HbgT	48189	4186	B5
Thatcham Ln				
46000	WynC	48111	4663	C6
Thatcher				
21400	DET	48219	4269	B1
Thatcher Ct				
24200	NOVI	48375	4192	E1
Thatcher Dr				
24300	NOVI	48375	4192	D1
Thatcher St				
6300	DET	48221	4199	D7
7400	DET	48221	4271	C1
12700	DET	48235	4271	A1
15500	DET	48235	4270	B1
Thayer Blvd				
600	NHVL	48167	4192	C6
Thayer Dr				
37600	HnTp	48164	4751	B1
Thayer St				
8700	DRBN	48126	4343	C4
N Thayer St				
100	AARB	48104	4406	C5
S Thayer St				
200	AARB	48104	4406	C6
The American Rd				
-	DRBN	48120	4417	B1
10	DRBN	48126	4417	B1
The Glade St				
3300	WasC	48103	4329	E6
Theisen St				
7200	DRBN	48126	4343	B3
Theodore Av				
1900	TNTN	48183	4669	D4
Theodore St				
200	PLYM	48170	4265	A7
500	DET	48202	4345	C2
1500	DET	48211	4345	D2
3600	DET	48211	4346	A1
6300	DET	48211	4274	A7
7000	DET	48213	4274	A7
Theresa Av				
35900	WTLD	48185	4338	C7
Theresa Pl				
4700	WIND	N8T	4422	C5
Theresa St				
35800	WTLD	48185	4338	D7
The Strand				
-	DET	48207	4347	A5
10	DET	48207	4346	D6
Thetford Ct E				
49900	CNTN	48187	4335	D4
Thetford Ct W				
50100	CNTN	48187	4335	D5
Theut Av				
7200	WRRN	48091	4202	A1
The Village Dr				
-	WIND	N8S	4347	E7
-	WIND	N8S	4348	A7
Thibault Ln				
-	SALN	48176	4572	C6
Thinbark Ct				
36700	WYNE	48184	4413	C5
Thinbark St				
36500	WYNE	48184	4413	B5
Thistle Ct				
1600	CNTN	48188	4411	C4
3100	WasC	48176	4572	C2
Thistle Dr				
1600	CNTN	48188	4411	C4
Thistle Ln				
25800	BNTN	48134	4753	C1
Thole Ct				
7400	DET	48238	4271	D2
Thomas Av				
14500	ALPK	48101	4500	B3
Thomas Cir				
29400	INKR	48141	4414	E7
Thomas Ct				
-	AARB	48103	4405	D5
24000	TYLR	48180	4583	A1
Thomas Pl				
1000	DRBN	48124	4415	E3
Thomas Rd				
-	Amhg	N9V	4671	E7
-	Amhg	N9V	4757	E1
5000	PTFD	48108	4574	A2
Thomas Rd CO-5				
-	Amhg	N9V	4671	E7
-	Amhg	N9V	4757	E1
Thomas St				
500	YPLT	48198	4492	B3
2200	LNPK	48101	4500	C4
2200	LNPK	48146	4500	C4
20200	BwTp	48183	4754	E2
23800	WRRN	48091	4201	B1
26000	FTRK	48134	4753	D2
32900	FMTN	48336	4195	A2
33200	FMTN	48336	4194	E2
33300	FMTN	48335	4194	E2
Thomas Lee Rd				
9000	WasC	48170	4333	B1
Thompson Blvd				
200	WIND	N8S	4347	B6
Thompson Ct				
4700	DET	48207	4346	A1
Thompson St				
300	AARB	48104	4406	C6
Thomson St				
13500	DET	48238	4272	B3
13500	HDPK	48203	4272	B3
13800	HDPK	48238	4272	B3
Thoreau Dr				
47700	PyTp	48170	4336	A3
Thoreau Ln				
500	SLYN	48178	4189	C3
Thorn Dr				
2800	MonC	48117	4839	A2
Thornapple Dr				
2500	WasC	48103	4405	B2
Thorn Apple Ln				
5500	WasC	48105	4333	A2
Thornapple Ln				
44400	NvlT	48167	4264	D1
Thornberry Ct				
6200	WIND	N8T	4422	D2
Thornbird Wy				
9300	WasC	48176	4658	E3
Thornbury Dr				
48700	NOVI	48374	4191	E1
Thornbush Dr				
21600	WDHN	48183	4668	C3
Thorncliffe St				
22500	SFLD	48034	4196	A2
Thorncroft Ct				
38600	WYNE	48184	4413	A5
Thorndyke Ct				
16100	NvlT	48167	4265	B3
Thorndyke St				
24600	SFLD	48034	4196	D2
Thornhill Ct				
500	BLVL	48111	4578	D3
45000	CNTN	48188	4411	D3
Thornhill Dr				
6600	YpTp	48197	4576	B4
Thornhill Pl				
1900	DET	48207	4346	A4
Thornhill Rd				
45100	CNTN	48188	4411	D3
Thornoaks Dr				
4000	AATp	48104	4490	D1
Thorn Ridge Av				
300	Amhg	N9V	4757	C4
Thornridge Ct				
200	YpTp	48197	4577	B5
Thornridge Dr				
200	YpTp	48197	4577	B5
14700	PyTp	48170	4265	C5
Thornton St				
13600	DET	48227	4270	E7
Thorn Tree Ct				
3500	WasC	48105	4260	C6
Thorntree Ct				
8100	WynC	48138	4670	D5
Thorntree Dr				
8300	WynC	48138	4670	C5
Thorn Tree Rd				
400	GSPW	48236	4276	E1
500	GSPW	48236	4204	E7
Thornwood Ct				
3900	AATp	48105	4333	A6
Thornwood Dr				
6200	VNBN	48111	4494	E2
7400	CNTN	48187	4335	C5
Thornwood St				
14100	RVVW	48192	4669	C1
Thorofare Rd				
19000	WynC	48138	4585	C7
19000	WynC	48138	4670	C1
Thorpe Ct				
26000	WynC	48138	4670	C7
Thorpe St				
8800	LVNA	48150	4340	A3
Thrush Av				
41600	CNTN	48188	4412	B4
Thuer Ct				
41100	PyTp	48170	4337	C2
Thurso Wy				
1000	WIND	N9G	4504	E5
Tiara Ln				
22000	TYLR	48180	4499	C5
Tibbitts Ct				
2000	AATp	48105	4406	D3
Ticknor Ct				
2800	AARB	48104	4489	E4
Tiffany Cir				
6700	CNTN	48187	4336	C6
Tiffany Dr				
21000	WDHN	48183	4669	A2
Tiffany Rd				
-	CNTN	48187	4336	C6
Tiger Lily Ct				
3100	PTFD	48103	4488	D4
Tiger Lily Dr				
3200	PTFD	48103	4488	D5
Tilford St				
35100	BwTp	48173	4841	D3
Tillbury Ct				
-	CNTN	48187	4335	C4
Tillman Ct				
10	WasC	48189	4259	A1
Tillman St				
1200	DRBN	48124	4416	D3
2800	DET	48216	4344	D6
4400	DET	48210	4344	D4
Tillotson Ct				
8100	CNTN	48187	4336	D4
Tillotson Dr				
44400	CNTN	48187	4336	D4
Tillson Dr				
11000	GOTp	48178	4187	E2
Tilman St				
31700	FNHL	48336	4195	B5
Tilsby Ct				
2200	AARB	48103	4489	A3
Tilston Dr				
1200	WIND	N9B	4420	C4
Timber Rdg				
1700	YpTp	48198	4492	D7
Timber Tr				
1600	AATp	48103	4405	E3
4500	WIND	N9G	4504	C4
8600	WasC	48178	4261	D2
26600	DBHT	48127	4415	B1
Timber Crest Ct				
48600	PyTp	48170	4263	E6
Timbercrest Ct				
2300	AARB	48105	4331	E7
Timbercrest Ln				
9000	WasC	48189	4186	E7
9000	WasC	48189	4258	E2
Timbergrove Ct				
11000	GOTp	48178	4188	B4
Timber Hill Dr				
2500	WasC	48103	4405	C2
Timberidge Cir				
30200	FNHL	48336	4195	C4
Timberidge Tr				
7000	WTLD	48185	4338	A5
Timberland Dr				
38000	WTLD	48185	4338	A4
Timberlane Ct				
10	DRBN	48126	4341	E7
Timberlane Dr				
300	WynC	48111	4662	D6
Timberlane St				
600	YPLT	48197	4491	D6
700	WasC	48103	4405	A4
46700	NvlT	48167	4192	B7
Timberline Ct				
3900	CNTN	48188	4411	C7
9300	PyTp	48170	4336	A2
Timberline Dr				
4200	CNTN	48188	4411	B7
22500	SFLD	48034	4196	B3
Timber Ridge Ct				
22400	WDHN	48183	4668	C3
Timber Ridge Dr				
-	DRBN	48126	4417	A1
3900	PTFD	48108	4488	D6
21300	WDHN	48183	4668	C3
Timber Ridge Tr				
24600	BNTN	48134	4667	E4
24600	BNTN	48134	4668	A4
Timbers Rd				
13200	MonC	48117	4749	A6
14100	MonC	48111	4749	A6
Timber Trace Blvd				
-	CNTN	48188	4412	D4
Timber Trail Ct				
800	SLYN	48178	4189	A4
Timberview Ct				
5000	WasC	48176	4572	C1
43800	VNBN	48111	4494	E4
43800	VNBN	48111	4495	A4
Timberview Dr				
-	VNBN	48111	4494	E5
-	VNBN	48111	4495	A5
Timberview Rd				
3000	WasC	48176	4572	B1
Timberwood Ct				
3300	WasC	48103	4330	B7
3300	WasC	48103	4405	B1
7500	SpTp	48198	4334	A7
Timberwood Dr				
47000	PyTp	48170	4336	B3
Timberwood Ln				
3300	WasC	48103	4330	B7
Times Dr				
49000	CNTN	48188	4410	E3
Times Sq				
1200	DET	48226	4345	C6
Times Square Blvd				
3400	CNTN	48188	4411	A6
Times Square Ct				
48500	CNTN	48188	4411	A6
Timken Av				
8000	WRRN	48091	4202	B1
12500	WRRN	48089	4202	D1
Timmins Rd				
1200	WasC	48103	4488	C1
Timothy Dr				
16100	SOGT	48195	4584	A4
Timothy Ln				
9900	GOTp	48178	4187	D2
Timothy Tr				
100	PTFD	48197	4574	E2
Tina Dr				
36800	FNHL	48335	4194	A3
Tioga Dr				
24600	SFLD	48034	4196	D1
Tipperary Cir				
5700	WasC	48105	4332	D2
Tireman				
22100	DET	48239	4341	B4
22700	DBHT	48127	4341	B4
Tireman Av				
-	DET	48228	4341	C3
-	DET	48239	4341	C3
Tireman St				
4200	DET	48204	4344	A3
4200	DET	48210	4344	A3
5900	DET	48204	4343	E3
5900	DET	48210	4343	E3
8100	DRBN	48126	4343	C3
8900	DET	48126	4343	C3
10800	DET	48228	4343	A3
13700	DET	48228	4342	E3
13700	DRBN	48126	4342	E3
15500	DET	48126	4342	D3
19000	DET	48228	4341	E3
20900	DET	48239	4341	D4
23200	DBHT	48127	4341	A4
25500	DBHT	48127	4340	D4
Titcombe Rd				
1300	WIND	N9C	4503	A1
1300	WIND	N9J	4503	A1
Tiverton Ct				
16100	NvlT	48167	4265	B3
Tobin Dr				
400	INKR	48141	4415	D2
Tobine St				
10000	RMLS	48174	4496	C6
Todd Av				
10	YpTp	48198	4492	E3
32300	WYNE	48184	4414	B5
Todd Ln				
1900	LSal	N9H	4503	C3
41000	NOVI	48375	4193	B4
Todds Ln				
11600	GOTp	48189	4187	A6
Toepfer Dr				
14600	EPTE	48021	4203	B3
18100	EPTE	48021	4204	A3
Toepfer Rd				
6700	WRRN	48091	4201	E3
7000	WRRN	48091	4202	A3
12300	WRRN	48089	4202	D3
13600	WRRN	48089	4203	A3
14500	WRRN	48021	4203	A3
Toledo Av				
2200	TNTN	48183	4755	C1
Toledo St				
3500	DET	48216	4344	D7
4400	DET	48209	4344	C7
5600	DET	48209	4419	C1
14800	BrTp	48134	4753	C4
Toles Ln				
20700	GSPW	48236	4204	D5
Tomahawk Dr				
34000	WTLD	48185	4338	E6
Tom Brown Ct				
36400	WTLD	48185	4338	B4
Tom Brown Dr				
8000	WTLD	48185	4338	B4
Tompkins St				
41400	VNBN	48111	4495	C6
Tomson Rd				
3300	TNTN	48183	4669	B7
Tonnacour Pl				
10	GSPF	48236	4276	E2
Tonquish Ct				
42100	CNTN	48187	4337	B5
Tonquish Tr				
34000	WTLD	48185	4338	E6
Tony St				
23500	WRRN	48091	4201	A1
Tony's Oaks				
18000	HnTp	48174	4666	D1
Topaz Cir				
400	WasC	48189	4186	E7
Top of Hill Ct				
50400	PyTp	48170	4335	D2
Top of Hill Dr				
50100	PyTp	48170	4335	D2
Topper Dr				
51100	CNTN	48187	4335	C5
Tor Ct				
100	PTFD	48197	4574	E2
Toronto St				
-	DET	48229	4418	C6
Torrey Av				
2500	PTFD	48108	4490	E3
30100	FTRK	48134	4754	B5
Torrey Ct				
3900	DET	48210	4344	C6
Torrey Rd				
1000	GSPW	48236	4204	D7
9000	AGST	48191	4748	A4
10500	AGST	48111	4748	A4
Torrey St				
4200	DET	48210	4344	C6
Torrington Dr N				
47400	CNTN	48188	4411	A3
Torrington Dr W				
300	CNTN	48188	4411	A3
Torry Pines St				
-	TYLR	48180	4583	A2
Totten St				
1100	WIND	N9B	4420	D5
Tottenham Ct				
24000	NOVI	48374	4192	A2
50000	CNTN	48187	4335	D5
Touchdown Ct				
2200	YPLT	48197	4491	A3
Touraine Ct				
300	GSPF	48236	4276	C2
Touraine Rd				
10	GSPF	48236	4276	C2
Tourangeau Rd				
1200	WIND	N8Y	4346	E7
1300	WIND	N8Y	4421	E1
1400	WIND	N8Y	4422	A1
2300	WIND	N8W	4422	B3
Tournament Ct				
4600	WIND	N9G	4504	D5
Tournament Dr				
-	NvlT	48167	4264	B3
Tournier St				
-	DET	48227	4270	B4
400	WIND	N9C	4420	A3
Tovenia Dr				
31700	BwTp	48173	4755	A6
Tower Ct				
22400	NOVI	48375	4193	D3
Tower Dr				
10	Lksr	N8N	4424	E3
10	SALN	48176	4572	C6
3000	AATp	48105	4332	D7
3000	AATp	48105	4407	D1
Tower Rd				
5200	WasC	48105	4333	E3
5200	WasC	48170	4333	E3
5900	WasC	48170	4261	E7
7300	WasC	48167	4261	E3
8500	WasC	48167	4189	E7
8500	WasC	48178	4189	E7
8500	WasC	48178	4261	E1
Town Ct				
2300	YpTp	48197	4491	B5
Town Ln				
6900	DBHT	48127	4341	D5
Town Center Dr				
10	DRBN	48126	4417	A1
100	HDPK	48203	4272	C3
Towne Rd				
24700	SFLD	48034	4196	E1
Towner Blvd				
2400	AARB	48104	4490	A3
Towner St				
500	YPLT	48198	4492	B5
Townley St				
16700	SOGT	48195	4584	C5
Townsend Av				
18200	BNTN	48192	4583	C7
Townsend Ct				
18100	BNTN	48192	4583	C6
49300	CNTN	48187	4410	D1
Townsend Dr				
800	SLYN	48178	4189	D2
Townsend St				
3600	DET	48214	4346	B1
4400	DET	48214	4274	B7
6400	DET	48213	4274	A5
Township Hall				
-	NvlT	48167	4265	B2
Township Hall Dr				
7200	YpTp	48197	4576	A1
Townsquare Blvd				
3600	MonC	48117	4753	B6
Town Square St				
3600	WYNE	48184	4413	D6
Towsley Ln				
900	SpTp	48105	4408	A7
Tracey St				
-	DET	48235	4270	E1
15300	DET	48227	4270	E4
18400	DET	48235	4198	E6
Tractor St				
-	DET	48229	4418	B6
-	DRBN	48120	4418	C2
Trade Center Dr				
3700	PTFD	48108	4490	C6
Tradition Blvd				
-	CNTN	48187	4335	E7
-	CNTN	48187	4410	E1
Tradition Dr				
1100	CNTN	48187	4410	E1
Trafalgar Ct				
2800	Tcmh	N0R	4505	C6
24100	NOVI	48374	4192	A2
Trafalgar Dr				
6400	CNTN	48187	4336	A6
Trafalgar Sq				
32900	WTLD	48186	4414	A2
Trafalgar St				
7500	TYLR	48180	4499	B3
Trafford Ct				
8100	CNTN	48187	4335	C4
Trail Dr				
1500	TNTN	48183	4669	C2
Trailbrooke Cir				
27600	WTLD	48185	4340	A3
Trail Creek Dr				
29400	HnTp	48164	4666	E6
Trail Ridge Ct				
18500	BNTN	48174	4583	B7
Trail Ridge Dr				
23600	BNTN	48174	4583	B7
Trails Ct				
44700	CNTN	48187	4336	D3
Trailside Ct				
22900	NOVI	48375	4193	D3
Trailwood Ct				
1800	WIND	N8W	4505	A1
Trailwood Ln				
2700	AATp	48105	4332	A6
Trailwood Rd				
10200	PyTp	48170	4336	D1
Tralee Tr				
37800	FNHL	48167	4194	A4
38100	FNHL	48167	4193	E4
Tranby Av				
6600	WIND	N8S	4422	D1
7100	WIND	N8S	4347	E7
Trancrest St				
29500	LVNA	48152	4267	D1
Tranquility Av				
2300	WIND	N8P	4423	D1
Trans X Rd				
24400	NOVI	48375	4193	A1
Trappers Av				
2300	WIND	N8P	4423	C1
Traskos St				
46000	WynC	48111	4663	C4
Traver Blvd				
2200	AARB	48105	4406	E2
2400	AARB	48105	4407	A2
Traver Ct				
1000	AARB	48105	4406	D3
Traver Knl				
1900	AARB	48105	4406	D3
Traver Rd				
1100	AARB	48105	4406	C4
2500	AARB	48105	4407	A2
2600	AATp	48105	4407	A2
Traverse St				
8000	DET	48213	4274	B4
Traverwood Dr				
2000	AARB	48105	4407	A3
2000	AATp	48105	4406	E2
2000	AATp	48105	4407	A3
Travis St				
15200	SOGT	48195	4584	B5
Travis Pointe Rd				
2600	WasC	48108	4572	B1
2600	WasC	48176	4572	B1
Traynor St				
16500	SOGT	48195	4584	C5
Treadway Pl				
8800	DET	48214	4346	D1
Treadwell Av				
1800	WTLD	48186	4413	B4
Treadwell St				
3100	WYNE	48184	4413	C5
4800	WYNE	48184	4496	C1
Tredwell Av				
21900	FNHL	48336	4196	A3
Treehill Blvd				
23300	FMTN	48335	4194	B2
Treeline Ct				
3300	WIND	N8R	4423	C3
Tree Side Ct				
1500	PTFD	48108	4573	A2
Tree Top Ct				
22800	LyTp	48178	4190	E2
Trego Cir				
500	AARB	48103	4405	C7
Tremmel Av				
2100	AARB	48104	4489	D2
Tremont Blvd				
7400	YpTp	48197	4576	E5
Tremont Dr				
3700	AARB	48105	4407	D4
Tremont Ln				
3700	AARB	48105	4407	C5
11100	PyTp	48170	4337	C2
Tremont Pl				
3700	AARB	48105	4407	D4
Tremont Rd				
1700	CNTN	48188	4411	D4
Trent Ct				
21500	NOVI	48375	4193	A4
41900	CNTN	48188	4412	B4
Trent Dr				
42000	CNTN	48188	4412	B3
Trenton Ct				
2400	AARB	48105	4407	B1
Trenton Dr N				
1700	TNTN	48183	4669	C3
Trenton Dr S				
1900	TNTN	48183	4669	C4
Trenton Rd				
-	SOGT	48195	4584	D3
16300	RVVW	48195	4584	D5
Trenton St				
2800	WIND	N8Y	4346	D7
3800	DET	48210	4343	D7
3800	DET	48210	4418	E1
Trenton Ter				
900	DRBN	48124	4416	A3
Trentwood Ct				
20000	BNTN	48183	4668	E1
Treverton Cres				
1000	WIND	N8P	4348	D6

STREET
Block City ZIP Map# Grid

Trevor Pl
1000 DET 48207 4346 A5
Triangle Dr
- AARB 48103 4405 D7
30500 GBTR 48173 4755 D5
Trillium Ct
1600 LSal N9H 4504 B5
33600 LVNA 48150 4338 E3
33600 LVNA 48185 4338 E3
Trillium Ct E
45500 PyTp 48170 4336 C3
Trillium Ct W
45700 PyTp 48170 4336 C3
Trillium Dr
8600 YpTp 48197 4576 C3
Trillium Ln
2700 WasC 48103 4488 A4
8800 PyTp 48170 4336 C3
10900 GOTp 48178 4187 D2
Trillium Tr
10 PTFD 48197 4574 E2
Trillium Woods Blvd
- AATp 48105 4407 D2
Trillium Woods Dr
2100 AATp 48105 4407 D2
Trinity Av
- LSal N9H 4503 C4
Trinity Ct
- NvlT 48167 4193 A6
Trinity St
8000 DET 48228 4341 C2
13900 DET 48223 4269 C5
16800 DET 48219 4269 C1
17500 DET 48219 4197 C7
Troester St
13600 DET 48205 4203 A7
Trojan St
18100 DET 48219 4198 A5
18100 DET 48235 4198 A5
19400 DET 48219 4197 D5
Trolley Industral Dr
20400 TYLR 48180 4499 C2
26400 TYLR 48174 4498 B4
26400 TYLR 48180 4498 B4
Trombley Rd
600 GPPK 48230 4276 A7
600 GPPK 48230 4348 A1
Trombley St
100 INKR 48141 4415 B2
Trombly St
1400 DET 48211 4273 C7
22500 STCS 48080 4204 E1
22600 STCS 48080 4205 A1
Troon Ct
4800 WasC 48103 4329 E3
4800 WasC 48103 4404 D6
15500 NvlT 48167 4264 D3
Troon Ln
300 CNTN 48188 4411 D2
Trotters Ln
7400 WasC 48189 4258 B4
Trotters Park St
7600 YpTp 48197 4576 B5
Trotwood Ct
42200 CNTN 48187 4337 B6
Trowbridge Ct
10 AARB 48108 4490 A6
Trowbridge Sq
26700 HnTp 48164 4751 B1
Trowbridge St
10 DET 48202 4272 E5
500 DET 48202 4273 A5
500 DET 48211 4273 A5
1900 HMTK 48212 4273 C4
5100 DET 48212 4273 C3
25000 DRBN 48124 4415 E4
25800 INKR 48141 4415 C4
Troy Av
15000 TYLR 48180 4583 A4
Troy Pl
19400 DET 48203 4200 B6
Troy St
10900 TYLR 48180 4498 E6
13100 OKPK 48237 4199 A2
14200 TYLR 48180 4583 A3
E Troy St
200 FRDL 48220 4199 E2
200 FRDL 48220 4200 A2
W Troy St
1200 FRDL 48220 4199 C2
Troyon Dr
13600 BwTp 48173 4841 D3
Truax St
10 TNTN 48183 4670 A3
300 TNTN 48183 4669 E3
Trudy Ln
3600 WasC 48105 4332 C2
Trufant Ct
21800 WDHN 48183 4669 A3
Truman Ct
24300 FNHL 48335 4194 B1
Truman Dr
6100 VNBN 48111 4577 C3
Truman Rd
32100 RKWD 48173 4754 E7
Trumbull Av
3000 TNTN 48183 4669 D5
Trumbull Ct
3900 TNTN 48183 4669 D6
Trumbull St
700 DET 48216 4345 B6
2200 DET 48201 4345 A4
3300 DET 48210 4345 A5
5000 DET 48202 4345 A3
6100 DET 48202 4344 E2
6100 DET 48210 4344 E2
13500 HDPK 48203 4272 C3
Truwood Av
2400 TNTN 48183 4669 C3
Truwood Ct
14800 SOGT 48195 4584 A3
Truwood St
16200 WDHN 48183 4669 A3
Tubbs Rd
3600 WasC 48103 4330 B6
3600 WasC 48105 4330 C6
Tuck Rd
21800 FNHL 48336 4195 C3
E Tucker St
10 HZLP 48030 4200 D2
Tucson Blvd
- RMLS 48174 4496 A2
Tucson Ct
9000 PyTp 48170 4337 B3
Tudor Ct
44100 CNTN 48187 4336 E6
Tudor Dr
1600 AARB 48103 4488 D2
Tudor St
14200 RVVW 48192 4669 D2
Tuebingen Pkwy
2700 AARB 48105 4406 E2
Tulane Av
22400 FNHL 48336 4195 D2
Tulane St
3900 DBHT 48124 4416 B6
3900 DBHT 48125 4416 B6
5800 TYLR 48125 4499 B1
7500 TYLR 48180 4499 B3
Tulip
10 WynC 48111 4664 B3
Tulip Ct
3800 WIND N9E 4504 E2
Tulip Dr
- CNTN 48187 4337 E5
- WTLD 48185 4337 E5
Tulip Ln
1600 WTLD 48186 4412 E4
Tulip Tree Ct
100 AARB 48103 4405 E6
Tulipwood St
21600 WDHN 48183 4668 D3
Tuller St
12200 DET 48204 4271 D6
15400 DET 48238 4271 D2
16100 DET 48221 4271 D2
Tumey St
8000 DET 48234 4274 A1
Tuomy Rd
2100 AARB 48104 4489 E1
Turbo St
5800 RMLS 48174 4498 A1
Turkey Run
11700 PyTp 48170 4336 D1
Turnberry Blvd
20700 NOVI 48167 4193 D5
20700 NOVI 48375 4193 D5
Turnberry Ct
7600 WasC 48189 4259 C4
42700 VNBN 48111 4495 B6
45000 CNTN 48188 4411 D3
Turnberry Dr
7800 WasC 48189 4259 C3
45100 CNTN 48188 4411 D3
Turnberry Ln
10 DRBN 48120 4417 C3
3000 PTFD 48108 4490 C4
Turnburry Dr
37000 LVNA 48152 4194 B7
Turner Cres
- Amhg N9V 4671 C4
Turner Ln
6600 BrTp 48166 4840 C6
6600 BrTp 48179 4840 C6
Turner Rd
1600 WIND N8W 4421 D2
3100 WIND N8W 4422 A7
3600 WIND N8W 4505 B1
3800 TNTN 48183 4669 B6
Turner St
12200 DET 48204 4271 D6
15300 DET 48238 4271 D4
16100 DET 48221 4271 D2
Turner Park Ct
600 AARB 48103 4406 A7
Turntable Ct
8100 WynC 48138 4670 C6
Turquoise Dr
400 WasC 48189 4186 D7
Turtle Club Pk
- LSal N9J 4502 D4
Turtlehead Ct N
45500 PyTp 48170 4336 C2
Turtlehead Ct S
45500 PyTp 48170 4336 D2
Turtlehead Dr
45000 PyTp 48170 4336 C2
Turtle Point Dr
5100 WasC 48105 4332 E3
Tuscany Av
22700 EPTE 48021 4203 E1
Tuscany Cres
300 Tcmh N8N 4424 B1
Tuscany Ct
38400 LVNA 48154 4265 E4
39400 NOVI 48375 4193 D2
Tuscany Valley Wy
9800 WasC 48178 4189 C6
Tuscarora St
10 WIND N9A 4420 E2
400 WIND N9A 4421 A1
1800 WIND N8Y 4346 B7
Tuscola Ct
31800 WTLD 48186 4414 C4
Tuson Wy
- WIND N9G 4504 D4
Tuthill Rd
10300 GOTp 48178 4187 D4
10300 GOTp 48189 4187 D4
Tutle Av
6100 LSal N9H 4503 C5
Tuttle Hill Rd
5400 YpTp 48197 4576 D3
8000 AGST 48197 4576 D7
8000 AGST 48197 4661 D2
9000 AGST 48191 4661 C4
Tuxedo St
10 HDPK 48203 4272 D5
1600 DET 48206 4272 B6
4000 DET 48204 4272 A6
5100 DET 48204 4271 D7
9900 DRBN 48120 4418 D3
Twining Ct
45100 CNTN 48187 4336 C4
Twining Dr
23000 SFLD 48075 4197 E2
45300 CNTN 48187 4336 C4
Twin Islands Ct
2100 PTFD 48108 4572 E2
Twin Lakes Dr
2400 PTFD 48197 4491 A3
Twin Oak Dr
25900 TYLR 48180 4498 D5
Twin Oaks
6200 WTLD 48185 4338 C6
Twin Oaks Dr
7700 WIND N8T 4423 B5
8000 WIND N8N 4423 B5
Twin Pond Dr
19900 BNTN 48183 4668 B1
Twin Towers St
700 YpTp 48198 4492 B3
Twin Valley Ct
24100 FMTN 48335 4194 E1
Twyckingham Ln
44500 CNTN 48187 4336 D6
E Tyler Dr
14100 PyTp 48170 4263 D6
S Tyler Dr
50400 PyTp 48170 4263 C6
Tyler Ln
300 CNTN 48188 4412 D3
Tyler Rd
500 YPLT 48198 4492 B6
1400 YpTp 48198 4492 D6
2200 YpTp 48198 4493 A6
3000 VNBN 48111 4493 C6
37400 RMLS 48174 4496 A5
38400 RMLS 48174 4495 D5
39400 VNBN 48111 4495 D5
39400 VNBN 48174 4495 D5
43600 VNBN 48111 4494 E5
Tyler St
- DET 48223 4269 D6
200 HDPK 48203 4272 C4
2900 DET 48238 4272 A5
3700 DET 48238 4271 E6
13600 DET 48227 4270 D6
31400 WYNE 48184 4497 C1
Tyndall Cir
6100 RMLS 48174 4496 D2
Tyndall Dr
900 CNTN 48187 4412 B1
Tyrone St
5000 YpTp 48197 4575 B3
19100 DET 48236 4204 B7
19200 HRWD 48225 4204 B7

U

Ulster St
100 LSal N9J 4502 C5
22000 DET 48219 4269 B2
N Umberland Cir
43900 CNTN 48187 4336 E6
S Umberland Cir
43900 CNTN 48187 4336 E6
N Umberland Dr
44300 CNTN 48187 4336 C4
Underdown Rd
10 BNHL 48105 4406 B1
Underwood St
4800 DET 48204 4343 E2
Unicorn Ln
33400 WTLD 48186 4414 A3
Union Ct
33600 WTLD 48186 4414 A3
Union Rd
36500 HnTp 48164 4751 C1
Union St
- DET 48201 4345 B5
10 ECRS 48229 4501 D2
2400 WIND N9B 4420 B3
24000 DRBN 48124 4416 A6
24300 DRBN 48124 4415 E6
50900 VNBN 48111 4577 C4
E Union St
100 PLYM 48170 4265 B7
N Union St
100 PLYM 48170 4265 A7
S Union St
100 PLYM 48170 4265 A7
200 PLYM 48170 4337 A2
Unity Dr
11100 WRRN 48089 4202 B1
Universal Av
20700 EPTE 48021 4203 C3
Universal Dr
12000 TYLR 48180 4583 A1
Universal St
- DRBN 48124 4417 A7
- DRBN 48125 4417 A7
4400 DBHT 48125 4417 A7
University Av
100 SLYN 48178 4189 B4
1300 LNPK 48146 4501 A2
1700 LNPK 48146 4500 D1
2200 LNPK 48101 4500 D1
E University Av
400 AARB 48104 4406 C7
N University Av
700 AARB 48104 4406 C6
S University Av
800 AARB 48104 4406 D7
University Av E
10 WIND N9A 4420 E1
500 WIND N9A 4421 A1
800 WIND N9A 4346 A7
University Av W
10 WIND N9A 4420 B2
1100 WIND N9B 4420 B2
2800 WIND N9C 4420 B2
University Ct
700 YPLT 48197 4491 C3
N University Ct
1300 AARB 48104 4406 D6
University Dr
6000 DBHT 48127 4341 C6
22000 WynC 48138 4670 B4
University Pl
200 GSPT 48230 4276 C5
800 DET 48230 4276 B4
4000 DET 48224 4276 A2
University St
- GDNC 48185 4413 E2
100 FRDL 48220 4199 C4
100 FRDL 48220 4200 A3
14500 ALPK 48101 4500 D1
34700 WTLD 48185 4413 D2
University Park Dr
17800 LVNA 48152 4266 A1
Upland Ct
19300 NvlT 48167 4193 B7
36400 WYNE 48184 4413 C5
Upland Dr
1800 AARB 48105 4406 E3
1800 AATp 48105 4406 E3
1800 WasC 48103 4488 C2
30500 HnTp 48164 4666 E5
Upland Hl
24700 NOVI 48375 4193 A1
Upper Glade Ct
4100 WasC 48103 4329 E7
4100 WasC 48103 4330 A7
Urbanek Av
20700 WRRN 48091 4201 A4
Ure St
5000 Tcmh N0R 4505 D5
Ursuline St
23700 STCS 48080 4204 C1
US-12
- VNBN 48111 4493 C3
- VNBN 48198 4493 C3
- YPLT - 4491 C7
- YPLT - 4492 C6
- YpTp - 4491 C7
- YpTp - 4492 C6
- YpTp 48198 4492 C6
- YpTp 48198 4493 C3
US-12 BUS
- VNBN 48111 4493 D2
US-12 Ecorse Rd
1900 YpTp 48198 4492 E5
2100 YpTp 48198 4493 A4
US-12 BUS S Hamilton St
- YPLT 48197 4492 A6
10 YPLT 48197 4491 E4
US-12 BUS S Huron St
- YPLT 48197 4491 E6
- YpTp 48197 4491 E6
10 YPLT 48197 4492 A4
US-12 Michigan Av
- DRBN 48128 4417 D1
10 DET 48226 4345 C6
1300 DET 48216 4345 C6
2500 DET 48216 4344 B6
4000 DET 48210 4344 B6
6900 DET 48210 4343 C7
9400 DET 48126 4343 C7
10000 DRBN 48126 4343 C7
13800 DRBN 48126 4342 E7
14200 DRBN 48126 4417 D1
16300 DRBN 48120 4417 D1
19000 DRBN 48124 4417 D1
20000 DRBN 48124 4416 B3
20000 DRBN 48128 4416 B3
24500 DRBN 48124 4415 A4
25400 DBHT 48125 4415 A4
25600 DBHT 48141 4415 A4
25800 INKR 48141 4415 A4
28900 INKR 48141 4414 D5
30400 WTLD 48141 4414 D5
30400 WTLD 48186 4414 D5
31200 WTLD 48184 4414 D5
39400 CNTN 48188 4412 B6
43600 CNTN 48188 4411 D7
45900 CNTN 48111 4494 B1
45900 CNTN 48188 4494 B1
47400 VNBN 48111 4494 B1
48800 CNTN 48111 4493 A4
48800 CNTN 48188 4493 A4
49100 VNBN 48111 4493 A4
US-12 BUS Michigan Av
50500 VNBN 48111 4493 D2
51300 VNBN 48198 4493 C2
51300 YpTp 48198 4493 C2
US-12 E Michigan Av
100 SALN 48176 4572 E7
6100 PTFD 48108 4574 C2
6100 PTFD 48176 4574 C2
6100 PTFD 48197 4574 C2
6400 PTFD 48176 4573 B5
7600 SALN 48176 4573 B5
US-12 BUS E Michigan Av
10 YPLT 48198 4492 C4
800 YpTp 48198 4492 C4
2100 YpTp 48198 4493 A3
US-12 W Michigan Av
100 SALN 48176 4657 A2
3100 PTFD 48197 4491 A7
3100 YpTp 48197 4491 A7
4700 PTFD 48197 4574 E1
4700 PTFD 48197 4575 A1
8600 WasC 48176 4657 A2
8800 WasC 48176 4656 C4
US-12 BUS W Michigan Av
10 YPLT 48197 4492 A4
10 YPLT 48198 4492 A4
US-12 Michigan Av E
31400 WYNE 48184 4414 C5
33800 WYNE 48184 4413 C6
38900 WYNE 48184 4412 E6
39200 WYNE 48188 4412 E6
US-12 Michigan Av W
31400 WYNE 48184 4414 C5
34000 WYNE 48184 4413 E6
38900 WYNE 48184 4412 E6
US-23
- AARB - 4331 E7
- AARB - 4332 B7
- AARB - 4407 C1
- AARB - 4490 D1
- AATp - 4331 C5
- AATp - 4332 B7
- AATp - 4407 D5
- AATp - 4490 D1
- GOTp - 4186 E7
- GOTp - 4187 B2
- PTFD - 4490 D4
- PTFD - 4574 C3
- WasC - 4186 E7
- WasC - 4258 E1
- WasC - 4259 A2
- WasC - 4331 C5
- WasC - 4574 C3
- WasC - 4659 D6
US-23 BUS E Huron St
100 AARB 48104 4406 B6
US-23 BUS N Main St
- AARB 48103 4406 B4
- AARB 48105 4406 B4
- AATp 48103 4406 B4
100 AARB 48104 4406 B4
US-23 BUS Washtenaw Av
- PTFD 48104 4490 C2
- PTFD 48105 4490 C2
- PTFD 48108 4490 C2
400 AARB 48104 4406 D7
1900 AARB 48104 4489 E1
2100 AARB 48104 4490 C2
US-24 Telegraph Rd
- DET 48034 4196 E3
- DET 48223 4268 E5
5800 TYLR 48180 4499 A5
8800 RDFD 48239 4341 A2
11600 RDFD 48239 4269 A7
12000 MonC 48117 4839 A1
12000 MonC 48179 4839 A1
12000 TYLR 48180 4583 A1
12600 DET 48223 4269 A7
12600 DET 48239 4269 A7
12600 RDFD 48223 4269 A7
13000 MonC 48117 4753 C5
13500 MonC 48134 4753 C5
14000 BrTp 48134 4753 C5
14200 RDFD 48223 4268 E5
14200 RDFD 48239 4268 E5
15000 FTRK 48134 4753 C5
15800 RDFD 48219 4268 E5
16100 DET 48219 4268 E5
16600 TYLR 48174 4583 A1
17000 BNTN 48174 4583 A1
18200 DET 48219 4196 E3
18500 BNTN 48174 4668 A2
20600 BNTN 48183 4668 A2
20700 SFLD 48034 4196 E3
21000 BNTN 48134 4668 A2
24800 BNTN 48134 4667 E7
25800 BNTN 48134 4753 C5
US-24 N Telegraph Rd
100 DRBN 48124 4416 A1
100 DRBN 48128 4416 A1
1500 DRBN 48128 4341 A4
2200 DRBN 48127 4341 A4
5600 DBHT 48127 4341 A4
8700 DBHT 48239 4341 A4
US-24 S Telegraph Rd
100 DRBN 48124 4416 A2
3800 DRBN 48125 4416 A6
3900 DBHT 48125 4416 A6
5600 DBHT 48125 4499 A1
5600 DBHT 48180 4499 A1
US Customs Dr
- DET 48226 4345 E6
US Turnpike Rd
9000 BrTp 48166 4840 E7
9900 BrTp 48179 4841 A5
Usufruct Av
7600 DRBN 48126 4343 C3
Utah
300 WynC 48111 4662 D2
Utah Ct
300 WynC 48111 4662 D3
Utah St
10 YpTp 48198 4492 E3
8800 LVNA 48150 4339 A3
Uthes St
4400 DET 48209 4344 D7
Utica Ln
- NvlT 48167 4193 B7
Utica St
- DET 48204 4271 D7

V

Vacri Ln
17100 LVNA 48152 4266 E1
22400 FNHL 48335 4194 B3
Vail Ct
2100 PTFD 48108 4488 E6
Vail Dr
16800 SOGT 48195 4584 A5
Valade St
17000 RVVW 48192 4584 E5
17000 RVVW 48195 4584 E5
Vale St
21900 OKPK 48237 4198 E3
Valebrook St
2400 WIND N9E 4503 D1
Valencia Dr
- GBTR 48173 4755 A4
Valencia St
18700 NvlT 48167 4192 C7
18700 NvlT 48167 4264 C1
Valente Ct
12000 Tcmh N8N 4348 E7
Valentine Ct
1500 CNTN 48188 4411 E4
Valentine Rd
3400 WasC 48189 4258 A3
3900 WasC 48130 4258 A3
Valerie St
22600 LyTp 48178 4189 C3
Valhalla Dr
10 WasC 48103 4489 B2
Valiant Ct
- NvlT 48167 4193 A6
Valiant St
1800 LSal N9H 4503 C5
Valley Av
24200 EPTE 48021 4203 B1
Valley Cir
1900 YpTp 48197 4491 C4
Valley Cr
35400 FNHL 48335 4194 C2
Valley Ct
3300 TNTN 48183 4669 B6
Valley Dr
10 YpTp 48197 4491 B4
2500 AARB 48103 4405 C5
2500 WasC 48103 4405 C5
23400 BNTN 48174 4583 B6
N Valley Dr
45900 NvlT 48167 4192 B6
Valley Rd
4500 TNTN 48183 4669 B6
20000 NvlT 48167 4192 C6
Valley St
5900 DBHT 48127 4341 C6
Valley Vw
8400 WasC 48178 4261 D2
Valley Cir Dr
700 SALN 48176 4657 B1
Valley Creek Dr
25600 FTRK 48134 4753 D1
25700 BNTN 48134 4753 D1
Valley Field Dr
6200 WasC 48170 4263 A7
6200 WasC 48170 4335 A1
Valley Forge Rd
7300 HbgT 48116 4186 B2
Valley Starr
23500 NOVI 48375 4193 C2
Valley View Cir
8100 WTLD 48185 4340 A3
32200 FMTN 48336 4195 A2
Valley View Dr
- DRBN 48126 4417 A2
- DRBN 48128 4417 A2
5800 CNTN 48187 4335 E7
5800 CNTN 48187 4336 A7
22900 SFLD 48034 4197 A2
38900 RMLS 48174 4580 A5
Valleyview Dr
1700 SpTp 48105 4408 A6
7800 YpTp 48197 4576 B1
Valley View St
31800 FMTN 48336 4195 B2
Valleyview St
18200 RVVW 48192 4584 B7
Van Ct
- LVNA 48150 4339 A1
36400 LVNA 48150 4338 C1
Van Rd
18300 LVNA 48152 4194 C7
18300 LVNA 48152 4266 C1
Van Allen Av
- VNBN 48111 4494 B6
12400 VNBN 48111 4578 B2
Van Alstyne Blvd
3000 WYDT 48192 4585 C3
Van Antwerp Av
1800 GSPW 48236 4204 C5
Van Antwerp Rd
9200 HbgT 48116 4186 B1
Van Antwerp St
19900 HRWD 48225 4204 A4
21100 HRWD 48236 4204 B4
Van Born Ct
5600 DBHT 48125 4498 E1
5600 DBHT 48180 4498 E1
Van Born Rd
18600 ALPK 48101 4499 A1
18600 ALPK 48125 4499 A1
18600 DBHT 48101 4499 A1
20000 TYLR 48101 4499 A1
20000 TYLR 48125 4499 A1
20000 TYLR 48180 4499 A1
23400 DBHT 48180 4499 A1
24600 DBHT 48125 4498 E1
24600 DBHT 48180 4498 E1
24600 TYLR 48180 4498 E1
27300 DBHT 48174 4498 A1
27300 DBHT 48186 4498 A1
27300 TYLR 48174 4498 A1
27400 RMLS 48174 4498 A1
27400 WTLD 48174 4498 A1
27400 WTLD 48186 4498 A1
28200 RMLS 48186 4498 A1
28700 RMLS 48174 4497 C1
28700 RMLS 48186 4497 C1
28700 WTLD 48186 4497 C1
30600 WTLD 48174 4497 C1
30800 RMLS 48184 4497 C1
30800 WTLD 48184 4497 C1
31400 WYNE 48184 4497 C1
32100 WYNE 48174 4497 C1
33900 RMLS 48174 4496 A1
33900 WYNE 48174 4496 A1
33900 WYNE 48184 4496 A1
34400 RMLS 48184 4496 A1
38600 RMLS 48174 4495 E1
38600 RMLS 48184 4495 E1
38600 WYNE 48184 4495 E1
39400 CNTN 48188 4495 D1
39400 VNBN 48111 4495 D1
39400 VNBN 48188 4495 D1
40900 CNTN 48111 4495 C1
45400 VNBN 48111 4494 C2
Van Buren Ct
9600 VNBN 48111 4495 B6
Van Buren Dr
50200 PyTp 48170 4263 C6
Van Buren Ln
10600 VNBN 48111 4495 B7
Van Buren Rd
23800 DBHT 48127 4341 A3
26700 DBHT 48127 4340 B3
Van Buren St
- DET 48228 4341 E3
6300 DET 48204 4343 D2
9400 VNBN 48111 4495 C6
13600 DET 48228 4342 E2
13600 DET 48228 4343 D2
20700 SFLD 48034 4196 B4
20700 SFLD 48240 4196 B4
Vance Av
23000 HZLP 48030 4200 E2
Vancourt St
5700 DET 48210 4344 A3
Vancouver St
- DET 48204 4344 A3
5500 DET 48204 4343 E3
Vanderbilt Cres
400 WIND N8P 4348 B5
Vanderbilt St
8000 DET 48209 4419 A4
Vandernoot Av
500 LSal N9J 4502 E5
Van Dusen Dr
1100 AARB 48103 4406 A7
1100 AARB 48103 4489 A1
Van Dyke Av
- WRRN 48234 4202 A1
20600 WRRN 48089 4202 A1
20600 WRRN 48091 4202 A1
23700 CTNL 48015 4202 A1
23700 WRRN 48015 4202 A1
Van Dyke Av SR-53
- WRRN 48234 4202 A1
20600 WRRN 48089 4202 A1
20600 WRRN 48091 4202 A1
23700 CTNL 48015 4202 A1
23700 WRRN 48015 4202 A1
Van Dyke Pl
7800 DET 48214 4346 D3
Van Dyke St
500 DET 48214 4346 C2
4400 DET 48214 4274 B7
5000 DET 48213 4274 B6
9700 DET 48234 4274 A2
17100 DET 48212 4202 A4
17100 DET 48212 4274 A2
17100 DET 48234 4202 A4
Van Dyke St SR-53
5300 DET 48213 4274 B6
9700 DET 48234 4274 A2
17100 DET 48212 4202 A4
17100 DET 48212 4274 A2
17100 DET 48234 4202 A4
Van Horn Rd
1500 TNTN 48183 4669 A6
18400 WDHN 48183 4669 A6
20000 WDHN 48183 4668 D7
23000 BNTN 48183 4668 A7
23700 BNTN 48134 4668 A7
23700 WDHN 48134 4668 A7
25000 BNTN 48134 4667 E7
27400 HnTp 48134 4667 A7
27400 HnTp 48164 4667 A7
29400 HnTp 48134 4666 D7
29400 HnTp 48164 4666 D7
Vanier St
500 WIND N8X 4421 C6
Vanilla St
100 WTLD 48186 4414 D7
Van K Dr
21000 GSPW 48236 4205 A4
Van Lawn St
300 WTLD 48186 4413 E3
Van Petten St
37400 RMLS 48174 4580 B1
Van Riper Av
29000 FTRK 48134 4753 E4
Van Riper Ct
23400 BNTN 48183 4668 B6
Vansull St
100 WTLD 48185 4413 E2
100 WTLD 48186 4413 E2
Vargo Dr
33400 LVNA 48152 4266 E2

STREET
Block City ZIP Map# Grid

Vargo St
27400 LVNA 48152 4268 A1
31400 LVNA 48152 4267 B2
36500 LVNA 48152 4266 B2
Varjo St
6700 DET 48212 4201 E7
6700 DET 48212 4202 A7
Varney St
6300 DET 48211 4273 E5
Varsity Dr
3500 AARB 48108 4489 D5
4000 PTFD 48108 4489 D6
Vasilos Ct
22800 NOVI 48374 4191 E3
Vassar
1000 SLYN 48178 4189 B3
Vassar Av
13200 DET 48235 4199 A6
18100 DET 48219 4198 A6
18100 DET 48235 4198 A6
18800 DET 48219 4197 D6
22900 HZLP 48030 4200 D1
25900 RDFD 48240 4196 B6
Vassar St
3000 DRBN 48124 4416 B6
3900 DBHT 48124 4416 B6
3900 DBHT 48125 4416 B6
27400 LVNA 48152 4196 A6
28800 LVNA 48152 4195 E6
43900 CNTN 48188 4411 E2
Vaughan St
3700 WIND N9C 4420 B5
6300 DET 48228 4341 E5
11600 DET 48228 4269 D7
14500 DET 48223 4269 D4
16400 DET 48219 4269 D2
19900 DET 48219 4197 D5
Vaughn St
900 AARB 48104 4406 C7
Veach St
20100 DET 48234 4202 B4
Vendome Ct
200 GSPF 48236 4276 D2
Vendome Rd
10 GSPF 48236 4276 D3
Venetian Av
45000 VNBN 48111 4578 D1
Venetian Dr
10 Amhg N9V 4757 D2
Venice Cir
4900 WasC 48167 4190 A6
Venice Ct
- NvlT 48167 4263 D4
Venice Dr
24300 NOVI 48374 4192 B1
Venice St
1300 DRBN 48124 4417 A5
6400 DET 48213 4274 D4
Venness St
15000 SOGT 48195 4584 C2
N Venoy Cir
200 GDNC 48135 4414 A2
S Venoy Cir
100 GDNC 48135 4414 A2
Venoy Rd
100 GDNC 48135 4414 A1
100 GDNC 48186 4414 A1
1700 GDNC 48135 4339 A6
2900 WYNE 48184 4414 A6
5100 WYNE 48174 4497 B1
5100 WYNE 48184 4497 B1
5600 WTLD 48185 4339 A6
6900 WTLD 48135 4339 A6
N Venoy Rd
7200 WTLD 48185 4339 A5
S Venoy Rd
100 WTLD 48186 4414 B4
Ventnor Av
10 Amhg N9V 4757 D2
Ventura Ct
400 AARB 48103 4405 E6
17800 LVNA 48152 4266 E1
Venture Dr
4500 PTFD 48108 4489 D7
4500 PTFD 48108 4573 D1
11000 GOTp 48189 4186 E6
22400 NOVI 48375 4193 A3
Vera Pl
400 WIND N9A 4420 D2
Veranda Dr
20700 NOVI 48375 4193 A5
Vercheres Av
2100 WIND N9B 4420 C3
Verdant Ct
12300 Tcmh N9K 4424 A4
Verdant Dr
24200 FNHL 48335 4194 B1
Verdun Av
1900 WIND N8W 4421 D4
Verdun Ct
43700 CNTN 48188 4411 E4
Verdun Dr
22000 HnTp 48174 4667 B4
Verdun St
21500 FNHL 48336 4196 A4
23600 DET 48219 4197 A6
23800 DET 48219 4196 E6
Veri Ct
35500 LVNA 48152 4194 C7
Veri St
35400 LVNA 48152 4194 C7
35500 LVNA 48152 4266 C1
Verle Av
2800 AARB 48108 4490 A5
Vermont
400 WynC 48111 4662 D2
Vermont Dr
10 Amhg N9V 4757 E2
Vermont St
- DET 48216 4420 B1
Vermont St
100 LSal N9J 4502 C4
2600 DET 48216 4345 A5
3500 DET 48210 4345 A5
5700 DET 48210 4344 D2
32500 LVNA 48150 4339 A2
Verna Av
2500 YpTp 48197 4491 B4
Verna Ln
19000 HnTp 48174 4666 C1
Verne St
- DET 48219 4270 A2
15500 DET 48235 4270 C2
22000 DET 48219 4269 C2
23800 DET 48219 4268 E2
Verner Hwy W
1900 DET 48216 4345 A6
Vernier Cir
20600 GSPW 48236 4204 E5
Vernier Rd
10 GSPS 48236 4205 A5
500 GSPW 48236 4205 A5
600 GSPW 48236 4204 D5
2100 GSPW 48225 4204 A4
17700 EPTE 48021 4203 E4
17700 EPTE 48225 4203 E4
17700 HRWD 48225 4203 E4
19100 HRWD 48225 4204 A4
Vernier Rd SR-102
1700 GSPW 48236 4204 A4
2100 GSPW 48225 4204 A4
17700 EPTE 48021 4203 E4
17700 EPTE 48225 4203 E4
17700 HRWD 48225 4203 E4
18000 HRWD 48225 4204 A4
Vernon
18500 BNTN 48192 4583 C7
Vernon Av
12200 WRRN 48089 4202 D3
Vernon Cres
200 WIND N8S 4347 C6
Vernon Ct
2000 TNTN 48183 4669 D3
Vernon St
1500 TNTN 48183 4669 D3
1500 TNTN 48192 4669 D3
5800 VNBN 48111 4493 C1
N Vernon St
100 DRBN 48128 4416 A1
1500 DRBN 48128 4340 E6
5600 DBHT 48128 4340 E6
6400 DBHT 48127 4340 E5
S Vernon St
100 DRBN 48124 4416 A2
Vernor Hwy
9800 DRBN 48120 4418 D3
9800 DRBN 48209 4418 D3
E Vernor Hwy
- GPPK 48230 4276 A5
- GSPT 48230 4276 A5
12500 DET 48214 4275 C7
15100 GPPK 48230 4275 E6
Vernor Hwy E
2100 DET 48207 4345 E4
2600 DET 48207 4346 A3
7000 DET 48214 4346 C2
10400 DET 48214 4347 A1
Vernor Hwy W
- DRBN 48209 4418 D3
2200 DET 48216 4345 A6
2700 DET 48216 4344 D7
4000 DET 48209 4344 D7
4200 DET 48209 4419 C1
8200 DET 48209 4418 D3
Vero Ct
43400 NOVI 48167 4192 E3
Verona Dr
2800 WasC 48167 4190 A7
Verona St
19100 DET 48205 4203 A6
Veronica Av
16000 EPTE 48021 4203 D3
17900 EPTE 48021 4204 A3
Veronica Ct
13100 Tcmh N8N 4349 B7
Veronica St
12700 SOGT 48195 4584 D3
35400 LVNA 48150 4266 C7
Versailles Av
- WasC 48103 4404 B6
Versailles Av E
5500 WasC 48103 4404 B6
Versailles Ln
27500 HnTp 48174 4667 A4
Versailles Rd
42700 CNTN 48187 4337 A4
Vesper Rd
800 AARB 48103 4406 A4
Vester St
100 FRDL 48220 4199 E2
300 FRDL 48220 4200 A2
Veterans Pkwy
- SOGT 48195 4584 B3
2600 TNTN 48183 4669 E4
Veterans Plz
34600 WYNE 48184 4413 E6
Veteran's Wy
- CNTN 48188 4411 D3
Viale Udine
10 WIND N9A 4420 E1
Via Plazza
19400 NvlT 48167 4191 D7
Via Sacra Dr
2600 AATp 48105 4407 D1
Via Vita St
2300 WIND N9E 4503 D2
Vicary Ln
36400 FMTN 48335 4194 B1
Vick Ct
400 WasC 48103 4489 A2
Vickery Ln
12300 Tcmh N9K 4424 A4
Vicksburg Ct
43800 CNTN 48188 4411 E3
Vicksburg St
2600 DET 48206 4344 B2
4000 DET 48204 4344 B2
Vicky Cir
1700 WIND N8W 4421 E7
Victor Ct
17200 NvlT 48167 4265 C2
Victor Dr
800 WIND N8S 4347 C6
17100 NvlT 48167 4265 C2
Victor Pkwy
19900 LVNA 48152 4194 A5
20500 LVNA 48167 4194 A5
Victor St
10 HDPK 48203 4272 D3
1600 DET 48203 4272 E2
1600 YpTp 48198 4492 E7
1800 DET 48203 4273 A2
Victoria
- TYLR 48180 4498 D5
Victoria Av
200 WIND N9A 4420 E1
1000 LNPK 48146 4501 A2
1200 WIND N8X 4420 E3
2100 WIND N8X 4421 A4
2400 AARB 48104 4489 E2
3400 WIND N9E 4504 C1
Victoria Cir
2100 AATp 48103 4405 E3
Victoria Ct
500 WasC 48176 4658 D2
16600 NvlT 48167 4264 A3
N Victoria Ct
- FNHL 48336 4196 B4
S Victoria Ct
- FNHL 48336 4196 B4
Victoria St
10 RVRG 48218 4418 E6
2000 DET 48212 4273 A2
2500 AARB 48104 4489 E3
5800 VNBN 48111 4493 C2
45500 WynC 48111 4663 D6
Victoria St N
10 Amhg N9V 4757 C1
Victoria St S
10 Amhg N9V 4757 C3
Victorian Blvd
- CNTN 48188 4411 B7
Victorian Ct
300 BLVL 48111 4578 E3
Victorian Ln
200 BLVL 48111 4578 E3
Victorian Sq E
4700 CNTN 48188 4411 B7
Victorian Sq N
47000 CNTN 48188 4411 B7
Victorian Sq S
47000 CNTN 48188 4411 B7
Victorian Sq W
4700 CNTN 48188 4411 B7
Victoria Park Dr N
13000 DET 48214 4347 D1
Victoria Park Dr S
13100 DET 48214 4347 D1
Victoria Park Dr W
500 DET 48214 4347 D1
Victor Lewis St
9400 WasC 48167 4262 D2
Victors Wy
700 AARB 48108 4489 C5
Victory Av
7000 WRRN 48091 4202 A3
Victory St
100 LSal N9J 4586 D1
28700 FNHL 48336 4195 E4
Viewpoint Ct
- NvlT 48167 4193 B6
Viking Blvd
20700 HZLP 48030 4200 C2
Viking Ct
10500 GOTp 48178 4187 C2
Viking Ln
9500 GOTp 48178 4187 D2
Villa
35300 BwTp 48173 4841 D3
Villa Dr
400 YpTp 48198 4491 E2
Villa Ln
100 STCS 48080 4204 E2
Villa Borghese Ct
2500 WIND N9G 4504 A4
Villa Borghese Dr
3800 WIND N9G 4504 A3
Villa France Av
- WasC 48103 4404 B6
Village Cir N
3000 PTFD 48108 4490 C4
Village Cir S
3000 PTFD 48108 4490 C4
Village Ct
14200 PyTp 48170 4265 B6
22000 WDHN 48183 4668 C7
44200 CNTN 48187 4336 E5
Village Dr
22100 WDHN 48183 4668 C7
Village Ln
10 GSPT 48230 4276 B6
1400 YpTp 48198 4492 D6
13800 RVVW 48192 4584 D6
W Village Ln
10 DRBN 48124 4416 C3
Village Rd
- DRBN 48120 4417 A3
1100 DRBN 48124 4416 E3
1100 DRBN 48124 4417 A3
5000 WasC 48176 4572 C2
Village Green Blvd
200 AATp 48105 4407 E6
1800 AARB 48105 4406 E3
13400 SOGT 48195 4584 B2
Village Green Blvd E
41000 CNTN 48187 4412 C2
Village Green Blvd W
41400 CNTN 48187 4412 B2
Village Green Ct
20000 BwTp 48183 4754 C2
20000 BwTp 48183 4755 A3
Village Green Dr
- RDFD 48240 4268 D1
Village Green Ln
46000 VNBN 48111 4578 C1
Village Grove Dr
300 Tcmh N8N 4424 B1
Village Lake St
41100 NOVI 48375 4193 B3
Village Oaks
40300 NOVI 48375 4193 C2
Village Oaks Ct
400 AARB 48103 4489 A3
Village Park Dr
13200 SOGT 48195 4584 B2
Villager
- RMLS 48174 4496 A4
Village Run Dr
39800 NvlT 48167 4265 C2
Village Square Dr
13500 SOGT 48195 4584 B1
Village Wood Ln
39600 NOVI 48375 4193 D3
Village Woode Cir
39700 NOVI 48375 4193 D2
Village Woode Rd
39400 NOVI 48375 4193 C2
Villaire Av
200 WIND N8S 4347 B6
1100 WIND N8S 4422 D1
Villa Maria Blvd N
1500 WIND N9G 4504 B3
Villa Maria Blvd S
1300 WIND N9G 4504 B4
Villa Paradiso Cres
4400 WIND N9G 4504 C4
Vimy Av
600 WIND N8X 4421 C4
2800 WIND N8W 4421 E3
Vince Dr
7900 WIND N8R 4423 A2
Vincennes Pl
200 GSPF 48236 4276 D2
Vincent Av
37000 WTLD 48186 4413 B5
Vincent St
- WTLD 48186 4413 B4
100 INKR 48141 4415 C2
5800 HMTK 48211 4273 D4
8800 DET 48211 4273 D4
8800 HMTK 48212 4273 D4
Vine Av
8200 ALPK 48101 4500 C4
Vine Ct
2600 WIND N8T 4422 E2
14600 ALPK 48101 4500 C4
Vine St
1300 YPLT 48197 4491 D6
Vineway Dr
1800 CNTN 48188 4411 E6
1800 CNTN 48188 4412 A5
Vinewood Av
1200 WYDT 48192 4585 A2
2200 WYDT 48192 4584 E2
2300 WYDT 48195 4584 E2
Vinewood Blvd
1800 AARB 48104 4406 E7
22000 TYLR 48180 4583 C2
Vinewood Ct
300 YPLT 48198 4492 B4
Vinewood Dr
- VNBN 48111 4494 E5
Vinewood Ln
29200 GBTR 48173 4755 A4
Vinewood Rd
29100 HnTp 48134 4753 A4
Vinewood St
100 DET 48216 4419 E1
1700 DET 48216 4344 D7
3300 DET 48210 4344 C5
35200 RMLS 48174 4496 D2
S Vinewood St
100 DET 48216 4419 E2
Vineyard Av
6000 PTFD 48108 4572 E4
6000 PTFD 48176 4572 E4
Vineyard St
17600 BNTN 48192 4583 C6
Vining Rd
- RMLS 48174 4497 A5
- RMLS 48242 4496 E7
- RMLS 48242 4497 A5
- RMLS 48242 4580 E1
16000 RMLS 48174 4581 A5
17000 HnTp 48174 4581 A7
18000 HnTp 48164 4581 A7
18000 HnTp 48164 4666 A1
18000 HnTp 48174 4666 A1
Vintage Dr
7000 WasC 48105 4258 D6
7000 WasC 48189 4258 D6
Vintage Valley Rd
3400 AARB 48105 4407 B4
Vinton St
9100 DET 48213 4274 C4
Violet Ln
45500 NOVI 48374 4192 C3
Violet St
22400 FMTN 48336 4195 B2
36500 HnTp 48164 4665 C1
Violetlawn St
10000 DET 48204 4343 B1
Virgil
8800 RDFD 48127 4341 A2
9600 RDFD 48239 4341 A1
11600 RDFD 48239 4269 A7
Virgil St
7900 DBHT 48127 4341 A3
12600 DET 48223 4269 A6
Virginia
700 WynC 48111 4662 D3
Virginia Av
10 Amhg N9V 4757 D2
100 AARB 48103 4405 E6
800 WIND N8S 4347 D6
1300 WIND N8S 4422 D1
21700 EPTE 48021 4203 C2
23800 WRRN 48091 4201 A1
Virginia Ct
300 CNTN 48187 4412 C2
3700 ECRS 48229 4501 D2
Virginia Ln
8000 WasC 48167 4262 B4
20700 GSPW 48236 4204 E5
Virginia Pk
2700 WIND N9E 4421 A7
3000 WIND N9E 4504 B1
Virginia Pl
700 YPLT 48198 4492 B3
Virginia St
500 PLYM 48170 4337 A1
2300 WYDT 48192 4585 C2
8900 LVNA 48150 4339 A2
20000 TYLR 48180 4583 E5
20000 TYLR 48195 4583 E5
Virginia Park St
10 DET 48202 4273 A7
1100 DET 48202 4272 E7
1200 DET 48206 4272 E7
2600 DET 48206 4344 B2
4000 DET 48204 4344 B2
Virnankay Cir
1800 AARB 48103 4405 E7
Visger Rd
10 ECRS 48229 4501 D2
100 RVRG 48218 4501 D2
Visger St
11800 DET 48229 4501 B1
Vista Av
- DET 48207 4347 A5
400 LSal N9J 4586 D5
Vista Ct
8500 WTLD 48185 4338 B3
Vista Dr
- LVNA 48152 4194 A6
6000 YpTp 48197 4575 C3
37100 WTLD 48185 4338 B3
Vista Dr N
38100 LVNA 48152 4193 E5
38100 LVNA 48152 4194 A5
Vista Dr S
38100 LVNA 48152 4193 E6
38100 LVNA 48152 4194 A6
Vista Ln
22000 NOVI 48167 4192 E4
Vista Pl
100 WIND N9B 4420 A2
Vistas Blvd
1300 CNTN 48188 4411 A4
Vistas Ct
47900 CNTN 48188 4411 A4
Vistas Cir Dr N
47400 CNTN 48188 4411 A4
Vistas Cir Dr S
47600 CNTN 48188 4411 A4
Vivian St
3900 DBHT 48125 4415 E6
7100 TYLR 48180 4498 E3
15000 TYLR 48180 4582 E4
Viviparous Wy
1000 AARB 48103 4405 D7
Vixen Ct
6000 CNTN 48187 4336 A7
Voight
- RVVW 48192 4584 D6
Voight St
14900 DET 48224 4275 D4
Voigt Av
8300 WynC 48138 4585 C7
Vollans St
1500 LSal N9H 4504 B5
Voltaire Pl
200 GSPF 48236 4276 D2
Volte St
9900 DET 48227 4342 E1
Vorhies Rd
3500 SpTp 48105 4333 C5
3500 SpTp 48198 4333 C5
5000 WasC 48105 4333 C2
5000 WasC 48170 4333 C2
Voss St
1500 DET 48209 4419 A5
Votrobeck Ct
20000 DET 48219 4197 D6
Votrobeck Dr
19100 DET 48219 4197 D6
Vought St
600 YPLT 48198 4492 B3
Vreeland Rd
2200 GBTR 48173 4755 B1
2200 TNTN 48183 4755 B1
3900 GBTR 48183 4755 B1
3900 TNTN 48173 4755 B1
5500 SpTp 48105 4408 B5
5800 SpTp 48198 4408 D5
8000 SpTp 48198 4409 C4
9000 SpTp 48198 4410 A4
16000 BwTp 48183 4755 A1
16000 WDHN 48183 4755 A1
19400 BwTp 48183 4754 C2
Vreeland Rd
19400 WDHN 48183 4754 C2
22000 FTRK 48183 4754 C2
22400 FTRK 48134 4754 C2
24800 FTRK 48134 4753 E2
24800 FTRK 48183 4753 E2
Vreeland St
12500 RVVW 48192 4584 D6
12500 RVVW 48192 4585 A6
Vulcan St
2000 DET 48211 4273 C6

W

Wabash St
2500 DET 48216 4345 A6
3300 DET 48210 4345 A5
5400 DET 48210 4344 D2
15700 DET 48238 4272 A2
36800 RMLS 48174 4580 B2
38400 RMLS 48174 4579 E2
39500 VNBN 48174 4579 E2
E Wabash St
10 BLVL 48111 4578 D3
N Wabash St
2600 MVDL 48122 4418 A6
S Wabash St
2300 MVDL 48122 4418 A7
W Wabash St
10 BLVL 48111 4578 D3
Wabeek Ct
43600 NvlT 48167 4264 E3
Wabeek Ln
43600 NvlT 48167 4264 E3
Wachna Dr
3100 WIND N8T 4422 D4
Waco Dr
13100 LVNA 48150 4266 A6
Waddington Rd
46500 CNTN 48187 4336 A6
Wade Rd
38400 RMLS 48174 4580 A3
39000 RMLS 48174 4579 E3
Wade St
11200 DET 48213 4274 E4
12200 DET 48213 4275 A3
14400 DET 48224 4275 C2
Wade Bridge Ct
47900 CNTN 48187 4336 A5
Wade Bridge Dr
7200 CNTN 48187 4336 A5
Wadsworth
23200 DET 48239 4269 B7
23200 RDFD 48239 4269 A7
26600 RDFD 48239 4268 B7
Wadsworth St
- LVNA 48150 4268 A7
- LVNA 48239 4268 A7
10300 DET 48204 4271 A7
12900 DET 48227 4271 A7
13600 DET 48227 4270 E7
18600 DET 48223 4270 A7
18600 DET 48228 4270 A7
20500 DET 48228 4269 D7
34800 LVNA 48150 4338 D1
Wagar Ct
23400 BNTN 48183 4668 B5
Wager St
3400 DET 48206 4272 B7
3400 DET 48206 4344 B1
27100 FTRK 48134 4753 D2
Wagner Av
23000 WRRN 48089 4202 D1
Wagner Ct
500 DRBN 48124 4416 C2
2700 WasC 48103 4405 B1
N Wagner Rd
100 WasC 48103 4405 B3
S Wagner Rd
100 WasC 48103 4405 B6
400 AARB 48103 4405 B6
800 WasC 48103 4488 B6
4000 WasC 48108 4488 B6
Wagner St
6300 DET 48210 4344 A4
6400 DET 48210 4343 E5
Wagner Ridge Ct
3500 WasC 48103 4405 A3
Wagner Woods Ct
3400 WasC 48103 4405 B3
Wagoneer Ct
5500 WasC 48103 4487 C1
Wagon Wheel Dr
5700 WasC 48176 4572 B2
Wagonwheel Dr
23000 BNTN 48183 4668 B2
Wagon Wheel Rd
1300 CNTN 48188 4412 B3
Wahketa St
300 WIND N8X 4420 E4
Wahl St
24000 WRRN 48089 4202 E1
Wahneta St
10 LSal N9J 4502 C6
Wahrman Rd
15000 RMLS 48174 4580 D6
17000 HnTp 48164 4580 D7
17000 HnTp 48174 4580 D7
18400 HnTp 48164 4665 D2
Wahrman St
8200 RMLS 48174 4496 D4
11200 RMLS 48174 4580 D1
Wakedon St
20700 SFLD 48034 4196 C4
Wakefield Av
1400 AARB 48103 4405 E7
Wakefield Ct
2900 CNTN 48188 4411 B6
38600 FNHL 48167 4193 E3
Wakefield Dr
2800 CNTN 48188 4411 B5
Wakefield St
20100 DET 48221 4199 D5
Wakenden
15300 RDFD 48239 4268 C3
16600 RDFD 48240 4268 C2
19700 RDFD 48240 4196 C5
Wakerobin Ct
1600 WasC 48103 4488 C1
Walbridge St
8000 DET 48213 4274 B5
Walden Blvd
9300 VNBN 48111 4494 E5
Walden Ct
23700 SFLD 48034 4196 E1
23700 SFLD 48034 4197 B1
Walden Dr
4200 SpTp 48105 4333 E5
E Walden Dr
9200 VNBN 48111 4494 E5
W Walden Dr
8600 VNBN 48111 4494 E5
Walden Ln
500 SLYN 48178 4189 C3
Walden Rd E
24600 SFLD 48034 4197 A1
Walden Rd W
24600 SFLD 48034 4196 E1
Walden St
8000 DET 48213 4274 A5
Waldenhill Ct
5400 SpTp 48198 4408 B2
Waldenwood Dr
3700 AARB 48105 4407 C5
Walden Woods
24400 FNHL 48335 4194 B1
Waldo St
6800 DET 48210 4344 A7
7100 DET 48210 4343 E7
Waldron St
21100 FNHL 48336 4195 E4
Wales Av
6100 LSal N9J 4502 E4
Wales Ct
6200 LSal N9J 4502 E4
Wales St
39600 CNTN 48188 4412 D3
Walker Ct
39700 NvlT 48167 4265 C2
Walker Rd
- WIND N8W 4422 A6
200 WIND N8Y 4346 C7
900 WIND N8Y 4421 D2
1300 WIND N8W 4421 D2
3600 WIND N8W 4505 B1
4700 WIND N9G 4505 C3
4900 Tcmh N0R 4505 B4
Walker Run
7100 WasC 48167 4261 E1
7100 WasC 48178 4261 E1
Walker St
100 DET 48207 4346 B5
4600 WYNE 48184 4413 C7
Wall Av
3500 ALPK 48101 4417 E7
3600 ALPK 48101 4500 D1
Wall St
900 AARB 48104 4406 C5
900 AARB 48105 4406 C5
3200 CNTN 48188 4411 A6
17800 MVDL 48122 4418 A6
18800 MVDL 48122 4417 E7
Wallace
- TNTN 48183 4669 E2
Wallace Av
500 WIND N9G 4504 E3
900 WIND N9G 4505 A3
35000 WTLD 48186 4413 D4
N Wallace Blvd
10 YPLT 48197 4491 D4
S Wallace Blvd
10 YPLT 48197 4491 D5
10 YpTp 48197 4491 D5
Wallace Ct
34400 LVNA 48150 4338 E2
Wallace Dr
100 SALN 48176 4572 C6
21200 SFLD 48075 4197 B3
26500 FTRK 48134 4753 C1
Wallace St
8300 DET 48213 4274 A5
32900 WTLD 48186 4414 A4
Wall Gene Rd
9000 WasC 48178 4189 A7
Wallingford Ct S
47400 CNTN 48188 4411 B4
Wallingford Rd
2100 AARB 48104 4489 E1
Wallingford St
- DET 48224 4276 A4
Wallis St
- NHVL 48167 4192 E6
Walnut
- CNTN 48188 4411 D6
Walnut Av
1100 YpTp 48198 4492 C3
Walnut Cr
- FTRK 48134 4754 A4
Walnut Ct
4600 PTFD 48197 4574 E2
Walnut Dr
300 SLYN 48178 4189 B1
400 Amhg N9V 4757 C4
9000 WasC 48189 4259 B1
Walnut Rd
2500 WasC 48103 4405 C2
Walnut Rdg
11200 PyTp 48170 4336 A2
12700 GOTp 48178 4188 C1

Detroit & Wayne County Street Index

STREET
Block City ZIP Map# Grid

Walnut St
- HnTp 48134 4752 E3
10 RVRG 48218 4501 E1
10 WYDT 48192 4585 C2
10 WynC 48111 4578 B7
100 NHVL 48167 4192 D5
100 TNTN 48183 4669 E5
100 TNTN 48183 4670 A5
500 AARB 48104 4406 D7
600 WTLD 48186 4414 C7
1000 DRBN 48124 4417 B5
2100 WYDT 48192 4584 E2
2100 WYDT 48195 4584 E2
2900 INKR 48141 4415 A5
14500 SOGT 48195 4584 C2
19200 SOGT 48195 4583 D2
25800 TYLR 48180 4582 D2
29000 FTRK 48134 4753 E4
38000 RMLS 48174 4580 A3
Walnut Hall
5600 SpTp 48105 4408 B4
Walnut Ridge Cir
1400 CNTN 48187 4412 B1
Walnut Ridge Ct
44900 NvIT 48167 4264 D3
Walnut Ridge Dr
2700 WasC 48103 4405 C3
Walnut Woods Dr
4900 AATp 48105 4333 A5
Walsingham Dr
22400 FNHL 48335 4194 B3
Walter Dr
2200 AARB 48103 4405 D5
24400 BNTN 48134 4668 A6
Walter St
10 BrTp 48134 4753 C6
16400 SOGT 48195 4584 B5
Walters Wy
2700 WasC 48103 4329 E7
2700 WasC 48103 4330 A7
2700 WasC 48103 4405 A1
Waltham Dr
1500 AARB 48103 4488 D2
Waltham Rd
20600 WRRN 48089 4202 D3
Waltham St
12100 DET 48205 4274 E1
12600 DET 48205 4202 D7
Walton Blvd
8600 CNTN 48187 4337 D3
Walton St
6300 DET 48210 4343 E4
N Walton St
100 WTLD 48185 4413 C2
1700 WTLD 48185 4338 C7
S Walton St
1400 WTLD 48186 4413 C4
Waltz Av
1900 WRRN 48091 4200 E2
2200 WRRN 48091 4201 A2
Waltz Rd
19300 HnTp 48164 4665 B2
19300 HnTp 48174 4665 B2
25400 HnTp 48164 4751 C3
Walwit St
4500 DRBN 48126 4417 D1
4700 DRBN 48126 4342 D7
Wanamaker Pl
22400 DET 48223 4269 B4
Wanda St
400 FRDL 48220 4200 B3
17100 DET 48203 4272 D1
17700 DET 48203 4200 D7
Wapiti Wy
6900 PTFD 48176 4573 B5
Warbler
- PTFD 48197 4574 E2
Warbler Wy
300 PTFD 48197 4574 D2
Ward Av
3200 TNTN 48183 4669 B5
Ward Ct
2900 AARB 48108 4489 E4
Ward St
8000 DET 48228 4343 A3
9500 DET 48227 4343 A2
12800 SOGT 48195 4584 D1
13000 DET 48227 4271 A5
17100 DET 48235 4271 A1
19400 DET 48235 4199 A5
24300 TYLR 48180 4498 E3
24300 TYLR 48180 4499 A3
24800 DRBN 48124 4415 E2
Ware Ct
1000 YpTp 48198 4492 E2
Wareham
46800 CNTN 48187 4411 B1
Warfield St
8000 CNTN 48187 4336 E4
S Waring St
- LNPK 48229 4501 B1
400 DET 48229 4418 C5
2900 DET 48229 4501 B1
Warner Av
20700 WRRN 48091 4201 A3
Warner Ct
- LVNA 48150 4267 C6
14000 LVNA 48154 4267 C6
Warner Pl
200 WasC 48176 4658 E2
2400 AARB 48104 4489 D3
Warner Rd
10 GSPF 48236 4276 D5
6500 PTFD 48176 4573 E4
8000 WasC 48176 4573 E6
8000 WasC 48176 4658 E5
10000 WasC 48160 4658 E5
Warner St
1200 YpTp 48197 4491 D5
9300 DET 48214 4274 D7
22800 FMTN 48336 4194 E2
23600 FMTN 48336 4195 A2
W Warner St
10 YPLT 48197 4491 D5
10 YpTp 48197 4491 D5
Warner Creek Dr
1200 PTFD 48176 4574 B4
Warner Farms Dr
38000 WTLD 48185 4338 A7
W Warren Av
8100 DRBN 48126 4343 A4
13700 DRBN 48126 4342 D4
Warren Av E
10 DET 48201 4345 C2
10 DET 48202 4345 C2
900 DET 48207 4345 C2
900 DET 48211 4345 C2
3500 DET 48207 4346 A1
3500 DET 48211 4346 A1
6600 DET 48207 4274 A7
6600 DET 48211 4274 A7
7200 DET 48213 4274 C7
7200 DET 48214 4274 C7
11400 DET 48213 4275 A5
11400 DET 48214 4275 A5
14300 DET 48224 4275 B4
16800 DET 48224 4276 A3
18400 DET 48236 4276 A3
18500 GSPF 48236 4276 A3
Warren Av W
10 DET 48201 4345 A3
10 DET 48202 4345 A3
1400 DET 48210 4345 A3
1700 DET 48210 4344 C4
5900 DET 48210 4343 D4
8000 DET 48126 4343 D4
13600 DRBN 48126 4343 D4
15500 DET 48126 4342 C4
15500 DET 48228 4342 C4
19100 DET 48228 4341 C4
20200 DBHT 48127 4341 C4
20200 DBHT 48228 4341 C4
20500 DET 48127 4341 C4
20600 DET 48239 4341 C4
Warren Ct
3800 AATp 48105 4331 C6
Warren Dr
25200 BNTN 48134 4667 E5
Warren Rd
100 AATp 48105 4331 C6
1600 AATp 48105 4332 B6
4000 AATp 48105 4333 A6
5000 SpTp 48105 4333 A6
7100 SpTp 48105 4334 A5
8700 SpTp 48170 4334 D5
8700 SpTp 48170 4335 A5
8700 SpTp 48198 4334 D5
8700 SpTp 48198 4335 A5
27400 GDNC 48135 4340 A5
27400 GDNC 48185 4340 A5
27400 WTLD 48185 4340 A5
27500 WTLD 48135 4340 A5
28600 GDNC 48135 4339 D5
28600 WTLD 48135 4339 D5
28600 WTLD 48185 4339 D5
29600 GDNC 48185 4339 D5
33600 WTLD 48185 4338 C5
38400 WTLD 48185 4337 D6
39400 CNTN 48187 4337 D6
43600 CNTN 48187 4336 D5
48600 CNTN 48187 4335 E5
50800 CNTN 48170 4335 C5
N Warren St
100 SLYN 48178 4189 B2
S Warren St
100 SLYN 48178 4189 B3
W Warren St
24000 DBHT 48127 4341 A5
24400 DBHT 48127 4340 D5
Warren St W
23700 DBHT 48127 4341 A5
Warrendale Dr
- DBHT 48127 4341 A4
Warrington Cir
1400 AATp 48103 4405 E2
Warrington Ct
24200 NOVI 48374 4192 A1
Warrington Dr
1100 AATp 48103 4405 E2
1200 AATp 48103 4406 A2
1300 AARB 48103 4406 A1
17100 DET 48221 4271 D1
19100 DET 48221 4199 D4
47600 NOVI 48374 4192 A1
Warrington St
25800 DBHT 48127 4340 C6
Warsaw Pl
1900 DET 48207 4345 D2
Warwick Av
1300 LNPK 48146 4501 E4
1700 LNPK 48146 4500 D2
14500 ALPK 48101 4500 C1
Warwick Cir
48500 CNTN 48187 4336 A4
Warwick Ct
10 DRBN 48124 4415 E5
1500 AARB 48103 4488 D2
16900 NvIT 48167 4263 D3
Warwick Rd
200 Tcmh N8N 4424 D1
3000 AARB 48104 4490 B2
Warwick St
5600 DET 48228 4342 A6
5600 DRBN 48228 4342 A6
6700 DET 48228 4341 E3
15800 DET 48223 4269 E2
17100 DET 48219 4269 E1
19300 DET 48219 4197 E6
Washburn St
- CNTN 48188 4412 A7
11600 DET 48204 4271 B6
15700 DET 48238 4271 B3
16100 DET 48221 4271 B1
18000 DET 48221 4199 B7
Washington
100 WynC 48111 4662 D2
6200 VNBN 48111 4577 C3
Washington Av
2000 LNPK 48146 4501 A4
Washington Blvd
10 DET 48226 4345 D6
2000 LSal N9H 4503 C4
Washington Cir
1100 NHVL 48167 4192 A5
Washington Dr
13900 PyTp 48170 4263 D6
21600 BNTN 48192 4583 D6
Washington Hts
1500 AARB 48104 4406 D6
Washington Rd
200 GSPT 48230 4276 C5
900 DET 48224 4276 C3
900 DET 48230 4276 C3
Washington St
10 TNTN 48183 4585 A7
10 TNTN 48192 4585 A7
100 SALN 48176 4657 B2
100 SLYN 48178 4189 B2
100 TNTN 48183 4670 A1
1000 DRBN 48124 4416 B3
3700 INKR 48141 4415 B6
4900 WYNE 48184 4413 D7
7100 RMLS 48174 4496 D3
7300 HbgT 48189 4186 B3
12500 SRKW 48179 4840 C2
21700 RKWD 48173 4754 D7
32000 LVNA 48150 4339 A3
E Washington St
100 AARB 48104 4406 B6
N Washington St
10 YPLT 48197 4492 A4
S Washington St
10 YPLT 48197 4492 A5
W Washington St
100 AARB 48104 4406 A6
300 AARB 48103 4406 A6
1400 AARB 48103 4405 E6
Washington Wy
43100 CNTN 48187 4337 A5
Washtenaw Av
- PTFD 48104 4490 A2
100 YPLT 48197 4492 A4
300 YPLT 48197 4491 E4
400 AARB 48104 4406 D7
1700 YpTp 48197 4491 C3
1900 AARB 48104 4489 E1
2100 AARB 48104 4490 A2
2700 YpTp 48108 4491 C3
4000 PTFD 48105 4490 E3
4000 PTFD 48108 4490 E3
4300 PTFD 48197 4490 E3
4700 PTFD 48108 4491 C3
4700 PTFD 48197 4491 C3
Washtenaw Av I-94 BUS
- PTFD 48104 4490 A2
- PTFD 48105 4490 A2
- PTFD 48108 4490 A2
400 AARB 48104 4406 D7
1900 AARB 48104 4489 E1
2100 AARB 48104 4490 A2
Washtenaw Av SR-17
400 YPLT 48197 4491 C3
1700 YpTp 48197 4491 C3
2700 YpTp 48108 4491 C3
4000 PTFD 48105 4490 E3
4000 PTFD 48108 4490 E3
4300 PTFD 48197 4490 E3
4700 PTFD 48108 4491 C3
4700 PTFD 48197 4491 C3
Washtenaw Av US-23 BUS
- PTFD 48104 4490 A2
- PTFD 48105 4490 A2
- PTFD 48108 4490 A2
400 AARB 48104 4406 D7
1900 AARB 48104 4489 E1
2100 AARB 48104 4490 A2
Washtenaw Ct
1200 AARB 48104 4406 C6
Washtenaw St
18500 HRWD 48225 4203 D6
20200 HRWD 48225 4204 A7
Wasmund Av
2900 WRRN 48091 4201 B4
Wassanova Rd
11000 BrTp 48179 4841 A4
Water St
10 YPLT 48198 4492 A4
4700 WIND N9C 4419 D7
Waterbury Ct
100 WTLD 48186 4414 B2
400 BLVL 48111 4578 E3
Waterbury Wy
26000 WynC 48138 4670 B7
Watercrest Ct
23800 FNHL 48336 4195 C1
Waterfall Rd
41400 NvIT 48167 4265 B2
Waterfield Ct
5400 PTFD 48108 4573 A2
Waterford
- TYLR 48180 4582 D5
Waterford Av
2300 WIND N8P 4423 D1
Waterford Rd
42400 NvIT 48167 4265 A2
Waterland Dr
22200 NOVI 48167 4191 B4
Waterlily Dr
200 WasC 48189 4259 B1
Waterloo St
2200 DET 48207 4345 E4
2200 DET 48207 4346 A4
17000 GSPT 48230 4276 C4
Waterman Dr
600 WasC 48103 4405 A4
9100 WynC 48138 4670 B6
Waterman St
800 DET 48209 4419 B2
S Waterman St
100 DET 48209 4419 C3
Watermill Ln
3300 MonC 48117 4753 A7
W Waters Rd
1500 PTFD 48103 4488 E4
2400 WasC 48103 4488 A4
2700 PTFD 48108 4488 E4
2700 PTFD 48108 4489 A4
3700 WasC 48103 4487 E4
Watersedge Ct
600 AARB 48105 4407 C6
Watersedge Dr
600 AARB 48105 4407 B5
Watershed Ct
700 AARB 48105 4407 C5
Watershed Dr
700 AARB 48105 4407 C5
700 AATp 48105 4407 C5
Watershed Rd
700 AARB 48105 4407 C5
Water Side Ct
1600 PTFD 48108 4573 A2
Waterside Rd
- CNTN 48187 4411 C1
Waterstone Ct
50300 PyTp 48170 4263 C7
Waterview Ct
400 CNTN 48188 4411 A3
5400 PTFD 48108 4573 A2
Waterview Dr
23000 HnTp 48164 4666 E5
Waterview Rd
19500 WynC 48138 4670 D1
Waterway Dr
9500 WynC 48138 4670 B6
Waterways Dr
- PTFD 48108 4573 A2
Waterwheel Ct N
42000 NvIT 48167 4265 B1
Waterwheel Ct W
42300 NvIT 48167 4265 A1
Waterwheel Rd
41900 NvIT 48167 4265 B2
Watkins St
200 WIND N9C 4419 E4
400 WIND N9C 4420 A4
Watko St
3800 DET 48212 4201 B7
Watling St
800 YPLT 48197 4491 E6
Watson Av
200 WIND N8S 4347 D5
1100 YpTp 48198 4493 A6
4600 ALPK 48101 4417 A7
5600 ALPK 48101 4500 A1
Watson Cir
- WTLD 48186 4413 A5
Watson Rd
800 SALN 48176 4572 D6
Watson St
10 DET 48201 4345 C4
1300 DET 48207 4345 D4
Watsonia St
22000 DRBN 48128 4341 B7
Watt Dr
22500 FNHL 48336 4195 E2
Waveney St
12500 DET 48214 4275 C5
15300 DET 48224 4275 D4
16500 DET 48224 4276 A4
Waverly Dr
1500 TNTN 48183 4669 C2
1500 TNTN 48192 4669 C2
11300 PyTp 48170 4337 B1
Waverly Dr E
11200 PyTp 48170 4337 B2
Waverly Ln
10 GSPF 48236 4276 E2
Waverly Pl
4000 AATp 48105 4407 D2
Waverly Rd
1700 AARB 48103 4488 E2
Waverly St
300 HDPK 48203 4272 C4
1000 WIND N8X 4421 D6
2900 DET 48238 4272 A5
3200 DET 48238 4271 E5
15700 SOGT 48195 4584 A2
N Waverly St
100 DRBN 48128 4416 A1
1700 DRBN 48128 4341 A7
5600 DBHT 48127 4341 A5
S Waverly St
100 DRBN 48124 4416 A2
100 DRBN 48128 4416 A2
Wayburn St
1000 DET 48214 4275 D6
1000 DET 48230 4275 D6
1000 GPPK 48230 4275 D6
1400 GPPK 48214 4275 D6
11000 DET 48224 4275 D6
11400 DET 48224 4203 D7
Waycroft Dr
22600 NOVI 48375 4192 C3
Waycross
25000 SFLD 48034 4196 C1
Waycross Ct
24900 SFLD 48034 4196 B1
Wayland Ct
4100 INKR 48141 4414 E6
Waymarket Dr
300 AARB 48103 4489 A4
Wayne Av
- NvIT 48167 4265 C1
Wayne Rd
- RMLS 48242 4580 D2
5800 RMLS 48174 4496 D2
8800 LVNA 48150 4338 D1
10800 RMLS 48242 4496 D4
11400 RMLS 48174 4580 D1
12700 LVNA 48150 4266 D6
15000 RMLS 48174 4581 A5
16100 LVNA 48154 4266 C2
17100 LVNA 48152 4266 C1
19800 LVNA 48152 4194 C6
N Wayne Rd
100 WTLD 48185 4413 D1
1700 WTLD 48185 4338 D5
S Wayne Rd
100 WTLD 48185 4413 D3
100 WTLD 48186 4413 D3
2500 WTLD 48184 4413 D7
2900 WYNE 48184 4413 D7
5200 WYNE 48184 4496 D1
Wayne St
1900 AARB 48104 4406 E7
5700 LSal N9H 4503 D3
N Wayne St
2900 LNPK 48146 4500 C5
Waynecourse St
6800 RMLS 48174 4496 C3
Waynesboro St
- WYNE 48184 4414 A6
Waynewood Ct
10 DRBN 48124 4417 B5
Wayside
- WTLD 48185 4413 C2
Wayside Dr
400 WynC 48111 4662 D6
2600 AATp 48105 4405 D2
41500 CNTN 48187 4412 C2
WCRC Northgate Rd
- WasC 48130 4404 B3
Wear Rd
39700 WynC 48111 4664 E7
39700 WynC 48164 4664 E7
43400 WynC 48111 4663 E7
49400 WynC 48111 4662 D7
Wear St
100 WIND N8X 4421 A4
Weatherfield Dr
15900 NvIT 48167 4265 C3
Weatherfield Wy
6500 CNTN 48187 4336 B6
Weatherhill Dr
1500 WasC 48130 4404 B2
Weatherstone Dr
1500 PTFD 48108 4489 A5
1600 PTFD 48108 4488 E5
Weathervane Ct
24200 NOVI 48374 4192 C1
Weaver Rd
600 WIND N9J 4502 D2
Weaver St
18100 DET 48227 4342 A1
18100 DET 48228 4342 A1
18600 DET 48228 4270 A7
18700 DET 48223 4270 A7
Webb Ct
39000 WTLD 48185 4337 E6
Webb Dr
38400 WTLD 48185 4338 A7
38700 WTLD 48185 4337 E6
Webb St
1100 DET 48202 4272 C5
1100 DET 48203 4272 C5
1400 DET 48206 4272 C5
4000 DET 48204 4272 A7
5100 DET 48204 4271 D7
Webber Av
20700 EPTE 48021 4203 E3
Webber Dr
- EPTE 48225 4203 E4
- HRWD 48225 4203 E4
Webber Pl
10 GSPS 48236 4204 E7
10 GSPS 48236 4205 A7
Weber Rd
3500 WasC 48176 4572 A4
4300 WasC 48176 4571 D4
Webster Rd
100 GSPF 48236 4276 C2
44200 CNTN 48187 4336 E4
Webster St
2600 TNTN 48183 4669 C5
4400 ECRS 48229 4501 D5
23000 OKPK 48237 4199 A2
34900 WTLD 48185 4338 D5
E Webster St
100 FRDL 48220 4200 A4
W Webster St
100 FRDL 48220 4199 E4
100 FRDL 48220 4200 A4
Webster Church Rd
4900 WasC 48130 4329 E2
7700 WasC 48130 4258 A4
7700 WasC 48189 4258 A4
Weddel Av
27000 BwTp 48183 4754 E2
Weddel St
5800 TYLR 48125 4499 E1
5800 TYLR 48180 4499 E1
16000 TYLR 48180 4583 E4
Weddell St
3500 DRBN 48124 4416 E6
3900 DBHT 48124 4416 E6
3900 DBHT 48125 4416 E7
Wedgewood
29400 HnTp 48134 4753 A4
Wedgewood Cir
1200 PTFD 48176 4574 A4
Wedgewood Ct
3700 Tcmh N0R 4505 C6
19100 RVVW 48192 4584 D7
Wedgewood Dr
200 Tcmh N8N 4349 B7
1300 PTFD 48176 4574 B4
20600 GSPW 48236 4204 E5
21600 GSPW 48236 4205 A4
Wedgewood Rd
5600 CNTN 48187 4337 A7
19100 RVVW 48192 4584 D7
19100 RVVW 48192 4669 D1
Weeburn
3600 PTFD 48108 4490 C5
Weed Rd
6000 WasC 48170 4262 D7
S Weed Rd
5700 WasC 48170 4334 D1
Weeping Willow Dr
24900 BNTN 48134 4667 E4
Weigel Rd
26000 HnTp 48164 4751 C1
Weimer Dr
46600 WynC 48111 4663 C2
Weir St
- DET 48210 4343 C6
Weithoff Ct
2400 INKR 48141 4415 B4
Weitzel Ct
3600 DET 48211 4273 E7
3600 DET 48211 4274 A7
Welch Ct
2000 AARB 48103 4488 E2
Welch Rd
300 NHVL 48167 4192 D4
21600 NOVI 48167 4192 D4
Welch St
10000 DRBN 48120 4418 D3
Weldon Blvd
1700 AARB 48103 4488 D2
Weller Av
21700 WRRN 48089 4203 A2
Wellesley Av
2100 WIND N8W 4421 C4
Wellesley Blvd
- PTFD 48197 4574 C2
Wellesley Ct
47500 NOVI 48374 4192 A1
Wellesley Dr
10 PTRG 48069 4199 D1
1300 DET 48203 4200 A6
Wellesley Ln
5600 PTFD 48197 4574 C2
Wellesley St
1400 INKR 48141 4414 E4
13800 DRBN 48126 4417 E1
20100 RVVW 48192 4669 D1
Wellington
8600 WasC 48167 4262 C4
Wellington Av
300 WIND N9A 4420 C2
1200 WIND N8X 4420 D3
21700 WRRN 48089 4203 A2
Wellington Ct
800 CNTN 48187 4411 C2
1000 AARB 48104 4406 D7
9500 YpTp 48197 4576 E6
10200 PyTp 48170 4336 A2
Wellington Dr
5300 DBHT 48125 4415 B7
5500 DBHT 48125 4498 B1
5500 DBHT 48180 4498 B1
9600 PyTp 48170 4336 B2
Wellington Ln
7000 YpTp 48197 4576 E5
Wellington Pl
10 GSPT 48230 4276 C7
Wellington St
100 SLYN 48178 4189 C1
1100 DET 48211 4273 B6
3000 INKR 48141 4415 B5
6000 TYLR 48180 4498 B1
15500 TYLR 48180 4582 C4
21000 WDHN 48183 4669 A2
22700 DRBN 48124 4416 B2
Wellington Cross Rd
3600 AARB 48105 4407 D5
Wells St
1100 AARB 48104 4489 C1
3400 WIND N9C 4420 A4
N Wells St
100 SLYN 48178 4189 B2
S Wells St
100 SLYN 48178 4189 B2
Wellsley
37300 FNHL 48335 4194 A4
Wellsley Ct
48800 NvIT 48167 4263 E2
Wellwood Ct
500 Tcmh N8N 4424 D2
Welsh Rd
4300 AATp 48105 4490 D1
Welton St
5500 DET 48204 4343 C1
Wembley Ct
600 AARB 48103 4489 A2
4700 WIND N9G 4504 D5
Wendell Av
900 YpTp 48198 4492 C2
Wendell Ct
7600 WynC 48138 4670 D3
Wendell St
2300 DET 48209 4418 E2
Wendingo Ct
43500 NOVI 48375 4192 E2
Wendover Ct
9300 GOTp 48116 4186 E1
12400 PyTp 48170 4263 C7
Wendover Dr
51000 PyTp 48170 4263 C7
Wendy Ct
1100 AARB 48103 4406 A4
18500 RVVW 48192 4584 E7
N Wendy Ct
18200 RVVW 48192 4584 E7
Wendy Ln
20700 GSPW 48236 4204 D5
23600 SFLD 48075 4198 B2
Wendy St
15300 TYLR 48180 4582 C4
Wentworth Ct
1800 CNTN 48188 4411 C5
Wentworth Dr
1600 CNTN 48188 4411 C4
9600 YpTp 48197 4577 A5
Wentworth St
1400 WIND N9C 4503 B1
28400 LVNA 48154 4267 E3
Werner Av
4900 WIND N9C 4503 B1
Wesboro Dr
46000 PyTp 48170 4264 C7
Wesford Ct
46300 PyTp 48170 4336 C1
Wesley Av
300 AARB 48103 4406 A5
N Wesley Av
28200 FTRK 48134 4753 D3
S Wesley Av
29000 FTRK 48134 4753 D4
Wesley Pl
34400 FMTN 48335 4194 D1
Wesley St
12700 SOGT 48195 4584 D1
23500 FMTN 48335 4194 D1
Wessex Ct
5400 DRBN 48126 4341 E7
Wesson St
5100 DET 48210 4344 A4
West Rd
- DRBN 48124 4416 E4
- DRBN 48126 4342 B7
- DRBN 48126 4417 B1
- RDFD 48240 4268 B2
10 TNTN 48183 4670 A4
600 TNTN 48183 4669 E4
16000 WDHN 48183 4669 A4
20000 WDHN 48183 4668 C5
22700 BNTN 48183 4668 C5
23800 BNTN 48134 4668 C5
25000 BNTN 48134 4667 E5
27400 HnTp 48134 4667 A5
27400 HnTp 48164 4667 A5
29400 HnTp 48164 4666 C5
West St
100 NHVL 48167 4192 D6
500 DET 48201 4345 D4
2200 INKR 48141 4415 B4
3600 WasC 48103 4329 E6
9400 WasC 48189 4187 A7
Westaire Ct
2200 AARB 48103 4405 D4
Westaire Wy
1000 AARB 48103 4405 D4
Westbourne Ct
300 CNTN 48188 4411 A3
Westbriar Ct
46200 PyTp 48170 4336 C3
Westbrook
100 WasC 48189 4259 A2
Westbrook Ct
15000 LVNA 48154 4266 C4
21600 GSPW 48236 4204 D4
Westbrook Dr
- LVNA 48154 4266 C1
4000 PTFD 48108 4488 E6
4000 PTFD 48108 4489 A6
18300 LVNA 48152 4194 C7
18300 LVNA 48152 4266 B1
Westbrook Rd
13500 PyTp 48170 4264 C6
Westbrook St
13900 DET 48223 4269 C4
15500 LVNA 48154 4266 C3
17100 DET 48219 4269 C1
19100 DET 48219 4197 C6
Westbrooke Dr
700 SLYN 48178 4189 C4
Westbury Av
9100 PyTp 48170 4337 D2
Westbury Ct
10 AARB 48105 4407 A1
Westbury Dr
23100 STCS 48080 4204 E3
23200 STCS 48080 4205 A3
Westchester Ct
43000 NOVI 48375 4193 A5
Westchester Dr
500 WIND N8S 4348 A6
18200 LVNA 48152 4266 B1
Westchester Ln
8200 CNTN 48187 4336 E3
23200 BNTN 48174 4583 B6
38700 FNHL 48167 4193 E4
Westchester Rd
600 GPPK 48230 4348 A1
700 GPPK 48230 4276 A7
Westchester St
1300 WTLD 48186 4414 D4
Westcott Ct
13800 SOGT 48195 4584 A2
Westcott Dr
13500 SOGT 48195 4584 A2
18200 WynC 48111 4578 C7
18200 WynC 48111 4663 C1

STREET Block City ZIP Map# Grid

Westcott Rd
1100 WIND N8Y 4346 E7
1200 WIND N8Y 4421 E1
1700 WIND N8Y 4422 A2
1800 WIND N8W 4422 A2
Westcott St
300 WTLD 48186 4412 E3
Westcroft Dr
21600 WynC 48138 4670 B3
Westend St
100 DET 48209 4419 B3
100 FRDL 48030 4200 B3
100 FRDL 48220 4200 B3
100 HZLP 48030 4200 B3
Westend St S
100 DET 48209 4419 B4
Western Dr
1000 AARB 48103 4405 D4
Western St
- DET 48210 4343 C6
400 INKR 48141 4414 D2
2800 DET 48209 4418 D2
6000 VNBN 48111 4493 E2
Western Golf Dr
25800 RDFD 48239 4268 C4
27400 LVNA 48154 4268 A5
Westfarm Ct
21100 FNHL 48167 4193 E5
Westfarm Ln
20900 FNHL 48167 4193 E5
Westfield
23700 RDFD 48239 4341 A2
25200 RDFD 48239 4340 D2
Westfield Av
1400 AARB 48103 4488 E1
2500 TNTN 48183 4669 C4
Westfield Cir
40900 CNTN 48188 4412 C3
Westfield Ct
800 CNTN 48188 4412 C3
3000 TNTN 48183 4669 C4
Westfield Rd
1500 TNTN 48183 4669 C4
1500 TNTN 48192 4669 C4
Westfield St
- DET 48228 4341 E2
- DET 48228 4342 E2
- DET 48228 4343 A2
8200 DET 48204 4343 C2
28600 LVNA 48150 4340 A2
28800 LVNA 48150 4339 E2
E Westfield St
10 ECRS 48229 4501 D4
W Westfield St
10 ECRS 48229 4501 D3
Westgate Ct
2300 CNTN 48188 4411 B5
Westgate Dr
4900 WasC 48103 4329 D5
14000 RDFD 48239 4268 E5
Westhampton Av
18100 SFLD 48075 4198 A4
20000 SFLD 48075 4197 C4
Westhampton Rd
17100 SFLD 48075 4198 B4
Westhampton St
23900 OKPK 48237 4198 E1
Westhaven Av
18100 SFLD 48075 4198 A4
20100 SFLD 48075 4197 C4
Westhill St
19700 NvlT 48167 4192 B6
30800 FNHL 48336 4195 B1
West Hills Dr
700 SLYN 48178 4189 A3
Westlake Cir
1000 VNBN 48111 4494 D6
Westlake Dr
12000 Tcmh N8N 4423 E3
12200 Tcmh N8N 4424 A3
Westlake St
3900 DBHT 48125 4415 E6
7100 TYLR 48180 4498 E3
14000 TYLR 48180 4582 E3
Westland Av
18100 SFLD 48075 4198 A4
Westland Ct
6200 WTLD 48185 4339 A6
Westland Dr
6200 WTLD 48185 4338 E6
20000 SFLD 48075 4197 D4
Westland Rd
26900 RDFD 48240 4268 B2
27200 RDFD 48152 4268 B2
Westland St
4400 DRBN 48126 4417 C1
4700 DRBN 48126 4342 C7
Westland Estates Dr
35100 WTLD 48185 4338 D5
Westlawn St
400 YpTp 48197 4491 B3
2100 DRBN 48120 4418 D3
Westloch Cir
3100 SpTp 48198 4408 B2
Westmeath Ct
42100 NvlT 48167 4265 B3
Westmeath Rd
42200 NvlT 48167 4265 B3
Westminister Ct
19300 DRBN 48124 4416 E5
Westminister Rd
13600 SOGT 48195 4584 B2
Westminister St
13100 SOGT 48195 4584 B2
Westminister Wy
43400 CNTN 48187 4337 A7
43600 CNTN 48187 4336 E7
Westminster Av
6700 WRRN 48091 4201 E3
7000 WRRN 48091 4202 A3

Westminster Av
8000 WRRN 48089 4202 A3
Westminster Blvd
800 WIND N8S 4347 A7
800 WIND N8Y 4347 A7
1400 WIND N8T 4422 B2
1400 WIND N8Y 4422 B2
Westminster Cir
39400 FNHL 48375 4193 D2
39400 NOVI 48375 4193 D2
Westminster Dr
16400 NvlT 48167 4263 C4
Westminster Pl
1500 AARB 48104 4489 C1
Westminster St
10 DET 48202 4272 E6
200 DET 48202 4273 A5
1100 DET 48211 4273 A5
21100 FNHL 48336 4195 D4
Westmont Ct
24100 NOVI 48374 4192 C2
Westmont Dr
23900 NOVI 48374 4192 C2
Westmoorland St
1100 YPLT 48197 4491 C4
1400 YpTp 48197 4491 C4
Westmore Ct
15900 LVNA 48154 4267 A3
Westmore St
9600 LVNA 48150 4339 A1
12700 LVNA 48150 4267 A6
15300 LVNA 48154 4267 A4
18200 LVNA 48152 4267 A1
20000 LVNA 48152 4195 A5
Westmoreland Dr
24300 FNHL 48336 4195 C1
Westmoreland Rd
16200 DET 48223 4269 E2
17100 DET 48219 4269 E1
20200 DET 48219 4197 E5
Weston Dr
- NOVI 48375 4192 E3
50700 PyTp 48170 4335 C1
Westover Av
10 WasC 48103 4405 B5
18100 SFLD 48075 4198 A4
20000 SFLD 48075 4197 D4
Westover Rd
17300 SFLD 48075 4198 A4
Westover St
10400 DET 48204 4343 B3
Westpark Ct
4300 PTFD 48108 4488 E7
Westphal Av
3400 TNTN 48183 4669 B6
Westphal Dr
26300 DBHT 48127 4415 C1
26300 DBHT 48141 4415 C1
Westphalia St
12300 DET 48205 4274 E1
18000 DET 48205 4202 D6
West Point St
2600 DRBN 48124 4416 A4
10000 DET 48204 4343 B2
15000 TYLR 48180 4583 A4
24500 BNTN 48183 4668 B6
Westpoint St
3900 DBHT 48125 4416 A7
5600 DBHT 48125 4499 B2
5600 DBHT 48180 4499 B2
9000 TYLR 48180 4499 A5
14000 TYLR 48180 4583 A3
Westpointe St
24000 BNTN 48134 4668 A6
24000 BNTN 48183 4668 A6
Westport Rd
1100 AARB 48103 4405 E4
Westridge Ct
2300 FRDL 48220 4199 C2
3300 WYNE 48184 4413 A6
Westridge Ln
43500 NOVI 48167 4192 E4
Westridge Rd
1700 AATp 48105 4330 D7
Westvale St
38400 RMLS 48174 4580 A3
West Valley Dr
- FNHL 48336 4195 C5
Westview Av
20700 ROTp 48220 4199 C3
Westview Dr
19900 NvlT 48167 4191 E6
Westview St
10 YPLT 48197 4491 C2
Westview Wy
1000 WasC 48103 4405 A7
1200 WasC 48103 4488 A1
Westwick Dr
4700 WYNE 48184 4414 B7
Westwind Dr
- LVNA 48150 4338 A2
Westwind Ln
10 GSPF 48236 4276 E4
Westwood Av
200 AARB 48103 4405 E4
Westwood Cir
37700 WTLD 48185 4338 A3
Westwood Dr
23000 BNTN 48183 4668 B5
23000 WDHN 48183 4668 B5
Westwood St
2100 DRBN 48124 4415 E4
5800 DET 48228 4341 E5
11600 DET 48228 4269 E7
12500 DET 48223 4269 E6
21000 WDHN 48183 4668 D5
Wetherby St
7200 DET 48210 4343 D4
8000 DET 48204 4343 D3

Wexford Av
10 BLVL 48111 4578 E2
Wexford Ct
3400 AARB 48108 4489 D4
10000 GOTp 48178 4188 E2
Wexford Dr
- SpTp 48198 4409 E7
- SpTp 48198 4410 A7
- TYLR 48180 4582 E5
Wexford St
17800 DET 48212 4201 B7
18000 DET 48234 4201 B7
33400 WTLD 48185 4339 A5
Weyher St
9300 DET 48214 4274 D7
19100 LVNA 48152 4195 E6
Weymouth Dr
37000 LVNA 48152 4266 B1
44800 CNTN 48188 4411 D4
Whalen St
2300 HMTK 48212 4273 B3
Wharton Av
500 YpTp 48198 4492 D5
Wheat Grass Ln
9500 VNBN 48111 4494 C6
Wheatley Dr
41300 NvlT 48167 4265 B2
Wheaton Dr
7500 CNTN 48187 4336 D4
44300 NvlT 48167 4264 D2
Wheaton Ln
21000 NOVI 48375 4193 A5
Wheeler Ct
200 SALN 48176 4572 C7
Wheeler St
7100 DET 48210 4343 D4
9800 VNBN 48111 4495 C6
21400 FNHL 48336 4195 D3
Wheelock St
800 DET 48209 4419 B2
Wheelton Dr
3400 WIND N8W 4422 B6
Whelan Dr
- Amhg N9V 4671 C5
Whelpton St
2600 WIND N8Y 4346 C7
Wherle Dr
19200 BNTN 48192 4669 A1
Whimbrel Ct
- PTFD 48197 4575 A6
E Whipple Dr
20100 NvlT 48167 4192 B6
W Whipple Dr
20100 NvlT 48167 4192 B6
Whipple St
100 SLYN 48178 4189 A2
7700 DET 48213 4274 B7
Whippoorwill Ln
2800 WasC 48103 4405 D1
Whisler Dr
16600 BwTp 48173 4841 A1
Whisper Ct
29200 RMLS 48174 4581 E5
43000 NvlT 48170 4265 A3
Whispering Ln
39900 NOVI 48375 4193 D4
Whispering Pns
3900 WIND N8W 4422 A4
Whispering Wy
10 YpTp 48197 4577 B4
Whispering Maples Ct
1300 PTFD 48108 4573 B1
Whispering Maples Dr
1400 PTFD 48108 4573 A1
Whispering Oaks Dr
3500 PTFD 48108 4488 D5
Whispering Pines Ct
9600 WasC 48176 4658 A3
Whispering Pines Dr
9000 WasC 48176 4658 B2
Whispering Willow
7800 WTLD 48185 4337 E4
Whispering Willows Dr
26000 HnTp 48164 4751 B1
Whispering Woods Ct
2000 WasC 48103 4405 C2
Whispering Woods Dr
2700 WasC 48103 4405 C3
Whisperwood Dr
3000 AARB 48105 4407 B1
Whisperwood Ln
9700 GOTp 48116 4186 C2
9700 HbgT 48116 4186 C2
Whistler Cres
1000 WIND N8P 4348 D6
Whistler Ct
900 WIND N8P 4348 D6
Whistling Wy
100 YpTp 48197 4577 B4
Whitall Ln
9100 WynC 48138 4670 B2
Whitby Av
6400 GDNC 48135 4339 D6
23000 FTRK 48134 4754 B4
Whitby Ct
- NvlT 48167 4265 C3
20100 LVNA 48152 4194 E6
Whitby Dr
20000 LVNA 48152 4194 D6
Whitby St
16500 LVNA 48154 4266 E2
18200 LVNA 48152 4266 E1
18600 LVNA 48152 4194 E7
Whitcomb
21500 NOVI 48375 4193 C4
Whitcomb Dr
10 GSPF 48236 4276 E2
Whitcomb St
8000 DET 48228 4342 D3
9500 DET 48227 4342 D1

Whitcomb St
13900 DET 48227 4270 D5
16100 DET 48235 4270 D3
18400 DET 48235 4198 C6
27800 LVNA 48154 4267 E2
27800 LVNA 48154 4268 A2
35900 LVNA 48154 4266 B2
White Av
1000 LNPK 48146 4501 A4
1800 LNPK 48146 4500 D3
2200 LNPK 48101 4500 D3
14500 ALPK 48101 4500 B2
White Pn
3100 AARB 48105 4331 E7
White St
100 ECRS 48229 4501 C4
1100 AARB 48104 4406 C7
1100 AARB 48104 4489 C1
30000 GBTR 48173 4755 C4
White Birch Ct
25000 BNTN 48134 4667 E3
Whitefield Ct
300 DBHT 48125 4415 D2
Whitefield St
1100 DBHT 48127 4415 D1
8300 DBHT 48127 4340 D3
White Fir Ct
16200 NvlT 48167 4264 D3
Whitegate Dr
900 NHVL 48167 4192 B5
Whitehall Ct
2600 WRRN 48091 4201 A1
22100 WDHN 48183 4668 C5
Whitehall St
- WTLD 48185 4339 E4
23300 NOVI 48374 4192 A2
White Hart Blvd
- CNTN 48188 4412 A5
White Haven Ct
41000 NvlT 48167 4265 C3
Whitehaven Dr
16000 NvlT 48167 4265 C2
Whitehead St
6300 DET 48210 4344 A6
Whitehill St
11300 DET 48224 4275 C1
11500 DET 48224 4203 C7
Whitehorn St
8300 RMLS 48174 4496 D4
11200 RMLS 48174 4580 D1
Whitehurst Rd
6600 CNTN 48187 4336 C6
White Oak
6200 WTLD 48185 4338 C6
White Oak Ct
2600 AATp 48103 4405 E2
White Oak Dr
2600 AATp 48103 4405 E1
27700 BwTp 48183 4754 E2
White Oak Ln
300 AGST 48191 4661 B7
1900 SpTp 48198 4409 E7
White Pine Cir E
44400 NvlT 48167 4264 D1
White Pine Cir W
44400 NvlT 48167 4264 D2
White Pine Ct
4400 AATp 48105 4331 D5
4600 PTFD 48197 4574 E2
17500 NvlT 48167 4264 D1
White Pine Tr
34900 FNHL 48335 4194 D4
White Pines Dr
45300 NOVI 48375 4192 B3
45400 NOVI 48374 4192 B3
White Plains Dr
24700 NOVI 48374 4192 C1
Whiteside Dr
3400 WIND N9E 4504 C1
Whitestone Ct
42900 NvlT 48170 4265 A3
White Swan Ln
6000 PTFD 48108 4573 A3
White Tail Ct
2600 WasC 48178 4260 A4
12300 PyTp 48170 4263 E7
12300 PyTp 48170 4335 E1
White Tail Ln
41400 CNTN 48188 4412 C4
Whitetail Tr
5500 WasC 48130 4404 B2
White Tail Run Ct
2500 AARB 48105 4332 A7
Whitewood Pl
33800 WTLD 48185 4338 D4
Whitewood St
2600 AARB 48104 4490 C3
5900 DET 48210 4344 A3
Whitfield St
4800 DET 48204 4343 E2
Whithorn Ct
12500 PyTp 48170 4264 A7
Whithorn St
11000 DET 48205 4274 D2
Whitlock Av
8600 DRBN 48126 4343 C5
Whitlock Dr
20200 DBHT 48127 4341 D5
Whitlock St
- DET 48126 4342 C5
- DET 48228 4341 E5
100 SALN 48176 4657 B1
15800 DET 48228 4342 C5
20700 FNHL 48336 4195 A4
Whitman Av
1600 YpTp 48198 4492 D3
44500 CNTN 48187 4411 D1
N Whitman Cir
4700 WasC 48103 4329 D4

S Whitman Cir
4600 WasC 48103 4329 D4
Whitman Ct
19500 NvlT 48167 4193 C5
Whitmore Rd
300 DET 48203 4272 B1
Whitmore St
21200 DRBN 48124 4416 C5
21600 OKPK 48237 4198 D3
Whitmore Lake Rd
2400 AATp 48105 4406 B2
2400 BNHL 48105 4406 B2
3000 AATp 48105 4331 B5
3000 BNHL 48105 4331 B5
5000 WasC 48105 4331 B1
5000 WasC 48189 4331 B1
6100 WasC 48105 4259 A6
6100 WasC 48189 4259 A6
7000 WasC 48189 4258 E5
8200 GOTp 48116 4187 A1
11000 GOTp 48189 4186 E6
11000 GOTp 48189 4187 A6
Whitney Av
3700 WIND N9C 4420 B6
Whitney Ct
48000 CNTN 48187 4336 A5
Whitney Dr
37400 WYNE 48184 4413 B5
Whitney St
2600 DET 48206 4344 C2
4000 DET 48204 4344 B2
Whittaker Ct
34700 FMTN 48335 4194 D1
Whittaker Rd
1800 YpTp 48197 4575 E2
5500 YpTp 48197 4576 B7
8000 AGST 48191 4661 B1
8000 AGST 48197 4576 B7
8000 AGST 48197 4661 B1
10000 AGST 48160 4661 B4
Whittaker St
7000 DET 48209 4419 A2
8300 DET 48209 4418 E2
23500 FMTN 48335 4194 D1
Whittier Ct
700 SALN 48176 4572 D6
2900 AARB 48104 4489 D4
Whittier Dr
200 SLYN 48178 4189 B3
900 CNTN 48187 4411 E1
Whittier Pl
1300 DRBN 48124 4415 E3
Whittier Rd
700 GPPK 48230 4276 A5
1200 YPLT 48197 4491 C3
2400 YpTp 48197 4491 B3
Whittier St
10 WasC 48189 4259 A1
1100 WIND N9G 4504 B3
5700 DET 48224 4275 E2
Whittington St
9900 DRBN 48120 4418 D3
22400 FNHL 48336 4195 E2
Whittlesey Lake Dr
8800 PyTp 48170 4336 C3
Wiard Blvd
1300 YpTp 48198 4493 A2
1400 SpTp 48198 4492 E1
1400 SpTp 48198 4493 A2
Wiard Ct
2300 YpTp 48198 4493 A4
Wiard Rd
- SpTp 48198 4492 E1
1300 YpTp 48198 4493 A5
N Wick Ct
10 AARB 48105 4407 B1
Wick Rd
14700 ALPK 48101 4500 B4
19200 ALPK 48101 4499 C4
20000 TYLR 48101 4499 C4
20000 TYLR 48180 4499 C4
24500 TYLR 48180 4498 E5
27000 TYLR 48174 4498 A5
27400 RMLS 48174 4498 A5
28400 RMLS 48174 4497 E5
33900 RMLS 48174 4496 D5
Wickfield Ct
800 AARB 48105 4406 D3
42200 CNTN 48187 4337 B6
Wickham Rd
8200 RMLS 48174 4497 C4
Wicks Ln
20700 GSPW 48236 4204 D5
Wiclif Ct
44100 CNTN 48187 4336 E6
Widman Pl
6200 DET 48211 4273 C7
Wight St
2600 DET 48207 4346 B5
Wigle Rd
1000 WIND N9C 4420 B4
Wigle St
500 Amhg N9V 4757 B4
Wilber
- WynC 48138 4756 A3
Wilbur Ct
15300 RDFD 48239 4268 E3
Wilbur St
- DET 48202 4344 E2
Wilcox Av
3700 WIND N9E 4504 C2
Wilcox Rd
- PyTp 48170 4265 C6
100 PLYM 48170 4265 C6
Wildberry Cres
2500 Tcmh N9K 4424 A6
Wildbranch Dr
- DRBN 48126 4417 A1
Wildbrook Dr
14300 VNBN 48111 4579 B3

Wilde St
800 DET 48209 4419 A4
Wildemere St
- DET 48210 4344 B1
7300 DET 48206 4344 B1
9700 DET 48206 4272 A6
13100 DET 48238 4272 A6
15400 DET 48238 4271 E2
16100 DET 48221 4271 E2
18000 DET 48221 4199 E6
Wilder Dr N
10 Lksr N8N 4424 E3
Wilder Dr S
10 Lksr N8N 4424 E3
Wilder Pl
400 AARB 48103 4406 A7
Wilderness Ct
6300 WasC 48178 4261 C1
Wilderness Park Dr
7200 WTLD 48185 4338 B5
Wilderness Park Dr E
7300 WTLD 48185 4338 C5
Wilderness Park Dr W
7200 WTLD 48185 4338 B5
Wildflower Ct
4700 PTFD 48108 4573 B1
9500 VNBN 48111 4494 C6
Wildflower Dr
17600 NvlT 48167 4264 E1
Wild Flower Ln
25600 BNTN 48134 4667 C7
25600 BNTN 48134 4753 C1
Wild Fox Ct
300 WasC 48103 4404 C6
Wildfox Ct
16200 RMLS 48174 4582 A5
Wild Ivy Ct
100 WasC 48103 4404 B5
Wild Meadow Cir
6600 WasC 48105 4260 C6
Wild Oak Ln
2200 AATp 48105 4331 E6
Wild Oaks Cir
9200 GOTp 48178 4188 B1
Wild Rose Ct
200 WasC 48103 4404 B6
Wildrose Ct
- GOTp 48178 4188 C3
Wildrose Dr
48500 CNTN 48187 4335 E7
48500 CNTN 48187 4336 A7
Wildrye Ct
45700 VNBN 48111 4494 D6
Wildt St
800 AARB 48103 4406 B5
Wild Turkey Ln
41400 CNTN 48188 4412 C5
Wild Turkey Rd
11000 GOTp 48178 4187 D5
Wildwing Rd
11700 PyTp 48170 4336 D1
Wildwood
- YpTp 48198 4493 A3
Wildwood Av
200 AARB 48103 4405 E5
N Wildwood Av
100 WTLD 48185 4413 E1
100 WTLD 48186 4413 E1
1700 WTLD 48185 4338 E6
Wildwood Ct
2900 SALN 48176 4572 D5
48800 PyTp 48170 4263 E7
Wildwood Dr
2900 WIND N8R 4423 B3
6800 PTFD 48197 4574 D5
20800 HRWD 48225 4204 B6
Wildwood Ln
800 CNTN 48188 4412 D3
1500 WasC 48176 4658 A2
Wildwood St
900 DET 48203 4200 B6
21700 DRBN 48128 4341 C7
23000 OKPK 48237 4198 D2
N Wildwood St
7700 WTLD 48185 4338 E4
S Wildwood St
100 WTLD 48186 4413 E4
Wildwood Tr
1300 SALN 48176 4572 C5
8600 WasC 48178 4260 C1
28400 FNHL 48336 4195 E1
Wildwood Lake Dr
9000 WasC 48189 4258 E1
9400 WasC 48189 4186 E7
Wilfred St
11400 DET 48213 4274 D2
13000 DET 48213 4275 A1
Wilke St
800 DET 48209 4419 A3
Wilkie St
7100 TYLR 48180 4498 D3
Wilkins St
400 DET 48201 4345 D4
900 DET 48207 4345 D4
Wilkinson Ct
10 Amhg N9V 4757 C2
Wilkinson St
3400 WIND N9C 4419 E4
3400 WIND N9C 4420 A4
Willard Av
23000 WRRN 48089 4202 E1
Willard Dr
1400 CNTN 48187 4412 A1
1500 CNTN 48187 4411 E1
N Willard Rd
100 CNTN 48187 4412 A2
S Willard Rd
4200 CNTN 48188 4412 A7
Willard St
1100 AARB 48104 4406 C7

Willard St
8000 DET 48214 4274 C7
Will Carleton Rd
10 HnTp 48117 4751 E4
10 HnTp 48164 4751 E4
10 MonC 48117 4751 E4
400 HnTp 48117 4752 C4
400 HnTp 48164 4752 C4
400 MonC 48117 4752 C4
1000 HnTp 48134 4752 C4
1200 MonC 48134 4752 C4
3100 HnTp 48134 4753 A4
3100 MonC 48134 4753 A4
4000 BrTp 48134 4753 A4
4000 FTRK 48134 4753 A4
Willette St
6300 DET 48210 4343 E5
6300 DET 48210 4344 A4
William Av
2100 YpTp 48198 4493 A7
2900 YpTp 48111 4493 B7
William Ct
31600 RKWD 48173 4754 C6
45300 CNTN 48188 4411 D3
William Ct E
19800 GSPW 48236 4204 D7
William Ct W
19800 GSPW 48236 4204 D7
William St
10 Amhg N9V 4757 C1
600 Tcmh N8N 4348 E7
600 Tcmh N8N 4423 E1
800 PLYM 48170 4265 A7
900 Tcmh N8N 4424 A1
1200 PLYM 48170 4264 E7
5800 TYLR 48125 4499 C1
7100 TYLR 48180 4499 C3
E William St
100 AARB 48104 4406 B6
W William St
100 AARB 48104 4406 B6
200 AARB 48103 4406 B6
William G Rogell Dr
- RMLS 48242 4497 C7
William M Kreger Dr
10 WYDT 48192 4585 C3
William R Av
2800 TNTN 48183 4669 D4
Williams
- DET 48210 4344 C3
Williams Av
10 GSPF 48236 4276 C3
E Williams Cir
1900 WTLD 48186 4413 A4
N Williams Cir
38200 WTLD 48186 4413 A4
S Williams Cir
38200 WTLD 48186 4413 A4
W Williams Cir
1900 WTLD 48186 4413 A4
Williams Ct
14800 GBTR 48173 4755 C5
18600 LVNA 48152 4266 B1
21900 STCS 48080 4204 D3
Williams St
100 SALN 48176 4572 D7
200 SALN 48176 4657 D1
2700 DET 48216 4344 D6
3000 DET 48210 4344 D6
3000 INKR 48141 4415 B5
3300 DRBN 48124 4416 C5
3900 DRBN 48124 4416 C5
3900 DBHT 48125 4416 C6
3900 WYNE 48184 4413 D6
5200 WYNE 48184 4496 D1
15600 LVNA 48154 4266 B3
18500 LVNA 48152 4266 B1
18600 LVNA 48152 4194 B7
22200 RKWD 48173 4754 C7
22200 RKWD 48173 4840 C1
Williamsburg Blvd
40900 CNTN 48187 4412 C2
Williamsburg Ct
- NvlT 48167 4263 E2
900 NHVL 48167 4192 A5
14700 RVWW 48192 4584 C6
20400 HRWD 48225 4204 A4
Williamsburg Dr
10 DRBN 48120 4417 D3
3000 AARB 48108 4490 B5
Williamsburg Rd
20300 DBHT 48127 4341 D6
Williamsburg Sq
23200 WDHN 48183 4669 A5
Williamsburg St
13700 RVWW 48192 4584 D6
Williamsburg on the River Rd
4300 WasC 48176 4571 E7
4300 WasC 48176 4572 A7
Williamsburg Towne St
10 SFLD 48075 4198 A2
Williams Mall
600 DET 48202 4345 A3
Williamson Ct
10 DRBN 48126 4342 E5
Williamson Ln
21200 WynC 48138 4670 B3
Williamson St
- DRBN 48126 4417 E2
5600 DRBN 48126 4342 E6
Willingham Dr
45700 NOVI 48374 4192 B2
Willis Ct
42900 WynC 48111 4664 B2
Willis Rd
200 SALN 48176 4657 D2
600 WasC 48176 4657 E2
3200 WasC 48160 4659 C2
3200 WasC 48197 4659 C2

INDEX 57

Willis Rd — Detroit & Wayne County Street Index — Woodruff Rd

STREET
Block City ZIP Map# Grid

Willis Rd
4600 WasC 48160 4660 A2
4600 WasC 48197 4660 A2
4800 AGST 48160 4660 B2
4800 AGST 48197 4660 B2
7000 AGST 48191 4661 C2
7000 AGST 48197 4661 C2
9000 AGST 48191 4662 A2
43400 WynC 48111 4663 E2
43400 WynC 48111 4664 A2
48900 WynC 48111 4662 E2
50100 WynC 48191 4662 E2
E Willis Rd
10 WasC 48176 4659 B2
3000 WasC 48160 4659 B2
3000 WasC 48197 4659 B2
W Willis Rd
10 WasC 48176 4659 A2
100 WasC 48176 4658 C2
1800 WasC 48176 4657 E2
Willis St E
10 DET 48201 4345 C3
1900 DET 48207 4345 E2
3300 DET 48207 4346 A2
Willis St W
1300 DET 48201 4345 A4
1400 DET 48210 4345 A4
Willison Rd
10 GSPS 48236 4205 A6
Willistead Cres
2000 WIND N8Y 4421 C1
Willmarth
22000 DET 48219 4269 B1
Willow
11200 SOGT 48195 4500 B7
Willow Ct
200 Tcmh N8N 4424 C1
16300 RMLS 48174 4581 E5
22000 WDHN 48183 4668 C4
Willow Dr
100 LSal N9J 4586 C1
500 SLYN 48178 4189 C1
Willow Ln
10 GSPF 48236 4276 E2
1600 AARB 48105 4406 D4
18200 BNTN 48174 4582 B7
20700 FNHL 48336 4195 E5
24300 NOVI 48375 4193 C1
37400 WTLD 48185 4413 B1
Willow Rd
- CNTN 48188 4411 D5
- HnTp 48134 4666 B7
- HnTp 48164 4666 B7
9500 AGST 48191 4748 C1
10700 AGST 48111 4748 C1
32900 HnTp 48134 4752 A1
32900 HnTp 48164 4752 A1
34100 HnTp 48164 4751 E1
38600 HnTp 48164 4750 E1
39000 WynC 48164 4750 E1
43400 WynC 48111 4749 D1
43400 WynC 48111 4750 A1
48400 WynC 48111 4748 D1
Willow St
- CNTN 48188 4410 C7
- CNTN 48188 4411 A7
900 AARB 48103 4406 A5
1900 DRBN 48124 4417 A6
Willow Wy
100 VNBN 48111 4494 E5
Willoway Ct
12300 PyTp 48170 4264 A7
Willoway Rd
21500 DRBN 48124 4416 C1
Willowbridge Rd
5800 YpTp 48197 4576 C2
Willowbrook
23200 NOVI 48375 4193 C1
Willowbrook Ct
25400 HnTp 48134 4666 D6
Willowbrook Dr
22900 FNHL 48335 4194 A2
Willowbrook Ln
15000 PyTp 48170 4265 C4
Willow Cove
26400 WDHN 48183 4755 A1
Willow Cove Blvd
4400 ALPK 48101 4417 C7
E Willow Cove Blvd
4500 ALPK 48101 4417 B7
W Willow Cove Blvd
4500 ALPK 48101 4417 B7
Willow Creek Dr
6800 CNTN 48187 4337 A5
7200 YpTp 48197 4576 A5
Willow Creek Rd
9200 GOTp 48178 4188 B1
Willowgreen Ct
- GOTp 48178 4188 B4
Willow Grove St
17400 BNTN 48174 4583 B6
Willow Pond Dr
4000 PTFD 48197 4574 D3
Willow Ridge Ct
17100 NvlT 48167 4264 E2
Willow Ridge Dr
5800 PTFD 48197 4574 D3
17100 NvlT 48167 4264 E2
Willow Run Airport
800 YpTp 48198 4493 C5
Willow Springs Rd
30100 FTRK 48173 4754 A5
Willow Tree Ct
22300 FNHL 48335 4194 B3
Willow Tree Ln
200 WasC 48103 4404 A4
Willowtree Ln
1800 AARB 48105 4406 E3
Willow Tree Pl
10 GSPS 48236 4205 A5

Willowtree St
28000 RMLS 48174 4582 B4
Willow Wood Ln
11300 PyTp 48170 4336 A1
Wilmarth St
23300 FMTN 48335 4194 E1
Wilmer St
2000 WTLD 48185 4338 B7
Wilmot Av
23300 EPTE 48021 4203 E1
Wilmot Ct
1300 AARB 48104 4406 D6
Wilmot Rd
19700 WynC 48111 4663 C3
Wilmot St
1300 AARB 48104 4406 D6
Wilshire Dr
10900 DET 48213 4274 D3
12500 DET 48213 4275 A2
Wilshire Pkwy
1800 WTLD 48186 4413 C4
Wilshire St
9000 LVNA 48150 4338 B3
Wilson Av
1200 LNPK 48146 4501 A3
4200 WYDT 48146 4501 A7
5400 TNTN 48183 4755 C1
11500 VNBN 48111 4578 E1
16900 EPTE 48021 4203 D1
22300 DRBN 48128 4416 B1
24400 DRBN 48128 4415 E1
Wilson Ct
18100 BNTN 48192 4583 C6
Wilson Dr
5700 WYNE 48184 4497 B1
13900 PyTp 48170 4263 D6
24100 BNTN 48183 4668 B6
25400 DBHT 48127 4415 D1
Wilson Rd
6000 PTFD 48108 4573 C3
Wilson St
200 YpTp 48197 4491 D5
29000 GBTR 48173 4755 D3
Wilton Ct
600 AARB 48103 4405 E5
Wilton St
300 AARB 48103 4405 E5
Wiltshire Ct
900 SALN 48176 4572 B5
2000 AARB 48103 4488 D2
Wiltshire Dr
- SpTp 48198 4409 B7
1800 AARB 48103 4488 D2
Wimpole
- AARB 48103 4488 D1
Winans Lake Rd
6700 HbgT 48116 4186 A1
7800 GOTp 48116 4186 D2
9000 GOTp 48116 4187 A1
Winchell Dr
2100 AARB 48104 4489 E2
Winchester E
900 DET 48203 4200 C4
Winchester W
10 DET 48203 4200 C4
Winchester Av
600 LNPK 48146 4501 A6
1000 LNPK 48146 4500 D6
Winchester Ct
16500 NvlT 48167 4265 B2
Winchester Dr
200 PTFD 48176 4573 E5
15400 NvlT 48170 4265 B2
15700 NvlT 48167 4265 B2
24700 DRBN 48124 4415 E3
Winchester St
200 SLYN 48178 4189 C1
5900 VNBN 48111 4493 C2
27000 BwTp 48183 4754 D2
33000 WTLD 48185 4339 A6
Winchester St E
- DET 48234 4200 E4
- DET 48234 4201 A4
Winchester Ter
27000 BwTp 48183 4754 D2
S Wind Cres
200 Tcmh N8N 4424 E1
Wind Crest Cir
10100 HbgT 48189 4186 B3
Windemere Cir
16100 SOGT 48195 4584 B5
Windemere Ct
3500 AARB 48105 4407 D4
Windemere Dr
- CNTN 48187 4336 C4
3500 AARB 48105 4407 C5
Windemere St
11600 SOGT 48195 4500 C7
13500 SOGT 48195 4584 C2
Winder St
10 DET 48201 4345 C5
900 DET 48207 4345 E4
Windermere Ct
22400 NOVI 48374 4192 B4
Windermere Dr
10 GSPF 48236 4276 E2
Windermere Rd
400 WIND N8Y 4346 B7
600 WIND N8Y 4421 C1
1700 WIND N8W 4421 C3
Windham Ln
10 DRBN 48120 4417 D3
Windham St
1100 WTLD 48186 4414 C3
Winding Creek Ct
15800 NvlT 48167 4264 D4
Winding Creek Dr
21200 LyTp 48178 4189 B5
25100 HnTp 48164 4665 D7
25700 HnTp 48164 4751 D1

Winding Pond Ln
13600 VNBN 48111 4579 A3
Winding Pond Tr
42400 VNBN 48111 4579 A3
Winding Valley Rd
10200 GOTp 48116 4186 D3
Windmill Ct
6100 PTFD 48176 4572 D3
43300 NOVI 48375 4193 A4
Windmill Dr
44200 CNTN 48187 4336 D5
Windmill Wy
2200 PTFD 48176 4572 D3
2400 WasC 48176 4572 D3
Windmill Pointe Dr
14900 DET 48214 4348 A1
14900 GPPK 48214 4348 A1
14900 GPPK 48230 4348 A1
15800 GPPK 48230 4276 B7
Windmoor Dr
13500 GOTp 48178 4188 E2
Windridge Blvd
- CNTN 48188 4411 B5
Windridge Dr
19100 NvlT 48167 4193 D7
Windridge Ln
24000 NOVI 48374 4192 B1
45900 CNTN 48188 4411 B4
Windshadow Dr
3300 AATp 48105 4330 D7
Windside Ct
2800 WasC 48103 4488 C2
Windsome Dr
39400 NvlT 48167 4193 D6
Windsor
- TYLR 48180 4582 E5
30200 GBTR 48173 4755 C5
Windsor Av
400 WIND N9A 4420 E1
800 WIND N9A 4421 A2
1200 WIND N8X 4421 A3
27400 GDNC 48135 4340 A5
29700 FTRK 48134 4754 B4
30900 WTLD 48185 4339 C5
32500 GDNC 48135 4339 B5
Windsor Ct
8500 SpTp 48198 4492 C1
22200 WDHN 48183 4668 C7
41300 NvlT 48167 4193 C6
Windsor Dr
2100 AARB 48103 4488 D2
Windsor St
- DET 48224 4275 D5
17200 DET 48224 4276 B4
Windsor Woods Dr
7200 CNTN 48187 4337 A5
Windward Ct
200 DET 48207 4346 C5
Windward Pl
10 GSPF 48236 4276 E4
Windwood Dr
2700 AARB 48105 4407 A1
37400 FNHL 48335 4194 A2
Windwood Pointe
- STCS 48080 4204 E1
100 STCS 48080 4205 A1
Windycrest Dr
- AATp 48104 4407 C6
300 AATp 48105 4407 C6
Windy Ridge Ct
1500 WasC 48176 4658 A2
Winekoff Dr
38400 WTLD 48186 4413 A5
Wines Dr
1100 AARB 48103 4405 E4
Winewood Av
2300 AARB 48103 4405 D6
Winfield Av
20700 WRRN 48091 4202 A4
Winfield Ct
37600 WTLD 48186 4413 A4
Winfield Dr
1600 LSal N9H 4504 C6
Winfield Rd
22500 NOVI 48375 4193 C3
40300 CNTN 48188 4412 D3
Winfield St
- DET 48234 4274 A4
8500 DET 48211 4274 A4
8500 DET 48213 4274 A4
9800 HMTK 48212 4273 C4
Wing Ct
200 NHVL 48167 4192 D7
Wing Dr
1000 WasC 48103 4404 C3
Wing Pl
2600 DET 48216 4345 A7
Wing St
500 PLYM 48170 4337 A1
1000 PLYM 48170 4336 E1
N Wing St
100 NHVL 48167 4192 D6
S Wing St
100 NHVL 48167 4192 D7
Wingate Blvd
1400 YpTp 48198 4492 D7
Wingate Ct
22100 FNHL 48335 4194 B4
Winged Foot Ct
2400 PTFD 48108 4572 D1
Winged Foot Wy
23400 LyTp 48178 4190 D2
Winifred Av
23800 WRRN 48091 4201 A1
Winifred St
1500 WTLD 48186 4414 B4
3000 WYNE 48184 4414 B6
Winkelman St
8100 DET 48211 4273 D5

Winner Cir
10700 HbgT 48189 4186 C4
Winnsborough Ln
23300 NOVI 48375 4192 E2
Winona Av
6300 ALPK 48101 4500 A1
Winona Ct
9000 AGST 48197 4661 D1
Winona Dr
4800 WasC 48130 4329 D4
Winona St
10 HDPK 48203 4272 D3
24400 DRBN 48124 4415 E3
32600 WTLD 48185 4339 A4
Winora Av
17300 SFLD 48075 4198 A3
Winsap St
- LVNA 48150 4337 D2
39400 PyTp 48170 4337 D2
Winslow Ct
5600 PTFD 48197 4574 E2
49500 PyTp 48170 4335 D1
Winslow Dr
26600 FTRK 48134 4753 C2
Winslow Rd
10600 WIND N8R 4423 C2
Winslow St
5700 DET 48210 4344 D3
33900 WYNE 48184 4413 E7
33900 WYNE 48184 4414 A7
Winsted Blvd
1600 AARB 48103 4488 E2
Winston
9100 RDFD 48239 4340 E1
15300 RDFD 48239 4268 E3
Winston Dr
- TYLR 48180 4582 D5
Winston Ln
8300 DBHT 48127 4340 E3
8400 DBHT 48239 4340 E3
Winston St
16100 DET 48219 4268 E1
19100 DET 48219 4196 E5
Winter Ct
10 WIND N9E 4504 A3
29500 GDNC 48135 4414 E2
41800 CNTN 48187 4337 B6
Winter Dr
6100 CNTN 48187 4337 B6
29500 GDNC 48135 4414 E2
Winter St
13500 MonC 48117 4753 A7
Winter Garden Ct
2700 AARB 48105 4407 B1
Wintergreen Cir
20500 NvlT 48167 4193 B5
23500 NOVI 48374 4192 B2
Wintergreen Ct
1800 WasC 48103 4488 B2
Wintergreen St
10 WTLD 48186 4414 C6
Winters Ln
8000 WasC 48189 4258 E2
8000 WasC 48189 4259 A3
Winterset Cir
9400 PyTp 48170 4335 E2
Winthrop Ct
2700 AARB 48104 4489 D3
23400 NOVI 48375 4192 D2
Winthrop Dr
43900 NOVI 48375 4192 D2
Winthrop Pl
10 GSPF 48236 4276 E3
Winthrop Rd
2200 TNTN 48183 4669 D4
Winthrop St
9100 DET 48228 4342 C2
9500 DET 48227 4342 C1
12800 DET 48227 4270 C6
16100 DET 48235 4270 C3
19700 DET 48235 4198 C5
Winwood Av
18200 BNTN 48192 4583 C7
Winwood Ct
18100 BNTN 48192 4583 C6
Wiscasset Rd
3300 DRBN 48120 4417 D3
Wisconsin St
7600 DRBN 48126 4343 C3
9300 DET 48204 4343 C1
11800 DET 48204 4271 C6
15400 DET 48238 4271 C3
17100 DET 48221 4271 C1
20400 DET 48221 4199 C4
32100 LVNA 48150 4339 A2
Wismer Av
1500 YpTp 48198 4492 D7
Wisner St
8000 DET 48234 4274 B2
Wistaria Dr
24400 FNHL 48336 4195 E1
Wisteria Dr
1200 AARB 48104 4489 C2
Witherell St
10 DET 48226 4345 D5
2000 DET 48201 4345 D5
Withington St
200 FRDL 48220 4199 D2
Witmire St
1800 YPLT 48197 4491 C3
Witt St
7900 DET 48209 4419 A3
9100 DET 48209 4418 E4
Wixom Rd
24600 NOVI 48374 4191 D1
Woburn Dr
500 YpTp 48198 4491 E2
600 YpTp 48197 4491 E2
Woe Be Tide
3200 PTFD 48108 4490 C5

Wohlfeil St
21300 TYLR 48180 4499 C4
25400 TYLR 48180 4498 D4
Wolcott St
2300 FRDL 48220 4200 A1
Wolfe Ct
3500 WIND N9C 4420 B5
Wolfe St
100 Amhg N9V 4757 C2
Wolff St
4000 DET 48209 4344 D7
Wolfriver Dr
10000 PyTp 48170 4337 D2
Wolverhampton Ln
1100 AARB 48105 4407 B5
E Wolverine Dr
3000 AARB 48108 4490 B5
W Wolverine Dr
2800 AARB 48108 4490 B5
Wolverine St
25800 BNTN 48134 4667 D6
Wood Av
7200 CTNL 48015 4202 A1
7200 WRRN 48091 4202 A1
Wood Ct
- CNTN 48188 4411 C5
1400 SALN 48176 4572 D5
Wood Dr
8000 WynC 48138 4670 D2
Wood Hvn
2200 AARB 48105 4331 D7
S Wood Ln
25300 TYLR 48180 4582 E4
Wood St
- DET 48234 4274 B3
12300 Tcmh N8N 4348 E7
17100 MVDL 48122 4417 E5
22700 STCS 48080 4204 B2
32700 RKWD 48173 4754 C7
33600 LVNA 48154 4266 E2
Woodale Av
1500 YpTp 48198 4493 B7
2000 YpTp 48198 4577 B1
Woodale Wy
39700 CNTN 48188 4412 E4
Woodbend Ct
46900 NvlT 48167 4192 B6
Wood Bend Dr
9500 WasC 48176 4658 A4
Woodbend Dr
20100 NvlT 48167 4192 B6
Woodberry Rd
8800 PyTp 48170 4336 B3
Woodbine
9500 RDFD 48239 4340 E1
15100 RDFD 48239 4268 E4
Woodbine Dr
1900 CNTN 48188 4412 B4
25800 INKR 48141 4415 D3
Woodbine St
8100 DBHT 48127 4341 A4
16100 DET 48219 4268 E2
19900 DET 48219 4196 E5
Woodbourne St
1400 WTLD 48186 4414 C3
Woodbridge
200 WasC 48176 4657 B2
Woodbridge Blvd
1000 AARB 48103 4406 A6
E Woodbridge Cir
7600 WTLD 48185 4338 C3
N Woodbridge Cir
37100 WTLD 48185 4338 B4
S Woodbridge Cir
37000 WTLD 48185 4338 B4
W Woodbridge Cir
7600 WTLD 48185 4338 C3
Woodbridge Ct
10 DRBN 48124 4416 C2
1600 CNTN 48188 4412 B4
Woodbridge Dr
300 Tcmh N8N 4349 A7
41800 CNTN 48188 4412 B4
Woodbridge Rd
- SALN 48176 4572 C6
24400 WRRN 48091 4201 A1
Woodbridge St
600 DET 48226 4345 E6
900 DET 48207 4345 E6
1300 DET 48207 4346 A6
1300 STCS 48080 4204 A3
Woodbridge Towne St
10 SFLD 48075 4198 B2
Woodbrook Dr
32300 WYNE 48184 4414 B5
41800 CNTN 48188 4412 B6
Woodburn Dr
20000 SFLD 48075 4197 C3
Woodbury Ct
18200 NvlT 48167 4264 B1
Woodbury Dr
- VNBN 48111 4579 C3
1800 AARB 48104 4489 C2
N Woodbury Dr
41100 VNBN 48111 4579 C3
S Woodbury Dr
41100 VNBN 48111 4579 C3
Woodbury Ln
10 DRBN 48120 4417 D2
Woodchester Ct
11200 GOTp 48178 4188 B5
Woodchip Wy
2300 PTFD 48197 4491 A3
Woodcreek Blvd
1400 AATp 48104 4490 C2
1800 AARB 48104 4490 C2
20200 NvlT 48167 4193 B6
Woodcreek Cir
600 SALN 48176 4572 B7

Woodcreek Ct
600 SALN 48176 4572 B7
700 YpTp 48198 4492 C3
2500 CNTN 48188 4412 B5
Woodcreek Dr
4000 PTFD 48197 4490 E6
22300 BNTN 48134 4667 E4
22700 TYLR 48180 4583 B2
Woodcreek Ln
42000 CNTN 48188 4412 B5
Woodcrest Ct
4200 PTFD 48197 4490 D6
21500 FNHL 48335 4194 B4
Woodcrest Dr
100 DRBN 48124 4416 C1
8000 WynC 48138 4670 D2
8200 WTLD 48185 4338 D4
Woodcrest St
12200 TYLR 48180 4583 B1
18500 HRWD 48225 4203 D5
19600 HRWD 48225 4204 A6
Woodcroft Dr
24500 DRBN 48124 4415 E3
Wooddale Ct
3400 AATp 48104 4490 C2
Woodfarm
59200 LyTp 48178 4189 D5
Woodfarm Dr
21100 FNHL 48167 4194 A4
Woodgate Dr
12400 PyTp 48170 4264 D7
Woodglen
41900 NOVI 48375 4193 A2
Woodglen Av
1000 YpTp 48198 4493 A6
Woodgreen Ct
2300 CNTN 48188 4411 B5
Woodgreen Dr
7600 WTLD 48185 4338 C4
Woodgrove Ct
- GOTp 48178 4188 C3
Woodgrove Dr
300 WasC 48103 4404 C6
9000 PyTp 48170 4335 E3
12900 GOTp 48178 4188 C3
27900 BwTp 48183 4755 A3
Woodhall St
5500 DET 48224 4276 A2
9100 DET 48224 4275 E1
Woodham Ct
48700 CNTN 48187 4335 E5
Woodham Rd
24100 NOVI 48374 4191 E1
Woodhaven Ct
23100 FMTN 48335 4194 C2
23100 FNHL 48335 4194 C2
Woodhill Cir
3300 SpTp 48198 4408 D1
Woodhill Dr
- NHVL 48167 4192 B6
500 SALN 48176 4657 E1
19900 NvlT 48167 4192 B6
21200 FNHL 48167 4193 E4
Woodingham Ct
100 SALN 48176 4657 D2
Woodingham Dr
15400 DET 48238 4271 C3
17100 DET 48221 4271 C1
20400 DET 48220 4199 C4
20400 DET 48221 4199 C4
Woodington Ct
2600 CNTN 48188 4412 B5
Woodland Av
3000 WIND N9E 4504 B1
Woodland Cr
41500 NOVI 48375 4193 B2
Woodland Ct
1200 SALN 48176 4572 B5
9600 YpTp 48197 4576 E4
9600 YpTp 48197 4577 A4
10000 OKPK 48237 4199 B1
Woodland Dr
- HnTp 48164 4665 C1
100 SLYN 48178 4189 A1
700 SALN 48176 4572 E5
1000 INKR 48141 4415 A3
1400 AARB 48103 4489 A1
1700 PTFD 48176 4572 E3
4000 WasC 48103 4329 E5
6200 CNTN 48187 4336 A7
15600 DRBN 48120 4417 D3
16200 WDHN 48183 4669 A3
17700 HnTp 48164 4580 D7
Woodland Dr E
200 SALN 48176 4572 C5
Woodland Dr W
300 SALN 48176 4572 B5
Woodland Pk
44500 NvlT 48167 4192 D7
Woodland Pl
10 GSPT 48230 4276 C6
10 LyTp 48167 4189 E6
1200 PLYM 48170 4336 E1
Woodland Rd
3400 AATp 48104 4490 C1
24000 BNTN 48134 4667 E7
Woodland St
10 DET 48202 4272 E5
10 DET 48203 4272 E5
1100 DET 48203 4273 A4
1100 DET 48211 4273 A4
1300 DET 48212 4273 A4
1600 HMTK 48212 4273 A4
18500 HRWD 48225 4203 D5
19600 HRWD 48225 4204 A6
E Woodland St
100 FRDL 48220 4199 E1
W Woodland St
100 FRDL 48220 4199 D1

Woodland Glen Dr
20700 NOVI 48167 4193 A5
20700 NOVI 48375 4193 A5
Woodland Hills Dr
3100 PTFD 48108 4490 E4
Woodland Ridge Blvd
- GOTp 48178 4188 B5
Woodland Ridge Cir
11900 GOTp 48178 4188 B5
Woodland Ridge Ct
- GOTp 48178 4188 B5
Woodlands Ct
12200 PyTp 48170 4335 E1
12300 PyTp 48170 4263 E7
Woodland Shores Dr
10 GSPS 48236 4276 E1
10 GSPS 48236 4277 A1
Woodlawn Av
300 YpTp 48198 4492 D5
900 AARB 48104 4489 C1
2100 WIND N8W 4421 C4
Woodlawn Ct
25400 TYLR 48180 4498 D6
Woodlawn St
8000 DET 48213 4274 B4
10000 TYLR 48180 4498 E6
Woodlea Dr
3300 WasC 48103 4405 B1
Woodleigh Ct
45200 PyTp 48170 4336 D1
Woodleigh Wy
45200 PyTp 48170 4336 C1
Woodlily Ct
1900 WasC 48103 4488 C2
Woodline Ct
26300 FTRK 48134 4753 C1
Woodlong Dr
46900 CNTN 48187 4411 B2
Woodlore Ln
- PyTp 48170 4336 B2
Woodlore South Dr
8800 PyTp 48170 4336 B3
Woodmanor Ct
3000 AARB 48104 4490 A4
3000 AARB 48108 4490 A4
Woodmere Dr
6500 CNTN 48187 4336 C6
Woodmere St
2200 DET 48209 4418 E2
Woodmont E
2400 CNTN 48188 4411 E5
Woodmont W
1800 CNTN 48188 4411 D5
Woodmont Av
- TNTN 48183 4669 B4
8600 DET 48228 4342 B2
9500 DET 48227 4342 B1
13900 DET 48227 4270 B5
Woodmont Cres
1100 LSal N9J 4503 A4
N Woodmont Cres
5900 LSal N9J 4503 B4
Woodmont Ct
1800 CNTN 48188 4411 D5
15000 RMLS 48174 4582 A4
38600 WYNE 48184 4413 A5
Woodmont St
15000 RMLS 48174 4582 A5
19100 HRWD 48225 4203 E5
19600 HRWD 48225 4204 A5
Woodpecker Ct
6000 YpTp 48197 4576 B3
Woodpine Dr
12500 GOTp 48178 4188 C1
Woodridge Av
1000 AATp 48105 4407 E4
Woodridge Ct
5500 WasC 48103 4487 B1
41400 NvlT 48167 4193 B5
Woodridge Dr
- WTLD 48185 4338 A3
16900 BNTN 48192 4669 A1
Woodridge Wy
2300 PTFD 48197 4491 A2
Woodring Ct
16000 LVNA 48154 4267 A3
Woodring Dr
15700 LVNA 48154 4267 A3
Woodring St
11000 LVNA 48150 4339 A1
15300 LVNA 48154 4267 A3
18500 LVNA 48152 4267 A1
18900 LVNA 48152 4195 A7
Woodrising Ln
22500 FNHL 48335 4194 B2
Woodrow
26300 RDFD 48240 4268 C2
Woodrow St
2600 WasC 48103 4405 C3
5800 DET 48210 4344 B4
6500 DET 48204 4344 B4
Woodrow Wilson Av
23800 WRRN 48091 4201 A1
Woodrow Wilson St
7300 DET 48210 4344 E1
8200 DET 48206 4344 D1
8400 DET 48206 4272 D6
14000 DET 48238 4272 B3
15400 DET 48203 4272 B3
Woodruff Av
1900 WRRN 48091 4200 E2
2100 WRRN 48091 4201 A2
E Woodruff Av
10 HZLP 48030 4200 D2
W Woodruff Av
200 HZLP 48030 4200 C2
Woodruff Ln
2500 YpTp 48198 4493 B1
Woodruff Rd
15600 BwTp 48173 4755 A5

INDEX 58

Woodruff Rd — Detroit & Wayne County Street Index — 8 Mile Rd

STREET Block City ZIP Map# Grid

Woodruff Rd
15600 GBTR 48173 4755 A5
19000 GBTR 48173 4754 D6
19000 RKWD 48173 4754 D6
19000 RKWD 48173 4755 A5
20200 BwTp 48173 4754 D6
21500 FTRK 48134 4754 A5
21500 RKWD 48134 4754 D6
23500 FTRK 48173 4754 A5
25000 FTRK 48134 4753 E5
25000 FTRK 48173 4753 E5
Wood Run Cir
11000 GOTp 48178 4188 A4
Wood Run Ct
800 SLYN 48178 4189 A4
Woods Dr
10 PLYM 48170 4265 B7
10 PLYM 48170 4337 B1
Woods Ln
500 GSPW 48236 4205 A4
800 GSPW 48236 4204 E4
Woods Rd
900 YPLT 48197 4491 D5
Woods Tr
8000 WasC 48189 4258 A3
Woodsboro Ct
2600 CNTN 48188 4412 C5
Woods Cir Dr
3100 DET 48207 4346 B4
Woodsfield St
27300 INKR 48141 4415 B2
Woodshire Ct
23400 NOVI 48375 4193 D2
Woodshire St
25700 DBHT 48127 4340 C5
Woodside Av
4500 PTFD 48197 4490 E5
4600 PTFD 48197 4491 A5
21000 ROTp 48220 4199 B3
Woodside Ct
6400 VNBN 48111 4494 D2
21700 NOVI 48167 4192 D4
E Woodside Ct
24700 FNHL 48335 4194 D1
Woodside Dr
- DET 48207 4347 B5
1200 WTLD 48185 4413 A1
1800 DRBN 48124 4416 E5
8500 WynC 48138 4670 C7
14400 LVNA 48154 4266 B5
46400 CNTN 48187 4411 C2
Woodside Dr N
39600 NvlT 48167 4265 D3
Woodside Dr S
39700 NvlT 48167 4265 D3
Woodside Rd
1700 TNTN 48183 4669 B3
2000 AARB 48104 4489 E1
9000 WasC 48167 4190 E7
9000 WasC 48167 4262 E1
Woodside St
7100 RMLS 48174 4498 B3
9700 DET 48204 4343 E1
16500 LVNA 48154 4266 C2
17200 LVNA 48152 4266 C2
18500 HRWD 48225 4203 E6
19600 HRWD 48225 4204 A6
Woodside Park Dr
8700 OKPK 48237 4199 B1
Woods Ln Ct
900 GSPW 48236 4204 E4
Woodson Ct
12600 DET 48213 4275 B5
Woodstock Ct
22300 WDHN 48183 4668 C5
Woodstock Dr
2300 DET 48203 4200 A4
2500 DET 48203 4199 E4
3100 DET 48221 4199 E4
Woodstock St
1600 CNTN 48188 4412 B4
Woodston Rd
19100 DET 48203 4200 A6
19200 DET 48203 4199 E6
Woodstream Dr
4200 PTFD 48197 4490 E6
Woodvale Dr
34400 LVNA 48154 4266 D4
Woodvale St
13300 OKPK 48237 4198 E2
13300 OKPK 48237 4199 A2
Woodview Ct
5100 DRBN 48126 4341 D7
Woodview Dr
2200 YpTp 48198 4576 E1
2200 YpTp 48198 4577 A1
7300 WTLD 48185 4338 C4
21300 WDHN 48183 4669 A3
Woodview Ln
2100 PTFD 48108 4488 D7
17600 BNTN 48174 4583 B6
Woodwall Ct
6300 VNBN 48111 4494 D2
Woodward Av
- FRDL 48203 4200 A5
10 DET 48226 4345 C4
2100 DET 48201 4345 C4
5000 DET 48202 4345 B3
7400 DET 48202 4273 A7
8900 DET 48202 4272 D4
11700 DET 48203 4272 D4
17100 HDPK 48203 4272 C1
20400 DET 48203 4200 A5
21200 FRDL 48220 4200 A5
21800 FRDL 48220 4199 D1
23600 FRDL 48069 4199 D1
23600 PTRG 48069 4199 D1
23600 PTRG 48220 4199 D1
Woodward Av SR-1
- FRDL 48203 4200 A5
10 DET 48226 4345 C4
2100 DET 48201 4345 C4
5000 DET 48202 4345 B3
7400 DET 48202 4273 A7
8900 DET 48202 4272 D4
11700 HDPK 48203 4272 D4
17500 DET 48203 4272 C1
17900 DET 48203 4200 A5
21400 FRDL 48220 4200 A5
21800 FRDL 48220 4199 D1
23600 FRDL 48069 4199 D1
23600 PTRG 48069 4199 D1
23600 PTRG 48220 4199 D1
Woodward Blvd
3300 WIND N8W 4421 E7
3500 WIND N8W 4422 A7
3600 WIND N8W 4505 A1
Woodward Hts
500 FRDL 48069 4199 E1
500 FRDL 48220 4199 E1
800 FRDL 48220 4200 A1
2300 HZLP 48030 4200 A1
2300 HZLP 48220 4200 A1
Woodward Rd
100 CNTN 48188 4411 B2
Woodward St
100 YPLT 48197 4492 A5
4600 WYNE 48184 4413 D7
5200 WYNE 48184 4496 D1
E Woodward St
10 ECRS 48229 4501 D3
W Woodward St
10 ECRS 48229 4501 D3
Woodward Heights Blvd
10 PTRG 48069 4199 D1
10 PTRG 48220 4199 D1
E Woodward Heights Blvd
10 HZLP 48030 4200 C1
W Woodward Heights Blvd
10 HZLP 48030 4200 C1
Woodway Dr
48900 PyTp 48170 4335 E2
Woodwill St
22100 SFLD 48075 4197 E3
Woodwind Ct
2100 CNTN 48188 4412 B5
Woodwind Ln
42200 CNTN 48188 4412 A5
Woodworth
14700 RDFD 48239 4268 B4
16700 RDFD 48240 4268 C2
19900 RDFD 48240 4196 C5
Woodworth Av
20000 RDFD 48240 4196 C5
Woodworth Cir
26300 DBHT 48127 4340 C5
Woodworth Ct
32900 WTLD 48185 4339 A6
Woodworth St
3900 DRBN 48126 4417 D1
4700 DRBN 48126 4342 D7
S Woody Ct
700 YPLT 48197 4491 D6
Woody Ln
55300 LyTp 48178 4190 C3
Woolsey
22600 NOVI 48375 4193 D3
Woonsocket Dr
6600 CNTN 48187 4337 A5
Wooster Ct
49100 CNTN 48188 4410 E5
Wooster St
2200 CNTN 48188 4410 E5
Worcester Dr
21700 NOVI 48374 4192 B4
Worcester Pl
10 DET 48203 4200 C7
10 DET 48203 4272 C1
Worchester St
500 WTLD 48186 4413 A3
38800 WTLD 48186 4412 E3
Worden Av
100 AARB 48103 4405 E5
Worden St
300 YPLT 48197 4491 E5
10700 DET 48224 4203 E7
Wordsworth St
100 FRDL 48220 4199 C4
100 FRDL 48220 4200 A3
Wormer
9500 RDFD 48239 4340 E1
15300 RDFD 48239 4268 E3
Wormer St
8100 DBHT 48127 4340 E3
17600 DET 48219 4268 E1
18200 DET 48219 4196 E7
Worth St
30000 GBTR 48173 4755 D5
Worthington Ct
40300 CNTN 48188 4412 D2
Worthington Dr
11700 TYLR 48180 4583 E1
11700 TYLR 48195 4583 E1
Worthington Pl
600 AARB 48103 4489 A3
Worthington Rd
300 CNTN 48188 4412 D2
Wreford St
3200 DET 48210 4344 C3
Wren St
10500 DRBN 48120 4418 C2
Wrenson St
1800 FRDL 48220 4200 B2
Wrexford Dr
22500 SFLD 48034 4196 B2
Wright Av
- Amhg N9V 4671 C4
Wright Rd
4300 WasC 48160 4659 E3
4400 WasC 48160 4660 A3
4900 AGST 48160 4660 A3
Wright St
300 WIND N9C 4419 D7
1000 AARB 48105 4406 C4
13200 GBTR 48173 4755 D5
Wyandotte Pl
2200 WIND N8Y 4346 C7
Wyandotte St
- Amhg N9V 4671 B5
2200 HMTK 48212 4273 C5
Wyandotte St E
10 WIND N9A 4420 E1
400 WIND N9A 4421 A1
1500 WIND N8Y 4346 E7
1600 WIND N8Y 4346 E7
4500 WIND N8Y 4347 A7
5100 WIND N8S 4347 E6
8900 WIND N8S 4348 A6
11200 WIND N8P 4348 C6
Wyandotte St W
10 WIND N9A 4420 D2
1200 WIND N9B 4420 D2
2800 WIND N9C 4420 A3
Wyatt Av
27000 BwTp 48183 4754 D2
Wykes St
7200 DET 48210 4343 D4
8000 DET 48204 4343 D3
Wyman St
22200 DET 48219 4269 B2
Wyndchase Blvd
41000 CNTN 48188 4412 C2
41200 CNTN 48187 4412 C2
Wyndham Ct
13100 PyTp 48170 4264 C7
Wyngate Ct
25400 HnTp 48134 4666 E7
Wyngate Dr
44000 OakC 48167 4192 D3
Wynnstone Dr
1200 AARB 48105 4407 C4
Wyoming
200 WynC 48111 4662 E2
Wyoming Av
2600 LSal N9H 4503 E3
2700 DRBN 48120 4418 C1
4200 DRBN 48126 4343 C3
4200 DRBN 48126 4418 C1
5200 DET 48126 4343 C3
5300 DET 48210 4343 C3
20700 ROTp 48220 4199 B3
21600 OKPK 48220 4199 B3
21600 OKPK 48237 4199 B3
Wyoming Ct
21600 OKPK 48220 4199 B3
21600 OKPK 48237 4199 B3
Wyoming Dr
38600 RMLS 48174 4496 A3
39000 RMLS 48174 4495 E3
Wyoming Pl
21700 OKPK 48220 4199 B3
21700 OKPK 48237 4199 B3
Wyoming St
- ROTp 48221 4199 B7
2200 DRBN 48120 4418 C3
8000 DET 48204 4343 C2
11300 DET 48204 4271 C6
12600 DET 48238 4271 C6
16100 DET 48221 4271 B2
18000 DET 48221 4199 B7
31600 LVNA 48150 4339 B3
W Wyoming St
10400 DRBN 48120 4418 C3

Y

Yacama Rd
19100 DET 48203 4200 D6
Yacht Av
6700 WRRN 48091 4201 E3
7000 WRRN 48091 4202 A3
Yale Av
25800 INKR 48141 4415 C5
Yale Ct
38700 FNHL 48167 4193 E4
Yale St
- LVNA 48150 4266 D5
- LVNA 48150 4338 D1
100 CNTN 48187 4411 E2
100 CNTN 48188 4411 E2
5600 WTLD 48185 4338 D6
8400 OKPK 48237 4199 C1
13900 LVNA 48154 4266 D5
23400 DRBN 48124 4416 A5
25400 DBHT 48125 4415 D5
25400 DBHT 48141 4415 D5
S Yale St
400 DET 48209 4419 B4
Yarmouth Cross
4300 PTFD 48197 4574 E2
Yarmouth Ct
1100 CNTN 48188 4411 B4
Yarmouth Dr
46900 CNTN 48188 4411 B3
Yates St
8800 DET 48214 4274 C7
Yellowbrick Rd
1500 TNTN 48183 4669 B2
1500 TNTN 48192 4669 B2
Yellowood St
3800 WIND N9E 4504 E2
Yellowstone Dr
3300 AARB 48105 4407 B1
Yellowstone St
9200 DET 48204 4343 E1
9200 DET 48204 4344 A1
9900 DET 48204 4271 E7
Yellow Wood Tr
400 PTFD 48197 4574 D2
Yemans Av
1900 HMTK 48212 4273 C4
Yeoman Ct
2000 AARB 48103 4488 D2
Yerkes St
300 NHVL 48167 4192 E6
Yinger Av
7800 DRBN 48126 4342 D3
Yoder Dr
- FMTN 48336 4194 E2
Yolanda St
- WIND N8R 4423 A2
8000 DET 48234 4202 A5
Yonka St
17800 DET 48212 4201 B7
20100 DET 48234 4201 B4
York Av
- TNTN 48183 4669 D6
York Ct
8400 SpTp 48198 4409 C7
8400 SpTp 48198 4492 C1
York St
400 DET 48202 4345 A2
700 PLYM 48170 4265 B6
1400 WIND N8X 4420 E4
1500 WIND N8X 4421 A4
2000 WasC 48167 4190 A7
28800 INKR 48141 4414 E7
28800 INKR 48141 4415 A7
32200 RKWD 48173 4754 C7
N York St
100 DRBN 48128 4416 B1
1300 DRBN 48128 4341 B7
S York St
100 DRBN 48124 4416 B2
York Ter
1500 WasC 48176 4658 A1
Yorkdale Ct
6800 WTLD 48185 4339 A5
Yorkdale Dr
33000 WTLD 48185 4339 A5
York Mills Cir
21900 NOVI 48374 4192 B4
Yorkshire Blvd
100 DBHT 48127 4415 B1
100 DBHT 48141 4415 B1
Yorkshire Ct
10 DRBN 48126 4341 D7
1200 SALN 48176 4572 B5
9800 WasC 48167 4190 B6
18400 RVVW 48192 4584 B7
Yorkshire Dr
9000 WasC 48176 4658 B3
17600 RVVW 48192 4584 B6
18500 LVNA 48152 4195 B7
44000 CNTN 48187 4336 E7
44500 NOVI 48375 4192 D1
Yorkshire Pl
26000 WynC 48138 4670 C7
Yorkshire Rd
- DET 48224 4203 B7
1000 GPPK 48230 4276 B5
1400 GPPK 48224 4276 B5
2300 AARB 48104 4490 A3
3400 DET 48224 4276 A4
9100 DET 48224 4275 D1
Yorkshire Sq
27100 DBHT 48127 4415 B2
Yorkshire St
14500 SOGT 48195 4500 C7
16700 LVNA 48152 4267 B2
16700 LVNA 48154 4267 B2
Yorktown
- WynC 48138 4756 B1
Yorktown Ct
800 NHVL 48167 4192 A5
Yorktown Dr
2000 AARB 48105 4407 B2
Yorktown Rd
1200 GSPW 48236 4204 D4
1400 STCS 48080 4204 D4
1400 STCS 48236 4204 D4
Yorktown St
43600 CNTN 48188 4411 E3
43600 CNTN 48188 4412 A5
Yorkville Ct
4300 INKR 48141 4414 E6
43600 CNTN 48188 4412 A4
Yorkville Dr
43500 CNTN 48188 4412 A4
York Woods Dr
9300 WasC 48176 4658 B3
Yosemite St
9200 DET 48204 4343 E1
9200 DET 48204 4344 A1
9900 DET 48204 4271 E7
N Yost Av
14500 ALPK 48101 4500 C4
S Yost Av
14600 ALPK 48101 4500 C5
Yost Blvd
2200 AARB 48104 4490 C3
Yost Rd
42800 CNTN 48188 4495 A1
42800 VNBN 48111 4495 A1
44000 CNTN 48111 4495 A1
44400 CNTN 48111 4494 D1
44400 CNTN 48188 4494 D1
44400 VNBN 48111 4494 D1
44400 VNBN 48188 4494 D1
Young Dr
29700 GBTR 48173 4755 C4
Young Ln
20700 GSPW 48236 4204 E5
Young Pl
1000 AARB 48105 4407 B5
Young St
800 YPLT 48198 4492 B4
800 YpTp 48198 4492 B4
13300 DET 48205 4202 E7
13900 DET 48205 4203 B7
Youngstown St
2300 WIND N9E 4503 E1
Ypres Av
2800 WIND N8W 4421 E3
3200 WIND N8W 4422 A3
Ypres Blvd
800 WIND N8W 4421 C4
Ypsi Ct
10 YpTp 48198 4492 D4
Ypsilanti St
26100 FTRK 48134 4753 D3
Yuma St
33600 WTLD 48185 4338 E5
33600 WTLD 48185 4339 A5
Yvonne Dr
24000 BNTN 48134 4668 A7

Z

Zachary St
42000 VNBN 48111 4495 B5
Zeeb Rd
- WasC 48103 4404 C1
2000 WasC 48130 4404 C1
4000 WasC 48130 4329 C4
6000 WasC 48176 4571 C5
N Zeeb Rd
10 WasC 48103 4404 C3
200 WasC 48130 4404 C3
2800 WasC 48130 4329 C7
S Zeeb Rd
10 WasC 48103 4404 C5
1000 WasC 48103 4487 C1
4000 WasC 48103 4571 C1
4000 WasC 48176 4571 C1
Zellmer St
28600 RMLS 48174 4582 A4
Zender Pl
3600 DET 48207 4346 A2
Zephyr Av
1000 YpTp 48198 4492 E6
Zerita St
23500 WRRN 48091 4201 A1
Ziegler Av
- WDHN 48183 4668 E4
Ziegler St
3700 DRBN 48124 4416 E6
3900 DBHT 48124 4416 E6
3900 DBHT 48125 4416 E6
5800 TYLR 48125 4499 E1
6500 TYLR 48180 4499 E2
14000 TYLR 48180 4583 E3
Zina Pitcher Pl
100 AARB 48104 4406 D6
Zinow St
2300 HMTK 48212 4273 B3
Zisette Dr
21700 NOVI 48375 4193 D4
Zorn St
1400 WTLD 48186 4414 A4
Zug Island Rd
1000 DET 48209 4419 B4
Zurich Av
4100 WIND N9G 4505 A4

#

1st Av
300 YPLT 48197 4491 E5
1st Ct
500 YPLT 48197 4491 E6
1st St
- BNTN 48134 4753 E1
- DBHT 48127 4341 B5
- FTRK 48134 4753 E1
- WasC 48197 4659 C1
10 BLVL 48111 4578 D2
10 CNTN 48188 4493 C1
10 DBHT 48127 4340 C5
100 WYDT 48192 4501 C6
200 NHVL 48167 4192 D6
600 DET 48226 4345 C6
2100 WYDT 48192 4585 C2
2900 WRRN 48091 4201 A4
3900 WYNE 48184 4413 E6
4400 ECRS 48229 4501 C5
6000 SpTp 48105 4491 C1
6000 SpTp 48198 4491 C1
6800 SRKW 48179 4840 C2
12000 Tcmh N8N 4423 E2
12000 Tcmh N8P 4423 E2
26000 TYLR 48180 4498 D3
42700 NvlT 48167 4265 A2
N 1st St
100 AARB 48103 4406 B5
100 AARB 48104 4406 B5
S 1st St
100 AARB 48103 4406 B6
100 AARB 48104 4406 B6
2nd Av
- DET 48226 4345 C6
1800 WTLD 48186 4413 E5
2900 DET 48201 4345 B3
7300 DET 48202 4345 A1
7700 DET 48202 4273 A7
8300 DET 48202 4272 E6
11800 HDPK 48203 4272 E5
17100 DET 48203 4272 C1
2nd St
- BNTN 48134 4753 E1
- CNTN 48188 4493 C1
- FTRK 48134 4753 E1
10 BLVL 48111 4578 D2
10 DBHT 48127 4340 C5
200 DBHT 48127 4341 B6
200 WYDT 48192 4501 C6
300 AARB 48103 4406 B6
300 SLYN 48178 4189 A2
300 YPLT 48197 4491 D5
1400 WYDT 48192 4585 C1
2500 WTLD 48186 4413 E5
2900 WYNE 48184 4413 E6
4300 ECRS 48229 4501 C4
4700 WIND N9E 4503 C1
5300 WYNE 48184 4496 E1
5800 RMLS 48174 4496 E1
5800 RMLS 48184 4496 E1
26000 TYLR 48180 4498 D3
2nd Concession Rd
900 Amhg N9V 4671 E4
1800 Amhg N9V 4586 E7
2nd Concession Rd CO-5
900 Amhg N9V 4671 E4
1800 Amhg N9V 4586 E7
3 Mile Dr
800 GPPK 48230 4276 A5
3400 DET 48224 4276 A5
3600 DET 48224 4275 E4
3rd St
- CNTN 48188 4493 C1
10 BLVL 48111 4578 C2
10 DBHT 48127 4340 C5
100 AARB 48103 4406 A6
200 VNBN 48111 4494 B5
1100 WYDT 48192 4501 C7
1200 DET 48226 4345 C6
1700 WYDT 48192 4585 C1
2100 TNTN 48183 4670 A3
2200 LSal N9H 4503 C3
2300 TNTN 48183 4669 E5
2900 DET 48201 4345 B4
2900 WYNE 48184 4413 E5
4300 ECRS 48229 4501 C4
5800 DET 48202 4345 A2
7700 DET 48202 4344 E1
8000 DET 48202 4272 E7
11800 HDPK 48203 4272 D4
17100 DET 48203 4272 B1
25400 WynC 48138 4670 D7
26000 TYLR 48180 4498 D3
4th Av
- WynC 48138 4756 B1
N 4th Av
100 AARB 48104 4406 B5
S 4th Av
100 AARB 48104 4406 B6
4th St
- DET 48226 4345 C6
- VNBN 48111 4494 A4
- WasC 48197 4659 B1
10 BLVL 48111 4578 C2
10 DBHT 48127 4340 C5
10 WYDT 48192 4501 C5
300 AARB 48103 4406 A6
2100 TNTN 48183 4669 E3
2200 LSal N9H 4503 C3
2900 WYNE 48184 4413 E5
3900 WYDT 48192 4585 C3
4400 ECRS 48229 4501 C5
4500 DET 48201 4345 A3
5200 WYNE 48184 4496 E1
5700 DET 48202 4345 A2
5800 RMLS 48174 4496 E1
25400 WynC 48138 4670 C7
26000 TYLR 48180 4498 D3
5 Mile Rd
- NvlT 48170 4264 E4
- NvlT 48170 4265 A4
2000 WasC 48178 4259 E5
2000 WasC 48178 4260 A5
2000 WasC 48189 4259 E5
2000 WasC 48189 4260 A5
3000 WasC 48105 4260 A5
4500 WasC 48105 4261 A5
4500 WasC 48178 4261 A5
6100 WasC 48167 4261 D5
7000 WasC 48167 4262 A5
7000 WasC 48170 4261 E5
7000 WasC 48170 4262 A5
9500 WasC 48167 4263 A5
9500 WasC 48170 4263 A5
24000 RDFD 48239 4268 A4
27300 RDFD 48154 4268 A4
27400 LVNA 48154 4268 A4
31700 LVNA 48154 4267 A4
36900 LVNA 48154 4266 A4
38700 LVNA 48154 4265 E4
39200 LVNA 48170 4265 E4
39400 PyTp 48170 4265 E4
39600 NvlT 48167 4265 E4
43400 NvlT 48167 4264 E4
43400 PyTp 48167 4264 B4
43700 PyTp 48170 4264 B4
47400 NvlT 48167 4263 E4
47400 PyTp 48170 4263 E4
E 5 Mile Rd
10 WasC 48189 4258 E5
500 WasC 48189 4259 A5
W 5 Mile Rd
10 WasC 48189 4258 D5
5th Av
48500 CNTN 48188 4411 A6
N 5th Av
100 AARB 48104 4406 B5
S 5th Av
100 AARB 48104 4406 B6
5th St
- DET 48226 4345 B6
- WasC 48197 4659 C1
10 BLVL 48111 4578 C2
300 AARB 48103 4406 A6
600 WYDT 48192 4501 C6
2000 WYDT 48192 4585 C1
2200 LSal N9H 4503 C3
2300 TNTN 48183 4669 E4
2600 DET 48201 4345 B5
4200 ECRS 48229 4501 C5
4700 WIND N9E 4503 D1
25400 WynC 48138 4670 C7
26000 TYLR 48180 4498 D3
5th Av Ct
49000 CNTN 48188 4410 E6
6 Mile Rd
10 WasC 48189 4258 E4
100 WasC 48189 4259 A4
2300 WasC 48178 4259 B4
2300 WasC 48178 4260 B3
5000 WasC 48178 4261 A3
6000 WasC 48167 4261 D3
7400 WasC 48167 4262 B3
10000 WasC 48167 4263 A2
27400 LVNA 48152 4268 A2
27400 LVNA 48154 4268 A2
28000 LVNA 48152 4267 E2
28000 LVNA 48154 4267 E2
33400 LVNA 48152 4266 D2
35500 LVNA 48154 4266 B2
38000 LVNA 48152 4265 E2
38000 LVNA 48154 4265 E2
38900 LVNA 48167 4265 E2
39400 NvlT 48167 4265 E2
43300 NvlT 48167 4264 E2
48100 NvlT 48167 4263 C2
W 6 Mile Rd
25000 RDFD 48240 4268 C2
27200 RDFD 48152 4268 B2
6th St
- WasC 48197 4659 C1
100 WYDT 48192 4501 B6
500 AARB 48103 4406 A6
1000 DET 48226 4345 B6
2200 LSal N9H 4503 D3
3300 WYDT 48192 4585 C3
4200 ECRS 48229 4501 C4
25400 WynC 48138 4670 C7
6th Concession
3700 WIND N8W 4505 A2
3800 WIND N9G 4505 A4
6th Concession Rd
1100 LSal N9H 4504 B6
7 Mile Rd
- WasC 48189 4259 A2
400 NHVL 48167 4192 E7
700 WasC 48189 4187 B7
1900 WasC 48178 4259 D2
2500 WasC 48178 4188 C7
3500 WasC 48178 4260 D1
4700 WasC 48178 4261 B1
6900 WasC 48167 4261 E1
7400 WasC 48167 4262 A1
10000 WasC 48167 4191 B7
10000 WasC 48167 4263 A1
27400 LVNA 48152 4196 A7
27400 LVNA 48240 4196 A7
31100 LVNA 48152 4195 B7
33400 LVNA 48152 4194 E7
38000 LVNA 48152 4193 D7
38800 LVNA 48167 4193 D7
39400 NvlT 48167 4193 D7
43000 NvlT 48167 4192 E7
48300 NvlT 48167 4191 D7
W 7 Mile Rd
- RDFD 48219 4196 C7
25000 RDFD 48240 4196 C7
7 Mile Rd E
10 DET 48203 4200 D6
1800 DET 48234 4200 D6
2200 DET 48234 4201 C6
7100 DET 48234 4202 A6
11600 DET 48205 4202 D6
16000 DET 48205 4203 B6
16100 DET 48224 4203 B6
7 Mile Rd W
- DET 48221 4200 A6
10 DET 48203 4200 A6
2600 DET 48221 4199 D6
12700 DET 48235 4199 A6
13400 DET 48235 4198 D6
18100 DET 48219 4198 C6
18900 DET 48219 4197 C7
23900 DET 48219 4196 D7
7th St
800 WYDT 48192 4501 B7
2000 WYDT 48192 4585 B1
2300 WIND N9E 4503 D2
3900 ECRS 48229 4501 C3
6000 LSal N9H 4503 D4
25400 WynC 48138 4670 C7
N 7th St
100 AARB 48103 4406 A5
S 7th St
100 AARB 48103 4406 A6
1100 AARB 48103 4489 A1
2400 AARB 48103 4488 E3
7th Concession
4100 Tcmh N0R 4505 C2
4100 WIND N8W 4505 C2
8 Mile Rd
- NOVI 48152 4193 E5
- NvlT 48152 4193 E5
- NvlT 48167 4193 E5
- WasC 48189 4187 A6
400 GOTp 48189 4186 D6
400 WasC 48189 4186 D6
1100 HbgT 48189 4186 D6
37400 FNHL 48167 4194 A5
37400 LVNA 48152 4194 A5
37400 LVNA 48167 4194 A5
38400 FNHL 48167 4193 E5
38400 LVNA 48152 4193 E5
38400 LVNA 48167 4193 E5
43000 NOVI 48152 4193 A5
43000 NOVI 48375 4193 A5
43300 NOVI 48167 4192 A5

Detroit & Wayne County Street Index

STREET Block	City	ZIP	Map#	Grid
8 Mile Rd				
46300	NHVL	48167	4192	A5
46300	NvlT	48167	4192	A5
48200	NOVI	48167	4191	B6
48200	NvlT	48167	4191	B6
51400	LyTp	48167	4191	B6
51400	WasC	48167	4191	B6
52000	LyTp	48167	4190	E6
52000	WasC	48167	4190	E6
56800	LyTp	48167	4189	E6
56800	WasC	48167	4189	E6
58400	LyTp	48178	4189	E6
58400	WasC	48178	4189	E6
E 8 Mile Rd				
-	DET	48030	4200	D4
-	DET	48203	4200	D4
-	HZLP	48203	4200	D4
10	HZLP	48030	4200	D4
100	FRDL	48220	4200	D4
100	NHVL	48167	4192	D5
900	FRDL	48203	4200	D4
1500	FRDL	48030	4200	D4
1900	WRRN	48030	4200	D4
1900	WRRN	48091	4200	D4
2100	GSPW	48236	4204	C4
2100	STCS	48080	4204	C4
2100	STCS	48236	4204	C4
2200	HRWD	48236	4204	C4
2200	WRRN	48091	4201	E4
7000	WRRN	48091	4202	A4
8000	WRRN	48089	4202	A4
21000	HRWD	48225	4204	C4
21000	STCS	48225	4204	C4
58600	LyTp	48167	4189	D6
58600	LyTp	48178	4189	D6
58600	WasC	48167	4189	D6
58600	WasC	48178	4189	D6
E 8 Mile Rd SR-102				
-	DET	48030	4200	B4
-	DET	48203	4200	B4
-	HZLP	48203	4200	B4
10	HZLP	48030	4200	B4
100	FRDL	48220	4200	B4
900	FRDL	48203	4200	B4
1500	FRDL	48030	4200	B4
1900	WRRN	48030	4200	B4
1900	WRRN	48091	4200	B4
2200	WRRN	48091	4201	E4
7000	WRRN	48091	4202	A4
8000	WRRN	48089	4202	A4
W 8 Mile Rd				
-	DET	48203	4200	B4
10	HZLP	48030	4200	B4
100	FRDL	48203	4200	B4
100	FRDL	48220	4200	B4
100	NHVL	48167	4192	D5
700	NvlT	48167	4192	D5
18100	DET	48219	4198	A4
18100	DET	48235	4198	A4
18100	SFLD	48219	4198	A4
18100	SFLD	48235	4198	A4
18400	SFLD	48075	4198	A4
18600	DET	48219	4197	B5
18600	SFLD	48219	4197	B5
18800	SFLD	48075	4197	B5
20200	DET	48075	4197	B5
22000	SFLD	48034	4197	B5
22500	DET	48034	4197	B5
24500	DET	48034	4196	C5
24500	DET	48219	4196	C5
24600	SFLD	48034	4196	C5
24900	SFLD	48240	4196	C5
25000	RDFD	48240	4196	C5
27400	FNHL	48152	4196	C5
27400	FNHL	48336	4196	C5
27400	LVNA	48152	4196	C5
28000	LVNA	48336	4196	C5
28300	FNHL	48336	4195	B5
28300	LVNA	48152	4195	B5
28300	LVNA	48336	4195	B5
29100	FNHL	48152	4195	B5
32400	FMTN	48336	4195	B5
33200	FMTN	48336	4194	C5
33200	LVNA	48152	4194	C5
33200	LVNA	48336	4194	C5
33400	FNHL	48152	4194	C5
33400	FNHL	48335	4194	C5
33400	LVNA	48335	4195	C5
37000	FNHL	48167	4194	C5
37000	LVNA	48167	4194	C5
61000	LyTp	48178	4189	A6
61000	WasC	48178	4189	A6
63000	GOTp	48178	4188	D6
63000	GOTp	48178	4189	A6
63000	WasC	48178	4188	D6
68200	GOTp	48178	4187	E6
68200	GOTp	48189	4187	E6
68200	WasC	48178	4187	E6
68200	WasC	48189	4187	E6
W 8 Mile Rd SR-102				
-	DET	48203	4200	B4
-	FRDL	48203	4200	B4
-	FRDL	48220	4200	B4
10	HZLP	48030	4200	B4
18100	DET	48219	4198	A4
18100	DET	48235	4198	A4
18100	SFLD	48219	4198	A4
18100	SFLD	48235	4198	A4
18400	SFLD	48075	4198	A4
18600	DET	48219	4197	B5
18600	SFLD	48219	4197	B5
18800	SFLD	48075	4197	B5
20200	DET	48075	4197	B5
22000	SFLD	48034	4197	B5
22500	DET	48034	4197	B5
24000	DET	48034	4196	C5
24000	DET	48219	4196	C5
24000	SFLD	48034	4196	C5
25000	RDFD	48240	4196	C5
25000	SFLD	48240	4196	C5
W 8 Mile Rd SR-102				
27400	FNHL	48152	4196	C5
27400	FNHL	48336	4196	C5
27400	LVNA	48152	4196	C5
8 Mile Rd E				
1500	DET	48030	4200	C4
1500	DET	48203	4200	C4
1500	HZLP	48030	4200	C4
1500	HZLP	48203	4200	C4
1900	DET	48234	4200	C4
1900	WRRN	48030	4200	C4
1900	WRRN	48091	4200	C4
1900	WRRN	48203	4200	C4
1900	WRRN	48234	4200	C4
2000	DET	48234	4201	B4
2000	WRRN	48091	4201	B4
2000	WRRN	48234	4201	B4
7100	DET	48234	4202	C4
7100	WRRN	48091	4202	C4
7100	WRRN	48234	4202	C4
11300	DET	48089	4202	C4
11600	DET	48205	4202	C4
11600	WRRN	48205	4202	C4
11800	WRRN	48089	4202	C4
13800	DET	48205	4203	A4
13800	WRRN	48205	4203	A4
13900	WRRN	48089	4203	A4
14700	WRRN	48021	4203	A4
14800	EPTE	48021	4203	A4
14800	EPTE	48205	4203	A4
17300	DET	48225	4203	D4
17300	EPTE	48225	4203	D4
18000	EPTE	48021	4204	A4
18000	HRWD	48021	4203	D4
18000	HRWD	48021	4204	A4
18000	HRWD	48225	4203	D4
18000	HRWD	48225	4204	A4
19200	HRWD	48080	4204	A4
19200	STCS	48021	4204	A4
19200	STCS	48080	4204	A4
20600	STCS	48225	4204	A4
8 Mile Rd E SR-102				
1500	DET	48030	4200	E4
1500	DET	48203	4200	E4
1500	HZLP	48030	4200	E4
1500	HZLP	48203	4200	E4
1900	DET	48234	4200	E4
1900	WRRN	48030	4200	E4
1900	WRRN	48091	4200	E4
1900	WRRN	48203	4200	E4
1900	WRRN	48234	4200	E4
2000	DET	48234	4201	B4
2000	WRRN	48091	4201	B4
2000	WRRN	48234	4201	B4
7100	DET	48234	4202	C4
7100	WRRN	48091	4202	C4
7100	WRRN	48234	4202	C4
11300	DET	48089	4202	C4
11600	DET	48205	4202	C4
11600	WRRN	48205	4202	C4
11800	WRRN	48089	4202	C4
13800	DET	48205	4203	A4
13800	WRRN	48205	4203	A4
13900	WRRN	48089	4203	A4
14700	WRRN	48021	4203	A4
14800	EPTE	48021	4203	A4
14800	EPTE	48205	4203	A4
17300	DET	48225	4203	D4
17300	EPTE	48225	4203	D4
17300	HRWD	48225	4203	D4
8 Mile Rd W				
-	DET	48219	4197	C5
-	SFLD	48075	4197	C5
-	SFLD	48219	4197	C5
10	DET	48203	4200	C4
10	HZLP	48030	4200	C4
10	HZLP	48203	4200	C4
400	FRDL	48203	4199	B4
400	FRDL	48220	4199	B4
600	FRDL	48203	4200	B4
600	FRDL	48220	4200	B4
2600	DET	48203	4199	B4
3000	DET	48220	4199	B4
3000	DET	48221	4199	B4
4100	FRDL	48221	4199	B4
8100	ROTp	48220	4199	B4
8100	ROTp	48221	4199	B4
11000	ROTp	48235	4199	B4
11000	ROTp	48237	4199	B4
12700	DET	48235	4199	B4
12700	OKPK	48235	4199	B4
12700	OKPK	48237	4199	B4
13400	DET	48235	4198	A5
13400	OKPK	48235	4198	A5
13400	OKPK	48237	4198	A5
15500	DET	48075	4198	A5
15500	SFLD	48075	4198	A5
15500	SFLD	48235	4198	A5
15500	SFLD	48237	4198	A5
23900	SFLD	48034	4197	A5
24300	DET	48034	4196	E5
24300	DET	48219	4196	E5
24300	SFLD	48034	4196	E5
8 Mile Rd W SR-102				
-	DET	48075	4198	A5
-	DET	48219	4197	C5
-	SFLD	48075	4197	C5
-	SFLD	48219	4197	C5
-	SFLD	48235	4198	A5
10	DET	48203	4200	C4
10	HZLP	48030	4200	C4
10	HZLP	48203	4200	C4
400	FRDL	48203	4199	B4
400	FRDL	48220	4199	B4
600	FRDL	48203	4200	B4
600	FRDL	48220	4200	B4
2600	DET	48203	4199	B4
3000	DET	48220	4199	B4
3000	DET	48221	4199	B4
4100	FRDL	48221	4199	B4
8 Mile Rd W SR-102				
8100	ROTp	48220	4199	B4
8100	ROTp	48221	4199	B4
11000	ROTp	48235	4199	B4
11000	ROTp	48237	4199	B4
12700	DET	48235	4199	B4
12700	OKPK	48235	4199	B4
12700	OKPK	48237	4199	B4
13400	DET	48235	4198	A5
13400	OKPK	48235	4198	A5
13400	OKPK	48237	4198	A5
16800	SFLD	48075	4198	A5
23900	SFLD	48034	4197	A5
24300	DET	48034	4196	E5
24300	DET	48219	4196	E5
24300	SFLD	48034	4196	E5
8th St				
400	AARB	48103	4406	A6
600	WYDT	48192	4501	B7
1400	DET	48216	4345	B6
1400	DET	48226	4345	B6
3300	WYDT	48192	4585	B3
3700	ECRS	48229	4501	D3
25400	WynC	48138	4670	C7
8th Concession				
4200	Tcmh	N0R	4505	D2
8 1/2 Mile Rd				
21100	SFLD	48075	4197	B4
21400	SFLD	48034	4197	B4
9 Mile Rd				
8000	GOTp	48116	4186	C3
8000	GOTp	48189	4186	C3
9200	GOTp	48116	4187	C4
9200	GOTp	48189	4187	C4
10800	GOTp	48178	4187	C4
11100	GOTp	48178	4188	B4
13400	GOTp	48178	4189	A4
38100	FNHL	48167	4193	E3
38100	FNHL	48167	4194	A3
38100	FNHL	48335	4193	E3
38100	FNHL	48335	4194	A3
38800	FNHL	48375	4193	D3
51600	LyTp	48167	4191	A4
51600	LyTp	48178	4191	A4
51600	LyTp	48374	4191	A4
51700	LyTp	48167	4190	E4
51700	LyTp	48178	4190	E4
57700	LyTp	48167	4189	A4
57700	LyTp	48178	4189	A4
60000	SLYN	48178	4189	A4
9 Mile Rd SR-36				
8000	GOTp	48116	4186	C3
8000	GOTp	48189	4186	C3
9200	GOTp	48116	4187	A4
9200	GOTp	48189	4187	A4
E 9 Mile Rd				
-	STCS	48080	4205	A2
10	HZLP	48030	4200	E2
100	FRDL	48220	4199	E2
300	FRDL	48220	4200	E2
1900	WRRN	48091	4200	E2
2200	WRRN	48091	4201	B2
7000	WRRN	48091	4202	B2
8000	WRRN	48089	4202	B2
13900	WRRN	48089	4203	E2
14400	WRRN	48021	4203	E2
14500	EPTE	48021	4203	E2
18200	EPTE	48021	4204	A2
19000	EPTE	48080	4204	A2
19000	STCS	48080	4204	A2
19400	STCS	48021	4204	A2
W 9 Mile Rd				
10	HZLP	48030	4200	B2
100	FRDL	48220	4199	B2
600	FRDL	48220	4200	B2
600	HZLP	48220	4200	B2
1500	FRDL	48237	4199	B2
1500	OKPK	48220	4199	B2
1500	OKPK	48237	4199	B2
13200	OKPK	48237	4198	B3
15500	SFLD	48075	4198	B3
18400	SFLD	48075	4197	D3
22000	SFLD	48034	4197	A3
23800	SFLD	48034	4196	E3
27400	FNHL	48034	4196	A3
27400	FNHL	48336	4196	A3
28300	FNHL	48336	4195	E3
30700	FMTN	48336	4195	C3
33000	FMTN	48336	4194	C3
33400	FMTN	48335	4194	C3
33400	FNHL	48335	4194	C3
33400	FNHL	48336	4194	C3
37300	FNHL	48167	4194	C3
39400	NOVI	48375	4193	E3
42900	NOVI	48375	4192	E3
43400	NOVI	48167	4192	E3
45400	NOVI	48374	4192	B3
47700	NOVI	48167	4191	C4
47700	NOVI	48374	4191	C4
9th St				
100	AARB	48103	4406	A6
600	WYDT	48192	4501	B7
2000	WYDT	48192	4585	B2
3700	ECRS	48229	4501	C3
5700	LSal	N9H	4503	D4
10 Mile Rd				
12500	GOTp	48178	4188	C2
13900	GOTp	48178	4189	A2
51400	LyTp	48178	4191	A2
52200	LyTp	48178	4190	D2
57800	LyTp	48178	4189	D2
W 10 Mile Rd				
19000	SFLD	48075	4197	C1
22000	SFLD	48034	4197	A1
23800	SFLD	48034	4196	D1
27400	FNHL	48034	4196	A1
27400	FNHL	48336	4196	A1
28100	FNHL	48336	4195	E1
31400	FMTN	48336	4195	A1
38000	FNHL	48335	4193	E1
W 10 Mile Rd				
38000	FNHL	48335	4194	A1
38600	FNHL	48375	4193	E1
39400	NOVI	48375	4193	E1
42900	NOVI	48375	4192	E1
45400	NOVI	48374	4192	B1
48000	NOVI	48374	4191	C2
10th St				
1000	WYDT	48192	4501	B7
1400	WYDT	48192	4585	B1
1700	DET	48216	4345	B6
4000	ECRS	48229	4501	C3
5600	LSal	N9H	4503	E3
10th Concession Rd				
700	Lksr	N0R	4424	B7
11th St				
1000	WYDT	48192	4501	B7
1400	WYDT	48192	4585	B1
1900	DET	48216	4345	B6
3700	ECRS	48229	4501	C3
5900	LSal	N9H	4503	E4
11th Concession				
3400	Tcmh	N0R	4423	D7
12th St				
1000	WYDT	48192	4501	B7
1400	WYDT	48192	4585	B1
3700	ECRS	48229	4501	C3
12th Concession				
2600	Tcmh	N0R	4424	A7
13th St				
1000	WYDT	48146	4501	A7
1000	WYDT	48192	4501	A7
1400	WYDT	48192	4585	A1
4200	ECRS	48229	4501	C3
6000	LSal	N9H	4503	E4
14th St				
700	DET	48216	4420	B1
1700	WIND	N9J	4503	B3
1700	WYDT	48192	4585	A1
2400	DET	48216	4345	A5
3300	DET	48210	4344	E4
3700	ECRS	48229	4501	C2
7300	DET	48206	4344	C1
8700	DET	48206	4272	C7
15700	DET	48238	4272	A3
15th St				
-	DET	48216	4345	A6
700	DET	48216	4420	A1
1000	WYDT	48192	4501	A7
1400	WYDT	48192	4585	A1
3000	DET	48216	4344	E5
3700	ECRS	48229	4501	C2
5400	DET	48210	4344	D2
16th St				
1000	WYDT	48146	4501	A7
1000	WYDT	48192	4501	A7
1000	WYDT	48192	4585	A1
2300	DET	48216	4345	A6
2800	DET	48216	4344	E5
3700	ECRS	48229	4501	C2
5400	DET	48210	4344	D2
17th St				
700	DET	48216	4420	A1
1000	LNPK	48146	4501	A7
1000	WYDT	48146	4501	A7
1000	WYDT	48192	4501	A7
1000	WYDT	48192	4585	A1
2200	DET	48216	4345	A6
2700	DET	48216	4344	E5
3500	DET	48210	4344	E4
3700	ECRS	48229	4501	C2
18th St				
500	DET	48216	4420	A1
1000	LNPK	48146	4501	A7
1000	WYDT	48146	4501	A7
1000	WYDT	48192	4501	A7
1200	DET	48216	4345	A7
2000	WYDT	48192	4585	A1
2800	DET	48216	4344	E5
3300	DET	48210	4344	E5
3700	ECRS	48229	4501	C2
19th St				
1000	WYDT	48192	4501	A7
3700	ECRS	48229	4501	B2
4000	WYDT	48192	4585	A4
20th St				
1000	WYDT	48192	4501	A7
1000	WYDT	48192	4585	A1
1400	DET	48216	4344	E7
1400	DET	48216	4345	A7
21st St				
400	DET	48216	4420	A1
1000	WYDT	48192	4501	A7
1000	WYDT	48192	4585	A1
1400	DET	48216	4344	E7
22nd St				
-	DET	48216	4419	E1
700	DET	48216	4420	A1
1000	WYDT	48192	4500	E7
2500	DET	48216	4344	E6
2600	WYDT	48192	4585	A3
3300	WYDT	48192	4584	E3
23rd St				
300	DET	48216	4420	A1
700	DET	48216	4419	E1
1000	LNPK	48146	4500	E7
1000	WYDT	48146	4500	E7
1000	WYDT	48192	4500	E7
2600	DET	48216	4344	E6
2600	WYDT	48192	4584	E2
5400	DET	48210	4344	C3
24th St				
-	DET	48216	4420	A1
700	DET	48216	4419	E1
2200	DET	48216	4344	D6
3300	DET	48210	4344	D6
25th St				
700	DET	48216	4419	E1
2700	DET	48216	4344	D6
3500	DET	48210	4344	C5
28th St				
5400	DET	48210	4344	B4
29th St				
3300	DET	48210	4344	C5
30th St				
5600	DET	48210	4344	B3
31st St				
5300	DET	48210	4344	B4
32nd St				
5100	DET	48210	4344	B4
33rd St				
-	DET	48210	4344	B4
35th St				
-	DET	48210	4344	A5
51st St				
4300	DET	48210	4343	E6
52nd St				
4300	DET	48210	4343	E6

Detroit & Wayne County Points of Interest Index

Detroit & Wayne County Points of Interest Index

Detroit & Wayne County Points of Interest Index

Hospitals

FEATURE NAME Address City ZIP Code	MAP#	GRID
Bon Secours Hosp 468 Cadieux Rd, GSPT, 48230	4276	C6
Botsford General Hosp 28050 Botsford Dr, FNHL, 48336	4196	A4
Children's Hosp of Michigan 3901 Beaubien St, DET, 48201	4345	C3
Cottage Hosp 159 Kercheval Av, GSPF, 48236	4276	D4
Detroit Med Ctr DET, 48201	4345	C3
Detroit Receiving Hosp 4201 St. Antoine St, DET, 48201	4345	C3
Forest Health Med Ctr 135 S Prospect Rd, YPLT, 48198	4492	A5
Garden City Hosp 6245 N Inkster Rd, GDNC, 48135	4340	B6
Greater Detroit Hosp 3105 Carpenter St, DET, 48212	4273	B3
Harper University Hosp 3990 John R St, DET, 48201	4345	C3
Hawthorn Center 18471 Haggerty Rd, NvlT, 48167	4265	D1
Henry Ford Hosp 2799 Grand Blvd W, DET, 48202	4344	E1
Henry Ford Kingswood Hosp 10300 8 Mile Rd W, ROTp, 48220	4199	B4
Henry Ford Wyandotte Hosp 2333 Walnut St, WYDT, 48192	4585	D1
Hotel-Dieu Grace Hosp 1030 Ouellette Av, WIND, N9A	4420	E2
Hutzel Hosp 4707 St. Antoine St, DET, 48201	4345	C2
John D Dingell Veterans Affairs Med Ctr 4646 John R St, DET, 48201	4345	C3
Margaret Montgomery Hosp 28303 Joy Rd, WTLD, 48185	4340	A3
Oakwood Annapolis Hosp 33155 Annapolis St, WYNE, 48184	4414	A7
Oakwood Healthcare Center-Canton 7300 N Canton Center Rd, CNTN, 48187	4336	D5
Oakwood Healthcare Center-Lincoln Park 25650 Outer Dr, LNPK, 48146	4501	A1
Oakwood Heritage Hosp 10000 Haig St, TYLR, 48180	4498	E5
Oakwood Hosp-Dearborn 18101 Oakwood Blvd, DRBN, 48124	4417	B5
Oakwood Southshore Med Ctr 5450 Fort St, TNTN, 48183	4755	B1
Providence Hosp & Med Ctr 16001 W 9 Mile Rd, SFLD, 48075	4198	C3
Riverside Osteopathic Hosp 150 George St, TNTN, 48183	4670	A3
St. John Detroit Riverview Hosp 7733 Jefferson Av E, DET, 48214	4346	D4
St. John Gratiot Center 15000 Gratiot Av, DET, 48205	4203	B4
St. John Hosp & Med Ctr 22101 Moross Rd, DET, 48236	4276	B1
St. John Northeast Community Hosp 4777 Outer Dr E, DET, 48234	4202	B5
St. Joseph Mercy Hosp 5301 E Huron River Dr, SpTp, 48197	4491	A2
St. Joseph Mercy Saline Hosp 400 W Russell St, SALN, 48176	4572	B7
St. Mary Mercy Hosp 36475 5 Mile Rd, LVNA, 48154	4266	B4
Sinai-Grace Hosp 6071 Outer Dr W, DET, 48235	4270	E1
Sinai Hosp 6767 Outer Dr W, DET, 48235	4270	D1
University of Michigan Hosp 1500 E Medical Center Dr, AARB, 48104	4406	D5
Veterans Med Ctr 2215 Fuller Ct, AARB, 48105	4406	E5
Windsor Regional Hosp-Metropolitan Campus 1995 Lens Av, WIND, N8W	4421	D3
Windsor Regional Hosp-Western Campus 1453 Prince Rd, WIND, N9C	4420	B6

Law Enforcement

FEATURE NAME Address City ZIP Code	MAP#	GRID
Allen Park Police Dept 16850 Southfield Rd, ALPK, 48101	4500	A1
Amherstburg Police Station 532 Sandwich St S, Amhg, N9V	4757	C4
Ann Arbor Police Dept 100 N 5th Av, AARB, 48104	4406	B6
Belleville Police Dept 6 Main St, BLVL, 48111	4578	D2
Brownstown Twp Police Dept 21313 Telegraph Rd, BNTN, 48183	4668	A3
Canton Twp Police Dept 1150 S Canton Center Rd, CNTN, 48188	4411	D3
Dearborn Heights Police Dept 6045 Fenton St, DBHT, 48127	4340	E6
Dearborn Police Dept 16099 Michigan Av, DRBN, 48126	4417	C1
Detroit Police Dept 4747 Woodward Av, DET, 48201	4345	B3
Detroit Police Dept 1441 7 Mile Rd W, DET, 48203	4200	B6
Detroit Police Dept 12000 Livernois Av, DET, 48204	4271	E7
Detroit Police Dept 3300 Mack Av, DET, 48207	4346	A2
Detroit Police Dept 5100 Nevada St E, DET, 48212	4201	C7
Detroit Police Dept 11187 Gratiot Av, DET, 48213	4274	D2
Detroit Police Dept 11411 Jefferson Av E, DET, 48214	4347	B1
Detroit Police Dept 2801 Vernor Hwy W, DET, 48216	4344	E7
Detroit Police Dept 21400 Grand River Av, DET, 48219	4269	C2
Detroit Police Dept 1300 Beaubien St, DET, 48226	4345	D5
Detroit Police Dept 13530 Lesure St, DET, 48227	4270	E6
Detroit Police Dept 11450 Warwick St, DET, 48228	4341	E1
Eastpointe Police Dept 16083 E 9 Mile Rd, EPTE, 48021	4203	C2
Ecorse Police Dept 3869 W Jefferson Av, ECRS, 48229	4501	D3
Farmington Police Dept 23600 Liberty St, FMTN, 48335	4194	E2
Ferndale Police Dept 310 E 9 Mile Rd, FRDL, 48220	4199	E2
Flat Rock Police Dept 25500 Gibraltar Rd, FTRK, 48134	4753	E4
Garden City Police Dept 6000 Middlebelt Rd, GDNC, 48135	4339	E6
Gibraltar Police Dept 29450 Munro Av, GBTR, 48173	4755	D4
Grosse Ile Police Dept 24525 Meridian Rd, WynC, 48138	4670	B6
Grosse Pointe Park Police Dept 15115 Jefferson Av E, GPPK, 48230	4275	E7
Grosse Pointe Police Dept 17145 Maumee St, GSPT, 48230	4276	C5
Grosse Pointe Shores Police Dept 795 Lake Shore Rd, GSPS, 48236	4205	A5
Grosse Pointe Woods Police Dept 20025 Mack Plaza Dr, GSPW, 48236	4204	C6
Hamtramck Police Dept 3456 Evaline Av, HMTK, 48212	4273	C4
Harper Woods Police Dept 19617 Harper Av, HRWD, 48225	4204	A6
Hazel Park Police Dept 111 E 9 Mile Rd, HZLP, 48030	4200	C2
Highland Park Police Dept 25 Gerald St, HDPK, 48203	4272	D3
Inkster Police Dept 27301 S River Park Dr, INKR, 48141	4415	B4
La Salle Police Dept 5950 Malden Rd, LSal, N9H	4503	C4
Lincoln Park Police Dept 1427 Cleophus Pkwy, LNPK, 48146	4500	E3
Livonia Police Dept 33000 Civic Center Dr, LVNA, 48154	4267	A4
Lodi Twp Police Dept 1055 N Zeeb Rd, WasC, 48130	4404	C3
Melvindale Police Dept 3100 Oakwood Blvd, MVDL, 48122	4418	A6
Northfield Twp Police Dept 75 Barker Rd, WasC, 48189	4187	A7
Northville Police Dept 215 W Main St, NHVL, 48167	4192	D6
Northville Twp Police Dept 41600 Township Hall, NvlT, 48167	4265	B2
Novi Police Dept 45125 W 10 Mile Rd, NOVI, 48375	4192	D1
Oak Park Police Dept 13600 Oak Park Blvd, OKPK, 48237	4198	E1
Pleasant Ridge Police Dept 23925 Woodward Av, PTRG, 48069	4199	D1
Plymouth Police Dept 210 S Main St, PLYM, 48170	4265	A7
Redford Twp Police Dept 25833 Elsinore, RDFD, 48239	4268	C4
River Rouge Police Dept 10600 W Jefferson Av, RVRG, 48218	4418	E7
Riverview Police Dept 14100 Civic Park Dr, RVVW, 48192	4584	D6
Rockwood Police Dept 32409 Fort Rd, RKWD, 48173	4754	C7
Romulus Police Dept 11165 Olive St, RMLS, 48174	4496	C7
Royal Oak Twp Police 21149 Wyoming Av, ROTp, 48220	4199	B4
Saline Police Dept 100 N Harris St, SALN, 48176	4572	D7
Scio Twp Police Dept 1055 N Zeeb Rd, WasC, 48130	4404	C3
South Lyon Police Dept 214 W Lake St, SLYN, 48178	4189	B2
Taylor Police Dept 23515 Goddard Rd, TYLR, 48180	4499	B7
Tecumseh Police Dept 13677 St. Gregory's Rd, Tcmh, N8N	4424	C1
Trenton Police Dept 2872 W Jefferson Av, TNTN, 48183	4669	E4
Van Buren Twp Police Dept 46425 Tyler Rd, VNBN, 48111	4494	C5
Wayne Police Dept 34840 Sims St, WYNE, 48184	4413	E6
Webster Twp Police Dept 1055 N Zeeb Rd, WasC, 48130	4404	C3
Westland Police Dept 36701 Ford Rd, WTLD, 48185	4338	B7
Windsor Police Dept 150 Goyeau St, WIND, N9A	4420	E1
Woodhaven Police Dept 21869 West Rd, WDHN, 48183	4668	D5
Wyandotte Police Dept 2015 Biddle Av, WYDT, 48192	4585	C1
Ypsilanti Police Dept 505 W Michigan Av, YPLT, 48197	4491	E4

Libraries

FEATURE NAME Address City ZIP Code	MAP#	GRID
Allen Park 8100 Allen Rd, ALPK, 48101	4500	A3
Amherstburg 232 Sandwich St S, Amhg, N9V	4757	B3
Ann Arbor-5th Av 343 S 5th Av, AARB, 48104	4406	B6
Ann Arbor-Nellie Loving 3042 Creek Dr, AARB, 48108	4490	B4
Ann Arbor-Plymouth 2713 Plymouth Rd, AARB, 48105	4407	A3
Beacon Memorial Public 45 Biddle Av, WYDT, 48192	4585	D2
Bentley Historical 1150 Beal Av, AARB, 48105	4407	A5
Canton Public 1200 S Canton Center Rd, CNTN, 48188	4411	D4
Caroline Kennedy 24590 George St, DBHT, 48127	4340	E6
Detroit-Bowen 3648 Vernor Hwy W, DET, 48216	4344	E7
Detroit-Bryant 22100 Michigan Av, DRBN, 48124	4416	C3
Detroit-Campbell 6625 Fort St W, DET, 48209	4419	C3
Detroit-Chandler Park 12800 Harper Av, DET, 48213	4275	A3
Detroit-Chaney 16101 Grand River Av, DET, 48227	4270	C4
Detroit-Chase 17731 7 Mile Rd W, DET, 48235	4198	A7
Detroit-Conley 4600 Martin St, DET, 48210	4344	A6
Detroit-Douglass 3666 Grand River Av, DET, 48210	4345	A4
Detroit-Duffield 2507 Grand Blvd W, DET, 48206	4344	D2
Detroit-Edison 18400 Joy Rd, DET, 48228	4342	A2
Detroit-Elmwood Park 550 Chene St, DET, 48207	4346	A5
Detroit-Esper 12929 W Warren Av, DRBN, 48126	4343	A4
Detroit-Franklin 13651 McNichols Rd E, DET, 48205	4202	E7
Detroit-Gratiot Av 121 Gratiot Av, DET, 48226	4345	D6
Detroit-Gray Branch 7737 Kercheval St, DET, 48214	4346	C2
Detroit-Hubbard 12929 McNichols Rd W, DET, 48235	4271	A1
Detroit-Jefferson 12350 Outer Dr E, DET, 48224	4275	E3
Detroit-Knapp 13330 Conant St, DET, 48212	4273	C2
Detroit-Lincoln 1221 7 Mile Rd E, DET, 48203	4200	D6
Detroit-Lothrop 1529 Grand Blvd W, DET, 48210	4344	C4
Detroit-Mark Twain 8500 Gratiot Av, DET, 48213	4274	C6
Detroit-Monteith 14100 Kercheval St, DET, 48214	4275	D7
Detroit-Parkman 1766 Oakman Blvd, DET, 48238	4272	A4
Detroit Public 5201 Woodward Av, DET, 48202	4345	B2
Detroit-Redford 21200 Grand River Av, DET, 48219	4269	C2
Detroit-Richard 9876 Grand River Av, DET, 48204	4343	D1
Detroit-Sherwood Forest 7117 7 Mile Rd W, DET, 48221	4199	D6
Detroit-Snow 23950 Princeton St, DRBN, 48124	4416	A5
Detroit-Tavy Stone Fashion 5401 Woodward Av, DET, 48202	4345	B2
Detroit-Wilder 7140 7 Mile Rd E, DET, 48234	4202	A6
Eastpointe Memorial 15875 Oak Av, EPTE, 48021	4203	C2
Ecology Center 417 Detroit St, AARB, 48104	4406	B5
Ecorse Public 4184 W Jefferson Av, ECRS, 48229	4501	D4
Farmington Community 23550 Liberty St, FMTN, 48335	4194	E2
Ferndale 222 E 9 Mile Rd, FRDL, 48220	4199	E2
Flat Rock 26336 E Huron River Dr, FTRK, 48134	4753	D3
Fred C Fischer 167 4th St, BLVL, 48111	4578	C2
Garden City Public 2012 Middlebelt Rd, GDNC, 48135	4339	E7
Grosse Pointe Farms Public 10 Kercheval Av, GSPF, 48236	4276	C4
Grosse Pointe-Grosse Pointe Woods Branch 20600 Mack Av, GSPW, 48236	4204	C5
Grosse Pointe Public 15430 Kercheval St, GPPK, 48230	4275	E6
Hamburg Twp Public 7225 Stone St, HbgT, 48189	4186	B3
Hamtramck 2360 Caniff St, HMTK, 48212	4273	B4
Harper Woods City 19601 Harper Av, HRWD, 48225	4204	A6
Hazel Park 123 E 9 Mile Rd, HZLP, 48030	4200	C2
Henry Ford Centennial 16301 Michigan Av, DRBN, 48126	4417	C2
Highland Park-McGregor 12244 Woodward Av, HDPK, 48203	4272	D4
Inkster 2005 Inkster Rd, INKR, 48141	4415	B4
John F Kennedy 24602 Van Born Rd, DBHT, 48125	4498	E1
La Salle 5940 Malden Rd, LSal, N9H	4503	C4
Library Hanover St, DBHT, 48125	4415	E7
Livonia Civic Center 32777 5 Mile Rd, LVNA, 48154	4267	A4
Livonia Public 32901 Plymouth Rd, LVNA, 48150	4339	A1
Maybelle Burnette 22005 Van Dyke Av, WRRN, 48091	4202	A3
Melvindale Public 18650 Allen Rd, MVDL, 48122	4417	D6
Northfield Twp 125 Barker Rd, WasC, 48189	4187	A7
Northville Public 215 W Main St, NHVL, 48167	4192	D6
Novi Public 45245 W 10 Mile Rd, NOVI, 48375	4192	D1
Oak Park 14200 Oak Park Blvd, OKPK, 48237	4198	E1
Plymouth Public 223 S Main St, PLYM, 48170	4337	A1
Redford Twp 15150 Norborne, RDFD, 48239	4268	C4
River Rouge Public 221 Burke St, RVRG, 48218	4418	E7
Riverview Public 14300 Sibley Rd, RVVW, 48192	4584	D7
Royal Oak Twp 21272 Mendota Av, ROTp, 48220	4199	B4
Rudolf Steiner 1923 Geddes Av, AARB, 48104	4406	E6

Detroit & Wayne County Points of Interest Index

Parks & Recreation

Detroit & Wayne County Points of Interest Index

Detroit & Wayne County Points of Interest Index

Detroit & Wayne County Points of Interest Index

Schools

FEATURE NAME Address City ZIP Code	MAP#	GRID
Boyd W Arthurs Middle School 4000 Marian Dr, TNTN, 48183	4669	B5
Boykin Continuing Education Center 10225 3rd St, DET, 48202	4272	D5
Boynton Elementary School 12800 Visger St, DET, 48229	4501	B1
Brace-Lederle Elementary School 18575 W 9 Mile Rd, SFLD, 48075	4198	A3
Brady Elementary School 2920 Joy Rd, DET, 48206	4272	B7
Brake Middle School 13500 Pine Av, TYLR, 48180	4583	B2
Brewer Elementary School 12450 Hayes St, DET, 48205	4275	B1
Brick Elementary School 8970 Whittaker Rd, AGST, 48197	4661	B2
Brooks Middle School 16101 W Chicago St, DET, 48228	4342	C1
Brownstown Middle School 20135 Inkster Rd, BNTN, 48174	4667	B2
Bryant Elementary School 2150 Santa Rosa Dr, AARB, 48108	4489	E5
Bryant Middle School 460 N Vernon St, DRBN, 48128	4416	A1
Buchanan Elementary School 16400 Hubbard St, LVNA, 48154	4267	B3
Bulman Elementary School 15995 Delaware Av, RDFD, 48239	4268	B3
Bunche Elementary School 2601 Ellery St, DET, 48207	4346	B3
Burbank Middle School 15600 State Fair St E, DET, 48205	4203	C5
Burns Elementary School 14350 Terry St, DET, 48227	4270	D5
Burns Park Elementary School 1414 Wells St, AARB, 48104	4489	D1
Burroughs Middle School 8950 St. Cyril St, DET, 48213	4274	A4
Burt Elementary School 20710 Pilgrim St, DET, 48223	4269	D3
Burton International School 3420 Cass Av, DET, 48201	4345	C4
Butzel Middle School 2301 Van Dyke St, DET, 48214	4346	D2
Cabrini Elementary School 15300 Wick Rd, ALPK, 48101	4500	B4
Cabrini High School 15305 Wick Rd, ALPK, 48101	4500	B5
Cadillac Middle School 15125 Schoolcraft St, DET, 48227	4270	D5
Calvary Christian Academy 1007 Ecorse Rd, YpTp, 48198	4492	C5
Calvary Lutheran School 3320 Electric Av, LNPK, 48146	4501	A5
Campbell Elementary School 2301 Alexandrine St E, DET, 48207	4345	E2
Carleton Elementary School 11724 Casino St, DET, 48224	4203	D7
Carl T Renton Junior High School 31578 Huron River Dr, HnTp, 48164	4666	C7
Carpenter Elementary School 4250 Central Blvd, PTFD, 48108	4490	D3
Carstens Elementary School 2592 Coplin St, DET, 48214	4275	C6
Carver Elementary School 18701 Paul St, DET, 48228	4342	A5
Cass Elementary School 34663 Munger St, LVNA, 48154	4266	D2
Cass Technical High School 2421 2nd Av, DET, 48201	4345	C5
Catherine White Elementary School 5161 Charles St, DET, 48212	4273	D2
Catholic Central High School 441 Tecumseh Rd E, WIND, N8X	4421	B4
Centennial Elementary School 62500 9 Mile Rd, SLYN, 48178	4189	A4
Central Academy 2459 S Industrial Hwy, AARB, 48104	4489	D3
Central Christian School 670 Church St, PLYM, 48170	4265	A7
Central High School 2425 Tuxedo St, DET, 48206	4272	B6
Central Middle School 650 Church St, PLYM, 48170	4265	A7
Central Public School 700 Norfolk St, WIND, N9E	4504	B1
Century High School 1375 California Av, WIND, N9B	4420	C4
Cerveny Middle School 15850 Strathmoor St, DET, 48227	4270	E3
Cesar Chavez Academy 8126 Vernor Hwy W, DET, 48209	4419	A2
Cesar Chavez Middle School 1648 Porter St, DET, 48216	4345	B7
CG Desantis Catholic School 930 Marion Av, WIND, N9A	4421	B1
Chadsey High School 5335 Martin St, DET, 48210	4343	E5
Chandler Elementary School 9227 Chapin St, DET, 48213	4274	C6
Chandler Park Academy 15932 Warren Av E, DET, 48224	4275	E3
Chapelle Community Elementary School 111 S Wallace Blvd, YpTp, 48197	4491	D5
Charles C Rogers High School 16400 Tireman St, DET, 48228	4342	C3
Charles Drew Middle School 9600 Wyoming St, DET, 48204	4343	C1
Charles H Wright Academy 19299 Berg Rd, DET, 48219	4197	A6
Chatterton Middle School 24330 Ryan Rd, WRRN, 48091	4201	B1
Cheney Elementary School 1500 Stamford Rd, SpTp, 48198	4492	D1
Children's Village Int'l Ctr 14901 Meyers Rd, DET, 48227	4271	A4
Chormann Elementary School 15500 Howard St, SOGT, 48195	4584	E4
Christian Mont Sch Of Ann Arbr 5225 Jackson Rd, WasC, 48103	4404	C5
Christ the Good Shepherd School 1590 Riverbank St, LNPK, 48146	4500	E6
Christ the King Lutheran School 15600 Trenton Rd, SOGT, 48195	4584	D4
Christ the King School 16800 Trinity St, DET, 48219	4269	C2
Christ the King School 1200 Grand Marais Rd W, WIND, N9E	4504	A1
Chrysler Elementary School 1445 Lafayette St E, DET, 48207	4345	E5
Churchill High School 8900 Newburgh Rd, LVNA, 48150	4338	B3
City Day School of Detroit 22180 Parklawn St, OKPK, 48237	4198	E3
Clague Middle School 2616 Nixon Rd, AARB, 48105	4407	A2
Clara Barton Elementary School 8530 Joy Rd, DET, 48204	4343	C2
Clarence Randall Elementary School 8699 Robert St, TYLR, 48180	4499	B4
Clarenceville High School 20155 Middlebelt Rd, LVNA, 48152	4195	D6
Clarenceville Middle School 20210 Middlebelt Rd, LVNA, 48152	4195	D5
Clark Elementary School 15755 Bremen St, DET, 48224	4275	E4
Clark Elementary School 2500 Martin Rd, FRDL, 48220	4200	B1
Cleveland Elementary School 28030 Cathedral St, LVNA, 48150	4340	A2
Cleveland Middle School 13322 Conant St, DET, 48212	4273	C2
Clinton Elementary School 8145 Chalfonte St, DET, 48238	4271	C4
Clippert Academy 1981 McKinstry St, DET, 48209	4419	D1
Clonlara School 1289 Jewett Av, AARB, 48104	4489	D2
Coffey Middle School 17210 Cambridge Av, DET, 48235	4198	B6
Coleman Young Elementary School 15715 Hubbell St, DET, 48227	4270	D3
Colin Powell Academy 4800 Coplin St, DET, 48214	4275	C5
Columbian Primary School 4700 Vinewood St, DET, 48210	4344	C5
Columbus Middle School 18025 Brock St, DET, 48205	4203	B7
Commonwealth Community Development Academy 8735 Schoolcraft St, DET, 48238	4271	C5
Communication & Media Arts High School 14771 Mansfield St, DET, 48227	4270	B4
Concord Public School 6700 Raymond Av, WIND, N8S	4347	C7
Congreg Shaarey Zedek/Clintn St Grtr Beth Ch 2901 Rochester St, DET, 48206	4272	B7
Cooke Elementary School 18800 Puritan St, DET, 48219	4270	A2
Cooke Junior High School 21200 Taft Rd, NHVL, 48167	4192	C5
Cooley High School 15055 Hubbell St, DET, 48227	4270	D3
Coolidge Elementary School 16501 Elmira St, DET, 48227	4342	B1
Coolidge Elementary School 30500 Curtis Rd, LVNA, 48152	4267	C1
Coolidge Intermediate School 2521 Bermuda St, FRDL, 48220	4199	E1
Cooper Elementary School 6836 Georgia St, DET, 48211	4274	A5
Cooper Elementary School 28550 Ann Arbor Tr, WTLD, 48185	4340	A3
Cornerstone Academy 15633 Pennsylvania Rd, RVVW, 48192	4584	B5
Cornerstone Middle School 9333 Linwood St, DET, 48206	4272	B7
Cornerstone School 2411 Iroquois St, DET, 48214	4346	D2
Cornerstone School West 9333 Linwood St, DET, 48206	4272	B7
Coronation Elementary School 5400 Coronation Av, WIND, N8T	4422	C1
Cortland Academy of Integrated Learning 138 Cortland St, HDPK, 48203	4272	D4
Cory Elementary School 35200 Smith Rd, RMLS, 48174	4496	D4
Courtis Elementary School 8100 Davison W, DET, 48238	4271	C5
Crary Elementary School 16164 Asbury Pk, DET, 48235	4270	B2
Creative Montessori Center 3804 Hazel Av, LNPK, 48146	4500	C6
Crescent Academy International 40440 Palmer Rd, CNTN, 48188	4412	D4
Crescentwood Elementary School 14500 Crescentwood Av, WRRN, 48021	4203	B2
Crestwood High School 1501 N Beech Daly Rd, DBHT, 48127	4340	C7
Crockett Technical High School 571 Mack Av, DET, 48201	4345	C3
Daly Elementary School 25824 Michigan Av, INKR, 48141	4415	D4
Dar-Ul Arqam Islamic School 4612 Lonyo St, DET, 48210	4343	D7
David Maxwell Elementary School 1648 Francois Rd, WIND, N8Y	4422	A1
Davidson Middle School 13940 Leroy St, SOGT, 48195	4584	D4
Davison Elementary School 2800 Davison St E, DET, 48212	4273	B2
Davis Technical High School 10200 Erwin St, DET, 48234	4274	B3
Daycroft Montessori School 100 Oakbrook Dr, AARB, 48103	4489	B4
Dearborn Academy 19310 Ford Rd, DRBN, 48228	4341	E6
Dearborn Christian School 21360 Donaldson St, DRBN, 48124	4416	D4
Dearborn Heights Montessori Center 466 N John Daly Rd, DBHT, 48127	4415	C1
Dearborn High School 19501 Outer Dr, DRBN, 48124	4416	B2
Defer Elementary School 15425 Kercheval St, GPPK, 48230	4275	E6
Denby High School 12800 Kelly Rd, DET, 48224	4203	C7
Detroit Academy of Arts & Sciences 2985 Jefferson Av E, DET, 48207	4346	B5
Detroit Academy of Science 5020 John R St, DET, 48202	4345	B2
Detroit Acad For Sci Math-Tech 8401 Woodward Av, DET, 48202	4273	A7
Detroit Catholic Central High School 14200 Breakfast Dr, RDFD, 48239	4268	B5
Detroit City High School 3500 McGraw St, DET, 48210	4344	C3
Detroit Community High School 9331 Grandville Av, DET, 48228	4341	E2
Detroit High School of Arts 4333 Rosa Parks Blvd, DET, 48210	4344	E4
Detroit Open Elementary School 24601 Frisbee St, DET, 48219	4196	E6
Detroit School of Industrial Arts 11055 Glenfield St, DET, 48213	4274	D2
Detroit Urban Lutheran School 8181 Greenfield Rd, DET, 48228	4342	D3
Detroit Waldorf School 2555 Burns St, DET, 48214	4346	D2
Dewey Center for Urban Education 3550 John C Lodge Frwy, DET, 48201	4345	B5
Dicken Elementary School 2135 Runnymede Blvd, AARB, 48103	4488	D1
Dickinson East High School 3385 Norwalk St, HMTK, 48212	4273	C4
Dickinson West High School 2650 Caniff St, HMTK, 48212	4273	B4
Discovery Middle School 45083 Hanford Rd, CNTN, 48187	4336	D6
Divine Child Elementary School 25001 Hollander St, DRBN, 48128	4415	E1
Divine Child High School 1001 N Silvery Ln, DRBN, 48128	4415	E1
Dixon Elementary School 19500 Tireman St, DET, 48228	4341	E3
DM Eagle Elementary School 14194 Tecumseh Rd, Tcmh, N8N	4424	D2
Dodson Elementary School 205 N Beck Rd, CNTN, 48187	4411	B2
Dominican Academy 9740 McKinney St, DET, 48224	4275	D2
Dominican High School 9740 McKinney St, DET, 48224	4275	D2
Dossin Elementary School 16650 Glendale St, DET, 48227	4270	B6
Dougall Elementary School 811 Dougall Av, WIND, N9A	4420	E2
Douglas Elementary School 6400 Hartel St, GDNC, 48135	4340	A6
Douglass Academy 2600 Leland St, DET, 48207	4345	E2
Dove Academy of Detroit 11055 Glenfield St, DET, 48213	4274	D2
Dow Elementary School 19900 McIntyre St, DET, 48219	4197	B5
Downriver High School 33211 McCann Rd, BwTp, 48173	4841	C1
Duffield Elementary School 2715 Macomb St, DET, 48207	4346	A4
Dunn Middle School 163 Burke St, RVRG, 48218	4418	E7
Durfee Middle School 2470 Collingwood St, DET, 48206	4272	B6
Duvall Elementary School 22561 Beech St, DRBN, 48124	4416	C3
Earhart Middle School 1000 Scotten St, DET, 48209	4419	E1
Earl F Carr Elementary School 3901 Ferris Av, LNPK, 48146	4501	A6
East Bethlehem Lutheran School 3510 Outer Dr E, DET, 48234	4201	D5
East Catholic High School 5206 Field St, DET, 48213	4274	B7
East Detroit High School 15501 Couzens Av, EPTE, 48021	4203	C2
East Middle School 1042 S Mill St, PLYM, 48170	4337	B2
East Middle School 510 Emerick St, YPLT, 48198	4492	B5
East River Elementary School 23276 E River Rd, WynC, 48138	4670	D5
Eastside Academy 1095 Hibbard St, DET, 48214	4346	E2
Eastside Vicariate School 4230 McDougall St, DET, 48207	4345	E2
Eastwood Elementary School 3555 Forest Glade Dr, WIND, N8T	4423	B3
Eberwhite Elementary School 800 Soule Blvd, AARB, 48103	4405	E7
Ecole Georges P Vanier 6200 Edgar St, WIND, N8S	4347	C7
Ecole L'Envolee 1799 Iroquois St, WIND, N8Y	4421	C2
Ecole Monseigneur Jean Noel 3225 California Av, WIND, N9E	4503	E2
Ecole St. Antoine 1317 Lesperance Rd, Tcmh, N8N	4423	E2
Ecole St. Edmond 1562 Rossini Blvd, WIND, N8Y	4422	A1
Ecole Ste. Marguerite D'Youville 13025 St. Thomas St, Tcmh, N8N	4349	B7
Ecole Ste. Therese 5305 Tecumseh Rd E, WIND, N8T	4422	C2
Ecorse High School 27385 7th St, ECRS, 48229	4501	C3
Edgemont Elementary School 125 S Edgemont St, BLVL, 48111	4578	E2
Edison Elementary School 17045 Grand River Av, DET, 48227	4270	B4
Edison Elementary School 1700 Shevlin St, FRDL, 48220	4200	A1
Edison Elementary School 34505 Hunter Av, WTLD, 48185	4338	E6
Edmonson Elementary School 1300 Canfield St W, DET, 48201	4345	A4
Edmund Atkinson Elementary School 4900 Hildale St E, DET, 48234	4201	C7
Edsel Ford High School 20601 Rotunda Dr, DRBN, 48124	4416	E5
Edwin S Sherrill Elementary School 7300 Garden St, DET, 48204	4343	D3
Einstein Elementary School 14001 Northend Av, OKPK, 48237	4198	E3

Schools | Detroit & Wayne County Points of Interest Index | **Schools**

Detroit & Wayne County Points of Interest Index

FEATURE NAME Address City ZIP Code	MAP#	GRID
University Liggett School 1045 Cook Rd, GSPW, 48236	4204	D7
University of Detroit High School 8400 Cambridge Av N, DET, 48221	4199	C6
University Public School 2727 2nd Av, DET, 48201	4345	B5
Vandenberg Elementary School 15000 Trojan St, DET, 48235	4198	D5
Vandenberg Elementary School 32101 Stellwagen St, WYNE, 48184	4414	B7
Vandenburg Elementary School 24901 Cathedral, RDFD, 48239	4340	E2
Van Zile Elementary School 2915 Outer Dr E, DET, 48234	4201	C5
Vernor Elementary School 13726 Pembroke Av, DET, 48235	4198	E5
Vernor Primary School 13735 7 Mile Rd W, DET, 48235	4198	E6
Vetal School 14200 Westwood St, DET, 48223	4269	E5
Victoria Elementary School 12433 Dillon Dr, Tcmh, N8N	4348	E6
Victors Center 1200 Alter Rd, DET, 48214	4275	E7
Village Oaks Elementary School 23333 Willowbrook, NOVI, 48375	4193	C2
Vincent Continuing Education Center 1095 Hibbard St, DET, 48214	4346	E3
Von Stueben Middle School 12300 Linnhurst St, DET, 48205	4202	D6
Waldo F Lessenger Middle School 8401 Trinity St, DET, 48228	4341	C3
Walkerville High School 2100 Richmond St, WIND, N8Y	4421	B1
Walker-Winter Elementary School 39932 Michigan Av, CNTN, 48188	4412	D6
Wareing Elementary School 24800 Hayes St, TYLR, 48180	4498	E3
Warrendale Elementary School 14170 Couwlier Av, WRRN, 48089	4203	A3
Washington Elementary School 1201 Livernois St, FRDL, 48220	4199	D3
Washington Elementary School 9449 Hix Rd, LVNA, 48150	4338	A2
Washington Elementary School 11400 Continental Av, WRRN, 48089	4202	C2
Washington Elementary School 1440 Superior Blvd, WYDT, 48192	4585	A2
Wayne Elementary School 10633 Courville St, DET, 48224	4275	C1
Wayne Memorial High School 3001 4th St, WYNE, 48184	4413	E5
Weatherby Elementary School 20500 Wadsworth St, DET, 48228	4269	D7
Webber Middle School 4700 Tireman St, DET, 48204	4344	B3
Webb Middle School 2100 Woodward Hts, FRDL, 48220	4200	B1
Webster Elementary School 1450 25th St, DET, 48216	4419	E1
Webster Elementary School 431 W Jarvis Av, HZLP, 48030	4200	C3
Webster Elementary School 37855 Lyndon St, LVNA, 48154	4266	A5
Wegienka Elementary School 23925 Arsenal Rd, BNTN, 48134	4667	D6
Western International High School 1500 Scotten St, DET, 48209	4419	D1
West Middle School 44401 W Ann Arbor Tr, PyTp, 48170	4264	D7
West Middle School 105 N Mansfield St, YpTp, 48197	4491	C4
Westside Christian Academy 9540 Bramell, DET, 48239	4341	B1
Westview Elementary School 24077 Warner Av, WRRN, 48091	4201	A1
West Wayne Christian Academy 5039 Woodward St, WYNE, 48184	4413	D7
WF Herman Secondary School 1930 Rossini Blvd, WIND, N8W	4422	A2
WG Davis Elementary School 2855 Rivard Av, WIND, N8T	4422	C4
Whitmore Bolles Elementary School 21501 Whitmore St, DRBN, 48124	4416	C5
Whitmore Lake Elementary School 1077 Barker Rd, WasC, 48189	4186	D7
Whitmore Lake High School 8877 Main St, WasC, 48189	4259	A1
Whitmore Lake Middle School 8877 Main St, WasC, 48189	4259	A2
Wick Elementary School 36900 Wick Rd, RMLS, 48174	4496	C5
Wildwood Elementary School 500 N Wildwood Av, WTLD, 48185	4413	E2
Wilkins Elementary School 12400 Nashville St, DET, 48205	4274	D1
William A Brummer Elementary School 9919 N Rushton St, GOTp, 48178	4188	C2
William Allan Academy 44555 Galway Dr, NOVI, 48167	4192	D4
William A Nowlin Elementary School 23600 Penn St, DRBN, 48124	4416	A5
William C Taylor Elementary School 3700 Benson Rd, TNTN, 48183	4669	B7
William Ford Elementary School 14749 Alber St, DRBN, 48126	4342	E6
William Grace Elementary School 29040 Shiawassee Rd, FNHL, 48336	4195	E3
William J Beckham Academy 9860 Park Dr, DET, 48213	4275	A3
William Taft Elementary School 891 Goddard Rd, WYDT, 48192	4501	B7
Willow Run High School 235 Spencer Ln, YpTp, 48198	4492	E3
Wilson Elementary School 1244 Paxton St, FRDL, 48220	4200	A3
Winchester Elementary School 16141 Winchester Dr, NvlT, 48167	4265	B3
Windsor Adventist Elementary School 5350 Haig Av, WIND, N8T	4422	C3
Wines Elementary School 1701 Newport Rd, AARB, 48103	4405	E3
Winship Elementary School 14717 Curtis St, DET, 48235	4198	D7

FEATURE NAME Address City ZIP Code	MAP#	GRID
Winterhalter Elementary School 12121 Broadstreet Av, DET, 48204	4271	E7
WJ Langlois Elementary School 3110 Rivard Av, WIND, N8T	4422	D4
WL Bonner Christian Academy 2326 7 Mile Rd E, DET, 48234	4201	A6
Wonderland Primary School 4719 7 Mile Rd E, DET, 48234	4201	C6
Woodhaven High School 24787 Van Horn Rd, BNTN, 48134	4668	A7
Woodland Elementary School 23750 David Av, EPTE, 48021	4203	E1
Woodland Meadows Elementary School 350 Woodland Dr E, SALN, 48176	4572	C5
Woodrow Wilson Middle School 1275 15th St, WYDT, 48192	4501	A7
Woodward Academy 951 Lafayette St E, DET, 48207	4345	E5
Woodward Elementary School 2900 Wreford St, DET, 48210	4344	C3
Woodworth Elementary School 4951 Ternes St, DRBN, 48126	4342	D7
Wyandotte Catholic Consolidated 3051 4th St, WYDT, 48192	4585	C3
Yake Elementary School 16400 Carter Rd E, WDHN, 48183	4669	A3
Yeshiva Gedolah High School 24600 Greenfield Rd, OKPK, 48237	4198	C1
Yost Elementary School 16161 Winston St, DET, 48219	4268	E2
Young Magnet Middle School 2757 Macomb St, DET, 48207	4346	A4
Ypsilanti High School 2095 Packard Rd, YpTp, 48197	4491	C4

Shopping Centers

FEATURE NAME Address City ZIP Code	MAP#	GRID
Bel Air Centre 8 Mile Rd E, DET, 48234	4202	B4
Briarwood Mall 100 Briarwood Cir, AARB, 48108	4489	B4
Devonshire Mall 3100 Howard Av, WIND, N8X	4421	C7
Eastland Shopping Center 18000 Vernier Rd, HRWD, 48225	4204	A4
Fairlane Green Outer Dr, ALPK, 48101	4417	C6
Fairlane Meadows 16221 Meadows Dr, DRBN, 48126	4342	C7
Fairlane Town Center 1 Town Center Dr, DRBN, 48126	4417	A1
Fort Malden Mall 400 Sandwich St S, Amhg, N9V	4757	B4
Independence Marketplace Outer Dr, ALPK, 48101	4417	B6
Laurel Park Place Mall 37700 6 Mile Rd, LVNA, 48152	4266	A2
Lincoln Park Plaza Shopping Center 3584 Fort Park Blvd, LNPK, 48146	4500	D6
Lincoln Park Shopping Center Dix Hwy, LNPK, 48146	4500	D2
Livonia Mall 29514 7 Mile Rd, LVNA, 48152	4195	D7
Maple Village N Maple Rd, AARB, 48103	4405	D5
Northland Mall 21500 Northwestern Hwy, SFLD, 48075	4198	B3
RioCan Centre Legacy Park Dr, WIND, N8W	4505	B3
Southland Shopping Center 23000 Eureka Rd, TYLR, 48180	4583	B3
Tecumseh Mall 7654 Tecumseh Rd E, WIND, N8T	4422	E1
Westland Mall 35000 Warren Rd, WTLD, 48185	4338	D5
West Ridge Shopping Center Warren Rd, WTLD, 48185	4338	D5
Wonderland Village Center 29859 Plymouth Rd, LVNA, 48150	4339	D1
Woodhaven Commons West Rd, WDHN, 48183	4669	A4

Subdivisions & Neighborhoods

FEATURE NAME Address City ZIP Code	MAP#	GRID
Canton, CNTN	4412	A2
Cherry Hill, CNTN	4410	D2
Delhi, WasC	4329	E6
Dixboro, SpTp	4408	A2
Highland Lakes, LVNA	4193	E6
Northfield, AATp	4331	D5
Northville Commons, NvlT	4265	D3
Willow Run, SpTp	4492	D1

Transportation

FEATURE NAME Address City ZIP Code	MAP#	GRID
Amtrak-Ann Arbor Station, AARB	4406	C5
Amtrak-Dearborn Station, DRBN	4417	C1
Amtrak-Detroit Station, DET	4345	A1
Greyhound-Detroit Station, DET	4346	E3
Greyhound-Detroit Station, DET	4345	C6
Greyhound-Lincoln Park Station, LNPK	4501	A2
Greyhound-Washtenaw Station, AARB	4406	B6
Greyhound-Wayne Station, WYNE	4414	B5
Greyhound-Windsor Station, WIND	4420	E1
People Mover-Bricktown Station, DET	4345	E6
People Mover-Broadway Station, DET	4345	D6
People Mover-Cadillac Station, DET	4345	D6
People Mover-Cobo Center Station, DET	4345	D6
People Mover-Financial District Station, DET	4345	D6
People Mover-Fort Cass Station, DET	4345	C6
People Mover-Grand Circus Station, DET	4345	D6
People Mover-Greektown Station, DET	4345	D6
People Mover-Joe Louis Arena Station, DET	4345	C7
People Mover-Michigan Station, DET	4345	C6
People Mover-Millender Center Station, DET	4345	D6
People Mover-Renaissance Center Station, DET	4345	E6
People Mover-Times Square Station, DET	4345	C6
VIA Rail-Windsor Station, WIND	4346	C6

Visitor Information

FEATURE NAME Address City ZIP Code	MAP#	GRID
Metropolitan Detroit Visitors Bureau 100 Renaissance Center, DET, 48226	4345	E6
Ontario Tourist Information 110 Park St E, WIND, N9A	4420	E1

FEATURE NAME Address City ZIP Code	MAP#	GRID
Ontario Tourist Information WIND, N9C	4420	B4
Tourist Information Sandwich St N, Amhg, N9V	4757	B1
Visitor Bureau of Windsor & Area 333 Riverside Dr E, WIND, N9A	4420	E1
Ypsilanti Visitors Bureau 125 N Huron St, YPLT, 48197	4492	A4

RAND McNALLY

Thank you for purchasing this Rand McNally Street Guide!
We value your comments and suggestions.

Please help us serve you better by completing this postage-paid reply card.
This information is for internal use ONLY and will not be distributed or sold to any external third party.

Missing pages? Maybe not... Please refer to the "Using Your Street Guide" page for further explanation.

Street Guide Title: Detroit including Wayne County   ISBN# 0-528-85503-4   Edition: 5th   MKT: DET

Today's Date: _____   Gender: ☐M ☐F   Age Group: ☐18-24 ☐25-31 ☐32-40 ☐41-50 ☐51-64 ☐65+

1. What type of industry do you work in?
   ☐Real Estate   ☐Trucking   ☐Delivery   ☐Construction   ☐Utilities   ☐Government
   ☐Retail   ☐Sales   ☐Transportation ☐Landscape   ☐Service & Repair
   ☐Courier   ☐Automotive   ☐Insurance   ☐Medical   ☐Police/Fire/First Response
   ☐Other, please specify: _____

2. What type of job do you have in this industry?_____

3. Where did you purchase this Street Guide? (store name & city) _____

4. Why did you purchase this Street Guide? _____

5. How often do you purchase an updated Street Guide? ☐Annually ☐2 yrs. ☐3-5 yrs. ☐Other:_____

6. Where do you use it? ☐Primarily in the car ☐Primarily in the office ☐Primarily at home ☐Other: _____

7. How do you use it? ☐Exclusively for business ☐Primarily for business but also for personal or leisure use
   ☐Both work and personal evenly ☐Primarily for personal use ☐Exclusively for personal use

8. What do you use your Street Guide for?
   ☐Find Addresses ☐In-route navigation ☐Planning routes ☐Other: _____
   Find points of interest: ☐Schools ☐Parks ☐Buildings ☐Shopping Centers ☐Other:_____

9. How often do you use it? ☐Daily ☐Weekly ☐Monthly ☐Other: _____

10. Do you use the internet for maps and/or directions? ☐Yes ☐No

11. How often do you use the internet for directions? ☐Daily ☐Weekly ☐Monthly ☐Other:_____

12. Do you use any of the following mapping products in addition to your Street Guide?
    ☐Folded paper maps ☐Folded laminated maps ☐Wall maps ☐GPS ☐PDA ☐In-car navigation ☐Phone maps

13. What features, if any, would you like to see added to your Street Guide? _____
    _____

14. What features or information do you find most useful in your Rand McNally Street Guide? (please specify)
    _____
    _____

15. Please provide any additional comments or suggestions you have. _____
    _____
    _____

We strive to provide you with the most current updated information available if you know of a map correction, please notify us here.

Where is the correction?   Map Page #:_____   Grid #:_____   Index Page #:_____

Nature of the correction: ☐Street name missing   ☐Street name misspelled   ☐Street information incorrect
    ☐Incorrect location for point of interest   ☐Index error   ☐Other: _____
Detail: _____

I would like to receive information about updated editions and special offers from Rand McNally
   ☐via e-mail   E-mail address: _____
   ☐via postal mail
   Your Name: _____   Company (if used for work): _____
   Address:_____   City/State/ZIP: _____

Thank you for your time and help. We are working to serve you better.
This information is for internal use ONLY and will not be distributed or sold to any external third party.

get directions at
randmcnally.com

NO POSTAGE
NECESSARY
IF MAILED
IN THE
UNITED STATES

BUSINESS REPLY MAIL
FIRST-CLASS MAIL   PERMIT NO. 388   CHICAGO IL
POSTAGE WILL BE PAID BY ADDRESSEE

**RAND MCNALLY
CONSUMER AFFAIRS
PO BOX 7600
CHICAGO IL   60680-9915**

✸ RAND M^cNALLY
The most trusted name on the map.

**You'll never need to ask for directions again with these
Rand McNally products!**

- EasyFinder® Laminated Maps
- Folded Maps
- Street Guides
- Wall Maps
- CustomView Wall Maps
- Road Atlases
- Motor Carriers' Road Atlases